TEXAS COMMERCIAL CAUSES OF ACTION

TEXAS COMMERCIAL CAUSES OF ACTION

Claims, Defenses and Remedies

Jim Wren
Elizabeth Fraley
2020

Copyright © 2020 Fastcase. All Rights Reserved.

No part of this publication may be reproduced or transmitted in any form or by any means, electronic or mechanical, including photocopy, recording, or utilized by any information storage or retrieval system, without written permission from the publisher. For information about permissions or to request permissions online, visit us at www.fastcase.com, or a written request may be e-mailed to our permissions department at support@fastcase.com.

Printed in the United States of America

1 2 3 4 5 6 7 8 9 0

ISBN 978-1-949884-48-7

Summary of Contents

Table of Contents	vii
About this Book	lv
About the Authors	lvii
Acknowledgements	lix

SECTION I	**TEXAS BUSINESS AND CONTRACT CAUSES OF ACTION**	**1**
Chapter 1	BUSINESS TORTS LITIGATION	3
Chapter 2	BUSINESS MANAGEMENT LITIGATION	67
Chapter 3	CONTRACT AND COMMERCIAL LITIGATION	145
Chapter 4	PROFESSIONAL LIABILITY AND FIDUCIARY LITIGATION	205
Chapter 5	INSURANCE LITIGATION	213
Chapter 6	EMPLOYMENT LITIGATION	235
Chapter 7	OIL AND GAS LITIGATION	251
Chapter 8	EQUITABLE AND EXTRAORDINARY RELIEF	301
Chapter 9	MISCELLANEOUS BUSINESS CAUSES OF ACTION—BUSINESS CAUSES OF ACTION EXPRESSLY NOT RECOGNIZED IN TEXAS	361
SECTION II	**PLEADING DAMAGES**	**379**
Chapter 10	GENERAL PLEADING REQUIREMENTS FOR DAMAGES IN BUSINESS LITIGATION	381
Chapter 11	COMMON BUSINESS LITIGATION DAMAGES MODELS	387
Chapter 12	DEFENSIVE ISSUES RELATING TO DAMAGES	419

SECTION III	PLEADING DEFENSES	429
Chapter 13	PLEADING BURDENS	431
Chapter 14	SPECIAL AND VERIFIED DENIALS	451
Chapter 15	INFERENTIAL REBUTTAL DEFENSES	457
Chapter 16	AFFIRMATIVE DEFENSES	461
Chapter 17	STATUTES OF LIMITATIONS AND REPOSE	479
Chapter 18	PROPORTIONATE RESPONSIBILITY, CONTRIBUTION, AND INDEMNITY	495

SECTION IV	SPECIAL PLEADING ISSUES	505
Chapter 19	TEXAS PLEADING STANDARDS	507
Chapter 20	PLEADING TEXAS STATE COURT DISCOVERY LEVEL	515
Chapter 21	PLEADING SUBJECT MATTER JURISDICTION IN TEXAS STATE TRIAL COURTS	525
Chapter 22	PLEADING TEXAS VENUE	535
Chapter 23	PLEADING PARTIES AND METHODS OF SERVICE	547
Chapter 24	PLEADING CHOICE OF LAW	553
Chapter 25	PLEADING TO AVOID OR COMPEL ARBITRATION	563
Chapter 26	PLEADING TO RESIST OR ENFORCE A FORUM SELECTION CLAUSE	571
Chapter 27	PLEADING REMOVAL AND REMAND	575
Chapter 28	MOTIONS AND RESPONSES TO MOTIONS ATTACKING PLEADINGS	587
Chapter 29	AMENDMENT OF PLEADINGS	595
Chapter 30	MAKING AND RESPONDING TO MOTIONS FOR SUMMARY JUDGMENT	603

Table of Cases   615
Index   719

Table of Contents

About this Book   lv
About the Authors   lvii
Acknowledgements   lix

SECTION I   TEXAS BUSINESS AND CONTRACT CAUSES OF ACTION

Chapter 1   BUSINESS TORTS LITIGATION   3

1-1	Tortious Interference with Existing Contract			3
	1-1:1	Overview		3
		1-1:1.1	Related Causes of Action	3
	1-1:2	Elements		3
	1-1:3	Damages and Remedies		5
		1-1:3.1	Actual Damages	5
			1-1:3.1a Pecuniary Loss	6
			1-1:3.1b Mental Anguish	6
			1-1:3.1c Injury to Reputation	6
			1-1:3.1d Lost Profits and Loss of Value of a Business	6
		1-1:3.2	Exemplary Damages	6
		1-1:3.3	Injunctive Relief	7
		1-1:3.4	Interest	7
		1-1:3.5	Court Costs	7
	1-1:4	Defenses		7
		1-1:4.1	Statute of Limitations	7
		1-1:4.2	Comparative Fault	7
		1-1:4.3	Privilege and Justification	7
		1-1:4.4	Void Ab Initio	8
1-2	Tortious Interference with Prospective Business Relationship			8
	1-2:1	Overview		8
		1-2:1.1	Related Causes of Action	8
	1-2:2	Elements		8
	1-2:3	Damages and Remedies		9
		1-2:3.1	Actual Damages	9
			1-2:3.1a Pecuniary Loss	10
			1-2:3.1b Mental Anguish	10

			1-2:3.1c	Injury to Reputation	10
			1-2:3.1d	Lost Profits and Loss of Value of a Business	10
		1-2:3.2	Exemplary Damages		11
		1-2:3.3	Injunctive Relief		11
		1-2:3.4	Interest		11
		1-2:3.5	Court Costs		11
	1-2:4	Defenses			11
		1-2:4.1	Statute of Limitations		11
		1-2:4.2	Comparative Fault		12
		1-2:4.3	Privilege and Justification		12
		1-2:4.4	Void Ab Initio		12
1-3	Conversion				12
	1-3:1	Introduction			12
		1-3:1.1	Related Causes of Action		12
	1-3:2	Elements			12
	1-3:3	Damages and Remedies			14
		1-3:3.1	Actual Damages		14
			1-3:3.1a	Loss of Value	14
			1-3:3.1b	Loss of Use	14
			1-3:3.1c	Loss of Profits	15
		1-3:3.2	Exemplary Damages		15
		1-3:3.3	Injunctive Relief		15
		1-3:3.4	Interest		15
		1-3:3.5	Court Costs		15
	1-3:4	Defenses			15
		1-3:4.1	Qualified Good Faith Refusal		15
		1-3:4.2	Statute of Limitations		15
		1-3:4.3	Good Faith Purchaser		16
		1-3:4.4	Buyer in the Ordinary Course of Business		16
		1-3:4.5	Possession After Repair		16
		1-3:4.6	Comparative Fault		16
		1-3:4.7	Express or Implied Consent		17
1-4	Common Law Fraud				17
	1-4:1	Overview			17
		1-4:1.1	Related Causes of Action		17
	1-4:2	Elements			17
	1-4:3	Damages and Remedies			19
		1-4:3.1	Actual Damages		19
			1-4:3.1a	Benefit-of-the-Bargain	19

TABLE OF CONTENTS ix

			1-4:3.1b	Out-of-Pocket	19
			1-4:3.1c	Damages to Personal Property	19
			1-4:3.1d	Mental Anguish	19
		1-4:3.2	Exemplary Damages		20
		1-4:3.3	Equitable Remedies		20
			1-4:3.3a	Rescission	20
			1-4:3.3b	Reformation	20
		1-4:3.4	Interest		20
		1-4:3.5	Costs		20
	1-4:4	Defenses			20
		1-4:4.1	Statute of Limitations		20
		1-4:4.2	Disclaimer of Reliance Contractual Disclaimer		21
		1-4:4.3	Ratification		21
		1-4:4.4	Statute of Frauds		22
		1-4:4.5	Attacking Justifiable Reliance		22
1-5	Statutory Fraud				22
	1-5:1	Overview			22
		1-5:1.1	Related Causes of Action		22
	1-5:2	Elements			23
	1-5:3	Damages and Remedies			23
		1-5:3.1	Actual Damages		23
			1-5:3.1a	Benefit-of-the-Bargain	23
			1-5:3.1b	Out-of-Pocket	24
		1-5:3.2	Exemplary Damages		24
		1-5:3.3	Rescission and Reformation		24
		1-5:3.4	Specific Performance		24
		1-5:3.5	Attorney's Fees		24
		1-5:3.6	Interest		24
		1-5:3.7	Court Costs		24
	1-5:4	Defenses			24
		1-5:4.1	Statute of Limitations		24
		1-5:4.2	Disclaimer of Reliance		25
		1-5:4.3	Statute of Frauds		25
1-6	Fraud by Non-Disclosure				25
	1-6:1	Overview			25
		1-6:1.1	Related Causes of Action		25
	1-6:2	Elements			25
	1-6:3	Damages and Remedies			28
		1-6:3.1	Actual Damages		28
			1-6:3.1a	Benefit-of-the-Bargain	28

		1-6:3.1b	Out-of-Pocket	28
		1-6:3.1c	Damages to Personal Property	28
		1-6:3.1d	Mental Anguish	28
	1-6:3.2	Exemplary Damages		28
	1-6:3.3	Equitable Remedies		28
		1-6:3.3a	Rescission	28
		1-6:3.3b	Reformation	29
	1-6:3.4	Interest		29
	1-6:3.5	Court Costs		29
1-6:4	Defenses			29
	1-6:4.1	Statute of Limitations		29
	1-6:4.2	Contractual Disclaimer		29
	1-6:4.3	Ratification		29
	1-6:4.4	Statute of Frauds		29
	1-6:4.5	Sovereign Immunity		30
1-7 Negligent Misrepresentation				30
1-7:1	Introduction			30
	1-7:1.1	Related Causes of Action		30
1-7:2	Elements			30
1-7:3	Damages and Remedies			32
	1-7:3.1	Actual Damages		32
	1-7:3.2	Exemplary Damages		32
	1-7:3.3	Interest		32
	1-7:3.4	Court Costs		32
1-7:4	Defenses			32
	1-7:4.1	Statute of Limitations		32
	1-7:4.2	Existence of a Contract or Contractual Opportunity		33
	1-7:4.3	Statute of Frauds		33
	1-7:4.4	Disclaimer of Reliance		33
	1-7:4.5	Ratification and Waiver		33
1-8 Business Disparagement				33
1-8:1	Introduction			33
	1-8:1.1	Related Causes of Action		34
1-8:2	Elements			34
1-8:3	Damages and Remedies			35
	1-8:3.1	Actual Damages		35
		1-8:3.1a	Loss of Sale	36
		1-8:3.1b	Loss of Credit	36
		1-8:3.1c	Loss of Business	36

TABLE OF CONTENTS xi

			1-8:3.2	Exemplary Damages	36
			1-8:3.3	Interest	36
			1-8:3.4	Court Costs	36
	1-8:4	Defenses			36
			1-8:4.1	Privilege	36
			1-8:4.2	Prior Restraint	37
			1-8:4.3	Comparative Fault	37
			1-8:4.4	Statute of Limitations	37
			1-8:4.5	Texas Citizens Participation Act	37
			1-8:4.6	Interlocutory Appeal	37
1-9	Negligent Hiring				38
	1-9:1	Introduction			38
			1-9:1.1	Related Causes of Action	38
	1-9:2	Elements			38
	1-9:3	Damages and Remedies			40
			1-9:3.1	Actual Damages	40
			1-9:3.2	Exemplary Damages	40
			1-9:3.3	Interest	40
			1-9:3.4	Court Costs	40
	1-9:4	Defenses			40
			1-9:4.1	Statute of Limitations	40
			1-9:4.2	Limitation on Liability Statute	40
1-10	Negligence				41
	1-10:1	Introduction			41
			1-10:1.1	Related Causes of Action	41
	1-10:2	Elements			41
	1-10:3	Damages and Remedies			42
			1-10:3.1	Actual Damages	42
				1-10:3.1a Personal Property	42
				1-10:3.1b Real Property	43
				1-10:3.1c Economic Injury	43
			1-10:3.2	Exemplary Damages	43
			1-10:3.3	Interest	43
			1-10:3.4	Court Costs	43
	1-10:4	Defenses			43
			1-10:4.1	Statute of Limitations	43
			1-10:4.2	Comparative Fault	43
			1-10:4.3	Economic Loss Rule	43

1-11	Negligence Per Se			43
	1-11:1	Introduction		43
		1-11:1.1	Related Causes of Action	44
	1-11:2	Elements		44
	1-11:3	Damages and Remedies		45
		1-11:3.1	Actual Damages	45
			1-11:3.1a Damages for Injury to Personal Property	45
			1-11:3.1b Damages for Injury to Real Property	45
			1-11:3.1c Damages for Economic Injury	45
		1-11:3.2	Exemplary Damages	46
		1-11:3.3	Interest	46
		1-11:3.4	Court Costs	46
		1-11:3.5	Damages Caps	46
	1-11:4	Defenses		46
		1-11:4.1	Statute of Limitations	46
		1-11:4.2	Comparative Fault	46
1-12	Intellectual Property—Common Law Trademark Infringement			46
	1-12:1	Introduction		46
	1-12:2	Elements		47
	1-12:3	Damages and Remedies		49
		1-12:3.1	Injunction	49
	1-12:4	Defenses		49
		1-12:4.1	Statute of Limitations	49
		1-12:4.2	Laches	50
		1-12:4.3	Abandonment	50
		1-12:4.4	Acquiescence	50
		1-12:4.5	Fair Use	50
1-13	Intellectual Property—Statutory Trademark Infringement/ Texas Trademark Act			51
	1-13:1	Introduction		51
		1-13:1.1	Related Causes of Action	51
	1-13:2	Elements		51
		1-13:2.1	Infringement	51
		1-13:2.2	Dilution	53
		1-13:2.3	Fraudulent Registration	54
	1-13:3	Damages and Remedies		54
		1-13:3.1	Actual Damages	54
		1-13:3.2	Disgorgement	54
		1-13:3.3	Injunction	54

TABLE OF CONTENTS xiii

			1-13:3.4	Statutory Damages	55
			1-13:3.5	Attorney's Fees	55
		1-13:4	Defenses		55
			1-13:4.1	Statute of Limitations	55
			1-13:4.2	Invalidity of the Mark	55
			1-13:4.3	Abandonment	57
			1-13:4.4	Laches	57
			1-13:4.5	First Amendment	57
			1-13:4.6	Fair Use	57
			1-13:4.7	Non-Commercial Use	57
			1-13:4.8	News Reporting or Commentary	58
1-14		Intellectual Property—Misuse of A Trade Name			58
	1-14:1	Overview			58
			1-14:1.1	Related Causes of Action	58
	1-14:2	Elements			58
	1-14:3	Damages and Remedies			60
			1-14:3.1	Injunction	60
	1-14:4	Defenses			60
			1-14:4.1	Statute of Limitations	60
			1-14:4.2	Laches	61
			1-14:4.3	Abandonment	61
			1-14:4.4	Acquiescence	61
			1-14:4.5	First Amendment Concerns	61
			1-14:4.6	Fair Use	62
1-15		Intellectual Property—Misappropriation of Trade Secrets			62
	1-15:1	Introduction			62
	1-15:2	Elements			62
	1-15:3	Damages and Remedies			64
			1-15:3.1	Statute of Limitations	65

Chapter 2	**BUSINESS MANAGEMENT LITIGATION**				**67**
2-1		Officer and Director Liability—Breach of The Duty of Care			67
	2-1:1	Overview			67
			2-1:1.1	Related Causes of Action	67
	2-1:2	Elements			67
			2-1:2.1	Mismanagement	67
			2-1:2.2	Wrongful Distribution of Dividends	68
	2-1:3	Damages and Remedies			68
			2-1:3.1	Actual Damages	68

		2-1:3.2	Special Damages	69
		2-1:3.3	Exemplary Damages	69
	2-1:4	Defenses		69
		2-1:4.1	Statutory Safe Harbor for Directors	69
		2-1:4.2	Exculpatory Clauses	70
		2-1:4.3	Statute of Limitations	70
	2-1:5	Procedural Implications		70
		2-1:5.1	Who May Sue	70
2-2	Officer and Director Liability—Breach of The Duty of Loyalty			71
	2-2:1	Overview		71
		2-2:1.1	Related Causes of Action	71
	2-2:2	Elements		71
		2-2:2.1	Mismanagement	71
		2-2:2.2	Wrongful Distribution of Dividends	72
	2-2:3	Damages and Remedies		72
		2-2:3.1	Actual Damages	72
		2-2:3.2	Special Damages	72
		2-2:3.3	Exemplary Damages	72
	2-2:4	Defenses		73
		2-2:4.1	Statutory Safe Harbor	73
		2-2:4.2	Interested Transaction/Corporate Opportunity Validity Procedures	73
		2-2:4.3	Exculpatory Clauses	73
		2-2:4.4	Statute of Limitations	74
	2-2:5	Procedural Implications		74
		2-2:5.1	Who May Sue	74
2-3	Officer and Director Liability—Wrongful Distribution of Dividends			74
	2-3:1	Overview		74
		2-3:1.1	Related Causes of Action	74
	2-3:2	Elements		75
	2-3:3	Damages and Remedies		77
		2-3:3.1	Excess Distributions	77
		2-3:3.2	Joint and Several Liability	77
		2-3:3.3	Contribution	77
	2-3:4	Defenses		77
		2-3:4.1	Good Faith Reliance	77
		2-3:4.2	Subsequent Events Purge the Wrongfulness	78
		2-3:4.3	Statute of Limitations	78
	2-3:5	Procedural Implications		78
		2-3:5.1	Who May Sue	78

TABLE OF CONTENTS

2-4		Officer and Director Liability—Liability for Securities Fraud		79
	2-4:1	Overview		79
		2-4:1.1	Related Causes of Action	79
	2-4:2	Elements		79
		2-4:2.1	Rule 10b-5 General Fraud	79
		2-4:2.2	Rule 10b-5 Insider Trading	81
		2-4:2.3	Rule 14e-3 Tender Offers	82
		2-4:2.4	Short Swing Profits	83
		2-4:2.5	Common Law Fraud	84
	2-4:3	Damages and Remedies		84
		2-4:3.1	Out-of-Pocket	84
		2-4:3.2	Benefit-of-the-Bargain	84
		2-4:3.3	Disgorgement	84
		2-4:3.4	Rescission	85
		2-4:3.5	Exemplary Damages	85
		2-4:3.6	Consequential Damages	85
		2-4:3.7	Common Law Fraud Damages	85
	2-4:4	Defenses		85
		2-4:4.1	10b-5-1 Plan	85
		2-4:4.2	In Pari Delicto	86
		2-4:4.3	Statute of Limitations	86
		2-4:4.4	Certain Defenses Not Applicable	87
	2-4:5	Procedural Implications		87
		2-4:5.1	Pleading Burden	87
		2-4:5.2	Jurisdiction	87
		2-4:5.3	Short Swing Profits	87
2-5		Officer and Director Liability—Liability as an Agent		87
	2-5:1	Overview		87
		2-5:1.1	Related Causes of Action	88
	2-5:2	Elements		88
	2-5:3	Damages and Remedies		88
	2-5:4	Defenses		88
2-6		Officer and Director Liability—State Revocation of Corporate Status		88
	2-6:1	Overview		88
	2-6:2	Elements		88
		2-6:2.1	Administrative Termination by the Secretary of State	88
		2-6:2.2	Judicial Termination by the Attorney General	89

		2-6:2.3	Termination for Failure to Pay Franchise Taxes	90
	2-6:3	Damages and Remedies		91
		2-6:3.1	Termination of the Corporate Form	91
	2-6:4	Defenses		91
		2-6:4.1	Reinstatement	91
2-7	Shareholder Oppression			91
	2-7:1	Overview		91
		2-7:1.1	Related Causes of Action	92
	2-7:2	Elements		92
	2-7:3	Damages and Remedies		94
		2-7:3.1	Receivership	94
	2-7:4	Defenses		94
		2-7:4.1	Defenses, Generally	94
	2-7:5	Procedural Implications		94
		2-7:5.1	Fact Finder's Role	94
2-8	Derivate Shareholder Suits			94
	2-8:1	Overview		94
		2-8:1.1	Related Causes of Action	95
	2-8:2	Elements		95
	2-8:3	Damages and Remedies		96
		2-8:3.1	Generally	96
		2-8:3.2	Cost Shifting	97
		2-8:3.3	Indemnification	97
	2-8:4	Defenses		98
		2-8:4.1	Procedural Defenses	98
		2-8:4.2	Defenses Held by the Defendant Third Party	98
		2-8:4.3	Defenses Against the Shareholder-Plaintiff	99
	2-8:5	Procedural Implications		99
		2-8:5.1	Forum	99
		2-8:5.2	Venue	99
		2-8:5.3	Claim Joinder	100
		2-8:5.4	Demand	100
		2-8:5.5	Statutory Stay of the Derivative Proceedings	101
		2-8:5.6	Dismissal of Suit by the Board of Directors	101
		2-8:5.7	Limited Discovery	101
		2-8:5.8	Settlement	102
		2-8:5.9	Application to Foreign Corporations	102
		2-8:5.10	Closely Held Corporations	102

TABLE OF CONTENTS

2-9		Dissenting Shareholders Suits		103
	2-9:1	Overview		103
		2-9:1.1	Related Causes of Action	103
	2-9:2	Elements		103
	2-9:3	Damages and Remedies		106
		2-9:3.1	Dissent and Appraisal Right/Fair Value	106
		2-9:3.2	Prejudgment Interest	107
		2-9:3.3	Costs	107
		2-9:3.4	Exclusivity of Remedy	108
		2-9:3.5	Special Damages for Fraud	108
	2-9:4	Defenses		108
		2-9:4.1	Procedural Non-Compliance	108
	2-9:5	Procedural Implications		109
		2-9:5.1	Strict Compliance Requirement	109
		2-9:5.2	Interim Status of Ownership Interest	109
		2-9:5.3	Withdrawal of Demand	109
		2-9:5.4	Judicial Proceeding to Determine Fair Value	109
		2-9:5.5	Responsible Organization	110
2-10		Breach of Partnership Duty		110
	2-10:1	Overview		110
		2-10:1.1	Related Causes of Action	111
	2-10:2	Elements		111
	2-10:3	Damages and Remedies		113
		2-10:3.1	Actual Damages	113
		2-10:3.2	Interest	113
		2-10:3.3	Accounting	113
		2-10:3.4	Rescission	113
		2-10:3.5	Restitution	113
		2-10:3.6	Constructive Trust	113
		2-10:3.7	Forfeiture of Compensation	114
		2-10:3.8	Receivership	114
		2-10:3.9	Winding Up of Partnership	114
		2-10:3.10	Exemplary Damages	114
	2-10:4	Defenses		114
		2-10:4.1	Statute of Limitations	114
		2-10:4.2	Financial Incapability	115
		2-10:4.3	Abandonment of Business Opportunity	115
	2-10:5	Procedural Implications		115
		2-10:5.1	Who May Bring Suit	115

2-11	Usurpation of Business Opportunity			115
	2-11:1	Overview		115
		2-11:1.1	Related Causes of Action	115
	2-11:2	Elements		115
	2-11:3	Damages and Remedies		117
		2-11:3.1	Constructive Trust	117
		2-11:3.2	Turnover of Business Opportunity	117
		2-11:3.3	Forfeiture of Compensation	117
		2-11:3.4	Disgorgement	117
		2-11:3.5	Actual Damages	117
		2-11:3.6	Removal of Defendant from Office	117
		2-11:3.7	Exemplary Damages	117
	2-11:4	Defenses		118
		2-11:4.1	Statute of Limitations	118
		2-11:4.2	Financial Incapability	118
		2-11:4.3	Abandonment of Business Opportunity	118
		2-11:4.4	Ratification	119
2-12	Suit to Compel Inspection			119
	2-12:1	Overview		119
		2-12:1.1	Related Causes of Action	119
	2-12:2	Elements		119
		2-12:2.1	Corporation	119
		2-12:2.2	Limited Liability Company	121
		2-12:2.3	General Partnership	123
		2-12:2.4	Limited Partnership	124
		2-12:2.5	Public Offices Who May Compel Inspection	126
	2-12:3	Damages and Remedies		126
		2-12:3.1	Mandamus	126
		2-12:3.2	Costs	127
		2-12:3.3	Actual Damages	127
	2-12:4	Defenses—Corporations		127
		2-12:4.1	Improper Purpose	127
2-13	Suit to Pierce The Corporate Veil			128
	2-13:1	Overview		128
		2-13:1.1	Related Causes of Action	128
	2-13:2	Elements		129
		2-13:2.1	Contractual Obligations	129
		2-13:2.2	Tort Obligations	130
		2-13:2.3	Single Business Enterprise Theory	131
		2-13:2.4	Veil Piercing and Limited Liability Companies	131

TABLE OF CONTENTS

	2-13:3	Damages and Remedies		131
		2-13:3.1	Generally	131
	2-13:4	Defenses		132
		2-13:4.1	Statute of Limitations	132
	2-13:5	Trial by Jury		132
		2-13:5.1	The Jury's Role	132
2-14	Dissolution of Partnership—Judicial Expulsion of Partner			132
	2-14:1	Overview		132
		2-14:1.1	Related Causes of Action	132
	2-14:2	Elements		132
	2-14:3	Damages and Remedies		134
		2-14:3.1	Expulsion of the Partner	134
		2-14:3.2	Wrongful Withdrawal Remedies	134
	2-14:4	Defenses		134
		2-14:4.1	Unclean Hands	134
	2-14:5	Procedural Implications		134
		2-14:5.1	Effective Date of Expulsion	134
2-15	Dissolution of Partnership—Judicial Winding Up of Partnership			134
	2-15:1	Overview		134
		2-15:1.1	Related Causes of Action	135
	2-15:2	Elements		135
	2-15:3	Damages and Remedies		136
		2-15:3.1	Winding Up and Termination	136
		2-15:3.2	Receivership	136
		2-15:3.3	Attorney's Fees	137
	2-15:4	Defenses		137
		2-15:4.1	Unclean Hands	137
		2-15:4.2	Other Equitable Defenses	137
	2-15:5	Procedural Implications		137
		2-15:5.1	Venue	137
		2-15:5.2	Parties to be Named	137
2-16	Dissolution of Partnership—Wrongful Withdrawal of Partner			138
	2-16:1	Overview		138
		2-16:1.1	Related Causes of Action	138
	2-16:2	Elements		138
	2-16:3	Damages and Remedies		140
		2-16:3.1	Redemption/Contribution	140
		2-16:3.2	Damages	141
		2-16:3.3	Attorney's Fees	141

	2-16:3.4	Prior Partnership Liability	142
	2-16:3.5	Interest	142
	2-16:3.6	Setoff	142
	2-16:3.7	Additional Damages for Bad Faith Demand or Payment of Estimated Redemption	142
2-16:4	Defenses		142
	2-16:4.1	Statute of Limitations	142
2-16:5	Procedural Implications		143
	2-16:5.1	Who May Bring Suit	143
	2-16:5.2	What Issues May Be Litigated	143
	2-16:5.3	Effect of Partnership Agreement	143

Chapter 3 CONTRACT AND COMMERCIAL LITIGATION 145

3-1	Breach of Contract		145
	3-1:1	Introduction	145
		3-1:1.1 Related Causes of Action	145
	3-1:2	Elements	145
	3-1:3	Damages and Remedies	147
		3-1:3.1 Actual Damages	147
		3-1:3.1a Benefit-of-the-Bargain	147
		3-1:3.1b Out-of-Pocket Damages	148
		3-1:3.1c Restitution and Rescission Damages	148
		3-1:3.2 Quantum Meruit	148
		3-1:3.3 Unjust Enrichment	149
		3-1:3.4 Liquidated Damages	149
		3-1:3.5 Nominal Damages	149
		3-1:3.6 Specific Performance	150
		3-1:3.7 Rescission	150
		3-1:3.8 Reformation	150
		3-1:3.9 Declaratory Judgment	150
		3-1:3.10 Interest	150
		3-1:3.11 Court Costs	151
		3-1:3.12 Attorney's Fees	151
		3-1:3.13 Lost Profits	151
	3-1:4	Defenses	152
		3-1:4.1 Statute of Limitations	152
		3-1:4.2 Standing	152
		3-1:4.3 Repudiation	152
		3-1:4.3a Plaintiff-Repudiated Contract	152

TABLE OF CONTENTS

		3-1:4.4	Revocation	152
		3-1:4.5	Lack of Capacity	152
		3-1:4.6	Illegality	153
		3-1:4.7	Void as Against Public Policy	153
		3-1:4.8	Fraud	153
		3-1:4.9	Failure of Consideration	154
		3-1:4.10	Lack of Consideration	154
		3-1:4.11	Duress	154
		3-1:4.12	Mutual Mistake	155
		3-1:4.13	Unilateral Mistake	155
		3-1:4.14	Statute of Frauds	155
		3-1:4.15	Failure to Perform Condition Precedent	156
		3-1:4.16	Impossibility	156
		3-1:4.17	Accord and Satisfaction	156
		3-1:4.18	Novation	157
		3-1:4.19	Unconscionability	157
		3-1:4.20	Modification	158
		3-1:4.21	Release	158
3-2	Suit for Rescission			158
	3-2:1	Overview		158
		3-2:1.1	Related Causes of Action	158
	3-2:2	Elements		158
		3-2:2.1	Equitable Rescission	158
		3-2:2.2	Rescission by Consent	161
		3-2:2.3	Rescission by Option	162
	3-2:3	Damages and Remedies		163
		3-2:3.1	Rescission	163
		3-2:3.2	Special Damages	163
		3-2:3.3	Interest	163
		3-2:3.4	Exemplary Damages	163
	3-2:4	Defenses		163
		3-2:4.1	Statute of Limitations	163
		3-2:4.2	Laches	163
		3-2:4.3	Waiver or Ratification	163
		3-2:4.4	Other Equitable Defenses	164
	3-2:5	Procedural Implications		164
		3-2:5.1	Parol Evidence Rule	164
3-3	Quantum Meruit			164
	3-3:1	Overview		164
		3-3:1.1	Related Causes of Action	164

	3-3:2	Elements		164
	3-3:3	Damages and Remedies		165
		3-3:3.1	Reasonable Value	165
		3-3:3.2	Interest	165
	3-3:4	Defenses		166
		3-3:4.1	Statute of Limitations	166
		3-3:4.2	Express Contract	166
		3-3:4.3	Offset	166
		3-3:4.4	Res Judicata	166
		3-3:4.5	Equitable Defenses	167
3-4	Unjust Enrichment			167
	3-4:1	Overview		167
		3-4:1.1	Related Causes of Action	167
	3-4:2	Elements		167
	3-4:3	Damages and Remedies		168
		3-4:3.1	Restitution	168
	3-4:4	Defenses		168
		3-4:4.1	Statute of Limitations	168
		3-4:4.2	Valid Contract	169
		3-4:4.3	Other Defenses, Generally	169
	3-4:5	Procedural Implications		169
		3-4:5.1	Characterization as a Cause of Action	169
3-5	Promissory Estoppel			170
	3-5:1	Overview		170
		3-5:1.1	Related Causes of Action	170
	3-5:2	Elements		170
		3-5:2.1	As a Cause of Action	170
		3-5:2.2	As a Means of Enforcing a Contract Within the Statute of Frauds	171
	3-5:3	Damages and Remedies		171
		3-5:3.1	Reliance Damages	171
		3-5:3.2	Enforcement of the Promise	171
	3-5:4	Defenses		172
		3-5:4.1	Statute of Limitations	172
		3-5:4.2	Other Defenses, Generally	172
3-6	Money had and Received			172
	3-6:1	Overview		172
		3-6:1.1	Related Causes of Action	173
	3-6:2	Elements		173

TABLE OF CONTENTS

	3-6:3	Damages and Remedies		173
		3-6:3.1	Restitution	173
		3-6:3.2	Attorney's Fees	174
	3-6:4	Defenses		174
		3-6:4.1	Statute of Limitations	174
		3-6:4.2	Other Defenses, Generally	174
3-7	Suit on A Sworn Account			175
	3-7:1	Overview		175
		3-7:1.1	Related Causes of Action	175
	3-7:2	Elements		175
	3-7:3	Damages and Remedies		176
		3-7:3.1	Generally	176
		3-7:3.2	Effect of Verified Petition	176
	3-7:4	Defenses		176
		3-7:4.1	Generally	176
	3-7:5	Procedural Implications		176
		3-7:5.1	Pleading	176
3-8	Suit on an Account			177
	3-8:1	Overview		177
		3-8:1.1	Related Causes of Action	177
	3-8:2	Elements		177
		3-8:2.1	Suit on an Open Account	177
		3-8:2.2	Suit on an Account Stated	178
	3-8:3	Damages and Remedies		179
		3-8:3.1	Actual Damages	179
		3-8:3.2	Prejudgment Interest	179
		3-8:3.3	Attorney's Fees	179
	3-8:4	Defenses		179
		3-8:4.1	Statute of Limitations	179
		3-8:4.2	Payment	180
		3-8:4.3	Accord and Satisfaction	180
		3-8:4.4	Failure of Consideration	180
		3-8:4.5	Other Affirmative Defenses	180
	3-8:5	Procedural Implications		181
		3-8:5.1	Pleading—As Sworn Account	181
3-9	Bailment Actions—Bailee's Liability			181
	3-9:1	Overview		181
		3-9:1.1	Related Causes of Action	181
	3-9:2	Elements		181

	3-9:3		Damages and Remedies	183
		3-9:3.1	Generally	183
		3-9:3.2	Actual Damages	183
		3-9:3.3	Liquidated Damages	184
		3-9:3.4	Attorney's Fees	184
		3-9:3.5	Lost Profits	184
		3-9:3.6	Interest	184
		3-9:3.7	Loss of Use	184
		3-9:3.8	Repossession	184
		3-9:3.9	Acceleration	184
		3-9:3.10	Exemplary Damages	185
	3-9:4		Defenses	185
		3-9:4.1	Statute of Limitations	185
		3-9:4.2	Failure of Consideration	185
		3-9:4.3	Denial of Execution	185
3-10			Bailment Actions—Bailor's Liability	186
	3-10:1		Overview	186
		3-10:1.1	Related Causes of Action	186
	3-10:2		Elements	186
		3-10:2.1	Liability for Defects in the Subject of the Bailment	186
		3-10:2.2	Liability to a Third Party/Negligent Entrustment	188
	3-10:3		Damages and Remedies	189
		3-10:3.1	Actual Damages	189
		3-10:3.2	Liquidated Damages	189
		3-10:3.3	Attorney's Fees	189
		3-10:3.4	Lost Profits	189
		3-10:3.5	Interest	189
		3-10:3.6	Exemplary Damages	189
	3-10:4		Defenses	190
		3-10:4.1	Statute of Limitations	190
		3-10:4.2	Failure of Consideration	190
		3-10:4.3	Denial of Execution	190
		3-10:4.4	Negligent Entrustment Defenses	190
3-11			Agency Actions—Agent's Action Binding on the Principal	190
	3-11:1		Overview	190
		3-11:1.1	Related Causes of Action	191
	3-11:2		Elements	191
		3-11:2.1	Contractual Liability	191
		3-11:2.2	Tort Liability	193

	3-11:3	Damages and Remedies		194
		3-11:3.1	Generally	194
		3-11:3.2	Exemplary Damages	194
	3-11:4	Defenses		195
		3-11:4.1	Statute of Conveyances	195
3-12	Agency Actions—Agent Personally Liable on Contract Between Principal And Third Party			195
	3-12:1	Overview		195
		3-12:1.1	Related Causes of Action	195
	3-12:2	Elements		196
		3-12:2.1	Partially Disclosed or Undisclosed Principal	196
		3-12:2.2	Disclosed Principal	197
		3-12:2.3	Nonexistent or Legally Incompetent Principal	197
		3-12:2.4	Assumption of Liability	197
		3-12:2.5	Agent's Breach of the Warranty of Authority	197
		3-12:2.6	Tort Liability	198
	3-12:3	Damages and Remedies		199
		3-12:3.1	Contractual Liability	199
		3-12:3.2	Tort Liability	199
	3-12:4	Defenses		199
		3-12:4.1	Indemnity	199
		3-12:4.2	Breach of Warranty—Actual Damages	199
		3-12:4.3	Breach of Warranty—Quantum Meruit	199
3-13	Agency Actions—Agent Personally Liable for Breach of Duty			199
	3-13:1	Overview		199
		3-13:1.1	Related Causes of Action	200
	3-13:2	Elements		200
	3-13:3	Damages and Remedies		201
		3-13:3.1	Actual Damages	201
		3-13:3.2	Forfeiture of Fee	201
		3-13:3.3	Disgorgement	202
		3-13:3.4	Avoidance of Contract	202
		3-13:3.5	Breach of the Duty of Obedience	202
		3-13:3.6	Exemplary Damages	202
	3-13:4	Defenses		203
		3-13:4.1	Ratification	203
		3-13:4.2	Estoppel	203
		3-13:4.3	Statute of Limitations	203

Chapter 4		**PROFESSIONAL LIABILITY AND FIDUCIARY LITIGATION**		**205**
4-1	Legal Malpractice			205
	4-1:1	Overview		205
	4-1:2	Elements		205
	4-1:3	Damages and Remedies		207
		4-1:3.1	Actual Damages	207
		4-1:3.2	Interest	208
		4-1:3.3	Court Costs	208
		4-1:3.4	Mental Anguish	208
		4-1:3.5	Exemplary Damages	208
	4-1:4	Defenses		209
		4-1:4.1	Statute of Limitations	209
			4-1:4.1a Two-Year Statute of Limitations	209
			4-1:4.1b Accrues When Client Suffers Legal Injury	209
			4-1:4.1c The Discovery Rule Applies	209
	4-1:5	Related Causes of Action		210
4-2	Attorneys and Fiduciary Litigation			210
	4-2:1	Overview		210
	4-2:2	Elements		210
	4-2:3	Damages and Remedies		211
		4-2:3.1	Actual Damages	211
		4-2:3.2	Attorneys' Fee Forfeiture	211
	4-2:4	Defenses		212
		4-2:4.1	Statute of Limitations	212
Chapter 5		**INSURANCE LITIGATION**		**213**
5-1	Unfair Insurance Practices—Violations of the Texas Prompt Payment of Claims			213
	5-1:1	Overview		213
		5-1:1.1	Related Causes of Action	213
		5-1:1.2	Notice	213
	5-1:2	Elements		213
	5-1:3	Damages and Remedies		215
		5-1:3.1	Actual Damages	215
		5-1:3.2	Statutory Damages	215
		5-1:3.3	Prejudgment Interest	216
		5-1:3.4	Post-judgment Interest	216
		5-1:3.5	Court Costs	216
		5-1:3.6	Attorney's Fees	216

TABLE OF CONTENTS

5-2		Unfair Insurance Practices—Deceptive Insurance Practices		217
	5-2:1	Overview		217
		5-2:1.1	Related Causes of Action	217
	5-2:2	Notice		217
	5-2:3	Elements		218
	5-2:4	Damages and Remedies		219
		5-2:4.1	Actual Damages	219
			5-2:4.1a Lost Profits	220
			5-2:4.1b Lost Income	220
			5-2:4.1c Damaged Credit Reputation	220
			5-2:4.1d Damages for Personal Injury	220
		5-2:4.2	Additional Damages	220
		5-2:4.3	Injunction	220
		5-2:4.4	Other Relief	220
		5-2:4.5	Interest	221
		5-2:4.6	Court Costs	221
		5-2:4.7	Attorney's Fees	221
	5-2:5	Defenses		221
		5-2:5.1	Statute of Limitations	221
		5-2:5.2	Reducing Damages with Settlement Offer	221
5-3		Insurance Bad Faith		222
	5-3:1	Overview		222
		5-3:1.1	Related Causes of Action	222
	5-3:2	Elements		222
	5-3:3	Damages and Remedies		222
		5-3:3.1	Actual Damages	222
			5-3:3.1a Mental Anguish	222
			5-3:3.1b Loss of Credit Reputation	223
			5-3:3.1c Increased Business Costs	223
		5-3:3.2	Exemplary Damages	223
		5-3:3.3	Interest	223
		5-3:3.4	Court Costs	224
	5-3:4	Defenses		224
		5-3:4.1	Statute of Limitations	224
		5-3:4.2	Reasonable Basis	224
		5-3:4.3	Fraudulent Inducement	224
5-4		Uninsured Motorist/Underinsured Motorist (UM/UIM) Coverage Claim		225
	5-4:1	Overview		225
		5-4:1.1	Related Causes of Action	225

		5-4:2	Elements	226
		5-4:3	Damages and Remedies	226
			5-4:3.1 Actual Damages	226
			5-4:3.2 Interest	226
			5-4:3.3 Attorney's Fees	226
			5-4:3.4 Court Costs	226
		5-4:4	Defenses	227
			5-4:4.1 Limitations	227
			5-4:4.2 Rejection of Coverage	227
5-5	Declaratory Judgment on Policy—Coverage Claim			227
		5-5:1	Overview	227
			5-5:1.1 Related Causes of Action	227
		5-5:2	Requirements to Bring a Declaratory Judgment Action	228
			5-5:2.1 Elements	228
		5-5:3	Damages and Remedies	228
			5-5:3.1 Declaratory Judgment	228
			5-5:3.2 Court Costs	228
			5-5:3.3 Attorney's Fees	228
		5-5:4	Defenses	229
			5-5:4.1 Statute of Limitations	229
5-6	Declaratory Judgment on Policy—Duty to Defend			229
		5-6:1	Overview	229
			5-6:1.1 Related Causes of Action	229
		5-6:2	Elements	229
		5-6:3	Damages and Remedies	230
			5-6:3.1 Declaratory Judgment	230
			5-6:3.2 Court Costs	230
			5-6:3.3 Attorney's Fees	230
		5-6:4	Defenses	230
			5-6:4.1 Statute of Limitations	230
			5-6:4.2 No Timely Notice of Claim or Occurrence	231
			5-6:4.3 Did Not Cooperate	231
			5-6:4.4 Known Loss	231
5-7	*Stowers* Claim			231
		5-7:1	Overview	231
			5-7:1.1 Related Causes of Action	231
		5-7:2	Elements	231
		5-7:3	Damages and Remedies	233
			5-7:3.1 Actual Damages	233
			5-7:3.2 Exemplary Damages	233

TABLE OF CONTENTS xxix

	5-7:3.3	Court Costs	233
	5-7:3.4	Interest	233
5-7:4	Defenses		234
	5-7:4.1	Statute of Limitations	234
	5-7:4.2	No *Stowers* Demand	234
	5-7:4.3	Policy Exhausted	234

Chapter 6   EMPLOYMENT LITIGATION   235

6-1	Wrongful Discharge—Breach of Employment Agreement		235
	6-1:1	Overview	235
		6-1:1.1 Related Causes of Action	235
	6-1:2	Elements	235
	6-1:3	Damages and Remedies	237
		6-1:3.1 Actual Damages	237
		6-1:3.2 Interest	237
		6-1:3.3 Court Costs	238
		6-1:3.4 Attorney's Fees	238
	6-1:4	Defenses	238
		6-1:4.1 Statute of Limitations	238
		6-1:4.2 Good Cause	238
		6-1:4.3 Statute of Frauds	238
		6-1:4.4 Payment	239
		6-1:4.5 Mitigation of Damages	239
		6-1:4.6 Failure to Exhaust Administrative Remedies	239
6-2	Wrongful Discharge Refusal to Perform an Illegal Act		239
	6-2:1	Overview	239
		6-2:1.1 Related Causes of Action	239
	6-2:2	Elements	240
	6-2:3	Damages and Remedies	242
		6-2:3.1 Actual Damages	242
		6-2:3.2 Prejudgment Interest	242
		6-2:3.3 Injunction	242
		6-2:3.4 Reinstatement	242
		6-2:3.5 Exemplary Damages	242
	6-2:4	Defenses	243
		6-2:4.1 Statute of Limitations	243
		6-2:4.2 Sovereign Immunity	243

6-3		Employment Discrimination		243
	6-3:1	Overview		243
		6-3:1.1	Related Causes of Action	243
	6-3:2	Elements		243
	6-3:3	Damages and Remedies		245
		6-3:3.1	Compensatory Damages	245
		6-3:3.2	Prejudgment Interest	246
		6-3:3.3	Equitable Relief	246
		6-3:3.4	Punitive Damages	246
		6-3:3.5	Damage Cap	247
	6-3:4	Defenses		247
		6-3:4.1	Statute of Limitations	247
		6-3:4.2	Failure to Exhaust Administrative Remedies	248
		6-3:4.3	Waiver	248
		6-3:4.4	Business Necessity	248
		6-3:4.5	Bona Fide Occupational Qualification	248
		6-3:4.6	Reliance on Commission Interpretation or Opinion	249
		6-3:4.7	Employment by Religious Organization	249
		6-3:4.8	Bona Fide Employee Benefit Plan	249
		6-3:4.9	Undue Hardship Defense	249
		6-3:4.10	Other Statutory Defenses	249

Chapter 7	**OIL AND GAS LITIGATION**			**251**
7-1	Action to Quiet Title			251
	7-1:1	Overview		251
		7-1:1.1	Related Causes of Action	251
	7-1:2	Elements		251
	7-1:3	Damages and Remedies		252
		7-1:3.1	Judicial Declaration	252
		7-1:3.2	Attorney's Fees	252
	7-1:4	Defenses		252
		7-1:4.1	Limitations	252
		7-1:4.2	Quieting or Vesting of Title in Defendant	253
		7-1:4.3	Claim for Improvements	253
		7-1:4.4	Other Equitable Defenses	253
	7-1:5	Procedural Implications		253
		7-1:5.1	Venue	253
		7-1:5.2	Pleading Slander of Title	253
		7-1:5.3	Recording the Judgment	254

7-2	Trespass to Try Title			254
	7-2:1	Overview		254
		7-2:1.1	Related Causes of Action	254
	7-2:2	Elements		254
	7-2:3	Damages and Remedies		256
		7-2:3.1	Judicial Declaration of Title	256
		7-2:3.2	Writ of Possession	256
		7-2:3.3	Damages for Defendant's Use and Occupation of the Premises	257
		7-2:3.4	Damages for Special Injury to the Property	257
	7-2:4	Defenses		257
		7-2:4.1	Statute of Limitations	257
		7-2:4.2	Plaintiff's Claim to Title Is Invalid	257
		7-2:4.3	Superior Title in Defendant	258
		7-2:4.4	Claim for Improvements	258
	7-2:5	Procedural Implications		258
		7-2:5.1	Venue	258
		7-2:5.2	Plaintiff's Pleading Requirements	258
		7-2:5.3	Defendant's Pleading Requirements	259
			7-2:5.3a Defendant's Plea of Not Guilty	259
			7-2:5.3b Defendant's Specifically Plead Adverse Possession	259
			7-2:5.3c Defendant's Pleading Requirements	259
		7-2:5.4	Proof Requirements	259
7-3	Declaratory Judgment Action			259
	7-3:1	Overview		259
		7-3:1.1	Related Causes of Action	260
	7-3:2	Elements		260
	7-3:3	Damages and Remedies		261
		7-3:3.1	Judicial Declaration	261
		7-3:3.2	Attorney's Fees	261
	7-3:4	Defenses		261
		7-3:4.1	Statute of Limitations	261
		7-3:4.2	No Justiciable Controversy	261
		7-3:4.3	Improper Use of Declaratory Judgment Act	261
	7-3:5	Procedural Implications		262
		7-3:5.1	Venue	262
		7-3:5.2	Joinder	262

7-4		Forcible Entry and Detainer Action		262
	7-4:1	Overview		262
		7-4:1.1	Must Read Authority	263
7-5		Breach of Contract		263
	7-5:1	Overview		263
		7-5:1.1	Related Causes of Action	264
	7-5:2	Elements		264
	7-5:3	Damages and Remedies		265
		7-5:3.1	Compensatory Damages	265
		7-5:3.2	Termination of Lease	265
		7-5:3.3	Attorney's Fees	265
	7-5:4	Defenses		265
		7-5:4.1	Temporary Cessation Doctrine	265
		7-5:4.2	Express Lease Provisions	266
	7-5:5	Procedural Implications		266
		7-5:5.1	Venue	266
7-6		Suit in Assumpsit		267
	7-6:1	Overview		267
		7-6:1.1	Related Causes of Action	267
	7-6:2	Elements		267
	7-6:3	Damages and Remedies		268
		7-6:3.1	Use and Occupation Damages	268
	7-6:4	Defenses		268
		7-6:4.1	Statute of Limitations	268
	7-6:5	Procedural Implications		269
		7-6:5.1	Venue	269
7-7		Breach of Fiduciary Duty		269
	7-7:1	Overview		269
		7-7:1.1	Related Causes of Action	269
	7-7:2	Elements		269
	7-7:3	Damages and Remedies		271
		7-7:3.1	Imposition of Constructive Trust	271
	7-7:4	Defenses		271
		7-7:4.1	Statute of Limitations	271
	7-7:5	Procedural Implications		271
		7-7:5.1	Venue	271
7-8		Tort Conversion		271
	7-8:1	Overview		271
		7-8:1.1	Related Causes of Action	272
	7-8:2	Elements		272

TABLE OF CONTENTS xxxiii

		7-8:3	Damages and Remedies	273
		7-8:3.1	Value of Converted Property	273
		7-8:3.2	Exemplary Damages	273
		7-8:4	Defenses	274
		7-8:4.1	Statute of Limitations	274
		7-8:4.2	Rule of Capture	274
		7-8:5	Procedural Implications	274
		7-8:5.1	Venue	274
7-9	Public Nuisance			275
	7-9:1	Overview		275
		7-9:1.1	Related Causes of Action	275
	7-9:2	Elements		275
	7-9:3	Damages and Remedies		276
		7-9:3.1	Special Damages	276
		7-9:3.2	Injunction	276
	7-9:4	Defenses		277
		7-9:4.1	Statute of Limitations	277
		7-9:4.2	Standing	277
		7-9:4.3	Political Question Doctrine	279
		7-9:4.4	Preemption	279
		7-9:4.5	No Particularized Injury	279
		7-9:4.6	Causation	279
	7-9:5	Procedural Implications		280
		7-9:5.1	Choice of Law	280
7-10	Slander of Title			280
	7-10:1	Overview		280
		7-10:1.1	Related Causes of Action	280
	7-10:2	Elements		280
	7-10:3	Damages and Remedies		282
		7-10:3.1	Special Damages	282
		7-10:3.2	Exemplary Damages	283
		7-10:3.3	Attorney's Fees	283
	7-10:4	Defenses		283
		7-10:4.1	Statute of Limitations	283
		7-10:4.2	Acting on Advice of Counsel	284
	7-10:5	Procedural Implications		284
		7-10:5.1	Venue	284
7-11	Negligence			284
	7-11:1	Overview		284
		7-11:1.1	Related Causes of Action	284

	7-11:2	Elements		285
	7-11:3	Damages and Remedies		286
		7-11:3.1	Compensatory Damages	286
		7-11:3.2	Exemplary Damages	287
	7-11:4	Defenses		287
		7-11:4.1	Statute of Limitations	287
		7-11:4.2	Duty Created by Contract, Not Imposed by Law	287
		7-11:4.3	Contributory Negligence	288
7-12	Breach of Implied Covenant to Protect Against Drainage			288
	7-12:1	Overview		288
		7-12:1.1	Related Causes of Action	288
	7-12:2	Elements		288
	7-12:3	Damages and Remedies		290
		7-12:3.1	Value of the Royalty Lost	290
		7-12:3.2	Exemplary Damages Not Recoverable	290
		7-12:3.3	Future Drainage	290
		7-12:3.4	Conditional Cancellation	291
	7-12:4	Defenses		291
		7-12:4.1	Pooling	291
		7-12:4.2	Express Lease Provisions	291
		7-12:4.3	Statute of Limitations	291
	7-12:5	Procedural Implications		292
		7-12:5.1	Cotenants	292
		7-12:5.2	Obligation to Exercise Reasonable Diligence in Protecting Interests	292
7-13	Breach of Implied Covenant to Market			292
	7-13:1	Overview		292
		7-13:1.1	Related Causes of Action	293
	7-13:2	Elements		293
	7-13:3	Damages and Remedies		294
		7-13:3.1	Royalty	294
		7-13:3.2	Conditional Cancellation	294
	7-13:4	Defenses		295
		7-13:4.1	Market Value Lease	295
		7-13:4.2	Take-or-Pay Provisions	295
	7-13:5	Procedural Implications		295
		7-13:5.1	Class Certification	295
7-14	Breach of Implied Covenant to Reasonably Develop			296
	7-14:1	Overview		296
		7-14:1.1	Related Causes of Action	296

		7-14:2	Elements		297
		7-14:3	Damages and Remedies		298
			7-14:3.1	Full Value of Lost Royalty	298
			7-14:3.2	Cancellation of the Lease	299
		7-14:4	Defenses		299
			7-14:4.1	Express Lease Provisions	299
			7-14:4.2	Opportunity to Cure	300
		7-14:5	Procedural Implications		300
			7-14:5.1	Jury Instructions	300
			7-14:5.2	Opportunity to Cure	300

Chapter 8		**EQUITABLE AND EXTRAORDINARY RELIEF**			**301**
8-1		Temporary Injunction			301
	8-1:1	Overview			301
		8-1:1.1	Related Causes of Action		301
	8-1:2	Elements			301
	8-1:3	Damages and Remedies			303
		8-1:3.1	Injunction Order		303
		8-1:3.2	Scope of Injunction		303
	8-1:4	Defenses			304
		8-1:4.1	Unclean Hands		304
		8-1:4.2	Laches		304
	8-1:5	Procedural Implications			304
		8-1:5.1	Jurisdiction		304
		8-1:5.2	Venue		304
		8-1:5.3	Petition		305
		8-1:5.4	Notice		305
		8-1:5.5	Hearing		305
		8-1:5.6	Appeal		306
8-2		Permanent Injunction			306
	8-2:1	Overview			306
		8-2:1.1	Related Causes of Action		306
	8-2:2	Elements			306
	8-2:3	Pleadings			308
8-3		Specific Performance			308
	8-3:1	Overview			308
		8-3:1.1	Related Causes of Action		308
	8-3:2	Elements			309
	8-3:3	Damages and Remedies			311
		8-3:3.1	Decree of Specific Performance		311

	8-3:4	Defenses		312
		8-3:4.1	Statute of Limitations	312
		8-3:4.2	Laches	312
		8-3:4.3	Contractual Defenses	312
		8-3:4.4	Waiver	312
		8-3:4.5	Estoppel	312
		8-3:4.6	Other Equitable Defenses	313
	8-3:5	Procedural Implications		313
		8-3:5.1	Express Right to Specific Performance	313
		8-3:5.2	Joinder of Parties	313
		8-3:5.3	Election of Remedies	313
8-4	Accounting			313
	8-4:1	Overview		313
		8-4:1.1	Related Causes of Action	313
	8-4:2	Elements		314
		8-4:2.1	Equitable Accounting	314
		8-4:2.2	Other Grounds for an Accounting	315
	8-4:3	Damages and Remedies		315
		8-4:3.1	Order Requiring Accounting	315
		8-4:3.2	Judgment for Payment	316
		8-4:3.3	Interest	316
		8-4:3.4	Attorney's Fees	316
	8-4:4	Defenses		316
		8-4:4.1	Statute of Limitations	316
		8-4:4.2	Laches	316
		8-4:4.3	Unclean Hands	316
		8-4:4.4	Other Equitable Defenses	317
	8-4:5	Procedural Implications		317
		8-4:5.1	Jurisdiction	317
		8-4:5.2	Appeal of Order Granting or Denying Accounting	317
		8-4:5.3	Abandonment of the Remedy	317
		8-4:5.4	Separate Trials	317
		8-4:5.5	Appointment of Auditor	317
8-5	Constructive Trust			318
	8-5:1	Overview		318
		8-5:1.1	Related Causes of Action	318
	8-5:2	Elements		318
	8-5:3	Damages and Remedies		320
		8-5:3.1	Imposition of Constructive Trust	320

TABLE OF CONTENTS

		8-5:3.2	Scope of Constructive Trust	321
		8-5:3.3	Exemplary Damages	321
	8-5:4	Defenses		321
		8-5:4.1	Statute of Limitations	321
		8-5:4.2	Laches	322
		8-5:4.3	Other Equitable Defenses	322
8-6	Sequestration			322
	8-6:1	Overview		322
		8-6:1.1	Related Causes of Action	322
	8-6:2	Elements		322
	8-6:3	Damages and Remedies		324
		8-6:3.1	Issuance of the Writ	324
		8-6:3.2	Levy upon the Writ	325
		8-6:3.3	Sale of Perishable Personal Property	325
		8-6:3.4	Plaintiff May Reply	325
	8-6:4	Defenses		325
		8-6:4.1	Defendant's Replevy Bond	325
		8-6:4.2	Failure to Strictly Comply with Statutes	325
		8-6:4.3	Exemption from Execution	325
	8-6:5	Procedural Implications		326
		8-6:5.1	Sworn Application	326
		8-6:5.2	Posting of Bond	326
		8-6:5.3	Ex Parte Relief	327
		8-6:5.4	Service	327
		8-6:5.5	Joinder of Parties	327
		8-6:5.6	Amendment	327
		8-6:5.7	Dissolution or Modification of the Writ	327
8-7	Attachment			328
	8-7:1	Overview		328
		8-7:1.1	Related Causes of Action	328
	8-7:2	Elements		328
	8-7:3	Damages and Remedies		329
		8-7:3.1	Issuance of the Writ	329
		8-7:3.2	Levy upon the Writ	330
		8-7:3.3	Sale of Perishable Personal Property	330
		8-7:3.4	Costs and Interest	330
	8-7:4	Defenses		330
		8-7:4.1	Replevy Bond	330
		8-7:4.2	Failure to Strictly Comply with Statutes	330
		8-7:4.3	Exemption from Execution	331

TABLE OF CONTENTS

	8-7:5		Procedural Implications	331
		8-7:5.1	Sworn Application	331
		8-7:5.2	Posting of Bond	331
		8-7:5.3	Ex Parte Relief	332
		8-7:5.4	Service	332
		8-7:5.5	Joinder of Parties	332
		8-7:5.6	Amendment	332
		8-7:5.7	Dissolution or Modification of the Writ	332
		8-7:5.8	Third-Party Claimants	333
8-8	Garnishment			333
	8-8:1	Overview		333
		8-8:1.1	Related Causes of Action	333
	8-8:2	Elements		333
		8-8:2.1	Prejudgment Garnishment	333
		8-8:2.2	Post-judgment Garnishment	335
	8-8:3	Damages and Remedies		335
		8-8:3.1	Issuance of the Writ	335
		8-8:3.2	Execution on the Writ	336
		8-8:3.3	Costs and Interest	336
	8-8:4	Defenses		336
		8-8:4.1	Replevy Bond	336
		8-8:4.2	Failure to Strictly Comply with Statutes	336
		8-8:4.3	Validity of Underlying Judgment	336
		8-8:4.4	Exemption from Execution	337
		8-8:4.5	Setoff	337
	8-8:5	Procedural Implications		337
		8-8:5.1	Posting of Bond	337
		8-8:5.2	Ex Parte Relief	338
		8-8:5.3	Service	338
		8-8:5.4	Garnishee's Answer	338
8-9	Receivership			338
	8-9:1	Overview		338
		8-9:1.1	Related Causes of Action	339
	8-9:2	Elements		339
		8-9:2.1	Common Law Appointment	339
		8-9:2.2	Statutory Appointment	340
	8-9:3	Damages and Remedies		344
		8-9:3.1	Appointment of Receiver	344
		8-9:3.2	Receivership Fees	344

TABLE OF CONTENTS

	8-9:4	Defenses		344
		8-9:4.1	Defenses, Generally	344
	8-9:5	Procedural Implications		344
		8-9:5.1	Ex Parte Relief	344
		8-9:5.2	Posting of Bond	345
		8-9:5.3	Venue	345
8-10	Declaratory Judgment			345
	8-10:1	Overview		345
		8-10:1.1	Related Causes of Action	346
	8-10:2	Elements for Declaratory Judgment		346
	8-10:3	Damages and Remedies		348
		8-10:3.1	Declaratory Judgment	348
		8-10:3.2	Attorney's Fees	349
	8-10:4	Defenses		350
		8-10:4.1	Absence of a Justiciable Controversy	350
		8-10:4.2	Other Active Proceeding	350
		8-10:4.3	Plaintiff has no Justiciable Interest in the Controversy	350
		8-10:4.4	Other Exclusive Remedy	351
		8-10:4.5	Defenses to the Underlying Action	351
	8-10:5	Procedural Implications		351
		8-10:5.1	Joinder of Parties	351
		8-10:5.2	Subsequent Relief	351
8-11	Forcible Entry and Detainer			351
	8-11:1	Overview		351
		8-11:1.1	Related Causes of Action	352
	8-11:2	Elements		352
		8-11:2.1	Elements of Forcible Entry and Detainer	352
		8-11:2.2	Elements of Forcible Detainer	353
	8-11:3	Damages and Remedies		357
		8-11:3.1	Writ of Possession	357
		8-11:3.2	Unpaid Rent	357
		8-11:3.3	Attorney's Fees and Costs of Court	357
	8-11:4	Defenses		358
		8-11:4.1	Resolving Issue of Possession Necessarily Requires Resolution of Title Dispute	358
		8-11:4.2	Injunctive Relief	359
	8-11:5	Procedural Implications		359
		8-11:5.1	Notice to Vacate	359
		8-11:5.2	Jurisdiction	359

		8-11:5.3	Sworn Statement		359
		8-11:5.4	Concurrent Claims for Damages, Title Issues, etc.		360
Chapter 9	**MISCELLANEOUS BUSINESS CAUSES OF ACTION—BUSINESS CAUSES OF ACTION EXPRESSLY NOT RECOGNIZED IN TEXAS**				**361**
9-1	Action Against Opposing Attorney				361
	9-1:1	Overview			361
		9-1:1.1	Related Causes of Action		361
	9-1:2	Expressly Rejected in Texas			362
9-2	Confession of Judgment in Pre-suit Instrument				362
	9-2:1	Overview			362
	9-2:2	Expressly Rejected in Texas			362
9-3	Conspiracy to Breach Contract				362
	9-3:1	Overview			362
		9-3:1.1	Related Causes of Action		363
	9-3:2	Expressly Rejected in Texas			363
9-4	Conversion of Real Property				363
	9-4:1	Overview			363
		9-4:1.1	Related Causes of Action		364
	9-4:2	Expressly Rejected in Texas			364
9-5	Detrimental Reliance as Independent Tort Claim				364
	9-5:1	Overview			364
		9-5:1.1	Related Causes of Action		364
	9-5:2	Expressly Rejected in Texas			365
9-6	Embracery (Jury Tampering)				365
	9-6:1	Overview			365
		9-6:1.1	Related Causes of Action		365
	9-6:2	Expressly Rejected in Texas			366
9-7	Common Law Shareholder Oppression				366
	9-7:1	Overview			366
		9-7:1.1	Related Causes of Action		366
	9-7:2	Expressly Rejected in Texas			366
9-8	Grossly Negligent Inducement of Contract				366
	9-8:1	Overview			366
		9-8:1.1	Related Causes of Action		367
	9-8:2	Expressly Rejected in Texas			367

TABLE OF CONTENTS

9-9		Invasion of Privacy (False Light)	367
	9-9:1	Overview	367
		9-9:1.1 Related Causes of Action	368
	9-9:2	Expressly Rejected in Texas	368
9-10		Negligent Defense of Insured by Insurer	368
	9-10:1	Overview	368
		9-10:1.1 Related Causes of Action	368
	9-10:2	Expressly Rejected in Texas	368
9-11		Negligent Infliction of Emotional Distress	369
	9-11:1	Overview	369
		9-11:1.1 Related Causes of Action	369
	9-11:2	Expressly Rejected in Texas	369
9-12		Negligent Investigation of Employee Misconduct	369
	9-12:1	Overview	369
		9-12:1.1 Related Causes of Action	370
	9-12:2	Expressly Rejected in Texas	370
9-13		Liability of Successor for Tortious Conduct of Predecessor	370
	9-13:1	Overview	370
	9-13:2	Expressly Rejected in Texas	370
9-14		Wrongful Expulsion of Whistleblowing Partner	371
	9-14:1	Overview	371
		9-14:1.1 Related Causes of Action	371
	9-14:2	Expressly Rejected in Texas	371
9-15		Perjury	371
	9-15:1	Overview	371
		9-15:1.1 Related Causes of Action	372
	9-15:2	Expressly Rejected in Texas	372
9-16		"Prima Facie Tort"	372
	9-16:1	Overview	372
		9-16:1.1 Related Causes of Action	372
	9-16:2	Expressly Rejected in Texas	373
9-17		Retaliatory Discharge for Perception of Participation in Protected Activity	373
	9-17:1	Overview	373
		9-17:1.1 Related Causes of Action	373
	9-17:2	Expressly Rejected in Texas	373
9-18		Retaliatory Discharge for Protected Act of Third Party	374
	9-18:1	Overview	374
		9-18:1.1 Related Causes of Action	374
	9-18:2	Expressly Rejected in Texas	374

9-19	Spoliation of Evidence		374
	9-19:1	Overview	374
	9-19:2	Expressly Rejected in Texas	375
9-20	Tortious Interference with Fiduciary Duty		375
	9-20:1	Overview	375
		9-20:1.1 Related Causes of Action	375
	9-20:2	Expressly Rejected in Texas	375
9-21	Breach of Implied Warranty of Professional Services		376
	9-21:1	Overview	376
		9-21:1.1 Related Causes of Action	376
	9-21:2	Expressly Rejected in Texas	376
9-22	Whistleblower Action: Protection of Private Sector Employee		376
	9-22:1	Overview	376
		9-22:1.1 Related Causes of Action	376
	9-22:2	Expressly Rejected in Texas	377
9-23	Oil and Gas Litigation—Implied Covenant to Further Explore		377
	9-23:1	Overview	377
		9-23:1.1 Related Causes of Action	377
	9-23:2	Expressly Rejected in Texas	377

SECTION II   PLEADING DAMAGES

Chapter 10   GENERAL PLEADING REQUIREMENTS FOR DAMAGES IN BUSINESS LITIGATION — 381

10-1	Necessity of Pleading Damage Amount	381
10-2	Necessity for Match Between Pleading and Proof of Damages	382
10-3	Effect of Pleading General Damages	383
10-4	Necessity of Pleading Special Damages	384
10-5	Distinguishing Between Direct and Consequential Damages	384
10-6	Interplay Between Pleadings and Requirements of Request for Disclosure	385
10-7	Pleading Requirements for Statutory Damages Cap	386

Chapter 11   COMMON BUSINESS LITIGATION DAMAGES MODELS — 387

11-1	Choosing the Right Damage Model	387
11-2	Benefit-of-the-Bargain Damages	388
11-3	Out-of-Pocket Damages	389
11-4	Restitution (Misappropriation)-Damages	390

TABLE OF CONTENTS xliii

11-5		Contractual Damages and Remedies	390
	11-5:1	Uniform Commercial Code Statutory Remedies	390
	11-5:2	Seller's Uniform Commercial Code Statutory Remedies	391
	11-5:3	Buyer's UCC Statutory Remedies	391
	11-5:4	Pleading UCC Statutory Remedies	392
		11-5:4.1 Seller's Remedies	392
		11-5:4.2 Buyer's Remedies	393
	11-5:5	Pleading Contractually Defined Damages	393
	11-5:6	Pleading Damages on Sworn Accounts	394
	11-5:7	Pleading Benefit-of-the-Bargain and Out-of-Pocket Damages	396
	11-5:8	Pleading Contractual Remedies Other Than Damages	397
11-6		Lost Profit	399
	11-6:1	When to Use a Lost Profits Damage Model	399
	11-6:2	Using a Discount Rate in a Lost Profits Calculation	400
	11-6:3	Pleading Lost Profits	401
11-7		Loss of Value of a Business	402
	11-7:1	When to Use a Loss of Business Value Damage Model	402
	11-7:2	Common Loss of Business Value Damage Models	403
	11-7:3	Pleading Loss of Value of a Business	405
11-8		Property Valuation and Damages	405
	11-8:1	Real Property Valuation and Damages	406
	11-8:2	Personal Property Valuation and Damages	407
11-9		Other Pecuniary and Intangible Damages	409
	11-9:1	Loss of Credit or Injury to Credit Reputation	409
	11-9:2	Reputation Damages to a Corporation	409
	11-9:3	Reputation and Mental Anguish Damages to an Individual	409
11-10		Statutory Damages Specific to the Cause of Action	409
11-11		Equitable Remedies for Recovery of Monetary Funds	410
	11-11:1	Constructive Trust	411
	11-11:2	Unjust Enrichment	411
	11-11:3	Rescission or Restitution	413
	11-11:4	Quantum Meruit Damages	413
	11-11:5	Forfeiture and Disgorgement	414
	11-11:6	Accounting	414
	11-11:7	Money Had and Received	415
11-12		Exemplary Damages	415
11-13		Interest, Costs, and Attorney's Fees	416
	11-13:1	Prejudgment and Post-judgment Interest	416

	11-13:2	Costs of Suit	417
	11-13:3	Attorney Fees	418

Chapter 12 DEFENSIVE ISSUES RELATING TO DAMAGES — 419

12-1	Mitigation of Damages		419
12-2	Issues of Excessive or Double Recovery		421
	12-2:1	Duplicative Damages	421
	12-2:2	Excessive Damages	423
12-3	Economic Loss Rule		424

SECTION III PLEADING DEFENSES

Chapter 13 PLEADING BURDENS — 431

13-1	Distinguishing Pleading Burdens from Substantive Defenses		431
13-2	Due Order of Pleading Requirement		431
	13-2:1	Due Order of Pleading—Special Appearance	432
	13-2:2	Defects in the Special Appearance: Unsworn Motion	433
	13-2:3	Defects in the Special Appearance: No "Subject to" Language	433
	13-2:4	Special Appearance: Due Order of Hearing Requirement	434
	13-2:5	Due Order of Pleading—Motion to Transfer Venue	436
	13-2:6	Motion to Transfer Venue—Due Order of Hearing Requirement	437
13-3	The General Denial		438
	13-3:1	General Denial Defined	438
	13-3:2	General Denial Extending to Amendments	438
	13-3:3	Deemed General Denial to Counterclaim or Crossclaim	438
	13-3:4	Deemed General Denial—Effect on Amendments Within Seven Days of Trial	439
	13-3:5	Deemed General Denial—No Waiver of Special Appearance or Motion to Transfer Venue	440
	13-3:6	General Denial—Not Subject to Prohibition Against Groundless, Bad Faith Pleadings	440
13-4	Verified and Special Denials		440
	13-4:1	Certain Pleas to be Verified	440
	13-4:2	Verification—Personal Knowledge Requirement	442
	13-4:3	Verification—Exceptions to the Personal Knowledge Requirement	442

TABLE OF CONTENTS   xlv

	13-4:4	Verification—Who May Verify	443
	13-4:5	Verification—Unless Such Matters Appear of Record	444
	13-4:6	Denial of the Occurrence or Performance of a Condition Precedent	444
13-5	Affirmative Defenses		445
	13-5:1	Rule 94 as a Nonexclusive List of Affirmative Defenses	445
	13-5:2	Satisfying the Pleading Burden for Affirmative Defenses	447
13-6	Inferential Rebuttal Defenses		448
	13-6:1	Inferential Rebuttal Defenses Defined	448
	13-6:2	Examples of Inferential Rebuttal Defenses	449
	13-6:3	Charging the Jury on Inferential Rebuttal Defenses	449
	13-6:4	Pleading Requirements for Inferential Rebuttal Defenses	450

Chapter 14 SPECIAL AND VERIFIED DENIALS   451

14-1	Lack of Capacity	451
14-2	Another Suit Pending Between Same Parties for Same Claim	452
14-3	Defect of Parties	452
14-4	Denial of Partnership or Corporate Status	453
14-5	Denial of Execution of Written Instrument	453
14-6	Denial of Genuineness of Indorsement or Assignment	454
14-7	Denial of Notice and Proof of Loss or Claim	454
14-8	Denial of Assumed Name	454
14-9	Denial of Sworn Account	454
14-10	Denial of Condition Precedent	455
14-11	Failure or Lack of Consideration	455
14-12	Usurious Contract	455
14-13	Form of Verified Denial	455

Chapter 15 INFERENTIAL REBUTTAL DEFENSES   457

15-1	Sole Proximate Cause	457
15-2	Superseding Cause (I.E., New, and Independent Cause)	457
15-3	Failure to Mitigate	458
15-4	Unavoidable Occurrence or Sudden Emergency	459
	15-4:1 Unavoidable Occurrence	459
	15-4:2 Sudden Emergency	459
15-5	Act of God	459

Chapter 16	AFFIRMATIVE DEFENSES	461
16-1	Pleading Rules and Their Effect	461
16-2	Payment	461
	16-2:1 Elements	461
	16-2:2 Elements: Voluntary Payment	461
	16-2:3 Other Substantive Issues	462
16-3	Accord and Satisfaction	462
	16-3:1 Elements—Common Law	462
	16-3:2 Elements—Statutory	463
	16-3:3 Other Substantive Issues	463
16-4	Arbitration and Award	464
	16-4:1 Elements	464
16-5	Release	464
	16-5:1 Elements	464
	16-5:2 Other Substantive Issues	465
16-6	Waiver	465
	16-6:1 Elements	465
16-7	Res Judicata and Collateral Estoppel	465
	16-7:1 Elements—Res Judicata	466
	16-7:2 Elements—Collateral Estoppel	466
	16-7:3 Other Substantive Issues	466
16-8	Discharge in Bankruptcy	467
	16-8:1 Elements	467
	16-8:2 Other Substantive Issues	467
16-9	License	467
	16-9:1 Elements	468
16-10	Assumption of The Risk and Contributory Negligence	468
	16-10:1 Elements—Express Assumption of the Risk	468
	16-10:2 Elements—Contributory Negligence	468
	16-10:3 Other Substantive Issues	469
16-11	Duress	469
	16-11:1 Elements	469
	16-11:2 Other Substantive Issues	469
16-12	Estoppel	470
	16-12:1 Elements—Equitable Estoppel	470
	16-12:2 Elements—Promissory Estoppel	470
	16-12:3 Elements—Judicial Estoppel	471
16-13	Illegality	471
	16-13:1 Elements	472
	16-13:2 Other Substantive Issues	472

16-14	Failure of Consideration		472
	16-14:1	Elements	472
	16-14:2	Other Substantive Issues	473
16-15	Fraud		473
	16-15:1	Elements	473
	16-15:2	Other Substantive Issues	474
16-16	Statute of Frauds		474
	16-16:1	Elements	474
	16-16:2	Other Substantive Issues	475
16-17	Statute of Limitations		476
16-18	Laches		476
	16-18:1	Elements	476
	16-18:2	Other Substantive Issues	476
16-19	Parental Immunity		477

Chapter 17 STATUTES OF LIMITATIONS AND REPOSE 479

17-1	One-Year Statute of Limitations		479
17-2	Two-Year Statute of Limitations		480
17-3	Three-Year Statute of Limitations		481
17-4	Four-Year Statute of Limitations		481
	17-4:1	The Residual Four-Year Limitations Period	482
17-5	Five-Year Statute of Limitations		482
17-6	Six-Year Statute of Limitations		483
17-7	Ten-Year Statute of Limitations		483
17-8	Fifteen-Year Statute of Limitations		483
17-9	Limitations Established or Modified By Agreement		484
17-10	Commencement of Limitation Period		484
17-11	Suspending and Extending the Limitations Period		486
	17-11:1	Fraudulent Concealment	486
	17-11:2	Discovery Rule	487
	17-11:3	Disabilities	488
	17-11:4	Death of Claimant	488
	17-11:5	Military Service	489
	17-11:6	Absence from Texas	490
	17-11:7	Savings Statute for Jurisdictional Dismissals	490
17-12	Satisfying The Statute of Limitations		490
	17-12:1	Misnomer and Misidentification of Defendants	491
	17-12:2	Suit Against Defendant in Assumed or Common Name	492

17-13	Statutes of Repose		492
	17-13:1	Ten-Year Repose for Suits Against Architects, Engineers, Designers, Inspectors, and Surveyors	492
	17-13:2	Fifteen-Year Repose for Product Liability Actions	493
	17-13:3	Healthcare Liability Claims	494

Chapter 18 PROPORTIONATE RESPONSIBILITY, CONTRIBUTION, AND INDEMNITY   495

18-1	Scope of Chapter 33		495
18-2	Determination of Percentage of Responsibility		496
	18-2:1	Determination Made as to "Each Cause of Action"	496
	18-2:2	Determination Made as to Each Claimant, Defendant, Settling Person, and Responsible Third Party	497
	18-2:3	Percentage of Responsibility	498
18-3	Determining Amount of Recovery		498
18-4	Joint and Several Liability		499
18-5	Procedure for Designation of Responsible Third Parties		500
	18-5:1	Motion for Leave to Designate a Responsible Third Party	500
	18-5:2	Objection to a Motion for Leave to Designate a Responsible Third Party	501
	18-5:3	Motion to Designate Unknown Criminal as Responsible Third Party	501
	18-5:4	Motion to Strike the Designation of a Responsible Third Party	501
	18-5:5	Effect of Designation of Responsible Third Party	502
18-6	Contribution and Indemnity		502
	18-6:1	Right of Contribution for Jointly and Severally Liable Defendants	502
	18-6:2	Right of Contribution for Other Liable Defendants; Claim Against Contribution Defendant	503
	18-6:3	Indemnity	503

SECTION IV   SPECIAL PLEADING ISSUES

Chapter 19 TEXAS PLEADING STANDARDS   507

19-1	Necessity of Pleadings to Support the Charge	507
19-2	Texas Pattern Jury Charges and Other Sources for the Charge	508
19-3	Texas "Fair Notice" Standard for Pleadings	510

TABLE OF CONTENTS xlix

| 19-4 | Comparing Texas and Federal Pleading Requirements | 511 |
| 19-5 | Additional Pleading Requirements for Equitable Remedies | 513 |

Chapter 20   PLEADING TEXAS STATE COURT DISCOVERY LEVEL   515

20-1	The Requirement to Plead Discovery Level	515
20-2	Considerations Before Pleading Level 1	516
20-3	Considerations Before Pleading Level 2	520
20-4	Considerations Before Pleading Level 3	523
20-5	Responding to Pleading of Discovery Level	524

Chapter 21   PLEADING SUBJECT MATTER JURISDICTION IN TEXAS STATE TRIAL COURTS   525

21-1	The Subject Matter Jurisdiction of Texas Trial Courts	525
	21-1:1 Justice Courts	525
	21-1:2 Constitutional County Courts	525
	21-1:3 Statutory County Courts	526
	21-1:4 District Courts	527
	21-1:5 Statutory Probate Courts	528
21-2	Pleading and Determining Amount in Controversy	528
	21-2:1 Aggregation of Claims	528
	21-2:2 Presumption in Favor of Jurisdiction	529
	21-2:3 Judgment in Excess of Jurisdictional Maximum	530
21-3	Subject Matter Jurisdiction for Counter, Cross, and Third-Party Claims	530
21-4	Case or Controversy Requirement	531
21-5	Ecclesiastical Disputes	531
21-6	Exclusive Jurisdiction Lying with Agency	531
21-7	Exclusive Jurisdiction in Federal Court	531
21-8	Sovereign Immunity	532
21-9	Attacking Subject Matter Jurisdiction	532

Chapter 22   PLEADING TEXAS VENUE   535

22-1	Presumptions Accorded to Pleaded Venue Facts	535
22-2	Overview of the Texas Venue Scheme	536
22-3	General Venue Options	537
22-4	Mandatory Venue Options	540
22-5	Permissive Venue Options	542
22-6	Derivative Venue Options	543
22-7	Pleadings Attacking and Supporting Venue	544

TABLE OF CONTENTS

Chapter 23   PLEADING PARTIES AND METHODS OF SERVICE   547

23-1	Pleading Requirements for Parties	547
23-2	Addressing the Mispleading of Parties	549
23-3	Pleading Personal Jurisdiction over Nonresident Defendants	550
23-4	Pleading Method of Service	551

Chapter 24   PLEADING CHOICE OF LAW   553

24-1		General Principles Governing Choice of Law in Texas	553
	24-1:1	Texas Procedural Rules Applicable	553
	24-1:2	Necessity of a Conflict	553
	24-1:3	The Most Significant Relationship Test	554
	24-1:4	Most Significant Relationship Test in Tort Cases	554
	24-1:5	Most Significant Relationship Test in a Contract Case	555
	24-1:6	Most Significant Relationship Test in Property Cases	556
	24-1:7	Choice of Law Under the Uniform Commercial Code	556
	24-1:8	Other Texas Statutes Affecting Choice of Law	557
	24-1:9	The "Internal Affairs" Doctrine	558
	24-1:10	Application of Law Contrary to Fundamental Public Policy	558
24-2		Enforcing A Choice of Law Clause	559
24-3		Pleading and Proving Choice of Law	560
	24-3:1	Presumption in Favor of Texas Law	560
	24-3:2	Pleading and Proving Law of Other Jurisdiction	560

Chapter 25   PLEADING TO AVOID OR COMPEL ARBITRATION   563

25-1		Choice of Arbitration Law	563
	25-1:1	The Federal Arbitration Act	563
	25-1:2	The Texas Arbitration Act	564
	25-1:3	Texas Common Law of Arbitration	564
25-2		Compelling Arbitration	565
25-3		Resisting Arbitration	566
	25-3:1	Dispute Outside the Scope of the Agreement	566
	25-3:2	Resisting on Grounds Agreement Is Unconscionable	567
	25-3:3	Resisting on Ground of Fraud	567
	25-3:4	Waiver of Right to Arbitrate	568
25-4		Post Arbitration Proceedings	568
	25-4:1	Confirmation of an Award	569
	25-4:2	Vacating an Award	569
	25-4:3	Modifying or Correcting an Award	570

TABLE OF CONTENTS

Chapter 26	PLEADING TO RESIST OR ENFORCE A FORUM SELECTION CLAUSE		571
26-1	Enforcing A Forum Selection Clause		571
	26-1:1	Enforceability of Forum Selection Clauses Generally	571
	26-1:2	Distinguishing Forum Selection Clauses from Venue Selection Clauses	572
26-2	Resisting A Forum Selection Clause		573
	26-2:1	Fraud	573
	26-2:2	Waiver	574

Chapter 27	PLEADING REMOVAL AND REMAND			575
27-1	Removal Generally			575
27-2	Removal on Federal Question Grounds			575
	27-2:1	Federal Question Jurisdiction Defined		575
	27-2:2	Joinder of Federal and State Law Claims		576
27-3	Removal on Diversity of Citizenship Grounds			577
	27-3:1	Determining the Amount in Controversy Requirement		577
	27-3:2	The Complete Diversity Requirement		577
	27-3:3	Determining the Citizenship of the Parties		577
		27-3:3.1	Citizenship for Natural Persons	578
		27-3:3.2	Citizenship for Corporations	579
		27-3:3.3	Citizenship for Unincorporated Business Entities	579
		27-3:3.4	Citizenship Determined at the Time the Complaint Is Filed	580
	27-3:4	The Forum State Defendant Rule		581
	27-3:5	The Improperly (Also Known as Fraudulently) Joined Defendant		581
	27-3:6	Prohibition on Removal on Diversity Grounds After One Year		583
27-4	Cases made Non Removable by Statute			583
27-5	Removal Procedure			584
	27-5:1	Removal Venue		584
	27-5:2	The Contents of the Notice of Removal		584
	27-5:3	Deadline to Remove		585
	27-5:4	Unanimity of Consent Rule		585
	27-5:5	Deadline to Answer Following Removal		585
27-6	Remand			586

Chapter 28	**MOTIONS AND RESPONSES TO MOTIONS ATTACKING PLEADINGS**	**587**

28-1	Motions to Dismiss Baseless Causes of Action		587
	28-1:1	Scope of Application	587
	28-1:2	No Basis in Law or Fact	587
	28-1:3	Contents of Motion	588
	28-1:4	Timing of Motion, Response, and Hearing	588
	28-1:5	Ruling on the Motion	589
	28-1:6	Award of Costs and Attorney Fees Required	589
	28-1:7	Effect on Venue and Personal Jurisdiction	590
28-2	Special Exceptions		590
28-3	Pleas in Abatement		591
28-4	Texas Anti-SLAPP Act		592

Chapter 29	**AMENDMENT OF PLEADINGS**	**595**

29-1	Distinguishing Between Amended and Supplemental Pleadings	595
29-2	Effect of Amendment on Superseded Pleadings	596
29-3	Time Limits for Amendment of Pleadings	597
29-4	Motion for leave to Amend Pleadings	598
29-5	Trial Amendment to Pleadings	599
29-6	Trial by Consent	600
29-7	Post-Verdict Amendment of Pleadings	601

Chapter 30	**MAKING AND RESPONDING TO MOTIONS FOR SUMMARY JUDGMENT**	**603**

30-1	The Traditional Motion for Summary Judgment		603
	30-1:1	Timing of Motion and Response	603
	30-1:2	Burden of Persuasion	604
	30-1:3	Movant's Burden of Pleading	604
	30-1:4	Movant's Burden of Production	605
	30-1:5	Effect of a Legally Insufficient Motion	606
	30-1:6	Nonmovant's Burden of Pleading	606
	30-1:7	Nonmovant's Burden of Production	606
30-2	The No-Evidence Motion for Summary Judgment		607
	30-2:1	Timing of Motion and Response	607
	30-2:2	Availability of No-Evidence Motion	608
	30-2:3	Movant's Burden of Pleading	608
	30-2:4	Nonmovant's Burden of Production	609

TABLE OF CONTENTS

30-3		Summary Judgment Evidence	609
	30-3:1	Prohibition on Oral Testimony	609
	30-3:2	Deadlines for Filing Summary Judgment Evidence	609
	30-3:3	Affidavits: Personal Knowledge Requirement	610
	30-3:4	Affidavits: Requirement to Set Forth Facts Admissible at Trial	610
	30-3:5	Affidavits: Interested Witnesses	611
	30-3:6	Affidavits: Exhibits to Affidavits	611
	30-3:7	Sham and Bad Faith Affidavits	612
	30-3:8	Use of Discovery	612
	30-3:9	Pleadings as Summary Judgment Evidence	613
	30-3:10	Objecting to Summary Judgment Evidence	613
30-4		The Ruling	614
	30-4:1	Written	614
	30-4:2	Final Judgment	614

Table of Cases   615
Index   719

About this Book

Texas Commercial Causes of Action provides a single-volume source and pleading guide for both plaintiffs and defendants in Texas business litigation. The book presents the most common business litigation pleading issues in the order in which both plaintiff and defense counsel are likely to consider them. The first section identifies potential causes of action (along with their essential elements) that plaintiffs may want to plead. Each cause of action subsection concisely details the liability elements which must be pleaded and proven, the recoverable damage elements that are available, and the leading case law and statutory authority for these elements. The key defenses applicable to the cause of action are also noted. This format provides a method for efficiently reviewing and selecting the potential causes of action and damage elements which best fit the facts, while simultaneously considering or anticipating the most likely defenses to be raised.

The remaining sections of the book delve more fully into the detailed pleading and proof requirements for damages, defenses, and special pleading issues. Section two explains the various categories of damages routinely encountered in business litigation and provides the leading sources of authority for these damage categories. Since certain types of defenses (such as affirmative defenses, equitable defenses, those requiring special or verified denials, and those involving joinder of additional parties and designation of responsible third parties) require specific pleading, detailed guidance for pleading these defenses are discussed in the third section of this book.

The fourth section of the book addresses special pleading issues specific to business litigation in Texas state courts, including subject matter jurisdiction in the various Texas trial courts, pleading of parties and personal jurisdiction, pleading of venue, and Texas pleading standards generally. The overlapping grants of subject matter jurisdiction and venue options in Texas state courts offer strategic advantages for those familiar with the options and the different locales. Texas rules and statutes set forth a variety of requirements for pleading of parties in Texas. When out-of-state parties are involved, personal jurisdiction pleading requirements need to be considered. Texas rules also specify the interrelationship between the pleading of damages and the extent of discovery allowed. All of these issues are addressed in section four.

For the practitioner in Texas business litigation (and for courts hearing these cases), this book provides a concise and efficient reference point for drafting and determining the adequacy of pleadings in business litigation cases.

About the Authors

Jim Wren is the Leon Jaworski Chair of Practice & Procedure at Baylor Law School. He has 40 years of trial experience and is the Director of Baylor Law's nationally renowned Practice Court Program (comprising the civil procedure, evidence and advocacy courses required of all third-year Baylor students). Together with co-author Elizabeth Fraley, he is also Co-Director of Baylor Law's innovative Executive LL.M. in Litigation Management.

Prior to joining the Baylor Law faculty, Jim was designated annually as a Texas Super Lawyer in Business Litigation. He is the former National President of the National Board of Trial Advocacy (the largest ABA-accredited national certifying board for civil trial, criminal trial, and other legal specializations), and is board certified as a specialist in Civil Trial Law by both the National Board of Trial Advocacy and the Texas Board of Legal Specialization.

Jim is also the co-author with Jeremy Counseller and Elizabeth Fraley of *Texas Trial Procedure and Evidence* (ALM Publication, New York, 2020), and with Laura Brown of *Proving Damages to the Jury* (James Publishing, San Francisco, 2020).

Elizabeth M. Fraley is an Associate Professor of Law at Baylor Law School with 32 years of trial experience. She teaches in the nationally renowned Practice Court program and is co-director of Executive LL.M. in litigation management. Liz is past president of the Waco Chapter of ABOTA, serves as a national board member and on the editorial board for ABOTA's Voir Dire Magazine. She has published and lectured extensively on evidence, civil procedure and trial tactics and strategy. She has been designated as a Texas Super Lawyer annually since 2004 and has been named one of D Magazine's Best Lawyers in Dallas annually since 2011. In addition to her teaching and publishing responsibilities, Liz maintains an active trial practice.

Acknowledgements

Jim Wren gratefully acknowledges the continuing patience of his long-suffering wife Mindy, who knows that "mountain vacations" are really covers for extended work and writing sessions, and who still professes to love him anyway.

Liz Fraley appreciates her family's support during the creation of this book and their endless supply of breakfast tacos to fuel the writing process.

SECTION I
Texas Business and Contract Causes of Action

CHAPTER 1

Business Torts Litigation*

1-1 Tortious Interference with Existing Contract

1-1:1 Overview

A party to a contract does not commit a tort by merely breaching that agreement, absent some other duty imposed by law. However, a third party (a non-party to the contract) may incur tort liability when it intentionally interferes with an existing contract of another. A plaintiff will prevail on a cause of action for tortious interference with an existing contract if he can establish that a valid contract exists, that the defendant knew about the contract and intentionally interfered with it, and that the plaintiff suffered damages as a proximate result of the defendant's interference.

1-1:1.1 Related Causes of Action

Tortious Interference with Prospective Business Relations, Breach of Contract, Breach of Covenant not to Compete, Business Disparagement

MUST READ CASES

Prudential Ins. Co. of Am. v. Fin. Rev. Servs., Inc., 29 S.W.3d 74, 77 (Tex. 2000)

ACS Investors v. McLaughlin, 943 S.W.2d 426, 430 (Tex. 1997)

Juliette Fowler Homes, Inc. v. Welch Assocs., 793 S.W.2d 660 (Tex. 1990)

1-1:2 Elements

(1) The plaintiff must show a contract exists that is subject to interference.[1]

- A contract which is void, illegal or unenforceable on grounds of public policy cannot validly be the subject of a claim for tortious interference with existing contract.[2]

---

* The authors thank Miranda Chavez and Juan Antonio Solis for their assistance in the updating of this chapter.
[1] *Community Health Sys. Prof'l Servs. Corp. v. Hansen*, 525 S.W.3d 671, 689 (Tex. 2017).
[2] *Juliette Fowler Homes, Inc. v. Welch Assocs.*, 793 S.W.2d 660, 664–65 (Tex. 1990).

- A contract which is voidable but not void may still be the subject of a claim for tortious interference with existing contract.[3]

- Unenforceability of a contract pursuant to the statute of frauds has been held to eliminate an action for interference with a contract.[4]

- An employment contract terminable at will may or may not be sufficient to support an action for interference with a contract.[5]

- The plaintiff must present evidence that the defendant interfered with a specific contract, beyond simply showing that contracts generally exist.[6]

- A party generally cannot interfere with its own contract, but the corporate agent of the party who is motivated only by his own personal interests can be liable for tortious interference.[7]

(2) The defendant committed a willful and intentional act of interference with the contract.[8]

- The plaintiff must prove that the defendant had actual knowledge of the contract and the plaintiff's interest in it, or sufficient knowledge to lead a reasonable person to believe in the existence of the contract.[9]

- The plaintiff must prove that the defendant committed an act of interference with the plaintiff's contract by intentionally inducing or causing a party to the contract to breach.[10]

---

[3] *SJW Prop. Commerce, Inc. v. Sw. Pinnacle Props., Inc.*, 328 S.W.3d 121, 151–52 (Tex. App.—Corpus Christi–Edinburg 2010, pet. denied) *abrogated by Zorrilla v. Aypco Constr., II, LLC*, 469 S.W.3d 143 (Tex. 2015).

[4] *Overton v. Bengel*, 139 S.W.3d 754 (Tex. App.—Texarkana 2004, no pet.) (no claim for tortious interference with a contract which is unenforceable under the statute of frauds).

[5] *Sterner v. Marathon Oil Co.*, 767 S.W.2d 686, 688 (Tex. 1989) (a cause of action exists for tortious interference with a contract of employment terminable at will); *see also AmeriPath, Inc. v. Hebert*, 447 S.W.3d 319, 342 (Tex. App.—Dallas 2014, pet. denied) (the terminable-at-will status of a contract is no defense to a claim for tortious interference with existing contract); *but see Lazer Spot, Inc. v. Hiring Partners, Inc.*, 387 S.W.3d 40, 51 (Tex. App.—Texarkana 2012, pet. denied) (a claim of tortious interference with contract cannot be premised merely on the hiring of an at-will employee, without more).

[6] *Better Bus. Bureau of Metro. Houston, Inc. v. John Moore Servs., Inc.*, 441 S.W.3d 345, 361 (Tex. App.—Houston [1st Dist.] 2013, pet. denied).

[7] *Swank v. Sverdlin*, 121 S.W.3d 785, 800 (Tex. App.—Houston [1st Dist.] 2003, pet. denied) (citing Texas Supreme Court authority).

[8] *Washington Square Fin., LLC v. RSL Funding, LLC*, 418 S.W.3d 761, 767 (Tex. App.—Houston [14th Dist.] 2013, pet. denied) (citing Texas Supreme Court authority). To prove the willful and intentional interference element of a tortious interference claim, the plaintiff must show that the defendant was legally capable of tortious interference. *See Holloway v. Skinner*, 898 S.W.2d 793, 795–96 (Tex. 1995). To be legally capable of tortious interference, the defendant must be a stranger to the contract with which he allegedly interfered. *Holloway v. Skinner*, 898 S.W.2d 793, 794–95 (Tex. 1995); *Community Health Sys. Prof'l Servs. Corp. v. Hansen*, 525 S.W.3d 671, 690 (Tex. 2017).

[9] *Exxon Corp. v. Allsup*, 808 S.W.2d 648, 656 (Tex. App.—Corpus Christi 1991, writ denied).

[10] *John Paul Mitchell Sys. v. Randalls Food Mkts., Inc.*, 17 S.W.3d 721, 730–31 (Tex. App.—Austin 2000, pet. denied) (necessary that there be some act of interference or of persuading party to breach for tort liability to arise; merely participating in transaction does not

- A defendant interferes with a contract when the act makes performance more difficult and defendant intends to cause a breach.[11]
- The defendant's interference with the contract must have been intentional.[12]

(3) The willful and intentional act was a proximate cause of damage.[13]

- To establish tortious interference with contract requires meeting the classic proximate cause test with the component elements of cause in fact and foreseeability.[14]

(4) Actual damage or loss occurred to the plaintiff.[15]

- The measure of damages for tortious interference is the same as for breach of contract, to put plaintiff in the same economic position as if the contract had not been breached.[16]
- Despite the general rule equating tortious interference with contract and breach of contract damages, the rule is not without exception; damages for tortious interference with contract are necessarily limited to damages proximately caused by the act of interference and do not extend to any other breach of the contract that the contracting party happened to commit.[17]

1-1:3 Damages and Remedies

1-1:3.1 Actual Damages

Restatement (Second) of Torts § 774A provides:

One who is liable to another for interference with a contract or prospective contractual relation is liable for damages for

(a) the pecuniary loss of the benefits of the contract or the prospective relation;

(b) consequential losses for which the interference is a legal cause; and

(c) emotional distress or actual harm to reputation, if they are reasonably to be expected to result from the interference.[18]

---

constitute knowing inducement required to impose liability for tortious interference with contract); *see also Davis v. HydPro, Inc.*, 839 S.W.2d 137, 139 (Tex. App.—Eastland 1992, writ denied).

[11] *Moore v. Bushman*, 559 S.W.3d 645 (Tex. App.—Houston [14th Dist.] 2018, no pet.).
[12] *Southwestern Bell Tel. Co. v. John Carlo Tex., Inc.*, 843 S.W.2d 470, 472 (Tex. 1992).
[13] *Community Health Sys. Prof'l Servs. Corp. v. Hansen*, 525 S.W.3d 671, 690 (Tex. 2017).
[14] *Tex. Campaign for the Env't v. Partners Dewatering Int'l, LLC*, 485 S.W.3d 184 (Tex. App.—Corpus Christi 2016, no pet.).
[15] *Community Health Sys. Prof'l Servs. Corp. v. Hansen*, 525 S.W.3d 671, 690 (Tex. 2017).
[16] *Hill v. Heritage Res., Inc.*, 964 S.W.2d 89, 123 (Tex. App.—El Paso 1997, pet. denied).
[17] *Palla v. Bio-One, Inc.*, 424 S.W.3d 722, 726 (Tex. App.—Dallas 2014, no pet.).
[18] Restatement (Second) of Torts § 774A (1) (1979); *see Browning-Ferris, Inc. v. Reyna*, 852 S.W.2d 540, 549 (Tex. App.—San Antonio 1992), *rev'd on other grounds*, 865 S.W.2d 925 (Tex. 1993).

1-1:3.1a Pecuniary Loss

The measure of actual damages in tortious interference cases is the same as for breach of contract—to put the plaintiff back in the same economic position he would have occupied had the contract been performed.[19] See Chapter 11.

1-1:3.1b Mental Anguish

Mental anguish damages are recoverable.[20]

1-1:3.1c Injury to Reputation

Damages are potentially recoverable for actual harm to reputation resulting from the tortious interference.[21]

1-1:3.1d Lost Profits and Loss of Value of a Business

Lost profits are recoverable when they are reasonably calculable.[22]

When a plaintiff cannot show his own lost profits with a reasonable degree of certainty, a plaintiff may still be entitled to recover lost profits based upon the amount of profits the defendant realized on the contract.[23]

Where the result of interference is to put the plaintiff out of business, damages are the difference between the value of the plaintiff's business in the absence of the interference and the amount realized by liquidation.[24] See Chapter 11, Sections 11-4, 11-6, and 11-7.

1-1:3.2 Exemplary Damages

Exemplary damages are available in an action for tortious interference with a contract.[25] The Texas Supreme Court has recognized that "[e]xemplary damages are authorized under the Texas Civil Practice and Remedy Code when the claimant proves by clear and convincing evidence that the harm results from fraud, malice or gross negligence."[26] See Chapter 11, Section 11-12.

---

[19] *American Nat'l Petroleum Co. v. Transcon. Gas Pipe Line Corp.*, 798 S.W.2d 274, 278 (Tex. 1990).

[20] *Exxon Corp. v. Allsup*, 808 S.W.2d 648, 660–61 (Tex. App.—Corpus Christi 1991, writ denied); *Comstock Silversmiths, Inc. v. Carey*, 894 S.W.2d 56, 57 n.2 (Tex. App.—San Antonio 1995, no writ) (mental anguish damages are an available element of damages for an intentional tort).

[21] *See* Restatement (Second) of Torts § 774A (1)(c) (1979); *see also Knox v. Taylor*, 992 S.W.2d 40, 60 (Tex. App.—Houston [14th Dist.] 1999, no pet.).

[22] *Horizon Health Corp. v. Acadia Healthcare Co.*, 520 S.W.3d 848, 859–60 (Tex. 2017) (the amount of loss must be shown by competent evidence); *Fluor Enters., Inc. v. Conex Int'l, Corp.*, 273 S.W.3d 426, 447 (Tex. App.—Beaumont 2008, pet. denied).

[23] *Sandare Chem. Co. v. WAKO Int'l*, 820 S.W.2d 21, 24 (Tex. App.—Fort Worth 1991, no writ).

[24] *Gonzales v. Gutierrez*, 694 S.W.2d 384, 390 (Tex. App.—San Antonio 1985, no writ).

[25] *Exxon Corp. v. Allsup*, 808 S.W.2d 648, 661 (Tex. App.—Corpus Christi 1991, writ denied); *see also Texas Beef Cattle Co. v. Green*, 921 S.W.2d 203, 210 (Tex. 1996).

[26] *Dillard Dep't Stores, Inc. v. Silva*, 148 S.W.3d 370, 372–73 (Tex. 2004) (citing Tex. Civ. Prac. & Rem. Code Ann. § 41.003(a)).

BUSINESS TORTS LITIGATION

1-1:3.3 Injunctive Relief

A claim for tortious interference with contract can support a claim for injunctive relief.[27]

1-1:3.4 Interest

See Chapter 11, Section 11-13:1.

1-1:3.5 Court Costs

See Chapter 11, Section 11-13:2.

1-1:4 Defenses

1-1:4.1 Statute of Limitations

The two-year limitations period applies.[28] However, the one-year limitations period applies when the sole basis of the plaintiff's claim is a defamatory statement.[29]

- The cause of action accrues when the defendant interferes with the contract, and harm is caused to the plaintiff.[30]
- The discovery rule may apply if the injury is inherently undiscoverable and objectively verifiable.[31]

See Chapter 17.

1-1:4.2 Comparative Fault

An action for tortious interference is subject to proportionate responsibility.[32]

1-1:4.3 Privilege and Justification

A defendant may exercise his own legal rights or a good faith claim to a colorable legal right without incurring liability.[33] Unlike other jurisdictions, which require claimants to disprove privilege and justification, Texas treats privilege and justification as an affirmative defense that must be pleaded and proved by the defendant.

---

[27] *DP Sols., Inc. v. Rollins, Inc.*, 34 Fed. Appx. 150 (5th Cir. 2002); *Graham v. Mary Kay Inc.*, 25 S.W.3d 749, 755 (Tex. App.—Houston [14th Dist.] 2000, pet. denied).

[28] Tex. Civ. Prac. & Rem. Code Ann. § 16.003(a); *First Nat'l Bank of Eagle Pass v. Levine*, 721 S.W.2d 287, 288–89 (Tex. 1986).

[29] *Nath v. Tex. Children's Hosp.*, 446 S.W.3d 355, 370 (Tex. 2014) *reh'g denied* (Nov. 21, 2014); *Nationwide Bi-Weekly Admin., Inc. v. Belo Corp.*, 512 F.3d 137, 146–47 (5th Cir. 2007).

[30] *See Hill v. Heritage Res., Inc.*, 964 S.W.2d 89, 116 (Tex. App.—El Paso 1997, pet. denied).

[31] *Carl M. Archer Tr. No. Three v. Tregellas*, 566 S.W.3d 281, 290 (Tex. 2018).

[32] *See* Tex. Civ. Prac. & Rem. Code, Ch. 33; *see also White v. Zhou Pei*, 452 S.W.3d 527, 543 (Tex. App.—Houston [14th Dist.] 2014).

[33] *Wal-Mart Stores v. Sturges*, 52 S.W.3d 711, 727 (Tex. 2001).

1-1:4.4 Void Ab Initio

A defendant may avoid liability by proving that the contract at issue in the dispute is void ab initio (e.g., it is against public policy or attempts to carry out an illegal act).[34] However, it is not a defense that a contract is merely voidable.

1-2 Tortious Interference with Prospective Business Relationship

1-2:1 Overview

Tortious Interference with a Prospective Business Relationship is closely related to the cause of action for Tortious Interference with an Existing Contract. The biggest difference is the requirement that the defendant's conduct must be independently tortious to sustain a cause of action for Tortious Interference with a Prospective Business Relationship.

1-2:1.1 Related Causes of Action

Tortious Interference with Existing Contract, Breach of Contract, Breach of Covenant not to Compete, Business Disparagement

MUST READ CASE

Wal-Mart Stores, Inc. v. Sturges, 52 S.W.3d 711 (Tex. 2001)

1-2:2 Elements

(1) A reasonable probability that the plaintiff would have entered into a business relationship with a third party.[35]

- Although it is not necessary to prove that a contract would have certainly been made but for the interference, the transaction must have been reasonably probable, considering all of the facts and circumstances.[36]

- To establish a claim for tortious interference, a plaintiff must prove that more than mere negotiations occurred.[37]

- An existing business relationship may properly fall within this category of prospective business relationship.[38]

---

[34] E.g., *Jetall Cos. v. Four Seasons Distribs.*, 474 S.W.3d 780, 784 (Tex. App.—Houston [14th Dist.], no pet.).

[35] *Coinmach Corp. v. Aspenwood Apartment Corp.*, 417 S.W.3d 909, 923 (Tex. 2013).

[36] *Richardson-Eagle, Inc. v. William M. Mercer, Inc.*, 213 S.W.3d 469, 475–76 (Tex. App.—Houston [1st Dist.] 2006, pet. denied); *Hill v. Heritage Res., Inc.*, 964 S.W.2d 89, 109 (Tex. App.—El Paso 1997, pet. denied).

[37] See *Milam v. Nat'l Ins. Crime Bureau*, 989 S.W.2d 126, 132 (Tex. App.—San Antonio 1999, no pet.); *Caller–Times Publ'g Co. v. Triad Commc'ns, Inc.*, 855 S.W.2d 18, 24 (Tex. App.—Corpus Christi 1993, no writ).

[38] *Faucette v. Chantos*, 322 S.W.3d 901, 915 (Tex. App.—Houston [14th Dist.] 2010, no pet.).

BUSINESS TORTS LITIGATION

(2) The defendant either acted with a conscious desire to prevent the relationship from occurring or knew the interference was certain or substantially certain to occur as a result of the conduct.[39]

- Interference which is the incidental result of conduct undertaken for another purpose but with knowledge that interference would likely occur does not make it improper.[40]

(3) The defendant's conduct was independently tortious or unlawful.[41]

- "Independently tortious" does not mean the plaintiff must be able to prove all elements of an independent tort, but only that the defendant's conduct would be actionable under a recognized tort.[42]

- Conduct that is merely "sharp" or perceived as "unfair competition" is not actionable as the basis for tortious interference with prospective business relations.[43]

(4) The interference proximately caused the plaintiff's injury.[44]

- Conduct that results in delaying but not preventing the execution of a contract does not constitute tortious interference with a prospective business relationship.[45]

- At a minimum, the tortious conduct must constitute a cause in fact which prevented the prospective business relationship from coming to fruition, i.e. whether the act or omission was a substantial factor in causing the injury "without which the harm would not have occurred."[46]

(5) The plaintiff suffered actual damage or loss as a result.[47]

1-2:3 Damages and Remedies

1-2:3.1 Actual Damages

Restatement (Second) of Torts § 774A provides:

One who is liable to another for interference with a contract or prospective contractual relation is liable for damages for

---

[39] *Coinmach Corp. v. Aspenwood Apartment Corp.*, 417 S.W.3d 909, 923 (Tex. 2013).
[40] *Bradford v. Vento*, 48 S.W.3d 749, 757 (Tex. 2001); *Larson v. Family Violence & Sexual Assault Prevention Ctr.*, 64 S.W.3d 506, 517 (Tex. App.—Corpus Christi 2001, pet. denied).
[41] *Coinmach Corp. v. Aspenwood Apartment Corp.*, 417 S.W.3d 909, 923 (Tex. 2013); *Day v. Fed'n of State Med. Bds. of the U.S., Inc.*, 579 S.W.3d 810, 823–24 (Tex. App.—San Antonio 2019, no pet. h.) (analyzing tortious interference claim when defamation is the allegedly independent tortious conduct).
[42] *Wal-Mart Stores, Inc. v. Sturges*, 52 S.W.3d 711, 726 (Tex. 2001).
[43] *Wal-Mart Stores, Inc. v. Sturges*, 52 S.W.3d 711, 726 (Tex. 2001).
[44] *Coinmach Corp. v. Aspenwood Apartment Corp.*, 417 S.W.3d 909, 923 (Tex. 2013).
[45] *Texas Disposal Sys. Landfill, Inc. v. Waste Mgmt. Holdings, Inc.*, 219 S.W.3d 563, 590–91 (Tex. App.—Austin 2007, pet. denied).
[46] *COC Servs. v. Comp. U.S.A., Inc.*, 150 S.W.3d 654, 679 (Tex. App.—Dallas 2004, pet. denied); *Van Der Linden v. Khan*, 535 S.W.3d 179 (Tex. App.—Fort Worth 2017, no pet.).
[47] *Coinmach Corp. v. Aspenwood Apartment Corp.*, 417 S.W.3d 909, 923 (Tex. 2013).

(a) the pecuniary loss of the benefits of the contract or the prospective relation;

(b) consequential losses for which the interference is a legal cause; and

(c) emotional distress or actual harm to reputation, if they are reasonably to be expected to result from the interference.[48]

1-2:3.1a Pecuniary Loss

The measure of actual damages in tortious interference cases is the same as for breach of contract—to put the plaintiff back in the same economic position he would have occupied had the contract been performed.[49] *See* Chapter 11.

1-2:3.1b Mental Anguish

Mental anguish damages are recoverable.[50]

1-2:3.1c Injury to Reputation

Damages are potentially recoverable for actual harm to reputation resulting from the tortious interference.[51]

1-2:3.1d Lost Profits and Loss of Value of a Business

Lost profits are recoverable when they are reasonably calculable.[52]

A plaintiff may recover both lost profits and the loss of potential profits, thus allowing recovery for the loss of the future growth of the plaintiff's business.[53]

When a plaintiff cannot show lost profits with a reasonable degree of certainty, a plaintiff may still be entitled to recover lost profits based upon the amount of profits the defendant realized on the contract.[54]

Where the result of interference is to put the plaintiff out of business, damages are the difference between the value of the plaintiff's business in the absence of the

---

[48] Restatement (Second) of Torts § 774A (1) (1979); *see King v. Acker*, 725 S.W.2d 750, 754 (Tex. App.—Houston [1st Dist.] 1987, no writ). Texas has since rejected tortious interference with an inheritance as a cause of action. *See Archer v. Anderson,* 556 S.W.3d 228 (Tex. 2018). However, *King v Acker's* discussion on damages still applies to other interference causes of action.

[49] *American Nat'l Petroleum Co. v. Transcon. Gas Pipe Line Corp.*, 798 S.W.2d 274, 278 (Tex. 1990).

[50] *Exxon Corp. v. Allsup*, 808 S.W.2d 648, 660–61 (Tex. App.—Corpus Christi 1991, writ denied); *Comstock Silversmiths, Inc. v. Carey*, 894 S.W.2d 56, 57 n.2 (Tex. App.—San Antonio 1995, no writ) (mental anguish damages are an available element of damages for an intentional tort).

[51] *See* Restatement (Second) of Torts § 774A (1)(c) (1979); *see also Knox v. Taylor*, 992 S.W.2d 40, 60 (Tex. App.—Houston [14th Dist.] 1999, no pet.).

[52] *Horizon Health Corp. v. Acadia Healthcare Co.*, 520 S.W.3d 848, 859–60 (Tex. 2017) (the amount of loss must be shown by competent evidence); *Fluor Enters., Inc. v. Conex Int'l Corp.*, 273 S.W.3d 426, 447 (Tex. App.—Beaumont 2008, pet. denied).

[53] *Champion v. Wright*, 740 S.W.2d 848, 856 (Tex. App.—San Antonio 1987, writ denied).

[54] *Sandare Chem. Co. v. WAKO Int'l*, 820 S.W.2d 21, 24 (Tex. App.—Fort Worth 1991, no writ).

interference and the amount realized by liquidation.[55] *See* Chapter 11, Sections 11-4, 11-6 and 11-7.

1-2:3.2 Exemplary Damages

Exemplary damages are available in an action for tortious interference with prospective business relations.[56] The Texas Supreme Court has recognized that "[e]xemplary damages are authorized under the Texas Civil Practice and Remedy Code when the claimant proves by clear and convincing evidence that the harm results from fraud, malice or gross negligence."[57] *See* Chapter 11, Section 11-12.

1-2:3.3 Injunctive Relief

A claim for tortious interference with prospective business relations can support a claim for injunctive relief.[58]

1-2:3.4 Interest

See Chapter 11, Section 11-13:1.

1-2:3.5 Court Costs

See Chapter 11, Section 11-13:2.

1-2:4 Defenses

1-2:4.1 Statute of Limitations

The two-year limitations period applies.[59]

However, the one-year limitations period applies when the sole basis of the plaintiff's claim is a defamatory statement.[60]

The cause of action accrues when the defendant interferes with the contract.[61]

The discovery rule may apply if the injury is inherently undiscoverable.[62] *See* Chapter 17.

---

[55] *Gonzales v. Gutierrez*, 694 S.W.2d 384, 390 (Tex. App.—San Antonio 1985, no writ).
[56] *McGowan & Co., Inc. v. Bogan*, No. CIV.A. H-12-1716, 2015 WL 3422366 n.6 (S.D. Tex. May 27, 2015).
[57] *Dillard Dep't Stores, Inc. v. Silva*, 148 S.W.3d 370, 372–73 (Tex. 2004) (citing Tex. Civ. Prac. & Rem. Code Ann. § 41.003(a)).
[58] *Reagan Nat'l Advert. v. Vanderhoof Family Trust*, 82 S.W.3d 366, 369 (Tex. App.—Austin 2002, no pet.).
[59] Tex. Civ. Prac. & Rem. Code Ann. § 16.003(a); *First Nat'l Bank of Eagle Pass v. Levine*, 721 S.W.2d 287, 288–89 (Tex. 1986).
[60] *Nath v. Tex. Children's Hosp.*, 446 S.W.3d 355, 370 (Tex. 2014) *reh'g denied* (Nov. 21, 2014); *Nationwide Bi-Weekly Admin., Inc. v. Belo Corp.*, 512 F.3d 137, 146–47 (5th Cir. 2007).
[61] *See Hill v. Heritage Res. Inc.*, 964 S.W.2d 89, 116 (Tex. App.—El Paso 1997, pet. denied).
[62] *Carl M. Archer Tr. No. Three v. Tregellas*, 566 S.W.3d 281, 290 (Tex. 2018).

1-2:4.2 Comparative Fault

An action for tortious interference is subject to proportionate responsibility.[63]

1-2:4.3 Privilege and Justification

A defendant may exercise his own legal rights or a good faith claim to a colorable legal right without incurring liability.[64] Unlike other jurisdictions, which require claimants to disprove privilege and justification, Texas treats privilege and justification as an affirmative defense that must be pleaded and proved by the defendant.

1-2:4.4 Void Ab Initio

A defendant may avoid liability by proving that the contract at issue in the dispute is void ab initio (e.g., it is against public policy or attempts to carry out an illegal act).[65] However, it is not a defense that a contract is merely voidable.

1-3 Conversion

1-3:1 Introduction

The unauthorized and wrongful assumption and exercise of dominion and control over the personal property of another, to the exclusion of or inconsistent with the owner's rights, is in law a conversion. To constitute a conversion, it is not necessary that there be a manual taking of the property in question.

1-3:1.1 Related Causes of Action

Fraud, Breach of Fiduciary Duty, Money had and received, Negotiable Instruments, Quantum Meruit, Security Deposit Statute (Texas Property Code Section 92.109), Texas Theft Liability Act (Civil Practice and Remedies Code Sections 134.001–134.005)

1-3:2 Elements

(1) The plaintiff must have either ownership, possession, or the right to immediate possession of the property.[66]

- The property in question must be personal property because Texas does not recognize a cause of action for conversion of real property.[67]

---

[63] *See* Tex. Civ. Prac. & Rem. Code Ann., Ch. 33; *see also White v. Zhou Pei*, 452 S.W.3d 527, 543 (Tex. App.—Houston [14th Dist.] 2014).

[64] *Wal-Mart Stores v. Sturges*, 52 S.W.3d 711, 727 (Tex. 2001).

[65] *E.g., Jetall Cos. v. Four Seasons Distribs.*, 474 S.W.3d 780, 784 (Tex. App.—Houston [14th Dist.] 2014, no pet.).

[66] *FCLT Loans, L.P. v. Estate of Bracher*, 93 S.W.3d 469, 482 (Tex. App.—Houston [14th Dist.] 2002, no pet.).

[67] *Lucio v. John G. & Marie Stella Kenedy Mem'l Found.*, 298 S.W.3d 663, 672 (Tex. App.—Corpus Christi–Edinburg 2009, pet. denied); *see also Augillard v. Madura*, 257 S.W.3d 494, 500–03 n.15 (Tex. App.—Austin 2008, no pet.) (recognizing that animals, whether owned as pets or livestock, are personal property subject to conversion).

- The property in question must be tangible personal property because Texas generally does not recognize a cause of action for conversion of intangible property[68] or money.[69]

(2) The defendant wrongfully exercised dominion and control over the plaintiff's property in denial of or inconsistent with the plaintiff's rights.[70]

- Defendant does not have to manually take the property for an act of conversion to occur, provided there is an unauthorized and wrongful exercise of control over the property to the exclusion of or inconsistent with the owner's rights.[71]

- Property initially obtained legally may still be the basis of a suit for conversion when the property departs so far from the conditions under which it was received as to amount to an assertion of right inconsistent with the owner's.[72]

- However, there is authority for the argument that where a defendant's conduct would give rise to liability only because it breaches the parties' agreement, the plaintiff's claim ordinarily sounds only in contract, and the tort of conversion can be barred by the economic loss rule.[73]

- A wrongful intent by the defendant is not necessary; it suffices that the defendant intends to assert a right in the property.[74]

(3) Plaintiff made a demand for the property which the defendant refused.[75]

- An exception to the demand requirement exists when the defendant's acts of control constitute a clear repudiation of the plaintiff's rights which would excuse a demand[76] or when the demand would be useless.[77]

---

[68] *Robin Singh Educ. Servs., Inc. v. Test Masters Educ. Servs., Inc.*, 401 S.W.3d 95, 97–98 (Tex. App.—Houston [14th Dist.] 2011, no pet.) ("Texas law has never recognized a cause of action for conversion of intangible property except in cases where an underlying intangible right has been merged into a document and that document has been converted.").

[69] *Houston Nat'l Bank v. Biber*, 613 S.W.2d 771, 774–75 (Tex. App.—Houston [14th Dist.] 1981, writ ref'd n.r.e.) (action for conversion of money only when there is an obligation resting on the defendant not to convert specific coin or notes to his own use, as opposed to a general debt to pay money).

[70] *Waisath v. Lack's Stores, Inc.*, 474 S.W.2d 444, 446 (Tex. 1971).

[71] *Waisath v. Lack's Stores, Inc.*, 474 S.W.2d 444, 447 (Tex. 1971).

[72] *Pierson v. GFH Fin. Servs. Corp.*, 829 S.W.2d 311, 314 (Tex. App.—Austin 1992, no writ).

[73] *Exxon Mobil Corp. v. Kinder Morgan Operating L.P.*, 192 S.W.3d 120, 126–28 (Tex. App.—Houston [14th Dist.] 2006, no pet.) (referring to the economic loss rule as the independent injury rule); *Lincoln General Ins. Co. v. U.S. Auto Ins. Servs.*, 787 F. 3d 716, 726 (5th Cir. 2015) (economic loss rule generally bars a tort claim when no factual basis for the tort claim would exist had the defendant complied with the contract). See discussion of the Texas economic loss rule in Chapter 12, Section 12-3.

[74] *Winkle Chevy-Olds-Pontiac v. Condon*, 830 S.W.2d 740, 746 (Tex. App.—Corpus Christi 1992, writ dism'd).

[75] *Wise v. SR Dallas, LLC*, 436 S.W.3d 402, 412 (Tex. App.—Dallas 2014, no pet.).

[76] *Automek, Inc. v. Orandy*, 105 S.W.3d 60, 63–64 (Tex. App.—Houston [1st Dist.] 2003, no pet.); *Whitaker v. Bank of El Paso*, 850 S.W.2d 757, 760 (Tex. App.—El Paso 1993, no writ).

[77] *First State Bank, N.A. v. Morse*, 227 S.W.3d 820, 827 (Tex. App.—Amarillo 2007, no pet.).

(4) The plaintiff suffered actual loss or injury as a natural and proximate result of the defendant's conversion.[78]

1-3:3 Damages and Remedies

1-3:3.1 Actual Damages

Actual damages and the return of property are recoverable.[79] They are measured by the sum of money necessary to compensate the plaintiff for all actual losses, not merely the reasonable market value of the property.[80] *See* Chapters 10 and 11.

1-3:3.1a Loss of Value

General measure of damages for loss of value is the fair market value of the property at the time and place of the conversion.[81]

When conversion involves fraud, willful wrong, or gross negligence, and the property converted was of a changing value, damages for conversion may be measured by the fair market value at its highest rate for the period between the date of conversion and the date of filing suit.[82]

Measure of damages for stocks and bonds is the highest intermediate value of the stock between the time of conversion and a reasonable time after the owner has received notice of the conversion.[83]

Damages are measured by intrinsic value of the property when the converted property is without market value.[84]

1-3:3.1b Loss of Use

If the plaintiff recovers the converted property, damages for loss of use may be obtained for the period during which the plaintiff was deprived of its use.[85]

---

[78] *Wells Fargo Bank Nw., N.A. v. RPK Capital XVI, L.L.C.*, 360 S.W.3d 691, 706 (Tex. App—Dallas 2012, no pet.).

[79] *See Winkle Chevy-Olds-Pontiac, Inc. v. Condon*, 830 S.W.2d 740, 746 (Tex. App.—Corpus Christi 1992, writ dism'd) (plaintiff establishing conversion is entitled to return of the property and damages for loss of use during the tort-feasor's detention).

[80] *Alan Reuber Chevrolet, Inc. v. Grady Chevrolet, Ltd.*, 287 S.W.3d 877, 889 (Tex. App.—Dallas 2009, no pet.).

[81] *Imperial Sugar Co. v. Torrans*, 604 S.W.2d 73, 74 (Tex. 1980); *United Mobile Networks, L.P. v. Deaton*, 939 S.W.2d 146, 147–48 (Tex. 1997) ("Generally, the measure of damages for conversion is the fair market value of the property at the time and place of the conversion."). *Perdue v. Pfeifer*, No. 04-16-00396-CV, 2017 WL 1337645, at *3 (Tex. App.—San Antonio Apr. 12, 2017); *see also Violet Rose Holdings, Ltd. v. Spinning Star Energy, LLC*, No. 01-17-00022-CV, 2018 WL 1526169, at *2 (Tex. App.—Houston [1st Dist.] Mar. 29, 2018).

[82] *Imperial Sugar Co. v. Torrans*, 604 S.W.2d 73, 74 (Tex. 1980).

[83] *Reed v. White, Weld & Co., Inc.*, 571 S.W.2d 395, 397 (Tex. Civ. App.—Texarkana 1978, no writ).

[84] *Williams v. Dodson*, 976 S.W.2d 861, 864 (Tex. App.—Austin 1998, no pet.).

[85] *Luna v. N. Star Dodge Sales, Inc.*, 667 S.W.2d 115, 119 (Tex. 1984).

1-3:3.1c Loss of Profits

A party who loses the opportunity to accrue earnings from the use of its converted property may also be entitled to recover loss of use damages in the form of lost profits.[86] See Chapter 11, Sections 11-4, 11-6, and 11-7.

1-3:3.2 Exemplary Damages

Exemplary damages may be recovered in a conversion action, in which case attorney's fees may be considered when determining the amount of exemplary damages.[87] See Chapter 11, Section 11-12.

1-3:3.3 Injunctive Relief

Injunction and temporary restraining orders are available.[88] See Chapter 8, Sections 8-1, 8-2, and 8-3.

1-3:3.4 Interest

See Chapter 11, Section 11-13:1.

1-3:3.5 Court Costs

See Chapter 11, Section 11-13:2.

1-3:4 Defenses

1-3:4.1 Qualified Good Faith Refusal

While an absolute refusal to transfer possession to one entitled to it generally constitutes conversion, a refusal to deliver property on request may be justified in order to investigate the rights of the parties, and no conversion results if such refusal is made in good faith to resolve a doubtful matter.[89] Any reasons for refusing to turn over the property which are not mentioned at the time of the refusal are lost and may not be raised later.[90]

1-3:4.2 Statute of Limitations

The two-year statute of limitations applies.[91]

---

[86] *Wiese v. Pro Am. Servs., Inc.*, 317 S.W.3d 857, 863 (Tex. App.—Houston [14th Dist.] 2010, no pet.); *see Amelia's Auto., Inc. v. Rodriguez*, 921 S.W.2d 767, 771 (Tex. App.—San Antonio 1996, no pet.).

[87] *R.J. Suarez Enters. Inc. v. PNYX L.P.*, 380 S.W.3d 238, 249 (Tex. App.—Dallas 2012, no pet.).

[88] *See Taiwan Shrimp Farm Vill. Ass'n v. U.S.A. Shrimp Farm Dev., Inc.*, 915 S.W.2d 61, 65 (Tex. App.—Corpus Christi 1996, writ denied).

[89] *Edmunds v. Sanders*, 2 S.W.3d 697, 703–04 (Tex. App.—El Paso 1999, pet. denied).

[90] *Edmunds v. Sanders*, 2 S.W.3d 697, 703–04 (Tex. App.—El Paso 1999, pet. denied).

[91] Tex. Civ. Prac. & Rem. Code Ann. § 16.003(a); *Burns v. Rochon*, 190 S.W.3d 263, 271 (Tex. App.—Houston [1st Dist.] 2006, no pet.).

1-3:4.3 Good Faith Purchaser

- Defendant purchased the goods for value;[92]
- The goods were purchased from a seller who received the goods under a transaction of purchase;[93] and
- The purchase was made in good faith.[94]
- The seller's transaction of purchase must have been voluntary.[95]
- Good faith means honesty in fact and observance of reasonable commercial standards of fair dealing.[96]

1-3:4.4 Buyer in the Ordinary Course of Business

The plaintiff entrusted the property to a third party;

- The seller is a merchant who deals in the kind of goods that were sold to the buyer; and
- The defendant was a buyer in the ordinary course of business.

Defense that defendant entrusted goods to a merchant who deals in goods of that kind and that the buyer was in the ordinary course of business.[97]

1-3:4.5 Possession After Repair

Defense that the defendant took possession of an article it repaired after the plaintiff did not pay for the work.[98]

1-3:4.6 Comparative Fault

Although the proportionate responsibility statute by its terms applies to "any cause of action based on tort," and would therefore apply to a common law tort claim for conversion, it has been found not to apply to statutory conversion claims where its application would be disruptive of the statutory fault-allocation scheme.[99] *See* Chapter 18, Section 18-2:3.

---

[92] *See* Tex. Bus. & Com. Code Ann. § 2.403(a).
[93] *See* Tex. Bus. & Com. Code Ann. § 2.403(a).
[94] *See* Tex. Bus. & Com. Code Ann. § 2.403(a).
[95] *Kotis v. Nowlin Jewelry, Inc.*, 844 S.W.2d 920, 922 (Tex. App.—Houston [14th Dist.] 1992, no writ).
[96] *Carter v. Cookie Coleman Cattle Co., Inc.*, 271 S.W.3d 856, 859–60 (Tex. App.—Amarillo 2008, no pet.).
[97] Tex. Bus. & Com. Code Ann. § 2.403(b).
[98] Tex. Prop. Code Ann. § 70.001(a); *Smith v. Maximum Racing, Inc.*, 136 S.W.3d 337, 341–42 (Tex. App.—Austin 2004, no pet.).
[99] *Challenger Gaming Sols., Inc. v. Earp*, 402 S.W.3d 290, 293–99 (Tex. App.—Dallas 2013, no pet.) (declining to apply proportionate responsibility in a UFTA conversion claim), citing *Sw. Bank v. Info. Support Concepts, Inc.*, 149 S.W.3d 104, 111 (Tex. 2004) (concluding proportionate responsibility statute does not apply to conversion claims under article 3 of the Uniform Commercial Code because article 3 has its own loss-allocation scheme).

1-3:4.7 Express or Implied Consent

The owner's express or implied consent to the taking of the property is a bar to a claim for conversion.[100]

1-4 Common Law Fraud

1-4:1 Overview

Common law fraud in the United States is a tort that is derived from the original English action of deceit. In sum, a plaintiff bringing a common law fraud claim must plead with specificity and particularity that the opposing party intentionally or recklessly represented a material and false past or existing fact with the intent to cause the plaintiff to act in accordance with the representation and that the plaintiff ignorantly and reasonably relied upon the representation to her injury.

1-4:1.1 Related Causes of Action

Statutory Fraud, Fraud by Non-Disclosure, Uniform Fraudulent Transfer Act (UFTA), Negligent Misrepresentation, Breach of Fiduciary Duty

MUST READ CASES

Italian Cowboy Partners, Ltd. v. Prudential Ins. Co. of Am., 341 S.W.3d 323 (Tex. 2011)

Grant Thornton LLP v. Prospect High Income Fund, 314 S.W.3d 913 (Tex. 2010)

Formosa Plastics Corp. U.S.A. v. Presidio Eng'rs & Contractors, Inc., 960 S.W.2d 41 (Tex. 1998)

1-4:2 Elements

(1) A material representation was made.[101]

- A fraudulent representation may be made to the plaintiff either directly or indirectly, and a person intending to defraud another may make the representation to that person, or he may make such representation to another with the intent that it should be repeated to the intended party for the purpose of deceiving him,[102] or with knowledge of "an especial likelihood" that it will reach and influence the conduct of a specific party.[103]

---

[100] *See Gronberg v. York*, 568 S.W.2d 139, 144–45 (Tex. Civ. App.—Tyler 1978, writ ref'd n.r.e.).

[101] *Italian Cowboy Partners, Ltd. v. Prudential Ins. Co. of Am.*, 341 S.W.3d 323, 337 (Tex. 2011). An actionable representation is one concerning a material fact; a pure expression of opinion will not support an action for fraud. *Trenholm v. Ratcliff*, 646 S.W.2d 927, 930 (Tex. 1983). *See also Transport Ins. Co. v. Faircloth*, 898 S.W.2d 269, 276 (Tex. 1995).

[102] *Neuhaus v. Kain*, 557 S.W.2d 125, 138 (Tex. Civ. App.—Corpus Christi 1977, writ ref'd n.r.e.).

[103] *Ernst & Young, L.L.P. v. Pac. Mut. Life Ins. Co.*, 51 S.W.3d 573, 581 (Tex. 2001).

(2) The representation was false.[104]

- A promise of future performance constitutes an actionable misrepresentation only if the promise was made with no intention of performing at the time it was made and with the intent to deceive.[105]
- An actionable misrepresentation may be expressed by conduct or by a combination of words and conduct.[106]

(3) When the representation was made, the defendant knew it was false or made it recklessly without any knowledge of the truth and as a positive assertion of fact.[107]

- Proof that a defendant made a statement knowing of its falsity or without knowledge of its truth may be proved by direct or circumstantial evidence.[108]

(4) The defendant made the representation with the intent that the other party should act upon it.[109]

- The requirement of showing an intent to induce reliance is not satisfied by evidence that a misrepresentation may be read in the future by some unknown member of the public or of a specific industry; the "reason-to-expect standard requires more than mere foreseeability . . . ."[110]

(5) The plaintiff acted in reliance on the representation.[111]

- The plaintiff must show actual and justifiable reliance on the misrepresentation, and "a person may not justifiably rely on a representation if 'there are "red flags" indicating such reliance is unwarranted.'"[112]
- Evidence the plaintiff conducted an independent investigation can indicate the absence of reliance, but evidence only of the opportunity to investigate, by itself, does not negate reliance.[113]

(6) The plaintiff thereby suffered injury.[114]

- Damages for fraud may vary from what is recoverable for fraudulent inducement, which is a particular species of fraud that arises only in the context of an existent contract.[115]

---

[104] *Italian Cowboy Partners, Ltd. v. Prudential Ins. Co. of Am.*, 341 S.W.3d 323, 337 (Tex. 2011).
[105] *Formosa Plastics Corp. U.S.A. v. Presidio Eng'rs & Contractors, Inc.*, 960 S.W.2d 41, 48 (Tex. 1998).
[106] *Douglas v. Neill*, 545 S.W.2d 903, 905–06 (Tex. Civ. App.—Texarkana 1977, writ ref'd n.r.e.).
[107] *Italian Cowboy Partners, Ltd. v. Prudential Ins. Co. of Am.*, 341 S.W.3d 323, 337 (Tex. 2011).
[108] *Johnson & Higgins of Tex., Inc. v. Kenneco Energy, Inc.*, 962 S.W.2d 507, 526 (Tex. 1998).
[109] *Italian Cowboy Partners, Ltd. v. Prudential Ins. Co. of Am.*, 341 S.W.3d 323, 337 (Tex. 2011).
[110] *Exxon Corp. v. Emerald Oil & Gas Co.*, 348 S.W.3d 194, 219 (Tex. 2011) (quoting *Ernst & Young, L.L.P. v. Pac. Mut. Life Ins. Co.*, 51 S.W.3d 573, 580 (Tex. 2001)).
[111] *Italian Cowboy Partners, Ltd. v. Prudential Ins. Co. of Am.*, 341 S.W.3d 323, 337 (Tex. 2011).
[112] *Grant Thornton LLP v. Prospect High Income Fund*, 314 S.W.3d 913, 923 (Tex. 2010) (quoting *Lewis v. Bank of Am. NA*, 343 F.3d 540, 546 (Tex. 2003)).
[113] *Pleasant v. Bradford*, 260 S.W.3d 546, 553–55 (Tex. App.—Austin 2008, pet. denied).
[114] *Italian Cowboy Partners, Ltd. v. Prudential Ins. Co. of Am.*, 341 S.W.3d 323, 337 (Tex. 2011).
[115] *Haase v. Glazner*, 62 S.W.3d 795, 798–99 (Tex. 2001).

- Tort damages for fraudulent inducement are recoverable regardless of whether the representations are later subsumed in a contract or whether the defrauded party suffers only economic loss related to the contract.[116]
- The economic loss rule may bar recovery of damages for fraud other than fraudulent inducement when the damages are the subject of a contract.[117]

1-4:3 Damages and Remedies

1-4:3.1 Actual Damages

Actual damages for fraud may be either the direct damages which compensate for the necessary and usual result of the fraud (including benefit-of-the-bargain damages or out-of-pocket damages), or consequential damages which result naturally, but not necessarily, from the act and which must be specially pleaded.[118] *See* Chapters 10 and 11.

1-4:3.1a Benefit-of-the-Bargain

Under the benefit-of-the-bargain measure, lost profits on the fraudulent bargain may be recovered if proved with reasonable certainty, but only to the extent of profits that would have been made if the bargain had been performed as promised.[119] *See* Chapter 11, Section 11-2. The benefit-of-the-bargain measure of damages may be barred by the economic loss rule, however, unless the plaintiff can demonstrate a source of duty independent of the contract.[120] *See* Chapter 12, Section 12-3.

1-4:3.1b Out-of-Pocket

Out-of-pocket damages are recoverable to the extent they are caused by the fraud.[121] *See* Chapter 11, Section 11-3.

1-4:3.1c Damages to Personal Property

Damages for repair costs of personal property are recoverable.[122]

1-4:3.1d Mental Anguish

Mental anguish damages are recoverable.[123]

---

[116] *Scott v. Sebree*, 986 S.W.2d 364, 370–71 (Tex. App.—Austin 1999, pet. denied).

[117] *Heil Co. v. Polar Corp.*, 191 S.W.3d 805, 815–17 (Tex. App.—Fort Worth 2006, pet. denied) (referring to the economic loss rule as the independent injury rule).

[118] *Anderson v. Durant*, 550 S.W.3d 605, 614 (Tex. 2018).

[119] *Formosa Plastics Corp. U.S.A. v. Presidio Eng'rs & Contractors, Inc.*, 960 S.W.2d 41, 50 (Tex. 1998).

[120] *James J. Flanagan Shipping Corp. v. Del Monte Fresh Produce N.A., Inc.*, 403 S.W.3d 360, 365–66 (Tex. App.—Houston [1st Dist.] 2013, no pet.).

[121] *Ghosh v. Grover*, 412 S.W.3d 749, 757–758 (Tex. App.—Houston [14th Dist.] 2013, no pet.).

[122] *See Trenholm v. Ratcliff*, 646 S.W.2d 927, 933 (Tex. 1983).

[123] *Tony Gullo Motors I, L.P. v. Chapa*, 212 S.W.3d 299, 304 (Tex. 2006).

1-4:3.2 Exemplary Damages

Exemplary damages are recoverable.[124]

Exemplary damages are not recoverable for constructive fraud.[125] *See* Chapter 11, Section 11-12.

1-4:3.3 Equitable Remedies

For the equitable remedies of rescission or reformation of contracts obtained through fraud, *see* Chapter 8, Sections 8-4 and 8-5.

1-4:3.3a Rescission

Rescission is available to avoid the defendant's unjust enrichment.[126] A party must rescind within a reasonable time from discovering the grounds for rescission.[127] *See* Chapter 8, Section 8-4.

1-4:3.3b Reformation

Reformation is available as an equitable remedy to conform the contract to the original intent of the parties.[128] *See* Chapter 8, Section 8-5.

1-4:3.4 Interest

See Chapter 11, Section 11-13:1.

1-4:3.5 Costs

See Chapter 11, Section 11-13:2.

1-4:4 Defenses

1-4:4.1 Statute of Limitations

Limitations:

- The four-year limitations period applies.[129]

- Generally, causes of action accrue, and statutes of limitation begin to run, when facts come into existence that authorize a claimant to seek a judicial remedy,

---

[124] Tex. Civ. Prac. & Rem. Code Ann. § 41.003(a)(1); *Tony Gullo Motors I, L.P. v. Chapa*, 212 S.W.3d 299, 304 (Tex. 2006).
[125] Tex. Civ. Prac. & Rem. Code Ann. § 41.001(6).
[126] *See Italian Cowboy Partners, Ltd. v. Prudential Ins. Co. of Am.*, 341 S.W.3d 323, 344 (Tex. 2011).
[127] *Italian Cowboy Partners, Ltd. v. Prudential Ins. Co. of Am.*, 341 S.W.3d 323, 344 (Tex. 2011).
[128] *Gilbane Bldg. Co. v. Keystone Structural Concrete, Ltd.*, 263 S.W.3d 291, 301 (Tex. App.—Houston [1st Dist.] 2007).
[129] Tex. Civ. Prac. & Rem. Code Ann. § 16.004(a)(4); *Shannon v. Law-Yone*, 950 S.W.2d 429, 433 (Tex. App.—Fort Worth 1997, pet. denied).

but a person cannot be permitted to avoid liability for his actions by deceitfully concealing wrongdoing until limitations period has run.[130] Limitations period applicable to claim of fraudulent inducement does not start to run until the fraud with respect to the contract is discovered or the exercise of reasonable diligence would discover it.[131]

See Chapter 17.

1-4:4.2 Disclaimer of Reliance Contractual Disclaimer

A defendant may avoid liability if the plaintiff's fraud claim is barred by a contractual disclaimer expressing clear and unequivocal intent to disclaim reliance on specific representations.[132] This defense, if successfully proved, negates the justifiable reliance element of a plaintiff's fraud claim.

A party must clearly and specifically disclaim reliance to bar an action for fraud.[133] If this threshold issue is met, courts will balance other factors, such as whether the contract was negotiated or boilerplate[134] and whether the complaining party was represented by counsel during the negotiations.[135] A merger clause without more, however, is insufficient to clearly and unequivocally disclaim reliance.[136]

Although Texas historically recognized this defense only when the underlying agreement ended a long-running dispute (e.g., settlement agreement[137]), the Texas Supreme Court recently enforced a disclaimer of reliance when the underlying agreement symbolized the start of a business relationship.[138]

1-4:4.3 Ratification

Ratification may be asserted against a plaintiff who continues to accept the benefits of fraudulent dealings after learning of the fraud.[139] See Chapter 8, Section 8-4:4.4.

---

[130] *Hooks v. Samson Lone Star, Ltd. P'Ship*, 457 S.W.3d 52, 57 (Tex. 2015), *reh'g denied* (May 1, 2015).

[131] *Hooks v. Samson Lone Star, Ltd. P'Ship*, 457 S.W.3d 52, 57 (Tex. 2015), *reh'g denied* (May 1, 2015); *Little v. Smith*, 943 S.W.2d 414, 420 (Tex. 1997).

[132] *Italian Cowboy Partners, Ltd. v. Prudential Ins. Co. of Am.*, 341 S.W.3d 323, 337 (Tex. 2011) (defense that the plaintiff's fraud claim is barred by contractual disclaimer expressing clear and unequivocal intent to disclaim reliance on specific representations); *see also Armstrong v. Am. Home Shield Corp.*, 333 F.3d 566, 571 (5th Cir. 2003) (applying Texas law).

[133] *Sclumberger Tech. Corp. v. Swanson*, 959 S.W.2d 171, 179 (Tex. 1997); *Citizens Nat'l Bank v. Allen Rae Invs., Inc.*, 142 S.W.3d 459, 475 (Tex. App.—Fort Worth 2004, no pet.).

[134] Note, however, that the disclaimer of reliance itself need not have been negotiated as long as other "deal points" are negotiated. *Int'l Bus. Machs. Corp. v. Lufkin Indus. LLC*, 573 S.W.3d 224, 229 n.4 (Tex. 2019).

[135] *Forest Oil Corp. v. McAllen*, 268 S.W.3d 51, 60 (Tex. 2008).

[136] *Italian Cowboy Partners, Ltd. v. Prudential Ins. Co. of Am.*, 341 S.W.3d 323, 338 (Tex. 2011).

[137] *E.g., Forest Oil Corp. v. McAllen*, 268 S.W.3d 51, 60–61 (Tex. 2008).

[138] *Int'l Bus. Machs. Corp. v. Lufkin Indus. LLC*, 573 S.W.3d 224, 229 n.4 (Tex. 2019).

[139] *Fortune Prod. v. Conoco, Inc.*, 52 S.W.3d 671, 678 (Tex. 2000).

1-4:4.4 Statute of Frauds

The statute of frauds defense is only available where the plaintiff seeks benefit-of-the-bargain damages based upon an unenforceable contract.[140]

1-4:4.5 Attacking Justifiable Reliance

Although fraud plaintiffs have no general duty to investigate the truth of representations, in arm's length transactions, they will be presumed to have knowledge of facts that a reasonably prudent person similarly situated would have discovered.[141] Thus, a plaintiff's fraud claim may fail if she has information, or reasonably could have discovered information, that would serve as a danger signal.[142]

For example, in a claim for fraudulent inducement predicated upon an agreement that is negotiated at arm's length, a plaintiff cannot justifiably rely on an oral misrepresentation that the agreement directly contradicts, even if no other "red flags" indicate fraud that may have occurred.[143]

1-5 Statutory Fraud

1-5:1 Overview

Statutory fraud is specific to fraud in real estate and stock transactions,[144] with essentially all except one of the same elements as common-law fraud (excluding the requirement that the defendant's knowledge of falsity or recklessness must be proven).[145] Statutory fraud allows recovery of the same actual damages as common-law fraud[146] but with the additional ability to also recover attorney fees and other litigation fees.[147]

1-5:1.1 Related Causes of Action

Common Law Fraud, Fraud by Non-Disclosure, Uniform Fraudulent Transfer Act (UFTA), Negligent Misrepresentation, DTPA, Breach of Fiduciary Duty, Breach of Contract

---

[140] *Baylor Univ. v. Sonnichsen*, 221 S.W.3d 632, 636 (Tex. 2007).
[141] *Thigpen v. Locke*, 363 S.W.2d 247, 251 (Tex. 1962).
[142] Although there has been considerable disagreement among Texas courts as to whether a failure to use due diligence can bar a claim for fraudulent inducement, the Texas Supreme Court's recent decisions suggest that it can. *See, e.g., JPMorgan Chase Bank, N.A. v. Orca Assets, G.P., LLC*, 546 S.W.3d 648, 660 (Tex. 2018).
[143] *Mercedes-Benz USA, LLC v. Carduco, Inc.*, 583 S.W.3d 553, 558–59 (Tex. 2019).
[144] Tex. Bus. & Com. Code Ann. § 27.01.
[145] *Trinity Indus., Inc. v. Ashland, Inc.*, 53 S.W.3d 852, 867 (Tex. App.—Austin 2001, pet. denied).
[146] *Scott v. Sebree*, 986 S.W.2d 364, 368 (Tex. App.—Austin 1999, pet. denied).
[147] Tex. Bus. & Com. Code Ann. § 27.01(e).

1-5:2 Elements

(1) There was a transaction involving real estate or stock in a corporation or joint stock company.[148]

- A transaction occurs if there is either a sale or a contract to sell real estate or stock.[149]

(2) During the transaction, the defendant either:

- (1) made a false representation of past or existing material fact, and (2) for the purpose of inducing the person to enter into a contract;[150] or

- (1) made a false promise to do an act which was material, (2) made with the intention of not fulfilling it, and (3) for the purpose of inducing the person to enter into a contract;[151] or

- (1) had actual awareness of the falsity of a representation or promise made by another person, (2) failed to disclose the falsity of the representation or promise to the person defrauded, and (3) benefitted from the false representation or promise.[152]

(3) The plaintiff relied on the false representation or promise in entering into the contract.[153]

- Reliance is a necessary element of a statutory fraud claim, and a disclaimer of reliance can conclusively negate an allegation of reliance.[154]

(4) Actual damages to the plaintiff from the false representation or promise.[155]

1-5:3 Damages and Remedies

1-5:3.1 Actual Damages

The same damages recoverable for common law fraud are recoverable for statutory fraud, with the addition of attorney's fees and other litigation fees.[156]

1-5:3.1a Benefit-of-the-Bargain

Benefit-of-the-bargain damages are recoverable for statutory fraud.[157]

---

[148] Tex. Bus. & Com. Code Ann. § 27.01(a).
[149] *Tukua Invs., LLC v. Spenst*, 413 S.W.3d 786, 796–97 (Tex. App.—El Paso 2013, pet. denied); *Texas Commerce Bank Reagan v. Lebco Constructors, Inc.*, 865 S.W.2d 68, 82 (Tex. App.—Corpus Christi 1993, writ denied).
[150] Tex. Bus. & Com. Code Ann. § 27.01(a)(1).
[151] Tex. Bus. & Com. Code Ann. § 27.01(a)(2).
[152] Tex. Bus. & Com. Code Ann. § 27.01(d).
[153] Tex. Bus. & Com. Code Ann. § 27.01(a).
[154] *Schlumberger Tech. Corp. v. Swanson*, 959 S.W.2d 171, 179 (Tex. 1997).
[155] Tex. Bus. & Com. Code Ann. § 27.01(b); *Scott v. Sebree*, 986 S.W.2d 364, 368 (Tex. App.—Austin 1999, pet. denied).
[156] Tex. Bus. & Com. Code Ann. § 27.01(b); *Scott v. Sebree*, 986 S.W.2d 364, 369 (Tex. App.—Austin 1999, pet. denied).
[157] *Rhey v. Redic*, 408 S.W.3d 440, 454–55 (Tex. App.—El Paso 2013, no pet.).

1-5:3.1b Out-of-Pocket

Out-of-pocket damages, the difference between the value paid and the value received, are recoverable for statutory fraud.[158]

1-5:3.2 Exemplary Damages

Exemplary damages are recoverable.[159] *See* Chapter 11, Section 11-2. The plaintiff must prove the defendant's actual awareness by clear and convincing evidence.[160]

1-5:3.3 Rescission and Reformation

The equitable remedies of rescission or reformation of contracts obtained through fraud are available.[161] *See* Chapter 8, Sections 8-4 and 8-5.

1-5:3.4 Specific Performance

Specific performance is available in lieu of actual damages as a remedy for statutory fraud in real estate transactions.[162] *See* Chapter 8, Section 8-6.

1-5:3.5 Attorney's Fees

Plaintiff may recover attorney's fees, expert witness fees and deposition copy costs.[163] *See* Chapter 11, Section 11-13:3.

1-5:3.6 Interest

See Chapter 11, Section 11-13:1.

1-5:3.7 Court Costs

See Chapter 11, Section 11-13:2.

1-5:4 Defenses

1-5:4.1 Statute of Limitations

The four-year limitations period applies.[164] *See* Chapter 17.

---

[158] *Harstan, Ltd. v. Si Kyu Kim*, 441 S.W.3d 791, 802 (Tex. App.—El Paso 2014, no pet.); *Rhey v. Redic*, 408 S.W.3d 440, 454–55 (Tex. App.—El Paso 2013, no pet.).

[159] Tex. Bus. & Com. Code Ann. § 27.01(c); *Woodlands Land Dev. Co., L.P. v. Jenkins*, 48 S.W.3d 415, 423 (Tex. App.—Beaumont 2001, no pet.).

[160] Tex. Civ. Prac. & Rem. Code Ann. § 41.004(c).

[161] *Brush v. Reata Oil & Gas Corp.*, 984 S.W.2d 720, 729 (Tex. App.—Waco 1998, pet. denied).

[162] *Scott v. Sebree*, 986 S.W.2d 364, 368 (Tex. App.—Austin 1999, pet. denied).

[163] Tex. Bus. & Com. Code Ann. § 27.01(e).

[164] Tex. Civ. Prac. & Rem. Code Ann. § 16.004(a)(4); *Sullivan v. Hoover*, 782 S.W.2d 305, 306 (Tex. App.—San Antonio 1989, no writ).

1-5:4.2 Disclaimer of Reliance

A defendant may avoid liability if the plaintiff's fraud claim is barred by a contractual disclaimer expressing clear and unequivocal intent to disclaim reliance on specific representations.[165]

1-5:4.3 Statute of Frauds

The defendant may assert the statute of frauds as a defense only when the plaintiff seeks to obtain the benefit of the bargain that he would have obtained had the defendant's promise been performed.[166]

1-6 Fraud by Non-Disclosure

1-6:1 Overview

Fraud by non-disclosure is a subcategory of fraud.[167] Generally, a failure to disclose information does not constitute fraud unless a duty to disclose the information exists.[168] Circumstances giving rise to a duty to disclose include when there is a fiduciary or special relationship, when newly discovered information makes previous disclosures misleading or untrue, when a partial disclosure creates a false impression, or when voluntary disclosure of some information requires the disclosure of the entire truth. When a defendant has a duty to disclose but fails to do so, the defendant's non-disclosure is equally as actionable as an affirmative misrepresentation.

1-6:1.1 Related Causes of Action

Common Law Fraud, Statutory Fraud, Uniform Fraudulent Transfer Act (UFTA), Negligent Misrepresentation, DTPA, Breach of Warranty, Breach of Fiduciary Duty, Breach of Contract

MUST READ CASE

Schlumberger Tech. Corp. v. Swanson, 959 S.W.2d 171 (Tex. 1997)

1-6:2 Elements

(1) The defendant deliberately failed to disclose material facts.[169]

- The fact question of deliberate conduct or intent to deceive is almost always made by circumstantial evidence, for which the jury can look to the circumstances, relationship and interests of the parties, the nature of

---

[165] *Italian Cowboy Partners, Ltd. v. Prudential Ins. Co. of Am.*, 341 S.W.3d 323, 337 (Tex. 2011) (defense that the plaintiff's fraud claim is barred by contractual disclaimer expressing clear and unequivocal intent to disclaim reliance on specific representations).

[166] *See Hawkins v. Walker*, 233 S.W.3d 380, 396 (Tex. App.—Fort Worth 2007, no pet.).

[167] *Schlumberger Tech. Corp. v. Swanson*, 959 S.W.2d 171, 181 (Tex. 1997).

[168] *Bradford v. Vento*, 48 S.W.3d 749, 755 (Tex. 2001).

[169] *Wise v. SR Dallas, LLC*, 436 S.W.3d 402, 409 (Tex. App.—Dallas 2014, no pet.).

the transaction, the failure to perform, and the nature of any efforts to perform.[170]

- Information is considered "material" if a reasonable person would attach importance to it and would be induced to act on it in determining his choice of actions in the matter.[171]

(2) The defendant had a duty to disclose such facts to the plaintiff.[172]

- The existence of a duty to disclose is a question of law.[173]
- A duty to disclose arises when:
  - The defendant is in a fiduciary relationship with the plaintiff;[174]
    - Formal fiduciary relationships arise as a matter of law.[175]
    - Informal fiduciary relationships are a question of fact when the evidence is disputed.[176]
  - New information is discovered that makes the defendant aware than an earlier representation was false or misleading;[177]
  - The defendant makes a partial disclosure which leaves a substantially false impression,[178] or voluntarily discloses some information and therefore has a duty to disclose the whole truth.[179]

(3) The plaintiff was ignorant of the facts and did not have an equal opportunity to discover them.[180]

---

[170] *See Duval Cty. Ranch Co. v. Wooldridge*, 667 S.W.2d 887, 894–95 (Tex. App.—Austin 1984, no writ). *Chase Commercial Corp. v. Datapoint Corp.*, 774 S.W.2d 359, 367 (Tex. App.—Dallas 1989, no writ), *abrogated by Greathouse v. Charter Nat'l Bank Sw.*, 851 S.W.2d 173 (Tex. 1992) (abrogated as to requirement that deposition of collateral in commercially reasonable manner must be specifically plead).

[171] *White v. Zhou Pei*, 452 S.W.3d 527, 538 (Tex. App.—Houston [14th Dist.] 2014, no pet.); *Citizens Nat'l Bank v. Allen Rae Invs., Inc.*, 142 S.W.3d 459, 478–79 (Tex. App.—Fort Worth 2004, no pet.) (citing *Am. Med. Int'l, Inc. v. Giurintano*, 821 S.W.2d 331, 338 (Tex. App.—Houston [14th Dist.] 1991, no writ)).

[172] *Wise v. SR Dallas, LLC*, 436 S.W.3d 402, 409 (Tex. App.—Dallas 2014, no pet.).

[173] *Bradford v. Vento*, 48 S.W.3d 749, 755 (Tex. 2001).

[174] *Hoggett v. Brown*, 971 S.W.2d 472, 487 (Tex. App.—Houston [14th Dist.] 1997, pet. denied).

[175] *Meyer v. Cathey*, 167 S.W.3d 327, 330 (Tex. 2005); *National Med. Enters. v. Godbey*, 924 S.W.2d 123, 147 (Tex.1996) (quoting *Lacy v. Ticor Title Ins. Co.*, 794 S.W.2d 781, 787 (Tex. App.—Dallas 1990), *writ denied per curiam*, 803 S.W.2d 265 (Tex.1991)).

[176] *Lee v. Hasson*, 286 S.W.3d 1, 14 (Tex. App.—Houston [14th Dist.] 2007, pet. denied).

[177] *Four Bros. Boat Works, Inc. v. Tesoro Petroleum Co., Inc.*, 217 S.W.3d 653, 670–71 (Tex. App.—Houston [14th Dist.] 2006, pet. denied).

[178] *Anderson, Greenwood & Co. v. Martin*, 44 S.W.3d 200, 213 (Tex. App.—Houston [14th Dist.] 2001, pet. denied).

[179] *White v. Zhou Pei*, 452 S.W.3d 527, 537–38 (Tex. App.—Houston [14th Dist.] 2014, no pet.). No duty will arise, however, if the disclosures or representations are not made to the plaintiff's "decision-maker." *See Mercedes-Benz USA, LLC v. Carduco, Inc.*, 583 S.W.3d 553, 562–53 (Tex. 2019).

[180] *Wise v. SR Dallas, LLC*, 436 S.W.3d 402, 409 (Tex. App.—Dallas 2014, no pet.).

- The plaintiff must prove that the defendant knew of the plaintiff's ignorance of the facts and lack of equal opportunity to discover the truth.[181]

(4) The defendant intended for the plaintiff to act or refrain from acting as a result of the non-disclosure.[182]

- The defendant's intent may be shown by circumstantial evidence.[183]

- Failure to perform, standing alone, is no evidence of the promisor's intent not to perform when the promise was made.[184] However, that fact is a circumstance to be considered with other facts to establish intent.[185] Because intent to defraud is not usually susceptible to direct proof, in most cases it must be proven by circumstantial evidence.[186] "Slight circumstantial evidence" of fraud, when considered with the breach of promise to perform, is sufficient to support a finding of fraudulent intent.[187] If a party denies ever having made the promise in question, that is a factor showing no intent to perform at the time the promise was made.[188] The fact that the defendant makes no pretense of performance may also be considered in showing a lack of intent.[189]

(5) The plaintiff relied on the non-disclosure resulting in injury.[190]

- The plaintiff's reliance on the non-disclosure must be justifiable.[191]

- A showing of reliance may not be required when the non-disclosure is by a fiduciary.[192]

- The plaintiff must show that it suffered injury as a result of acting without knowledge of the undisclosed fact.[193]

---

[181] *Holland v. Thompson*, 338 S.W.3d 586, 597 (Tex. App—El Paso 2010, pet. denied).
[182] *Wise v. SR Dallas, LLC*, 436 S.W.3d 402, 409 (Tex. App.—Dallas 2014, no pet.).
[183] *See Spoljaric v. Percival Tours, Inc.*, 708 S.W.2d 432, 435 (Tex. 1986) (addressing intent to defraud generally).
[184] *Spoljaric v. Percival Tours, Inc.*, 708 S.W.2d 432, 435 (Tex. 1986).
[185] *Spoljaric v. Percival Tours, Inc.*, 708 S.W.2d 432, 435 (Tex. 1986).
[186] *Spoljaric v. Percival Tours, Inc.*, 708 S.W.2d 432, 435 (Tex. 1986).
[187] *Spoljaric v. Percival Tours, Inc.*, 708 S.W.2d 432, 435 (Tex. 1986).
[188] *Spoljaric v. Percival Tours, Inc.*, 708 S.W.2d 432, 435 (Tex. 1986).
[189] *Spoljaric v. Percival Tours, Inc.*, 708 S.W.2d 432, 435 (Tex. 1986). *W & F Transp., Inc. v. Wilhelm*, 208 S.W.3d 32, 48 (Tex. App.—Houston [14th Dist.] 2006).
[190] *Wise v. SR Dallas, LLC*, 436 S.W.3d 402, 409 (Tex. App.—Dallas 2014, no pet.).
[191] *BP Am. Prod. Co. v. Zaffirini*, 419 S.W.3d 485, 506 (Tex. App—San Antonio 2013, pet. denied); *see Horizon Shipbuilding, Inc. v. Blyn II Holding, LLC*, 324 S.W.3d 840, 850 (Tex. App.—Houston [14th Dist.] 2010, no pet.); *see also Bradford v. Vento*, 48 S.W.3d 749, 754–55 (Tex. 2001).
[192] *PAS, Inc. v. Engel*, 350 S.W.3d 602, 614 n.8 (Tex. App.—Houston [14th Dist.] 2011, no pet.).
[193] *UMLIC VP, LLC v. T&M Sales & Envtl. Sys. Inc.*, 176 S.W.3d 595, 604 (Tex. App.—Corpus Christi 2005, pet. denied).

1-6:3 Damages and Remedies

1-6:3.1 Actual Damages

Actual damages are the same for fraud by non-disclosure as for common law fraud. Fraud by non-disclosure (e.g., fraud by omission) is simply a subcategory of fraud because the omission or non-disclosure may be as misleading as a positive misrepresentation of fact where a party has a duty to disclose.[194] *See* Chapter 1, Section 1-4:3.

1-6:3.1a Benefit-of-the-Bargain

Benefit-of-the-bargain damages, the difference between the value as represented and the value received, are recoverable for fraud by non-disclosure.[195] *See* Chapter 11, Section 11-2.

1-6:3.1b Out-of-Pocket

Out-of-pocket damages, the difference between the value paid and the value received, are recoverable for fraud by omission.[196] *See* Chapter 11, Section 11-3.

1-6:3.1c Damages to Personal Property

See Chapter 11, Section 11-8:2.

1-6:3.1d Mental Anguish

Mental anguish damages are recoverable.[197]

1-6:3.2 Exemplary Damages

See Chapter 11, Section 11-12.

1-6:3.3 Equitable Remedies

1-6:3.3a Rescission

Rescission is available to avoid unjust enrichment.[198] *See* Chapter 8, Section 8-4.

---

[194] *Four Bros. Boat Works, Inc. v. Tesoro Petroleum Co., Inc.*, 217 S.W.3d 653, 670 (Tex. App.—Houston [14th Dist.] 2006, pet. denied).

[195] *K.A. West, LLC v. GK Invs., Inc.*, No. 05-11-00617-CV, 2013 WL 5270861, at *5 (Tex. App.—Dallas Sept. 17, 2013, no pet.).

[196] *K.A. West, LLC v. GK Invs., Inc.*, No. 05-11-00617-CV, 2013 WL 5270861, at *5 (Tex. App.—Dallas Sept. 17, 2013, no pet.); *Solutioneers Consulting, Ltd. v. Gulf Greyhound Partners, Ltd.*, 237 S.W.3d 379, 386 (Tex. App.—Houston [14th Dist.] 2007, no pet.).

[197] *Tony Gullo Motors I, L.P. v. Chapa*, 212 S.W.3d 299, 304 (Tex. 2006).

[198] *See Italian Cowboy Partners, Ltd. v. Prudential Ins. Co. of Am.*, 341 S.W.3d 323, 344 (Tex. 2011).

1-6:3.3b *Reformation*

Reformation is available as an equitable remedy to conform the contract to the original intent of the parties.[199] *See* Chapter 8, Section 8.5.

1-6:3.4 Interest

See Chapter 11, Section 11-13:1.

1-6:3.5 Court Costs

Reasonable court costs are available.[200] *See* Chapter 11, Section 11-13:2.

1-6:4 Defenses

1-6:4.1 Statute of Limitations

The four-year limitations period applies.[201] *See* Chapter 17.

1-6:4.2 Contractual Disclaimer

A defendant may avoid liability if the plaintiff's fraud claim is barred by a contractual disclaimer expressing clear and unequivocal intent to disclaim reliance on specific representations.[202]

A party must clearly and specifically disclaim reliance to bar an action for fraud.[203]

1-6:4.3 Ratification

Ratification may be asserted against a plaintiff who continues to accept the benefits of fraudulent dealings after learning of the fraud.[204] *See* Chapter 8, Section 8-4:4.4

1-6:4.4 Statute of Frauds

The statute of frauds defense is only available where the plaintiff seeks benefit-of-the-bargain damages based on an unenforceable contract.[205]

---

[199] *Gilbane Bldg. Co. v. Keystone Structural Concrete, Ltd.*, 263 S.W.3d 291, 301 (Tex. App.—Houston [1st Dist.] 2007).

[200] Tex. Bus. & Com. Code Ann. § 27.01(e).

[201] Tex. Civ. Prac. & Rem. Code Ann. § 16.004(a)(4).

[202] *Italian Cowboy Partners, Ltd. v. Prudential Ins. Co. of Am.*, 341 S.W.3d 323, 337 (Tex. 2011) (defense that the plaintiff's fraud claim is barred by contractual disclaimer expressing clear and unequivocal intent to disclaim reliance on specific representations); *see also Armstrong v. Am. Home Shield Corp.*, 333 F.3d 566, 571 (5th Cir. 2003) (applying Texas law).

[203] *Citizens Nat'l Bank v. Allen Rae Invs., Inc.*, 142 S.W.3d 459, 457 (Tex. App.—Fort Worth 2004, no pet.).

[204] *Fortune Prod. Co. v. Conoco, Inc.*, 52 S.W.3d 671, 678 (Tex. 2000).

[205] *Baylor Univ. v. Sonnichsen*, 221 S.W.3d 632, 636 (Tex. 2007).

1-6:4.5 Sovereign Immunity

Where applicable, defendant may assert sovereign immunity.[206]

1-7 Negligent Misrepresentation

1-7:1 Introduction

The claim of negligent misrepresentation allows plaintiffs to recover for misrepresentations made, absent a contractual relationship, that proximately cause pecuniary harm in the course of business.[207] This cause of action is nearly identical to fraud, except that it has a lower scienter, ordinary negligence, and is narrower in scope.[208] Only those defendants who fail to exercise reasonable care in obtaining or supplying information to known parties for a known purpose are potentially liable under this tort.[209]

1-7:1.1 Related Causes of Action

Breach of Contract, Business Disparagement, Statutory Fraud, Common Law Fraud, Fraud by Non-Disclosure, DTPA, Negligence

MUST READ CASES

D.S.A., Inc. v. Hillsboro Indep. Sch. Dist., 973 S.W.2d 662 (Tex. 1998)

McCamish, Martin, Brown & Loeffler v. F.E. Appling Interests, 991 S.W.2d 787 (Tex. 1999)

Grant Thornton LLP v. Prospect High Income Fund, 314 S.W.3d 913 (Tex. 2010)

LAN/STV v. Martin K. Eby Constr. Co., Inc., 435 S.W.3d 234 (Tex. 2014)

1-7:2 Elements

(1) The defendant made a representation to the plaintiff in the course of the defendant's business or in a transaction in which the defendant had a pecuniary interest.[210]

(2) The defendant supplied false information for the guidance of others in their business.[211]

---

[206] *Sanders v. City of Grapevine*, 218 S.W.3d 772, 778–79 (Tex. App.—Fort Worth 2007, pet. denied).

[207] *Affordable Power, L.P. v. Buckeye Ventures, Inc.*, 347 S.W.3d 825, 830 (Tex. App.—Dallas 2011, no pet.).

[208] *See Grant Thornton LLP v. Prospect High Income Fund*, 314 S.W.3d 913, 920 (Tex. 2010).

[209] *Grant Thornton LLP v. Prospect High Income Fund*, 314 S.W.3d 913, 920 (Tex. 2010).

[210] *Blankinship v. Brown*, 399 S.W.3d 303, 308 (Tex. App—Dallas 2013, pet. denied) (citing Texas Supreme Court authority).

[211] *Blankinship v. Brown*, 399 S.W.3d 303, 308 (Tex. App—Dallas 2013, pet. denied) (citing Texas Supreme Court authority).

- The "false information" contemplated in a negligent misrepresentation case must be a misstatement of an existing fact rather than a promise of future conduct.[212]
- Negligent misrepresentation action is available only when information is transferred to a known party for a known purpose.[213]
- Negligent misrepresentation can be based on silence rather than an affirmative misrepresentation when there is a duty to speak.[214]
- Negligent misrepresentation is not analogous to either a professional malpractice or negligence claim because liability is based on the defendant's awareness and intention that the non-client rely on the defendant's representations, rather than on the breach of a duty owed by law or contract.[215]

(3) The defendant did not exercise reasonable care or competence in obtaining or communicating the information.[216]

(4) The plaintiff suffered pecuniary loss by justifiably relying on the representation.[217]

- The plaintiff must show actual and justifiable reliance based on the "plaintiff's individual characteristics, abilities, and appreciation of facts and circumstances at or before the time of the alleged fraud" as well as any "'red flags' indicating such reliance is unwarranted."[218]
- Unlike fraudulent inducement, with negligent misrepresentation the benefit-of-the-bargain measure of damages is not available; the plaintiff is limited to out-of-pocket pecuniary damages.[219]
- There must be an independent injury, other than a breach of contract, to support negligent misrepresentation (in order to avoid converting every contract interpretation dispute into a negligent misrepresentation claim).[220]

---

[212] *Scherer v. Angell*, 253 S.W.3d 777, 781 (Tex. App.—Amarillo 2007, no pet.); *Miller v. Raytheon Aircraft Co.*, 229 S.W.3d 358, 379 (Tex. App.—Houston [1st Dist.] 2007, no pet.).

[213] *McCamish, Martin, Brown & Loeffler v. F.E. Appling Interests*, 991 S.W.2d 787, 794 (Tex. 1999).

[214] *Brown & Brown of Tex., Inc. v. Omni Metals, Inc.*, 317 S.W.3d 361, 384 (Tex. App.—Houston [1st Dist.] 2010, pet. denied) (citing circumstances in which a duty to disclose arises).

[215] *Ervin v. Mann Frankfort Stein & Lipp CPAS*, 234 S.W.3d 172, 176–77 (Tex. App.—San Antonio 2007, no pet.) ("Thus, an accountant can be subject to a negligent misrepresentation claim when he is not subject to a professional negligence claim.").

[216] *Blankinship v. Brown*, 399 S.W.3d 303, 308 (Tex. App.—Dallas 2013, pet. denied) (citing Texas Supreme Court authority).

[217] *Blankinship v. Brown*, 399 S.W.3d 303, 308 (Tex. App.—Dallas 2013, pet. denied) (citing Texas Supreme Court authority).

[218] *Grant Thornton LLP v. Prospect High Income Fund*, 314 S.W.3d 913, 923 (Tex. 2010).

[219] *D.S.A., Inc. v. Hillsboro Indep. Sch. Dist.*, 973 S.W.2d 662, 663–64 (Tex. 1998).

[220] *Scherer v. Angell*, 253 S.W.3d 777, 781 (Tex. App.—Amarillo 2007, no pet.) (citing *D.S.A., Inc. v. Hillsboro Indep. Sch. Dist.*, 973 S.W.2d 662, 663–64 (Tex. 1998)).

- The economic loss rule may bar recovery for negligent misrepresentation in a contractual setting, depending "on an analysis of [the economic loss rule's] rationales in a particular situation."[221]

1-7:3 Damages and Remedies

1-7:3.1 Actual Damages

Defendant may only recover for pecuniary loss.[222] *See* Chapter 11, Sections 11-3 and 11-9.

1-7:3.2 Exemplary Damages

Exemplary damages are recoverable in accordance with Chapter 41 of the Texas Civil Practice and Remedies Code.[223] For negligent misrepresentation, however, the Texas Supreme Court has stated that exemplary damages are not recoverable for grossly negligent misrepresentations posing an extreme degree of risk in the absence of evidence of actual physical harm.[224]

1-7:3.3 Interest

See Chapter 11, Section 11-13:1.

1-7:3.4 Court Costs

See Chapter 11, Section 11-13:2.

1-7:4 Defenses

1-7:4.1 Statute of Limitations

Two-year statute of limitations applies.[225]

---

[221] *LAN/STV v. Martin K. Eby Constr. Co., Inc.*, 435 S.W.3d 234, 245–46 (Tex. 2014); *see* discussion of the Texas economic loss rule at section 12-3.

[222] *D.S.A., Inc. v. Hillsboro Indep. Sch. Dist.*, 973 S.W.2d 662, 663–64 (Tex. 1998); *CCE, Inc. v. PBS&J Constr. Servs., Inc.*, 461 S.W.3d 542, 549–50 (Tex. App.—Houston [1st Dist.] 2011). As noted by the Texas Supreme Court, "damages recoverable for a negligent misrepresentation are those necessary to compensate the plaintiff for the pecuniary loss to him of which the misrepresentation is a legal cause," including:

(a) the difference between the value of what he has received in the transaction and its purchase price or other value given for it; and
(b) pecuniary loss suffered otherwise as a consequence of the plaintiff's reliance upon the misrepresentation.

Federal Land Bank Ass'n of Tyler v. Sloane, 825 S.W.2d 439, 442 (Tex. 1991) (emphasis added) (quoting Restatement (Second) of Torts § 552B (1977)).

[223] *See* Tex. Civ. P. & Rem. Code Ann. § 41.003.

[224] *D.S.A., Inc. v. Hillsboro Indep. Sch. Dist.*, 973 S.W.2d 662, 664 (Tex. 1998) (citing Restatement (Second) of Torts § 311 (1965)).

[225] Tex. Civ. Prac. & Rem. Code Ann. § 16.003; *Hendricks v. Thornton*, 973 S.W.3d 348, 364 n.19 (Tex. App.—Beaumont 1998, pet. denied).

1-7:4.2 Existence of a Contract or Contractual Opportunity

Defense that the plaintiff does not have a valid negligent misrepresentation claim because of a contract, or because of the reasonable opportunity to allocate risks contractually (even if no contractual allocation of risks was actually made).[226]

1-7:4.3 Statute of Frauds

Defendant can assert statute of frauds if the plaintiff's claim is that an oral communication created a contract and that the defendant breached that contract.[227]

1-7:4.4 Disclaimer of Reliance

Defense that the plaintiff's fraud claim is barred by contractual disclaimer expressing clear and unequivocal intent to disclaim reliance on specific representations.[228]

Party must clearly and specifically disclaim reliance to bar an action for fraud.[229]

1-7:4.5 Ratification and Waiver

Like in a common law fraud claim, a plaintiff may waive her claim for negligent misrepresentation if, with full knowledge of the misrepresentation, she continues to accept benefits under the arrangement instead of filing suit.[230]

1-8 Business Disparagement

1-8:1 Introduction

The Texas Supreme Court has explained that "[a] business disparagement claim is similar in many respects to a defamation action, [but] the two torts differ in that defamation actions chiefly serve to protect the personal reputation of an injured party, while a business disparagement claim protects economic interests . . .

[A] business disparagement defendant may be held liable 'only if he knew of the falsity or acted with reckless disregard concerning it, or *if he acted with ill will or intended to interfere in the economic interest of the plaintiff in an unprivileged fashion.*'"[231]

---

[226] *LAN/STV v. Constr. Co.*, 435 S.W.3d 234, 247–48 (Tex. 2014); *D.S.A., Inc. v. Hillsboro Indep. Sch. Dist.*, 973 S.W.2d 662, 663–64 (Tex. 1998).

[227] *Federal Land Bank Ass'n of Tyler v. Sloane*, 825 S.W.2d 439, 442 (Tex. 1991).

[228] *Italian Cowboy Partners, Ltd. v. Prudential Ins. Co. of Am.*, 341 S.W.3d 323, 337 (Tex. 2011); see also *Armstrong v. Am. Home Shield Corp.*, 333 F.3d 566, 571 (5th Cir. 2003) (applying Texas law).

[229] *Citizens Nat'l Bank v. Allen Rae Invs., Inc.*, 142 S.W.3d 459, 475 (Tex. App.—Fort Worth 2004, no pet.).

[230] *See, e.g., Williams v. City of Midland*, 932 S.W.2d 679, 685 (Tex. App.—El Paso 1996, no writ).

[231] *Forbes, Inc. v. Granada Biosciences, Inc.*, 124 S.W.3d 167, 170 (Tex. 2003) (quoting in part from Restatement (Second) of Torts § 623A, cmt. g (1977)).

MUST READ CASES & AUTHORITY

Restatement (Second) of Torts §§ 623A, 629–635, 646A-652

Hurlbut v. Gulf Atl. Life Ins. Co., 749 S.W.2d 762 (Tex. 1987)

Forbes, Inc. v. Granada Biosciences, Inc., 124 S.W.3d 167 (Tex. 2003)

Waste Mgmt. of Tex., Inc. v. Tex. Disposal Sys. Landfill, Inc., 434 S.W.3d 142 (Tex. 2014)

In re Lipsky, 460 S.W.3d 579 (Tex. 2015)

1-8:1.1 Related Causes of Action

Defamation, Slander of Title, Tortious Interference with Existing Contract, Tortious Interference with Prospective Relations, Texas False Disparagement of Perishable Food Products Act[232]

1-8:2 Elements

(1) The defendant published false and disparaging words about the plaintiff.[233]

- The action for business disparagement is to protect the economic interests of the plaintiff against pecuniary loss, rather than the personal reputation of the plaintiff.[234]

- A plaintiff ultimately must prove that the defendant published false, disparaging information, but whether the words used in a publication are reasonably capable of defamatory meaning is initially a question of law for the court to decide.[235]

- The false and disparaging information must amount to a statement of fact.[236]

- "A statement is disparaging if it is understood to cast doubt upon the quality of another's land, chattels or intangible things, or upon the existence or extent of his property in them, and the publisher intends the statement to cast the doubt, or the recipient's understanding of it as casting the doubt was reasonable."[237]

---

[232] *See* Tex. Civ. Prac. & Rem. Code Ann. §§ 96.001–.004 (imposing liability for defendants who knowingly disseminate false information implying that a perishable food product is not safe for human consumption); *see also Tex. Beef Group v. Winfrey*, 201 F.3d 680 (5th Cir. 2000) (interpreting the Act in light of declining beef prices following a discussion about "Mad Cow Disease" on the Oprah Winfrey Show).

[233] *Forbes, Inc. v. Granada Biosciences, Inc.*, 124 S.W.3d 167, 170 (Tex. 2003).

[234] *Hurlbut v. Gulf Atl. Life Ins. Co.*, 749 S.W.2d 762, 766 (Tex. 1987). The tort does not seek to redress dignitary harms to the business owner, but rather redresses aspersions cast on the business's commercial product or activity that diminishes those interests. *Hurlbut v. Gulf Atl. Life Ins. Co.*, 749 S.W.2d 762, 766–67 (Tex. 1987); *In re Lipsky*, 460 S.W.3d 579, 591 (Tex. 2015).

[235] *Astoria Indus. of Iowa, Inc. v. SNF, Inc.*, 223 S.W.3d 616, 639 n.83 (Tex. App.—Fort Worth 2007, pet. denied); *Turner v. KTRK Television, Inc.*, 38 S.W.3d 103, 114 (Tex. 2000).

[236] *Community Initiatives, Inc. v. Chase Bank of Tex.*, 153 S.W.3d 270, 284 (Tex. App.—El Paso 2004, no pet.); *see also Prudential Ins Co. v. Fin. Rev. Servs.*, 29 S.W.3d 74, 82 (Tex. 2000).

[237] Restatement (Second) of Torts § 629 (1977).

(2) The defendant published the information with malice.[238]

- For plaintiffs generally, to meet the malice requirement for a business disparagement claim, there must be proof that the statements were made with knowledge of their falsity, with reckless disregard as to the statements' truth, or with ill will or an intent to interfere with the plaintiff's economic interest.[239]

- Public figures cannot recover for damaging statements made about them absent proof of "actual malice" which "requires proof that the defendant made the statement 'with knowledge that it was false or with reckless disregard of whether it was true or not.'"[240]

(3) The defendant published the information without privilege.[241]

- "In the context of a tort such as business disparagement or injurious falsehood, only absolute privileges have relevance to the defendant. This is because the tort itself incorporates malice as an element of recovery; hence, if the plaintiff carries his burden, he likewise defeats any conditional privilege."[242]

(4) The publication of information resulted in special damages to the plaintiff.[243]

- "[P]ecuniary loss to the plaintiff must always be proved to establish a cause of action for business disparagement."[244]

- The element of special damages requires proof that the false communication played a substantial part in inducing the loss of trade or other dealings and requires plaintiff to "establish pecuniary loss that has been realized or liquidated as in the case of specific lost sales."[245]

- Out-of-pocket expenses incurred with consultants in an effort to remedy the fallout from false statements are special damages which may be recovered.[246]

1-8:3 Damages and Remedies

1-8:3.1 Actual Damages

Actual damages must be specifically pleaded.[247] Although the jury generally has broad latitude in determining defamation damages, it must consist of more than

---

[238] *Forbes, Inc. v. Granada Biosciences, Inc.*, 124 S.W.3d 167, 170 (Tex. 2003).
[239] *Fluor Enters., Inc. v. Conex Int'l Corp.*, 273 S.W.3d 426, 438–39 (Tex. App—Beaumont 2008, pet. denied); *Hurlbut v. Gulf Atl. Life Ins. Co.*, 749 S.W.2d 762, 766 (Tex. 1987).
[240] *Forbes, Inc. v. Granada Biosciences, Inc.*, 124 S.W.3d 167, 171 (Tex. 2003).
[241] *Forbes, Inc. v. Granada Biosciences, Inc.*, 124 S.W.3d 167, 170 (Tex. 2003).
[242] *Hurlbut v. Gulf Atl. Life Ins. Co.*, 749 S.W.2d 762, 768 (Tex. 1987).
[243] *Forbes, Inc. v. Granada Biosciences, Inc.*, 124 S.W.3d 167, 170 (Tex. 2003).
[244] *Hurlbut v. Gulf Atl. Life Ins. Co.*, 749 S.W.2d 762, 766 (Tex. 1987).
[245] *Hurlbut v. Gulf Atl. Life Ins. Co.*, 749 S.W.2d 762, 767 (Tex. 1987).
[246] *Waste Mgmt. of Tex., Inc. v. Tex. Disposal Sys. Landfill, Inc.*, 434 S.W.3d 142, 161 (Tex. 2014).
[247] *See Hurlbut v. Gulf Atl. Life Ins. Co.*, 749 S.W.2d 762, 767 (Tex. 1987).

simply stating the value of the business which has been attacked.[248] See Chapter 10 and Chapter 11.

1-8:3.1a Loss of Sale

Damages for loss of a specific sale are recoverable.[249] See Chapter 11, Section 11-6:3.

1-8:3.1b Loss of Credit

Loss of credit damages are recoverable.[250] See Chapter 11, Section 11-9:1.

1-8:3.1c Loss of Business

Loss of business damages are recoverable if the plaintiff's business is destroyed.[251] See Chapter 11, Section 11-7.

1-8:3.2 Exemplary Damages

Exemplary damages are potentially recoverable for business disparagement.[252] See Chapter 11, Section 11-2.

1-8:3.3 Interest

See Chapter 11, Section 11-13:1.

1-8:3.4 Court Costs

See Chapter 11, Section 11-13:2.

1-8:4 Defenses

1-8:4.1 Privilege

See *Hurlbut v. Gulf Atlantic Life Insurance Co.*,[253] discussing privilege to defamation actions in the context of a business disparagement claim.

---

[248] *Burbage v. Burbage*, 447 S.W.3d 249, 259 (Tex. 2014).
[249] Restatement (Second) of Torts § 633 (1977); *Hurlbut v. Gulf Atl. Life Ins. Co.*, 749 S.W.2d 762, 767 (Tex. 1987).
[250] *Commonwealth Lloyd's Ins. Co. v. Thomas*, 825 S.W.2d 135, 146–47 (Tex. App.—Dallas 1992), *writ granted, set aside, dism'd per parties' settlement*, 843 S.W.2d 486 (Tex. 1993).
[251] *Gulf Atl. Life Ins. Co. v. Hurlbut*, 696 S.W.2d 83, 99 (Tex. App.—Dallas 1985), *rev'd on other grounds*, 749 S.W.2d 762 (Tex. 1987); *Sawyer v. Fitts*, 630 S.W.2d 872, 873–74 (Tex. App.—Fort Worth 1982, no writ).
[252] See *Burbage v. Burbage*, 447 S.W.3d 249, 263 (Tex. 2014).
[253] *Hurlbut v. Gulf Atl. Life Ins. Co.*, 749 S.W.2d 762, 768 (Tex. 1987).

1-8:4.2 Prior Restraint

A permanent injunction that would require the removal of public statements that have been adjudicated defamatory would not be a prior restraint of speech, but a permanent injunction prohibiting a competitor from making similar statements in the future would be a prior restraint prohibited by the Texas Constitution.[254] Damages, not injunctive relief, are generally the proper remedy for defamation.[255]

1-8:4.3 Comparative Fault

See Chapter 18, Section 18-2:3.

1-8:4.4 Statute of Limitations

Two-year statute of limitations applies.[256]

A defamation suit must be brought not later than one year after the cause of action accrues.[257] An injured party may sue for both personal defamation and business disparagement in the same suit so long as he avoids duplication of damages.[258] If the shorter limitation period bars the defamation claim, it will not bar the disparagement claim so long as the plaintiff does not plead allegations typical of an action for defamation.[259]

1-8:4.5 Texas Citizens Participation Act

The Texas Citizens Participation Act (TCPA)[260] protects citizens who petition or speak on matters of public concern from retaliatory lawsuits that seek to intimidate or silence them, by means of a special motion for expedited consideration asking the trial court to dismiss the suit unless "clear and specific evidence" establishes the plaintiffs' "prima facie case."[261]

1-8:4.6 Interlocutory Appeal

Interlocutory appeal is permitted from the denial of a motion for summary judgment involving a claim or defense arising under the free speech clause of the U.S. Constitution or Texas Constitution, when asserted by or against a member of the elec-

---

[254] *Kinney v. Barnes*, 443 S.W.3d 87 (Tex. 2014).
[255] *Kinney v. Barnes*, 443 S.W.3d 87, 99–100 (Tex. 2014).
[256] Tex. Civ. Prac. & Rem. Code Ann. § 16.003; *Procter & Gamble Co. v. Amway Corp.*, 80 F. Supp. 2d 639, 653 (S.D. Tex. 1999), *aff'd in part, rev'd in part on other grounds*, 242 F.3d 539 (5th Cir. 2001); *Dwyer v. Sabine Min. Co.*, 890 S.W.2d 140, 142 (Tex. App.—Texarkana 1994, writ denied).
[257] Tex. Civ. Prac. & Rem. Code Ann. § 16.002.
[258] *Dwyer v. Sabine Mining Co.*, 890 S.W.2d 140, 142–43 (Tex. App.—Texarkana 1994, writ denied).
[259] *Dwyer v. Sabine Mining Co.*, 890 S.W.2d 140, 142–43 (Tex. App.—Texarkana 1994, writ denied).
[260] Tex. Civ. Prac. & Rem. Code Ann. §§ 27.001-27.011.
[261] Tex. Civ. Prac. & Rem. Code Ann. § 27.005(c); *In re Lipsky*, 460 S.W.3d 579, 590 (Tex. 2015); *Lippincott v. Whisenhunt*, 462 S.W.3d 507, 510 (Tex. 2015).

tronic or print media.[262] Texas appellate courts are split on how to interpret "electronic media."[263]

1-9 Negligent Hiring

1-9:1 Introduction

A claim for negligent hiring, retention, and supervision "is not the type of tort that depends on proof of an employee performing a negligent or intentional act within the course of his employment. This tort arises instead from the simple negligence of the employer. An employer is negligent if the employer hires, retains, or supervises an employee whom the employer knows, or by the exercise of reasonable care should have known, is unfit or incompetent, and whose unfitness or incompetence creates an unreasonable risk of harm to others because of the employee's job-related duties."[264]

1-9:1.1 Related Causes of Action

Negligence, Negligence per se, Negligent Entrustment, Negligent Referral

MUST READ CASE

Wansey v. Hole, 379 S.W.3d 246 (Tex. 2012)

1-9:2 Elements

(1) The defendant has a legal duty to hire competent employees.[265]

- The existence of a duty is a question of law for the court to decide.[266]

- The duty of an employer to hire competent employees has been routinely recognized, and has been observed to be "absolute and nondelegable."[267]

- "An employer owes a duty to its other employees and to the general public to ascertain the qualifications and competence of the employees it hires, especially when the employees are engaged in occupations that require skill or experience and that could be hazardous to the safety of others."[268]

---

[262] Tex. Civ. Prac. & Rem. Code Ann. § 51.014(a)(6).

[263] *Service Emps. Int'l Union Local 5 v. Prof'l Janitorial Serv. of Houston, Inc.*, 481 S.W.3d 210 (Tex. 2014, mem. op.).

[264] *Mindi M. v. Flagship Hotel, Ltd.*, 439 S.W.3d 551, 557 (Tex. App.—Houston [14th Dist.] 2014), *review granted, judgment vacated, and remanded by agreement* (Apr. 10, 2015); *see also Pagayon. v. ExxonMobil Corp.*, 536 S.W.3d 499, 504–06 (Tex. 2017).

[265] *Moore v. Strike, LLC*, No. 04-16-00324-CV, 2017 WL 96130, at *7 (Tex. App.—San Antonio Jan. 11, 2017, no. pet.).

[266] *Barton v. Whataburger, Inc.*, 276 S.W.3d 456, 462 (Tex. App.—Houston [1st Dist.] 2008, pet. denied).

[267] *See Fort Worth Elevators Co. v. Russell*, 70 S.W.2d 397, 401 (1934), *overruled on other grounds by Wright v. Gifford–Hill & Co.*, 725 S.W.2d 712 (Tex. 1987).

[268] *Wise v. Complete Staffing Servs. Inc.*, 56 S.W.3d 900, 902 (Tex. App.—Texarkana 2001, no pet.).

- The Texas Supreme Court has "never expressly set out what duty an employer has in hiring employees, or said that a negligent hiring claim requires more than just negligent hiring practices."[269]
- A party engaging an independent contractor is required to use ordinary care in hiring the contractor.[270]

(2) The defendant breached the duty to hire competent employees.[271]

- An employer is liable for negligent hiring if it "hires an incompetent or unfit employee whom it knows, or by the exercise of reasonable care should have known, was incompetent or unfit, thereby creating an unreasonable risk of harm to others."[272]

(3) Damages to the plaintiff were proximately caused as a result of the defendant's breach.[273]

- For an employer to be found liable for negligently hiring, retaining, or supervising its employee, the plaintiff must "suffer some damages from the foreseeable misconduct of an employee hired pursuant to the defendant's negligent practices."[274]
- A claim of negligent hiring, supervision, or retention is not dependent upon a finding that the employee was acting in the course and scope of his employment when the tortious act occurred,[275] but there must be some connection between the plaintiff's injury and the fact of employment.[276]
- "In a negligent-hiring or negligent-entrustment claim, a plaintiff must show that the risk that caused the entrustment or hiring to be negligent also proximately caused plaintiff's injuries," rather than simply furnishing the employment which made the injury possible.[277]
- "The proximate cause element of a negligent hiring claim consists of cause in fact and foreseeability. A plaintiff establishes cause in fact if she demonstrates that the negligent act or omission was a substantial factor in bringing about the injury, without which the harm would not have occurred. Cause

---

[269] *Wansey v. Hole*, 379 S.W.3d 246, 247 (Tex. 2012).
[270] *Mireles v. Ashley*, 201 S.W.3d 779, 782 (Tex. App—Amarillo 2006, no pet.).
[271] *Moore v. Strike, LLC*, No. 04-16-00324-CV, 2017 WL 96130, at *7 (Tex. App.—San Antonio Jan. 11, 2017, no. pet. h.).
[272] *Martinez v. Hays Constr., Inc.*, 355 S.W.3d 170, 180 (Tex. App.—Houston [1st Dist.] 2011, no pet.), *disapproved of on other grounds by Gonzalez v. Ramirez*, 463 S.W.3d 499 (Tex. 2015); *Morris v. JTM Materials, Inc.*, 78 S.W.3d 28, 49 (Tex. App.—Fort Worth 2002, no pet.).
[273] *Fifth Club, Inc., v. Ramirez*, 196 S.W.3d 788, 796 (Tex. 2006); *Moore v. Strike, LLC*, No. 04-16-00324-CV, 2017 WL 96130, at *7 (Tex. App.—San Antonio Jan. 11, 2017, no. pet. h.).
[274] *Wansey v. Hole*, 379 S.W.3d 246, 247 (Tex. 2012).
[275] *Wrenn v. G.A.T.X. Logistics, Inc.*, 73 S.W.3d 489, 496 (Tex. App—Fort Worth 2002, no pet.).
[276] *Robertson v. Church of God, Int'l*, 978 S.W.2d 120, 125 (Tex. App.—Tyler 1997, pet. denied). "[W]e focus on the issue whether the Boys Club's failure to investigate, screen, or supervise its volunteers proximately caused the injuries the plaintiffs allege. The components of proximate cause are cause in fact and foreseeability." *Travis v. City of Mesquite*, 830 S.W.2d 94, 98 (Tex. 1992); *Doe v. Boys Clubs of Greater Dallas, Inc.*, 907 S.W.2d 472, 477 (Tex. 1995).
[277] *TXI Transp. Co. v. Hughes*, 306 S.W.3d 230, 240–41 (Tex. 2010).

in fact is not shown if the defendant's negligence did no more than furnish a condition which made the injury possible."[278]

- "The plaintiff's harm must be foreseeable in the sense that it is brought about by conduct that was in some manner job-related."[279]

1-9:3 Damages and Remedies

1-9:3.1 Actual Damages

A negligent hiring claim requires that the plaintiff suffer some direct damages from the foreseeable misconduct of an employee hired pursuant to the defendant's negligent practices, other than pure economic harm in the form of loss to the subject matter of the contract which is only recoverable under a breach of contract claim.[280]

1-9:3.2 Exemplary Damages

Exemplary damages are recoverable for harm that results from gross negligence.[281] *See* Chapter 11, Section 11-12.

1-9:3.3 Interest

See Chapter 11, Section 11-13:1.

1-9:3.4 Court Costs

See Chapter 11, Section 11-13:2.

1-9:4 Defenses

1-9:4.1 Statute of Limitations

Two-year statute of limitations applies.[282]

1-9:4.2 Limitation on Liability Statute

Texas Civil Practice and Remedies Code Section 142.002 provides limitations on liability for an employer based solely on evidence that the employee had been convicted of an offense.[283]

---

[278] *Martinez v. Hays Constr., Inc.*, 355 S.W.3d 170, 180 (Tex. App.—Houston [1st Dist.] 2011, no pet.), *disapproved of on other grounds by Gonzalez v. Ramirez*, 463 S.W.3d 499 (Tex. 2015).

[279] *Moore v. Strike, LLC*, No. 04-16-00324-CV, 2017 WL 96130, at *7 (Tex. App.—San Antonio Jan. 11, 2017, no. pet. h.).

[280] *Wansey v. Hole*, 379 S.W.3d 246, 247–48 (Tex. 2012).

[281] *See* Tex. Civ. Prac. & Rem. Code Ann. § 41.003(a)(3).

[282] Tex. Civ. Prac. & Rem. Code Ann. § 16.003(a); *H.D.N. Corp. v. Autozone Tex., L.P.*, No. 4:12-CV-3723, 2014 WL 4471537, at *5 (S.D. Tex. Sept. 9, 2014).

[283] Tex. Civ. Prac. & Rem. Code Ann. § 142.002.

Employers have no duty to check the criminal histories of its employees unless it is directly related to the duties of the job at hand; but if undertaken, the check must not be inadequate or negligent.[284]

1-10 Negligence

1-10:1 Introduction

Negligence actions are often pleaded in a commercial litigation setting, and often run into difficulty in Texas in pure economic loss cases (unaccompanied by injury to person or tangible property) because of the economic loss rule, although numerous exceptions and limitations to the economic loss rule exist (such as for negligence occurring in the setting of professional relationships).[285]

1-10:1.1 Related Causes of Action

DTPA, Legal Malpractice, Negligent Entrustment, Negligent Hiring, Negligent Misrepresentation, Negligent Undertaking

1-10:2 Elements

(1) Defendant owed a legal duty of care to the Plaintiff.[286]

- "Every person has a duty to exercise reasonable care to avoid a foreseeable risk of injury to others."[287]

- Courts apply a balancing test in determining whether a legal duty exists under common law, considering the risk, foreseeability, and likelihood of injury, weighed against the social utility of the actor's conduct, the magnitude of the burden of guarding against the injury, and the consequences of placing the burden on the defendant.[288]

- The existence of a duty is a question of law for the court to decide from the facts surrounding the occurrence in question.[289]

- All that is required for foreseeability is [1] "that the injury be of such a general character as might reasonably have been anticipated; and [2] that the injured party should be so situated with relation to the wrongful act that injury to him or to one similarly situated might reasonably have been foreseen."[290]

---

[284] *See Wise v. Complete Staffing Servs., Inc.*, 56 S.W.3d 900, 903–04 (Tex. App.—Texarkana 2001, no pet.).

[285] *See* discussion of the Texas economic loss rule in Chapter 12, § 12-3.

[286] *Firestone Steel Prods. Co. v. Barajas*, 927 S.W.2d 608, 613 (Tex. 1996); *Midwest Emp'rs Cas. Co. ex rel. English v. Harpole*, 293 S.W.3d 770, 776 (Tex. App.—San Antonio 2009, no pet.).

[287] *Midwest Emp'rs Cas. Co. ex rel. English v. Harpole*, 293 S.W.3d 770, 776 (Tex. App.—San Antonio 2009, no pet.).

[288] *J.P. Morgan Chase Bank, N.A. v. Tex. Contract Carpet, Inc.*, 302 S.W.3d 515, 533 (Tex. App—Austin 2009, no pet.).

[289] *Greater Houston Transp. Co. v. Phillips*, 801 S.W.2d 523, 525 (Tex. 1990).

[290] *Mellon Mortg. Co. v. Holder*, 5 S.W.3d 654, 655 (Tex. 1999); *Nixon v. Mr. Prop. Mgmt. Co., Inc.*, 690 S.W.2d 546, 551 (Tex. 1985).

- In determining duty the court may also consider "whether one party would generally have superior knowledge of the risk or a right to control the actor who caused the harm."[291]

- In some cases a duty will exist as a matter of law based upon the existence of a special relationship.[292]

(2) Defendant breached the duty of care to the plaintiff.[293]

- In determining whether a party exercised the ordinary prudence expected under the same or similar circumstances, it is appropriate to consider any knowledge, skill, or even intelligence superior to that of the ordinary person and whether the party acted in accordance with those circumstances.[294]

(3) Damages to the plaintiff proximately resulted from the breach.[295]

- Proximate cause has two elements: cause in fact and foreseeability. The test for cause in fact is whether the act or omission was a substantial factor in causing the injury without which the harm would not have occurred. If the defendant's negligence merely furnished a condition that made the injuries possible, there can be no cause in fact.[296]

- Foreseeability means that the actor, as a person of ordinary intelligence, should have anticipated the dangers that his negligent act created for others... "[I]t is not required that the particular accident complained of should have been foreseen. All that is required is 'that the injury be of such a general character as might reasonably have been anticipated.'"[297]

- "Usually, the criminal conduct of a third party is a superseding cause relieving the negligent actor from liability. However, the tortfeasor's negligence will not be excused where the criminal conduct is a foreseeable result of such negligence."[298]

1-10:3 Damages and Remedies

1-10:3.1 Actual Damages

See Chapter 10 and Chapter 11.

1-10:3.1a Personal Property

See Chapter 11, Section 11-8:2.

---

[291] *Nabors Drilling, U.S.A. Inc. v. Escoto*, 288 S.W.3d 401, 410 (Tex. 2009).
[292] *Golden Spread Council, Inc. v. Akins*, 926 S.W.2d 287, 292 (Tex. 1996); *Van Horn v. Chambers*, 970 S.W.2d 542, 546–47 (Tex. 1998).
[293] *Firestone Steel Prods. Co. v. Barajas*, 927 S.W.2d 608, 613 (Tex. 1996); *Midwest Emp'rs Cas. Co. ex rel. English v. Harpole*, 293 S.W.3d 770, 776 (Tex. App.—San Antonio 2009, no pet.).
[294] *Jackson v. Axelrad*, 221 S.W.3d 650, 655–56 (Tex. 2007).
[295] *Firestone Steel Prods. Co. v. Barajas*, 927 S.W.2d 608, 613 (Tex. 1996).
[296] *Western Invs., Inc. v. Urena*, 162 S.W.3d 547, 551 (Tex. 2005).
[297] *Nixon v. Mr. Prop. Mgmt. Co., Inc.*, 690 S.W.2d 546, 550–51 (Tex. 1985); *Ryder Integrated Logistics, Inc. v. Fayette Cty.*, 453 S.W.3d 922 (Tex. 2015).
[298] *Nixon v. Mr. Prop. Mgmt. Co., Inc.*, 690 S.W.2d 546, 550 (Tex. 1985).

1-10:3.1b Real Property

See Chapter 11, Section 11-8:1.

1-10:3.1c Economic Injury

See generally Chapter 11. *But also see* Chapter 12, Section 12-3 for a discussion of the economic loss rule in Texas.

1-10:3.2 Exemplary Damages

Exemplary damages are recoverable for harm that results from gross negligence.[299] *See* Chapter 11, Section 11-12.

1-10:3.3 Interest

See Chapter 11, Section 11-13:1.

1-10:3.4 Court Costs

See Chapter 11, Section 11-13:2.

1-10:4 Defenses

1-10:4.1 Statute of Limitations

Two-year statute of limitations applies.[300]

1-10:4.2 Comparative Fault

See Chapter 18, Section 18-2:3.

1-10:4.3 Economic Loss Rule

See Economic Loss Rule, Chapter 12, Section 12-3.

1-11 Negligence Per Se

1-11:1 Introduction

Negligence per se is a tort concept whereby a legislatively imposed standard of conduct is adopted by a civil court as defining the conduct of a reasonably prudent person.

---

[299] Tex. Civ. Prac. & Rem. Code Ann. § 41.003(a)(3); *Bennett v. Reynolds*, 315 S.W.3d 867, 871 n.13 (Tex. 2010).

[300] Tex. Civ. Prac. & Rem. Code Ann. § 16.003(a); *G.T. Leach Builders, LLC v. Sapphire V.P., LP*, 458 S.W.3d 502, 510 (Tex. 2015); *KPMG Peat Marwick v. Harrison Cty. Housing Fin. Corp.*, 988 S.W.2d 746, 750 (Tex. 1999).

1-11:1.1 Related Causes of Action

Negligence, Negligent Hiring, Negligent Misrepresentation, Negligent Undertaking

MUST READ CASES

Moughon v. Wolf, 576 S.W.2d 603 (Tex. 1978)

Nixon v. Mr. Prop. Mgmt. Co., Inc., 690 S.W.2d 546 (Tex. 1985)

Perry v. S.N., 973 S.W.2d 301 (Tex. 1998)

1-11:2 Elements

(1) The plaintiff belongs to the class that the statute was designed to protect, and the plaintiff's injury is of a type that the statute was designed to prevent.[301]

- All persons have a duty to obey the criminal law in the sense that they may be prosecuted for not doing so, but this is not equivalent to a duty in tort.[302]

(2) It is appropriate to impose tort liability for violations of the statute.[303]

- This is a question of law for the court to determine.[304]

- Factors which may be considered by the court include: (1) whether the statute is the sole source of any tort duty from the defendant to the plaintiff or merely supplies a standard of conduct for an existing common law duty; (2) whether the statute puts the public on notice by clearly defining the required conduct; (3) whether the statute would impose liability without fault; (4) whether negligence per se would result in ruinous damages disproportionate to the seriousness of the statutory violation, particularly if the liability would fall on a broad and wide range of collateral wrongdoers; and (5) whether the plaintiff's injury is a direct or indirect result of the violation of the statute.[305]

(3) The defendant violated the statute without legal excuse.[306]

- The violator may excuse his conduct, but he must produce some evidence of a legally acceptable excuse. If some evidence of a legally acceptable excuse such as emergency, incapacity or impossibility is produced in the case by the violator, the litigant charging statutory violation must assume a further burden of requesting an issue which inquires whether the litigant charged is guilty of negligence as measured by the common law or reasonable person standard. The evidence adduced must be more than a mere

---

[301] *Perry v. S.N.*, 973 S.W.2d 301, 305 (Tex. 1998); *Moughon v. Wolf*, 576 S.W.2d 603, 604 (Tex. 1978).

[302] *Perry v. S.N.*, 973 S.W.2d 301, 304 (Tex. 1998); *see, e.g., Smith v. Merritt*, 940 S.W.2d 602, 607–08 (Tex. 1997).

[303] *Perry v. S.N.*, 973 S.W.2d 301, 305 (Tex. 1998); *Smith v. Merritt*, 940 S.W.2d 602, 607–08 (Tex. 1997).

[304] *Perry v. S.N.*, 973 S.W.2d 301, 305 (Tex. 1998); *Smith v. Merritt*, 940 S.W.2d 602, 607–08 (Tex. 1997).

[305] *Perry v. S.N.*, 973 S.W.2d 301, 309 (Tex. 1998).

[306] *Southern Pac. Co. v. Castro*, 493 S.W.2d 491, 497 (Tex. 1973).

scintilla and the excuse must be legally acceptable; otherwise, this additional burden does not arise and the common law negligence theory should not be submitted.[307]

(4) The violative conduct was the proximate cause of plaintiff's injury.[308]

- To establish foreseeability, the plaintiff must show that the defendant should have anticipated the dangers that its negligent act or omission created for others, but only with regard to the general danger, not the exact sequence of events that produced the harm.[309]
- The test for cause in fact is whether the negligent act or omission was a substantial factor in bringing about the injury, without which the harm would not have occurred.[310]

1-11:3 Damages and Remedies

1-11:3.1 Actual Damages

Actual damages recoverable for negligence actions are also recoverable for negligence per se. Negligence per se is not a separate cause of action that exists independently of a common-law negligence cause of action, but is merely one method of proving the breach of duty element of a negligence cause of action.[311] *See* Chapter 10 and Chapter 11.

1-11:3.1a Damages for Injury to Personal Property

See Chapter 11, Section 11-8:2.

1-11:3.1b Damages for Injury to Real Property

See Chapter 11, Section 11-8:1.

1-11:3.1c Damages for Economic Injury

Recover for pure economic loss may be problematic in negligence-based torts as a result of the economic loss rule. *See* Chapter 11, Section 11-1 and Chapter 12, Section 12-3.

---

[307] *Moughon v. Wolf*, 576 S.W.2d 603, 604–05 (Tex. 1978).
[308] *Moughon v. Wolf*, 576 S.W.2d 603, 604 (Tex. 1978).
[309] *Ambrosio v. Carter's Shooting Ctr., Inc.*, 20 S.W.3d 262, 265 (Tex. App.—Houston [14th Dist.] 2000, pet denied).
[310] *Ambrosio v. Carter's Shooting Ctr., Inc.*, 20 S.W.3d 262, 266 (Tex. App.—Houston [14th Dist.] 2000, pet denied).
[311] *Weirich v. IESI Corp.*, No. 03-14-00819-CV, 2016 WL 4628066, at *2 (Tex. App.—Austin Aug. 31, 2016, no pet.); *Thomas v. Uzoka*, 290 S.W.3d 437, 445 (Tex. App.—Houston [14th Dist.] 2009, pet. denied).

1-11:3.2 Exemplary Damages

Exemplary damages are recoverable for harm that results from gross negligence.[312] *See* Chapter 11, Section 11-12.

1-11:3.3 Interest

See Chapter 11, Section 11-13:1.

1-11:3.4 Court Costs

See Chapter 11, Section 11-13:2.

1-11:3.5 Damages Caps

1-11:4 Defenses

1-11:4.1 Statute of Limitations

Two-year statute of limitations applies.[313]

1-11:4.2 Comparative Fault

See Chapter 18, Section 18-2:3.

1-12 Intellectual Property—Common Law Trademark Infringement

1-12:1 Introduction

Similar to statutory trademark infringement under the Lanham Act or the Texas Trademark Act, a Common Law Trademark Infringement suit protects a person's ability to distinguish his goods and services from others' goods or services by eliminating similar uses which might prove confusing, deceptive, or dilutive. In fact, the issues in a Common Law Trademark Infringement suit under Texas law are no different than a trademark infringement suit under federal law.[314] The elements in common law

---

[312] Tex. Civ. Prac. & Rem. Code Ann. § 41.003(a)(3); *Bennett v. Reynolds*, 315 S.W.3d 867, 871 n.13 (Tex. 2010).

[313] Tex. Civ. Prac. & Rem. Code Ann. § 16.003(a); *G.T. Leach Builders, LLC v. Sapphire V.P., LP*, 458 S.W.3d 502, 510 (Tex. 2015); *KPMG Peat Marwick v. Harrison Cty. Housing Fin. Corp.*, 988 S.W.2d 746, 750 (Tex. 1999).

[314] *Keane v. Fox Television Stations, Inc.*, 297 F. Supp. 2d 921, 937 (S.D. Tex. 2004) *aff'd*, 129 Fed. Appx. 874 (5th Cir. 2005); *Condom Sense, Inc. v. Alshalabi*, 390 S.W.3d 734, 738 (Tex. App.—Dallas 2012, no pet.); *All Am. Builders, Inc. v. All Am. Siding of Dallas, Inc.*, 991 S.W.2d 484, 488 (Tex. App.—Fort Worth 1999, no pet.) ("To succeed on a common law claim for service mark infringement, the party seeking an injunction must show: (1) the name it seeks to protect is eligible for protection; (2) it is the senior user of the name; (3) there is a likelihood of confusion between its mark and that of its competitor; and (4) the likelihood of confusion will cause irreparable injury for which there is no adequate legal

trademark or service mark infringement under Texas law are the same as those under federal trademark law.[315]

MUST READ CASES

Union Nat'l Bank of Tex., Laredo, Tex. v. Union Nat'l Bank of Tex., Austin, Tex., 909 F.2d 839 (5th Cir. 1990)

All Am. Builders, Inc. v. All Am. Siding of Dallas, Inc., 991 S.W.2d 484 (Tex. App.—Fort Worth 1999, no pet.)

Zapata Corp. v. Zapata Trading Int'l, Inc., 841 S.W.2d 45 (Tex. App.—Houston [14th Dist.] 1992, no writ)

1-12:2 Elements

(1) The proposed mark is eligible for protection

- The proposed mark is eligible for protection.[316]

- Whether a proposed mark is eligible for protection turns on which of four categories it belongs in:

    - Arbitrary/Fanciful;
    - Suggestive;
    - Descriptive; or
    - Generic.[317]

- The categorization of a proposed mark is a question of fact[318] which seeks to answer where on the spectrum each proposed mark lies.[319]

---

remedy."); *All Am. Builders, Inc. v. All Am. Siding of Dallas, Inc.*, 991 S.W.2d 484, 488 (Tex. App.—Fort Worth 1999, no pet.).

[315] *Hot-Hed, Inc. v. Safehouse Habitats (Scotland), Ltd.*, 333 S.W.3d 719, 730 (Tex. App.—Houston [1st Dist.] 2010, pet. denied); *Restrepo v. All. Riggers & Constructors, Ltd.*, 538 S.W.3d 724, 743–44 (Tex. App.—El Paso, 2017).

[316] *Horseshoe Bay Resort Sales Co. v. Lake Lyndon B. Johnson Improvement Corp.*, 53 S.W.3d 799, 806 (Tex. App.—Austin 2001, pet. denied); *All Am. Builders, Inc. v. All Am. Siding of Dallas, Inc.*, 991 S.W.2d 484, 488 (Tex. App.—Fort Worth 1999, no pet.).

[317] *All Am. Builders, Inc. v. All Am. Siding of Dallas, Inc.*, 991 S.W.2d 484, 489–90 (Tex. App.—Fort Worth 1999, no pet.) (An arbitrary mark is either coined, such as "Xerox," or not suggestive of the product, such as "Ivory" for soaps. A suggestive mark is one that requires the consumer to draw a conclusion based upon their imagination, such as "Igloo" for water coolers. A descriptive mark is one that identifies one or more characteristics or qualities of the good or service, such as "speedy." A generic mark is the name of a particular genus or class of which an individual article or service is but a member, for instance using the term "fruit" which applies equally to apples, oranges, or grapes.).

[318] *Union Nat'l Bank of Tex., Laredo, Tex. v. Union Nat'l Bank of Tex., Austin, Tex.*, 909 F.2d 839, 846 (5th Cir. 1990); *All Am. Builders, Inc. v. All Am. Siding of Dallas, Inc.*, 991 S.W.2d 484, 489 (Tex. App.—Fort Worth 1999, no pet.).

[319] *Union Nat'l Bank of Tex., Laredo, Tex. v. Union Nat'l Bank of Tex., Austin, Tex.*, 909 F.2d 839, 846 (5th Cir. 1990).

- Arbitrary and suggestive marks are given the greatest amount of protection because they are distinctive; they require no proof of secondary meaning.[320]
- Descriptive terms are only eligible for trademark protection if they have developed secondary meaning.[321]
  - In order to establish secondary meaning, the plaintiff must show that the primary significance of the term in the minds of the consuming public is not the product but the producer.[322]
- Generic terms are not eligible for trademark protection.[323]

(2) The plaintiff is the senior user of the mark

- The plaintiff is the senior user of the mark.[324]
- The first person to use the mark is deemed to be the senior user. Registration of a mark is not determinative.[325]

(3) There is a likelihood of confusion between the plaintiff's mark and that of the other user

- There is a likelihood of confusion between the plaintiff's mark and that of the other user.[326]
- Whether a defendant's use is likely to deceive or cause confusion is a factor-based test which looks to:
  - The category of trademark;
    - Arbitrary, Suggestive, Descriptive, or Generic;
  - The similarity of design;
  - The similarity of the products;
  - The identity of retail outlets and purchasers;

---

[320] *Union Nat'l Bank of Tex., Laredo, Tex. v. Union Nat'l Bank of Tex., Austin, Tex.*, 909 F.2d 839, 844 (5th Cir. 1990); *All Am. Builders, Inc. v. All Am. Siding of Dallas, Inc.*, 991 S.W.2d 484, 489 (Tex. App.—Fort Worth 1999, no pet.).

[321] *All Am. Builders, Inc. v. All Am. Siding of Dallas, Inc.*, 991 S.W.2d 484, 489 (Tex. App.—Fort Worth 1999, no pet.).

[322] *Kellogg Co. v. Nat'l Biscuit Co.*, 305 U.S. 111, 118 (1938). One Texas court seemed to heighten the burden, requiring a plaintiff to prove that in the minds of the public, the proposed mark identifies a "single thing coming from a single source." See *Zapata Corp. v. Zapata Trading Int'l, Inc.*, 841 S.W.2d 45, 48 (Tex. App.—Houston [14th Dist.] 1992, no writ).

[323] *All Am. Builders, Inc. v. All Am. Siding of Dallas, Inc.*, 991 S.W.2d 484, 489 (Tex. App.—Fort Worth 1999, no pet.).

[324] *Horseshoe Bay Resort Sales Co. v. Lake Lyndon B. Johnson Improvement Corp.*, 53 S.W.3d 799, 806 (Tex. App.—Austin 2001, pet. denied); *All Am. Builders, Inc. v. All Am. Siding of Dallas, Inc.*, 991 S.W.2d 484, 488 (Tex. App.—Fort Worth 1999, no pet.).

[325] *Union Nat'l Bank of Tex., Laredo, Tex. v. Union Nat'l Bank of Tex., Austin, Tex.*, 909 F.2d 839, 842–43 (5th Cir. 1990).

[326] *Horseshoe Bay Resort Sales Co. v. Lake Lyndon B. Johnson Improvement Corp.*, 53 S.W.3d 799, 806 (Tex. App.—Austin 2001, pet. denied); *All Am. Builders, Inc. v. All Am. Siding of Dallas, Inc.*, 991 S.W.2d 484, 488 (Tex. App.—Fort Worth 1999, no pet.).

BUSINESS TORTS LITIGATION

- The identity of advertising media utilized;
- The defendant's intent;
- Whether actual confusion occurred.[327]
- A finding of likelihood of confusion does not need to be supported by a majority of these factors.[328]
- Parody is an additional factor to consider regarding whether a likelihood of confusion exists.[329]

(4) The likelihood of confusion will cause irreparable injury for which there is no adequate legal remedy

- The likelihood of confusion will cause irreparable injury for which there is no adequate legal remedy.[330]
- Likely damage to the plaintiff's goodwill and reputation are sufficient to prove irreparable injury.[331]

1-12:3 Damages and Remedies

1-12:3.1 Injunction

The exclusive remedy for common law Trademark Infringement is an injunction. A successful plaintiff may only enjoin a defendant from use in areas where he is currently doing business and areas he is likely to expand into.[332]

1-12:4 Defenses

1-12:4.1 Statute of Limitations

The two-year limitations period controls.[333]

Trademark infringement is a continuing tort.[334]

---

[327] *Zapata Corp. v. Zapata Trading Int'l, Inc.*, 841 S.W.2d 45, 49 (Tex. App.—Houston [14th Dist.] 1992, no writ).
[328] *Zapata Corp. v. Zapata Trading Int'l, Inc.*, 841 S.W.2d 45, 49 (Tex. App.—Houston [14th Dist.] 1992, no writ).
[329] *Elvis Presley Enters., Inc. v. Capece*, 141 F.3d 188, 194 (5th Cir. 1998).
[330] *Horseshoe Bay Resort Sales Co. v. Lake Lyndon B. Johnson Improvement Corp.*, 53 S.W.3d 799, 806 (Tex. App.—Austin 2001, pet. denied); *All Am. Builders, Inc. v. All Am. Siding of Dallas, Inc.*, 991 S.W.2d 484, 488 (Tex. App.—Fort Worth 1999, no pet.).
[331] *See Zapata Corp. v. Zapata Trading Int'l, Inc.*, 841 S.W.2d 45, 50 (Tex. App.—Houston [14th Dist.] 1992, no writ).
[332] *Union Nat'l Bank of Tex., Laredo, Tex. v. Union Nat'l Bank of Tex., Austin, Tex.*, 909 F.2d 839, 843 (5th Cir. 1990).
[333] Tex. Civ. Prac. & Rem. Code Ann. § 16.003; *Thompson v. Thompson Air Conditioning & Heating, Inc.*, 884 S.W.2d 555, 561 (Tex. App.—Texarkana 1994, no writ); *but see Mary Kay, Inc. v. Weber*, 601 F. Supp. 2d 839, 859–60 (N.D. Tex. 2009) (holding a federal Lanham Act violation is governed by a four-year limitations period under Texas law).
[334] *Horseshoe Bay Resort Sales Co. v. Lake Lyndon B. Johnson Improvement Corp.*, 53 S.W.3d 799, 812 (Tex. App.—Austin 2001, pet. denied).

1-12:4.2 Laches

Laches is an available affirmative defense.[335]

Laches consists of three elements:

1. An unreasonable delay in asserting a right or claim;
2. That is not excused; and
3. That results in undue prejudice to the defendant.[336]

1-12:4.3 Abandonment

Abandonment of a trademark is a defense to a common law Trademark Infringement suit.[337]

Abandonment is established by proof:

- That the plaintiff discontinued use of the mark; and
- Intended to abandon the mark.[338]

1-12:4.4 Acquiescence

Acquiescence is an available defense.[339]

Acquiescence occurs if the plaintiff makes implicit or explicit assurances to the defendant which induces the defendant's reliance.[340]

1-12:4.5 Fair Use

Fair use is an affirmative defense.[341]

Fair use allows for:

- The ability of a copyist who legally copied to tell the public that he has copied;[342] and
- The ability of a person to compare his goods and services with that of the markholder.[343]

Fair use is limited by these principles:

---

[335] *Condom Sense, Inc. v. Alshalabi*, 390 S.W.3d 734, 758 (Tex. App.—Dallas 2012, no pet.).
[336] *Condom Sense, Inc. v. Alshalabi*, 390 S.W.3d 734, 758 (Tex. App.—Dallas 2012, no pet.).
[337] *Condom Sense, Inc. v. Alshalabi*, 390 S.W.3d 734, 751 (Tex. App.—Dallas 2012, no pet.).
[338] *Condom Sense, Inc. v. Alshalabi*, 390 S.W.3d 734, 751 (Tex. App.—Dallas 2012, no pet.).
[339] *Elvis Presley Enters., Inc. v. Capece*, 141 F.3d 188, 206 (5th Cir. 1998).
[340] *Elvis Presley Enters., Inc. v. Capece*, 141 F.3d 188, 206 (5th Cir. 1998).
[341] *Board of Supervisors for Louisiana State Univ. Agric. & Mech. Coll. v. Smack Apparel Co.*, 550 F.3d 465, 488 (5th Cir. 2008).
[342] *Pebble Beach Co. v. Tour 18 I Ltd.*, 155 F.3d 526, 545 (5th Cir. 1998), *abrogated on other grounds by Traffix Devices, Inc., v. Mktg. Displays, Inc.*, 532 U.S. 23 (2001).
[343] *Pebble Beach Co. v. Tour 18 I Ltd.*, 155 F.3d 526, 545 (5th Cir. 1998), *abrogated on other grounds by Traffix Devices, Inc., v. Mktg. Displays, Inc.*, 532 U.S. 23 (2001).

- The defendant may only use so much of the mark as is necessary to identify the product or service; and

- The defendant may not do anything that suggests affiliation, sponsorship or endorsement by the markholder.[344]

Federal and Texas statutes provide more protections for "fair use" in a statutory trademark infringement context.[345]

1-13 Intellectual Property—Statutory Trademark Infringement/Texas Trademark Act

1-13:1 Introduction

The law of trademark infringement has three sources: The Lanham Act, the Texas Trademark Act, and the common law. All three areas of law are similar in that they protect a person's ability to distinguish his goods or services from others' goods or services by eliminating similar uses which might prove confusing, deceptive or dilutive. The crux of the Texas Trademark Act is that, in order to bring suit upon it, the plaintiff must have registered his trademark with the Secretary of State.

1-13:1.1 Related Causes of Action

Common Law Trademark Infringement, Federal Trademark Infringement,[346] Misuse of a Trade Name, Misappropriation of Trade Secrets

MUST READ CASES

Condom Sense, Inc. v. Alshalabi, 390 S.W.3d 734 (Tex. App.—Dallas 2012, no pet.)

Horseshoe Bay Resort Sales Co. v. Lake Lyndon B. Johnson Improvement. Corp., 53 S.W.3d 799 (Tex. App.—Austin 2001, pet. denied)

Zapata Corp. v. Zapata Trading Int'l, Inc., 841 S.W.2d 45 (Tex. App.—Houston [14th Dist.] 1992, no writ)

1-13:2 Elements

1-13:2.1 Infringement

(1) The plaintiff holds a registered mark.[347]

- A certificate of registration is prima facie proof of the validity and ownership of the mark.[348]

---

[344] *Board of Supervisors for Louisiana State Univ. Agric. & Mech. Coll. v. Smack Apparel Co.*, 550 F.3d 465, 489 (5th Cir. 2008).
[345] *See* 15 U.S.C.A. § 1125(c)(3)(A); Tex. Bus. & Com. Code Ann. § 16.103(d).
[346] Federal Trademark Infringement is largely governed by the Lanham Act (15 U.S.C.A. §§ 1051–1127). This publication does not address Federal Trademark Infringement.
[347] Tex. Bus. & Com. Code Ann. § 16.102(a)(1).
[348] Tex. Bus. & Com. Code Ann. § 16.060(c)(1)–(2).

(2) The defendant uses the mark without the plaintiff's consent.[349]

- The "mark" used by the defendant is one that is a:
  - Reproduction of the registered mark;
  - Counterfeit of the registered mark;
  - Copy of the registered mark; or
  - Colorable imitation of the registered mark.[350]
- The defendant's "use" means:
  - A mark is considered to be in use in this state in connection with goods when:
    - The mark is placed in any manner on:

    (A) the goods;

    (B) containers of the goods;

    (C) displays associated with the goods;

    (D) tags or labels affixed to the goods; or

    (E) documents associated with the goods or sale of the goods, if the nature of the goods makes placement described by Paragraphs (A) through (D) impracticable; and
  - The goods are sold or transported in commerce in this state.[351]
  - A mark is considered to be in use in this state in connection with services when:
    - The mark is used or displayed in this state in connection with selling or advertising the services; and
    - The services are rendered in this state.[352]

(3) In connection with selling, distributing, offering for sale, or advertising goods or services

- In connection with selling, distributing, offering for sale, or advertising goods or services.[353]

(4) Such use is likely to deceive or cause confusion as to the origin of the goods or services

- Such use is likely to deceive or cause confusion as to the origin of the goods or services.[354]

---

[349] Tex. Bus. & Com. Code Ann. § 16.102(a)(1).
[350] Tex. Bus. & Com. Code Ann. § 16.102(a)(1).
[351] Tex. Bus. & Com. Code Ann. § 16.003(a).
[352] Tex. Bus. & Com. Code Ann. § 16.003(b).
[353] Tex. Bus. & Com. Code Ann. § 16.003(b).
[354] Tex. Bus. & Com. Code Ann. § 16.102(a)(1).

- Whether a defendant's use is likely to deceive or cause confusion is a factor-based test[355] which looks to:
    - Type of trademark;
    - Arbitrary, suggestive, descriptive or generic;
    - The similarity of design;
    - The similarity of the product;
    - The identity of retail outlets and purchasers;
    - The identity of advertising media utilized;
    - The defendant's intent;
    - Whether actual confusion occurred.[356]

OR

(1) The plaintiff holds a registered mark.[357]
   - A certificate of registration is prima facie proof of the validity and ownership of the mark.[358]

(2) The defendant reproduces, counterfeits, copies or colorably imitates the mark.[359]

(3) The defendant applies the reproduction to goods or services to be sold or distributed in Texas.[360]

1-13:2.2 Dilution

(1) The plaintiff holds a famous, distinctive and registered mark.[361]
   - A certificate of registration is prima facie proof of the validity and ownership of the mark.[362]

---

[355] The factors in this test are referred to colloquially as the Dupont Factors. The United States Court of Customs and Patent Appeals issued the *In Re E.I. Du Pont de Nemours & Co.* opinion in 1973 where it gave a list of 12 factors to be considered when determining likelihood of confusion in trademark infringement cases. *In re E. I. Du Pont de Nemours & Co.*, 476 F.2d 1357, 1361 (Cust. & Pat. App 1973). Since that time the various federal circuits and state court systems have issued opinions stating the factors they find most relevant in trademark infringement cases. They do not typically include all 12 Dupont Factors. However, those lists are normally non-exhaustive. The lesser-used Dupont Factors can prove useful in strengthening a claim or in providing factors that show infringement even if the more commonly-used factors do not.
[356] *Zapata Corp. v. Zapata Trading Int'l, Inc.*, 841 S.W.2d 45, 49 (Tex. App.—Houston [14th Dist.] 1992, no writ).
[357] Tex. Bus. & Com. Code Ann. § 16.102(a)(2).
[358] Tex. Bus. & Com. Code Ann. § 16.060(c)(1)–(2).
[359] Tex. Bus. & Com. Code Ann. § 16.102(a)(2).
[360] Tex. Bus. & Com. Code Ann. § 16.102(a)(2).
[361] Tex. Bus. & Com. Code Ann. § 16.103(a).
[362] Tex. Bus. & Com. Code Ann. § 16.060(c)(1)–(2).

- Whether a mark is famous is determined by factors including:
  - The duration, extent and geographic reach of the advertisement and publicity of the mark in this state, regardless of whether the mark is advertised or publicized by the owner or a third party;
  - The amount, volume and geographic extent of sales of goods or services offered under the mark in this state;
  - The extent of actual recognition of the mark in this state; and
  - Whether the mark is registered in this state or in the United States Patent and Trademark Office.[363]
(2) The defendant's use of a mark or trade name is likely to cause dilution of the plaintiff's mark.[364]

1-13:2.3 Fraudulent Registration

(1) A person files for or obtains registration of a mark.[365]
(2) By knowingly making a false or fraudulent representation or declaration, oral or written, or by any other fraudulent means.[366]

1-13:3 Damages and Remedies

1-13:3.1 Actual Damages

An infringement plaintiff may be able to recover his actual damages resulting from the defendant's infringement if the defendant acted with intent to cause confusion or mistake or with intent to deceive.[367]

A fraudulent registration plaintiff may recover all damages resulting from the fraudulent filing or registration.[368]

1-13:3.2 Disgorgement

An infringement plaintiff may be able to recover the defendant's profits resulting from the infringement.[369]

1-13:3.3 Injunction

An infringement plaintiff is entitled to an injunction if he prevails.[370]

---

[363] Tex. Bus. & Com. Code Ann. § 16.103(b).
[364] Tex. Bus. & Com. Code Ann. § 16.103(a).
[365] Tex. Bus. & Com. Code Ann. § 16.101.
[366] Tex. Bus. & Com. Code Ann. § 16.101.
[367] Tex. Bus. & Com. Code Ann. § 16.102(c)(1), (e).
[368] Tex. Bus. & Com. Code Ann. § 16.101.
[369] Tex. Bus. & Com. Code Ann. § 16.102(c)(1).
[370] Tex. Bus. & Com. Code Ann. § 16.104(b).

A dilution plaintiff is entitled to an injunction in the areas of the state in which the plaintiff's mark was famous before the defendant began using the dilutive mark.[371]

1-13:3.4 Statutory Damages

A court may award an infringement plaintiff up to three times the combined amount of the defendant's profits and the plaintiff's damages if the defendant acted:

- With one of the following:
  - With actual knowledge of the plaintiff's mark; or
  - In bad faith;[372] and
- With the intent to cause confusion or mistake or with intent to deceive.[373]

1-13:3.5 Attorney's Fees

A court may award an infringement plaintiff reasonable attorney's fees if the defendant acted:

- With one of the following:
  - With actual knowledge of the plaintiff's mark; or
  - In bad faith;[374] and
- With the intent to cause confusion or mistake or with intent to deceive.[375]

1-13:4 Defenses

1-13:4.1 Statute of Limitations

The two-year limitations period controls.[376]

Trademark infringement is a continuing tort.

1-13:4.2 Invalidity of the Mark

A defendant may put on evidence to counter the validity of a mark.[377]

---

[371] Tex. Bus. & Com. Code Ann. § 16.103(c).
[372] Tex. Bus. & Com. Code Ann. § 16.102(d).
[373] Tex. Bus. & Com. Code Ann. § 16.102(e).
[374] Tex. Bus. & Com. Code Ann. § 16.102(d)(2).
[375] Tex. Bus. & Com. Code Ann. § 16.102(e).
[376] Tex. Civ. Prac. & Rem. Code Ann. § 16.003; *Thompson v. Thompson Air Conditioning & Heating, Inc.*, 884 S.W.2d 555, 561 (Tex. App.—Texarkana 1994, no writ); *but see Mary Kay, Inc. v. Weber*, 601 F. Supp. 2d 839, 859–60 (N.D. Tex. 2009) (holding a federal Lanham Act violation is governed by a four-year limitations period under Texas law).
[377] *See Horseshoe Bay Resort Sales Co. v. Lake Lyndon B. Johnson Improvement Corp.*, 53 S.W.3d 799, 806 (Tex. App.—Austin 2001, pet. denied) (deciding validity of a trademark under common law, where the registration of a mark is not prima facie proof of its validity).

An invalid mark is one that:

- Does not distinguish the goods or services it is attached to;[378] or
- One that:
  - Consists of or comprises matter that is immoral, deceptive or scandalous;
  - Consists of or comprises matter that may disparage,[379] falsely suggest a connection with, or bring into contempt or disrepute:
    - A person, whether living or dead;
    - An institution;
    - A belief; or
    - A national symbol;
  - Depicts, comprises, or simulates the flag, the coat of arms or other insignia of:
    - The United States;
    - A state;
    - A municipality; or
    - A foreign nation;
  - Consists of or comprises the name, signature or portrait of a particular living individual who has not consented in writing to the mark's registration;
  - When used on or in connection with the applicant's goods or services:
    - Is merely descriptive or deceptively misdescriptive of the applicant's goods or services; or
    - Is primarily geographically descriptive or deceptively misdescriptive of the applicant's goods or services;
  - Is primarily merely a surname; or
  - Is likely to cause confusion or mistake, or to deceive, because, when used on or in connection with the applicant's goods or services, it resembles:
    - A mark registered in this state; or
    - An unabandoned mark registered with the United States Patent and Trademark Office.[380]

A mark that is merely descriptive or deceptively misdescriptive, primarily geographically descriptive or deceptively misdescriptive, or is primarily a surname is a valid mark if it has acquired distinctiveness through secondary meaning.[381]

---

[378] *See* Tex. Bus. & Com. Code Ann. § 16.051(a).
[379] In June 2017, the Supreme Court decided *Matal v. Tam*, where it struck down the disparagement clause within Section 2(a) of the Lanham Act as facially unconstitutional under the Free Speech Clause of the First Amendment. 137 S. Ct. 1744, 1765 (2017). As a result, the Texas statute will likely also have to change.
[380] Tex. Bus. & Com. Code Ann. § 16.051(a).
[381] Tex. Bus. & Com. Code Ann. § 16.051(b).

1-13:4.3 Abandonment

A holder of a mark abandons the mark if:

- The mark's use has been discontinued[382] with intent not to resume the use;[383] or
- The owner's conduct, including an omission or commission of an act, causes the mark to lose its significance as a mark.[384]

1-13:4.4 Laches

Laches is an available affirmative defense.[385]

Laches consists of three elements:

- An unreasonable delay in asserting a right or claim;
- That is not excused; and
- That results in undue prejudice to the defendant.[386]

1-13:4.5 First Amendment

First Amendment protections are a defense to trademark infringement.[387]

Most of the statutory defenses provide co-equal protection with the First Amendment.[388]

1-13:4.6 Fair Use

Fair use is a defense to a dilution claim.[389]

Fair use includes:

- Advertising or promoting that permits consumers to compare goods or services; or
- Identifying and parodying, criticizing, or commenting on the famous mark owner or the famous mark owner's goods or services.[390]

1-13:4.7 Non-Commercial Use

Non-commercial use is a defense to a dilution claim.[391]

---

[382] Nonuse of a mark for three consecutive years constitutes prima facie evidence of the mark's abandonment. Tex. Bus. & Com. Code Ann. § 16.004(c).

[383] Tex. Bus. & Com. Code Ann. § 16.004(a)(1).

[384] Tex. Bus. & Com. Code Ann. § 16.004(a)(2).

[385] *Condom Sense, Inc. v. Alshalabi*, 390 S.W.3d 734, 758 (Tex. App.—Dallas 2012, no pet.).

[386] *Condom Sense, Inc. v. Alshalabi*, 390 S.W.3d 734, 758 (Tex. App.—Dallas 2012, no pet.).

[387] *Abraham v. Alpha Chi Omega*, 708 F.3d 614, 628 (5th Cir. 2013).

[388] *Compare* Tex. Bus. & Com. Code Ann. § 16.103(d)(1)–(2) *with Abraham v. Alpha Chi Omega*, 708 F.3d 614, 628 (5th Cir. 2013).

[389] Tex. Bus. & Com. Code Ann. § 16.103(d)(1).

[390] Tex. Bus. & Com. Code Ann. § 16.103(d)(1).

[391] Tex. Bus. & Com. Code Ann. § 16.103(d)(2).

1-13:4.8 News Reporting or Commentary

News reporting or commentary is a defense to a dilution claim.[392]

1-14 Intellectual Property—Misuse of a Trade Name

1-14:1 Overview

Trade names are not permitted to be registered with Texas or the Patent and Trademark Office unless they also qualify as a trade or service mark. However, the common law recognizes a property interest in a trade name and the corollary cause of action for Misuse of Trade Name. The common law cause of action is nearly identical to that for common law trademark infringement, with the most significant difference being that descriptive names are not eligible for protection. Courts, and the authors of this publication, cite trademark and trade name cases for the same propositions.

1-14:1.1 Related Causes of Action

Common Law Trademark Infringement, Texas Trademark Act, Federal Trademark Infringement,[393] Misappropriation of Trade Secrets

MUST READ CASES

Union Nat'l Bank of Tex., Laredo, Tex. v. Union Nat'l Bank of Tex., Austin, Tex., 909 F.2d 839 (5th Cir. 1990)

All Am. Builders, Inc. v. All Am. Siding of Dallas, Inc., 991 S.W.2d 484 (Tex. App.—Fort Worth 1999, no pet.)

Zapata Corp. v. Zapata Trading Int'l, Inc., 841 S.W.2d 45 (Tex. App.—Houston [14th Dist.] 1992, no writ)

1-14:2 Elements

(1) The proposed name is eligible for protection.[394]

- Whether a proposed name is eligible for protection turns on which of four categories it belongs in:
  - Arbitrary/Fanciful;
  - Suggestive;
  - Descriptive; or
  - Generic.[395]

---

[392] Tex. Bus. & Com. Code Ann. § 16.103(d)(2).

[393] Federal Trademark Infringement is largely governed by the Lanham Act (15 U.S.C.A. §§ 1051–1127). This publication does not address Federal Trademark Infringement.

[394] *Horseshoe Bay Resort Sales Co. v. Lake Lyndon B. Johnson Improvement Corp.*, 53 S.W.3d 799, 806 (Tex. App.—Austin 2001, pet. denied); *All Am. Builders, Inc. v. All Am. Siding of Dallas, Inc.*, 991 S.W.2d 484, 488 (Tex. App.—Fort Worth 1999, no pet.).

[395] *All Am. Builders, Inc. v. All Am. Siding of Dallas, Inc.*, 991 S.W.2d 484, 489–90 (Tex. App.—Fort Worth 1999, no pet.) (An arbitrary mark is either coined, such as "Xerox," or not

- The categorization of a proposed name is a question of fact[396] which seeks to answer where on the spectrum each proposed name lies.[397]
- Arbitrary and suggestive marks are given the greatest amount of protection because they are distinctive; they require no proof of secondary meaning.[398]
- Descriptive terms are not eligible for trade name protection.[399]
- Generic terms are not eligible for trade name protection.[400]

(2) The plaintiff is the senior user of the name.[401]
- The first person to use the name is deemed to be the senior user. Registration of a trade name as a trade or service mark is not determinative.[402]

(3) There is a likelihood of confusion between the plaintiff's name and that of the other user.[403]
- Whether a defendant's use is likely to deceive or cause confusion is a factor-based test which looks to:
    - Type of name;
        - Arbitrary, suggestive, descriptive or generic;
    - The similarity of design;
    - The similarity of the product;
    - The identity of retail outlets and purchasers;

---

suggestive of the product, such as "Ivory" for soaps. A suggestive mark is one that requires the consumer to draw a conclusion based upon their imagination, such as "Igloo" for water coolers. A descriptive mark is one that identifies one or more characteristics or qualities of the good or service, such as "speedy." A generic mark is the name of a particular genus or class of which an individual article or service is but a member, for instance using the term "fruit" which applies equally to apples, oranges, or grapes.).

[396] *Union Nat'l Bank of Tex., Laredo, Tex. v. Union Nat'l Bank of Tex., Austin, Tex.*, 909 F.2d 839, 846 (5th Cir. 1990); *All Am. Builders, Inc. v. All Am. Siding of Dallas, Inc.*, 991 S.W.2d 484, 489 (Tex. App.—Fort Worth 1999, no pet.).

[397] *Union Nat'l Bank of Tex., Laredo, Tex. v. Union Nat'l Bank of Tex., Austin, Tex.*, 909 F.2d 839, 846 (5th Cir. 1990).

[398] *Union Nat'l Bank of Tex., Laredo, Tex. v. Union Nat'l Bank of Tex., Austin, Tex.*, 909 F.2d 839, 844 (5th Cir. 1990); *All Am. Builders, Inc. v. All Am. Siding of Dallas, Inc.*, 991 S.W.2d 484, 489 (Tex. App.—Fort Worth 1999, no pet.).

[399] *Thompson v. Thompson Air Conditioning & Heating, Inc.*, 884 S.W.2d 555, 559 (Tex. App.—Texarkana 1994, no writ); *Pipe Linings, Inc. v. Inplace Linings, Inc.*, 349 S.W.2d 279, 280 (Tex. Civ. App.—Fort Worth 1961, writ ref'd n.r.e.).

[400] *All Am. Builders, Inc. v. All Am. Siding of Dallas, Inc.*, 991 S.W.2d 484, 489 (Tex. App.—Fort Worth 1999, no pet.).

[401] *Horseshoe Bay Resort Sales Co. v. Lake Lyndon B. Johnson Improvement Corp.*, 53 S.W.3d 799, 806 (Tex. App.—Austin 2001, pet. denied); *All Am. Builders, Inc. v. All Am. Siding of Dallas, Inc.*, 991 S.W.2d 484, 488 (Tex. App.—Fort Worth 1999, no pet.).

[402] *Union Nat'l Bank of Tex., Laredo, Tex. v. Union Nat'l Bank of Tex., Austin, Tex.*, 909 F.2d 839, 842 (5th Cir. 1990).

[403] *Horseshoe Bay Resort Sales Co. v. Lake Lyndon B. Johnson Imp. Corp.*, 53 S.W.3d 799, 806 (Tex. App.—Austin 2001, pet. denied); *All Am. Builders, Inc. v. All Am. Siding of Dallas, Inc.*, 991 S.W.2d 484, 488 (Tex. App.—Fort Worth 1999, no pet.).

- The identity of advertising media utilized;
- The defendant's intent;
- Whether actual confusion occurred.[404]
- A finding of likelihood of confusion does not need to be supported by a majority of these factors.[405]
- The First Amendment requires a court to inquire into whether the complained-of use was a parody. Parody is an additional factor to consider in whether a likelihood of confusion exists.[406]
- An individual may use his legal name in all instances, unless such use operates as a fraud, is contractually barred, or he is estopped from so using it.[407]
  - Fraud means a use which is calculated to mislead the public as to the identity of the businesses.[408]

(4) The likelihood of confusion will cause irreparable injury for which there is no adequate legal remedy.[409]
- Likely damage to the plaintiff's goodwill and reputation are sufficient to prove irreparable injury.[410]

1-14:3 Damages and Remedies

1-14:3.1 Injunction

The exclusive remedy for Misuse of Trade Name is an injunction.[411]

1-14:4 Defenses

1-14:4.1 Statute of Limitations

The two-year limitations period controls.[412]

---

[404] *Zapata Corp. v. Zapata Trading Int'l, Inc.*, 841 S.W.2d 45, 49 (Tex. App.—Houston [14th Dist.] 1992, no writ).

[405] *Zapata Corp. v. Zapata Trading Int'l, Inc.*, 841 S.W.2d 45, 49 (Tex. App.—Houston [14th Dist.] 1992, no writ).

[406] *Elvis Presley Enters., Inc. v. Capece*, 141 F.3d 188, 194 (5th Cir. 1998).

[407] *Hanover Mfg. Co. Inc. v. Ed Hanover Trailers, Inc.*, 434 S.W.2d 109, 112 (Tex. 1968); *Goidl v. Advance Neckwear Co.*, 123 S.W.2d 865, 866 (Tex. 1939).

[408] *Goidl v. Advance Neckwear Co.*, 123 S.W.2d 865, 867 (Tex. 1939).

[409] *Horseshoe Bay Resort Sales Co. v. Lake Lyndon B. Johnson Imp. Corp.*, 53 S.W.3d 799, 806 (Tex. App.—Austin 2001, pet. denied); *All Am. Builders, Inc. v. All Am. Siding of Dallas, Inc.*, 991 S.W.2d 484, 488 (Tex. App.—Fort Worth 1999, no pet.).

[410] *Zapata Corp. v. Zapata Trading Int'l., Inc.*, 841 S.W.2d 45, 50 (Tex. App.—Houston [14th Dist.] 1992, no writ).

[411] *See Douglas v. Walker*, 707 S.W.2d 733 (Tex. App.—Beaumont 1986, no writ).

[412] Tex. Civ. Prac. & Rem. Code Ann. § 16.003; *Thompson v. Thompson Air Conditioning & Heating, Inc.*, 884 S.W.2d 555, 561 (Tex. App.—Texarkana 1994, no writ); *but see Mary Kay, Inc. v. Weber*, 601 F. Supp. 2d 839, 859–60 (N.D. Tex. 2009) (holding a federal Lanham Act violation is governed by a four-year limitations period under Texas law).

Trade name infringement is a continuing tort.[413]

1-14:4.2 Laches

Laches is an available affirmative defense.[414]

Laches consists of three elements:

- An unreasonable delay in asserting a right or claim;
- That is not excused; and
- That results in undue prejudice to the defendant.[415]

1-14:4.3 Abandonment

Abandonment of a trade name is a defense to a trademark infringement suit.[416]

Abandonment is established by proof:

- That the plaintiff discontinued use of the name; and
- Intended to abandon the name.[417]

A person is presumed to have not intended to abandon the use of his own legal name as a trade name.[418] There must be express language establishing the intention to abandon one's own legal name.[419]

1-14:4.4 Acquiescence

Acquiescence is an available defense.[420]

Acquiescence occurs if the plaintiff makes implicit or explicit assurances to the defendant which induces the defendant's reliance.[421]

1-14:4.5 First Amendment Concerns

Parody, although not an affirmative defense, is a factor to be considered in determining whether a likelihood of confusion exists.[422]

---

[413] *Horseshoe Bay Resort Sales Co. v. Lake Lyndon B. Johnson Improvement Corp.*, 53 S.W.3d 799, 812 (Tex. App.—Austin 2001, pet. denied) (discussing the related cause of action for trademark infringement).
[414] *Condom Sense, Inc. v. Alshalabi*, 390 S.W.3d 734, 758 (Tex. App.—Dallas 2012, no pet.).
[415] *Condom Sense, Inc. v. Alshalabi*, 390 S.W.3d 734, 758 (Tex. App.—Dallas 2012, no pet.).
[416] *Condom Sense, Inc. v. Alshalabi*, 390 S.W.3d 734, 751 (Tex. App.—Dallas 2012, no pet.).
[417] *Condom Sense, Inc. v. Alshalabi*, 390 S.W.3d 734, 751 (Tex. App.—Dallas 2012, no pet.).
[418] *Haltom v. Haltom's Jewelers, Inc.*, 691 S.W.2d 823, 826 (Tex. App.—Fort Worth 1985, writ ref'd n.r.e.).
[419] *Haltom v. Haltom's Jewelers, Inc.*, 691 S.W.2d 823, 826 (Tex. App.—Fort Worth 1985, writ ref'd n.r.e.).
[420] *Elvis Presley Enters., Inc. v. Capece*, 141 F.3d 188, 206 (5th Cir. 1998).
[421] *Elvis Presley Enters., Inc. v. Capece*, 141 F.3d 188, 206 (5th Cir. 1998).
[422] *Elvis Presley Enters., Inc. v. Capece*, 141 F.3d 188, 194 (5th Cir. 1998).

1-14:4.6 Fair Use

Fair use is an affirmative defense.[423]

Fair use allows for:

- The ability of a copyist who legally copied to tell the public that he has copied;[424] and

- The ability of a person to compare his goods and services with that of the name holder.[425]

Fair use is limited by these principles:

- The defendant may only use so much of the mark as necessary to identify the product or service; and

- The defendant may not do anything that suggests affiliation, sponsorship or endorsement by the name holder.[426]

  - Federal and Texas statutes governing trademarks provide more protections for "fair use" in the statutory infringement context.[427]

1-15 Intellectual Property—Misappropriation of Trade Secrets

1-15:1 Introduction

For trade-secret misappropriations commencing on or after September 1, 2013, the new governing state law is provided by the Texas Uniform Trade Secrets Act (TUTSA).[428]

1-15:2 Elements

(1) A trade secret exists.[429]

"Trade secret" means information, including a formula, pattern, compilation, program, device, method, technique, process, financial data, or list of actual or potential customers or suppliers, that:

derives independent economic value, actual or potential, from not being generally known to, and not being readily ascertainable by proper means by, other persons who can obtain economic value from its disclosure or use; and

---

[423] *Board of Supervisors for Louisiana State Univ. Agric. & Mech. Coll. v. Smack Apparel Co.*, 550 F.3d 465, 488 (5th Cir. 2008).
[424] *Pebble Beach Co. v. Tour 18 I Ltd.*, 155 F.3d 526, 545 (5th Cir. 1998), *abrogated on other grounds by Traffix Devices, Inc., v. Mktg. Displays, Inc.*, 532 U.S. 23 (2001).
[425] *Pebble Beach Co. v. Tour 18 I Ltd.*, 155 F.3d 526, 545 (5th Cir. 1998), *abrogated on other grounds by Traffix Devices, Inc., v. Mktg. Displays, Inc.*, 532 U.S. 23 (2001).
[426] *Board of Supervisors for Louisiana State Univ. Agric. & Mech. Coll. v. Smack Apparel Co.*, 550 F.3d 465, 489 (5th Cir. 2008).
[427] *See* 15 U.S.C.A. § 1125(c)(3)(A); Tex. Bus. & Com. Code Ann. § 16.103(d).
[428] Tex. Civ. Prac. & Rem. Code Ann. § 134A.001 *et seq.*
[429] Tex. Civ. Prac. & Rem. Code Ann. § 134A.002(6).

is the subject of efforts that are reasonable under the circumstances to maintain its secrecy.[430]

(2) Misappropriation of the trade secret has occurred (or is threatened) by:

(A) acquisition of a trade secret of another by a person who knows or has reason to know that the trade secret was acquired by improper means; or

(B) disclosure or use of a trade secret of another without express or implied consent by a person who:

(i) used improper means to acquire knowledge of the trade secret; or

(ii) at the time of disclosure or use, knew or had reason to know that the person's knowledge of the trade secret was:

(a) derived from or through a person who had utilized improper means to acquire it;

(b) acquired under circumstances giving rise to a duty to maintain its secrecy or limit its use; or

(c) derived from or through a person who owed a duty to the person seeking relief to maintain its secrecy or limit its use; or

(iii) before a material change of the person's position, knew or had reason to know that it was a trade secret and that knowledge of it had been acquired by accident or mistake.[431]

"Improper means" includes theft, bribery, misrepresentation, breach or inducement of a breach of a duty to maintain secrecy, to limit use, or to prohibit discovery of a trade secret, or espionage through electronic or other means.[432]

(3) The defendant's misappropriation has injured (or threatens to injure) the plaintiff, for which the granting of injunctive relief and/or the recovery of damages is appropriate.

For injunctive relief:

Actual or threatened misappropriation may be enjoined. On application to the court, an injunction shall be terminated when the trade secret has ceased to exist, but the injunction may be continued for an additional reasonable period of time in order to eliminate commercial advantage that otherwise would be derived from the misappropriation.[433]

In exceptional circumstances, an injunction may condition future use upon payment of a reasonable royalty for no longer than the period of time for which use could have been prohibited. Exceptional circumstances include a material and prejudicial change of position before acquiring knowledge or

---

[430] Tex. Civ. Prac. & Rem. Code Ann. § 134A.002(6).
[431] Tex. Civ. Prac. & Rem. Code Ann. § 134A.002(3).
[432] Tex. Civ. Prac. & Rem. Code Ann. § 134A.002(2).
[433] Tex. Civ. Prac. & Rem. Code Ann. § 134A.003(a).

reason to know of misappropriation that renders a prohibitive injunction inequitable.[434]

In appropriate circumstances, affirmative acts to protect a trade secret may be compelled by court order.[435]

In an action under TUTSA, a court shall preserve the secrecy of an alleged trade secret by reasonable means. There is a presumption in favor of granting protective orders to preserve the secrecy of trade secrets. Protective orders may include provisions limiting access to confidential information to only the attorneys and their experts, holding in camera hearings, sealing the records of the action, and ordering any person involved in the litigation not to disclose an alleged trade secret without prior court approval.[436]

For the recovery of damages:

In addition to or in lieu of injunctive relief, a claimant is entitled to recover damages for misappropriation. Damages can include both the actual loss caused by misappropriation and the unjust enrichment caused by misappropriation that is not taken into account in computing actual loss. In lieu of damages measured by any other methods, the damages caused by misappropriation may be measured by imposition of liability for a reasonable royalty for a misappropriator's unauthorized disclosure or use of a trade secret.[437]

If willful and malicious misappropriation is proven by clear and convincing evidence, the fact finder may award exemplary damages in an amount not exceeding twice any award made under Tex. Civ. Prac. & Rem. Code Ann. § 134A.004(a).[438]

The court may award reasonable attorney's fees to the prevailing party if:

a claim of misappropriation is made in bad faith;

a motion to terminate an injunction is made or resisted in bad faith; or

willful and malicious misappropriation exists.[439]

1-15:3 Damages and Remedies

In 2016, the Texas Supreme Court discussed the flexibility and fact-specific nature of damages for these cases.[440] Below is a portion of the discussion:

A "flexible and imaginative" approach is applied to the calculation of damages in misappropriation-of-trade-secrets cases. *Univ. Computing Co. v. Lykes–Youngstown Corp.*, 504 F.2d 518, 538 (5th Cir.1974). Damages in misappropria-

---

[434] Tex. Civ. Prac. & Rem. Code Ann. § 134A.003(b).
[435] Tex. Civ. Prac. & Rem. Code Ann. § 134A.003(c).
[436] Tex. Civ. Prac. & Rem. Code Ann. § 134A.006.
[437] Tex. Civ. Prac. & Rem. Code Ann. § 134A.004(a).
[438] Tex. Civ. Prac. & Rem. Code Ann. § 134A.004(b).
[439] Tex. Civ. Prac. & Rem. Code Ann. § 134A.005.
[440] *Southwestern Energy Prod. Co. v. Berry-Helfand*, 491 S.W.3d 699, 710–11 (Tex. 2016).

tion cases can therefore take several forms, including the value of the plaintiff's lost profits, the defendant's actual profits from the use of the secret, the value a reasonably prudent investor would have paid for the trade secret, the development costs the defendant avoided by the misappropriation, and a reasonable royalty.[441]

See discussion of injunctive relief and damages in Section 1-15:2.

1-15:3.1 Statute of Limitations

Three-year statute of limitations.[442]

A misappropriation of trade secrets that continues over time is a single cause of action and the limitations period begins running without regard to whether the misappropriation is a single or continuing act.[443]

---

[441] *Bohnsack v. Varco, L.P.*, 668 F.3d 262, 280 (5th Cir. 2012).

[442] Tex. Civ. Prac. & Rem. Code Ann. § 16.010(a). *Southwestern Energy Prod. Co. v. Berry-Helfand*, 491 S.W.3d 699, 721–22 (Tex. 2016). As a general proposition, a cause of action accrues when a wrongful act causes a legal injury, even if the fact of injury is not discovered until later, and even if all resulting damages have not yet occurred. *See Trinity River Auth. v. URS Consultants, Inc.*, 889 S.W.2d 259, 262 (Tex.1994). A cause of action for trade-secret misappropriation accrues "when the trade secret is actually used." *Computer Assocs. Int'l, Inc. v. Altai, Inc.*, 918 S.W.2d 453, 455 (Tex.1996); *Southwestern Energy Prod. Co. v. Berry-Helfand*, 491 S.W.3d 699, 721–22 (Tex. 2016).

[443] Tex. Civ. Prac. & Rem. Code Ann. § 16.010(b).

CHAPTER 2

Business Management Litigation*

2-1 Officer and Director Liability—Breach of the Duty of Care

2-1:1 Overview

Corporate officers and directors owe a fiduciary duty of care to the corporation which they serve. This duty may be limited by the certificate of formation, but not altogether eliminated. The duty encompasses mismanagement as well as wrongful distributions. This subtopic solely discusses mismanagement.

2-1:1.1 Related Causes of Action

Shareholder Derivative Suits, Breach of Duty of Loyalty, Wrongful Distribution of Dividends, Breach of Partnership Duty

MUST READ CASES

Gearhart Indus., Inc. v. Smith Int'l., Inc., 741 F.2d 707 (5th Cir. 1984)

Meyers v. Moody, 693 F.2d 1196 (5th Cir. 1982)

2-1:2 Elements

2-1:2.1 Mismanagement

(1) The defendant is an officer or director of a corporation

- Officers and directors owe their corporations duties.[1]

(2) The defendant owes a duty of care to the corporation

- Generally, all officers and directors owe their corporations a duty of care.[2]
- The duty of care requires an officer or director to act "as an ordinarily prudent man would under similar circumstances."[3]

---

* The authors thank Robyn Leatherwood for her assistance in the updating of this chapter.
[1] *Meyers v. Moody*, 693 F.2d 1196, 1209 (5th Cir. 1982).
[2] *Meyers v. Moody*, 693 F.2d 1196, 1209 (5th Cir. 1982).
[3] *Gearhart Indus., Inc. v. Smith Intern., Inc.*, 741 F.2d 707, 720 (5th Cir. 1984) (quoting *McCollum v. Dollar*, 213 S.W. 259 (Tex. Comm'n App. 1919)).

- However, the corporation's certificate of formation may limit the scope of the duty of care.[4]

(3) The defendant breaches that duty of care

- The Texas Supreme Court has never directly addressed the applicable standard of care. However, the majority of courts have held the applicable standard of care to be gross negligence.[5]
- The Texas Supreme Court has generally defined gross negligence as conduct that involves an extreme degree of risk, and the defendant was aware of the extreme risk created by his or her conduct.[6]
- The plaintiff must affirmatively negate the business judgment rule, which insulates an officer or director who acts in good faith, despite how mistaken those actions might later be.[7]
- The business judgment rule is not a defense, but rather a substantive rule of law.[8]

(4) Which proximately causes damages to the corporation

- The officer or director's gross negligence must proximately cause the corporation damages.[9]

2-1:2.2 Wrongful Distribution of Dividends

For elements, damages and remedies, and defenses of a Usurpation of Business Opportunity cause of action, *see* Wrongful Distribution of Dividends.

2-1:3 Damages and Remedies

2-1:3.1 Actual Damages

Actual damages are an appropriate remedy.[10]

---

[4] Tex. Bus. Orgs. Code Ann. § 7.001(b)–(c).

[5] *See, e.g., In re Life Partners Holdings, Inc.*, No. DR-11-CV-43-AM, 2015 WL 8523103, at *7 (W.D. Tex. Nov. 9, 2015) (Texas law); *F.D.I.C. v. Schreiner*, 892 F. Supp. 869, 881–82 (W.D. Tex. 1995) (Texas law); *Resolution Tr. Corp. v. Acton*, 844 F. Supp. 307, 313 (N.D. Tex. 1994), aff'd, 49 F.3d 1086 (5th Cir. 1995) (Texas law); *Smith v. Van Gorkom*, 488 A.2d 858, 873 (Del. 1985), *overruled on other grounds by Gantler v. Stephens*, 965 A.2d 695 (Del. 2009); *Elloway v. Pate*, 238 S.W.3d 882, 891 (Tex. App.—Houston [14th Dist.] 2007, no pet.). *But see Floyd v. Hefner*, No. CIV.A. H03-5693, 2006 WL 2844245, at *26–28 (S.D. Tex. Sept. 29, 2006), *on reconsideration in part*, 556 F. Supp. 2d 617 (S.D. Tex. 2008) (rejecting unequivocally the proposition that directors can be held liable for gross negligence under Texas law as it exists now).

[6] *Transp. Ins. Co. v. Moriel*, 879 S.W.2d 10, 22 (Tex. 1994).

[7] *Gearhart Indus., Inc. v. Smith Int'l, Inc.*, 741 F.2d 707, 721 (5th Cir. 1984) (Texas law); *F.D.I.C. v. Benson*, 867 F. Supp. 512, 521 (S.D. Tex. 1994) (explaining that the plaintiff must plead and prove bad faith in order to overcome the business judgment rule).

[8] *F.D.I.C. v. Benson*, 867 F. Supp. 512, 521 (S.D. Tex. 1994).

[9] *See F.D.I.C. v. Niblo*, 821 F. Supp. 441, 460 (N.D. Tex. 1993).

[10] *Meyers v. Moody*, 693 F.2d 1196, 1212 (5th Cir. 1982).

2-1:3.2 Special Damages

Special damages are an appropriate remedy if the plaintiff proves fraud.[11]

2-1:3.3 Exemplary Damages

Exemplary damages are available if the defendant acts:

- Maliciously;
- Fraudulently; or
- With gross negligence.[12]

Willful breaches suffice for the imposition of exemplary damages.[13]

Exemplary damages may be predicated upon an equitable remedy alone.[14]

2-1:4 Defenses

2-1:4.1 Statutory Safe Harbor for Directors

In discharging the duty of care, a director may, in good faith and with ordinary care, rely on information prepared or presented by:

- An officer or employee of the entity;
- Legal counsel;
- A certified public accountant;
- An investment banker;
- A person who the officer or director reasonably believes possesses professional expertise in the matter; or
- A committee of the board of directors of which the director is not a member.[15]

A director may not in good faith rely on prepared or presented information if the director has knowledge of the matter that makes the reliance unwarranted.[16]

The Statutory Safe Harbor for Directors might not be an affirmative defense.[17]

---

[11] *Meyers v. Moody*, 693 F.2d 1196, 1212 (5th Cir. 1982).
[12] Tex. Civ. Prac. & Rem. Code Ann. § 41.003(a).
[13] *International Bankers Life Ins. Co. v. Holloway*, 368 S.W.2d 567, 583–84 (Tex. 1963).
[14] *Mack v. Newton*, 737 F.2d 1343, 1363 (5th Cir. 1984).
[15] Tex. Bus. Orgs. Code Ann. § 3.102(a). This is essentially a codification of the business judgment rule.
[16] Tex. Bus. Orgs. Code Ann. § 3.102(b).
[17] *See Elloway v. Pate*, 238 S.W.3d 882, 897 (Tex. App.—Houston [14th Dist.] 2007, no pet.) (assuming Delaware's statutory safe harbor was not an affirmative defense, but not deciding the issue).

2-1:4.2 Exculpatory Clauses

Exculpatory clauses in a corporation's certificate of formation are to be treated as affirmative defenses.[18]

A corporation may limit all liabilities, except for:

- A breach of the person's duty of loyalty, if any, to the organization or its owners or members;

An act or omission not in good faith that:

- Constitutes a breach of duty of the person to the organization; or
- Involves intentional misconduct or a knowing violation of law;

A transaction from which the person received an improper benefit, regardless of whether the benefit resulted from an action taken within the scope of the person's duties; or

An act or omission for which the liability of a governing person is expressly provided by an applicable statute.[19]

2-1:4.3 Statute of Limitations

The four-year limitations period applies to a breach of fiduciary duty claim.[20]

The statute of limitations accrues when the disinterested and independent agents of the entity have actual or constructive notice of the defendant's breach.[21]

A majority of the disinterested and independent agents must have actual or constructive notice of the defendant's breach; although, it is not necessary that such notice come to such members in a board meeting.[22]

The discovery rule applies to breaches sounding in tort.[23]

2-1:5 Procedural Implications

2-1:5.1 Who May Sue

Who may sue:

- The cause of action lies with the corporation.[24]
- However, shareholders may sue derivatively.[25]

---

[18] *Elloway v. Pate*, 238 S.W.3d 882, 889–90 (Tex. App.—Houston [14th Dist.] 2007, no pet.).
[19] Tex. Bus. Orgs. Code Ann. § 7.001(c).
[20] Tex. Civ. Prac. & Rem. Code Ann. § 16.004(a)(5); *Rowe v. Rowe*, 887 S.W.2d 191, 201 (Tex. App.—Fort Worth 1994, writ denied).
[21] *International Bankers Life Ins. Co. v. Holloway*, 368 S.W.2d 567, 580 (Tex. 1963).
[22] *Allen v. Wilkerson*, 396 S.W.2d 493, 500 (Tex. Civ. App.—Austin 1965, writ ref'd n.r.e.).
[23] *F.D.I.C. v. Howse*, 736 F. Supp. 1437, 1441 (S.D. Tex. 1990).
[24] *Meyers v. Moody*, 693 F.2d 1196, 1209 (5th Cir. 1982).
[25] See Shareholder Derivative Suits.

2-2 Officer and Director Liability—Breach of the Duty of Loyalty

2-2:1 Overview

Corporate officers and directors owe a fiduciary duty of loyalty to the corporation which they serve. The duty encompasses mismanagement as well as wrongful distributions. This subtopic solely discusses mismanagement.

2-2:1.1 Related Causes of Action

Shareholder Derivative Suits, Breach of Duty of Care, Wrongful Distribution of Dividends, Breach of Partnership Duty

MUST READ CASES

Gearhart Indus., Inc. v. Smith Int'l, Inc., 741 F.2d 707 (5th Cir. 1984)

International Bankers Life Ins. Co. v. Holloway, 368 S.W.2d 567 (Tex. 1963).

2-2:2 Elements

2-2:2.1 Mismanagement

(1) The defendant is an officer or director of a corporation

- Officers and directors owe their corporations duties.[26]

(2) The defendant owes a duty of loyalty to the corporation

- Generally, all officers and directors owe their corporations a duty of loyalty.[27]

(3) The defendant breaches that duty of loyalty

- The Texas Supreme Court has never directly addressed the applicable standard of care. However, the majority of courts have held the applicable standard of care to be gross negligence.[28]

- The Texas Supreme Court has generally defined gross negligence as conduct that involves an extreme degree of risk, and the defendant was aware of the extreme risk created by his or her conduct.[29]

---

[26] *Meyers v. Moody*, 693 F.2d 1196, 1209 (5th Cir. 1982).

[27] *Gearhart Indus., Inc. v. Smith Int'l*, Inc., 741 F.2d 707, 719 (5th Cir. 1984).

[28] *See, e.g., In re Life Partners Holdings, Inc.*, No. DR-11-CV-43-AM, 2015 WL 8523103, at *7 (W.D. Tex. Nov. 9, 2015) (Texas law); *F.D.I.C. v. Schreiner*, 892 F. Supp. 869, 881–82 (W.D. Tex. 1995) (Texas law); *Resolution Tr. Corp. v. Acton*, 844 F. Supp. 307, 313 (N.D. Tex. 1994), *aff'd*, 49 F.3d 1086 (5th Cir. 1995) (Texas law); *Smith v. Van Gorkom*, 488 A.2d 858, 873 (Del. 1985), *overruled on other grounds by Gantler v. Stephens*, 965 A.2d 695 (Del. 2009); *Elloway v. Pate*, 238 S.W.3d 882, 891 (Tex. App.—Houston [14th Dist.] 2007, no pet.). *But see Floyd v. Hefner*, No. CIV.A. H03-5693, 2006 WL 2844245, at *26–28 (S.D. Tex. Sept. 29, 2006), *on reconsideration in part*, 556 F. Supp. 2d 617 (S.D. Tex. 2008) (rejecting unequivocally the proposition that directors can be held liable for gross negligence under Texas law as it exists now).

[29] *Transp. Ins. Co. v. Moriel*, 879 S.W.2d 10, 22 (Tex. 1994).

- The plaintiff must affirmatively negate the business judgment rule, which insulates an officer or director who acts in good faith, despite how mistaken those actions might later be.[30]
- The business judgment rule is not a defense, but rather a substantive rule of law.[31]

(4) Which proximately causes damages to the corporation

- The officer or director's gross negligence must proximately cause the corporation damages.[32]

2-2:2.2 Wrongful Distribution of Dividends

For elements, damages and remedies, and defenses of a Usurpation of Business Opportunity cause of action, *see* Wrongful Distribution of Dividends.

2-2:3 Damages and Remedies

2-2:3.1 Actual Damages

Actual damages are an appropriate remedy.[33]

2-2:3.2 Special Damages

Special damages are an appropriate remedy if the plaintiff proves fraud.[34]

2-2:3.3 Exemplary Damages

Exemplary damages are available if the defendant acts:

- Maliciously;
- Fraudulently; or
- With gross negligence.[35]
- Willful breaches suffice for the imposition of exemplary damages.[36]
- Exemplary damages may be predicated upon an equitable remedy alone.[37]

---

[30] *Gearhart Indus., Inc. v. Smith Int'l, Inc.*, 741 F.2d 707, 721 (5th Cir. 1984) (Texas law).
[31] *F.D.I.C. v. Benson*, 867 F. Supp. 512, 521 (S.D. Tex. 1994).
[32] *See F.D.I.C. v. Niblo*, 821 F. Supp. 441, 460 (N.D. Tex. 1993).
[33] *Meyers v. Moody*, 693 F.2d 1196, 1212 (5th Cir. 1982).
[34] *Meyers v. Moody*, 693 F.2d 1196, 1212 (5th Cir. 1982).
[35] Tex. Civ. Prac. & Rem. Code Ann. § 41.003(a).
[36] *International Bankers Life Ins. Co. v. Holloway*, 368 S.W.2d 567, 583–84 (Tex. 1963).
[37] *Mack v. Newton*, 737 F.2d 1343, 1363 (5th Cir. 1984).

2-2:4 Defenses

2-2:4.1 Statutory Safe Harbor

In discharging a duty, a director may, in good faith and with ordinary care, rely on information prepared or presented by:

- An officer or employee of the entity;
- Legal counsel;
- A certified public accountant;
- An investment banker;
- A person who the officer or director reasonably believes possesses professional expertise in the matter; or
- A committee of the board of directors of which the director is not a member.[38]
- The Statutory Safe Harbor for Directors might not be an affirmative defense.[39]

2-2:4.2 Interested Transaction/Corporate Opportunity Validity Procedures

Interested-director transactions will be deemed valid notwithstanding the director's interest in the transaction or participation in the meeting at which the transaction is approved when the director fully discloses the director's interest in the transaction and approval is granted by disinterested directors or the shareholders.[40]

A director may pursue a corporate opportunity so long as the opportunity is fully disclosed to and declined by the corporation.[41]

2-2:4.3 Exculpatory Clauses

A corporation's certificate of formation may not limit officer or director liability for a breach of the person's duty of loyalty, if any, to the organization or its owners or members.[42]

---

[38] Tex. Bus. Orgs. Code Ann. § 3.102(a). This is essentially a codification of the business judgment rule.

[39] *See Elloway v. Pate*, 238 S.W.3d 882, 897 (Tex. App.—Houston [14th Dist.] 2007, no pet.) (assuming Delaware's statutory safe harbor was not an affirmative defense, but not deciding the issue).

[40] *See* Tex. Bus. Orgs. Code Ann. § 21.418. If one of the procedures outlined in the Business Organizations Code is not followed, the transaction will nevertheless withstand challenge if it passes scrutiny for "fairness" to the corporation.

[41] *See Imperial Grp. (Tex.), Inc. v. Scholnick*, 709 S.W.2d 358, 365 (Tex. App.—Tyler 1986, writ ref'd n.r.e.).

[42] Tex. Bus. Orgs. Code Ann. § 7.001(c)(1).

2-2:4.4 Statute of Limitations

The four-year limitations period applies to a breach of fiduciary duty claim.[43]

The statute of limitations accrues when the disinterested and independent agents of the entity have actual or constructive notice of the defendant's breach.[44]

A majority of the disinterested and independent agents

must have actual or constructive notice of the defendant's breach.[45]

The discovery rule applies to breaches sounding in tort.[46]

The corporation's certificate of formation may limit the scope of the director's duty of care and limit the director's liability for breaches of that duty of care.

2-2:5 Procedural Implications

2-2:5.1 Who May Sue

The cause of action lies with the corporation.[47] However, shareholders may sue derivatively.[48]

2-3 Officer and Director Liability—Wrongful Distribution of Dividends

2-3:1 Overview

The corporate board of directors has the sole authority to make distributions to shareholders. The Business Organizations Code limits the board's authority by holding the directors personally liable for wrongful distributions.[49] A distribution in excess of the limits imposed by the Business Organizations Code is recoverable by the corporation.

2-3:1.1 Related Causes of Action

Shareholder Derivative Suits, Breach of Duty of Loyalty, Breach of Duty of Care, Fraudulent Transfer

MUST READ CASES

Henry I. Siegel Co., Inc. v. Holliday, 663 S.W.2d 824 (Tex. 1984)

Smith v. Chapman, 897 S.W.2d 399 (Tex. App.—Eastland 1995, no writ)

Renger Mem'l Hosp. v. State, 674 S.W.2d 828 (Tex. App.—Austin 1984, no writ)

---

[43] Tex. Civ. Prac. & Rem. Code Ann. § 16.004(a)(5); *Rowe v. Rowe*, 887 S.W.2d 191, 201 (Tex. App.—Fort Worth 1994, writ denied).
[44] *International Bankers Life Ins. Co. v. Holloway*, 368 S.W.2d 567, 580 (Tex. 1963).
[45] *Allen v. Wilkerson*, 396 S.W.2d 493, 500 (Tex. Civ. App.—Austin 1965, writ ref'd n.r.e.).
[46] *F.D.I.C. v. Howse*, 736 F. Supp. 1437, 1441 (S.D. Tex. 1990).
[47] *Meyers v. Moody*, 693 F.2d 1196, 1209 (5th Cir. 1982).
[48] *See Shareholder Derivative Suits.*
[49] Tex. Bus. Orgs. Code Ann. § 21.316

2-3:2 Elements

(1) The boards of directors authorize

- A corporation's board of directors may authorize a distribution.[50]
- Each director who votes for or assents to the distribution may be held liable.[51]
- A director who is present at the relevant meeting is deemed to have assented to the distribution, unless:
  - The director's dissent has been entered in the minutes of the meeting;
  - The director has filed a written dissent to the action with the person acting as the secretary of the meeting before the meeting is adjourned; or
  - The director has sent a written dissent by registered mail to the secretary of the corporation immediately after the meeting has been adjourned.[52]

(2) A distribution

- "Distribution" means a transfer of property, including cash, or issuance of debt, by a corporation to its shareholders in the form of:
  - A dividend on any class or series of its outstanding shares;
  - A purchase or redemption, directly or indirectly, of any of its own shares; or
  - A payment by the corporation in liquidation of all or a portion of its assets.[53]
- "Distribution" does not include:
- A split-up or division of the issued shares of a class of a corporation into a larger number of shares within the same class that does not increase the stated capital of the corporation; or
- A transfer of the corporation's own shares or rights to acquire its own shares.[54]

(3) That is wrongful

- A distribution is wrongful if it:
  - Exceeds the distribution limit;
  - Would render the corporation insolvent; or
  - Is not authorized by the corporation's certificate of formation.[55]

---

[50] Tex. Bus. Orgs. Code Ann. § 21.302.
[51] Tex. Bus. Orgs. Code Ann. § 21.316(a).
[52] Tex. Bus. Orgs. Code Ann. § 21.414(a).
[53] Tex. Bus. Orgs. Code Ann. § 21.002(6)(A).
[54] Tex. Bus. Orgs. Code Ann. § 21.002(6)(B).
[55] Tex. Bus. Orgs. Code Ann. § 21.303(a)–(b).

- The distribution limit is one of the following:
- Net assets of a corporation engaging in:
    - A redemption of its own shares;
    - A purchase of its own shares; or
    - Any action by a "consuming assets corporation;"[56] or
- Surplus of a corporation:
    - For any corporation which does not qualify for the net assets distribution limit.[57]

"Net assets" means the amount by which the total assets of a corporation exceed the total debts of the corporation.[58]

"Surplus" means the amount by which the net assets of a corporation exceed the stated capital of the corporation.[59]

"Net assets," "surplus," and a corporation's solvency are to be determined based upon:

(1) financial statements of the corporation, including financial statements that:
- Include subsidiary corporations or other corporations accounted for on a consolidated basis or on the equity method of accounting; or
- Present the financial condition of the corporation in accordance with generally accepted accounting principles;

(2) financial statements prepared using the method of accounting used to file the corporation's federal income tax return or using any other accounting practices and principles that are reasonable under the circumstances;

(3) financial information, including condensed or summary financial statements, that is prepared on the same basis as financial statements described by Subdivision (1) or (2);

(4) projection, forecast, or other forward-looking information relating to the future economic performance, financial condition, or liquidity of the corporation that is reasonable under the circumstances;

(5) a fair valuation or information from any other method that is reasonable under the circumstances; or

(6) a combination of a statement, valuation or information authorized by this section.[60]

---

[56] Tex. Bus. Orgs. Code Ann. § 21.301(1)(A).
[57] Tex. Bus. Orgs. Code Ann. § 21.301(1)(B).
[58] Tex. Bus. Orgs. Code Ann. § 21.002(9).
[59] Tex. Bus. Orgs. Code Ann. § 21.002(12).
[60] Tex. Bus. Orgs. Code Ann. § 21.314(a).

2-3:3 Damages and Remedies

2-3:3.1 Excess Distributions

Directors are liable to the corporation for the amount the distribution:

- Exceeds the authorized amount within the corporation's certificate of formation;
- Exceeds the distribution limit; or
- Renders the corporation insolvent.[61]

2-3:3.2 Joint and Several Liability

Directors who voted for or assented to the distribution are jointly and severally liable for the distribution.[62]

2-3:3.3 Contribution

A director who is held liable for a wrongful distribution is entitled to receive contributions from shareholders who accepted or received the wrongful distribution knowing that it was wrongful. The amount of contribution is to be in proportion to the amounts received by the shareholders.[63]

A director who is liable for a claim for a wrongful distribution is entitled to receive contributions from each of the other directors who are liable with respect to that claim in an amount appropriate to achieve equity.[64]

2-3:4 Defenses

2-3:4.1 Good Faith Reliance

A director is not jointly and severally liable for a wrongful distribution if, in voting for or assenting to the distribution, the director:

- Relies in good faith and with ordinary care on:
  - The statements, valuations, or information described by Section 21.314; or
  - Other information, opinions, reports or statements, including financial statements and other financial data, concerning the corporation or another person that are prepared or presented by:
    - One or more officers or employees of the corporation;
    - A legal counsel, public accountant, investment banker or other person relating to a matter the director reasonably believes is within the person's professional or expert competence; or

---

[61] Tex. Bus. Orgs. Code Ann. § 21.316(a).
[62] Tex. Bus. Orgs. Code Ann. § 21.316(a).
[63] Tex. Bus. Orgs. Code Ann. § 21.318(a).
[64] Tex. Bus. Orgs. Code Ann. § 21.318(b).

- A committee of the board of directors of which the director is not a member;
- Acting in good faith and with ordinary care, considers the assets of the corporation to be valued at least at their book value; or
- In determining whether the corporation made adequate provision for payment, satisfaction or discharge of all of the corporation's liabilities and obligations, as provided by Sections 11.053 and 11.356, relies in good faith and with ordinary care on financial statements of, or other information concerning, a person who was or became contractually obligated to pay, satisfy or discharge some or all of the corporation's liabilities or obligations.[65]

2-3:4.2 Subsequent Events Purge the Wrongfulness

A director is not liable for a wrongful distribution if, at a later date, the distribution was not prohibited by the certificate of formation, distribution limits or solvency limits.[66]

If only a portion of the wrongful distribution is purged, the director is liable only for that portion which remains wrongful.[67]

2-3:4.3 Statute of Limitations

The two-year statute of limitations applies. The cause of action accrues at the time of the wrongful distribution.[68]

2-3:5 Procedural Implications

2-3:5.1 Who May Sue

Generally, the cause of action lies with the corporation.[69]

Exceptions to the general rule allow others to pursue the corporation's cause of action on behalf of the corporation:

- Shareholder Derivative Suits;[70]
- Corporate creditors who have:
  - Been assigned the corporation's cause of action; or
  - Obtained the cause of action through judicial means, such as seizure or turnover;[71] or

---

[65] Tex. Bus. Orgs. Code Ann. § 21.316(c).
[66] Tex. Bus. Orgs. Code Ann. § 21.316(b).
[67] Tex. Bus. Orgs. Code Ann. § 21.316(b).
[68] Tex. Bus. Orgs. Code Ann. § 21.317.
[69] *Smith v. Chapman*, 897 S.W.2d 399, 401 (Tex. App.—Eastland 1995, no writ).
[70] For the requirements for a shareholder to bring a Shareholder Derivative Suit, *see Shareholder Derivative Suits*.
[71] *Renger Mem'l Hosp. v. State*, 674 S.W.2d 828, 830 (Tex. App.—Austin 1984, no writ).

BUSINESS MANAGEMENT LITIGATION

Corporate creditors pursuing a trust-fund theory on behalf of a dissolved corporation.[72]

2-4 Officer and Director Liability—Liability for Securities Fraud[73]

2-4:1 Overview

2-4:1.1 Related Causes of Action

Fraud by Non-Disclosure, Common Law Fraud, Statutory Fraud, Officer and Director Liability, Breach of the Duty of Loyalty, Breach of Partnership Duty, Antitrust

MUST READ CASES

Basic Inc. v. Levinson, 485 U.S. 224, 108 S. Ct. 978, 99 L. Ed. 2d 194 (1988)

Dirks v. S.E.C., 463 U.S. 646, 103 S. Ct. 3255, 77 L. Ed. 2d 911 (1983)

2-4:2 Elements

2-4:2.1 Rule 10b-5 General Fraud

(1) A person uses any means or instrumentality of interstate commerce or of the mails or of any facility of any national securities exchange to:

- This jurisdictional hook is to be interpreted flexibly and broadly.[74]
- It is sufficient that any portion of the transaction utilize the means or instrumentality of interstate commerce.[75]
- The intrastate use of telephones is sufficient to confer jurisdiction.[76]

(1) (a) Make a misrepresentation or fail to disclose

- The defendant must make a misrepresentation or fail to disclose a fact.[77]
    - However, silence absent a duty to disclose is not considered to be misleading.[78]
- Mere mismanagement or breach of fiduciary duty will not suffice.[79]

(1) (b) A material fact

---

[72] *Henry I. Siegel Co., Inc. v. Holliday*, 663 S.W.2d 824, 827–28 (Tex. 1984).
[73] This subtopic does not include causes of action for violations of the Securities Act of 1933 involving the registration of securities and the initial offer and sale of securities.
[74] *Dupuy v. Dupuy*, 511 F.2d 641, 643 (5th Cir. 1975).
[75] *Stevens v. Vowell*, 343 F.2d 374, 378–79 (10th Cir. 1965).
[76] *Dupuy v. Dupuy*, 511 F.2d 641, 643 (5th Cir. 1975).
[77] 17 C.F.R. § 240.10b–5.
[78] *Matrixx Initiatives, Inc. v. Siracusano*, 563 U.S. 27, 45 (2011).
[79] *Schreiber v. Burlington N., Inc.*, 472 U.S. 1, 7 (1985).

- There must be a substantial likelihood that the disclosure of the omitted fact would have been viewed by the reasonable investor as having significantly altered the total mix of information made available.[80]
- When analyzing future events, materiality will depend at any given time upon a balancing of both the indicated probability that the event will occur and the anticipated magnitude of the event in light of the totality of the company's activities.[81]
- A finding of materiality does not require proof that the plaintiff would have changed her mind.[82]
  - However, proving reliance might require such a showing.[83]

(1)(c) In connection with the purchase or sale of any security

- This language is to be construed broadly[84]
- However, a plaintiff must have actually purchased or sold securities.[85]

(1)(d) With scienter

- The defendant must:
  - Know of the falsity of the information; and
  - Intend to deceive, manipulate, or defraud.[86]
  - An opinion or prediction is actionable if there is a gross disparity between prediction and fact.[87]

(2) Which the plaintiff reasonably relies upon

- A plaintiff must establish his reasonable reliance on the misrepresentation or omission.[88]
- The relevant question in determining reliance is: had the investor known the truth, would he have acted differently?[89]
- A plaintiff is afforded a rebuttable presumption of reliance if the securities are traded in an open and developed market.[90]

---

[80] *Matrixx Initiatives, Inc. v. Siracusano,* 563 U.S. 27, 38 (2011).
[81] *In re Magnum Hunter Res. Corp. Sec. Litig.,* 26 F. Supp. 3d 278, 291 (S.D.N.Y. 2014), aff'd, 616 Fed. Appx. 442 (2d Cir. 2015).
[82] *Mills v. Elec. Auto-Lite Co.,* 396 U.S. 375, 384 (1970).
[83] *See Huddleston v. Herman & MacLean,* 640 F.2d 534, 549 (5th Cir. 1981), *aff'd in part, rev'd in part on other grounds,* 459 U.S. 375 (1983).
[84] *S.E.C. v. Zandford,* 535 U.S. 813, 819, 122 S. Ct. 1899, 1903, 153 L. Ed. 2d 1 (2002).
[85] *See Blue Chip Stamps v. Manor Drug Stores,* 421 U.S. 723, 749 (1975) (adopting the rule from *Birnbaum v. Newport Steel Corp.,* 193 F.2d 461 (2d Cir. 1952)).
[86] *Tellabs, Inc. v. Makor Issues & Rights, Ltd.,* 551 U.S. 308, 319 (2007).
[87] *Spitzberg v. Houston Am. Energy Corp.,* 758 F.3d 676, 691 (5th Cir. 2014).
[88] *First Virginia Bankshares v. Benson,* 559 F.2d 1307, 1314 (5th Cir. 1977).
[89] *Huddleston v. Herman & MacLean,* 640 F.2d 534, 549 (5th Cir. 1981), *aff'd in part, rev'd in part on other grounds,* 459 U.S. 375 (1983).
[90] *Stoneridge Inv. Partners, LLC v. Sci.-Atlanta,* 552 U.S. 148, 159 (2008).

BUSINESS MANAGEMENT LITIGATION

- A plaintiff is afforded a rebuttable presumption of reliance if the defendant fails to disclose a material fact.[91]
- A plaintiff must also exercise due diligence in examining other information available to the plaintiff with regard to the transaction.[92]
- This element is often referred to as "transaction causation."[93]

(3) Which proximately causes the plaintiff injury

- This element is often referred to as "loss causation."[94]
- The misrepresentation or omission must touch upon the reasons for the investment's decline in value.[95]

2-4:2.2 Rule 10b-5 Insider Trading

(1) A person uses any means or instrumentality of interstate commerce or of the mails or of any facility of any national securities exchange to

- This jurisdictional hook is to be interpreted flexibly and broadly.[96]
- It is sufficient that any portion of the transaction utilize the means or instrumentality of interstate commerce.[97]
- The intrastate use of telephones is sufficient to confer jurisdiction.[98]

(2) Purchase or sell any security

- The defendant must purchase or sell a security.[99]

(3) On the basis of information which is:

- "On the basis of" means awareness of that information.[100]

(3)(a) Material

- There must be a substantial likelihood that the disclosure of the omitted fact would have been viewed by the reasonable investor as having significantly altered the total mix of information made available.[101]
- When analyzing future events, materiality will depend at any given time upon a balancing of both the indicated probability that the event will occur

---

[91] *Stoneridge Inv. Partners, LLC v. Sci.-Atlanta*, 552 U.S. 148, 159 (2008).
[92] *First Virginia Bankshares v. Benson*, 559 F.2d 1307, 1314 (5th Cir. 1977).
[93] *Erica P. John Fund, Inc. v. Halliburton Co.*, 563 U.S. 804, 812 (2011).
[94] *See* 15 U.S.C. § 78u-4(b)(4); *Erica P. John Fund, Inc. v. Halliburton Co.*, 563 U.S. 804, 812 (2011).
[95] *Huddleston v. Herman & MacLean*, 640 F.2d 534, 549 (5th Cir. 1981), *aff'd in part, rev'd in part on other grounds*, 459 U.S. 375 (1983).
[96] *Dupuy v. Dupuy*, 511 F.2d 641, 643 (5th Cir. 1975).
[97] *Stevens v. Vowell*, 343 F.2d 374, 378–79 (10th Cir. 1965).
[98] *Dupuy v. Dupuy*, 511 F.2d 641, 643 (5th Cir. 1975).
[99] 17 C.F.R. § 240.10b5-1(a).
[100] 17 C.F.R. § 240.10b5-1(b).
[101] *Matrixx Initiatives, Inc. v. Siracusano*, 563 U.S. 27, 38 (2011).

and the anticipated magnitude of the event in light of the totality of the company's activities.[102]

- A finding of materiality does not require proof that the plaintiff would have changed his mind.[103]
- However, proving reliance might require such proof.[104]

(3)(b) Non-public

- The information must be non-public.[105]
- Non-public information is information intended to be available only for a corporate purpose and not for the personal benefit of anyone.[106]

(4) In violation of a fiduciary duty owed to the issuer or the source of the information

There is a duty to disclose information when:

- The insider occupies a fiduciary relationship to the corporation; or
- The corporation had placed their trust and confidence in that person.[107]

(5) The insider does not publicly disclose the information before trading on it.

- The insider does not publicly disclose the information before trading on it.[108]

2-4:2.3 Rule 14e-3 Tender Offers

(1) A person trades in securities

- A defendant must:
  - Purchase or sell securities; or
  - Cause securities to be purchased or sold.[109]

(2) On this basis of information that is reasonably known to be material, non-public information

- On this basis of information that is reasonably known to be material, non-public information.[110]
- Materiality:

---

[102] *In re Magnum Hunter Res. Corp. Sec. Litig.*, 26 F. Supp. 3d 278, 291 (S.D.N.Y. 2014), aff'd, 616 Fed. Appx. 442 (2d Cir. 2015).
[103] *Mills v. Elec. Auto-Lite Co.*, 396 U.S. 375, 384 (1970).
[104] *See Huddleston v. Herman & MacLean*, 640 F.2d 534, 549 (5th Cir. 1981), *aff'd in part, rev'd in part on other grounds*, 459 U.S. 375 (1983).
[105] *Dirks v. SEC*, 463 U.S. 646, 654 (1983).
[106] *Dirks v. SEC*, 463 U.S. 646, 658–60 (1983).
[107] *See* 17 C.F.R. § 240.10b5-1(a); *Dirks v. SEC*, 463 U.S. 646, 654 (1983).
[108] *Dirks v. SEC*, 463 U.S. 646, 654 (1983).
[109] 17 C.F.R. § 240.14e–3(a).
[110] 17 C.F.R. § 240.14e–3(a).

- There must be a substantial likelihood that the disclosure of the omitted fact would have been viewed by the reasonable investor as having significantly altered the total mix of information made available.[111]
- When analyzing future events, materiality will depend at any given time upon a balancing of both the indicated probability that the event will occur and the anticipated magnitude of the event in light of the totality of the company's activities.[112]
- A finding of materiality does not require proof that the plaintiff would have changed his mind.[113]
- However, proving reliance might require such proof.[114]
- Non-public:
  - Non-public information is information intended to be available only for a corporate purpose and not for the personal benefit of anyone.[115]

(3) With reason to believe such information was acquired from: (a) the offering person; (b) the issuer; or (c) any agent of the offering person or issuer

- With reason to believe such information was acquired from
  - The offering person;
  - The issuer; or
  - Any agent of the offering person or issuer.[116]

(4) Not publicly disclosing such information

- The person does not publicly disclose the information before trading on it.[117]

2-4:2.4 Short Swing Profits

(1) An insider

- An insider means:
  - A director;
  - An officer; or
  - A beneficial owner of 10% of any class of any security.[118]

---

[111] *Matrixx Initiatives, Inc. v. Siracusano*, 563 U.S. 27, 38 (2011).
[112] *In re Magnum Hunter Res. Corp. Sec. Litig.*, 26 F. Supp. 3d 278, 291 (S.D.N.Y. 2014), aff'd, 616 Fed. Appx. 442 (2d Cir. 2015).
[113] *Mills v. Elec. Auto-Lite Co.*, 396 U.S. 375, 384 (1970).
[114] *See Huddleston v. Herman & MacLean*, 640 F.2d 534, 549 (5th Cir. 1981), *aff'd in part, rev'd in part on other grounds*, 459 U.S. 375 (1983).
[115] *Dirks v. SEC*, 463 U.S. 646, 658–60 (1983).
[116] 17 C.F.R. § 240.14e–3.
[117] *Dirks v. SEC*, 463 U.S. 646, 654 (1983).
[118] 15 U.S.C. § 78p(a)(1).

(2) Of a corporation which must register its securities

- A covered corporation is one which must register its securities under Section 12 of the Securities Act of 1933.[119]

(3) (a) Who purchases and then sells his corporation's securities within six months of each other.[120]

(3) (b) Who sells and then purchases his corporation's securities within six months of each other.[121]

2-4:2.5 Common Law Fraud

See Fraud by Non-Disclosure, Common Law Fraud.

Special Note On Duty

The general rule is that an officer or director owes no duty to disclose information to shareholders.[122]

However, an officer or director must disclose any knowledge of special matters relating to the corporate business—e.g., merger, assured sale, etc.—that may affect the value of the stock.[123]

2-4:3 Damages and Remedies

2-4:3.1 Out-of-Pocket

Out-of-pocket damages are the traditional measure of damages for a Rule 10b-5—General Fraud violation.[124]

2-4:3.2 Benefit-of-the-Bargain

Benefit-of-the-bargain damages are available for a Rule 10b-5 violation.[125]

2-4:3.3 Disgorgement

Disgorgement in favor of the issuing corporation is an appropriate remedy for a Short Swing Profits suit.[126]

---

[119] 15 U.S.C. § 78p(a)(1).
[120] 15 U.S.C. § 78p(b).
[121] 15 U.S.C. § 978p(b).
[122] *Miller v. Miller*, 700 S.W.2d 941, 946 (Tex. App.—Dallas 1985, writ ref'd n.r.e.).
[123] *Miller v. Miller*, 700 S.W.2d 941, 946 (Tex. App.—Dallas 1985, writ ref'd n.r.e.).
[124] *James v. Meinke*, 778 F.2d 200, 205 (5th Cir. 1985); *Abell v. Potomac Ins. Co.*, 858 F.2d 1104, 1136 (5th Cir. 1988), *cert. granted, judgment vacated sub nom. Fryar v. Abell*, 492 U.S. 914 (1989).
[125] *Abell v. Potomac Ins. Co.*, 858 F.2d 1104, 1136, 1137–38 (5th Cir. 1988), *cert. granted, judgment vacated sub nom.*
[126] 15 U.S.C. § 78p(b).

Profits to be disgorged are calculated by using the highest sale price and lowest purchase price, or highest purchase price and lowest sale price, in any given six month period.[127]

Disgorgement of profits or loss avoided is the appropriate measure of damages for a Rule 10b-5—Insider Trading violation.[128]

Each person who traded in the security during the relevant time frame shares in the recovery pro rata.[129]

2-4:3.4 Rescission

Rescission is available for Securities Exchange Act violations, such as:

- Rule 10b-5—General Fraud;
- Rule 10b-5—Insider Trading;
- Tender Offers; and
- Short Swing Profits.[130]

2-4:3.5 Exemplary Damages

Generally, exemplary damages are not available for a federal cause of action.[131]

However, exemplary damages are available for common law fraud.[132]

2-4:3.6 Consequential Damages

Consequential damages are available for a Rule 10b-5 violation.[133]

2-4:3.7 Common Law Fraud Damages

For a complete list of common law fraud damages, *See* Fraud by Non-disclosure, Common Law Fraud.

2-4:4 Defenses

2-4:4.1 10b-5-1 Plan

A sale of shares in accordance with a 10b-5-1 plan is an affirmative defense to suit alleging a violation of Rule 10b-5.[134]

---

[127] *Smolowe v. Delendo Corp.*, 136 F.2d 231, 235–39 (2d Cir. 1943).
[128] 15 U.S.C. § 78t-1(b).
[129] 15 U.S.C. § 78t-1(b).
[130] *See Regional Props., Inc. v. Fin. & Real Estate Consulting Co.*, 678 F.2d 552, 558 (5th Cir. 1982).
[131] 15 U.S.C. § 78bb(a)(1).
[132] Tex. Civ. Prac. & Rem. Code Ann. § 41.003(a)(1); *Tony Gullo Motors I, L.P. v. Chapa*, 212 S.W.3d 299, 304 (Tex. 2006).
[133] *James v. Meinke*, 778 F.2d 200, 205 (5th Cir. 1985).
[134] 17 C.F.R. § 240.10b5-1(c).

A person's purchase or sale is not "on the basis of" material non-public information if the person making the purchase or sale demonstrates that:

- Before becoming aware of the information, the person had:
  - Entered into a binding contract to purchase or sell the security;
  - Instructed another person to purchase or sell the security for the instructing person's account; or
  - Adopted a written plan for trading securities;
- The contract, instruction, or plan:
  - Specified the amount of securities to be purchased or sold and the price at which and the date on which the securities were to be purchased or sold;
  - Included a written formula or algorithm, or computer program, for determining the amount of securities to be purchased or sold and the price at which and the date on which the securities were to be purchased or sold; or
  - Did not permit the person to exercise any subsequent influence over how, when, or whether to effect purchases or sales; provided, in addition, that any other person who, pursuant to the contract, instruction, or plan, did exercise such influence must not have been aware of the material non-public information when doing so; and
  - The purchase or sale that occurred was pursuant to the contract, instruction, or plan.[135]

2-4:4.2 In Pari Delicto

In pari delicto is an available defense to a Rule 10b-5 violation if the plaintiff's fault is equal to or greater than the defendant's.[136]

2-4:4.3 Statute of Limitations

A litigant must bring suit within two years from the discovery of a Rule 10b-5 or Rule 14e-3 violation, but in no case more than five years after the violation.[137]

The Discovery Rule applies to private securities fraud complaints.[138]

A litigant must bring suit within two years after the date the profits were realized to recover short swing profits.[139]

---

[135] 17 C.F.R. § 240.10b5-1(c).
[136] *Pinter v. Dahl*, 486 U.S. 622, 633 (1988).
[137] 28 U.S.C. § 1658(b).
[138] *See Merck & Co. v. Reynolds*, 559 U.S. 633, 637 (2010) (A private securities fraud complaint is timely if filed no more than two years after the plaintiffs discovered the facts constituting the violation. A cause of action accrues (1) when the plaintiff did in fact discover, or (2) when a reasonably diligent plaintiff would have discovered, the facts constituting the violation—whichever comes first. The facts constituting the violation include the fact of scienter, a mental state embracing intent to deceive, manipulate, or defraud.).
[139] 15 U.S.C. § 78p(b).

2-4:4.4 Certain Defenses Not Applicable

Equitable defenses may not be utilized in a Short Swing Profits suit.[140]

2-4:5 Procedural Implications

2-4:5.1 Pleading Burden

The complaint shall specify each statement alleged to have been misleading, the reason or reasons why the statement is misleading, and, if an allegation regarding the statement or omission is made on information and belief, the complaint shall state with particularity all facts on which that belief is formed.[141]

2-4:5.2 Jurisdiction

Federal courts have exclusive jurisdiction over Securities Exchange Act causes of action, such as:

- Rule 10b-5—General Fraud;
- Rule 10b-5—Insider Trading;
- Tender Offers; and
- Short Swing Profits[142]

2-4:5.3 Short Swing Profits

The proper plaintiff in a Short Swing Profits suit is the corporation.[143]

However, a shareholder may bring a shareholder derivative suit on behalf of the corporation if:

- 60 days have passed since the shareholder requested the corporation take action; and
- The shareholder owns shares in the corporation at the time of the lawsuit.[144]

2-5 Officer and Director Liability—Liability as an Agent

2-5:1 Overview

A corporation's officers and directors are normally protected from personal liability by the corporate form. However, as agents of the corporation they may be liable to the corporation or to third parties based upon an agency theory.

---

[140] *Texas Int'l Airlines v. Nat'l Airlines, Inc.*, 714 F.2d 533, 536 (5th Cir. 1983).
[141] 15 U.S.C. § 78u-4(b)(1).
[142] 15 U.S.C. § 78aa(a).
[143] 15 U.S.C. § 78p(b).
[144] 15 U.S.C. § 78p(b).

2-5:1.1 Related Causes of Action

Agency Actions: Agent's Breach of Duty, Agency Actions: Agent's Liability to Third Parties, Agency Actions: Agent's Actions Binding upon Principal

2-5:2 Elements

For the elements to establish an officer or director's liability based upon an agency theory, *see* Agency Actions: Agent's Breach of Duty, Agency Actions: Agent's Liability to Third Parties.

2-5:3 Damages and Remedies

For the damages and remedies applicable to an officer or director's liability based upon an agency theory, *see* Agency Actions: Agent's Breach of Duty, Agency Actions: Agent's Liability to Third Parties.

2-5:4 Defenses

For the defenses applicable to an officer or director's liability based upon an agency theory, *see* Agency Actions: Agent's Breach of Duty, Agency Actions: Agent's Liability to Third Parties.

2-6 Officer and Director Liability—State Revocation of Corporate Status

2-6:1 Overview

A corporation's officers and directors are normally protected from personal liability by the corporate form. State revocation of corporate status, although not a cause of action in which a private litigant will initiate proceedings, can be a valuable exception to the general rule regarding officer and director liability. Locating the certificate of termination is the only concern of a litigant attempting to establish officer and director liability based upon state revocation of corporate status.

2-6:2 Elements

2-6:2.1 Administrative Termination by the Secretary of State

(1) A filing entity defaults on a required act
  - The Secretary of State may terminate a filing entity's existence if the Secretary finds that:
    - The entity has failed to file a report within the period required by law;
    - The entity has failed to pay a fee or penalty prescribed by law when due and payable;
    - The entity has failed to maintain a registered agent or registered office in this state as required by law; or

BUSINESS MANAGEMENT LITIGATION

- The entity has failed to pay a fee required in connection with the filing of its certificate of formation, or payment of the fee was dishonored when presented by the state for payment.[145]

(2) The Secretary of State notifies the filing entity of the specific default.
- Before the Secretary of State may terminate a filing entity, the Secretary must send notice to the filing entity of the specific default.[146]

(3) The filing entity does not timely cure its default.
- The filing entity has until the 91st day after the Secretary of State mails the notice to cure the following defects:
  - The entity has failed to file a report within the period required by law;
  - The entity has failed to pay a fee or penalty prescribed by law when due and payable; and
  - The entity has failed to maintain a registered agent or registered office in this state as required by law.[147]
- The filing entity has until the 16th day after the Secretary of State mails the notice to cure the following defect:
  - The entity has failed to pay a fee required in connection with the filing of its certificate of formation, or payment of the fee was dishonored when presented by the state for payment.[148]

(4) The Secretary of State issues a certificate of termination.[149]
- The certificate will be on file with the Secretary of State.

2-6:2.2 Judicial Termination by the Attorney General

(1) A filing entity defaults
- The Attorney General may terminate a filing entity's existence if it proves:
  - The filing entity or its organizers did not comply with a condition precedent to its formation;
  - The certificate of formation of the filing entity or any amendment to the certificate of formation was fraudulently filed;
  - A misrepresentation of a material matter has been made in an application, report, affidavit or other document submitted by the filing entity under this code;
  - The filing entity has continued to transact business beyond the scope of the purpose of the filing entity as expressed in its certificate of formation; or

---

[145] Tex. Bus. Orgs. Code Ann. § 11.251(b).
[146] Tex. Bus. Orgs. Code Ann. § 11.251(a)–(b).
[147] Tex. Bus. Orgs. Code Ann. § 11.251(b)(1).
[148] Tex. Bus. Orgs. Code Ann. § 11.251(b)(2).
[149] Tex. Bus. Orgs. Code Ann. § 11.252(a).

- Public interest requires winding up and termination of the filing entity because:
  - The filing entity has been convicted of a felony or a high managerial agent of the filing entity has been convicted of a felony committed in the conduct of the filing entity's affairs;
  - The filing entity or high managerial agent has engaged in a persistent course of felonious conduct; and
  - Termination is necessary to prevent future felonious conduct of the same character.[150]

(2) The Attorney General institutes a lawsuit.
- The Attorney General shall file an action against a filing entity in the name of the state seeking termination of the entity's existence if:
  - The filing entity has not cured the problems for which winding up and termination is sought before the 31st day after the date the notice under Section 11.302(b) is mailed; and
  - The Attorney General determines that cause exists for the involuntary winding up of a filing entity's business and termination of the entity's existence under Section 11.301.[151]

(3) The filing entity does not cure the default
- The filing entity may cure its default before the 31st day after the date notice is mailed.[152]

(4) The court issues a decree requiring the winding up and termination of the entity
- The court issues a decree requiring the winding up and termination of the entity.[153]
- Termination is effective on the date the decree is filed.[154]

2-6:2.3 Termination for Failure to Pay Franchise Taxes

(1) A corporation defaults on a required act
- The Comptroller shall forfeit the corporate privileges of a corporation on which the franchise tax is imposed if the corporation:
  - Does not file a report required by this chapter;
  - Does not pay a tax imposed by Texas Tax Code Chapter 171;
  - Does not pay a penalty imposed by Texas Tax Code Chapter 171 relating to that tax; or

---

[150] Tex. Bus. Orgs. Code Ann. § 11.301(a).
[151] Tex. Bus. Orgs. Code Ann. § 11.303.
[152] Tex. Bus. Orgs. Code Ann. § 11.303(1).
[153] Tex. Bus. Orgs. Code Ann. § 11.315(a).
[154] Tex. Bus. Orgs. Code Ann. § 11.315(c).

BUSINESS MANAGEMENT LITIGATION

- Does not permit the Comptroller to examine under Section 171.211 of this code the corporation's records.[155]

(2) The Comptroller notifies the corporation of the specific default
   - The Comptroller notifies the corporation of the specific default.[156]

(3) The corporation does not timely cure the default
   - The corporation may cure the following defaults within 45 days after the Comptroller mails the required notice:
     - Does not file a report required by this chapter;
     - Does not pay a tax imposed by Texas Tax Code Chapter 171; and
     - Does not pay a penalty imposed by Texas Tax Code Chapter 171 relating to that tax;

(4) The Comptroller effectuates the forfeiture of corporate privileges.[157]

2-6:3 Damages and Remedies

2-6:3.1 Termination of the Corporate Form

The filing entity is terminated and the officers and directors of the corporation are personally liable.[158]

2-6:4 Defenses

2-6:4.1 Reinstatement

A filing entity may be reinstated or have its privileges revived.[159]

However, any personal liability which attached while corporate privileges were forfeited or the entity was terminated is unaffected by reinstatement.[160]

2-7 Shareholder Oppression

2-7:1 Overview

There is no common law cause of action for minority shareholder oppression.[161] The statutory cause of action for the appointment of a receiver is the exclusive statutory remedy available to an oppressed shareholder. Moreover, the definition of "oppression" in the receivership context is less inclusive than the definition of oppression

---

[155] Tex. Tax Code Ann. § 171.251.
[156] Tex. Tax Code Ann. § 171.256.
[157] Tex. Tax Code Ann. § 171.257.
[158] Tex. Tax Code Ann. § 171.252; Tex. Bus. Orgs. Code Ann. §§ 11.252, 11.313.
[159] Tex. Tax Code Ann. § 171.258; Tex. Bus. Orgs. Code Ann. § 11.253.
[160] Tex. Tax Code Ann. § 171.258(d); Tex. Bus. Orgs. Code Ann. § 11.253(d).
[161] *Ritchie v. Rupe*, 443 S.W.3d 856, 878 (Tex. 2014).

under the defunct reasonable-expectations or fair-dealings test.[162] Despite this exclusive definition, a governing person's actions which constitute "oppression" in the receivership context might also constitute an actionable breach of fiduciary duty owed to the corporation.[163] Therefore, the Supreme Court of Texas's rejection of the common law cause of action for minority shareholder oppression did not completely eliminate a plaintiff's ability to obtain a money judgment. Rather, it only limited the causes of actions available for such a plaintiff.

2-7:1.1 Related Causes of Action

Receivership, Derivative Shareholder Suits, Officer and Director Liability: Breach of the Duty of Loyalty, Accounting, Fraud and Constructive Fraud, Conversion, Fraudulent Transfer, Unjust Enrichment

MUST READ CASE

Ritchie v. Rupe, 443 S.W.3d 856 (Tex. 2014)

2-7:2 Elements

(1) A governing person

- A governing person must be the person who engages in "oppressive" conduct.[164]

(2) Engages in oppressive conduct by

- A governing person only engages in oppressive conduct if they abuse their authority over the corporation with the intent to harm the interests of one or more of the shareholders, in a manner that does not comport with the honest exercise of their business judgment, and by doing so create a serious risk of harm to the corporation.[165]

- The definition of "oppression" in the receivership context is less inclusive than the definition of oppression under the defunct reasonable-expectations or fair-dealings test.[166]

(2) (a) Abusing their authority over the corporation

- An officer or shareholder must abuse their authority over the corporation.

---

[162] *See Ritchie v. Rupe*, 443 S.W. 3d 856, 870–71 (Tex. 2014) ("[W]e cannot accept a definition that would find oppression on either of [the fair-dealings or reasonable expectations tests] alone").

[163] For example, the Supreme Court reiterated that the malicious suppression of dividends will support a cause of action for breach of fiduciary duty, despite there not being a common law cause of action for shareholder oppression. *Ritchie v. Rupe*, 443 S.W.3d 856, 884 (Tex. 2014) (quoting *Patton v. Nicholas*, 279 S.W.2d 848, 853 (Tex. 1955)).

[164] Tex. Bus. Orgs. Code Ann. § 11.404(a)(1)(C).

[165] *Ritchie v. Rupe*, 443 S.W. 3d 856, 870 (Tex. 2014).

[166] *See Ritchie v. Rupe*, 443 S.W.3d 856, 870 (Tex. 2014) ("[W]e cannot accept a definition that would find oppression on either of [the fair-dealings or reasonable-expectations tests] alone").

(2) (b) With the intent to harm the interests of one or more of their shareholders
- An officer or shareholder must abuse such authority with the intent to harm the interests of one or more of their shareholders.

(2) (c) In a manner that does not comport with the honest exercise of their business judgment
- An officer or shareholder must abuse such authority in a manner that does not comport with the honest exercise of their business judgment.

(2) (d) Creates a serious risk of harm to the corporation
- Such abuse of authority must create a serious risk of harm to corporation.[167]

(3) The other requirements for the appointment of a receiver are met.
- For the appointment of a receiver of specific property:
  - The applicant shows that the property or fund is in danger of being lost, removed or materially injured;
  - Circumstances exist that are considered by the court to necessitate the appointment of a receiver to conserve the property or fund and avoid damage to interested parties;
  - All other requirements of law are complied with; and
  - The court determines that other available legal and equitable remedies are inadequate.[168]
- For the appointment of a rehabilitative receiver:
  - Circumstances exist that are considered by the court to necessitate the appointment of a receiver to conserve the property and business of the domestic entity and avoid damage to interested parties;
  - All other requirements of law are complied with; and
  - The court determines that all other available legal and equitable remedies, including the appointment of a receiver for specific property of the domestic entity under Section 11.402(a), are inadequate.[169]
- For the appointment of a receiver to liquidate the corporation:
  - The circumstances demand liquidation to avoid damage to interested persons;
  - All other requirements of law are complied with; and
  - The court determines that all other available legal and equitable remedies, including the appointment of a receiver for specific property of the domestic entity and appointment of a receiver to rehabilitate the domestic entity, are inadequate.[170]

---

[167] *Ritchie v. Rupe*, 443 S.W.3d 856, 870 (Tex. 2014).
[168] Tex. Bus. Orgs. Code Ann. § 11.403(b).
[169] Tex. Bus. Orgs. Code Ann. § 11.404(b).
[170] Tex. Bus. Orgs. Code Ann. § 11.405(b).

2-7:3 Damages and Remedies

2-7:3.1 Receivership

Receivership is the only remedy available to a plaintiff.[171]

A receiver may be appointed for specific corporate assets[172] or to either rehabilitate[173] or liquidate the corporation.[174]

For more information on receivership as a remedy, *see* Chapter 8, Section 8-12—Receivership.

2-7:4 Defenses

2-7:4.1 Defenses, Generally

Receiverships, even statutory ones, are equitable in nature and are likely subject to equitable defenses.

2-7:5 Procedural Implications

2-7:5.1 Fact Finder's Role

It is the fact finder's role to determine what actions the controlling shareholders took.[175]

It is the court's role to determine whether those actions constitute "oppression" under the receivership statute.[176]

2-8 Derivate Shareholder Suits

2-8:1 Overview

Corporate shareholders have no say in the day to day decisions affecting the corporation they own. However, when the corporation refuses to rectify a wrong done to it by a third party—often a member of the board of directors or a corporate officer—shareholders may step in and litigate on behalf of the corporation. The current framework for Derivative Shareholder Suits strikes a balance between the autonomy of the corporate board of directors and the need for shareholders to police the corporation they own.

---

[171] *Ritchie v. Rupe*, 443 S.W.3d 856, 872–73 (Tex. 2014).
[172] Tex. Bus. Orgs. Code Ann. § 11.403(b)(3).
[173] Tex. Bus. Orgs. Code Ann. § 11.404(a)(1)(C).
[174] Tex. Bus. Orgs. Code Ann. § 11.405(a)(3).
[175] *Davis v. Sheerin*, 754 S.W.2d 375, 380 (Tex. App.—Houston [1st Dist.] 1988, writ denied), *disapproved of on other grounds by Ritchie v. Rupe*, 443 S.W.3d 856 (Tex. 2014).
[176] *Davis v. Sheerin*, 754 S.W.2d 375, 380 (Tex. App.—Houston [1st Dist.] 1988, writ denied), *disapproved of on other grounds by Ritchie v. Rupe*, 443 S.W.3d 856 (Tex. 2014).

BUSINESS MANAGEMENT LITIGATION

2-8:1.1 Related Causes of Action

Officer and Director Liability, Breach of Partnership Duty, Usurpation of Business Opportunity, Securities Litigation, Class Action Suits

2-8:2 Elements

(1) Corporation suffers an injury

- Any action by a third party which has harmed the corporation.[177]

(2) Corporation does not enforce its right to redress the injury

- Corporation does not enforce its right to redress the injury. Essentially, the corporation refuses to act.[178]

(3) Shareholder has standing to sue

- The shareholder:
  - Satisfies one of the following:
    - Was a shareholder at the time the act or omission complained of occurred; or
    - Became a shareholder by operation of law from a person who was a shareholder at the time the act or omission complained of occurred; and
  - The shareholder fairly and adequately represents the interests of the corporation in enforcing the right of the corporation.[179]

(4) Shareholder makes written demand on the board of directors

- The shareholder must make a written demand of the board of directors which:
  - States with particularity the act, omission, or other matter which is the subject of the claim or challenge;[180]
  - Requests that the corporation take suitable action;[181] and
  - Identifies the shareholder(s) by name.[182]

---

[177] *See Commonwealth of Mass. v. Davis*, 140 Tex. 398, 407, 168 S.W.2d 216, 221 (1942).

[178] *Providential Inv. Corp. v. Dibrell*, 320 S.W.2d 415, 418 (Tex. Civ. App.—Houston 1959, no writ).

[179] Tex. Bus. Orgs. Code Ann. § 21.552; *Eye Site, Inc. v. Blackburn*, 796 S.W.2d 160, 162 (Tex. 1990) (equating "adequately represents" to the similar language found in Federal Rule of Civil Procedure 23.1 and Texas Rule of Civil Procedure 42.2 dealing with class actions); *but see* Tex. Bus. Orgs. Code Ann. § 21.563(b) (sections 21.552–21.560 do not apply to a closely held corporation); *Sneed v. Webre*, 465 S.W.3d 169 (Tex. 2015) (recognizing double-derivative standing).

[180] Tex. Bus. Orgs. Code Ann. § 21.553(a); *In re Schmitz*, 285 S.W.3d 451, 458 (Tex. 2009) (The degree of particularity required depends on "the circumstances of the corporation, the board, and the transaction involved in the complaint."); *but see* Tex. Bus. Orgs. Code Ann. § 21.563(b) (sections 21.552–21.560 do not apply to a closely held corporation).

[181] Tex. Bus. Orgs. Code Ann. § 21.553(a); *In re Schmitz*, 285 S.W.3d 451, 458 (Tex. 2009) (demand must provide a specific direction for the board of directors to follow); *but see* Tex. Bus. Orgs. Code Ann. § 21.563(b) (sections 21.552–21.560 do not apply to a closely held corporation).

[182] *In re Schmitz*, 285 S.W.3d 451, 455 (Tex. 2009).

- However, if the converted entity in a conversion is a corporation, a shareholder of that corporation may not institute or maintain in a derivative proceeding unless:
    - The proceeding is not based on an act or omission that occurred before the date of the conversion; or
    - The shareholder was an equity owner of the converting entity at the time of the act or omission and the shareholder fairly and adequately represents the interest of the corporation.[183]
- (5) 91 days have passed since the shareholder has made his written demand, unless: (a) the shareholder has been notified that the demand has been rejected by the corporation; (b) the corporation is suffering irreparable injury; or (c) irreparable injury to the corporation would result by waiting for the expiration of the 90-day period.
    - 91 days must pass after the shareholder makes his written demand.[184]

Exceptions:

- The shareholder has been notified that the demand has been rejected by the corporation;
- The corporation is suffering irreparable injury; or
- Irreparable injury to the corporation would result by waiting for the expiration of the 90-day period.[185]

2-8:3 Damages and Remedies

2-8:3.1 Generally

The damages and remedies available to a plaintiff will be determined by the underlying cause(s) of action.[186]

---

[183] Tex. Bus. Orgs. Code Ann. § 21.552(b); *but see* Tex. Bus. Orgs. Code Ann. § 21.563(b) (sections 21.552–21.560 do not apply to a closely held corporation).

[184] Tex. Bus. Orgs. Code Ann. § 21.553(a); *but see* Tex. Bus. Orgs. Code Ann. § 21.563(b) (sections 21.552–21.560 do not apply to a closely held corporation). This statute was amended in 2019 and now subsection b says the waiting period required by Subsection (a) before a derivative proceeding may be instituted is not required or, if applicable, shall terminate if:
  (1) the shareholder has been notified that the demand has been rejected by the corporation;
  (2) the corporation is suffering irreparable injury; or
  (3) irreparable injury to the corporation would result by waiting for the expiration of the 90-day period.

[185] Tex. Bus. Orgs. Code Ann. § 21.553(b); *but see* Tex. Bus. Orgs. Code Ann. § 21.563(b) (sections 21.552–21.560 do not apply to a closely held corporation).

[186] *See Wingate v. Hajdik*, 795 S.W.2d 717, 719 (Tex. 1990) (awarding damages to the corporation for multiple underlying liability findings, including fraud, breach of fiduciary duty, and misappropriation of assets).

BUSINESS MANAGEMENT LITIGATION

The corporation will recover any damages or receive the benefit of any equitable relief.[187]

There are circumstances where the court may award damages directly to the shareholder-plaintiff.[188]

2-8:3.2 Cost Shifting

- Any party may be ordered to pay the expenses of another party[189]
    - "Expenses" includes
    - Attorney's fees;
    - Costs in pursuing an investigation of the matter that was the subject of the derivative proceeding; or
    - Expenses for which the corporation or a corporate defendant may be required to indemnify another person.[190]

The corporation must pay the shareholder-plaintiff's expenses upon a court finding that the shareholder-plaintiff obtained a substantial benefit for the corporation.[191]

The shareholder-plaintiff must pay the corporation's expenses incurred in investigating and defending the proceeding upon a court finding that the litigation has been instituted or maintained without reasonable cause or for an improper purpose.[192]

Any party must pay the expenses incurred in relating to the filing of a motion, pleading or other paper if the motion, pleading or other paper was improper.[193]

2-8:3.3 Indemnification

A corporation shall indemnify a defendant director or officer for actual expenses incurred in a wholly successful defense.[194]

A corporation may indemnify an officer or director who is threatened to be named in a proceeding for reasonable expenses, in advance of the final disposition of the proceeding when:

(1) The corporation receives a written affirmation by the person of the person's good faith belief that the person has met the standard of conduct necessary for indemnification under Chapter 8 of the BOC;

and

---

[187] *See Wingate v. Hajdik*, 795 S.W.2d 717, 719 (Tex. 1990) ("The cause of action for injury to the property of a corporation, or the impairment or destruction of its business, is vested in the corporation.").

[188] Tex. Bus. Orgs. Code Ann. § 21.563(c) (allowing a shareholder of a closely held corporation to directly recover any damages if "justice requires"); *Wingate v. Hajdik*, 795 S.W.2d 717, 719 (Tex. 1990) (citing *Commonwealth of Mass. v. Davis*, 168 S.W.2d 216, 222 (1942)).

[189] Tex. Bus. Orgs. Code Ann. § 21.561(b).

[190] Tex. Bus. Orgs. Code Ann. § 21.561(a).

[191] Tex. Bus. Orgs. Code Ann. § 21.561(b)(1).

[192] Tex. Bus. Orgs. Code Ann. § 21.561(b)(2).

[193] Tex. Bus. Orgs. Code Ann. § 21.561(b)(3).

[194] Tex. Bus. Orgs. Code Ann. § 8.051(a).

(2) The corporation receives a written undertaking by or on behalf of the person to repay the amount paid or reimbursed if the final determination is that the person has not met that standard or that indemnification is prohibited by Section 8.102.[195]

2-8:4 Defenses

2-8:4.1 Procedural Defenses

No demand or an insufficient demand made on the board of directors is an appropriate defense.[196]

Premature filing of a lawsuit following the shareholder-plaintiff's demand is also an appropriate defense.[197]

2-8:4.2 Defenses Held by the Defendant Third Party

The defendant corporation may assert all of the defenses held by the defendant third party.

- Statute of Limitations:
  - The applicable limitations period is determined by the underlying cause of action.[198]
  - Statute of limitations accrues on the date of the legal injury to the corporation.[199]
  - A written demand filed with the corporation under Business Organizations Code Section 21.533 tolls the statute of limitations on the claim on which demand is made until the later of:
    (1) The 31st day after the expiration of any waiting period under Section 21.553; or
    (2) The 31st day after the expiration of any stay granted under Section 21.555, including all continuations of the stay.[200]
- Res Judicata:
  - Bars relitigation of derivative claims which arise out of the same subject matter and could have been brought in the first lawsuit.[201]

---

[195] Tex. Bus. Orgs. Code Ann. § 8.104(a).

[196] Tex. Bus. Orgs. Code Ann. § 21.553(a); *In re Schmitz*, 285 S.W.3d 451, 458 (Tex. 2009); *but see* Tex. Bus. Orgs. Code Ann. § 21.563(b) (sections 21.552–21.560 do not apply to a closely held corporation).

[197] Tex. Bus. Orgs. Code Ann. § 21.553(a); *but see* Tex. Bus. Orgs. Code Ann. § 21.563(b) (sections 21.552–21.560 do not apply to a closely held corporation).

[198] *Langston v. Eagle Publ'g. Co.*, 719 S.W.2d 612, 616–17 (Tex. App.—Waco 1986, writ ref'd n.r.e.) (applying the limitations period for a libel in the derivative shareholder suit context).

[199] *Crowley v. Coles*, 760 S.W.2d 347, 350 (Tex. App.—Houston [1st Dist.] 1988, no writ) (using the date of the complained of transaction as the date the statute of limitations accrued).

[200] Tex. Bus. Orgs. Code Ann. § 21.557.

[201] *Cervantes v. Ocwen Loan Servicing, L.L.C.*, 749 Fed. Appx. 242, 245 (5th Cir. 2018).

BUSINESS MANAGEMENT LITIGATION

- Res Judicata does not bar claims if the absent shareholders were not adequately represented.[202]

2-8:4.3 Defenses Against the Shareholder-Plaintiff

A defendant corporation and a defendant third party may assert the following defenses against the shareholder-plaintiff:

- Shareholder's standing to sue;
- The plaintiff participated in, consented to, or acquiesced in the misconduct he seeks to challenge on the corporation's behalf;[203]
- The plaintiff purchased his stock with knowledge of prior misconduct;[204]
- The plaintiff is guilty of laches in bringing the suit;[205] or
- The plaintiff purchased his shares from someone who participated in the misconduct in question.[206]

2-8:5 Procedural Implications

2-8:5.1 Forum

- Derivative shareholder suits may always be brought in state court.[207]
- Derivative shareholder suits may be brought in federal court given the proper jurisdictional facts.[208]
- Plaintiffs might prefer federal court because there are fewer procedural mechanisms.

2-8:5.2 Venue

- Corporations will generally be classified as plaintiffs for venue purposes.[209]
- If the corporation will be adversely affected by the lawsuit, the defendant corporation will be deemed to be a defendant for venue purposes.[210]

---

[202] *See Citizens Ins. Co. of Am. v. Daccach*, 217 S.W.3d 430, 450 (Tex. 2007) (discussing res judicata's effect on class actions); *Nacogdoches Cty. v. Marshall*, 469 S.W.2d 633, 637 (Tex. Civ. App.—Tyler 1971, no writ) (same).
[203] *Stubblefield v. Belco Mfg. Co., Inc.*, 931 S.W.2d 54, 55 (Tex. App.—Austin 1996, no writ).
[204] *Greenspun v. Greenspun*, 145 Tex. 374, 377, 198 S.W.2d 82, 84 (1946).
[205] *Laches of stockholders in attacking sale of corporate assets*, 70 A.L.R. 53 (originally published 1931).
[206] *Stubblefield v. Belco Mfg. Co., Inc.*, 931 S.W.2d 54, 55 (Tex. App.—Austin 1996, no writ).
[207] Tex. Const. art. V, § 8 (granting district courts general jurisdiction).
[208] 28 U.S.C. §§ 1331–32, 1367 (federal question, diversity, and supplemental jurisdiction).
[209] *National Bankers Life Ins. Co. v. Adler*, 324 S.W.2d 35, 37–38 (Tex. Civ. App.—San Antonio 1959, no writ).
[210] *National Bankers Life Ins. Co. v. Adler*, 324 S.W.2d 35, 37–38 (Tex. Civ. App.—San Antonio 1959, no writ).

2-8:5.3 Claim Joinder

- A shareholder-plaintiff must bring all direct claims arising out of the same subject matter.[211]

- Shareholders who are not an actual party to the lawsuit are not required to bring any direct claims.[212]

2-8:5.4 Demand

- The shareholder must make a written demand of the board of directors which:
  - States with particularity the act, omission or other matter which is the subject of the claim or challenge;[213]
  - Requests that the corporation take suitable action;[214] and
  - Identifies the shareholder(s) by name.[215]

A shareholder may not institute a derivative proceeding until the 91st day after the date the shareholder makes his written demand.[216]

Exceptions:

- The shareholder has been notified that the demand has been rejected by the corporation;
- The corporation is suffering irreparable injury; or
- Irreparable injury to the corporation would result by waiting for the expiration of the 90-day period.[217]

---

[211] *Amstadt v. U.S. Brass Corp.*, 919 S.W.2d 644, 652–53 (Tex. 1996) (discussing elements of res judicata).

[212] *See Amstadt v. U.S. Brass Corp.*, 919 S.W.2d 644, 653 (Tex. 1996) (discussing elements of res judicata). It appears that the element requiring identity of the parties would not be satisfied because the nominal party to the lawsuit could not adequately represent—or even litigate—the absentee shareholder's direct claims.

[213] Tex. Bus. Orgs. Code Ann. § 21.553(a); *In re Schmitz*, 285 S.W.3d 451, 458 (Tex. 2009) (The degree of particularity required depends on "the circumstances of the corporation, the board, and the transaction involved in the complaint."); *but see* Tex. Bus. Orgs. Code Ann. § 21.563(b) (sections 21.552–21.560 do not apply to a closely held corporation).

[214] Tex. Bus. Orgs. Code Ann. § 21.553(a); *In re Schmitz*, 285 S.W.3d 451, 458 (Tex. 2009) (demand must provide a specific direction for the board of directors to follow); *but see* Tex. Bus. Orgs. Code Ann. § 21.563(b) (sections 21.552–21.560 do not apply to a closely held corporation).

[215] *In re Schmitz*, 285 S.W.3d 451, 455 (Tex. 2009).

[216] Tex. Bus. Orgs. Code Ann. § 21.553(a); *but see* Tex. Bus. Orgs. Code Ann. § 21.563(b) (sections 21.552–21.560 do not apply to a closely held corporation).

[217] Tex. Bus. Orgs. Code Ann. § 21.553(b); *but see* Tex. Bus. Org. Code Ann. § 21.563(b) (sections 21.552–21.560 do not apply to a closely held corporation).

2-8:5.5 Statutory Stay of the Derivative Proceedings

The court shall stay the proceedings for not more than 60 days if the defendant corporation is conducting a good faith investigation into the allegations.[218]

This investigation must be conducted by a group of disinterested and independent directors. Such a group must consist of:

- A group of directors which constitute a quorum of the board of directors and a vote is taken outside of the presence of interested or dependent directors;
- A committee consisting of two or more independent and disinterested directors appointed by an affirmative vote of the majority of one or more independent and disinterested directors present at a meeting of the board of directors, regardless of whether the independent and disinterested directors constitute a quorum of the board of directors; or
- A panel of one or more independent and disinterested persons appointed by the court on a motion by the corporation listing the names of the persons to be appointed and stating that, to the best of the corporation's knowledge, the persons to be appointed are disinterested and qualified to make the determinations contemplated by Texas Business Organizations Code Section 21.558.[219]

The court shall grant a stay upon written application by the defendant corporation. The written application must include an agreement that the defendant corporation will promptly inform the court and the shareholder-plaintiff of the determinations of the investigation. Upon motion, which provides the court and the shareholder with a status of the review and why an extension is appropriate, the stay may be reviewed every 60 days for continuation. If the court determines that the continuation of the stay is appropriate in the interests of the corporation, an extension shall be granted for a period not to exceed 60 days.[220]

2-8:5.6 Dismissal of Suit by the Board of Directors

The disinterested and independent directors on the board of directors may dismiss a derivative shareholder suit if it determines the suit is not in the best interests of the corporation.[221]

The same group of disinterested and independent directors required to obtain a statutory stay of the proceedings must decide whether to dismiss the lawsuit.[222]

2-8:5.7 Limited Discovery

In this situation, a shareholder-plaintiff may only discover:

---

[218] Tex. Bus. Orgs. Code Ann. § 21.555(a); *but see* Tex. Bus. Orgs. Code Ann. § 21.563(b) (sections 21.552–21.560 do not apply to a closely held corporation).

[219] Tex. Bus. Orgs. Code Ann. § 21.554(a); *but see* Tex. Bus. Orgs. Code Ann. § 21.563(b) (sections 21.552–21.560 do not apply to a closely held corporation).

[220] Tex. Bus. Orgs. Code Ann. § 21.555.

[221] Tex. Bus. Orgs. Code Ann. § 21.558.

[222] Tex. Bus. Orgs. Code Ann. § 21.554(a); *but see* Tex. Bus. Orgs. Code Ann. § 21.563(b) (sections 21.552–21.560 do not apply to a closely held corporation).

- Facts relating to whether the person or group of persons described by Section 21.554 is independent and disinterested;
- The good faith of the inquiry and review by the person or group; and
- The reasonableness of the procedures followed by the person or group in conducting the review.[223]

The scope of discovery shall not be limited if the court determines after notice and hearing that a good faith review of the allegations has not been made by an independent and disinterested person or group in accordance with Sections 21.554 and 21.558.[224]

2-8:5.8 Settlement

Any settlement requires court approval.[225]

If a settlement substantially affects the interests of other shareholders, the court shall direct that notice of the proposed settlement be sent to the affected shareholders.[226]

2-8:5.9 Application to Foreign Corporations

A derivative shareholder suit against a foreign corporation is only subject to the procedural implications regarding:

- Cost shifting;
- Settlement; and
- The statutory stay, unless the law which governs the foreign corporation requires otherwise.[227]

When determining who constitutes the group of disinterested and independent directors for purposes of the statutory stay, the substantive law which governs the foreign corporation will control.[228]

2-8:5.10 Closely Held Corporations

A derivative shareholder suit against a closely held corporation is only subject to the procedural implications regarding:

- Cost shifting; and
- Applicability to foreign corporations.[229]

---

[223] Tex. Bus. Orgs. Code Ann. § 21.556(a); *but see* Tex. Bus. Orgs. Code Ann. § 21.563(b) (sections 21.552–21.560 do not apply to a closely held corporation).

[224] Tex. Bus. Orgs. Code Ann. § 21.556(b); *but see* Tex. Bus. Orgs. Code Ann. § 21.563(b) (sections 21.552–21.560 do not apply to a closely held corporation).

[225] Tex. Bus. Orgs. Code Ann. § 21.560(a); *but see* Tex. Bus. Orgs. Code Ann. § 21.563(b) (sections 21.552–21.560 do not apply to a closely held corporation).

[226] Tex. Bus. Orgs. Code Ann. § 21.560(b); *but see* Tex. Bus. Orgs. Code Ann. § 21.563(b) (sections 21.552–21.560 do not apply to a closely held corporation).

[227] Tex. Bus. Orgs. Code Ann. § 21.562(a).

[228] Tex. Bus. Orgs. Code Ann. § 21.562(b).

[229] Tex. Bus. Orgs. Code Ann. § 21.563(b).

A closely held corporation is a corporation that has:

- Fewer than 35 shareholders; and
- No shares listed on a national securities exchange or regularly quoted in an over-the-counter market by one or more members of a national securities association.[230]

A court may treat a derivative action involving a closely held corporation the same as a direct action, including payment of damages directly to the shareholder.[231]

2-9 Dissenting Shareholders Suits

2-9:1 Overview

During the course of its life, a business entity may undertake one or more fundamental transactions or changes. Owner approval is generally required for these fundamental actions. Because these fundamental actions do not normally require unanimous consent from the entity's owners, several owners might be compelled to acquiesce to a fundamental action which they don't want the entity to participate in. The Texas Legislature has enacted a remedy for these dissenting owners. A dissenting shareholder suit is a cause of action which seeks to provide a dissenting owner the fair value of his ownership interest. In order to receive fair value, the owner must strictly comply with the procedural rules outlined by the Texas Legislature.

2-9:1.1 Related Causes of Action

Shareholder Oppression, Breach of Fiduciary Duty, Breach of Partnership Duty, Derivative Shareholder Suits

MUST READ CASES & STATUTES

Farnsworth v. Massey, 365 S.W.2d 1 (Tex. 1963)

Gannon v. Baker, 807 S.W.2d 793 (Tex. App.—Houston [1st Dist.] 1991), *writ granted* (Nov. 6, 1991), *rev'd in part on other grounds*, 818 S.W.2d 754 (Tex. 1991)

Texas Business Organizations Code Annotated Sections 10.351-10.368

2-9:2 Elements

(1) An owner
- The owner can be:
  - A shareholder in a
    - Domestic for-profit corporation;
    - Professional corporation;
    - Professional association; or

---

[230] Tex. Bus. Orgs. Code Ann. § 21.563(a).
[231] Tex. Bus. Orgs. Code Ann. § 21.563(c).

- Real estate investment trust;[232]
- Partnership or LLC owners provided rights of dissent and appraisal within the organization's governing documents.[233]

(2) Of a qualifying entity
- To qualify, the entity must be one of the following:
  - A domestic for-profit corporation;
  - A professional corporation;
  - A professional association;
  - A real estate investment trust;[234] or
  - A partnership or limited liability company that expressly provides its owners a right of dissent and appraisal.[235]

(3) Which proposes to make a qualifying entity action
- An owner has dissent and appraisal rights from the following actions:
  - A plan of merger to which the domestic entity is a party if owner approval is required by this code and the owner owns in the domestic entity an ownership interest that was entitled to vote on the plan of merger;
  - A sale of all or substantially all of the assets of the domestic entity if owner approval is required by this code and the owner owns in the domestic entity an ownership interest that was entitled to vote on the sale;
  - A plan of exchange in which the ownership interest of the owner is to be acquired;
  - A plan of conversion in which the domestic entity is the converting entity if owner approval is required by this code and the owner owns in the domestic entity an ownership interest that was entitled to vote on the plan of conversion; or
  - A merger effected under Texas Business Organizations Code Section 10.006 (Short Form Merger) in which:
    - The owner is entitled to vote on the merger; or
    - The ownership interest of the owner is converted or exchanged;[236]
- An owner does not have dissent and appraisal rights from a merger or conversion where there is only one surviving entity, or from any plan of exchange in which:
  - The owner's ownership interest is:

---

[232] Tex. Bus. Orgs. Code Ann. § 10.351(b).
[233] Tex. Bus. Orgs. Code Ann. § 10.351(c).
[234] Tex. Bus. Orgs. Code Ann. § 10.351(b).
[235] Tex. Bus. Orgs. Code Ann. § 10.351(c).
[236] Tex. Bus. Orgs. Code Ann. § 10.354(a)(1).

BUSINESS MANAGEMENT LITIGATION

- Traded on a national stock exchange; or
- Held of record by at least 2,000 owners;
- The owner is not required to accept consideration that is different from consideration offered to other owners of the same class or series; and
- The owner is not required by the terms of the plan of merger, conversion or exchange, as appropriate, to accept for the owner's ownership interest any consideration other than:
  - (A) ownership interests, or depository receipts in respect of ownership interests, of a domestic entity or non-code organization of the same general organizational type that, immediately after the effective date of the merger, conversion or exchange, as appropriate, will be part of a class or series of ownership interests, or depository receipts in respect of ownership interests, that are:
    - Listed on a national securities exchange or authorized for listing on the exchange on official notice of issuance; or
    - Held of record by at least 2,000 owners;
  - (B) cash instead of fractional ownership interests or fractional depository receipts the owner would otherwise be entitled to receive; or
  - (C) any combination of the ownership interests or fractional depository receipts and cash described by Paragraphs (A) and (B).[237]

(4) Owner sends written notice objecting to that action
- If the proposed action is to be submitted to a vote of the owners at a meeting, the owner must give to the domestic entity a written notice of objection to the action that:
  - Is addressed to the entity's president and secretary;
  - States that the owner's right to dissent will be exercised if the action takes effect;
  - Provides an address to which notice of effectiveness of the action should be delivered or mailed; and
  - Is delivered to the entity's principal executive offices before the meeting;[238]

(5) Owner dissents from the action
- The owner must dissent from the action:
  - The owner must vote against the action if the owner is entitled to vote on the action and the action is approved at a meeting of the owners; and
  - The owner may not consent to the action if the action is approved by written consent;[239]

---

[237] Tex. Bus. Orgs. Code Ann. § 10.354(b).
[238] Tex. Bus. Orgs. Code Ann. § 10.356(b)(1).
[239] Tex. Bus. Orgs. Code Ann. § 10.356(b)(2).

(6) Owner makes a timely written demand on the responsible organization
- The owner must give to the responsible organization a demand in writing that:
    - Is addressed to the president and secretary of the responsible organization;
    - Demands payment of the fair value of the ownership interests for which the rights of dissent and appraisal are sought;
    - Provides to the responsible organization an address to which a notice relating to the dissent and appraisal procedures may be sent;
    - States the number and class of the ownership interests of the domestic entity owned by the owner and the fair value of the ownership interests as estimated by the owner; and
    - Is delivered to the responsible organization at its principal executive offices at the following time:
        - Not later than the 20th day after the date the responsible organization sends to the owner the notice required by Section 10.355(e) that the action has taken effect, if the action was approved by a vote of the owners at a meeting;
        - Not later than the 20th day after the date the responsible organization sends to the owner the notice required by Section 10.355(d)(2) that the action has taken effect, if the action was approved by the written consent of the owners; or
        - Not later than the 20th day after the date the responsible organization sends to the owner a notice that the merger was effected, if the action is a merger effected under Section 10.006.[240]

(7) Owner timely submits any certificates representing the owner's ownership interest to the responsible organization.
- Not later than the 20th day after the date an owner makes a demand for fair value of his ownership interest, the owner must submit to the responsible organization any certificates representing the ownership interest to which the demand relates.[241]

2-9:3 Damages and Remedies

2-9:3.1 Dissent and Appraisal Right/Fair Value

An owner is entitled to the "fair value" of his ownership interest.

"Fair value" means:

- Going concern value; and

---

[240] Tex. Bus. Orgs. Code Ann. § 10.356(b)(3).
[241] Tex. Bus. Orgs. Code Ann. § 10.356(d).

- An adjustment for the relative rights—other than voting rights—of a class or series of ownership interest.[242]

"Fair value" may not include:

- Any appreciation or depreciation in the value of the ownership interest occurring in anticipation of the proposed action or as a result of the action;[243]
- Any control premium;
- Any minority ownership discount; or
- Any discount for lack of marketability.[244]

"Fair value" is determined as of the date preceding the date of the action that is the subject of the appraisal.[245]

The responsible organization pays the owner the fair value of the ownership interest.[246]

2-9:3.2 Prejudgment Interest

Prejudgment interest is authorized.[247]

Interest accrues on the 91st day after the date the applicable action for which the owner elected to dissent was effected until the date of the judgment.[248]

Interest accrues at the same rate as is provided for the accrual of prejudgment interest in civil cases.[249]

2-9:3.3 Costs

Court costs are to be divided equitably between the parties.[250]

Costs include a reasonable fee for the appraiser appointed under Section 10.361(e)(2).[251]

Costs likely do not include attorney's fees.[252]

---

[242] Tex. Bus. Orgs. Code Ann. § 10.362(b). There are no Texas cases which discuss "fair value" in the dissent and appraisal context, but the Dallas Court of Appeals' discussion in *Ritchie v. Rupe*, is helpful. There, the court applied the "enterprise value" formulation in finding the fair value of an oppressed shareholder's shares. *Ritchie v. Rupe*, 339 S.W.3d 275, 300–01 (Tex. App.—Dallas 2011, pet. granted). The court went on to say, albeit in dicta, that the enterprise value approach is appropriate in the dissent and appraisal context.
[243] Tex. Bus. Orgs. Code Ann. § 10.362(a).
[244] Tex. Bus. Orgs. Code Ann. § 10.362(b).
[245] Tex. Bus. Orgs. Code Ann. § 10.362(a).
[246] Tex. Bus. Orgs. Code Ann. § 10.352(2).
[247] Tex. Bus. Orgs. Code Ann. § 10.364(b).
[248] Tex. Bus. Orgs. Code Ann. § 10.364(b).
[249] Tex. Bus. Orgs. Code Ann. § 10.364(c).
[250] Tex. Bus. Orgs. Code Ann. § 10.365(b).
[251] Tex. Bus. Orgs. Code Ann. § 10.365(a).
[252] *See Bay Area Thoracic & Cardiovascular Surgical Ass'n, P.A. v. Nathanson*, 908 S.W.2d 10, 12 (Tex. App.—Houston [1st Dist.] 1995, no writ) (interpreting similar language under Texas Business Corporations Act).

2-9:3.4 Exclusivity of Remedy

In the absence of fraud in the transaction, any right of an owner of an ownership interest to dissent from an action and obtain the fair value of the ownership interest under this subchapter is the exclusive remedy for recovery of:

- The value of the ownership interest; or
- Money damages to the owner with respect to the action.[253]

This exclusivity provision does not prohibit:

- Any cause of action unrelated to the qualifying entity action, such as:
  - Additional damages for fraud in the transaction.[254]
  - An owner derivative suit unrelated to the qualifying entity action;[255] or
  - A direct cause of action for wrongs done to the owner individually where the wrongdoer violates a duty arising from contract or otherwise, and owing directly by him to the stockholder.[256]

2-9:3.5 Special Damages for Fraud

Special damages for fraud in the transaction are available.[257]

2-9:4 Defenses

Failure of the owner to perfect dissent and appraisal rights

- An owner may only perfect his dissent and appraisal rights by following the procedures listed in Subchapter H of the Texas Business Organizations Code.[258]
- Failure to follow the procedures listed in Subchapter H of the Texas Business Organizations Code is a total bar to suit to recover the value of the ownership interest or money damages relating to the qualifying entity action.[259]
- *See* Procedural Implications below for specific procedural requirements.

2-9:4.1 Procedural Non-Compliance

Although not a traditional defense, an owner must strictly follow the procedures of the Texas Business Organizations Code.

---

[253] Tex. Bus. Orgs. Code Ann. § 10.368.
[254] Tex. Bus. Orgs. Code Ann. § 10.368; *Farnsworth v. Massey*, 365 S.W.2d 1, 5 (Tex. 1963).
[255] *See Gannon v. Baker*, 807 S.W.2d 793, 798 (Tex. App.—Houston [1st Dist.] 1991), *writ granted* (Nov. 6, 1991), *rev'd in part on other grounds*, 818 S.W.2d 754 (Tex. 1991) (holding that this type of cause of action belongs to the corporation, not the shareholder).
[256] *Gannon v. Baker*, 807 S.W.2d 793, 798 (Tex. App.—Houston [1st Dist.] 1991), *writ granted* (Nov. 6, 1991), *rev'd in part on other grounds*, 818 S.W.2d 754 (Tex. 1991).
[257] Tex. Bus. Orgs. Code Ann. § 10.368; *Farnsworth v. Massey*, 365 S.W.2d 1, 5 (Tex. 1963).
[258] Tex. Bus. Orgs. Code Ann. § 10.356(a).
[259] Tex. Bus. Orgs. Code Ann. § 10.356(e); *see* Tex. Bus. Orgs. Code Ann. § 10.367.

2-9:5 Procedural Implications

2-9:5.1 Strict Compliance Requirement

Failure to follow the procedures listed in Subchapter H of the Texas Business Organizations Code is a total bar to suit to recover the value of the ownership interest or money damages relating to the qualifying entity action.[260]

2-9:5.2 Interim Status of Ownership Interest

A dissenting owner seeking appraisal may not vote his ownership interest or exercise any other ownership right, except to:

- Receive payment for the ownership interest under this subchapter; and
- Bring an appropriate action to obtain relief on the ground that the action to which the demand relates would be or was fraudulent.[261]

An ownership interest for which payment has been demanded under Section 10.356 may not be considered outstanding for purposes of any subsequent vote or action.[262]

2-9:5.3 Withdrawal of Demand

An owner may withdraw his demand:

- At any time before payment for the ownership interest has been made under Sections 10.358 and 10.361;
- At any time before a petition has been filed under Section 10.361; or
- Upon consent of the responsible organization.[263]

2-9:5.4 Judicial Proceeding to Determine Fair Value

A dissenting owner may file suit only after both:

- The responsible organization rejects the owner's demand; and
- The responsible organization and the owner cannot agree on the fair value of the ownership interest within 90 days from the date the qualifying entity action took effect.[264]

The owner must file a petition not later than 150 days from the date the qualifying entity action took effect.[265]

Venue lies in:

- The county in which the organization's principal office is located in this state; or

---

[260] Tex. Bus. Orgs. Code Ann. § 10.356(e); see Tex. Bus. Orgs. Code Ann. § 10.367.
[261] Tex. Bus. Orgs. Code Ann. § 10.366(b).
[262] Tex. Bus. Orgs. Code Ann. § 10.366(c).
[263] Tex. Bus. Orgs. Code Ann. § 10.357(a)–(b).
[264] Tex. Bus. Orgs. Code Ann. § 10.361(a).
[265] Tex. Bus. Orgs. Code Ann. § 10.361(b).

- The county in which the organization's registered office is located in this state, if the organization does not have a business office in this state.[266]

The court shall appoint one or more appraisers to determine the fair value of the ownership interest.[267]

Either party may object to the appraisal, whereon the court will hold a hearing to determine the fair value.[268]

There is likely no right to jury trial in a hearing to determine fair value.[269]

2-9:5.5 Responsible Organization

The responsible organization is:

- The organization responsible for:
  - The provision of notices under this subchapter; and
  - The primary obligation of paying the fair value for an ownership interest held by a dissenting owner;
- With respect to a merger or conversion:
  - For matters occurring before the merger or conversion, the organization that is merging or converting; and
  - For matters occurring after the merger or conversion, the surviving or new organization that is primarily obligated for the payment of the fair value of the dissenting owner's ownership interest in the merger or conversion;
- With respect to an interest exchange, the organization the ownership interests of which are being acquired in the interest exchange; and
- With respect to the sale of all or substantially all of the assets of an organization, the organization the assets of which are to be transferred by sale or in another manner.[270]

2-10 Breach of Partnership Duty

2-10:1 Overview

General partners owe duties of loyalty and care and an obligation of good faith to both the partnership and other partners. These duties have historically been characterized as fiduciary duties. Despite the Texas Legislature's attempts to eliminate the fiduciary label of these duties and obligations, Texas courts still characterize them as fiduciary

---

[266] Tex. Bus. Orgs. Code Ann. § 10.361(a).
[267] Tex. Bus. Orgs. Code Ann. § 10.361(e)(2).
[268] Tex. Bus. Orgs. Code Ann. § 10.364(a)–(b).
[269] Determination of fair value, 20A Texas Practice Series, Business Organizations § 40:15 n. 12 (3d ed.) (Since the statute provides that the court shall determine fair value, *Farnsworth v. Massey*, 365 S.W.2d 1, 4 (Tex. 1963), which held that the jury should determine fair value, has presumably been superseded.).
[270] Tex. Bus. Orgs. Code Ann. § 10.352(2).

BUSINESS MANAGEMENT LITIGATION

ones. Relatively recent legislation has allowed for partners to curtail or even eliminate their duties.

2-10:1.1 Related Causes of Action

Officer and Director Liability, Usurpation of Business Opportunity, Securities Litigation, Class Action Suits, Derivative Shareholder Suits, Dissolution of Partnership, Breach of Fiduciary Duty

MUST READ CASES

Huffington v. Upchurch, 532 S.W.2d 576 (Tex. 1976)

Dunnagan v. Watson, 204 S.W.3d 30 (Tex. App.—Fort Worth 2006, pet. denied)

2-10:2 Elements

(1) Duty

- General partners owe fiduciary duties to other partners and the partnership.[271]
- Generally, limited partners do not owe each other a fiduciary duty.[272]
- The duty of loyalty includes:
  - Accounting to and holding for the partnership property, profit or benefit derived by the partner:
    - In the conduct and winding up of the partnership business; or
    - From use by the partner of partnership property;
  - Refraining from dealing with the partnership on behalf of a person who has an interest adverse to the partnership; and
  - Refraining from competing or dealing with the partnership in a manner adverse to the partnership.[273]
- In regards to the duty of care:
  - To act in the conduct and winding up of the partnership business with the care an ordinarily prudent person would exercise in similar circumstances.
  - An error in judgment does not by itself constitute a breach of the duty of care.

---

[271] *In re Gupta*, 394 F.3d 347, 351 (5th Cir. 2004) (quoting *M.R. Champion, Inc. v. Mizell*, 904 S.W.2d 617, 618 (Tex. 1995)).

[272] *Strebel v. Wimberly*, 371 S.W.3d 267, 279 (Tex. App.—Houston [1st Dist.] 2012, pet. denied) ("[S]tatus as a passive investor does not give rise to fiduciary duties, but a party's status as a limited partner does not insulate that party from the imposition of fiduciary duties that arise when a limited partner also takes on a nonpassive role by exercising control over the partnership in a way that justifies the recognition of such duties or by contract.").

[273] Tex. Bus. Orgs. Code Ann. § 152.205.

- A partner is presumed to satisfy the duty of care if the partner acts on an informed basis, in good faith, and in a manner the partner reasonably believes is in the best interests of the partnership.[274]
- Essentially, partners must satisfy the "business judgment rule" to discharge their duty of care.[275]
    - Obligation of good faith:
        - A partner shall discharge the partner's duties to the partnership and the other partners under this code or under the partnership agreement and exercise any rights and powers in the conduct or winding up of the partnership business:
            - In good faith; and
            - In a manner the partner reasonably believes to be in the best interest of the partnership.[276]
    - Partners may modify their duties and obligation of good faith. Partners may specify certain actions or conduct which do not violate their duties or obligation of good faith, so long as the actions or conduct are not manifestly unreasonable.[277]

(2) Breach

- The defendant breached a duty to the plaintiff.[278]
- Partners may specify certain actions or conduct which do not violate their duties or obligation of good faith, so long as the actions or conduct are not manifestly unreasonable.[279]

(3) Causation

- The defendant's breach resulted in harm to the partnership.[280]

(4) Damages/Harm

- "The defendant's breach resulted in either (a) an injury to the plaintiff; or (b) a benefit to the defendant."[281]

---

[274] Tex. Bus. Orgs. Code Ann. § 152.206.
[275] Partner duties under current statute, 19 Texas Practice Series, Business Organizations § 7:13 (3d ed.) (a partner shall discharge their duties in good faith and in a manner reasonably believed to be in the best interest of the partnership).
[276] Tex. Bus. Orgs. Code Ann. § 152.204(b).
[277] Tex. Bus. Orgs. Code Ann. § 152.002(a)–(b).
[278] *Matter of UTSA Apartments 8, L.L.C.*, 886 F.3d 473, 492 (5th Cir. 2018), *reh'g denied* (July 17, 2018).
[279] Tex. Bus. Orgs. Code Ann. § 152.002(a)–(b).
[280] Tex. Bus. Orgs. Code Ann. § 152.211(a) ("A partnership may maintain an action against a partner for a breach of the partnership agreement or for the violation of a duty to the partnership *causing* harm to the partnership.") (emphasis added).
[281] *Matter of UTSA Apartments 8, L.L.C.*, 886 F.3d 473, 492 (5th Cir. 2018), *reh'g denied* (July 17, 2018).

BUSINESS MANAGEMENT LITIGATION

2-10:3 Damages and Remedies

2-10:3.1 Actual Damages

A partner may pursue a claim for legal relief against another partner for breach of partnership duties.[282]

Legal damages are permitted.[283]

2-10:3.2 Interest

Post-judgment interest is available on money judgments.[284]

The default interest rate is governed by Texas Finance Code Annotated Section 302.002.[285]

2-10:3.3 Accounting

A partner may bring an action for an accounting to enforce partnership duties.[286]

2-10:3.4 Rescission

Rescission is an available equitable remedy.[287]

2-10:3.5 Restitution

Restitution is an available equitable remedy.[288]

2-10:3.6 Constructive Trust

A court may impose a constructive trust on property the breaching partner holds because of the breach.[289]

A constructive trust is proper when there is a:

- Breach of a special trust, fiduciary relationship, or actual fraud;
- Unjust enrichment of the wrongdoer; and
- Tracing to identifiable property.[290]

---

[282] Tex. Bus. Orgs. Code Ann. § 152.211(b).
[283] *Dunnagan v. Watson*, 204 S.W.3d 30, 47 (Tex. App.—Fort Worth 2006, pet. denied).
[284] Tex. Fin. Code Ann. § 304.005.
[285] Tex. Bus. Orgs. Code Ann. § 152.005.
[286] Tex. Bus. Orgs. Code Ann. § 152.211(b).
[287] *See Johnson v. Buck*, 540 S.W.2d 393, 416 (Tex. Civ. App.—Corpus Christi 1976, writ ref'd n.r.e.).
[288] *Matter of Bennett*, 989 F.2d 779, 790 (5th Cir. 1993), *opinion amended on reh'g*, 91-1059, 1993 WL 268299 (5th Cir. July 15, 1993).
[289] *Huffington v. Upchurch*, 532 S.W.2d 576, 577 (Tex. 1976).
[290] *Midwestern Cattle Mktg., L.L.C. v. Legend Bank, N. A.*, 800 Fed. Appx. 239, 247 (5th Cir. 2020).

2-10:3.7 Forfeiture of Compensation

A partner may be ordered to forfeit compensation because of his breach of partnership duties.[291]

2-10:3.8 Receivership

A partner may seek to have a receiver appointed.[292]

2-10:3.9 Winding Up of Partnership

A court may order the partnership to wind up upon application by a partner of the partnership if it finds that another partner in the partnership has engaged in conduct relating to the partnership's business that makes it not reasonably practical to carry on the business of the partnership with that partner.[293]

A court may also order the partnership to wind up upon application by a partner or owner in a partnership even if there is no finding that a partner breached his partnership duties when the economic purpose of the partnership is unreasonably frustrated or the partnership is unable to reasonably carry on in conformity with its governing documents.[294]

2-10:3.10 Exemplary Damages

Exemplary damages are recoverable for malicious, fraudulent, or grossly negligent breaches of partnership duties.[295]

A willful or intentional breach of a partnership duty is sufficient to support an award of exemplary damages.[296]

A receiver may be appointed to manage specific property held by the partnership, to rehabilitate the partnership, or to wind up the partnership.

2-10:4 Defenses

2-10:4.1 Statute of Limitations

The accrual of and a time limitation on a right of action for a remedy under this section is governed by other applicable law.[297]

A partner must bring an action for an accounting within four years after the partnership winds up.[298]

---

[291] *Russell v. Truitt*, 554 S.W.2d 948, 955 (Tex. Civ. App.—Fort Worth 1977, writ ref'd n.r.e.).
[292] Tex. Civ. Prac. & Rem. Code Ann. § 64.001(a)(3); Tex. Bus. Orgs. Code Ann. § 11.404.
[293] Tex. Bus. Orgs. Code Ann. § 11.314.
[294] Tex. Bus. Orgs. Code Ann. § 11.314; *Dunnagan v. Watson*, 204 S.W.3d 30, 39 (Tex. App.—Fort Worth 2006, pet. denied).
[295] Tex. Civ. Prac. & Rem. Code Ann. § 41.003(a); *Hawthorne v. Guenther*, 917 S.W.2d 924, 936 (Tex. App.—Beaumont 1996, writ denied).
[296] *Hawthorne v. Guenther*, 917 S.W.2d 924, 936 (Tex. App.—Beaumont 1996, writ denied).
[297] Tex. Bus. Orgs. Code Ann. § 152.211(c).
[298] Tex. Civ. Prac. & Rem. Code Ann. § 16.004(c).

BUSINESS MANAGEMENT LITIGATION

However, a right to an accounting does not revive a claim barred by law.[299]

2-10:4.2 Financial Incapability

A partnership's financial incapability is a defense to a usurpation claim.[300]

2-10:4.3 Abandonment of Business Opportunity

A partnership's abandonment of a business opportunity is a defense to a usurpation claim.[301]

2-10:5 Procedural Implications

2-10:5.1 Who May Bring Suit

A partnership may maintain an action against a partner for a breach of the partnership agreement or for the violation of a duty to the partnership which causes harm to the partnership.[302]

2-11 Usurpation of Business Opportunity

2-11:1 Overview

Corporate officers and directors—and their counterparts in LLCs and partnerships—owe a duty of loyalty to their principals. This duty encompasses the strict prohibition against usurpation of business opportunity.

2-11:1.1 Related Causes of Action

Officer and Director Liability, Class Action Suits, Derivative Shareholder Suits, Dissolution of Partnership, Breach of Fiduciary Duty

MUST READ CASE

International Bankers Life Ins. Co. v. Holloway, 368 S.W.2d 567 (Tex. 1963)

2-11:2 Elements

(1) An officer, director, manager, or partner

- Officers or directors of corporations are proper defendants.[303]

---

[299] Tex. Bus. Orgs. Code Ann. § 152.211(d).
[300] *Huffington v. Upchurch*, 532 S.W.2d 576, 579 (Tex. 1976); *BCOWW Holdings, LLC v. Collins*, SA-17-CA-00379-FB, 2017 WL 3868184, at *18 (W.D. Tex. Sept. 5, 2017).
[301] *BCOWW Holdings, LLC v. Collins*, SA-17-CA-00379-FB, 2017 WL 3868184, at *18 (W.D. Tex. Sept. 5, 2017).
[302] Tex. Bus. Orgs. Code Ann. § 152.211(a).
[303] *International Bankers Life Ins. Co. v. Holloway*, 368 S.W.2d 567, 583–84 (Tex. 1963); *Icom Sys., Inc. v. Davies*, 990 S.W.2d 408, 410 (Tex. App.—Texarkana 1999, no pet.).

- Partners in partnerships are proper defendants.[304]
- Officers, managers or member managers of LLCs are proper defendants.[305]

(2) Usurps a business opportunity

- The defendant must usurp a business opportunity/interest.[306]
- A defendant who diverts profits from the entity in violation of his fiduciary relationship is personally liable even though the profits are acquired by an agency controlled by the director.[307]

(3) Which properly belonged to the entity

- The defendant must usurp a business opportunity/interest.[308]
- A business opportunity which belongs to the plaintiff is one which:
    - The plaintiff has an "interest and expectancy" in;[309]
    - The financial resources to take advantage of the opportunity.[310]
    - Is in the plaintiff's "line of business."[311]
        - "Where a corporation is engaged in a certain business, and an opportunity is presented to it embracing an activity as to which it has fundamental knowledge, practical experience and ability to pursue, which, logically and naturally, is adaptable to its business having regard for its financial position, and is one that is consonant with its reasonable needs and aspirations for expansion, it may be properly said that the opportunity is in the line of the corporation's business."[312]
    - The "line of business" test is broader in scope than the "interest and expectancy" test.[313]

---

[304] *Lifshutz v. Lifshutz*, 199 S.W.3d 9, 19 (Tex. App.—San Antonio 2006, pet. denied).

[305] *See Pinnacle Data Servs., Inc. v. Gillen*, 104 S.W.3d 188, 191 (Tex. App.—Texarkana 2003, no pet.), *disapproved of on other grounds by Ritchie v. Rupe*, 443 S.W.3d 856 (Tex. 2014) (contemplating that persons with control over an LLC owe a duty of loyalty).

[306] *International Bankers Life Ins. Co. v. Holloway*, 368 S.W.2d 567, 577 (Tex. 1963).

[307] *International Bankers Life Ins. Co. v. Holloway*, 368 S.W.2d 567, 577 (Tex. 1963).

[308] *International Bankers Life Ins. Co. v. Holloway*, 368 S.W.2d 567, 577 (Tex. 1963).

[309] *In re Structual Software, Inc.*, 67 Fed. Appx. 253 (5th Cir. 2003).

[310] *Dyer v. Shafer, Gilliland, Davis, McCollum & Ashley, Inc.*, 779 S.W.2d 474, 477 (Tex. App.—El Paso 1989, writ denied).

[311] *Imperial Grp. (Tex.), Inc. v. Scholnick*, 709 S.W.2d 358, 365 (Tex. App.—Tyler 1986, writ ref'd n.r.e.).

[312] *Imperial Grp. (Tex.), Inc. v. Scholnick*, 709 S.W.2d 358, 365–66 (Tex. App.—Tyler 1986, writ ref'd n.r.e.).

[313] Corporate opportunities and unfair competition, 20A Texas Practice Series, Business Organizations § 36:9 (3d ed.).

2-11:3 Damages and Remedies

2-11:3.1 Constructive Trust

A plaintiff may seek a constructive trust.[314]

2-11:3.2 Turnover of Business Opportunity

A plaintiff may seek turnover of the business opportunity in the future.[315]

2-11:3.3 Forfeiture of Compensation

Forfeiture of compensation is appropriate.[316]

2-11:3.4 Disgorgement

Disgorgement is an appropriate remedy.[317]

2-11:3.5 Actual Damages

An entity may hold the defendant liable for any loss it suffers as a result of mismanagement.[318]

2-11:3.6 Removal of Defendant from Office

The shareholders of a corporation may call a special vote to remove a director from office.[319]

A partner may be expelled by other partners or by judicial decree.[320]

A member of an LLC may not be expelled[321] unless the company agreement modifies the statutory rule.[322]

A manager of an LLC may be removed.[323]

2-11:3.7 Exemplary Damages

Exemplary damages are available if the defendant acts:

- Maliciously;

---

[314] *In re Structural Software, Inc.*, 67 Fed. Appx. 253 (5th Cir. 2003).
[315] *See Thomas, Tr. of Performance Products, Inc. v. Hughes*, SA-16-CV-00951-DAE, 2020 WL 773444, at *3 (W.D. Tex. Feb. 18, 2020).
[316] *Saden v. Smith*, 415 S.W.3d 450, 469 (Tex. App.—Houston [1st Dist.] 2013, pet. denied); *Burrow v. Arce*, 997 S.W.2d 229, 237 (Tex. 1999).
[317] *ERI Consulting Eng'rs, Inc. v. Swinnea*, 318 S.W.3d 867, 873 (Tex. 2010).
[318] *Meyers v. Moody*, 693 F.2d 1196, 1215 (5th Cir.1982) (applying Texas law).
[319] Tex. Bus. Orgs. Code Ann. § 21.409(a).
[320] Tex. Bus. Orgs. Code Ann. § 152.501.
[321] Tex. Bus. Orgs. Code Ann. § 101.107.
[322] *See* Tex. Bus. Orgs. Code Ann. § 101.054.
[323] Tex. Bus. Orgs. Code Ann. § 101.304.

- Fraudulently; or
- With gross negligence.[324]

Willful usurpations suffice.[325]

Exemplary damages may be predicated upon an equitable remedy alone.[326]

2-11:4 Defenses

2-11:4.1 Statute of Limitations

The four-year limitations period applies to a breach of fiduciary duty claim.[327]

The period accrues when the disinterested and independent agents of the entity have actual or constructive notice of the defendant's usurpation.[328]

A majority of the disinterested and independent agents must have actual or constructive notice of the defendant's usurpation.[329]

The discovery rule applies to usurpations sounding in tort.[330]

2-11:4.2 Financial Incapability

A plaintiff's financial inability to pursue the business opportunity is a defense to a usurpation claim.[331]

This is an affirmative defense.[332]

Courts are hesitant to apply this defense.

Courts strictly limit the application of this defense because it is often the defendant who is to secure financial backing for the plaintiff.[333]

2-11:4.3 Abandonment of Business Opportunity

A plaintiff's abandonment of the business opportunity is a defense to a usurpation claim.[334]

---

[324] Tex. Civ. Prac. & Rem. Code Ann. § 41.003(a).
[325] *International Bankers Life Ins. Co. v. Holloway*, 368 S.W.2d 567, 583–84 (Tex. 1963).
[326] *International Bankers Life Ins. Co. v. Holloway*, 368 S.W.2d 567, 583 (Tex. 1963).
[327] Tex. Civ. Prac. & Rem. Code Ann. § 16.004(a)(5); *Rowe v. Rowe*, 887 S.W.2d 191, 201 (Tex. App.—Fort Worth 1994, writ denied).
[328] *International Bankers Life Ins. Co. v. Holloway*, 368 S.W.2d 567, 580 (Tex. 1963).
[329] *Allen v. Wilkerson*, 396 S.W.2d 493, 500 (Tex. Civ. App.—Austin 1965, writ ref'd n.r.e.).
[330] *F.D.I.C. v. Howse*, 736 F. Supp. 1437, 1441 (S.D. Tex. 1990).
[331] *BCOWW Holdings, LLC v. Collins*, SA-17-CA-00379-FB, 2017 WL 3868184, at *18 (W.D. Tex. Sept. 5, 2017).
[332] *See Canion v. Tex. Cycle Supply, Inc.*, 537 S.W.2d 510, 513 (Tex. Civ. App.—Austin 1976, writ ref'd n.r.e.) ("The burden of pleading and proving the corporate inability should be placed upon the officer or director.").
[333] *Huffington v. Upchurch*, 532 S.W.2d 576, 579 (Tex. 1976).
[334] *Landon v. S & H Mktg. Grp., Inc.*, 82 S.W.3d 666, 681 (Tex. App.—Eastland 2002, no pet.).

BUSINESS MANAGEMENT LITIGATION

This is an affirmative defense.[335]

A valid corporate/LLC relinquishment requires:

- Approval by a disinterested group of directors after full disclosure;
- Approval by the shareholders after full disclosure; or
- Proof of fairness.[336]

2-11:4.4 Ratification

Ratification might be a defense to a usurpation claim.[337]

A valid corporate/LLC ratification requires:

- Approval by a disinterested group of directors after full disclosure;
- Approval by the shareholders after full disclosure; or
- Proof of fairness.[338]

2-12 Suit to Compel Inspection

2-12:1 Overview

Suits to compel inspection are the means shareholders, partners, or members have to obtain information from their entity. There have not been many cases on the topic because, in most cases, the entity is required by law to make all information available and does not refuse an initial request.

2-12:1.1 Related Causes of Action

Officer and Director Liability, Class Action Suits, Derivative Shareholder Suits, Dissolution of Partnership, Breach of Fiduciary Duty

2-12:2 Elements

2-12:2.1 Corporation

(1) A shareholder

- Must be a shareholder:
    - For at least six months prior to demand;
    - Of at least 5% of the total outstanding shares; or

---

[335] *See Canion v. Tex. Cycle Supply, Inc.*, 537 S.W.2d 510, 513 (Tex. Civ. App.—Austin 1976, writ ref'd n.r.e.) ("The burden of pleading and proving the corporate inability should be placed upon the officer or director").

[336] Tex. Bus. Orgs. Code Ann. §§ 21.418, 101.255.

[337] *Lifshutz v. Lifshutz*, 199 S.W.3d 9, 21–22 (Tex. App.—San Antonio 2006, pet. denied).

[338] Tex. Bus. Orgs. Code Ann. § 21.418.

- Who obtains court permission.[339]
- A shareholder includes the holder of a beneficial interest in a trust who meets one of the requirements.[340]

(2) Makes a written demand on the corporation
- The demand must be written.[341]
- The demand must specify a reasonable time to inspect the records.[342]

(2)(a) For covered records
- Covered records include:
  - Books and records of accounts;
  - Minutes of the proceedings of the owners or members or governing authority of the filing entity and committees of the owners or members or governing authority of the filing entity;
  - A current record of the name and mailing address of each owner or member of the filing entity; and
  - Other books and records as required by the title of the Business Organizations Code governing the entity.[343]
  - In addition to the books and records required to be kept as listed above, a corporation shall keep at its registered office, principal place of business, or at the office of its transfer agent or registrar, a record of:
    - The original issuance of shares issued by the corporation;
    - Each transfer of those shares that have been presented to the corporation for registration of transfer;
    - The names and addresses of all past shareholders of the corporation; and
    - The number and class or series of shares issued by the corporation held by each current and past shareholder.[344]
- A shareholder, or the shareholder's agent, accountant, or attorney, is entitled to:
  - Examine the records; or
  - Copy the records.[345]

(2)(b) For a proper purpose

---

[339] Tex. Bus. Orgs. Code Ann. § 21.218(b)–(c).
[340] Tex. Bus. Orgs. Code Ann. § 21.218(a).
[341] Tex. Bus. Orgs. Code Ann. § 21.218(b). The Business Organizations Code defines "written." Tex. Bus. Orgs. Code Ann. § 1.002(89).
[342] Tex. Bus. Orgs. Code Ann. § 21.218(b).
[343] Tex. Bus. Orgs. Code Ann. § 3.151(a).
[344] Tex. Bus. Orgs. Code Ann. § 21.173.
[345] Tex. Bus. Orgs. Code Ann. § 21.218(b).

- A proper purpose is one that is:
  - Directed toward obtaining information bearing upon the protection of the shareholder's interest and that of other shareholders in the corporation.[346]
- An improper purpose includes one that is:
  - Designed to obtain a competitive advantage over the company; or
  - Intended to harass.[347]
- Whether the shareholder's purpose is a "proper purpose" is a jury question.[348]

(3) Which the corporation refuses

- The corporation must first refuse the demand.[349]

2-12:2.2 Limited Liability Company

(1) A member

- Requesting party must be:
  - A member; or
  - An assignee of a member.[350]

(2) Makes a written request

- The request must be written.[351]
- The request must specify a reasonable time to inspect the records.[352]

(2) (a) For covered records

- Covered records include:
  - Books and records of accounts;
  - Minutes of the proceedings of the owners or members or governing authority of the filing entity and committees of the owners or members or governing authority of the filing entity;
  - A current record of the name and mailing address of each owner or member of the filing entity; and

---

[346] What is a proper purpose?, 20 Texas Practice Series, Business Organizations § 33:8 (3d ed.) (citing William T. Blackburn, Comment, *Shareholder Inspection Rights*, 12 Sw. L.J. 61, 74–76 (1958)).
[347] *See Uvalde Rock Asphalt Co. v. Loughridge*, 425 S.W.2d 818, 819 (Tex. 1968).
[348] *Uvalde Rock Asphalt Co. v. Loughridge*, 425 S.W.2d 818, 820 (Tex. 1968).
[349] *See Chavco Inv. Co., Inc. v. Pybus*, 613 S.W.2d 806, 809 (Tex. Civ. App.—Houston [14th Dist.] 1981, writ ref'd n.r.e.) (requiring a corporation to first refuse a shareholder's demand).
[350] Tex. Bus. Orgs. Code Ann. § 101.502(a).
[351] Tex. Bus. Orgs. Code Ann. § 101.502(a). The Business Organizations Code defines "written." Tex. Bus. Orgs. Code Ann. § 1.002(89).
[352] Tex. Bus. Orgs. Code Ann. § 101.502(a).

- Other books and records as required by the title of the Business Organizations Code governing the entity.[353]
- An LLC shall keep at its principal office, or make available to a person at its principal office not later than the fifth day after the date the person submits a written request to examine the books and records of the company the following additional records:
- A current list that states:
  - The percentage or other interest in the limited liability company owned by each member; and
  - If one or more classes or groups of membership interests are established in or under the certificate of formation or company agreement, the names of the members of each specified class or group;
- A copy of the company's federal, state, and local tax information or income tax returns for each of the six preceding tax years;
- A copy of the company's certificate of formation, including any amendments to or restatements of the certificate of formation;
- If the company agreement is in writing, a copy of the company agreement, including any amendments to or restatements of the company agreement;
- An executed copy of any powers of attorney;
- A copy of any document that establishes a class or group of members of the company as provided by the company agreement; and, unless stated in a written company agreement, a written statement of:
  - The amount of a cash contribution and a description and statement of the agreed value of any other contribution made or agreed to be made by each member;
  - The dates any additional contributions are to be made by a member;
  - Any event the occurrence of which requires a member to make additional contributions;
  - Any event the occurrence of which requires the winding up of the company; and
  - The date each member became a member of the company.[354]
- Additionally, on written request and proper purpose a member, assignee of a member, or a member or assignee representative may examine and copy other information regarding the business, affairs, and financial condition of the company that is reasonable for the person to examine and copy.[355]

---

[353] Tex. Bus. Orgs. Code Ann. § 3.151(a).
[354] Tex. Bus. Orgs. Code Ann. § 101.501(a).
[355] Tex. Bus. Orgs. Code Ann. § 101.502(a)(2).

(2) (b) Stating a proper purpose

- A proper purpose is one that is:
  - Directed toward obtaining information bearing upon the protection of the member's interest and that of other members in the LLC.[356]
- An improper purpose includes a purpose that is:
  - Designed to obtain a competitive advantage over the company; or
  - Intended to harass.[357]
- Whether the member's purpose is a "proper purpose" is a jury question.[358]

(3) Which is refused by the company

- The company must first refuse the demand.[359]

2-12:2.3 General Partnership

(1) Denial of access

- A partnership shall provide a partner access to its books and records.[360]

(2) To partnership books and records

- A partnership shall provide a partner access to its books and records.[361]
  - A current partner is entitled to the books and records for all periods.[362]
  - A former partner is entitled to the books and records pertaining to when the former partner was a partner.[363]
  - A former partner must have a proper purpose for the books and records from any other time period.[364]
- A partnership may limit, but not unreasonably restrict, a partner's access to books and records.[365]

OR

(1) A partner

- Requesting party must be:
  - A partner;

---

[356] What is a proper purpose?, 20 Texas Practice Series, Business Organizations § 33:8 (3d ed.) (citing William T. Blackburn, Comment, Shareholder Inspection Rights, 12 Sw. L.J. 61, 74–76 (1958)).
[357] *See Uvalde Rock Asphalt Co. v. Loughridge*, 425 S.W.2d 818, 819 (Tex. 1968).
[358] *Uvalde Rock Asphalt Co. v. Loughridge*, 425 S.W.2d 818, 820 (Tex. 1968).
[359] *See Chavco Inv. Co., Inc. v. Pybus*, 613 S.W.2d 806, 809 (Tex. Civ. App.—Houston [14th Dist.] 1981, writ ref'd n.r.e.) (requiring a corporation first refuse a shareholder's demand).
[360] Tex. Bus. Orgs. Code Ann. § 152.212(c).
[361] Tex. Bus. Orgs. Code Ann. § 152.212(c).
[362] *See* Tex. Bus. Orgs. Code Ann. § 152.212(c).
[363] Tex. Bus. Orgs. Code Ann. § 152.212(d).
[364] Tex. Bus. Orgs. Code Ann. § 152.212(d).
[365] Tex. Bus. Orgs. Code Ann. § 152.002(b)(1).

- A representative of a deceased partner;
- A representative of a legally disabled partner; or
- An assignee.[366]

(2) Makes a request
- The request must be just and reasonable.[367]
- The request does not need to be written.[368]

(2)(a) For complete and accurate information concerning the partnership
- The request may be for "complete and accurate information concerning the partnership."[369]
- The information requested must be just and reasonable.[370]

(3) Which the partnership refuses
- The company must first refuse the demand.[371]

2-12:2.4 Limited Partnership

(1) A partner
- Requesting party must be:
  - A partner; or
  - An assignee of a partner.[372]

(2) Makes a written request
- The request must be written.[373]
- The request must specify a reasonable time to inspect the records.[374]

(2)(a) For covered records
- Covered records includes:
  - A current list that states:
    - The name and mailing address of each partner, separately identifying in alphabetical order the general partners and the limited partners;

---

[366] Tex. Bus. Orgs. Code Ann. § 152.213(a)–(b).
[367] Tex. Bus. Orgs. Code Ann. § 152.213(a).
[368] See Tex. Bus. Orgs. Code Ann. § 152.213(a).
[369] Tex. Bus. Orgs. Code Ann. § 152.213(a).
[370] Tex. Bus. Orgs. Code Ann. § 152.213(a).
[371] See Chavco Inv. Co., Inc. v. Pybus, 613 S.W.2d 806, 809 (Tex. Civ. App.—Houston [14th Dist.] 1981, writ ref'd n.r.e.) (requiring a corporation first refuse a shareholder's demand).
[372] Tex. Bus. Orgs. Code Ann. § 153.552(a).
[373] Tex. Bus. Orgs. Code Ann. § 153.552(a). The Business Organizations Code defines "written." Tex. Bus. Orgs. Code Ann. § 1.002(89).
[374] Tex. Bus. Orgs. Code Ann. § 153.552(b).

- The last known street address of the business or residence of each general partner;
- The percentage or other interest in the partnership owned by each partner; and
- If one or more classes or groups are established under the partnership agreement, the names of the partners who are members of each specified class or group;
- A copy of:
  - The limited partnership's federal, state, and local information or income tax returns for each of the partnership's six most recent tax years;
  - The partnership agreement and certificate of formation; and
  - All amendments or restatements;
- Copies of any document that creates, in the manner provided by the partnership agreement, classes or groups of partners;
- An executed copy of any powers of attorney under which the partnership agreement, certificate of formation, and all amendments or restatements to the agreement and certificate have been executed;
- Unless contained in the written partnership agreement, a written statement of:
  - the amount of the cash contribution and a description and statement of the agreed value of any other contribution made by each partner;
  - The amount of the cash contribution and a description and statement of the agreed value of any other contribution that the partner has agreed to make in the future as an additional contribution;
  - The events requiring additional contributions to be made or the date on which additional contributions are to be made;
  - The events requiring the winding up of the limited partnership; and
  - The date on which each partner in the limited partnership became a partner; and
- Books and records of the accounts of the limited partnership.[375]
- Additionally, on written request and proper purpose, a partner or an assignee of a partnership interest may examine and copy other information regarding the business, affairs, and financial condition of the limited partnership as is just and reasonable for the person to examine and copy.[376]

(2) (b) Stating a proper purpose

- A proper purpose is one that is:

---

[375] Tex. Bus. Orgs. Code Ann. § 153.551(a).
[376] Tex. Bus. Orgs. Code Ann. § 153.552(a).

- Directed toward obtaining information bearing upon the protection of the partner's interest and that of other partners in the partnership.[377]
- An improper purpose includes a purpose that is:
  - Designed to obtain a competitive advantage over the company; or
  - Intended to harass.[378]
- Whether the partner's purpose is a "proper purpose" is a jury question.[379]

(3) Which the partner/partnership refuses.
- The company must first refuse the demand.[380]

2-12:2.5 Public Offices Who May Compel Inspection

- The Secretary of State—The Secretary of State may compel inspection of a filing entity's records through interrogatories.[381]
- The Attorney General—The Attorney General may compel inspection of records.[382]
- The Texas Securities Commissioner—The Texas Securities Commissioner may compel inspection of records.[383]
- The Texas Comptroller of Public Accounts—The Texas Comptroller of Public Accounts may compel inspection of records.[384]
- The Texas Banking Commissioner—The Texas Banking Commissioner may compel inspection of records.[385]
- The Texas Department of Insurance—The Texas Department of Insurance may compel inspection of records.[386]

2-12:3 Damages and Remedies

2-12:3.1 Mandamus

Mandamus is an appropriate remedy to enforce an inspection right.[387]

---

[377] What is a proper purpose?, 20 Texas Practice Series, Business Organizations § 33:8 (3d ed.) (citing William T. Blackburn, Comment, Shareholder Inspection Rights, 12 Sw. L.J. 61, 74–76 (1958)).

[378] See Uvalde Rock Asphalt Co. v. Loughridge, 425 S.W.2d 818, 819 (Tex. 1968).

[379] Uvalde Rock Asphalt Co. v. Loughridge, 425 S.W.2d 818, 820 (Tex. 1968).

[380] See Chavco Inv. Co., Inc. v. Pybus, 613 S.W.2d 806, 809 (Tex. Civ. App.—Houston [14th Dist.] 1981, writ ref'd n.r.e.) (requiring a corporation first refuse a shareholder's demand).

[381] Tex. Bus. Orgs. Code Ann. § 12.002.

[382] Tex. Bus. Orgs. Code Ann. § 12.151.

[383] Tex. Rev. Civ. Stat. Ann. art. 581–28.

[384] Tex. Tax Code Ann. § 171.205.

[385] Tex. Fin. Code Ann. §§ 31.105, 107–08.

[386] Tex. Ins. Code Ann. §§ 36.152, 38.001.

[387] Uvalde Rock Asphalt Co. v. Loughridge, 425 S.W.2d 818, 819 (Tex. 1968); Shioleno v. Sandpiper Condos. Council of Owners, Inc. 13-07-00312-CV, 2008 WL 2764530, at *3 (Tex. App.—

BUSINESS MANAGEMENT LITIGATION

A shareholder, or the shareholder's agent, accountant or attorney, is entitled to:

- Examine the records; or
- Copy the records.[388]

2-12:3.2 Costs

A shareholder of a corporation is entitled to:

- Reasonable attorney's fees;
- Court costs; and
- Reasonable expenses.[389]

2-12:3.3 Actual Damages

Actual damages are available.[390]

2-12:4 Defenses—Corporations

2-12:4.1 Improper Purpose[391]

It is a defense to a suit to compel inspection if the shareholder:

(1) Has, within the two years preceding the date the action is brought, sold or offered for sale a list of shareholders or of holders of voting trust certificates for shares of the corporation or any other corporation;

(2) Has aided or abetted a person in procuring a list of shareholders or of holders of voting trust certificates for the purpose described by Subdivision (1);

(3) Has improperly used information obtained through a prior examination of the books and account records, minutes, or share transfer records of the corporation or any other corporation; or

(4) Was not acting in good faith or for a proper purpose in making the request for examination.[392]

- A proper purpose is one that is:

Corpus Christi July 17, 2008, no pet.); *Burton v. Cravey*, 759 S.W.2d 160, 161 (Tex. App.—Houston [1st Dist.] 1988, no writ), *disapproved of on other grounds by Huie v. DeShazo*, 922 S.W.2d 920 (Tex. 1996).

[388] Tex. Bus. Orgs. Code Ann. § 21.218(b).

[389] Tex. Bus. Orgs. Code Ann. § 21.222(a).

[390] *See* Tex. Bus. Orgs. Code Ann. § 21.222(a) (preserving any other damages or remedies available); Tex. Bus. Orgs. Code Ann. § 21.220 (expressly holding corporate agents liable to a shareholder who suffers damages because of the failure for the damage caused by the failure to prepare a shareholding voting list).

[391] An improper purpose is not always a defense. An improper purpose is a defense when the shareholder: (1) has been a shareholder for at least six months at the time of demand; or (2) owns at least 5% of the total outstanding shares. Who has the burden of proving a proper purpose?, 20 Texas Practice Series, Business Organizations § 33:7 (3d ed.).

[392] Tex. Bus. Orgs. Code Ann. § 21.222(b).

- Directed toward obtaining information bearing upon the protection of the shareholder's interest and that of other shareholders in the corporation.[393]
- An improper purpose includes one that is:
  - Designed to obtain a competitive advantage over the company.
  - Intended to harass.[394]
- Whether the shareholder acts with a "proper purpose" is a jury question.[395]
- A company must specifically plead facts which tend to establish the shareholder's improper purpose.[396]

2-13 Suit to Pierce the Corporate Veil

2-13:1 Overview

A suit to pierce the corporate veil is a remedial device available to a plaintiff that has sued a corporation or a limited liability company. When such a plaintiff successfully pierces the veil of a liability-protected entity, he may execute on the assets of the entity's owners. The controversial Supreme Court opinion in *Castleberry v. Branscum* made it easier for a plaintiff to pierce the veil of a liability-protected entity. This decision prompted a legislative reaction to restrict its reach, resulting in present-day Texas Business Organization Code Section 21.223. However, Section 21.223 has not entirely curtailed *Castleberry*.

2-13:1.1 Related Causes of Action

Uniform Fraudulent Transfer Act (UFTA), Officer and Director Liability, Derivative Shareholder Suits, Breach of Partnership Duty, Agency Actions

MUST READ CASES & STATUTES

Texas Business Organizations Code Annotated Section 21.223-21.225

Texas Business Organizations Code Annotated Section 101.002(a)

Castleberry v. Branscum, 721 S.W.2d 270 (Tex. 1986)

SSP Partners v. Gladstrong Inves. (USA) Corp., 275 S.W.3d 444 (Tex. 2008)

---

[393] What is a proper purpose?, 20 Texas Practice Series, Business Organizations § 33:8 (3d ed.) (citing William T. Blackburn, Comment, Shareholder Inspection Rights, 12 Sw. L.J. 61, 74–76 (1958)).
[394] *See Uvalde Rock Asphalt Co. v. Loughridge*, 425 S.W.2d 818, 819 (Tex. 1968).
[395] *Uvalde Rock Asphalt Co. v. Loughridge*, 425 S.W.2d 818, 820 (Tex. 1968).
[396] *Chavco Inv. Co., Inc. v. Pybus*, 613 S.W.2d 806, 809–10 (Tex. Civ. App.—Houston [14th Dist.] 1981, writ ref'd n.r.e.) (requiring a corporation first refuse a shareholder's demand).

BUSINESS MANAGEMENT LITIGATION

2-13:2 Elements

2-13:2.1 Contractual Obligations

(1) A recognized circumstance of injustice, including: (a) when the corporate fiction is used as a means of perpetrating actual fraud; (b) where the corporation is organized and operated as an alter ego; (c) where the corporate fiction is resorted to as a means of evading an existing legal obligation; (d) where the corporate fiction is employed to achieve or perpetrate monopoly; e) where the corporate fiction is used to circumvent a statute; (f) where the corporate fiction is relied upon as a protection of crime or to justify wrong; or (g) inadequate capitalization.[397]

- A "contractual obligation" includes purely contractual obligations as well as those obligations arising out of or related to a contract.[398]
- Recognized circumstances of injustice include:
  - When the corporate fiction is used as a means of perpetrating actual fraud.[399]
    - "Actual fraud" means "dishonesty of purpose or intent to deceive."[400]
  - Where the corporation is organized and operated as an alter ego.[401]
  - Where the corporate fiction is resorted to as a means of evading an existing legal obligation.[402]
  - Where the corporate fiction is employed to achieve or perpetrate monopoly.[403]
  - Where the corporate fiction is used to circumvent a statute.[404]
  - Where the corporate fiction is relied upon as a protection of crime or to justify wrong.[405]
  - Inadequate capitalization.[406]
- Failure to follow corporate formalities cannot be used as evidence in support of a veil piercing theory.[407]

---

[397] Tex. Bus. Orgs. Code Ann. § 21.223(a)(2); *Castleberry v. Branscum*, 721 S.W.2d 270, 272 (Tex. 1986).
[398] Tex. Bus. Orgs. Code Ann. § 21.223(a)(2).
[399] Tex. Bus. Orgs. Code Ann. § 21.223(a)(2); *Castleberry v. Branscum*, 721 S.W.2d 270, 272 (Tex. 1986).
[400] *Castleberry v. Branscum*, 721 S.W.2d 270, 273 (Tex. 1986); *Latham v. Burgher*, 320 S.W.3d 602, 607 (Tex. App.—Dallas 2010, no pet.).
[401] *Castleberry v. Branscum*, 721 S.W.2d 270, 272 (Tex. 1986).
[402] *Castleberry v. Branscum*, 721 S.W.2d 270, 272 (Tex. 1986).
[403] *Castleberry v. Branscum*, 721 S.W.2d 270, 272 (Tex. 1986).
[404] *Castleberry v. Branscum*, 721 S.W.2d 270, 272 (Tex. 1986).
[405] *Castleberry v. Branscum*, 721 S.W.2d 270, 272 (Tex. 1986).
[406] *Castleberry v. Branscum*, 721 S.W.2d 270, 272 (Tex. 1986).
[407] Tex. Bus. Orgs. Code Ann. § 21.223(a)(3).

(2) That the shareholder "caused the corporation to be used for the purpose of perpetrating and did perpetrate an actual fraud on the" contract creditor

- The shareholder "caused the corporation to be used for the purpose of perpetrating and did perpetrate an actual fraud on the" contract creditor.[408]

(3) The fraud was "primarily for the direct personal benefit of the" shareholder

- The fraud was "primarily for the direct personal benefit of the" shareholder.[409]

2-13:2.2 Tort Obligations

(1) A recognized circumstance of injustice, including:

(a) when the corporate fiction is used as a means of perpetrating fraud;

(b) where the corporation is organized and operated as an alter ego;

(c) where the corporate fiction is resorted to as a means of evading an existing legal obligation;

(d) where the corporate fiction is employed to achieve or perpetrate monopoly;

(e) where the corporate fiction is used to circumvent a statute;

(f) where the corporate fiction is relied upon as a protection of crime or to justify wrong; or

(g) inadequate capitalization.[410]

Recognized circumstances of injustice include:

- When the corporate fiction is used as a means of perpetrating fraud.[411]

  - "Actual fraud" means "dishonesty of purpose or intent to deceive."[412]

  - Constructive fraud, as defined in *Castleberry*, might be sufficient for a tort plaintiff to pierce the corporate veil.[413]

  - Constructive fraud is "the breach of some legal or equitable duty which, irrespective of moral guilt, the law declares fraudulent because of its tendency to deceive others, to violate confidence, or to injure public interests."[414]

- Where the corporation is organized and operated as an alter ego.[415]

---

[408] Tex. Bus. Orgs. Code Ann. § 21.223(b).
[409] Tex. Bus. Orgs. Code Ann. § 21.223(b).
[410] Tex. Bus. Orgs. Code Ann. § 21.223(a)(2); *Castleberry v. Branscum*, 721 S.W.2d 270, 272 (Tex. 1986).
[411] Tex. Bus. Orgs. Code Ann. § 21.223(a)(2); *Castleberry v. Branscum*, 721 S.W.2d 270, 272 (Tex. 1986).
[412] *Latham v. Burgher*, 320 S.W.3d 602, 607 (Tex. App.—Dallas 2010, no pet.).
[413] *Latham v. Burgher*, 320 S.W.3d 602, 607 (Tex. App.—Dallas 2010, no pet.).
[414] *Castleberry v. Branscum*, 721 S.W.2d 270, 273 (Tex. 1986).
[415] *Castleberry v. Branscum*, 721 S.W.2d 270, 272 (Tex. 1986).

BUSINESS MANAGEMENT LITIGATION

- Where the corporate fiction is resorted to as a means of evading an existing legal obligation.[416]
- Where the corporate fiction is employed to achieve or perpetrate monopoly.[417]
- Where the corporate fiction is used to circumvent a statute.[418]
- Where the corporate fiction is relied upon as a protection of crime or to justify wrong.[419]
- Inadequate capitalization.[420]

Failure to follow corporate formalities cannot be used as evidence in support of a veil piercing theory.[421]

2-13:2.3 Single Business Enterprise Theory

Texas does not recognize the single business enterprise theory.[422]

A single business enterprise occurs "whenever two corporations coordinate operations and combine resources in pursuit of the same business purpose."[423]

Two or more corporations may engage in such synchronous behavior that they would be jointly liable under a joint enterprise theory, rather than a veil piercing theory.[424]

2-13:2.4 Veil Piercing and Limited Liability Companies

The same principles which govern piercing the veil of a corporation apply when attempting to pierce the liability veil of a limited liability company.[425]

2-13:3 Damages and Remedies

2-13:3.1 Generally

The veil-piercing doctrine is itself a remedy. The damages and remedies available to a plaintiff will be determined by the underlying cause(s) of action.

---

[416] *Castleberry v. Branscum*, 721 S.W.2d 270, 272 (Tex. 1986).
[417] *Castleberry v. Branscum*, 721 S.W.2d 270, 272 (Tex. 1986).
[418] *Castleberry v. Branscum*, 721 S.W.2d 270, 272 (Tex. 1986).
[419] *Castleberry v. Branscum*, 721 S.W.2d 270, 272 (Tex. 1986).
[420] *Castleberry v. Branscum*, 721 S.W.2d 270, 272 (Tex. 1986).
[421] Tex. Bus. Orgs. Code Ann. § 21.223(a)(3).
[422] *SSP Partners v. Gladstrong Invs. (USA) Corp.*, 275 S.W.3d 444, 452 (Tex. 2008).
[423] *SSP Partners v. Gladstrong Invs. (USA) Corp.*, 275 S.W.3d 444, 452 (Tex. 2008).
[424] *SSP Partners v. Gladstrong Invs. (USA) Corp.*, 275 S.W.3d 444, 451 (Tex. 2008); *Texas Dep't of Transp. v. Able*, 35 S.W.3d 608, 613 (Tex. 2000) (describing the joint enterprise theory of liability).
[425] Tex. Bus. Orgs. Code Ann. § 101.002(a); *TecLogistics, Inc. v. Dresser-Rand Grp. Inc.*, 527 S.W.3d 589, 599–600 (Tex. App.—Houston [14th Dist.] 2017, no pet. h.) (citing Tex. Bus. Orgs. Code. Ann. § 101.002).

2-13:4 Defenses

2-13:4.1 Statute of Limitations

Ten year statute likely applies.[426]

Accrues when final judgment on the underlying cause of action is entered.[427]

2-13:5 Trial by Jury

2-13:5.1 The Jury's Role

Historically, determining whether to pierce the corporate veil was a question of law.[428]

The Supreme Court of Texas has since put the decision in the hands of jurors.[429]

2-14 Dissolution of Partnership—Judicial Expulsion of Partner

2-14:1 Overview

There are several methods a partnership may use to expel a partner. They are, in ascending order of difficulty and expense, expulsion according to the partnership agreement, statutory expulsion by a majority-in-interest of the partners, and judicial expulsion. Because judicial expulsion is far more difficult and expensive to accomplish, it is best used as a last resort.

2-14:1.1 Related Causes of Action

Breach of Formal Fiduciary Duty, Breach of Partnership Duty, Wrongful Withdrawal of Partner, Judicial Winding Up of Partnership, Usurpation of Business Opportunity

MUST READ STATUTE

Texas Business Organizations Code Annotated Section 152.502(b)(5)

2-14:2 Elements

(1) Application by the partnership or another partner

- The partnership or a partner must apply for judicial expulsion.[430]

(2) A judicial decree determining that the partner

- The requisite findings must be made in a judicial decree.[431]

---

[426] Tex. Civ. Prac. & Rem. Code Ann. § 34.001; *Matthews Constr. Co., Inc. v. Rosen*, 796 S.W.2d 692, 694 n. 3 (Tex. 1990); *In re Moore*, 379 B.R. 284, 298–99 (Bankr. N.D. Tex. 2007).
[427] *In re Moore*, 379 B.R. 284, 298–99 (Bankr. N.D. Tex. 2007).
[428] *Castleberry v. Branscum* and its aftermath, 20 Texas Practice Series, Business Organizations § 29:3 (3d ed.).
[429] *Castleberry v. Branscum*, 721 S.W.2d 270, 277 (Tex. 1986).
[430] Tex. Bus. Orgs. Code Ann. § 152.501(b)(5).
[431] Tex. Bus. Orgs. Code Ann. § 152.501(b)(5).

(2) (a) Engaged in wrongful conduct that adversely and materially affected the partnership business

- The partner must have engaged in wrongful conduct that adversely and materially affected the partnership business.[432]
- Such conduct might include:
  - Failing to pay rents to the partnership when the sole business of the partnership was to lease farmland.[433]
  - Misappropriating money from a company trust account.[434]

(2) (b) Willfully or persistently committed a material breach of: (i) The partnership agreement; or (ii) A duty owed to the partnership or the other partners under Sections 152.204-152.206

- The partner must have willfully or persistently committed a material breach of: (i) The partnership agreement; or (ii) A duty owed to the partnership or the other partners under Sections 152.204-152.206.[435]
- For conduct that constitutes a breach of a duty, *see* Chapter 2 Breach of Partnership Duty.

(2) (c) Engaged in conduct relating to the partnership business that made it not reasonably practicable to carry on the business in partnership with that partner

- The partner must have engaged in conduct relating to the partnership business that made it not reasonably practicable to carry on the business in partnership with that partner.[436]
- Such conduct might include:
  - Failing to pay rents to the partnership when the sole business of the partnership was to lease farmland.[437]
  - Partner's moral turpitude and criminal fraud, and failure to be honest in court as to the extent of his criminal wrongdoing.[438]
  - Misappropriating money from a company trust account.[439]

---

[432] Tex. Bus. Orgs. Code Ann. § 152.501(b)(5)(A).
[433] *Robertson v. Jacobs Cattle Co.*, 285 Neb. 859, 869, 830 N.W.2d 191, 201 (2013).
[434] *CCD, L.C. v. Millsap*, 2005 UT 42, ¶ 14, 116 P.3d 366, 370 (2005) (applying similar language in Utah's LLC expulsion statute).
[435] Tex. Bus. Orgs. Code Ann. § 152.501(b)(5)(B).
[436] Tex. Bus. Orgs. Code Ann. § 152.501(b)(5)(C).
[437] *Robertson v. Jacobs Cattle Co.*, 285 Neb. 859, 869, 830 N.W.2d 191, 201 (2013).
[438] *Brennen v. Lehn*, No. X10UWYCV044010222S, 2006 WL 2949111 at *13 (Conn. Super. Ct. Sept. 28, 2006).
[439] *CCD, L.C. v. Millsap*, 2005 UT 42, 116 P.3d 366, 370 (applying similar language in Utah's LLC expulsion statute).

2-14:3 Damages and Remedies

2-14:3.1 Expulsion of the Partner

The partner is expelled from the partnership.[440]

2-14:3.2 Wrongful Withdrawal Remedies

A partner's expulsion by judicial decree is a wrongful withdrawal.[441]

For a complete list of damages and remedies, *see* Chapter 2, Wrongful Withdrawal of Partner.

2-14:4 Defenses

2-14:4.1 Unclean Hands

Unclean hands might be an appropriate defense.[442]

2-14:5 Procedural Implications

2-14:5.1 Effective Date of Expulsion

The effective date of expulsion is the date of the judicial decree.[443]

2-15 Dissolution of Partnership—Judicial Winding Up of Partnership

2-15:1 Overview

Under the since-repealed Texas Uniform Partnership Act, one partner could compel the dissolution and termination of a partnership. Today, the Business Organizations Code employs a less permissive method, generally requiring a majority-in-interest vote to wind up and terminate a partnership. This less permissive method of voluntary winding up is supplemented by a partner's ability to bring an action for the judicial winding up of partnership.

---

[440] Tex. Bus. Orgs. Code Ann. § 152.501(b)(5).
[441] Tex. Bus. Orgs. Code Ann. § 152.503(b)(3).
[442] *Sister Initiative, LLC v. Broughton Maint. Ass'n, Inc.*, 02-19-00102-CV, 2020 WL 726785, at *29 (Tex. App.—Fort Worth Feb. 13, 2020, pet. filed).
[443] *Compare* Tex. Bus. Orgs. Code Ann. § 152.501(b)(5) ("An event of withdrawal of a partner occurs on the partner's expulsion by judicial decree."), *with* Utah Code Ann. § 48-2c-710(3) ("A member of a company may be expelled on application by the company or another member"). In Utah, courts have interpreted their statutory provision to mean the effective date withdrawal is the date of application, not the date of the judicial decree. *See Holladay v. Storey*, 2013 UT App 158, ¶ 12, 307 P.3d 584, 590–92 (2013).

2-15:1.1 Related Causes of Action

Judicial Expulsion of Partner, Breach of Fiduciary Duty, Breach of Partnership Duty, Usurpation of Business Opportunity, Breach of Contract, Wrongful Withdrawal, Shareholder Oppression

MUST READ CASE

Dunnagan v. Watson, 204 S.W.3d 30 (Tex. App.—Fort Worth 2006, pet. denied)

2-15:2 Elements

(1) Application by a partner

- A partner must submit an application.[444]

(2) A judicial determination

- The court must determine that the grounds for winding up exist.[445]

(2)(a) The economic purpose of the partnership is likely to be unreasonably frustrated

- One possible ground for winding up is:
  - The economic purpose of the partnership is likely to be unreasonably frustrated.[446]

(2)(b) Another partner has engaged in conduct relating to the partnership's business that makes it not reasonably practicable to carry on the business in partnership with that partner

- One possible ground for winding up is:
  - Another partner has engaged in conduct relating to the partnership's business that makes it not reasonably practicable to carry on the business in partnership with that partner.[447]
- The wrongdoing partner's actions need not rise to the level of a breach of fiduciary duty.[448]
- The following conduct is sufficient to support a finding that it is not reasonably practical to carry on partnership business:
  - When the purpose of a partnership was the operating of a horse racing track, a partner's:
    - Refusal to contribute additional capital to obtain a racing license;
    - Breaking through the ceiling of the partnership accountant's office to remove computer hardware;

---

[444] Tex. Bus. Orgs. Code Ann. § 11.314.
[445] Tex. Bus. Orgs. Code Ann. § 11.314.
[446] Tex. Bus. Orgs. Code Ann. § 11.314(1)(A).
[447] Tex. Bus. Orgs. Code Ann. § 11.314(1)(B).
[448] *Dunnagan v. Watson*, 204 S.W.3d 30, 40 (Tex. App.—Fort Worth 2006, pet. denied).

- Testimony that the wrongdoing partner said he could not work with the remaining partners anymore.[449]

(2)(c) It is not reasonably practicable to carry on the partnership's business in conformity with its governing documents

- It is not reasonably practicable to carry on the partnership's business in conformity with its governing documents.[450]

2-15:3 Damages and Remedies

2-15:3.1 Winding Up and Termination

The court may order the partnership to wind up and terminate.[451]

Winding up must be accomplished in a reasonably practical time.[452]

The assets of the partnership are to be applied toward the partnership's creditors' claims first.[453]

Whether a partner is entitled to a distribution or obligated to make a contribution depends on the final balance of that partner's capital account.[454]

To determine the balance of a partner's capital account:

- A partner's capital account is credited:
  - That partner's share of the profits;[455] and
  - That partner's contributions to the partnership;[456] and
- A partner's capital account is charged:
  - That partner's share of any losses;[457] and
  - That partner's distributions.[458]

Any distribution is to be paid in cash.[459]

2-15:3.2 Receivership

The court may appoint a receiver to rehabilitate[460] or liquidate[461] the partnership.

---

[449] *Dunnagan v. Watson*, 204 S.W.3d 30, 42–44 (Tex. App.—Fort Worth 2006, pet. denied) (decided using similar language in the Texas Revised Partnership Act).
[450] Tex. Bus. Orgs. Code Ann. § 11.314(2).
[451] Tex. Bus. Orgs. Code Ann. § 11.314.
[452] Tex. Bus. Orgs. Code Ann. § 152.703(a).
[453] Tex. Bus. Orgs. Code Ann. § 152.706(a).
[454] Tex. Bus. Orgs. Code Ann. § 152.707(d).
[455] Tex. Bus. Orgs. Code Ann. § 152.707(b).
[456] Tex. Bus. Orgs. Code Ann. § 151.001(1).
[457] Tex. Bus. Orgs. Code Ann. § 152.707(b).
[458] Tex. Bus. Orgs. Code Ann. § 151.001(1).
[459] Tex. Bus. Orgs. Code Ann. § 152.706(b).
[460] Tex. Bus. Orgs. Code Ann. § 11.404.
[461] Tex. Bus. Orgs. Code Ann. § 11.405.

2-15:3.3 Attorney's Fees

One could make the argument that attorney's fees are recoverable under:

- The partnership agreement;[462] or
- Chapter 38 of the Texas Civil Practice and Remedies Code.[463]

2-15:4 Defenses

2-15:4.1 Unclean Hands

Unclean hands is an appropriate defense[464]

However, the defense is likely not a practical one.[465]

2-15:4.2 Other Equitable Defenses

Judicial dissolution of a partnership is an equitable proceeding, subject to equitable defenses.[466]

2-15:5 Procedural Implications

2-15:5.1 Venue

Venue lies in the county in which the partnership had its registered office or principal place of business.[467]

2-15:5.2 Parties to be Named

The partnership itself does not need to be a party to the litigation if all beneficial owners of the partnership are joined in the suit.[468]

However, it would be a good idea to name the partnership as a party.[469]

---

[462] *See* Tex. Bus. Orgs. Code Ann. § 152.002(a)–(b).
[463] Tex. Civ. Prac. & Rem. Code Ann. § 38.001-006 (authorizing the recovery of attorney's fees under a written or oral contract).
[464] *Dunnagan v. Watson*, 204 S.W.3d 30, 41–42 (Tex. App.—Fort Worth 2006, pet. denied).
[465] *Dunnagan v. Watson*, 204 S.W.3d 30, 41–42 (Tex. App.—Fort Worth 2006, pet. denied).
[466] *See Collins v. Lewis*, 283 S.W.2d 258, 261 (Tex. Civ. App.—Galveston 1955, writ ref'd n.r.e.).
[467] Tex. Bus. Orgs. Code Ann. § 11.314.
[468] *Russell v. Campbell*, 725 S.W.2d 739, 743 (Tex. App.—Houston [14th Dist.] 1987, writ ref n.r.e.); *Matz v. Bennion*, 961 S.W.2d 445, 454 (Tex. App.—Houston [1st Dist.] 1997, pet. denied) (arriving at same answer with regard to pre-Business Organizations Code dissolution of a corporation).
[469] *See Dunnagan v. Watson*, 204 S.W.3d 30, 30 (Tex. App.—Fort Worth 2006, pet. denied) (partnership named as a party).

2-16 Dissolution of Partnership—Wrongful Withdrawal of Partner

2-16:1 Overview

A partner always has the power to withdraw from the partnership; however, he does not always have the right to do so. Upon withdrawal, the partner or the partnership may file suit to determine the extent of the partner's right to redemption or obligation for contribution. Although most of the rules discussed below are provided by statute, it is important to note that the partnership agreement will often have altered the statutory rules.

2-16:1.1 Related Causes of Action

Judicial Expulsion of Partner, Judicial Winding up of Partnership, Breach of Fiduciary Duty, Breach of Partnership Duty, Usurpation of Business Opportunity, Breach of Contract

MUST READ CASE

Bendalin v. Youngblood & Assocs., 381 S.W.3d 719 (Tex. App.—Texarkana 2012, pet. filed)

2-16:2 Elements

(1) An event of withdrawal

- The partner must withdraw from the partnership.[470]
- An event of withdrawal occurs on:
  - Receipt by the partnership of notice of the partner's express will to withdraw as a partner on:
    - The date on which the notice is received; or
    - A later date specified by the notice;
  - An event specified in the partnership agreement as causing the partner's withdrawal;
  - The partner's expulsion as provided by the partnership agreement;
  - The partner's expulsion by vote of a majority-in-interest of the other partners if:
    - It is unlawful to carry on the partnership business with that partner;
    - There has been a transfer of all or substantially all of that partner's partnership interest, other than:
      - A transfer for security purposes that has not been foreclosed; or

---

[470] Tex. Bus. Orgs. Code Ann. § 152.503(b).

- The substitution of a successor trustee or successor personal representative;
- Not later than the 90th day after the date on which the partnership notifies an entity partner, other than a nonfiling entity or foreign nonfiling entity partner, that it will be expelled because it has filed a certificate of termination or the equivalent, its existence has been involuntarily terminated or its charter has been revoked, or its right to conduct business has been terminated or suspended by the jurisdiction of its formation, if the certificate of termination or the equivalent is not revoked or its existence, charter or right to conduct business is not reinstated; or
- An event requiring a winding up has occurred with respect to a nonfiling entity or foreign nonfiling entity that is a partner;
• The partner's expulsion by judicial decree, on application by the partnership or another partner, if the judicial decree determines that the partner:
  - Engaged in wrongful conduct that adversely and materially affected the partnership business;
  - Wilfully or persistently committed a material breach of:
    - The partnership agreement; or
    - A duty owed to the partnership or the other partners under Sections 152.204-152.206; or
  - Engaged in conduct relating to the partnership business that made it not reasonably practicable to carry on the business in partnership with that partner;
• The partner's:
  - Becoming a debtor in bankruptcy;
  - Executing an assignment for the benefit of a creditor;
  - Seeking, consenting to, or acquiescing in the appointment of a trustee, receiver or liquidator of that partner or of all or substantially all of that partner's property; or
  - Failing, not later than the 90th day after the appointment, to have vacated or stayed the appointment of a trustee, receiver or liquidator of the partner or of all or substantially all of the partner's property obtained without the partner's consent or acquiescence, or not later than the 90th day after the date of expiration of a stay, failing to have the appointment vacated;
• If a partner is an individual:
  - The partner's death;
  - The appointment of a guardian or general conservator for the partner; or
  - A judicial determination that the partner has otherwise become incapable of performing the partner's duties under the partnership agreement;
• Termination of a partner's existence;

- If a partner has transferred all of the partner's partnership interest, redemption of the transferee's interest under Section 152.611; or

- An agreement to continue the partnership under Section 11.057(d) if the partnership has received a notice from the partner under Section 11.057(d) requesting that the partnership be wound up.[471]

(2) That is wrongful

- The withdrawal must be wrongful.[472]

(2)(a) Breaches an express provision of the partnership agreement

- A wrongful withdrawal includes one where the partner breaches an express provision of the partnership agreement.[473]

(2)(b) Prematurely withdraws

- A wrongful withdrawal includes when a partner prematurely withdraws from a partnership that (1) has a period of duration, (2) is for a particular undertaking, or (3) or is required under its partnership agreement to wind up the partnership on occurrence of a specified event by:

  - The partner withdraws by express will;

  - The partner withdraws by becoming a debtor in bankruptcy; or

  - In the case of a partner that is not an individual, a trust other than a business trust, or an estate, the partner is expelled or otherwise withdraws because the partner willfully dissolved or terminated.[474]

(2)(c) The partner is expelled by judicial decree

- A wrongful withdrawal includes one where the partner is expelled by judicial decree.[475]

- For more information on expulsion by judicial decree, see Chapter 2 Judicial Expulsion of Partner.

2-16:3 Damages and Remedies

2-16:3.1 Redemption/Contribution

A wrongfully withdrawn partner is entitled to the redemption of his partnership interest.[476]

The redemption price is:

- The "fair value" of the partnership interest at the time of the event of withdrawal;[477] or

---

[471] Tex. Bus. Orgs. Code Ann. § 152.501(b).
[472] Tex. Bus. Orgs. Code Ann. § 152.503(b).
[473] Tex. Bus. Orgs. Code Ann. § 152.503(b)(1).
[474] Tex. Bus. Orgs. Code Ann. § 152.503(b)(2).
[475] Tex. Bus. Orgs. Code Ann. § 152.503(b)(3).
[476] Tex. Bus. Orgs. Code Ann. § 152.601(a).
[477] Tex. Bus. Orgs. Code Ann. § 152.602(a).

- In the event of a partner who wrongfully withdraws before the expiration of the partnership's period of duration, the completion of a particular undertaking, or the occurrence of a specified event requiring a winding up of partnership business, is the lesser of:
  - The fair value of the withdrawn partner's interest on the date of withdrawal.[478]
  - The amount the withdrawn partner would have received if an event requiring winding up had occurred at the time of the withdrawal.[479]

In the event of a partner who wrongfully withdraws before the expiration of the partnership's period of duration, the completion of a particular undertaking, or the occurrence of a specified event requiring a winding up of partnership business, the partnership may:

- Defer payment of the redemption price.[480]
  - The deferred payment accrues interest.[481]
  - The wrongfully withdrawn partner may compel payment of the redemption price or adequate security for the redemption price.[482]
- The redemption price may be specified in the partnership agreement.[483]
- A partner may be required to contribute funds to the partnership.[484]

2-16:3.2 Damages

The remaining partners or partnership may recover damages caused by the withdrawal.[485]

The partnership agreement may specify an amount for a reasonable amount of liquidated damages.[486]

2-16:3.3 Attorney's Fees

A litigant may recover attorney's fees under:

- The partnership agreement;[487]
- Chapter 38 of the Texas Civil Practice and Remedies Code; and[488]
- Under the Business Organizations Code[489]

---

[478] Tex. Bus. Orgs. Code Ann. § 152.602(b)(1).
[479] Tex. Bus. Orgs. Code Ann. § 152.602(b)(2).
[480] Tex. Bus. Orgs. Code Ann. § 152.608(a).
[481] Tex. Bus. Orgs. Code Ann. § 152.608(b).
[482] Tex. Bus. Orgs. Code Ann. § 152.608(a), (c).
[483] *See* Tex. Bus. Orgs. Code Ann. § 152.002(a)–(b).
[484] Tex. Bus. Orgs. Code Ann. §§ 152.707-152.708.
[485] Tex. Bus. Orgs. Code Ann. § 152.503(c).
[486] *See* Tex. Bus. Orgs. Code Ann. § 152.002(a)–(b).
[487] *See* Tex. Bus. Orgs. Code Ann. § 152.002(a)–(b).
[488] Tex. Civ. Prac. & Rem. Code Ann. §§ 38.001–38.006 (authorizing the recovery of attorney's fees under a written or oral contract).
[489] Tex. Bus. Orgs. Code Ann. § 152.609(e).

2-16:3.4 Prior Partnership Liability

Withdrawal of a partner does not by itself discharge the partner's liability for an obligation of the partnership incurred before the date of withdrawal.[490]

The nature of the prior-existing liability determines if the plaintiffs may collect on this liability in the wrongful withdrawal suit.

2-16:3.5 Interest

Interest is payable on the redemption price.[491]

Interest accrues as of the date of withdrawal.[492]

2-16:3.6 Setoff

The partnership may set off against the redemption price payable to the withdrawn partner the damages for wrongful withdrawal and all other amounts owed by the withdrawn partner to the partnership, whether currently due, including interest.[493]

2-16:3.7 Additional Damages for Bad Faith Demand or Payment of Estimated Redemption

If the court finds that a party failed to tender payment or make an offer to pay or to comply with the requirements of Section 152.607(c) "Demand or Payment of Estimated Redemption" or otherwise acted arbitrarily, vexatiously or not in good faith, the court may assess damages against the party, including, if appropriate, in an amount the court finds equitable:

- A share of the profits of the continuing business;
- Reasonable attorney's fees; and
- Fees and expenses of appraisers or other experts for a party to the action.[494]

2-16:4 Defenses

2-16:4.1 Statute of Limitations

The action must be commenced not later than the first anniversary of the later of:

- The date of delivery of information required by Section 152.607(c); or
- The date written notice is given under Section 152.607(d).[495]

The limitations period is inherently flawed. There are two situations where the limitations period technically does not begin:

---

[490] Tex. Bus. Orgs. Code Ann. § 152.505(a).
[491] Tex. Bus. Orgs. Code Ann. § 152.602(c).
[492] Tex. Bus. Orgs. Code Ann. § 152.602(c).
[493] Tex. Bus. Orgs. Code Ann. § 152.604.
[494] Tex. Bus. Orgs. Code Ann. § 152.609(e).
[495] Tex. Bus. Orgs. Code Ann. § 152.609(b).

- Where a party entitled to request explanatory information in connection with a payment, offer or demand does not do so; and
- Where a withdrawn partner owes money to the partnership and makes a payment to the partnership claiming such payment is in full satisfaction of the partner's obligation.[496]

2-16:5 Procedural Implications

2-16:5.1 Who May Bring Suit

A withdrawn partner or the partnership may bring suit.[497]

2-16:5.2 What Issues May Be Litigated

The following issues may be litigated:
- The terms of the redemption of the withdrawn partner's interest;
- Any contribution obligation;
- Any setoff rights; and
- Any interest due.[498]

2-16:5.3 Effect of Partnership Agreement

The partnership agreement controls the relationship between the partnership and its partners.[499]

There are very few aspects of the statutorily-defined default relationship which cannot be altered by agreement.[500]

---

[496] Procedures for resolution of redemption of withdrawn partner's interest, 19 Texas Practice Series, Business Organizations § 10:16 (3d ed.).
[497] Tex. Bus. Orgs. Code Ann. § 152.610(a).
[498] Tex. Bus. Orgs. Code Ann. § 152.610(c).
[499] Tex. Bus. Orgs. Code Ann. § 152.002(a).
[500] Tex. Bus. Orgs. Code Ann. § 152.002(b).

CHAPTER 3

Contract and Commercial Litigation*

3-1 Breach of Contract

3-1:1 Introduction

Breach of contract is the failure by one party to a valid agreement (potentially written or oral) to fulfill the obligations of the agreement. The following sections set forth the requirements for and possible defenses against a cause of action to recover for breach of contract.

3-1:1.1 Related Causes of Action

Promissory Estoppel, Quantum Meruit, Breach of Covenant Not to Compete, Breach of Warranty, Fraud, Tortious Interference, Torts arising from contract, DTPA

MUST READ STATUTES AND AUTHORITY

Restatement (Second) of Contracts Section 1-385 (1981)

Texas Business and Commerce Code Chapter 2

3-1:2 Elements[1]

(1) The existence of a valid contract[2]

---

* The authors thank Miranda Chavez for her assistance in the updating of this chapter.
[1] *Williams v. First Tenn. Nat'l Corp.*, 97 S.W.3d 798, 802 (Tex. App.—Dallas 2003, no pet.) (listing these elements). For a discussion of the elements, *see* O'Connor, Michol, *Texas Causes of Action*, Chapter 5-B (2014). For charging the jury as to the cause of action, *see* Tex. P.J.C.—Business, Consumer, Insurance & Employment 101.2 (2012).
[2] *Lopez v. Bucholz*, No. 03-15-00034-CV, 2017 Tex. App. LEXIS 3071, at *17 (App.—Austin Apr. 7, 2017); *In re Staley*, 320 S.W.3d 490 (Tex. App.—Dallas 2010, no pet.); *Parker Drilling Co. v. Romfor Supply Co.*, 316 S.W.3d 68 (Tex. App.—Houston [14th Dist.] 2010), *review denied*, (Apr. 1, 2011); *Schriver v. Tex. Dept. of Transp.*, 293 S.W.3d 846 (Tex. App.—Fort Worth 2009, no pet.); *In re Green Tree Servicing LLC*, 275 S.W.3d 592 (Tex. App.—Texarkana 2008, no pet.); *City of The Colony v. N. Tex. Mun. Water Dist.*, 272 S.W.3d 699 (Tex. App.—Fort Worth 2008, no pet.); *Williams v. Unifund CCR Partners Assignee of Citibank*, 264 S.W.3d 231 (Tex. App.—Houston [1st Dist.] 2008, no pet.); *DeClaire v. G & B Mcintosh Family*

- A binding contract requires: (1) an offer; (2) an acceptance in strict compliance with the terms of the offer;[3] (3) a meeting of the minds; (4) each party's consent to the terms; (5) execution and delivery of the contract with the intent that it be mutual and binding;[4] and (6) consideration.[5]

(2) Plaintiff performed, tendered performance of, or was excused from performing

- Plaintiff must establish that it performed, tendered performance or was excused from performing its contractual obligation.[6]
- Where the plaintiff was prevented from satisfying its obligations under the contract by defendant or where the defendant repudiates the contract before the time for performance, the plaintiff need not establish performance or tender thereof.[7]

(3) Breach

- Plaintiff must establish that defendant breached the contract.[8]
- The damages the plaintiff sustains must be a result of that breach.[9]

Ltd. P'ship, 260 S.W.3d 34 (Tex. App.—Houston [1st Dist.] 2008, no pet.); *Winchek v. Am. Exp. Travel Related Servs. Co., Inc.*, 232 S.W.3d 197 (Tex. App.—Houston [1st Dist.] 2007, no pet.); *Vermont Info. Processing, Inc. v. Montana Beverage Corp.*, 227 S.W.3d 846 (Tex. App.—El Paso 2007, no pet.); *Texas Disposal Sys. Landfill, Inc. v. Waste Mgmt. Holdings, Inc.*, 219 S.W.3d 563 (Tex. App.—Austin 2007, no pet.).

[3] In a contract for the sale of goods, an expression of acceptance may still operate as an acceptance even though it adds additional or different terms unless acceptance is made expressly conditional on the assent to the additional or different terms. Tex. Bus. & Com. Code Ann. § 2.207.

[4] *In Re Capco Energy, Inc.*, 669 F.3d 274, 279–80 (5th Cir. 2012); *Lerma v. Border Demolition & Envtl., Inc.*, 459 S.W.3d 695, 703 (Tex. App.—El Paso 2015); *Expro Ams., LLC v. Sanguine Gas Expl., LLC*, 351 S.W.3d 915, 920 (Tex. App.—Houston [14th Dist] 2011, pet. denied) (citing *Parker Drilling Co. v. Romfor Supply Co.*, 316 S.W.3d 68, 72 (Tex. App.—Houston [14th Dist.] 2010, pet. denied).

[5] *Expro Ams., LLC v. Sanguine Gas Expl., LLC*, 351 S.W.3d 915, 920 (Tex. App. Houston [14th Dist.] 2011, pet. denied).

[6] *Mustang Amusements, Inc. v. Sinclair*, No. 10-07-00362-CV, 2009 Tex. App. LEXIS 8338, at *14 (App.—Waco Oct. 28, 2009).

[7] *Krayem v. USRP (PAC), L.P.*, 194 S.W.3d 91, 94 (Tex. App.—Dallas 2006, pet denied) (citing *17090 Parkway, Ltd. v. McDavid*, 80 S.W.3d 252, 256 (Tex. App.—Dallas 2002, pet. denied)).

[8] *Vega v. Compass Bank*, No. 04-13-00383-CV, 2014 Tex. App. LEXIS 2709, at *3–4 (App.—San Antonio Mar. 12, 2014).

[9] *AZZ Inc. v. Morgan*, 462 S.W.3d 284, 289 (Tex. App.—Fort Worth 2015, no pet.); *Vega v. Compass Bank*, No. 04-13-00383-CV, 2014 Tex. App. LEXIS 2709, at *3–4 (App.—San Antonio Mar. 12, 2014); *Southwell v. Univ. of the Incarnate Word*, 974 S.W.2d 351, 354–55 (Tex. App.—San Antonio 1998, pet. denied); *Mead v. Johnson Grp.*, 615 S.W.2d 685, 687 (Tex. 1981); *Allen v. Am. Gen. Fin. Inc.*, 251 S.W.3d 676, 685 (Tex. App.—San Antonio 2007, pet. granted).

3-1:3 Damages and Remedies

3-1:3.1 Actual Damages

In an action for breach of contract, the plaintiff can recover actual damages.[10]

3-1:3.1a Benefit-of-the-Bargain

"Benefit-of-the-bargain" damages serve to protect the promisee's "expectation interest," which is its interest in having the benefit of the bargain by being put in as good a position as he would have been had the contract or promise been fully performed.[11] Benefit-of-the-bargain damages are measured as the difference between the value as represented and the value received. When the harm caused by the breach of contract is difficult to estimate, the court may calculate damages based upon the market value or the price that would be offered by willing buyer to willing seller when neither is under compulsion to buy or sell.[12] For example, in a breach of contract for real estate, the measure of damages is the difference between the contract and the property's market value at the time of the breach.[13]

The UCC offers both buyers and seller various remedies for a breach of contract in the sale of goods. Upon breach of contract by the seller, the buyer may "cover" and have damages awarded as to the goods affected by the breach or recover damages for non-delivery, in addition to recovering the price that the buyer had already paid.[14] A buyer may also recover incidental or consequential damages.[15] When the buyer breaches the contract, the UCC permits the seller to elect to recover either "the difference between the market price at the time and place for tender and the unpaid contract price together with any incidental damages," less expenses saved in consequence of the buyer's breach;[16] or, if that is inadequate to put the seller in as good a position as performance would have done, the measure of the damages is the profit that the seller would have earned had the buyer fully performed the contract, plus any incidental damages with due allowance for costs reasonably incurred and due credit for payments or proceeds of resale.[17] *See* Chapter 11, Section 11-2 and Chapter 11, Section 11-5 for UCC buyer and seller remedies.[18]

---

[10] *Mead v. Johnson Grp.*, 615 S.W.2d 685, 687 (Tex. 1981); *Garden Ridge, L.P. v. Advance Int'l, Inc.*, 403 S.W.3d 432, 436–37 (Tex. App.—Houston [14th Dist.] 2013, pet. denied).

[11] *Transitional Entity LP v. Elder Care LP*, No. 05-14-01615-CV, 2016 Tex. App. LEXIS 5711, at *14 (App.—Dallas May 27, 2016); *8305 Broadway Inc. v. J&J Martindale Ventures, LLC*, No. 04-16-00447-CV, 2017 Tex. App. LEXIS 5926, at *6–7 (App.—San Antonio June 28, 2017).

[12] *Internacional Realty, Inc. v. 2005 RP W., Ltd.*, 449 S.W.3d 512, 542 (Tex. App.—Houston [1st Dist.] 2014, pet. denied).

[13] *Barry v. Jackson*, 309 S.W.3d 135, 140 (Tex. App.—Austin 2010, no pet.); *Elsas v. Yakkassippi, L.L.C.*, 746 Fed. Appx 344 (5th Cir. 2018).

[14] Tex. Bus. & Com. Code Ann. § 2.711(a).

[15] Tex. Bus. & Com. Code Ann. § 2.715.

[16] Tex. Bus. & Com. Code Ann. § 2.708(a).

[17] Tex. Bus. & Com. Code Ann. § 2.708(b).

[18] *Classic Superoof LLC v. Bean*, No. 05-12-00941-CV, 2014 Tex. App. LEXIS 11365, at *17–21 (App.—Dallas Oct. 14, 2014); *Qaddura v. Indo-European Foods, Inc.*, 141 S.W.3d 882, 888–89 (Tex. App.—Dallas 2004, pet. denied).

3-1:3.1b Out-of-Pocket Damages

In a breach of contract action, "out-of-pocket" damages protect a reliance interest by restoring the expenditures made in reliance on the contract to the non-breaching party.[19] "Out-of-pocket" damages are calculated based upon the difference between what the plaintiff paid in consideration and what he actually received.[20] Where liability is based on breach of contract, the non-breaching party can recover "out-of-pocket" damages as reimbursement for expenditures made to perform the contract, regardless of whether those expenditures were made before the contract was signed or during the course of performance.[21] *See* Chapter 11, Section 11-3.[22]

3-1:3.1c Restitution and Rescission Damages

Restitution is an appropriate measure of damages when one party to a contract advances the other party money and, upon repudiation of the contract, the latter has been unjustly enriched.[23] Principles of restitution normally require the party who has been unjustly enriched to refund that money.[24] Restitution damages are measured by the positive value to the defendant.[25] *See* Chapter 11, Sections 11-4 and 11-11:3.

3-1:3.2 Quantum Meruit

Quantum meruit is an equitable remedy that a plaintiff may recover when the plaintiff has partially performed but, due to defendant's breach, plaintiff is prevented from completing performance of the contract.[26] To recover under quantum meruit, a claimant must prove:

(1) valuable services or materials were rendered or furnished to the defendant;

(2) the defendant accepted, used, or enjoyed the services or materials; and

(3) the defendant had reasonable notice that the plaintiff expected to be paid for performing the services or furnishing the materials.[27]

---

[19] *Siam v. Mt. Vista Builders*, 544 S.W.3d 504, 516 (Tex. App.—El Paso 2018, no pet.); *see Wes-Tex Tank Rental, Inc. v. Pioneer Nat Res. USA, Inc.*, 327 S.W.3d 316, 320 n.4 (Tex. App.—Eastland 2010, no pet.).

[20] *Compaq Comput Corp. v. Lapray*, 135 S.W.3d 657, 679 (Tex. 2004).

[21] *Starkey v. Graves*, 448 S.W.3d 88, 109 n.28 (Tex. App.—Houston [14th Dist.] 2014, no pet.).

[22] *Mays v. Pierce*, 203 S.W.3d 564, 577 (Tex. App.—Houston [14th Dist.] 2006, pet. denied).

[23] *Mobil Oil Expl. & Producing Se. v. U.S.*, 530 U.S. 604, 624 (2000).

[24] *Mobil Oil Expl. & Producing Se. v. U.S.*, 530 U.S. 604, 624 (2000).

[25] *Miller v. Recovery Sys., Inc.*, No. 02-12-00468, 2013 WL 5303060, at *9 (Tex. App.—Fort Worth 2013, no pet.).

[26] *McFarland v. Sanders*, 932 S.W.2d 640, 645–46 (Tex. App.—Tyler 1996, no writ); *Lerma v. Border Demolition & Envtl., Inc.*, 459 S.W.3d 695, 507 (Tex. App.—El Paso 2015, pet. denied).

[27] *Hill v. Shamoun & Norman, LLP*, 544 S.W.3d 724, 732–33 (Tex. 2018); *Fulgham v. Fischer*, 349 S.W.3d 153, 159 (Tex. App.—Dallas 2011); *Vortt Expl. Co., Inc. v. Chevron U.S.A., Inc.*, 787 S.W.2d 942, 944 (Tex. 1990).

A party may recover quantum meruit, or the reasonable value of services rendered or material supplied, when there is no express contract covering the services or material furnished.[28] *See* Chapter 11, Section 11-11:4.

3-1:3.3 Unjust Enrichment

Unjust enrichment is an equitable remedy under an implied-contract theory providing that a party should make restitution if it would be unjust to retain received benefits.[29] Unjust enrichment requires that the beneficial services rendered were knowingly accepted with an expectation of payment.[30] When a valid contract already addresses the matter, recovery under the equitable theory of unjust enrichment would be inconsistent with the express agreement because the party seeking recovery has a legal remedy under the contract.[31] *See* Chapter 11, Section 11-11:2 and Chapter 3, Section 3-17.

3-1:3.4 Liquidated Damages

A contract may include a liquidated damages clause defining the damages calculation that, if found enforceable, provides the specific amount of damages that a claimant may recover in a breach of contract action. The court must make two indispensable findings to enforce contractual damages provisions: (1) "the harm caused by the breach is incapable or difficult of estimation," and (2) "the amount of liquidated damages called for is a reasonable forecast of just compensation"; these findings are made by the court from the perspective of the parties at the time of contracting.[32] The enforceability of a liquidated damages clause is ultimately a question of law for the court to decide.[33] Sometimes a provision not designed to be a penalty can nevertheless operate as one. Courts must now include a third step in the enforceability analysis, whether at the time of the breach an unbridgeable discrepancy exists between actual and liquidated damages.[34] "When the liquidated damages provisions operate with no rational relationship to actual damages, thus rendering the provision unreasonable in light of actual damages, they are unenforceable."[35] *See* Chapter 11, Section 11-5:5.

3-1:3.5 Nominal Damages

The plaintiff can recover at least nominal damages for a breach of contract regardless of whether the plaintiff proves actual damages.[36]

---

[28] *Truly v. Austin*, 744 S.W.2d 934, 937 (Tex. 1988).

[29] *Glass v. Gilbert*, No. 01-14-00643-CV, 2015 Tex. App. LEXIS 6494, at *10 (Tex. App.—Houston [1st Dist.] 2015, no pet. h.).

[30] *Christus Health v. Quality Infusion Care, Inc.*, 359 S.W.3d 719, 722–23 (Tex. App.—Houston [1st Dist.] 2011, no pet.).

[31] *Ledig v. Duke Energy Corp.*, 193 S.W.3d 167, 176 (Tex. App.—Houston [1st Dist.] 2006, no pet.); *Christus Health v. Quality Infusion Care, Inc.*, 359 S.W.3d 719, 723 (Tex. App.—Houston [1st Dist.] 2011, no pet.).

[32] *Phillips v. Phillips*, 820 S.W.2d 785, 788 (Tex. 1991).

[33] *FPL Energy, LLC v. TXU Portfolio Mgmt. Co.*, L.P., 426 S.W.3d 59, 69–70 (Tex. 2014).

[34] *Atrium Med. Ctr., LP v. Hous. Red C LLC*, 595 S.W.3d 188, 190 (Tex. 2020).

[35] *FPL Energy, LLC v. TXU Portfolio Mgmt. Co., L.P.*, 426 S.W.3d 59, 72 (Tex. 2014).

[36] *MBM Fin. Corp. v. Woodlands Operating Co.*, 292 S.W.3d 660, 664–65 (Tex. 2009).

3-1:3.6 Specific Performance

Specific performance is an equitable remedy in the form of injunctive relief that may be used as a substitute for monetary damages when such damages would not be adequate.[37] A plaintiff seeking specific performance to show: (1) that he was ready, willing, and able to perform at the relevant time; and (2) that he tendered that performance.[38] See Chapter 11, Section 11-5:8.

3-1:3.7 Rescission

Rescission is the common name for the composite remedy of rescission and restitution.[39] Rescission is not an independent cause of action but rather an equitable remedy available in a breach of contract action that requires each party to restore property received from the other, or mutual restitution to return the parties to their status quo.[40] See Chapter 11, Section 11-5:8 and Chapter 3, Section 3-2.

3-1:3.8 Reformation

The remedy of reformation is available to correct a contract if, owing to mutual mistake, the language used therein did not fully or accurately express the agreement and intention of the parties.[41] See Chapter 11, Section 11-5:8.

3-1:3.9 Declaratory Judgment

A declaratory judgment action provides a procedural device allowing judicial determination of the rights, status, and other legal relations of the parties involved in a breach of contract action without regard to whether or not relief is or could be prayed for by the parties.[42] The declaration, whether affirmative or negative in nature, has the force and effect of a final judgment or decree.[43] See Chapter 8, Section 13.

3-1:3.10 Interest

Prejudgment interest is compensation allowed by law for the lost use of the money due as damages during the time between the accrual of the claim and the judgment date.[44] In a contract claim, a money judgment that provides for interest or time price differential within its terms earns post-judgment interest at a rate equal to the lesser of the rate specified in the contract, which may be variable and 18% a year.[45] Prejudgment interest accrues at the same rate at the post-judgment interest rate and is computed as

---

[37] *Scott v. Sebree*, 986 S.W.2d 364, 368 (Tex. App.—Austin 1999, pet. denied); *Khan v. Chaudhry*, No. 09-14-00479-CV, 2016 Tex. App. LEXIS 3035, at *27–28 (App.—Beaumont Mar. 24, 2016).

[38] *DiGiuseppe v. Lawler*, 269 S.W.3d 588, 599 (Tex. 2008).

[39] *Cruz v. Andrews Restoration, Inc.*, 364 S.W.3d 817, 825 (Tex. 2012).

[40] *Morton v. Nguyen*, 412 S.W.3d 506, 510 (Tex. 2013).

[41] *Kansas v. Nebraska*, 135 S. Ct. 1042, 1071 (2015).

[42] Tex. Civ. Prac. & Rem. Code Ann. § 37.003.

[43] Tex. Civ. Prac. & Rem. Code Ann. § 37.003.

[44] *Ventling v. Johnson*, 466 S.W.3d 153 (Tex. 2015).

[45] Tex. Fin. Code Ann. § 304.002.

simple interest, while post-judgment interest is compounded annually.[46] Prejudgment interest accrues on the earlier date of the 180th day after the defendant receives written notice of a claim and the date that the suit is filed.[47] Post-judgment interest accrues on the date that judgment is rendered and ends on the date that judgment is satisfied except that, if a case is appealed and a motion for extension of time to file a brief is granted for a party who was a claimant at trial, interest does not accrue for the period of the extension.[48] *See* Chapter 11, Section 11-13:1.

3-1:3.11 Court Costs

Under the Texas Rules of Civil Procedure, costs of suit are made recoverable to the prevailing party without any stated requirement of pleading for costs.[49] "Costs" generally refers to the statutorily defined fees and charges required by law to be paid to the courts, such as filing and service fees.[50] *See* Chapter 11, Section 11-13:2.

3-1:3.12 Attorney's Fees

Attorney fees are not recoverable unless specifically authorized by contract or statute.[51] Therefore, a claimant must specifically plead and establish entitlement to attorney fees in order to support their recovery in a breach of contract action.[52] *See* Chapter 11, Section 11-13:3.

3-1:3.13 Lost Profits

Recovery of lost profits does not require the loss to be susceptible of exact calculation.[53] However, the amount of lost profits "must be shown by competent evidence with reasonable certainty."[54] Furthermore, lost profits must be based on objective facts, figures or data from which the lost profits amount may be ascertained.[55] *See* Chapter 11, Section 11-6.

---

[46] *Siam v. Mt. Vista Builders*, 544 S.W.3d 504, 512–13 (Tex. App.—El Paso 2018, no pet); *Landmark Org., L.P. v. Delphini Constr. Co.*, No. 13-04-371-CV, 2005 Tex. App. LEXIS 8414, at *15 (Tex. App.—Corpus Christi 2005, pet. denied).

[47] Tex. Fin. Code Ann. § 304.104.

[48] Tex. Fin. Code Ann. § 304.005.

[49] Tex. R. Civ. P. 131.

[50] *Hatfield v. Solomon*, 316 S.W.3d 50, 66 (Tex. App.—Houston [14th Dist.] 2010, no pet.).

[51] *Cytogenix, Inc. v. Waldroff*, 213 S.W.3d 479, 489 (Tex. App.—Houston [1st Dist.] 2006), pet denied).

[52] *Cadle Co. v. Int'l Bank of Commerce*, No. 04-06-00456-CV, 2007 Tex. App. LEXIS 1952, at *14 (App.—San Antonio Mar. 14, 2007).

[53] *Horizon Health Corp. v. Acadia Healthcare Co.*, 520 S.W.3d 848, 860 (Tex. 2017); *Saden v. Smith*, 415 S.W.3d 450, 466 (Tex. App.—Houston [1st Dist.] 2013, pet. denied).

[54] *Horizon Health Corp. v. Acadia Healthcare Co.*, 520 S.W.3d 848, 860 (Tex. 2017); *Saden v. Smith*, 415 S.W.3d 450, 466 (Tex. App.—Houston [1st Dist.] 2013, pet. denied).

[55] *Saden v. Smith*, 415 S.W.3d 450, 466 (Tex. App.—Houston [1st Dist.] 2013, pet. denied); *see Natural Gas Pipeline Co. v. Justiss*, 397 S.W.3d 150, 157 (Tex. 2012).

3-1:4 Defenses

3-1:4.1 Statute of Limitations

Four-year statute of limitations applies, and generally the cause of action accrues at the time of breach.[56,57] See Chapter 17, Sections 17-4 and 17-9.

3-1:4.2 Standing

Defendant can assert that the plaintiff lacks standing to sue, for example, by being an incidental (rather than intended) third-party beneficiary.[58]

3-1:4.3 Repudiation

3-1:4.3a Plaintiff-Repudiated Contract

Repudiation is effected by words or actions by a party to a contract that indicate it will not perform the contract.[59]

To effectively repudiate a contract by conduct, a party's conduct must show a "fixed intention to abandon, renounce, and refuse to perform the contract;" to repudiate a contract by statement, a party's language must be "sufficiently positive to be reasonably interpreted to mean that the party will not or cannot perform."[60]

3-1:4.4 Revocation

An offeror can revoke the offer before acceptance (including acceptance by partial performance) but this revocation must be communicated to the offeree.[61] This notice is not required where the offeror acts inconsistently with holding open the offer and the offeree has knowledge of the act[62] (such as selling the property that is the subject of the offer). Revocation sent by mail is effective only upon receipt by the offeree, not upon sending.[63]

3-1:4.5 Lack of Capacity

A person who lacks capacity at the time of contracting may elect, as a general rule, to void the contract; the contract is not automatically void but rather voidable at the election of the party lacking capacity at the time of formation. A person lacks capacity if he

---

[56] Tex. Civ. Prac. & Rem. Code Ann. § 16.051.
[57] *Via Net v. TIG Ins.*, 211 S.W.3d 310, 314 (Tex. 2006).
[58] *Stine v. Stewart*, 80 S.W.3d 586, 592 (Tex. 2002).
[59] *City of The Colony v. N. Tex. Mun. Water Dist.*, 272 S.W.3d 699, 738 (Tex. App.—Fort Worth 2008, pet. dism'd); *Tubb v. Aspect Int'l, Inc.*, No. 12-14-00323-CV, 2017 Tex. App. LEXIS 362, at *5–6 (App.—Tyler Jan. 18, 2017).
[60] *City of The Colony v. N. Tex. Mun. Water Dist.*, 272 S.W.3d 699, 738 (Tex. App.—Fort Worth 2008, pet. dism'd); *Tubb v. Aspect Int'l, Inc.*, No. 12-14-00323-CV, 2017 Tex. App. LEXIS 362, at *5–6 (App.—Tyler Jan. 18, 2017).
[61] *Sunshine v. Manos*, 496 S.W.2d 195, 198–199 (Tex. Civ. App.—Tyler 1973).
[62] *Antwine v. Reed*, 199 S.W.2d 482, 485 (Tex. 1947).
[63] *Bowles v. Fickas*, 167 S.W.2d 741, 742–43 (Tex. 1943).

is a minor[64] or is mentally incapacitated (meaning that the person cannot appreciate the effect of and understand the nature of the person's acts in relation to the contract).[65]

A minor may elect to void a contract even after reaching the age or majority (18) so long as the election occurs within a reasonable time of the minor reaching the age of 18.[66]

However, a minor cannot void a contract which the minor ratified after turning 18.[67]

3-1:4.6 Illegality

A contract that cannot be performed without violation of the law violates public policy and is void.[68] The defense of illegality may be pursued when the contract is: (1) illegal; or (2) against public policy.[69] A court may deem a contract unenforceable when the agreement is based upon gambling debts, unreasonable restraints on trade, or furthering criminal activity. *See* Chapter 16, Section 16-13.

3-1:4.7 Void as Against Public Policy

Enforcement of the contract may be against public policy[70] but a court might only void that provision and enforce the rest of the contract.[71]

3-1:4.8 Fraud

The defense of fraud bars recovery under a contract. To prove fraud as an affirmative defense, a party must show that:

(1) A material representation was made;

(2) The representation was false;

(3) When the speaker made the representation, he knew it was false or made it recklessly without knowledge of the truth and as a positive assertion;

(4) The speaker made it with the intention that is should be acted upon by the party;

(5) The party acted in reliance upon it; and

(6) The party thereby suffered injury.[72]

See Chapter 16, Section 16-15.

---

[64] *See In re H.V.*, 252 S.W.3d 319, n.55 (Tex. 2008) (collecting TX cases holding contract of a minor is voidable at minor's election and not void).
[65] *Mandell & Wright v. Thomas*, 441 S.W.2d 841, 845 (Tex. 1969).
[66] *Searcy v. Hunter*, 17 S.W. 372, 372–73 (Tex. 1891).
[67] *Knandel v. Cameron*, 263 S.W.2d 184, 185 (Tex. Civ. App.—San Antonio 1953, no writ.); *Evans v. Henry*, 230 S.W.2d 620, 621 (Tex. Civ. App.—San Antonio 1950, no writ); *Johnson v. Newberry*, 267 S.W. 476, 478 (Tex. Comm'n App. 1924, holding approved).
[68] *Villanueva v. Gonzalez*, 123 S.W.3d 461, 464 (Tex. App.—San Antonio 2003, no pet.).
[69] *Lewkowicz v. El Paso Apparel Corp.*, 625 S.W.2d 301, 304 (Tex. 1981).
[70] *Sacks v. Dallas Gold & Silver Exch. Inc.*, 720 S.W.2d 177, 180 (Tex. App.—Dallas 1986, no writ).
[71] *Bristol-Myers-Squibb Co. v. Goldston*, 957 S.W.2d 671, 674 (Tex. App.—Fort Worth 1997, pet. denied).
[72] *Anderson, Greenwood & Co. v. Martin*, 44 S.W.3d 200, 212 (Tex. App.—Houston [14th Dist.] 2001, pet. denied).

3-1:4.9 Failure of Consideration

Failure of consideration may be an affirmative defense when the promised performance fails.[73] A failure of consideration may be either partial or total.[74] A party is released from further obligations to perform under the contract if the other party materially breaches the contract.[75] Only the non-breaching party's future performance (not past) is excused by a material breach. The Restatement (Second) of Contracts section 241 provides factors to use to determine whether a failure is material. A total failure of consideration provides for cancellation or rescission of the contract; whereas, a partial failure of consideration will not invalidate the contract and prevent recovery thereon, but is a defense pro tanto.[76] To prove failure of consideration, a party must show:

(1) The parties entered into an agreement;

(2) The consideration consisted of promises for future performance; and

(3) The plaintiff does not fulfill its promise to perform.

See Chapter 16, Section 16-14.

3-1:4.10 Lack of Consideration

Lack of consideration occurs when the contract does not impose obligations upon both parties at its inception.[77] Thus, a lack of consideration exists where a purported contract lacks mutuality of obligation.[78] The existence of a written contract presumes consideration, so the party alleging the lack of consideration defense must rebut this presumption.[79] A defendant may only allege a lack of consideration to a written contract if the defendant submits a verified pleading to that affect.[80] *See* Chapter 16, Section 16-14.

3-1:4.11 Duress

A party may use the defense of duress in a contract action when evidence exists that a person threatened another to enter the contract in such a manner as to destroy the free will of the party against whom the threat was issued.[81] Duress creates the power of avoidance when:

(1) The opposing party threatens to do something he has no legal right to do;

---

[73] *Cheung-Loon, LLC v. Cergon, Inc.*, 392 S.W.3d 738, 747 (Tex. App.—Dallas 2012, no pet.); *Fortitude Energy, LLC v. Sooner Pipe LLC*, 564 S.W.3d 167 (Tex. App.—Houston [1st Dist.] 2018, no pet.).

[74] *Cheung-Loon, LLC v. Cergon, Inc.*, 392 S.W.3d 738, 747–48 (Tex. App.—Dallas 2012, no pet.); *Fortitude Energy, LLC v. Sooner Pipe LLC*, 564 S.W.3d 167 (Tex. App.—Houston [1st Dist.] 2018, no pet.).

[75] *Bartush-Schnitzius Foods Co. v. Cimco Refrigeration, Inc.*, 518 S.W.3d 432, 436 (Tex. 2017).

[76] *Cheung-Loon, LLC v. Cergon, Inc.*, 392 S.W.3d 738, 747–48 (Tex. App.—Dallas 2012, no pet.).

[77] *Cheung-Loon, LLC v. Cergon, Inc.*, 392 S.W.3d 738, 747–48 (Tex. App.—Dallas 2012, no pet.).

[78] *Burges v. Mosley*, 304 S.W.3d 623, 628 (Tex. App.—Tyler 2010, no pet.).

[79] *Burges v. Mosley*, 304 S.W.3d 623, 628 (Tex. App.—Tyler 2010, no pet.).

[80] Tex. R. Civ. P. 93.

[81] *First Tex Sav. Ass'n v. Dicker Ctr.*, 631 S.W.2d 179, 184 (Tex. App.—Tyler 1982).

CONTRACT AND COMMERCIAL LITIGATION

(2) The threat was of such a character to destroy the free will of the party against whom it was issued and thereby overcome his will and cause him to do what he would not otherwise have done.

(3) The threatened injury was imminent; and

(4) The party against whom the threat was issued had no immediate means of protection.

A party may claim economic duress only when the party against whom it is claimed is responsible for the financial distress.[82] *See* Chapter 16, Section 16-1.

3-1:4.12 Mutual Mistake

Mutual mistake may be employed as a defense when the parties shared a basic assumption at the time they entered into the contract that was a mistaken fact.[83] When a mutual mistake exists, the parties are allowed to rescind their contract.[84] To prove the mutual mistake:

(1) Both parties must share the mistake of fact;

(2) The fact must be material or central to the contract; and

(3) The party availing itself of the defense must show that it did not bear the risk of that mistake.

See Chapter 3, Section 3-16:21.

3-1:4.13 Unilateral Mistake

A unilateral mistake by a party to the agreement may not constitute grounds for relief when the mistake was not known to or induced by the other party.[85] However, equitable relief will be granted for a party against a unilateral mistake, when a party shows:

(1) the mistake is of so great a consequence that to enforce the contract as made would be unconscionable;

(2) the mistake relates to a material feature of the contract;

(3) the mistake must have been made regardless of the exercise of ordinary care; and the parties can be placed in status quo in the equity sense.[86]

See Chapter 3, Section 3-16:21.

3-1:4.14 Statute of Frauds

See Chapter 16, Section 16-16.

---

[82] *Berry v. Encore Bank*, No. 01-14-00246-CV, 2015 Tex. App. LEXIS 5551, at *33 (Tex. App.—Houston [1st Dist.] 2015, no pet. h.); *First Tex. Sav. Ass'n of Dallas v. Dicker Ctr.*, 631 S.W.2d 179, 185–86 (Tex. App.—Tyler 1982, no writ).

[83] *Green v. Morris*, 43 S.W.3d 604, 606 (Tex. App.—Waco 2001, no pet.).

[84] *Bolle, Inc. v. Am. Greetings Corp.*, 109 S.W.3d 827, 835 (Tex. App.—Dallas 2003, pet. denied).

[85] *Welkener v. Welkener*, 71 S.W.3d 364, 366 (Tex. App.—Corpus Christi 2001, no pet.).

[86] *Flores v. Medline Indus., Inc.*, No. 13-14-00436-CV, 2015 Tex. App. LEXIS 12719, at *18 (App.—Corpus Christi 2015, no pet. h.).

3-1:4.15 Failure to Perform Condition Precedent

When a party breaches a contract by failure to perform a condition precedent, then the provision to which the condition is attached may be deemed unenforceable.[87] Under the defense of failure to perform condition precedent, the party claiming the defense must specially deny the satisfaction of conditions precedent to performance under the contract in order to require another party to the contract to prove those conditions occurrence or performance.[88] The defendant must specifically describe the conditions precedent that have not been met. *See* Chapter 14, Section 14-10.

3-1:4.16 Impossibility

The impossibility defense is based upon "supervening circumstances" that render a party's performance impracticable or impossible.[89] These "supervening circumstances" may include: supervening illegality, supervening death or incapacity of a person whose existence is essential to performance of the contract, or supervening destruction of a thing whose existence is essential to the performance of the contract.[90] The impossibility of a party being able to perform also precludes specific performance as an available remedy.[91] *See* Chapter 8, Section 8-6:2.

3-1:4.17 Accord and Satisfaction

The defense of accord and satisfaction, based upon an express or implied contract, discharges an existing obligation by means of a lesser payment tendered and accepted.[92] An accord, the new agreement, and satisfaction, the performance of that agreement, constitutes a complete bar to any action on the original obligation.[93]

Under the common law, the defense of accord and satisfaction may be established upon proof of:

(1) An express or implied agreement between the parties;

(2) In which the parties agree to the discharge of an existing obligation by means of a lesser payment tendered and accepted; and

(3) the agreement is performed.[94]

Under the Texas Business and Commerce Code, the defense of accord and satisfaction may be established, subject to certain statutory exceptions, upon proof that:

---

[87] *Beard Family P'ship v. Commercial Indem. Ins. Co.*, 116 S.W.3d 839, 855 (Tex. App.—Austin 2003, no pet.).

[88] Tex. R. Civ. P. 54.

[89] *Hollis v. Gallagher*, No. 03-11-00278-CV, 2012 Tex. App. LEXIS 7547, at *12 (Tex. App.—Austin 2012, no pet.).

[90] *Centex Corp. v. Dalton*, 840 S.W.2d 952 (Tex. 1992); *Tractebel Energy Mktg., Inc. v. E.I. Du Pont de Nemours & Co.*, 118 S.W.3d 60 (Tex. App.—Houston [14th Dist.] 2003, pet. denied).

[91] *See Nash v. Conaster*, 410 S.W.2d 512, 520 (Tex. Civ. App.—Dallas 1966, no writ).

[92] *Lopez v. Munoz, Hockema & Reed, L.L.P.*, 22 S.W.3d 857, 863 (Tex. 2000).

[93] *Harris v. Rowe*, 593 S.W.2d 303, 306 (Tex. 1979); *Bagwell v. Ridge at Alta Vista Invs. I, LLC*, 440 S.W.3d 287, 291–292 (Tex. App.—Dallas 2014).

[94] *Lopez v. Munoz, Hockema & Reed, L.L.P.*, 22 S.W.3d 857, 863 (Tex. 2000).

(1) A person in good faith tendered an instrument to the claimant as full satisfaction of the claim;

(2) The instrument or accompanying written communication contains a conspicuous statement to the effect that the instrument was tendered as full satisfaction of the claim.

(3) The amount of the claim was unliquidated or subject to a bona fide dispute; and

(4) The claimant obtained payment of the instrument.[95]

See Chapter 16, Section 16-3.

3-1:4.18 Novation

Elements:[96]

A valid novation requires:

- a previous valid contract;
- a mutual agreement of all parties to accept the new contract;
- the extinguishment of the old contract or obligation; and
- the new contract to be valid and enforceable.

Intent to accept new obligation in lieu of and in discharge of old obligation may be inferred from facts and circumstances surrounding transaction and conduct of parties.[97]

If reasonable minds differ on the evidence of a new express agreement, its function as a novation is a question of fact.[98]

3-1:4.19 Unconscionability

Unconscionability may be either procedural or substantive. Neither aspect has a precise legal definition, but procedural unconscionability focuses on "shocking abuse" arising from the making of the contract while substantive unconscionability focuses on the terms itself.[99] Factors considered to determine procedural unconscionability: (1) presence of deception, overreaching and sharp business practices; (2) absence of a viable alternative; and (3) relative acumen, knowledge, education, and financial ability of parties involved.[100]

---

[95] Tex. Bus. & Com. Code Ann. § 3.311(a) and (b).
[96] *CDB Software, Inc. v. Kroll*, 992 S.W.2d 31, 38 (Tex. App.—Houston [1st Dist.] 1999).
[97] *Bank of N. Am. v. Bluewater Maint., Inc.*, 578 S.W.2d 841, 842 (Tex. Civ. App.—Houston [1st Dist.] 1979, writ ref'd n.r.e.).
[98] *In the Interest of B.N.L.-B.*, 375 S.W.3d 557, 562–563 (Tex. App.—Dallas 2012).
[99] *Delfingen US-Tex., L.P. v. Valenzuela*, 407 S.W.3d 791, 797–8 (Tex. App.—El Paso 2013, no pet.) (citing *In re Olshan Foundation Repair Co., LLC*, 328 S.W.3d 883, 892 (Tex. 2010)).
[100] *El Paso Nat. Gas Co. v. Minco Oil & Gas Co.*, 964 S.W.2d 54, 61 (Tex. App.—Amarillo 1997, rev'd on other grounds, 8 S.W.3d 309 (Tex. 1999)).

3-1:4.20 Modification[101]

3-1:4.21 Release

A release is a contractual agreement between the parties that dissipates any claim to liability the plaintiff may have.[102] The actual language used in the release determines its scope.[103] The release may cover both known and unknown injuries. Id. To prove the release defense, the defendant must show:

(1) The parties entered into contract; and

(2) The contract releases the defendant from liability.[104]

See Chapter 16, Section 16-5.

3-2 Suit for Rescission

3-2:1 Overview

A suit for rescission can be either a defense to a breach of contract claim or a stand-alone lawsuit. In both instances, the party seeking rescission looks to the equity powers of the court to set aside a contract. A party seeking rescission will be successful if he can prove that grounds for rescission exist, that he has offered to reestablish the status quo, and that he has no adequate remedy at law.

3-2:1.1 Related Causes of Action

Breach of Contract, Quantum Meruit, Assumpsit, Unjust Enrichment, Common Law Fraud, Statutory Fraud, Fraud by Non-disclosure, DTPA Action

3-2:2 Elements

3-2:2.1 Equitable Rescission

(1) Grounds for rescission exist:

(1)(a) Fraud

- Fraud is a ground for rescission.[105]

- For the elements of a fraud cause of action, *See* Chapter 1: Fraud: Common Law Fraud; Chapter 1: Fraud: Statutory Fraud; Chapter 1: Fraud: Fraud by Non-disclosure.

(1)(b) Constructive Fraud

- "[C]onstructive fraud is the breach of some legal or equitable duty which, irrespective of moral guilt, the law declares fraudulent because of

---

[101] Tex. P.J.C. 101.31-Business, Consumer, Insurance & Employment (2012) (citing *Mandril v. Kasishke*, 620 S.W.2d 238, 244 (Tex. Civ. App.—Amarillo 1981 writ ref'd n.r.e.).
[102] *Williams v. Glash*, 789 S.W.2d 261, 264 (Tex. 1990).
[103] *Williams v. Glash*, 789 S.W.2d 261, 264 (Tex. 1990).
[104] *Williams v. Glash*, 789 S.W.2d 261, 264 (Tex. 1990).
[105] *Dallas Farm Mach. Co. v. Reaves*, 307 S.W.2d 233, 238–239 (Tex. 1957).

its tendency to deceive others, to violate confidence, or to injure public interest."[106]

- A duty to deal fairly often arises because of some type of special relationship.[107]
- Constructive fraud exists when there is an entire failure of consideration.[108]

(1)(c) Mistake

- Mistake may qualify as a ground for rescission, depending on the type of mistake and other circumstances.
- Mutual mistake is a ground for rescission when the mistake:
    - is a mistake of fact;[109]
    - is held mutually by the parties;[110]
    - materially affects the agreed-upon exchange;[111] and
    - is not the result of the party seeking rescission's negligence.[112]
- Unilateral mistake is a ground for rescission when:
- Either, there is a unilateral mistake of fact by the party seeking rescission and inequitable conduct by the opposing party;[113] or
    - The mistake is of such magnitude that enforcement of the contract would be unconscionable;
    - The mistake relates to a material element of the contract;
    - The mistake occurred regardless of the exercise of ordinary care; and

---

[106] *Archer v. Griffith*, 390 S.W.2d 735, 740 (Tex. 1964).

[107] *Miller v. Miller*, 700 S.W.2d 941, 946–947 (Tex. App.—Dallas 1985, writ ref'd n.r.e.).

[108] *Radford v. Snyder Nat'l Farm Loan Ass'n*, 121 S.W.2d 478, 480 (Tex. Civ. App.—Austin 1938, no writ).

[109] *Green v. Morris*, 43 S.W.3d 604, 606–07 (Tex. App.—Waco 2001, no pet.); *de Monet v. PERA*, 877 S.W.2d 352, 357 (Tex. App.—Dallas 1994, no writ); *Community Mut. Ins. Co. v. Owen*, 804 S.W.2d 602, 604–05 (Tex. App.—Houston [1st Dist.] 1991, writ denied) (defining a mistake of law as "a mistake as to the legal consequences of an assumed state of facts," and a mistake of facts as a "state of mind not in accord with the facts"). A party's mistaken belief as to private contractual rights is deemed a mistake of fact or a mixed mistake of law and fact and may serve as the grounds for rescission. *Ferguson v. Mounts*, 281 S.W. 616, 620 (Tex. Civ. App.—Amarillo 1926, writ dism'd w.o.j.), *disapproved of on other grounds by United States Fid. & Guar. Co. v. Bimco Iron & Metal Corp.*, 464 S.W.2d 353 (Tex. 1971).

[110] *Green v. Morris*, 43 S.W.3d 604, 606–07 (Tex. App.—Waco 2001, no pet.); *de Monet v. PERA*, 877 S.W.2d 352, 357 (Tex. App.—Dallas 1994, no writ).

[111] *Green v. Morris*, 43 S.W.3d 604, 606–07 (Tex. App.—Waco 2001, no pet.); *de Monet v. PERA*, 877 S.W.2d 352, 357 (Tex. App.—Dallas 1994, no writ).

[112] *Zapatero v. Canales*, 730 S.W.2d 111, 113 (Tex. App.—San Antonio 1987, writ ref'd n.r.e.).

[113] *Cambridge Cos., Inc. v. Williams*, 602 S.W.2d 306, 308 (Tex. Civ. App.—Texarkana 1980), *aff'd*, 615 S.W.2d 172 (Tex. 1981).

- The relief does not result in prejudice to the other party beyond the loss of its bargain.[114]
- Absent misrepresentation about the contents of a contract, a party's mistaken belief about a contract based upon that party's failure to read the contract is not an actionable mistake.[115]

(1)(d) Duress

- Duress exists when:
  - The opposing party threatens to do something he has no legal right to do;
  - The threat was of such a character as to destroy the free will of the party against whom it was issued and thereby overcome his will and cause his to do what he would not otherwise have done;
  - The threatened injury was imminent; and
  - The party against whom the threat was issued had no immediate means of protection.[116]

(1)(e) Incapacity

- A party has the capacity to contract when he can appreciate "the effect of what he [is] doing and [understands] the nature and consequences of his acts and the business he [is] transacting."[117]
- Common forms of incapacity are: minority,[118] intoxication,[119] and insanity/lack of mental capacity.[120]

(2) The party seeking rescission offers to reestablish the status quo.

- The party seeking rescission usually must offer to reestablish the status quo.[121]
- The party seeking rescission may not be required to reestablish the status quo if such reestablishment would result in an inequitable result.[122]

---

[114] *Colvin v. Baskett*, 407 S.W.2d 19, 20 (Tex. Civ. App.—Amarillo 1966, no writ); *see also B.D. Holt Co. v. OCE Inc.*, 971 S.W.2d 618, 62 (Tex. App.—San Antonio 1998, pet. denied); *Kendziorski v. Saunders*, 191 S.W.3d 395, 407 (Tex. App.—Austin 2006).

[115] *Thigpen v. Locke*, 363 S.W.2d 247, 253 (Tex. 1962).

[116] *Dale v. Simon*, 267 S.W. 467, 470 (Tex. Comm'n App. 1924).

[117] *Mandell & Wright v. Thomas*, 441 S.W.2d 841, 845 (Tex. 1969).

[118] *Ulmer v. John Hancock Mut. Life Ins. Co.*, 161 S.W.2d 862, 865 (Tex. Civ. App.—Eastland 1942, writ ref'd w.o.m.).

[119] *Portwood v. Portwood*, 109 S.W.2d 515, 523 (Tex. Civ. App.—Eastland 1937, writ dism'd).

[120] *Ulmer v. John Hancock Mut. Life Ins. Co.*, 161 S.W.2d 862, 865 (Tex. Civ. App.—Eastland 1942, writ ref'd w.o.m.).

[121] *Texas Co. v. State*, 281 S.W.2d 83, 91 (Tex. 1955).

[122] *Turner v. Houston Agr. Credit Corp.*, 601 S.W.2d 61, 65 (Tex. Civ. App.—Houston [1st Dist.] 1980, writ ref'd n.r.e.) (holding that when the status quo cannot be reestablished because of some wrongdoing of the opposing party, the party seeking rescission is not required to reestablish the status quo).

- The inability of the party seeking rescission to restore the status quo is a factor to consider in whether the court will grant rescission.[123]

(3) The party seeking rescission has no adequate remedy at law.

- The party seeking rescission must establish that it has no adequate remedy at law.[124]

3-2:2.2 Rescission by Consent[125]

(1) The parties mutually agree to the rescission

- Such an agreement may be express or implied by the circumstances.[126]
- Contracts that are required to be written may only be rescinded by written agreement to rescind.[127]
- Contracts that are not required to be written may be rescinded orally.[128]
- Only contracts for the sale of goods may expressly prohibit oral rescission.[129]
- There are several ways in which the parties may agree to rescind:
  - The parties may mutually and expressly agree to rescind the contract;[130]
  - One party may acquiesce to the other's repudiation of the contract;[131] or
  - The parties may form a second contract which is complete in itself while being substantially inconsistent with the first contract.[132]

(2) An agreement to rescind a contract must be supported by consideration.

- The mutual promise between the parties to release the other party/parties from the contract is sufficient consideration to create an enforceable agreement to rescind a contract.[133]

---

[123] *Ennis v. Interstate Distribs., Inc.*, 598 S.W.2d 903, 906 (Tex. Civ. App.—Dallas 1980, no writ).
[124] *Chenault v. Cty. of Shelby*, 320 S.W.2d 431, 433 (Tex. Civ. App.—Austin 1959, writ ref'd n.r.e.).
[125] Although the elements are listed, the remaining Damages and Remedies and Defenses listed only apply to Equitable Rescission.
[126] *Marsh v. Orville Carr Assocs., Inc.*, 433 S.W.2d 928, 931 (Tex. Civ. App.—San Antonio 1968, writ ref'd n.r.e.).
[127] *Givens v. Dougherty*, 671 S.W.2d 877, 878 (Tex. 1984).
[128] *Pinson v. Odom*, 250 S.W.2d 609, 611 (Tex. Civ. App.—Eastland 1952, no writ).
[129] *See* Tex. Bus. & Com. Code Ann. § 2.209(b).
[130] *Marsh v. Orville Carr Assocs., Inc.*, 433 S.W.2d 928, 931 (Tex. Civ. App.—San Antonio 1968, writ ref'd n.r.e.).
[131] *Marsh v. Orville Carr Assocs., Inc.*, 433 S.W.2d 928, 931 (Tex. Civ. App.—San Antonio 1968, writ ref'd n.r.e.).
[132] *Ed Hoffman Motors v. G.F.C. Corp.*, 304 S.W.2d 216, 217–218 (Tex. Civ. App.—San Antonio 1957, writ ref'd n.r.e.).
[133] *Texas Gas Util. Co. v. Barrett*, 460 S.W.2d 409, 414 (Tex. 1970).

3-2:2.3 Rescission by Option[134]

Generally:

- The parties to a contract may prospectively grant one or more parties the option to rescind.[135]

An effective rescission accomplishes:

- The setting aside of the contract;
- The return of all consideration; and
- The return of the parties to the status quo.[136]

Special Damages:

- In addition to the return of consideration, the party seeking rescission is entitled to special damages.[137]

Interest:

- The party seeking rescission may be entitled to prejudgment interest.[138]
- The party seeking rescission is entitled to interest as a matter of right if he can show that the measure of damages is fixed by conditions existing at the time the claim arose.[139]
- Although the measure of damages must be fixed, the amount of damages does not need to be fixed.[140]

Exemplary Damages:

- A party seeking rescission may recover exemplary damages.[141] Such damages are available if the defendant acts:
  - Maliciously;
  - Fraudulently; or
  - With gross negligence.[142]

---

[134] Although the elements are listed, the remaining Damages and Remedies and Defenses listed only apply to Equitable Rescission.
[135] *Jones v. Chester*, 363 S.W.2d 150, 155 (Tex. Civ. App.—Austin 1962, writ ref'd n.r.e.).
[136] *Humphrey v. Camelot Ret. Cmty.*, 893 S.W.2d 55, 59 (Tex. App.—Corpus Christi 1994, no writ).
[137] *Smith v. Nat'l Resort Cmtys., Inc.*, 585 S.W.2d 655, 660 (Tex. 1979).
[138] *Smith v. Nat'l Resort Cmtys., Inc.*, 585 S.W.2d 655, 660 (Tex. 1979).
[139] *City of Ingleside v. Stewart*, 554 S.W.2d 939, 946–47 (Tex. Civ. App.—Corpus Christi 1977, writ ref'd n.r.e.).
[140] *City of Ingleside v. Stewart*, 554 S.W.2d 939, 946–47 (Tex. Civ. App.—Corpus Christi 1977, writ ref'd n.r.e.).
[141] *Consolidated Tex. Fin. v. Shearer*, 739 S.W.2d 477, 479–80 (Tex. App.—Fort Worth 1987, writ ref'd).
[142] Tex. Civ. Prac. & Rem. Code Ann. § 41.003(a).

CONTRACT AND COMMERCIAL LITIGATION

3-2:3 Damages and Remedies

3-2:3.1 Rescission

Rescission sets aside the contract, returns any consideration, and returns the parties to the status quo.

3-2:3.2 Special Damages

In addition to the return of consideration, the party seeking rescission is entitled to special damages.

3-2:3.3 Interest

Interest may be available as a matter of right.

3-2:3.4 Exemplary Damages

See Chapter 11, Section 11-2.

3-2:4 Defenses

3-2:4.1 Statute of Limitations

The four-year limitations period controls.[143] The cause of actions accrues when the contract for which rescission is sought is formed.[144] However, the discovery rule applies when the party seeking rescission is seeking rescission based upon a fraud-based theory.[145]

3-2:4.2 Laches

An unreasonable delay in bringing suit which causes harm to the defendant may preclude a suit for rescission.[146]

3-2:4.3 Waiver or Ratification

A party seeking rescission may waive any claim for rescission by ratifying the contract.[147]

In order to ratify the contract and thus waive a claim for rescission, the party seeking rescission must accept the benefits of the contract.

---

[143] Tex. Civ. Prac. & Rem. Code Ann. § 16.051; *Williams v. Khalaf*, 802 S.W.2d 651, 658 (Tex. 1990).

[144] *S.V. v. R.V.*, 933 S.W.2d 1, 4 (Tex. 1996).

[145] *S.V. v. R.V.*, 933 S.W.2d 1, 4 (Tex. 1996).

[146] *Vandervoort v. Sansom*, 293 S.W.2d 271, 275 (Tex. Civ. App.—Fort Worth 1956, writ ref'd n.r.e.).

[147] *DePuy v. Bodine*, 509 S.W.2d 698, 699 (Tex. Civ. App.—San Antonio 1974, writ ref'd n.r.e.).

3-2:4.4 Other Equitable Defenses

Other equitable defenses would be appropriate, given the equitable nature of the cause of action.[148]

3-2:5 Procedural Implications

3-2:5.1 Parol Evidence Rule

Parol evidence may be used to prove the grounds for rescission.[149]

3-3 Quantum Meruit

3-3:1 Overview

Quantum meruit is an equitable cause of action which implies the existence of a contract to avoid the unjust enrichment of the defendant. Although an express contract generally precludes recovery in quantum meruit, there are several exceptions. A plaintiff is entitled to the reasonable value of his services rendered or materials furnished if he can prove he gave something of value to the defendant, which the defendant accepted, used and enjoyed, and for which the defendant reasonably understood the plaintiff expected to be paid.

3-3:1.1 Related Causes of Action

Assumpsit, Unjust Enrichment, Money had and received, Breach of Contract, Trover, Conversion, Restitution, Constructive Trust

MUST READ CASES

Vortt Expl. Co., Inc. v. Chevron U.S.A., Inc., 787 S.W.2d 942 (Tex. 1990)

Truly v. Austin, 744 S.W.2d 934 (Tex. 1988)

Bashara v. Baptist Mem'l Hosp. Sys., 685 S.W.2d 307 (Tex. 1985)

3-3:2 Elements

(1) The plaintiff gave either services or materials of value.[150,151]

(2) The service or materials must have been given for the defendant.[152]

- The value must be given for the defendant. Incidental benefits to the defendant are not sufficient.[153]

---

[148] *See, e.g., Isaacs v. Bishop*, 249 S.W.3d 100, 109 (Tex. App.—Texarkana 2008, pet. denied) (describing a Suit for Rescission as an equitable remedy).
[149] *Santos v. Mid-Continent Refrigerator Co.*, 471 S.W.2d 568, 569 (Tex. 1971).
[150] *Bashara v. Baptist Mem'l Hosp. Sys.*, 685 S.W.2d 307, 310 (Tex. 1985).
[151] *Bashara v. Baptist Mem'l Hosp. Sys.*, 685 S.W.2d 307, 310 (Tex. 1985).
[152] *Bashara v. Baptist Mem'l Hosp. Sys.*, 685 S.W.2d 307, 310 (Tex. 1985).
[153] *Bashara v. Baptist Mem'l Hosp. Sys.*, 685 S.W.2d 307, 310 (Tex. 1985).

- It is not necessary that the defendant own the improved property, so long as the plaintiff's services benefitted the defendant.[154]
- A plaintiff who gives value so that he is also directly benefitted is precluded from recovery.[155]

(3) The defendant accepted, used, and enjoyed the valuable thing.[156]

- Equity imposes upon the defendant an obligation to pay because, if the defendant does not pay the plaintiff, the defendant would be unjustly enriched at the plaintiff's expense.[157]

(4) The defendant reasonably understood the plaintiff expected to be paid.[158]

- The plaintiff may expect any form of payment, including non-monetary forms.[159]

3-3:3 Damages and Remedies

3-3:3.1 Reasonable Value

A plaintiff may recover the reasonable value of the services rendered or materials furnished.[160]

A defendant may offset a plaintiff's recovery because of any defects in the services rendered or materials furnished.[161]

3-3:3.2 Interest

A plaintiff is entitled to interest as a matter of right if he can show that the measure of damages is fixed by conditions existing at the time the claim arose.[162]

The measure of damages must be fixed, but the amount of damages does not need to be fixed.[163]

---

[154] *Concept Gen. Contracting, Inc. v. Asbestos Maint. Servs., Inc.*, 346 S.W.3d 172, 182 (Tex. App.—Amarillo 2011, pet. denied).

[155] *Truly v. Austin*, 744 S.W.2d 934, 937 (Tex. 1988) (plaintiff who owned 40% stake in a joint venture was precluded from recovering in Quantum Meruit for services rendered to the joint venture).

[156] *Bashara v. Baptist Mem'l Hosp. Sys.*, 685 S.W.2d 307, 310 (Tex. 1985).

[157] *See Truly v. Austin*, 744 S.W.2d 934, 938 (Tex. 1988) (requiring a plaintiff prove the defendant would be unjustly enriched at the plaintiff's expense).

[158] *Bashara v. Baptist Mem'l Hosp. Sys.*, 685 S.W.2d 307, 310 (Tex. 1985).

[159] *Vortt Expl. Co., Inc. v. Chevron U.S.A., Inc.*, 787 S.W.2d 942, 945 (Tex. 1990).

[160] *Vortt Expl. Co., Inc. v. Chevron U.S.A., Inc.*, 787 S.W.2d 942, 945 (Tex. 1990).

[161] *City of Ingleside v. Stewart*, 554 S.W.2d 939, 946 (Tex. Civ. App.—Corpus Christi 1977, writ ref'd n.r.e.).

[162] *City of Ingleside v. Stewart*, 554 S.W.2d 939, 946–47 (Tex. Civ. App.—Corpus Christi 1977, writ ref'd n.r.e.).

[163] *City of Ingleside v. Stewart*, 554 S.W.2d 939, 946–47 (Tex. Civ. App.—Corpus Christi 1977, writ ref'd n.r.e.).

3-3:4 Defenses

3-3:4.1 Statute of Limitations

The four-year limitations period applies to quantum meruit claims.[164] The cause of action accrues when the plaintiff renders services or furnishes materials.[165]

The discovery rule likely does not apply to a claim for quantum meruit.[166]

3-3:4.2 Express Contract

As a general rule, a plaintiff may not recover in quantum meruit when an express agreement covers the services rendered or materials provided.[167] Where the existence or terms of such an agreement is in dispute, it is the burden of the party seeking to preclude recovery in quantum meruit to secure findings from the trial court that an express contract exists that covers the subject matter of the dispute.[168]

However, a plaintiff may recover in quantum meruit despite the existence of an express contract if:

(1) the plaintiff partially performed, but could not substantially perform, because of the defendant's breach,[169] or

(2) if the contract imposes unilateral obligations on the plaintiff.[170]

Further, a breaching plaintiff may recover in quantum meruit on a construction contract.[171]

3-3:4.3 Offset

A defendant may offset a plaintiff's recovery in the amount of any defects in the services rendered or materials furnished.[172]

3-3:4.4 Res Judicata

Res judicata is an applicable defense.[173]

---

[164] *Pepi Corp. v. Galliford*, 254 S.W.3d 457, 460–61 (Tex. App.—Houston [1st Dist.] 2007, pet. denied); *Lamajak, Inc. v. Frazin*, 230 S.W.3d 786, 796 (Tex. App.—Dallas 2007, no pet.).

[165] *See Quigley v. Bennett*, 256 S.W.3d 356, 360 (Tex. App.—San Antonio 2008, no pet.) (holding the plaintiff's cause of action accrued on the last date the plaintiff rendered services).

[166] *See Quigley v. Bennett*, 256 S.W.3d 356, 361–62 (Tex. App.—San Antonio 2008, no pet.).

[167] *Fortune Prod. Co. v. Conoco, Inc.*, 52 S.W.3d 671, 684 (Tex. 2000); *Christus Health v. Quality Infusion Care, Inc.*, 359 S.W.3d 719, 723 (Tex. App.—Houston [1st Dist.] 2011, no pet.) (stating an express contract would provide the plaintiff a legal remedy, which would preclude a recovery in equity).

[168] *Fortune Prod. Co. v. Conoco, Inc.*, 52 S.W.3d 671, 685 (Tex. 2000).

[169] *Truly v. Austin*, 744 S.W.2d 934, 936 (Tex. 1988).

[170] *Truly v. Austin*, 744 S.W.2d 934, 937 (Tex. 1988).

[171] *Truly v. Austin*, 744 S.W.2d 934, 937 (Tex. 1988).

[172] *Rasa Floors, L.P. v. Spring Vill. Partners, Ltd.*, No. 01-08-00918-CV, 2010 Tex. App. LEXIS 9253 at *15–18 (App.—Houston [1st Dist.] Nov. 18, 2010).

[173] *See Barr v. Resolution Tr. Corp.*, 837 S.W.2d 627 (Tex. 1992).

CONTRACT AND COMMERCIAL LITIGATION

3-3:4.5 Equitable Defenses

Quantum meruit is an equitable cause of action[174] and is therefore subject to equitable defenses, including:

- Unclean Hands;[175]
- Waiver;[176] or
- Estoppel.[177]

3-4 Unjust Enrichment

3-4:1 Overview

Unjust enrichment is a cause of action founded in quasi-contract. Founded in equity, unjust enrichment seeks to restore a benefit conferred on an undeserving person. Such a benefit will be restored if the plaintiff proves the defendant obtained it from the plaintiff by means of fraud, duress, undue advantage, or passively obtaining a benefit that it would be unconscionable to retain.

3-4:1.1 Related Causes of Action

Assumpsit, Quantum Meruit, Money had and received, Breach of Contract, Trover, Conversion, Restitution, Constructive Trust

MUST READ CASES

Fortune Prod. Co. v. Conoco, Inc., 52 S.W.3d 671 (Tex. 2000)

Heldenfels Bros., Inc. v. City of Corpus Christi, 832 S.W.2d 39 (Tex. 1992)

3-4:2 Elements

(1) The defendant obtains a benefit

- The defendant, rather than a third party, obtains a benefit.[178]

(2) From the plaintiff[179]

- The benefit must come from the plaintiff.[180]

AND

(3) By means of

---

[174] *Truly v. Austin*, 744 S.W.2d 934, 938 (Tex. 1988).
[175] *Truly v. Austin*, 744 S.W.2d 934, 938 (Tex. 1988).
[176] *Concept Gen. Contracting, Inc. v. Asbestos Maint. Servs., Inc.*, 346 S.W.3d 172, 187 (Tex. App.—Amarillo 2011, pet. denied).
[177] *Concept Gen. Contracting, Inc. v. Asbestos Maint. Servs., Inc.*, 346 S.W.3d 172, 187 (Tex. App.—Amarillo 2011, pet. denied).
[178] *Heldenfels Bros., Inc. v. City of Corpus Christi*, 832 S.W.2d 39, 41 (Tex. 1992).
[179] *Heldenfels Bros., Inc. v. City of Corpus Christi*, 832 S.W.2d 39, 41 (Tex. 1992).
[180] *HECI Expl. Co. v. Neel*, 982 S.W.2d 881, 891 (Tex. 1998).

(a) Fraud

- By means of fraud.[181]
- It is not enough that the conferral of a benefit is generally unfair or would yield a windfall; rather, there must be some level of wrongdoing.[182]

(b) Duress[183]

- It is not enough that the conferral of a benefit is generally unfair or would yield a windfall; rather, there must be some level of wrongdoing.[184]

(c) Taking an undue advantage[185]

- An unfair advantage may be the failure of consideration.[186]
- It is not enough that the conferral of a benefit is generally unfair or would yield a windfall; rather, there must be some level of wrongdoing.[187]

OR

(d) Passively obtaining a benefit which is unconscionable to retain.[188]

- One means of passively receiving a benefit is when an oil company mistakenly overpays one royalty owner while underpaying another.[189]
- This passive receipt is likely the sub-element several cases refer to when they say recovery does not depend upon the defendant's wrongful act.[190]

3-4:3 Damages and Remedies

3-4:3.1 Restitution

Restitution may be an available remedy.[191]

3-4:4 Defenses

3-4:4.1 Statute of Limitations

The two-year limitations period applies.[192]

---

[181] *Heldenfels Bros., Inc. v. City of Corpus Christi*, 832 S.W.2d 39, 41 (Tex. 1992).
[182] *HECI Expl. Co. v. Neel*, 982 S.W.2d 881, 891 (Tex. 1998).
[183] *Heldenfels Bros., Inc. v. City of Corpus Christi*, 832 S.W.2d 39, 41 (Tex. 1992).
[184] *HECI Expl. Co. v. Neel*, 982 S.W.2d 881, 891 (Tex. 1998).
[185] *Heldenfels Bros., Inc. v. City of Corpus Christi*, 832 S.W.2d 39, 41 (Tex. 1992).
[186] *See Oxford Fin. Cos., Inc. v. Velez*, 807 S.W.2d 460, 465 (Tex. App.—Austin 1991, writ denied).
[187] *HECI Expl. Co. v. Neel*, 982 S.W.2d 881, 891 (Tex. 1998).
[188] *Stewart Title Guar. Co. v. Mims*, 405 S.W.3d 319, 339 (Tex. App.—Dallas 2013, no pet.).
[189] *HECI Expl. Co. v. Neel*, 982 S.W.2d 881, 891 (Tex. 1998).
[190] *Oxford Fin. Cos., Inc. v. Velez*, 807 S.W.2d 460, 465 (Tex. App.—Austin 1991, writ denied); *Fun Time Ctrs., Inc. v. Cont'l Nat'l Bank*, 517 S.W.2d 877, 884 (Tex. Civ. App. 1974, writ ref'd n.r.e.).
[191] *See Mowbray v. Avery*, 76 S.W.3d 663, 680 (Tex. App.—Corpus Christi 2002, pet. denied); *but see Excess Underwriters at Lloyd's v. Frank's Casing Crew & Rental Tools, Inc.*, 246 S.W.3d 42 (Tex. 2008).
[192] *Elledge v. Friberg-Cooper Water Supply Corp.*, 240 S.W.3d 869, 870 (Tex. 2007).

3-4:4.2 Valid Contract

A valid contract generally precludes recovery under a quasi-contract theory.[193]

In addition, any adequate legal remedy may preclude recovery.[194]

A plaintiff may recover under a quasi-contract theory despite the existence of a valid contract when the plaintiff has (1) overpaid on the contract;[195] or (2) sued on a construction contract.[196]

3-4:4.3 Other Defenses, Generally

Other applicable defenses could include:

- Unclean hands;[197]
- Voluntary payment;[198] and
- Material change of position.[199]

3-4:5 Procedural Implications

3-4:5.1 Characterization as a Cause of Action

Some courts do not characterize unjust enrichment as an independent cause of action, but rather as a justification for a claim of restitution or the imposition of a constructive trust.[200]

Therefore, it is prudent to plead restitution, constructive trust and unjust enrichment as separate causes of action.[201]

---

[193] *Fortune Prod. Co. v. Conoco, Inc.*, 52 S.W.3d 671, 684 (Tex. 2000).
[194] *BMG Direct Mktg., Inc. v. Peake*, 178 S.W.3d 763, 770 (Tex. 2005).
[195] *Southwestern Elec. Power Co. v. Burlington N. R.R. Co.*, 966 S.W.2d 467, 469–70 (Tex. 1998).
[196] *Pepi Corp. v. Galliford*, 254 S.W.3d 457, 462–63 (Tex. App.—Houston [1st Dist.] 2007, pet. denied).
[197] *Best Buy Co. v. Barrera*, 248 S.W.3d 160, 163 (Tex. 2007).
[198] *BMG Direct Mktg., Inc. v. Peake*, 178 S.W.3d 763, 768 (Tex. 2005) (holding that voluntary payment exists when a person: (1) pays money on a claim of right; (2) in the absence of fraud, deception, duress, or compulsion; (3) with full knowledge of the facts; (4) because the person was ignorant or mistaken about the law).
[199] *Bryan v. Citizens Nat'l Bank in Abilene*, 628 S.W.2d 761, 763 (Tex. 1982) (holding that a defendant who, in reliance on the money, materially changes his position, will generally be immune from recovery).
[200] *Casstevens v. Smith*, 269 S.W.3d 222, 229 (Tex. App.—Texarkana 2008, pet. denied); *Friberg-Cooper Water Supply Corp. v. Elledge*, 197 S.W.3d 826, 832 (Tex. App.—Fort Worth 2006), rev'd on other grounds, 240 S.W.3d 869 (Tex. 2007); *Walker v. Cotter Props., Inc.*, 181 S.W.3d 895, 900 (Tex. App.—Dallas 2006, no pet.); *Mowbray v. Avery*, 76 S.W.3d 663, 680 (Tex. App.—Corpus Christi 2002, pet. denied).
[201] 16 Tex. Prac., West's Texas Elements of an Action § 10:1 (maintaining that Unjust Enrichment is an independent cause of action based upon Texas Supreme Court precedent).

3-5 Promissory Estoppel

3-5:1 Overview

As a cause of action, promissory estoppel does not create a contract where one does not exist. Rather, a suit for promissory estoppel merely prevents the defendant from strictly enforcing his legal rights regarding the enforceability of promises. As a means of enforcing a contract within the statute of frauds, Promissory Estoppel allows a plaintiff to enforce an otherwise unenforceable promise.

3-5:1.1 Related Causes of Action

Breach of Contract, Assumpsit, Quantum Meruit, Unjust Enrichment

MUST READ CASES

Walker v. Walker, No. 14-16-00357-CV, 2017 Tex. App. LEXIS 2719 (App.—Houston [14th Dist.] Mar. 30, 2017)

English v. Fischer, 660 S.W.2d 521 (Tex. 1983)

3-5:2 Elements

3-5:2.1 As a Cause of Action[202]

(1) The defendant makes a promise.[203]

- The promise must be sufficiently definite.[204]

- If the promise is subject to two interpretations (one of which would not be inconsistent with the defendant's position at trial), there can be no estoppel.[205]

(2) It is foreseeable that the plaintiff will rely upon the promise.[206]

(3) The plaintiff substantially relies on the promise to his detriment.[207]

- The plaintiff's reliance must be reasonable.[208]

---

[202] *Henry Schein v. Stromboe*, 102 S.W.3d 675, n.25 (Tex. 2002).

[203] *English v. Fischer*, 660 S.W.2d 521, 524 (Tex. 1983).

[204] *David McDavid Nissan, Inc. v. Subaru of Am., Inc.*, 10 S.W.3d 56, 74 (Tex. App.—Dallas 1999), *aff'd in part, rev'd in part on other grounds*, 84 S.W.3d 212 (Tex. 2002).

[205] *Lloyd v. Singleton*, 16 S.W.2d 891, 894 (Tex. Civ. App.—Amarillo 1929, no writ).

[206] *English v. Fischer*, 660 S.W.2d 521, 524 (Tex. 1983); *Adams v. Petrade Intern., Inc.*, 754 S.W.2d 696, 708 (Tex. App.—Houston [1st Dist.] 1988, writ denied).

[207] *English v. Fischer*, 660 S.W.2d 521, 524 (Tex. 1983).

[208] *Wheeler v. White*, 398 S.W.2d 93, 96 (Tex. 1965); *Adams v. Petrade Intern., Inc.*, 754 S.W.2d 696, 708 (Tex. App.—Houston [1st Dist.] 1988, writ denied) (discussing reasonable reliance).

3-5:2.2 As a Means of Enforcing a Contract Within the Statute of Frauds[209]

(1) The defendant promises to sign a writing that would satisfy the Statute of Frauds.[210]

- The defendant may also promise that the agreement falls outside of the Statute of Frauds.[211]

(2) The defendant should have expected that his promise would lead the plaintiff to experience a definite and substantial injury.[212]

(3) Such an injury occurred; and[213]

(4) The court must enforce the promise to avoid injustice.[214]

3-5:3 Damages and Remedies

3-5:3.1 Reliance Damages

A plaintiff may only recover reliance damages.[215]

Reliance damages are those damages that would put the plaintiff back into the position he would have been but for his reliance on the defendant's promise.[216]

Reliance damages may never include lost profits or benefit-of-the-bargain damages.[217]

A plaintiff may not sue on a theory of promissory estoppel if the promise made was part of a valid and enforceable contract.[218]

3-5:3.2 Enforcement of the Promise

The court may enforce the otherwise unenforceable promise.[219]

---

[209] This is a means of enforcing a contract, and as such we have only included the elements necessary to prove promissory estoppel as a means of enforcing a contract within the Statute of Frauds. In addition, promissory estoppel can function as a substitute for consideration. *Citizens Nat'l Bank at Brownwood v. Ross Const. Co.*, 206 S.W.2d 593, 595 (Tex. 1947). The rest of this subtopic addresses the damages defenses, and remedies available when there is no contract.

[210] *Nagle v. Nagle*, 633 S.W.2d 796, 800 (Tex. 1982); *Old Tin Roof Steakhouse, LLC v. Haskett*, No. 04-12-00363-CV, 2013 Tex. App. LEXIS 2874, at *27 (Tex. App.—San AntonioMar. 20, 2013, no pet.).

[211] *Ford v. City State Bank of Palacios*, 44 S.W.3d 121, 139 (Tex. App.—Corpus Christi 2001, no pet.).

[212] *Nagle v. Nagle*, 633 S.W.2d 796, 800 (Tex. 1982).

[213] *Nagle v. Nagle*, 633 S.W.2d 796, 800 (Tex. 1982).

[214] *Nagle v. Nagle*, 633 S.W.2d 796, 800 (Tex. 1982).

[215] *Wheeler v. White*, 398 S.W.2d 93, 97 (Tex. 1965).

[216] *Wheeler v. White*, 398 S.W.2d 93, 97 (Tex. 1965).

[217] *Wheeler v. White*, 398 S.W.2d 93, 97 (Tex. 1965).

[218] *Guaranty Bank v. Lone Star Life Ins. Co.*, 568 S.W.2d 431, 434 (Tex. Civ. App.—Dallas 1978, writ ref'd n.r.e.); *Severs v. Mira Vista Homeowners Ass'n*, 559 S.W.3d 684, 701 (Tex. App.—Fort Worth 2018, pet denied.).

[219] *Nagle v. Nagle*, 633 S.W.2d 796, 800 (Tex. 1982).

3-5:4 Defenses

3-5:4.1 Statute of Limitations

The four-year limitations period applies.[220] The cause of action accrues when the defendant breaches its promise to the plaintiff.[221]

3-5:4.2 Other Defenses, Generally

Because of the equitable nature of the cause of action, equitable defenses need not be pleaded to be asserted.[222]

Rather, a defendant may put on proof of any fact or defense which might rebalance the equities.[223]

Such equitable defenses could include:

- Unclean hands;[224]
- Voluntary payment;[225]
- Material change of position;[226] and
- Any facts which tend to negate the essential elements of the plaintiff's claim.[227]

Other than limitations, there are no silver bullet defenses. Each equitable defense and fact proven is attributed to the equity of the case.

3-6 Money Had and Received

3-6:1 Overview

Money had and received is a cause of action rooted in assumpsit and unjust enrichment. The only inquiry to be made is whether the defendant has money which in equity belongs to the plaintiff.

---

[220] Tex. Civ. Prac. & Rem. Code Ann. § 16.051; *Prestige Ford Garland Ltd. P'ship v. Morales*, 336 S.W.3d 833, 836 (Tex. App.—Dallas 2011, no pet.).

[221] *Prestige Ford Garland Ltd. P'ship v. Morales*, 336 S.W.3d 833, 837 (Tex. App.—Dallas 2011, no pet.).

[222] *See Best Buy Co. v. Barrera*, 248 S.W.3d 160, 163 (Tex. 2007) (discussing defenses to the equitable cause of action for money had and received).

[223] *See Best Buy Co. v. Barrera*, 248 S.W.3d 160, 163 (Tex. 2007) (discussing defenses to the equitable cause of action for money had and received).

[224] *Best Buy Co. v. Barrera*, 248 S.W.3d 160, 163 (Tex. 2007).

[225] *BMG Direct Mktg., Inc. v. Peake*, 178 S.W.3d 763, 768 (Tex. 2005) (Voluntary payment exists when a person: (1) pays money on a claim of right; (2) in the absence of fraud, deception, duress or compulsion; (3) with full knowledge of the facts; (4) because the person was ignorant or mistaken about the law.).

[226] *Bryan v. Citizens Nat'l Bank in Abilene*, 628 S.W.2d 761, 763 (Tex. 1982) (A defendant who, in reliance on the money, materially changes his position, will generally be immune from recovery.).

[227] *Best Buy Co. v. Barrera*, 248 S.W.3d 160, 163 (Tex. 2007).

CONTRACT AND COMMERCIAL LITIGATION 173

3-6:1.1 Related Causes of Action

Assumpsit, Quantum Meruit, Unjust Enrichment, Breach of Contract, Trover, Conversion

MUST READ CASES

Best Buy Co. v. Barrera, 248 S.W.3d 160 (Tex. 2007)

H.E.B., L.L.C. v. Ardinger, 369 S.W.3d 496 (Tex. App.—Fort Worth 2012)

3-6:2 Elements

(1) The defendant has money or a substitute for money.[228]

    (1)(a) Money.[229]

    (1)(b) An equivalent of money

- Equivalents for money include:
  - Cashier's checks;[230]
  - Other financial instruments;[231] and
  - Property converted into money before trial.[232]

(2) Which in equity, justice and law belongs to the plaintiff.[233]

- To recover, the plaintiff need not prove the defendant acted wrongfully. Rather, the plaintiff merely must establish the equities balance in his favor.[234]
- Where the plaintiff and defendant are both innocent, the one who could have avoided the loss must bear the loss.[235]

3-6:3 Damages and Remedies

3-6:3.1 Restitution

Restitution is an available remedy.[236]

---

[228] *Staats v. Miller*, 243 S.W.2d 686, 687 (1951).
[229] *H.E.B., L.L.C. v. Ardinger*, 369 S.W.3d 496, 507 (Tex. App.—Fort Worth 2012); *First Tech Fed. Credit Union v. Fisher*, No. 14-18-00140-CV, 2020 Tex. App. LEXIS 1424, at *10 (Tex. App.—Houston [14th Dist.] Feb. 20, 2020, no pet. h.).
[230] *First Nat'l Bank of Mineola, Tex. v. Farmers & Merchs. State Bank of Athens, Tex.*, 417 S.W.2d 317, 324 (Tex. Civ. App.—Tyler 1967, writ ref'd n.r.e.).
[231] *First Nat'l Bank of Mineola, Tex. v. Farmers & Merch. State Bank of Athens, Tex.*, 417 S.W.2d 317, 324 (Tex. Civ. App.—Tyler 1967, writ ref'd n.r.e.).
[232] *Tri-State Chems. v. W. Organics*, 83 S.W.3d 189, 195 (Tex. App.—Amarillo 2002).
[233] *Miller-Rogaska, Inc. v. Bank One, N.A.*, 931 S.W.2d 655, 662 (Tex. App.—Dallas 1996, no writ).
[234] *London v. London*, 192 S.W.3d 6, 13 (Tex. App.—Houston [14th Dist.] 2005, pet. denied).
[235] *Gonzales Motor Co. v. Buhidar*, 348 S.W.2d 376, 378 (Tex. Civ. App.—Eastland 1961, writ ref'd n.r.e.).
[236] *Amoco Prod. Co. v. Smith*, 946 S.W.2d 162, 164 (Tex. App.—El Paso 1997, no writ).

3-6:3.2 Attorney's Fees

Attorney's fees may be recoverable under Chapter 38 of the Texas Civil Practice and Remedies Code.[237]

It is likely that attorney's fees, to be recoverable, must be recoverable under Section 38.001(1).[238]

3-6:4 Defenses

3-6:4.1 Statute of Limitations

The limitations period may be two years[239] or four years.[240] The cause of action accrues when the money is paid to the defendant.[241] The discovery rule may apply.[242]

3-6:4.2 Other Defenses, Generally

Because of the equitable nature of the cause of action, equitable defenses need not be pleaded to be asserted.[243]

Rather, a defendant may put on proof of any fact or defense which might rebalance the equities.[244]

Such equitable defenses could include:

- Unclean hands;[245]
- Voluntary payment;[246]

---

[237] *Ferrous Prods. Co. v. Gulf States Trading Co.*, 323 S.W.2d 292, 297 (Tex. Civ. App.—Houston 1959), *aff'd*, 160 Tex. 399, 332 S.W.2d 310 (1960).

[238] Section 38.001(8) authorizes the payment of attorney's fees based upon an oral or written contract. Because Money had and received is an action in quasi-contract—as opposed to a contract in fact—it is likely that Section 38.001(8) does not apply.

[239] *Elledge v. Friberg-Cooper Water Supply Corp.*, 240 S.W.3d 869 (Tex. 2007) (The main cause of action in this case is for unjust enrichment. However, the Court discusses two-year vs. four-year limitations periods and how to classify which causes of action belong in which categories.); *Tanglewood Terrace, Ltd. v. City of Texarkana*, 996 S.W.2d 330, 342 (Tex. App.—Texarkana 1999, no pet.); *Pelto Oil Co. v. CSX Oil & Gas Corp.*, 804 S.W.2d 583, 586 (Tex. App.—Houston [1st Dist.] 1991, writ denied).

[240] *Amoco Prod. Co. v. Smith*, 946 S.W.2d 162, 165 (Tex. App.—El Paso 1997, no writ) (characterizing a suit for Money had and received as one for "debt.").

[241] *Tanglewood Terrace, Ltd. v. City of Texarkana*, 996 S.W.2d 330, 337 (Tex. App.—Texarkana 1999, no pet.); *First City Bank of Plano, N.A.*, 794 S.W.2d 537, 542–43 (Tex. App.—Dallas 1990, writ denied); *Vickory v. Summit Nat'l Bank*, 702 S.W.2d 324 (Tex. App.—Fort Worth 1986, writ ref'd n.r.e.).

[242] *Tanglewood Terrace, Ltd. v. City of Texarkana*, 996 S.W.2d 330, 342 (Tex. App.—Texarkana 1999, no pet.).

[243] *Best Buy Co. v. Barrera*, 248 S.W.3d 160, 163 (Tex. 2007).

[244] *Best Buy Co. v. Barrera*, 248 S.W.3d 160, 163 (Tex. 2007).

[245] *Best Buy Co. v. Barrera*, 248 S.W.3d 160, 163 (Tex. 2007).

[246] *BMG Direct Mktg., Inc. v. Peake*, 178 S.W.3d 763, 768 (Tex. 2005) (Voluntary payment exists when a person: (1) pays money on a claim of right; (2) in the absence of fraud, deception,

CONTRACT AND COMMERCIAL LITIGATION

- Material change of position;[247] and
- Any facts which tend to establish the money or its equivalent belongs to the defendant.[248]

3-7 Suit on A Sworn Account

3-7:1 Overview

A sworn account is not a type of account parties prospectively enter into, but rather refers to the plaintiff's use of Texas Rule of Civil Procedure 185.[249] When a plaintiff files a verified petition that conforms to Rule 185, the defendant must file a verified denial or the account is deemed to exist as the plaintiff swore.

3-7:1.1 Related Causes of Action

Suit on an account, Usury, Breach of Contract, Quantum Meruit

MUST READ CASES

Powers v. Adams, 2 S.W.3d 496 (Tex. App.—Houston [14th Dist.] 1999, no pet.)

Woodhaven Partners, Ltd. v. Shamoun & Norman, L.L.P., 422 S.W.3d 821 (Tex. App.—Dallas 2014)

3-7:2 Elements

(1) The account must be one for goods, wares, merchandise, or services rendered.[250]

- Open accounts and stated accounts fall within the scope of Rule 185.[251]
- Although some courts have held that a credit-card account is an "open account" for limitations purposes,[252] a credit-card account is likely not within the scope of Rule 185.[253]

---

duress, or compulsion; (3) with full knowledge of the facts; (4) because the person was ignorant or mistaken about the law.).

[247] *Bryan v. Citizens Nat'l Bank in Abilene*, 628 S.W.2d 761, 763 (Tex. 1982) (A defendant who, in reliance on the money, materially changes his position, will generally be immune from recovery.).

[248] *Best Buy Co. v. Barrera*, 248 S.W.3d 160, 163 (Tex. 2007).

[249] *Meaders v. Biskamp*, 316 S.W.2d 75, 78 (Tex. 1958).

[250] Tex. R. Civ. P. 185; *Hollingsworth v. Nw. Nat'l Ins. Co.*, 522 S.W.2d 242, 245 (Tex. Civ. App.—Texarkana 1975, no writ).

[251] *Long v. Miken Oil, Inc.*, No. 12-13-00252-CV, 2014 Tex. App. LEXIS 9189, at *29–30 (App.—Tyler Aug. 20, 2014).

[252] *Bank of Am. v. Jeff Taylor LLC*, 358 S.W.3d 848, 859 (Tex. App.—Tyler 2012, no pet.); *Capital One Bank (USA), N.A. v. Conti*, 345 S.W.3d 490, 491 (Tex. App.—San Antonio 2011, no pet.); *Eaves v. Unifund CCR Partners*, 301 S.W.3d 402, 408–09 (Tex. App.—El Paso 2009, no pet.).

[253] E.g. *Dulong v. Citibank (South Dakota), N.A.*, 261 S.W.3d 890, 893 n.3 (Tex. App.—Dallas 2008, no pet.); *Williams v. Unifund CCR Partners Assignee of Citibank*, 264 S.W.3d 231, 234 (Tex. App.—Houston [1st Dist.] 2008, no pet.).

(2) The account was systematically recorded.[254]

AND

(3) The account is sworn to in a verified petition.[255]
- The plaintiff files a verified petition stating:
  - The account is just and true;
  - The account is due; and
  - That all just and lawful offsets, payments and credits have been applied.[256]

3-7:3 Damages and Remedies

3-7:3.1 Generally

The damages and remedies available on the underlying account apply. For a list of available damages and remedies, *see*

Chapter 3—suit on an account.

3-7:3.2 Effect of Verified Petition

An account will be deemed to exist if the defendant does not file a verified denial of the account.[257]

3-7:4 Defenses

3-7:4.1 Generally

The defenses available to the underlying account apply. For a list of available defenses, *see* Chapter 3—suit on an account. In order to put on proof disputing the existence of the account, the defendant must file a verified denial of the account.[258] A defendant need not file a verified denial in response to a plaintiff's verified petition in order to assert a confession and avoidance defense.[259]

3-7:5 Procedural Implications

3-7:5.1 Pleading

The plaintiff's verified petition must include:

---

[254] Tex. R. Civ. P. 185.
[255] Tex. R. Civ. P. 185.
[256] Tex. R. Civ. P. 185.
[257] Tex. R. Civ. P. 185; *Rizk v. Fin. Guardian Ins. Agency, Inc.*, 584 S.W.2d 860, 862 (Tex. 1979).
[258] Tex. R. Civ. P. 185.
[259] *Wauson & Williams, Architects, Inc. v. Reeder Dev. Corp.*, 572 S.W.2d 24, 26 (Tex. Civ. App.—Houston [1st Dist.] 1978, no writ).

CONTRACT AND COMMERCIAL LITIGATION

- An itemized statement of the goods or services sold;[260]
- Facts which show the account was kept systematically;[261]
- A statement that he account is just and true;[262]
- A statement that any offsets, payments, or credits have been applied;[263] and
- A statement that the balance is due and owing.[264]

3-8 Suit on an Account

3-8:1 Overview

Parties may keep open or stated accounts to record transactions between them. When the debtor defaults on a payment, the creditor may pursue a suit on an account. Plaintiffs should always attempt to file a verified petition for a Suit on a Sworn Account under Texas Rule of Civil Procedure 185.

3-8:1.1 Related Causes of Action

Suit on a Sworn Account, Usury, Breach of Contract, Quantum Meruit

MUST READ CASES

Capital One Bank (USA), N.A. v. Conti, 345 S.W.3d 490 (Tex. App.—San Antonio 2011, no pet.)

Wing Aviation, L.L.C. v. Balmanno, No. 09-06-022-CV, 2006 Tex. App. LEXIS 7447 (App.—Beaumont Aug. 24, 2006)

Livingston Ford Mercury, Inc. v. Haley, 997 S.W.2d 425 (Tex. App.—Beaumont 1999, no pet.)

3-8:2 Elements

3-8:2.1 Suit on an Open Account

(1) An open account exists.

(1)(a) Transactions between the parties.[265]

---

[260] Tex. R. Civ. P. 185; *Powers v. Adams*, 2 S.W.3d 496, 498 (Tex. App.—Houston [14th Dist.] 1999, no pet.) (An itemized statement of the goods and services sold is only required if the court sustains a defendant's exception to the pleadings.).

[261] Tex. R. Civ. P. 185; *Powers v. Adams*, 2 S.W.3d 496, 498 (Tex. App.—Houston [14th Dist.] 1999, no pet.).

[262] *Powers v. Adams*, 2 S.W.3d 496, 498 (Tex. App.—Houston [14th Dist.] 1999, no pet.).

[263] *Powers v. Adams*, 2 S.W.3d 496, 498 (Tex. App.—Houston [14th Dist.] 1999, no pet.).

[264] *Powers v. Adams*, 2 S.W.3d 496, 498 (Tex. App.—Houston [14th Dist.] 1999, no pet.).

[265] *Capital One Bank (USA), N.A. v. Conti*, 345 S.W.3d 490, 491 (Tex. App.—San Antonio 2011, no pet.); *McJam, Inc. v. CD Auto Serv.*, No. 04-17-00849-CV, 2018 Tex. App. LEXIS 9966, at *6 (Tex. App.—San Antonio Dec. 5, 2018, no pet.).

- The transactions may be sales of personal property or completion of services.[266]
- The goods or services do not necessarily have to pass between the two parties to the account, but could pass between third parties.[267]

(1)(b) Creating a creditor-debtor relationship through the general course of dealing.[268]

(1)(c) With the account still being open.[269]

- An "open" account is one in which nothing has occurred to bind either party to price or time of payment.[270]
- A "stated" account is one in which each item within it has been agreed to as to the price and time of payment.[271]

(1)(d) With the expectation of further dealing.[272]

(2) The amount due on the account is just or the amount due is reasonable, customary and usual.[273]

- A "just" amount is one that is expressly agreed to by the parties.[274]

(3) The account is due and owing.[275]

3-8:2.2 Suit on an Account Stated

(1) The sale and delivery of merchandise or performance of services.[276]

- A "stated" account is one in which each item within it has been agreed to as to the price and time of payment.[277]

---

[266] *Eaves v. Unifund CCR Partners*, 301 S.W.3d 402, 408 (Tex. App.—El Paso 2009).

[267] *Bank of Am. v. Jeff Taylor LLC*, 358 S.W.3d 848, 859 (Tex. App.—Tyler 2012, no pet.).

[268] *Capital One Bank (USA), N.A. v. Conti*, 345 S.W.3d 490, 491 (Tex. App.—San Antonio 2011, no pet.); *McJam, Inc. v. CD Auto Serv.*, No. 04-17-00849-CV, 2018 Tex. App. LEXIS 9966, at *6 (Tex. App.—San Antonio Dec. 5, 2018, no pet.).

[269] *Capital One Bank (USA), N.A. v. Conti*, 345 S.W.3d 490, 491 (Tex. App.—San Antonio 2011, no pet.); *McJam, Inc. v. CD Auto Serv.*, No. 04-17-00849-CV, 2018 Tex. App. LEXIS 9966, at *6 (Tex. App.—San Antonio Dec. 5, 2018, no pet.).

[270] *Schucht v. Stidham*, 37 S.W.2d 214, 215 (Tex. Civ. App.—Fort Worth 1930, no writ).

[271] *Schucht v. Stidham*, 37 S.W.2d 214, 215 (Tex. Civ. App.—Fort Worth 1930, no writ).

[272] *Capital One Bank (USA), N.A. v. Conti*, 345 S.W.3d 490, 491 (Tex. App.—San Antonio 2011, no pet.); *McJam, Inc. v. CD Auto Serv.*, No. 04-17-00849-CV, 2018 Tex. App. LEXIS 9966, at *6 (Tex. App.—San Antonio Dec. 5, 2018, no pet.).

[273] *Powers v. Adams*, 2 S.W.3d 496, 499 (Tex. App.—Houston [14th Dist.] 1999, no pet.).

[274] *Powers v. Adams*, 2 S.W.3d 496, 499 (Tex. App.—Houston [14th Dist.] 1999, no pet.).

[275] *Powers v. Adams*, 2 S.W.3d 496, 499 (Tex. App.—Houston [14th Dist.] 1999, no pet.).

[276] *Powers v. Adams*, 2 S.W.3d 496, 499 (Tex. App.—Houston [14th Dist.] 1999, no pet.); *Breakwater Advanced Mfg., LLC v. E. Tex. Mach. Works, Inc.*, No. 12-19-00013-CV, 2020 Tex. App. LEXIS 1437, at *11–12 (Tex. App.—Tyler Feb. 19, 2020, no pet. h.).

[277] *Schucht v. Stidham*, 37 S.W.2d 214, 215 (Tex. Civ. App.—Fort Worth 1930, no writ).

CONTRACT AND COMMERCIAL LITIGATION

(2) The amount due on the account is just or the amount due is reasonable, customary and usual.[278]

- A "just" amount is one that is expressly agreed to by the parties.[279]

(3) The account is due and owing[280]

3-8:3 Damages and Remedies

3-8:3.1 Actual Damages

The plaintiff may recover the amount due and owing.[281]

3-8:3.2 Prejudgment Interest

In the absence of contract, a creditor may recover prejudgment interest at the statutory rate.[282]

3-8:3.3 Attorney's Fees

Attorney's fees are appropriate under Texas Civil Practice and Remedies Code Section 38.001.[283]

3-8:4 Defenses

3-8:4.1 Statute of Limitations

The four-year limitations period applies.[284] The cause of action accrues at the time the dealings in which the parties were interested together cease.[285] To establish when dealings have ceased, a defendant must prove more than the date of last payment.[286] A defendant need not file a verified denial in response to a plaintiff's verified petition in order to assert a confession and avoidance defense.[287]

---

[278] *Powers v. Adams*, 2 S.W.3d 496, 499 (Tex. App.—Houston [14th Dist.] 1999, no pet.); *Breakwater Advanced Mfg., LLC v. E. Tex. Mach. Works, Inc.*, No. 12-19-00013-CV, 2020 Tex. App. LEXIS 1437, at *11–12 (Tex. App.—Tyler Feb. 19, 2020, no pet. h.).

[279] *Powers v. Adams*, 2 S.W.3d 496, 499 (Tex. App.—Houston [14th Dist.] 1999, no pet.).

[280] *Powers v. Adams*, 2 S.W.3d 496, 499 (Tex. App.—Houston [14th Dist.] 1999, no pet.); *Breakwater Advanced Mfg., LLC v. E. Tex. Mach. Works, Inc.*, No. 12-19-00013-CV, 2020 Tex. App. LEXIS 1437, at *11–12 (Tex. App.—Tyler Feb. 19, 2020, no pet. h.).

[281] *See Bank of Am. v. Jeff Taylor LLC*, 358 S.W.3d 848, 855 (Tex. App.—Tyler 2012, no pet.).

[282] Tex. Fin. Code Ann. § 302.002.

[283] Tex. Civ. Prac. & Rem. Code Ann. § 38.001; *Great Global Assurance Co. v. Keltex Properties*, 904 S.W.2d 771, 775–776 (Tex. App.—Corpus Christi 1995).

[284] Tex. Civ. Prac. & Rem. Code Ann. § 16.004(c).

[285] Tex. Civ. Prac. & Rem. Code Ann. § 16.004(c).

[286] *Capital One Bank (USA), N.A. v. Conti*, 345 S.W.3d 490, 492 (Tex. App.—San Antonio 2011, no pet.).

[287] *Wauson & Williams, Architects, Inc. v. Reeder Dev. Corp.*, 572 S.W.2d 24, 26 (Tex. Civ. App.—Houston [1st Dist.] 1978, no writ).

3-8:4.2 Payment

Payment on an account is an appropriate defense.[288] A defendant need not file a verified denial in response to a plaintiff's verified petition in order to assert a confession and avoidance defense.[289]

3-8:4.3 Accord and Satisfaction

Accord and satisfaction is an appropriate defense.[290] A defendant need not file a verified denial in response to a plaintiff's verified petition in order to assert a confession and avoidance defense.[291]

3-8:4.4 Failure of Consideration

Failure of consideration is an appropriate defense.[292] A defendant need not file a verified denial in response to a plaintiff's verified petition in order to assert a confession and avoidance defense.[293]

3-8:4.5 Other Affirmative Defenses

Other affirmative defenses likely available include:

- Fraud;
- Discharge in bankruptcy;
- Release;
- Duress; and
- Statute of frauds.[294]

A defendant need not file a verified denial in response to a plaintiff's verified petition in order to assert a confession and avoidance defense.[295]

---

[288] Tex. R. Civ. P. 94; *Chapin & Chapin v. Tex. Sand & Gravel*, 844 S.W.2d 664, 664–65 (Tex. 1992).

[289] *Wauson & Williams, Architects, Inc. v. Reeder Dev. Corp.*, 572 S.W.2d 24, 26 (Tex. Civ. App.—Houston [1st Dist.] 1978, no writ).

[290] Tex. R. Civ. P. 94; *Jeffrey v. Larry Plotnick Co., Inc.*, 532 S.W.2d 99, 101 (Tex. Civ. App.—Dallas 1975, no writ).

[291] *Wauson & Williams, Architects, Inc. v. Reeder Dev. Corp.*, 572 S.W.2d 24, 26 (Tex. Civ. App.—Houston [1st Dist.] 1978, no writ).

[292] Tex. R. Civ. P. 94; *Wauson & Williams, Architects, Inc. v. Reeder Dev. Corp.*, 572 S.W.2d 24, 26 (Tex. Civ. App.—Houston [1st Dist.] 1978, no writ).

[293] *Wauson & Williams, Architects, Inc. v. Reeder Dev. Corp.*, 572 S.W.2d 24, 26 (Tex. Civ. App.—Houston [1st Dist.] 1978, no writ).

[294] Tex. R. Civ. P. 94.

[295] *Wauson & Williams, Architects, Inc. v. Reeder Dev. Corp.*, 572 S.W.2d 24, 26 (Tex. Civ. App.—Houston [1st Dist.] 1978, no writ).

CONTRACT AND COMMERCIAL LITIGATION

3-8:5 Procedural Implications

3-8:5.1 Pleading—As Sworn Account

A suit on an account may be pleaded as a sworn account.[296] Special pleading requirements apply when swearing to an account.[297]

3-9 Bailment Actions—Bailee's Liability

3-9:1 Overview

Parties may enter into a bailment agreement in which the bailor delivers possession of real property to a bailee, who in turn promises to return the property to the bailor. Despite the relationship's contractual nature, the bailor may sue the bailee for negligence and conversion, as well as breach of the bailment agreement.

3-9:1.1 Related Causes of Action

Conversion, Breach of Contract, Trespass to Personalty, Trover, Negligence

MUST READ CASES

Prime Prods., Inc. v. S.S.I. Plastics, Inc., 97 S.W.3d 631 (Tex. App.—Houston [1st Dist.] 2002, pet. denied)

Maddux v. Reid, No. 10-13-00174-CV, 2015 Tex. App. LEXIS 6245, at *4–6 (App.—Waco June 18, 2015)

3-9:2 Elements

(1) A bailment agreement exists.[298]

(1) (a) Delivery of personal property for a specific purpose

- The property which is the subject of the bailment must be delivered to the bailee.[299]
- Specific purposes may include:
- Those solely benefitting the bailee or the bailor;[300] or
- Those mutually benefitting each party.[301]

---

[296] Tex. R. Civ. P. 185.
[297] Tex. R. Civ. P. 185.
[298] *See Cessna Aircraft Co. v. Aircraft Network, L.L.C.*, 213 S.W.3d 455, 462 (Tex. App.—Dallas 2006, pet. denied).
[299] *Smith v. Radam, Inc.*, 51 S.W.3d 413, 418–419 (Tex. App.—Houston [1st Dist.] 2001).
[300] A gratuitous bailment is one that is not for the mutual benefit of both parties. *See Andrews v. Allen*, 724 S.W.2d 893, 895–96 (Tex. App.—Austin 1987).
[301] A bailment benefits both parties if the purpose of the bailment is for the bailee and bailor to obtain some benefit or profit from the bailment. *Bill Bell, Inc. v. Ramsey*, 284 S.W.2d 244, 247 (Tex. Civ. App.—Waco 1955, no writ).

(1) (b) Acceptance by the transferee of such delivery;

- The property which is the subject of the bailment must be accepted by the bailee.[302]
- A bailee accepts property which it knows, or should know, has been delivered.[303]

(1) (c) An agreement that the purpose will be fulfilled

- A bailment agreement may be express or implied.[304] A bailment agreement may be oral.[305]

(1) (d) An understanding that property will be returned

- The bailee may not expect to permanently keep the property which is the subject of the bailment.[306]
- The bailee must return the property to the bailor, or dispose of the property as directed by the bailor.[307]

(2) The bailee breached a duty under the agreement

- The common law imposes varying standards of care for the different classifications of bailments.[308]
- In a bailment for mutual benefit, the bailee is held to a negligence standard of care.[309]
- In a bailment solely for the benefit of the bailor, the bailee is held to a gross negligence standard.[310]
- In a bailment solely for the benefit of the bailee, the bailee is responsible for "slight neglect."[311]

---

[302] *Allright Auto Parks, Inc. v. Moore*, 560 S.W.2d 129, 130 (Tex. Civ. App.—San Antonio 1977, writ ref'd n.r.e.).

[303] *Shamrock Hilton Hotel v. Caranas*, 488 S.W.2d 151, 155 (Tex. Civ. App.—Houston [14th Dist.] 1972, writ ref'd n.r.e.).

[304] *Sanroc Co. Intern. v. Roadrunner Transp., Inc.*, 596 S.W.2d 320, 322 (Tex. Civ. App.—Houston [1st Dist.] 1980, no writ).

[305] *Stewart & Stevenson Servs., Inc. v. Kratochvil*, 737 S.W.2d 65, 66 (Tex. App.—San Antonio 1987, no writ).

[306] *English v. Dhane*, 294 S.W.2d 709, 711 (Tex. 1956).

[307] *English v. Dhane*, 294 S.W.2d 709, 711 (Tex. 1956).

[308] *See Prime Prods., Inc. v. S.S.I. Plastics, Inc.*, 97 S.W.3d 631, 635 (Tex. App.—Houston [1st Dist.] 2002, pet. denied).

[309] *Prime Prods., Inc. v. S.S.I. Plastics, Inc.*, 97 S.W.3d 631, 635 (Tex. App.—Houston [1st Dist.] 2002, pet. denied).

[310] *Granberry v. Tex. Pub. Serv. Co.*, 171 S.W.2d 184, 187 (Tex. Civ. App.—Amarillo 1943, no writ).

[311] *Citizens' Nat'l Bank of Jasper v. Ratcliff & Lanier*, 253 S.W. 253, 258 (Tex. Comm'n App. 1923).

CONTRACT AND COMMERCIAL LITIGATION

- In a bailment for mutual benefit where the plaintiff has established a prima facie case,[312] the plaintiff is afforded a rebuttable presumption that the bailee acted negligently.[313]
  - The rebuttable presumption might not apply to losses caused by fire or theft.[314]
  - The bailee's standard of care may be enlarged or limited by the bailment agreement.[315]
  - To enlarge or limit the bailee's standard of care, the parties must use express and clear language in the agreement.[316]
  - A bailee is only responsible for that property it knows, or should know, it possesses.[317]
- (3) Which proximately caused damages to the plaintiff
  - Generally, a bailee is liable only for the consequence of his breach.[318]
  - A bailment agreement may modify the general rule and make the bailee an insurer.[319]

3-9:3 Damages and Remedies

3-9:3.1 Generally

A bailor-plaintiff may seek damages based upon the bailee's breach of the bailment agreement or upon the bailee's conversion of the bailor's property.[320]

3-9:3.2 Actual Damages

Actual costs or expenses of replacement are available for a conversion.[321]

---

[312] A prima facie case involves proof of: (1) bailment; (2) that the property was delivered to the bailee in good condition; and (3) that the property was either damaged or not returned by the bailee. *Trammell v. Whitlock*, 150 Tex. 500, 504, 242 S.W.2d 157, 159 (1951).

[313] *Sanroc Co. Intern. v. Roadrunner Transp., Inc.*, 596 S.W.2d 320, 322 (Tex. Civ. App.—Houston [1st Dist.] 1980, no writ).

[314] *Lufkin Indus., Inc. v. Mission Chevrolet, Inc.*, 614 S.W.2d 596, 597–99 (Tex. App.—Waco 1981).

[315] *Prime Prods., Inc. v. S.S.I. Plastics, Inc.*, 97 S.W.3d 631, 635–36 (Tex. App.—Houston [1st Dist.] 2002, pet. denied).

[316] *Bank One, Tex., N.A. v. Stewart*, 967 S.W.2d 419, 432 (Tex. App.—Houston [14th Dist.] 1998, pet. denied).

[317] *Shamrock Hilton Hotel v. Caranas*, 488 S.W.2d 151, 155 (Tex. Civ. App.—Houston [14th Dist.] 1972, writ ref'd n.r.e.).

[318] *Prime Prods., Inc. v. S.S.I. Plastics, Inc.*, 97 S.W.3d 631, 636 (Tex. App.—Houston [1st Dist.] 2002, pet. denied).

[319] *Prime Prods., Inc. v. S.S.I. Plastics, Inc.*, 97 S.W.3d 631, 636 (Tex. App.—Houston [1st Dist.] 2002, pet. denied).

[320] *Barker v. Eckman*, 213 S.W.3d 306, 310 (Tex. 2006).

[321] *International Freight Forwarding, Inc. v. Am. Flange*, 993 S.W.2d 262, 271 (Tex. App.—San Antonio 1999, no pet.).

Actual damages are available for any property damage or holdover by the bailee.[322]

3-9:3.3 Liquidated Damages

A bailment agreement may specify a rental rate in the event of the bailee's holdover.[323]

3-9:3.4 Attorney's Fees

A litigant may recover attorney's fees under Chapter 38 of the Texas Civil Practice and Remedies Code.[324]

3-9:3.5 Lost Profits

Lost profits are available as a special damages element.[325]

3-9:3.6 Interest

Prejudgment interest is available for a conversion.[326] Prejudgment interest is required for any property damage.[327]

3-9:3.7 Loss of Use

Loss of use is an appropriate damages measure.

3-9:3.8 Repossession

A bailment agreement may grant a bailor the right to repossess his property.[328]

3-9:3.9 Acceleration

A bailment agreement may grant a bailor the right to accelerate any payments due under the agreement.[329]

---

[322] *Anchor Cas. Co. v. Robertson Transp. Co.*, 389 S.W.2d 135, 138 (Tex. Civ. App.—Corpus Christi 1965, writ ref'd n.r.e.).

[323] *Page v. Marshall*, 347 S.W.2d 656, 657 (Tex. Civ. App.—Austin 1961, no writ).

[324] Tex. Civ. Prac. & Rem. Code Ann. §§ 38.001-38.006 (authorizing the recovery of attorney's fees under a written or oral contract and providing for applicable presumptions and exceptions to such an authorization).

[325] *Smith-Hamm, Inc. v. Equip. Connection*, 946 S.W.2d 458, 461 (Tex. App.—Houston [14th Dist.] 1997, no writ).

[326] *International Freight Forwarding, Inc. v. Am. Flange*, 993 S.W.2d 262, 271 (Tex. App.—San Antonio 1999, no pet.).

[327] Tex. Fin. Code Ann. § 304.102.

[328] *Young v. J. F. Zimmerman & Sons, Inc.*, 434 S.W.2d 926, 927–28 (Tex. Civ. App.—Waco 1968, writ dism'd).

[329] *Young v. J. F. Zimmerman & Sons, Inc.*, 434 S.W.2d 926, 927–28 (Tex. Civ. App.—Waco 1968, writ dism'd).

CONTRACT AND COMMERCIAL LITIGATION

3-9:3.10 Exemplary Damages

Exemplary damages are available if the plaintiff proves the bailee converted his property.[330]

Exemplary damages are available if the bailee acts:

- Maliciously;
- Fraudulently; or
- With gross negligence.[331]

3-9:4 Defenses

3-9:4.1 Statute of Limitations

- The two-year limitations period applies to conversions.[332] The four-year limitations period applies to breach of contract damages.[333]
- Cause of action accrues at the earlier of the time:
  - When the bailor makes demand upon the bailee; or
  - If demand is nonexistent or ineffective, then when the bailor receives actual notice of conduct by the bailee which is inconsistent with the bailor's rights.[334]
- The discovery rule may apply.[335]

3-9:4.2 Failure of Consideration

Failure of consideration is a valid defense and must be verified.[336]

3-9:4.3 Denial of Execution

- Denial of execution is a valid defense to a bailment.[337]
- Denial of execution must be verified.[338]

---

[330] *McVea v. Verkins*, 587 S.W.2d 526, 531 (Tex. Civ. App.—Corpus Christi 1979, no writ).
[331] Tex. Civ. Prac. & Rem. Code Ann. § 41.003(a).
[332] Tex. Civ. Prac. & Rem. Code Ann. § 16.003.
[333] Tex. Civ. Prac. & Rem. Code Ann. §§ 16.004(a)(3), 16.051.
[334] *Barker v. Eckman*, 213 S.W.3d 306, 311 (Tex. 2006).
[335] *Barker v. Eckman*, 213 S.W.3d 306, 311 (Tex. 2006).
[336] Tex. R. Civ. P. 93(9).
[337] *Safway Scaffolds Co. of Hous. v. Sharpstown Realty Co.*, 409 S.W.2d 883, 885 (Tex. Civ. App.—Waco 1966, no writ).
[338] Tex. R. Civ. P. 93(7).

3-10 Bailment Actions—Bailor's Liability

3-10:1 Overview

Parties may enter into a bailment agreement in which the bailor delivers possession of property to a bailee, who in turn promises to return the property to the bailor. A bailor's liability is often tied to negligent entrustment, a defect in the subject of the bailment or contractual duties.

3-10:1.1 Related Causes of Action

Negligent Entrustment, Breach of Contract, Implied Warranty of Fitness, Implied Warranty of Merchantability, Implied Warranty of Suitability, Products Liability[339]

MUST READ CASES

Prime Prods., Inc. v. S.S.I. Plastics, Inc., 97 S.W.3d 631 (Tex. App.—Houston [1st Dist.] 2002, pet. denied)

Maddux v. Reid, No. 10-13-00174-CV, 2015 Tex. App. LEXIS 6245, at *4-6 (App.—Waco June 18, 2015)

3-10:2 Elements

3-10:2.1 Liability for Defects in the Subject of the Bailment

(1) A bailment agreement exists

- A bailment agreement must exist for a plaintiff to bring suit on the bailment.[340]

(1)(a) Delivery of personal property for a specific purpose

- The property which is the subject of the bailment must be delivered to the bailee.[341]
- Specific purposes may include:
  - Those solely benefitting the bailee or the bailor;[342] or
  - Those mutually benefitting each party.[343]

(1)(b) Acceptance by the transferee of such delivery;

---

[339] Not included in this publication.
[340] *See Cessna Aircraft Co. v. Aircraft Network, L.L.C.*, 213 S.W.3d 455, 462 (Tex. App.—Dallas 2006, pet. denied).
[341] *Allright Auto Parks, Inc. v. Moore*, 560 S.W.2d 129, 130 (Tex. Civ. App.—San Antonio 1977, writ ref'd n.r.e.).
[342] A gratuitous bailment is one that is not for the mutual benefit of both parties. *See Bill Bell, Inc. v. Ramsey*, 284 S.W.2d 244, 247 (Tex. Civ. App.—Waco 1955, no writ).
[343] *Bill Bell, Inc. v. Ramsey*, 284 S.W.2d 244, 247 (Tex. Civ. App.—Waco 1955, no writ) (A bailment benefits both parties if the purpose of the bailment is for the bailee and bailor to obtain some benefit or profit from the bailment.).

CONTRACT AND COMMERCIAL LITIGATION

- The property which is the subject of the bailment must be accepted by the bailee.[344]
- A bailee accepts property which it knows, or should know, has been delivered.[345]

(1)(c) An agreement that the purpose will be fulfilled

- A bailment agreement may be express or implied.[346]
- A bailment agreement may be oral.[347]

(1)(d) An understanding that property will be returned

- The bailee may not expect to permanently keep the property which is the subject of the bailment.[348]
- The bailee must return the property to the bailor, or dispose of the property as directed by the bailor.[349]

(2) The bailor breached a duty under the agreement or at common law

- The common law imposes a varying standard of care for the different classifications of bailments.[350]
- In a bailment for mutual benefit, the bailor must make a reasonable inspection of the bailed property and warn the bailee of any defects in the property about which the bailor knows, or should know.[351]
- In a bailment solely for the benefit of the bailee, the bailor must disclose only those defects which he is aware of and which make the use of the property perilous.[352]
- The bailor's standard of care may be enlarged or limited by the bailment agreement.[353]
- If the bailment falls under Article 2 of the Uniform Commercial code, the bailor makes these contractual implied warranties:
  - Fitness[354]
  - Merchantability[355]

---

[344] *Allright Auto Parks, Inc. v. Moore*, 560 S.W.2d 129, 130 (Tex. Civ. App.—San Antonio 1977, writ ref'd n.r.e.).
[345] *Russell v. Am. Real Estate Corp.*, 89 S.W.3d 204, 210–11 (Tex. App.—Corpus Christi 2002).
[346] *Sanroc Co. Intern. v. Roadrunner Transp., Inc.*, 596 S.W.2d 320, 322 (Tex. Civ. App.—Houston [1st Dist.] 1980, no writ).
[347] *Stewart & Stevenson Servs., Inc. v. Kratochvil*, 737 S.W.2d 65, 66 (Tex. App.—San Antonio 1987, no writ).
[348] *English v. Dhane*, 294 S.W.2d 709, 711 (Tex. 1956).
[349] *English v. Dhane*, 294 S.W.2d 709, 711 (Tex. 1956).
[350] *See Prime Prods., Inc. v. S.S.I. Plastics, Inc.*, 97 S.W.3d 631, 635 (Tex. App.—Houston [1st Dist.] 2002, pet. denied).
[351] 8A Am. Jur. 2d, Bailments § 102.
[352] 8A Am. Jur. 2d, Bailments § 99.
[353] *See Prime Prods., Inc. v. S.S.I. Plastics, Inc.*, 97 S.W.3d 631, 635–36 (Tex. App.—Houston [1st Dist.] 2002, pet. denied).
[354] *See* Chapter 3, Section 3-10.
[355] *See* Chapter 3, Section 3-9.

- To enlarge or limit the bailor's standard of care, the parties must use express and clear language in the agreement.[356]

(3) Which proximately caused damages to the plaintiff[357]

- Generally, a bailee is liable only for the consequence of his breach.[358]
- A bailment agreement may modify the general rule and make the bailor an insurer.[359]

3-10:2.2 Liability to a Third Party/Negligent Entrustment

(1) Entrustment of a chattel by the owner.[360] Generally, the chattel must be a vehicle.[361]

(2) To an incompetent person.[362]

(3) That the owner knew or should have known to be incompetent.[363]

(4) That the person was negligent on the occasion in question.[364]

(5) That the person's negligence proximately caused the accident.[365]

Proximate cause exists when the defendant entrustor should be reasonably able to anticipate that an injury would result as a natural and probable consequence of the entrustment.[366]

---

[356] *See Bank One, Tex., N.A. v. Stewart*, 967 S.W.2d 419, 432 (Tex. App.—Houston [14th Dist.] 1998, pet. denied).

[357] Proximate cause would not be a required element if the parties agreed the bailee would act as an insurer of the bailed property.

[358] *Prime Prods., Inc. v. S.S.I. Plastics, Inc.*, 97 S.W.3d 631, 636 (Tex. App.—Houston [1st Dist.] 2002, pet. denied).

[359] *Prime Prods., Inc. v. S.S.I. Plastics, Inc.*, 97 S.W.3d 631, 636 (Tex. App.—Houston [1st Dist.] 2002, pet. denied).

[360] *Schneider v. Esperanza Transmission Co.*, 744 S.W.2d 595, 596 (Tex. 1987); *National Convenience Stores, Inc. v. T.T. Barge Cleaning Co.*, 883 S.W.2d 684, 687 (Tex. App.—Dallas 1994, writ denied).

[361] *National Convenience Stores, Inc. v. T.T. Barge Cleaning Co.*, 883 S.W.2d 684, 687 (Tex. App.—Dallas 1994, writ denied).

[362] *Schneider v. Esperanza Transmission Co.*, 744 S.W.2d 595, 596 (Tex. 1987); *National Convenience Stores, Inc. v. T.T. Barge Cleaning Co.*, 883 S.W.2d 684, 687 (Tex. App.—Dallas 1994, writ denied).

[363] *Schneider v. Esperanza Transmission Co.*, 744 S.W.2d 595, 596 (Tex. 1987); *National Convenience Stores, Inc. v. T.T. Barge Cleaning Co.*, 883 S.W.2d 684, 687 (Tex. App.—Dallas 1994, writ denied).

[364] *Schneider v. Esperanza Transmission Co.*, 744 S.W.2d 595, 596 (Tex. 1987); *National Convenience Stores, Inc. v. T.T. Barge Cleaning Co.*, 883 S.W.2d 684, 687 (Tex. App.—Dallas 1994, writ denied).

[365] *Schneider v. Esperanza Transmission Co.*, 744 S.W.2d 595, 596 (Tex. 1987); *National Convenience Stores, Inc. v. T.T. Barge Cleaning Co.*, 883 S.W.2d 684, 687 (Tex. App.—Dallas 1994, writ denied).

[366] *Schneider v. Esperanza Transmission Co.*, 744 S.W.2d 595, 596 (Tex. 1987).

CONTRACT AND COMMERCIAL LITIGATION

3-10:3 Damages and Remedies

3-10:3.1 Actual Damages

Actual damages are available for the bailor's wrongful withholding of the subject of the bailment.[367]

A bailee may also recover expenses for remodeling or formatting the subject of the bailment.[368]

Actual damages are available for negligent entrustment.[369]

3-10:3.2 Liquidated Damages

A bailment agreement may contain a liquidated damages provision.[370]

3-10:3.3 Attorney's Fees

A litigant may recover attorney's fees under Chapter 38 of the Texas Civil Practice and Remedies Code.[371]

3-10:3.4 Lost Profits

Lost profits are available to a bailee as a special damages element.[372]

3-10:3.5 Interest

Prejudgment interest is available for a conversion.[373]

Prejudgment interest is required for any property damage.[374]

3-10:3.6 Exemplary Damages

Exemplary damages are available for a negligent entrustment or otherwise available if the entrustor acts:

- Maliciously;

- Fraudulently; or

---

[367] *See Barker v. Eckman*, 213 S.W.3d 306 (Tex. 2006).
[368] *Hubbard v. Goode*, 335 P.2d 1063, 1065 (N.M. 1959).
[369] *See Schneider v. Esperanza Transmission Co.*, 744 S.W.2d 595, 596 (Tex. 1987).
[370] *Robinson v. Granite Equip. Leasing Corp.*, 553 S.W.2d 633, 637 (Tex. Civ. App.—Houston [1st Dist.] 1977, writ ref'd n.r.e.).
[371] Tex. Civ. Prac. & Rem. Code Ann. §§ 38.001-38.006 (authorizing the recovery of attorney's fees under a written or oral contract).
[372] *Hubbard v. Goode*, P.2d 1063, 1065 (N.M. 1959).
[373] *International Freight Forwarding, Inc. v. Am. Flange*, 993 S.W.2d 262, 271 (Tex. App.—San Antonio 1999, no pet.).
[374] Tex. Fin. Code Ann. § 304.102.

- With gross negligence.[375,376]

3-10:4 Defenses

3-10:4.1 Statute of Limitations

- The two-year limitations period applies to conversion, damage to property and personal injury claims.[377]
- The four-year limitations period applies to breach of contract damages.[378]
- The cause of action accrues at the earlier of the time:
  - When the bailee makes demand upon the bailor; or
  - If demand is nonexistent or ineffective, then when the bailor receives actual notice of conduct by the bailee which is inconsistent with the bailee's rights.[379]
- The discovery rule may apply.[380]

3-10:4.2 Failure of Consideration

Failure of consideration is a valid defense and must be verified.[381]

3-10:4.3 Denial of Execution

Denial of execution is a valid defense to a bailment.[382]

Denial of execution must be verified.[383]

3-10:4.4 Negligent Entrustment Defenses

For a complete list of negligent entrustment defenses, *see* Chapter 1: Negligence.

3-11 Agency Actions—Agent's Action Binding on the Principal

3-11:1 Overview

In this context, whether a person is an agent is not a cause of action in itself, but is rather a means to ascertain whether the agent, principal or both are liable on an obligation. As a general rule, the principal is bound to the contracts an agent enters into

---

[375] Tex. Civ. Prac. & Rem. Code Ann. § 41.003(a); *Schneider v. Esperanza Transmission Co.*, 744 S.W.2d 595, 596 (Tex. 1987).
[376] Tex. Civ. Prac. & Rem. Code Ann. § 41.003(a); *Schneider v. Esperanza Transmission Co.*, 744 S.W.2d 595, 596 (Tex. 1987).
[377] Tex. Civ. Prac. & Rem. Code Ann. § 16.003.
[378] Tex. Civ. Prac. & Rem. Code Ann. §§ 16.004(a)(3), 16.051.
[379] *Barker v. Eckman*, 213 S.W.3d 306, 311 (Tex. 2006).
[380] *Barker v. Eckman*, 213 S.W.3d 306, 311 (Tex. 2006).
[381] Tex. R. Civ. P. 93(9).
[382] *Bauer v. Valley Bank of El Paso*, 560 S.W.2d 520, 522 (Tex. Civ. App.—El Paso 1977).
[383] Tex. R. Civ. P. 93(7).

CONTRACT AND COMMERCIAL LITIGATION

on the principal's behalf. Moreover, a principal may be liable for its agent's tortious conduct.

3-11:1.1 Related Causes of Action

Agency Actions: Agent's Liability to Third Parties, Agency Actions: Agent's Breach of Duty of Duty, Respondeat Superior

MUST READ CASES

In re Merrill Lynch Tr. Co. FSB, 235 S.W.3d 185 (Tex. 2007)

Celtic Life Ins. Co. v. Coats, 885 S.W.2d 96 (Tex. 1994)

Nears v. Holiday Hospitality Franchising, Inc., 295 S.W.3d 787 (Tex. App.—Texarkana 2009, no pet.)

3-11:2 Elements

3-11:2.1 Contractual Liability

(1) An agency relationship exists

- An agency exists when the principal manifests assent to the agent that the agent shall act on the principal's behalf and subject to the principal's control, and the agent consents.[384]
- The law does not presume agency.[385]
- The party alleging agency has the burden of proving it.[386]
- Agency formation does not require consideration.[387]
- For an agency agreement to be enforceable as between the principal and agent, there must be consideration.[388]

(2) The agent enters into an agreement with a third party

- The agent must enter into an agreement on the principal's behalf to bind the principal.[389]

(3) The agent acts with:

---

[384] *Carr v. Hunt*, 651 S.W.2d 875, 879 (Tex. App.—Dallas 1983, writ ref'd n.r.e.).
[385] *IRA Res., Inc. v. Griego*, 221 S.W.3d 592, 597 (Tex. 2007); *Cmty. Health Sys. Prof'l Servs. Corp. v. Hansen*, 525 S.W.3d 671 (Tex. 2017).
[386] *IRA Res., Inc. v. Griego*, 221 S.W.3d 592, 597 (Tex. 2007); *Cmty. Health Sys. Prof'l Servs. Corp. v. Hansen*, 525 S.W.3d 671 (Tex. 2017).
[387] *J.M. Radford Grocery Co. v. Estelline State Bank*, 66 S.W.2d 1110 (Tex. Civ. App.—Amarillo 1933, writ dism'd).
[388] *Gulf States Paint Co. v. Kornblee Co.*, 390 S.W.2d 356, 359 (Tex. Civ. App.—Texarkana 1965, writ ref'd n.r.e.).
[389] *Nears v. Holiday Hosp. Franchising, Inc.*, 295 S.W.3d 787, 793 (Tex. App.—Texarkana 2009, no pet.) ("An agent acting within the scope of apparent authority binds a principal as though the principal performed the action").

(3) (a) Actual Authority

- Actual authority is found when a principal:
    - Intentionally confers authority upon an agent;
    - Intentionally allows the agent to believe that he possesses authority; or
    - Negligently allows the agent to believe that he possesses authority.[390]
- Actual authority may be either express or implied.[391]
- Express authority is delegated through words that expressly authorize the agent to do an act or series of acts on behalf of the principal.[392]
- Implied authority is that which is proper, usual and necessary to exercise the agent's express authority.[393]
    - Implied authority cannot exist without express authority.[394]
- Parol evidence may be used to prove an agent's authority.[395]

(3) (b) Apparent Authority

- Apparent authority exists when:
    - The principal, by its conduct;
    - Caused the third party to reasonably believe that the putative agent was an employee or agent of the principal; and
    - The third party justifiably relied on the appearance of agency.[396]
- Apparent authority ordinarily does not exist when an agent is attempting to sell real estate.[397]
- Texas has expressly rejected the approach taken by the Restatement (Second) of Torts Section 429.[398]

---

[390] *Nears v. Holiday Hosp. Franchising, Inc.*, 295 S.W.3d 787, 795 (Tex. App.—Texarkana 2009, no pet.); *Spring Garden 79U, Inc. v. Stewart Title Co.*, 874 S.W.2d 945, 948 (Tex. App.—Houston [1st Dist.] 1994, no writ).

[391] *Spring Garden 79U, Inc. v. Stewart Title Co.*, 874 S.W.2d 945, 948 (Tex. App.—Houston [1st Dist.] 1994, no writ); *LandAmerica Commonwealth Title Co. v. Wido*, No. 05-14-00036-CV, 2015 Tex. App. LEXIS 11201, at *14 (Tex. App.—Dallas Oct. 29, 2015, no pet.).

[392] *Nears v. Holiday Hosp. Franchising, Inc.*, 295 S.W.3d 787, 795 (Tex. App.—Texarkana 2009, no pet.).

[393] *Spring Garden 79U, Inc. v. Stewart Title Co.*, 874 S.W.2d 945, 948 (Tex. App.—Houston [1st Dist.] 1994, no writ).

[394] *Nears v. Holiday Hosp. Franchising, Inc.*, 295 S.W.3d 787, 795 (Tex. App.—Texarkana 2009, no pet.); *Spring Garden 79U, Inc. v. Stewart Title Co.*, 874 S.W.2d 945, 948 (Tex. App.—Houston [1st Dist.] 1994, no writ).

[395] *Pitman v. Lightfoot*, 937 S.W.2d 496, 521 (Tex. App.—San Antonio 1996).

[396] *Baptist Mem'l Hosp. Sys. v. Sampson*, 969 S.W.2d 945, 949 (Tex. 1998) (citing Restatement (Second) of Agency, § 267); *Gaines v. Kelly*, 235 S.W.3d 179, 183–84 (Tex. 2007).

[397] *Placemaker, Inc. v. Greer*, 654 S.W.2d 830, 834 (Tex. App.—Tyler 1983).

[398] *Baptist Mem'l Hosp. Sys. v. Sampson*, 969 S.W.2d 945, 949 (Tex. 1998) (citing Restatement (Second) of Agency, § 267).

CONTRACT AND COMMERCIAL LITIGATION

(3) (c) Substitute for Authority

- Ratification:
    - A principal ratifies an unauthorized contract when:
        (1) He gives approval by act, word or conduct;
        (2) With full knowledge of the facts of the earlier contract; and
        (3) With the intention of giving validity to the earlier contract.[399]

3-11:2.2 Tort Liability

(1) An agency relationship exists

- An agency exists when the principal manifests assent to the agent that the agent shall act on the principal's behalf and subject to the principal's control, and the agent consents.[400]
- The law does not presume agency.[401]
- The party alleging agency has the burden of proving it.[402]
- Agency formation does not require consideration.[403]
- For an agency agreement to be enforceable as between the principal and agent, there must be consideration.[404]

(2) The agent commits a tort

- The agent commits a tort.[405]
- A principal is vicariously liable for an intentional tort if the action was within the scope of the agent's authority.[406]
- A principal is vicariously liable for an intentional tort even if the principal has no knowledge of it.[407]

(3) Within the scope and course of his agency

- A principal is liable for an agent's misconduct which is within the course and scope of his agency.[408]

---

[399] *Providian Nat'l Bank v. Ebarb*, 180 S.W.3d 898, 901 (Tex. App.—Beaumont 2005, no pet.).
[400] *Carr v. Hunt*, 651 S.W.2d 875, 879 (Tex. App.—Dallas 1983, writ ref'd n.r.e.).
[401] *IRA Res., Inc. v. Griego*, 221 S.W.3d 592, 597 (Tex. 2007); *Cmty. Health Sys. Prof'l Servs. Corp. v. Hansen*, 525 S.W.3d 671 (Tex. 2017).
[402] *IRA Res., Inc. v. Griego*, 221 S.W.3d 592, 597 (Tex. 2007); *Cmty. Health Sys. Prof'l Servs. Corp. v. Hansen*, 525 S.W.3d 671 (Tex. 2017).
[403] *J.M. Radford Grocery Co. v. Estelline State Bank*, 66 S.W.2d 1110 (Tex. Civ. App.—Amarillo 1933, writ dism'd).
[404] *Gulf States Paint Co. v. Kornblee Co.*, 390 S.W.2d 356, 359 (Tex. Civ. App.—Texarkana 1965, writ ref'd n.r.e.).
[405] See *Robertson Tank Lines, Inc. v. Van Cleave*, 468 S.W.2d 354, 356–57 (Tex. 1971).
[406] *Miller v. Towne Servs., Inc.*, 665 S.W.2d 143, 145 (Tex. App.—Houston [1st Dist.] 1983, no writ).
[407] *Campbell v. Hamilton*, 632 S.W.2d 633, 634–635 (Tex. App.—Dallas 1982, writ ref'd n.r.e.).
[408] *Celtic Life Ins. Co. v. Coats*, 885 S.W.2d 96, 98 (Tex. 1994).

- It does not matter whether the principal authorized the specific wrongful act.[409]
- An agent is acting within the scope and course of his agency when the action is:
  - Within the scope of the agent's general authority;
  - In furtherance of the principal's business; and
  - For the accomplishment of the object for which the agent is employed.[410]
- A plaintiff is afforded a rebuttable presumption that the tortfeasor was acting within the scope and course of his agency if he can prove:
  - The tortfeasor was the principal's agent; and
  - The tortfeasor was driving the principal's vehicle.[411]

3-11:3 Damages and Remedies

3-11:3.1 Generally

The damages and remedies available will be determined by the underlying contractual obligation or tort liability.

3-11:3.2 Exemplary Damages

Exemplary damages are available when it can fairly be said that the principal engaged in the requisite level of wrongdoing.

A principal is only liable for exemplary damages if:

(1) The principal authorized the doing and the manner of the act;[412]

(2) The agent was unfit and the principal was reckless in employing him;[413]

(3) The agent was employed in a managerial capacity and was acting in the scope of employment;[414]

(4) The employer or a manager of the employer ratified or approved the act;[415] or

(5) The agent was a vice principal.[416]

Vice principals are:

- Corporate officers;

---

[409] *Celtic Life Ins. Co. v. Coats*, 885 S.W.2d 96, 99 (Tex. 1994).
[410] *Goodyear Tire & Rubber Co. v. Mayes*, 236 S.W.3d 754, 757 (Tex. 2007).
[411] *Goodyear Tire & Rubber Co. v. Mayes*, 236 S.W.3d 754, 757 (Tex. 2007).
[412] *Purvis v. Prattco, Inc.*, 595 S.W.2d 103, 103–04 (Tex. 1980).
[413] *Purvis v. Prattco, Inc.*, 595 S.W.2d 103, 103–04 (Tex. 1980).
[414] *Purvis v. Prattco, Inc.*, 595 S.W.2d 103, 103–04 (Tex. 1980).
[415] *Purvis v. Prattco, Inc.*, 595 S.W.2d 103, 103–04 (Tex. 1980).
[416] *Bennett v. Reynolds*, 315 S.W.3d 867, 883 (Tex. 2010); *Crossroads Hospice, Inc. v. FC Compassus, LLC*, No. 01-19-00008-CV, 2020 Tex. App. LEXIS 2216, at *25–26 (Tex. App.—Houston [1st Dist.] Mar. 17, 2020, no pet. h.).

CONTRACT AND COMMERCIAL LITIGATION

- Those who have authority to employ, direct and discharge servants of the master;
- Those engaged in the performance of nondelegable or absolute duties of the master; and
- Those to whom a master has confided the management of the whole or a department or division of his business.[417]

3-11:4 Defenses

3-11:4.1 Statute of Conveyances

- An agent's authority must be in writing to accomplish:
  - The conveyance of an estate of inheritance, a freehold or an estate for more than one year.[418]
- However, written authority is not necessary to enable an agent to bind the principal in an executory contract for the sale of land.[419]

3-12 Agency Actions—Agent Personally Liable on Contract Between Principal and Third Party

3-12:1 Overview

In this context, whether a person is an agent is not a cause of action in itself, but is rather a means to ascertain whether the agent, principal or both are liable on an obligation. As a general rule, agents are not liable to third parties based upon contracts entered into on the principal's behalf. However, agents are liable to third parties for their own tortious conduct.

3-12:1.1 Related Causes of Action

Agency Actions: Agent's Liability to Third Parties, Agency Actions: Agent's Actions Binding upon Principal, Breach of Formal Fiduciary Duty, Breach of Formal Fiduciary Duty from Special Relationship

MUST READ CASES

Davis v. Chaparro, 431 S.W.3d 717, 721–24 (Tex. App. El Paso 2014).

Gordon v. Leasman, 365 S.W.3d 109 (Tex. App.—Houston [1st Dist.] 2011, no pet.)

---

[417] *Bennett v. Reynolds*, 315 S.W.3d 867, 884 (Tex. 2010); *Crossroads Hospice, Inc. v. FC Compassus, LLC*, No. 01-19-00008-CV, 2020 Tex. App. LEXIS 2216, at *25–26 (Tex. App.—Houston [1st Dist.] Mar. 17, 2020, no pet. h.).
[418] Tex. Prop. Code Ann. § 5.021.
[419] *Little v. Clark*, 592 S.W.2d 61, 64 (Tex. Civ. App.—Fort Worth 1979, writ ref'd n.r.e.).

3-12:2 Elements

3-12:2.1 Partially Disclosed or Undisclosed Principal

(1) An agent acting for a principal

- An agency exists when the principal manifests assent to the agent that the agent shall act on the principal's behalf and subject to the principal's control, and the agent consents.[420]
- The law does not presume agency.[421]
- The party alleging agency has the burden of proving it.[422]
- Agency formation does not require consideration.[423]
- For an agency agreement to be enforceable as between the principal and agent, there must be consideration.[424]

(2) Enters into an agreement with a third party

- The agent must enter into an agreement with a third party.[425]

(3) Without fully disclosing his agency.

- To avoid liability on a contract, an agent must disclose his status as an agent and the identity of his principal.[426]
- Full disclosure of the principal's identity requires disclosure of the principal's legal name or designation; trade names do not suffice.[427]
- Whether an agent fully disclosed his agency depends on whether the third party knew or should have known of the principal's existence and identity at the time of agreement.[428]
  - It does not matter how the third party learns of the existence and identity of the principal.[429]
- A contractual provision seeking to disclaim the agent's liability is not effective unless the agent also discloses the name of his principal.[430]

---

[420] *Carr v. Hunt*, 651 S.W.2d 875, 879 (Tex. App.—Dallas 1983, writ ref'd n.r.e.).
[421] *IRA Res., Inc. v. Griego*, 221 S.W.3d 592, 597 (Tex. 2007).
[422] *IRA Res., Inc. v. Griego*, 221 S.W.3d 592, 597 (Tex. 2007).
[423] *J.M. Radford Grocery Co. v. Estelline State Bank*, 66 S.W.2d 1110 (Tex. Civ. App.—Amarillo 1933, writ dism'd).
[424] *Gulf States Paint Co. v. Kornblee Co.*, 390 S.W.2d 356, 359 (Tex. Civ. App.—Texarkana 1965, writ ref'd n.r.e.).
[425] *See Carter v. Walton*, 469 S.W.2d 462, 471–72 (Tex. Civ. App.—Corpus Christi 1971, writ ref'd n.r.e.).
[426] *A to Z Rental Ctr. v. Burris*, 714 S.W.2d 433, 435 (Tex. App.—Austin 1986, writ ref'd. n.r.e.).
[427] *Burch v. Hancock*, 56 S.W.3d 257, 261–62 (Tex. App.—Tyler 2001, no pet.).
[428] *Gordon v. Leasman*, 365 S.W.3d 109, 115 (Tex. App.—Houston [1st Dist.] 2011, no pet.).
[429] *Gordon v. Leasman*, 365 S.W.3d 109, 115 (Tex. App.—Houston [1st Dist.] 2011, no pet.).
[430] *Dorman v. Boehringer*, 195 S.W. 669, 670, *rev'd on reh'g*, 195 S.W. 1183 (Tex. Civ. App.—San Antonio 1917, no writ).

3-12:2.2 Disclosed Principal

- An agent acting within the scope of his authority for a fully disclosed principal is not contractually liable to a third party.[431]
- Whether an agent fully disclosed his agency depends on whether the third party knew or should have known of the principal's existence and identity at the time of agreement.[432]
  - It does not matter how the third party learns of the existence and identity of the principal.[433]
- However, this general rule may be altered by agreement and an agent may expressly bind himself to the contract.[434]

3-12:2.3 Nonexistent or Legally Incompetent Principal

- Agent is liable for a contract when he purports to be an agent for a nonexistent or legally incompetent principal.[435]
- The relevant time period is the time the agreement between the agent and third party is made.[436]

3-12:2.4 Assumption of Liability

An agent may assume an obligation under a contract.[437] Such consent can be express, or it can arise impliedly from the circumstances.[438]

3-12:2.5 Agent's Breach of the Warranty of Authority

(1) A person acts as an agent without authority from his principal

- Any person who acts as an agent without authority from his principal may be liable.[439]

---

[431] *Instone Travel Tech. Marine & Offshore v. Int'l Shipping Partners, Inc.*, 334 F.3d 423, 428 (5th Cir. 2003).

[432] *Gordon v. Leasman*, 365 S.W.3d 109, 115 (Tex. App.—Houston [1st Dist.] 2011, no pet.).

[433] *Gordon v. Leasman*, 365 S.W.3d 109, 115 (Tex. App.—Houston [1st Dist.] 2011, no pet.).

[434] *Instone Travel Tech. Marine & Offshore v. Int'l Shipping Partners, Inc.*, 334 F.3d 423, 428 (5th Cir. 2003).

[435] *Carter v. Walton*, 469 S.W.2d 462, 471 (Tex. Civ. App.—Corpus Christi 1971, writ ref'd n.r.e.); Restatement (Third) of Agency, § 6.04 (2006).

[436] *See Gordon v. Leasman*, 365 S.W.3d 109, 114–15 (Tex. App.—Houston [1st Dist.] 2011, no pet.); *Carter v. Walton*, 469 S.W.2d 462, 472 (Tex. Civ. App.—Corpus Christi 1971, writ ref'd n.r.e.).

[437] *Instone Travel Tech. Marine & Offshore v. Int'l Shipping Partners, Inc.*, 334 F.3d 423, 428 (5th Cir. 2003).

[438] *Hull v. S. Coast Catamarans, L.P.*, 365 S.W.3d 35, 45 (Tex. App.—Houston [1st Dist.] 2011, pet. denied).

[439] *Hur v. City of Mesquite*, 893 S.W.2d 227, 233 (Tex. App.—Amarillo 1995, writ denied).

- The agent's good faith belief that he possesses the requisite authority is immaterial. It only matters that the agent exceeded his authority.[440]

(2) A third party relied on the agent

- The third party must reasonably rely upon the agent's representation of authority.[441]
- If the third party knows the agent lacks authority, there can be no reasonable reliance.[442]
- If the third party knows all of the facts surrounding the agent's authority so that the third party may make an assessment of the scope of the agent's authority, there can be no reasonable reliance.[443]

(3) Proximately causes damages.

- Liability is not on the contract itself, but for a breach of warranty.[444]
- There can be no liability if the principal ratified the contract.
- A principal ratifies an unauthorized contract when:
    (1) He gives approval by act, word, or conduct;
    (2) With full knowledge of the facts of the earlier contract; and
    (3) With the intention of giving validity to the earlier contract.[445]

3-12:2.6 Tort Liability

- An agent is always liable for his own tortious conduct.[446]
- When both the principal and agent are liable on a contract, the third party must make an election to take a judgment against the principal or the agent, but not both.[447]

---

[440] *Thomas, Richardson, Runden & Co., Inc. v. State*, 683 S.W.2d 100, 102 (Tex. App.—Tyler 1984, writ ref'd n.r.e.).

[441] *First State Bank of Roby v. Hilbun*, 61 S.W.2d 521, 522 (Tex. Civ. App.—Eastland 1933, no writ).

[442] *First State Bank of Roby v. Hilbun*, 61 S.W.2d 521, 522 (Tex. Civ. App.—Eastland 1933, no writ).

[443] *First State Bank of Roby v. Hilbun*, 61 S.W.2d 521, 522 (Tex. Civ. App.—Eastland 1933, no writ).

[444] *First State Bank of Roby v. Hilbun*, 61 S.W.2d 521, 522 (Tex. Civ. App.—Eastland 1933, no writ).

[445] *Providian Nat'l Bank v. Ebarb*, 180 S.W.3d 898, 901 (Tex. App.—Beaumont 2005, no pet.).

[446] *Miller v. Keyser*, 90 S.W.3d 712, 717 (Tex. 2002); *State v. Morello*, 547 S.W.3d 881, 887 (Tex. 2018); *Hull v. S. Coast Catamarans, L.P.*, 365 S.W.3d 35, 45 (Tex. App.—Houston [1st Dist.] 2011, pet. denied).

[447] *Glendon Invs., Inc. v. Brooks*, 748 S.W.2d 465, 468 (Tex. App.—Houston [1st Dist.] 1988, writ denied).

CONTRACT AND COMMERCIAL LITIGATION 199

3-12:3 Damages and Remedies

3-12:3.1 Contractual Liability

The damages and remedies available for an agent's breach of contract are determined by the underlying contract.[448]

For a list of damages and remedies available for a breach of contract, *see* Section 3-1 of this chapter.

3-12:3.2 Tort Liability

The damages and remedies available for an agent's tortious conduct are determined by the underlying cause of action.[449]

3-12:4 Defenses

3-12:4.1 Indemnity

- A principal must indemnify its agent against contractual liabilities the agent incurs while acting on behalf of the principal.[450]
- A principal must indemnify its agent against tort liabilities the agent incurs while acting on behalf of the principal.[451]

3-12:4.2 Breach of Warranty—Actual Damages

A third party may recover actual damages.[452]

3-12:4.3 Breach of Warranty—Quantum Meruit

A third party may recover in quantum meruit.[453]

3-13 Agency Actions—Agent Personally Liable for Breach of Duty

3-13:1 Overview

The agency relationship places several fiduciary duties upon the agent. The agent must act with care, loyalty, and obedience, in the execution of his agency and must

---

[448] *See Latch v. Gratty, Inc.*, 107 S.W.3d 543, 546 (Tex. 2003).
[449] *Miller v. Keyser*, 90 S.W.3d 712, 717–18 (Tex. 2002) (awarding DTPA damages for an agent's DTPA violation).
[450] *Butler v. Cont'l Oil Co.*, 182 S.W.2d 843, 846 (Tex. Civ. App.—Galveston 1944, no writ).
[451] *Mercedes-Benz of N. Am., Inc. v. Dickenson*, 720 S.W.2d 844, 858 (Tex. App.—Fort Worth 1986, no writ).
[452] *Angroson, Inc. v. Indep. Commc'ns, Inc.*, 711 S.W.2d 268, 271 (Tex. App.—Dallas 1986, writ ref'd n.r.e.).
[453] *Angroson, Inc. v. Indep. Commc'ns, Inc.*, 711 S.W.2d 268, 271 (Tex. App.—Dallas 1986, writ ref'd n.r.e.).

fully disclose material information to his principal. If the agent breaches any of those duties to the principal, the principal may seek a wide variety of remedies.

3-13:1.1 Related Causes of Action

Agency Actions: Agent's Liability to Third Parties, Agency Action: Agent's Actions Binding upon Principal, Breach of Partnership Duty, Breach of Formal Fiduciary Duty, Officer and Director Liability: Breach of the Duty of Care, Officer and Director Liability: Breach of the Duty of Loyalty

MUST READ CASES

Johnson v. Brewer & Pritchard, P.C., 73 S.W.3d 193 (Tex. 2002)

KCM Fin. LLC v. Bradshaw, 457 S.W.3d 70 (Tex. 2015)

3-13:2 Elements

(1) An agency relationship exists

- An agency exists when the principal manifests assent to the agent that the agent shall act on the principal's behalf and subject to the principal's control, and the agent consents.[454]

- The law does not presume agency.[455]

- The party alleging agency has the burden of proving it.[456]

- Agency formation does not require consideration.[457]

- For an agency agreement to be enforceable as between the principal and agent, there must be consideration.[458]

(2) The agent breaches a duty of

- An agent's duties are characterized as fiduciary in nature.[459]

(2) (a) Care

- An agent is held to a reasonable standard of care regarding:
  - The principal's property[460]

- An agent is held to a high standard of care regarding:

---

[454] *Carr v. Hunt*, 651 S.W.2d 875, 879 (Tex. App.—Dallas 1983, writ ref'd n.r.e.).
[455] *IRA Res., Inc. v. Griego*, 221 S.W.3d 592, 597 (Tex. 2007).
[456] *IRA Res., Inc. v. Griego*, 221 S.W.3d 592, 597 (Tex. 2007).
[457] *J.M. Radford Grocery Co. v. Estelline State Bank*, 66 S.W.2d 1110 (Tex. Civ. App.—Amarillo 1933, writ dism'd).
[458] *Gulf States Paint Co. v. Kornblee Co.*, 390 S.W.2d 356, 359 (Tex. Civ. App.—Texarkana 1965, writ ref'd n.r.e.).
[459] *See Johnson v. Brewer & Pritchard, P.C.*, 73 S.W.3d 193, 200 (Tex. 2002).
[460] *American Indem. Co. v. Baumgart*, 840 S.W.2d 634, 639 (Tex. App.—Corpus Christi 1992, no writ).

CONTRACT AND COMMERCIAL LITIGATION

- The principal's funds which are to be paid to a third party.[461]
- An agent may be held to a reasonable standard of care regarding:
  - The quality of a contract the agent executes on the principal's behalf.[462]

(2)(b) Loyalty

- An agent may not compete with his principal while still an agent, without first making full disclosure to the principal.[463]
- Conduct that would violate the duty of loyalty includes:
  - Appropriating trade secrets;[464]
  - Soliciting the principal's customers while still an agent;[465]
  - Carrying away customer lists;[466] and
  - Referring a customer to a competitor for a fee.[467]

(2)(c) Obedience

- An agent must obey all of the principal's lawful instructions.[468]

(2)(d) Full Disclosure

- An agent must disclose all known material facts which might affect the principal's rights.[469]

3-13:3 Damages and Remedies

3-13:3.1 Actual Damages

Actual damages are an appropriate remedy for an agent's breach of duty.[470]

3-13:3.2 Forfeiture of Fee

A principal may recover any fee paid to the agent.[471]

---

[461] *Douglas v. Aztec Petroleum Corp.*, 695 S.W.2d 312, 318 (Tex. App.—Tyler 1985, no writ).

[462] *American Indem. Co. v. Baumgart*, 840 S.W.2d 634, 639 (Tex. App.—Corpus Christi 1992, no writ); *Hartford Cas. Ins. Co. v. Walker Cty. Agency, Inc.*, 808 S.W.2d 681, 688 (Tex. App.—Corpus Christi 1991, no writ).

[463] *Lang v. Lee*, 777 S.W.2d 158, 161-163 (Tex. App.—Dallas 1989).

[464] *Johnson v. Brewer & Pritchard, P.C.*, 73 S.W.3d 193, 202 (Tex. 2002).

[465] *Johnson v. Brewer & Pritchard, P.C.*, 73 S.W.3d 193, 202 (Tex. 2002).

[466] *Johnson v. Brewer & Pritchard, P.C.*, 73 S.W.3d 193, 202 (Tex. 2002).

[467] *Johnson v. Brewer & Pritchard, P.C.*, 73 S.W.3d 193, 202 (Tex. 2002).

[468] *General Motors Acceptance Corp./Crenshaw, Dupree & Milam, L.L.P. v. Crenshaw, Dupree & Milam, L.L.P./Gen. Motors Acceptance Corp.*, 986 S.W.2d 632, 636 (Tex. App.—El Paso 1998, pet. denied).

[469] *Huie v. DeShazo*, 922 S.W.2d 920, 923 (Tex. 1996); *Home Loan Corp. v. Tex. Am. Title Co.*, 191 S.W.3d 728, 731 (Tex. App.—Houston [14th Dist.] 2006, pet. denied).

[470] *Hartford Cas. Ins. Co. v. Walker Cty. Agency, Inc.*, 808 S.W.2d 681, 688 (Tex. App.—Corpus Christi 1991, no writ) (affirming award of actual damages).

[471] *ERI Consulting Eng'rs, Inc. v. Swinnea*, 318 S.W.3d 867, 872 (Tex. 2010).

The applicability and extent of forfeiture will depend upon the facts of each case.[472]

3-13:3.3 Disgorgement

Disgorgement is an appropriate remedy for breach of an agency duty.[473]

3-13:3.4 Avoidance of Contract

A contract entered into by a self-interested agent is voidable by the principal.[474] A principal may not avoid a contract if he ratified the transaction.[475]

3-13:3.5 Breach of the Duty of Obedience

A breach of the duty of obedience imposes personal liability on the agent for any unauthorized contracts entered into.[476]

An agent who is authorized to purchase property is liable for any payments due on the purchase that are in excess of the agreed purchase price.[477]

If an agent is merely authorized to collect money, the agent is liable for any unauthorized expenditure of that money.[478]

If an agent remits funds to its principal in an unauthorized manner, it assumes any risk of loss of such funds.[479]

3-13:3.6 Exemplary Damages

Exemplary damages are available if the breach of duty is accomplished:

- Maliciously;
- Fraudulently; or
- With gross negligence.[480]

---

[472] *ERI Consulting Eng'rs, Inc. v. Swinnea*, 318 S.W.3d 867, 874 (Tex. 2010).
[473] *ERI Consulting Eng'rs, Inc. v. Swinnea*, 318 S.W.3d 867, 873 (Tex. 2010).
[474] *Burrow v. Arce*, 997 S.W.2d 229, 239 n.35 (Tex. 1999) (quoting *Anderson v. Griffith*, 501 S.W.2d 695, 701 (Tex. Civ. App.—Fort Worth 1973, writ ref'd n.r.e)).
[475] *Thomson Oil Royalty, LLC v. Graham*, 351 S.W.3d 162, 166 (Tex. App.—Tyler 2011, no pet.).
[476] *Albright v. Lay*, 474 S.W.2d 287, 291 (Tex. Civ. App.—Corpus Christi 1971, no writ); *See also* Chapter 3, Sections 3-36:1, 3-26:2.5.
[477] *Western Union Tel. Co. v. Chihuahua Exch.*, 206 S.W. 364 (Tex. Civ. App.—El Paso 1918, no writ).
[478] *Dowlen v. C.W. Georgs Mfg. Co.*, 59 Tex. Civ. App. 124, 125 S.W. 931 (1910).
[479] *Kerr v. Cotton*, 23 Tex. 411, 1859 WL 6291 (1859).
[480] Tex. Civ. Prac. & Rem. Code Ann. § 41.003(a).

CONTRACT AND COMMERCIAL LITIGATION

3-13:4 Defenses

3-13:4.1 Ratification

A principal may ratify a breach of the duty of loyalty.[481]

A principal ratifies an unauthorized contract when:

(1) He gives approval by act, word, or conduct;

(2) With full knowledge of the facts of the earlier contract; and

(3) With the intention of giving validity to the earlier contract.[482]

A principal may not avoid a contract if he ratified the transaction.[483]

3-13:4.2 Estoppel

Equitable estoppel is an appropriate defense to an agent's breach of duty.[484]

3-13:4.3 Statute of Limitations

- The four-year limitations period applies to a breach of fiduciary duty claim.[485] The discovery rule may apply to breaches sounding in tort.[486]

---

[481] *Allison v. Harrison*, 137 Tex. 582, 588, 156 S.W.2d 137, 140 (Tex. Comm'n App. 1941) (making full disclosure and the principal's acquiescence in full awareness thereof relieves the agent of liability).

[482] *Providian Nat'l Bank v. Ebarb*, 180 S.W.3d 898, 901 (Tex. App.—Beaumont 2005, no pet.).

[483] *Thomson Oil Royalty, LLC v. Graham*, 351 S.W.3d 162, 166 (Tex. App.—Tyler 2011, no pet.).

[484] *Daniel v. Falcon Interest Realty Corp.*, 190 S.W.3d 177, 188 (Tex. App.—Houston [1st Dist.] 2005, no pet.).

[485] Tex. Civ. Prac. & Rem. Code Ann. § 16.004(a)(5); *Rowe v. Rowe*, 887 S.W.2d 191, 201 (Tex. App.—Fort Worth 1994, writ denied).

[486] *FDIC v. Howse*, 736 F. Supp. 1437, 1441 (S.D. Tex. 1990).

CHAPTER 4

Professional Liability and Fiduciary Litigation*

4-1 Legal Malpractice

4-1:1 Overview

A cause of action for legal malpractice generally is in the nature of a tort.[1] Claims relating to the quality of a lawyer's representation of his client are professional negligence claims.[2] When the claim arises due to the lawyer's obtaining an improper benefit from representing a client, however, the client may also sue for breach of fiduciary duty.[3] A violation of the Texas Disciplinary Rules of Professional Conduct alone does not give rise to a private cause of action.[4] The client may also have a claim from breach of contract depending on the nature of the agreement (written versus oral); the enforceability may be affected by application of the Statute of Frauds.

MUST READ CASES

Cosgrove v. Grimes, 744 S.W.2d 662 (Tex. 1989) (Supreme Court rejected concept of judgmental immunity, which protects lawyers who exercise professional judgment in subjective good faith); *Willis v. Maverick*, 760 S.W.2d 642 (Tex. 1988)

Cook v. Brundidge, Fountain, Elliott & Churchill, 533 S.W.2d 751, 758 (Tex. 1976) (basic principles of agency apply to law firm's liability for its lawyers and staff in malpractice action)

4-1:2 Elements[5]

(1) Attorney owed plaintiff a duty:

---

* The authors thank Robyn Leatherwood for her assistance in the updating of this chapter.
[1] *Cosgrove v. Grimes*, 774 S.W.2d 662, 664 (Tex. 1989).
[2] *Murphy v. Gruber*, 241 S.W.3d 689, 696–97 (Tex. App.—Dallas 2008, pet. denied).
[3] *See Aiken v. Hancock*, 115 S.W.3d 26 (Tex. App.—San Antonio 2003, pet. denied). The statute of limitations for a breach of fiduciary duty claim is four years. Tex. Civ. Prac. & Rem. Code Ann. § 16.004(a)(5).
[4] Tex. Disciplinary R. Prof'l Conduct preamble § 15; *see McGuire, Craddock, Strother & Hale, P.C. v. Transcon. Realty Inv'rs, Inc.*, 251 S.W.3d 890, 896 (Tex. App.—Dallas 2008, pet. denied).
[5] *Starwood Mgt., LLC by and through Gonzalez v. Swaim*, 530 S.W.3d 673, 678 (Tex. 2017); *Stanfield v. Neubaum*, 494 S.W.3d 90, 96 (Tex. 2016).

- This duty is established by proving the existence of an attorney-client relationship.[6]
- A lawyer owes a duty to a non-client if the lawyer should have reasonably expected that the non-client would believe the lawyer represented him and the lawyer failed to advise of non-representation.[7]
- An excess carrier may bring a legal malpractice claim against the insured's lawyer based on an equitable subrogation claim.[8]
- A lawyer does not owe the beneficiaries of a decedent's estate a duty on which the beneficiaries could sue for legal malpractice.[9] However, an estate's personal representative may bring a legal malpractice claim against the decedent's estate planning attorney on behalf of the estate.[10]

(2) Attorney breached that duty:

- A lawyer's standard of care is that which would be exercised by a reasonably prudent lawyer.[11]
- Board certified lawyers may be expected to possess a higher degree of skill and learning than a general practitioner.[12]

(3) The breach proximately caused plaintiff's injuries:

- When couched as a negligence claim, the plaintiff must prove that the legal malpractice was the proximate cause of the injury.[13] The plaintiff must show that the malpractice was a substantial factor in bringing about the injury and without which no harm would have occurred.[14] The plaintiff must also prove that the lawyer should have anticipated the dangers to his client by the negligent act.[15] Mere differences in decision making are judgment may not be sufficient. If the attorney makes a decision that a reasonably prudent attorney could make in the same or similar circumstance, then it is not an act of negligence, even if the result is undesirable.[16]
- When a plaintiff's malpractice claim alleges that the attorney's negligence caused an adverse result in prior litigation, the plaintiff must prove that it

---

[6] *Barcelo v. Elliott*, 923 S.W.2d 575, 577 (Tex. 1996).
[7] *Border Demolition & Envtl., Inc. v. Pineda*, 535 S.W.3d 140, 152 (Tex. App.—El Paso 2017).
[8] *American Centennial Ins. Co. v. Canal Ins. Co.*, 843 S.W.2d 480, 484 (Tex. 1992); *Keck, Mahin & Cate v. Nat'l Union Fire Ins. Co.*, 20 S.W.3d 692, 698, 700 (Tex. 2000).
[9] *Barcelo v. Elliott*, 923 S.W.2d 575, 579 (Tex. 1996).
[10] *Belt v. Oppenheimer, Blend, Harrison & Tate, Inc.*, S.W.3d 780, 786–87 (Tex. 2006); *see Smith v. O'Donnell*, 288 S.W.3d 417, 419 (Tex. 2009) (An executor may bring suit against a decedent's attorneys for malpractice committed outside of the estate-planning context.).
[11] *Cosgrove v. Grimes*, 774 S.W.2d 662, 665 (Tex. 1989); *Zenith Star Ins. Co. v. Wilkerson*, 150 S.W.3d 525, 530 (Tex. App.—Austin 2004, no pet.).
[12] *See, e.g., Rhodes v. Batilla*, 848 S.W.2d 833, 842 (Tex. App.—Houston [14th Dist.] 1993, writ denied) (Attorney who holds himself out as an expert will be held to the standard of care of a reasonably prudent expert in that field.).
[13] *Cosgrove v. Grimes*, 774 S.W.2d 662, 665 (Tex. 1989).
[14] *Rogers v. Zanetti*, 518 S.W.3d 394, 402 (Tex. 2017).
[15] *Rogers v. Zanetti*, 518 S.W.3d 394, 402 (Tex. 2017).
[16] *Cunningham v. Hughes & Luce, L.L.P.*, 312 S.W.3d 62, 67–68 (Tex. App.—El Paso 2010).

would have prevailed in the underlying case but for the attorney's negligence.[17] the plaintiff must prove that the client would have obtained a more favorable result in the underlying litigation had the attorney conformed to the proper standard of care.[18] This unique requirement of legal malpractice is known as the "suit-within-a-suit" requirement.[19]

- Traditionally, the suit within a suit necessitates recreating the underlying case[20],[21]

(4) Damages occurred

- The plaintiff may seek to recover foreseeable damages proximately caused by the malpractice. When the alleged malpractice is based on the attorney's wrongful conduct in the prior litigation, the foreseeable damages are usually the amount the client would have collected, or would have avoided paying, if the litigation had been competently handled.[22]

4-1:3 Damages and Remedies

4-1:3.1 Actual Damages

A malpractice plaintiff may recover actual damages.[23]

[24] The general measure of damages in a legal-malpractice case is the difference between the amount plaintiff probably would have recovered in the absence of the malpractice, and the amount recovered.[25] The plaintiff may recover attorneys' fees from the underlying suit as damages if the malpractice proximately caused the additional fees.[26] For example, the plaintiff may recover attorneys' fees for separate counsel retained for post-trial proceedings caused by the defendant attorney's malpractice.[27]

---

[17] *Green v. McKay*, 376 S.W.3d. 891, 898 (Tex. App.—Dallas 2012, pet. denied). *See also Jackson v. Urban Coolidge, Pennington & Scott*, 516 S.W.2d 948, 949 (Tex. App.—Houston [1st Dist.] 1974, writ ref'd n.r.e.).

[18] *Elizondo v. Krist*, 415 S.W.3d 259, 263 (Tex. 2013).

[19] *Kelley v. Witherspoon, L.L.P. v. Hoover*, 401 S.W.3d 841, 847 (Tex. App.—Dallas 2013, no pet.).

[20] 4 Ronald E. Mallen, Legal Malpractice § 33:7, at 673 (2017).

[21] 4 Ronald E. Mallen, Legal Malpractice § 37:87, at 1695 (2015). Where the injury claimed does not depend on the merits of the underlying action, however, the case-within-a-case methodology does not apply. *Rogers v. Zanetti*, 518 S.W.3d 394, 401 (Tex. 2017).

[22] *Cosgrove v. Grimes*, 774 S.W.2d 662, 666 (Tex. 1989); *Keck, Mahin & Cate v. Nat'l Union Fire Ins. Co.*, 20 S.W.3d 692, 703 (Tex. 2000).

[23] *Cosgrove v. Grimes*, 774 S.W.2d 662, 665–66 (Tex. 1989).

[24] *Keck, Mahin & Cate v. Nat'l Union Fire Ins. Co.*, 20 S.W.3d 692, 703 (Tex. 2000).

[25] *Elizondo v. Krist*, 415 S.W.3d 259, 270 (Tex. 2013).

[26] *Akin, Gump, Strauss, Hauer & Feld, L.L.P. v. Nat'l Dev. & Research Corp.*, 299 S.W.3d 106, 122 (Tex. 2009).

[27] *Akin, Gump, Strauss, Hauer & Feld, L.L.P. v. Nat'l Dev. & Research Corp.*, 299 S.W.3d 106, 119–24 (Tex. 2009).

4-1:3.2 Interest

Prejudgment interest is recoverable.[28]

4-1:3.3 Court Costs

Under the Texas Rules of Civil Procedure, the successful party in a suit is entitled to recover all the taxable costs incurred, without any stated requirement of pleading for costs.[29] In a legal malpractice claim, a "successful party," one who obtains a judgment of a competent court of jurisdiction vindicating a civil claim of right, may recover court costs.[30] See Chapter 11, Section 11-13:2. Typically, however, the party should plead for all relief, both at law and in equity, which the party may be justly entitled.[31]

4-1:3.4 Mental Anguish

In 1989, the Texas Supreme Court allowed a mental anguish award in a legal malpractice case without discussion of the issue.[32] However, 10 years later in 1999, the Supreme Court held that mental anguish damages caused by economic losses due to an attorney's negligence are not recoverable.[33] The Court left open the question of whether mental anguish damages are recoverable in noneconomic loss cases or when heightened culpability is alleged.[34]

Mental anguish damages may be recoverable for intentional or malicious conduct.[35]

4-1:3.5 Exemplary Damages

Exemplary damages are available if the plaintiff proves harm resulted from fraud, malice, or gross negligence.[36]

Unless alleged malpractice constitutes felony, exemplary damages are capped at two times the economic damages plus not more than $750,000 of any noneconomic damages, or $200,000, whichever is greater.[37]

---

[28] *Sample v. Freeman*, 873 S.W.2d 470, 476 (Tex. App.—Beaumont 1994, writ denied); *Rhodes v. Batilla*, 848 S.W.2d 833, 849 (Tex. App.—Houston [14th Dist.] 1993, writ denied).

[29] Tex. R. Civ. P. 131.

[30] *Mora v. Villalobos*, No. 13-02-00691-CV, 2005 Tex. App. LEXIS 6787, at *15, (Tex. App.—Corpus Christi 2005, pet. denied) (mem. op.) (finding that the defendants did not commit legal malpractice and ordering all costs to be taxed against plaintiffs).

[31] Tex. R.Civ. P. 301

[32] *Cosgrove v. Grimes*, 774 S.W.2d 662, 666 (Tex. 1989).

[33] *Douglas v. Delp*, 987 S.W.2d 879, 885 (Tex. 1999).

[34] *Douglas v. Delp*, 987 S.W.2d 879, 885 (Tex. 1999).

[35] *See, e.g., Parenti v. Moberg*, No. 04-06-00497-CV, 2007 WL 1540952, at *3 (Tex. App.—San Antonio May 30, 2007, pet. denied).

[36] Tex. Civ. Prac. & Rem. Code Ann. § 41.003.

[37] Tex. Civ. Prac. & Rem. Code Ann. § 41.008.

4-1:4 Defenses

4-1:4.1 Statute of Limitations

4-1:4.1a Two-Year Statute of Limitations

A two-year limitations period applies to legal malpractice claims regardless of whether plaintiff pleads in tort, contract, fraud or some other theory.[38] A claim regarding the quality of the lawyer's representation is a legal malpractice claim and courts will treat it as such, regardless of the label.[39] A client cannot mask or fracture a claim that is, at the bottom, a claim for legal malpractice.[40]

Fraudulent concealment is an affirmative defense to the legal malpractice statute of limitations.[41]

4-1:4.1b Accrues When Client Suffers Legal Injury

A legal malpractice cause of action accrues when the facts that authorize a claimant to seek a judicial remedy come into existence.[42] For example, a plaintiff suffers legal injury from faulty professional advice when the advice is taken.[43] This is known as the legal injury rule.[44]

4-1:4.1c The Discovery Rule Applies

The accrual of a legal malpractice claim is governed by the discovery rule.[45] While tort claims generally are subject to a two year statute of limitations, the client may not know of or discover the harm or wrong until more than two years from the breach or tort. Similarly, malpractice by the attorney might be remedied or reversed during the appellate process. As such, Teas applies the *Hughes* tolling rule. The rule states when an attorney commits malpractice in the prosecution or defense of a claim that results in litigation, the statute of limitations on the malpractice claim against the attorney is tolled until all appeals on the underlying claim are exhausted.[46] The client need not have been represented continuously by the allegedly negligent attorney to receive the benefit of tolling.[47] The *Hughes* rule does not apply, however, to DTPA claims against attorneys or in transactional malpractice claims.[48]

---

[38] *Willis v. Maverick*, 760 S.W.2d 642, 644 (Tex. 1988).
[39] *Klein v. Reynolds, Cunningham, Peterson, & Cordell*, 923 S.W.2d 45, 49 (Tex. App.—Houston [1st Dist.] 1995, no writ).
[40] *Black v. Wills*, 758 S.W.2d 809, 814 (Tex. App.—Dallas 1988, no writ); *Sledge v. Alsup*, 759 S.W.2d 1, 2 (Tex. App.—El Paso 1988, no writ).
[41] *Haas v. George*, 71 S.W.3d 904, 913 (Tex. App.—Texarkana 2002, no pet.); *Nichols v. Smith*, 507 S.W.2d 518, 522 (Tex. 1974).
[42] *Willis v. Maverick*, 760 S.W.2d 642, 644 (Tex. 1988).
[43] *Murphy v. Campbell*, 964 S.W.2d 265, 270 (Tex. 1997).
[44] *Murphy v. Campbell*, 964 S.W.2d 265, 270 (Tex. 1997).
[45] *Murphy v. Campbell*, 964 S.W.2d 265, 270–71 (Tex. 1997).
[46] *Erikson v. Renda*, 590 S.W.3d 55, 564 (Tex. 2019) (quoting *Hughes v. Mahaney & Higgens*, 821 S.W.2d 154, 157 (Tex. 1991)).
[47] *Apex Towing Co. v. Tolin*, 41 S.W.3d 118, 121–22 (Tex. 2001).
[48] *Murphy v. Mullin, Hoard & Brown, L.L.P.*, 168 S.W.3d 288, 292 (Tex. App.—Dallas 2005, no pet.); *Underkofler v. Vanasek*, 53 S.W.3d 343, 346–47 (Tex. 2001).

4-1:5 Related Causes of Action

Breach of Contract (allegation that lawyer charged excessive legal fees only), Breach of Fiduciary Duty, Fraud, DTPA Violation, Negligent Misrepresentation, Malicious Prosecution, Conspiracy to Defraud, Federal Fair Debt Collection Practices Act, Texas Debt Collection Act (DCA), Securities Exchange Act of 1934.

4-2 Attorneys and Fiduciary Litigation

4-2:1 Overview

While a claim related to the quality of a lawyer's representation is a negligence claim, a fiduciary-duty claim focuses on whether the attorney's conduct violated the duties of trust, integrity and fidelity, including whether the attorney obtained an improper benefit from representing the client.[49] The attorney must put the client's interest ahead of his own interest or he risks breaching his fiduciary obligation. If a jury finds breach of fiduciary duty, the range of damages are more expansive than with merely a negligence finding.

MUST READ CASE

Burrow v. Arce, 997 S.W.2d 229 (Tex. 1999) (an attorney who breaches his fiduciary duty to his client may be required to forfeit all or part of his fee, whether or not there were actual damages)

4-2:2 Elements[50]

(1) A fiduciary relationship existed

- An attorney owes his client a fiduciary duty as a matter of law, but the attorney-client relationship must first exist before a fiduciary duty arises.[51]

(2) The attorney breached its fiduciary duty

- An attorney commits a fiduciary breach when he or she benefits improperly from the attorney-client relationship by, among other things, subordinating his or her client's interests to his or her own, retaining the client's funds, engaging in self-dealing, improperly using client confidences, failing to disclose conflicts of interest, or making misrepresentations to achieve those ends.[52]

- As a fiduciary, an attorney is obligated to render a full and fair disclosure of facts material to the client's representation.[53] However, this duty to inform does not extend to matters beyond the scope of representation.[54]

---

[49] *Neese v. Lyon*, 479 S.W.3d 368, 387 (Tex. App.—Dallas 2015, no pet.).
[50] *Dollahite v. Howry, Breen & Herman, L.L.P.*, 03-19-00011-CV, 2019 WL 6720997, at *2 (Tex. App.—Austin Dec. 11, 2019, no pet.).
[51] *Willis v. Maverick*, 760 S.W.2d 642, 645 (Tex. 1988).
[52] *Neese v. Lyon*, 479 S.W.3d 368, 387 (Tex. App.—Dallas 2015, no pet.).
[53] *Willis v. Maverick*, 760 S.W.2d 642, 645 (Tex.1988).
[54] *Joe v. Two Thirty Nine Joint Venture*, 145 S.W.3d 150, 159–60 (Tex. 2004).

- When a fiduciary profits or benefits in any way from a *transaction* with the beneficiary, a presumption of unfairness arises that shifts the burden of persuasion to the fiduciary or the party claiming the validity or benefits of the transaction to show that the transaction was fair and equitable to the beneficiary.[55]

- A presumption of unfairness also arises and the burden of proof shifts to the fiduciary if the fiduciary places himself in a position in which his self-interest might conflict with his obligations as a fiduciary.[56]

(3) The attorney's breach resulted in injury or benefit

- A fiduciary litigation plaintiff needs to show one of the following: (1) the attorney's breach resulted in injury to the plaintiff or (2) the attorney's breach resulted in benefit to the attorney.[57]

- As a fiduciary, an attorney cannot take a profit or benefit from a fiduciary breach, even if the client has no damages.[58]

4-2:3 Damages and Remedies

4-2:3.1 Actual Damages

Actual damages are available for breach of fiduciary duty,[59] but actual damages are no required to receive fee disgorgement damages. "A client need not prove actual damages in order to obtain forfeiture of an attorney's fee for the attorney's breach of fiduciary duty to the client."[60] Similarly, the client need not show causation and actual damages to be entitled to equitable remedies[61] including but not limited to constructive trust.[62]

4-2:3.2 Attorneys' Fee Forfeiture

A client can seek an attorneys' fee forfeiture, even in the absence of actual damages.[63] This is sometimes referred to as disgorgement of fees.[64] This remedy is restricted to "clear and serious" violations of duty.[65] The Texas Supreme Court identified the

---

[55] *Archer v. Griffith*, 390 S.W.2d 735, 739 (Tex. 1964); *Keck, Mahin & Cate v. Nat'l Union Fire Ins. Co. of Pittsburgh, Pa.*, 20 S.W.3d 692, 699 (Tex. 2000); *Texas Bank & Trust Co. v. Moore*, 595 S.W.2d 502, 509 (Tex. 1980).

[56] *Stephens Cty. Museum, Inc. v. Swenson*, 517 S.W.2d 257, 260–61 (Tex. 1974).

[57] *Burrow v. Arce*, 997 S.W.2d 229, 240 (Tex. 1999).

[58] *Burrow v. Arce*, 997 S.W.2d 229, 240 (Tex. 1999).

[59] *Manges v. Guerra*, 673 S.W.2d 180, 184 (Tex. 1984).

[60] *First United Pentecostal Church of Beaumont v. Parker*, 514 S.W.3d 214, 220 (Tex. 2017) (quoting *Burrow v. Arce*, 997 S.W.2d 229, 240 (Tex. 1999)).

[61] *First United Pentecostal Church of Beaumont v. Parker*, 514 S.W.3d 214, 221 (Tex. 2017).

[62] *See Miller v. Huebner*, 474 S.W.2d 587, 591 (Tex. Civ. App.—Houston [14th Dist.] 1971, writ ref'd n.r.e.).

[63] *Burrow v. Arce*, 997 S.W.2d 229, 232 (Tex. 1999).

[64] *Burrow v. Arce*, 997 S.W.2d 229 (Tex. 1999).

[65] *Burrow v. Arce*, 997 S.W.2d 229, 241 (Tex. 1999).

following factors for considering whether a breach is the kind "clear and serious" violation prime for fee forfeiture:[66]

(1) the gravity and timing of the violation,

(2) its willfulness,

(3) its effect on the value of the lawyer's work for the client,

(4) any other threatened or actual harm to the client,

(5) the adequacy of other remedies,

(6) and the public interest in maintaining the integrity of attorney-client relationships.

Depending on the circumstances, fees may be fully forfeited, partially forfeited, or not at all.[67]

4-2:4 Defenses

4-2:4.1 Statute of Limitations

A four-year statute of limitations applies to breach of fiduciary duty claims.[68]

Although breach of fiduciary duty claims have a four-year statute of limitations, Texas courts will impose the two-year legal malpractice statute of limitations when the substance of the claim is tort-based and largely about the quality of the lawyer's representation.[69]

---

[66] *Burrow v. Arce*, 997 S.W.2d 229, 243 (Tex. 1999).
[67] *Burrow v. Arce*, 997 S.W.2d 229, 243 (Tex. 1999).
[68] Tex. Civ. Prac. & Rem. Code Ann. § 16.004(a)(5).
[69] *Murphy v. Gruber*, 241 S.W.3d 689, 697–98 (Tex. App.—Dallas 2007, pet. denied).

CHAPTER 5

Insurance Litigation*

5-1 Unfair Insurance Practices—Violations of the Texas Prompt Payment of Claims

5-1:1 Overview

5-1:1.1 Related Causes of Action

Bad Faith, Breach of Contract, Breach of *Stowers* Duty, DTPA, Chapter 541 Insurance Code Violations

5-1:1.2 Notice

Similar to the DTPA, chapter 541 requires a plaintiff to give notice of their intent to file suit claiming a 541 violation. If they fail to give notice, the suit is abated.

MUST READ CASES & STATUTES

The Texas Prompt Payment of Claims Act (TPPCA)—Texas Insurance Code Chapter 542 Subchapter B (requiring insurers to follow certain procedures and meet certain deadlines when it receives, accepts, rejects or pays insurance claim)[1]

Lamar Homes, Inc. v. Mid-Continent Cas. Co., 242 S.W.3d 1 (Tex. 2007)

Barbara Techs. Corp. v. State Farm Lloyds, 589 S.W.3d 806 (Tex. 2019)

Ortiz v. State Farm Lloyds, 589 S.W.3d 127 (Tex. 2019)

Allstate Ins. v. Bonner, 51 S.W.3d 289, 291 (Tex. 2001)

5-1:2 Elements

(1) Chapter 542 applies to claims that are personal to the insured; therefore, Chapter 542 does not apply to third-party claims.[2] The proper party plaintiff may be either the policy holder or a beneficiary making a claim under the policy.[3]

---

* The authors thank Caylin Craig for her assistance in the updating of this chapter.
[1] Formerly found in Article 21.55 of the Texas Insurance Code.
[2] *See Evanston Ins. v. ATOFINA Pets., Inc.*, 256 S.W.3d 660, 674 (Tex. 2008).
[3] Tex. Ins. Code Ann. § 542.060(a).

"Claimant" means a person making a claim.[4]

(2) The insurer is liable for a claim under the insurance policy.

Chapter 542 Subchapter B applies to any insurer authorized to engage in business as an insurance company or to provide insurance in Texas.[5] For a non-exhaustive list of insurers this subchapter applies to see § 542.052.[6]

"Claim" means a first-party claim that (a) is made by an insured or policyholder under an insurance policy or contract or by a beneficiary named in the policy or contract; and (b) must be paid by the insurer directly to the insured or beneficiary.[7]

An insurer is not liable for a claim under an insurance policy "until it (1) has completed its investigation, evaluated the claim, and come to a determination to accept and pay the claim or some part of it; or (2) been adjudicated liable by a court or arbitration panel."[8]

(3) The insurer failed to follow one or more of the statutory deadlines with respect to the claim.[9]

Within 15 days of receiving notice of a claim[10], the insurer must acknowledge receipt of the claim, commence any investigation of the claim, and request from the claimant all items, statements, and forms that the insurer reasonably believes, at that time, will be required from the claimant.[11]

Within 15 business days of the insurer receiving all items, statements, and forms required to secure final proof of loss, the insurer must notify the insured in writing of acceptance or rejection of the claim.[12] If an insurer

---

[4] Tex. Ins. Code Ann. § 542.051(3).
[5] Tex. Ins. Code Ann. § 542.052.
[6] *Id.*
[7] Tex. Ins. Code Ann. § 542.051(2).
[8] *Barbara Techs. Corp. v. State Farm Lloyds*, 589 S.W.3d 806, 819 (Tex. 2019).
[9] *See* Tex. Ins. Code Ann. §§ 542.055 - 542.057. Note: The deadlines found in Subchapter B of Chapter 542 are subject to an extension for good cause by the court and are automatically extended by 15 days in the event of a weather-related catastrophe or major natural disaster. Tex. Ins. Code. Ann. § 542.059.
[10] "Notice of Claim" is defined as "any written notification provided by a claimant to an insurer that reasonably apprises the insurer of the facts relating to the claim." Tex. Ins. Code. Ann. § 542.051(4).
[11] Tex. Ins. Code Ann. § 542.055(a); *Lee v. Catlin Specialty Ins.*, 766 F. Supp. 2d 812, 825–26 (S.D. Tex. 2011). If the insurer is an eligible surplus lines insurer meeting certain statutory requisites, the deadlines are extended to the 30th business day after the insurer receives notice of the claim. Tex. Ins. Code Ann. § 542.055(a).
[12] Tex. Ins. Code Ann. § 542.056(a); However, if an insurer has a reasonable basis to believe that a loss resulted from arson, the insurer's deadline to notify the insured of acceptance or rejection is extended to the 30th day after the date the insurer receives all items, statements, and forms required by the insurer. Tex. Ins. Code Ann. § 542.055(b). Furthermore, the statute allows for the insurer to extend the deadline to accept or reject if the insurer is unable to accept or reject the claim within the time periods specified by § 542.056(a) or (b). Tex. Ins. Code Ann. § 542.056(c). To take advantage of this extension, the insurer must notify the claimant of the reasons that the insurer needs additional time within the applicable time period either under § 542.056(a) or (b). *Id.* Once the notice to extend is sent, the

rejects a claim, its written notice of rejection to the insured must state the reasons for rejection.[13] If the insurer notifies insured that it will pay all or part of a claim, the insurer must make the payment within five business days after the date notice is made.[14] However, if payment of the claim or part of the claim is conditioned on the performance of an act by the claimant, the insurer must pay the claim not later than the fifth business day after the date the act is performed.[15]

If an insurer, after receiving all items, statements, and forms reasonably requested and required under Section 542.055, delays payment of the claim for a period exceeding the period specified by other applicable statutes or, if other statutes do not specify a period, for more than 60 days, the insurer shall pay damages and other items as provided by Section 542.060.[16] However, this provision does not apply in a case in which it is found as a result of arbitration or litigation that a claim received by an insurer is invalid and should not be paid by the insurer.[17]

5-1:3 Damages and Remedies

5-1:3.1 Actual Damages

The amount of the claim is recoverable by the policy holder or beneficiary making the claim under the policy for the insurer's violation of any provision in Chapter 542 Subchapter B.[18]

5-1:3.2 Statutory Damages

An insurer found liable for a TPPCA violation must pay statutory damages of 18% interest per year on the amount of the claim.[19] The accrual date of this statutory penalty is subject to some uncertainty in Texas courts.[20]

---

insurer's new deadline to send its notice of acceptance or rejection is the 45th day after the date the insurer notifies a claimant of its need for an extension. *Id.*

[13] Tex. Ins. Code. Ann. § 542.056(c).

[14] Tex. Ins. Code Ann. § 542.057(a). However, if the insurer is an eligible surplus lines insurer, the insurer's deadline to pay the claim is extended to the 20th business day after the notice or the date the act which the payment is conditioned on is performed. Tex. Ins. Code. Ann. § 542.057(c).

[15] Tex. Ins. Code. Ann. § 542.057(b).

[16] Tex. Ins. Code Ann. § 542.058(a).

[17] Tex. Ins. Code Ann. § 542.058(b).

[18] Tex. Ins. Code Ann. § 542.060(a); *see* Tex. Ins. Code Ann. § 542.051(2) for the definition of "Claim"; *Republic Underwriters Ins. Co. v. Mex-Tex, Inc.*, 150 S.W.3d 423, 426 (Tex. 2004) (discussing the definition of "claim" under Chapter 542 Subchapter B as one limited to the "amount ultimately determined to be owed, which of course would be net of any partial payments made prior to that determination").

[19] Tex. Ins. Code Ann. § 542.060(a); *see* Tex. Ins. Code Ann. § 542.051(2) for the definition of "Claim."

[20] *Cox Operating, L.L.C. v. St. Paul Surplus Lines Ins. Co.*, No. H-07-2724, 2013 U.S. Dist. LEXIS 116098, at *8 (S.D. Tex. 2013) (discussing the different approaches taken by Texas courts on accrual dates for the statutory penalty).

If the insurer tendered partial payment to the insured, and that payment is not unconditional, the statutory penalty of 18% interest is calculated on the difference between amount of insured's claim as determined by the jury and amount tendered by the insurer.[21]

5-1:3.3 Prejudgment Interest

In addition to the statutory penalty of 18% interest on the amount of the claim, prejudgment interest on amount of claim is recoverable.[22]

Prejudgment interest accrues 30 days after the policy sum is due and continues to accrue until judgment date.[23]

Texas appellate courts disagree on whether to permit prejudgment interest to be calculated on the 18% statutory damages.[24]

5-1:3.4 Post-judgment Interest

Post-judgment interest is recoverable.[25]

5-1:3.5 Court Costs

The Texas Rules of Civil Procedure permit the prevailing party to recover all adversary costs incurred.[26] In a TPPCA action, the trial court may award court costs, and the trial court has discretion to allocate the court costs under Rule 141 as it deems appropriate and will not be overturned on appeal unless the trial court abused its discretion.[27] *See* Chapter 11, Section 11–13:2.

5-1:3.6 Attorney's Fees

Reasonable attorney's fees are recoverable in a Chapter 542 action.[28] *See* Chapter 11, Section 11–13:3. Contingency fee issue

---

[21] *Id.* at 425–28.

[22] Tex. Ins. Code Ann. 542.060(a). *See Certain Underwriters at Lloyd's v. Prime Nat. Res., Inc.*, No. 01-17-00881-CV, 2019 Tex. App. LEXIS 10275, at *64 (Tex. App.—Houston [1st Dist.] Nov. 26, 2019) (explaining that prejudgment interest is not recoverable on partial payments made on the claim by the insurer).

[23] Tex. Fin. Code Ann. § 302.002.

[24] *See Texas Farmers Ins. v. Cameron*, 24 S.W.3d 386, 399 (Tex. App.—Dallas 2000, pet. denied); *Dunn v. S. Farm Bur. Cas. Ins.*, 991 S.W.2d 467, 478–79 (Tex. App.—Tyler 1999, pet. denied).

[25] *Mid-Century Ins. Co. v. Barclay*, 880 S.W.2d 807, 813 (Tex. App.—Austin 1994, writ denied).

[26] Tex. R. Civ. P. 131.

[27] Tex. R. Civ. P. 141; *Ware v. United Fire Lloyds*, No. 09-12-00061-CV, 2013 Tex. App. LEXIS 5730, at *8–9 (Tex. App.—Beaumont 2013, no pet.) (recognizing that the trial court may award court costs in a action under Chapter 542 of the Texas Insurance Code).

[28] Tex. Ins. Code Ann. § 542.060(b).

5-2 Unfair Insurance Practices—Deceptive Insurance Practices

5-2:1 Overview

5-2:1.1 Related Causes of Action

Bad Faith, Breach of Contract, Breach of *Stowers* Duty, Texas Prompt Payment of Claims Act Violation, DTPA

MUST READ CASES & STATUTES

USAA Texas Lloyds Co. v. Menchaca, 545 S.W.3d 479 (Tex. 2018)

Ortiz v. State Farm Lloyds, 589 S.W.3d 127 (Tex. 2019)

Crown Life Ins. Co. v. Casteel, 22 S.W.3d 378 (Tex. 2000)

Rocor Int'l v. Nat'l Union Fire Ins. Co., 77 S.W.3d 253 (Tex. 2002)

Texas Insurance Code Chapter 541 (regulates insurance trade practices and provides a private cause of action for unfair or deceptive insurance practices).[29]

5-2:2 Notice

A person seeking damages in an action against another person under Chapter 541 must provide written notice to the other person not later than the 61st day before the date the action is filed.[30] This notice must advise the other person of: the specific complaint; and the amount of actual damages and expense, including attorney's fees reasonably incurred in asserting the claim against the other person.[31]

The notice is not required if giving notice is impracticable because the action: must be filed to prevent the statute of limitations from expiring; or is asserted as a counterclaim.[32]

A person who has had a claim under Chapter 151 filed against them but did not receive the required notice under § 541.154 may file a plea in abatement.[33] The deadline to file a plea in abatement is not later than the 30th day after the date the person files an original answer in the court in which the action is pending.[34]

The action is automatically abated beginning on the 11th day after the plea in abatement is filed if the plea is (1) verified and alleges that the person against whom the action is pending did not receive the required notice; and (2) is not controverted by an affidavit filed by the claimant before the 11th day after the date the plea in abatement is filed.[35] If the action is not automatically abated, the court shall abate the action if,

---

[29] Formerly found in Article 21.21 of the Texas Insurance Code.
[30] Tex. Ins. Code Ann. § 541.154(a).
[31] Tex. Ins. Code Ann. § 541.154(b).
[32] Tex. Ins. Code Ann. § 541.154(c).
[33] Tex. Ins. Code Ann. § 541.155(a).
[34] *Id.*
[35] Tex. Ins. Code Ann. § 541.155(c).

after a hearing, the court finds that the person is entitled to an abatement because the claimant did not provide the required notice.[36]

If the action is abated under § 541.155, the abatement continues until the 60th day after the date notice is provided in compliance with § 541.154.[37]

5-2:3 Elements

(1) The claimant is a person who has sustained actual damages.[38]

"Person" for the purposes of Chapter 541 is defined as: an individual, corporation, association, partnership, reciprocal or interinsurance exchange, Lloyd's plan, fraternal benefit society, or other legal entity engaged in the business of insurance, including an agent, broker, adjuster or life and health insurance counselor.[39]

The insured or a beneficiary of the insurance policy has standing to sue under Chapter 541.[40] A third party claimant does not have a right to recover under Chapter 541.[41]

Note that if the claimant is alleging allegations of the DTPA as the basis for recovery under Chapter 541, the claimant may have to prove that she is a consumer as defined by the DTPA depending on which provisions of the DTPA she is alleging were violated.[42]

(2) The party against whom the Chapter 541 action is brought is a "person."[43]

"Person" can include employees of an insurance company whose job duties call for them to engage in the business of insurance—meaning that these employees can both sue and be sued for violations of the Texas Insurance Code.[44]

An insurance company may be liable for any acts of its employees or agents that is within the actual or apparent scope of the agent's authority.[45]

(3) Defendant violated at least one of three categories of statutes.[46]

---

[36] Tex. Ins. Code Ann. § 541.155(b).
[37] Tex. Ins. Code Ann. § 541.155(d).
[38] Tex. Ins. Code Ann. § 541.151.
[39] Tex. Ins. Code Ann. § 541.002(2); see *Ceshker v. Bankers Commercial Life Ins. Co.*, 568 S.W.2d 128, 129 (Tex. 1978).
[40] *Chaffin v. Transamerica Ins. Co.*, 731 S.W.2d 728, 731 (Tex. App.—Houston [14th Dist.] 1987, writ ref'd n.r.e.).
[41] *Allstate Ins. Co. v. Watson*, 876 S.W.2d 145, 149 (Tex. 1994).
[42] *Crown Life Ins. Co. v. Casteel*, 22 S.W.3d 378, 386–87 (Tex. 2000).
[43] Tex. Ins. Code Ann. § 541.151; see Tex. Ins. Code Ann. § 541.002(2) for the definition of "person"; *Dallas Fire Ins. Co. v. Texas Contractors Sur. & Cas. Agency*, 159 S.W.3d 895, 897 (Tex. 2004).
[44] *Crown Life Ins. v. Casteel*, 22 S.W.3d 378, 384–85 (Tex. 2000); *Liberty Mut. Ins. Co. v. Garrison Contractors*, 966 S.W.2d 482, 487 (Tex. 1998).
[45] *Celtic Life Ins. v. Coats*, 885 S.W.2d 96, 98 (Tex. 1994).
[46] Tex. Ins. Code Ann. § 541.151 (West).

INSURANCE LITIGATION

Violation of Texas Insurance Code chapter 541, subchapter B.[47]

Violation of § 17.46(b) of the Texas DTPA and the person bringing the action relied on the act or practice to their detriment.[48]

Violation of a tie-in provision of the Texas Insurance Code.[49]

(4) Defendant's act or practice was a producing cause of actual damages.[50]

"Producing cause" means a cause that was a substantial factor in bringing about an injury, and without which the injury would not have occurred.[51]

5-2:4 Damages and Remedies

5-2:4.1 Actual Damages

Actual damages are recoverable.[52] *See* Chapter 10 and Chapter 11.

The General Rule: An insured cannot recover policy benefits as damages for an insurer's statutory violation if the policy does not provide the insured right to receive those benefits.

The Entitled-To-Benefits Rule: An insured who establishes a right to receive benefits under the policy can recover those benefits as actual damages under the Insurance code if the insurer's statutory violation causes the loss of the benefits.[53]

The Benefits-Lost Rule: Even if the insured cannot establish a present contractual right to policy benefits, the insured can recover benefits as actual damages under the Insurance code if the insurer's statutory violation caused the insured to lose that contractual right.[54]

The Independent Injury Rule: If an insurer's statutory violation causes an injury independent of the loss of policy benefits, the insured may recover damages for that injury even if the policy does not grant the insured a right to benefits.[55]

---

[47] Tex. Ins. Code Ann. § 541.151(1).

[48] *See* Tex. Bus. & Comm. Code Ann. § 17.46(b); *Guardian Life Ins. Co. v. Kinder*, 663 F. Supp. 2d 544, 552 (S.D. Tex. 2009); *Crown Life Ins. Co. v. Casteel*, 22 S.W.3d 378, 386–87 (Tex. 2000).

[49] Examples of tie-in statues include Tex. Ins. Code Ann. § 1501.357 (making a violation of 1501.352, regulating the marketing of small employer health benefits plans, an unfair method of competition and an unfair or deceptive practice under Chapter 541); Tex. Ins. Code Ann. § 843.051 (applying Chapter 541 to certain HMOs); and Tex. Ins. Code Ann. § 544.254 (defining a violation of § 544.253, prohibiting certain insurance practices as to church property, as an unfair or deceptive act or practice under Chapter 541).

[50] While the statute itself does not provide a causation standard, Texas courts have seemed to accept producing cause as the correct standard. *See State Farm Fire & Cas. Co. v. Miller*, 713 S.W.2d 700, 704 (Tex. App.—Dallas 1986, writ ref'd n.r.e.); *Provident Am. Ins. Co. v. Castaneda*, 988 S.W.2d 189, 193 (Tex. 1998).

[51] *Ford Motor Co. v. Ledesma*, 242 S.W.3d 32, 46 (Tex. 2007).

[52] Tex. Ins. Code Ann. § 541.152(a)(1).

[53] *USAA Tex. Lloyds Co. v. Menchaca*, 545 S.W.3d 479, 497 (Tex. 2018).

[54] *Id.*

[55] *Id.* at 499.

The No-Recovery Rule: An insured cannot recover any damages based on an insurer's statutory Violation if the insured had no right to receive benefits under the policy and sustained no injury independent of a right to benefits.[56]

5-2:4.1a Lost Profits

Lost Profits are recoverable.[57] See Chapter 11, Section 11-6.

5-2:4.1b Lost Income

Lost income is recoverable.[58]

5-2:4.1c Damaged Credit Reputation

More than nominal damages are available for a plaintiff's damaged credit reputation if plaintiff was denied a loan which in turn was proved to have caused a financial injury, or was charged a higher interest rate.[59] See Chapter 11, Section 11–19:1.

5-2:4.1d Damages for Personal Injury

Personal injury damages are recoverable for mental anguish only if the defendant acted knowingly.[60]

5-2:4.2 Additional Damages

Additional damages up to three times the amount of actual damages are recoverable where the defendant acted knowingly.[61]

5-2:4.3 Injunction

Equitable relief in the form of an injunction is available.[62]

5-2:4.4 Other Relief

Other equitable relief the court deems proper is available.[63]

---

[56] *Id.* at 500.
[57] *Southland Lloyd's Ins. v. Tomberlain*, 919 S.W.2d 822, 830 (Tex. App.—Texarkana 1996, writ denied).
[58] *Southland Lloyd's Ins. v. Tomberlain*, 919 S.W.2d 822, 830 (Tex. App.—Texarkana 1996, writ denied).
[59] *St. Paul Surplus Lines Ins. Co. v. Dal-Worth Tank Co.*, 974 S.W.2d 51, 53 (Tex. 1998).
[60] Tex. Bus. & Com. Code Ann. § 17.50(a); Tex. Ins. Code Ann. § 541.152(b). *State Farm Life Ins. Co. v. Beaston*, 907 S.W.2d 430, 436 (Tex. 1995) ("We therefore hold that mental anguish damages are not recoverable . . . without an express finding of knowing conduct.").
[61] Tex. Ins. Code Ann. § 541.152(b).
[62] Tex. Ins. Code Ann. § 541.152(a)(2).
[63] Tex. Ins. Code Ann. § 541.152(a)(3).

INSURANCE LITIGATION

5-2:4.5 Interest

Prejudgment and post-judgment interest are recoverable.[64]

5-2:4.6 Court Costs

Court costs are available for prevailing plaintiff.[65]

Court costs are available for the defendant if the court finds that plaintiff's suit was groundless and brought in bad faith or for purpose of harassment.[66]

5-2:4.7 Attorney's Fees

Reasonable attorney's fees are recoverable for a plaintiff who recovers damages.[67]

Reasonable attorney's fees may be recoverable for defendant if the plaintiff's suit was groundless and brought in bad faith or for the purpose of harassment.[68]

5-2:5 Defenses

5-2:5.1 Statute of Limitations

Two-year statute of limitations for violation of Chapter 541.[69]

Discovery rule applies to Chapter 541.[70]

Deadline for filing suit can be extended for 180 days if the plaintiff proves suit was filed late as result of conduct by defendant that was solely calculated to induce plaintiff to postpone or refrain from filing action.[71]

5-2:5.2 Reducing Damages with Settlement Offer

If a defendant makes a settlement offer in compliance with § 541.157 that is the same as or substantially same as the damages awarded by the trier of fact, the claimant may not recover damages any amount in excess of the lessor of: (1) the amount of damages stated in the settlement offer; or (2) the amount of damages found by the trier of fact.[72]

---

[64] *St. Paul Surplus Lines Ins. Co. v. Dal-Worth Tank Co.*, 974 S.W.2d 51, 54–55 (Tex. 1998). Tex. Fin. Code Ann. § 304.001 (West 2015).
[65] Tex. Ins. Code Ann. § 541.152(a)(1).
[66] Tex. Ins. Code Ann. § 541.153.
[67] Tex. Ins. Code Ann. § 541.152(a)(1).
[68] Tex. Ins. Code Ann. § 541.153.
[69] Tex. Ins. Code Ann. § 541.162.
[70] Tex. Ins. Code Ann. § 541.162.
[71] Tex. Ins. Code Ann. § 541.162(b).
[72] Tex. Ins. Code Ann. § 541.159.

5-3 Insurance Bad Faith

5-3:1 Overview

An insurer's breach of its duty of good faith and fair dealing is a cause of action that sounds in tort and is distinct from a contract action for the breach of the terms of the underlying insurance policy.[73]

5-3:1.1 Related Causes of Action

Breach of Contract, Breach of *Stowers* Duty, Late Payment of Claims, DTPA, Deceptive Trade Practices

5-3:2 Elements

(1) A contract between insurer and insured giving rise to the duty of good faith and fair dealing.[74]

> An insurer owes a duty of good faith and fair dealing to the insured because of the special relationship arising out of the insurance contract.[75]

> An insurer's duty of good faith and fair dealing does not extend to third party claimants.[76]

(2) An insurer violates its duty of good faith and fair dealing by denying or delaying payment of claim if insurer knew or should have known that it was reasonably clear that claim was covered.[77]

(3) The insurer's breach was the proximate cause of the insured's damages.[78]

5-3:3 Damages and Remedies

5-3:3.1 Actual Damages

5-3:3.1a Mental Anguish

Mental anguish damages are recoverable upon a showing that the denial or delay in payment of a claim seriously disrupted the insured's life; they are not available in all cases.[79] See Chapter 11, Section 11-9:3.

---

[73] *See Twin City Fire Ins. v. Davis*, 904 S.W.2d 663, 666 (Tex. 1995).

[74] *Hudspeth v. Enter. Life Ins.*, 358 S.W.3d 373, 389 (Tex. App.—Houston [1st Dist.] 2011, no pet.); *see also Arnold v. Nat'l Cty. Mut. Fire Ins.*, 725 S.W.2d 165, 167 (Tex. 1987).

[75] *Transport Ins. v. Faircloth*, 898 S.W.2d 269, 279 (Tex. 1995).

[76] *Transport Ins. v. Faircloth*, 898 S.W.2d 269, 279–80 (Tex. 1995).

[77] *Universe Life Ins. Co. v. Giles*, 950 S.W.2d 48, 56 (Tex. 1997).

[78] *Provident Am. Ins. v. Castañeda*, 988 S.W.2d 189, 193 n.13 (Tex. 1998); *Aranda v. Ins. Co. of N. Am.*, 748 S.W.2d 210, 215 (Tex. 1988), *overruled on other grounds, Texas Mut. Ins. v. Ruttiger*, 381 S.W.3d 430 (Tex. 2012).

[79] *Universe Life Ins. Co. v. Giles*, 950 S.W.2d 48, 54 (Tex. 1997).

5-3:3.1b Loss of Credit Reputation

Loss of credit reputation is recoverable as actual damages in a suit where damage to credit was the necessary and usual result of the defendant's actions.[80] The amount of damages need only be established with the degree of certainty to which it is susceptible.[81] *See* Chapter 11, Section 11-9:1.

5-3:3.1c Increased Business Costs

Increased business costs may be recoverable as actual damages.[82] *See* Chapter 11, Section 11-3.

5-3:3.2 Exemplary Damages

Exemplary damages are only available in exceptional bad faith cases.[83] The plaintiff must show that the insurer's conduct rose to the level of malicious, intentional, fraudulent, or grossly negligent conduct to receive exemplary damages.[84] Therefore, the plaintiff must show that the insurer was actually aware that its action would probably result in extraordinary harm not ordinarily associated with breach of contract or bad faith denial of a claim—such as death, grievous physical injury, or financial ruin.[85]

Exemplary damage awards serve to punish the wrongdoer and set a public example to prevent the repetition of the act.[86] The punishment imposed through exemplary damages is to be directed at the wrongdoer, and an award of exemplary damages must be specific as to each defendant.[87] A defendant's liability for exemplary damages is limited based on the conduct of employees, agents, and associates.[88] *See* Chapter 11, Section 11-2.

5-3:3.3 Interest

A party may recover prejudgment and post-judgment interest on an award in an insurance bad faith claim.[89] Prejudgment interest is compensation allowed by law for the lost use of the money due as damages during the time between the accrual of the claim and the judgment date.[90] If no statute requires prejudgment interest, then the

---

[80] *EMC Mortg. Corp. v. Jones*, 252 S.W.3d 857, 872 (Tex. App.—Dallas 2008, no pet.). *See also Mead v. Johnson Grp., Inc.*, 615 S.W.2d 685, 688 (Tex. 1991).

[81] *Id.*

[82] *St. Paul Surplus Lines Ins. Co. v. Dal-Worth Tank Co.*, 974 S.W.2d 51, 53 (Tex. 1998) (upholding award for "increased business costs" founded upon evidence that defendant's vendors insisted on payment in advance, which resulted in increased costs to defendant).

[83] *Universe Life Ins. Co. v. Giles*, 950 S.W.2d 48, 54 (Tex. 1997).

[84] *Id.*

[85] *Id.*

[86] *Fairfield Ins. Co. v. Stephens Martin Paving, LP*, 246 S.W.3d 653, 666 (Tex. 2008).

[87] Tex. Civ. Prac. & Rem. Code Ann. § 41.006.

[88] Tex. Civ. Prac. & Rem. Code Ann. § 41.005.

[89] *Southland Lloyds Ins. Co. v. Cantu*, 399 S.W.3d 558, 580 (Tex. App.—San Antonio 2011, pet. denied) (permitting prevailing party to recover with interest in bad faith claim).

[90] *Johnson & Higgins, Inc. v. Kenneco Energy*, 962 S.W.2d 507, 528 (Tex. 1998).

trial court generally has discretion whether to award prejudgment interest.[91] For a recovery of interest to be sustained it must have a basis in the pleadings; interest must be asked for specifically or be embraced in the aggregate amount laid as damages.[92]

A money judgment that provides for interest or time price differential within its terms earns post-judgment interest at a rate equal to the lesser of the rate specified in the contract and 18%.[93] Prejudgment interest accrues at the same rate at the post-judgment interest rate and is computed as simple interest, while post-judgment interest is compounded annually.[94] Prejudgment interest accrues on the earlier date of the 180th day after the defendant receives written notice of a claim and the date that the suit is filed.[95] Post-judgment interest accrues on the date that judgment is rendered and ends on the date that judgment is satisfied.[96] *See* Chapter 11, Section 11–13:1.

5-3:3.4 Court Costs

A judgment creditor to insurance bad faith claim may recover reasonable court costs.[97] *See* Chapter 11, Section 11–13:2.

5-3:4 Defenses

5-3:4.1 Statute of Limitations

Two-year statute of limitations.[98]

5-3:4.2 Reasonable Basis

Reasonable basis for denying or delaying payment of a claim exists where insurer's decision was based on bona fide coverage dispute.[99]

Reasonable basis exists when insurer's decision was based on objective and reliable information prepared by expert.[100]

5-3:4.3 Fraudulent Inducement

Defense that plaintiff secured insurance policy through fraud.[101]

---

[91] *Hoelscher v. Kilman*, No. 03-04-00440-CV, 2006 Tex. App. LEXIS 1351, at *16 (Tex. App.—Austin 2006, no pet.).

[92] *Zuider Zee Oyster Bar, Inc. v. Martin*, 503 S.W.2d 292, 299 (Tex. Civ. App.—Fort Worth 1973, writ ref'd n.r.e.).

[93] Tex. Fin. Code Ann. § 304.002.

[94] *Landmark Org., L.P. v. Delphini Constr. Co.*, No. 13-04-371-CV, 2005 Tex. App. LEXIS 8414, at *15 (Tex. App.—Corpus Christi 2005, pet. denied).

[95] *See* Tex. Fin. Code Ann. § 304.104.

[96] *See* Tex. Fin. Code Ann. § 304.005.

[97] Tex. Civ. Prac. & Rem. Code Ann. § 31.002; *Universe Life Ins. Co. v. Giles*, 982 S.W.2d 488, 493 (Tex. App.—Texarkana 1998, pet. denied) (permitting a judgment creditor to recover reasonable court costs).

[98] Tex. Civ. Prac. & Rem. Code Ann. § 16.003(a).

[99] *Provident Am. Ins. v. Castaneda*, 988 S.W.2d 189, 194 (Tex. 1998).

[100] *Lyons v. Millers Cas. Ins.*, 866 S.W.2d 597, 601 (Tex. 1993).

[101] *Koral Indus. v. Security-Conn. Life Ins.*, 802 S.W.2d 650, 651 (Tex. 1990).

5-4 Uninsured Motorist/Underinsured Motorist (UM/UIM) Coverage Claim

5-4:1 Overview

The Texas Insurance Code requires every insurer issuing automobile liability insurance policies to provide uninsured or underinsured motorist (UM/UIM) coverage in the policy or as a supplement to the policy.[102] However, uninsured or underinsured motorist coverage is not required to be provided if the insured rejects the covered in writing.[103]

The insured must establish the liability of an uninsured/underinsured motorist and the extent of the damages before becoming legally entitled to recover benefits under a UM/UIM policy.[104]

5-4:1.1 Related Causes of Action

Bad Faith, Breach of Contract, Breach of *Stowers* Duty, DTPA, Insurance Code Violations, Late Payment of Claims, Duty to Defend

MUST READ CASES & STATUTES

Texas Insurance Code Section 1952.101 (Texas Motor Vehicle Safety Responsibility Act)

Dryden v. Dairyland Cty. Mut. Ins. Co., 633 S.W.2d 912, 914 (Tex. App.—Beaumont 1982, no pet.) (Elements 1—3)

Brainard v. Trinity Universal Ins. Co., 216 S.W.3d 809 (Tex. 2006) (An insurer has no contractual duty to pay benefits until the insured "obtains a judgment establishing the liability and underinsured status of the other motorist."[105] Since *Brainard* stands for the proposition that an insurer cannot breach the insurance contract until it refuses to pay a judgment, a number of courts have held that a breach of contract claim is no longer the proper vehicle to prove up a UM/UIM claim. *See Stoyer v. State Farm Mut. Auto. Ins. Co.*, 2009 U.S. Dist. LEXIS 15571 at *5 (N. D. Tex. Feb. 24, 2009); *Owen v. Empr's Mut. Cas. Co.*, 2008 U.S. Dist. LEXIS 24893 at *5 (N. D. Tex. Mar. 28, 2008). In the wake of *Brainard*, the proper vehicle may be a declaratory judgment action under Chapter 37 of the Texas Civil Practices and Remedies Code. *See Allstate Ins. Co. v. Jordan*, 503 S.W.3d 450, 456 (Tex. App.—Texarkana 2016, no pet.); *Farmers Ins. Exch. v. Rodriguez*, 366 S.W.3d 216, 219 (Tex. App.—Houston [14th Dist.] 2012, rev. denied)

---

[102] Tex. Ins. Code Ann. § 1952.101.
[103] *Id.*
[104] *See Henson v. S. Farm Bureau Cas. Ins. Co.*, 17 S.W.3d 652, 654 (Tex. 2000).
[105] *Brainard, v. Trinity Universal Ins. Co.*, 216 S.W.3d 809, 818 (Tex. 2006).

5-4:2 Elements

(1) Insured is legally entitled to recover from the uninsured motorist;[106]

(2) The injury sustained was caused by the accident;[107] and

(3) The injury arises out of the ownership, maintenance or use of such uninsured automobile.[108]

5-4:3 Damages and Remedies

5-4:3.1 Actual Damages

Actual Damages: recovery from under-insured motorist coverage may be had only for damages sustained in amount in excess of total amount of tortfeasor's liability coverage.[109]

5-4:3.2 Interest

Prejudgment interest available.[110]

5-4:3.3 Attorney's Fees

Prevailing plaintiff entitled to reasonable and necessary attorney's fees.[111]

Plaintiff must suffer actual damages in order to prevail.[112]

Prevailing defendant entitled to reasonable attorney's fees and costs necessary to defend a DTPA claim if the court finds the suit was groundless, brought in bad faith or brought for purpose of harassment.[113]

5-4:3.4 Court Costs

Court costs are available.[114]

---

[106] *Dryden v. Dairyland Cty. Mut. Ins. Co.*, 633 S.W.2d 912, 914 (Tex. App.—Beaumont 1982, no pet.) (Elements 1—3).
[107] *Dryden v. Dairyland Cty. Mut. Ins. Co.*, 633 S.W.2d 912, 914 (Tex. App.—Beaumont 1982, no pet.) (Elements 1—3).
[108] *Dryden v. Dairyland Cty. Mut. Ins. Co.*, 633 S.W.2d 912, 914 (Tex. App.—Beaumont 1982, no pet.) (Elements 1—3).
[109] *Olivas v. State Farm Mut. Auto. Ins. Co.*, 850 S.W.2d 564, 565–66 (Tex. App.—El. Paso 1993, writ denied).
[110] *Brainard v. Trinity Universal Ins. Co.*, 216 S.W.3d 809, 812 (Tex. 2006).
[111] Tex. Bus. & Com. Code Ann. § 17.50(d).
[112] *Guzman v. Ugly Duckling Car Sales*, 63 S.W.3d 522, 526 (Tex. App.—San Antonio 2001, pet. denied).
[113] Tex. Bus. & Com. Code Ann. § 17.50(c).
[114] Tex. Bus. & Com. Code Ann. § 17.50(d).

INSURANCE LITIGATION

5-4:4 Defenses

5-4:4.1 Limitations

Four-year statute of limitations applies to both uninsured and underinsured motorist claims since the insured's cause of action is a contract cause of action.[115]

Statute of limitations runs when insurance company denies claim, not on date of accident giving rise to claim.[116]

5-4:4.2 Rejection of Coverage

Defense that insured rejected coverage in writing.[117]

5-5 Declaratory Judgment on Policy—Coverage Claim

5-5:1 Overview

"The Declaratory Judgments Act does not confer new substantive rights upon the parties nor additional jurisdiction on the courts but merely provides a procedural device for determination of controversies which are already within the jurisdiction of the courts."[118]

Texas courts construe insurance policies using ordinary rules of contract interpretation.[119] Therefore, Declaratory Judgment actions can be a useful tool to settle disputes on insurance coverage.

5-5:1.1 Related Causes of Action

Bad Faith, Breach of Contract, Breach of *Stowers* Duty, DTPA, Insurance Code Violations

MUST READ CASES & STATUTES

Texas Civil Practice and Remedies Code Section 37.004 (Uniform Declaratory Judgments Act)

Texas Ass'n of Bus. v. Tex. Air Control Bd., 852 S.W.2d 440, 446 (Tex. 1993)

---

[115] *Franco v. Allstate Ins. Co.*, 505 S.W.2d 789 (Tex. 1974).
[116] *Webster v. Allstate Ins. Co.*, 833 S.W.2d 747, 750 (Tex. App.—Houston [1st Dist.] 1992, no writ).
[117] Tex. Ins. Code Ann. § 1952.101(c); *Ortiz v. State Farm Mut. Auto Ins. Co*, 955 S.W.2d 353, 357 (Tex. App.—San Antonio, 1997).
[118] *Hous. Auth. of City of Harlingen v. Valdez*, 841 S.W.2d 860, 864 (Tex. App.—Corpus Christi 1992, writ denied).
[119] *Nassar v. Liberty Mut. Fire Ins. Co.*, 508 S.W.3d 254, 257 (Tex. 2017).

5-5:2 Requirements to Bring a Declaratory Judgment Action[120]

(1) A justiciable controversy (to constitute a justiciable controversy, there must exist a real and substantial controversy involving a genuine conflict of tangible interests and not merely a theoretical dispute).[121] exists as to the rights and status of the parties; and

(2) A declaration will resolve the controversy.

5-5:2.1 Elements

To prove coverage under the policy, the insured must establish that:

(1) the injury or damage is the type covered by the policy,

(2) the injury or damage was incurred at a time covered by the policy, and

(3) the injury or damage was incurred by a person whose injuries are covered by the policy.[122]

If the insured establishes coverage, the insurer then has the burden to plead and prove that the loss falls within an exclusion to the policy's coverage.[123]

5-5:3 Damages and Remedies

5-5:3.1 Declaratory Judgment

Texas Civil Practice and Remedies Code Section 37.004 (Uniform Declaratory Judgments Act).

5-5:3.2 Court Costs

Court can award court costs to either party in declaratory judgment action.[124]

5-5:3.3 Attorney's Fees

Court can award reasonable and necessary attorney's fees in declaratory judgment action.[125]

---

[120] *Texas Ass'n of Bus. v. Tex. Air Control Bd.*, 852 S.W.2d 440, 446 (Tex. 1993); *see also Bonham State Bank v. Beadle*, 907 S.W.2d 465, 467 (Tex. 1995).

[121] *Bexar-Medina-Atascosa Ctys. Water Control & Improvement Dist. No. 1 v. Medina Lake Prot. Ass'n*, 640 S.W.2d 778, 779–80 (Tex. App.—San Antonio 1982, writ ref'd n.r.e).

[122] *Seger v. Yorkshire Ins. Co.*, 503 S.W.3d 388, 400 (Tex. 2016).

[123] *Id.* at 400–01.

[124] Tex. Civ. Prac. & Rem. Code Ann. § 37.009.

[125] Tex. Civ. Prac. & Rem. Code Ann. § 37.009; *Warrantech Corp. v. Steadfast Ins.*, 210 S.W.3d 760, 769 (Tex. App.—Fort Worth 2006, pet. denied).

INSURANCE LITIGATION

5-5:4 Defenses

5-5:4.1 Statute of Limitations

Because declaratory judgment action is a procedural device used to vindicate substantive rights, it is generally governed by the statute of limitations for the legal remedy underlying the claim.[126]

5-6 Declaratory Judgment on Policy—Duty to Defend

5-6:1 Overview

5-6:1.1 Related Causes of Action

Bad Faith, Breach of Duty of Prompt Payment, Breach of Contract, DTPA, Insurance Code Violations, Claims Against Contractual and Statutory Indemnitors

MUST READ CASES & STATUTES

Texas Civil Practice and Remedies Code Sections 37.001–37.011 (Texas Declaratory Judgments Act)

Nat'l County Mut. Fire Ins. Co. v. Johnson, 829 S.W.2d 322, 324 (Tex. App.—Austin 1992), aff'd, 879 S.W.2d 1 (Tex. 1993)

5-6:2 Elements

(1) Plaintiff is insured or beneficiary under the policy[127]

   Insured has the burden to prove coverage under the terms of the insurance policy.[128]

(2) A third party sues the insured[129]

(3) Insured notifies insurer that a defense is expected[130]

   Insured must comply with the notice of suit provision in the insurance policy.[131]

(4) A claim alleged falls within the scope of policy coverage[132]

---

[126] *Northwest Austin Mun. Util. Dist. No. 1 v. City of Austin*, 274 S.W.3d 820, 836 (Tex. App.—Austin 2008).

[127] *See King v. Dallas Fire Ins.*, 85 S.W.3d 185, 188 (Tex. 2002).

[128] *Gilbert Tex. Constr., L.P. v. Underwriters at Lloyd's London*, 327 S.W.3d 118, 124 (Tex. 2010).

[129] *Gehan Homes, Ltd. v. Emp'rs Mut. Cas. Co.*, 146 S.W.3d 833, 838 (Tex. App.—Dallas 2004, pet. denied).

[130] *National Union Fire Ins. v. Crocker*, 246 S.W.3d 603, 608 (Tex. 2008).

[131] *Harwell v. State Farm Mut. Auto. Ins.*, 896 S.W.2d 170, 173–74 (Tex. 1995).

[132] *Archon Invs. v. Great Am. Lloyds Ins.*, 174 S.W.3d 334, 339 (Tex. App.—Houston [1st Dist.] 2005, pet. denied).

Once the duty to defend arises as to one claim, the insurer must defend the entire suit.[133]

Courts follow the "eight corners" rule to determine if an insurer has the duty to defend by analyzing the third-party plaintiff's pleadings, considered in light of the insurance policy provisions, without regard to the truth or falsity of those allegations.[134]

Courts interpret insurance policies using the same rules of construction as ordinary contracts.[135]

Pleadings must allege a claim within the policy period.[136]

To trigger the duty to defend, the insured must allege an injury.[137]

5-6:3 Damages and Remedies

5-6:3.1 Declaratory Judgment

Duty to defend is a justiciable issue suitable for declaratory judgment.[138]

5-6:3.2 Court Costs

Court can award court costs to either party in declaratory judgment action.[139]

5-6:3.3 Attorney's Fees

Court can award reasonable and necessary attorney's fees in declaratory judgment action.[140]

5-6:4 Defenses

5-6:4.1 Statute of Limitations

Because a suit over an insured's duty to defend is a contractual dispute, limitations period for bringing a declaratory judgment action is four years.[141]

---

[133] *Archon Invs. v. Great Am. Lloyds Ins.*, 174 S.W.3d 334, 339 (Tex. App.—Houston [1st Dist.] 2005, pet. denied).

[134] *GuideOne Elite Ins. Co. v. Fielder Rd. Baptist Church*, 197 S.W.3d 305, 308 (Tex. 2006).

[135] *Trinity Universal Ins. v. Cowan*, 945 S.W.2d 819, 823 (Tex. 1997).

[136] *American Physicians Ins. Exch. v. Garcia*, 876 S.W.2d 842, 848 (Tex. 1994).

[137] *King v. Dallas Fire Ins.*, 85 S.W.3d 185, 188 (Tex. 2002); *see also U.S. Metals, Inc. v. Libert Mut. Grp.*, 490 S.W.3d 20, 24 (Tex. 2016).

[138] *See Firemen's Ins. Co. v. Burch*, 442 S.W.2d 331, 332 (Tex. 1969); *J.E.M. v. Fidelity & Cas. Co. of N.Y.*, 928 S.W.2d 688, 671 (Tex. App.—Houston [1st Dist.] 1996, no writ).

[139] Tex. Civ. Prac. & Rem. Code Ann. § 37.009.

[140] Tex. Civ. Prac. & Rem. Code Ann. § 37.009; *Warrantech Corp. v. Steadfast Ins.*, 210 S.W.3d 760, 769 (Tex. App.—Fort Worth 2006, pet. denied).

[141] *See Whatley v. City of Dallas*, 758 S.W.2d 301, 310 (Tex. App.—Dallas 1988, writ denied).

INSURANCE LITIGATION

5-6:4.2 No Timely Notice of Claim or Occurrence

Insurer can assert defense that insured did not provide timely notice of claim or occurrence[142]

5-6:4.3 Did Not Cooperate

Insurer can assert the defense that insured did not cooperate in the investigation, defense or settlement of the insurance claim[143]

5-6:4.4 Known Loss

Under the Fortuity Doctrine, insurer can assert the defense that the insured knew about the claim that gave rise to suit when it purchased the policy.[144]

5-7 *Stowers* Claim

5-7:1 Overview

5-7:1.1 Related Causes of Action

Bad Faith, Breach of Contract, Late Payment of Claims, DTPA, Deceptive Insurance Practices

MUST READ CASES

G. A. Stowers Furniture Co. v. Am. Indem. Co., 15 S.W.2d 544, 547–48 (Tex. Comm'n App. 1929, holding approved)

Am. Physicians Ins. Exch. v. Garcia, 876 S.W.2d 842 (Tex. 1994)

Seger v. Yorkshire Ins. Co., Ltd., 503 S.W.3d 388 (Tex. 2016)

OneBeacon Ins. Co. v. T. Wade Welch & Assocs., 841 F.3d 669 (5th Cir. 2016).

5-7:2 Elements

The Stowers Doctrine holds that a liability insurer that undertakes the defense of an insured has a duty to act in good faith in settling a liability claim.[145] The "duty to defend" language in standard insurance policies gives liability insurers absolute control over the conduct of the defense, and absent a consent to settle provision, complete discretion whether to settle the claim and for what amount. The carrier is not obligated to accept pretrial settlement demands for an amount within the liability policy limit and has the contractual right to take the claim to trial. The Stowers Doctrine imposes an extracontractual duty on insurers to act in good faith related to settlement

---

[142] *Employers Cas. Co. v. Glens Falls Ins.*, 484 S.W.2d 570, 575 (Tex. 1972).
[143] *Martinez v. ACCC Ins.*, 343 S.W.3d 924, 929 (Tex. App.—Dallas 2011, no pet.).
[144] *See Two Pesos, Inc. v. Gulf Ins.*, 901 S.W.2d 495, 501 (Tex. App.—Houston [14th Dist.] 1995, no writ).
[145] *G.A. Stowers Furniture Co. v. American Indem. Co.*, 15 S.W.2d 544 (Tex. Comm'n App. 1929).

demands within policy limits. If the insurer unreasonably rejects a pretrial settlement offer within policy limits resulting in a trial and an excess verdict against the insured for an amount above policy limits, the insurer may be liable to pay the entire judgment, even in amounts above policy limits. An insurer has a *Stowers* duty when the insurance policy requires the following: (1) the insurer to defend any claim within the scope of coverage; (2) the insurer is to indemnify the insured for any damages awarded against insured within the scope of coverage up to the policy limits; and (3) insurer has control over insured's defense.[146]

These contractual duties give rise to the implied Stowers duty to accept reasonable settlement demands within policy limits.[147] **5-7:2 Elements**

(1) The claim against the insured was within the scope of coverage[148]

An insurer has no duty to settle a claim that is not covered under its policy.[149]

The initial burden is on the plaintiff to prove coverage.[150] To prove coverage, the plaintiff must establish that (1) the injury or damage is the type covered by the policy, (2) the injury or damage was incurred at a time covered by the policy, and (3) that the injury or damage was incurred by a person whose injuries are covered by the policy.[151]

(2) There was a settlement demand within the policy limits[152]

Insured must establish that a third party offered to settle its claims against insured within policy limits.[153]

A *Stowers* settlement demand must release the insured fully in exchange for a specified amount of money or the policy limits.[154]

(3) The terms of the demand were such that an ordinary prudent insurer would have accepted, considering the likelihood and degree of the insured's potential exposure to an excess judgment[155]

Insured must also offer evidence that insurer's negligent failure to settle proximately caused damages to the insured.[156]

The injury producing event in a Stowers action is the underlying judgment in excess of policy limits.[157]

---

[146] *American Physicians Ins. Exch. v. Garcia*, 876 S.W.2d 842, 846 (Tex. 1994).
[147] *Am. Physicians Ins. Exch. v. Garcia*, 876 S.W.2d 842, 846 (Tex. 1994).
[148] *Seger v. Yorkshire Ins. Co., Ltd.*, 503 S.W.3d 388, 395 (Tex. 2016).
[149] *Am. Physicians Ins. Exch. v. Garcia*, 848.
[150] *Seger v. Yorkshire Ins. Co., Ltd.*, 503 S.W.3d 388, 396 (Tex. 2016).
[151] *Seger v. Yorkshire Ins. Co., Ltd.*, 503 S.W.3d 388, 400 (Tex. 2016).
[152] *Seger v. Yorkshire Ins. Co., Ltd.*, 503 S.W.3d 388, 395 (Tex. 2016).
[153] *State Farm Lloyds Ins. v. Maldonado*, 963 S.W.2d 38, 41 (Tex. 1998).
[154] *American Physicians Ins. Exch. v. Garcia*, 876 S.W.2d 842, 848–49 (Tex. 1994).
[155] *Seger v. Yorkshire Ins. Co., Ltd.*, 503 S.W.3d 388, 396 (Tex. 2016).
[156] *Texas Farmers Ins. v. Soriano*, 881 S.W.2d 312, 316 n.4 (Tex. 1994).
[157] *Murray v. San Jacinto Agency, Inc.*, 800 S.W.2d 826, 829 (Tex. 1990).

5-7:3 Damages and Remedies

5-7:3.1 Actual Damages

Insured can recover actual damages, which are fixed as a matter of law as the amount of the excess judgment rendered against the insured over the policy limit.[158] However, if the insured assigns her Stowers action to the plaintiff in the underlying suit, the underlying judgment is inadmissible as evidence of damages unless rendered as the result of a fully adversarial trial.[159]

5-7:3.2 Exemplary Damages

Exemplary damage awards serve to punish the wrongdoer and set a public example to prevent the repetition of the act.[160] The punishment imposed through exemplary damages is to be directed at the wrongdoer, and an award of exemplary damages must be specific as to each defendant.[161] A claimant may recover exemplary damages in a Stowers claim, so long as it does not violate an express statutory definition of exemplary damages.[162] *See* Chapter 11, Section 11–12.

5-7:3.3 Court Costs

The trial court has discretion to allocate the court costs under Rule 141 as it deems appropriate and will not be overturned on appeal unless the trial court abused its discretion.[163] Furthermore, a trial court may award a defendant court costs if the court finds that the *Stowers* action was brought in bad faith or brought for the purpose of harassment.[164] *See* Chapter 11, Section 11–13:2.

5-7:3.4 Interest

Prejudgment interest is compensation allowed by law for the lost use of the money due as damages during the time between the accrual of the claim and the judgment date.[165] If no statute requires prejudgment interest, then the trial court generally has discretion whether to award prejudgment interest.[166] For a recovery of interest to be

---

[158] *Yorkshire Ins. Co. v. Seger*, 279 S.W.3d 755, 772 (Tex. App.—Amarillo 2007, pet. denied); *Allstate Ins. v. Kelly*, 680 S.W.2d 595, 606 (Tex. App.—Tyler 1984, writ n.r.e.).

[159] *Yorkshire Ins. Co. v. Seger*, 279 S.W.3d 755, 772 (Tex. App.—Amarillo 2007, pet. denied).

[160] *Fairfield Ins. Co. v. Stephens Martin Paving, LP*, 246 S.W.3d 653, 666 (Tex. 2008).

[161] Tex. Civ. Prac. & Rem. Code Ann. § 41.006.

[162] *Westchester Fire Ins. Co. v. Admiral Ins. Co.*, 152 S.W.3d 172, 190 n.9 (Tex. App.—Fort Worth 2004, pet. denied) (holding that insurance coverage for punitive damages was not void as against Texas public policy).

[163] Tex. R. Civ. P. 141; *Welch v. McLean*, 191 S.W.3d 147, 173 (Tex. App.—Fort Worth 2005, no pet.) (holding that prevailing party was entitled to reasonable court costs).

[164] Tex. Ins. Code Ann. § 541.153; Tex. Bus. & Com. Code Ann. § 17.50(c); *Vela v. Catlin Specialty Ins. Co.*, No. 13-13-00475-CV, 2015 Tex. App. LEXIS 3743, at *39–40 (Tex. App.—Corpus Christi 2015, pet. denied) (stating that a trial court could abuse its discretion for failing to award court costs).

[165] *Johnson & Higgins, Inc. v. Kenneco Energy*, 962 S.W.2d 507, 528 (Tex. 1998).

[166] *Hoelscher v. Kilman*, No. 03-04-00440-CV, 2006 Tex. App. LEXIS 1351, at *16 (Tex. App.—Austin 2006, no pet.); *Welch v. McLean*, 191 S.W.3d 147, 154 (Tex. App.—Fort Worth 2005, no pet.) (holding that the trial court erred in failing award prejudgment interest).

sustained it must have a basis in the pleadings; interest must be asked for specifically or be embraced in the aggregate amount laid as damages.[167]

A money judgment that provides for interest or time price differential within its terms earns post-judgment interest at a rate equal to the lesser of the rate specified in the contract and 18%.[168] Prejudgment interest accrues at the same rate at the post-judgment interest rate and is computed as simple interest, while post-judgment interest is compounded annually.[169] Prejudgment interest accrues on the earlier date of the 180th day after the defendant receives written notice of a claim and the date that the suit is filed.[170] Post-judgment interest accrues on the date that judgment is rendered and ends on the date that judgment is satisfied.[171] *See* Chapter 11, Section 11–13:1.

5-7:4 Defenses

5-7:4.1 Statute of Limitations

Two-year statute of limitations applies.[172]

Limitations will bar the suit two years after the excess judgment becomes final.[173]

5-7:4.2 No *Stowers* Demand

Defense that no *Stowers* duty triggered because the third party demand was above policy limits.[174]

5-7:4.3 Policy Exhausted

If the policy provides, the insurer can assert the defense that its coverage limits under the policy have been exhausted.[175]

---

[167] *Zuider Zee Oyster Bar, Inc. v. Martin*, 503 S.W.2d 292, 299 (Tex. Civ. App.—Fort Worth 1973, writ ref'd n.r.e.).

[168] Tex. Fin. Code Ann. § 304.002.

[169] *Landmark Org., L.P. v. Delphini Constr. Co.*, No. 13-04-371-CV, 2005 Tex. App. LEXIS 8414, at *15 (Tex. App.—Corpus Christi 2005, pet. denied).

[170] *See* Tex. Fin. Code Ann. § 304.104.

[171] *See* Tex. Fin. Code Ann. § 304.005.

[172] *See Street v. Second Ct. of Appeals*, 756 S.W.2d 299, 301 (Tex. 1988); *see also Hernandez v. Truck Ins. Exch.*, 553 S.W.3d 689, 702 (Tex. App.—Fort Worth 2018).

[173] *Id.*

[174] *American Physicians Ins. Exch. v. Garcia*, 876 S.W.2d 842, 849 (Tex. 1994); *see also G.A. Stowers Furniture Co. v. Am. Indem. Co.*, 15 S.W.2d 544, 547 (Tex. Comm'n App. 1929, holding approved).

[175] *See Mid-Century Ins. Co. v. Childs*, 15 S.W.3d 187, 189–90 (Tex. App.—Texarkana 2000, no pet.).

CHAPTER 6

Employment Litigation*

6-1 Wrongful Discharge—Breach of Employment Agreement

The long-standing rule in Texas provides for employment at will, terminable at any time by either party, with or without cause, absent an express agreement to the contrary.[1] There exists a presumption that employees in Texas are hired at will.[2] An employment contract is an exception to the employment-at-will doctrine.[3]

6-1:1 Overview

6-1:1.1 Related Causes of Action

Tortious Interference with Employment Contract, Invasion of Privacy, Intentional Infliction of Emotional Distress, Defamation, Negligent Misrepresentation, Fraud, Breach of Contract.

6-1:2 Elements

(1) Plaintiff had an enforceable employment contract[4]

- A written employment contract signed by the employer is enforceable.[5]

- An oral employment contract is enforceable if the contract can be performed within one year.[6]

---

* The authors thank Miranda Chavez and Robyn Leatherwood for their assistance in the updating of this chapter.
[1] *Hillman v. Nueces County*, 579 S.W.3d 354, 358 (Tex. 2019), *reh'g denied* (Aug. 30, 2019).
[2] *Midland Judicial Dist. Cmty. Supervision & Corr. Dep't v. Jones*, 92 S.W.3d 486, 487 (Tex. 2002).
[3] *Montgomery Cty. Hosp. Dist. v. Brown*, 965 S.W.2d 501, 502 (Tex. 1998).
[4] The Texas Pattern Jury Charge commentary discusses the elements of this cause of action and the proper submission of the issue to the jury. See Tex. P.J.C—Business, Consumer, Insurance & Employment, 107.1 (2018).
[5] *Webber v. M.W. Kellogg Co.*, 720 S.W.2d 124, 127 (Tex. App.—Houston [14th Dist.] 1986, writ ref'd n.r.e.) ("To establish his cause of action for wrongful termination appellant must prove (1) that he and his employer had a contract that specifically provided that the employer did not have the right to terminate the employment contract at will, and (2) that the employment contract was in writing."); *see also* Tex. Bus. & Com. Code Ann. § 26.01(a)(1).
[6] Tex. Bus. & Com. Code Ann. § 26.01(b)(6); *Cruikshank v. Consumer Direct Mortg., Inc.*, 138 S.W.3d 497, 501 (Tex. App.—Houston [14th Dist.] 2004, pet. denied); *see also*

(2) The employment contract must restrict the employer's right to discharge plaintiff at will.[7]

- A written employment contract may restrict the employer's right to discharge the plaintiff by requiring the employer to give the employee notice before discharge.[8]
- An oral employment contract qualifies if the employer "unequivocally indicate[s] a definite intent to be bound not to terminate the employee except under clearly specific circumstances."[9]
- Employee handbook language must directly limit the employer's right to terminate without cause in a "meaningful and special way".[10]
- An employment contract restricts an employer's right to discharge if the contract is for a stated term unless the agreement allows for termination for "any reason."[11]

(3) Plaintiff "performed or tendered performance."[12]

(4) Defendant breached the contract by discharging plaintiff contrary to the contract terms.[13]

(5) Plaintiff was damaged as a result of the breach.[14]

- The evidence must show that the damages are the natural, probable, and foreseeable consequence of the defendant's conduct.[15]

Henriquez v. Cemex Mgmt., 177 S.W.3d 241, 248–49 (Tex. App.—Houston [1st Dist.] 2005, pet. denied).

[7] *Williams v. First Tenn. Nat'l Corp.*, 97 S.W.3d 798, 803 (Tex. App.—Dallas 2003, no pet.); *Montgomery Cty. Hosp. Dist. v. Brown*, 965 S.W.2d 501, 502 (Tex. 1998); *Hussong v. Schwan's Sales Enter.*, 896 S.W.2d 320, 324–25 (Tex. App.—Houston [1st Dist.] 1995, no writ).

[8] See *Cushman & Wakefield, Inc. v. Fletcher*, 915 S.W.2d 538, 544–45 (Tex. App.—Dallas 1995, writ denied); see also *Hussong v. Schwan's Sales Enter.*, 896 S.W.2d 320, 324–25 (Tex. App.—Houston [1st Dist.] 1995, no writ).

[9] *Montgomery Cty. Hosp. Dist. v. Brown*, 965 S.W.2d 501, 502 (Tex. 1998), *but see Goodyear Tire & Rubber Co. v. Portilla*, 879 S.W.2d 47, 51–52 n.8 (Tex. 1994) (refusing to decide the question of whether oral modifications of an at will employment are effective).

[10] *Williams v. First Tenn. Nat'l Corp.*, 97 S.W.3d 798, 803 (Tex. App.—Dallas 2003, no pet.) (quoting *Reyna v. First Nat'l Bank in Edinburg*, 55 S.W.3d 58, 71 (Tex. App—Corpus 2001, no pet.)).

[11] *C.S.C.S., Inc. v. Carter*, 129 S.W.3d 584, 591 (Tex. App.—Dallas 2003, no pet.); *see also Curtis v. Ziff Energy Grp., Ltd.*, 12 S.W.3d 114, 118 (Tex. App.—Houston [14th Dist.] 1999, no pet.).

[12] *Garcia v. Corpus Christi Indep. Sch. Dist.*, 866 F. Supp. 2d 646, 659 (S.D. Tex. 2011).

[13] *Hussong v. Schwan's Sales Enter.*, 896 S.W.2d 320, 326 (Tex. App.—Houston [1st Dist.] 1995, no writ).

[14] *Henriquez v. Cemex Mgmt.*, 177 S.W.3d 241, 248 n.6 (Tex. App.—Houston [1st Dist.] 2005, pet. denied); *Prudential Sec., Inc. v. Haughland*, 973 S.W.2d 394, 396–97 (Tex. App.—El Paso 1998, pet. denied).

[15] *Prudential Sec., Inc. v. Haughland*, 973 S.W.2d 394, 396–97 (Tex. App.—El Paso 1998, pet. denied) (citing *Mead v. Johnson Grp., Inc.*, 615 S.W.2d 685, 687 (Tex. 1981)); *Winograd v. Clear Lake City Water Auth.*, 811 S.W.2d 147, 156 (Tex. App.—Houston [1st Dist.] 1991, writ denied).

EMPLOYMENT LITIGATION

- The absence of a causal connection between the alleged breach and the alleged damages will preclude recovery.[16]

6-1:3 Damages and Remedies

6-1:3.1 Actual Damages

The measure of actual damages is the present cash value of the contract to the employee if the contract had not been breached less any amounts that the employee should in the exercise of reasonable diligence be able to earn through other employment.[17]

6-1:3.2 Interest

Prejudgment interest is compensation allowed by law for the lost use of the money due as damages during the time between the accrual of the claim and the judgment date.[18] If no statute requires prejudgment interest, then the trial court may award prejudgment interest.[19] An award of equitable prejudgment interest is within the trial court's discretion.[20] For a recovery of interest to be sustained it must be based in the pleadings; interest must be asked for specifically or be[21,22]

A money judgment that provides for interest or time price differential within its terms earns post-judgment interest at a rate equal to the lesser of the rate specified in the contract or 18%.[23] Prejudgment interest accrues at the same rate as the post-judgment interest rate.[24] Prejudgment interest accrues on the earlier of the 180th day after the defendant receives written notice of a claim or the date that the suit is filed.[25] Prejudgment interest is computed as simple interest and does not compound.[26] Post-judgment interest accrues on the date that judgment is rendered and ends on the date that judgment is satisfied.[27] Post-judgment interest compounds annually.[28] *See* Chapter 11, Section 11-13:1.

---

[16] *Prudential Sec., Inc. v. Haughland*, 973 S.W.2d 394, 396–97 (Tex. App.—El Paso 1998, pet. denied) (citing *Nelson Cash Register, Inc. v. Data Terminal Sys., Inc.*, 671 S.W.2d 594, 500 (Tex. App.—San Antonio 1984, no writ)).

[17] *Gulf Consol. Intern., Inc. v. Murphy*, 658 S.W.2d 565, 566 (Tex. 1983).

[18] *J & D Towing, LLC v. Am. Alt. Ins. Corp.*, 478 S.W.3d 649, 677 (Tex. 2016).

[19] *Hoelscher v. Kilman*, No. 03-04-00440-CV, 2006 LEXIS 1351, at *16 (Tex. App.—Austin 2006, no pet.).

[20] *Kurtz v. Kurtz*, 14-08-00351-CV, 2010 WL 1293769, at *11 (Tex. App.—Houston [14th Dist.] Apr. 6, 2010, no pet.)

[21] *Zuider Zee Oyster Bar, Inc. v. Martin*, 503 S.W.2d 292, 299 (Tex. Civ. App.—Fort Worth 1973, writ ref'd n.r.e.).

[22] *Mansfield Heliflight, Inc. v. Bell/Agusta Aero. Co.*, No. 4:06-CV-425-A, 2007 U.S. Dist. LEXIS 79548, at *15 (N.D. Tex. Oct. 26, 2007).

[23] Tex. Fin. Code Ann. § 304.002.

[24] *Landmark Org., L.P. v. Delphini Constr. Co.*, No. 13-04-371-CV, 2005 LEXIS 8414, at *15 (Tex. App.—Corpus Christi Oct. 13, 2005, pet. denied).

[25] Tex. Fin. Code Ann. § 304.104.

[26] Tex. Fin. Code Ann. § 304.104.

[27] Tex. Fin. Code Ann. § 304.005.

[28] Tex. Fin. Code Ann. § 304.006.

6-1:3.3 Court Costs

The award and allocation of court costs under Texas Rules of Civil Procedure 131 and 141 are matters for the trial court's discretion and may be awarded in a wrongful discharge claim.[29] *See* Chapter 11, Section 11-13:2.

6-1:3.4 Attorney's Fees

A person may recover reasonable attorney's fees if the claim is for an oral or written contract.[30]

6-1:4 Defenses

6-1:4.1 Statute of Limitations

The limitations period is four years for a breach of contract action.[31] The action accrues at the time of the breach.[32]

6-1:4.2 Good Cause

Express Discharge Conditions—good cause from conditions expressly listed in the contract.[33]

Implied Discharge Conditions—good cause implied under the law[34]

(1) Plaintiff failed to perform duties that "a person of ordinary prudence would have done under the same or similar circumstances"; or

(2) Plaintiff committed an act "inconsistent with the continued existence of the employer-employee relationship."

6-1:4.3 Statute of Frauds

Defendant may assert statute of frauds as an affirmative defense.[35]

Elements:

(1) Contract was oral; and

(2) Contract could not be performed within one year.

---

[29] *Power Reps, Inc. v. Cates*, No. 01-13-00856-CV, 2015 LEXIS 8384, at *54–55 (Tex. App.—Houston [1st Dist.] 2015, no pet.); Tex. R. Civ. P. 131; Tex. R. Civ. P. 141.

[30] Tex. Civ. Prac. & Rem. Code Ann. § 38.001(8); *Gordon v. Leasman*, 365 S.W.3d 109, 116 (Tex. App.—Houston [1st Dist.] 2011, no pet.).

[31] Tex. Civ. Prac. & Rem. Code Ann. § 16.051.

[32] *Carl M. Archer Trust v. Tregellas*, 566 S.W.3d 281, 288 (Tex.2018).

[33] *Pinnacle Anesthesia Consultants v. Fisher*, 309 S.W.3d 93, 99 (Tex. App.—Dallas 2009, pet. denied); *see Cushman & Wakefield, Inc. v. Fletcher*, 915 S.W.2d 538, 543 n.1 (Tex. App.—Dallas 1995, writ denied).

[34] *See Lee-Wright, Inc. v. Hall*, 840 S.W.2d 572, 580 (Tex. App.—Houston [1st Dist.] 1992, no writ).

[35] Tex. R. Civ. P. 94; *Baylor Univ. v. Sonnichsen*, 221 S.W.3d 632, 635 (Tex. 2007); Tex. Bus. & Com. Code Ann. § 26.01(b)(6).

6-1:4.4 Payment

Defendant may assert as an affirmative defense that plaintiff was paid the amounts due under the contract.[36]

6-1:4.5 Mitigation of Damages

Defendant may assert the defense that the plaintiff should have mitigated damages by seeking other employment.[37]

6-1:4.6 Failure to Exhaust Administrative Remedies

Government employer may raise the defense of failure to exhaust administrative remedies.[38]

6-2 Wrongful Discharge Refusal to Perform an Illegal Act

6-2:1 Overview

Texas has long recognized that at-will employment relationships may be terminated by either party with or without cause.[39] The Supreme Court of Texas crafted a narrow exception to this long-standing rule by creating the common law cause of action for Refusal to Perform an Illegal Act. Courts require strict compliance with the Supreme Court's initial framework as laid out in *Sabine Pilot Service Inc. v. Hauck*.[40]

6-2:1.1 Related Causes of Action

Wrongful Discharge: Breach of Employment Agreement, Suit for Retaliatory Treatment: Filing a Workers' Compensation Claim, Employment Discrimination, Breach of Contract

MUST READ CASES

Sabine Pilot Serv., Inc. v. Hauck, 687 S.W.2d 733 (Tex. 1985)

Marx v. Elec. Data Sys. Corp., 418 S.W.3d 626 (Tex. App.—Amarillo 2009, no pet.)

---

[36] *Hussong v. Schwan's Sales Enter.*, 896 S.W.2d 320, 326 (Tex. App.—Houston [1st Dist.] 1995, no writ); *Craddock v. McAfee*, 151 S.W.2d 936, 937 (Tex. Civ. App.—El Paso 1941, no writ) (requiring the defense to be pled).

[37] *Hertz Equip. Rental Corp. v. Barousse*, 365 S.W.3d 46, 59 (Tex. App.—Houston [1st Dist.] 2011, pet. denied); *Gulf Consol. Int'l v. Murphy*, 658 S.W.2d 565, 566 (Tex. 1983); *Professional Servs., Inc. v. Amaitis*, 592 S.W.2d 396 (Tex. Civ. App.—Dallas 1979, writ ref'd n.r.e.); *see* Tex. Patttern Jury Charges 115.25.

[38] *Ogletree v. Glen Rose ISD*, 314 S.W.3d 450, 453–54 (Tex. App.—Waco 2010, pet. denied); *Essenburg v. Dallas Cty.*, 988 S.W.2d 188, 189 (Tex. 1998) (holding that the plaintiff's failure to exhaust administrative remedies deprives the trial court of subject matter jurisdiction to determine the case). *See also Matagorda Cty. Appraisal Dist. v. Coastal Liquids Partners, L.P.*, 165 S.W.3d 329, 331 (Tex. 2005); *Van Indep. Sch. Dist. v. McCarty*, 165 S.W.3d 351, 354 (Tex. 2005); *University of Tex. Sw. Med. Ctr. at Dall. v. Loutzenhiser*, 140 S.W.3d 351, 361 (Tex. 2004).

[39] *East Line & R.R.R. Co. v. Scott*, 10 S.W. 99, 102 (Tex. 1888).

[40] *Sabine Pilot Serv., Inc. v. Hauck*, 687 S.W.2d 733 (Tex. 1985).

6-2:2 Elements

(1) The plaintiff was an at-will employee.[41]

- Texas presumes all employment relationships are at-will employment relationships.[42]

(2) The plaintiff refused to perform an illegal act.[43]

- In order to satisfy this element, the plaintiff must produce evidence which establishes:
  - The employer either ordered or required the employee to perform the act;[44] and
  - The plaintiff refused to do so.[45]
- The act must be one that could result in criminal penalties against the plaintiff.[46]
- The plaintiff's refusal may be multifaceted and encompass more than merely refusing to perform.[47]
- An employer may terminate an employee without incurring civil liability for:
  - Requiring an employee to perform a legal act;[48]
  - Requiring an employee to perform a legal act pending the employee's further investigation into the legality of the act;[49]

---

[41] *Simmons Airlines v. Lagrotte*, 50 S.W.3d 748, 753 (Tex. App.—Dallas 2001, pet. denied); *see Sabine Pilot Serv., Inc. v. Hauck*, 687 S.W.2d 733 (Tex. 1985).

[42] *Montgomery Cty. Hosp. Dist. v. Brown*, 965 S.W.2d 501, 502 (Tex. 1998).

[43] *Hillman v. Nueces County*, 579 S.W.3d 354, 358 (Tex. 2019), reh'g denied (Aug. 30, 2019).

[44] *Coe v. Sienna Fin. Servs., LLC*, No. 14-18-00338-CV, 2019 Tex. App. LEXIS 7054 (Tex. App. Aug. 13, 2019); *see Winters v. Houston Chronicle Publ'g Co.*, 795 S.W.2d 723, 724 (Tex. 1990) (stating that an employee must be "unacceptably forced to choose between risking criminal liability and being discharged from his livelihood").

[45] *Laredo Med. Grp. Corp. v. Mireles*, 155 S.W.3d 417, 421 (Tex. App.—San Antonio 2004, pet. denied).

[46] *Thompson v. Cherokee Water Co.*, 6 S.W.3d 343, 347–48 (Tex. App.—Texarkana 1999, no pet.).

[47] *Hawthorne v. Star Enter., Inc.*, 45 S.W.3d 757, 761 (Tex. App.—Texarkana 2001, pet. denied) (A plaintiff's personal refusal to perform, his directive to subordinates not to perform, and report to the Occupational Safety and Health Administration together constituted his "refusal to perform" under *Sabine Pilot*.).

[48] *Ran Ken, Inc. v. Schlapper*, 963 S.W.2d 102, 106–07 (Tex. App.—Austin 1998, pet. denied).

[49] *Ran Ken, Inc. v. Schlapper*, 963 S.W.2d 102, 106–07 (Tex. App.—Austin 1998, pet. denied); *Camunes v. Frontier Enters.*, 61 S.W.3d 579, 580–81 (Tex. App.—San Antonio 2011, pet. denied); *Mayfield v. Lockheed Eng'g & Scis. Co.*, 970 S.W.2d 185, 187 (Tex. App.—Houston [14th Dist.] 1998, pet. denied); *but see Johnston v. Del Mar Distrib. Co.*, 776 S.W.2d 768, 771–72 (Tex. App.—Corpus Christi 1989, writ denied) (authorizing such a lawsuit). It appears that the Austin Court of Appeals' holding is correct, in that it takes into account the Texas Supreme Court's express limitation on its holding in *Sabine Pilot*.

- Requiring an employee to perform a legal act which, in good faith, the employee believes to be illegal;[50] or
- Requiring an employee to not report an illegal act.[51]

(3) The plaintiff's refusal was the sole reason for the plaintiff's termination.[52]

- An employer who discharges an employee both for refusing to perform an illegal act and for a legitimate reason or reasons cannot be liable for wrongful discharge—likely regardless of pretext.[53]
- Termination may be direct or constructive.[54]
  - Constructive discharge occurs when job conditions are made so difficult or unpleasant that a reasonable person in the employee's shoes would feel compelled to resign.[55]
  - Constructive termination looks into the conditions imposed by the employer, not the employer's subjective state of mind.[56]
- In a constructive termination situation, the relevant inquiry is whether the employer imposed the conditions solely because of the plaintiff's refusal to perform an illegal act.[57]
- Regarding whether the plaintiff's refusal to perform an illegal act was the sole reason for the plaintiff's termination:
  - Mere temporal proximity between an employee's protected conduct and the employee's termination is insufficient to show a causal link.[58]
  - The plaintiff's subjective opinion of the employer's motivation is no evidence.[59]

---

[50] *Ran Ken, Inc. v. Schlapper*, 963 S.W.2d 102, 107 (Tex. App.—Austin 1998, pet. denied) (refusing to expand the Supreme Court's holding in *Sabine Pilot*).

[51] *Ed Rachal Found. v. D'Unger*, 207 S.W.3d 330, 332 (Tex. 2006).

[52] *Marx v. Elec. Data Sys. Corp.*, 418 S.W.3d 626, 632 (Tex. App.—Amarillo 2009, no pet.); *Hawthorne v. Star Enter., Inc.*, 45 S.W.3d 757, 760 (Tex. App.—Texarkana 2001, pet. denied).

[53] *See Texas Dept. of Human Servs. of State of Tex. v. Hinds*, 904 S.W.2d 629, 633 (Tex. 1995) (indicating that pretext may not be a relevant inquiry).

[54] *See Sabine Pilot Serv., Inc. v. Hauck*, 687 S.W.2d 733, 734 (Tex. 1985) (discussing direct termination, or "firing"); *see also Marx v. Elec. Data Sys. Corp.*, 418 S.W.3d 626, 631 (Tex. App—Amarillo 2009, no pet.) (discussing constructive termination).

[55] *Kosa v. Dall. Lite & Barricade, Inc.*, 228 S.W.3d 428, 430 (Tex. App.—Dallas 2007, no pet.).

[56] *Marx v. Elec. Data Sys. Corp.*, 418 S.W.3d 626, 634 (Tex. App.—Amarillo 2009, no pet.) (citing *Bourque v. Powell Elec. Mfg. Co.*, 617 F.2d 61, 65 (5th Cir.1980)).

[57] *Marx v. Elec. Data Sys. Corp.*, 418 S.W.3d 626, 634–35 (Tex. App.—Amarillo 2009, no pet.).

[58] *Marx v. Elec. Data Sys. Corp.*, 418 S.W.3d 626, 635 (Tex. App.—Amarillo 2009, no pet.) (borrowing from the Title VII context); *e.g., Peine v. Hit Servs.*, 479 S.W.3d 445, 455 (Tex. App.—Houston [14th Dist.] 2015, pet. denied).

[59] *Nichols v. Loral Vought Sys. Corp.*, 81 F.3d 38, 42 (5th Cir. 1996); *Gold v. Exxon Corp.*, 960 S.W.2d 378, 385 (Tex. App.—Houston [14th Dist.] 1998, no pet.).

6-2:3 Damages and Remedies

6-2:3.1 Actual Damages

The plaintiff may recover actual damages, including:

- Back pay;
- Future pay;
- Mental anguish;[60] and
- Lost benefits.[61]

6-2:3.2 Prejudgment Interest

The plaintiff may recover prejudgment interest.[62]

6-2:3.3 Injunction

Injunction may be a viable remedy.[63] *See* Chapter 8, Sections 8–1, 8–2 and 8–3.

6-2:3.4 Reinstatement

Reinstatement may be a viable remedy.[64]

6-2:3.5 Exemplary Damages

The plaintiff may recover exemplary damages if he proves the employer acted with malice.[65] Malice means consciously ignoring a risk of some additional serious harm.[66]

---

[60] *Rescar, Inc. v. Ward*, 60 S.W.3d 169, 178–79 (Tex. App.—Houston [1st Dist.] 2001, pet. granted, *judgm't vacated w.r.m.*); *Safeshred, Inc. v. Martinez*, 365 S.W.3d 655, 658–59 (Tex. 2012).

[61] *Ed Rachal Found. v. D'Unger*, 117 S.W.3d 348, 370 (Tex. App.—Corpus Christi 2003), *judgm't rev'd on other grounds*, 207 S.W.3d 330 (Tex. 2006).

[62] *Rescar, Inc. v. Ward*, 60 S.W.3d 169, 175 (Tex. App.—Houston [1st Dist.] 2001, *pet. granted, judgm't vacated w.r.m.*).

[63] Tex. Lab. Code Ann. § 451.003; *see Sabine Pilot Serv., Inc. v. Hauck*, 687 S.W.2d 733, 736 (Tex. 1985) (Concurrence, Kilgarin, J.).

[64] *See* Tex. Lab. Code Ann. § 451.002(b); *see Sabine Pilot Serv., Inc. v. Hauck*, 687 S.W.2d 733, 736 (Tex. 1985) (Concurrence, Kilgarin, J.).

[65] *Safeshred, Inc. v. Martinez*, 365 S.W.3d 655, 663 (Tex. 2012), as corrected (June 8, 2012).

[66] *Safeshred, Inc. v. Martinez*, 365 S.W.3d 655, 663 (Tex. 2012), as corrected (June 8, 2012).

EMPLOYMENT LITIGATION 243

6-2:4 Defenses

6-2:4.1 Statute of Limitations

A two-year limitations period controls.[67] The cause of action accrues when the employee is terminated.[68]

6-2:4.2 Sovereign Immunity

Sovereign Immunity is an applicable defense.[69]

6-3 Employment Discrimination

6-3:1 Overview

A claim for Employment Discrimination under the Texas Commission on Human Rights Act (TCHRA) is analogous to a lawsuit brought under federal anti-discrimination laws. The relationship is so close that Texas courts may use federal case law interpreting federal law as authority.[70] A claim for Employment Discrimination is purely statutory in respect to its elements, damages, remedies, and defenses.

6-3:1.1 Related Causes of Action

Americans with Disabilities Act (ADA) Claims,[71] Wrongful Discharge: Breach of Employment Agreement; Wrongful Discharge: Refusal to Perform an Illegal Act, Suit for Retaliatory Treatment: Filing a Workers' Compensation Claim; Texas Whistleblower Act.[72]

MUST READ CASES & STATUTES

Chapter 21 Texas Labor Code; *McDonnell Douglas Corp. v. Green*, 411 U.S. 792 (1973); *Nichols v. Loral Vought Sys. Corp.*, 81 F.3d 38 (5th Cir. 1996); *Gold v. Exxon Corp.*, 960 S.W.2d 378 (Tex. App.—Houston [14th Dist.] 1998, no pet.)

6-3:2 Elements

(1) The plaintiff must establish a prima facie case of discrimination.[73]

- The burden of establishing a prima facie case is easy to meet.[74]

---

[67] Tex. Civ. Prac. & Rem. Code Ann. § 16.003(a); *Stroud v. VBFSB Holding Corp.*, 917 S.W.2d 75, 79 (Tex. App.—San Antonio 1996, writ denied).
[68] *Stroud v. VBFSB Holding Corp.*, 917 S.W.2d 75, 81 (Tex. App.—San Antonio 1996, writ denied).
[69] *Hillman v. Nueces County*, 579 S.W.3d 354, 357 (Tex. 2019), reh'g denied (Aug. 30, 2019).
[70] *In re United Services Auto. Ass'n*, 307 S.W.3d 299, 308 (Tex. 2010).
[71] The state cause of action for Employment Discrimination is modeled after the federal cause of action under the ADA. This publication does not discuss the ADA.
[72] Tex. Gov't. Code 554.001.
[73] *Kaplan v. City of Sugar Land*, 525 S.W.3d 297, 302 (Tex. App.—Hous. [14th Dist.] 2017).
[74] *Young v. United Parcel Serv., Inc.*, 575 U.S. 206 (2015).

The plaintiff establishes a prima case by showing the following:

(a) The plaintiff is a member of a protected class;[75]

- The following is an exclusive list of protected classes under the TCHRA:
  - Race;
  - Color;
  - Disability;
  - Religion;
  - Sex;
  - National origin; or
  - Age.[76]
- Age may only be asserted if the plaintiff was at least 40 years old.[77]

(b) The plaintiff was qualified for his employment position.[78]

- Generally, the inquiry is whether the plaintiff could do the work the employment position required, not whether he could do it well.[79]

(c) The employer made an adverse employment decision regarding the plaintiff.[80]

- Adverse employment decisions include:
  - Failing or refusing to hire an individual;
  - Discharging an individual;
  - Discriminating in any other manner against an individual in connection with:
    - Compensation; or
    - The terms, conditions, or privileges of employment;
  - Limiting, segregating or classifying an employee or applicant for employment in a manner that would:
    - Deprive or tend to deprive an individual of any employment opportunity; or
    - Adversely affect in any other manner the status of an employee.[81]

(d) Employer treated plaintiff less favorably than similarly qualified persons.[82]

---

[75] *Kaplan v. City of Sugar Land*, 525 S.W.3d 297, 302 (Tex. App.—Hous. [14th Dist.] 2017).
[76] Tex. Lab. Code Ann. § 21.051.
[77] Tex. Lab. Code Ann. § 21.101.
[78] *Kaplan v. City of Sugar Land*, 525 S.W.3d 297, 302 (Tex. App.—Hous. [14th Dist.] 2017).
[79] *Kaplan v. City of Sugar Land*, 525 S.W.3d 297, 302 (Tex. App.—Hous. [14th Dist.] 2017).
[80] *Kaplan v. City of Sugar Land*, 525 S.W.3d 297, 302 (Tex. App.—Hous. [14th Dist.] 2017).
[81] Tex. Lab. Code Ann. § 21.051.
[82] *Kaplan v. City of Sugar Land*, 525 S.W.3d 297, 302 (Tex. App.—Hous. [14th Dist.] 2017).

EMPLOYMENT LITIGATION

- A plaintiff must provide specific reasons that establish his disparate treatment.[83]
- An employee's subjective opinion that he was treated less favorably than similarly qualified persons is no evidence.[84]

(2) If the employer articulates a legitimate reason for its adverse employment decision regarding the plaintiff, the plaintiff's prima facie case is rebutted, and the burden shifts back to the plaintiff to establish the employer's reason was a pretext for unlawful discrimination.[85]

- The plaintiff must establish that the plaintiff's status as a protected class member was a "motivating factor" for the adverse employment decision.[86]
  - "Motivating factor" means that the plaintiff's status as a protected class member was one of the reasons for the adverse employment decision.[87]

6-3:3 Damages and Remedies

6-3:3.1 Compensatory Damages

Compensatory damages are available.[88]

Compensatory damages include:

- Future pecuniary loss;
- Emotional pain;
- Suffering, inconvenience;
- Mental anguish;
- Loss of enjoyment of life; and
- Other nonpecuniary losses.[89]

Compensatory damages might also include:

- Past pecuniary loss.[90]

---

[83] *Nichols v. Loral Vought Sys. Corp.*, 81 F.3d 38, 42 (5th Cir. 1996).
[84] *Nichols v. Loral Vought Sys. Corp.*, 81 F.3d 38, 42 (5th Cir. 1996); *Gold v. Exxon Corp.*, 960 S.W.2d 378, 385 (Tex. App.—Houston [14th Dist.] 1998, no pet.).
[85] *McDonnell Douglas Corp. v. Green*, 411 U.S. 792, 804–05 (1973); *Elgaghil v. Tarrant Cty. Junior Coll.*, 45 S.W.3d 133, 139 (Tex. App.—Fort Worth 2000, pet. denied).
[86] Tex. Lab. Code Ann. § 21.125(a); *Quantum Chem. Corp. v. Toennies*, 47 S.W.3d 473, 479–80 (Tex. 2001).
[87] *Quantum Chem. Corp. v. Toennies*, 47 S.W.3d 473, 477 (Tex. 2001).
[88] Tex. Lab. Code Ann. §21.2585(a)(1); *Autozone, Inc. v. Reyes*, 272 S.W.3d 644, 655 (Tex. App.—Corpus Christi 2006), *judgm't rev'd on other grounds*, 272 S.W.3d 588 (Tex. 2008).
[89] *Autozone, Inc. v. Reyes*, 272 S.W.3d 644, 655 (Tex. App.—Corpus Christi 2006), *judgm't rev'd on other grounds*, 272 S.W.3d 588 (Tex. 2008).
[90] Despite the *Autozone* court's exclusion of past pecuniary loss from the realm of recoverable compensatory damages, it would appear that past pecuniary loss is recoverable under Section 21.2585 as compensatory damages. Section 21.2585(a) authorizes compensatory damages, subsection, (c) explicitly excludes back pay, interest on back pay, and equitable

Attorneys' fees.[91]

Compensatory damages does not include:

- Back pay;
- Interest on back pay; or
- Any relief granted under Section 21.258(b).[92]

6-3:3.2 Prejudgment Interest

Prejudgment interest is appropriate.[93]

6-3:3.3 Equitable Relief

The following equitable remedies are available:

- Enjoining the defendant from an unlawful employment practice;
- Hiring or reinstating the employee with or without back pay;
- Upgrading an employee with or without pay;
- Admitting to or restoring union membership;
- Admitting to or participating in a guidance program, apprenticeship, or on-the-job training or other training or retraining program, using objective job-related criteria in admitting an individual to a program;
- Reporting on the manner of compliance with the terms of a final order issued under Chapter 21 of the Texas Labor Code; and
- Paying court costs.[94]

Any back pay awarded must be from a period no more than two years prior to the date the plaintiff filed his complaint with the Texas Workforce Commission.[95]

6-3:3.4 Punitive Damages

Punitive damages are available if the defendant acted with:

- Malice; or
- Reckless indifference to the plaintiff's rights.[96]

---

relief granted under Section 21.258(b), and subsection (d) merely caps punitive damages and certain types of compensatory damages. Therefore, it would seem as if past pecuniary loss is recoverable under Section 21.2585 as a compensatory damage.

[91] *See Apache Corp. v. Davis*, 573 S.W.3d 475, 502–03 (Tex. App.—Hous. [14th Dist.] 2019) & Tex. Labor Code Ann. § 21.259.

[92] Tex. Lab. Code Ann. § 21.2585(c).

[93] *City of Austin v. Gifford*, 824 S.W.2d 735, 743 (Tex. App.—Austin 1992, no writ); *see also Pegues v. Miss. State Emp't Serv.*, 899 F.2d 1449, 1453 (5th Cir. 1990).

[94] Tex. Lab. Code Ann. § 21.258(a)–(b).

[95] Tex. Lab. Code Ann. § 21.258(c).

[96] Tex. Lab. Code Ann. § 21.2585(b).

EMPLOYMENT LITIGATION

Punitive damages are not available against a governmental entity.[97]

Chapter 21 of the Texas Labor Code does not define "governmental entity[98]

6-3:3.5 Damage Cap

The sum of the amount of compensatory damages awarded under Section 21.2585 for future pecuniary losses, emotional pain, suffering, inconvenience, mental anguish, loss of enjoyment of life and other nonpecuniary losses and the amount of punitive damages awarded may not exceed, for each complainant:

- $50,000 in the case of a respondent that has fewer than 101 employees;
- $100,000 in the case of a respondent that has more than 100 and fewer than 201 employees;
- $200,000 in the case of a respondent that has more than 200 and fewer than 501 employees; and
- $300,000 in the case of a respondent that has more than 500 employees.[99]

The following measurements of damages are not to be capped:

- Past pecuniary losses;[100]
- Back pay;[101]
- Interest on back pay;[102] or
- Other equitable relief granted under Section 21.258(b).[103]

6-3:4 Defenses

6-3:4.1 Statute of Limitations

There are two cumulative statutes of limitation.[104]

- A plaintiff must file a complaint with the Texas Workforce Commission Civil Rights Division within 180 days of when the unlawful employment practice occurred.[105]

---

[97] Tex. Lab. Code Ann. § 21.2585(b).

[98] *Dallas/Fort Worth Intern. Airport Bd. v. Funderburk,* 188 S.W.3d 233 (Tex. App.—Fort Worth 2006, pet. granted).

[99] Tex. Lab. Code Ann. § 21.2585(d).

[100] *See* Tex. Lab. Code Ann. § 21.2585(d).

[101] Tex. Lab. Code Ann. § 21.2585(c); *Texas Comm'n on Human Rights v. Morrison,* 346 S.W.3d 838, 848 (Tex. App.—Austin 2011), *rev.granted, judgm't rev'd on other grounds,* 381 S.W.3d 533 (Tex. 2012) (back pay is considered equitable relief, rather than compensatory damages, and is thus not subject to the statutory cap on compensatory damages).

[102] Tex. Lab. Code Ann. § 21.2585(c).

[103] Tex. Lab. Code Ann. § 21.2585(c).

[104] *See* Tex. Lab. Code Ann. §§ 21.202(a), 21.256.

[105] Tex. Lab. Code Ann. § 21.202(a).

- If a plaintiff opts to file a lawsuit, he must do so within two years of filing his complaint with the Commission.[106]

The unlawful employment practice "occurs" when the employer discriminates and informs the employee of the employment decision.[107]

- It does not matter when the employee feels the consequences of the discrimination.[108]

6-3:4.2 Failure to Exhaust Administrative Remedies

A plaintiff's failure to exhaust his administrative remedies under Chapter 21 of the Texas Labor Code is a jurisdictional defect.[109]

6-3:4.3 Waiver

A plaintiff may only litigate those unlawful employment practices which are:

- Raised in the plaintiff's administrative complaint; or
- Like or related to an unlawful employment practice which was raised in the plaintiff's administrative complaint.[110]

6-3:4.4 Business Necessity

An employer does not commit an unlawful employment practice by engaging in a practice that has a discriminatory effect and that would otherwise be prohibited if the employer establishes that the practice:

- Is not intentionally devised or operated to contravene the prohibitions of this chapter; and
- Is justified by business necessity.[111]

6-3:4.5 Bona Fide Occupational Qualification

An employer does not commit a violation if the plaintiff's age, disability, national origin, sex or religion is a bona fide occupational qualification.[112]

---

[106] Tex. Lab. Code Ann. § 21.256.
[107] *Specialty Retailers, Inc. v. DeMoranville*, 933 S.W.2d 490, 493 (Tex. 1996).
[108] *See Specialty Retailers, Inc. v. DeMoranville*, 933 S.W.2d 490, 492 (Tex. 1996).
[109] Tex. Lab. Code Ann. § 21.201; *Schroeder v. Tex. Iron Works, Inc.*, 813 S.W.2d 483, 487 (Tex. 1991), *overruled in part on other grounds*, 307 S.W.3d 299, 310 (Tex. 2010); *Waffle House, Inc. v. Williams*, 313 S.W.3d 796, 804 (Tex. 2010).
[110] *University of Tex. v. Poindexter*, 306 S.W.3d 798, 807 (Tex. App.—Austin 2009, no pet.); *Elgaghil v. Tarrant Cty. Junior Coll.*, 45 S.W.3d 133, 141 (Tex. App.—Fort Worth 2000, pet. denied).
[111] Tex. Lab. Code Ann. § 21.115(a).
[112] Tex. Lab. Code Ann. § 21.119; *Poteet v. City of Palestine*, 620 S.W.2d 181, 184 (Tex. Civ. App.—Tyler 1981, no writ).

6-3:4.6 Reliance on Commission Interpretation or Opinion

An employer may in good faith conform with and rely upon a written interpretation or opinion of the Texas Workforce Commission.[113]

6-3:4.7 Employment by Religious Organization

Religious organizations do not commit an unlawful employment practice if they:

- Limit employment to members of the organization's religion; or
- Give preference to members of the religious organization's religion.[114]

Religious organizations are not subject to liability under the TCHRA in relation to any employee which:

- Performs work connected with the performance of religious activities.[115]

6-3:4.8 Bona Fide Employee Benefit Plan

An employer may treat employees differently pursuant to a bona fide employee benefit plan.[116] The U.S. Supreme Court, however, has recently ruled that employers cannot discriminate on the basis of sexual orientation or gender identity without violating Title VII of the Civil Rights Act of 1964.[117]

6-3:4.9 Undue Hardship Defense

Undue hardship on the employer is a defense to a claim under the TCHRA.[118]

6-3:4.10 Other Statutory Defenses

Other statutory defenses include:

- Workforce diversity programs;[119]
- Use of controlled substance;[120]
- Plan to end discriminatory school practices;[121] and
- Treatment of employees at different locations.[122]

---

[113] Tex. Lab. Code Ann. § 21.116.
[114] Tex. Lab. Code Ann. § 21.109(a).
[115] Tex. Lab. Code Ann. § 21.109(b).
[116] Tex. Lab. Code Ann. § 21.102.
[117] *Bostock v. Clayton County*, 590 U.S. ___, 140 S.Ct.173, 2020 U.S. Lexis 3252.
[118] Tex. Lab. Code Ann. § 21.260.
[119] Tex. Lab. Code Ann. § 21.121.
[120] Tex. Lab. Code Ann. § 21.120.
[121] Tex. Lab. Code Ann. § 21.114.
[122] Tex. Lab. Code Ann. § 21.112.

NOTE: Texas law does not permit at-will employees to bring fraud claims against their employer for loss of their employment.[123] Recently, plaintiffs have tried to assert that their termination was a due process violation, and the courts have said in order to do so there must be a property interest in the employment à "A property interest in employment only arises when the employer "abrogat[es] its right to terminate an employee without cause," modifying the at-will status of the employment relationship."[124]

---

[123] *See PAS, Inc. v. Engel,* 350 S.W.3d 602, 612–13 (Tex. App.—Houston [14th Dist.] 2011, no pet.); *Cahak v. Rehab Care Group, Inc.,* No. 10–06–00399–CV, 2008 WL 3112083, at *3, 2008 Tex. App. LEXIS 6011, at *7 (Tex. App.—Waco Aug. 6, 2008, no pet.).

[124] *Wei-Ping Zeng v. Texas Tech U. Health Sci. Ctr. at El Paso,* EP-19-CV-99-KC, 2020 WL 1074810, at *19 (W.D. Tex. Mar. 4, 2020).

CHAPTER 7
Oil and Gas Litigation*

7-1 Action to Quiet Title

7-1:1 Overview

An Action to Quiet Title is an equitable cause of action that nullifies an adverse party's disputed claim to the mineral estate, thereby removing any "cloud" impairing title to the property. It does not establish the superiority of the plaintiff's title or declare the invalidity of some instrument the plaintiff was induced to sign. Successful prosecution of the action will result in a declaration that the adverse claim is invalid, clearing the title to the property. No money damages are recoverable on an action to quiet title. A party should only resort to an action to quiet title if other remedies are not available.

7-1:1.1 Related Causes of Action

Trespass to Try Title, Rescission, Reformation, Slander of Title, Trespass to Real Property

7-1:2 Elements

The effect of a suit to quiet title is to declare invalid or ineffective the defendant's claim to title.[1] The plaintiff has the burden of supplying the proof necessary to establish his superior equity and right to relief.[2] The elements of the cause of action to quiet title are that the plaintiff must show (1) an interest in a specific property, (2) title to the property is affected by a claim by the defendant, and (3) the claim, although facially valid, is invalid or unenforceable.[3]

---

* The authors thank Grant McDonald for his assistance in the updating of this chapter.
[1] *See, e.g., Vernon v. Perrien*, 390 S.W.3d 47, 61 (Tex. App.—El Paso 2012, pet. denied).
[2] *Vernon v. Perrien*, 390 S.W.3d 47, 61 (Tex. App.—El Paso 2012, pet. denied).
[3] *Vernon v. Perrien*, 390 S.W.3d 47, 61 (Tex. App.—El Paso 2012, pet. denied); *see also Wright v. Matthews*, 26 S.W.3d 575, 578 (Tex. App.—Beaumont 2000, pet. denied) (showing of equitable title based on performance under contract can constitute showing of greater right in the property). *Rhodes v. Kelly*, No. 05-16-00888-CV, 2017 WL 2774452, at *10 (Tex. App.—Dallas June 27, 2017).

7-1:3 Damages and Remedies

7-1:3.1 Judicial Declaration

The primary form of relief is a judicial declaration that the claim clouding the title is invalid or unenforceable.[4]

7-1:3.2 Attorney's Fees

Attorney's fees are available in actions under the Declaratory Judgments Act.[5]

The DJA applies to any person "interested" under a deed or other writing constituting a contract and any person whose rights or other legal relations are "affected" by a contract.[6] Accordingly, a suit to quiet title falls within the literal language of the DJA.

Plaintiffs have successfully brought quiet title actions under the DJA in the past, typically with no apparent argument from the opposing party that the DJA was inapplicable.[7]

Recent case law complicates the availability of the DJA in real property causes of action.[8]

The propriety of bringing an action to quiet title under the DJA has not been addressed in a case involving an interest in oil and gas.

7-1:4 Defenses

7-1:4.1 Limitations

A cloud on title is a continuous injury to property.[9]

Therefore, an equitable cause of action to remove the cloud on title is not subject to limitations if the deed is void ab initio or has expired by its own terms.[10]

---

[4] *Duncan Land & Exploration, Inc. v. Littlepage*, 984 S.W.2d 318, 333–34 (Tex. App.—Fort Worth 1998, pet. denied).

[5] Tex. Civ. Prac. & Rem. Code § 37.009.

[6] Tex. Civ. Prac. & Rem. Code § 37.004(a).

[7] *E.g., Duncan Land & Expl., Inc. v. Littlepage*, 984 S.W.2d 318, 333–34 (Tex. App.—Fort Worth 1998, pet. denied); *Exploracion De La Estrella Soloataria Incorporacion v. Birdwell*, 858 S.W.2d 549, 551 (Tex. App.—Eastland 1993, no writ).

[8] *Martin v. Amerman*, 133 S.W.3d 262, 267–68 (Tex. 2004). The Texas Supreme Court held in *Martin v. Amerman* that a trespass to try title suit cannot be brought as an action under the DJA. However, that decision focused on the exclusivity of the statutory remedy of a trespass to try title action. An action to quiet title is an equitable remedy that is not governed by statute. Case authority decided after *Martin* indicates that if the incidental effect of the declaratory relief is to quiet title then the DJA is proper, but if the true intent of the suit is to clear title, a quiet title action cannot be recharacterized as a declaratory judgment action in order to obtain attorney's fees. *E.g., Florey v. Estate of McConnell*, 212 S.W.3d 439, 448 (Tex. App.—Austin 2006, pet. denied); *Elijah Ragira/Vip Lodging Grp., Inc. v. Vip Lodging Grp., Inc.*, 301 S.W.3d 747, 757 (Tex. App.—El Paso 2009, pet. denied).

[9] *Watson v. Rochmill*, 155 S.W.2d 783, 785 (Tex. 1941).

[10] *Watson v. Rochmill*, 155 S.W.2d 783, 785 (Tex. 1941).

OIL AND GAS LITIGATION

However, when a deed is voidable, rather than void ab initio, then a party is subject to the general four-year limitations period.[11]

In addition, if the removal of the cloud on title depends on a tort or a contract, then the limitations period for the underlying basis of the claim controls.[12]

7-1:4.2 Quieting or Vesting of Title in Defendant

A defendant can choose to counterclaim to establish the validity of their own claim to the property interest in question. The defendant has the burden to prove their own interest in the property and the invalidity or unenforceability of the plaintiff's interest.[13]

7-1:4.3 Claim for Improvements

If a defendant's claim was possessory and the defendant made good faith improvements, the defendant may counterclaim for recovery of the fair value of the improvements.[14]

7-1:4.4 Other Equitable Defenses

An action to quiet title is an equitable proceeding, subject to equitable defenses such as laches and estoppel.[15]

7-1:5 Procedural Implications

7-1:5.1 Venue

Venue is mandatory in the county in which all or part of the real property is located.[16]

7-1:5.2 Pleading Slander of Title

Slander of title is a tort action that is often pleaded with an action to quiet title because it allows for money damages.[17]

---

[11] *Ford v. Exxon Mobil Chem. Co.*, 235 S.W.3d 615, 618 (Tex. 2007).
[12] *Ditta v. Conte*, 298 S.W.3d 187, 192 (Tex. 2009).
[13] *Dittmar v. Alamo Nat'l Co.*, 132 Tex. 44, 118 S.W.2d 298, 299–301 (1938).
[14] *Eubank v. Twin Mountain Oil Corp.*, 406 S.W.2d 789, 792 (Tex. Civ. App.—Eastland 1966, writ ref'd n.r.e.).
[15] *See Teledyne Isotopes, Inc. v. Bravenec*, 640 S.W.2d 387, 391 (Tex. App.—Houston [1st Dist.] 1982, writ ref'd n.r.e.); *Exploracion De La Estrella Soloataria Incorporacion v. Birdwell*, 858 S.W.2d 549, 554–55 (Tex. App.—Eastland 1993, no writ).
[16] Tex. Civ. Prac. & Rem. Code Ann. § 15.011; *Madera Prod. Co. v. Atl. Richfield Co.*, 107 S.W.3d 652, 656–58 (Tex. App.—Texarkana 2003, pet. denied).
[17] *Pampell Interests v. Wolle*, 797 S.W.2d 392, 395 (Tex. App.—Austin 1990, no writ).

The plaintiff must plead and prove that the defendant acted with legal malice when placing the cloud on the title and that it caused the plaintiff to lose a specific sale of property.[18]

7-1:5.3 Recording the Judgment

After the judgment becomes final, the county clerk of the county where the land is located should record a copy.[19]

7-2 Trespass to Try Title

7-2:1 Overview

A Trespass to Try Title Action is the sole method of determining title to real property in Texas.[20] It is a purely statutory cause of action and is governed by special pleading and proof requirements.[21] A Trespass to Try Title Action affords a legal remedy and should be distinguished from the equitable Quiet Title Action. A Trespass to Try Title Action is appropriate when multiple parties claim conflicting possessory rights to real property. A Trespass to Try Title Action cannot be used to determine rights to non-possessory mineral interests, such as royalty interests and possibilities of reverter. To recover in a Trespass to Try Title Action, the plaintiff is required to prevail on the superiority of his own title, not on the weakness of the defendant's title. The trespass-to-try-title statute, however, only applies when the claimant is seeking to establish or obtain *the claimant's* ownership or possessory right in the land at issue.[22] A trespass-to-try-title plaintiff, in other words, "must recover upon the strength of his own title."[23] If successful, a plaintiff acquires title to the disputed property and actual damages. If properly pleaded, a defendant can recover for value of improvements.

7-2:1.1 Related Causes of Action

Action to Quiet Title, Rescission, Reformation, Slander of Title, Trespass to Real Property

MUST READ CASE

Martin v. Amerman, 133 S.W.3d 262 (Tex. 2004) (elements)

7-2:2 Elements

(1) Plaintiff must establish a prima facie right of title by proving:

---

[18] *Duncan Land & Expl., Inc. v. Littlepage*, 984 S.W.2d 318, 332–33 (Tex. App.—Fort Worth 1998, pet. denied).
[19] Tex. Prop. Code Ann. § 12.013.
[20] *Martin v. Amerman*, 133 S.W.3d 262, 265 (Tex. 2004).
[21] *See* Tex. R. Civ. P. § 783-809; Tex. Prop. Code Ann. §§ 22.001-22.045.
[22] *Lance v. Robinson*, 543 S.W.3d 723, 735 (Tex. 2018).
[23] *Rogers v. Ricane Enters., Inc.*, 884 S.W.2d 763, 768 (Tex. 1994); *Lance v. Robinson*, 543 S.W.3d 723, 735 (Tex. 2018).

- A plaintiff must establish title to the mineral estate in themselves and cannot rely on the inferiority of the defendant's claim.[24]

(a) A regular chain of conveyances from the sovereign;

- The plaintiff must establish a land grant or patent from the state or sovereignty showing that the title vested in the original grantee or patentee and has passed by successive conveyances to the plaintiff.[25]
    - Courts strictly apply this method. A plaintiff should only utilize this method if there is no connection between the competing chains of title.[26]

(b) A superior title out of a common source;

- The plaintiff must connect his title and the defendant's title through complete chains of title to the common source and then show that his title is superior to the one that the defendant derived from the common source.[27]
- The rule of common source of title is one of evidence, not of estoppel. Therefore, a defendant can challenge the title to the plaintiff's alleged common source.[28] However, once the plaintiff establishes a common source, either by proof or agreement, the plaintiff only needs to prove good title in herself to establish a prima facie case of superior title.[29]

(c) Title by limitation; or

- The plaintiff must meet the requirements of the three-, five-, or ten, or twenty-five year statutes of limitations.[30]
- When adverse possession commences before a severance of the mineral estate, the adverse possession includes both the surface and mineral estate.[31]
- Once the mineral estate is severed from the surface estate, possession of the surface alone will not constitute adverse possession of minerals. Actual possession of the minerals must occur.[32]
- In the case of oil and gas, this requires drilling and production of oil or gas.[33]

---

[24] *Friedman Oil Corp. v. S. Oil Ref. Co.*, 73 S.W.2d 137, 138 (Tex. Civ. App.—Waco 1934, writ dism'd).
[25] *Friedman Oil Corp. v. Southern Oil Refining Co.*, 73 S.W.2d 137, 138 (Tex. Civ. App.—Waco 1934, writ dism'd).
[26] *Kilpatrick v. McKenzie*, 230 S.W.3d 207, 213–15 (Tex. App.—Houston [14th Dist.] 2006, no pet.).
[27] *Wolfe v. Devon Energy Prod. Co., LP*, 382 S.W.3d 434, 445–46 (Tex. App.—Waco 2012, pet. filed).
[28] *Johnson v. Johnson*, 275 S.W.2d 146, 147 (Tex. Civ. App.—Texarkana 1955, writ ref'd n.r.e.).
[29] *Rogers v. Ricane Enters., Inc.*, 884 S.W.2d 763, 768 (Tex. 1994).
[30] Tex. Civ. Prac. & Rem. Code Ann. §§ 16.024-16.028; *Friedman Oil Corp. v. S. Oil Ref. Co.*, 73 S.W.2d 137, 138 (Tex. Civ. App.—Waco 1934, writ dism'd).
[31] *Gulley v. Davis*, 321 S.W.3d 213, 220 (Tex. App.—Houston [1st Dist.] 2010, pet. denied) (reh'g op.).
[32] *Natural Gas Pipeline Co. of Am. v. Pool*, 124 S.W.3d 188, 192–93 (Tex. 2003).
[33] *Natural Gas Pipeline Co. of Am. v. Pool*, 124 S.W.3d 188, 193 (Tex. 2003).

(d) Prior possession which has not been abandoned.
- If the plaintiff's actual possession of the mineral estate was prior in time to that of the defendants' possession, a rebuttable presumption arises that the party having prior possession has a better right.[34]
  - To rebut the presumption, the defendant must prove a superior title.[35]
  - The defense that title is in a third party is not sufficient to rebut the plaintiff's title by prior possession.[36]

7-2:3 Damages and Remedies

7-2:3.1 Judicial Declaration of Title

The primary form of relief is a judicial declaration that the plaintiff recover of the defendant the title, possession, or both.[37]

- The judgment must describe the land.[38]
- This title is conclusive "against the party from whom the property is recovered and against a person claiming the property through that party by a title that arises after the action is initiated."[39]

If the plaintiff does not prove a superior right to the land, the court will enter a take-nothing judgment.[40]

The effect of a take-nothing judgment is to divest the plaintiff of any claim or title to the mineral interest and to vest title to the mineral interest in the defendant.[41] The scope of the take-nothing judgment is limited to the mineral interest put into issue by the parties, pleadings, and proof.[42]

7-2:3.2 Writ of Possession

If the plaintiff recovers possession of the contested property, the court must issue a writ of possession.[43]

- If the defendant obtains a judgment for the value of the defendant's improvements in excess of the defendant's liability for use, occupation and damages, the court may not issue a writ of possession until the first anniversary of the judgment unless the plaintiff pays to the clerk of the court for the benefit of the defendant the amount of the judgment in favor of the defendant plus interest.[44]

---

[34] *Teon Mgmt., LLC v. Turquoise Bay Corp.*, 357 S.W.3d 719, 728–29 (Tex. App.—Eastland 2011, pet. denied).

[35] *Teon Mgmt., LLC v. Turquoise Bay Corp.*, 357 S.W.3d 719, 728 (Tex. App.—Eastland 2011, pet. denied).

[36] *Reiter v. Coastal States Gas Producing Co.*, 382 S.W.2d 243, 251 (Tex. 1964).

[37] Tex. R. Civ. P. 804.

[38] Tex. R. Civ. P. 804.

[39] Tex. Prop. Code Ann. § 22.003.

[40] *Henderson v. Hall*, 174 S.W.2d 985, 990 (Tex. Civ. App.—Galveston 1943, writ ref'd w.o.m.).

[41] *Lile v. Smith*, 291 S.W.3d 75, 79 (Tex. App.—Texarkana 2009, no pet.).

[42] *See Poth v. Roosth*, 202 S.W.2d 442 (Tex. 1947).

[43] Tex. R. Civ. P. 804.

[44] Tex. Prop. Code Ann. § 22.022.

7-2:3.3 Damages for Defendant's Use and Occupation of the Premises

A plaintiff is entitled to damages for use and occupation of the premises.[45]

- When a defendant extracts oil, gas or other minerals, the method by which damages are calculated depends on whether the defendant's actions are in good faith.[46] An oil producer acts in good faith when the producer has an honest and reasonable belief in the superiority of his title.[47]
    - If a defendant trespasses in good faith, the measure of damages is the value of the minerals minus drilling and operating costs.[48]
    - If a defendant trespasses in bad faith, the measure of damages is the value of the minerals, without deduction of drilling and operating costs.[49]

7-2:3.4 Damages for Special Injury to the Property

A plaintiff is entitled to recover damages for any alleged and proved special injury to the property.[50]

7-2:4 Defenses

7-2:4.1 Statute of Limitations

A plaintiff can bring a trespass to try title cause of action when the plaintiff has the right to title or possession.[51] A limitations defense is only available when a party claims the right to title based on adverse possession under the three-, five-, ten-, or twenty-five-year limitations.[52] A party must specially plead the defense of title by limitations.[53] The general four-year statute of limitations is not applicable in a trespass to try title cause of action because it is a suit involving real property.[54]

7-2:4.2 Plaintiff's Claim to Title Is Invalid

Proof of a legal title outstanding in a third person constitutes a defense to plaintiff's suit, even though defendant cannot connect himself with such outstanding legal title.[55]

---

[45] Tex. R. Civ. P. 805.
[46] *Moore v. Jet Stream Invs., Ltd.*, 261 S.W.3d 412, 428 (Tex. App.—Texarkana 2008, pet. denied).
[47] *Moore v. Jet Stream Invs., Ltd.*, 261 S.W.3d 412, 428 (Tex. App.—Texarkana 2008, pet. denied).
[48] *Moore v. Jet Stream Invs., Ltd.*, 261 S.W.3d 412, 428 (Tex. App.—Texarkana 2008, pet. denied).
[49] *Moore v. Jet Stream Invs., Ltd.*, 261 S.W.3d 412, 428 (Tex. App.—Texarkana 2008, pet. denied).
[50] Tex. R. Civ. P. 805.
[51] Tex. R. Civ. P. 783.
[52] Tex. Civ. Prac. & Rem. Code Ann. §§ 16.024-16.028.
[53] Tex. R. Civ. P. 789.
[54] Tex. Civ. Prac. & Rem. Code Ann. § 16.051.
[55] *McShan v. Pitts*, 554 S.W.2d 759, 763 (Tex. App.—San Antonio 1977, no writ).

7-2:4.3 Superior Title in Defendant

A defendant may establish superior title in himself via:

- Superior title out of a common source;[56] or
- Title by limitation.[57]

7-2:4.4 Claim for Improvements

A defendant who is not the rightful owner of the property, but who has possessed the property in good faith and made permanent and valuable improvements to it, is entitled to offset damages owed with the value of the defendant's improvements.[58]

- A good faith developer of oil or gas must have an honest and reasonable belief in the superiority of their title.[59]

7-2:5 Procedural Implications

7-2:5.1 Venue

Venue is mandatory in the county in which all or part of the real property is located.[60]

7-2:5.2 Plaintiff's Pleading Requirements

A plaintiff's petition is subject to heightened pleading requirements.[61]

---

[56] *See Socony Mobil Oil Corp. v. Belveal*, 430 S.W.2d 529, 533–34 (Tex. Civ. App.—El Paso 1968, writ ref'd n.r.e.).

[57] *Moran v. Stanolind Oil & Gas Co.*, 127 S.W.2d 1012, 1016 (Tex. Civ. App.—Fort Worth 1939, writ dism'd).

[58] Tex. Prop. Code Ann. § 22.021(a).

[59] *Moore v. Jet Stream Invs., Ltd.*, 261 S.W.3d 412, 428 (Tex. App.—Texarkana 2008, pet. denied).

[60] Tex. Civ. Prac. & Rem. Code Ann. § 15.011; *Madera Production Co. v. Atlantic Richfield Co.*, 107 S.W.3d 652, 656–58 (Tex. App.—Texarkana 2003, pet. denied).

[61] *See* Tex. R. Civ. P. 783 (Plaintiff's petition must state: (1) The real names of the plaintiff and defendant and their residences, if known; (2) A description of the premises by metes and bounds, or with sufficient certainty to identify the same, so that from such description possession thereof may be delivered, and state the county or counties in which the same are situated; (3) The interest which the plaintiff claims in the premises, whether it be a fee simple or other estate; and, if he claims an undivided interest, the petition shall state the same and the amount thereof; (4) That the plaintiff was in possession of the premises or entitled to such possession; (5) That the defendant afterward unlawfully entered upon and dispossessed him of such premises, stating the date, and withholds from him the possession thereof; (6) If rents and profits or damages are claimed, such facts as show the plaintiff to be entitled thereto and the amount thereof; (7) It shall conclude with a prayer for the relief sought.).

OIL AND GAS LITIGATION

7-2:5.3 Defendant's Pleading Requirements

7-2:5.3a Defendant's Plea of Not Guilty

Defendant should file a plea of "not guilty" as opposed to a general denial.[62]

- This puts the burden of proof on the plaintiff to establish all necessary elements and allows defendant to assert any equitable or legal defense.[63]

7-2:5.3b Defendant's Specifically Plead Adverse Possession

Pleading Requirements—Specifically Plead Adverse Possession

A defendant must specifically plead the defense of limitations.[64]

7-2:5.3c Defendant's Pleading Requirements

Defendant's Pleading Requirements—Specifically Plead Claim for Improvements.

The defendant's claim for improvements is subject to heightened pleading requirements.[65]

7-2:5.4 Proof Requirements

Plaintiff proving prima facie right of title through regular chain of conveyances through sovereign or superior title out of a common source must establish a chain of title through documentary evidence. Testimonial evidence is insufficient.[66]

7-3 Declaratory Judgment Action

7-3:1 Overview

The Declaratory Judgment Act states that a "person interested under a deed . . . may have determined any question of construction or validity arising under the instrument . . . and obtain a declaration of rights, status, or other legal relations thereunder."[67] A Declaratory Judgment Action is proper if the dispute involves non-possessory mineral interests, such as royalty interests and possibilities of reverter. A Declaratory Judgment Action is also proper when the validity or construction of a contract or deed

---

[62] Tex. R. Civ. P. 788.
[63] Tex. R. Civ. P. 789; *Socony Mobil Oil Corp. v. Belveal*, 430 S.W.2d 529, 533 (Tex. Civ. App.—El Paso 1968, writ ref'd n.r.e.).
[64] Tex. R. Civ. P. 789.
[65] *See* Tex. Prop. Code Ann. § 22.021 (The defendant who makes a claim for improvements must plead: (1) That the defendant and those under whom the defendant claims have had good faith adverse possession of the property in controversy for at least one year before the date the action began; (2) That they or the defendant made permanent and valuable improvements to the property while in possession; (3) The grounds for the claim; (4) The identity of the improvements; and (5) The value of each improvement.).
[66] *McCammon v. Ischy*, No. 03-06-00707-CV, 2010 Tex. App. LEXIS 3642 (Tex. App.—Austin May 12, 2010, pet. filed).
[67] Tex. Civ. Prac. & Rem. Code Ann. § 37.004(a).

is at issue. A Trespass to Try Title Action, rather than a Declaratory Judgment Action, is proper when the immediate issue is determination of a title dispute.[68]

7-3:1.1 Related Causes of Action

Trespass to Try Title, Rescission, Reformation, Slander of Title, Trespass to Real Property, Action to Quiet Title

MUST READ CASES

Martin v. Amerman, 133 S.W.3d 262 (Tex. 2004)

Richmond v. Wells, 395 S.W.3d 262 (Tex. App.—Eastland 2012, no pet.)

7-3:2 Elements

(1) An interest under a deed or other writing constituting a contract

- A plaintiff must have an interest "under a deed . . . or other writings constituting a contract" or be a person whose "legal relations are affected by a . . . contract."[69]

(2) A question of construction or validity arising under the instrument

- A question of construction or validity arising under the deed or lease must exist.[70]
    - A plaintiff cannot use a Declaratory Judgment Action to obtain a declaration that they have title to certain mineral rights.[71]
    - A plaintiff can use a Declaratory Judgment Action to ascertain the meaning and/or validity of a deed or lease.[72]

(3) A justiciable controversy as to the rights and status of the parties

- A justiciable controversy as to the rights and status of the parties must exist.[73]

(4) A judicial declaration will resolve the controversy

- A judicial declaration must resolve the controversy.[74]

---

[68] Tex. Prop. Code Ann. § 22.001(a). A Trespass to Try Title Action is the sole method of determining title to real property in Texas. However, construing the terms of contracts and deeds frequently implicates the ultimate issue of title. As a result, courts struggle to reconcile the Declaratory Judgment Act with the Property Code.

[69] Tex. Civ. Prac. & Rem. Code Ann. § 37.004(a).

[70] Tex. Civ. Prac. & Rem. Code Ann. § 37.004(a).

[71] *Wolfe v. Devon Energy Prod. Co.*, 382 S.W.3d 434, 451–52 (Tex. App.—Waco 2012, pet. denied).

[72] *Richmond v. Wells*, 395 S.W.3d 262, 267 (Tex. App.—Eastland 2012, no pet.).

[73] *See Phillips Petroleum Co. v. Bivins*, 423 S.W.2d 340, 345 (Tex. Civ. App.—Amarillo 1967, writ ref'd n.r.e.).

[74] *Shannon v. Barbee*, No. 10-06-00414-CV, 2008 WL 802266, at *3 (Tex. App.—Waco Mar. 26, 2008, pet. denied).

7-3:3 Damages and Remedies

7-3:3.1 Judicial Declaration

The primary form of relief is a judicial declaration that determines any question of construction or validity arising under the deed or lease and sets forth any rights, status or other legal relations thereunder.[75]

7-3:3.2 Attorney's Fees

In any proceeding under the Declaratory Judgments Act, the court may award costs and reasonable and necessary attorney's fees as are equitable and just.[76]

7-3:4 Defenses

7-3:4.1 Statute of Limitations

A declaratory judgment action is a procedural device to determine substantive rights. Therefore, the applicable limitations period depends on the underlying cause of action.[77]

- The cause of action begins to accrue when there is an actual controversy between the parties.[78]

7-3:4.2 No Justiciable Controversy

A justiciable controversy is essential to subject matter jurisdiction and the issue can be raised at any time during the proceedings.[79]

A defendant can successfully show a lack of justiciable controversy if fact determinations render an issue moot.[80]

7-3:4.3 Improper Use of Declaratory Judgment Act

Mineral rights are subject to the Real Property Code, which states that a Trespass to Try Title Action is the sole method of determining title to real property.[81]

- The court must distinguish between actions brought to determine title to the mineral estate and actions brought to determine the construction or validity of a deed or oil and gas lease.[82]

---

[75] Tex. Civ. Prac. & Rem. Code Ann. § 37.004(a).
[76] Tex. Civ. Prac. & Rem. Code Ann. § 37.009.
[77] *In re Estate of Denman*, 362 S.W.3d 134, 144 (Tex. App.—San Antonio 2011, pet. granted).
[78] *In re Estate of Denman*, 362 S.W.3d 134, 144 (Tex. App.—San Antonio 2011, pet. granted).
[79] *Phillips Petroleum Co. v. Bivins*, 423 S.W.2d 340, 345 (Tex. Civ. App.—Amarillo 1967, writ ref'd n.r.e.).
[80] *Phillips Petroleum Co. v. Bivins*, 423 S.W.2d 340, 344–346 (Tex. Civ. App.—Amarillo 1967, writ ref'd n.r.e.).
[81] Tex. Prop. Code Ann. § 22.001(a).
[82] *See Wolfe v. Devon Energy Prod. Co.*, 382 S.W.3d 434, 452 (Tex. App.—Waco 2012, pet. denied); *Richmond v. Wells*, 395 S.W.3d 262 (Tex. App.—Eastland 2012, no pet.).

- A Trespass to Try Title Action is never proper to determine the validity of a royalty interest or possibility of reverter under an oil and gas lease.[83]

7-3:5 Procedural Implications

7-3:5.1 Venue

Venue is mandatory in the county in which all or part of the real property is located.[84]

7-3:5.2 Joinder

The Declaratory Judgment Act requires all persons who have or claim any interest that would be affected by the declaration must be made parties.[85]

- A declaration of rights under an oil and gas lease affects all lessees under the lease; therefore, joinder is necessary for a just adjudication.[86]
- If a defendant requests the joinder of the lessees and joinder is feasible, the trial court must require joinder of all parties to the lease.[87]

7-4 Forcible Entry and Detainer Action

7-4:1 Overview

The primary purpose of a Forcible Entry and Detainer Action is to determine who has the right to immediate possession of real property in a traditional landlord-tenant relationship.[88] An oil and gas lease is not a "lease" in the traditional sense of a lease of the surface of real property and does not create a traditional landlord-tenant relationship. Rather, the lessor is a grantor and grants a fee simple determinable interest to the lessee, who is actually a grantee. The lessee has possession so long as the "lease" remains in effect.[89] Consequently, any determination of possession would first require a determination of title to the mineral estate. The statute places jurisdiction over Forcible Entry and Detainer in the justice and county courts.[90] If possession may not be determined without first determining title, justice and county courts are without jurisdiction to make any determinations regarding title, which are in sole jurisdiction of district courts.[91] While some of the early case law excluded from a county court's subject matter jurisdiction only those cases in which the court's judgment

---

[83] *Richmond v. Wells*, 395 S.W.3d 262, 267 (Tex. App.—Eastland 2012, no pet.). A royalty interest and possibility of reverter are non-possessory interests. Generally, non-possessory interests are not proper subjects of a trespass-to-try-title action.

[84] Tex. Civ. Prac. & Rem. Code Ann. § 15.011; *Madera Prod. Co. v. Atl. Richfield Co.*, 107 S.W.3d 652, 656–58 (Tex. App.—Texarkana 2003, pet. denied).

[85] Tex. Civ. Prac. & Rem. Code Ann. § 37.006(a).

[86] *Kodiak Res., Inc. v. Smith*, 361 S.W.3d 246, 251–52 (Tex. App.—Beaumont 2012, no pet.).

[87] Tex. R. Civ. P. 39(a); Tex. Civ. Prac. & Rem. Code Ann. § 37.006(a); *Kodiak Res., Inc. v. Smith*, 361 S.W.3d 246, 251–52 (Tex. App.—Beaumont 2012, no pet.).

[88] Tex. Prop. Code Ann. § 24.002.

[89] *Natural Gas Pipeline Co. of Am. v. Pool*, 124 S.W.3d 188, 192 (Tex. 2003).

[90] Tex. Prop. Code Ann. § 24.004.

[91] *Mitchell v. Armstrong Capital Corp.*, 911 S.W.2d 169, 171 (Tex. App.—Houston [1st Dist.] 1995, writ denied); *see Yarbrough v. Household Fin. Corp. III*, 455 S.W.3d 277, 280 (Tex.,

would include an award of title to land,[92] under *Coughran* the district courts also have exclusive jurisdiction over cases in which a judicial determination of a title dispute between the parties is necessary to render the judgment, even if the judgment itself does not include an express grant of relief with respect to title.[93]

But when the gist of a cause of action, whether in the form of trespass to try title or in any other form, rests upon the proposition that the title to land asserted by the plaintiff is superior to that of the defendant, the district court alone has jurisdiction to adjudicate the matter.[94]

Thus, a Forcible Entry and Detainer Action is not a proper method for adjudicating a mineral-ownership dispute. Forcible entry is an entry upon property without the consent of the person in actual possession of the property, without the consent of the tenant (at will or at sufferance); or without the consent of the person who acquired possession by forcible entry.[95] Forcible detainer, on the other hand, occurs when a person who refuses to surrender possession of real property upon demand and the person is a holdover tenant or subtenant, is a tenant at will or by sufferance, or is a tenant of a person who acquired possession by forcible entry.[96]

7-4:1.1 Must Read Authority

Texas Property Code Sections 24.001, 24.002, 24.004

7-5 Breach of Contract

7-5:1 Overview

Under Texas law, mineral leases are considered contracts. Therefore, Breach of Contract is a viable cause of action in oil and gas litigation. Courts apply the usual rules of construction when determining the parties' intent, subject to certain mineral-specific rules. A mineral lease creates a contractual relationship as well as an interest in real property. Mineral leases contain covenants, which impose express or implied contractual obligations on the parties, as well as conditions, which determine how long the real property interest will last. The plaintiff's remedy depends on whether the defendant breached a covenant or a condition. Courts favor the creation of covenants in the absence of specific language creating a condition.

App.—Houston [14th Dist.] 20 15, no pet.) (concluding that the issue of title was so intertwined with the issue of possession that it precluded jurisdiction in the justice court).

[92] *See, e.g., Victoria v. Schott*, 29 S.W. 681 (Tex. Civ. App.—Houston 1895, no writ).

[93] *See Kegans v. White*, 131 S.W.2d 990, 994–95 (Tex. Civ. App.—Eastland 1939, writ ref'd); *see Chinyere v. Wells Fargo Bank, N.A.*, 440 S.W.3d 80, 85 (Tex. App.—Houston [1st Dist.] 2012) (concluding that the lower courts did not have jurisdiction over the forcible detainer action because the plaintiff's claims relied upon disputed title rights).

[94] *Edwards v. Hefley*, 22 S.W. 659, 661 (Tex. Civ. App.—Austin 1893, no writ); *Merit Mgmt. Partners I, L.P. v. Noelke*, 266 S.W.3d 637, 647 (Tex. App.—Austin, 2008).

[95] Tex. Prop. Code Ann. § 24.001(b)(1)–(3).

[96] Tex. Prop. Code Ann. § 24.002(b)(1)–(3).

7-5:1.1 Related Causes of Action

Rescission, Reformation, Estoppel, Unjust Enrichment, Declaratory Judgment Action, Trespass to Try Title, Breach of Implied Covenant to Further Explore (not recognized in Texas), Breach of Implied Covenant to Market, Breach of Implied Covenant to Protect Against Drainage

MUST READ CASES

Anadarko Petroleum Corp. v. Thompson, 94 S.W.3d 550, 560 (Tex. 2002)

Rogers v. Ricane Enters., Inc., 772 S.W.2d 76, 79 (Tex. 1989)

7-5:2 Elements

(1) The existence of a valid contract;

- A valid contract must exist.[97]

(2) Performance or tendered performance by the plaintiff;

- The plaintiff must have performed or tendered performance under the contract.[98]

(3) Breach of the contract by the defendant; and

- The defendant must breach the contract.[99]

- Courts apply ordinary rules of construction when ascertaining the meaning of lease provisions, subject to several mineral-specific rules.[100]

  - A mineral lease is to be strictly construed against the lessee and in favor of the lessor.[101]

  - In construing mineral leases, the habendum clause will control unless properly modified by other provisions.[102]

(4) Damages sustained by the plaintiff as a result of the breach.

- The plaintiff must sustain damages as a result of the defendant's breach.[103]

---

[97] *Pathfinder Oil & Gas, Inc. v. Great Western Drilling, Ltd.*, 574 S.W.3d 882, 890 (Tex. 2019).
[98] *Pathfinder Oil & Gas, Inc. v. Great Western Drilling, Ltd.*, 574 S.W.3d 882, 890 (Tex. 2019).
[99] *Pathfinder Oil & Gas, Inc. v. Great Western Drilling, Ltd.*, 574 S.W.3d 882, 890 (Tex. 2019).
[100] See *Anadarko Petroleum Corp. v. Thompson*, 94 S.W.3d 550, 554 (Tex. 2002).
[101] *Clark v. Perez*, 679 S.W.2d 710 (Tex. App.—San Antonio 1984, no writ)
[102] *Gulf Oil Corp. v. Southland Royalty Co.*, 496 S.W.2d 547, 552 (Tex. 1973); *BP Am. Prod. Co. v. Red Deer Res., LLC*, 526 S.W.3d 389, 394–95 (Tex. 2017).
[103] *Pathfinder Oil & Gas, Inc. v. Great Western Drilling, Ltd.*, 574 S.W.3d 882, 890 (Tex. 2019).

OIL AND GAS LITIGATION

7-5:3 Damages and Remedies

7-5:3.1 Compensatory Damages

Breach of a covenant does not automatically terminate the estate, but instead subjects the breaching party to liability for monetary damages.[104]

- Since forfeitures are not favored, courts are inclined to construe the provisions in a contract as covenants rather than as conditions.[105]
- The measure of damages varies depending on the covenant breached.[106]

7-5:3.2 Termination of Lease

Breach of a condition results in automatic termination of the leasehold estate upon the happening of stipulated events.[107]

- Courts will only construe provisions in a contract as conditions if a lease expressly provides for termination.[108]

When damages do not provide adequate relief, the court can conditionally terminate the lease if actual production does not occur within a reasonable time.[109]

7-5:3.3 Attorney's Fees

A plaintiff who recovers damages for breach of contract is entitled to attorney's fees.[110]

7-5:4 Defenses

7-5:4.1 Temporary Cessation Doctrine

Temporary cessation of production in paying quantities does not terminate a lease if the lessee exercises diligent efforts to restore production and there is a reasonable expectation of success within a reasonable period of time.[111]

---

[104] *Rogers v. Ricane Enters., Inc.*, 772 S.W.2d 76, 79 (Tex. 1989).

[105] *Rogers v. Ricane Enters., Inc.*, 772 S.W.2d 76, 79 (Tex. 1989).

[106] *See Coastal Oil & Gas Corp. v. Garza Energy Tr.*, 268 S.W.3d 1, 19 (Tex. 2008) (For a breach of the covenant of reasonable development, the lessee is entitled to recover the full value of royalty lost.); *Phillips Petroleum Co. v. Yarbrough*, 405 S.W.3d 70, 78 (Tex. 2013) (For a breach of the covenant to market, the measure of damages is based on sales of gas at the well, or the price received by the lessee.).

[107] *Rogers v. Ricane Enters., Inc.*, 772 S.W.2d 76, 79 (Tex. 1989).

[108] *Riley v. Meriwether*, 780 S.W.2d 919, 923 (Tex. App.—El Paso 1989, no writ).

[109] *Anadarko Petroleum Corp. v. Thompson*, 94 S.W.3d 550, 560 (Tex. 2002).

[110] Tex. Civ. Prac. & Rem. Code Ann. §§ 38.001–38.006; *Hideca Petroleum Corp. v. Tampimex Oil Int'l, Ltd.*, 740 S.W.2d 838 (Tex. App.—Houston [1st Dist.] 1987, no writ); *Ohrt v. Union Gas Corp.* 398 S.W.3d 315, 333 (Tex, App.—Corpus Christi- Edinburg 2012, pet. denied) ("However, in order to qualify for fees under the statute, a litigant must prevail on a breach of contract claim and recover damages.").

[111] *Ridge Oil Co., Inc. v. Guinn Invs., Inc.*, 148 S.W.3d 143, 150 (Tex. 2004).

- What constitutes a reasonable time depends on the facts of each case.[112]
- The burden is on the lessee to prove that the cessation in production fell within the temporary cessation doctrine.[113]
- The Temporary Cessation of Production Doctrine is meant to alleviate lessees of the harsh effects of the strict construction rule.[114]

7-5:4.2 Express Lease Provisions

Courts do not imply covenants unless it appears from the express provisions in the contract that it was within the contemplation of the parties or it appears necessary to effectuate the purpose of the contract.[115]

Most mineral leases contain clauses that specifically address common situations that would otherwise constitute breaches of implied covenants.[116]

7-5:5 Procedural Implications

7-5:5.1 Venue

Venue is mandatory in the county in which all or part of the real property is located.[117]

- A Breach of Contract Action under a mineral lease is ultimately dependent upon proof of ownership rights in the mineral lease. Thus, the only proper venue is the county in which the mineral estate is located.[118]

---

[112] *See, e.g. Midwest Oil Corp. v. Winsauer*, 323 S.W.2d 944, 948 (1959) (Cessation in production lasting six months held to be reasonable period of time); *Scarborough v. New Domain Oil & Gas Co.*, 276 S.W. 331, 336 (Tex. Civ. App.—El Paso 1925, writ dism'd w.o.j.) (In finding that lease did not terminate, the court considered the provisions of the lease, production in paying quantities in the primary term, the cause of cessation of production was unforeseen and unavoidable, the lessees in good faith used reasonable diligence to resume production, and did resume production after great expense).

[113] *Krabbe v. Andarko Petroleum Corp.*, 46 S.W.3d 308, 316 (Tex. App.—Amarillo, 2001, pet. denied).

[114] *Ridge Oil Co., Inc. v. Guinn Invs., Inc.*, 148 S.W.3d 143, 150 (Tex. 2004).

[115] *HECI Expl. Co. v. Neel*, 982 S.W.2d 881, 888–89 (Tex. 1998) ("We have imposed implied covenants only when they are fundamental to the purposes of a mineral lease and when the lease does not expressly address the subject matter of the covenant sought to be implied.").

[116] *See Stanolind Oil & Gas Co. v. Newman Bros. Drill. Co.*, 305 S.W.2d 169, 173–74 (Tex. 1957) ("Habendum clause . . . is both modified and enlarged by the recital that it is subject to the other lease provisions, and is required to yield to any and all other provisions which affect the duration of the lease. It is clear then that the lease may be kept in force after the end of the primary term either by production or by the operation of its other provisions.").

[117] Tex. Civ. Prac. & Rem. Code Ann. § 15.011.

[118] *Madera Prod. Co. v. Atl. Richfield Co.*, 107 S.W.3d 652, 659–60 (Tex. App.—Texarkana 2003, pet. denied). *Retamco Operating, Inc. v. Republic Drilling Co.*, 278 S.W.3d 333, 339 (Tex. 2009) ("Oil and Gas interests are real property interests.").

7-6 Suit in Assumpsit

7-6:1 Overview

Texas belongs to a minority of states that permit a plaintiff to waive a Trespass Action and bring a Suit in Assumpsit under an implied contract. A Suit in Assumpsit allows a plaintiff to recover for the reasonable value of the use and occupation of the mineral estate in the event that there is no actual injury. Courts use a reasonable market value measure when determining the value for the use and occupation of the mineral estate.

7-6:1.1 Related Causes of Action

Trespass, Breach of Contract, Unjust Enrichment[119]

MUST READ CASE

Phillips Petroleum Co. v. Cowden, 241 F.2d 586 (5th Cir.1957)

7-6:2 Elements

(1) The plaintiff owns or has a lawful right to possess real property;

- The plaintiff must own or have a lawful right to possess real property.[120]
    - The plaintiff must have title to the mineral estate. The title-holder of the surface estate cannot maintain a Trespass or Assumpsit action.[121]
    - A lessor who has leased the mineral estate may still maintain a Suit in Assumpsit, provided they did not grant the lessee an exclusive right to prospect.[122]

(2) The defendant physically and intentionally entered the plaintiff's land.[123]

- Texas recognizes geophysical subsurface trespass, such as unauthorized seismic testing of a mineral estate.[124]

---

[119] A plaintiff cannot recover under unjust enrichment if the court rejects a trespass or assumpsit action. If a defendant did not trespass, they did not wrongfully secure a benefit which would be unconscionable to retain. *Villarreal v. Grant Geophysical, Inc.*, 136 S.W.3d 265, 270 (Tex. App.—San Antonio 2004, pet. denied).

[120] *Baker v. Energy Transfer Co.*, No. 10–09–00214–CV, 2011 WL 4978287, at *7 (Tex. App.—Waco Oct. 19, 2011, no pet. h.) (mem. op.).

[121] *Phillips Petroleum Co. v. Cowden*, 241 F.2d 586, 591–92 (5th Cir. 1957).

[122] *See Phillips Petroleum Co. v. Cowden*, 241 F.2d 586, 592 (5th Cir. 1957) (The lessor has at least a prospective interest in the mineral estate and thus a legitimate interest even while the lease is in effect).

[123] *Baker v. Energy Transfer Co.*, No. 10–09–00214–CV, 2011 WL 4978287, at *7 (Tex. App.—Waco Oct. 19, 2011, no pet. h.) (mem. op.).

[124] *Villarreal v. Grant Geophysical, Inc.*, 136 S.W.3d 265, 268 (Tex. App.—San Antonio 2004, pet. denied).

- However, there must be physical entry or injury upon the surface estate.[125]

(3) The defendant's trespass caused injury to the plaintiff.

- Under a Suit in Assumpsit, a plaintiff does not need to establish actual physical injury to the land.[126]
    - Plaintiff may recover under an implied contract basis for value of the right to conduct exploratory testing on their own terms.[127]
    - Plaintiff is entitled to this recovery even if the defendant does not receive any actual benefit from the testing.[128]

7-6:3 Damages and Remedies

7-6:3.1 Use and Occupation Damages

A plaintiff is entitled to the value of the use and occupation of the mineral estate.[129]

- The value of the use and occupation of the mineral estate is the reasonable market value of exploratory testing.[130]

7-6:4 Defenses

7-6:4.1 Statute of Limitations

The statute of limitations for permanent injury to land is two years from the date of the first injury. However, the damages for temporary injury to land may be recovered for the two years prior to filing suit.[131]

- The cause of action begins to accrue on the date the trespass is committed.[132]
- Texas courts reject application of the discovery rule to claims involving oil and gas operations, since owners of oil, gas and mineral interests have a duty to exercise reasonable diligence in protecting their interests.[133]

---

[125] *See Kennedy v. Gen. Geophysical Co.*, 213 S.W.2d 707, 709, 711 (Tex. Civ. App.—Galveston 1948, writ ref'd n.r.e) (Trespass may not be committed by mere vibrations from neighboring lands.).

[126] *Villarreal v. Grant Geophysical, Inc.*, 136 S.W.3d 265, 269 (Tex. App.—San Antonio 2004, pet. denied).

[127] *Phillips Petroleum Co. v. Cowden*, 241 F.2d 586, 593–94 (5th Cir. 1957).

[128] *Phillips Petroleum Co. v. Cowden*, 241 F.2d 586, 593–94 (5th Cir. 1957).

[129] *Phillips Petroleum Co. v. Cowden*, 241 F.2d 586, 593–94 (5th Cir. 1957).

[130] *See Phillips Petroleum Co. v. Cowden*, 241 F.2d 586, 593–94 (5th Cir. 1957) (Recovery is based on an implied promise whose assumed terms should conform fairly closely to the sort of agreement that might actually have been reached by reasonable parties.).

[131] *EnerQuest Oil & Gas, LLC v. Plains Expl. & Prod. Co.*, 981 F. Supp. 2d 575, 618 (W.D. Tex. Nov. 7, 2013).

[132] *EnerQuest Oil & Gas, LLC v. Plains Expl. & Prod. Co.*, 981 F. Supp. 2d 575, 618 (W.D. Tex. Nov. 7, 2013).

[133] *EnerQuest Oil & Gas, LLC v. Plains Expl. & Prod. Co.*, 981 F. Supp. 2d 575, 618 (W.D. Tex. Nov. 7, 2013).

7-6:5 Procedural Implications

7-6:5.1 Venue

Venue is mandatory in the county in which all or part of the real property is located.[134]

7-7 Breach of Fiduciary Duty

7-7:1 Overview

A cause of action for Breach of Fiduciary Duty is not available in the oil and gas context unless a fiduciary relationship existed prior to the creation of the mineral lease or joint operating agreement. A partnership, joint venture, agency or tenancy in common could create a fiduciary relationship. The scope of the pre-existing fiduciary relationship must encompass the interest under the mineral lease or joint operating agreement. Courts impose a constructive trust upon the mineral lease or joint operating agreement that reflects the pre-existing fiduciary relationship. The constructive trust will not extend past the development and activities of the particular lease or agreement.

7-7:1.1 Related Causes of Action

Breach of Contract, Unjust Enrichment, Declaratory Judgment Action, Breach of Informal Fiduciary Duty from Special Relationship, Breach of Formal Fiduciary Duty

MUST READ CASES

Rankin v. Naftalis, 557 S.W.2d 940 (Tex. 1977)

Consolidated Gas & Equip. Co. of Am. v. Thompson, 405 S.W.2d 333 (Tex. 1966)

7-7:2 Elements

(1) Existence of a fiduciary relationship;

- A fiduciary relationship does not arise from a contractual agreement between lessors and lessees under a mineral lease or operators and working-interest owners under a joint operating agreement, unless specifically set forth in the contract.[135]

- For a constructive trust to arise there must be a fiduciary relationship before and apart from the agreement made the basis of the suit.[136]

---

[134] Tex. Civ. Prac. & Rem. Code Ann. § 15.011; *Madera Prod. Co. v. Atl. Richfield Co.*, 107 S.W.3d 652, 656–58 (Tex. App.—Texarkana 2003, pet. denied); *Retamco Operating, Inc. v. Republic Drilling Co.*, 278 S.W.3d 333, 339 (Tex. 2009) ("Oil and Gas interests are real property interests.").

[135] *Norman v. Apache Corp.*, 19 F.3d 1017, 1024 (5th Cir. 1994).

[136] *Consolidated Gas & Equip. Co. of Am. v. Thompson*, 405 S.W.2d 333, 336 (Tex. 1966).

- A fiduciary relationship can arise between joint adventurers, particularly when there is an agreement to share financial gains and losses.[137]
- General partners owe fiduciary duties to other partners and the partnership.[138]
- An informal fiduciary relationship could arise from "moral, social, domestic or purely personal relationships," but subjective trust alone is not enough to transform arms-length dealing into a fiduciary relationship.[139]
- The mineral lease or joint operating agreement at issue in the suit can expressly impose a fiduciary relationship between the parties thereto.[140]

(2) Lease or agreement in question is within the scope of that fiduciary relationship;

- The scope of the pre-existing fiduciary relationship must encompass the interests under the particular mineral lease or joint operating agreement at issue.[141]
    - The terms of any resulting constructive trust will not extend past those specific activities and interests under the lease or agreement.[142]

(3) Breach of fiduciary duty.

- In general, a fiduciary owes a duty of good faith and fair dealing and an additional duty of loyalty by which the fiduciary must place the interest of the beneficiary above his/her own.[143]
    - The exact parameters of the duties owed by fiduciaries vary based on the type of relationship and the agreement of the parties.[144]

---

[137] *Consolidated Gas & Equip. Co. of Am. v. Thompson*, 405 S.W.2d 333, 336–37 (Tex. 1966).

[138] *See Crowder v. Tri–C Res., Inc.*, 821 S.W.2d 393, 399 (Tex. App.—Houston [1st Dist.] 1991, no writ) (determining that the relationship between the non-operators and the operator pursuant to the joint operating agreement between them did not give rise to the duty of good faith and fair dealing that would arise in a partnership).

[139] *Thigpen v. Locke*, 363 S.W.2d 247, 253 (Tex. 1962). For a more detailed analysis of informal fiduciary duties, *see* Chapter 4: Breach of Informal Fiduciary Duties.

[140] *Norman v. Apache Corp.*, 19 F.3d 1017, 1024 (5th Cir. 1994).

[141] *Smith v. Bolin*, 271 S.W.2d 93, 97 (Tex. 1954).

[142] *See Rankin v. Naftalis*, 557 S.W.2d 940, 945 (Tex. 1977) ("The fiduciary relationship created by a joint drilling venture does not forbid further acquisition and development of leases in the general area by individual venturers so long as these leases are not embraced within the scope of the enterprise or are not a natural outgrowth therefrom. . . . Such a holding would discourage the financing of new oil and gas leases.").

[143] *Crim Truck & Tractor Co. v. Navistar Int'l Transp. Corp.*, 823 S.W.2d 591, 593–94 (Tex. 1992).

[144] *See Smith v. Bolin*, 271 S.W.2d 93, 97 (Tex. 1954) (Partner breached fiduciary duty under pre-existing partnership agreement when he took new leases on the partnership's leases, but did not breach duty when he did not include partners in farmout agreements as to two other leases not embraced in the written contract between the partners.).

7-7:3 Damages and Remedies

7-7:3.1 Imposition of Constructive Trust

A constructive trust is an equitable remedy. As such, there is no specific formula to determine its terms. The equity of the transaction will shape the measure of relief granted.[145]

7-7:4 Defenses

7-7:4.1 Statute of Limitations

The four-year statute of limitations is applicable.[146]

In the case of a constructive trust, limitations begin running at the inception of the trust.[147]

If a plaintiff proves fraudulent concealment, the statute of limitations will be tolled from the time the concealed fraud is discovered, or could have been discovered by reasonable diligence.[148]

7-7:5 Procedural Implications

7-7:5.1 Venue

If the plaintiff wishes to impose a constructive trust on the mineral estate, venue is mandatory in the county in which all or part of the real property is located.[149]

However, if the primary nature of a constructive trust action is one for specific performance of a contract, the general venue rule applies.[150]

7-8 Tort Conversion

7-8:1 Overview

Conversion is an intentional exercise of dominion or control over personal property which so seriously interferes with the right of another to control it that the actor may justly be required to pay the other the full value of the property. Oil and gas is considered real property when in place and personal property when severed from the ground. Thus, a plaintiff may only bring a Conversion Action if the defendant brings the minerals to the surface. Conversion and Trespass to Chattel and Personalty are distinguished by the degree of control the defendant exercises over the property.

---

[145] *Magee v. Young*, 198 S.W.2d 883, 885–86 (Tex. 1946).
[146] Tex. Civ. Prac. & Rem. Code Ann. § 16.051; *Dunmore v. Chicago Title Ins. Co.*, 400 S.W.3d 635, 640 (Tex. App.—Dallas 2013, no pet.).
[147] *Carr v. Weiss*, 984 S.W.2d 753, 761 (Tex. App.—Amarillo 1999).
[148] *Mowbray v. Avery*, 76 S.W.3d 633, 690 (Tex. App.—Corpus Christi 2002, pet. denied).
[149] Tex. Civ. Prac. & Rem. Code Ann. § 15.011; *Brown v. Gilmore*, 267 S.W.2d 908, 911 (Tex. Civ. App.—El Paso 1954, writ dism'd).
[150] Tex. Civ. Prac. & Rem. Code Ann. § 15.002; *Energy Reserves Grp., Inc. v. Tarina Oil Co.*, 664 S.W.2d 169, 171–72 (Tex. App.—San Antonio 1983, no writ).

Trespass to Chattel and Personalty only requires interference with the plaintiff's use of the chattel. Conversion requires affirmative control over the chattel. The importance of the distinction lies in the measure of damages. In trespass the plaintiff may recover for the diminished value of his chattel because of any damage to it. In conversion the measure of damages is the full value of the chattel, which is typically more than a recovery for diminished value. Removal of minerals from the ground is irreparable and always constitutes affirmative control over chattel.[151] Therefore, Conversion is always an available cause of action that entitles a plaintiff to a greater recovery. For these reasons, a Conversion Action subsumes Trespass to Chattel and Personalty Actions and is the only appropriate method for adjudicating dispossession of minerals.

7-8:1.1 Related Causes of Action

Trespass to Chattel, Trespass to Real Property, Fraud, Negligence

MUST READ CASES

Pan Am. Petroleum Corp. v. Long, 340 F.2d 211 (5th Cir. 1964)

Harrington v. Texaco, Inc., 339 F.2d 814 (5th Cir. 1964)

7-8:2 Elements

(1) An intentional exercise of control over the personal property of another;

- A distinct act of dominion or control over the personal property of another must occur.[152]

- The convertor may either have actual or constructive possession of the property.[153]

    - Control must be intentional, but a wrongful or fraudulent intent or purpose is not required.[154]

---

[151] *See* Restatement (Second) of Torts § 222A (1965) ("Normally any dispossession is so clearly a serious interference with the right of control that it amounts to a conversion; and it is frequently said that any dispossession is a conversion."); *Hastings Oil Co. v. Tex. Co.*, 234 S.W.2d 389, 398 (Tex. 1950) (Trespass to mining property is irreparable "since the injury goes to the immediate destruction of the minerals which constitute the chief value of this species of property.").

[152] *See* Restatement (Second) of Torts § 222A (1965) (Defining conversion as "an intentional exercise of dominion over property which so seriously interfered with the right of another to control it that the actor may justly be required to pay the other the full value of the property").

[153] *See Pan Am. Petroleum Corp. v. Long*, 340 F.2d 211, 220–21 (5th Cir. 1964) (Financial institution received sales proceeds of converted oil and applied proceeds towards converter's balance on note. Although financial institution never had actual possession of the oil, the terms of the payment instruments and division orders invested them with broad operational power over the converter. This power sufficiently created the necessary amount of control over the oil to constitute conversion by the financial institution.).

[154] *See, e.g., Pan Am. Petroleum Corp. v. Long*, 340 F.2d 211, 220–21 (5th Cir. 1964) (Financial institution liable for conversion to the same extent as operator who fraudulently concealed a slant-hole drilling operation); *Bankers Life Ins. Co. of Neb. v. Scurlock Oil Co.*, 447 F.2d 997,

(2) To the exclusion of the same rights by the owner.

- The defendant must actually exclude the owner from exercising control over the property. Temporary interference with the property is not sufficient.[155]

7-8:3 Damages and Remedies

7-8:3.1 Value of Converted Property

The measure of damages for a Conversion Action is the value of the converted property.[156]

- In oil and gas cases, this is the market value of the oil at the surface.[157]
  - Market value is defined as the price property would bring when it is offered for sale by one who desires, but is not obligated, to sell and is bought by one who is under no necessity of buying it.[158]
  - Market value may be calculated by using sales of gas that are comparable in time, quality, quantity and availability of marketing outlets.[159]
- A defendant who is guilty of conversion but acted without fraudulent intent is entitled to set off the costs of production.[160]
  - The defendant has the burden of pleading and proving that the conversion was not willful, and the dollar amount of the claimed costs of production.[161]

7-8:3.2 Exemplary Damages

Exemplary damages are recoverable for conversion accompanied by fraud or oppression, or by willfulness and malice.[162]

1005 (5th Cir. 1971) (Principal liable for fraudulent conversion by its agent, even though the principal had no knowledge of the fraud, did not consent to it, and was a victim of the fraud himself.).

[155] *See* Restatement (Second) of Torts § 222A (1965), cmt. a ("Conversion is an exercise of the defendant's dominion or control over the chattel, as distinguished from a mere interference with the chattel itself, or with the possession of it. Since any interference with the chattel is to some extent an exercise of "dominion," the difference between the two becomes almost entirely a matter of degree.").

[156] *Harrington v. Texaco, Inc.*, 339 F.2d 814, 821 (5th Cir. 1964).

[157] *Harrington v. Texaco, Inc.*, 339 F.2d 814, 821 (5th Cir. 1964).

[158] *Exxon Corp. v. Middleton*, 613 S.W.2d 240, 246 (Tex. 1981).

[159] *Exxon Corp. v. Middleton*, 613 S.W.2d 240, 246 (Tex. 1981).

[160] *Harrington v. Texaco, Inc.*, 339 F.2d 814, 821 (5th Cir. 1964).

[161] *Harrington v. Texaco, Inc.*, 339 F.2d 814, 821 (5th Cir. 1964).

[162] Tex. Civ. Prac. & Rem. Code Ann. § 41.003; *Mauriceville Nat'l Bank v. Zernial*, 880 S.W.2d 282, 289 (Tex. App.—Beaumont 1994), *rev'd on other grounds*, 892 S.W.2d 858 (Tex. 1995), citing *Craddock v. Goodwin*, 54 Tex. 578 (1881).

7-8:4 Defenses

7-8:4.1 Statute of Limitations

A person must bring a suit for conversion of personal property not later than two years after the day the cause of action accrues.[163]

- The cause of action accrues on the date the conversion takes place.[164]
- Limitation does not run and the statute is tolled in circumstances where the cause of action has been fraudulently concealed by the defendant and is not discovered by the plaintiff two years before filing suit if the plaintiff exercised reasonable diligence in seeking to discover the fraud after being put on inquiry.[165]

7-8:4.2 Rule of Capture

The Rule of Capture gives a mineral rights owner title to the oil and gas produced from a lawful well bottomed on the property, even if the oil and gas flowed to the well from beneath another owner's tract.[166]

However, the Rule of Capture does not protect against slant-hole drilling.[167]

7-8:5 Procedural Implications

7-8:5.1 Venue

The general venue rule is applicable.[168]

- The mandatory venue statute for suits for recovery of land would only apply if the plaintiff sought additional relief, such as a declaratory judgment, that would require the court to determine an ownership interest in real property.[169]

---

[163] Tex. Civ. Prac. & Rem. Code Ann. § 16.003(a).

[164] *Marathon Oil Co. v. Gulf Oil Corp.*, 130 S.W.2d 365 (Tex. Civ. App.—El Paso, 1939), *rev'd in part Gulf Oil Corp. v. Marathon Oil Co.*, 152 S.W.2d 711 (1941).

[165] *Pan Am. Petroleum Corp. v. Orr*, 319 F.2d 612, 613 (5th Cir. 1963); *Cass v. Stephens*, 156 S.W.3d 38, 67–68 (Tex. App.—El Paso 2004, pet. denied),

[166] *Coastal Oil & Gas Corp. v. Garza Energy Tr.*, 268 S.W.3d 1, 13 (Tex. 2008).

[167] *See Coastal Oil & Gas Corp. v. Garza Energy Tr.*, 268 S.W.3d 1, 13–14 (Tex. 2008) (Slant-hole drilling involves drilling from a well that departs from the vertical significantly and bottoms on another's property. The gas produced through slant-hole drilling does not migrate to the wellbore from another's property. It is taken directly from another's property and thus constitutes conversion.).

[168] Tex. Civ. Prac. & Rem. Code Ann. § 15.002; *Powell v. Forest Oil Corp.*, 392 S.W.2d 549, 551–52 (Tex. Civ. App.—Texarkana 1965, no writ).

[169] *See W.B. Johnson Drilling Co. v. Lacy*, 336 S.W.2d 230, 234–35 (Tex. Civ. App.—Eastland 1960, no writ) (All the relief sought could have been properly granted without a determination of the present ownership of the mineral estate. The court could have granted them judgment for the proceeds of the sale of oil produced prior to the trial by determining only that they were owners of such leasehold interest during the period that the oil was produced.).

OIL AND GAS LITIGATION

7-9 Public Nuisance

7-9:1 Overview

A public nuisance is an unreasonable interference with a right common to the general public. An individual or distinct class may bring a Public Nuisance Action for monetary damages only if the individual or class has suffered significant harm different in kind from that suffered by the general public. A representative of a state or political subdivision may bring a Public Nuisance Action on behalf of the general public. In this instance, recovery is limited to an injunction. Public Nuisance Actions are becoming increasingly popular methods of addressing global warming, which is allegedly caused by increased production of oil and gas. Recent case law in this area addresses numerous procedural issues. However, courts handling these cases have yet to reach final decisions on the merits.

7-9:1.1 Related Causes of Action

Private Nuisance, Trespass to Real Property, Conversion

MUST READ CASES

Comer v. Murphy Oil U.S.A., 585 F.3d 855 (5th Cir. 2009)[170]

Comer v. Murphy Oil U.S.A., 839 F. Supp. 2d 849 (S.D. Miss. 2012), *aff'd*, 718 F.3d 460 (5th Cir. 2013)[171]

7-9:2 Elements

(1) An unreasonable interference by the defendant

- There must be an unreasonable interference by the defendant.[172]

---

[170] In this case, plaintiffs filed a class action public nuisance lawsuit against a group of oil companies, alleging that the oil company defendants released by-products that led to the development and increase of global warming. The district court held that plaintiffs lacked standing because their injuries were not fairly traceable to the defendants' actions and that the claims were non-justiciable political questions. On appeal, a panel of the Fifth Circuit reversed in part with regard to plaintiffs' claims of public and private nuisance. The Fifth Circuit granted rehearing *en banc*, but then lost a quorum, which meant it was not authorized to transact judicial business, and the appeal was dismissed. The panel opinion was lawfully vacated and could not be reinstated, leaving the district court dismissal as the controlling law.

[171] Subsequent to the vacating of the 5th Circuit *Comer* opinion, the *Comer* class action plaintiffs filed a new lawsuit, again asserting public and private nuisance. The district court found that the claims were barred by res judicata and collateral estoppel. It also held again that the plaintiffs lacked standing, that the claims presented non-justiciable political questions, and that the claim was preempted by the Clean Air Act. On appeal, the Fifth Circuit affirmed the district court's judgment, but expressly did so solely on the basis of res judicata.

[172] *Louisiana v. Rowan Cos. Inc.*, 728 F. Supp. 2d 896, 905 (S.D. Tex. 2010); *Crosstex North Texas Pipeline, L.P. v. Gardiner*, 505 S.W.3d 580, 595 (Tex. 2016).

- Circumstances that may sustain a holding that an interference with a public right is unreasonable include the following:
  - Whether the conduct involves a significant interference with the public health, the public safety, the public peace, the public comfort or the public convenience;[173]
  - Whether the conduct is proscribed by a statute, ordinance or administrative regulation;[174] or
  - Whether the conduct is of a continuing nature or has produced a permanent or long-lasting effect, and, as the actor knows or has reason to know, has a significant effect upon the public right.[175]

(2) With a right common to the general public
- The defendant must interfere with a right common to the general public.[176]

7-9:3 Damages and Remedies

7-9:3.1 Special Damages

A plaintiff who successfully establishes the elements of a Public Nuisance Action and the existence of a particularized injury is entitled to monetary damages that proximately, naturally and reasonably result from the alleged injury.[177]

- Special damages can encompass physical injury, property damage and pecuniary loss.[178]
- Damages are the appropriate remedy if it is unreasonable to allow the defendant to engage in the conduct without paying for the harm done.[179]

7-9:3.2 Injunction

When a representative of the state or political subdivision brings a Public Nuisance Action, the traditional remedy is an injunction.[180]

- An injunction is the appropriate remedy if the activity itself is so unreasonable that it must be stopped.[181]

---

[173] Restatement (Second) of Torts § 821B (1979).
[174] Restatement (Second) of Torts § 821B (1979).
[175] Restatement (Second) of Torts § 821B (1979).
[176] *Louisiana v. Rowan Cos. Inc.*, 728 F. Supp. 2d 896, 905 (S.D. Tex. 2010).
[177] Restatement (Second) of Torts § 821C (1979), cmts. a, b.
[178] Restatement (Second) of Torts § 821C (1979), cmts. d, h.
[179] Restatement (Second) of Torts § 821B (1979), cmt. 1.
[180] Restatement (Second) of Torts § 821C (1979), cmt. j.
[181] Restatement (Second) of Torts § 821B (1979), cmt. i.

7-9:4 Defenses

7-9:4.1 Statute of Limitations

A Public Nuisance Action is governed by the two-year period of limitations.[182]

The accrual of the period of limitations depends upon whether the nuisance is temporary or permanent.

- A nuisance is permanent if (a) it cannot be repaired, fixed, or restored, or (b) even though the injury can be repaired, fixed, or restored, it is substantially certain that the injury will repeatedly, continually, and regularly recur, such that future injury can be reasonably evaluated.[183]

    - An action for permanent damages accrues upon discovery of the first actionable injury and not on the date when the extent of the damages to the land are fully ascertainable.[184]

- A nuisance is temporary if (a) it can be repaired, fixed, or restored, and (b) any anticipated recurrence would be only occasional, irregular, intermittent, and not reasonably predictable, such that future injury could not be estimated with reasonable certainty.[185]

    - An action for temporary injury accrues upon each injury.[186]

Limitations is not a defense to an action seeking to enjoin a continuing nuisance, as opposed to a suit for damages.[187]

7-9:4.2 Standing

Federal Constitutional standing requires plaintiffs to demonstrate that:

- They have suffered an "injury in fact";[188]

---

[182] Tex. Civ. Prac. & Rem. Code Ann. § 16.003(a); *Schneider Nat'l Carriers, Inc. v. Bates*, 147 S.W.3d 264, 270 (Tex. 2004).

[183] *Schneider Nat'l Carriers, Inc. v. Bates*, 147 S.W.3d 264, 271–72 (Tex. 2004); *Gilbert Wheeler, Inc. v. Enbridge Pipelines (E.Tex.), L.P.*, 449 S.W.3d 474, 480 (Tex.2014). *Gilbert Wheeler* modified the definitions in *Schneider* and stated that these definitions apply to cases in which entry onto real property is physical (as in a trespass) and to cases in which entry onto real property is not physical (as with a nuisance).

[184] *Schneider Nat'l Carriers, Inc. v. Bates*, 147 S.W.3d 264, 271–72 (Tex. 2004).

[185] *Schneider Nat'l Carriers, Inc. v. Bates*, 147 S.W.3d 264, 271–72 (Tex. 2004); *Gilbert Wheeler, Inc. v. Enbridge Pipelines (E.Tex.), L.P.*, 449 S.W.3d 474, 480 (Tex.2014). *Gilbert Wheeler* modified the definitions in *Schneider* and stated that these definitions apply to cases in which entry onto real property is physical (as in a trespass) and to cases in which entry onto real property is not physical (as with a nuisance).

[186] *Schneider Nat'l Carriers, Inc. v. Bates*, 147 S.W.3d 264, 271–72 (Tex. 2004).

[187] *City of Dallas v. Early*, 281 S.W. 883, 885 (Tex. Civ. App.—Dallas 1926, writ dism'd); *International & G.N. Ry. Co. v. Davis*, 29 S.W. 483, 484 (Tex. Civ. App.—1895, writ ref'd).

[188] *Lujan v. Defenders of Wildlife*, 504 U.S. 555, 560 (1992); *Meyers v. JDC/Firethorne, LTD.*, 548 S.W.3d 477, 485 (Tex. 2018).

- A past causation link must lead to particularized damage without speculation as to the defendant's future actions.[189]
- The injury is "fairly traceable" to the defendant's actions;[190] and
  - The plaintiff must show that it is substantially probable that the challenged acts of the defendant, not of some absent third party, will cause the particularized injury of the plaintiff.
  - The more indirect the chain of causation between the defendant's conduct and the plaintiff's injury, the less likely the plaintiff will be able to establish a causal link sufficient for standing.[191]
  - However, the traceability requirement need not be as close as the proximate causation needed to succeed on the merits of a tort claim.[192]
- The injury will "likely . . . be redressed by a favorable decision."[193]
  - State common-law tort claims in which plaintiffs allege that they sustained actual, concrete injury in fact to their particular lands and property can be redressed by the compensatory and punitive damages they seek for those injuries.[194]

The test for constitutional standing in Texas requires:

- A real controversy between the parties;[195]
- Which will be actually determined by the judicial declaration sought.[196]

---

[189] *See Center for Biological Diversity v. U.S. Dep't of Interior*, 563 F.3d 466, 489 (D.C. Cir. 2009) (The D.C. Circuit found that the plaintiffs could only speculate that the damages *will* occur only if many different actors (oil companies, consumers, car manufacturers, and the Department of Interior) all acted in a way that would increase global warming to cause damage.).

[190] *Lujan v. Defs. of Wildlife*, 504 U.S. 555, 560–61 (1992); *Meyers v. JDC/Firethorne, LTD.*, 548 S.W.3d 477, 485 (Tex. 2018).

[191] *See Center for Biological Diversity v. U.S. Dep't of Interior*, 563 F.3d 466, 479 (D.C. Cir. 2009) (Plaintiffs sued the Department of Interior for permitting drilling on the Outer Continental Shelf, arguing that more drilling will increase oil consumption, causing more emissions, and, in turn, increase global warming and hurt animals and their habitats, thereby harming the plaintiffs' enjoyment. The court stated, "such a causal chain cannot adequately establish causation because Petitioners rely on the speculation that various different groups of actors not present in this case—namely, oil companies, individuals using oil in their cars, cars actually dispersing carbon dioxide—might act in a certain way in the future.").

[192] *Comer v. Murphy Oil USA*, 585 F.3d 855, 864 (5th Cir. 2009).

[193] *Lujan v. Defs. of Wildlife*, 504 U.S. 555, 560 (1992); *Meyers v. JDC/Firethorne, LTD.*, 548 S.W.3d 477, 485 (Tex. 2018).

[194] *Comer v. Murphy Oil USA*, 585 F.3d 855, 863 (5th Cir. 2009).

[195] *Texas Ass'n of Bus. v. Tex. Air Control Bd.*, 852 S.W.2d 440, 446 (Tex. 1993), citing *Bd. of Water Eng'rs v. City of San Antonio*, 283 S.W.2d 722, 724 (Tex. 1955).

[196] *Texas Ass'n of Bus. v. Tex. Air Control Bd.*, 852 S.W.2d 440, 446 (Tex. 1993), citing *Bd. of Water Eng'rs v. City of San Antonio*, 283 S.W.2d 722, 724 (Tex. 1955).

7-9:4.3 Political Question Doctrine

The political question doctrine excludes from judicial review those controversies which:

- Contain no judicially discoverable and manageable standards for resolving the issues presented;[197] and
- Require the court to make initial policy determinations that have been entrusted to Congress.[198]

7-9:4.4 Preemption

A federal act preempts state common law when the language of the statute expressly or impliedly authorizes preemption.[199]

- There is conflicting case law regarding preemption under the Clean Air Act.[200]

7-9:4.5 No Particularized Injury

To recover damages, a plaintiff must have suffered a particularized injury.[201]

- "Particularized injury" is defined as significant harm different in kind from that suffered by the general public.[202]
- The inherent harmfulness to the environment of oil and gas production is not a particularized injury.[203]

7-9:4.6 Causation

A defendant is not liable for a plaintiff's particularized injury unless the defendant's action proximately caused the injury.[204]

---

[197] *See Comer v. Murphy Oil USA*, 839 F. Supp. 2d 849, 864 (S.D. Miss. 2012), *aff'd*, 718 F.3d 460 (5th Cir. 2013) ("It is unclear how this Court or any jury, regardless of its level of sophistication, could determine whether the defendants' emissions unreasonably endanger the environment or the public without making policy determinations that weigh the harm caused by the defendants' actions against the benefits of the products they produce.").

[198] *See Comer v. Murphy Oil USA*, 839 F. Supp. 2d 849, 864 (S.D. Miss. 2012), *aff'd*, 718 F.3d 460 (5th Cir. 2013) (Congress designated an expert agency, here, EPA, as best suited to serve as primary regulator of greenhouse gas emissions.).

[199] *Comer v. Murphy Oil USA*, 839 F. Supp. 2d 849, 865 (S.D. Miss. 2012), *aff'd*, 718 F.3d 460 (5th Cir. 2013).

[200] *See Comer v. Murphy Oil USA*, 839 F. Supp. 2d 849, 865 (S.D. Miss. 2012), *aff'd*, 718 F.3d 460 (5th Cir. 2013) (A Public Nuisance Action aimed at oil and gas production requires courts to determine what amount of pollution is unreasonable as well as what level of reduction is practical, feasible and economically viable. However, these determinations are properly left to the Environmental Protection Agency under the Clean Air Act.); *Gutierrez v. Mobil Oil Corp.*, 798 F. Supp. 1280 (W.D. Tex. 1992) (A nuisance claim under state law is not preempted by the Clean Air Act.).

[201] *Louisiana v. Rowan Cos. Inc.*, 728 F. Supp. 2d 896, 905 (S.D. Tex. 2010).

[202] *Louisiana v. Rowan Cos. Inc.*, 728 F. Supp. 2d 896, 905 (S.D. Tex. 2010).

[203] *Louisiana v. Rowan Cos. Inc.*, 728 F. Supp. 2d 896, 905 (S.D. Tex. 2010).

[204] Restatement (Second) of Torts § 281 (1965).

- The causal link sufficient to fulfill the "fairly traceable" standing requirement is likely insufficient to meet the proximate cause requirement of tort causation.[205]

7-9:5 Procedural Implications

7-9:5.1 Choice of Law

When a state representative brings a Public Nuisance Action seeking to enjoin widespread oil and gas pollution, the court must apply the law of the state in which the pollution source is located, rather than the law of the state that is affected by the pollution.[206]

7-10 Slander of Title

7-10:1 Overview

A Slander of Title Action is aimed at obtaining compensation for a property owner's loss caused by another's malicious disparagement of the property's title. "Slander of title" is defined as a false and malicious statement made in disparagement of a person's title to property, which causes special damages.[207] Ordinarily the action is joined with a Quiet Title Action. The matters that disparage a property title are the same matters that cloud the title. A plaintiff who successfully establishes Slander of Title may recover compensation for the loss of a specific lease of the mineral estate. A plaintiff might also recover exemplary damages and attorney's fees.

7-10:1.1 Related Causes of Action

Action to Quiet Title, Declaratory Judgment Action, Trespass to Try Title, Conversion, Trespass to Real Property, Fraud, Tortious Interference with Business Relations

MUST READ CASES

Kidd v. Hoggett, 331 S.W.2d 515 (Tex. Civ. App.—San Antonio 1959, writ ref'd n.r.e.)

Williams v. Jennings, 755 S.W.2d 874 (Tex. App.—Houston [14th Dist.] 1988, writ denied)

Duncan Land & Expl., Inc. v. Littlepage, 984 S.W.2d 318 (Tex. App.—Fort Worth 1998, pet. denied)

7-10:2 Elements

(1) The plaintiff has an interest in the specific real estate claimed to have been slandered

---

[205] *Comer v. Murphy Oil U.S.A.*, 585 F.3d 855, 864 (5th Cir. 2009).
[206] *International Paper Co. v. Ouellette*, 479 U.S. 481, 487 (1987).
[207] *Sadler v. Duvall*, 815 S.W.2d 285, 293 (Tex. App.—Texarkana 1991, writ denied); *Allen-Pieroni v. Pieroni*, 535 S.W.3d 887 (Tex. 2017), *citing Marrs & Smith P'ship v. D.K. Boyd Oil & Gas Co., Inc.*, 223 S.W.3d 1, 20 (Tex. App.—El Paso, 2005).

- A plaintiff must have an interest in the mineral estate claimed to have been slandered.[208]
- Fee simple ownership or actual possession are not necessary.
  - Ordinarily, offering proof of record title to the mineral estate is sufficient for the lessor.[209]
  - Offering proof of an interest in an oil and gas lease is sufficient for the lessee.[210]

(2) The defendant published a statement disparaging the plaintiff's property

- The defendant must "publish" a statement disparaging the plaintiff's property.[211]
  - This is historical language that courts continue to employ. Practically, the plaintiff must show that the defendant somehow interfered with the plaintiff's interest in the mineral estate.[212] This might consist of:
    - The defendant placing a document in deed records that clouds plaintiff's title;[213] or
    - The defendant failing to record a release upon the termination of an oil and gas lease.[214]

(3) The defendant's statement was false

- The plaintiff must prove that the defendant's right or interest in the property is invalid or unenforceable.[215]

(4) The defendant's statement was malicious

- The plaintiff must establish that the defendant acted with legal malice.[216]

---

[208] *Williams v. Jennings*, 755 S.W.2d 874, 879–80 (Tex. App.—Houston [14th Dist.] 1988, writ denied).

[209] *Watson v. Rochmill*, 155 S.W.2d 783, 785 (Tex. 1941).

[210] *Amarillo Oil Co. v. Energy-Agri Prods.*, 794 S.W.2d 20, 22 (Tex. 1990).

[211] *Duncan Land & Expl., Inc. v. Littlepage*, 984 S.W.2d 318, 332 (Tex. App.—Fort Worth 1998, pet. denied).

[212] *Duncan Land & Expl., Inc. v. Littlepage*, 984 S.W.2d 318, 332 (Tex. App.—Fort Worth 1998, pet. denied).

[213] *See, e.g., Duncan Land & Expl., Inc. v. Littlepage*, 984 S.W.2d 318, 323 (Tex. App.—Fort Worth 1998, pet. denied) (defendant signed and recorded an affidavit saying that the plaintiff's oil and gas lease had terminated due to the lack of production in commercial quantities); *Williams v. Jennings*, 755 S.W.2d 874, 882 (Tex. App.—Houston [14th Dist.] 1988, writ denied) (oil and gas lease containing false claim of interest in property was recorded); *A.H. Belo Corp. v. Sanders*, 632 S.W.2d 145, 145 (Tex. 1982) (defendant obtained and filed an abstract of judgment in an effort to perfect a lien on the plaintiff's property).

[214] *Kidd v. Hoggett*, 331 S.W.2d 515, 517–18 (Tex. Civ. App.—San Antonio 1959, writ ref'd n.r.e.).

[215] *See Williams v. Jennings*, 755 S.W.2d 874, 882 (Tex. App.—Houston [14th Dist.] 1988, writ denied) (Lessee executed oil and gas lease reciting that the lessor owned an interest in the property when the lessor in fact owned no interest.).

[216] *Duncan Land & Expl., Inc. v. Littlepage*, 984 S.W.2d 318, 332 (Tex. App.—Fort Worth 1998, pet. denied).

- Legal malice exists when the defendant engages in deliberate conduct without reasonable cause.[217]
  - This should be distinguished from actual malice, necessary for recovery of exemplary damages.[218]
(5) The defendant's statement caused the loss of a specific sale of an interest in real property.
  - The plaintiff must establish that the disparagement created by the defendant caused the loss of a specific sale of an interest in real property.[219]
  - The requisite elements include the uttering and publishing of disparaging words that were false and malicious; that the plaintiff sustained special damages thereby; and that the plaintiff possessed an interest in the property disparaged.[220] The plaintiff must demonstrate the loss of a specific sale in order to recover.[221]
    - A mineral lease is a conveyance of an interest in real estate. Therefore, the loss of a definite oil lease is equivalent to the loss of a specific sale.[222]

7-10:3 Damages and Remedies

7-10:3.1 Special Damages

Special damages are those damages that proximately, naturally and reasonably result from the alleged slander.[223]

- In order to recover special damages, the plaintiff must prove the loss of a specific, pending sale that was defeated by the slander.[224]
- A plaintiff may recover the amount he would have realized from the sale less the amount for which he could have sold the lease at the time of the trial with the cloud removed.[225]

---

[217] *Duncan Land & Expl., Inc. v. Littlepage*, 984 S.W.2d 318, 332 (Tex. App.—Fort Worth 1998, pet. denied).

[218] *Duncan Land & Expl., Inc. v. Littlepage*, 984 S.W.2d 318, 332 (Tex. App.—Fort Worth 1998, pet. denied).

[219] *Duncan Land & Expl., Inc. v. Littlepage*, 984 S.W.2d 318, 332 (Tex. App.—Fort Worth 1998, pet. denied).

[220] *Clayton Williams Energy, Inc. v. BMT O&G TX, L.P.*, 473 S.W.3d 341, 354 (Tex. App.—El Paso 2015) (quoting *Hill v. Heritage Res., Inc.*, 964 S.W.2d 89, 109–10 (Tex. App.—El Paso 1997, pet. denied)).

[221] *Hill v. Heritage Res., Inc.*, 964 S.W.2d 89, 115–16 (Tex. App.—El Paso 1997, pet. denied); *Marrs & Smith P'ship v. D.K. Boyd Oil & Gas Co., Inc.*, 223 S.W.3d 1, 20 (Tex. App.—El Paso, 2005).

[222] *Williams v. Jennings*, 755 S.W.2d 874, 885 (Tex. App.—Houston [14th Dist.] 1988, writ denied).

[223] *Duncan Land & Expl., Inc. v. Littlepage*, 984 S.W.2d 318, 333 (Tex. App.—Fort Worth 1998, pet. denied).

[224] *Duncan Land & Expl., Inc. v. Littlepage*, 984 S.W.2d 318, 333 (Tex. App.—Fort Worth 1998, pet. denied).

[225] E.g. *Duncan Land & Expl., Inc. v. Littlepage*, 984 S.W.2d 318, 333 (Tex. App.—Fort Worth 1998, pet. denied); *A.H. Belo Corp. v. Sanders*, 632 S.W.2d 145, 146 (Tex. 1982); *Reaugh v. McCollum Exploration Co.*, 139 Tex. 485, 163 S.W.2d 620, 622 (1942).

OIL AND GAS LITIGATION

7-10:3.2 Exemplary Damages

A plaintiff may recover exemplary damages if the defendant acted either:

- with a specific intent to cause substantial injury; or
- with a conscious indifference to the rights of others and an actual, subjective awareness of the extreme risk of potential harm.[226]

This should be distinguished from legal malice, which comprises an element of an Action for Slander of Title.[227]

7-10:3.3 Attorney's Fees

When a Slander of Title Action is joined with an Action to Quiet Title brought under the Declaratory Judgments Act, the plaintiff is entitled to recover attorney's fees for the Quiet Title portion of the litigation.[228]

- The attorney's efforts to prove the elements of the quiet title action should be segregated from the work performed to establish malice and damages, which are elements of the slander action only.[229]
  - However, if the causes of action are so intertwined as to be more or less inseparable, the court may award total amount of attorney's fees incurred.[230]

7-10:4 Defenses

7-10:4.1 Statute of Limitations

An action for slander of title to realty is governed by the two-year statute of limitations.[231]

- The cause of action accrues the day the plaintiff loses a specific lease because of the defendant's disparaging statement.[232]

---

[226] Tex. Civ. Prac. & Rem. Code Ann. § 41.001(11).

[227] *See Williams v. Jennings*, 755 S.W.2d 874, 886 (Tex. App.—Houston [14th Dist.] 1988, writ denied) (The required malice to justify exemplary damages resulted not from the defendant's initial act of uttering a false document disparaging title, but from the unjustified refusal to promptly deliver a release of the offending claim.).

[228] Tex. Civ. Prac. & Rem. Code Ann. § 38.001; *Duncan Land & Exploration, Inc. v. Littlepage*, 984 S.W.2d 318, 333–34 (Tex. App.—Fort Worth 1998, pet. denied).

[229] *American Nat'l Bank & Tr. Co. v. First Wis. Mortg. Tr.*, 577 S.W.2d 312, 319–20 (Tex. Civ. App.—Beaumont 1979, writ ref'd n.r.e.).

[230] *See Duncan Land & Expl., Inc. v. Littlepage*, 984 S.W.2d 318, 333–34 (Tex. App.—Fort Worth 1998, pet. denied) (upholding attorney's fees for slander of title and quiet title action).

[231] Tex. Civ. Prac. & Rem. Code Ann. § 16.003.

[232] *Kidd v. Hoggett*, 331 S.W.2d 515, 520 (Tex. Civ. App.—San Antonio 1959, writ ref'd n.r.e.).

7-10:4.2 Acting on Advice of Counsel

To rebut the plaintiff's contention that the defendant's adverse claim was malicious, the defendant may show that they consulted with counsel and acted with a bona fide belief that the claim asserted was valid.[233]

- Evidence of reliance on counsel may not establish good faith as a matter of law, but is a consideration for the fact finder in deciding the malice issue.[234]

- This defense is not applicable if the attorney based the advice on facts related by the defendant and the defendant recklessly disregarded the truth when ascertaining and relating those facts.[235]

7-10:5 Procedural Implications

7-10:5.1 Venue

Venue is mandatory in the county in which all or part of the real property is located.[236]

7-11 Negligence

7-11:1 Overview

A cause of action for negligence in Texas requires three elements: (1) a legal duty owed by one person to another; (2) a breach of that duty; and (3) damages proximately caused by the breach. The law imposes a duty on a well operator to avoid the negligent waste or destruction of oil and gas wells and of the minerals themselves. A plaintiff who establishes the elements of negligence is entitled to compensatory damages. If the plaintiff can prove gross negligence, the plaintiff is also entitled to exemplary damages.

7-11:1.1 Related Causes of Action

Breach of Contract, Breach of Fiduciary Duty, Conversion, Wrongful Death, Fraud, Breach of Implied Covenant to Protect Against Drainage, Breach of Implied Covenant to Market, Breach of Implied Covenant to Reasonably Develop

MUST READ CASES

Elliff v. Texon Drilling Co., 210 S.W.2d 558 (Tex. 1948)

Dowell, Inc. v. Cichowski, 540 S.W.2d. 342 (Tex. Civ. App.—San Antonio 1976, no writ)

---

[233] *Humble Oil & Ref. Co. v. Luckel*, 171 S.W.2d 902, 906 (Tex. Civ. App.—Galveston 1943, writ ref'd w.o.m.).

[234] *Murren v. Foster*, 674 S.W.2d 406, 412 (Tex. App.—Amarillo 1984, no writ).

[235] *Duncan Land & Expl., Inc. v. Littlepage*, 984 S.W.2d 318, 332–33 (Tex. App.—Fort Worth 1998, pet. denied).

[236] Tex. Civ. Prac. & Rem. Code Ann. § 15.011; *Madera Prod. Co. v. Atl. Richfield Co.*, 107 S.W.3d 652, 656–58 (Tex. App.—Texarkana 2003, pet. denied).

7-11:2 Elements

(1) A legal duty owed by defendant to plaintiff

- The defendant must owe a legal duty to the plaintiff.[237]
    - The law imposes a duty to exercise ordinary care to avoid the negligent waste or destruction of the property of others.[238]
        - This includes negligent waste or destruction of oil and gas wells.[239]
        - This includes waste or destruction of the minerals themselves.[240]

(2) A breach of that duty

- The defendant's conduct must breach the legal duty owed to the plaintiff.[241]
    - The standard of conduct to which the defendant must conform to avoid being negligent is that of a reasonable man under like circumstances.[242]

(3) The breach was a proximate cause of the plaintiff's damages.

- The breach must proximately cause the plaintiff's damages.[243]
    - Proximate cause requires both cause in fact and foreseeability.[244]
        - The test for cause in fact is whether the act or omission was a substantial factor in causing the injury without which the harm would not have occurred.[245]

---

[237] *D. Houston, Inc. v. Love*, 92 S.W.3d 450, 454 (Tex. 2002).

[238] *Elliff v. Texon Drilling Co.*, 210 S.W.2d 558, 563 (Tex. 1948).

[239] *Bay Rock Operating Co. v. St. Paul Surplus Lines Ins. Co.*, 298 S.W.3d 216, 230 (Tex. App.—San Antonio 2009, pet. denied).

[240] *See Elliff v. Texon Drilling Co.*, 210 S.W.2d 558, 562–63 (1948) (Although there is no liability for legitimate and reasonable drainage from a common pool under the law of capture, each owner of land over a common oil supply has duties to the other owners not to exercise his privileges of taking so as to injure the common source of supply.).

[241] *D. Houston, Inc. v. Love*, 92 S.W.3d 450, 454 (Tex. 2002).

[242] Restatement (Second) of Torts § 283 (1965) *See, e.g., Elliff v. Texon Drilling Co.*, 210 S.W.2d 558, 559 (1948) (Jury found that reasonable drilling operator would have used drilling mud of a sufficient weight in drilling their well in order to prevent cratering of offset wells in the event of a blow-out.); *Bay Rock Operating Co. v. St. Paul Surplus Lines Ins. Co.*, 298 S.W.3d 216, 227 (Tex. App.—San Antonio 2009, pet. denied) (Jury found that reasonable operator would not drill ahead without running a true formation integrity test ("FIT") to ensure that the intermediate casing seat and surrounding formation could withstand the anticipated higher pressures as they drilled further down-hole.).

[243] *D. Houston, Inc. v. Love*, 92 S.W.3d 450, 454 (Tex. 2002).

[244] *Union Pump Co. v. Allbritton*, 898 S.W.2d 773, 776 (Tex. 1995).

[245] *See Union Pump Co. v. Allbritton*, 898 S.W.2d 773, 774–76 (Tex. 1995) (Plaintiff alleged that Union Pump caused her injuries by manufacturing a defective pump which caused the fire, which in turn led to the pipe rack being wet and slippery, and ultimately caused her injuries. The circumstances surrounding her injuries were too remotely connected with the defective pump to constitute the cause in fact of her injuries. The pump, by causing a fire, did no more than create the condition which made the plaintiff's injuries possible.).

- Foreseeability means that the defendant, as a person of ordinary intelligence, should have anticipated the dangers that his negligent act created for others.[246]

7-11:3 Damages and Remedies

7-11:3.1 Compensatory Damages

To recover well site damages the plaintiff must demonstrate that the well was capable of producing in paying quantities.[247]

- The phrase "capable of production in paying quantities" means a well that will produce in paying quantities without additional equipment or repair.[248]

- Whether production is in paying quantities is determined by ascertaining whether or not under all relevant circumstances, a reasonably prudent operator would continue to operate a well in the manner in which it is being operated for the purpose of making a profit and not merely for speculation.[249]

The measure of compensatory damages for negligent destruction of a well depends on whether the well could be reproduced by drilling another well.[250]

- If the jury finds that the cost of the reproduction of the well exceeds the value of the damaged well or that the well could not have been reproduced, the damage measure should be the reasonable cash market value of the well as equipped immediately preceding its destruction, less any salvage value.[251]

- The measure of damages for negligent injury to an oil or gas well that can be reproduced is the lesser of two values:[252]

  - The cash market value of the old well;[253] or

  - The cost of reproducing the well with a new well equipped like the old one, less any salvage value of the old well.[254]

---

[246] *Travis v. City of Mesquite*, 830 S.W.2d 94, 98 (Tex. 1992); *See Elliff v. Texon Drilling Co.*, 210 S.W.2d 558, 563 (Tex. 1948) (Defendants had knowledge that a failure to use due care in drilling their well might result in a blowout with the consequent waste and dissipation of the oil, gas and distillate from the common reservoir.).

[247] *Dowell, Inc. v. Cichowski*, 540 S.W.2d. 342, 347–49 (Tex. Civ. App.—San Antonio 1976, no writ).

[248] *Anadarko Petroleum Corp. v. Thompson*, 94 S.W.3d 550, 558 (Tex. 2002).

[249] *Clifton v. Koontz*, 325 S.W.2d 684, 690–91 (Tex. 1959).

[250] *Dowell, Inc. v. Cichowski*, 540 S.W.2d 342, 350 (Tex. Civ. App.—San Antonio 1976, no writ).

[251] *Dowell, Inc. v. Cichowski*, 540 S.W.2d 342, 350 (Tex. Civ. App.—San Antonio 1976, no writ).

[252] E.g. *Dresser Ind., Inc. v. Page Petroleum, Inc.*, 853 S.W.2d 505, 511–12 (Tex. 1993); *Basic Energy Serv., Inc. v. D-S-B Prop., Inc.*, 367 S.W.3d 254, 262 (Tex. App.—Tyler 2011, no pet.).

[253] E.g. *Dresser Ind., Inc. v. Page Petroleum, Inc.*, 853 S.W.2d 505, 511–12 (Tex. 1993); *Basic Energy Serv., Inc. v. D-S-B Prop., Inc.*, 367 S.W.3d 254, 262 (Tex. App.—Tyler 2011, no pet.).

[254] E.g. *Dresser Ind., Inc. v. Page Petroleum, Inc.*, 853 S.W.2d 505, 511–12 (Tex. 1993); *Basic Energy Serv., Inc. v. D-S-B Prop., Inc.*, 367 S.W.3d 254, 262 (Tex. App.—Tyler 2011, no pet.).

OIL AND GAS LITIGATION

Parties seeking damages for the repair of an oil or gas well must present sufficient evidence to justify findings that the costs of repair were reasonable, and the repairs were necessary.[255]

7-11:3.2 Exemplary Damages

Exemplary damages may be awarded if the plaintiff proves by clear and convincing evidence that the defendant's conduct was grossly negligent.[256]

- Gross negligence presumes a negligent act or omission and includes two further elements:
  - Viewed objectively from the standpoint of the defendant, the act or omission must involve an extreme degree of risk, considering the probability and magnitude of the potential harm to others;[257] and
  - The defendant must have actual, subjective awareness of the risk involved, but nevertheless proceed in conscious indifference to the rights, safety or welfare of others.[258]

7-11:4 Defenses

7-11:4.1 Statute of Limitations

A person must bring a suit for negligence not later than two years after the day the cause of action accrues.[259]

- The cause of action for negligence accrues on the day the duty of care is breached, even though the injury may not be apparent, and the plaintiff may be unaware of the breach until a later date.[260]

7-11:4.2 Duty Created by Contract, Not Imposed by Law

The duties to protect against drainage, to reasonably develop, and to market are considered implied contractual covenants. Breach of these duties are actions sounding in contract and not in tort.[261]

---

[255] *Baker Hughes Oilfield Operations, Inc. v. Hennig Prod. Co., Inc.*, 164 S.W.3d 438, 446 (Tex. App.—Houston [14th Dist.] 2005, no pet.).
[256] Tex. Civ. Prac. & Rem. Code Ann. § 41.003(a)(3).
[257] *Reeder v. Wood County Energy, LLC*, 395 S.W.3d 789, 796–797 (Tex. 2012).
[258] *Reeder v. Wood County Energy, LLC*, 395 S.W.3d 789, 796–797 (Tex. 2012).
[259] Tex. Civ. Prac. & Rem. Code Ann. § 16.003; *Morriss v. Enron Oil & Gas Co.*, 948 S.W.2d 858, 869 (Tex. App.—San Antonio 1997, no writ).
[260] *Dunmore v. Chicago Title Ins. Co.*, 400 S.W.3d 635, 641 (Tex. App.—Dallas 2013) (Note that the Discovery Rule will toll the limitations accrual if the injury is inherently undiscoverable.).
[261] *Amoco Prod. Co. v. Alexander*, 622 S.W.2d 563, 571 (Tex. 1981).

7-11:4.3 Contributory Negligence

A plaintiff may not recover damages if his percentage of responsibility is greater than 50%.[262]

7-12 Breach of Implied Covenant to Protect Against Drainage

MUST READ CASE

Amoco Prod. Co. v. Alexander, 622 S.W.2d 563 (Tex. 1981)

7-12:1 Overview

Texas courts recognize implied covenants in fact that extend beyond the express terms of an oil and gas lease. These covenants describe certain duties required of the lessee if the lease is silent regarding those duties. The oil and gas lease has an Implied Covenant to Protect the Leasehold.[263] The Implied Covenant to Protect Against Drainage is part of the Implied Covenant to Protect the Leasehold.[264]

7-12:1.1 Related Causes of Action

Breach of Implied Covenant to Further Explore (not recognized in Texas), Breach of Implied Covenant to Reasonably Develop, Breach of Implied Covenant to Market

7-12:2 Elements

(1) Substantial uncompensated drainage

- The lessee has a duty to protect from local drainage and field-wide drainage.[265]
  - Local drainage occurs when oil migrates from under one lease "to the well bore of a producing well on an adjacent lease."[266]
  - Local drainage begins, increases and decreases based on the rate of production of wells in a specific area in a field.[267]
  - Field-wide drainage depends on the water-drive and production from every well in a field.[268]

---

[262] Tex. Civ. Prac. & Rem. Code Ann. § 33.001; *Abalos v. Oil Dev. Co. of Tex.*, 544 S.W.2d 627, 632 (Tex. 1976).
[263] *Amoco Prod. Co. v. Alexander*, 622 S.W.2d 563, 567 (Tex. 1981).
[264] *Amoco Prod. Co. v. Alexander*, 622 S.W.2d 563, 568 (Tex. 1981).
[265] *Amoco Prod. Co. v. Alexander*, 622 S.W.2d 563, 567–68 (Tex. 1981).
[266] *Amoco Prod. Co. v. Alexander*, 622 S.W.2d 563, 567 (Tex. 1981).
[267] *Amoco Prod. Co. v. Alexander*, 622 S.W.2d 563, 567 (Tex. 1981).
[268] *Amoco Prod. Co. v. Alexander*, 622 S.W.2d 563, 567 (Tex. 1981).

- It is more difficult to protect against field-wide drainage, but production lost by field-wide drainage is as important as production lost by local drainage.[269]

- Substantial drainage has been defined as "the drainage of a sufficient quantity of oil that would cause a reasonably prudent operator, with the expectation of making a reasonable profit, to take action to protect it from that drainage."[270]

(2) A reasonable operator would act to prevent the drainage

- The standard of care is that of the reasonably prudent operator under the same or similar facts and circumstances.[271]

- The lessee must perform *any* act that a reasonably prudent operator would perform to protect from substantial local and substantial field-wide drainage.[272]

- The duties of a reasonably prudent operator include:

    (1) drilling replacement wells;

    (2) re-working existing wells;

    (3) drilling additional wells;

    (4) seeking field-wide regulatory action;

    (5) seeking Rule 37 exceptions from the Railroad Commission;

    - The Railroad Commission promulgates rules regarding distance and spacing requirements for oil, gas and natural resource wells.[273]

    - Operators can file applications for an exception to Rule 37.[274]

    (6) seeking voluntary unitization; and

    (7) seeking other available administrative relief.[275]

- A lessee may be able to protect against drainage by drilling offset wells.[276]

(3) The proposed solution would yield a reasonable expectation of profit

- There is no duty to protect against field-wide drainage "unless such an amount of oil can be recovered to equal the cost of administrative expenses, drilling or re-working and equipping a protection well, producing and marketing the oil, and yield to the lessee a *reasonable expectation of profit*."[277]

---

[269] *Amoco Prod. Co. v. Alexander*, 622 S.W.2d 563, 568 (Tex. 1981).

[270] *Amoco Prod. Co. v. Alexander*, 622 S.W.2d 563, 568 (Tex. 1981); *Petroleum Synergy Grp., Inc. v. Occidental Permian, Ltd.*, 331 S.W.3d 14, 17 (Tex. App.—Amarillo 2010, pet. denied).

[271] *Amoco Prod. Co. v. Alexander*, 622 S.W.2d 563, 567–68 (Tex. 1981).

[272] *Amoco Prod. Co. v. Alexander*, 622 S.W.2d 563, 568 (Tex. 1981).

[273] 16 Tex. Admin. Code § 3.37.

[274] 16 Tex. Admin. Code § 3.37(f).

[275] *Amoco Prod. Co. v. Alexander*, 622 S.W.2d 563, 568 (Tex. 1981).

[276] *Coastal Oil & Gas Corp. v. Garza Energy Tr.*, 268 S.W.3d 1, 17 (Tex. 2008).

[277] *Amoco Prod. Co. v. Alexander*, 622 S.W.2d 563, 568 (Tex. 1981) (emphasis added), citing *Clifton v. Koontz*, 325 S.W.2d 684, 695–96 (Tex. 1959).

- A reasonable expectation of profit exists if (1) the quantity is sufficient to warrant the use of the product in the market; (2) the income exceeds the actual marketing costs; and (3) production occurs in paying quantities.
  - The standard by which production is measured is "paying quantities," which means if "a well pays a profit, even small, over operating expenses, it produces in paying quantities, though it may never repay its costs, and the enterprise as a whole may prove unprofitable."[278]

7-12:3 Damages and Remedies

7-12:3.1 Value of the Royalty Lost

The measure of damages for breach of the Implied Covenant to Protect Against Drainage is the amount that will fully compensate, but not overcompensate, the lessor for the breach, which means "the value of the royalty lost to the lessor because of the lessee's failure to act as a reasonably prudent operator."[279]

- The amount of royalties that the lessor would have received from the offset well would overcompensate the lessor when production from the offset well exceeded the drainage.[280]
- Similarly, the value of royalty on the drained gas would also overcompensate if the drainage could not have been fully prevented.[281]

7-12:3.2 Exemplary Damages Not Recoverable

The Implied Covenant to Protect Against Drainage is contractual in nature.[282]

Exemplary damages are not allowed for breach of contract.[283]

- Breach of the Implied Covenant to Protect Against Drainage will not support recovery of exemplary damages unless there exists proof of an independent tort.[284]

7-12:3.3 Future Drainage

"A party may not recover damages if those damages are remote, speculative, or conjectural."[285]

Proof of future drainage and recovery for future drainage requires evidence of present drainage.[286]

---

[278] *Clifton v. Koontz*, 325 S.W.2d 684, 690–91 (Tex. 1959).
[279] *Coastal Oil & Gas Corp. v. Garza Energy Tr.*, 268 S.W.3d 1, 18–19 (Tex. 2008).
[280] *Coastal Oil & Gas Corp. v. Garza Energy Tr.*, 268 S.W.3d 1, 18 (Tex. 2008).
[281] *Coastal Oil & Gas Corp. v. Garza Energy Tr.*, 268 S.W.3d 1, 18 (Tex. 2008).
[282] *Amoco Prod. Co. v. Alexander*, 622 S.W.2d 563, 571 (Tex. 1981).
[283] *Amoco Prod. Co. v. Alexander*, 622 S.W.2d 563, 571 (Tex. 1981).
[284] *Amoco Prod. Co. v. Alexander*, 622 S.W.2d 563, 571 (Tex. 1981).
[285] *Cone v. Fagadau Energy Corp.*, 68 S.W.3d 147, 159 (Tex. App.—Eastland 2001, pet. denied).
[286] *Cone v. Fagadau Energy Corp.*, 68 S.W.3d 147, 159 (Tex. App.—Eastland 2001, pet. denied).

OIL AND GAS LITIGATION

7-12:3.4 Conditional Cancellation

A mineral lease grants a fee simple determinable, which will "terminate automatically if the event upon which it is limited occurs."[287]

- Breach of an implied covenant may subject the breaching party to "a conditional decree of cancellation."[288]

- When damages do not provide adequate relief, the court can conditionally terminate the lease.[289]

7-12:4 Defenses

7-12:4.1 Pooling

A lessee can protect itself from the duty to protect against drainage by exercising contractual pooling authority.[290]

- "Pooling" means to combine tracts from two or more leases into a single unit around a well that is already producing.[291]

- "The primary legal consequence of pooling is that production and operations anywhere on the pooled unit are treated as if they have taken place on each tract within the unit."[292]

7-12:4.2 Express Lease Provisions

Courts do not imply covenants unless it appears from the express provisions in the contract that it was within the contemplation of the parties or it appears necessary to effectuate the purpose of the contract.[293]

Lessees can protect themselves against the Implied Covenant to Protect Against Drainage by including within the lease a specific provision made for drilling offset wells to prevent drainage.[294]

7-12:4.3 Statute of Limitations

Breach of the Implied Covenant to Protect Against Drainage is part of the written lease and is governed by the four-year statute of limitations.[295]

---

[287] *Anadarko Petroleum Corp. v. Thompson*, 94 S.W.3d 550, 554 (Tex. 2002).
[288] *Anadarko Petroleum Corp. v. Thompson*, 94 S.W.3d 550, 560 (Tex. 2002).
[289] *Anadarko Petroleum Corp. v. Thompson*, 94 S.W.3d 550, 560 (Tex. 2002).
[290] *Southeastern Pipe Line Co. v. Tichacek*, 997 S.W.2d 166, 170 (Tex. 1999).
[291] *Southeastern Pipe Line Co. v. Tichacek*, 997 S.W.2d 166, 170 (Tex. 1999).
[292] *Southeastern Pipe Line Co. v. Tichacek*, 997 S.W.2d 166, 170 (Tex. 1999).
[293] *HECI Expl. Co. v. Neel*, 982 S.W.2d 881, 888–89 (Tex. 1998) ("We have imposed implied covenants only when they are fundamental to the purposes of a mineral lease and when the lease does not expressly address the subject matter of the covenant sought to be implied.").
[294] *Danciger Oil & Ref. Co. of Tex. v. Powell*, 154 S.W.2d 632, 636 (Tex. 1941).
[295] *HECI Expl. Co. v. Neel*, 982 S.W.2d 881, 885 (Tex. 1998).

- "A royalty owner who makes no inquiry for years on end cannot then sue for breaches of contract that could have been discovered within the limitations period if reasonable diligence had been exercised."[296]

7-12:5 Procedural Implications

7-12:5.1 Cotenants

There is no cause of action for the Implied Covenant to Protect Against Drainage between cotenants because each tenant has a right to capture the minerals.[297]

7-12:5.2 Obligation to Exercise Reasonable Diligence in Protecting Interests

Owners of an interest in a mineral estate have an obligation to exercise reasonable diligence in protecting their interests.[298]

Reasonable diligence includes determining whether operators have inflicted damage.[299]

Reasonable diligence also includes determining whether a common reservoir exists because "when there are other wells drilled in a common reservoir, there is the potential for drainage."[300]

7-13 Breach of Implied Covenant to Market

7-13:1 Overview

Texas courts recognize certain duties in an oil and gas lease that extend beyond the express terms of the lease if the lease is silent regarding those duties. These duties are implied covenants in fact. One implied covenant that Texas courts recognize is the implied covenant to manage and administer the lease.[301] Within the implied covenant to manage and administer the lease is the duty to reasonably market oil and gas.[302]

The Implied Covenant to Market serves to protect the lessor from the lessee's bad faith or negligence. The implied covenant to market is only assumed in proceeds leases where royalty calculations are based on the price received by the lessee.[303] When the parties enter into market value leases, requiring royalties to be paid at market value, the courts do not imply a covenant to market.[304]

---

[296] *HECI Expl. Co. v. Neel*, 982 S.W.2d 881, 887 (Tex. 1998).
[297] *Cone v. Fagadau Energy Corp.*, 68 S.W.3d 147, 159 (Tex. App.—Eastland 2001, pet. denied).
[298] *HECI Expl. Co. v. Neel*, 982 S.W.2d 881, 886 (Tex. 1998).
[299] *HECI Expl. Co. v. Neel*, 982 S.W.2d 881, 886 (Tex. 1998).
[300] *HECI Expl. Co. v. Neel*, 982 S.W.2d 881, 886 (Tex. 1998).
[301] *Yzaguirre v. KCS Res., Inc.*, 53 S.W.3d 368, 373 (Tex. 2001).
[302] *Yzaguirre v. KCS Res., Inc.*, 53 S.W.3d 368, 373 (Tex. 2001).
[303] *Phillips Petroleum Co. v. Yarbrough*, 405 S.W.3d 70, 78 (Tex. 2013).
[304] *Yzaguirre v. KCS Res., Inc.*, 53 S.W.3d 368, 374 (Tex. 2001) ("Because the lease provides an objective basis for calculating royalties that is independent of the price the lessee actually obtains, the lessor does not need the protection of an implied covenant.").

OIL AND GAS LITIGATION

7-13:1.1 Related Causes of Action

Breach of Implied Covenant to Further Explore (not recognized in Texas), Breach of Implied Covenant to Reasonably Develop, Breach of Implied Covenant to Protect Against Drainage

MUST READ CASE

Yzaguirre v. KCS Res., Inc., 53 S.W.3d 368 (Tex. 2001)

7-13:2 Elements

(1) Failure to market the production with due diligence

- The lessee has a duty to market the production with due diligence.[305]
    - The standard of care is that of a reasonably prudent operator under the same or similar circumstances.[306]
    - The court focuses on the behavior of the lessee.[307]

(2) Failure to obtain the best price reasonably possible

- The lessee has a duty to obtain the best current price reasonably available.[308]
    - Production should be sold for the best price or under the best terms.[309]
    - The standard of care is that of a reasonably prudent operator under the same or similar circumstances.[310]
- Failure to sell at market value is probative but not conclusive evidence of a breach of the covenant to market.[311]
    - Market value is the "prevailing market price at the time of delivery and is not affected by a price set at the time the lessee enters into a long-term sales contract with the buyer."[312]
    - Market value may not be related to the price the lessee receives as proceeds.[313]

---

[305] *Cabot Corp. v. Brown*, 754 S.W.2d 104, 106 (Tex. 1987).
[306] *Cabot Corp. v. Brown*, 754 S.W.2d 104, 106 (Tex. 1987).
[307] *Union Pacific Res. Grp., Inc. v. Hankins*, 111 S.W.3d 69, 71 (Tex. 2003).
[308] *Cabot Corp. v. Brown*, 754 S.W.2d 104, 106 (Tex. 1987).
[309] *Condra v. Quinoco Petroleum, Inc.*, 954 S.W.2d 68, 73 (Tex. App.—San Antonio 1997, pet. denied).
[310] *Cabot Corp. v. Brown*, 754 S.W.2d 104, 106 (Tex. 1987).
[311] *Yzaguirre v. KCS Res., Inc.*, 53 S.W.3d 368, 374–75 (Tex. 2001).
[312] *Yzaguirre v. KCS Res., Inc.*, 53 S.W.3d 368, 374 (Tex. 2001).
[313] *Yzaguirre v. KCS Res., Inc.*, 53 S.W.3d 368, 372 (Tex. 2001).

7-13:3 Damages and Remedies

7-13:3.1 Royalty

There are two common methods for determining the royalties due to royalty owners.[314]

Under a market value lease, courts do not imply a covenant to market. A cause of action for breach of implied covenant to market is not available under a market value lease.[315]

Under a proceeds lease, the courts imply a covenant to market to protect the lessor from the lessee's negligence or self-dealing.[316]

Under a proceeds lease, the measure of royalty is based on sales of gas at the well, or the price received by the lessee.[317]

Failure to sell at market value is probative but not conclusive evidence of a breach of the covenant to market.[318]

Thus, in a proceeds lease, a lessee can be held liable for acting in bad faith and selling the product at a rate substantially below market value.[319]

"The same plain terms that fix the lessee's duty to pay royalty also define the benefit the lessor is entitled to receive."[320]

7-13:3.2 Conditional Cancellation

A mineral lease grants a fee simple determinable, which will "terminate automatically if the event upon which it is limited occurs."[321]

Breach of the implied covenant to market does not automatically terminate the estate.[322]

Breach of the implied covenant may subject the breaching party to "a conditional decree of cancellation."[323]

When damages do not provide adequate relief, the court can conditionally terminate the lease if actual production does not occur within a reasonable time.[324]

---

[314] *Yzaguirre v. KCS Res., Inc.*, 53 S.W.3d 368, 372 (Tex. 2001).
[315] *Yzaguirre v. KCS Res., Inc.*, 53 S.W.3d 368, 374 (Tex. 2001) ("Because the lease provides an objective basis for calculating royalties that is independent of the price the lessee actually obtains, the lessor does not need the protection of an implied covenant.").
[316] *Phillips Petroleum Co. v. Yarbrough*, 405 S.W.3d 70, 78 (Tex. 2013).
[317] *Phillips Petroleum Co. v. Yarbrough*, 405 S.W.3d 70, 78 (Tex. 2013).
[318] *Yzaguirre v. KCS Res., Inc.*, 53 S.W.3d 368, 374–75 (Tex. 2001).
[319] *Yzaguirre v. KCS Res., Inc.*, 53 S.W.3d 368, 373 (Tex. 2001).
[320] *Yzaguirre v. KCS Res., Inc.*, 53 S.W.3d 368, 373 (Tex. 2001).
[321] *Anadarko Petroleum Corp. v. Thompson*, 94 S.W.3d 550, 554 (Tex. 2002).
[322] *Anadarko Petroleum Corp. v. Thompson*, 94 S.W.3d 550, 560 (Tex. 2002).
[323] *Anadarko Petroleum Corp. v. Thompson*, 94 S.W.3d 550, 560 (Tex. 2002).
[324] *Anadarko Petroleum Corp. v. Thompson*, 94 S.W.3d 550, 560 (Tex. 2002).

OIL AND GAS LITIGATION

7-13:4 Defenses

7-13:4.1 Market Value Lease

Under a market value lease, the measure of royalties due to the royalty owner is based on the market value for sales that occurred off the premises.[325]

When the parties enter into a lease requiring royalties to be paid at market value, the courts do not imply a covenant to market.[326]

The implied covenant to market is only assumed in "proceeds" leases where royalty calculations are based on the price received by the lessee.[327]

Under market value leases, royalties are based on the prevailing market price at the time of sale.[328]

Under a market value lease, the lessee must pay market-value royalty even if the lessee received less than market value in sales.[329]

7-13:4.2 Take-or-Pay Provisions

Royalty owners are not entitled to settlement proceeds arising from the breach of take-or-pay contracts.[330]

Royalties are tied to production, and royalties are not due unless and until actual production occurs.[331]

7-13:5 Procedural Implications

7-13:5.1 Class Certification

The Implied Covenant to Market raises concerns regarding certifying classes for class actions.[332]

Texas law requires typicality, meaning the claim arises from the same event or course of conduct that gives rise to the claims of other class members.[333]

Breach of the implied covenant to market depends on factors such as where the product is sold and the actions of the lessee, raising concerns about typicality.[334]

---

[325] *Yzaguirre v. KCS Res., Inc.*, 53 S.W.3d 368, 372 (Tex. 2001).
[326] *Yzaguirre v. KCS Res., Inc.*, 53 S.W.3d 368, 374 (Tex. 2001) ("Because the lease provides an objective basis for calculating royalties that is independent of the price the lessee actually obtains, the lessor does not need the protection of an implied covenant.").
[327] *Phillips Petroleum Co. v. Yarbrough*, 405 S.W.3d 70, 78 (Tex. 2013).
[328] *Yzaguirre v. KCS Res., Inc.*, 53 S.W.3d 368, 372 (Tex. 2001).
[329] *Yzaguirre v. KCS Res., Inc.*, 53 S.W.3d 368, 373 (Tex. 2001).
[330] *Alameda Corp. v. Transam. Nat. Gas Corp.*, 950 S.W.2d 93, 97 (Tex. App.—Houston [14th Dist.] 1997, writ denied).
[331] *Alameda Corp. v. Transam. Nat. Gas Corp.*, 950 S.W.2d 93, 97 (Tex. App.—Houston [14th Dist.] 1997, writ denied).
[332] *Phillips Petroleum Co. v. Yarbrough*, 405 S.W.3d 70, 79 (Tex. 2013).
[333] Tex. R. Civ. P. 42(a)(3).
[334] *Phillips Petroleum Co. v. Yarbrough*, 405 S.W.3d 70, 80 (Tex. 2013).

The predominance requirement ensures that questions of law or fact common to the class predominate over any questions relating only to individual members.[335]

A predominance issue occurs when some members of a class have leases containing express market value clauses and other members have proceeds leases because the leases require different duties from the lessee.[336]

7-14 Breach of Implied Covenant to Reasonably Develop

7-14:1 Overview

Courts imply certain covenants in fact based on the nature of oil and gas transactions. Texas courts recognize an implied covenant to reasonably develop the premises after production begins.[337] The covenant to reasonably develop requires a lessee to conduct further development with reasonable diligence.[338] Texas courts have recognized an implied covenant to reasonably develop and protect the leased premises, once production has been obtained.[339] A lessee's duty under this covenant is to act as a reasonably prudent operator under the same or similar circumstances.[340] The covenant to develop is only implicated after production is secured and requires the lessee to act with reasonable diligence so that the operations result in a profit to both lessor and lessee.[341] The lessee must drill as many wells to develop the property as would a reasonably prudent operator.[342]

7-14:1.1 Related Causes of Action

Breach of Implied Covenant to Further Explore (not recognized in Texas), Breach of Implied Covenant to Market, Breach of Implied Covenant to Protect Against Drainage

MUST READ CASES

Sun Expl. & Prod. Co. v. Jackson, 783 S.W.2d 202 (Tex. 1989)

Clifton v. Koontz, 325 S.W.2d 684 (Tex. 1959)

---

[335] Tex. R. Civ. P. 42(b)(3).
[336] *Phillips Petroleum Co. v. Yarbrough*, 405 S.W.3d 70, 80 (Tex. 2013).
[337] *Clifton v. Koontz*, 325 S.W.2d 684, 693–94 (Tex. 1959).
[338] *Clifton v. Koontz*, 325 S.W.2d 684, 693–94 (Tex. 1959).
[339] *Amoco Prod. Co. v. Alexander*, 622 S.W.2d 563, 567 (Tex. 1981); *Grayson v. Crescendo Res., L.P.*, 104 S.W.3d 736, 739 (Tex. App.—Amarillo 2003, pet. denied); *Hardin-Simmons Univ. v. Hunt Cimarron Ltd. P'ship*, No. 07-15-00303-CV, 2017 WL 3197920, at *9 (Tex. App.—Amarillo July 25, 2017, pet. denied).
[340] *Amoco Prod. Co. v. Alexander*, 622 S.W.2d 563, 567–68 (Tex. 1981).
[341] *Clifton v. Koontz*, 325 S.W.2d 684, 693 (Tex. 1959); *Hardin-Simmons Univ. v. Hunt Cimarron Ltd. P'ship*, No. 07-15-00303-CV, 2017 WL 3197920, at *9 (Tex. App.—Amarillo July 25, 2017).
[342] *Clifton v. Koontz*, 325 S.W.2d 684, 695 (Tex. 1959) (standard of care used to judge whether a breach occurs is the standard of the reasonably prudent operator).

7-14:2 Elements

(1) Proof of additional wells in an already producing stratum or additional wells in those strata different from that where production already occurs

- The burden is on the lessor to prove "that producing stratum required additional wells, or that strata different from that from which production is being obtained, in reasonable probability exist."[343]

    - For example, there could be evidence that reasonable development requires an extra well to be drilled in a formation that is already producing.[344]

    - Alternatively, there must be evidence that a geological formation exists in the area of the lease, other than the formation from which production is already being obtained, where a well can be drilled to obtain more production of either oil or gas.[345]

- Courts will take into account rules promulgated by the Railroad Commission when determining whether a lessee reasonably developed a leasehold.[346]

    - For example, the Railroad Commission promulgates rules defining the allowable acreage and distance between wells, as well as the amount of production that shall be allowable to each well.[347]

        - The lessee does not violate the implied covenant to reasonably develop when drilling a second well would not result in greater production than a single well.[348]

(2) Substantial delay in developing

- Substantial delay in developing.[349]

    - A reasonable amount of delay in proceeding to develop or drill new wells is allowable.[350]

    - The courts will consider the reasonableness of the delay in determining whether the lessor is owed damages on account of the delay.[351]

(3) A reasonably prudent operator would develop

- A reasonably prudent operator would develop.[352]

---

[343] *Clifton v. Koontz*, 325 S.W.2d 684, 695 (Tex. 1959).
[344] *Clifton v. Koontz*, 325 S.W.2d 684, 695 (Tex. 1959).
[345] *Clifton v. Koontz*, 325 S.W.2d 684, 695 (Tex. 1959).
[346] *Clifton v. Koontz*, 325 S.W.2d 684, 691 (Tex. 1959).
[347] *Clifton v. Koontz*, 325 S.W.2d 684, 695 (Tex. 1959).
[348] *Clifton v. Koontz*, 325 S.W.2d 684, 695 (Tex. 1959).
[349] *Clifton v. Koontz*, 305 S.W.2d 782, 788 (Tex. Civ. App.—Fort Worth 1957), *aff'd by* 325 S.W.2d 684 (Tex. 1959).
[350] *Clifton v. Koontz*, 305 S.W.2d 782, 788 (Tex. Civ. App.—Fort Worth 1957), *aff'd by* 325 S.W.2d 684 (Tex. 1959).
[351] *Clifton v. Koontz*, 305 S.W.2d 782, 788 (Tex. Civ. App.—Fort Worth 1957), *aff'd by* 325 S.W.2d 684 (Tex. 1959).
[352] *Sun Expl. & Prod. Co. v. Jackson*, 783 S.W.2d 202, 204 (Tex. 1989).

- The courts interpret an express agreement in a lease to develop with "due diligence" to require the same standard that is required in the implied covenant to develop.[353]

(4) There exists a reasonable expectation of profit

- A reasonable expectation of profit must exist for both the lessor and the lessee.[354]

- The lessee's duty under that covenant is to act as a reasonably prudent operator under the same or similar circumstances.[355]

- The covenant to develop is only implicated after production is secured and requires the lessee to act with reasonable diligence so that the operations result in a profit to both lessor and lessee.[356]

- A reasonable expectation of profit exists if (1) the quantity is sufficient to warrant the use of the product in the market; (2) the income exceeds the actual marketing costs; and (3) production occurs in paying quantities.

    - The standard by which production is measured is "paying quantities," which means if "a well pays a profit, even small, over operating expenses, it produces in paying quantities, though it may never repay its costs, and the enterprise as a whole may prove unprofitable."[357]

- If, under the same or similar circumstances, a reasonably prudent operator would continue to operate a well or drill new wells, for the purpose of making a profit, then the lessee must continue to operate the well or drill new wells.[358]

- The obligation to drill additional wells depends on the facts of each particular case.[359] The covenant requires a balance between a lessor's desire for rapid production and the lessee's desire to keep production costs down.[360]

7-14:3 Damages and Remedies

7-14:3.1 Full Value of Lost Royalty

The usual remedy for breach of the implied covenant for reasonable development is an action for money damages.[361]

---

[353] *Atlantic Richfield Co. v. Gruy*, 720 S.W.2d 121, 123 (Tex. App.—San Antonio 1986, writ ref'd n.r.e.).
[354] *Clifton v. Koontz*, 325 S.W.2d 684, 695 (Tex. 1959).
[355] *Clifton v. Koontz*, 325 S.W.2d 684, 693 (Tex. 1959).
[356] *Clifton v. Koontz*, 325 S.W.2d 684, 693 (Tex. 1959); *Grayson v. Crescendo Res., L.P.*, 104 S.W.3d 736, 739 (Tex. App.—Amarillo, 2003).
[357] *Clifton v. Koontz*, 325 S.W.2d 684, 690–91 (Tex. 1959).
[358] *Clifton v. Koontz*, 325 S.W.2d 684, 691 (Tex. 1959).
[359] *Senter v. Shanafelt*, 233 S.W.2d 202, 206 (Tex. Civ. App.—Fort Worth 1950, no writ).
[360] *Clifton v. Koontz*, 325 S.W.2d 684, 693 (Tex. 1959); *Grayson v. Crescendo Res., L.P.*, 104 S.W.3d 736, 739 (Tex. App.—Amarillo, 2003).
[361] *W.T. Waggoner Estate v. Sigler Oil Co.*, 19 S.W.2d 27, 29 (Tex. 1929).

OIL AND GAS LITIGATION

For a breach of the covenant of reasonable development, the lessee is entitled to recover the full value of royalty lost.[362]

The damages calculation depends upon past and projected production rates, prices, and the time value of money.[363]

Where damages result from failure to develop, the amount and value of oil or gas production must be proven with reasonable certainty.[364]

7-14:3.2 Cancellation of the Lease

Under extraordinary circumstances, when damages do not provide adequate relief, the court can cancel the lease in whole or in part.[365]

- The implied covenant to develop is not a condition on the lease. Rather, it is a mere covenant, the breach of which will not automatically trigger termination.[366]

- To avoid forfeiture, the court typically will not cancel the lease without first allowing an opportunity to cure.[367]

7-14:4 Defenses

7-14:4.1 Express Lease Provisions

Courts do not imply covenants unless it appears from the express provisions in the contract that it was within the contemplation of the parties or it appears necessary to effectuate the purpose of the contract.[368]

The existence of the implied covenant for development will not be assumed when the parties have expressly agreed to a plan to proceed with development.[369]

Parties can protect themselves against the covenant of reasonable development by including a provision in the lease specifying the drilling operations that will satisfy the covenant of reasonable development for a reasonable period of time.[370]

For example, where the parties include provisions (1) agreeing that the lease will continue so long as delay rentals are paid; and (2) agreeing that no forfeiture will result from any breach of any implied covenant, the express language of the contract directly contradicts the implied covenant of development.[371]

---

[362] *Coastal Oil & Gas Corp. v. Garza Energy Tr.*, 268 S.W.3d 1, 19 (Tex. 2008).
[363] *Coastal Oil & Gas Corp. v. Garza Energy Tr.*, 268 S.W.3d 1, 20 (Tex. 2008).
[364] *Texas Pacific Coal & Oil Co. v. Barker*, 6 S.W.2d 1031, 1034 (Tex. 1928).
[365] *W.T. Waggoner Estate v. Sigler Oil Co.*, 19 S.W.2d 27, 29 (Tex. 1929).
[366] *W.T. Waggoner Estate v. Sigler Oil Co.*, 19 S.W.2d 27, 31 (Tex. 1929).
[367] *Slaughter v. Cities Serv. Oil Co.*, 660 S.W.2d 860, 862 (Tex. App.—Amarillo 1983, no writ).
[368] *HECI Expl. Co. v. Neel*, 982 S.W.2d 881, 888–89 (1998) ("We have imposed implied covenants only when they are fundamental to the purposes of a mineral lease and when the lease does not expressly address the subject matter of the covenant sought to be implied.").
[369] *Gulf Prod. Co. v. Kishi*, 103 S.W.2d 965, 969 (Tex. Comm'n App. 1937); *see Union Pac. Res. Group Inc., v. Neinast* 67 S.W.3d 275, 282 (Tex. App.—Houston [1st Dist.] 2001, no pet.).
[370] *Dallas Power & Light Co. v. Cleghorn*, 623 S.W.2d 310, 311 (Tex. 1981).
[371] *Dallas Power & Light Co. v. Cleghorn*, 623 S.W.2d 310, 311 (Tex. 1981).

7-14:4.2 Opportunity to Cure

Since lessors cannot pursue an action for breach of the implied covenant to reasonably develop without first giving lessees an opportunity to cure, lessees can argue that they have not been given an opportunity to cure.[372]

7-14:5 Procedural Implications

7-14:5.1 Jury Instructions

Attorneys should be careful to draft a charge with the appropriate instructions.

The charge should include a question asking the jury whether the lessee failed to reasonably develop the lease.[373]

The language of the accompanying instruction should define "to reasonably develop" as "the development which a prudent operator would do with respect to the lease."[374]

7-14:5.2 Opportunity to Cure

Lessors cannot pursue an action for breach of the implied covenant to reasonably develop without first giving lessees an opportunity to cure.[375]

---

[372] *Slaughter v. Cities Serv. Oil Co.*, 660 S.W.2d 860, 862 (Tex. App.—Amarillo 1983, no writ).
[373] *Sun Expl. & Prod. Co. v. Jackson*, 783 S.W.2d 202, 204 (Tex. 1989).
[374] *Sun Expl. & Prod. Co. v. Jackson*, 783 S.W.2d 202, 204 (Tex. 1989).
[375] *Slaughter v. Cities Serv. Oil Co.*, 660 S.W.2d 860, 862 (Tex. App.—Amarillo 1983, no writ).

CHAPTER 8

Equitable and Extraordinary Relief*

8-1 Temporary Injunction

8-1:1 Overview

The purpose of a temporary injunction is to maintain the status quo of the litigation's subject matter and to prevent probable, irreparable injury pending trial of the case on its merits. Injunctive relief may be based on the application of general equitable principles or on express authorization contained in statute. Only after notice and a hearing may a temporary injunction be issued to maintain the status quo. A temporary injunction remains in force until, and expires upon, entry of final judgment if not previously dissolved by the court. In the context of business litigation, equitable relief is the usual remedy for the use or disclosure of trade secrets.

8-1:1.1 Related Causes of Action

Permanent Injunction, Temporary Restraining Order, Breach of Covenant not to Compete, Misappropriation of Trade Secrets, Tortious Interference with Business Relations, Statutory Trademark Infringement

MUST READ CASES

Butnaru v. Ford Motor Co., 84 S.W.3d 198 (Tex. 2002) (elements)

In re Texas Nat. Res. Conservation Comm'n, 85 S.W.3d 201 (Tex. 2002)

Walling v. Metcalfe, 863 S.W.2d 56 (Tex. 1993)

8-1:2 Elements

(1) A pleaded and proven cause of action against the defendant[1]:

- The applicant must plead and prove a cause of action against the defendant.[2]

---

* The authors thank Robyn Leatherwood for her assistance in the updating of this chapter.
[1] *Butnaru v. Ford Motor Co.*, 84 S.W.3d 198, 204 (Tex. 2002).
[2] *Butnaru v. Ford Motor Co.*, 84 S.W.3d 198, 204 (Tex. 2002).

301

- A trial court may grant a temporary injunction to preserve the status quo pending trial even though the applicant's prayer does not include a claim for equitable relief following determination of the merits.[3]

(2) A probable right to the relief sought[4], and

- A probable right of recovery is shown by alleging a cause of action and presenting evidence tending to sustain it.[5]
- A party does not have to establish it will prevail on final trial, rather the court must decide whether the applicant is entitled to preservation of the status quo pending trial on the merits.[6]

(3) A probable, imminent, and irreparable injury in the interim[7]:

- Probable injury includes the elements of imminent harm, irreparable injury and no adequate remedy at law.[8]
    - In equity, the general rule is that before injunctive relief can be obtained, it must appear that there does not exist an adequate remedy at law.[9]
- An adequate remedy is one that is as complete, practical, and efficient to the prompt administration of justice as is equitable relief.[10]
- An injury is irreparable if the injured party cannot be adequately compensated in damages, or if the damages cannot be measured by any certain pecuniary standard.[11]
    - Disruption to a business can be irreparable harm.[12]
    - A showing of irreparable injury is not required to obtain a temporary injunction to enforce a covenant not to compete.[13]
- The claimed injury cannot be merely speculative, as fear and apprehension of injury are not sufficient to support a temporary injunction.[14]

---

[3] *See Walling v. Metcalfe*, 863 S.W.2d 56, 57 (Tex. 1993).
[4] *Butnaru v. Ford Motor Co.*, 84 S.W.3d 198, 204 (Tex. 2002).
[5] *Fox v. Tropical Warehouses, Inc.*, 121 S.W.3d 853, 857 (Tex. App.—Fort Worth 2003, no pet.).
[6] *See Patel v. St. Luke's Sugar Land P'ship, L.L.P.*, No. 01-13-00273-CV, 2013 WL 5947500 (Tex. App.—Houston [1st Dist.] Nov. 7, 2013, pet. filed).
[7] *Butnaru v. Ford Motor Co.*, 84 S.W.3d 198, 204 (Tex. 2002).
[8] *4415 W Lovers Lane, LLC v. Stanton*, 05-17-01363-CV, 2018 WL 3387384, at *3 (Tex. App.—Dallas July 12, 2018, no pet.).
[9] *See Butnaru v. Ford Motor Co.*, 84 S.W.3d 198, 210 (Tex. 2002).
[10] *Shor v. Pelican Oil & Gas Mgt., LLC*, 405 S.W.3d 737, 750 (Tex. App.—Hous. [1st Dist.] 2013).
[11] *Butnaru v. Ford Motor Co.*, 84 S.W.3d 198, 204 (Tex. 2002).
[12] *Al-Wahban v. Hamdan*, 10-19-00026-CV, 2019 WL 2479894, at *3 (Tex. App.—Waco June 12, 2019, no pet.).
[13] Tex. Bus. & Com. Code Ann. §§ 15.51-15.52.
[14] *Al-Wahban v. Hamdan*, No. 10-19-00026-CV, 2019 Tex. App. LEXIS 4849, at *8 (Tex. App. June 12, 2019).

8-1:3 Damages and Remedies

8-1:3.1 Injunction Order

Texas Rules of Civil Procedure 683 and 684 set forth the specific requirements for every order granting an injunction:

- Set forth the reasons for its issuance;
- Be specific in terms;
- Describe in reasonable detail, and not by reference to the complaint or other document, the act or acts sought to be restrained; and
- Include an order setting the cause for trial on the merits with respect to the ultimate relief sought.

Further, in the order granting the temporary injunction, the court shall fix the amount of security to be given by the applicant; such an order is binding only upon the parties to the action, their officers, agents, servants, employees, and attorneys, and upon those persons in active concert or participation with them who receive actual notice of the order by personal service or otherwise.[15]

These procedural requirements are mandatory, and an order that does not meet them is subject to being declared void and dissolved.[16]

8-1:3.2 Scope of Injunction

The court must set out in the temporary injunction order the reasons it believes the applicant will suffer injury if it does not grant the injunction.[17]

The reasons must be specific and legally sufficient, not merely conclusory statements.[18]

An injunction should be broad enough to prevent a repetition of the wrong sought to be corrected, but not so broad that it enjoins a party from lawful activities.[19]

A temporary injunction operates until dissolved by an interlocutory order or until the final hearing of the case.[20]

---

[15] Tex. R. Civ. P. 683, 684.
[16] *Qwest Commc'n Corp. v. AT&T Corp.*, 24 S.W.3d 334, 337 (Tex. 2000).
[17] *Maldonado v. Franklin*, 04-18-00819-CV, 2019 WL 4739438, at *3 (Tex. App.—San Antonio Sept. 30, 2019, no pet.).
[18] *Maldonado v. Franklin*, 04-18-00819-CV, 2019 WL 4739438, at *3 (Tex. App.—San Antonio Sept. 30, 2019, no pet.).
[19] *Super Starr Int'l, LLC v. Fresh Tex Produce, LLC*, 531 S.W.3d 829, 849 (Tex. App.—Corpus Christi 2017, no pet.).
[20] *In re Texas Nat. Res. Conservation Comm'n*, 85 S.W.3d 201, 205 (Tex. 2002).

8-1:4 Defenses

8-1:4.1 Unclean Hands

Courts recognize that one who comes seeking equity must come with clean hands.[21]

A party may not obtain injunctive relief if its own wrongful conduct injured the other party.[22]

The complaining party must have been the party harmed by the allegedly improper conduct.[23]

8-1:4.2 Laches

Delay, coupled with disadvantage to another, are the essential elements of laches.[24]

Latches does not bar recovery unless allowing the action would work a grave injustice. If a party, knowing its rights, takes no steps to enforce those rights, and the condition of the other party, in good faith, has become so changed that the other party cannot be resorted to its former state, laches may bar equitable relief.[25]

8-1:5 Procedural Implications

8-1:5.1 Jurisdiction

When an injunction is sought against a resident of this state, jurisdiction is proper in either a district or county court in the county of that party.[26]

A district court may hear and grant any relief that could be granted by either courts of law or equity.[27]

8-1:5.2 Venue

Venue lies in the county of the defendant's domicile.[28]

The injunction venue statute, which is mandatory, applies only to suits in which the relief sought is primarily injunctive.[29]

---

[21] *See Jones v. Whatley*, No. 13-09-00355-CV, 2011 Tex. App. LEXIS 4380, at *9 (Tex. App.—Corpus Christi June 9, 2011).

[22] *See Omohundro v. Matthews*, 341 S.W.2d 401, 410 (Tex. 1960).

[23] *See Dunnagan v. Watson*, 204 S.W.3d 30, 41 (Tex. App.—Fort Worth 2006, pet. denied).

[24] *See City of Dallas v. Ellis*, No. 05-16-00348-CV, 2017 Tex. App. LEXIS 1408, at *9–10 (App.—Dallas Feb. 17, 2017); *Culver v. Pickens*, 176 S.W.2d 167 (Tex. 1943).

[25] *See Keene v. Reed*, 340 S.W.2d 859, 860 (Tex. Civ. App.—Waco 1960, writ ref'd).

[26] Tex. Civ. Prac. & Rem. Code Ann. § 65.023(a).

[27] Tex. Gov't Code Ann. § 24.008.

[28] *In re Fox River Real Estate Holdings*, Inc., 18-0913, 2020 WL 501702, at *4 (Tex. Jan. 31, 2020), *reh'g denied* (Apr. 17, 2020).

[29] *In re Fox River Real Estate Holdings, Inc.*, 18-0913, 2020 WL 501702, at *4 (Tex. Jan. 31, 2020), *reh'g denied* (Apr. 17, 2020).

When an injunction is merely ancillary to the main purpose of the suit, the mandatory venue provision does not apply.[30]

8-1:5.3 Petition

An injunction may be granted only on the basis of a verified petition that sets out a plain and intelligible statement of grounds for relief.[31]

The petition must show a probable injury and a probable right of recovery.[32]

The petition should name as defendants all persons whose interests will be affected and whose joinder is needed to make the order effective.[33]

8-1:5.4 Notice

No temporary injunction may be issued without notice to the party being restrained.[34]

Reasonable notice of day and time of the temporary injunction hearing must be given.[35]

8-1:5.5 Hearing

As a prerequisite to a temporary injunction, probable right and probable injury must be established by competent evidence adduced at a hearing.[36]

An injunction may not issue on sworn pleadings alone.[37]

When a temporary restraining order is granted without notice, the hearing for a temporary injunction must be set at the earliest possible date and takes precedence over all matters except older matters of the same character.[38]

To warrant an injunction, an applicant must plead a cause of action, show probable right to recovery, and show probable injury in the interim.[39]

A probable right of success is shown by alleging a cause of action and presenting evidence that tends to sustain it.[40]

---

[30] *In re Fox River Real Estate Holdings, Inc.*, 18-0913, 2020 WL 501702, at *5 (Tex. Jan. 31, 2020), *reh'g denied* (Apr. 17, 2020).

[31] Tex. R. Civ. P. 682.

[32] *See Walling v. Metcalfe*, 863 S.W.2d 56, 57 (Tex. 1993).

[33] Tex. R. Civ. P. 39; *In re Texas. Educ. Agency*, 442 S.W.3d 753 (Tex. App.—Austin 2014).

[34] Tex. R. Civ. P. 681.

[35] Tex. R. Civ. P. 686.

[36] *Town of Flower Mound v. Eagleridge Operating, LLC*, 02-18-00392-CV, 2019 WL 3955197, at *3 (Tex. App.—Fort Worth Aug. 22, 2019, no pet.).

[37] *See Goldthorn v. Goldthorn*, 242 S.W.3d 797, 798 (Tex. App.—San Antonio 2007, no pet.).

[38] Tex. R. Civ. P. 680.

[39] *City of Palmview v. Agua Special Util. Dist.*, 13-18-00416-CV, 2019 WL 1066423, at *7 (Tex. App.—Corpus Christi Mar. 7, 2019, no pet.) (quoting *Sun Oil Co. v. Whitaker*, 424 S.W.2d 216, 218 (Tex. 1968)).

[40] *Efremov v. GeoSteering, LLC*, 01-16-00358-CV, 2017 WL 976072, at *2 (Tex. App.—Houston [1st Dist.] Mar. 14, 2017, pet. denied).

Probable injury is shown by demonstrating imminent harm, irreparable injury and no adequate remedy at law for damages.[41]

8-1:5.6 Appeal

By statute, an order granting or refusing a temporary injunction, or granting or overruling a motion to dissolve a temporary injunction, is appealable.[42] A reviewing court should reverse an order granting or denying injunctive relief only if the trial court abused that discretion.[43]

8-2 Permanent Injunction

8-2:1 Overview

A permanent injunction is not a cause of action, but an equitable remedy. Unlike a temporary injunction, a permanent injunction provides permanent relief. A permanent injunction is intended to give final or permanent relief after a trial on the merits. Unlike a temporary injunction, a permanent injunction may be perpetual in nature, or may extend until a particular date set by the trial court. Permanent injunctions do not depend on any further action by the trial court and grant all the relief that the court intends to grant in the case.

8-2:1.1 Related Causes of Action

Temporary Injunction, Temporary Restraining Order, Breach of Covenant Not to Compete, Misappropriation of Trade Secrets, Tortious Interference with Business Relations

MUST READ CASES

Triantaphyllis v. Gamble, 93 S.W.3d 398 (Tex. App.—Houston [14th Dist.] 2002, pet. denied) (outlining the elements required for permanent injunctive relief)

1717 Bissonnet, LLC v. Loughhead, 500 S.W.3d 488 (Tex. App.—Houston [14th Dist.] 2016)

Webb v. Glenbrook Owners Ass'n, Inc., 298 S.W.3d 374 (Tex. App.—Dallas 2009, no pet.)

8-2:2 Elements

(1) The existence of a wrongful act

- The applicant must prove that the defendant has attempted to, or intends to harm the plaintiff in the future.[44]

---

[41] *Telephone Equip. Network, Inc. v. TA/Westchase Place, Ltd.*, 80 S.W.3d 601, 607 (Tex. App.—Houston [1st Dist.] 2002, no pet. h.).

[42] Tex. Civ. Prac. & Rem. Code Ann. § 51.014(a)(4).

[43] *Butnaru v. Ford Motor Co.*, 84 S.W.3d 198, 204 (Tex. 2002).

[44] *See Morris v. Collins*, 881 S.W.2d 138, 140 (Tex. App.—Houston [1st Dist.] 1994, pet. denied).

- Fear or apprehension of the possibility of injury is not sufficient.[45]

(2) The existence of imminent harm

- An injunction will not issue unless it is shown that the defendant will engage in the activity enjoined.[46]

(3) The existence of irreparable injury, and

- A permanent injunction will not be issued to prevent an injury that is purely conjectural or speculative.[47]
- An irreparable injury is one for which actual damages will not adequately compensate the injured party or the damages cannot be measured by any certain pecuniary standard.[48]
  - Disruption to a business can be irreparable harm.[49]
  - Courts can enforce contractual rights by permanent injunction if the injured party shows an inadequate remedy at law and an irreparable injury.[50]
  - For example, when a competitor acquired a plaintiff's trade secrets, used those trade secrets to drive away a particular company's business, and a large part of the plaintiff's business came from that one company, the plaintiff suffered an irreparable injury.[51]
- When a party's actions would disrupt the organized business dealings of a company, threaten customer confidence in the company, and probably cause the company to lose customers and profits, the company suffers an irreparable harm.[52]

(4) The absence of an adequate remedy at law.

- A permanent injunction issues only if a party does not have an adequate legal remedy.[53]
- If there is an adequate legal remedy (normally monetary damages), then a party is not entitled to injunctive relief as well.[54]

---

[45] *Frey v. DeCordova Bend Estates Owners Ass'n*, 647 S.W.2d 246, 248 (Tex. 1983); *Spangle v. McGee*, No. 03-08-00054-CV, 2009 Tex. App. LEXIS 312, at *10 (App.—Austin Jan. 15, 2009).

[46] *Farkas v. Wells Fargo Bank, N.A.*, No. 03-14-00716-CV, 2016 Tex. App. LEXIS 12956, at *28–29 (App.—Austin Dec. 8, 2016).

[47] *Lynd v. Bass Pro Outdoor World, Inc.*, 05-12-00968-CV, 2014 WL 1010120, at *8 (Tex. App.—Dallas Mar. 12, 2014, pet. denied).

[48] *Butnaru v. Ford Motor Co.*, 84 S.W.3d 198, 204 (Tex. 2002).

[49] *Frequent Flyer Depot, Inc. v. Am. Airlines, Inc.*, 281 S.W.3d 215, 228 (Tex. App.—Fort Worth 2009, pet. denied).

[50] *Luv N' Care, Ltd. v. Royal King Infant Products Co. Ltd.*, 2:10-CV-461-JRG, 2016 WL 3617776, at *9 (E.D. Tex. July 6, 2016).

[51] *See Fox v. Tropical Warehouses, Inc.*, 121 S.W.3d 853 (Tex. App.—Fort Worth 2003, pet. denied).

[52] *See David v. Bache Hlasey Stuart Shields, Inc.*, 630 S.W.2d 754, 757 (Tex. App.—Houston [1st Dist.] 1982, no writ).

[53] *Schneider Nat. Carriers, Inc. v. Bates*, 147 S.W.3d 264, 284 (Tex. 2004).

[54] *Schneider Nat. Carriers, Inc. v. Bates*, 147 S.W.3d 264, 284 (Tex. 2004).

- The Texas Supreme Court has noted that future damages cannot be recovered if a permanent injunction issues to abate them in the context of cases involving covenants not to compete, trade secrets, wrongful discharge and real estate contracts.[55]
- An adequate remedy is one that is as complete, practical and efficient to the prompt administration of justice as is equitable relief.[56]
  - A remedy is not adequate simply because some of the proven damages are calculable.[57]
  - Intangible types of injuries, such as a company's loss of good will, are the types of injuries to which a dollar value may not easily be assigned.[58]

8-2:3 Pleadings

Persons seeking a permanent injunction must be specific in pleading the relief sought, and courts are without authority to grant relief beyond that so specified in the pleadings. Yet, an injunction should be broad enough to prevent a repetition of the evil sought to be corrected.[59] A pleading is sufficient if it gives the opposing party adequate information to enable him to prepare a defense.[60]

8-3 Specific Performance

8-3:1 Overview

Specific performance is an equitable remedy used as a substitute for monetary damages that compels a party who has failed or refused to perform a valid contractual obligation to fulfill that obligation by performing the contract.[61] To obtain specific performance, there must be a valid and enforceable agreement between the parties. A plaintiff must establish that the contract sought to be enforced is valid and complete, and that it possesses the essentials of a binding legal obligation.

8-3:1.1 Related Causes of Action

Breach of Contract, Assumpsit, Declaratory Judgment, Suit for Rescission, Common Law Fraud, Statutory Fraud, Fraud by Non-disclosure, Constructive Fraud, Fraudulent Concealment, Breach of Covenant not to Compete

---

[55] *Schneider Nat. Carriers, Inc. v. Bates*, 147 S.W.3d 264, 285 (Tex. 2004).
[56] *Cheniere Energy, Inc. v. Parallax Enters., LLC*, 585 S.W.3d 70, 76 (Tex. App.—Houston [14th Dist.] 2019).
[57] *Cheniere Energy, Inc. v. Parallax Enters., LLC*, 585 S.W.3d 70, 76 (Tex. App.—Houston [14th Dist.] 2019).
[58] *See Frequent Flyer Depot, Inc. v. Am. Airlines, Inc.*, 281 S.W.3d 215, 229 (Tex. App.—Fort Worth 2009, pet. denied).
[59] *Livingston v. Livingston*, 537 S.W.3d 578, 588 (Tex. App.—Houston [1st Dist.] 2017, no pet.).
[60] *King v. Lyons*, 457 S.W.3d 122, 126 (citing *Roark v. Allen*, 633 S.W.2d 804, 809–10 (Tex. 1982)).
[61] *Tamuno Ifiesimama v. Haile*, 522 S.W.3d 675, 685 (Tex. App.—Houston [1st Dist.] 2017, pet. denied).

EQUITABLE AND EXTRAORDINARY RELIEF

MUST READ CASES

DiGiuseppe v. Lawler, 269 S.W.3d 588 (Tex. 2008)

Stafford v. S. Vanity Magazine, Inc., 231 S.W.3d 530 (Tex. App.—Dallas 2007)

8-3:2 Elements

(1) The existence of a valid and binding contract

- There must be an enforceable contract to be performed for a party to seek specific performance.[62]

- The contract must have precise terms capable of enforcement.[63] The essential terms of the contract must be clear and certain enough to be understood without recourse to parol evidence.[64]

- However, small ambiguities will not preclude a decree for specific performance if they can be made clear with extrinsic evidence.[65]

- The contract must contain all of the material terms to be enforced.[66] The absence of some terms will not preclude specific performance if those terms were non-essential.[67]

- The contract does not need to be in writing unless the statute of frauds requires it to be written.[68]

(2) The plaintiff has performed all obligations imposed by the contract or is ready, willing, and able to perform

- A party must show that it has satisfied its obligations under the contract to be entitled to specific performance.[69]

- The party seeking specific performance must demonstrate its own readiness, willingness, and ability to perform its obligations under the contract.[70]

- A plaintiff seeking specific performance must actually tender performance as a prerequisite to obtaining specific performance.[71]

---

[62] *Barham v. McGraw*, 342 S.W.3d 716, 718 (Tex. App.—Amarillo 2011, pet. denied).

[63] *Cytogenix, Inc. v. Waldroff*, 213 S.W.3d 479, 488 (Tex. App.—Houston [1st Dist.] 2006, pet. denied).

[64] *TLC Hosp., LLC v. Pillar Income Asset Mgmt., Inc.*, 570 S.W.3d 749, 768 (Tex. App.—Tyler 2018, pet. denied).

[65] *Burrus v. Reyes*, 516 S.W.3d 170, 188 (Tex. App.—El Paso 2017, pet. denied).

[66] *Condovest Corp. v. John Street Builders*, 662 S.W.2d 138, 140 (Tex. App.—Austin 1983, writ ref'd n.r.e.).

[67] *Burris v. Hastert*, 191 S.W.2d 811, 814 (Tex. Civ. App.—San Antonio 1945, writ ref'd).

[68] Tex. Bus. & Com. Code Ann. §§ 2.201(a)-26.01(b).

[69] *Glass v. Anderson*, 596 S.W.2d 507, 514 (Tex. 1980).

[70] *DiGiuseppe v. Lawler*, 269 S.W.3d 588, 595 (Tex. 2008).

[71] *DiGiuseppe v. Lawler*, 269 S.W.3d 588, 594 (Tex. 2008).

- When a defendant refuses to perform or repudiates a contract, the plaintiff may be excused from actually tendering performance before filing suit for specific performance.[72]
  - The general rule requiring actual tender is relaxed, based on equitable considerations, when tender would be a useless act.[73]
- In 2019, the Texas Supreme Court stated that a party seeking the equitable remedy of specific performance in lieu of money damages may, in some circumstances, be excused from pleading and proving that the plaintiff performed or tendered performance as contractually required, but must additionally plead and prove that, at all relevant times, it was ready, willing, and able to perform under the contract.[74] The Court did not elaborate, however, regarding the circumstances in which pleading and proof of performance or tender would be excused.

(3) The plaintiff has no adequate remedy at law

- The plaintiff must have no adequate remedy at law.[75]
- If the subject matter of the contract is the conveyance of real property, specific performance is more readily available as a remedy for the sale of real estate than for the sale of personal property, because damages are generally believed to be inadequate in connection with real property.[76]
- If the subject matter of the contract is the sale of personal property, specific performance may be available if the personal property has a "special, peculiar, or unique value or character."[77]
- If the subject matter of the contract is the performance of services, courts will not grant specific performance because there is no mutuality of remedy.[78] However, courts are more likely to grant specific performance when the contract requires a party to refrain from doing something.[79]

---

[72] *DiGiuseppe v. Lawler*, 269 S.W.3d 588, 594 (Tex. 2008).

[73] *Lyons v. Ortego*, 01-17-00092-CV, 2018 WL 4014218, at *5 (Tex. App.—Houston [1st Dist.] Aug. 23, 2018, pet. denied).

[74] *Pathfinder Oil & Gas, Inc. v. Great W. Drilling, Ltd.*, 574 S.W.3d 882, 890 (Tex. 2019).

[75] *L Series, L.L.C. v. Holt*, 571 S.W.3d 864, 876 (Tex. App.—Fort Worth 2019, pet. denied), *reh'g denied* (Mar. 28, 2019).

[76] *Rus-Ann Dev., Inc. v. ECGC, Inc.*, 222 S.W.3d 921, 927 (Tex. App.—Tyler 2007, no pet.); *see also Kress v. Soules*, 152 Tex. 595, 597, 261 S.W.2d 703, 704 (1953) (specific performance of a contract for the sale of realty is ordinarily granted where the suit is based on a valid contract, but it is not a remedy which exists as a matter of right); *Horner v. Bourland*, 724 F.2d 1142, 1144–45 (5th Cir. 1984) (in a case involving a contract for the sale of real estate that is otherwise subject to enforcement and where justification on the ground of inequity is lacking, it is an abuse of the trial court's discretion to refuse specific performance).

[77] *Stafford v. S. Vanity Magazine, Inc.*, 231 S.W.3d 530, 535 (Tex. App.—Dallas 2007, pet. denied).

[78] *Berryman's S. Fork, Inc. v. J. Baxter Brinkmann Intern. Corp.*, 418 S.W.3d 172, 188 (Tex. App.—Dallas 2013, pet. denied); *Gage v. Wimberley*, 476 S.W.2d 724, 731 (Tex. Civ. App.—Tyler 1972).

[79] *Electronic Data Sys. Corp. v. Kinder*, 360 F. Supp. 1044, 1051 (N.D. Tex. 1973), *aff'd* 497 F.2d 222 (enforcing non-compete provision); *McCormick v. Hines*, 498 S.W.2d 58, 64 (Tex. Civ. App.—Amarillo 1973, writ dism'd) (enforcing written agreement by trustees to resign).

(4) Equitable principles support the decree of specific performance
- specific performance will not be granted if the court deems the remedy inequitable under the circumstances.[80]
- Factors which a court may consider in determining whether to award specific performance include, but are not limited to:
  - The hardship such a decree would place on the parties;[81]
  - Whether long-continued supervision by the court will be required;[82]
  - Whether complete relief can be rendered by the remedy sought;[83] and
  - If the remedy sought is granted it can be adequately enforced.[84]
- Although mere hardship to the defendant does not preclude a decree for specific performance, excessive hardship might.[85] The impossibility of a defendant being able to perform precludes specific performance.[86]
- Courts will refuse to grant specific performance if:
  - The contract term is illegal;[87]
  - The contract was obtained through fraud, duress or coercion;[88] or
  - The contract was formed based upon a mutual mistake which precluded a meeting of the minds.[89]

8-3:3 Damages and Remedies

8-3:3.1 Decree of Specific Performance

A court will issue a decree compelling the defendant to perform.[90]

---

[80] *Gordin v. Shuler*, 704 S.W.2d 403, 408 (Tex. App.—Dallas 1985, writ ref'd n.r.e.).

[81] *In re Baerg Real Prop. Tr.*, 585 B.R. 373, 391 (Bankr. N.D. Tex. 2018); *Bennett v. Copeland*, 235 S.W.2d 605, 609 (Tex. 1951) (stating that "mere hardship" to the defendant will not preclude a decree of specific performance).

[82] *McKinney/Pearl Rest. Partners, L.P. v. Metro. Life Ins. Co.*, 241 F. Supp. 3d 737, 774 (N.D. Tex. 2017).

[83] *S. Plains Switching, Ltd. Co. v. BNSF Ry. Co.*, 255 S.W.3d 690, 703 (Tex. App.—Amarillo 2008, pet. denied).

[84] *McKinney/Pearl Rest. Partners, L.P. v. Metro. Life Ins. Co.*, 241 F. Supp. 3d 737, 775 (N.D. Tex. 2017).

[85] *Claflin v. Hillock Homes, Inc.*, 645 S.W.2d 629, 633 (Tex. App.—Austin 1983).

[86] *See Nash v. Conatser*, 410 S.W.2d 512, 520 (Tex. Civ. App.—Dallas 1966, no writ). However, the defense of impossibility is not available if the impossibility was created by a voluntary act. *Stafford v. S. Vanity Magazine, Inc.*, 231 S.W.3d 530, 537 (Tex. App.—Dallas 2007, pet. denied).

[87] *Montgomery v. Browder*, 930 S.W.2d 772, 779 (Tex. App.—Amarillo 1996).

[88] *Lloyd v. Holland*, 659 S.W.2d 103, 105–06 (Tex. App.—Houston [14th Dist.] 1983).

[89] *Lubel v. J.H. Uptmore & Assocs.*, 680 S.W.2d 518, 520 (Tex. App.—San Antonio 1984, no writ).

[90] *South Plains Switching, Ltd. v. BNSF Ry.*, 255 S.W.3d 690, 703 (Tex. App.—Amarillo 2008).

The decree must specifically detail those things which the defendant must do.[91]

The decree must be in conformity with the terms of the agreement made by the parties.[92]

Courts are reluctant to issue decrees in which they maintain ongoing supervision.[93]

8-3:4 Defenses

8-3:4.1 Statute of Limitations

The applicable limitations period is four years.[94]

The cause of action accrues immediately when there is a failure to perform the agreement.[95]

8-3:4.2 Laches

Laches is an available affirmative defense.[96]

8-3:4.3 Contractual Defenses

If the defendant may avoid the obligation on the underlying contract, the plaintiff may not obtain an order requiring specific performance.[97]

For more information on available defenses, *see* Chapter 15: Affirmative Defenses; Chapter 16: Statute of Limitations; Chapter 18: Miscellaneous Defenses.

8-3:4.4 Waiver

The plaintiff may either expressly or impliedly waive the right to specific performance.[98]

8-3:4.5 Estoppel

A plaintiff may be estopped from asserting a right to specific performance when his conduct makes it impossible to perform a condition precedent to the contract.[99]

---

[91] *Various Opportunities, Inc. v. Sullivan Invs., Inc.*, 677 S.W.2d 115, 118 (Tex. App.—Dallas 1984, no writ).

[92] *Brantley v. Etter*, 662 S.W.2d 752, 757 (Tex. App.—San Antonio 1983), writ ref'd n.r.e., 677 S.W.2d 503 (Tex. 1984).

[93] *American Hous. Resources Inc. v. Slaughter*, 597 S.W.2d 13, 15 (Tex. Civ. App.—Dallas 1980, writ ref'd n.r.e.).

[94] Tex. Civ. Prac. & Rem. Code Ann. §§ 16.004(a)(1), 16.051; Tex. Bus. & Com. Code § 2.725.

[95] *F.D. Stella Products Co. v. Scott*, 875 S.W.2d 462, 464 (Tex. App.—Austin 1994, no writ).

[96] *Air Park-Dallas Zoning Comm. v. Crow Billingsley Airpark, Ltd.*, 109 S.W.3d 900, 911 (Tex. App.—Dallas 2003, no pet.).

[97] *Cate v. Woods*, 299 S.W.3d 149, 152–53 (Tex. App.—Texarkana 2009).

[98] *Limestone Grp., Inc. v. Sai Thong, L.L.C.*, 107 S.W.3d 793, 796–797 (Tex. App.—Amarillo 2003, no pet.) (parties may expressly agree that specific performance is an applicable remedy even when not available in equity).

[99] *Sharifi v. Steen Auto., LLC*, 370 S.W.3d 126, 146 (Tex. App.—Dallas 2012).

EQUITABLE AND EXTRAORDINARY RELIEF

8-3:4.6 Other Equitable Defenses

Other equitable defenses would be appropriate, given the remedy's equitable nature.[100]

8-3:5 Procedural Implications

8-3:5.1 Express Right to Specific Performance

Even if specific performance is not available in equity, the parties may expressly agree that specific performance is an available remedy for breach.[101]

8-3:5.2 Joinder of Parties

A third party who purchases property from the defendant, knowing that the property is subject to a contract for sale, may be joined in the lawsuit as a defendant and ordered to convey the property to the plaintiff.[102]

8-3:5.3 Election of Remedies

A plaintiff must either elect to sue for breach of contract or for specific performance and may not recover for both.[103]

8-4 Accounting

8-4:1 Overview

A suit for an accounting is an equitable remedy which seeks to ascertain the amount or the identity of property one party owes another. A plaintiff must first obtain an order authorizing an accounting, which may then be carried through to final judgment following the formal accounting. An action for accounting may be a suit in equity or a particular remedy sought in conjunction with or as a remedy for another cause of action.

8-4:1.1 Related Causes of Action

Sworn Account, Account, Judicial Winding up of Partnership, Breach of Formal Fiduciary Duty, Breach of Contract, Attorney Breach of Fiduciary Duty

---

[100] *DiGiuseppe v. Lawler*, 269 S.W.3d 588, 593 (Tex. 2008).
[101] *Singh v. Skibicki*, 01-14-00825-CV, 2015 WL 7785566, at *6 (Tex. App.—Houston [1st Dist.] Dec. 3, 2015, no pet.).
[102] *Sterling v. Apple*, 513 S.W.2d 255, 257 (Tex. Civ. App.—Houston [1st Dist.] 1974, writ ref'd n.r.e.).
[103] *City of McAllen v. Casso*, 13-11-00749-CV, 2013 WL 1281992, at *15 (Tex. App.—Corpus Christi Mar. 28, 2013, no pet.); *Hamon v. Allen*, 457 S.W.2d 384, 391 (Tex. Civ. App.—Corpus Christi 1970, no writ).

MUST READ CASES

Sauceda v. Kerlin, 164 S.W.3d 892 (Tex. App.—Corpus Christi 2005), review granted, judgment vacated, 05-0653, 2006 WL 4706002 (Tex. Mar. 10, 2006), rev'd, 263 S.W.3d 920 (Tex. 2008)

T.F.W. Mgmt., Inc. v. Westwood Shores Prop. Owners Ass'n, 79 S.W.3d 712 (Tex. App.—Houston [14th Dist.] 2002, pet. denied)

8-4:2 Elements

8-4:2.1 Equitable Accounting

(1) The parties must usually have a pre-existing contractual or fiduciary relationship.[104]

(2) The facts and accounts presented are so complex that there is no adequate remedy at law, such as:[105]

(2)(a) A close fiduciary relationship

- A close fiduciary relationship is a situation in which a court may order an accounting, such as:
  - Executor of an estate and beneficiaries or heirs;[106]
  - Partners;[107]
  - Remaindermen and holder of a life estate.[108]
- However, there must be such complexity within the account(s) that no adequate remedy at law exists.[109]
  - When a party can obtain adequate relief at law through the use of standard discovery procedures, a trial court does not err in refusing to order an accounting.[110]

(2)(b) Mutual accounts between the parties

- Parties having mutual accounts between them is a situation in which a court may order an accounting.[111]

---

[104] *T.F.W. Mgmt., Inc. v. Westwood Shores Prop. Owners Ass'n*, 79 S.W.3d 712, 717 (Tex. App.—Houston [14th Dist.] 2002, pet. denied).

[105] *T.F.W. Mgmt., Inc. v. Westwood Shores Prop. Owners Ass'n*, 79 S.W.3d 712, 717 (Tex. App.—Houston [14th Dist.] 2002, pet. denied); *Hutchings v. Chevron U.S.A.*, 862 S.W.2d 752, 762 (Tex. App.—El Paso 1993, writ denied).

[106] *See In re Estate of Bateman*, 528 S.W.2d 86, 89 (Tex. Civ. App.—Tyler 1975, writ ref'd n.r.e.).

[107] *See Thelander v. Moore*, 684 S.W.2d 192, 194 (Tex. App.—Houston [14th Dist.] 1984, no writ).

[108] *See Hamman v. Ritchie*, 547 S.W.2d 698, 706 (Tex. Civ. App.—Fort Worth 1977, writ ref'd n.r.e.).

[109] *Richardson v. First Nat. Life Ins. Co.*, 419 S.W.2d 836, 838 (Tex. 1967).

[110] *T.F.W. Mgmt., Inc. v. Westwood Shores Prop. Owners Ass'n*, 79 S.W.3d 712, 717–18 (Tex. App.—Houston [14th Dist.] 2002, pet. denied).

[111] *Richardson v. First Nat. Life Ins. Co.*, 419 S.W.2d 836, 838 (Tex. 1967).

EQUITABLE AND EXTRAORDINARY RELIEF

- However, there must be such complexity within the account(s) that no adequate remedy at law exists.[112]
  - Where parties can obtain adequate relief at law through the use of standard discovery procedures, a trial court does not err in refusing to order an accounting.[113]

(2)(c) Non-mutual accounts

- When the parties have non-mutual accounts is a situation in which a court may order an accounting.[114]
- However, there must be such complexity within the account(s) that no adequate remedy at law exists.[115]
  - When a party can obtain adequate relief at law through the use of standard discovery procedures, a trial court does not err in refusing to order an accounting.[116]

8-4:2.2 Other Grounds for an Accounting

(1) Certain statutes authorize or require an accounting

- Certain statutes authorize an accounting, including but not limited to:
  - Trustees of an express trust;[117]
  - Custodians under the Uniform Transfers to Minors Act;[118]
  - Guardians of the estate of an incapacitated person;[119] and
  - Partners in a business venture.[120]

8-4:3 Damages and Remedies

8-4:3.1 Order Requiring Accounting

The order requiring an accounting is a means of ascertaining the amount or the identity of property one party owes another.[121]

---

[112] *Richardson v. First Nat. Life Ins. Co.*, 419 S.W.2d 836, 838 (Tex. 1967).
[113] *Henry v. Carrington Mortgage Services, LLC*, CV H-18-4414, 2019 WL 2491950, at *4 (S.D. Tex. June 14, 2019).
[114] *Richardson v. First Nat. Life Ins. Co.*, 419 S.W.2d 836, 838 (Tex. 1967).
[115] *Hoodye v. Wells Fargo Bank*, No. 2:12-CV-402, 2013 U.S. Dist. LEXIS 25438, at *4 (S.D. Tex. 2013).
[116] *T.F.W. Mgmt., Inc. v. Westwood Shores Prop. Owners Ass'n*, 79 S.W.3d 712, 717–18 (Tex. App.—Houston [14th Dist.] 2002, pet. denied).
[117] Tex. Prop. Code Ann. § 113.151-.52.
[118] Tex. Prop. Code Ann. § 141.020.
[119] Tex. Est. Code Ann. § 1163.002.
[120] Tex. Bus. Orgs. Code Ann. § 152.211(b) (authorizing partners to maintain an accounting against other partners or the partnership).
[121] *Sw. Livestock & Trucking Co. v. Dooley*, 884 S.W.2d 805, 810 (Tex. App.—San Antonio 1994, writ denied).

Whether a court will grant a request for an accounting is within the court's discretion.[122]

8-4:3.2 Judgment for Payment

A plaintiff must first establish his right to an accounting before a judgment for payment can be rendered.[123]

Final judgment will be entered on the amount determined to be owed by one party to the other.[124]

8-4:3.3 Interest

Prejudgment interest is an appropriate remedy.[125]

8-4:3.4 Attorney's Fees

Attorney's fees are only appropriate if the underlying controversy allows for their recovery.[126]

8-4:4 Defenses

8-4:4.1 Statute of Limitations

The four-year limitations period controls a suit for an accounting between partners.[127]

8-4:4.2 Laches

Laches is an appropriate equitable defense.[128]

8-4:4.3 Unclean Hands

Unclean hands is an appropriate equitable defense.[129]

---

[122] *Williams v. Wells Fargo Bank*, N.A., 560 Fed. Appx. 233, 243 (5th Cir. 2014).

[123] *Ferguson v. Ferguson*, 327 S.W.2d 787, 789 (Tex. Civ. App.—Fort Worth 1959) *rev'd on other grounds*, 338 S.W.2d 945 (Tex. 1960).

[124] *See Ferguson v. Ferguson*, 327 S.W.2d 787, 789 (Tex. Civ. App.—Fort Worth 1959) *rev'd on other grounds*, 338 S.W.2d 945 (Tex. 1960) (making a distinction between the order authorizing an accounting and the final judgment rendered thereon).

[125] *Sauceda v. Kerlin*, 164 S.W.3d 892 (Tex. App.—Corpus Christi 2005) *rev'd on other grounds*, 263 S.W.3d 920 (Tex. 2008).

[126] Tex. Civ. Prac. & Rem. Code Ann. § 38.001.

[127] Tex. Civ. Prac. & Rem. Code Ann. § 16.004(c).

[128] *York Group, Inc. v. York S., Inc.*, CIV.A. H-06-0262, 2006 WL 2883373, at *2 (S.D. Tex. Oct. 10, 2006).

[129] *Shwiff v. Priest*, 650 S.W.2d 894, 903 (Tex. App.—San Antonio 1983, writ ref'd n.r.e.).

EQUITABLE AND EXTRAORDINARY RELIEF

8-4:4.4 Other Equitable Defenses

Other equitable defenses would be appropriate, given the remedy's equitable nature.[130]

8-4:5 Procedural Implications

8-4:5.1 Jurisdiction

A suit for an accounting is to be brought in an appropriate court determined in accordance with the amount in controversy.[131]

- Specifically, the amount in controversy pleaded must be within the jurisdiction of the district court.[132]

8-4:5.2 Appeal of Order Granting or Denying Accounting

Generally, an order granting or denying an accounting is interlocutory in nature and is not appealable.[133]

An order that denies an accounting and disposes of all parties and claims is final and appealable.[134]

8-4:5.3 Abandonment of the Remedy

If the petition for an accounting contains a specific prayer for relief in the form of legal damages, any related claim for an accounting will be deemed to have been abandoned.[135]

8-4:5.4 Separate Trials

A party may move for a separate trial on the issue of whether the plaintiff has a right to an accounting.[136]

8-4:5.5 Appointment of Auditor

- The court shall appoint an auditor when it appears such an appointment is necessary for the purpose of justice between the parties.[137]

---

[130] *See Donnelly v. JP Morgan Chase, NA*, CIV.A. H-13-1376, 2014 WL 429246, at *3 (S.D. Tex. Feb. 4, 2014) (discussing the equitable nature of an accounting); *Richardson v. First Nat. Life Ins. Co.*, 419 S.W.2d 836, 838 (Tex. 1967).

[131] *See Peek v. Equip. Serv. Co. of San Antonio*, 779 S.W.2d 802, 804 (Tex. 1989).

[132] *See Peek v. Equip. Serv. Co. of San Antonio*, 779 S.W.2d 802, 804 (Tex. 1989).

[133] *Estate of Farmer*, 09-18-00314-CV, 2018 WL 5660339 (Tex. App.—Beaumont Nov. 1, 2018, no pet.).

[134] *Estate of Farmer*, 09-18-00314-CV, 2018 WL 5660339, at *1 (Tex. App.—Beaumont Nov. 1, 2018, no pet.) (quoting *Crowson v. Wakeham*, 897 S.W.2d 779, 783 (Tex. 1995)).

[135] *Nortman v. Itex Engery Corp.*, 84 C 421, 1986 WL 9564, at *8 (N.D. Ill. Aug. 26, 1986); *Mamlin v. Fairfield-Noble Corp.*, 433 F. Supp. 317, 319 (N.D. Tex. 1977).

[136] Tex. R. Civ. P. 174(b).

[137] Tex. R. Civ. P. 172.

- The auditor's verified report may be admitted into evidence by either party.[138]
- If neither party objects to specific items in the auditor's report, it serves as conclusive evidence of the account.[139]
    - However, if a party objects to one or more specific items in the report, the report only serves as prima facie evidence and may be rebutted.[140]
- The auditor must be paid a reasonable fee, which is to be taxed as costs of the action.[141]
    - The amount of the auditor's fee must be reasonable in light of the circumstances of the case and the complexity of the audit.[142]

8-5 Constructive Trust

8-5:1 Overview

A constructive trust is an equitable remedy which a plaintiff may utilize when he has been wrongfully deprived of property. The remedy is available when a plaintiff proves that he was wrongfully deprived of property, the defendant was unjustly enriched because of the wrongdoing, and the plaintiff can trace back to the identifiable property which was wrongfully taken from her. The most difficult aspect of obtaining a constructive trust is the element which requires traceability to identifiable property. The law will not impose a constructive trust upon any property which is not wrongfully acquired or commingled with the defendant's own property.

8-5:1.1 Related Causes of Action

Unjust Enrichment, Money had and received, Common Law Fraud, Statutory Fraud, Fraud by Non-disclosure, Breach of Partnership Duty, Officer and Director Liability: Breach of the Duty of Loyalty, Usurpation of Business Opportunity, Attorney Breach of Fiduciary Duty, Breach of Formal Fiduciary Duty, Breach of Informal Fiduciary Duty from Confidential Relationship, Oil and Gas Litigation: Breach of Fiduciary Duty

MUST READ CASES

Wilz v. Flournoy, 228 S.W.3d 674 (Tex. 2007)

KCM Fin. LLC v. Bradshaw, 457 S.W.3d 70 (Tex. 2015)

8-5:2 Elements

(1) A wrong done to the plaintiff[143]

---

[138] Tex. R. Evid. 706.
[139] *Eagle Mfg. Co. v. Hannaway*, 40 S.W. 13, 13-14 (Tex. 1897).
[140] *Eagle Mfg. Co. v. Hannaway*, 40 S.W. 13, 13-14 (Tex. 1897).
[141] Tex. R. Civ. P. 172.
[142] *Villiers v. Republic Fin. Servs., Inc.*, 602 S.W.2d 566, 571 (Tex. Civ. App.—Texarkana 1980, writ ref'd n.r.e.).
[143] *KCM Fin. LLC v. Bradshaw*, 457 S.W.3d 70, 87 (Tex. 2015).

- The defendant must wrong the plaintiff by "breach of a special trust or fiduciary relationship or actual or constructive fraud,"[144] i.e.:
  - Breaching a formal fiduciary duty;[145]
  - Breaching a confidential relationship;[146]
  - Committing actual fraud;[147] or
  - Committing constructive fraud[148]
- A constructive trust may be sought by a plaintiff in any instance where property has been obtained through bad faith.[149] Including, but not limited to the following causes of action:
  - Unjust enrichment;
  - Money had and received;
  - Common Law Fraud, Statutory Fraud;
  - Fraud by Non-disclosure;
  - Breach of Partnership Duty;
  - Officer and Director Liability: Breach of the Duty of Loyalty;
  - Usurpation of Business Opportunity;
  - Attorney Breach of Fiduciary Duty;
  - Breach of Formal Fiduciary Duty;
  - Breach of Informal Fiduciary Duty from Confidential Relationship; and
  - Oil and Gas Litigation: Breach of Fiduciary Duty.

(2) Which results in the unjust enrichment of the wrongdoer[150]
- The defendant must be unjustly enriched because of the wrong done to the plaintiff.[151]

(3) Traceable to identifiable property[152]
- The plaintiff must be able to identify and trace the property which is to be subject to the constructive trust.[153]

---

[144] *KCM Fin. LLC v. Bradshaw*, 457 S.W.3d 70, 87 (Tex. 2015); *Matter of Haber Oil Co., Inc.*, 12 F.3d 426, 437 (5th Cir.1994).

[145] *Lincoln Gen. Ins. Co. v. U.S. Auto Ins. Services, Inc.*, 787 F.3d 716, 728 (5th Cir. 2015) (citing *Meadows v. Bierschwale*, 516 S.W.2d 125, 128 (Tex. 1974)).

[146] *Meadows v. Bierschwale*, 516 S.W.2d 125, 128 (Tex. 1974); *Hubbard v. Shankle*, 138 S.W.3d 474, 485 (Tex. App.—Fort Worth 2004, pet. denied).

[147] *Meadows v. Bierschwale*, 516 S.W.2d 125, 128 (Tex. 1974); *Hubbard v. Shankle*, 138 S.W.3d 474, 485 (Tex. App.—Fort Worth 2004, pet. denied).

[148] *KCM Fin. LLC v. Bradshaw*, 457 S.W.3d 70, 87 (Tex. 2015).

[149] *Kinsel v. Lindsey*, 526 S.W.3d 411, 426 (Tex. 2017).

[150] *KCM Fin. LLC v. Bradshaw*, 457 S.W.3d 70, 87 (Tex. 2015).

[151] *Armstrong v. Armstrong*, 570 S.W.3d 783, 792 (Tex. App.—El Paso 2018, pet. denied).

[152] *KCM Fin. LLC v. Bradshaw*, 457 S.W.3d 70, 87 (Tex. 2015).

[153] *Longview Energy Co. v. Huff Energy Fund LP*, 533 S.W.3d 866, 873 (Tex. 2017).

- The plaintiff may recover from the defendant:
  - The very same property which the plaintiff was wrongfully parted from;[154] or
  - Property which was acquired with the property the plaintiff was wrongfully parted from.[155]
- In order to impose a constructive trust on property which was acquired with the property the plaintiff was wrongfully parted from, the plaintiff must trace such property to the wrongfully acquired property.[156]
- If the plaintiff proves that the defendant commingled its own property with wrongfully acquired property, the plaintiff may impose a constructive trust on either the commingled funds or property acquired with the commingled funds.[157]
  - The defendant may then put on proof that distinguishes between wrongfully acquired property and the defendant's own property.[158]
- If the defendant sells the wrongfully acquired property to a bona fide purchaser, the plaintiff's only option is to seek to impose a constructive trust on the proceeds of the sale.[159]
- If a third party is a knowing or unknowing participant in the defendant's wrongful conduct, the third party is not entitled to retain ownership of the property if the third party is unjustly enriched.[160]

8-5:3 Damages and Remedies

8-5:3.1 Imposition of Constructive Trust

The imposition of a constructive trust generally requires the defendant to convey the wrongfully acquired property to the plaintiff.[161]

The imposition of a constructive trust may also result in:

- The plaintiff and defendant being awarded joint ownership of the property in proportion to the amount of consideration each provided;[162] or
- Imposition of an equitable lien.[163]

---

[154] *KCM Fin. LLC v. Bradshaw*, 457 S.W.3d 70, 87–88 (Tex. 2015).
[155] *See Meadows v. Bierschwale*, 516 S.W.2d 125, 129–30 (Tex. 1974).
[156] *See Meadows v. Bierschwale*, 516 S.W.2d 125, 129–30 (Tex. 1974).
[157] *Sackheim v. Lynch*, CV SA-11-CA-794-FB, 2013 WL 12394007, at *5 (W.D. Tex. Mar. 8, 2013).
[158] *Wilz v. Flournoy*, 228 S.W.3d 674, 676–77 (Tex. 2007).
[159] *Meadows v. Bierschwale*, 516 S.W.2d 125, 129 (Tex. 1974).
[160] *Ginther v. Taub*, 675 S.W.2d 724, 728 (Tex. 1984).
[161] *Talley v. Howsley*, 176 S.W.2d 158, 160 (Tex. 1943).
[162] *Parr v. Duval Cty.*, 304 S.W.2d 957, 958–59 (Tex. Civ. App.—Eastland 1957, writ ref'd n.r.e.).
[163] *Meadows v. Bierschwale*, 516 S.W.2d 125, 129 (Tex. 1974).

EQUITABLE AND EXTRAORDINARY RELIEF

8-5:3.2 Scope of Constructive Trust

Generally, the scope of the constructive trust is left to the discretion of the court.[164] However, a constructive trust must not place the plaintiff in a more advantageous position than he would have been if the plaintiff had not been wronged.[165] A constructive trust must not be used as a means of completely defeating the statute of frauds.[166]

8-5:3.3 Exemplary Damages

Even if no actual damages are awarded, the plaintiff may recover exemplary damages if the conduct which necessitates the imposition of a constructive trust is sufficiently culpable.[167]

8-5:4 Defenses

8-5:4.1 Statute of Limitations

The applicable limitations period is determined by the type of property which is to be subject to the constructive trust.[168]

If the property which is to be subject to the constructive trust is personal property, the applicable limitations period is:

- Four years.[169]

If the property which is to be subject to the constructive trust is real property, the applicable limitations period is:

- Three years;[170]
- Five years;[171]
- 10 years;[172] or
- 25 years.[173]

The limitations period accrues when the alleged wrongful act affects an injury.[174]

---

[164] *Everett v. TK-Taito, L.L.C.*, 178 S.W.3d 844, 859 (Tex. App.—Fort Worth 2005, no pet.).

[165] *Placer Energy Corp. v. E & S Oil Co., Inc.*, 692 S.W.2d 197, 200 (Tex. App.—Fort Worth 1985, no writ).

[166] *Tyra v. Woodson*, 495 S.W.2d 211, 213 (Tex. 1973).

[167] *Lesikar v. Rappeport*, 33 S.W.3d 282, 310 (Tex. App.—Texarkana 2000, pet. denied); *see Int'l Bankers Life Ins. Co. v. Holloway*, 368 S.W.2d 567, 584 (Tex. 1963).

[168] Angus McSwain, *Limitations Statutes and the Constructive Trust in Texas*, 41 Baylor L. Rev. 429, 436–37 (1989).

[169] Tex. Civ. Prac. & Rem. Code Ann. § 16.051; *In re Estate of Melchior*, 365 S.W.3d 794, 798–801 (Tex. App.—San Antonio 2012, pet. denied).

[170] Tex. Civ. Prac. & Rem. Code Ann. § 16.024 (defendant's possession under color of title).

[171] Tex. Civ. Prac. & Rem. Code Ann. § 16.024 (defendant's possession plus other acts indicating legal ownership).

[172] Tex. Civ. Prac. & Rem. Code Ann. § 16.024 (defendant's bare possession).

[173] Tex. Civ. Prac. & Rem. Code Ann. § 16.024 (statute of repose).

[174] *York v. Boatman*, 487 S.W.3d 635, 647 (Tex. App.—Texarkana 2016, no pet.); *In re Estate of Melchior*, 365 S.W.3d 794, 799 (Tex. App.—San Antonio 2012, pet. denied).

The discovery rule applies.[175]

A plaintiff may impose a constructive trust even if the applicable statute of limitations for legal damages has run.[176]

8-5:4.2 Laches

Laches is an applicable affirmative defense.[177]

8-5:4.3 Other Equitable Defenses

Other equitable defenses would be appropriate, given the remedy's equitable nature.[178]

8-6 Sequestration

8-6:1 Overview

Sequestration is a statutorily created remedy that has no basis in the common law. The remedy is purely ancillary, in that there must be an underlying lawsuit pending in order for a court to issue a writ of sequestration. Sequestration is generally only available to secured creditors, but certain other claimants or unsecured creditors may pursue sequestration as well. As a summary proceeding, a plaintiff seeking to obtain a writ of sequestration must strictly comply with the statutes and rules governing the remedy. Such a writ may only be issued after a suit is filed but before judgment is rendered. Once the plaintiff has obtained a writ of sequestration, the sheriff or constable takes possession of the property to preserve it pending the outcome of the underlying litigation.

8-6:1.1 Related Causes of Action

Garnishment, Attachment, Receivership, Injunction: Temporary

8-6:2 Elements

(1) The underlying lawsuit is for title to real property

- The underlying lawsuit is:
  - For title to real property.[179]

(2) Specific grounds for sequestration exist.

- Specific grounds for sequestration exist:

---

[175] *In re Estate of Melchior*, 365 S.W.3d 794, 799 (Tex. App.—San Antonio 2012, pet. denied).
[176] *Austin Lake Estates, Inc. v. Meyer*, 557 S.W.2d 380, 383 (Tex. Civ. App.—Austin 1977, no writ).
[177] *Culver v. Pickens*, 176 S.W.2d 167, 170–71 (Tex. 1943).
[178] *KCM Fin. LLC v. Bradshaw*, 457 S.W.3d 70, 87–8 (Tex. 2015).
[179] Tex. Civ. Prac. & Rem. Code Ann. § 62.001(1)–(3).

- The plaintiff has previously been ejected from the property by force or violence;[180]
- A reasonable conclusion may be drawn that there is immediate danger that the defendant or the party in possession of the property will conceal, dispose of, ill-treat, waste, or destroy the property or remove it from the county during the suit;[181] or
- A reasonable conclusion may be drawn that there is immediate danger that the defendant or the party in possession of the property will use his possession to injure or ill-treat the property or waste or convert to his own use the timber, rents, fruits or revenue of the property.[182]

Or

(1) The underlying lawsuit is for possession of real property or fixtures or foreclosure or enforcement of a mortgage or lien on real property.

- The underlying lawsuit is:
  - For possession of real property or fixtures;[183] or
  - For foreclosure or enforcement of a mortgage or lien on real property.[184]

(2) Specific grounds for sequestration exist.

- Specific grounds for sequestration exist:
  - A reasonable conclusion may be drawn that there is immediate danger that the defendant or the party in possession of the property will use his possession to injure or ill-treat the property or waste or convert to his own use the timber, rents, fruits or revenue of the property.

Or

(1) The underlying lawsuit is for foreclosure or enforcement of a mortgage, lien or security interest on personal property or fixtures

- The underlying lawsuit is
  - For foreclosure or enforcement of a mortgage, lien or security interest on personal property or fixtures.[185]

(2) Specific grounds for sequestration exist

- Specific grounds for sequestration exist:
  - A reasonable conclusion may be drawn that there is immediate danger that the defendant or the party in possession of the property will conceal,

---

[180] Tex. Civ. Prac. & Rem. Code Ann. § 62.001(3).
[181] Tex. Civ. Prac. & Rem. Code Ann. § 62.001(1).
[182] Tex. Civ. Prac. & Rem. Code Ann. § 62.001(2).
[183] Tex. Civ. Prac. & Rem. Code Ann. § 62.001(1).
[184] Tex. Civ. Prac. & Rem. Code Ann. § 62.001(1).
[185] Tex. Civ. Prac. & Rem. Code Ann. § 62.001(2).

dispose of, ill-treat, waste, or destroy the property or remove it from the county during the suit.[186]

Or

(1) The underlying lawsuit is to try title to real property, to remove a cloud from the title of real property, to foreclose a lien on real property, or to partition real property

- The underlying lawsuit is:
  - To try title to real property;[187]
  - To remove a cloud from the title of real property;[188]
  - To foreclose a lien on real property;[189] or
  - To partition real property.[190]

(2) Specific grounds for sequestration exist

- Specific grounds for sequestration exist:
  - The plaintiff makes an oath that one or more of the defendants is a non-resident of this state.[191]

8-6:3 Damages and Remedies

8-6:3.1 Issuance of the Writ

The plaintiff may obtain a writ of sequestration from a district or county court judge or a justice of the peace.[192]

The writ of sequestration must:

- Prominently display a statement of the defendant's rights;[193]
- A description of the property to be sequestered;[194] and
- The value of the property to be sequestered.[195]

---

[186] Tex. Civ. Prac. & Rem. Code Ann. § 62.001(1).
[187] Tex. Civ. Prac. & Rem. Code Ann. § 62.001(4).
[188] Tex. Civ. Prac. & Rem. Code Ann. § 62.001(4).
[189] Tex. Civ. Prac. & Rem. Code Ann. § 62.001(4).
[190] Tex. Civ. Prac. & Rem. Code Ann. § 62.001(4).
[191] Tex. Civ. Prac. & Rem. Code Ann. § 62.001(4).
[192] Tex. Civ. Prac. & Rem. Code Ann. § 62.021.
[193] Tex. Civ. Prac. & Rem. Code Ann. § 62.023.
[194] See Tex. R. Civ. P. 699 (requiring the writ of sequestration to describe the property as it is described in the application or affidavit supporting the application).
[195] See Tex. R. Civ. P. 699.

EQUITABLE AND EXTRAORDINARY RELIEF

8-6:3.2 Levy upon the Writ

The sheriff or constable must be required to take possession of the property to be sequestered.[196]

8-6:3.3 Sale of Perishable Personal Property

Either the plaintiff or defendant may compel the sale of perishable goods likely to be wasted, destroyed, or depreciated if:

- 10 days have elapsed from the levy upon the writ of sequestration;
- Either party makes an affidavit in writing that the property levied upon, or any portion thereof, is likely to be wasted or destroyed or greatly depreciated in value by keeping; and
- The sheriff or constable certifies the truth of the party's affidavit.[197]

8-6:3.4 Plaintiff May Reply

The plaintiff may replevy the property from the sheriff or constable's possession if:

- 10 days have elapsed since the levy upon the writ of sequestration; and
- The plaintiff executes a bond payable to the defendant.[198]

8-6:4 Defenses

8-6:4.1 Defendant's Replevy Bond

If the defendant loses the underlying lawsuit, final judgment shall include a provision holding the defendant and sureties jointly and severally liable for the value of the property as of the date of the bond's execution, plus the value of the property's fruits, hire, revenue or rent.[199]

8-6:4.2 Failure to Strictly Comply with Statutes

A plaintiff seeking a writ of sequestration must strictly comply with both the statutes and rules governing attachments.[200]

8-6:4.3 Exemption from Execution

If the plaintiff has a security interest in the property, the defendant may not assert any exemption.[201]

---

[196] Tex. R. Civ. P. 699.
[197] Tex. R. Civ. P. 710.
[198] Tex. R. Civ. P. 708.
[199] Tex. R. Civ. P. 704.
[200] *Musterman v. Acme Engine Rebuilding Co.*, 383 S.W.2d 620, 622 (Tex. Civ. App.—Houston 1964).
[201] Tex. Prop. Code Ann. § 42.001(c) (secured creditors of personal property are not subject to any exemptions); Tex. Prop. Code Ann. § 41.001 (certain types of liens may be fixed upon

If the defendant is able to assert exemptions, property that is exempt from sequestration includes:

- Homestead property;[202]
- Certain personal property;[203]
- Certain money owed to original contractors or subcontractors;[204]
- Money owed under certain types of retirement, pension or savings plans;[205]

8-6:5 Procedural Implications

8-6:5.1 Sworn Application

An application for a writ of attachment must be supported by affidavits.[206]

The application must set out:

- The specific facts stating the nature of the plaintiff's claim;
- The amount in controversy, if any; and
- The facts justifying issuance of the writ.[207]

The application must also set out:

- A description of the property to be sequestered;[208] and
- The value of the property to be sequestered.[209]

8-6:5.2 Posting of Bond

A plaintiff must post a bond before obtaining a writ of sequestration.[210]

The bond must be:

- Made payable to the defendant;[211]
- In an amount fixed by the court;[212]
- With sufficient sureties;[213] and

---

homestead property, thereby rendering such plaintiff outside of the scope of the homestead exemption).

[202] Tex. Prop. Code Ann. § 41.001.
[203] Tex. Prop. Code Ann. § 42.001.
[204] Tex. Prop. Code Ann. § 53.151.
[205] Tex. Prop. Code Ann. § 42.0021.
[206] Tex. Civ. Prac. & Rem. Code Ann. § 62.022; Tex. R. Civ. P. 696.
[207] Tex. Civ. Prac. & Rem. Code Ann. § 62.022.
[208] Tex. R. Civ. P. 696.
[209] Tex. R. Civ. P. 696.
[210] Tex. R. Civ. P. 592a; Tex. Civ. Prac. & Rem. Code Ann. § 61.023.
[211] Tex. R. Civ. P. 698.
[212] Tex. R. Civ. P. 698.
[213] Tex. R. Civ. P. 698; Tex. Ins. Code Ann. § 3503.002 (bond executed by a surety company is "sufficient.").

EQUITABLE AND EXTRAORDINARY RELIEF

- Conditioned on the fact that the plaintiff will prosecute his suit to effect and pay to the extent of the penal amount of the bond all damages and costs as may be adjudged against him for wrongfully suing out such writ of sequestration.[214]

The amount of the bond may be increased or reduced.[215]

8-6:5.3 Ex Parte Relief

A plaintiff may obtain a writ of sequestration in an *ex parte* hearing.[216]

8-6:5.4 Service

Service of the writ of sequestration is a separate undertaking from the levy upon the writ.[217]

Service of the writ on the defendant is to be accomplished in the manner for serving citation or as prescribed under Rule 21a the Texas Rules of Civil Procedure.[218]

8-6:5.5 Joinder of Parties

When there is more than one plaintiff in the underlying lawsuit, a single plaintiff acting alone may apply for a writ of sequestration.[219]

8-6:5.6 Amendment

Clerical errors in the affidavit, bond or writ of sequestration may be amended if:

- The amendment does not change or add to the grounds for sequestration stated in the affidavit; and
- The amendment is in the furtherance of justice.[220]

8-6:5.7 Dissolution or Modification of the Writ

A defendant or interested third party may seek to dissolve or modify the writ of sequestration by submitting a sworn, written motion.[221]

The writ of sequestration will dissolve unless the plaintiff proves the grounds for the writ's issuance.[222]

---

[214] Tex. R. Civ. P. 698a.
[215] Tex. R. Civ. P. 698.
[216] Tex. R. Civ. P. 696.
[217] *See* Tex. R. Civ. P. 699, 700a (different rules and procedures for levy upon and service of the writ).
[218] Tex. R. Civ. P. 700a.
[219] *Lindsey v. Williams*, 228 S.W.2d 243, 250 (Tex. Civ. App.—Texarkana 1950, no writ). (Compare to the rule requiring joinder of all plaintiffs for an application for a writ of attachment; *see Haley v. Pearson*, 14 S.W.2d 313, 315 (Tex. Civ. App.—Dallas 1929, no writ)).
[220] Tex. R. Civ. P. 700.
[221] Tex. R. Civ. P. 712a.
[222] Tex. R. Civ. P. 712a.

The court may modify the writ of sequestration even if the plaintiff makes the proper proof.[223]

The movant has the burden of establishing that the value of the sequestered property exceeds the combined amount of the debt, interest for one year, and probable costs.[224]

8-7 Attachment

8-7:1 Overview

A proceeding to obtain a writ of attachment is ancillary to a pending lawsuit and is essentially a prejudgment execution on property; in Texas, the writ of attachment is purely of statutory origin.[225] Such a writ may only be issued after a suit is filed but before judgment is rendered.[226] The extraordinary remedy of attachment is purely statutory and is therefore strictly construed.[227]

8-7:1.1 Related Causes of Action

Garnishment, Sequestration, Receivership, Injunction: Temporary

8-7:2 Elements[228]

(1) The defendant is justly indebted to the plaintiff.[229]

- For resident defendants, the debt must be:
  - Liquidated, as opposed to contingent;
  - Based upon an express or implied contract; and
  - Not based upon debt arising from tort liability.[230]
- For defendants whom personal service cannot be accomplished:
  - The debt could be based on contract, tort or another unliquidated debt.[231]

(2) The attachment is not sought for the purpose of injuring or harassing the defendant.[232]

(3) The plaintiff will probably lose his debt unless the writ of attachment is issued.[233]

---

[223] Tex. R. Civ. P. 712a.
[224] Tex. R. Civ. P. 712a.
[225] *E.E. Maxwell Co. v. Arti Decor, Ltd.*, 638 F. Supp. 749, 753 (N.D. Tex. 1986).
[226] Tex. Civ. Prac. & Rem. Code Ann. § 61.003.
[227] *E.E. Maxwell Co. v. Arti Decor, Ltd.*, 638 F. Supp. 749, 753 (N.D. Tex. 1986).
[228] *See 3 Kids, Inc. v. Am. Jewel, LLC*, 3:18-MC-096-S (BH), 2019 WL 462781, at *2 (N.D. Tex. Jan. 15, 2019).
[229] Tex. Civ. Prac. & Rem. Code Ann. § 61.001(1).
[230] *Cleveland v. San Antonio Bldg. & Loan Ass'n*, 223 S.W.2d 226, 228–29 (Tex. 1949).
[231] Tex. Civ. Prac. & Rem. Code Ann. § 61.005.
[232] Tex. Civ. Prac. & Rem. Code Ann. § 61.001(2).
[233] Tex. Civ. Prac. & Rem. Code Ann. § 61.001(3).

EQUITABLE AND EXTRAORDINARY RELIEF

(4) Specific grounds for the writ exist.[234] There are nine listed specific grounds, but a plaintiff need only satisfy one.[235]

(4)(a) The defendant is not a resident of this state or is a foreign corporation or is acting as such;[236]

(4)(b) The defendant is about to move from this state permanently and has refused to pay or secure the debt due the plaintiff;[237]

(4)(c) The defendant is in hiding so that ordinary process of law cannot be served on him;[238]

(4)(d) The defendant has hidden or is about to hide his property for the purpose of defrauding his creditors;[239]

(4)(e) The defendant is about to remove his property from this state without leaving an amount sufficient to pay his debts;[240]

(4)(f) The defendant is about to remove all or part of his property from the county in which the suit is brought with the intent to defraud his creditors;[241]

(4)(g) The defendant has disposed of or is about to dispose of all or part of his property with the intent to defraud his creditors;[242]

(4)(h) The defendant is about to convert all or part of his property into money for the purpose of placing it beyond the reach of his creditors;[243]

(4)(i) The defendant owes the plaintiff for property obtained by the defendant under false pretenses[244] and the plaintiff must have relied upon the false pretenses.[245]

8-7:3 Damages and Remedies

8-7:3.1 Issuance of the Writ

The plaintiff may obtain a writ of attachment.[246]

The following form of writ may be issued:

"The State of Texas. To the Sheriff or any Constable of any County of the State of Texas, greeting: "We command you that you attach forthwith so much of the property of C. D., if it be found in your county, repleviable on security, as shall

---

[234] Tex. Civ. Prac. & Rem. Code Ann. § 61.001(4).
[235] *3 Kids, Inc. v. Am. Jewel, LLC*, 3:18-MC-096-S (BH), 2019 WL 462781, at *2 (N.D. Tex. Jan. 15, 2019).
[236] Tex. Civ. Prac. & Rem. Code Ann. § 61.002(1).
[237] Tex. Civ. Prac. & Rem. Code Ann. § 61.002(2).
[238] Tex. Civ. Prac. & Rem. Code Ann. § 61.002(3).
[239] Tex. Civ. Prac. & Rem. Code Ann. § 61.002(4).
[240] Tex. Civ. Prac. & Rem. Code Ann. § 61.002(5).
[241] Tex. Civ. Prac. & Rem. Code Ann. § 61.002(6).
[242] Tex. Civ. Prac. & Rem. Code Ann. § 61.002(7).
[243] Tex. Civ. Prac. & Rem. Code Ann. § 61.002(8).
[244] Tex. Civ. Prac. & Rem. Code Ann. § 61.002(9).
[245] *Gray & Wallace v. Steedman Bros.*, 63 Tex. 95, 99 (1885).
[246] Tex. Civ. Prac. & Rem. Code Ann. § 61.021; Tex. R. Civ. P. 594.

be of value sufficient to make the sum of _____ dollars, and the probable costs of suit, to satisfy the demand of A. B., and that you keep and secure in your hands the property so attached, unless replevied, that the same may be liable to further proceedings thereon to be had before our court in _____, County of _____. You will true return make of this writ on or before 10 a. m. of Monday, the _____ day of _____, 20___, showing how you have executed the same."[247]

8-7:3.2 Levy upon the Writ

The sheriff or constable may levy upon the writ in the same way that the sheriff or constable would levy upon a writ of execution.[248]

8-7:3.3 Sale of Perishable Personal Property

A plaintiff may submit an application to sell attached property if the attached property is perishable personal property.[249]

8-7:3.4 Costs and Interest

The plaintiff may recover costs and interest if:

- The plaintiff is successful in the underlying action and the defendant has replevied the property;[250]

8-7:4 Defenses

8-7:4.1 Replevy Bond

The defendant may replevy attached property.[251]

8-7:4.2 Failure to Strictly Comply with Statutes

A plaintiff seeking a writ of attachment must strictly comply with both the statutes and rules governing attachments.[252]

Substantial compliance (generally found when there has been a typographical error or small omission) is sufficient.[253]

---

[247] Tex. R. Civ. P. 594.
[248] Tex. R. Civ. P. 598.
[249] Tex. R. Civ. P. 600.
[250] Tex. Civ. Prac. & Rem. Code Ann. § 61.063.
[251] Tex. R. Civ. P. 599.
[252] *In re Warrior Energy Services Corp.*, 14-19-01010-CV, 2020 WL 1679344 (Tex. App.—Houston [14th Dist.] Apr. 7, 2020).
[253] *Jewett State Bank v. Evans*, 129 S.W.2d 1202, 1203 (Tex. Civ. App.—Waco 1939, no writ).

8-7:4.3 Exemption from Execution

A defendant may assert that the property is exempt from attachment because it is exempted from execution.[254]

Property that is exempt from attachment includes:

- Homestead property;[255]
- Certain personal property;[256]
- Certain money owed to original contractors or subcontractors;[257]
- Money owed under certain types of retirement, pension or savings plans;[258]
- Property acquired after the levy of a writ of attachment is not subject to the writ of attachment.[259]

8-7:5 Procedural Implications

8-7:5.1 Sworn Application

A plaintiff may only obtain a writ of attachment via a written application supported by affidavit.[260]

8-7:5.2 Posting of Bond

A plaintiff must post a bond before obtaining a writ of attachment.[261]

The bond must be:

- Made payable to the defendant;[262]
- In an amount fixed by the court;[263]
- With two or more sureties;[264] and
- Conditioned on the fact that the plaintiff will prosecute his suit to effect and pay to the extent of the penal amount of the bond all damages and costs as may be adjudged against him for wrongfully suing out such writ of attachment.[265]

The amount of the bond may be increased or reduced.[266]

---

[254] Tex. Civ. Prac. & Rem. Code Ann. § 61.041.
[255] Tex. Prop. Code Ann. § 41.001.
[256] Tex. Prop. Code Ann. § 42.001.
[257] Tex. Prop. Code Ann. § 53.151.
[258] Tex. Prop. Code Ann. § 42.0021.
[259] *Texas Oil & Gas Corp. v. U.S.*, 466 F.2d 1040, 1047–48 (5th Cir. 1972).
[260] Tex. R. Civ. P. 592; Tex. Civ. Prac. & Rem. Code Ann. § 61.022.
[261] Tex. R. Civ. P. 592a; Tex. Civ. Prac. & Rem. Code Ann. § 61.023.
[262] Tex. R. Civ. P. 592a; Tex. Civ. Prac. & Rem. Code Ann. § 61.023.
[263] Tex. R. Civ. P. 592a; Tex. Civ. Prac. & Rem. Code Ann. § 61.023.
[264] Tex. R. Civ. P. 592a; Tex. Civ. Prac. & Rem. Code Ann. § 61.023.
[265] Tex. R. Civ. P. 592a; Tex. Civ. Prac. & Rem. Code Ann. § 61.023.
[266] Tex. R. Civ. P. 592a.

Defects in bonds are not fundamental or jurisdictional and must be objected to.[267]

8-7:5.3 Ex Parte Relief

A plaintiff may obtain a writ of attachment in an ex parte hearing.[268]

8-7:5.4 Service

Service of the writ of attachment is a separate undertaking from levying upon the writ.[269]

Service of the writ on the defendant is to be accomplished in the manner for serving citation or as prescribed under Rule 21a of the Texas Rules of Civil Procedure.[270]

8-7:5.5 Joinder of Parties

A plaintiff must be the sole owner of the debt in order to solely sue for attachment.[271]

If there are joint payees on the debt, all of the joint payees must join in the application to obtain a writ of attachment.[272]

8-7:5.6 Amendment

Either party may amend clerical errors in the affidavit, bond, writ of attachment or the officer's return of the writ of attachment by:

- Submitting a written application to the judge of the court where the suit is filed;
- Providing notice to the opponent;
- Establishing the amendment to be in the furtherance of justice; and
- Obtaining an order entered into the minutes of court.[273]

Failure to strictly follow the procedures outlined in Rule 609 renders the writ of attachment void.[274]

8-7:5.7 Dissolution or Modification of the Writ

A defendant or interested third party may seek to dissolve or modify the writ of attachment by submitting a sworn, written motion.[275]

---

[267] *Smith v. Miller*, 298 S.W.2d 845, 847 (Tex. Civ. App.—Galveston 1957, writ ref'd n.r.e.).
[268] Tex. R. Civ. P. 592.
[269] *See* Tex. R. Civ. P. 598–598a (different rules and procedures for levy upon and service of the writ).
[270] Tex. R. Civ. P. 598a.
[271] *See Haley v. Pearson*, 14 S.W.2d 313, 315 (Tex. Civ. App.—Dallas 1929, no writ).
[272] *Haley v. Pearson*, 14 S.W.2d 313, 315 (Tex. Civ. App.—Dallas 1929, no writ).
[273] Tex. R. Civ. P. 609.
[274] *Carpenter v. Carpenter*, 476 S.W.2d 469, 470 (Tex. Civ. App.—Dallas 1972, no writ).
[275] Tex. R. Civ. P. 608.

EQUITABLE AND EXTRAORDINARY RELIEF

The writ of attachment will dissolve unless the plaintiff proves the grounds for the writ's issuance.[276]

The court may modify the writ of attachment even if the plaintiff makes the proper proof.[277]

The movant has the burden of establishing that the value of the attached property exceeds the combined amount of the debt, interest for one year, and probable costs.[278]

8-7:5.8 Third-Party Claimants

Because third parties may make a claim to the attached property and have priority over the plaintiff, a plaintiff should not elect the remedy of attachment unless there is equity in the property.[279]

8-8 Garnishment

8-8:1 Overview

Garnishment is a statutory proceeding[280] which is governed by neither the common law[281] nor equitable principles.[282] A garnishment proceeding involves three parties, the plaintiff or garnishor, the defendant, and the third-party or garnishee.[283] The plaintiff seeks to obtain payment on the defendant's debt by suing the third party.[284] This is allowed because the third party must be indebted to the defendant.[285] A writ of garnishment may be obtained either prejudgment or post-judgment.[286]

8-8:1.1 Related Causes of Action

Attachment, Sequestration, Receivership

8-8:2 Elements

8-8:2.1 Prejudgment Garnishment

(1) Grounds for garnishment exist:

- The plaintiff must establish that the statutory grounds for garnishment exist.[287]

---

[276] Tex. R. Civ. P. 608.
[277] Tex. R. Civ. P. 608.
[278] Tex. R. Civ. P. 608.
[279] *See* Tex. Civ. Prac. & Rem. Code Ann. § 61.044.
[280] *Bank One, Tex., N.A. v. Sunbelt Sav.*, F.S.B., 824 S.W.2d 557, 558 (Tex. 1992).
[281] *Walnut Equip. Leasing Co. v. J-V Dirt & Loam, a Div. of J-V Marble Mfg., Inc.*, 907 S.W.2d 912, 915 (Tex. App.—Austin 1995, writ denied).
[282] *Smith v. Rogers*, 147 S.W.2d 934, 935 (Tex. Civ. App.—San Antonio 1941, no writ).
[283] 17 Tex. Jur. 3d Creditors' Rights and Remedies § 349.
[284] 17 Tex. Jur. 3d Creditors' Rights and Remedies § 349.
[285] 17 Tex. Jur. 3d Creditors' Rights and Remedies § 349.
[286] *See* Tex. Civ. Prac. & Rem. Code Ann. § 63.001.
[287] Tex. Civ. Prac. & Rem. Code Ann. § 63.001; *Fogel v. White*, 745 S.W.2d 444, 446 (Tex. App.—Houston [14th Dist.] 1988, no writ).

(1) (a) A plaintiff sues for a debt

- The plaintiff must sue on a debt that is:
    - Liquidated, meaning a debt that is not contingent, is capable of ascertainment by the usual means of evidence, and does not rest in the discretion of the jury.[288]
- A tort action may never be the basis of a prejudgment garnishment.[289]

(1) (a) (i) The debt is just, due and unpaid

- The debt is just, due and unpaid.[290]
- The plaintiff must swear to this fact in an affidavit accompanying the petition.[291]

(1) (a) (ii) Within the plaintiff's knowledge, the defendant does not possess property in Texas subject to execution sufficient to satisfy the debt

- Within the plaintiff's knowledge, the defendant does not possess property in Texas subject to execution sufficient to satisfy the debt.[292]
- The plaintiff must swear to this fact in an affidavit accompanying the petition.[293]

(1) (a) (iii) The garnishment is not sought to injure the defendant or the garnishee

- The garnishment is not sought to injure the defendant or the garnishee.[294]
- The plaintiff must swear to this fact in an affidavit accompanying the petition.[295]

(1) (b) An original attachment has been issued

- An original attachment has been issued.[296]
- In suing for garnishment on an original attachment, the attachment does not need to be returned before the writ of garnishment is issued.[297]
- A writ of garnishment issued based upon a writ of attachment is dependent upon that writ of attachment. If the writ of attachment is dissolved, the writ of garnishment must also be dissolved.[298]

---

[288] *Albright v. Regions Bank*, 13-08-262-CV, 2009 WL 3489853, at *2 (Tex. App.—Corpus Christi 2009, no pet.).

[289] *Albright v. Regions Bank*, 13-08-262-CV, 2009 WL 3489853, at *2 (Tex. App.—Corpus Christi 2009, no pet.).

[290] Tex. Civ. Prac. & Rem. Code Ann. § 63.001(2)(A).

[291] Tex. Civ. Prac. & Rem. Code Ann. § 63.001(2).

[292] Tex. Civ. Prac. & Rem. Code Ann. § 63.001(2)(B).

[293] Tex. Civ. Prac. & Rem. Code Ann. § 63.001(2).

[294] Tex. Civ. Prac. & Rem. Code Ann. § 63.001(2)(C).

[295] Tex. Civ. Prac. & Rem. Code Ann. § 63.001(2).

[296] Tex. Civ. Prac. & Rem. Code Ann. § 63.001(2).

[297] Tex. R. Civ. P. 606; *E.L. Wilson Hardware Co. v. Anderson Knife & Bar Co.*, 54 S.W. 928, 929 (Tex. Civ. App. 1899, writ ref'd).

[298] *Gill v. Oak Cliff Bank & Trust Co.*, 331 S.W.2d 832, 834 (Tex. Civ. App.—Amarillo 1959, no writ).

8-8:2.2 Post-judgment Garnishment

(1) Grounds for garnishment exist

- The plaintiff must establish that the statutory grounds for garnishment exist.[299]

(1) (a) A plaintiff has a judgment against the defendant and the defendant does not possess property in Texas subject to execution sufficient to satisfy the judgment

- The plaintiff must have a final, valid and subsisting judgment against the defendant.[300]
    - Unlike the word "debt" in prejudgment garnishment, this judgment may be based upon any cause of action.[301]
    - A judgment is final when it has been signed, unless the defendant files a supersedeas bond.[302]
- The plaintiff must submit an affidavit which states, to the best of the plaintiff's knowledge, the defendant does not possess property in Texas subject to execution sufficient to satisfy the judgment.[303]

8-8:3 Damages and Remedies

8-8:3.1 Issuance of the Writ

A plaintiff may obtain a writ of garnishment.[304]

The writ of garnishment must:

- Be in the form mandated by TRCP 661.[305]
- State the amount which is to be recoverable from the garnishee;[306]
- Command the garnishee to appear in court;[307] and
- Command the garnishee to refrain from paying the defendant any indebtedness.[308]

---

[299] Tex. Civ. Prac. & Rem. Code Ann. § 63.001; *Fogel v. White*, 745 S.W.2d 444, 446 (Tex. App.—Houston [14th Dist.] 1988, no writ).
[300] Tex. Civ. Prac. & Rem. Code Ann. § 63.001(3).
[301] Tex. R. Civ. P. 657.
[302] Tex. R. Civ. P. 657.
[303] Tex. Civ. Prac. & Rem. Code Ann. § 63.001(3).
[304] Tex. R. Civ. P. 661.
[305] Tex. R. Civ. P. 661.
[306] Tex. R. Civ. P. 661.
[307] Tex. R. Civ. P. 661.
[308] Tex. R. Civ. P. 661.

8-8:3.2 Execution on the Writ

The sheriff or constable must execute the writ of garnishment by delivering a copy of the writ to the garnishee.[309] The garnishee will ultimately be required to liquidate any of the defendant's assets which it holds and make payment to the plaintiff.[310] The amount of the payment may not exceed the amount of the plaintiff's judgment.[311]

8-8:3.3 Costs and Interest

If a default judgment is entered against the garnishee:

- The court may award the plaintiff all interest and costs which have accrued in both the garnishment proceeding and the underlying proceeding.[312]

If the garnishee owes the defendant more than the amount of the garnishment judgment:

- The court may award the plaintiff all interest and costs which have accrued in both the garnishment proceeding and the underlying proceeding.[313]

If the garnishee owes the defendant less than the amount of the garnishment judgment:

- The court may only enter an award for the amount the garnishee owes to the defendant.[314]

8-8:4 Defenses

8-8:4.1 Replevy Bond

A defendant may execute a replevy bond in order to obtain possession of the property which has been or will be garnished.[315]

8-8:4.2 Failure to Strictly Comply with Statutes

A court may not issue a writ of garnishment unless the plaintiff has strictly complied with statutory requirements.[316]

8-8:4.3 Validity of Underlying Judgment

The judgment underlying a writ of garnishment must be valid.[317]

---

[309] Tex. R. Civ. P. 663.
[310] Tex. R. Civ. P. 669.
[311] Tex. R. Civ. P. 669.
[312] Tex. R. Civ. P. 667.
[313] Tex. R. Civ. P. 668.
[314] Tex. R. Civ. P. 668; *Vick v. Merchants' Fast Motor Lines*, 151 S.W.2d 293, 297 (Tex. Civ. App.—Eastland 1941, no writ).
[315] Tex. R. Civ. P. 664.
[316] *Marsoft, Inc. v. United LNG, L.P.*, CIV.A. H-13-2332, 2014 WL 5386094, at *9 (S.D. Tex. Oct. 21, 2014).
[317] Tex. Civ. Prac. & Rem. Code Ann. § 63.001(3).

EQUITABLE AND EXTRAORDINARY RELIEF

Only the defendant may challenge the validity of the underlying judgment.[318]

8-8:4.4 Exemption from Execution

A garnishee or defendant may assert that the property is exempt from garnishment.[319]

Property that is exempt from garnishment includes:

- Current wages for personal services;[320]
- Homestead property;[321]
- Certain personal property;[322]
- Certain money owed to original contractors or subcontractors;[323] and
- Money owed under certain types of retirement, pension or savings plans.[324]

8-8:4.5 Setoff

The garnishee may set-off any amount the defendant owes the garnishee.[325]

8-8:5 Procedural Implications

8-8:5.1 Posting of Bond

A plaintiff must post a bond before obtaining a prejudgment writ of attachment.[326]

The bond must be:

- Made payable to the defendant;[327]
- In an amount fixed by the court;[328]
- With adequate surety or sureties;[329] and
- Conditioned on the fact that the plaintiff will prosecute his suit to effect and pay to the extent of the penal amount of the bond all damages and costs as may be adjudged against him for wrongfully suing out such writ of garnishment.[330]

---

[318] *Zeecon Wireless Internet, LLC v. Am. Bank of Tex., N.A.*, 305 S.W.3d 813, 818 (Tex. App.—Austin 2010).

[319] *General Elec. Capital Corp. v. ICO, Inc.*, 230 S.W.3d 702, 705 (Tex. App.—Houston [14th Dist.] 2007, pet. denied).

[320] Tex. Const. art. XVI, § 28.

[321] Tex. Prop. Code Ann. § 41.001.

[322] Tex. Prop. Code Ann. § 42.001.

[323] Tex. Prop. Code Ann. § 53.151.

[324] Tex. Prop. Code Ann. § 42.0021.

[325] *See First Nat. Bank of Fabens v. Pac. Cotton Agency*, 329 S.W.2d 504, 505 (Tex. Civ. App.—San Antonio 1959, no writ).

[326] Tex. R. Civ. P. 658a.

[327] Tex. R. Civ. P. 658a.

[328] Tex. R. Civ. P. 658a.

[329] Tex. R. Civ. P. 658a.

[330] Tex. R. Civ. P. 658a.

The amount of the bond may be increased or reduced.[331]

Defects in bonds are not fundamental or jurisdictional, and must be objected to.[332]

8-8:5.2 Ex Parte Relief

A writ of garnishment may be issued in an *ex parte* hearing.[333]

8-8:5.3 Service

The plaintiff must serve the writ of garnishment, the application, accompanying affidavits and orders of the court on the defendant in a manner specified by TRCP 21a.[334]

- Service of a writ of garnishment on a financial institution is governed by Section 59.008, Finance Code.[335]

8-8:5.4 Garnishee's Answer

The garnishee's answer to the writ of garnishment must be:

- In writing;
- Sworn; and
- With complete answers to any inquiries made in the writ.[336]

If the garnishee does not answer by the time stated in the writ, the plaintiff may take a default judgment.[337]

- The time to answer is the same as a defendant would have to answer in a lawsuit.[338]

8-9 Receivership

8-9:1 Overview

A receiver is a person, appointed by the court, who receives and preserves property that is the subject of ongoing litigation.[339] The appointment of a receiver is necessarily ancillary to another substantive cause of action. Because of the ancillary nature of receiverships, all receiverships are temporary in the eyes of the law and terminate following the adjudication of the dispute.[340] Once appointed, a receiver acts as the agent

---

[331] *See* Tex. R. Civ. P. 658a.
[332] *Smith v. Miller*, 298 S.W.2d 845, 847 (Tex. Civ. App.—Galveston 1957, writ ref'd n.r.e.).
[333] Tex. R. Civ. P. 658.
[334] Tex. R. Civ. P. 663a.
[335] Tex. Civ. Prac. & Rem. Code Ann. § 63.008.
[336] Tex. R. Civ. P. 665.
[337] Tex. R. Civ. P. 667.
[338] *See* Tex. R. Civ. P. 661 (specifying that the writ of garnishment must include the words "at 10 o'clock a.m. on the Monday next following the expiration of twenty days from the date of service hereof").
[339] *See Ritchie v. Rupe*, 443 S.W.3d 856 (Tex. 2014).
[340] *Lynn v. First Nat'l Bank*, 40 S.W. 228 (Tex. Civ. App. 1897, no writ).

EQUITABLE AND EXTRAORDINARY RELIEF 339

of the trial court.[341] A receiver only has authority over property expressly mentioned in the trial court's order appointing the receiver.[342]

8-9:1.1 Related Causes of Action

Judicial Winding up of Partnership, Bankruptcy

MUST READ CASES & STATUTES

Tex. Civ. Prac. & Rem. Code Ann. §§ 64.001-64.108

Ritchie v. Rupe, 443 S.W.3d 856 (Tex. 2014)

8-9:2 Elements

8-9:2.1 Common Law Appointment

(1) The receivership is necessary to preserve property or protect the rights of persons having claim to that property.

- The receivership is necessary to preserve property or protect the rights of persons having claim to that property.[343]
    - This element requires findings that:
        - The property is in danger of being lost, removed or materially injured; and
        - The extraordinary remedy of receivership is necessary to preserve the property.[344]
- All circumstances bearing on the necessity of the receivership must be considered by the court.
- A receiver is not necessary when:
    - No advantage may be gained from the receiver's appointment;[345]
    - There is an adequate remedy at law;[346] or
    - A less intrusive equitable remedy is available.[347]

(2) There is no adequate remedy at law.

- A receiver may only be appointed if there is no adequate remedy at law.[348]

---

[341] *Glasstex, Inc. v. Arch Aluminum & Glass Co. Inc.*, 13-07-00483-CV, 2016 WL 747893, at *5 (Tex. App.—Corpus Christi Feb. 25, 2016, no pet.).
[342] *Ex parte Hodges*, 625 S.W.2d 304, 306 (Tex. 1981).
[343] *Texas & P. Ry. Co. v. Gay*, 26 S.W. 599, 601–02 (Tex. 1894) *aff'd sub nom. Texas & P Ry. Co v. Gay*, 167 U.S. 745 (Tex. 1897).
[344] *Hughes v. Marshall Nat. Bank*, 538 S.W.2d 820, 824 (Tex. Civ. App.—Tyler 1976, writ dism'd w.o.j.).
[345] *Grandfalls Mut. Irr. Co. v. White*, 131 S.W. 233, 235 (Tex. Civ. App. 1910, no writ).
[346] *Elliott v. Weatherman*, 396 S.W.3d 224, 228 (Tex. App.—Austin 2013, no pet.).
[347] *See Benefield v. State*, 266 S.W.3d 25, 31 (Tex. App.—Houston [1st Dist.] 2008, no pet.).
[348] *Elliott v. Weatherman*, 396 S.W.3d 224, 228 (Tex. App.—Austin 2013, no pet.).

8-9:2.2 Statutory Appointment

(1) Statutory grounds exist

- The appointment of a receiver may be governed by statute.
- Despite the legal nature of the statutes which authorize the appointment of receivers, an ex parte appointment of a receiver is also governed by the rules of equity.[349]

(1)(a) The Texas Civil Practice and Remedies Code

- A court of competent jurisdiction may appoint a receiver:
    - In an action by a vendor to vacate a fraudulent purchase of property;[350]
        - The applicant must:
            - Be the plaintiff or a party to such suit;
            - Have a probable interest in or right to the property or fund; and
            - The property or fund must be in danger of being lost, removed or materially injured.[351]
    - In an action by a creditor to subject any property or fund to his claim;[352]
        - The applicant must:
            - Be the plaintiff or a party to such suit;
            - Have a probable interest in or right to the property or fund; and
            - The property or fund must be in danger of being lost, removed or materially injured.[353]
    - In an action between partners or others jointly owning or interested in any property or fund;[354]
        - The applicant must:
            - Be the plaintiff or a party to such suit;
            - Have a probable interest in or right to the property or fund; and
            - The property or fund must be in danger of being lost, removed or materially injured.[355]
    - In an action by a mortgagee for the foreclosure of the mortgage and sale of the mortgaged property, only if;[356]

---

[349] *Morris v. N. Fort Worth State Bank*, 300 S.W.2d 314, 315 (Tex. Civ. App.—Fort Worth 1957, no writ).
[350] Tex. Civ. Prac. & Rem. Code Ann. § 64.001(a).
[351] Tex. Civ. Prac. & Rem. Code Ann. § 64.001(b).
[352] Tex. Civ. Prac. & Rem. Code Ann. § 64.001(a).
[353] Tex. Civ. Prac. & Rem. Code Ann. § 64.001(b).
[354] Tex. Civ. Prac. & Rem. Code Ann. § 64.001(a).
[355] Tex. Civ. Prac. & Rem. Code Ann. § 64.001(b).
[356] Tex. Civ. Prac. & Rem. Code Ann. § 64.001(a).

- It appears that the mortgaged property is in danger of being lost, removed or materially injured; or
- The condition of the mortgage has not been performed and the property is probably insufficient to discharge the mortgage debt.[357]
- For a corporation that is insolvent, is in imminent danger of insolvency, has been dissolved, or has forfeited its corporate rights;[358] or
- In any other case in which a receiver may be appointed under the rules of equity.[359]
- In all cases, the court has considerable discretion in appointing a receiver.[360]

(1)(b) The Business Organizations Code—Specific Property

- A court that has jurisdiction over specific property of a domestic or foreign entity may appoint a receiver in an action:

    (1) By a vendor to vacate a fraudulent purchase of the property;[361]

    (2) By a creditor to subject the property or fund to the creditor's claim;[362]

    (3) Between partners or others jointly owning or interested in the property or fund;[363]

    (4) By a mortgagee of the property for the foreclosure of the mortgage and sale of the property, when:[364]

    - It appears that the mortgaged property is in danger of being lost, removed or materially injured;[365] or
    - It appears that the mortgage is in default and that the property is probably insufficient to discharge the mortgage debt;[366] and

    (5) In which receivers for specific property have been previously appointed by courts of equity:[367]

- Additionally, a court may only appoint a receiver in one of the abovementioned actions if:
    - In (1), (2), or (3):

---

[357] Tex. Civ. Prac. & Rem. Code Ann. § 64.001(c).
[358] Tex. Civ. Prac. & Rem. Code Ann. § 64.001(a).
[359] Tex. Civ. Prac. & Rem. Code Ann. § 64.001(a).
[360] *Baptist Missionary & Educ. Convention of State of Tex. v. Knox*, 23 S.W.2d 781, 784 (Tex. Civ. App.—Fort Worth 1929, no writ).
[361] Tex. Bus. Orgs. Code Ann. § 11.403(a).
[362] Tex. Bus. Orgs. Code Ann. § 11.403(a).
[363] Tex. Bus. Orgs. Code Ann. § 11.403(a).
[364] Tex. Bus. Orgs. Code Ann. § 11.403(a).
[365] Tex. Bus. Orgs. Code Ann. § 11.403(a).
[366] Tex. Bus. Orgs. Code Ann. § 11.403(a).
[367] Tex. Bus. Orgs. Code Ann. § 11.403(a).

- The applicant shows that the property or fund is in danger of being lost, removed or materially injured;[368]

- Circumstances exist that are considered by the court to necessitate the appointment of a receiver to conserve the property or fund and avoid damage to interested parties;[369]

- All other requirements of law are complied with;[370] and

- The court determines that other available legal and equitable remedies are inadequate.[371]

(1)(c) The Business Organizations Code—Rehabilitation

- A district court in the county of the entity's registered office or principal place of business may appoint a receiver to rehabilitate an entity if:

    - In an action by an owner or member of the domestic entity, it is established that:

    - The entity is insolvent or in imminent danger of insolvency;

    - The governing persons of the entity are deadlocked in the management of the entity's affairs, the owners or members of the entity are unable to break the deadlock, and irreparable injury to the entity is being suffered or is threatened because of the deadlock;

    - The actions of the governing persons of the entity are illegal, oppressive or fraudulent;

    - The property of the entity is being misapplied or wasted; or

    - With respect to a for-profit corporation, the shareholders of the entity are deadlocked in voting power and have failed, for a period of at least two years, to elect successors to the governing persons of the entity whose terms have expired or would have expired on the election and qualification of their successors;

    - In an action by a creditor of the domestic entity, it is established that:

        - The entity is insolvent, the claim of the creditor has been reduced to judgment, and an execution on the judgment was returned unsatisfied; or

        - The entity is insolvent and has admitted in writing that the claim of the creditor is due and owing;

        - Courts of equity have traditionally appointed a receiver.[372]

- A court may only appoint a receiver in one of the abovementioned actions if:

---

[368] Tex. Bus. Orgs. Code Ann. § 11.403(b).
[369] Tex. Bus. Orgs. Code Ann. § 11.403(b).
[370] Tex. Bus. Orgs. Code Ann. § 11.403(b).
[371] Tex. Bus. Orgs. Code Ann. § 11.403(b).
[372] Tex. Bus. Orgs. Code Ann. § 11.404(a).

- Circumstances exist that are considered by the court to necessitate the appointment of a receiver to conserve the property and business of the domestic entity and avoid damage to interested parties;
- All other requirements of law are complied with; and
- The court determines that all other available legal and equitable remedies, including the appointment of a receiver for specific property of the domestic entity under Section 11.402(a) of the Texas Business Organizations Code, are inadequate.[373]

(1) (d) The Business Organizations Code—Liquidation

- A district court in the county the entity's registered office or principal place of business may appoint a receiver to liquidate an entity if:
  - When an action has been filed by the attorney general under this chapter to terminate the existence of the entity and it is established that liquidation of the entity's business and affairs should precede the entry of a decree of termination;
  - On application of the entity to have its liquidation continued under the supervision of the court;
  - The entity is in receivership and the court does not find that any plan presented before the first anniversary of the date the receiver was appointed is feasible for remedying the condition requiring appointment of the receiver;
  - On application of a creditor of the entity if it is established that irreparable damage will ensue to the unsecured creditors of the domestic entity as a class, generally, unless there is an immediate liquidation of the property of the domestic entity; or
  - On application of a member or director of a nonprofit corporation or cooperative association and it appears the entity is unable to carry out its purposes.[374]
- A court may only appoint a receiver in one of the abovementioned situations if:
  - The circumstances demand liquidation to avoid damage to interested persons;
  - All other requirements of law are complied with; and
  - The court determines that all other available legal and equitable remedies, including the appointment of a receiver for specific property of the domestic entity and appointment of a receiver to rehabilitate the domestic entity, are inadequate.[375]

---

[373] Tex. Bus. Orgs. Code Ann. § 11.404(b).
[374] Tex. Bus. Orgs. Code Ann. § 11.405(a).
[375] Tex. Bus. Orgs. Code Ann. § 11.405(b).

8-9:3 Damages and Remedies

8-9:3.1 Appointment of Receiver

The appointment of a receiver is temporary, pending the outcome of the underlying litigation.[376]

The scope of a receivership is limited to the language of the court order appointing the receiver.[377]

8-9:3.2 Receivership Fees

Receivers may be paid fees and expenses out of the proceeds from the sale of receivership property.[378]

Generally, a lienholder's interest in property held in receivership has priority over the receiver's right to payment from the proceeds of the sale of property.[379]

There are two exceptions to the general rule:

- When the lienholder has either sought the appointment of the receiver, or has acquiesced to the receiver's appointment and seeks the benefits of the receivership;[380] or

- When the lienholder knows of and consents to the receivership, and fees, expenses and debts are incurred from a receiver's operation of a business important to the public.[381]

8-9:4 Defenses

8-9:4.1 Defenses, Generally

Receiverships, even statutory ones, are equitable in nature and are likely subject to equitable defenses.

8-9:5 Procedural Implications

8-9:5.1 Ex Parte Relief

A receiver may be appointed in an *ex parte* hearing.[382] However, if the property for which a receivership is sought is "fixed and immovable," the court must provide notice and a hearing.[383]

---

[376] *Rudasill v. Rudasill*, 206 S.W. 983 (Tex. Civ. App.—Dallas 1918, no writ).
[377] *Matter of Mandel*, 747 Fed. Appx. 955, 961 (5th Cir. 2018), cert. denied sub nom. *Mastrogiovanni Schorsch & Mersky, P.C. v. Mandel*, 139 S. Ct. 1333, 203 L. Ed. 2d 568 (2019).
[378] *Chase Manhattan Bank v. Bowles*, 52 S.W.3d 871, 880 (Tex. App.—Waco 2001, no pet.).
[379] *Chase Manhattan Bank v. Bowles*, 52 S.W.3d 871, 880 (Tex. App.—Waco 2001, no pet.).
[380] *Chase Manhattan Bank v. Bowles*, 52 S.W.3d 871, 880 (Tex. App.—Waco 2001, no pet.).
[381] *Chase Manhattan Bank v. Bowles*, 52 S.W.3d 871, 880 (Tex. App.—Waco 2001, no pet.).
[382] *Krumnow v. Krumnow*, 174 S.W.3d 820, 828 (Tex. App.—Waco 2005, pet. denied).
[383] Tex. R. Civ. P. 695.

EQUITABLE AND EXTRAORDINARY RELIEF

Such an *ex parte* appointment is an extreme option and is only available upon a showing of "absolutely and imperatively necessary" to prevent loss, waste, destruction, irreparable injury or the defeat of the petitioner's rights.[384]

When proving the necessity of the appointment of a receiver in an *ex parte* action, the petitioner must either submit a verified petition or present evidence to the court.[385]

8-9:5.2 Posting of Bond

The applicant must post a good and sufficient bond that is payable to the defendant in the amount set by the court.[386]

Failure to post this bond is reversible error.

Before a person assumes the duties of a receiver, he must execute a good and sufficient bond that is:

- Approved by the appointing court;
- In an amount fixed by the court; and
- Conditioned on faithful discharge of his duties as receiver in the named action and obedience to the orders of the court.[387]

8-9:5.3 Venue

Any court may appoint a receiver under the Civil Practice and Remedies Code.[388]

> A court with subject matter jurisdiction over specific property may appoint a receiver for that specific property under the Business Organizations Code.[389]

> Only a district court in the county of the entity's registered office or principal place of business may appoint a receiver under the Business Organizations Code to:

- Rehabilitate an entity; or
- Liquidate an entity.[390]

8-10 Declaratory Judgment

8-10:1 Overview

An action for declaratory relief is governed by Chapter 37 of the Texas Civil Practice and Remedies Code, also referred to as the Uniform Declaratory Judgment Act (UDJA). Neither legal or equitable in nature, the Act provides a procedural device allowing judicial determination of controversies within a court's jurisdiction. The

---

[384] *Krumnow v. Krumnow*, 174 S.W.3d 820, 828 (Tex. App.—Waco 2005, pet. denied).
[385] *Hunt v. State*, 48 S.W.2d 466, 468 (Tex. Civ. App.—Austin 1932, no writ).
[386] Tex. R. Civ. P. 695a.
[387] Tex. Civ. Prac. & Rem. Code Ann. § 64.023.
[388] Tex. Civ. Prac. & Rem. Code Ann. § 64.001(a).
[389] Tex. Bus. Orgs. Code Ann. §§ 11.402(a), 11.403(a).
[390] Tex. Bus. Orgs. Code Ann. § 11.402(b).

purpose of the Act is to settle and afford relief from uncertainty and insecurity with respect to rights, status and other legal relations.

8-10:1.1 Related Causes of Action

Injunction, Specific Performance

8-10:2 Elements for Declaratory Judgment

(1) A justiciable controversy exists as to the rights, status or legal relations between the parties;

- To bring an action for declaratory judgment, a justiciable controversy must exist between the parties involved.[391]

- "To constitute a justiciable controversy, there must exist a real and substantial controversy involving genuine conflict of tangible interests and not merely a theoretical dispute."[392]

- As long as there is a justiciable controversy, the party seeking relief need not have incurred actual injury.[393]

- An actual controversy need not exist if the "ripening seeds" of a controversy are present.[394] Ripening seeds of controversy exist when facts and circumstances indicate imminent and inevitable litigation, as opposed to a hypothetical or abstract conflict.[395]

- "A person interested under a deed, will, written contract, or other writings constituting a contract or whose rights, status, or other legal relations are affected by a statute, municipal ordinance, contract, or franchise may have determined any question of construction or validity arising under the instrument, statute, ordinance, contract, or franchise and obtain a declaration of rights, status, or other legal relations thereunder."[396]

- However, declaratory judgment is not limited solely to disputes regarding written instruments and statutes. It encompasses a wide variety of factual situations and applies whenever there is a justiciable controversy involving uncertainty or insecurity as to the rights, legal relations or status of parties and declaratory relief will resolve the controversy.[397]

---

[391] Tex. Civ. Prac. & Rem. Code Ann. § 37.002(b); *Etan Indus., Inc. v. Lehmann*, 359 S.W.3d 620, 624–25 (Tex. 2011); *Robinson v. Parker*, 353 S.W.3d 753, 756 (Tex. 2011).

[392] *Fort Bend Cty. v. Martin-Simon*, 177 S.W.3d 479, 483 (Tex. App.—Houston [1st Dist.] 2005) (quoting *Bexar-Medina-Atascosa Ctys. Water Control & Improvement Dist. No. 1 v. Medina Lake Prot. Ass'n*, 640 S.W.2d 778, 779–80 (Tex. App.—San Antonio 1982, writ ref'd n.r.e.)).

[393] *City of San Antonio v. Greater San Antonio Builders Ass'n*, 04-12-00745-CV, 2013 WL 2247468, at *3 (Tex. App.—San Antonio May 22, 2013, no pet.).

[394] *Harris Cty. Dist. 156 v. United Somerset*, 274 S.W.3d 133, 139–40 (Tex. App.—Houston [1st Dist.] 2008, no pet).

[395] *Monk v. Pomberg*, 263 S.W.3d 199, 207–08 (Tex. App.—Houston [1st Dist.] 2007, no pet.).

[396] Tex. Civ. Prac. & Rem. Code Ann. § 37.004(a).

[397] *Bartoo v. Dallas Area Rapid Transit*, 05-02-00828-CV, 2003 WL 751812, at *2 (Tex. App.—Dallas Mar. 6, 2003, no pet.).

- Declaratory relief is proper when the sole issue concerning title to real property is the determination of the proper boundary line between adjoining properties.[398] If the controversy also requires determination of proper title to the land, however, declaratory judgment is not available.[399]

- Relief may also be obtained when a controversy exists regarding various aspects of administration of a trust.[400]

- A court may not render a declaratory judgment that rules on a hypothetical fact situation.[401]

- Declaratory relief is not available for the interpretation of a prior judgment entered by that or any other court.[402]

(2) The party seeking relief has a justiciable interest in the subject matter of the suit.

- To maintain an action for declaratory judgment, a plaintiff must have a justiciable interest in the subject matter of the suit.[403] Consistent with the usual rules of standing, the party seeking relief must demonstrate a particularized interest in a conflict distinct from the public at large.[404]

(3) The controversy will be resolved by the declaratory judgment sought;

- The judgment or decree sought must terminate the uncertainty or controversy giving rise to the proceeding.[405]

- A judgment that provides specific relief to a litigant or otherwise affects legal relationship terminates the uncertainty or controversy.[406]

- A court may not render a declaratory judgment that amounts to an advisory opinion.[407]

(4) The controversy's subject matter is:

- An action under the UDJA must fall within the specified subject matters outlined in Chapter 37 of the Act.[408]

- A potential defendant may not use a declaratory judgment action to determine potential tort liability; declaratory judgments were not intended to

---

[398] Tex. Civ. Prac. & Rem. Code Ann. § 37.004.
[399] *Texas Parks & Wildlife Dep't v. Sawyer Trust*, 354 S.W.3d 384, 389–90 (Tex. 2011); *Basley v. Adoni Holdings, LLC*, 373 S.W.3d 577, 588 (Tex. App.—Texarkana 2012, no pet.).
[400] Tex. Civ. Prac. & Rem. Code Ann. § 37.005.
[401] *Brooks v. Northglen Ass'n.*, 141 S.W.3d 158, 164 (Tex. 2004).
[402] *See Envision Realty Group, LLC v. Chuan Chen*, 05-18-00613-CV, 2020 WL 1060698, at *4 (Tex. App.—Dallas Mar. 5, 2020, no pet. h.).
[403] *Rawlings v. Gonzalez*, 407 S.W.3d 420, 425–26 (Tex. App.—Dallas 2013, no pet.); *Webb v. Voga*, 316 S.W.3d 809, 813 (Tex. App.—Dallas 2010, no pet.).
[404] *South Tex. Water Auth. v. Lomas*, 223 S.W.3d 304, 307–09 (Tex. 2007).
[405] Tex. Civ. Prac. & Rem. Code Ann. § 37.008.
[406] Loya Ins. Co. v. Avalos, 18-0837, 2020 WL 2089752, at *4 (Tex. May 1, 2020).
[407] *Brooks v. Northglen Ass'n.*, 141 S.W.3d 158, 164 (Tex. 2004).
[408] *See Trantham v. Isaacks*, 218 S.W.3d 750, 753 (Tex. App.—Fort Worth 2007, pet. denied).

deprive a potential tort plaintiff of the right to decide whether, when and where to sue.[409]

(4)(a) Determination of one of following questions arising in administration of estate or trust:

    (i) Ascertainment of class of creditors, devisees, legatees, heirs, next of kin or other persons interested in matter;

    (ii) Direction that executors, administrators or trustees do or abstain from doing a particular act in fiduciary capacity; or

    (iii) Any question arising in administration of trust or estate, including construction of will or other writing.[410]

(4)(b) Declaration of client's rights, status or other legal relations under deed, will, written contract, statute, municipal ordinance or franchise.

- Declaration of client's rights, status or other legal relations under deed, will, written contract, statute, municipal ordinance or franchise.[411]

- Whether an insurer is required to provide defense and indemnity may be included within this category.[412]

(4)(c) Determination of the proper boundary line between adjoining properties.

- Determination of the proper boundary line between adjoining properties.[413]

8-10:3 Damages and Remedies

8-10:3.1 Declaratory Judgment

A court of record within its jurisdiction has power to declare rights, status and other legal relations whether or not further relief is or could be claimed.[414]

The declaration may be either affirmative or negative in form and effect, and the declaration has the force and effect of a final judgment or decree.[415]

A declaratory judgment has the same force and effect as a final judgment or decree.[416] Declaratory relief is not available for the interpretation of a prior judgment entered by that or any other court.[417] An action for a declaratory judgment cannot be used to set aside a final judgment that is not void because it would constitute an impermissible collateral attack on the judgment.[418]

---

[409] *In re Estate of Bessire*, 399 S.W.3d 642, 651 (Tex. App.—Amarillo 2013, pet. denied).
[410] Tex. Civ. Prac. & Rem. Code Ann. § 37.005.
[411] Tex. Civ. Prac. & Rem. Code Ann. § 37.004(b).
[412] *In re Essex Ins. Co.*, 450 S.W.3d 524, 527 (Tex. 2014).
[413] Tex. Civ. Prac. & Rem. Code Ann. § 37.004(c).
[414] Tex. Civ. Prac. & Rem. Code Ann. § 37.003.
[415] Tex. Civ. Prac. & Rem. Code Ann. § 37.003.
[416] Tex. Civ. Prac. & Rem. Code Ann. § 37.003(b).
[417] *See Envision Realty Group, LLC v. Chuan Chen*, 05-18-00613-CV, 2020 WL 1060698, at *4 (Tex. App.—Dallas Mar. 5, 2020, no pet. h.).
[418] *Dallas Cty. Tax Collector v. Andolina*, 303 S.W.3d 926, 930 (Tex. App.—Dallas 2010, no pet.); *Sutherland v. Sutherland*, 560 S.W.2d 531, 533 (Tex. Civ. App.—Texarkana 1978, writ ref'd n.r.e.); *Cohen v. Cohen*, 632 S.W.2d 172, 173 (Tex. App.—Waco 1982, no writ).

8-10:3.2 Attorney's Fees

In any proceeding under the UDJA, the court may award costs and reasonable and necessary attorney's fees as are equitable and just.[419]

However, a declatory judgment may not be used solely to obtain attorney's fees.[420]

A party must file an affirmative pleading requesting attorney's fees, unless the issue was waived or tried by consent.[421]

The DJA places the grant or denial of attorney's fees in declaratory judgment actions within the discretion of the trial court.[422]

A prevailing party in a declaratory judgment action is not entitled to fees as a matter of law.[423]

A non-prevailing party may be awarded attorney's fees if it is equitable and just under the circumstances.[424]

The court may award attorney's fees even if a case does not go to trial or does not result in a judgment.[425]

In determining whether attorney's fees are equitable and just, the court should consider the following factors:

- The time and labor required, the novelty and difficulty of the questions involved, and the skill required to perform the legal service properly.
- The likelihood that the acceptance of the particular employment will preclude other employment by the lawyer.
- The fee customarily charged in the locality for similar legal services.
- The amount involved and the results obtained.
- The time limitations imposed by the client or by the circumstances.
- The nature and length of the professional relationship with the client.
- The experience, reputation and ability of the lawyer or lawyers performing the services.
- Whether the fee is fixed or contingent on results obtained or uncertainty of collection before the legal services have been rendered.[426]

---

[419] Tex. Civ. Prac. & Rem. Code Ann. § 37.009.
[420] *Tex. Dep't of Pub. Safety v. Alexander*, 300 S.W.3d 62, 78 (Tex. App.—Austin 2009, pet. denied).
[421] *Nowlin v. Davis*, 03-18-00694-CV, 2019 WL 2440103, at *2 (Tex. App.—Austin June 12, 2019, no pet.)
[422] *Neeley v. W. Orange-Cove Consol. Indep. Sch. Dist.*, 176 S.W.3d 746, 799 (Tex. 2005).
[423] *Anderton v. City of Cedar Hill*, 583 S.W.3d 188, 195 (Tex. App.—Dallas 2018, no pet.).
[424] *Bailey v. Smith*, 581 S.W.3d 374, 399 (Tex. App.—Austin 2019, pet. filed).
[425] *Nabers v. Nabers*, 14-18-00968-CV, 2020 WL 830025, at *3 (Tex. App.—Houston [14th Dist.] Feb. 20, 2020, no pet. h.).
[426] *Arthur Andersen v. Perry Equip. Corp.*, 945 S.W.2d 812, 818 (Tex. 1997).

8-10:4 Defenses

8-10:4.1 Absence of a Justiciable Controversy

A court may refuse to render a declaratory judgment or decree only if the judgment would not remove the uncertainty giving rise to the proceeding.[427]

A court does not have power to rule on hypothetical or contingent situations, or to determine questions not essential to the decision of an actual controversy, even though the questions may require adjudication in the future.[428]

8-10:4.2 Other Active Proceeding

As a general rule an action for declaratory judgment will not be entertained if there is pending, at the time it is filed, another action or proceeding between the same parties in which the same issues involved in the declaratory action may be adjudicated.[429]

Arguably, a plaintiff's claim for a declaratory judgment is not a bar to another party's assertion of a counterclaim or crossclaim for declaratory judgment in the same action,[430] but this is not a definitive rule.[431]

8-10:4.3 Plaintiff has no Justiciable Interest in the Controversy

A plaintiff must have standing in order to bring an action for declaratory judgment.[432]

To have standing an individual must demonstrate a particularized interest in a conflict distinct from that sustained by the public at large.[433]

---

[427] Tex. Civ. Prac. & Rem. Code Ann. § 37.008; *Longoria v. Exxon Mobil Corp.*, 255 S.W.3d 174, 180 (Tex. App.—San Antonio 2008, pet. denied).

[428] *Waldrop v. Waldrop*, 552 S.W.3d 396, 411 (Tex. App.—Fort Worth 2018, no pet.).

[429] *Tex. Mun. Power Agency v. Pub. Util. Comm'n of Tex.*, 253 S.W.3d 184, 200 (Tex. 2007).

[430] *Hawkins v. Tex. Oil and Gas Corp.*, 724 S.W.2d 878, 891 (Tex. App.—Waco 1987, writ ref'd n.r.e.).

[431] This idea and the holding of *Hawkins v. Tex. Oil and Gas Corp.*, 724 S.W.2d 878, 891 (Tex. App.—Waco 1987, writ ref'd n.r.e.) is expressly rejected in *Matter of Estate of Kidd*, 812 S.W.2d 356, 359 (Tex. App.—Amarillo 1991, writ denied). The Supreme Court has never cleared up which holding is correct. However, the majority of cases say counterclaims of this nature are impermissible. *See SW Loan A, L.P. v. Duarte-Viera*, 487 S.W.3d 697, 707 (Tex. App.—San Antonio 2016, no pet.); *Brush v. Reata Oil & Gas Corp.*, 984 S.W.2d 720, 730 (Tex. App.—Waco 1998, pet. denied); *Thomas v. Thomas*, 902 S.W.2d 621, 626 (Tex. App.—Austin 1995, writ denied).

[432] *Hawkins v. Tex. Oil and Gas Corp.*, 724 S.W.2d 878, 891 (Tex. App.—Waco 1987, writ ref'd n.r.e.).
316 S.W.3d 809, 813 (Tex. App.—Dallas 2010, no pet.)"*Webb v. Voga*, 316 S.W.3d 809, 813 (Tex. App.—Dallas 2010, no pet.).

[433] *South Tex. Water Auth. v. Lomas*, 223 S.W.3d 304, 307–09 (Tex. 2007).

8-10:4.4 Other Exclusive Remedy

A court may not award a declaratory judgment if the subject matter of the controversy has an exclusive remedy.[434]

8-10:4.5 Defenses to the Underlying Action

A defendant may raise any substantive defenses to the underlying claim which could be raised in a traditional trial.[435]

8-10:5 Procedural Implications

8-10:5.1 Joinder of Parties

All persons who have a claim or an interest that would be affected by the declaratory judgment must be made a party to the action.[436]

Any person that is not made a party may not be prejudiced by the declaratory judgment.[437]

8-10:5.2 Subsequent Relief

After a party has obtained a declaratory judgment, a subsequent suit may be brought for further relief if it is necessary or proper.[438]

If the subsequent relief was actually considered by the court in the declaratory judgment action, res judicata will bar its re-litigation.[439]

8-11 Forcible Entry and Detainer

8-11:1 Overview

Governed by Chapter 24 of the Texas Property Code and Rule 510 of the Texas Rules of Civil Procedure, a forcible entry and detainer action provides a lawful means to dispossess an individual who will not abandon nor voluntarily surrender possession of real property. It is a speedy, simple and inexpensive means to determine who has the right to immediate possession of real property without resorting to an action on the title.[440] Though a judgment on such an action determines who has the right to

---

[434] *FLCT, Ltd. v. City of Frisco*, 493 S.W.3d 238, 256–60 (Tex. App.—Fort Worth 2016, pet. denied).

[435] *See, e.g., Transportation Ins. Co. v. Franco*, 821 S.W.2d 751, 754–55 (Tex. App.—Amarillo 1992, writ denied) (defendant asserted statute of limitations defense on the underlying claim.)

[436] Tex. Civ. Prac. & Rem. Code Ann. § 37.006(a).

[437] Tex. Civ. Prac. & Rem. Code Ann. § 37.006(a).

[438] Tex. Civ. Prac. & Rem. Code Ann. § 37.011.

[439] *Jay Petroleum, L.L.C. v. EOG Resources, Inc.*, 332 S.W.3d 534, 540–41 (Tex. App.—Houston [1st Dist.] 2009, pet. denied).

[440] *In re High Pointe Investments, LLC*, 552 S.W.3d 384, 388 (Tex. App.—Waco 2018, no pet.).

immediate possession, it does not determine any issue regarding the merits of the title to the property.[441]

Though forcible entry and detainer is a term broadly used in legal parlance, a "forcible entry and detainer" action and a "forcible detainer" action are separate and distinct causes of action.[442] Forcible entry and detainer applies where *both* the initial entry onto the property and its continued possession are illegal.[443] Forcible detainer applies where the initial entry onto the property was legal, but its ongoing possession is illegal.[444]

8-11:1.1 Related Causes of Action

Trespass, Trespass to Try Title, Breach of Contract, DTPA, Tortious Interference with Prospective Business Relations

MUST READ CASES

Rice v. Pinney, 51 S.W.3d 705 (Tex. App.—Dallas 2001, no pet.)

Hong Kong Dev., Inc. v. Nguyen, 229 S.W.3d 415 (Tex. App.—Houston [1st Dist.] 2007)

8-11:2 Elements

8-11:2.1 Elements of Forcible Entry and Detainer

(1) The party bringing the suit has the right to possession of the property at the time of the forcible entry;

- No landlord-tenant relationship exists in a forcible entry and detainer action. The action may be brought by anyone with the right to possession of the property at the time of the unlawful entry.[445]

(2) A person commits a forcible entry on the property by:

(2)(a) Entering by force; or

(2)(b) Entering without legal authority by:

(2)(b)(i) Entering without the consent of the person in actual possession of the property;

(2)(b)(ii) Entering without the consent of a tenant at will or by sufferance; or

(2)(b)(iii) Entering without the consent of a person who acquired possession by forcible entry.

---

[441] *Jelinis, LLC v. Hiran*, 557 S.W.3d 159, 166 (Tex. App.—Houston [14th Dist.] 2018), cert. denied, 140 S. Ct. 244, 205 L. Ed. 2d 130 (2019).
[442] *Johnson v. Mohammed*, No. 03-10-00763-CV, 2013 Tex. App. LEXIS 5808, at *10–12 (App.—Austin May 10, 2013).
[443] Tex. Prop. Code Ann. § 24.001.
[444] Tex. Prop. Code Ann. § 24.002.
[445] *See* Tex. Prop. Code Ann. § 24.001.

"Force" includes a display of physical power that is reasonably calculated to inspire fear of physical harm in those who seek to oppose the trespasser.[446] Actual physical combat is not necessary.[447] A forcible entry is an entry without the consent of the person in actual possession of the property.[448]

A plaintiff must show that he was in actual possession of the property at the time of the entry.[449]

- Actual possession means:
  - A person who uses the premises as a place to keep his or her household goods and who claims dominion and control of the premises in connection with such use.[450]
  - Physical presence is not necessary to establish actual possession.[451]
  - A forcible entry is an entry without the consent of a tenant at will or by sufferance.[452]
  - A forcible entry is an entry without the consent of a person who acquired possession by forcible entry.[453]

(3) The person entitled to possession of the property gives oral or written notice to vacate immediately or by a specified deadline in compliance with Texas Property Code Section 24.005(d); and

- The plaintiff must give the occupant oral or written notice to vacate before the landlord files a forcible entry and detainer suit.[454]
- The notice to vacate under this subsection may be to vacate immediately or by a specified deadline.[455]

(4) The possessor refuses to surrender possession upon demand.

- The person enters the real property of another and refuses to surrender possession on demand.[456]

8-11:2.2 Elements of Forcible Detainer

(1) A person commits a forcible detainer when the person:

---

[446] *Smith v. Sinclair Ref. Co.*, 77 S.W.2d 894, 895 (Tex. Civ. App.—Fort Worth 1934, no writ).
[447] *Smith v. Sinclair Ref. Co.*, 77 S.W.2d 894, 895 (Tex. Civ. App.—Fort Worth 1934, no writ).
[448] Tex. Prop. Code Ann. § 24.001(b)(1).
[449] 41 Tex. Jur. 3d Forcible Entry and Detainer § 6 (2014) (citing *Benevides v. Lucio*, 13 S.W.2d 71, 72 (Tex. Comm'n App. 1929)).
[450] 41 Tex. Jur. 3d Forcible Entry and Detainer § 6 (2014) (citing *Benevides v. Lucio*, 13 S.W.2d 71, 72 (Tex. Comm'n App. 1929)).
[451] 41 Tex. Jur. 3d Forcible Entry and Detainer § 6 (2014) (citing *Benevides v. Lucio*, 13 S.W.2d 71, 72 (Tex. Comm'n App. 1929)).
[452] Tex. Prop. Code Ann. § 24.001(b)(2).
[453] Tex. Prop. Code Ann. § 24.001(b)(3).
[454] Tex. Prop. Code Ann. § 24.005(d).
[455] Tex. Prop. Code Ann. § 24.005(d).
[456] Tex. Prop. Code Ann. § 24.001(a).

- If there was no unlawful entry, the procedure to determine the right to immediate possession of real property is the action of forcible detainer.[457]

(1)(a) Is a tenant or a subtenant willfully and without force holding over after the termination of the tenant's right of possession;

- A person commits a forcible detainer if the person is a tenant or a subtenant willfully and without force holding over after the termination of the tenant's right of possession.[458]

- Any landlord-tenant relationship is sufficient for a forcible detainer action, including:

- Express leases;

  - Those that arise due to other contractual provisions between the parties; or

  - Those that arise by operation of law."[459]

(1)(b) Is a tenant at will or by sufferance, including an occupant at the time of foreclosure of a lien superior to the tenant's lease; or

- A person commits a forcible detainer if the person is a tenant at will or by sufferance, including an occupant at the time of foreclosure of a lien superior to the tenant's lease.[460]

- A tenant at sufferance does not have privity with the landlord but is merely an occupant in naked possession after his right to possession has ceased.[461]

- A plaintiff seeking possession against a tenant at sufferance after foreclosing a superior lien must prove that: (1) the plaintiff is indeed the owner; (2) the tenant at sufferance was an occupant at the time of foreclosure; and (3) the foreclosure was of a lien superior to the tenant's lien.[462]

- A property owners' association or other person who purchases occupied property at a sale foreclosing a property owners' association's assessment lien must commence and prosecute a forcible entry and detainer action under Chapter 24 to recover possession of the property.[463]

(1)(c) Is a tenant of a person who acquired possession by forcible entry;

- A person commits a forcible detainer if the person is a tenant of a person who acquired possession by forcible entry.[464]

(2) A written demand for possession was made in writing, by a person entitled to possession, and in compliance with the requirements for notice to vacate under Texas Property Code Section 24.005;

---

[457] *Murray v. U.S. Bank Nat'l Ass'n*, 411 S.W.3d 926, 928 (Tex. App.—El Paso 2013).
[458] Tex. Prop. Code Ann. § 24.002(a)(1).
[459] Dorsaneo, Texas Litigation Guide § 282.41.
[460] Tex. Prop. Code Ann. § 24.002(a)(2).
[461] *Jimenez v. McGeary*, 542 S.W.3d 810, 814 (Tex. App.—Fort Worth 2018, pet. denied).
[462] *Goggins v. Leo*, 849 S.W.2d 373, 377 (Tex. App.—Houston [14th Dist.] 1993, no writ).
[463] Tex. Prop. Code Ann. § 209.011(a).
[464] Tex. Prop. Code Ann. § 24.002(a)(3).

EQUITABLE AND EXTRAORDINARY RELIEF

- If the occupant is a tenant under a written lease or oral rental agreement, the landlord must give the tenant:
    - Written notice to vacate the premises;
    - At least three days before the landlord files a forcible detainer suit; unless:
        - The parties have contracted for a shorter or longer notice period in a written lease or agreement.[465]
- "A landlord who files a forcible detainer suit on grounds that the tenant is holding over beyond the end of the rental term or renewal period must also comply with the tenancy termination requirements of Section 91.001."[466]
- If the occupant is a tenant at will or by sufferance, the landlord must give the tenant:
    - Written notice to vacate the premises;
    - At least three days before the landlord files a forcible detainer suit; unless:
        - The parties have contracted for a shorter or longer notice period in a written lease or agreement.[467]
- "If a building is purchased at a tax foreclosure sale or a trustee's foreclosure sale under a lien superior to the tenant's lease and the tenant timely pays rent and is not otherwise in default under the tenant's lease after foreclosure, the purchaser must give a residential tenant of the building at least 30 days' written notice to vacate if the purchaser chooses not to continue the lease. The tenant is considered to timely pay the rent under this subsection if, during the month of the foreclosure sale, the tenant pays the rent for that month to the landlord before receiving any notice that a foreclosure sale is scheduled during the month or pays the rent for that month to the foreclosing lienholder or the purchaser at foreclosure not later than the fifth day after the date of receipt of a written notice of the name and address of the purchaser that requests payment. Before a foreclosure sale, a foreclosing lienholder may give written notice to a tenant stating that a foreclosure notice has been given to the landlord or owner of the property and specifying the date of the foreclosure."[468]
- If the occupant is a tenant of a person who acquired possession by forcible entry, the landlord must give the person:
    - Written notice to vacate;
    - At least three days before the landlord files a forcible detainer suit.[469]

---

[465] Tex. Prop. Code Ann. § 24.005(a).
[466] Tex. Prop. Code Ann. § 24.005(a); Tex. Prop. Code Ann. § 91.001.
[467] Tex. Prop. Code Ann. § 24.005(b).
[468] Tex. Prop. Code Ann. § 24.005(b).
[469] Tex. Prop. Code Ann. § 24.005(c).

- If the lease or applicable law requires the landlord to give a tenant an opportunity to respond to a notice of proposed eviction, a notice to vacate may not be given until the period provided for the tenant to respond to the eviction notice has expired.[470]
- The notice to vacate shall be given:
  - In person;
    - Notice in person may be by personal delivery to the tenant or any person residing at the premises who is 16 years of age or older or personal delivery to the premises and affixing the notice to the inside of the main entry door.
  - By mail at the premises in question.
    - Notice by mail may be by regular mail, by registered mail or by certified mail, return receipt requested, to the premises in question.
    - If the dwelling has no mailbox and has a keyless bolting device, alarm system or dangerous animal that prevents the landlord from entering the premises to leave the notice to vacate on the inside of the main entry door, the landlord may securely affix the notice on the outside of the main entry door."[471]

(3) The defendant refuses to surrender possession of real property; and

- A person who refuses to surrender possession of real property on demand commits a forcible detainer.[472]

(4) The plaintiff shows sufficient evidence of ownership to demonstrate a superior right to immediate possession of the property on the date possession was actually in dispute.

- A plaintiff does not need to present evidence verifying title, since good title is not an essential element of the action.[473]
- To prevail, the plaintiff need only show sufficient evidence of ownership to demonstrate a superior right to immediate possession.[474]

---

[470] Tex. Prop. Code Ann. § 24.005(e).
[471] Tex. Prop. Code Ann. § 24.005(f).
[472] Tex. Prop. Code Ann. § 24.002.
[473] *Hernandez v. Martinez*, 04-19-00076-CV, 2019 WL 5580261 (Tex. App.—San Antonio Oct. 30, 2019, no pet.).
[474] *Padilla v. NCJ Dev., Inc.*, 218 S.W.3d 811, 814 (Tex. App.—El Paso 2007, pet. dism'd w.o.j.) (citing *Dormady v. Dinero Land & Cattle Co., L.C.*, 61 S.W.3d 555, 557 (Tex. App.—San Antonio 2001, pet. dism'd w.o.j.); *Rice v. Pinney*, 51 S.W.3d 705, 709 (Tex. App.—Dallas 2001, no pet.)).

EQUITABLE AND EXTRAORDINARY RELIEF

8-11:3 Damages and Remedies

8-11:3.1 Writ of Possession[475]

The sole issue to be decided in a forcible entry and detainer or forcible detainer suit is who has the right to immediate possession of the property.[476]

"Except as provided by Rule 510.5, no writ of possession may issue before the 6th day after the date a judgment for possession is signed or the day following the deadline for the defendant to appeal the judgment, whichever is later. A writ of possession may not issue more than 60 days after a judgment for possession is signed. For good cause, the court may extend the deadline for issuance to 90 days after a judgment for possession is signed."[477]

A bond may be filed with the court to request immediate possession of the premises.[478]

8-11:3.2 Unpaid Rent[479]

A claim for rent within the justice court's jurisdiction may be asserted in an eviction case.[480]

On appeal to the county court, the appellant may recover damages suffered for withholding possession of the premises during the pendency of the appeal.[481]

The correct measure of damages is the market value of the property during the time possession is withheld from the landlord, not the rental provided in the lease.[482]

8-11:3.3 Attorney's Fees and Costs of Court[483]

A prevailing landlord in a forcible entry and detainer or forcible detainer suit may recover attorney's fees and all costs of court.[484]

To be eligible to recover attorney's fees in an eviction suit, a landlord must give a tenant who is unlawfully retaining possession of the landlord's premises a written demand to vacate the premises. The demand must state that if the tenant does not vacate the premises before the 11th day after the date of receipt of the notice and if the landlord files suit, the landlord may recover attorney's fees. The demand must be

---

[475] Tex. Prop. Code Ann. § 24.0061.
[476] *Holloway v. Guild Mortgage Co.*, 05-19-00491-CV, 2020 WL 582284, at *1 (Tex. App.—Dallas Feb. 6, 2020, no pet.).
[477] Tex. R. Civ. P. 510.8(d)(1).
[478] Tex. R. Civ. P. 510.5.
[479] Tex. Prop. Code Ann. § 24.0051, .0053–.0054 (Vernon).
[480] Tex. R. Civ. P. 510.3(d); *see* Tex. Gov't. Code Ann. § 27.031.
[481] Tex. R. Civ. P. 510.11.
[482] *Volume Millwork, Inc. v. W. Hous. Airport Corp.*, 218 S.W.3d 722, 725–26 (Tex. App.—Houston [1st Dist.] 2006).
[483] Tex. Prop. Code Ann. § 24.006.
[484] Tex. Prop. Code Ann. § 24.006.

sent by registered mail or by certified mail, return receipt requested, at least 10 days before the date the suit is filed.[485]

If a written lease entitles the landlord to recover attorney's fees, a prevailing landlord is entitled to recover reasonable attorney's fees from the tenant.[486]

The reasonableness of an attorney's fee award is determined according to the following non-exclusive factors: (1) the time and labor required, the novelty and difficulty of the questions involved, and the skill required to perform the legal service properly; (2) the likelihood that the acceptance of the particular employment will preclude other employment by the lawyer; (3) the fee customarily charged in the locality for similar legal services; (4) the amount involved and the results obtained; (5) the time limitations imposed by the client or by the circumstances; (6) the nature and length of the professional relationship with the client; (7) the experience, reputation and ability of the lawyer or lawyers performing the services; and (8) whether the fee is fixed or contingent on results obtained or uncertainty of collection before the legal services have been rendered.[487]

8-11:4 Defenses

8-11:4.1 Resolving Issue of Possession Necessarily Requires Resolution of Title Dispute

Justice courts are expressly denied jurisdiction to adjudicate title to land.[488]

When resolving the question of right to immediate possession also necessarily requires the resolution of a title dispute, the justice court lacks jurisdiction to consider the case.[489]

A justice court attempting to enter judgment on a case where the resolution of possession and title are intertwined may be enjoined from doing so.[490]

One indication that a justice court, and county court on appeal, is called on to adjudicate title to real estate in a forcible detainer case—and, thus exceed its jurisdiction—is when a landlord-tenant relationship is lacking.[491]

Specific evidence of a title dispute is required to raise an issue of a justice court's jurisdiction.[492]

---

[485] Tex. Prop. Code Ann. § 24.006(a).
[486] Tex. Prop. Code Ann. § 24.006.
[487] *Padilla v. NCJ Dev., Inc.*, 218 S.W.3d 811, 816 (Tex. App.—El Paso 2007, pet. dism'd w.o.j.), *Andersen & Co. v. Perry Equipment Corp.*, 945 S.W.2d 812, 818 (Tex. 1997).
[488] *See* Tex. Gov't Code Ann. § 27.031(b)(4); *Rice v. Pinney*, 51 S.W.3d 708 (Tex. App.—Dallas 2001, no pet.).
[489] *Wells Fargo Bank, N.A. v. Ezell*, 410 S.W.3d 919, 922 (Tex. App.—El Paso 2013, no pet.); *Padilla v. NCJ Dev., Inc.*, 218 S.W.3d 811, 815 (Tex. App.—El Paso 2007, pet. dism'd w.o.j.); *Ward v. Malone*, 115 S.W.3d 267, 271 (Tex. App.—Corpus Christi 2003, pet. denied); *Rice v. Pinney*, 51 S.W.3d 705, 709 (Tex. App.—Dallas 2001, no pet.).
[490] *Ward v. Malone*, 115 S.W.3d 267, 270 (Tex. App.—Corpus Christi 2003, pet. denied).
[491] *Ward v. Malone*, 115 S.W.3d 267, 270 (Tex. App.—Corpus Christi 2003, pet. denied).
[492] *Padilla v. NCJ Dev., Inc.*, 218 S.W.3d 811, 815 (Tex. App.—El Paso 2007).

A justice court does not have jurisdiction in a forcible entry and detainer or forcible detainer suit and shall dismiss the suit if the defendant files a sworn statement alleging the suit is based on a deed executed in violation of Chapter 21A, Business & Commerce Code.[493]

8-11:4.2 Injunctive Relief

A limited injunction preventing the landlord from interfering with the tenant's enjoyment of the property may be obtained.[494]

8-11:5 Procedural Implications

8-11:5.1 Notice to Vacate

Prior to filing an eviction suit, notice to vacate must be served upon the defendant prior to filing a forcible entry and detainer or forcible detainer suit.[495] The notice must comply with the requirements put forth in Texas Property Code Section 24.005(a). Generally, the landlord must give at tenant at least three days written notice of eviction before filing suit, unless a shorter period of time was agreed to between tenant and landlord in a written lease agreement.[496]

8-11:5.2 Jurisdiction

Justice courts have original jurisdiction over forcible entry and detainer and forcible detainer suits.[497] They may, however, be deprived of their jurisdiction if resolving the issue of possession necessarily requires resolving a title dispute.[498] The justice court in the precinct in which the real property is located has jurisdiction.[499]

8-11:5.3 Sworn Statement

A landlord should file a sworn statement in justice court seeking judgment against a tenant for possession of the premises and unpaid rent and personally serve the tenant in accordance with Texas Rule of Civil Procedure 742a because, in the event of default,

---

[493] Tex. Prop. Code Ann. § 24.004.
[494] *Breceda v. Whi*, 224 S.W.3d 237, 239–40 (Tex. App.—El Paso 2005, no pet.).
[495] Tex. Prop. Code Ann. § 24.005(a).
[496] Tex. Prop. Code Ann. § 24.005(a), (b). (Notice of eviction, though not necessarily written notice, must be given to an occupant who acquired possession by forcible entry prior to filing suit for eviction, but three days' notice is not required.); Tex. Prop. Code Ann. § 24.005(c).
[497] *See* Tex. Prop. Code Ann. § 24.004; *see also* Tex. Gov't Code Ann. § 27.031(a)(2); *Hong Kong Dev., Inc. v. Nguyen*, 229 S.W.3d 415, 433 (Tex. App.—Houston [1st Dist.] 2007, no pet.).
[498] *Wells Fargo Bank, N.A. v. Ezell*, 410 S.W.3d 919, 922 (Tex. App.—El Paso 2013, no pet.); *Yarto v. Gilliland*, 287 S.W.3d 83, 89–94 (Tex. App.—Corpus Christi 2009, no pet.); *Ward v. Malone*, 115 S.W.3d 267, 270 (Tex. App.—Corpus Christi 2003, pet. denied); *Rice v. Pinney*, 51 S.W.3d 705, 713 (Tex. App.—Dallas 2001, no pet.).
[499] Tex. Prop. Code Ann. § 24.004 (Vernon Supp. 1993); *Goggins v. Leo*, 849 S.W.2d 373, 375 (Tex. App.—Houston [14th Dist.] 1993, no writ).

such a sworn statement will support a default judgment for the possession of the premises and the amount of the alleged unpaid rent.[500]

8-11:5.4 Concurrent Claims for Damages, Title Issues, etc.

Forcible entry and detainer and forcible detainer actions are cumulative of any other remedy that may be had by a party. Therefore, parties are entitled to bring separate and concurrent actions in district court on title disputes, trespass, damages, waste, rent, or profits relating to the property.[501]

---

[500] Tex. Prop. Code Ann. § 24.0051.
[501] Tex. Prop. Code Ann. § 24.008; *Rice v. Pinney*, 51 S.W.3d 705, 709 (Tex. App.—Dallas 2001, no pet.); *Scott v. Hewitt*, 90 S.W.2d 816, 818–19 (Tex. 1936).

CHAPTER 9

Miscellaneous Business Causes of Action — Business Causes of Action Expressly not Recognized in Texas*

9-1 Action Against Opposing Attorney

9-1:1 Overview

Normally, a plaintiff must be in privity with an attorney to bring suit based upon the attorney's legal services.[1] Attorneys owe their clients a fiduciary duty[2] that likely is stricter than those duties other fiduciaries owe.[3] Attorneys also owe their clients a duty of care not to engage in professional negligence.[4] A client may maintain a cause of action for legal malpractice if the attorney commits a breach of that duty of care.[5] In some very limited circumstances, a third party may maintain an action against another's attorney if that attorney negligently furnished false information to a known third party for a known purpose and the third party justifiably relied upon that information.[6]

9-1:1.1 Related Causes of Action

Attorney Breach of Fiduciary Duty, Legal Malpractice

MUST READ CASES

McCamish, Martin, Brown & Loeffler v. F.E. Appling Interests, 991 S.W.2d 787 (Tex. 1999)

Mitchell v. Chapman, 10 S.W.3d 810 (Tex. App.—Dallas 2000, pet. denied)

---

* The authors thank Max Moran for his assistance in the updating of this chapter.
[1] *McCamish, Martin, Brown & Loeffler v. F.E. Appling Interests*, 991 S.W.2d 787, 792 (Tex. 1999).
[2] *Daniels v. Empty Eye, Inc.*, 368 S.W.3d 743, 749 (Tex. App.—Houston [14th Dist.] 2012, pet. denied); *Johnson v. Brewer & Pritchard, P.C.*, 73 S.W.3d 193, 199 (Tex. 2002).
[3] *See Trousdale v. Henry*, 261 S.W.3d 221, 229 (Tex. App.—Houston [14th Dist.] 2008, pet. denied) (The duties which an attorney owes her client require "absolute perfect candor, openness and honesty, and the absence of any concealment or deception.").
[4] *Duerr v. Brown*, 262 S.W.3d 63, 76 (Tex. App.—Houston [14th Dist.] 2008, no pet.).
[5] *Duerr v. Brown*, 262 S.W.3d 63, 76 (Tex. App.—Houston [14th Dist.] 2008, no pet.).
[6] *McCamish, Martin, Brown & Loeffler v. F.E. Appling Interests*, 991 S.W.2d 787, 794 (Tex. 1999).

9-1:2 Expressly Rejected in Texas

As a general rule, Texas courts expressly limit attorney liability to those persons in privity with the attorney.[7] The Supreme Court of Texas has recognized one exception to the general rule, authorizing a third party to maintain an action against another's attorney if that attorney negligently furnished false information to a known third party for a known purpose and the third party justifiably relied upon that information.[8] However, this avenue for a third party not in privity with the defendant-attorney is not open to opposing parties because an opposing party cannot justifiably rely upon an opposing counsel's statements.[9]

9-2 Confession of Judgment in Pre-Suit Instrument

9-2:1 Overview

A defendant may enter a confession of judgment in any judicial proceeding, thereby admitting the plaintiff's petition is true.[10] A pre-suit contract provision attempting to authorize acceptance of service and waiver of process or to confess judgment is void; such waiver is effective only after the lawsuit is filed.[11]

MUST READ STATUTE

Tex. Civ. Prac. & Rem. Code Ann. § 30.001

9-2:2 Expressly Rejected in Texas

In an instrument executed before suit is brought, a person may not accept service and waive process, enter an appearance in open court or confess a judgment.[12]

9-3 Conspiracy to Breach Contract

9-3:1 Overview

A civil conspiracy consists of "a combination by two or more persons to accomplish an unlawful purpose or to accomplish a lawful purpose by unlawful means."[13] A plaintiff who pleads and proves a civil conspiracy may hold the defendants jointly and sev-

---

[7] *McCamish, Martin, Brown & Loeffler v. F.E. Appling Interests*, 991 S.W.2d 787, 792 (Tex. 1999); *Mitchell v. Chapman*, 10 S.W.3d 810, 812 (Tex. App.—Dallas 2000, pet. denied).

[8] *McCamish, Martin, Brown & Loeffler v. F.E. Appling Interests*, 991 S.W.2d 787, 793–94 (Tex. 1999); *Blakenship v. Brown*, 399 S.W.3d 303, 309–10 (Tex. App.—Dallas 2013. pet. denied) (The duty owed by an attorney to a non-client, for purposes of a negligent misrepresentation claim, arises only when: (1) the attorney is aware of the non-client and intends that the non-client rely on the representation, and (2) the non-client justifiably relies on the attorney's representation of a material fact.).

[9] *Mitchell v. Chapman*, 10 S.W.3d 810, 812 (Tex. App.—Dallas 2000, pet. denied).

[10] 47 Tex. Jur. 3d Judgments § 11.

[11] Tex. Civ. Prac. & Rem. Code Ann. § 30.001.

[12] Tex. Civ. Prac. & Rem. Code Ann. § 30.001.

[13] *Firestone Steel Products Co. v. Barajas*, 927 S.W.2d 608, 617 (Tex. 1996); *Triplex Commc'ns, Inc. v. Riley*, 900 S.W.2d 716, 719 (Tex. 1995).

erally liable[14] and recover actual as well as exemplary damages.[15] Texas recognizes a distinction between tortious interference with existing contract and conspiracy to breach contract. Tortious interference with an existing contract is a valid cause of action which seeks to hold the third-party tortfeasor(s) liable,[16] whereas conspiracy to breach a contract of which the plaintiff is a party is not a viable cause of action in Texas.[17]

9-3:1.1 Related Causes of Action

Breach of Contract, Contract, Combination or Conspiracy, Tortious Interference with Existing Contract

MUST READ CASE

San Saba Energy, L.P. v. McCord, 167 S.W.3d 67 (Tex. App.—Waco 2005, pet. denied)

9-3:2 Expressly Rejected in Texas

While the Supreme Court of Texas has not expressly rejected this cause of action, it has done so impliedly.[18] Moreover, several courts of appeal have expressly rejected a cause of action for conspiracy to breach a contract to which the plaintiff is a party.[19]

9-4 Conversion of Real Property

9-4:1 Overview

A defendant converts personal property when he exercises an unlawful control and dominion over that property to the exclusion of and inconsistent with the property's rightful possessor.[20] However, Texas courts have clearly stated that an action only lies when the defendant converts personal property.[21]

---

[14] 12 Tex. Jur. 3d Civil Conspiracy § 3.
[15] 12 Tex. Jur. 3d Civil Conspiracy § 19.
[16] *Holloway v. Skinner*, 898 S.W.2d 793, 795 (Tex. 1995); *Prudential Ins. Co. of America v. Financial Review Servs., Inc.*, 29 S.W.3d 74, 79 (Tex. 2000). *Morgan Stanley & Co., Inc. v. Tex. Oil Co.*, 958 S.W.2d 178, 179 (Tex. 1997).
[17] *San Saba Energy, L.P. v. McCord*, 167 S.W.3d 67, 73 (Tex. App.—Waco 2005, pet. denied).
[18] *Morgan Stanley & Co., Inc. v. Tex. Oil Co.*, 958 S.W.2d 178, 179 (Tex. 1997) ("[A] person must be a stranger to a contract to tortiously interfere with it."); *Prudential Ins. Co. of America v. Financial Review Servs., Inc.*, 29 S.W.3d 74, 79 (Tex. 2000)
[19] *E.g., San Saba Energy, L.P. v. McCord*, 167 S.W.3d 67, 73 (Tex. App.—Waco 2005, pet. denied); *Grizzle v. Tex. Commerce Bank, N.A.*, 38 S.W.3d 265, 284–85 (Tex. App.—Dallas 2001), *rev'd in part on other grounds*, 96 S.W.3d 240 (Tex. 2002); *Deaton v. United Mobile Networks, L.P.*, 926 S.W.2d 756, 760–61 (Tex. App.—Texarkana 1996), *rev'd on other grounds*, 939 S.W.2d 146 (Tex. 1997); *MMR Int'l Ltd. v. Waller Marine, Ltd.*, No. H-11-1188, 2013 WL 3864271 (S.D. Tex. 2013).
[20] *Smith v. Maximum Racing, Inc.*, 136 S.W.3d 337, 341 (Tex. App.—Austin 2004, no pet.).
[21] *E.g., Cage Bros. v. Whiteman*, 139 Tex. 522, 526, 163 S.W.2d 638, 641 (Tex. [Comm'n Op.] 1942); *Lucio v. John G. & Marie Stella Kenedy Mem'l Found.*, 298 S.W.3d 663, 672 (Tex. App.—Corpus Christi 2009, pet. denied); *Lighthouse Church of Cloverleaf v. Tex. Bank*, 889 S.W.2d 595, 599 n.4 (Tex. App.—Houston [14th Dist.] 1994, writ denied).

9-4:1.1 Related Causes of Action

Oil and Gas Litigation: Conversion, Business Tort Litigation: Conversion, Trespass to Real Property

MUST READ CASES

Cage Bros. v. Whiteman, 163 S.W.2d 638 (Tex. Comm'n App. 1942)

Lucio v. John G. & Marie Stella Kenedy Mem'l Found., 298 S.W.3d 663 (Tex. App.—Corpus Christi 2009, pet. denied)

9-4:2 Expressly Rejected in Texas

The Texas Commission of Appeals impliedly rejected a cause of action for conversion of real property.[22] Recent courts of appeals decisions have expressly rejected such a cause of action.[23] The correct cause of action to bring in such a situation is a trespass to real property cause of action.[24] Some minerals, once removed from the mineral estate, become personal property and may be converted.[25]

9-5 Detrimental Reliance as Independent Tort Claim

9-5:1 Overview

Detrimental reliance occurs when a person reasonably relies upon another's representation to that person's detriment.[26] However, detrimental reliance is merely an element of another tort or contract cause of action, rather than an independent tort.[27] At its most extreme, one person's detrimental reliance upon another is treated as a Promissory Estoppel, effectively creating a contract where no express contract actually existed.[28]

9-5:1.1 Related Causes of Action

Promissory Estoppel, Fraud: Common Law Fraud, Fraud: Fraud by Non-disclosure, Fraud: Statutory Fraud, Oil and Gas Litigation: Fraud

---

[22] *Cage Bros. v. Whiteman*, 163 S.W.2d 638, 641 (Tex. Comm'n App. 1942).

[23] *E.g., Lucio v. John G. & Marie Stella Kenedy Mem'l Found.*, 298 S.W.3d 663, 672 (Tex. App.—Corpus Christi 2009, pet. denied); *Lighthouse Church of Cloverleaf v. Tex. Bank*, 889 S.W.2d 595, 599 n.4 (Tex. App.—Houston [14th Dist.] 1994, writ denied).

[24] *See Wilen v. Falkenstein*, 191 S.W.3d 791, 797 (Tex. App.—Fort Worth 2006, pet. denied) ("Trespass to real property occurs when a person enters another's land without consent.").

[25] *See Cage Bros. v. Whiteman*, 163 S.W.2d 638, 641 (Tex. Comm'n App. 1942).

[26] *English v. Fischer*, 660 S.W.2d 521, 524 (Tex. 1983); *Wheeler v. White*, 398 S.W.2d 93, 96 (Tex. 1965); *Adams v. Petrade Int'l, Inc.*, 754 S.W.2d 696, 708 (Tex. App.—Houston [1st Dist.] 1988, writ denied) (case discussing reasonable reliance).

[27] *Garner v. Corpus Christi Nat'l Bank*, 944 S.W.2d 469, 480 (Tex. App.—Corpus Christi 1997, writ denied), *holding modified by Allied Capital Corp. v. Cravens*, 67 S.W.3d 486 (Tex. App.—Corpus Christi 2002, no pet.).

[28] *Roberts v. Geosource Drilling Servs., Inc.*, 757 S.W.2d 48, 50 (Tex. App.—Houston [1st Dist.] 1988, no writ).

MISCELLANEOUS BUSINESS CAUSES OF ACTION

MUST READ CASES

Garner v. Corpus Christi Nat'l Bank, 944 S.W.2d 469 (Tex. App.—Corpus Christi 1997, writ denied), *holding modified by Allied Capital Corp. v. Cravens*, 67 S.W.3d 486 (Tex. App.—Corpus Christi 2002, no pet.)

University of Tex. Sys. v. Courtney, 946 S.W.2d 464 (Tex. App.—Fort Worth 1997, writ denied)

9-5:2 Expressly Rejected in Texas

The Supreme Court of Texas has not expressly rejected detrimental reliance as an independent tort, but several courts of appeals have.[29] Despite these courts' holdings, it appears that similar facts would support the contract-based cause of action for Promissory Estoppel.[30]

9-6 Embracery (Jury Tampering)

9-6:1 Overview

Embracery is an attempt to influence a jury corruptly to one side or the other.[31] Like spoliation of evidence and civil perjury, embracery involves the improper conduct by a party or a witness within the context of an underlying lawsuit.[32] In determining whether embracery has occurred, a juror may testify as to whether any outside influence was brought to bear on the jury.[33]

9-6:1.1 Related Causes of Action

Spoliation of Evidence (Expressly Rejected in Texas), Perjury (Expressly Rejected in Texas)

MUST READ CASE

Trevino v. Ortega, 969 S.W.2d 950 (Tex. 1998)

---

[29] *Garner v. Corpus Christi Nat'l Bank*, 944 S.W.2d 469, 480 (Tex. App.—Corpus Christi 1997, writ denied), *holding modified by Allied Capital Corp. v. Cravens*, 67 S.W.3d 486 (Tex. App.—Corpus Christi 2002, no pet.); *University of Tex. Sys. v. Courtney*, 946 S.W.2d 464, 468 (Tex. App.—Fort Worth 1997, no pet.).

[30] *See English v. Fischer*, 660 S.W.2d 521, 524 (Tex. 1983); *See also, Ford v. City State Bank of Palacios*, 44 S.W.3d 121, 138 (Tex. App.—Corpus Christi 2001); Chapter 4: Promissory Estoppel.

[31] *Trevino v. Ortega*, 969 S.W.2d 950, 953 (Tex. 1998) ((quoting Black's Law Dictionary 522 (6th ed.1990)).

[32] *Trevino v. Ortega*, 969 S.W.2d 950, 953 (Tex. 1998).

[33] Tex. R. Civ. P. 327.

9-6:2 Expressly Rejected in Texas

Although the Supreme Court of Texas has not expressly rejected the cause of action, the Court has assumed its invalidity in dicta.[34] When a litigant suspects another of engaging in embracery, it is likely that the claimant will be limited to pursuing sanctions in the underlying lawsuit.[35]

9-7 Common Law Shareholder Oppression

9-7:1 Overview

Common law shareholder oppression first gained traction in Texas in the 1988 case of *Davis v. Sheerin*.[36] The *Davis* courts and several other courts of appeals erroneously relied upon Section 11.404(b)(3) of the Business Organizations Code to create a cause of action which provided oppressed shareholders multiple equitable remedies.

9-7:1.1 Related Causes of Action

Statutory Shareholder Oppression, Receivership, Officer and Director Liability: Breach of the Duty of Loyalty

MUST READ CASE

Ritchie v. Rupe, 443 S.W.3d 856 (Tex. 2014)

9-7:2 Expressly Rejected in Texas

The Supreme Court of Texas recently rejected the common-law cause of action for shareholder oppression.[37] However, an oppressed shareholder may still seek the appointment of a receiver under the Business Organizations Code.[38] Furthermore, a governing person's actions, which constitute "oppression" in the receivership context might also constitute an actionable breach of fiduciary duty owed to the corporation.[39]

9-8 Grossly Negligent Inducement of Contract

9-8:1 Overview

As a general rule, a party that was fraudulently induced to enter into a contract is not bound by that contract.[40] Moreover, a party that fraudulently induces another to enter

---

[34] *Trevino v. Ortega*, 969 S.W.2d 950, 953 (Tex. 1998).
[35] *See Trevino v. Ortega*, 969 S.W.2d 950, 953 (Tex. 1998) (discussing sanctions for spoliation of evidence).
[36] *Davis v. Sheerin*, 754 S.W.2d 375, 378 (Tex. App.—Houston [1st Dist.] 1988, writ denied).
[37] *Ritchie v. Rupe*, 443 S.W. 3d 856, 878 (Tex. 2014).
[38] *See* Tex. Bus. Orgs. Code Ann. § 11.404(a)(1)(C).
[39] For example, the Supreme Court reiterated that the malicious suppression of dividends will support a cause of action for breach of fiduciary duty, despite there not being a common-law cause of action for shareholder oppression. *Ritchie v. Rupe*, 443 S.W.3d 856, 884–85 (Tex. 2014) (quoting *Patton v. Nicholas*, 279 S.W.2d 848, 853 (Tex. 1955)).
[40] *Formosa Plastics Corp. U.S.A. v. Presidio Eng'rs & Contractors, Inc.*, 960 S.W.2d 41, 46 (Tex. 1998).

into a contract has breached a separate legal duty and is liable for tort damages.[41] Courts have been hesitant to extend the cause of action for fraudulent inducement to lesser levels of culpability.[42] In determining whether a defendant's negligence or gross negligence gives rise to a contractual cause of action or rather one sounding in tort, courts look to the nature of the damages.[43] Where the injury is an economic loss to the subject matter of the contract, that loss sounds in contract, not in tort.[44]

9-8:1.1 Related Causes of Action

Rescission, Fraud: Common Law Fraud, Fraud: Statutory Fraud, Fraud: Fraud by Non-disclosure, Negligent Misrepresentation, Fraudulent Inducement

MUST READ CASES

D.S.A., Inc. v. Hillsboro Indep. Sch. Dist., 973 S.W.2d 662 (Tex. 1998)

Yzaguirre v. KCS Res., Inc., 47 S.W.3d 532 (Tex. App.—Dallas 2000), *aff'd*, 53 S.W.3d 368 (Tex. 2001)

9-8:2 Expressly Rejected in Texas

The Supreme Court of Texas has expressly rejected the cause of action for grossly negligent inducement to contract.[45] The Court had previously acknowledged a separate cause of action for fraudulent inducement and saw no reason to extend the fraudulent inducement cause of action as such an extension would potentially convert every breach of contract action into a tort claim.[46]

9-9 Invasion of Privacy (False Light)

9-9:1 Overview

The umbrella of "invasion of privacy" contains four discrete categories of proposed causes of action,[47] including false light.[48] In jurisdictions which do acknowledge false light as a tort, the plaintiff must prove that the defendant made false statements which caused publicity that unreasonably portrayed the plaintiff in a false light.[49]

---

[41] *Formosa Plastics Corp. U.S.A. v. Presidio Eng'rs & Contractors, Inc.*, 960 S.W.2d 41, 46 (Tex. 1998).
[42] *See D.S.A., Inc. v. Hillsboro Indep. Sch. Dist.*, 973 S.W.2d 662, 664 (Tex. 1998).
[43] *Yzaguirre v. KCS Res., Inc.*, 47 S.W.3d 532, 543 (Tex. App.—Dallas 2000) *aff'd*, 53 S.W.3d 368 (Tex. 2001).
[44] *Yzaguirre v. KCS Res., Inc.*, 47 S.W.3d 532, 543 (Tex. App.—Dallas 2000) *aff'd*, 53 S.W.3d 368 (Tex. 2001).
[45] *D.S.A., Inc. v. Hillsboro Indep. Sch. Dist.*, 973 S.W.2d 662, 664 (Tex. 1998).
[46] *D.S.A., Inc. v. Hillsboro Indep. Sch. Dist.*, 973 S.W.2d 662, 664 (Tex. 1998).
[47] *Cain v. Hearst Corp.*, 878 S.W.2d 577, 578 (Tex. 1994) (citing Restatement (Second) of Torts, § 652E).
[48] *Cain v. Hearst Corp.*, 878 S.W.2d 577, 578 (Tex. 1994) (citing Restatement (Second) of Torts, § 652E).
[49] *Cain v. Hearst Corp.*, 878 S.W.2d 577, 580 (Tex. 1994).

9-9:1.1 Related Causes of Action

Defamation, Libel, Slander

MUST READ CASE

Cain v. Hearst Corp., 878 S.W.2d 577 (Tex. 1994)

9-9:2 Expressly Rejected in Texas

The Supreme Court expressly rejected the common law tort of invasion of privacy by placing the plaintiff in a false light.[50] The Court held a false light claim duplicated a plaintiff's cause of action for defamation while unduly restricting the defendant's First Amendment protection.[51]

9-10 Negligent Defense of Insured by Insurer

9-10:1 Overview

An insurer owes a duty of good faith to effectuate claims made by the insured or the policy holder.[52] When a third-party makes a demand for payment, however, the insurer's duties are greatly diminished.[53] In the third-party demand context, an insurer must only abide by the duties imposed by *Stowers* or by contract.

9-10:1.1 Related Causes of Action

Insurance Litigation: *Stowers* Claims, Declaratory Judgment on Policy: Duty to Defend, Declaratory Judgment on Policy: Coverage Claim

MUST READ CASE

Mid-Continent Ins. Co. v. Liberty Mut. Ins. Co., 236 S.W.3d 765 (Tex. 2007)

9-10:2 Expressly Rejected in Texas

The Supreme Court has expressly rejected a cause of action for negligent defense of a third-party claim against the insured by the insurer.[54] The exclusive remedies available to an insured are those offered under the *Stowers* doctrine and any contractual remedies.[55]

---

[50] *Cain v. Hearst Corp.*, 878 S.W.2d 577, 579 (Tex. 1994).
[51] *Cain v. Hearst Corp.*, 878 S.W.2d 577, 579–80 (Tex. 1994).
[52] Tex. Ins. Code Ann. § 542.003.
[53] *See Mid-Continent Ins. Co. v. Liberty Mut. Ins. Co.*, 236 S.W.3d 765, 776 (Tex. 2007).
[54] *Mid-Continent Ins. Co. v. Liberty Mut. Ins. Co.*, 236 S.W.3d 765, 776 (Tex. 2007).
[55] *Mid-Continent Ins. Co. v. Liberty Mut. Ins. Co.*, 236 S.W.3d 765, 776 (Tex. 2007).

9-11 Negligent Infliction of Emotional Distress

9-11:1 Overview

Courts have struggled with the availability of emotional distress damages for quite some time. Texas has gone through several different standards in determining whether a plaintiff may recover for emotional distress.[56] There is no general duty in Texas not to negligently inflict emotional distress; claimant may recover mental anguish damages only in connection with defendant's breach of some other legal duty.[57]

9-11:1.1 Related Causes of Action

Intentional Infliction of Emotional Distress, Breach of Informal Fiduciary Duty from Confidential Relationship,[58] Bystander Emotional Distress, Negligence

MUST READ CASE

Boyles v. Kerr, 855 S.W.2d 593 (Tex. 1993)

9-11:2 Expressly Rejected in Texas

The Supreme Court has expressly rejected the cause of action for negligent infliction of emotional distress.[59] The Court accomplished this by rejecting a general duty to refrain from negligently inflicting emotional distress.[60] A plaintiff may, however, maintain a cause of action for negligently inflicted emotional distress if, and only if, the defendant violated some other pre-existing duty.[61]

9-12 Negligent Investigation of Employee Misconduct

9-12:1 Overview

Employment-at-will is deeply rooted in the Texas common law, and Texas courts have been reluctant to create exceptions to the employment-at-will doctrine. The Texas Legislature, however, has created several specific exceptions to advance public policy, including discharge of a public employee whistleblower, employment discrimination,

---

[56] See *St. Elizabeth Hosp. v. Garrard*, 730 S.W.2d 649, 653 (Tex. 1987), *overruled* by *Boyles v. Kerr*, 855 S.W.2d 593 (Tex. 1993) (creating a tort for negligently inflicted emotional distress); *Boyles v. Kerr*, 855 S.W.2d 593, 598 (Tex. 1993) (citing *Dillon v. Legg*, 441 P.2d 912, 920 (Cal. 1968) for the proposition that bystanders may recover for negligently inflicted emotional distress in certain circumstances); *Boyles v. Kerr*, 855 S.W.2d 593, 594 (Tex. 1993) (holding there is no general duty to refrain from the negligent infliction of emotional distress).

[57] *Patel v. Hussain*, 485 S.W.3d 153 (Tex. App.—Houston [14th Dist.] 2016, no pet.).

[58] Funeral Directors have a duty to preserve the dignity of any corpse entrusted to them. *Cox Texas Newspapers, L.P. v. Wootten*, 59 S.W.3d 717, 722 (Tex. App.—Austin 2001, pet. denied).

[59] *Boyles v. Kerr*, 855 S.W.2d 593, 597 (Tex. 1993).

[60] *Boyles v. Kerr*, 855 S.W.2d 593, 597 (Tex. 1993).

[61] *Boyles v. Kerr*, 855 S.W.2d 593, 597 (Tex. 1993).

and other statutory exceptions. The only court-created exception has been Wrongful Discharge: Refusal to Perform Illegal Act.

9-12:1.1 Related Causes of Action

Wrongful Discharge: Breach of Employment Agreement; Suit for Retaliatory Treatment: Filing a Worker's Compensation Claim, Wrongful Discharge: Refusal to Perform Illegal Act, Employment Discrimination, Breach of Contract

MUST READ CASE

Texas Farm Bureau Mut. Ins. Cos. v. Sears, 84 S.W.3d 604 (Tex. 2002)

9-12:2 Expressly Rejected in Texas

The Supreme Court of Texas expressly rejected a cause of action for Negligent Investigation of Employee Misconduct.[62] In *Texas Farm Bureau*, the Supreme Court held that when an at-will employment relationship exists, an employer may terminate its employee because of good reasons, bad reasons or carelessly formed reasons based upon a negligent investigation into employee misconduct without liability.[63]

9-13 Liability of Successor for Tortious Conduct of Predecessor

9-13:1 Overview

The form of an entity takeover will generally dictate whether a successor entity is liable for the tortious conduct of its predecessor. In Texas, an entity takeover may occur through merger, share exchange, conversion or sale of the entity's assets.[64] When an entity merges,[65] executes a share exchange[66] or converts,[67] all of the predecessor's liabilities are allocated to the surviving or new entities.

MUST READ CASE

Lockheed Martin Corp. v. Gordon, 16 S.W.3d 127 (Tex. App.—Houston [1st Dist.] 2000, pet. denied)

9-13:2 Expressly Rejected in Texas

When an entity purchases property from a predecessor entity, the general rule is that the successor assumes none of the predecessor's liabilities[68] unless the successor

---

[62] *Texas Farm Bureau Mut. Ins. Cos. v. Sears*, 84 S.W.3d 604, 610 (Tex. 2002).
[63] *Texas Farm Bureau Mut. Ins. Cos. v. Sears*, 84 S.W.3d 604, 609 (Tex. 2002).
[64] Tex. Bus. Orgs. Code Ann. §§ 10.001–10.254.
[65] Tex. Bus. Orgs. Code Ann. § 10.008(a)(3).
[66] Tex. Bus. Orgs. Code Ann. § 10.055.
[67] Tex. Bus. Orgs. Code Ann. § 10.106.
[68] Tex. Bus. Orgs. Code Ann. § 10.254.

expressly assumes the predecessor's liabilities.[69] A successor's assumption of the predecessor's tort liability must expressly include the words "tort liability."[70]

9-14 Wrongful Expulsion of Whistleblowing Partner

9-14:1 Overview

A partner's status within the partnership is governed under employment-at-will concepts.[71] Partners always have the *power* to withdraw from the partnership but only sometimes have the *right* to withdrawal.[72] In contrast, there are no substantive limitations on when a partnership may expel a partner from its ranks.[73]

9-14:1.1 Related Causes of Action

Breach of Partnership Duty, Judicial Expulsion of Partner, Wrongful Withdrawal of Partner

MUST READ CASE

Bohatch v. Butler & Binion, 977 S.W.2d 543 (Tex. 1998)

9-14:2 Expressly Rejected in Texas

The Supreme Court has expressly rejected the cause of action for wrongful expulsion of whistleblowing partner.[74] The Court reasoned that trust among the partners would be irreparably harmed if the Court were to recognize such a cause of action[75] even if the whistleblowing partner acted in good faith and was entirely accurate in her accusations.[76]

9-15 Perjury

9-15:1 Overview

Generally, a person perjures himself when he makes a false statement while under oath with the intent to deceive.[77] Simple perjury is a Class A misdemeanor, while aggravated perjury is a third degree felony.[78]

---

[69] *Lockheed Martin Corp. v. Gordon*, 16 S.W.3d 127, 139 (Tex. App.—Houston [1st Dist.] 2000, pet. denied). In contrast, other jurisdictions have a more permissive approach to successor liability. *See Lockheed Martin Corp. v. Gordon*, 16 S.W.3d 127, 134 (Tex. App.—Houston [1st Dist.] 2000, pet. denied) (quoting the four exceptions recognized in the Restatement (Third) of the Law of Torts, Products Liability § 12 (1998)).

[70] *Lockheed Martin Corp. v. Gordon*, 16 S.W.3d 127, 139–40 (Tex. App.—Houston [1st Dist.] 2000, pet. denied) (holding that a purchase agreement's assumption of "ordinary course of business" liabilities and obligations does not include tort liabilities).

[71] *Bohatch v. Butler & Binion*, 977 S.W.2d 543, 545 (Tex. 1998).

[72] *See* Tex. Bus. Orgs. Code Ann. § 152.503 (discussing wrongful withdrawal of a partner).

[73] *See Bohatch v. Butler & Binion*, 977 S.W.2d 543, 545 (Tex. 1998).

[74] *See Bohatch v. Butler & Binion*, 977 S.W.2d 543, 546 (Tex. 1998).

[75] *Bohatch v. Butler & Binion*, 977 S.W.2d 543, 546–47 (Tex. 1998).

[76] *Bohatch v. Butler & Binion*, 977 S.W.2d 543, 547 (Tex. 1998).

[77] Tex. Pen. Code Ann. § 37.02.

[78] Tex. Pen. Code Ann. §§ 37.02-37.03.

9-15:1.1 Related Causes of Action

Common Law Fraud, Statutory Fraud

MUST READ CASES

Long v. Tanner, 170 S.W.3d 752 (Tex. App.—Waco 2005, pet. denied)

Prostok v. Browning, 112 S.W.3d 876 (Tex. App.—Dallas 2003), *aff'd in part, rev'd in part*, 165 S.W.3d 336 (Tex. 2005)

9-15:2 Expressly Rejected in Texas

Texas courts have expressly rejected an independent cause of action for perjury[79] based on the well settled premise that the Texas Penal Code does not create private causes of action.[80] Courts will look to both the form and substance of a plaintiff's pleadings to determine whether the plaintiff has pleaded the non-existent cause of action for perjury.[81] Moreover, perjury is a form of intrinsic fraud and therefore cannot be used as a means to collaterally attack a final judgment.[82]

9-16 "Prima Facie Tort"

9-16:1 Overview

Prima facie tort is the infliction of an intentional harm without excuse or justification by an act or series of acts which otherwise would be lawful and which results in special damage.[83] The concept has its roots in a United States Supreme Court opinion,[84] but has not gained traction in Texas.

9-16:1.1 Related Causes of Action

Intentional Infliction of Emotional Distress, Malicious Prosecution, Abuse of Process

MUST READ CASE

Martin v. Trevino, 578 S.W.2d 763 (Tex. App.—Corpus Christi 1978, writ ref'd n.r.e.)

---

[79] *Long v. Tanner*, 170 S.W.3d 752, 755 (Tex. App.—Waco 2005, pet. denied); *Spurlock v. Johnson*, 94 S.W.3d 655, 658 (Tex. App.—San Antonio 2002, no pet.); *see Trevino v. Ortega*, 969 S.W.2d 950, 953 (Tex. 1998) (dicta).

[80] *Spurlock v. Johnson*, 94 S.W.3d 655, 658 (Tex. App.—San Antonio 2002, no pet.).

[81] *Prostok v. Browning*, 112 S.W.3d 876, 915 (Tex. App.—Dallas 2003) *aff'd in part, rev'd in part*, 165 S.W.3d 336 (Tex. 2005).

[82] *Browning v. Prostok*, 165 S.W.3d 336, 347–48 (Tex. 2005).

[83] *Martin v. Trevino*, 578 S.W.2d 763, 772 (Tex. App.—Corpus Christi 1978, writ ref'd n.r.e.).

[84] *Aikens v. State of Wis.*, 195 U.S. 194, 204 (1904).

9-16:2 Expressly Rejected in Texas

Those Texas courts writing on the issue expressly rejected prima facie tort as a cause of action.[85] Other sources of law provide a remedy, and any creation of a cause of action should be left to the legislature.[86]

9-17 Retaliatory Discharge for Perception of Participation in Protected Activity

9-17:1 Overview

Both Congress and the Legislature have passed statutory schemes aimed at protecting employees from discriminatory tactics in the workplace. These statutes also protect employees which have filed a complaint or otherwise reported discriminatory tactics from retaliation.

9-17:1.1 Related Causes of Action

Wrongful Discharge: Breach of Employment Agreement, Suit for Retaliatory Treatment: Filing a Worker's Compensation Claim, Wrongful Discharge: Refusal to Perform Illegal Act, Employment Discrimination, Breach of Contract

MUST READ CASES

Dias v. Goodman Mfg. Co., L.P., 214 S.W.3d 672 (Tex. App.—Houston [14th Dist.] 2007, pet. denied)

Salay v. Baylor Univ., 115 S.W.3d 625 (Tex. App.—Waco 2003, pet. denied)

9-17:2 Expressly Rejected in Texas

Texas courts have expressly rejected a retaliation cause of action based upon the employer's perception that an employee engaged in a protected activity.[87] Rather, these courts have held that the relevant statutes require the employee's actual participation in a protected activity before an employer may retaliate.[88]

---

[85] *E.g., A.G. Servs, Inc. v. Peat, Marwick, Mitchell & Co.*, 757 S.W.2d 503, 507 (Tex. App.—Houston [1st Dist.] 1988, writ denied); *Martin v. Trevino*, 578 S.W.2d 763, 772–73 (Tex. App.—Corpus Christi 1978, writ ref'd n.r.e.).

[86] *Martin v. Trevino*, 578 S.W.2d 763, 772–73 (Tex. App.—Corpus Christi 1978, writ ref'd n.r.e.).

[87] *Dias v. Goodman Mfg. Co., L.P.*, 214 S.W.3d 672, 678–79 (Tex. App.—Houston [14th Dist.] 2007, pet. denied); *Salay v. Baylor Univ.*, 115 S.W.3d 625, 627 (Tex. App.—Waco 2003, pet. denied).

[88] *Dias v. Goodman Mfg. Co., L.P.*, 214 S.W.3d 672, 678–79 (Tex. App.—Houston [14th Dist.] 2007, pet. denied); *Salay v. Baylor Univ.*, 115 S.W.3d 625, 627 (Tex. App.—Waco 2003, pet. denied).

9-18 Retaliatory Discharge for Protected Act of Third Party

9-18:1 Overview

Both Congress and the Legislature have passed statutory schemes aimed at protecting employees from discriminatory tactics in the workplace. These statutes also protect employees who have filed a complaint or otherwise reported discriminatory tactics from retaliation.

9-18:1.1 Related Causes of Action

Wrongful Discharge: Breach of Employment Agreement, Suit for Retaliatory Treatment: Filing a Worker's Compensation Claim; Wrongful Discharge: Refusal to Perform Illegal Act, Employment Discrimination; Breach of Contract

MUST READ CASES

Holt v. JTM Indus., Inc., 89 F.3d 1224 (5th Cir. 1996)

Dias v. Goodman Mfg. Co., L.P., 214 S.W.3d 672 (Tex. App.—Houston [14th Dist.] 2007, pet. denied)

9-18:2 Expressly Rejected in Texas

Texas and federal courts alike have expressly rejected a cause of action based upon an employer's retaliation for a third party's protected act.[89] These courts have done so based upon deference to the respective legislative intent as evidenced in the plain meaning of the statute.[90] Accordingly, a plaintiff in a retaliatory discharge lawsuit must have been the person who engaged in the protected act.[91]

9-19 Spoliation of Evidence

9-19:1 Overview

Spoliation of Evidence occurs when a party to a lawsuit has a duty to preserve evidence, culpably destroys or alters the evidence, and such destruction or alteration prejudices the non-spoliating party.[92] When the non-spoliating party establishes that spoliation has occurred, he may request an evidentiary sanction appropriate for the circumstances.[93]

---

[89] *Holt v. JTM Indus., Inc.*, 89 F.3d 1224, 1227 (5th Cir. 1996); *Dias v. Goodman Mfg. Co., L.P.*, 214 S.W.3d 672, 677-78 (Tex. App.—Houston [14th Dist.] 2007, pet. denied).

[90] *Holt v. JTM Indus., Inc.*, 89 F.3d 1224, 1227 (5th Cir. 1996); *Dias v. Goodman Mfg. Co., L.P.*, 214 S.W.3d 672, 677-78 (Tex. App.—Houston [14th Dist.] 2007, pet. denied).

[91] *Holt v. JTM Indus., Inc.*, 89 F.3d 1224, 1227 (5th Cir. 1996); *Dias v. Goodman Mfg. Co., L.P.*, 214 S.W.3d 672, 677-78 (Tex. App.—Houston [14th Dist.] 2007, pet. denied).

[92] *Trevino v. Ortega*, 969 S.W.2d 950, 954-55 (Tex. 1998) (Baker, J., Concurring).

[93] *Trevino v. Ortega*, 969 S.W.2d 950, 959 (Tex. 1998) (Baker, J., Concurring).

MISCELLANEOUS BUSINESS CAUSES OF ACTION

MUST READ CASES

Brookshire Bros., Ltd. v. Aldridge, 438 S.W.3d 9 (Tex. 2014)

Trevino v. Ortega, 969 S.W.2d 950 (Tex. 1998)

9-19:2 Expressly Rejected in Texas

The Supreme Court has expressly rejected an independent cause of action for spoliation of evidence.[94] The Court's rejected an independent cause of action based upon the speculative nature of damages, the ability of litigants to rectify the spoliation within the underlying lawsuit, and an analogy to the Court's rejection of independent causes of action for perjury and embracery.[95]

9-20 Tortious Interference with Fiduciary Duty

9-20:1 Overview

Tortious Interference with Fiduciary Duty, as contrasted by Knowing Participation in Breach of Fiduciary Duty, is not a viable cause of action in Texas.

9-20:1.1 Related Causes of Action

Knowing Participation in Breach of Fiduciary Duty, Civil Conspiracy, Tortious Interference with Existing Contract

MUST READ CASES

Taylor v. Allstate Ins. Co., 356 S.W.3d 92, 100 (Tex. App.—Houston [1st Dist.] 2011, pet. denied)

Alpert v. Crain, Caton & James, P.C., 178 S.W.3d 398, 407 (Tex. App.—Houston [1st Dist.] 2005, pet. denied)

9-20:2 Expressly Rejected in Texas

Tortious interference with fiduciary duty is not recognized as a cause of action in Texas.[96] There is no Supreme Court of Texas opinion on this point. There is a claim for knowing participation in a breach of fiduciary duty.[97]

---

[94] *Trevino v. Ortega*, 969 S.W.2d 950, 952 (Tex. 1998). *See also Brookshire Bros, Ltd. v. Aldridge*, 438 S.W.3d 9, 19 (Tex. 2014) ("In Texas, spoliation is an evidentiary concept rather than a separate cause of action.").

[95] *Trevino v. Ortega*, 969 S.W.2d 950, 952–53 (Tex. 1998).

[96] *Taylor v. Allstate Ins. Co.*, 356 S.W.3d 92, 100 (Tex. App.—Houston [1st Dist.] 2011, pet. denied); *Alpert v. Crain, Caton & James, P.C.*, 178 S.W.3d 398, 407 (Tex. App.—Houston [1st Dist.] 2005, pet. denied); W. McDonald & Carlson Tex. Civ. Prac. § 2:35 (2d. ed.).

[97] "[W]here a third party knowingly participates in the breach of duty of a fiduciary, such third party becomes a joint tortfeasor with the fiduciary and is liable as such." *Meadows v. Hartford Life Ins. Co.*, 492 F.3d 634, 639 (5th Cir. 2007) (quoting *Kinzbach Tool Co. v. Corbett-Wallace Corp.*, 138 Tex. 565, 160 S.W.2d 509, 514 (Tex. 1942)).

9-21 Breach of Implied Warranty of Professional Services

9-21:1 Overview

There exist several implied warranties to protect consumers in sales transactions, and a smaller number of implied warranties to protect consumers in service transactions.[98] However, Texas courts have been reluctant to impose implied warranties against providers of services.[99]

9-21:1.1 Related Causes of Action

Breach of Implied Warranty, Breach of Express Warranty

MUST READ CASE

Murphy v. Campbell, 964 S.W.2d 265 (Tex. 1997)

9-21:2 Expressly Rejected in Texas

The Supreme Court expressly rejected a cause of action for breach of implied warranty of professional services,[100] since the facts which would give rise to such a breach would also give rise to causes of action for professional negligence or breach of contract.[101] Implied warranties are imposed, however, on the provision of some nonprofessional services.[102]

9-22 Whistleblower Action: Protection of Private Sector Employee

9-22:1 Overview

Employment-at-will is rarely abrogated by Texas courts. The Texas Legislature, however, has created several specific exceptions to advance public policy, including discharge of a public employee whistleblower and several occupation-specific private sector whistleblower statutes. There is no general private sector whistleblower statute in Texas.

9-22:1.1 Related Causes of Action

Discharge of a Public Employee Whistleblower

---

[98] *See* Chapter 3.
[99] *Dennis v. Allison*, 698 S.W.2d 94, 96 (Tex. 1985) (Ray, J., dissenting).
[100] *Murphy v. Campbell*, 964 S.W.2d 265, 268–69 (Tex. 1997).
[101] *Murphy v. Campbell*, 964 S.W.2d 265, 269 (Tex. 1997).
[102] *See Melody Home Mfg. Co. v. Barnes*, 741 S.W.2d 349, 354 (Tex. 1987) (imposing the implied warranty of good and workmanlike construction on a provider of repair services to existing goods).

MISCELLANEOUS BUSINESS CAUSES OF ACTION

MUST READ CASES

Austin v. HealthTrust, Inc.—The Hosp. Co., 967 S.W.2d 400 (Tex. 1998)

Winters v. Houston Chronicle Pub. Co., 795 S.W.2d 723 (Tex. 1990)

9-22:2 Expressly Rejected in Texas

The Texas Legislature created several whistleblower exceptions to the general common-law doctrine of employment-at-will.[103] However, the Legislature has not granted general whistleblower protection for private sector employees,[104] and Texas does not recognize a cause of action for a private sector employee who reports illegal activities.[105]

9-23 Oil and Gas Litigation—Implied Covenant to Further Explore

9-23:1 Overview

In some jurisdictions, a lessee can be sued for not further exploring the leasehold for oil and gas within a reasonable time.[106] The covenant is based on the principles of promoting development and preventing delay. In jurisdictions that recognize the covenant, the lessee is under a duty to test and to explore other areas of the leasehold or risk cancellation of the lease. However, Texas courts have held that there is no implied covenant to further explore that exists independent of the implied covenant of reasonable development.[107]

9-23:1.1 Related Causes of Action

Breach of the Implied Covenant to Reasonably Develop

MUST READ CASES

Sun Expl. & Prod. Co. v. Jackson, 783 S.W.2d 202 (Tex. 1989)

Clifton v. Koontz, 325 S.W.2d 684 (Tex. 1959)

9-23:2 Expressly Rejected in Texas

Texas courts recognize an implied covenant to reasonably develop the premises after production begins.[108] The covenant to reasonably develop requires a lessee to conduct

---

[103] *See, e.g.*, Tex. Gov't Code Ann. § 554.002 (public employee); Tex. Health & Safety Code Ann. § 161.134 (hospital employee); Tex. Agric. Code Ann. § 125.013 (agricultural laborer); Tex. Labor Code Ann. § 21.055 (public or private employee who reports discrimination).

[104] *Austin v. HealthTrust, Inc.—The Hosp. Co.*, 967 S.W.2d 400, 403 (Tex. 1998).

[105] *Austin v. HealthTrust, Inc.—The Hosp. Co.*, 967 S.W.2d 400, 403 (Tex. 1998); *Winters v. Houston Chronicle Pub. Co.*, 795 S.W.2d 723, 724–25 (Tex. 1990).

[106] *Davis v. Ross Prod. Co.*, 910 S.W.2d 209, 213 (1995) (finding that an implied covenant exists such that the lessee must explore the property with reasonable diligence).

[107] *Sun Expl. & Prod. Co. v. Jackson*, 783 S.W.2d 202, 204 (Tex. 1989).

[108] *Clifton v. Koontz*, 325 S.W.2d 684, 693–94 (Tex. 1959).

further development with reasonable diligence.[109] The Texas Supreme Court has held that there is no implied covenant to further explore that is distinct from the implied covenant to reasonably develop. While the lessee has the right to further explore, the lessee is not under a duty to further explore.[110]

---

[109] *Clifton v. Koontz*, 325 S.W.2d 684, 693–94 (Tex. 1959).
[110] *Clifton v. Koontz*, 325 S.W.2d 684, 696–97 (Tex. 1959).

SECTION II
Pleading Damages

CHAPTER 10

General Pleading Requirements for Damages in Business Litigation*

10-1 Necessity of Pleading Damage Amount

Tex. R. Civ. P. 47(c) requires each new petition (other than suits governed by the Family Code) to plead into the jurisdiction of the Court using one of five categories specifying the relief sought:

- *Only* monetary relief of $100,000 or less, including damages of any kind, penalties, costs, expenses, prejudgment interest and attorney fees;

- Monetary relief of $100,000 or less *and* non-monetary relief;

- Monetary relief over $100,000 but not more than $200,000;

- Monetary relief over $200,000 but not more than $1,000,000; or,

- Monetary relief over $1,000,000.

Tex. R. Civ. P. 169 allows fast tracking of cases using the mandatory expedited case rules and apply to those matters seeking relief in the first category above. Rule 169 expressly exempts cases governed by the Family Code, the Property Code, the Tax Code, or Chapter 74 of the Civil Practice & Remedies Code.[1]

If a plaintiff fails to comply with Rule 47's pleading requirements, the defendant may specially except, and the plaintiff is barred from conducting discovery until the plaintiff's pleading is amended to comply.[2] Not uncommonly, the petition either includes a discovery request (such as a request for disclosure) or sends discovery shortly after filing suit. If the petition does not conform to Rule 47, the defendant faces a dilemma: answer the discovery to avoid waiving objections or stand on the procedural rights afforded by Rule 47. Best practices suggest that the defendant promptly specially except, as the Court can hear the exception on only 3 days' notice—substantially less than the 30 days afforded for objecting to discovery. Prompt action by the defendant protects against the dilemma. While the plaintiff may require a hearing with a ruling

---

* The authors thank Max Moran for his assistance in the updating of this chapter.
[1] Tex. R. Civ. P. 169(a); *see* Comment 2 (2013) to Rule 169. Although Tex. R. Civ. P. 47(c) only references a pleading exemption for suits governed by the Family Code, these other exemptions from the mandatory expedited trial rules are set forth in Tex. R. Civ. P. 169(a)(2).
[2] Tex. R. Civ. P. 47(d).

and order from the trial court,[3] frequently, the plaintiff will voluntarily amend to conform to Rule 47's damage stratums.

The plaintiff also must specify a discovery control plan depending in part on the amount of damages sought, electing either a Level 1, Level 2 or Level 3 discovery plan. Expedited actions are governed by Level 1 discovery plans and sharply curtail the amount of discovery which can be conducted.[4] Level 1 cases must be set for trial within 90 days of the end of the discovery period if any party so requests, and the parties are limited to 8 hours per side for jury selection, opening statement, presentation of evidence and closing argument.[5] For other cases, plaintiff may select either Level 2[6] or Level 3[7] depending on the anticipated complexity of the issues and amount of discovery needed. Level 2 discovery is governed by the limits on deposition time and discovery requests set out in Tex. R. Civ. P. 190.3(b). A Level 3 case requires entry of a docket control order that conforms to Tex. R. Civ. P. 190.4.

10-2 Necessity for Match Between Pleading and Proof of Damages

To understand the pleading requirements for damages, it is important to understand the distinction between the *character* of damages and the *measure* of damages.[8]

Damages are *characterized* as either general (direct) damages or as special (consequential) damages. Theoretically, general damages are not required to be specifically pleaded, since these are the damages which naturally and necessarily result from the kind of wrongful conduct alleged by the claimant (and can therefore be anticipated by the defendant without specific pleading).[9] Special damages, on the other hand, are required by Tex. R. Civ. P. 56 to be specifically pleaded so as to provide fair notice to the defendant of each kind of damages being claimed.[10] Sections 10–2, 10–3 and 10–4 of this Chapter discuss pleading general and special damages.

The *measure* of damages is the particular formula or method for calculating a specific kind of damages, although there may be more than one way to measure or calculate damages for a specific cause of action.

---

[3] Michael Morrison, James Wren, and Chris Galeczka, *Expedited Civil Actions in Texas and the U.S.: A Survey of State Procedures and a Guide to Implementing Texas's New Expedited Actions Process*, 65 Baylor L. Rev. 826, n. 263 (2013).

[4] *See* Tex. R. Civ. P. 190.1 (requiring designation of discovery level in the first numbered paragraph) and Tex. R. Civ. P. 190.2 (making Level 1 discovery applicable to expedited actions).

[5] Tex. R. Civ. P. 169(d).

[6] Level 2 provides a series of default discovery limitations and deadlines, as set forth in Tex. R. Civ. P. 190.3, and leaves other default deadlines in place, such as for pleading amendments without leave of court (Tex. R. Civ. P. 63), for designation of expert witnesses (Tex. R. Civ. P. 195.2), and to avoid presumed untimeliness of discovery supplementation (Tex. R. Civ. P. 193.5).

[7] Pursuant to Tex. R. Civ. P. 190.4, Level 3 requires the trial court to provide a specific scheduling order.

[8] *Drury Sw., Inc. v. Louie Ledeaux No. 1, Inc.*, No. 04-12-0087-CV, 2013 WL 5812989, at *11 (Tex. App.—San Antonio Oct. 30, 2013, no pet.).

[9] *See* discussion of general damages in Chapter 10, Section 10–3.

[10] *See* discussion of special damages in Chapter 10, Section 10–3.

PLEADING REQUIREMENTS

Generally, a plaintiff is not entitled to submit evidence or obtain recovery on a measure of damages that differs from the measure of damages actually pleaded (assuming a timely and specific objection by the defendant), because the variance between pleading and proof fails to provide the defendant with fair notice of the measure of damages actually relied upon.[11]

Courts construe the pleading requirement liberally, however, finding adequate notice despite the lack of an accurate damages pleading. For example, a pleading seeking punitive damages which referred to the wrong statute did not invalidate the damages pleading since the error was apparent, and the defendant had fair notice of the intended claim for punitive damages.[12] A pleading which affirmatively states an erroneous measure of damages may still support recovery of the correct measure of damages when that correct measure can be ascertained from other language. Where the contract at issue in the pleadings specifies the correct measure of damages, the defendant was found to have notice.[13] A vague reference to attorney fees sought in connection with enforcing a contractual right supports recovery of those contractual attorney fees even when the petition specifically alleged a claim of attorney's fees sought for violation of the DTPA, since "an attorney of reasonable competence with the pleadings before him" could ascertain that contractual attorney fees were being sought.[14]

When the pleaded measure of damages misstates the actual calculation or measure of damages sought at trial, the trial court should exclude proof of the unpleaded measure of damages. Defendants should be careful, however, about relying too strictly on the pleading if discovery responses or other pleaded matters put the defendant on notice.

10-3 Effect of Pleading General Damages

Although a pleading which affirmatively misstates the measure of damages may bar submission of a different measure of damages,[15] Texas pleading rules do not always require detail about what damages are sought. An allegation of the wrong committed by the defendant accompanied by a general prayer for relief and damages[16] will support the recovery of "general damages."[17]

---

[11] *Kissman v. Bendix Home Sys., Inc.*, 587 S.W.2d 675, 677 (Tex. 1979) (evidence of cost of repairs is not admissible if pleadings allege only the difference in the market value before and after a collision).

[12] *Horizon/CMS Healthcare Corp. v. Auld*, 34 S.W.3d 887, 896 (Tex. 2000).

[13] *Rowan Companies, Inc. v. Transco Expl. Co., Inc.*, 679 S.W.2d 660, 665–66 (Tex. App.—Houston [1st Dist.] 1984, writ ref'd n.r.e., *cert. denied*, 474 U.S. 822, 106 S.Ct. 74, 88 L.Ed.2d 61).

[14] *Daugherty v. Highland Capital Mgmt., L.P.*, No. 05-14-01215-CV, 2016 WL 4446158, at *3 (Tex. App.—Dallas Aug. 22, 2016, reh'g denied).

[15] *See* Chapter 10, Section 10–2.

[16] A general prayer for relief may be phrased "for recovery of all damages and other legal and equitable relief to which plaintiff may show himself to be entitled," accompanied by a categorization of the amount of damages being sought as required by Tex. R. Civ. P. 47(c).

[17] *Pringle v. Nowlin*, 629 S.W.2d 154, 157 (Tex. App.—Fort Worth 1982, writ ref'd n.r.e.) (general damages need not be specially pleaded and prayer for general relief will authorize judgment).

General damages are those damages which so usually flow from the kind of wrongdoing alleged in the petition that merely alleging the wrong provides sufficient notice of the damages.[18] Assuming, however, that a particular form of damages—such as lost profits—uniformly will or will not be considered "general damages" and therefore need not pleaded is risky. Lost profits may take the form of direct damages (considered as general damages) in one case but take the form of consequential (special) damages in another case.[19] Contract and business litigation damages often do not fall into the general damage category, so the safer course is to specifically plead special damages.

Itemizing damages carries its own risk since the proof must match the pleading.[20] Pleading with sufficient specificity, combined with thorough responses to requests for disclosure or expert designations, minimizes the likelihood a needed category of damages will be excluded on notice grounds.

10-4 Necessity of Pleading Special Damages

Special damages proximately result from the defendant's conduct but are not of such a usual nature that their occurrence would be routinely expected; instead, their occurrence would normally vary with the circumstances of an individual case.[21] Because the damages are not routinely incurred, the pleading must provide fair notice of the special damages re required by Tex. R. Civ. P. 56.

If plaintiff fails to properly plead an item of special damages, the defendant must object when placed on notice of the plaintiff's intent to seek recovery for the unpleaded special damages in order to avoid waiving the error.[22]

10-5 Distinguishing Between Direct and Consequential Damages

Courts in contract disputes and business litigation often refer to and distinguish between direct and consequential damages,[23] utilizing essentially the same definitions for general and direct damages, and essentially the same definitions for special and consequential damages. Direct (or general) damages compensate for the loss that necessarily and usually results from the wrongful act[24] and encompasses the loss that is conclusively presumed to have been foreseen by the defendant from his wrongful act.[25] Consequential (special) damages are "those damages which result naturally, but

---

[18] *Sherrod v. Bailey*, 580 S.W.2d 24, 28 (Tex. App.—Houston [1st Dist.] 1979, writ ref'd n.r.e.).
[19] *Continental Holdings, Ltd. v. Leahy*, 132 S.W.3d 471, 475 (Tex. App.—Eastland 2003, no pet.); *see also Harper v. Wellbeing Genomics Pty Ltd.*, 03-17-00035-CV, 2018 WL 6318876, at *11 (Tex. App.—Austin Dec. 4, 2018, pet. denied).
[20] *Weingartens, Inc. v. Price*, 461 S.W.2d 260, 263 (Tex. App.—Houston [14th Dist.] 1970, writ ref'd n.r.e.).
[21] *Sherrod v. Bailey*, 580 S.W.2d 24, 28 (Tex. App.—Houston [1st Dist.] 1979, writ red'd n.r.e.).
[22] *Italian Cowboy Partners, Ltd. v. Prudential Ins. Co. of Am.*, 341 S.W.3d 323, 345 (Tex. 2011), citing Tex. R. Civ. P. 90.
[23] *See, e.g., Arthur Andersen & Co. v. Perry Equip. Corp.*, 945 S.W.2d 812, 816 (Tex. 1997).
[24] *Baylor Univ. v. Sonnichsen*, 221 S.W.3d 632, 636 (Tex. 2007).
[25] *Arthur Andersen & Co. v. Perry Equip. Corp.*, 945 S.W.2d 812, 816 (Tex. 1997).

not necessarily" from the defendant's wrongful act[26] but must be both foreseeable and directly caused by the wrongful act.[27]

Direct damages may include either recovery of out-of-pocket losses (to obtain recovery of expenses incurred in reliance upon the defendant's promise or misrepresentation)[28] or benefit-of-the-bargain losses (to obtain the direct contractual expectancy that was lost due to the defendant's conduct),[29] to the extent these kinds of damages are directly and routinely foreseeable from the defendant's conduct.[30]

Consequential damages must be specifically pleaded[31] and require specific proof of foreseeability as a prerequisite to recovery.[32] For example, consequential damage could include foreseeable lost profits from other business opportunities (separate from the transaction in question) which were lost as a result of the defendant's misrepresentation.[33]

10-6 Interplay Between Pleadings and Requirements of Request for Disclosure

Tex. R. Civ. P. 194.2(d) requires a party who seeks damages to disclose "the amount and any method of calculating economic damages." This discovery disclosure requirement is in addition to the requirements for pleading damages. A failure to properly respond to this requirement, including a failure to timely supplement a response pursuant to Tex. R. Civ. P. 193.5, can result in exclusion of evidence of the economic damages.[34]

Because the calculations of the economic damages may change as more information is obtained in discovery or to address the passage of time, Tex. R. Civ. P. 194.6 states, "A response to [a request under Rule 194.2(d)] that has been changed by an amended or supplemental response is not admissible and may not be used for impeachment." Additionally, Tex. R. Civ. P. 197.3 states, "An answer to an interroga-

---

[26] *Baylor Univ. v. Sonnichsen*, 221 S.W.3d 632, 636 (Tex. 2007).

[27] *Arthur Andersen & Co. v. Perry Equip. Corp.*, 945 S.W.2d 812, 816 (Tex. 1997).

[28] The out-of-pocket measure computes the difference between the value paid and the value received. (*Formosa Plastics Corp. USA v. Presidio Eng'rs & Contractors, Inc.*, 960 S.W.2d 41, 49 (Tex. 1998)).

[29] The benefit-of-the-bargain measure computes the difference between the value as represented and the value received. (*Formosa Plastics Corp. U.S.A. v. Presidio Eng'rs & Contractors, Inc.*, 960 S.W.2d 41, 49 (Tex. 1998)).

[30] *Compare Formosa Plastics Corp. U.S.A. v. Presidio Eng'rs & Contractors, Inc.*, 960 S.W.2d 41, 49 (Tex. 1998) (referring to out-of-pocket restitution damages as direct damages); *Statewide Bank & SN Servicing Corp. v. Keith*, 301 S.W.3d 776, 786 (Tex. App.—Beaumont 2009, petition for review abated) (treating restitution and reliance damages in the case as consequential damages which must be specifically pleaded).

[31] *Statewide Bank & SN Servicing Corp. v. Keith*, 301 S.W.3d 776, 786 (Tex. App.—Beaumont 2009, petition for review abated).

[32] *AZZ Inc. v. Morgan*, 462 S.W.3d 284, 289 (Tex. App.—Fort Worth 2015, no pet.); *Stuart v. Bayless*, 964 S.W.2d 920, 921 (Tex. 1998).

[33] *Formosa Plastics Corp. USA v. Presidio Eng'rs & Contractors, Inc.*, 960 S.W.2d 41 n.1 (Tex. 1998).

[34] Tex. R. Civ. P. 193.6 and 215; see also *Allan v. Nersesova*, 307 S.W.3d 564, 576–78 (Tex. App.—Dallas 2010, no pet.) (excluding undisclosed diminution of market value of residence).

tory inquiring about matters described in Rule . . . 194.2(d) that has been amended or supplemented is not admissible and may not be used for impeachment." This protects both plaintiffs and defendants who initially answered the disclosure with the information available but needed to alter the calculations to more closely track the evidence.

This same protection does not apply to superseded pleadings which may constitute admissions by a party-opponent and thus admissible at trial by the opposing party.[35] As such, detailing the amount of economic damages is best done in response to a request for disclosure or interrogatory than in the pleadings.

10-7 Pleading Requirements for Statutory Damages Cap

Generally, statutory damage caps are to applied irrespective of whether the defendant has pleaded them as the cap is not a factual issue to be decided by the jury but rather a legally mandated limitation to be applied by the Court. The cap on exemplary damages set forth in Tex. Civ. Prac. & Rem. Code Ann. § 41.008(b) applies without any proof burden on the defendant; it is not "an avoidance or affirmative defense" pursuant to Tex. R. Civ. P. 94.[36] On the other hand, an opposing party is charged with knowledge of the statutory cap, including the necessity of pleading and proving any "cap-busting conduct."[37]

Presumably, the same reasoning applies to other forms of statutory caps on damages.

---

[35] *Bay Area Healthcare Grp., Ltd. V. McShane*, 239 S.W.3d 231, 235 (Tex. 2007).
[36] *Zorrilla v. Aypco Constr. II, LLC*, 469 S.W.3d 143, 155–58 (Tex. 2015).
[37] *Zorrilla v. Aypco Constr. II, LLC*, 469 S.W.3d 143, 157–58 (Tex. 2015).

CHAPTER 11

Common Business Litigation Damages Models*

11-1 Choosing the Right Damage Model

A plaintiff may plead alternatively into more than one cause of action which different remedies available depending on the jury's findings. It is thus important to determine the appropriate damage model for each cause of action, especially where more than one damage model can be pleaded for the same cause of action, such as "benefit-of-the-bargain" and "out-of-pocket" damages which may be alternative for remedies for breach of contract. Even within a broad category such as benefit-of-the-bargain are more discrete damage models like lost profits or the loss of value of a business that can be employed to determine the amount of benefit-of-the-bargain damages.

Alternative pleading is available for both alternate causes of action and alternate damage models, which requires knowledge and awareness of the "economic loss rule" and its application in Texas. The economic loss rule is actually an amalgamation of judicially created limitations on the recovery of economic damages in some tort actions.[1] The economic loss rule is not an affirmative defense that must be pleaded but is instead a principle for determining the proper measure of damages.[2] Thus, the economic loss rule may be raised by the defendant for the first time after the close of discovery or after the close of evidence. Depending on the timing, the defendant can raise the issue by summary judgment, directed verdict or via objection to a proposed damage submission in the jury charge.[3] The economic loss rule is discussed in Chapter 11, Section 11-1 and Chapter 12, Section 12-3.

The various Restatements of the Law (for contracts, economic torts, etc.) each categorize damages into conceptual frameworks appropriate for that particular area of

---

* The authors thank Juan Antonio Solis for his assistance in the updating of this chapter.
[1] "[T]here is not one economic loss rule broadly applicable throughout the field of torts, but rather several more limited rules that govern recovery of economic losses in selected areas of the law." Vincent R. Johnson, *The Boundary-Line Function of the Economic Loss Rule*, 66 Washington & Lee L. Rev. 523, 534–35 (2009), quoted in *Sharyland Water Supply Corp. v. City of Alton*, 354 S.W.3d 407, 415 (Tex. 2011).
[2] *Tarrant Cty. Hosp. Dist. v. GE Automation Servs.*, 156 S.W.3d 885, 895 (Tex. App.—Fort Worth 2005, no pet.) ("Economic loss rule is not an affirmative defense . . . but is a court-adopted rule for interpreting whether a party is barred from seeking damages in an action alleging tort injuries resulting from a contract between the parties.").
[3] Jim Wren, *Applying the Economic Loss Rule in Texas*, 64 Baylor L. Rev. 204, 208–09 (2012).

law.⁴ This book takes a broader approach recognizing that many of these conceptual frameworks have overlapping applications (e.g., a "lost profits" damage model works within multiple conceptual frameworks), and focuses on the common damage models which apply in business litigation, suggesting which damage models might best fit particular business litigation cases.

11-2 Benefit-of-the-Bargain Damages

A party's "expectation interest" is his interest in having the benefit of his bargain, and attempts to put the wronged party in an equivalent position to that he would have enjoyed without the breach of the contract or reliance on a fraudulent misrepresentation.⁵ The measure of damages is typically stated as the difference between the value as represented and the value received.⁶

Benefit-of-the-bargain damages are available for breach of contract and for fraudulent inducement of an enforceable agreement but not for fraud that induces a non-binding contract.⁷ When the fraud that does not induce an enforceable contract, out-of-pocket damages rather than benefit-of-the-bargain damages should be submitted.⁸

The expectancy value may have been expressly stated between the parties such as where the defendant promised delivery of property with a stated value. In this situation, the measure of damage is straightforward: the difference between the value as represented and the value received.⁹ The amount paid for the business opportunity is irrelevant to the calculation unless the amount paid is a factor in determining the net value represented. A party cannot both retain all the benefits of the transaction (i.e., recover on a benefit-of-the-bargain theory) and escape all of the obligations (i.e., simultaneously recover all out-of-pocket costs incurred to obtain the bargain).¹⁰

Where the business transactions does not expressly state the value to be received, the plaintiff must plead and prove the value of the lost opportunity, often using the lost profit measure of damages. Although theoretically this measure of damages still seeks to assess the difference between the value as represented and the value received, the value "as represented" must be assessed indirectly, from an estimation of likely profits rather than from a directly-stated dollar amount.

This lost profit measure of damages may qualify as either direct damages or as consequential damages. When the anticipated profits are the direct subject of the transaction, the failure of the transaction due to breach of contract or fraud will naturally

---

⁴ For example, Restatement (Second) of Contracts § 344 classifies contract damages as addressing a claimant's "expectation interest," "reliance interest," or "restitution interest." The more recent Restatement Third, Restitution and Unjust Enrichment, formally adopted in 2010 and published in 2011, modifies these classifications somewhat, particularly in §§ 37, 38, 39, and 54.

⁵ *See* Restatement (Second) of Contracts § 344(a) (expectancy damages for breach of contract); *Formosa Plastics Corp. USA v. Presidio Eng'rs. & Contractors, Inc.*, 960 S.W.2d 41, 49 (Tex. 1998) (benefit-of-the-bargain damages for fraud).

⁶ *Arthur Andersen & Co. v. Perry Equip. Corp.*, 945 S.W.2d 812, 817 (Tex. 1997).

⁷ *Zorrilla v. Aypco Constr. II, LLC*, 469 S.W.3d 143, 153 (Tex. 2015).

⁸ *Zorrilla v. Aypco Constr. II, LLC*, 469 S.W.3d 143, 153–54 (Tex. 2015).

⁹ *Formosa Plastics Corp. USA v. Presidio Eng'rs. & Contractors, Inc.*, 960 S.W.2d 41, 49 (Tex. 1998).

¹⁰ *Sharifi v. Steen Auto., LLC*, 370 S.W.3d 126, 151 (Tex. App.—Dallas 2012, no pet.).

and necessarily result in lost profits, constituting direct damages.[11] Conversely, the plaintiff may foreseeably have engaged in the transaction to generate profits in other business pursuits, with a reasonable expectancy of achieving those profits. The loss of those profits in other transactions will not be direct damages, but they may qualify as consequential damages subject to pleading and proof.[12] Lost profits are discussed in Chapter 11, Section 11-6.

Sometimes the lost opportunity (i.e., anticipated "benefit-of-the-bargain") is not just a stream of anticipated profits, but is instead a fully operational business, or the lost opportunity has caused a loss to the value of an existing business of the plaintiff. A methodology exists for determining the loss of value of a business that is separate and distinct from valuing a stream of lost profits. This distinction is discussed later in Chapter 11, Section 11-7:1, and the separate methodology for determining the loss of value of a business is discussed in Chapter 11, Section 11-7:2.

11-3 Out-of-Pocket Damages

"Out-of-pocket" damages seek to restore to the claimant the out-of-pocket costs he has incurred as a result of relying[13] on the contractual or fraudulent representations of the defendant, by measuring the difference between the value of that which was parted with and the value of that which was received.[14]

In most cases, a plaintiff will have anticipated receiving a greater "benefit-of-the-bargain" than the "out-of-pocket" costs being incurred, so "out-of-pocket" damages are usually sought as an alternate remedy when it will be difficult to prove the actual "benefit-of-the-bargain" damages.

Calculation of out-of-pocket damages may simply involve totaling the sum of all expenditures made by the claimant. Alternatively, where a plaintiff has delivered a business or business opportunity due to the fraud of the defendant, the out-of-pocket damages may require valuing the business or lost business opportunity to determine what has been "parted with."[15] Likewise, if real property has been sacrificed in reliance upon and as a cost of the transaction, the calculation of out-of-pocket damages may involve valuation of the real property. As a result, any one of several of the common damage calculations discussed in Chapter 11, Section 11-5:7 may be applicable as an out-of-pocket damages model.

Recovering both benefit-of-the-bargain damages and out-of-pocket damages for the same loss is inconsistent and an impermissible double recovery.[16] They are inconsistent because the first measure of damages seeks to affirm the transaction while the second measure of damages seeks to disaffirm it.[17] A plaintiff may recover under the damages theory that provides the greater recovery.[18] Both measures of damages

---

[11] *See Arthur Andersen & Co. v. Perry Equip. Corp.*, 945 S.W.2d 812, 816–17 (Tex. 1997).

[12] *See* Chapter 10, Section 10-2; *see Formosa Plastics Corp. U.S.A. v. Presidio Eng'rs & Contractors, Inc.*, 960 S.W.2d 41, 49 n.1 (Tex. 1998).

[13] *See* Restatement (Second) of Contracts § 344(b) (reliance damages for breach of contract).

[14] *Baylor Univ. v. Sonnichsen*, 221 S.W.3d 632, 636 (Tex. 2007).

[15] *Rogers v. Alexander*, 244 S.W.3d 370, 385–87 (Tex. App.—Dallas 2007, pet. denied).

[16] *Yeng v. Zou*, 407 S.W.3d 485, 491 (Tex. App.—Houston [14th Dist.] 2013, no pet.).

[17] *Sharifi v. Steen Auto., LLC*, 370 S.W.3d 126, 151 (Tex. App.—Dallas 2012, no pet.).

[18] *Arthur Andersen & Co. v. Perry Equip. Corp.*, 945 S.W.2d 812, 817 (Tex. 1997).

may be submitted to the jury, but an election of remedies is required for the entry of judgment.[19]

11-4 Restitution (Misappropriation)-Damages

The term "restitution damages" appears in a variety of contexts and with various meanings attached, but as used here—in a misappropriation context—the term references an alternative measure of damages to either benefit-of-the-bargain damages or out-of-pocket damages. While both benefit-of-the-bargain damages and out-of-pocket damages focus on recovery of the loss to the claimant, restitution damages are *measured by the positive value to the defendant* of what has been misappropriated by the defendant or provided by the claimant.[20]

Restitution damages often constitute an appropriate measure of damages in cases of breach of contract,[21] fraud,[22] breach of fiduciary duty,[23] misappropriation of trade secrets,[24] unjust enrichment,[25] or quantum meruit.[26] The valuation method for determining the positive value to the defendant may involve valuation of property acquired, or valuation of a business or of a stream of profits acquired.

11-5 Contractual Damages and Remedies

11-5:1 Uniform Commercial Code Statutory Remedies

Both sellers and buyers are afforded a wide ranging set of remedies for the breach of a contract for the sale of goods. Several of these remedies are more in line with self-help rights, as opposed to remedies that must be pleaded in a lawsuit.[27] This topic

---

[19] *Yeng v. Zou*, 407 S.W.3d 485, 491 (Tex. App.—Houston [14th Dist.] 2013, no pet.).

[20] *Atrium Med. Ctr., LP v. Houston Red C LLC*, 595 S.W.3d 188, 193 (Tex. 2020).

[21] See *McFarland v. Sanders*, 932 S.W.2d 640, 645–46 (Tex. App.—Tyler 1996, no writ).

[22] *Casstevens v. Smith*, 269 S.W.3d 222, 230 n.3 (Tex. App.—Texarkana 2008, pet. denied) ("Texas courts have allowed restitution for these types of claims in a variety of cases: by a defrauded party against the party who committed the fraud [citations omitted]; by a party that made an overpayment [citation omitted]; and by a party that paid or credited money to the wrong person or account [citations omitted].").

[23] *Kinzbach Tool Co. v. Corbett-Wallace Corp.*, 138 Tex. 565, 573–74, 160 S.W.2d 509, 514 (1942).

[24] *Sw. Energy Prod. Co. v. Berry-Helfand*, 491 S.W.3d 699, 710–12 (Tex. 2016) (raising question as to whether equitable disgorgement is available under either contract or trade-secret law absent a fiduciary relationship and, if so, whether it is cumulative of other remedies or available only to the exclusion of other remedies).

[25] *Sherer v. Sherer*, 393 S.W.3d 480, 491 n.22 (Tex. App.—Texarkana 2013, pet. denied). But note the disagreement between courts as to whether or not unjust enrichment is a distinct cause of action. See *Pepi Corp. v. Galliford*, 254 S.W.3d 457, 460 (Tex. App.—Houston [1st Dist.] 2007, pet. denied); *compare with Lilani v. Noorali*, No. H-09-2617, 2011 U.S. Dist. LEXIS 440, at *36–38 (S.D. Tex. Jan. 3, 2011) and *Davis v. OneWest Bank N.A.*, No. 02-14-00264-CV, 2015 Tex. App. LEXIS 3470, at *1–3 (Tex. App.—Fort Worth Apr. 9, 2015, pet. denied).

[26] *Eun Bok Lee v. Ho Chang Lee*, 411 S.W.3d 95, 111–12 (Tex. App.—Houston [1st Dist.] 2013, no pet.).

[27] *See, e.g.*, Tex. Bus. & Com. Code Ann. § 2.703(1) (seller may withhold delivery of goods); Tex. Bus. & Com. Code Ann. § 2.703(2) (seller may stop delivery of goods); Tex. Bus. & Com. Code Ann. § 2.703(3) (seller may resell goods); Tex. Bus. & Com. Code Ann. § 2.703(6)

will first briefly outline all of the rights and remedies that the Uniform Commercial Code (UCC) makes available to aggrieved sellers and buyers. This topic will conclude by outlining any pleading requirements for those remedies that must be pleaded in a lawsuit to be obtained.

11-5:2 Seller's Uniform Commercial Code Statutory Remedies

When the seller discovers that the buyer is insolvent, the seller may refuse or stop delivery[28] or may reclaim goods sold on credit.[29] If the buyer wrongfully rejects or revokes acceptance of goods, fails to make a payment or repudiates the contract, the seller may withhold delivery of such goods,[30] stop delivery,[31] identify previously unidentified goods and resell them,[32] resell and recover damages,[33] recover damages for non-acceptance,[34] in a proper case recover the contract price,[35] or cancel the contract.[36] A seller may rescind the contract if the buyer fraudulently induced the seller to enter into it.[37]

A seller may also recover incidental damages in connection with the return or resale of goods resulting from the buyer's breach.[38]

11-5:3 Buyer's UCC Statutory Remedies

When the seller fails to deliver the goods, repudiates the contract, or the buyer rightfully rejects goods, a buyer may cancel the contract,[39] cover and have damages awarded,[40] or recover damages.[41] A buyer may also recover incidental or consequential damages.[42] When the seller fails to deliver goods or repudiates the contract, the buyer may recover the goods,[43] obtain specific performance,[44] or replevy the goods.[45] A buyer may rescind the contract if it was fraudulently induced to enter into it.[46]

(seller may cancel the contract); Tex. Bus. & Com. Code Ann. § 2.716(c) (buyer may replevy goods).
[28] Tex. Bus. & Com. Code Ann. § 2.702(a).
[29] Tex. Bus. & Com. Code Ann. § 2.702(b).
[30] Tex. Bus. & Com. Code Ann. § 2.703(1).
[31] Tex. Bus. & Com. Code Ann. § 2.703(2).
[32] Tex. Bus. & Com. Code Ann. §§ 2.703(3), 2.704.
[33] Tex. Bus. & Com. Code Ann. § 2.703(4).
[34] Tex. Bus. & Com. Code Ann. §§ 2.703(5), 2.708.
[35] Tex. Bus. & Com. Code Ann. §§ 2.703(5), 2.709.
[36] Tex. Bus. & Com. Code Ann. § 2.703(6).
[37] *See* Tex. Bus. & Com. Code Ann. § 2.721.
[38] Tex. Bus. & Com. Code Ann. § 2.710.
[39] Tex. Bus. & Com. Code Ann. § 2.711(a).
[40] Tex. Bus. & Com. Code Ann. § 2.711(a)(1).
[41] Tex. Bus. & Com. Code Ann. § 2.711(a)(2).
[42] Tex. Bus. & Com. Code Ann. § 2.715.
[43] Tex. Bus. & Com. Code Ann. § 2.711(b)(1).
[44] Tex. Bus. & Com. Code Ann. § 2.711(b)(2).
[45] Tex. Bus. & Com. Code Ann. § 2.711(b)(2).
[46] *See* Tex. Bus. & Com. Code Ann. § 2.721.

11-5:4 Pleading UCC Statutory Remedies

11-5:4.1 Seller's Remedies

A plaintiff must generally only provide the defendant with fair notice of its cause of action.[47] Moreover, a plaintiff may generally aver that all conditions precedent to the contract have been performed or have occurred.[48] However, a plaintiff must specifically plead special damage elements.[49] A plaintiff must also plead into one of four ranges of monetary and non-monetary relief.[50] Generally in the Uniform Commercial Code context, a plaintiff may plead more than one remedy without making a prejudgment election.[51] However, whether the pursuit of one remedy bars another remedy is entirely dependent on the facts of each case.[52]

When pleading for seller's remedies under the Uniform Commercial Code, a plaintiff may generally plead:

- The existence of a contract;[53]

- The performance or occurrence of conditions precedent, including whether the resale was commercially reasonable;[54]

- One or more Uniform Commercial Code remedies.[55]

When pleading for seller's remedies under the Uniform Commercial Code, a plaintiff must specifically plead:

- For special damage elements, including incidental and consequential damages;[56]

- That the plaintiff's claim for relief falls into one of four ranges of monetary relief;[57]

- For attorney's fees;[58]

- Grounds establishing fraud.[59]

---

[47] Tex. R. Civ. P. 45(b); Tex. R. Civ. P. 47(a).
[48] Tex. R. Civ. P. 54.
[49] Tex. R. Civ. P. 56.
[50] Tex. R. Civ. P. 47(c).
[51] Tex. Bus. & Com. Code Ann. § 2.703, cmt. 1 (describing the seller's remedies under the Uniform Commercial Code as "cumulative").
[52] Tex. Bus. & Com. Code Ann. § 2.703, cmt. 1.
[53] See Tex. R. Civ. P. 45(b); Tex. R. Civ. P. 47(a).
[54] Tex. R. Civ. P. 54.
[55] See Tex. R. Civ. P. 45(b); Tex. R. Civ. P. 47(a).
[56] Tex. R. Civ. P. 56; Naegeli Transp. v. Gulf Electroquip, Inc., 853 S.W.2d 737, 739 (Tex. App.—Houston [14th Dist.] 1993, writ denied) (incidental and consequential damages must be specifically pleaded).
[57] Tex. R. Civ. P. 47(c).
[58] Ellis v. Waldrop, 656 S.W.2d 902, 905 (Tex. 1983) (a party must "plead and prove" its entitlement to attorney's fees under the predecessor to Chapter 38 of the Civil Practice and Remedies Code).
[59] See Tex. R. Civ. P. 94 (requiring the affirmative defense of fraud to be affirmatively pleaded).

11-5:4.2 Buyer's Remedies

A plaintiff must generally only provide the defendant with fair notice of its cause of action.[60] Moreover, a plaintiff may generally aver that all conditions precedent to the contract have been performed or have occurred.[61] However, a plaintiff must specifically plead special damage elements.[62] A plaintiff must also plead into one of five ranges of monetary and non-monetary relief.[63]

When pleading for buyer's remedies under the Uniform Commercial Code, a plaintiff may generally plead:

- The existence of a contract;[64]
- The performance or occurrence of conditions precedent, including whether the resale was commercially reasonable;[65]
- One or more Uniform Commercial Code remedies.[66]

When pleading for buyer's remedies under the Uniform Commercial Code, a plaintiff must specifically plead:

- For special damage elements, including incidental and consequential damages;[67]
- That the plaintiff's claim for relief falls into one of five ranges of monetary relief;[68]
- For attorney's fees;[69]
- Grounds establishing fraud;[70]
- Grounds supporting specific performance.[71]

11-5:5 Pleading Contractually Defined Damages

The contract in question may define the damages calculation, either by stating a formula for the determination of damages or by means of a liquidated damages clause. When the contract specifies the damages, plead the contractual terms by detailing them in the pleading or by attaching the contract to the pleading and incorporating its

---

[60] Tex. R. Civ. P. 45(b); Tex. R. Civ. P. 47(a).
[61] Tex. R. Civ. P. 54.
[62] Tex. R. Civ. P. 56.
[63] Tex. R. Civ. P. 47(c).
[64] *See* Tex. R. Civ. P. 45(b); Tex. R. Civ. P. 47(a).
[65] Tex. R. Civ. P. 54.
[66] *See* Tex. R. Civ. P. 45(b); Tex. R. Civ. P. 47(a).
[67] Tex. R. Civ. P. 56; *Naegeli Transp. v. Gulf Electroquip, Inc.*, 853 S.W.2d 737, 739 (Tex. App.—Houston [14th Dist.] 1993, writ denied) (incidental or consequential damages must be specifically pleaded).
[68] Tex. R. Civ. P. 47(c).
[69] *Archer v. Tregellas*, 566 S.W.3d 281, 287 n.8 (Tex. 2018) ("To be entitled to specific performance, the party seeking such relief must plead and prove he was ready, willing, and able to timely perform his obligations under the contract.").
[70] *See* Tex. R. Civ. P. 94 (requiring the affirmative defense of fraud to be affirmatively pleaded).
[71] *See DiGiuseppe v. Lawler*, 269 S.W.3d 588, 593 (Tex. 2008) (a party "must plead and prove he was ready, willing, and able to timely perform his obligations under the contract").

terms by reference.[72] When the contract specifies the formula for the calculation of damages, the specified formula can potentially override even an incorrect statement of the measure of damages in the pleadings.[73] When the contract includes a liquidated damages clause, the liquidated damages clause is enforceable (i.e. overrides the applicability of damage models based on benefit-of-the-bargain or out-of-pocket amounts) provided (1) the harm caused by the breach is incapable or difficult to estimate, and (2) the amount of liquidated damages called for is a reasonable forecast of just compensation.[74]

The party asserting that a liquidated damages clause is an unenforceable penalty bears the burden of pleading penalty as an affirmative defense (unless the illegality of the penalty is apparent from the opponent's pleadings) and of proving any fact issues necessary for the issue to be decided by the court as a question of law.[75]

11-5:6 Pleading Damages on Sworn Accounts

Tex. R. Civ. P. 185 specifies that a claim "founded upon an open account or other claim for goods, wares and merchandise, including any claim for a liquidated money demand based upon written contract or founded on business dealings between the parties, or is for personal service rendered, or labor done or labor or materials furnished, *on which a systematic record has been kept*,"[76] qualifies for a special sworn account procedure which can simplify the proof needed for a prima facie case.

The plaintiff's pleadings must include:

- An itemization reflecting the details for each charge and including any offsets, payments, and credits;[77]

- A sworn affidavit of the party, his agent, or his attorney "to the effect that such claim is, within the knowledge of affiant, just and true, that it is due, and that all just and lawful offsets, payments and credits have been allowed;"[78]

- A request for attorney's fees pursuant either to the contract or Texas Civil Practice and Remedies Code Section 38.001.

---

[72] Tex. R. Civ. P. 59 (exhibit to pleading deemed a part thereof for all purposes).

[73] *Rowan Cos., Inc. v. Transco Expl. Co., Inc.*, 679 S.W.2d 660, 665–66 (Tex. App.—Houston [1st Dist.] 1984, writ ref'd n.r.e.), *cert. denied*, 474 U.S. 822, 106 S. Ct. 74, 88 L. Ed. 2d 61 (1985).

[74] *GPA Holding, Inc. v. Baylor Health Care Sys.*, 344 S.W.3d 467, 475 (Tex. App.—Dallas 2011, pet. denied); *but see Bunker v. Strandhagen*, No. 03-14-00510-CV, 2017 Tex. App. LEXIS 1803, at *18 n.14 (Tex. App.—Austin Mar. 3, 2017) (setting forth circumstances in which courts are allowed to reject facial unreasonableness claims). In a contract for the sale of goods governed by the UCC, *see* the factors set forth in Tex. Bus. & Com. Code Ann. § 2.718(a).

[75] *Phillips v. Phillips*, 820 S.W.2d 785, 788–90 (Tex. 1991).

[76] Tex. R. Civ. P. 185 (emphasis added).

[77] *See Woodhaven Partners, Ltd. v. Shamoun & Norman, L.L.P.*, 422 S.W.3d 821, 834 (Tex. App.—Dallas 2014, no pet.) (itemized information held sufficient which reflected the date of each charge, initials of the individual who performed the service, a brief description of the work performed, hours billed, the billing rate, and the specific charges).

[78] Tex. R. Civ. P. 185.

Although the details for each charge should be itemized, Tex. R. Civ. P. 185 was amended in 1984 to place the burden on the defendant to specially except to any asserted deficiency in that regard.[79]

Once the plaintiff pleads a sworn account, the pleading burden shifts to the defendant to properly deny under oath the details of the sworn account in whole or in part. In the absence of a sworn denial meeting the requirements of Tex. R. Civ. P. 185, the plaintiff is entitled to rely upon the sworn account petition as prima facie evidence, and the defendant is not entitled to dispute the sworn account or present controverting evidence.[80]

In order to destroy the evidentiary effect of the sworn account and force the plaintiff to put on proof of his claim, the defendant's pleadings must include:

- A specific denial of each item disputed by the defendant;[81]

- A special exception to any item that defendant asserts has not been described with sufficient particularity;[82] and

- A sworn affidavit of the party, his agent, or his attorney, that each specific denial is true and correct, and within the knowledge of the affiant.[83]

Neither a general denial nor a sworn general denial will be sufficient to destroy the prima facie effect of the plaintiff's sworn account.[84] It can be sufficient, however, to specifically deny under oath each item in the plaintiff's sworn account, to wit: "Each

---

[79] Tex. R. Civ. P. 185 ("No particularization or description of the nature of the component parts of the account or claim is necessary unless the trial court sustains special exceptions to the pleadings."); *see Enernational Corp. v. Exploitation Eng'rs., Inc.*, 705 S.W.2d 749, 750–51 (Tex. App.—Houston [1st Dist.] 1986, writ ref'd n.r.e.) (defendant with any question regarding the dates of account required to file special exception asking for particularity, and in absence of special exception the sworn account is not deficient for lack of specificity).

[80] *Rizk v. Fin. Guardian Ins. Agency, Inc.*, 584 S.W.2d 860, 862 (Tex. 1979) ("Rule 185 is not a rule of substantive law but is a rule of procedure with regard to the evidence necessary to establish a prima facie right of recovery.").

[81] *Woodhaven Partners, Ltd. v. Shamoun & Norman, L.L.P.*, 422 S.W.3d 821, 833 (Tex. App.—Dallas 2014, no pet.) ("A sworn general denial does not constitute a denial of the account and is insufficient to remove the evidentiary presumption created by a properly worded and verified suit on an account.").

[82] Tex. R. Civ. P. 185 ("No particularization or description of the nature of the component parts of the account or claim is necessary unless the trial court sustains special exceptions to the pleadings."); *see Enernational Corp. v. Exploitation Eng'rs., Inc.*, 705 S.W.2d 749, 750–51 (Tex. App.—Houston [1st Dist.] 1986, writ ref'd n.r.e.) (defendant with any question regarding the dates of account required to file special exception asking for particularity, and in absence of special exception the sworn account is not deficient for lack of specificity).

[83] Tex. R. Civ. P. 185 (If defendant "does not timely file a written denial, under oath, he shall not be permitted to deny the claim, or any item therein, as the case may be."); Tex. R. Civ. P. 93(10) (requiring verification of a denial of an account that is the foundation of the plaintiff's action, supported by affidavit).

[84] *Woodhaven Partners, Ltd. v. Shamoun & Norman, L.L.P.*, 422 S.W.3d 821, 833 (Tex. App.—Dallas 2014, no pet.) ("A sworn general denial does not constitute a denial of the account and is insufficient to remove the evidentiary presumption created by a properly worded and verified suit on an account.").

and every item in Plaintiff's account attached to the Original Petition as Exhibit is not just or true in whole or in part. Defendant did not request Plaintiff to furnish the items listed therein or agree or promise to pay plaintiff for the charges shown therein."[85] Often only specific charges will be disputed, in which case the sworn denial should be specific regarding which items are in dispute.[86]

11-5:7 Pleading Benefit-of-the-Bargain and Out-of-Pocket Damages

In most cases in which benefit-of-the-bargain damages are sought, the anticipated profits are the direct subject of the transaction and the failure of the transaction due to breach of contract or fraud will naturally and necessarily result in lost profits, constituting direct damages.[87] This means that details of the damages do not have to be pleaded.[88] Likewise, out-of-pocket damages usually constitute direct damages.[89]

Benefit-of-the-bargain damages will need to be specified in the rarer circumstance where the plaintiff foreseeably engaged in the transaction to generate profits in other separate business pursuits, with a reasonable expectancy of achieving those profits.[90]

Benefit-of-the-bargain damages and out-of-pocket damages may be pleaded in the alternative, and both theories of recovery may be submitted to the jury, although an election will be required for purposes of the judgment.[91]

Benefit-of-the-bargain and out-of-pocket damages may be proved by means of various measures of damage, such as lost profits, loss of value of a business, or property valuation.[92] A party is not required to plead the specific measure of damages.[93]

When pleading for benefit-of-the-bargain and/or out-of-pocket damages for breach of contract, a plaintiff should plead:

- The existence of a contract and breach by the defendant;[94]
- The performance or occurrence of conditions precedent;[95]

---

[85] *Rizk v. Fin. Guardian Ins. Agency, Inc.*, 584 S.W.2d 860, 862 (Tex. 1979).
[86] *Sarandos v. Dave Seline Roofing Co.*, 498 S.W.2d 393, 394 (Tex. Civ. App.—Houston [1st Dist.] 1973, no writ) (when defendant files sworn denial questioning only part of the items, those not challenged are admitted, but upon proper pleadings a defendant may defend on other grounds).
[87] *See* Chapter 7, Section 7-14:3.1.
[88] *Myers v. Walker*, 61 S.W.3d 722, 729–30 (Tex. App.—Eastland 2001, pet. denied) (holding that plaintiff's inartful allegations of being damaged as a result of defendant's fraud and that the damages were within the trial court's jurisdictional limits sufficed to recover benefit-of-the-bargain damages).
[89] *Walker & Assocs. Surveying, Inc. v. Austin*, 301 S.W.3d 909, 918 (Tex. App.—Texarkana 2009, no pet.) (out-of-pocket loss constitutes direct rather than consequential economic loss).
[90] *See* Chapter 11, Section 11-2.
[91] *See* Chapter 11, Sections 11-2 and 11-3.
[92] *See* Chapter 11, Sections 11-2 and 11-3.
[93] *Bowen v. Robinson*, 227 S.W.3d 86, 94–95 (Tex. App.—Houston [1st Dist.] 2006, pet. denied) (a party is not required to plead his measure of damages).
[94] *See* Tex. R. Civ. P. 45(b); Tex. R. Civ. P. 47(a).
[95] Tex. R. Civ. P. 54.

- For damages generally, specifying that the claim for relief falls into one of four ranges of monetary relief;[96]

- For any special damage elements, specifying the consequential damages;[97]

- For attorney's fees pursuant to contract or Texas Civil Practice and Remedies Code Section 38.001;[98] and

- A general prayer for relief.[99]

Although the specific measure of damages does not have to be detailed in the pleadings, an adverse party is entitled to discovery of the amount and method of calculation of economic damages pursuant to Tex. R. Civ. P. 194.2(d).

11-5:8 Pleading Contractual Remedies Other Than Damages

A party to a contract may pursue any number of forms of relief in connection to a contract other than legal damages. A plaintiff may seek reformation,[100] rescission,[101] and specific performance[102] of a contract. A plaintiff may seek relief based upon unjust enrichment,[103] quantum meruit[104] or promissory estoppel.[105] A plaintiff may seek the extraordinary remedies of garnishment,[106] attachment,[107] and sequestration.[108] Also, various equitable remedies for the recovery of monetary funds exist in specific circumstances.[109]

---

[96] Tex. R. Civ. P. 47(c).

[97] Tex. R. Civ. P. 56; *Naegeli Transp. v. Gulf Electroquip, Inc.*, 853 S.W.2d 737, 739 (Tex. App.—Houston [14th Dist.] 1993, writ denied) (Incidental or consequential damages must be specifically pleaded.).

[98] *Ellis v. Waldrop*, 656 S.W.2d 902, 905 (Tex. 1983) (a party must "plead and prove" its entitlement to attorney's fees under the predecessor to Chapter 38 of the Civil Practice and Remedies Code).

[99] *Salomon v. Lesay*, 369 S.W.3d 540, 553 (Tex. App.—Houston [1st Dist.] 2012, no pet.) ("A prayer for general relief will support any relief raised by the evidence and consistent with the allegations in the petition.").

[100] *Continental Oil Co. v. Doornbos*, 402 S.W.2d 879, 883 (Tex. 1966). For more information on reformation as an equitable remedy, *see* Chapter 8, Section 8-5 Reformation.

[101] *Humphrey v. Camelot Ret. Cmty.*, 893 S.W.2d 55, 59 (Tex. App.—Corpus Christi 1994, no pet.). For more information on rescission as an equitable remedy, *see* Chapter 3: Suit for Rescission; Chapter 8, Section 8-4 Rescission.

[102] *DiGiuseppe v. Lawler*, 269 S.W.3d 588, 593–94 (Tex. 2008). For more information on specific performance as an equitable remedy, *see* Chapter 8, Section 8-6 Specific Performance.

[103] *HECI Expl. Co. v. Neel*, 982 S.W.2d 881, 891 (Tex. 1998). For more information on unjust enrichment as a cause of action authorizing the equitable remedy of restitution, *see* Chapter 3, Section 3-18 Unjust Enrichment.

[104] *Bashara v. Baptist Mem'l Hosp. Sys.*, 685 S.W.2d 307, 310 (Tex. 1985). For more information on quantum meruit as an equitable cause of action, *see* Chapter 3, Section 3-17 Quantum Meruit.

[105] *Wheeler v. White*, 398 S.W.2d 93, 97 (Tex. 1965). For more information on promissory estoppel as an equitable cause of action, *see* Chapter 3, Section 3-19 Promissory Estoppel.

[106] Tex. R. Civ. P. 658.

[107] Tex. R. Civ. P. 592.

[108] Tex. R. Civ. P. 696.

[109] *See* Chapter 6, Section 6-3:3.3.

A plaintiff must generally only provide the defendant with fair notice of his cause of action,[110] but to entitle the plaintiff to equitable relief he must show a proper case for a court of equity to exercise its equitable jurisdiction.[111] Specific pleading is required when seeking extraordinary relief.[112]

Additionally, a plaintiff must specifically plead special damage elements,[113] and must include within his pleadings any other matter that may be required by law or rule.[114] A plaintiff may generally aver that all conditions precedent to the contract have been performed or have occurred.[115] A plaintiff must also plead into one of four ranges of monetary and non-monetary relief.[116] Generally, a plaintiff may plead more than one remedy without making a prejudgment election.[117]

When pleading for one or more extraordinary forms of relief, a plaintiff should plead:

- The existence of a contract;[118]

- The applicable cause(s) of action;[119]

- The performance or occurrence of conditions precedent (if seeking to enforce the contract);[120]

- Specific grounds for any quasi-contractual remedy;[121]

- Specific grounds for any equitable remedy, including no adequate remedy at law;[122]

- The specific relief sought;[123] and

- That the plaintiff's claim for relief falls into one of four ranges of relief.[124]

---

[110] Tex. R. Civ. P. 45(b); Tex. R. Civ. P. 47(a).

[111] *Rogers v. Daniel Oil & Royalty Co.*, 130 Tex. 386, 392, 110 S.W.2d 891, 894 (1937).

[112] *See, e.g., Ryan v. Collins*, 496 S.W.2d 205 (Tex. Civ. App.—Tyler 1973, writ refused n.r.e.) (request for rescission must be specifically pleaded and prayed for, and equitable relief requires averment of no adequate remedy at law); *but see Omega Energy Corp. v. Gulf States Petroleum Corp.*, No. 13-03-275-CV, 2005 WL 977573, at *3 (Tex. App.—Corpus Christi-Edinburg Apr. 28, 2005, pet. denied) (allowing rescission despite failure to specifically plead for rescission).

[113] Tex. R. Civ. P. 56.

[114] Tex. R. Civ. P. 45(c).

[115] Tex. R. Civ. P. 54.

[116] Tex. R. Civ. P. 47(c).

[117] *International Piping Sys., Ltd. v. M.M. White & Assoc., Inc.*, 831 S.W.2d 444, 452–53 (Tex. App.—Houston [14th Dist.] 1992, writ denied).

[118] *See* Tex. R. Civ. P. 45(b); Tex. R. Civ. P. 47(a).

[119] *See* Tex. R. Civ. P. 45(b); Tex. R. Civ. P. 47(a).

[120] Tex. R. Civ. P. 54.

[121] *See, e.g., Pepi Corp. v. Galliford*, 254 S.W.3d 457, 460 (Tex. App.—Houston [1st Dist.] 2005, pet. denied) (discussing pleading distinctions between unjust enrichment and quantum meruit).

[122] *Ryan v. Collins*, 496 S.W.2d 205, 209 (Tex. Civ. App.—Tyler 1973, writ ref'd n.r.e.) (request for rescission must be specifically pleaded and prayed for, and equitable relief requires averment of no adequate remedy at law).

[123] *See* Tex. R. Civ. P. 45(b); Tex. R. Civ. P. 47(a).

[124] Tex. R. Civ. P. 47(c).

COMMON BUSINESS LITIGATION DAMAGES MODELS

When pleading for the extraordinary remedies of garnishment, attachment, or sequestration, a plaintiff must:

- Specifically include and outline the statutory grounds for the remedy;[125]
- Strictly follow the procedural requirements for the remedy;[126] and
- Specifically plead that the plaintiff's claim for relief falls into one of four ranges of relief.[127]

11-6 Lost Profit

11-6:1 When to Use a Lost Profits Damage Model

Generally, either the value of the business enterprise as a whole is being valued, or the stream of lost profits is being valued, but not both. Since a major factor in the valuation of a business enterprise is the valuation of the stream of income it is expected to generate, seeking recovery both for diminished value of the business and for lost profits would typically constitute double counting.[128] However, occasionally a damages expert will correctly build both computations into the damages model. For example, the expert may compute the value of a stream of lost profits for a defined period and then compute the reduction in the value of the business enterprise at the *end* of that defined period.[129]

A lost profits measure of damages is commonly utilized in breach of contract cases[130] and in tort cases, other than those cases in which an existing business is completely destroyed (in which event a loss of business value calculation may be required).[131]

A lost profits damage model is appropriate if there is enough data from which to determine the likely net profit (not just lost income[132]) that would have been received by the plaintiff but for the wrongful conduct of the defendant. Recovery for lost profits does not require that the loss be susceptible to exact calculation, but the injured party must do more than show that it suffered some lost profits.[133] Lost profits must be shown by

---

[125] *In re Argyll Equities, LLC*, 227 S.W.3d 268, 273 (Tex. App.—San Antonio 2007, no pet.) (attachment); *Fogel v. White*, 745 S.W.2d 444, 446 (Tex. App.—Houston [14th Dist.] 1988, no writ) (garnishment); *American Mortg. Corp. v. Samuell*, 130 Tex. 107, 111-12, 108 S.W.2d 193, 196 (1937) (sequestration).

[126] *In re Argyll Equities, LLC*, 227 S.W.3d 268, 273 (Tex. App.—San Antonio 2007, no pet.) (attachment); *Fogel v. White*, 745 S.W.2d 444, 446 (Tex. App.—Houston [14th Dist.] 1988, no writ) (garnishment); *American Mortg. Corp. v. Samuell*, 130 Tex. 107, 111-12, 108 S.W.2d 193, 196 (1937) (sequestration).

[127] Tex. R. Civ. P. 47(c).

[128] *Fraud-Tech, Inc. v. Choicepoint, Inc.*, 102 S.W.3d 366, 380 n.43 (Tex. App.—Fort Worth 2003, pet. denied) (citing to authority that recovery of both lost profits and loss of business value for the same time period would be duplicative).

[129] Excerpted from Jim Wren, Proving Damages to the Jury, 2d ed., § 6:30 of Chapter 6 "Valuations and Damages Models" (James Publishing, San Francisco, 2013).

[130] *Interceramic, Inc. v. S. Orient R.R. Co., Ltd.*, 999 S.W.2d 920, 927-28 (Tex. App.—Texarkana 1999, pet. denied).

[131] *Sawyer v. Fitts*, 630 S.W.2d 872, 874-75 (Tex. App.—Fort Worth 1982, no writ).

[132] *Holt Atherton Indus., Inc. v. Heine*, 835 S.W.2d 80, 83-84 (Tex. 1992).

[133] *Horizon Health Corp. v. Acadia Healthcare*, 520 S.W.3d 848, 860 (Tex. 2017) ("Rather the general rule is that recovery of lost profit damages is allowed 'where it is shown that a loss of profits is the natural and probable consequence of the act or omission complained of,

competent evidence with reasonable certainty, based on objective facts, figures or data from which the lost profits amount may be ascertained,[134] with a complete calculation.[135]

"Where the business is shown to have been already established and making a profit at the time when the contract was breached or the tort committed, such pre-existing profit, together with other facts and circumstances, may indicate with reasonable certainty the amount of profits lost."[136]

Unlike other jurisdictions, Texas permits a recovery for lost profits even by new businesses. However, where no such track record of profit exists (which invariably is the case with a new business), other methods exist for demonstrating lost profits with reasonable certainty, such as focusing on specific business activities with a proven track record rather than on the profits of the new business as a whole,[137] producing future contracts to show objectively that the opportunity for future revenue existed,[138] or measuring the opportunities of the new business by comparison to another established business also owned and operated by the plaintiff.[139] However, when a lost profits calculation depends on speculative future assumptions, lost profits are not recoverable.[140] "The mere hope for success of an untried enterprise, even when that hope is realistic, is not enough for recovery of lost profits. When there are firmer reasons to expect a business to yield a profit, the enterprise is not prohibited from recovering merely because it is new."[141]

11-6:2 Using a Discount Rate in a Lost Profits Calculation

There are multiple methods for proving lost profits[142] and not all lost profit calculations involve the use of a discount rate, nor do all lost profit calculations require expert testimony.[143] However, discount rates are commonly used for two purposes: to account for risk by discounting the certainty of future profits,[144] and to account for the time value of money by discounting future profits to present value.[145] A major issue in a lost profits analysis is the determination of a risk adjusted discount rate, because of how

---

and their amount is shown with sufficient certainty.'"); *see also Texas Instruments, Inc. v. Teletron Energy Mgmt., Inc.*, 877 S.W.2d 276, 279 (Tex. 1994).

[134] *Helena Chem. Co. v. Wilkins*, 47 S.W.3d 486, 504 (Tex. 2001).

[135] *Holt Atherton Indus., Inc. v. Heine*, 835 S.W.2d 80, 85 (Tex. 1992).

[136] *Texas Instruments, Inc. v. Teletron Energy Mgmt., Inc.*, 877 S.W.2d 276, 279 (Tex. 1994).

[137] *DaimlerChrysler Motors Co., LLC v. Manuel*, 362 S.W.3d 160, 191 (Tex. App.—Fort Worth 2012, no pet.).

[138] *Helena Chem. Co. v. Wilkins*, 47 S.W.3d 486, 505 (Tex. 2001).

[139] *DaimlerChrysler Motors Co., LLC v. Manuel*, 362 S.W.3d 160, 190–91 (Tex. App.—Fort Worth 2012, no pet.).

[140] *M & A Technology, Inc. v. iValue Grp., Inc.*, 295 S.W.3d 356, 366–67 (Tex. App.—El Paso 2009, pet. denied).

[141] *Texas Instruments, Inc. v. Teletron Energy Mgmt., Inc.*, 877 S.W.2d 276, 280 (Tex. 1994).

[142] *Holt Atherton Indus., Inc. v. Heine*, 835 S.W.2d 80, 85 (Tex. 1992).

[143] *Southwestern Bell Media, Inc. v. Lyles*, 825 S.W.2d 488, 499 (Tex. App.—Houston [1st Dist.] 1992, writ denied).

[144] *See City of Harlingen v. Estate of Sharboneau*, 48 S.W.3d 177, 184 n.3 (Tex. 2001) (criticizing discount rate which fails to adequately account for risk).

[145] For the requirement of discounting a future stream of payments to present value in order to account for the time value of money, *see Republic Bankers Life Ins. Co. v. Jaeger*, 551 S.W.2d 30 (Tex. 1976).

significant the effect can be. Discount rates on lost profits is often as high as 15–20% per year and can be much higher.[146]

The higher the discount rate, the greater the reduction in present value for future years, with the present value number falling rapidly for each additional year into the future. Even when some level of profit is reasonably certain (which is often not the case with an untested business), expect to defend against claims of future risk to the flow of profits based on changing economic conditions, changing industry conditions, entry of new competitors, vulnerability to excessive dependence on one or a few key customers, etc.[147]

A question often arises regarding how many years of lost profits should be sought. Sometimes the answer is clear from the facts, such as with a contract for a defined number of years. But if the defendant has caused a loss of profits for an indeterminate number of years into the future, often the best answer is to seek recovery for a relatively limited number of years, such as five years into the future. Because lost profit calculations often have a higher discount rate, each year further out has a significantly lower present value, and issues of mitigation and credibility can quickly overwhelm the value of years too far into the future.[148]

11-6:3 Pleading Lost Profits

When pleading for lost profits, a plaintiff must specifically plead:

- For special damage elements, including lost profits constituting consequential damages;[149] and
- That the plaintiff's claim for relief falls into one of four ranges of monetary relief.[150]

Neither the specific amount of lost profits nor the method of calculating lost profits need be pleaded (only the fact that lost profits are being sought and the total damage range of the case), but discovery of the amount and method of calculation of lost profits may be required by a request for disclosure.[151]

---

[146] See, e.g., *Bishop v. Miller*, 412 S.W.3d 758, 779 n.32 (Tex. App.—Houston [14th Dist.] 2013, no pet.).

[147] Excerpted from Jim Wren, Proving Damages to the Jury, 2d ed., § 6:31 of Chapter 6 "Valuations and Damages Models" (James Publishing, San Francisco, 2013).

[148] See Jim Wren, Proving Damages to the Jury, 2d ed., § 6:32 of Chapter 6 "Valuations and Damages Models" (James Publishing, San Francisco, 2013).

[149] Tex. R. Civ. P. 56; *Naegeli Transp. v. Gulf Electroquip, Inc.*, 853 S.W.2d 737, 739 (Tex. App.—Houston [14th Dist.] 1993, writ denied) (Lost profits constituting "consequential" damages must be specifically pleaded.).

[150] Tex. R. Civ. P. 47(c).

[151] Tex. R. Civ. P. 194.2(d).

11-7 Loss of Value of a Business

11-7:1 When to Use a Loss of Business Value Damage Model

While a lost profits calculation is generally simpler than a loss of value of business calculation, the latter may be appropriate because an existing business has been destroyed in its entirety by wrongful conduct,[152] or because a lost profits calculation alone does not capture the totality of harm.[153] Damages in a breach of contract case will more commonly be measured by lost profits rather than a loss of value of business calculation, unless loss of business value constitutes an out-of-pocket reliance cost that was contemplated or anticipated by the parties.[154]

Obviously anticipated future profits are crucially important in valuing a business, but other things such as the cost of the assets of a business can be part of a business valuation as well. Since the valuation of future profits is already considered in the valuation of a business (subject to the same requirement as for lost profits that the future profits not be remote or speculative[155]), the recovery of both lost profits and lost business value for the same time period would constitute a double recovery.[156] Conversely, two different measures of damages can be used to assess damages for two different time periods.[157]

Although the requirement of "reasonable certainty" for lost profits exists when the lost profits are not sought as damages themselves but are used to determine the lost market value of property for which recovery is sought, "the law should not require greater certainty in projecting those profits than the market itself would."[158] This means that if the market places a positive value on what might otherwise be considered a speculative opportunity, that positive value may be considered in determining the market value of the business property that owns the opportunity.[159]

Rather than valuing lost profits over a range of time, a "loss of value of business" is calculated as of a specific point in time, or more likely two points in time (before and after an event).[160] Pick the valuation date carefully.[161]

---

[152] *Sawyer v. Fitts*, 630 S.W.2d 872, 874–75 (Tex. App.—Fort Worth 1982, no writ).

[153] *See Cessna Aircraft Co. v. Aircraft Network, L.L.C.*, 213 S.W.3d 455, 464–65 (Tex. App.—Dallas 2006, pet. denied).

[154] *Nelson v. Data Terminal Sys., Inc.*, 762 S.W.2d 744, 747–48 (Tex. App.—San Antonio 1988, writ denied).

[155] *Southwest Bank & Trust Co. v. Exec. Sportsman Ass'n*, 477 S.W.2d 920, 929 (Tex. Civ. App.—Dallas 1972, writ ref'd n.r.e.).

[156] *Fraud-Tech, Inc. v. Choicepoint, Inc.*, 102 S.W.3d 366, 380 n.43 (Tex. App.—Fort Worth 2003, pet. denied) (citing to authority that recovery of both lost profits and loss of business value for the same time period would be duplicative).

[157] *Checker Bag Co. v. Wash.*, 27 S.W.3d 625, 641–42 (Tex. App.—Waco 2000, pet. denied).

[158] *Phillips v. Carlton Energy Grp., LLC*, 475 S.W.3d 265, 280 (Tex. 2015).

[159] *Phillips v. Carlton Energy Grp., LLC*, 475 S.W.3d 265, 280 (Tex. 2015) (allowing evidence of market valuation of a three-year concession to explore for coalbed methane in an unproven field in Bulgaria).

[160] *Sawyer v. Fitts*, 630 S.W.2d 872, 874–75 (Tex. App.—Fort Worth 1982, no writ).

[161] *Rojas v. Duarte*, 393 S.W.3d 837, 845–46 (Tex. App.—El Paso 2012, pet. denied) (excellent business valuation analysis utilizing wrong date provides no evidence to support a judgment).

11-7:2 Common Loss of Business Value Damage Models

As with valuation of real property, since business valuation is seeking to determine market value, most business valuation analysis is based on one or a combination of three market value models: the income approach, the asset-based cost approach, or the market approach.[162] Subject to the court's legal determination as to what constitutes a proper measure of damages,[163] when different experts present different valuation methods to the court or jury, the fact finder is not bound by any one specific approach.[164] These are some of the most common measures of damages for determining the loss of value of a business:

> Book Value of Investment [asset-based cost approach]: "Book value" was once the dominant method of valuing a business. Before computers, the most readily available information came from the accountants for a business, and accountants tracked the assets and liabilities of a business in their "books," with the difference between assets and liabilities reflecting the "net worth" or "equity" in the business. Since this book value number was available, it was commonly used in litigation. Book value often does not truly answer the question of business market value, however, because book value is based on historical cost, not necessarily reflective of current market value, and because the value of the whole is often greater than the sum of the component parts due to the earning power associated with the business operating as a going concern.[165]
>
> Multiple of Book Value [hybrid market and asset-based cost approach]: In some industries, it is common for businesses to be valued and sold on a "multiple of book." A multiple of book is the multiplier commonly used for sales of businesses in that industry (such as in banking), but the usefulness of this approach depends upon whether it is historically utilized in the particular industry. The multiple is typically derived through comparable sales from the industry, after "normalization" of the balance sheet (to more accurately restate historical numbers).[166]
>
> Multiple of Earnings [hybrid market and income approach]: A "multiple of earnings" is a variation of a "multiple of book" which values a business by applying a multiplier to the annual earnings of the business rather than to the book value of the business. Again, the usefulness of this approach depends upon the historical use of this method for buying and selling businesses in a particular industry. The multiple is typically derived through comparable sales from the industry, after "normalization" of the earnings (to remove extraordinary one-

---

[162] *See City of Harlingen v. Estate of Sharboneau*, 48 S.W.3d 177, 182–83 (Tex. 2001) (discussing the three models for determining market value).

[163] *Sawyer v. Fitts*, 630 S.W.2d 872, 875 (Tex. App.—Fort Worth 1982, no writ).

[164] *Grand Prairie Indep. Sch. Dist. v. Missouri Pac. R.R. Co.*, 730 S.W.2d 761, 762 (Tex. App.—Dallas 1986, writ ref'd n.r.e.).

[165] Excerpted from Jim Wren, Proving Damages to the Jury, 2d ed., § 6:21 of Chapter 6 "Valuations and Damages Models" (James Publishing, San Francisco, 2013).

[166] Excerpted from Jim Wren, Proving Damages to the Jury, 2d ed., § 6:22 of Chapter 6 "Valuations and Damages Models" (James Publishing, San Francisco, 2013).

time events, or the effects of taxes or non-cash events like amortization and depreciation).[167]

Capitalization Rate of Net Cash Flow [income approach]: With businesses that tend to produce a steady cash flow, particularly income-producing real estate and established business franchises, the "cap rate" is a method for valuing the capital cost (the price of investment) that is being paid to buy an asset. The cap rate is the multiple of the years of the net annual cash flow that is paid to buy the investment.[168] For further explanation of the calculation and defense of a cap rate, and illustrations of the inverse relationship between cap rates and interest rates, see Jim Wren, *Proving Damages to the Jury*, 2d ed., § 6:23 of Chapter 6 "Valuations and Damages Models" (James Publishing, San Francisco, 2013).

Discounted Cash Flow Analysis of Projected Future Earnings [income approach]: In simplest terms, discounted cash flow (DCF) analysis takes projections of future earnings and discounts them to present values based on their probabilities of occurring. It has been the advent of personal computers since the late 1970s and early 1980s that has allowed DCF analysis to develop more fully, with increasingly sophisticated projection and discounting of future earnings. There are many variations on DCF analysis, with the choice of methodology dependent on either the specifics of the business opportunity or the preferences of the valuation expert or both. DCF calculations are infinitely adaptable to the specifics of any given business opportunity because the inherent risk of projected but uncertain future cash flows can be dealt with by examining various possible scenarios and discounting each of those projected cash flow scenarios to present value. As a result of being able to consider and weigh multiple scenarios, this method is the one most likely to be applicable to analysis of new enterprises with projections of possible future earnings but with little or no past earnings history. Because DCF analysis is adaptable for uncertain future cash flows, the level of discounting is often high, and this quickly drives down the present value of those future cash flows. That is why you will often see the valuation of lost profits or of a lost business opportunity based only on five years (or less) of projected cash flows, since the present value of cash flows after five years of discounting is so low that it simply makes no sense to project out any further.[169]

Market Value Based on Comparable Businesses [market approach]: This approach determines the value of the business by comparing it to comparable investments that have been bought or sold during a relatively recent period of time. It is not as easily applied to more complex business enterprises because of the inevitable difficulties of trying to compare businesses with so many differences (although relatively complex enterprises are valued with the Guideline Public Companies method), but it is more commonly used with simpler, more fungible types of businesses. When used, it is common to make adjustments based on (1) the size of the business, revenues, numbers of customers, or what-

---

[167] Excerpted from Jim Wren, Proving Damages to the Jury, 2d ed., § 6:22 of Chapter 6 "Valuations and Damages Models" (James Publishing, San Francisco, 2013).

[168] Excerpted from Jim Wren, Proving Damages to the Jury, 2d ed., § 6:23 of Chapter 6 "Valuations and Damages Models" (James Publishing, San Francisco, 2013).

[169] Excerpted from Jim Wren, Proving Damages to the Jury, 2d ed., § 6:24 of Chapter 6 "Valuations and Damages Models" (James Publishing, San Francisco, 2013).

ever other type of size comparison is relevant; and (2) the comparison of sales price in relation to the quality of management as revealed by return on assets.[170]

Common Discounts and Premiums [adjustment to these approaches]: All of the valuation approaches assume that the business enterprise as a whole is being valued and that the business is freely marketable. Those assumptions, however, are not always true. Sometimes the ownership interest at issue in the lawsuit is only for a fractional portion of the enterprise and sometimes the ownership interest is not freely marketable. In these situations, valuation discounts and premiums are used to account for differences in control and liquidity.[171]

11-7:3 Pleading Loss of Value of a Business

When pleading for loss of value of a business, a plaintiff must specifically plead:

- For special damage elements, including the loss of value of a business constituting special or consequential damages;[172] and
- That the plaintiff's claim for relief falls into one of four ranges of monetary relief.[173]

Neither the specific amount of the loss of value of the business nor the method of calculating lost profits need be pleaded (only the fact that the loss of value of the business is being sought and the total damage range of the case), but discovery of the amount and method of calculation of the loss of value of the business may be required by a request for disclosure.[174]

11-8 Property Valuation and Damages

Damages to or loss of tangible property (real property or tangible personal property) may be assessed by determining the market value or diminishment in market value of the property, the remedial cost of repair, the value of the temporary loss of use of the property, the intrinsic value of the property lost, or some combination of these.

Note that under the Property-Owner Rule, a property owner is qualified to testify as to the market value of her property, whether real or personal, even though she would

---

[170] Excerpted from Jim Wren, Proving Damages to the Jury, 2d ed., § 6:25 of Chapter 6 "Valuations and Damages Models" (James Publishing, San Francisco, 2013).

[171] Excerpted from Jim Wren, Proving Damages to the Jury, 2d ed., § 6:25 of Chapter 6 "Valuations and Damages Models" (James Publishing, San Francisco, 2013). For further explanation, see the discussion in that section and authority cited there.

[172] Tex. R. Civ. P. 56; *Sw. Bank & Trust Co. v. Exec. Sportsman Ass'n*, 477 S.W.2d 920, 929 (Tex. Civ. App.—Dallas 1972, writ ref'd n.r.e.) (damages to a business such as loss of profits or loss of goodwill resulting from tort of wrongful sale must be specifically pleaded as special or consequential damages); *Nelson v. Data Terminal Sys., Inc.*, 762 S.W.2d 744, 747–48 (Tex. App.—San Antonio 1988, writ denied) (recovery for diminution in value of business not allowed because it could not be conclusively presumed to have been foreseen or contemplated by parties as a consequence of breach of contract, and the loss in value of the business was not pleaded and proved as a "special damage").

[173] Tex. R. Civ. P. 47(c).

[174] Tex. R. Civ. P. 194.2(d).

not otherwise be qualified to testify about the value of other property.[175] Available to natural persons and organizations alike, the rule is premised on the idea that a property owner is familiar with her own property and its value.[176] As such, the property owner's testimony must be based on a familiarity with the market value of the property, rather than speculation or conclusory statements.

11-8:1 Real Property Valuation and Damages

When dealing with real property, a distinction is commonly made between those damages that are permanent and those that are temporary in nature.[177] Whether an injury to real property is temporary or permanent is a question of law (although the determination may turn on the jury's answer to a predicate question of fact).[178] An injury to real property is considered permanent if it cannot be repaired, fixed, or restored, *or* it is substantially certain that the injury will repeatedly, continually, and regularly recur; it is considered temporary if it can be repaired, fixed, or restored, *and* any anticipated recurrence would be only occasional, irregular, intermittent, and not reasonably predictable.[179]

Damages for permanent injuries to realty are normally measured by the difference in value of the property before and after the permanent injury,[180] or by the difference in value of the property with and without the permanent nuisance.[181]

There are multiple methods for assessing the value of real property (and of property rights such as access rights, easements, and water rights) that correspond to the three approaches used in business valuations (i.e., income approach, market approach, and cost approach). In most valuations, all three methods are considered, although one method may be found to be the most determinative of value in that particular situation. Appraisers will typically state which method is being relied upon primarily and why, but they will then describe the analysis under the other methods to serve as a reality check on the primary method. If each method has more or less equal applicability, the appraiser will essentially average the valuations of all three.[182] In most circumstances, these methods are seeking to assess "fair market value" as that term is historically defined, which is the price a willing buyer would pay a willing seller when neither party is acting under any compulsion to buy or sell.[183]

---

[175] *See Reid Road Mun. Util. Dist. No. 2 v. Speedy Stop Food Stores*, 337 S.W.3d 846, 853–54 (Tex. 2011).

[176] *See Reid Road Mun. Util. Dist. No. 2 v. Speedy Stop Food Stores*, 337 S.W.3d 846, 852–53 (Tex. 2011).

[177] *See Schneider Nat'l Carriers, Inc. v. Bates*, 147 S.W.3d 264, 281 (Tex. 2004) (defining permanent versus temporary damage to land); *Gilbert Wheeler, Inc. v. Enbridge Pipelines (E. Tex.), L.P.*, 449 S.W.3d 474 (Tex. 2014).

[178] *Gilbert Wheeler, Inc. v. Enbridge Pipelines (E. Tex.), L.P.*, 449 S.W.3d 474, 480–81 (Tex. 2014).

[179] *Gilbert Wheeler, Inc. v. Enbridge Pipelines (E. Tex.), L.P.*, 449 S.W.3d 474, 480 (Tex. 2014).

[180] *Kraft v. Langford*, 565 S.W.2d 223, 227 (Tex. 1978), *disapproved on other grounds*.

[181] *Natural Gas Pipeline Co. of Am. v. Justiss*, 397 S.W.3d 150, 155 (Tex. 2012).

[182] Excerpted from Jim Wren, Proving Damages to the Jury, 2d ed., § 6:40 of Chapter 6 "Valuations and Damages Models" (James Publishing, San Francisco, 2013).

[183] *Houston Unlimited, Inc. Metal Processing v. Mel Acres Ranch*, 443 S.W.3d 820, 831 (Tex. 2014). On occasion, however, fair market value is defined differently; *see, e.g., PlainsCapital Bank v. Martin*, 459 S.W.3d 550, 555–56 (Tex. 2015).

Damages for temporary injuries to realty usually include costs of repair and recovery for the intervening loss of use of the property.[184] The valuation for loss of use of property can be calculated in various ways depending on the circumstances of the case[185] and can be based on reduced rental value,[186] the lost value of produce from the land,[187] the amount of out-of-pocket expenditures incurred during the time of lost use,[188] or loss of profits.[189] In addition, if some amount of diminished market value remains after repairs are made, that diminution in value may also be recovered.[190]

The Texas Supreme Court has recognized an "economic feasibility exception" to these general rules. In cases involving temporary injury, when the cost of required repairs or restoration exceeds the diminution in the property's market value to such a disproportionately high degree that the repairs are no longer economically feasible, a temporary injury is deemed permanent, and damages are limited to the loss in fair market value.[191] (There is also, however, an exception to the exception; specifically when trees have been destroyed but there is no loss—or only nominal loss—to the land's fair market value, the intrinsic value of the trees may be recovered.)[192]

11-8:2 Personal Property Valuation and Damages

Damages for injury to chattels may potentially involve both direct and consequential damages. Direct damages will be determined by the cost to repair or replace the chattel. Consequential damages may involve reasonable compensation for loss of use of the chattel for some period of time.[193]

For the direct damage component, the measure of damage will routinely turn on whether repair of the injury is economically feasible.[194] If repairs are economically feasible (in relation to the market value of the property), the direct damages are calculated by the cost of repair (plus any residual loss of market value remaining from the injury after repairs), or alternatively the difference in market value before and after the injury. If repair of the injury is not economically feasible, usually the direct damages are determined by the lost market value of the property.[195]

---

[184] *City of Abilene v. Walker*, 309 S.W.2d 494, 495 (Tex. Civ. App.—Eastland 1958, no writ); *Gilbert Wheeler, Inc. v. Enbridge Pipelines (E. Tex.), L.P.*, 449 S.W.3d 474, 481 (Tex. 2014).
[185] *Hall v. Robbins*, 790 S.W.2d 417, 418 (Tex. App.—Houston [14th Dist.] 1990, no writ).
[186] *City of Abilene v. Walker*, 309 S.W.2d 494, 495 (Tex. Civ. App.—Eastland 1958, no writ).
[187] *City of Abilene v. Walker*, 309 S.W.2d 494, 495 (Tex. Civ. App.—Eastland 1958, no writ).
[188] *City of Carrollton v. RIHR, Inc.*, 308 S.W.3d 444, 452–53 (Tex. App.—Dallas 2010, pet. denied).
[189] *San Antonio River Auth. v. Garrett Bros.*, 528 S.W.2d 266, 274 (Tex. Civ. App.—San Antonio 1975, writ ref'd n.r.e.).
[190] *Parkway Co. v. Woodruff*, 901 S.W.2d 434, 441 (Tex. 1995); *Houston Unlimited, Inc. v. Mel Acres Ranch*, 443 S.W.3d 820 (Tex. 2014).
[191] *Gilbert Wheeler, Inc. v. Enbridge Pipelines (East Tex.), L.P.*, 449 S.W.3d 474, 481 (Tex. 2014).
[192] *Gilbert Wheeler, Inc. v. Enbridge Pipelines (East Tex.), L.P.*, 449 S.W.3d 474, 482–83 (Tex. 2014).
[193] *J & D Towing, LLC v. Am. Alt. Ins. Corp.*, 478 S.W.3d 649, 655–56 (Tex. 2016).
[194] See discussion of economic feasibility in Chapter 12, Section 12-2:2.
[195] *Gilbert Wheeler, Inc. v. Enbridge Pipelines (East Texas), LP*, 449 S.W.3d 474, 481 (Tex. 2014).

For the consequential damage component, the plaintiff is entitled to plead and prove loss-of-use damages in addition to the cost to repair or the lost market value of the property.

By design, loss-of-use damages compensate a property owner for damages that result from "a reasonable period of lost use" of the personal property. The amount of damages may thus be measured according to the particular loss experienced, such as the amount of lost profits, the cost of renting a substitute chattel, or the rental value of the owner's own chattel.[196]

Traditionally, numerous Texas court of appeal decisions allowed loss-of-use damages only in partial-destruction cases and not for total-destruction cases.[197] In 2016, the Texas Supreme Court overruled these cases.[198] Loss-of-use damages are potentially recoverable in both partial-destruction and total-destruction cases. The question of consequential damages for loss-of-use is "wholly independent of the measure of [direct] property damage."[199]

The Supreme Court emphasizes, however, that recovery of loss-of-use damages in total-destruction cases remains subject to reasonable limitations and commonsense rules. The loss-of-use damages must not be "too remote." They are not required to necessarily be "the usual result of the wrong," but they must be foreseeable and directly traceable to the tortious act.[200]

Although mathematical exactness is not required, the evidence offered must rise above the level of pure conjecture. Moreover, the damages may not be awarded for an unreasonably long period of lost use. Whether framed as a duty of mitigation or a doctrine of avoidable consequences, the principle is the same: A plaintiff may not recover loss-of-use damages for a period longer than that reasonably needed to replace the personal property. That principle compels a plaintiff's diligence in remedying his loss and deters an opportunistic plaintiff from dilly-dallying at the expense of the defendant.[201]

In some cases, a different question arises as to whether improvements to real property constitute personal property or fixtures to be valued as part of the real property. The answer to this question turns on the mode and sufficiency of annexation to the realty, the adaptation of the article to the use or purpose of the realty, and especially the intention of the party who annexed the chattel to the realty.[202]

---

[196] *J & D Towing, LLC v. Am. Alt. Ins. Corp.*, 478 S.W.3d 649, 653 (Tex. 2016).
[197] *See, e.g., Hartley v. Schwab*, 564 S.W.2d 829 (Tex. Civ. App.—Amarillo 1978, writ ref'd n.r.e.).
[198] *J & D Towing, LLC v. Am. Alt. Ins. Corp.*, 478 S.W.3d 649, 676 (Tex. 2016).
[199] *J & D Towing, LLC v. Am. Alt. Ins. Corp.*, 478 S.W.3d 649, 659 (Tex. 2016).
[200] *J & D Towing, LLC v. Am. Alt. Ins. Corp.*, 478 S.W.3d 649, 656 (Tex. 2016).
[201] *J & D Towing, LLC v. Am. Alt. Ins. Corp.*, 478 S.W.3d 649, 677 (Tex. 2016).
[202] *Logan v. Mullis*, 686 S.W.2d 605, 607–08 (Tex. 1985); *see also State v. Clear Channel Outdoor, Inc.*, 463 S.W.3d 488, 493 (Tex. 2015).

11-9 Other Pecuniary and Intangible Damages

11-9:1 Loss of Credit or Injury to Credit Reputation

"[A]ctual damages for loss of credit or injury to credit reputation in an action for breach of contract may be recovered when there is evidence that loss of credit was a natural, probable, and foreseeable consequence of the defendant's breach."[203] Loss of credit or injury to credit reputation can also be a compensable injury in tort cases, such as for defamation[204] and fraud.[205]

11-9:2 Reputation Damages to a Corporation

A corporation may recover general damages for loss of reputation, which constitute noneconomic rather than economic damages.[206] "[T]hese non-pecuniary damages do not require certainty of actual monetized loss. Instead, they are measured by an amount that 'a reasonable person could possibly estimate as fair compensation.'"[207]

11-9:3 Reputation and Mental Anguish Damages to an Individual

These noneconomic damages "cannot be determined by mathematical precision; by their nature, they can be determined only by the exercise of sound judgment."[208] Compensation for mental anguish can only be assessed for evidence of "substantial disruption in ... daily routine" or "a high degree of mental pain and distress."[209] Mental anguish is recoverable for fraud,[210] but is rarely compensable in a breach of contract case or a tortious interference with contract case.[211] Damages for mental anguish resulting from the breach of a "special relationship" between the plaintiff and defendant can be compensable when the mental anguish is the necessary and foreseeable result of the defendant's conduct.[212]

11-10 Statutory Damages Specific to the Cause of Action

For some causes of action, applicable damages are specified by statute. These often provide potential damages that would otherwise be unavailable and are intended to discourage particular conduct. Leading examples include:

---

[203] *Mead v. Johnson Grp., Inc.*, 615 S.W.2d 685, 688 (Tex. 1981).
[204] *Blanche v. First Nationwide Mortg. Corp.*, 74 S.W.3d 444, 456 (Tex. App.—Dallas 2002, no pet.).
[205] *Duval Cty. Ranch Co. v. Wooldridge*, 674 S.W.2d 332, 336 (Tex. App.—Austin 1984, no writ).
[206] *Waste Mgmt. of Tex., Inc. v. Tex. Disposal Sys. Landfill, Inc.*, 434 S.W.3d 142, 149–51 (Tex. 2014).
[207] *Waste Mgmt. of Tex., Inc. v. Tex. Disposal Sys. Landfill, Inc.*, 434 S.W.3d 142, 153 (Tex. 2014).
[208] *Bentley v. Bunton*, 94 S.W.3d 561, 605 (Tex. 2002).
[209] *Parkway Co. v. Woodruff*, 901 S.W.2d 434, 444 (Tex. 1995).
[210] *Tony Gullo Motors I, L.P. v. Chapa*, 212 S.W.3d 299, 304 (Tex. 2006).
[211] *Soukup v. Sedgwick Claims Mgmt. Servs., Inc.*, No. 01-11-00871-CV, 2012 WL 3134223, at *6–7 (Tex. App.—Houston [1st Dist.] Aug. 2, 2012, pet. dism'd).
[212] *City of Tyler v. Likes*, 962 S.W.2d 489, 496 (Tex. 1997).

Damages for deceptive trade practices, which include the amount of economic damages found by the trier of fact (often by means of one of the damage models discussed in the preceding sections above), plus mental anguish damages and potential trebling of economic damages for conduct of the defendant committed knowingly,[213] plus potential trebling of mental anguish damages for conduct of the defendant committed intentionally, plus court costs and reasonable and necessary attorney's fees.[214]

Damages for violation of Texas usury law including triple the amount of excess interest or the lesser of 20 percent of the principal or $2000,[215] or totaling the entire amount of principal and interest if the rate charged and received was more than twice the amount allowed by law.[216]

Damages for violation of the Texas Debt Collection Act, including actual damages and injunctive relief, plus attorney's fees and costs.[217]

Damages for violation of the prompt payment requirements in the Texas Insurance Code including, in addition to the amount of the claim, interest on the amount of the claim at the rate of 18 percent a year as damages, together with reasonable attorney's fees.[218]

Employment law damages or damages specific to other causes of action covered in this book.

A statutory remedy can also restrict the recovery of damages. For example, when a covenant not to compete is part of an otherwise enforceable agreement but contains unreasonable restraints, "the court may not award the promisee damages for a breach of the covenant before its reformation and the relief granted to the promisee shall be limited to injunctive relief."[219]

11-11 Equitable Remedies for Recovery of Monetary Funds

For a variety of causes of action often seen in business litigation, such as fraud, breach of contract, breach of fiduciary duty, constructive fraud, and unjust enrichment, equi-

---

[213] Note, however, the split among Texas courts as to whether the DTPA authorizes up to three or up to four times actual damages total for knowing violations of the DTPA. *Compare Bossier Chrysler-Dodge II, Inc. v. Riley*, 221 S.W.3d 749, 752 (Tex. App.—Waco 2007, pet. denied) (interpreting the DTPA to allow actual damages plus trebling of three times actual damages), *with Reyelts v. Cross*, 968 F. Supp. 2d 835, 845 n.3 (N.D. Tex. 2013) (discussing the split among Texas courts but interpreting the DTPA to allow actual damages plus trebling of two times actual damages).

[214] Tex. Bus. & Com. Code Ann. § 17.50.

[215] Tex. Fin. Code Ann. § 305.001.

[216] Tex. Fin. Code Ann. § 305.002.

[217] Tex. Fin. Code Ann. § 392.403.

[218] Tex. Ins. Code Ann. § 542.060 (An alternate damages computation of interest, for suits arising under the new Tex. Ins. Code 542A applicable to first-party insurance claims resulting from weather and natural disasters, has been added to this section by HB 1774, effective Sept. 1, 2017).

[219] Tex. Bus. & Com. Code § 15.51(c).

11-11:1 Constructive Trust

Imposition of a constructive trust is an equitable remedy to prevent unjust enrichment when there is: (1) a breach of a special trust or fiduciary relationship, or actual or constructive fraud; (2) unjust enrichment of the wrongdoer; and (3) tracing of funds to an identifiable res.[221] It is an equitable means of requiring a wrongdoer, who holds legal title to wrongfully acquired property, to convey the property to the party that is deemed to hold equitable title, in order to avoid unjust enrichment.[222]

The first element may be satisfied by either a demonstration of actual fraud (without regard to the nature of the relationship between the parties),[223] or by demonstration of breach of a relationship of trust. The relationship of trust may exist due to a formal fiduciary relationship or due to an informal confidential relationship of trust.[224]

The second element is not limited solely to enrichment of the wrongdoer, but includes enrichment of a party who claims through the wrongdoer.[225] However, a party's mere receipt of funds from a wrongdoer does not necessarily constitute unjust enrichment when the receiving party is also a victim of the wrongdoer.[226]

The third element places the initial burden on the party who seeks to impose a constructive trust to trace funds into the specific property sought to be recovered.[227] Once the claimant has met that burden, the burden then shifts to the holder of the property to demonstrate what portion of the property came from his own funds; if that burden is not met, the entirety of the property is subject to the constructive trust.[228] The fact that the nature of the property changes form does not affect the power of the court to impose a constructive trust over it if the tracing burden is met.[229]

11-11:2 Unjust Enrichment

"A person is unjustly enriched when he obtains a 'benefit from another by fraud, duress, or the taking of an undue advantage.' Unjust enrichment is an equitable principle holding that one who receives benefits unjustly should make restitution for

---

[220] *See* Chapter 11, Section 11-5:7.
[221] *Hahn v. Love*, 321 S.W.3d 517, 533 (Tex. App.—Houston [1st Dist.] 2009, pet. denied).
[222] *Wheeler v. Blacklands Prod. Credit Ass'n*, 627 S.W.2d 846, 849 (Tex. App.—Fort Worth 1982, no writ).
[223] *Hahn v. Love*, 321 S.W.3d 517, 533 (Tex. App.—Houston [1st Dist.] 2009, pet. denied).
[224] *Hatton v. Turner*, 622 S.W.2d 450, 458 (Tex. Civ. App.—Tyler 1981, no writ).
[225] *Hamblet v. Coveney*, 714 S.W.2d 126, 130 (Tex. App.—Houston [1st Dist.] 1986, writ ref'd n.r.e.). (constructive trust imposed on property held by wife of wrongdoer that would unjustly enrich her, despite lack of wrongdoing by her).
[226] *Cote v. Texcan Ventures II*, 271 S.W.3d 450, 454 (Tex. App.—Dallas 2008, no pet.) (money transferred from one victim of Ponzi scheme to another).
[227] *Wilz v. Flournoy*, 228 S.W.3d 674, 676 (Tex. 2007).
[228] *Wilz v. Flournoy*, 228 S.W.3d 674, 676 (Tex. 2007).
[229] *Paschal v. Great W. Drilling Ltd.*, 215 S.W.3d 437 (Tex. App.—Eastland 2006, pet. denied) (constructive trust imposed on life insurance proceeds of policy purchased with traced funds).

those benefits."[230] Unjust enrichment has been variously described as a remedy,[231] as a cause of action[232] and as a doctrine justifying the imposition of various other equitable or quasi-contractual remedies such as constructive trust,[233] quantum meruit,[234] and restitution.[235]

Although unjust enrichment can result in the enforcement of a constructive trust (e.g., for fraud, or for duress that takes advantage of a confidential relationship), a remedy for unjust enrichment can also result in recovery in circumstances that would not justify imposition of a constructive trust. While a constructive trust requires breach of a special trust or fiduciary relationship, or actual or constructive fraud,[236] restitution for unjust enrichment can result from a business dealing without fraud or special relationship, but where the retention of benefits would constitute unjust enrichment.

Unjust enrichment will not simply relieve a party from a bad bargain[237] where the enrichment results from the terms of an express contract, especially when the contractual duty at issue has been performed,[238] but the finding of an agreement does not defeat all restitution remedies grounded in the principle of unjust enrichment.[239] "Indeed, the principle of unjust enrichment suggests that restitution is an appropriate remedy in circumstances where the agreement contemplated is unenforceable, impossible, not fully performed, thwarted by mutual mistake, or void for other legal reasons" and the retention of funds would constitute an unjust enrichment.[240] Likewise, unjust enrichment applies principles of restitution where there is no express contract at all, yet the retention of unjust benefits implies an obligation to make restitution.[241]

Although unjust enrichment can result in imposition of a constructive trust, it is not limited to the circumstances that would justify a constructive trust. This means there is no requirement that funds be traced to a specific res, but in the absence of tracing

---

[230] *Villarreal v. Grant Geophysical, Inc.*, 136 S.W.3d 265, 270 (Tex. App.—San Antonio 2004, pet. denied); but note the disagreement between courts as to whether or not unjust enrichment is a distinct cause of action. *See Pepi Corp. v. Galliford*, 254 S.W.3d 457, 460 (Tex. App.—Houston [1st Dist.] 2007, pet. denied); *compare with Lilani v. Noorali*, No. H-09-2617, 2011 U.S. Dist. LEXIS 440, at *36–38 (S.D. Tex. Jan. 3, 2011) and *Davis v. OneWest Bank N.A.*, No. 02-14-00264-CV, 2015 Tex. App. LEXIS 3470, at *1–3 (Tex. App.—Fort Worth Apr. 9, 2015, pet. denied).
[231] *Burlington N.R.R. Co. v. Sw. Elec. Power Co.*, 925 S.W.2d 92, 96–97 (Tex. App.—Texarkana 1996, *affirmed by*, 966 S.W.2d 467).
[232] *HECI Expl. Co. v. Neel*, 982 S.W.2d 881, 891 (Tex. 1998).
[233] *Mowbray v. Avery*, 76 S.W.3d 663, 680–81 (Tex. App.—Corpus Christi 2002, pet. denied).
[234] *Vortt Exploration Co., Inc. v. Chevron USA, Inc.*, 787 S.W.2d 942, 944 (Tex. 1990).
[235] *Walker v. Cotter Properties, Inc.*, 181 S.W.3d 895, 900 (Tex. App.—Dallas 2006, no pet.).
[236] *See* Chapter 8, Section 8-8:4.1.
[237] *Freeman v. Harleton Oil & Gas, Inc.*, 528 S.W.3d 708, 740 (Tex. App.—Texarkana 2017, pet. denied).
[238] *Burlington N. R.R. Co. v. Sw. Elec. Power Co.*, 925 S.W.2d 92, 97 (Tex. App.—Texarkana 1996, *affirmed by* 966 S.W.2d 467).
[239] *City of Harker Heights v. Sun Meadows Land, Ltd.*, 830 S.W.2d 313, 318 (Tex. App.—Austin 1992, no writ).
[240] *City of Harker Heights v. Sun Meadows Land, Ltd.*, 830 S.W.2d 313, 319 (Tex. App.—Austin 1992, no writ).
[241] *Walker v. Cotter Properties, Inc.*, 181 S.W.3d 895, 900 (Tex. App.—Dallas 2006, no pet.).

11-11:3 Rescission or Restitution

"Restitution" and "rescission" refer to the same remedy (although as with the term "unjust enrichment," the terms "restitution" and "rescission" have each been variously described as a cause of action[242] or as a remedy[243]). "[R]escission is the common name for the composite remedy of rescission and restitution."[244]

The remedy involves a mutual unwinding of a transaction, restoring both parties to their original positions.[245] Rather than requiring a party to a contract to prove expectation damages, the remedy can be used as an alternative measure of recovery simply requiring each party to restore to the other what has been received.[246] It is particularly useful as a remedy for recovering the defendant's wrongful gain in excess of the plaintiff's loss.[247]

11-11:4 Quantum Meruit Damages

Quantum meruit damages, as distinguished from a quasi-contractual cause of action for quantum meruit, constitute a remedy based on equity.[248] While a quantum meruit *cause of action* is inconsistent with an express contract, quantum meruit *damages* may be recovered consistently with an express contract when a plaintiff has partially performed but, because of the *defendant's* breach, the plaintiff is prevented from completing the contract,[249] when the contract is unilateral in nature,[250] or in building or construction contracts (less any damages resulting from the plaintiff's breach of the contract).[251] As with a quantum meruit cause of action, the remedy is for the value of the services or materials furnished,[252] or in the event of a breaching plaintiff in the setting of a construction contract, the value of the services or materials furnished less any damages resulting from the plaintiff's breach of the contract.[253]

---

[242] *Miller v. Recovery Sys., Inc.*, No. 02-12-00468-CV, 2013 WL 5303060, at *26–27 (Tex. App.—Fort Worth Sept. 19, 2013, pet. denied) (describing restitution as a cause of action); *Leonard v. Eskew*, 731 S.W.2d 124, 131–33 (Tex. App.—Austin 1987, writ ref'd n.r.e.) (describing rescission as a remedy).

[243] *City of Harker Heights v. Sun Meadows Land, Ltd.*, 830 S.W.2d 313, 317 (Tex. App.—Austin 1992, no writ) (describing restitution as a measure of recovery); *Morton v. Nguyen*, 412 S.W.3d 506, 510 (Tex. 2013) (describing rescission as a remedy).

[244] *Morton v. Nguyen*, 412 S.W.3d 506, 510 (Tex. 2013).

[245] *Morton v. Nguyen*, 412 S.W.3d 506, 510–12 (Tex. 2013).

[246] *City of Harker Heights v. Sun Meadows Land, Ltd.*, 830 S.W.2d 313, 317 (Tex. App.—Austin 1992, no writ).

[247] *Miller v. Recovery Sys., Inc.*, No. 02-12-00468-CV, 2013 WL 5303060, at *27 (Tex. App.—Fort Worth Sept. 19, 2013, pet. denied).

[248] *Truly v. Austin*, 744 S.W.2d 934, 938 (Tex. 1988).

[249] *McFarland v. Sanders*, 932 S.W.2d 640, 646 (Tex. App.—Tyler 1996, no writ).

[250] *Truly v. Austin*, 744 S.W.2d 934, 937 (Tex. 1988).

[251] *Truly v. Austin*, 744 S.W.2d 934, 937 (Tex. 1988).

[252] *McFarland v. Sanders*, 932 S.W.2d 640, 646 (Tex. App.—Tyler 1996, no writ).

[253] *Truly v. Austin*, 744 S.W.2d 934, 937 (Tex. 1988).

11-11:5 Forfeiture and Disgorgement

The equitable remedies of forfeiture (of the right to receive funds) and disgorgement (of funds received) require a fiduciary, or one in a position of trust, to account for and turn over any funds acquired from his position of trust that have profited him personally in violation of his duty to the beneficiary.[254] The remedies do not require the plaintiff to show harm, but only the profit received by the fiduciary in violation of duty.[255] "The main purpose of forfeiture is not to compensate an injured principal, even though it may have that effect. Rather, the central purpose of the equitable remedy of forfeiture is to protect relationships of trust by discouraging agents' disloyalty."[256]

Upon a showing of breach of duty, forfeiture and disgorgement do not automatically result in payment by the fiduciary of all profits received. Instead, based on determination of fact issues by the jury regarding the extent and seriousness of the breach, the court is charged with determining the extent of forfeiture or disgorgement.[257]

Forfeiture and disgorgement may be used to recover a fiduciary's fee,[258] contractual consideration to a fiduciary[259] or any other funds received in violation of duty.

11-11:6 Accounting

An equitable accounting is used to examine the accounts between parties, often of partners or other fiduciaries, preparatory to providing further relief. The court is authorized by Tex. R. Civ. P. 172 to appoint an auditor "to state the accounts between the parties and to make report thereof to the court as soon as possible." Thereafter, the court may award a monetary judgment reflecting a full reconciliation of accounts and injunctive relief, if appropriate, including a receivership.

To obtain an equitable accounting, a party must demonstrate that no adequate remedy at law exists without the accounting, or that there exists a close fiduciary relationship with a complication of accounts.[260]

---

[254] *Johnson v. Brewer & Pritchard, P.C.*, 73 S.W.3d 193, 200 (Tex. 2002) (Courts may disgorge any profit where "an agent diverted an opportunity from the principal or engaged in competition with the principal, [and] the agent or an entity controlled by the agent profited or benefitted in some way.").

[255] *Johnson v. Brewer & Pritchard, P.C.*, 73 S.W.3d 193, 200 (Tex. 2002).

[256] *Burrow v. Arce*, 997 S.W.2d 229, 238 (Tex. 1999).

[257] *Deutsch v. Hoover, Bax & Slovacek, L.L.P*, 97 S.W.3d 179, 196 (Tex. App.—Houston [14th Dist.] 2002, no pet.) (setting forth factors to be considered).

[258] *Burrow v. Arce*, 997 S.W.2d 229 (Tex. 1999) (forfeiture of fee received by fiduciary in violation of fiduciary duties, in amount determined by court, without regard to any harm suffered by plaintiff); *First United Pentecostal Church of Beaumont v. Parker*, No. 15-0708, 60 Tex. Sup. Ct. J. 608, 2017 WL 1032754, at *5 (Mar. 17, 2017) ("It is the agent's disloyalty, not any resulting harm, that violates the fiduciary relationship and thus impairs the basis for compensation.").

[259] *ERI Consulting Eng'rs, Inc. v. Swinnea*, 318 S.W.3d 867 (Tex. 2010) (forfeiture of contractual consideration fraudulently induced by fiduciary in knowing violation of fiduciary duties, without regard to any harm suffered by plaintiff).

[260] *Richardson v. First Nat'l Life Ins. Co.*, 419 S.W.2d 836, 838 (Tex. 1967).

Tex. R. Civ. P. 172 allows exceptions to the auditor's report to be filed by the parties. The report is admissible in evidence, and may only be contradicted to the extent that an exception has been filed.[261]

11-11:7 Money Had and Received

As a subcategory of unjust enrichment, money had and received is equitable in nature, but it is not premised on any wrongdoing by the defendant. Rather, all a claimant must prove is that the defendant holds money which, in equity and good conscience, belongs to him.[262] Courts focus on the retention, rather than the acquisition, as the basis of unjust enrichment. However, like most other equitable remedies, courts will balance the equities in determining whether a claimant is entitled to this remedy in the first place.

11-12 Exemplary Damages

Exemplary damages in Texas are governed by Chapter 41 of the Texas Civil Practice and Remedies Code. To obtain exemplary damages, a plaintiff must plead and prove by clear and convincing evidence that the harm forming the basis for the award of exemplary damages resulted from fraud, malice, or gross negligence.[263] Evidence of ordinary negligence, bad faith, or a deceptive trade practice will not suffice.[264]

Exemplary damages may not be awarded to a claimant who elects to have his recovery multiplied under another statute.[265]

Under specified circumstances, exemplary damages may be assessed against an employer for the criminal conduct of an employee.[266]

Subject to specified exceptions, exemplary damages against a defendant may not exceed an amount equal to the greater of:

- two times the amount of economic damages; plus
- an amount equal to any noneconomic damages found by the jury, not to exceed $750,000; or $200,000.[267]

This cap on exemplary damages does not apply to specified forms of felony conduct, including (among other felony conduct) forgery, commercial bribery, misapplication of fiduciary property or property of a financial institution, securing execution of a document by deception, fraudulent destruction or removal or concealment of a writing, and theft.[268] Exemplary damage awards excepted from and in excess of the

---

[261] *Villiers v. Republic Fin. Servs., Inc.*, 602 S.W.2d 566, 570 (Tex. Civ. App.—Texarkana 1980, writ ref'd n.r.e.).
[262] *Plains Expl. & Prod. Co. v. Torch Energy Advisors Inc.*, 473 S.W.3d 296, 302 n.4 (Tex. 2015).
[263] Tex. Civ. Prac. & Rem. Code § 41.003(a).
[264] Tex. Civ. Prac. & Rem. Code § 41.003(b).
[265] Tex. Civ. Prac. & Rem. Code § 41.004(b).
[266] Tex. Civ. Prac. & Rem. Code § 41.005.
[267] Tex. Civ. Prac. & Rem. Code § 41.008(b).
[268] Tex. Civ. Prac. & Rem. Code § 41.008(c).

caps, despite being statutorily authorized, are still subject to federal constitutional due process guidelines and limitations.[269]

Plaintiff must specifically plead the basis for exemplary damages, as well as providing fair notice of any specified exception to the exemplary damage caps.[270] Although for the sake of clarity it may be helpful for the defendant to plead any caps to exemplary damages, the caps do not constitute an affirmative defense and apply as a matter of law.[271] The defendant should plead federal constitutional due process limitations on any exemplary damages in excess of the caps, plus pleading for bifurcation of the exemplary damages phase of the case if desired.[272]

11-13 Interest, Costs, and Attorney's Fees

11-13:1 Prejudgment and Post-judgment Interest

Prejudgment interest falls into three basic categories, based on its source of authorization:

- Prejudgment interest provided by statute[273]
- Prejudgment interest provided by contract[274]
- Prejudgment interest provided by common law (equitable)[275]

"As a general rule, a plaintiff is required to plead for prejudgment interest sought at common law as an element of damages, whereas statutory or contractual interest may be predicated on a prayer for general relief."[276]

The safer course, however, is to always specifically plead for prejudgment interest rather than simply relying on a prayer for general relief, even in cases in which it would appear that prejudgment interest is provided by contract or statute. In many

---

[269] *Harris v. Archer*, 134 S.W.3d 411, 435–41 (Tex. App.—Amarillo 2004, pet. denied); *see* Jim Wren, Proving Damages to the Jury, 2d ed., Chapter 19 "Punitive Damages" (James Publishing, San Francisco, 2013).

[270] *Marin v. IESI TX Corp.*, 317 S.W.3d 314, 332 (Tex. App.—Houston [1st Dist.] 2010, pet. denied, *overruled on other grounds by Zorrilla v. Aypco Constr. II, LLC*, 469 S.W.3d 143 (Tex. 2015)).

[271] *Zorrilla v. Aypco Constr. II, LLC*, 469 S.W.3d 143, 155–58 (Tex. 2015).

[272] Tex. Civ. Prac. & Rem. Code § 41.009.

[273] *See, e.g.*, Tex. Fin. Code Ann. § 302.002 (specifying interest rate between creditor and obligor when no rate specified); §§ 304.101-304.108 (applying to judgments in wrongful death, personal injury, and property damage cases); Tex. Prop. Code Ann. §§ 28.002-28.004 (requiring prompt payment for construction and specifying interest on overdue payment).

[274] *Pegasus Energy Grp., Inc. v. Cheyenne Petroleum Co.*, 3 S.W.3d 112, 124 (Tex. App.—Corpus Christi 1999, pet. denied) (party entitled to prejudgment interest because contract provided for prejudgment interest).

[275] *Johnson & Higgins of Tex., Inc. v. Kenneco Energy, Inc.*, 962 S.W.2d 507, 528–33 (Tex. 1998, *superseded by statute on other grounds*, Tex. Fin. Code Ann. § 304.1045) (conforming common law equitable prejudgment interest to legislative principles).

[276] *Mason v. Mason*, 07-12-00007-CV, 2014 WL 199649, at *17 (Tex. App.—Amarillo Jan. 13, 2014, no pet.), citing *Republic Nat'l Bank v. Northwest Nat'l Bank*, 578 S.W.2d 109, 116–17 (Tex. 1978); *see Benavides v. Isles Const. Co.*, 726 S.W.2d 23, 25 (Tex. 1987) (general prayer for relief does not support a claim at common law for prejudgment interest).

cases, a claim for breach of contract is merely one of the causes of action alleged, and if the judgment ultimately granted is based on a tort cause of action, there is no basis for recovery of prejudgment interest without a specific allegation and prayer for prejudgment interest.[277] Even when the judgment enforces a contract, if the contract is silent regarding prejudgment interest, any assessment of prejudgment interest must then find its source in an enabling statute or the common law, and the enabling statute relevant to contractual causes of action does not necessarily apply to all contracts.[278]

A failure to adequately plead for prejudgment interest can be cured by a post-verdict trial amendment.[279] The opportunity to amend expires, however, once judgment is rendered.[280]

Post-judgment interest is mandated by statute and sets forth no pleading requirement as a predicate to recovery.[281]

11-13:2 Costs of Suit

Although it is customary and appropriate to include a prayer for recovery of costs in a general prayer for relief, a specific pleading of taxable court costs does not appear to be required. In the same way that post-judgment interest is made recoverable by statute without stating any pleading requirement, "costs" of suit are made recoverable by Tex. R. Civ. P. 131 without any stated requirement of a pleading for costs.[282]

"Texas statutes and common law delineate which items the court may and may not include as taxable costs . . . 'Costs' usually refers to fees and charges required by law to be paid to the courts or some of their officers, the amount of which is fixed by statute or the court's rules, for example filing and service fees. Costs within the meaning of Rules 125 through 149 are those items in the clerk's bill of costs."[283] In addition to filing and service fees, the certified original cost of taking depositions are included as taxable court costs[284] (but deposition copy costs and video costs are not included).[285] "If the trial court taxes costs other than those customarily taxed, it may do so only for good cause stated on the record."[286]

---

[277] *Mobil Producing Tex. & New Mexico, Inc. v. Cantor*, 93 S.W.3d 916, 920 (Tex. App.—Corpus Christi 2002, no pet.).

[278] *Bufkin v. Bufkin*, 259 S.W.3d 343, 356-58 (Tex. App.—Dallas 2008, pet. denied) (Tex. Fin. Code Ann. § 302.002 is silent on contracts not involving extensions of credit, and equitable prejudgment interest cannot be recovered in absence of specific pleading and prayer).

[279] *Benavides v. Isles Constr. Co.*, 726 S.W.2d 23, 25 (Tex. 1987) (interpreting Tex. R. Civ. P. 266).

[280] *Mitchell v. La Flamme*, 60 S.W.3d 123, 132 (Tex. App.—Houston [14th Dist.] 2000, no pet.) (trial court cannot grant motion to amend pleadings after it has rendered judgment).

[281] Tex. Fin. Code Ann. § 304.001; *see also DeGroot v. DeGroot*, 369 S.W.3d 918, 926-27 (Tex. App.—Dallas 2012, no pet.) (holding post-judgment interest to be recoverable on general prayer for relief even if not specifically awarded in the judgment).

[282] Tex. R. Civ. P. 131 ("successful party to a suit shall recover of his adversary all costs incurred therein, except where otherwise provided").

[283] *Hatfield v. Solomon*, 316 S.W.3d 50, 66 (Tex. App.—Houston [14th Dist.] 2010, no pet.).

[284] *Wallace v. Briggs*, 162 Tex. 485, 491, 348 S.W.2d 523, 527 (1961).

[285] *Gumpert v. ABF Freight Sys., Inc.*, 312 S.W.3d 237, 240-42 (Tex. App.—Dallas 2010, no pet.).

[286] *Headington Oil Co., L.P. v. White*, 287 S.W.3d 204, 212 (Tex. App.—Houston [14th Dist.] 2009, no pet.) (good cause did not exist to award recovery of expert witness fees as costs); *see* Tex. R. Civ. P. 141.

Rather than depending upon pleading for recovery of costs, the recoverability of costs is instead dependent upon qualifying as the successful party[287] subject to the court's exercise of discretion to assess costs other than in favor of the successful party.[288]

For some causes of action, however, statutes allow recovery of costs beyond those normally considered as taxable court costs.[289] When costs are sought based upon a specific statutory provision, the statutory basis for the claim should be pleaded.[290] By pleading violation of the statute, presumably the defendant is placed on notice of the damages, including costs of suit, expressly provided by the statute,[291] but the wiser course would be to plead the recoverable costs specifically.

11-13:3 Attorney Fees

Generally, attorney fees are not recoverable unless specifically authorized by contract or statute.[292] Furthermore, as a general rule, attorney fees must be specifically pleaded in order to support their recovery.[293]

When pleaded, various statutes make attorney fees recoverable for particular causes of action and proceedings.[294] In addition, Texas Civil Practice and Remedies Code Section 38.001 makes attorney fees recoverable for a variety of actions.[295]

---

[287] *Moore v. Trevino*, 94 S.W.3d 723, 729 (Tex. App.—San Antonio 2002, pet. denied) (party is "successful" based upon its success on the merits and not on whether damages are awarded).

[288] Tex. R. Civ. P. 141; *Furr's Supermarkets, Inc. v. Bethune*, 53 S.W.3d 375, 376–77 (Tex. 2001) (discretion to award costs other than to successful party requires good cause stated on the record).

[289] *See, e.g.*, Tex. Bus. & Com. Code Ann. § 27.01(e) (providing for recovery of reasonable and necessary attorney's fees, expert witness fees, costs for copies of depositions, and costs of court for statutory real estate and stock fraud).

[290] *Zavala v. Trujillo*, 883 S.W.2d 242, 248 (Tex. App.—El Paso 1994, writ denied) (general rule is that a party relying upon a statutory violation should plead such reliance and should reasonably identify the statute relied upon).

[291] *See Prudential Securities Inc. v. Shoemaker*, 981 S.W.2d 791, 793–94 (Tex. App.—Houston [1st Dist.] 1998, no pet.) (pleading a fraud claim under Tex. Bus. & Com. Code Ann. § 27.01 held sufficient to plead punitive damages expressly recoverable under § 27.01).

[292] *Wells Fargo Bank, N.A. v. Murphy*, 458 S.W.3d 912, 915 (Tex. 2015); *Cytogenix, Inc. v. Waldroff*, 213 S.W.3d 479, 489 (Tex. App.—Houston [1st Dist.] 2006, pet. denied).

[293] *Wells Fargo Bank, N.A. v. Murphy*, 458 S.W.3d 912, 915 (Tex. 2015); *Good v. Baker*, 339 S.W.3d 260, 266 (Tex. App.—Texarkana 2011, pet. denied).

[294] *See, e.g.*, Tex. Ins. Code Ann. § 541.152; Tex. Bus. & Com. Code Ann. § 17.50(d); Tex. Civ. Prac. & Rem. Code Ann. § 37.009.

[295] Tex. Civ. Prac. & Rem. Code § 38.001 (making attorney fees recoverable for oral or written contracts, sworn accounts, killed or injured stock, lost or damaged freight or express or overcharges for freight or express, or labor or services or material furnished).

CHAPTER 12

Defensive Issues Relating to Damages*

12-1 Mitigation of Damages

The duty to mitigate damages, sometimes called the doctrine of avoidable consequences,[1] reduces the damages recoverable by a plaintiff if the defendant can plead and prove that the plaintiff failed to act reasonably and limit the extent of loss.[2] Mitigation of damages is distinct from contributory negligence. Contributory negligence addresses conduct which caused or contributed to cause the losses claim; mitigation deals with post-occurrence negligence that prolonged or enhanced the extent of damage.[3] Failing to wear a seatbelt does not cause the motor vehicle accident but it does cause or contribute to cause the personal injuries sustained in the wreck and is thus contributory negligence.[4] Refusing to take needed antibiotics post-accident which then leads to infection is a failure to mitigate. "A mitigation of damages instruction is proper when the negligence complained of merely contributed to or added to the extent of the losses or injuries but has no part in causing the incident in question."[5]

The duty to mitigate damages includes taking affirmative steps to minimize the loss,[6] although there are limits on this duty. The plaintiff need not accept financial

---

[*] The authors thank Max Moran for his contributions to this chapter.
[1] *Pulaski Bank & Tr. Co. v. Tex. Am. Bank/Fort Worth, N.A.*, 759 S.W.2d 723, 735 (Tex. App.—Dallas 1988, writ denied).
[2] *Walker v. Salt Flat Water Co.*, 128 Tex. 140, 143–44, 96 S.W.2d 231, 232 (1936) (when a party can save himself from damages resulting from a breach of contract "at a trifling expense or with reasonable exertions, it is his duty to incur such expense and make such exertions").
[3] *Nabors Well Services Ltd. v. Romero*, 456 S.W.3d 553 (Tex. 2015).
[4] *Id.*; *see also* Tex. Civ. Prac. & Rem. Code sec. 33.004.
[5] *Hygeia Dairy Co. v. Gonzalez*, 994 S.W.2d 220, 224 (Tex. App.—San Antonio 1999, no pet.), citing *Elbaor v. Smith*, 845 S.W.2d 240, 245 (Tex. 1992); *see also Thota v. Young*, 366 S.W.3d 678, 684 (Tex. 2012).
[6] *David H. v. Spring Branch Indep. Sch. Dist.*, 569 F. Supp. 1324, 1340 (S.D. Tex. 1983) (Plaintiff cannot sit still and let damages pile up when reasonable steps would prevent further losses.).

risks,[7] sacrifice contractual rights[8] or accept an inadequate settlement offer in order to mitigate damages.[9]

During the time that a contract or duty to perform is in effect, if the defendant has equal opportunity with the plaintiff to perform, and equal knowledge of the consequences of nonperformance, the defendant cannot reduce the recovery of damages by insisting the plaintiff mitigate damages.[10] An "injured party is not required to minimize damages resulting from . . . fraud."[11]

The duty to mitigate arises in both contract and tort cases.[12] In contract and business tort litigation, the defendant generally must plead a failure to mitigate damages as an affirmative defense.[13] In personal injury litigation, the Texas Supreme Court has rejected mitigation as an affirmative defense because a failure to mitigate does not defeat the plaintiff's claim for damages "in whole or in specific part" as required by Tex. R. Civ. P. 94.[14] "There is a strong policy reason for holding that a failure to mitigate damages in a personal injury case is not an affirmative defense" because it "would result in a proliferation of special issues in an area already mired in a prolixity of complicated issues."[15]

In contract and business tort litigation, however, failure to mitigate more likely results in a specifically identifiable and quantifiable increase in damages, and thus the

---

[7] *Austin Hill Country Realty, Inc. v. Palisades Plaza, Inc.*, 948 S.W.2d 293, 298 (Tex. 1997); *but see White v. Harrison*, 390 S.W.3d 666, 675 n.5 (Tex. App.—Dallas 2012, no pet.), noting the subsequent limiting provision of Tex. Prop. Code Ann. § 91.006(b).

[8] *Texas Gas Expl. Corp. v. Broughton Offshore Ltd. II*, 790 S.W.2d 781, 789 (Tex. App.—Houston [14th Dist.] 1990, no writ).

[9] *Gunn Infiniti, Inc. v. O'Byrne*, 996 S.W.2d 854, 858 (Tex. 1999).

[10] *Williston on Contracts* § 64:27 (4th ed.), citing *Walker v. Salt Flat Water Co.*, 128 Tex. 140, 96 S.W.2d 231 (Tex. 1936); *see Mondragon v. Austin*, 954 S.W.2d 191 (Tex. App.—Austin 1997, pet. denied) (Plaintiff mitigated damages for loss of use of car by submitting claim to insurance company for repair of car, providing opportunity to insurance company to honor the claim and repair the car.).

[11] *Formosa Plastics Corp., USA v. Kajima Intern., Inc.*, 216 S.W.3d 436, 459 (Tex. App.—Corpus Christi-Edinburg 2006, pet. denied) (citing authority).

[12] *Formosa Plastics Corp., USA v. Kajima Intern., Inc.*, 216 S.W.3d 436, 458–59 (Tex. App.—Corpus Christi-Edinburg 2006, pet. denied).

[13] *Austin Hill Country Realty, Inc. v. Palisades Plaza, Inc.*, 948 S.W.2d 293, 299 (Tex. 1997) (burden on defendant to affirmatively prove mitigation defense); *Gunn Infiniti, Inc. v. O'Byrne*, 996 S.W.2d 854, 856 (Tex. 1999) (mitigation of damages is affirmative defense in a DTPA claim); *Allen v. Am. Gen. Fin., Inc.*, 251 S.W.3d 676, 686 (Tex. App.—San Antonio 2007, pet. granted, judgm't vacated w.r.m.) (mitigation-of-damages doctrine is affirmative defense in lender liability case).

[14] *Moulton v. Alamo Ambulance Serv., Inc.*, 414 S.W.2d 444, 448 (Tex. 1967).

[15] *Moulton v. Alamo Ambulance Serv., Inc.*, 414 S.W.2d 444, 448–49 (Tex. 1967) (explaining the policy reason as the desire to avoid a proliferation of jury questions).

defendant must specifically plead a plaintiff's failure to mitigate,[16] as well as prove the extent of avoidable loss resulting from the plaintiff's failure to mitigate.[17]

Where the defendant contends the plaintiff actually has mitigated losses by some amount (such as by leasing property vacated prematurely by the defendant), the defendant is not required to plead the actual mitigation as an affirmative defense.[18] "Rather, the [defendant's] evidence of the [plaintiff's] mitigation tends to rebut the measure of damages under the [plaintiff's] claim of breach and may be admitted under a general denial."[19] The defendant retains the burden to produce evidence of the extent of actual mitigation which should be offset against damages.[20]

12-2 Issues of Excessive or Double Recovery

12-2:1 Duplicative Damages

A party is generally entitled to sue and to seek damages on alternative theories[21] but cannot receive a double recovery, i.e. more than one recovery for the same injury.[22] Double recovery exists when the same measure of damages is presented to the jury for alternate theories of recovery, such as for Insurance Code violations and DTPA violations. It may be appropriate to submit both theories of recovery in the court's charge, but the Court cannot, when applying the law to the verdict, include the duplicate damage amounts in the judgment.[23] "Appellate courts have applied the one satisfaction rule when the defendants commit the same act as well as when the defendants commit technically differing acts which result in a single injury."[24]

---

[16] *Brazos River Auth. v. City of Graham*, 163 Tex. 167, 184, 354 S.W.2d 99, 111 (1961) (failure to mitigate property damage is an affirmative defense that the defendant waives by not pleading it); *Rauscher Pierce Refsnes, Inc. v. Great Sw. Savs., F.A.*, 923 S.W.2d 112, 117 (Tex. App.—Houston [14th Dist.] 1996, no pet.) (burden on defendant to plead failure to mitigate in breach of contract and breach of fiduciary duty case).

[17] *Formosa Plastics Corp., U.S.A. v. Kajima Intern., Inc.*, 216 S.W.3d 436, 459 (Tex. App.—Corpus Christi-Edinburg 2006, pet. denied) (defendant required to present some evidence from which the jury can make a reasoned calculation of the losses that occurred due to the plaintiff's decision not to mitigate); *but see Hygeia Dairy Co. v. Gonzalez*, 994 S.W.2d 220, 225 (Tex. App.—San Antonio 1999, no pet.) (law does not require exact showing of amount of damages attributable to failure to mitigate, provided evidence is sufficient to guide the jury in determining which damages are attributable to plaintiff's failure to mitigate).

[18] *Austin Hill Country Realty, Inc. v. Palisades Plaza, Inc.*, 948 S.W.2d 293, 300 (Tex. 1997).

[19] *Austin Hill Country Realty, Inc. v. Palisades Plaza, Inc.*, 948 S.W.2d 293, 300 (Tex. 1997).

[20] *Landry's Seafood House-Addison, Inc. v. Snadon*, 233 S.W.3d 430, 436 (Tex. App.—Dallas 2007, pet. denied) (defaulting tenant bears burden of proof to show landlord has "mitigated or failed to mitigate damages and the amount by which landlord reduced or could have reduced its damages").

[21] *Boyce Iron Works v. Sw. Bell Tel.*, 747 S.W.2d 785, 787 (Tex. 1988) (plaintiff may try and submit case to jury on alternative theories of recovery but is only entitled to judgment on theory that permits greatest recovery).

[22] *Waite Hill Servs., Inc. v. World Class Metal Works, Inc.*, 959 S.W.2d 182, 184 (Tex. 1998).

[23] *Waite Hill Servs., Inc. v. World Class Metal Works, Inc.*, 959 S.W.2d 182 (Tex. 1998).

[24] *Waite Hill Servs., Inc. v. World Class Metal Works, Inc.*, 959 S.W.2d 182, 185 (Tex. 1998), quoting *Stewart Title Guar. Co. v. Sterling*, 822 S.W.2d 1, 7 (Tex. 1991).

Not all potentially duplicative damages are so clear. Allowing the jury to assess both lost profits and loss of value of a business for the same contract or business tort injury may result in a double counting of damages[25] since anticipated profits are a primary component of the value of a business.[26] If the two measures of damage cover two distinct time periods[27] or two different markets of the business,[28] they are not necessarily duplicative. Business reputation, another significant component of the value of a business, may impact both loss of business reputation and loss of value of the business, but allowing recovery for both constitutes an impermissible double recovery.[29] Conversely, a party may simultaneously allege breach of contract and business tort claims (breach of fiduciary duty, intentional interference with a contract, civil conspiracy and exemplary damages) and recover for both the contractual and tort damages when they result from separate and distinct injuries.[30]

Recovering both benefit-of-the-bargain damages and out-of-pocket damages for the same loss is inconsistent and an impermissible double recovery[31] because the first measure of damages seeks to affirm the transaction while the second measure seeks to disaffirm it.[32] In the same regard, the damage amounts for two theories of recovery such as damages for misrepresentation and breach of contract which rely on benefit-of-the-bargain or out-of-pocket damage models, cannot both be incorporated into the judgment.[33]

A potential double counting of damages can arise in property damage cases. When personal property has not been completely destroyed, the proper damage model is either (1) the loss of market value measured by the difference in the immediate pre-injury value of the property and the immediate post-injury value before repairs, or (2) damages for cost of repair and loss of use.[34] "Generally, a property owner cannot recover both because it would constitute a double recovery, which is prohibited. However, damages for diminished value and damages for cost of repairs are not duplicative if the diminished value is calculated based on a comparison of the original value of the property and the property's post-repair value."[35]

---

[25] *See Sawyer v. Fitts*, 630 S.W.2d 872, 874–75 (Tex. App.—Fort Worth 1982, no writ).

[26] *C.A. May Marine Supply Co. v. Brunswick Corp.*, 649 F.2d 1049, 1053 (5th Cir. 1981) (both business goodwill and future profits are computed into the "going concern" value of a business, so compensating for both lost profits and loss of value of the business constitutes duplicative damages).

[27] *City of San Antonio v. Guidry*, 801 S.W.2d 142, 150 (Tex. App.—San Antonio 1990, no writ) (allowing recovery of lost profits during period of time in which business was interrupted and recuperating, and loss of value of business after period of recovery).

[28] *Checker Bag Co. v. Wash.*, 27 S.W.3d 625, 641–42 (Tex. App.—Waco 2000, pet. denied).

[29] *Nelson v. Data Terminal Sys., Inc.*, 762 S.W.2d 744, 748 (Tex. App.—San Antonio 1988, writ denied).

[30] *Diep Tuyet Vo v. Vu*, No. 02-15-00188-CV, 2016 WL 2841286, at *6–7 (Tex. App.—Fort Worth May 12, 2016, no pet.).

[31] *Yeng v. Zou*, 407 S.W.3d 485, 491 (Tex. App.—Houston [14th Dist.] 2013, no pet.).

[32] *Sharifi v. Steen Auto., LLC*, 370 S.W.3d 126, 151 (Tex. App.—Dallas 2012, no pet.).

[33] *Hart v. Moore*, 952 S.W.2d 90, 97 (Tex. App.—Amarillo 1997, pet. denied).

[34] *Noteboom v. Farmers Tex. Cty. Mut. Ins. Co.*, 406 S.W.3d 381, 384–85 (Tex. App.—Fort. Worth 2013, no pet.).

[35] *Noteboom v. Farmers Tex. Cty. Mut. Ins. Co.*, 406 S.W.3d 381, 385 (Tex. App.—Fort. Worth 2013, no pet.).

Allowing recovery for both loss of value and loss of use (measured by cost of replacement) results in duplicate damages if they compensate a party for the same injury (i.e. the value of the property as reflected by the use to which it can be put).[36] Conversely, compensating a plaintiff for the cost of repairs and loss of use (often measured by the cost of a replacement whether rented or not[37]) during the time that the damaged property is out of use is not a duplicate damage award because two separate components of the injury are being compensated.[38]

12-2:2 Excessive Damages

Separate from duplicative damages, excessive damages can occur when a plaintiff seeks judgment on the larger of two potential measures of damage.

While a plaintiff may submit a case to the jury on alternative theories of recovery and elect judgment on the theory that permits the greatest recovery,[39] on a single theory of recovery, a plaintiff may not be entitled to select the measure of damages which will result in the greatest recovery if that measure would constitute an unreasonable or excessive recovery.[40] This does not mean that a plaintiff is necessarily limited to the lesser of two measures of damage. "We are aware of no case which holds that the amount of recovery for repairs to [a] chattel plus loss of use of a chattel is limited by the fair market value of the chattel prior to the negligent act which caused the damage."[41] The rule is best understood as entitling a party to seek full recovery provided the recovery is economically feasible. When, for example, damaged personal property can be repaired, the property owner may recover the reasonable costs of such replacements and repairs as needed to restore the property to its condition immediately prior to the accident without regard to diminution in value, but only if repair is economically feasible.[42] Likewise, with a temporary injury to real property, the proper measure of damages "is the amount necessary to place the owner of the property in the same position he occupied prior to the injury,"[43] but subject to a limitation of physical and economic feasibility.[44] "When repairs are economically feasible, the proper measure of damages is the cost of repair; the diminution in market value of the property is the

---

[36] *Cessna Aircraft Co. v. Aircraft Network, L.L.C.*, 213 S.W.3d 455, 464–65 (Tex. App.—Dallas 2006, pet. denied).
[37] *Luna v. N. Star Dodge Sales, Inc.*, 667 S.W.2d 115, 119 (Tex. 1984).
[38] *City of Abilene v. Walker*, 309 S.W.2d 494, 495 (Tex. Civ. App.—Eastland 1958, no writ).
[39] *Boyce Iron Works v. Sw. Bell Tel.*, 747 S.W.2d 785, 787 (Tex. 1988).
[40] *Coastal Transp. Co., Inc. v. Crown Cent. Petroleum Corp.*, 136 S.W.3d 227, 235 (Tex. 2004) (plaintiff could not elect higher damages for diminution in property value when repair was feasible and would result in a lower recovery).
[41] *McCullough-Baroid Petroleum Serv. NL Indus. v. Sexton*, 618 S.W.2d 119, 120 (Tex. App.—Corpus Christi 1981, writ ref'd n.r.e.).
[42] *Hartley v. Schwab*, 564 S.W.2d 829, 831 (Tex. App.—Amarillo 1978, writ ref'd n.r.e.) (when accident caused vehicle to depreciate in value from only $525 to $75, a cost of repair, plus storage and loss of use, recovery of $1,558.25 was not economically feasible and thus, plaintiff did not have an election).
[43] *Kraft v. Langford*, 565 S.W.2d 223, 227 (Tex. 1978).
[44] *Greene v. Bearden Enters., Inc.*, 598 S.W.2d 649, 652 (Tex. App.—Fort. Worth 1980, writ ref'd n.r.e.).

correct measure only when it is less than the cost of repairs."[45] "If the cost to restore land is excessive or not economically feasible, the injury may be deemed to be permanent," limiting the plaintiff to recovery of the diminution in market value.[46]

Economic feasibility is judged by a "prudent owner" standard.[47] In the context of a construction contract on real property, feasibility versus "unreasonable economic waste" is determined by whether repairs "would impair the entire structure or require the expenditure of sums in excess of the value of the structure."[48] If the defendant believes that the remedial cost of repairs is an excessive measure of damages because it exceeds the diminution in market value, the burden is on the defendant to plead and prove the alternate measure of damage.[49]

Alternatively, if the defendant contends that repairs have enhanced the market value of property beyond its pre-injury state, the defendant has the burden to plead and prove that enhancement defensively.[50] Without pleading and proof by the defendant of an alternate measure, the plaintiff is entitled to recover the cost of repairs as long as those repairs to personal property would be considered economically feasible by a prudent owner. In the case of a structure, the costs of repairs must not impair the entire structure or require the expenditure of sums in excess of the total value of the structure.

Even when the proof establishes that damages for repairs and loss of use of personal property exceed the diminution in value of the property, the plaintiff is not necessarily limited to the lesser recovery of diminution in market value. Damages for repairs and loss of use in excess of diminution in market value have been held recoverable when, for example, the loss is due to delay in payment by the insurance company,[51] to the plaintiff's inability to obtain a replacement,[52] and to unfairly leaving the plaintiff without an effective remedy.[53] The Texas Supreme Court has expanded the rationale for enhanced recovery, upholding consequential loss-of-use damages in addition to direct damages for repair costs or lost market value of the property in both partial-destruction and total-destruction cases.[54] For further discussion of personal property valuation and damages, *see* Chapter 11, Section 11-8.2.

12-3 Economic Loss Rule

The economic loss rule has been a source of confusion for attorneys and judges, but understanding its application is vital for attorneys involved in contract and business

---

[45] *Wheelbarger v. Landing Council of Co-Owners*, 471 S.W.3d 875, 893 (Tex. App.—Houston [1st Dist.] 2015, pet. denied).
[46] *Primrose Operating Co. v. Senn*, 161 S.W.3d 258, 261 (Tex. App.—Eastland 2005, no pet.).
[47] *Hartley v. Schwab*, 564 S.W.2d 829, 831 (Tex. App.—Amarillo 1978, writ ref'd n.r.e.).
[48] *Hartley v. Schwab*, 564 S.W.2d 829, 831 (Tex. App.—Amarillo 1978, writ ref'd n.r.e.).
[49] *Hartley v. Schwab*, 564 S.W.2d 829, 831 (Tex. App.—Amarillo 1978, writ ref'd n.r.e.).
[50] *Pasadena State Bank v. Isaac*, 149 Tex. 47, 228 S.W.2d 127, 129 (1950).
[51] *Mondragon v. Austin*, 954 S.W.2d 191 (Tex. App.—Austin 1997, pet. denied).
[52] *Metro Ford Truck Sales, Inc. v. Davis*, 709 S.W.2d 785 (Tex. App.—Fort Worth 1986), *aff'd on rehearing*, 711 S.W.2d 145 (Tex. App.—Fort Worth 1986, writ ref'd n.r.e.).
[53] *B. A. Mortg. Co. v. McCullough*, 590 S.W.2d 955, 957 (Tex. App.—Fort Worth 1979, no writ).
[54] *J & D Towing, LLC v. Am. Alt. Ins. Corp.*, 478 S.W.3d 649 (Tex. 2016).

litigation in Texas.⁵⁵ In actions for unintentional torts, the economic loss rule restricts recovery of purely economic damages unaccompanied by injury to the plaintiff or his property.⁵⁶ "But the rule is not generally applicable in every situation; it allows recovery of economic damages in tort, or not, according to its underlying principles."⁵⁷ Instead of there being a single economic loss rule that applies to all torts, several more limited "economic loss" rules apply in selected areas of the law.⁵⁸

Those seeking to recover economic losses must anticipate the economic loss rule before it is formally raised by the defense *because the economic loss rule is not an affirmative defense that must be pleaded*.⁵⁹ It is a stealth weapon that may be asserted for the first time in a motion for summary judgment after the close of discovery, via directed verdict after the plaintiff rests or as an objection to the charge during the formal charge conference.⁶⁰ Pleading and proving a tort cause of action (such as negligence) when the case should be submitted as a contract cause of action will result in judgment for the defendant as a matter of law.⁶¹

Four Texas Supreme Court cases shape the contours of the economic loss rule: the 2011 *Sharyland* opinion,⁶² the 2012 *El Paso Marketing* opinion,⁶³ and the 2014 opinions in *LAN/STV* opinion⁶⁴ and *Chapman*.⁶⁵

Prior to the *Sharyland* opinion, Texas courts recognized an economic loss rule in three circumstances:

(1) In the setting of a defective product: The economic loss rule bars tort recovery of economic losses from a defective product where the damage or loss is limited to the product itself. Recovery is generally limited to contractual or contract-based statutory remedies.⁶⁶

(2) In the setting of a failure to perform a contract: The economic loss rule bars tort recovery of economic losses resulting from the negligent failure to per-

---

⁵⁵ For a detailed analysis and explanation of the economic loss rule in Texas, *see* Jim Wren, *Applying the Economic Loss Rule in Texas*, 64 Baylor L. Rev. 204 (2012); for developments from a national perspective, *see* Jim Wren, *Proving Damages to the Jury*, Chapter 22 "Economic Loss Rule" (James Publishing, San Francisco, 2016).

⁵⁶ *See LAN/STV v. Martin K. Eby Constr. Co.*, 435 S.W.3d 234, 235–36 (Tex. 2014); *Waste Mgmt. of Tex., Inc. v. Tex. Disposal Sys. Landfill, Inc.*, 434 S.W.3d 142, 153–54 (Tex. 2014), citing *Restatement (Third) of Torts: Liability for Economic Harm* § 2 (Tentative Draft No. 1, 2012) (approved at ALI Annual Meeting, May 2012).

⁵⁷ *LAN/STV v. Martin K. Eby Constr. Co.*, 435 S.W.3d 234, 236 (Tex. 2014).

⁵⁸ *Sharyland Water Supply Corp. v. City of Alton*, 354 S.W.3d 407, 415 (Tex. 2011).

⁵⁹ *Equistar Chem., L.P. v. Dresser-Rand Co.*, 240 S.W.3d 864, 867–68 (Tex. 2007).

⁶⁰ *See Tarrant Cty. Hosp. v. GE Automation Serv.*, 156 S.W.3d 885, 895 (Tex. App.—Fort Worth 2005, no pet.) (allowing defendant to assert economic loss rule on motion for summary judgment without pleading it as an affirmative defense); *Caldwell v. Wright*, No. 10-14-00244-CV, 2016 WL 4249136, at *3–4 (Tex. App.—Waco Aug. 10, 2016, no pet. h.) (defendant must object to a jury question on the grounds of the economic loss rule in the charge conference at the latest or the objection is waived).

⁶¹ *Southwestern Bell Tel. Co. v. DeLanney*, 809 S.W.2d 493, 494–95 (Tex. 1991).

⁶² *Sharyland Water Supply Corp. v. City of Alton*, 354 S.W.3d 407 (Tex. 2011).

⁶³ *El Paso Mktg., L.P. v. Wolf Hollow I, L.P.*, 383 S.W.3d 138 (Tex. 2012).

⁶⁴ *LAN/STV v. Martin K. Eby Constr. Co.*, 435 S.W.3d 234 (Tex. 2014).

⁶⁵ *Chapman Custom Homes, Inc. v. Dallas Plumbing Co.*, 445 S.W.3d 716 (Tex. 2014).

⁶⁶ *Equistar Chem., L.P. v. Dresser-Rand Co.*, 240 S.W.3d 864, 867–68 (Tex. 2007).

form the contract, when the source of the duty to perform arises from the contract. Recovery is generally limited to contractual or contract-based statutory remedies, rather than tort remedies.[67]

(3) In the setting of a tort claim with purely economic loss: A few Texas courts of appeal decisions, but not the Supreme Court, had held that the economic loss rule barred tort recovery generally for pure economic losses, without regard to a contractual relationship.[68]

The third category has generated the most controversy. In *Sharyland*, the Texas Supreme Court agreed that contractual privity is not always required for application of the economic loss rule[69] but noted numerous cases in which purely economic losses have properly been recovered in tort claims.[70] As a result, the Supreme Court rejected this breadth of the third version in favor of a more nuanced approach.[71]

The economic loss rule exists to preclude imposition of tort liability on purely contractual duties or on duties for which contract remedies better address the harm than do tort remedies. As such, the Court should look to the source of the duty at issue to determine whether the duty is solely a creature of contract (in which case the economic loss rule will typically apply),[72] whether the duty is one which contractual remedies best address (in which case the economic loss rule will probably apply),[73] or whether the duty is one that exists independently of a contract and is best left to tort law (in which case the economic loss rule will not bar recovery of economic losses).[74]

In *El Paso Marketing*, the plaintiff negotiated a contractual allocation of risk with the defendant and then assigned the contract. Despite lack of contractual privity at the time of suit, the Supreme Court held that the duty at issue in the case had been directly addressed by the contract; therefore, the economic loss rule barred tort recovery of purely economic losses.[75]

In *LAN/STV*, the plaintiff and defendant both contracted with the project owner for work on the same project during the same time frame but had no contractual relationship with each other. Despite the lack of any contractual relation

---

[67] *Southwestern Bell Tel. Co. v. DeLanney*, 809 S.W.2d 493 (Tex. 1991).
[68] *City of Alton v. Sharyland Water Supply Corp.*, 277 S.W.3d 132, 152–53 (Tex. App.—Corpus Christi 2009), *rev'd* 354 S.W.3d 407 (Tex. 2011).
[69] *Sharyland Water Supply Corp. v. City of Alton*, 354 S.W.3d 407, 419 (Tex. 2011).
[70] *Sharyland Water Supply Corp. v. City of Alton*, 354 S.W.3d 407, 418–19 (Tex. 2011).
[71] *Sharyland Water Supply Corp. v. City of Alton*, 354 S.W.3d 407, 419 (Tex. 2011) ("Merely because the sewer was the subject of a contract does not mean that a contractual stranger is necessarily barred from suing a contracting party for breach of an independent duty. If that were the case, a party could avoid tort liability to the world simply by entering into a contract with one party. The economic loss rule does not swallow all claims between contractual and commercial strangers.").
[72] *Southwestern Bell Tel. Co. v. DeLanney*, 809 S.W.2d 493, 494–95 (Tex. 1991) (duty to correctly publish information existed only because of contract, and therefore economic losses could not be recovered in a negligence action).
[73] *LAN/STV v. Martin K. Eby Constr. Co.*, 435 S.W.3d 234, (Tex. 2014).
[74] *Formosa Plastics Corp. U.S.A. v. Presidio Eng'rs & Contractors, Inc.*, 960 S.W.2d 41, 44–47 (Tex. 1998) (independent duty not to fraudulently induce a party into a contract exists outside of contract, and therefore economic loss rule does not bar tort recovery of economic losses).
[75] *El Paso Mktg., L.P. v. Wolf Hollow I, L.P.*, 383 S.W.3d 138 (Tex. 2012).

between the plaintiff and defendant, the Supreme Court held that the risk of loss should be contemplated and dealt with contractually by the parties since the risk of loss was one best addressed by contract remedies. The economic loss rule, then, barred tort recovery of purely economic losses.[76]

In *Sharyland*, the plaintiff and defendant both contracted with the city but not with each other. The city contracts were during time periods that were years apart. Because a duty of care existed independent of the contract and the contract did not allocate the risk of loss, the Supreme Court held that the duty independent of the contract was best addressed by tort remedies rather than to the economic loss rule.[77]

In *Chapman*, a landowner and general contractor brought suit against the plumbing subcontractor for negligently flooding and damaging the landowner's house. The Supreme Court declined to apply the economic loss rule, holding that the subject of the plumbing contract was the installation of the plumbing (rather than construction of the entire house), and the economic loss rule "does not bar all tort claims arising out of a contractual setting." The plumbing subcontractor had a contractual duty to properly install the plumbing but also an independent duty in tort not to negligently damage other property.[78]

Applying this principle attempting to separate tort liability from contractual duties can be challenging, but there are many examples that help explain the division between those situations which are and are not subject to the economic loss rule:

- When the only injury is to the product that is the subject of the contract or sale, the economic loss rule applies because the only loss is the contractual expectancy of a working product, so contractual or UCC remedies should suffice.[79] On the other hand, when physical injury occurs to the plaintiff's person or other property, the economic loss rule does not apply because a general tort duty exists independently of contract not to negligently harm a person or property.[80]

- When a party creates economic loss on another through fraudulent inducement of a contract, the economic loss rule does not apply because a general tort duty exists not to fraudulently induce a person to sign a contract.[81] On the other hand, when a party misrepresents that they have performed a duty which exists only

---

[76] *LAN/STV v. Martin K. Eby Constr. Co.*, 435 S.W.3d 234 (Tex. 2014).

[77] *Sharyland Water Supply Corp. v. City of Alton*, 354 S.W.3d 407 (Tex. 2011).

[78] *Chapman Custom Homes, Inc. v. Dallas Plumbing Co.*, 445 S.W.3d 716, 718 (Tex. 2014).

[79] *Equistar Chem., L.P. v. Dresser-Rand Co.*, 240 S.W.3d 864 (Tex. 2007) (recognizing economic loss rule precludes tort recovery when losses arise from failure of a product and the damage or loss is limited to the product itself).

[80] *Sharyland Water Supply Corp. v. City of Alton*, 354 S.W.3d 407 (Tex. 2011) (holding economic loss rule does not apply when contractor has caused injury to other property by negligent placement of sewer lines, and stating that repair costs necessarily imply that physical injury to property has occurred); *Chapman Custom Homes, Inc. v. Dallas Plumbing Co.*, 445 S.W.3d 716 (Tex. 2014) (plumber's duty in tort not to physically damage the house was independent of any contractual obligation, and the damages caused by the breach of that tort duty extended beyond the economic loss of any anticipated benefit under the plumbing contract).

[81] *Formosa Plastics Corp. USA v. Presidio Eng'rs & Contractors, Inc.*, 960 S.W.2d 41, 44–47 (Tex. 1998) (independent duty not to fraudulently induce a party into a contract exists out-

because of a contract and the only losses are to the subject of the contract, the economic loss rule may bar recovery in tort, forcing the plaintiff to rely on contractual remedies.[82]

- When a party converts property by failing to account and pay for it as contractually agreed, the economic loss rule applies because the duty to account has been created by contract and the nature of the loss is the subject of the contract, for which contractual remedies should suffice.[83] On the other hand, when a party converts property by using it for personal gain in a manner not contemplated by any contractual relationship, the economic loss rule does not apply because a general tort duty exists independently not to take the property of another.[84]

- When a party, such as a fiduciary or a first-party insurer, abuses a special relationship of trust and loyalty, the economic loss rule does not apply because a general tort duty exists independently of contract not to take advantage of another to whom a special duty of trust and loyalty is owed.[85] On the other hand, when a party in an arms-length transaction abuses the trust of the opposite party and the loss is to the subject of the contract, the economic loss rule applies because all duties have been created by contract and contractual remedies should suffice.[86]

- When the only duty governing the conduct of the parties stems from their contractual relationship, the economic loss rule will apply.[87] On the other hand, when a separate duty is defined by statute and is violated, the economic loss rule will not bar the claim for economic loss.[88]

---

side of contract, and therefore economic loss rule does not bar tort recovery of economic losses).

[82] *Classical Vacations, Inc. v. Air France*, No. 01-01-01137-CV, 2003 WL 1848247 (Tex. App.—Houston [1st Dist.] Apr. 10, 2003, no pet.) (mem. op.) (failure to pay money due under terms of a contract not recoverable on a post-contract fraud theory because there was no fraudulent inducement of contract and the damages are simply the subject of the contract).

[83] *Castle Tex. Prod. Ltd. P'ship v. Long Trs.*, 134 S.W.3d 267 (Tex. App.—Tyler 2003, pet. denied) (failing to account for gas production as required by contract does not provide basis for tort recovery based on conversion, and plaintiff must rely on contractual remedies).

[84] *Cass v. Stephens*, 156 S.W.3d 38, 68–69 (Tex. App.—El Paso 2004, pet. denied) (the duty not to convert jointly-owned equipment for personal gain is a duty that exists independently of a contract and therefore will support a conversion claim that is not barred by the economic loss rule).

[85] *James J. Flanagan Shipping vs. Del Monte Fresh Produce*, 403 S.W.3d 360 (Tex. App.—Houston [1st Dist.] 2013, no pet.) (participation by defendant in breach of fiduciary duty by employee of plaintiff involves violation of duty existing independently of contract and therefore prevents application of economic loss rule).

[86] *Atrium Cos., Inc. v. ESR Assocs., Inc.*, No. CIV.A. H-11-1288, 2012 WL 5355754, at *10–11 (S.D. Tex. Oct. 29, 2012, no pet.) (professional negligence may prevent application of economic loss rule, but only if the professional relationship exists prior to and apart from the contractual relationship).

[87] *Southwestern Bell Tel. Co. v. DeLanney*, 809 S.W.2d 493, 494 (Tex. 1991).

[88] *McCaig v. Wells Fargo Bank, N.A.*, 788 F.3d 463, 474–75 (5th Cir. 2015) (declining to apply the economic loss rule to bar a Texas Debt Collection Act claim).

SECTION III
Pleading Defenses

CHAPTER 13

Pleading Burdens*

13-1 Distinguishing Pleading Burdens from Substantive Defenses

This chapter discusses how to raise defenses and differentiate between those automatically implicated by a general denial and those which require specific pleading to avoid waiver of the issue. The nature of the defense (i.e., its substance) and the pleading requirements associated with the defense are related and tend to determine whether the defense must be specifically pleaded.

In Section 13.2 we discuss the Due Order of Pleading requirement which notes that certain defenses are waived if not presented in "due order." These defenses are dilatory in nature, attacking the propriety of the forum rather than the merits of the plaintiff's case.

Section 13.3 discusses the general denial, a Texas defensive pleading that denies all of the plaintiff's allegations and puts the plaintiff to his proof.[1] This broad language effectively places into issue all of the plaintiff's allegations, except for those that must be specially denied (i.e., specifically denied) or raised with a verified pleading. Special and verified pleadings are discussed in Section 13.4. Unlike in federal court, the general denial is not subject to the substantiality of pleading requirements. While Tex. R. Civ. P. 13 requires a pleading to be filed "in good faith," the general denial is exempted from this requirement. Section 13.3 discusses this exemption in more detail.

Section 13.5 of this chapter discusses the pleading of affirmative defenses. A denial (whether special, verified, or general) will not raise an affirmative defense. The nature of an affirmative defense is that it is a defense in "confession and avoidance." In other words, the defense precludes or reduces liability, not because the plaintiff's allegations are false, but because the elements of the affirmative defense are true.

13-2 Due Order of Pleading Requirement

The Due Order of Pleading rule provides that certain defenses are waived if not presented in "due order." As a general rule, the defendant's answer may include any

---

* The authors thank Robyn Leatherwood for her assistance in the updating of this chapter.
[1] The general denial language tracks the following: The defendant generally denies each and every, all and singular, the allegations of Plaintiff's petition and demands strict proof thereof.

defenses he has, whether of law or fact, dilatory or merits-based,[2] and the trial court may take up these issues in any order it directs.[3] The due order of pleading requirement, however, stands as an exception and requires special appearances and motions to transfer venue to be filed and heard in this order. If these defenses are not presented in the proper order, they are waived.

13-2:1 Due Order of Pleading—Special Appearance

A special appearance must be filed before a motion to transfer venue and any other plea, pleading, or motion.[4] Other pleas, pleadings, and motions, however, may be filed in the same instrument as the special appearance without waiving the special appearance.[5] If any other plea, pleading, or motion is filed before the special appearance, the special appearance is waived. This insures that any challenges to the court's jurisdiction over the party is heard as a threshold matter.

Any appearance not in conformity with this rule is a general appearance (waiving the challenge to personal jurisdiction),[6] and case law makes clear that Rule 120a requires "strict compliance."[7] A special appearance filed just one minute behind a motion to transfer venue and original answer constituted a general appearance and waived the challenge to personal jurisdiction.[8]

Despite the requirement that a special appearance must be filed before any other plea, pleading, or motion, a notice of removal filed before a special appearance does not constitute a general appearance.[9] A notice of removal is not a general appearance whereby the defendant subjects himself to the jurisdiction of the trial court but is instead an instrument that removes the case from state to federal court.[10]

Agreements pursuant to Tex. R. Civ. P. 11 which extend the defendant's time to appear do not waive the defendant's special appearance, even when the agreement is not expressly made subject to the special appearance.[11] TA Rule 11 agreement is not a "plea, pleading or motion" that, under Rule 120a, would constitute a general appear-

---

[2] Tex. R. Civ. P. 85.
[3] Tex. R. Civ. P. 84.
[4] Tex. R. Civ. P. 120a(1).
[5] Tex. R. Civ. P. 120a(1).
[6] Tex. R. Civ. P. 120a(1).
[7] *Grynberg v. M-I, LLC*, 398 S.W.3d 864, 876 (Tex. App.—Corpus 2012).
[8] *Allianz Risk Transfer (Bermuda), Ltd. v. S.J. Camp & Co.*, 117 S.W.3d 92, 96–97 (Tex. App.—Tyler 2003, no pet.) ("When Allianz Bermuda filed its motion to transfer venue and original answer at 5:03 p.m. on August 16, it made its special appearance, filed in a separate instrument one minute later, a nullity. Accordingly, we hold that Allianz Bermuda has made a general appearance in this suit, thereby waiving its special appearance.").
[9] *Antonio v. Marino*, 910 S.W.2d 624, 629 (Tex. App.—Houston [14th Dist.] 1995, no pet.); *Bramblett v. El Paso County*, EP-11-CV-167-PRM, 2011 WL 11741275, at *2 (W.D. Tex. June 13, 2011).
[10] *Bramblett v. El Paso County*, EP-11-CV-167-PRM, 2011 WL 11741275, at *2 (W.D. Tex. June 13, 2011).
[11] *Exito Elec. Co., Ltd. v. Trejo*, 142 S.W.3d 302, 306 (Tex. 2004) ("We therefore hold that a Rule 11 Agreement that extends a defendant's time to file an initial responsive pleading and is filed in the trial court before the defendant files a special appearance, even if the agreement is not expressly made subject to the special appearance, does not violate Rule 120a's 'due-order-of-pleading' requirement and thus does not constitute a general appearance.").

ance if filed before a special appearance, A Rule 11 agreement extending the time to file a response to the petition does not acknowledge that the trial court is a proper court for the adjudication of the dispute.[12] A letter to the court inquiring about the need to hire local counsel and indicating an intention to file a motion to dismiss did not constitute a general appearance.[13]

Merely filing a Rule 11 agreement is not a request that the trial court enforce the agreement (which would require the court to have jurisdiction to do so).[14] This rationale implies that a defendant may waive a special appearance by asking the trial court to enforce the agreement, such as when the plaintiff seeks a default judgment before the deadline set forth in the motion.

13-2:2 Defects in the Special Appearance: Unsworn Motion

A special appearance must be made by sworn motion, but Rule 120a also provides that a special appearance may be amended to cure defects.[15] In light of the amendment and cure language in Rule 120a, the failure to verify the special appearance does not, standing alone, constitute a general appearance and waiver, so long as the defect is cured before a general appearance is made.[16] The defect can even be cured after the trial court has ruled on the special appearance.[17]

13-2:3 Defects in the Special Appearance: No "Subject to" Language

When filing other pleas, pleadings or motions, either with the special appearance or after it, Texas lawyers commonly (perhaps even obsessively) make the pleadings and motions "subject to the special appearance." While this is undoubtedly a good practice and will prevent a trial court judge accustomed to the practice from wondering whether the absence of the language constitutes a general appearance, the Supreme Court of Texas has held that the failure to *expressly* make other pleas, pleadings and motions subject to the special appearance does not constitute a general appearance and waiver.[18]

---

[12] *Exito Elec. Co., Ltd. v. Trejo*, 142 S.W.3d 302, 305 (Tex. 2004).

[13] *Hegwer v. Edwards*, 527 S.W.3d 337, 341 (Tex. App.—Dallas 2017, no pet.).

[14] *Moore v. Elektro–Mobil Tecknik GmbH*, 874 S.W.2d 306 (Tex. App.—El Paso 1994, writ denied).

[15] Tex. R. Civ. P. 120a(1).

[16] *Dawson-Austin v. Austin*, 968 S.W.2d 319, 322 (Tex. 1998) (citing *Villalpando v. De La Garza*, 793 S.W.2d 274, 275–76 (Tex. App.—Corpus Christi 1990, no writ); *Carbonit Houston, Inc. v. Exch. Bank*, 628 S.W.2d 826, 828 (Tex. App.—Houston [14th Dist.] 1982, writ ref'd n.r.e.); *Stegall & Stegall v. Cohn*, 592 S.W.2d 427, 429 (Tex. App.—Fort Worth 1979, no writ); *Dennett v. First Cont'l Inv. Corp.*, 559 S.W.2d 384, 385–86 (Tex. App.—Dallas 1977, no writ).

[17] *Dennett v. First Cont'l Inv. Corp.*, 559 S.W.2d 384, 385–86 (Tex. App.—Dallas 1977, no writ); *Horowitz v. Berger*, 377 S.W.3d 115, 123 (Tex. App.—Houston [14th Dist.] 2012, no pet.).

[18] *Horowitz v. Berger*, 377 S.W.3d 115, 123 (Tex. App.—Houston [14th Dist.] 2012, no pet.) ("The rule makes matters in the same instrument and subsequent matters subject to the special appearance without an express statement to that effect for each matter."), *overruling Portland Sav. & Loan Ass'n v. Bernstein*, 716 S.W.2d 532, 534–35 (Tex. App.—Corpus Christi 1985, writ ref'd n.r.e.).

13-2:4 Special Appearance: Due Order of Hearing Requirement

A party may waive a special appearance even after complying with the due order of pleading requirements, if the party fails to comply with the due order of hearing requirement.

Rule 120a provides that "every appearance, prior to judgment, not in compliance with this rule is a general appearance." Rule 120a(2) provides that a special appearance shall be heard and determined before a motion to transfer venue or any other plea, pleading or motion.

The Supreme Court has quoted the following language from the El Paso Court of Appeals with approval:

> A party enters a general appearance whenever it invokes the judgment of the court on any question other than the court's jurisdiction; if a defendant's act recognizes that an action is properly pending or seeks affirmative action from the court, that is a general appearance.[19]

As such, a party generally appears when he (1) invokes the judgment of the court on any question other than the court's jurisdiction, (2) recognizes by his acts that an action is properly pending, or (3) seeks affirmative action from the court.[20] Citing this language from the Texas Supreme Court, the Fort Worth Court of Appeals held that a defendant generally appeared even after the trial court sustained its special appearance when the defendant moved for attorney fees under the Uniform Declaratory Judgment Act, obtained a hearing on the motion, and attended the hearing to argue its merits.[21]

The following activities have been held to constitute general appearances:

- Filing a motion to strike pleadings and having it heard prior to the determination of the special appearance.[22]

- Filing and arguing a motion for new trial prior to the determination of the special appearance.[23]

---

[19] *Dawson-Austin v. Austin*, 968 S.W.2d 319, 322 (Tex. 1998) (quoting *Moore v. Elektro-Mobil Technik GmbH*, 874 S.W.2d 327 (Tex. App.—El Paso 1994)).

[20] *Exito Elecs. Co., Ltd. v. Trejo*, 142 S.W.3d 302, 304 (Tex. 2004); *Dawson-Austin v. Austin*, 968 S.W.2d 322 (Tex. 1998).

[21] *Composite Cooling Sols., L.P. v. Larrabee Air Conditioning, Inc.*, No. 02-17-00006-CV, 2017 WL 2979918, at *5 (Tex. App.—Fort Worth July 13, 2017, no pet.).

[22] *SBG Dev. Servs., L.P. v. Nurock Grp., Inc.*, No. 02-11-00008-CV, 2011 WL 5247873, at *3 (Tex. App.—Fort Worth Nov. 3, 2011, no pet.).

[23] *Glob. Paragon Dallas, LLC v. SBM Realty, LLC*, 448 S.W.3d 607, 613 (Tex. App.—Houston [14th Dist.] 2014, no pet.); *Vertex Indus., Inc. v. Allstate Fire & Cas. Ins. Co.*, No. 12-16-00303-CV, 2017 WL 2464698, at *3 (Tex. App.—Tyler June 7, 2017, no pet.) (Holding that even an agreed motion for a new trial can constitute a general appearance.).

- Moving for an award of attorney fees under the Uniform Declaratory Judgment Act, obtaining a hearing on the matter, and appearing in court to argue the motion's merits after the trial court sustained the movant's special appearance.[24]

In contrast, the following post appearance actions have been held not to constitute general appearances:

- Taking depositions and serving discovery requests going to the merits of the action.[25]
- Conducting discovery related to the jurisdictional issue.[26]
- Filing a motion for continuance as to hearings on other defensive matters.[27]
- A motion for a protective order to limit discovery matters to the jurisdictional issue following the filing of a special appearance.[28]
- Filing a motion to dismiss on forum *non conveniens* grounds, which was made expressly subject to the special appearance.[29]
- Seeking a ruling on a discovery related issue that could affect the evidence presented at the special appearance hearing.[30]

Rule 120a provides that that the issuance of process for witnesses, the taking of depositions, the serving of requests for admissions and the use of discovery processes do not constitute a general appearance and waiver. This language is not limited to discovery regarding the jurisdictional issue.[31]

When the specially appearing party conducts merits-based discovery, however, and seeks relief related to that discovery (whether an assertion of privilege, a motion to compel, ruling on objections), that may constitute waiver. Requesting such relief conflicts with Rule 120a's requirement that the special appearance be heard and determined before any other plea, pleading or motion. Despite a considerable body of case law holding that conducting even merits related discovery does not waive a special appearance, practitioners should be cautious when seeking a ruling on a discovery related motion. Waiver can occur when a party obtains a ruling on a motion to compel discovery on the merits of the case because it violated the due order of hearing

---

[24] *Composite Cooling Sols., L.P. v. Larrabee Air Conditioning, Inc.*, No. 02-17-00006-CV, 2017 WL 2979918, at *5 (Tex. App.—Fort Worth July 13, 2017, no pet.).

[25] *Lisitsa v. Flit*, 419 S.W.3d 672, 678 (Tex. App.—Houston [14th Dist.] 2013, pet. filed); *Horowitz v. Berger*, 377 S.W.3d 123, 124 (Tex. App.—Houston [14th Dist.] 2012, no pet.); *Silbaugh v. Ramirez*, 126 S.W.3d 88, 93 (Tex. App.—Houston [1st Dist.] 2002, no pet.).

[26] *Exito Elecs. Co., Ltd. v. Trejo*, 142 S.W.3d 302, 307 (Tex. 2004).

[27] *Dawson-Austin v. Austin*, 968 S.W.2d 321, 322 (Tex. 1998).

[28] *International Turbine Serv., Inc. v. Lovitt*, 881 S.W.2d 805, 809 (Tex. App.—Fort Worth 1994, writ denied).

[29] *Antonio v. Marino*, 910 S.W.2d 624, 628 (Tex. App.—Houston [14th Dist.] 1995, no writ).

[30] *Huynh v. Nguyen*, 180 S.W.3d 608 (Tex. App.—Houston [14 Dist.] 2005, no pet.) (the discovery ruling was sought prior to filing the special appearance but is analogous to the post-appearance discovery related dispute).

[31] *Lisitsa v. Flit*, 419 S.W.3d 672, 678 (Tex. App.—Houston [14th Dist.] 2013, pet. filed); *Horowitz v. Berger*, 377 S.W.3d 123, 124 (Tex. App.—Houston [14th Dist.] 2012, no pet.); *Silbaugh v. Ramirez*, 126 S.W.3d 88, 93 (Tex. App.—Houston [1st Dist.] 2002, no pet.).

requirement and waived the special appearance.[32] The party specially appearing "did not waive its special appearance merely by participating in discovery processes. . . . It waived its special appearance by obtaining affirmative relief from the trial court that was entirely unrelated to the jurisdictional challenge."[33]

Tex. R. Civ. P. 91a provides that a party may move to dismiss a baseless cause of action. Rule 91a.8 specifically states that filing and seeking a ruling on a motion to dismiss made pursuant to the rule does not waive a special appearance or a motion to transfer venue (by filing or seeking a ruling on the motion). Rule 91a.8, however, states that it is not "an exception to the pleading requirements" for motions to transfer venue and special appearances. With little case law yet interpreting this apparent conflict in the rule, the careful practitioner will not file a Rule 91a motion before a special appearance, or else waiver of the special appearance may occur. The plain language of the rule suggest that filing a Rule 91a motion at the same time or after a special appearance will not waive the special appearance, nor will seeking a ruling on the Rule 91a motion even though the Court might have to assert jurisdiction to do so.

13-2:5 Due Order of Pleading—Motion to Transfer Venue

An objection to improper venue is waived if not made by written motion filed before or concurrently with any other plea, pleading or motion, except a special appearance.[34] In a multiple defendant case, one defendant's waiver of an objection to venue does not waive the objection as to other defendants.[35] Thus, as long as one defendant timely asserts its motion to transfer venue to a proper county, the entire case can still be transferred. An exception to the due order of pleading requirement is found in Tex. R. Civ. P. 86.1 which provides that the parties can file a written consent to transfer the case to another county at any time. Likewise, a motion to transfer venue on the ground that an impartial jury cannot be had in the county in which the case was filed is governed by Texas Rule of Civil Procedure 257 rather Rule 86 and is not subject to the due order of pleading requirement.

Not all actions taken in the trial court waive the motion to transfer venue,[36] but the motion to transfer venue is waived by failing to file the motion at all, by failing to

---

[32] *Nationwide Dist. Serv., Inc. v. Jones*, 496 S.W.3d 221, 228 (Tex. App.—Houston [1st Dist.] 2016, no pet.).

[33] *Nationwide Dist. Serv., Inc. v. Jones*, 496 S.W.3d 221, 228 (Tex. App.—Houston [1st Dist.] 2016, no pet.).

[34] Tex. R. Civ. P. 86(1).

[35] Tex. Civ. Prac. & Rem. Code Ann. § 16.0641 ("In a suit in which two or more defendants are joined, any action or omission by one defendant in relation to venue, including a waiver of venue by one defendant, does not operate to impair or diminish the right of any other defendant to properly challenge venue.").

[36] *See, e.g., Gentry v. Tucker*, 891 S.W.2d 766, 768 (Tex. App.—Texarkana 1995, no writ) (defendant's filing of a motion for continuance on a temporary injunction hearing before the trial court ruled on defendant's motion to transfer venue did not waive defendant's objections to venue).

file it in a timely manner[37] and by taking action in the trial court inconsistent with the motion.[38]

13-2:6 Motion to Transfer Venue—Due Order of Hearing Requirement

The trial court is required to determine the motion to transfer venue "promptly" and in a "reasonable time" before trial.[39] The movant has a duty to request a setting on the motion to transfer.[40] The rule does not set a specific deadline, but the failure to set the hearing promptly can result in waiver of the venue complaint. The movant "may not sit on his rights indefinitely."[41] The trial court may overrule the motion to transfer venue solely on the basis that the defendant did not promptly seek a hearing on the motion. The passage of one year between the making of the motion and seeking a hearing has been held to constitute a complete lack of diligence permitting the trial court to deny the motion,[42] although a delay of four years from the filing of the motion until a hearing was sought was held not to be unreasonable and did not constitute a

---

[37] *See, e.g., In re M.V.*, 343 S.W.3d 543, 550 (Tex. App.—Dallas 2011, no pet.) (failure to file motion to transfer venue in a parental rights termination lawsuit waives any objection to venue); *Jarvis v. Feild*, 327 S.W.3d 918, 925 (Tex. App.—Corpus Christi 2010, no pet.) (beneficiary under a will who waited until after final judgment was rendered to object to venue waived her objection to venue); *Union Carbide Corp. v. Loftin*, 256 S.W.3d 869, 875 (Tex. App.—Beaumont 2008, pet. dism'd) (when two of 100 defendants failed to file a motion to transfer venue either before or contemporaneously with their answer, those two defendants waived their objections to venue); *Kshatrya v. Tex. Workforce Commc'n*, 97 S.W.3d 825, 832 (Tex. App.—Dallas 2003, no pet.) (when defendants' first objections to venue were made in a plea to the jurisdiction submitted after their original answer, defendants waived their objections to improper venue).

[38] *See, e.g., Gentry v. Tucker*, 891 S.W.2d 766, 769 (Tex. App.—Texarkana 1995, no writ) (defendant waived its objection to venue when defendant properly filed a motion to transfer venue, but participated in the trial on the merits without insisting the trial court rule on its motion to transfer venue); *Grozier v. L-B Sprinkler & Plumbing Repair*, 744 S.W.2d 306, 310 (Tex. App.—Fort Worth 1988, writ denied) (even though defendant properly filed and set a hearing on its motion to transfer venue, defendant's attorney's filing of a motion to withdraw as counsel at the venue hearing, without pursuing the motion to transfer venue, is conduct inconsistent with the defendant's objections to venue); *O'Neal v. Tex. Bank & Trust Co. of Sweetwater*, 118 Tex. 133, 137, 11 S.W.2d 791, 792 (Tex. Comm'n App. 1929) (defendant's pursuit of a plea in abatement before a determination on a plea of privilege is conduct inconsistent with the defendant's objections to venue). *See also Smith v. Smith*, 541 S.W.3d 251, 257 (Tex. App.—Houston [14th Dist.] 2017, no pet.) ("In failing to make the summary judgment response and continuance motion subject to his venue motion or to reurge his venue objection in these filings, David acted inconsistently with an intent to urge his venue motion and invoked the jurisdiction of the trial court.").

[39] Tex. R. Civ. P. 87(1).

[40] Tex. R. Civ. P. 87(1).

[41] *Whitworth v. Kuhn*, 734 S.W.2d 108 (Tex. App.—Austin 1987, no pet.).

[42] *Whitworth v. Kuhn*, 734 S.W.2d 108 (Tex. App.—Austin 1987, no pet.). *See also Smith v. Smith*, 541 S.W.3d 251, 257 (Tex. App.—Houston [14th Dist.] 2017, no pet.) (passage of 11 months indicated a lack of diligence).

waiver.[43] Whether the trial court considers the motion after such a delay is within its discretion.[44]

Rule 91a provides that a party may move to dismiss a baseless cause of action. The rule specifically states that filing and seeking a ruling on a motion to dismiss made pursuant to the rule does not waive a special appearance or a motion to transfer venue by filing or seeking a ruling on the motion.

13-3 The General Denial

13-3:1 General Denial Defined

A general denial is a defensive pleading that denies all of the plaintiff's allegations and places into issue all of the plaintiff's allegations, except for those that must be specifically denied or raised with a verified pleading. A denial (whether special, verified or general) will not raise an affirmative defense. The nature of an affirmative defense is that it is a defense in "confession and avoidance." In other words, the defense precludes or reduces liability, not because the plaintiff's allegations are false, but because the elements of the affirmative defense are true. Any allegation by the plaintiff that is not denied, is deemed admitted.

13-3:2 General Denial Extending to Amendments

A defendant's initial general denial extends to any amended pleading of the plaintiff.[45] The general denial does not raise defenses that require a verified or special denial, nor does the extended general denial raise affirmative defenses to new claims in the amended pleadings.[46] Allegations raised in an amended pleading which would require a verified, special or specific denial must be denied in response to that amended pleading.

13-3:3 Deemed General Denial to Counterclaim or Crossclaim

When a counterclaim or crossclaim is served on a party that has already appeared, the party is deemed to have pleaded a general denial of the counterclaim or crossclaim in

---

[43] *In re Eastman Chem. Co.*, 13-18-00268-CV, 2019 WL 2529042 (Tex. App.—Corpus Christi June 20, 2019, no pet.).

[44] *Whitworth v. Kuhn*, 734 S.W.2d 108 (Tex. App.—Austin 1987, no pet.).

[45] Tex. R. Civ. P. 92.

[46] *MacDonald v. Bank of Kerrville*, 849 S.W.2d 371, 372 (Tex. App.—San Antonio 1993, writ dism'd) (general denial extended to amended pleading but did not satisfy Rule 54's requirement to specifically deny that any condition precedent to performance has occurred or been performed); *Fortinberry v. Freeway Lumber Co.*, 453 S.W.2d 849, 851–52 (Tex. Civ. App.—Houston [1st Dist.] 1970, no writ) (general denial extended to amended petition but did not satisfy Rule 185's requirements for a denying a suit on an open account under oath, though the defendant's sworn denial to the original petition served to satisfy Rule 185 with respect to the amended petition).

PLEADING BURDENS

the absence of a responsive pleading.[47] Where a party has not appeared in the action, the party is not deemed to have pleaded a general denial.[48]

The deemed general denial precludes entry of a no-answer default judgment against a party who has already appeared but either failed to respond to the counterclaim or crossclaim or filed a defective response.[49] Similarly, the deemed general denial precludes judgment against a party as a sanction in the absence of a merits determination or the striking of the defendant's pleadings.[50] The deemed general denial does not, however, preclude a post-answer default judgment.[51]

The deemed general denial does not raise any affirmative defense nor does it raise any matter that must be specially denied or denied under oath.[52]

13-3:4 Deemed General Denial—Effect on Amendments Within Seven Days of Trial

Rule 63 requires leave of court in order to file an amended pleading within seven days of trial. Answers to counterclaims or crossclaims require leave of court within seven days of trial even if the answer is the first written answer to the counterclaim or crossclaim.[53] The Supreme Court of Texas reasoned that because a party that has appeared is deemed to have denied the counterclaim or crossclaim and are, therefore, in no danger of default, allowing them to file their first written answer within seven days of trial, as if it were an original answer as opposed to an amended answer, would encourage parties to delay filing such an answer.[54] For purposes of seeking leave of court, answers to counterclaims and crossclaims are treated as amended pleadings for purposes of Rule 63.

---

[47] Tex. R. Civ. P. 92.
[48] *MEI, Inc. v. Griffin*, No. 05-10-00071-CV, 2012 WL 1537460, at *1 n.1 (Tex. App.—Dallas May 1, 2012, no pet.) (Defendant never appeared in the case and, therefore, was not deemed to have filed a general denial with respect to co-defendant's crossclaim.).
[49] *Jackson v. Textron Fin. Corp.*, No. 14-07-01011-CV, 2009 WL 997484, at *5 (Tex. App.—Houston [14th Dist.] 2009, no pet.) (trial court erred in signing a default judgment against a defendant on counterclaim where defendant had already appeared because defendant was deemed to have generally denied the allegations in the counter-petition).
[50] *See, e.g., Nelson v. Britt*, 241 S.W.3d 672 (Tex. App.—Dallas 2007, no pet.) (deemed denial not struck by the trial court as a sanction precluding judgment against the defendant where plaintiff had failed to prove liability).
[51] *See, e.g., Tex. Sting, Ltd. v. R.B. Foods, Inc.*, 82 S.W.3d 644, 650 n.7 (Tex. App.—San Antonio 2002, pet denied) (court of appeals evaluated *propriety* of setting aside default judgment and considered the default judgment a post-answer default because of the deemed denial to the counterclaim at issue).
[52] Tex. R. Civ. P. 92 ("a party who has made an appearance in the action . . . shall be deemed to have pleaded a general denial of the counterclaim or crossclaim . . . *In all other respects the rules prescribed for pleadings of defensive matter are applicable to answers to counterclaims and crossclaims.*") (emphasis added).
[53] *Lee v. Key West Towers, Inc.*, 783 S.W.2d 586, 588 (Tex. 1989).
[54] *Lee v. Key West Towers, Inc.*, 783 S.W.2d 586, 588 (Tex. 1989).

13-3:5 Deemed General Denial—No Waiver of Special Appearance or Motion to Transfer Venue

A written general denial filed before a special appearance or motion to transfer venue waives a special appearance and a motion to transfer venue, but a deemed general denial does not.[55]

13-3:6 General Denial—Not Subject to Prohibition Against Groundless, Bad Faith Pleadings

Rule 13 authorizes courts to impose sanctions on attorneys who sign pleadings that are groundless and/or brought in bad faith as well as on the parties those attorneys represent.[56] By signing a pleading, motion or other paper, an attorney is certifying to the court that the pleading, motion or paper complies with Rule 13. Rule 13 excepts the general denial out of this rule, stating that a general denial "does not constitute a violation of this rule."[57] A defending party may, therefore, plead a general denial even though the effect is to deny allegations the party knows are true.

13-4 Verified and Special Denials

Some allegations must be denied under oath or specifically rather than generally denied in order to require the plaintiff to prove the matter. Failure to follow the verification and special denial requirements in response to an allegation that requires it relieves the claimant from the obligation of proving the allegation. The substance of these defenses is discussed in Chapter 16. This section addresses requirements to raise the defenses subject to the verification and/or special denial requirement.

13-4:1 Certain Pleas to be Verified

Tex. R. Civ. P. 93 requires certain matters to be verified by affidavit unless "the truth of such matters appear of record." Fifteen matters must be verified by affidavit, along with a sixteenth "catch-all" provision that captures statutes that require pleadings to be made under oath.

(1) That the plaintiff has not legal capacity to sue or that the defendant has not legal capacity to be sued.

(2) That the plaintiff is not entitled to recover in the capacity in which he sues, or that the defendant is not liable in the capacity in which he is sued.

(3) That there is another suit pending in this State between the same parties involving the same claim.

(4) That there is a defect of parties, plaintiff or defendant.

(5) A denial of partnership as alleged in any pleading as to any party to the suit.

---

[55] Tex. R. Civ. P. 92 (Providing that "the party shall not be deemed to have waived any special appearance or motion to transfer venue.").

[56] Tex. R. Civ. P. 13.

[57] Tex. R. Civ. P. 13.

(6) That any party alleged in any pleading to be a corporation is not incorporated as alleged (Note: Rule 52 also requires denying the existence of a corporation under oath.[58]).

(7) Denial of the execution by himself or by his authority of any instrument in writing, upon which any pleading is founded, in whole or in part and charged to have been executed by him or by his authority, and not alleged to be lost or destroyed.

(8) A denial of the genuineness of the indorsement or assignment of a written instrument upon which suit is brought by an indorsee or assignee.

(9) That a written instrument upon which a pleading is founded is without consideration, or that the consideration of the same has failed in whole or in part.

(10) A denial of an account which is the foundation of the plaintiff's action, and supported by affidavit.

(11) That a contract sued upon is usurious.

(12) That notice and proof of loss or claim for damage has not been given as alleged.

(13) In the trial of any case appealed to the court from the Industrial Accident Board the following, if pleaded, shall be presumed to be true as pleaded and have been done and filed in legal time and manner, unless denied by verified pleadings:

- Notice of injury.
- Claim for compensation.
- Award of the Board.
- Notice of intention not to abide by the award of the Board.
- Filing of suit to set aside the award.
- That the insurance company alleged to have been the carrier of the workers' compensation insurance at the time of the alleged injury was in fact the carrier thereof.
- That there was good cause for not filing claim with the Industrial Accident Board within the one year period provided by statute.
- Wage rate.

---

[58] Tex. R. Civ. P. 52 ("An allegation that a corporation is incorporated shall be taken as true, unless denied by the affidavit of the adverse party, his agent or attorney, whether such corporation is a public or private corporation and however created."). *See, e.g., Coffin v. Finnegan's, Inc.*, No. 06-01-00171-CV, 2003 WL 21756653, at *2 (Tex. App.—Texarkana July 31, 2003, no pet.) (stating that the requirement to deny the existence of a corporation stems from both Rules 52 and 93(6) and that the failure to deny the same dispense with the requirement to prove corporate status). *See also Ginther Davis Constr. Co. v. Bryant Curington, Inc.*, 614 S.W.2d 923, 925 (Tex. App.—Waco 1981, no writ); *Galleria Bank v. Sw. Props., Inc.*, 498 S.W.2d 5, 7 (Tex. Civ. App.—Houston [1st Dist.] 1973, no writ).

(14) That a party plaintiff or defendant is not doing business under an assumed name or trade name as alleged.

(15) In the trial of any case brought against an automobile insurance company by an insured under the provisions of an insurance policy in force providing protection against uninsured motorists, an allegation that the insured has complied with all the terms of the policy as a condition precedent to bringing the suit shall be presumed to be true unless denied by verified pleadings which may be upon information and belief.

(16) Any other matter required by statute to be pleaded under oath.

13-4:2 Verification—Personal Knowledge Requirement

Generally, Rule 93 verifications must be based on personal knowledge, although some of the subsections specifically state the verification may be based on information and belief.[59] Those subsections that do not explicitly state that they may be based on information and belief default to the requirement that the verification be based on personal knowledge.[60]

13-4:3 Verification—Exceptions to the Personal Knowledge Requirement

Certain defenses may be verified with an affidavit that is based upon information and belief. In the trial of cases appealed from the Industrial Accident Board, certain matters, if pleaded, are presumed true and to have been done timely, unless denied by verified pleadings.[61] Matters in paragraphs (a) or (g) of Rule 93(16)—notice of injury

---

[59] Tex. R. Civ. P. 93(7) (only when the signatory is deceased); (8) (a denial of the genuineness of an indorsement or assignment in a suit brought by the indorsee or assignee); (13) (only with respect to denials of Notice of Injury and Good Cause for failing to file a claim with the Industrial Accident Board within the one year period); (15) (denials of conditions precedent to performance under an automobile insurance policy in a suit brought by the insured against the insurer under the uninsured motorist provisions of the policy).

[60] *Twist v. Nat'l Bank*, 294 S.W.3d 255, 260 (Tex. App.—Corpus Christi-Edinburgh 2009, no writ) (citing and quoting *Cantu v. Holiday Inns, Inc.*, 910 S.W.2d 113, 116 (Tex. App.—Corpus Christi 1995, writ denied) ("[W]e therefore agree with our sister court that Rule 93(13), which explicitly provides for verifications upon information and belief, logically indicates that the remainder of Rule 93 requires a verification based upon personal knowledge."); *Reyna v. Nat'l Union Fire Ins. Co. of Pittsburgh*, Pa., 883 S.W.2d 368, 370–73 (Tex. App.—El Paso 1994) ("We believe the provisions of Rule 93 which allow affidavits based upon information and belief regarding certain specified matters effectively require personal knowledge for matters involving the remaining subsections of Rule 93."), *rev'd on other grounds*, 897 S.W.2d 777, 778–79 (Tex. 1995)).

[61] Tex. R. Civ. P. 93(13) (The matters presumed to be true and timely are notice of the injury, claim for compensation, award of the Board, notice of intention not to abide by the award of the Board, filing of suit to set aside the award, that insurance carrier alleged to have been the carrier at the time of the accident was in fact the carrier, that there was good cause for not filing claim within the Industrial Accident Board with the one year period provided by statute, and the wage rate).

PLEADING BURDENS

and good cause for not filing a claim with the Accident Board within the one year period, respectively—may be denied on information and belief.[62]

Generally, a party's denial of the execution of any instrument in writing upon which a pleading is founded must be denied under oath.[63] Where the written instrument is charged to have been executed by someone who is deceased, however, the affidavit is sufficient if it states that the affiant has "reason to believe and does believe that such instrument was not executed by the decedent or by his authority."[64]

The denial of the genuineness (i.e., authenticity) of an indorsement or assignment of a written instrument where suit is brought by the endorsee or assignee must be verified.[65] Otherwise, the endorsement or assignment is "held as fully proved."[66] The denial required by this subdivision of Rule 93, however, may be made in all cases upon information and belief.[67]

The denial of the performance of conditions precedent in an automobile insurance policy in a suit brought by the insured against the insurer under the uninsured motorist provisions of an insurance policy must be verified, but such verification may be based on information and belief.[68]

13-4:4 Verification—Who May Verify

The verifications required by Rule 93 must be made by a person with personal knowledge of the facts required to be verified unless Rule 93 explicitly states that the

---

[62] *Reyna v. Nat'l Union Fire Ins. Co. of Pittsburgh, Pa.*, 883 S.W.2d 368, 370–73 (Tex. App.—El Paso 1994) ("A denial of any of the matters set forth in subdivisions (a) or (g) of paragraph 13 may be made on information and belief."); *see, e.g., National Union v. Reyna*, 897 S.W.2d 777, 779 (Tex. 1995) ("... McLean's affidavit adequately verified National Union's denial of Reyna's compensation claim, based on Reyna's failure to file his claim on time and his lack of good cause for untimely filing.").

[63] Tex. R. Civ. P. 93(7).

[64] *National Union v. Reyna*, 897 S.W.2d 777, 779 (Tex. 1995). *See, e.g., Pilot Travel Ctrs v. McCray*, 416 S.W.3d 168, 178 (Tex. App—Dallas 2013, no pet.) (In wrongful death case, arbitration agreement signed by decedent could not be challenged as inauthentic where plaintiffs failed to deny authenticity with affidavit, though court acknowledges that the denial could have been based on reasonable and actual belief due to death of alleged signatory.).

[65] Tex. R. Civ. P. 93(8).

[66] Tex. R. Civ. P. 93(8).

[67] Tex. R. Civ. P. 93(8).

[68] Tex. R. Civ. P. 93(15). *See, e.g., Burson v. Emp'rs Cas. Co.*, 558 S.W.2d 547, 549 (Tex. Civ. App.—Fort Worth 1977, no writ) ("Since the defendant-insurer has not brought into issue whether Maxey was insured as required by Tex. R. Civ. P. 93(p), it is presumed to be true since it is a condition precedent to bringing the suit against the uninsured motorist insurer. The effect of Tex. R. Civ. P. 93(p) in an uninsured motorist suit is to give the defendant an opportunity to contest the conditions precedent to plaintiff's initiation of the suit. When these conditions precedent are in dispute, the defendant may bring them into issue through his denial by verified pleadings which may be upon information and belief. Since the defendant did not bring the uninsured status of the driver into issue as required by Tex. R. Civ. P. 93(p), we hold that plaintiffs have sufficiently proved that Maxey was an uninsured motorist at the time of the accident.").

verification may be upon information and belief.[69] Tex. R. Civ. P. 14 allows the attorney for a party to a civil suit to make an affidavit whenever the party is required to make such an affidavit.[70] Despite this rule, attorneys are not typically able properly to verify the defense in Rule 93 because they lack personal knowledge, and Rule 14 does not excuse the personal knowledge requirement.[71]

13-4:5 Verification—Unless Such Matters Appear of Record

The list of matters in rule 93 must be verified by affidavit, unless "such matters appear of record." As one court stated, there is "a dearth of case law" on the meaning of this exception to the verification requirement. It appears, however, that if the facts Rule 93 requires to be verified have otherwise been sworn to, the facts "appear of record."[72] For example, the facts appeared of record when a witness with personal knowledge testified in a deposition that the defendant was not liable in the capacity in which it was sued based on his personal knowledge of the ownership of the hotel the witness worked for.[73] Also, copies of documents attached to an affidavit setting up workers' compensation matters ordinarily required to be verified "appeared of record" because they were "sworn documents" since attached to the affidavit.[74]

13-4:6 Denial of the Occurrence or Performance of a Condition Precedent

To properly plead the performance or occurrence of a condition precedent, a party need only plead generally that all conditions precedent have been performed or have occurred.[75] Once this has been pled, however, the party denying the occurrence or

---

[69] *Cantu v. Holiday Inns, Inc.*, 910 S.W.2d 113, 116 (Tex. App.—Corpus Christi 1995, writ denied) ("[W]e therefore agree with our sister court that Rule 93(13), which explicitly provides for verifications upon information and belief, logically indicates that the remainder of Rule 93 requires a verification based upon personal knowledge.").

[70] Tex. R. Civ. P. 14 ("Whenever it may be necessary or proper for any party to a civil suit or proceeding to make an affidavit, it may be made by either the party or his agent or his attorney.").

[71] *Cantu v. Holiday Inns, Inc.*, 910 S.W.2d 113, 116 (Tex. App.—Corpus Christi 1995, writ denied) (Citing Texas Rule 14, the court stated, "A party's attorney may verify the pleading where he has knowledge of the facts, but does not have authority to verify based merely on his status as counsel."); *Landscape Design & Const., Inc. v. Warren*, 566 S.W.2d 66, 66 (Tex. Civ. App.—Dallas 1978, no writ) ("While Rule 14 of the Texas Rules of Civil Procedure permits an affidavit to be made by a party's attorney or agent, this rule does not obviate the necessity of showing that the attorney has personal knowledge of the facts, as distinguished from information obtained from the client. Ordinarily, an attorney's knowledge of the facts of a case is obtained from the client.").

[72] *Cantu v. Holiday Inns, Inc.*, 910 S.W.2d 113, 116 (Tex. App.—Corpus Christi 1995, writ denied) ("There is a dearth of case law in Texas dealing with the 'of record' exception to the verification requirement in Rule 93.").

[73] *Cantu v. Holiday Inns, Inc.*, 910 S.W.2d 116, 117 (Tex. App.—Corpus Christi 1995, writ denied).

[74] *Lechuga v. Tex. Emp'rs Ins. Assoc.*, 791 S.W.2d 182, 184 (Tex. App.—Amarillo 1990, writ denied).

[75] Tex. R. Civ. P. 54.

PLEADING BURDENS

performance of a condition precedent must deny them specifically.[76] The party with the burden of proof on the conditions precedent is required to prove only those that have been specifically denied.[77] Merely denying that all conditions precedent have been performed or occurred to satisfy the rule isn't sufficient. Instead, the party denying the performance or occurrence of a condition precedent must specifically state the ones that have not occurred.[78]

13-5 Affirmative Defenses

Affirmative defenses must be pleaded, or they are waived.[79] A general denial does not raise an affirmative defense because an affirmative defense is one that precludes or reduces liability even if the plaintiff's allegations are true and is a defense in "confession and avoidance." In other words, an affirmative defense is one that does not controvert the facts asserted by the plaintiff but rather seeks to establish an independent reason why the plaintiff should not recover.[80] The defendant could (though he is not required to) confess the truth of the plaintiff's allegations and still avoid or reduce liability because the elements of the affirmative defense are true. The requirement to plead affirmative defenses applies to all parties, not just defendants (e.g., parties defending a counterclaim, crossclaim, or third-party claim).[81]

13-5:1 Rule 94 as a Nonexclusive List of Affirmative Defenses

Rule 94 provides a list of affirmative defenses that must be pled or else are waived. If the defense is in Rule 94, the attorney will waive it by failing to plead it. Rule 94 requires the following defenses to be pled:

- Accord and Satisfaction
- Arbitration and Award
- Assumption of Risk

---

[76] Tex. R. Civ. P. 54.

[77] Tex. R. Civ. P. 54. *See, e.g., Sunbelt Const. Corp., Inc. v. S & D Mech. Contractors, Inc.*, 668 S.W.2d 415 (Tex. App.—Corpus 1983, writ ref'd n.r.e.) (Failure to specifically deny perfection of mechanic's lien precluded need for proof of perfection); *Dairyland Cty. Mut. Ins. Co. v. Roman*, 498 S.W.2d 154, 157 (Tex. 1973) (failure to specifically deny the that the plaintiff had failed to comply with the notice requirement in the policy meant plaintiff was excused from proving he had provided proper notice as a condition precedent to performance under the policy).

[78] *Dairyland Cty. Mut. Ins. Co. v. Roman*, 498 S.W.2d 154, 157 (Tex. 1973) (A denial that all conditions precedent had occurred without naming the one or ones that had not was not sufficient to require plaintiff to prove them even where the defendant attached a list of the conditions precedent to his denial.).

[79] Tex. R. Civ. P. 94 (listing defenses that must be "set forth affirmatively" and also requiring the pleading of any other defense "constituting an avoidance or affirmative defense.").

[80] *Tex. Tax Sols., LLC v. City of El Paso*, 593 S.W.3d 903, 909 (Tex. App.—El Paso 2019, no pet.) (quoting *Gorman v. Life Ins. Co. of N. Am.*, 811 S.W.2d 542, 546 (Tex. 1991)).

[81] *Simmons v. Compania Financiera Libano, S.A.*, 830 S.W.2d 789, 792 ((Tex. App.—Houston [1st Dist.] 1992, writ denied) (citing *Royal Typewriter Co. v. Vestal*, 572 S.W.2d 377, 378 (Tex. App.—Houston [14th Dist.] 1978, no writ); *Sustala v. North Side Ready-Mix Concrete Co.*, 317 S.W.2d 64, 67–68 (Tex. Civ. App.—Houston [1st Dist.] 1958, no writ)).

- Contributory Negligence
- Discharge in Bankruptcy
- Duress
- Estoppel
- Failure of Consideration
- Fraud
- Illegality
- Injury by Fellow Servant
- Laches
- License
- Payment
- Release
- Res Judicata
- Statute of Frauds
- Statute of Limitations
- Waiver

Rule 94 is, however, a nonexclusive list of affirmative defenses. While the defenses listed in Rule 94 must be pled affirmatively, the rule states that a party should plead "any other matter constituting an avoidance or affirmative defense." The Supreme Court of Texas has also made clear that the list is not exclusive.[82] Any other defense that is one of confession and avoidance should be affirmatively pled. Recently, the Texas Supreme Court drew a distinction between affirmative defenses and defenses in confession and avoidance:

> [A confession-and-avoidance plea] is one of justification. It is based on a different set of facts from those establishing [the cause of action]. As an affirmative defense it [acknowledges] the existence of prima facie liability but [asserts] a proposition which, if established, avoids such liability. Rather than being in conflict with the [cause of action], the [confession and avoidance] admits it but asserts the existence of other facts which justify or excuse it.[83]

The court also noted that "avoidance and affirmative defenses are used interchangeably.[84] The following defenses have been held to be affirmative defenses, even though they do not appear in Rule 94:

- Penalty[85]

---

[82] *Phillips v. Phillips*, 820 S.W.2d 785, 789 (Tex. 1991) ("although penalty is not among the affirmative defenses enumerated in Rule 94 the listing in that rule is not exclusive").
[83] *Zorrilla v. Aypco Constr. II, LLC*, 469 S.W.3d 143, 156 (Tex. 2015).
[84] *Zorrilla v. Aypco Constr. II, LLC*, 469 S.W.3d 143, 156 (Tex. 2015).
[85] *Phillips v. Phillips*, 820 S.W.2d 785, 789 (Tex. 1991).

- Insolvency[86]
- Disclaimer of the Implied Warranty of Merchantability[87]
- Disclaimer of the Implied Warranty of Fitness[88]
- Parental Immunity[89]
- The Unconstitutionality of Statute[90]
- Preemption[91]
- Unconscionable Contract Provision[92]
- Limitation of Liability under Liquidated Damages Clause[93]

Where the attorney is uncertain whether a particular defense constitutes an affirmative defense, the attorney should err on the side of affirmatively pleading the defense. This will ensure the attorney does not waive the defense.

13-5:2 Satisfying the Pleading Burden for Affirmative Defenses

Rule 45 requires that affirmative defenses be pled in "plain and concise language" and must give "fair notice" to the opponent.[94] The question is whether or not the opposing party can "ascertain from the pleading the nature and basic issues of the controversy and what testimony will be relevant."[95] Moreover, the opposing party cannot complain

---

[86] *Sorbus, Inc. v. UHW Corp.*, 855 S.W.2d 771, 775 (Tex. App.—El Paso 1993, writ denied) (insolvency that prevented performance described as an affirmative defense in a claim for tortious interference).

[87] *Man Engines & Components, Inc. v. Shows*, 434 S.W.3d 132, 57 Tex. Sup. Ct. J. 661 (Tex. 2014).

[88] *Johnston v. McKinney Am., Inc.*, 9 S.W.3d 271, 279 (Tex. App.—Houston [14th Dist.] 1999, pet. denied).

[89] *Shoemaker v. Fogel, Ltd.*, 826 S.W.2d 933, 937 (Tex. 1990) (holding that parental immunity is an affirmative defense but also that it is not waived if "apparent on the face of the petition and established as a matter of law").

[90] *Scurlock Permian Corp. v. Brazos Cty.*, 869 S.W.2d 478, 483–84 (Tex. App.—Houston [1st Dist.] 1993, writ denied); *Houston Chronicle Publ'g Co. v. City of Houston*, 531 S.W.2d 177, 183 (Tex. App.—Houston [14th Dist.] 1975, writ ref'd n.r.e.).

[91] *Gorman v. Life Ins. Co. of N.A.*, 811 S.W.2d 542, 547 (Tex. 1991) ("Where ERISA's preemptive effect would result only in a change of the applicable law, preemption is an affirmative defense which must be set forth in the defendant's answer or it is waived.").

[92] *Parks v. Developers Sur. & Indem. Co.*, 302 S.W.3d 920, 923-4 (Tex. App.—Dallas 2010, no pet.) ("An allegation that a provision in a contract is void, unenforceable, or unconscionable is a matter in the nature of an avoidance and must be pleaded.").

[93] *Borders v. KRLB, Inc.*, 727 S.W.2d 357, 360 (Tex. App.—Amarillo 1987, writ ref'd n.r.e.) (failure to plead a $25,000 limit on liability in liquidated damages clause of contract waived the defense).

[94] Tex. R. Civ. P. 45(b).

[95] *Horizon/CMS Healthcare Corp. v. Auld*, 34 S.W.3d 887, 896–97 (Tex. 2000) (pleading gave fair notice of damage cap even though it cited the cap provision incorrectly).

about a defect in the pleadings on appeal unless the opposing party has excepted to the pleading in writing and obtained a ruling.[96]

Prudent attorneys will also keep the federal pleading standard in mind in cases that may be removed to federal court. Federal courts apply a more rigorous pleading standard called the "plausibility" pleading standard, which requires that the plaintiff plead facts sufficient to show that recovery is plausible.[97] *Bell Atlantic Corp. v. Twombly* and its progeny require the pleading of factual matters that demonstrate plausibility.[98] Though United States Supreme Court precedent applies the plausibility pleading standard only to claims for relief, not to affirmative defenses, some of the lower federal courts are applying a similar standard to defensive pleadings.[99] In cases that may be removed to federal court, the prudent attorney may want to plead defenses with this standard in mind.

13-6 Inferential Rebuttal Defenses

This subsection defines inferential rebuttal defenses and discusses the associated pleading requirements and proper submission of such defenses to the jury. The substance of inferential rebuttal defenses is discussed in Chapter 15.

13-6:1 Inferential Rebuttal Defenses Defined

An inferential rebuttal defense is a defense that negates an element or elements of the plaintiff's claim through proof of a separate set of facts.[100] It is, therefore, distinguishable from an affirmative defense in that it does not confess and avoid the truth of the plaintiff's allegations, but rather negates an essential element of the plaintiff's claim. "The basic characteristic of an inferential rebuttal is that it presents a contrary or inconsistent theory from the claim relied upon for recovery."[101]

---

[96] *Horizon/CMS Healthcare Corp. v. Auld*, 34 S.W.3d 887, 897 (Tex. 2000) (stating that pleadings should be liberally construed when opposing party fails to except); Tex. R. Civ. P. 90 ("Every defect omission or fault in a pleading either of form or of substance, which is not specifically pointed out by exception in writing and brought to the attention of the judge in the trial court before instruction or charge to the jury or, in a non-jury case, before the judgment is signed, shall be deemed to have been waived by the party seeking reversal on such account.").

[97] *Bell Atl. Corp. v. Twombly*, 550 U.S. 544, 557 (2007).

[98] *Bell Atl. Corp. v. Twombly*, 550 U.S. 544, 557 (2007); *see generally, Ashcroft v. Iqbal*, 556 U.S. 662 (2009).

[99] *See, e.g., Vargas v. HWC Gen. Maint., LLC*, No. H-11-875, 2012 WL 948892, at *2 (S.D. Tex. Mar. 20, 2012) (stating that plausibility standard should apply to pleading of affirmative defenses); *but see EEOC v. Courtesy Bldg. Serv., Inc.*, No. 3:10-CV-1911-D, 2011 WL 208408, at *2 (N.D. Tex. Jan. 21, 2011) ("... the court declines in today's case, and in the absence of complete briefing and guidance from the Fifth Circuit or the Supreme Court, to extend the *Iqbal* and *Twombly* plausibility standard to the pleading of affirmative defenses.").

[100] *Dillard v. Tex. Elec. Co-Op*, 157 S.W.3d 429 (Tex. 2005) ("An inferential rebuttal defense operates to rebut an essential element of the plaintiff's case by proof of other facts.").

[101] *Select Ins. Co. v. Boucher*, 561 S.W.2d 474, 477 (Tex. 1978).

13-6:2 Examples of Inferential Rebuttal Defenses

The following defenses have been held to be inferential rebuttal defenses:

- Partial Incapacity in Workmen's Compensation Case (where claimant claims only Total Incapacity)[102]
- Unavoidable Accident[103]
- New and Independent Cause[104]
- Sole Proximate Cause[105]
- Act of God[106]
- Emergency
- Failure to Mitigate Damages[107]

13-6:3 Charging the Jury on Inferential Rebuttal Defenses

An inferential rebuttal defense should not be submitted as a question to the jury[108] but instead, the charge should include an instruction on the inferential rebuttal defense when supported by the evidence and the pleadings.[109] An inferential rebuttal defense should not be submitted as an instruction to the jury, however, when the defense is nothing more than an alternate theory of liability that the plaintiff also wants submitted to the jury as a question. For example, partial incapacity may be submitted in a workmen's compensation case when the claimant's only theory of liability is total incapacity, but not when the claimant contends, in the alternative, that he is partially incapacitated.[110]

---

[102] *Select Ins. Co. v. Boucher*, 561 S.W.2d 474, 478–79 (Tex. 1978).

[103] *Bed, Bath & Beyond, Inc. v. Urista*, 211 S.W.3d 753, 756–57 (Tex. 2006) ("Unavoidable accident is not an alternative theory of liability but is 'an inferential rebuttal issue that requires plaintiffs to prove the nonexistence of an affirmative defense', or 'seeks to disprove the existence of an essential element submitted in another issue.") (internal citations omitted).

[104] *Dew v. Crown Derrick Erectors, Inc.*, 208 S.W.3d 448, 450–51 (Tex. 2006) (recognizing new and independent cause as inferential rebuttal defenses but holding that it was not error for the trial court to refuse to submit instruction on the defense).

[105] *Dillard v. Tex. Elec. Co-Op*, 157 S.W.3d 429, 432 (Tex. 2005) (recognizing sole proximate cause as an inferential rebuttal defense but finding no error in refusing to instruct juror on the defense).

[106] *Scott v. Atchison T & S.F.R Co.*, 572 S.W.2d 273, 279 (Tex. 1979) (recognizing "Act of God" as having "all of the aspects of an inferential rebuttal issue").

[107] *Moulton v. Alamo Ambulance Serv., Inc.*, 414 S.W.2d 444, 448 (Tex. 1967) (holding that failure to mitigate damages is an inferential rebuttal defense rather than an affirmative defense).

[108] Tex. R. Civ. P. 277 ("Inferential rebuttal questions shall not be submitted in the charge.").

[109] *Dillard v. Tex. Elec. Co-Op*, 157 S.W.3d 429, 432 (Tex. 2005); *see, e.g.*, Comm. on Pattern Jury Charges, State Bar of Tex., Texas Pattern Jury Charges—General Negligence & Intentional Personal Torts PJC 3.2 (2003) (sole proximate cause).

[110] *Select Ins. Co. v. Boucher*, 561 S.W.2d 474, 477 (Tex. 1978).

13-6:4 Pleading Requirements for Inferential Rebuttal Defenses

Generally, a defendant need not plead an inferential rebuttal defense in order to obtain an instruction in the charge on the defense.[111] The general denial may raise the issue from a pleading perspective, but the defendant still has the burden on production on any inferential rebuttal issue and must timely disclose the theory in response to Requests for Disclosure.

---

[111] *Columbia Rio Grande Healthcare, L.P. v. Hawley*, 284 S.W.3d 851 (Tex. 2009).

CHAPTER 14

Special and Verified Denials*

This chapter addresses the substantive elements for certain defensive pleas, listed in Tex. R. Civ. P. 93, that must be verified by affidavit.

14-1 Lack of Capacity

The issue of capacity concerns a party's personal right to come into court, whereas standing concerns the question of whether a party has a justiciable interest.[1] Capacity "is conceived of as a procedural issue dealing with the personal qualifications of a party to litigate."[2] A party has capacity when it has the legal authority to act, regardless of whether it has a justiciable interest in the controversy.[3] Lack of capacity must be challenged by a verified pleading, based on personal knowledge, or it is waived.[4]

The issue of capacity to sue is traditionally raised by a verified plea in abatement, but it may also be raised in a verified denial.[5] If the issue is raised by a verified denial, the plaintiff bears the burden of proving at trial that it is entitled to recover in the capacity in which it has filed suit, and as the party with the burden of proof, the plaintiff must obtain a jury finding on the particular capacity issue.[6]

A pleading alleging the a defect in capacity must point to specific facts and must be verified by affidavit, unless the truth of the matter appears of record:[7]

---

* The authors thank Kimberly Trimble for her assistance in the updating of this chapter.
[1] *Basic Energy Serv., Inc. v. D-S-B Props., Inc.*, 367 S.W.3d 254, 261 (Tex. App.—Tyler 2011, no pet.).
[2] *John C. Flood of DC, Inc. v. SuperMedia, L.L.C.*, 408 S.W.3d 645, 650 (Tex. App.—Dallas 2013, *rehearing overruled*) (quoting *Austin Nursing Ctr., Inc. v. Lovato*, 171 S.W.3d 845, 848–49 (Tex. 2005)).
[3] *Rhey v. Redic*, 408 S.W.3d 440, 456 (Tex. App.—El Paso 2013, no pet.).
[4] *Basic Energy Serv., Inc. v. D-S-B Props., Inc.*, 367 S.W.3d 254, 261 (Tex. App.—Tyler 2011, no pet.).
[5] *Bossier Chrysler Dodge II, Inc. v. Rauschenberg*, 201 S.W.3d 787 (Tex. App.—Waco 2006, *aff'd in part, rev'd in part* by *Bossier Chrysler Dodge II, Inc. d/b/a Bossier Country v. Rauschenberg*, 238 S.W.3d 376 (Tex. 2007) (Mem. Op.)).
[6] *Bossier Chrysler Dodge II, Inc. v. Rauschenberg*, 201 S.W.3d 787 (Tex. App.—Waco 2006, *aff'd in part, rev'd in part* by *Bossier Chrysler Dodge II, Inc. d/b/a Bossier Country v. Rauschenberg*, 238 S.W.3d 376 (Tex. 2007) (Mem. Op.)).
[7] *John C. Flood of DC, Inc. v. SuperMedia, L.L.C.*, 408 S.W.3d 645, 650 (Tex. App.—Dallas 2013, *rehearing overruled*).

That the plaintiff has not legal capacity to sue or that the defendant has not legal capacity to be sued;[8] and

That the plaintiff is not entitled to recover in the capacity in which he sues, or that the defendant is not liable in the capacity in which he is sued.[9]

14-2 Another Suit Pending Between Same Parties for Same Claim

Rule 93 requires verification by affidavit of a plea that "there is another suit pending in this State between the same parties involving the same claim."[10] A party's failure to verify a pleading required to be verified generally waives any complaint on appeal.[11] Pendency of a prior suit between the same parties involving the same subject matter must be raised by plea in abatement or the objection is waived.[12] Rule 93 requires that the plea in abatement be verified.[13]

A pleading alleging the following matters regarding pending suits must be verified:

Pending suit between the same parties; and

Involving the same claim.

14-3 Defect of Parties

A "defect of parties" generally refers to joinder problems involving necessary or indispensable parties, plaintiff or defendant, and must be raised by a verified pleading.[14] The party must plead that there is a defect of parties in that a particular absent party is a necessary party and has not been joined.[15] This verification must be based on personal knowledge.[16] Any defect of parties not raised and objected to in a verified denial is waived on appeal.[17]

A pleading alleging the following matters regarding a defect of parties must be verified:

An absent party is necessary; and

Has not been joined in the claim.

---

[8] Tex. R. Civ. P. 93(1).

[9] Tex. R. Civ. P. 93(2).

[10] Tex. R. Civ. P. 93(3); *S. Cty. Mut. Ins. Co. v. Ochoa*, 19 S.W.3d 452, 461 (Tex. App.—Corpus Christi 2000).

[11] *Southern Cty. Mut. Ins. Co. v. Ochoa*, 19 S.W.3d 452, 461 (Tex. App.—Corpus Christi 2000, no writ).

[12] *Day v. State*, 489 S.W.2d 368, 371 (Tex. App.—Austin 1972, writ ref'd n.r.e.).

[13] *Day v. State*, 489 S.W.2d 368, 371 (Tex. App.—Austin 1972, writ ref'd n.r.e.).

[14] *CHCA East Houston, L.P. v. Henderson*, 99 S.W.3d 630, 633 (Tex. App.—Houston [14th Dist.] 2003).

[15] *See* Tex. R. Civ. P. 93(4); 1 West's Tex. Forms, Cred. Rem. & Debt. Rights § 11:76 (4th ed. 2014).

[16] *Cantu v. Holiday Inns, Inc.*, 910 S.W.2d 113, 116 (Tex. App.—Corpus Christi 1995, writ denied).

[17] *Santa Fe Petroleum, L.L.C. v. Star Canyon Corp.*, 156 S.W.3d 630, 641 (Tex. App.—Tyler 2004, no pet.).

14-4 Denial of Partnership or Corporate Status

Rule 93 requires that a verified pleading be filed to assert "a denial of partnership as alleged in any pleading as to any party to the suit," and "that any party alleged in any pleading to be a corporation is not incorporated as alleged."[18]

Allegations of a partnership are deemed admitted when not denied by a verified affidavit.[19] When a petition alleges a claim against a partnership and the defendants never deny the existence of partnership status, the admission of the partnership's existence cannot be controverted at trial.[20] Defendant must plead that, although the plaintiff's petition alleges that defendant is a partnership, defendant is not a partnership.[21] Although plaintiff's petition alleges defendant is a partnership, the defendant must deny, by a verified pleading, that defendant is not a partnership.

A denial, verified by affidavit, of corporate status is necessary when any party alleged in any pleading to be a corporation is not actually incorporated as alleged. As with the denial of the existence of a partnership, the defendant must plead, by verified denial, that although plaintiff's petition alleged that defendant is a corporation, defendant is not a corporation.[22] Accordingly, any pleading alleging the following matters regarding the defendant's status as a corporation must be verified:

> Although plaintiff's petition alleges defendant is a corporation, defendant must deny, in a verified pleading, that defendant is a corporation.

14-5 Denial of Execution of Written Instrument

Defendant must deny, in a verified pleading, that the written instrument upon which plaintiff's petition is founded in whole or in part and which is charged to have been executed by a particular defendant or party, was executed by him or her or under his or her authority.[23]

When a claim is based on the execution of a written instrument and the defendant does not deny under oath the execution of the instrument, "the instrument shall be received as evidence as fully proved."[24]

---

[18] Tex. R. Civ. P. 93(5), (6) (2013).

[19] *Kirby Forest Indus., Inc. v. Dobbs*, 743 S.W.2d 348, 352 (Tex. App.—Beaumont 1987, writ denied).

[20] *Fincher v. B & D Air Conditioning and Heating Co.*, 816 S.W.2d 509, 512 (Tex. App.—Houston [1st Dist.] 1991); *Washburn v. Krenek*, 684 S.W.2d 187, 191 (Tex. App.—Houston [14th Dist.] 1984, writ ref'd n.r.e.).

[21] See *Washburn v. Krenek*, 684 S.W.2d 187, 191 (Tex. App.—Houston [14th Dist.] 1984, writ ref'd n.r.e.) ("A failure to deny partnership status by a verified denial results in an admission of the existence of a partnership which cannot be controverted at trial.").

[22] Tex. R. Civ. P. 93(6); *Bituminous Cas. Corp. v. Commercial Standard Ins. Co.*, 639 S.W.2d 25, 26 (Tex. App.—Tyler 1982, no writ).

[23] Tex. R. Civ. P. 93(7); *Sec. & Commc'ns Sys., Inc. v. Hooper*, 575 S.W.2d 606, 608 (Tex. Civ. App.—Dallas 1978, no writ) (defendant must specifically deny an agent's authority to enter into a written agreement in a verified denial).

[24] *Escalante v. Luckie*, 77 S.W.3d 410, 418 (Tex. App.—Eastland 2002, pet. denied).

14-6 Denial of Genuineness of Indorsement or Assignment

Defendant must deny, in a verified pleading, that the indorsement or assignment of the written instrument upon which the plaintiff brings suit is not genuine, upon the defendant's information and belief.[25]

A party who fails to plead by verified denial the genuineness of its signature on written instruments cannot contest the genuineness of its signatures at trial by way of proving the instruments are not genuine.[26] However, it would seem that, even in the absence of a verified denial, a defendant may produce evidence contesting the genuineness of an indorsement at the summary judgment stage.[27]

14-7 Denial of Notice and Proof of Loss or Claim

Defendant must deny, in a verified pleading, that the plaintiff gave the required notice or proof of loss or claim. Under Rule 93, defendant must verify by affidavit that notice and proof of loss or claim for damage has not been given as plaintiff alleged.[28] "Unless such plea is filed such notice and proof shall be presumed and no evidence to the contrary shall be admitted."[29] Defendant's denial of notice and proof shall be specific and made with particularity.[30] Failure to file a verified denial of the opposing party's allegation of notice or proof of loss or claim is waived on appeal.[31]

14-8 Denial of Assumed Name

Defendant must specifically deny, in a verified denial, pursuant to Tex. R. Civ. P. 93(14) that the plaintiff is doing business under an assumed or trade name, as plaintiff alleged in its petition, and must describe the basis for the denial, such as the business is neither owned nor operated by the defendant.[32]

14-9 Denial of Sworn Account

Defendant must specifically deny, in a verified denial, pursuant to Tex R. Civ. P. 93(10) and 18, that the alleged account which forms the basis of the plaintiff's claim against defendant, as alleged in the plaintiff's original petition.[33] A verified denial of an alleged

---

[25] Tex. R. Civ. P. 93(8); *Guardian Bank v. San Jacinto Sav. Ass'n*, 593 S.W.2d 860, 862–63 (Tex. Civ. App.—Houston [1st Dist.] 1980, writ ref'd n.r.e.).

[26] *Overall v. Sw. Bell Yellow Pages, Inc.*, 869 S.W.2d 629, 632 (Tex. App.—Houston [14th Dist.] 1994, pet. denied).

[27] *Guardian Bank v. San Jacinto Sav. Ass'n*, 593 S.W.2d 860, 863 (Tex. Civ. App.—Houston [1st Dist.] 1980, writ ref'd n.r.e.).

[28] Tex. R. Civ. P. 93(12); *Livingston Ford Mercury, Inc. v. Haley*, 997 S.W.2d 425, 430 (Tex. App.—Beaumont 1999, no pet.).

[29] Tex. R. Civ. P. 93(12).

[30] Tex. R. Civ. P. 93(12).

[31] *Sanchez v. Jary*, 768 S.W.2d 933, 936 (Tex. App.—San Antonio 1989, no writ).

[32] Tex. R. Civ. P. 93(14); *Condry v. Mantooth*, 460 S.W.2d 513, 516 (Tex. Civ. App.—Houston [1st Dist.] 1970, no writ).

[33] Tex. R. Civ. P. 93(10); Tex. R. Civ. P. 185; *Day Cruises Mar., L.L.C v. Christus Spohn Health Sys.*, 267 S.W.3d 42, 53 (Tex. App.—Corpus Christi 2008, pet. denied).

SPECIAL AND VERIFIED DENIALS

account may contest the justness and truth of the alleged account.[34] Defendant must also describe the basis for its denial of the justness or truth of the alleged account, such as plaintiff failing to credit the defendant for any payments already made.[35] In the absence of a defendant's verified denial, a defendant may prove that the account has been paid, or that it is barred by limitation, or matters of confession and avoidance, or set up a proper counterclaim.[36]

14-10 Denial of Condition Precedent

Conditions precedent to performance under a contract must be specially (i.e. specifically) denied or the plaintiff is not required to prove their occurrence or performance, per Texas Rules of Civil Procedure 54. For further discussion, *see* Chapter 13, Section 13-4:6. In a case against an automobile insurance company, filed by an insured under a policy, an allegation that the insured has complied with all conditions precedent to filing suit are presumed to be true unless denied by the defendant, by verified pleadings, which may be based upon information and belief.[37] Furthermore, defendant must specifically describe the conditions precedent that have not been met.

14-11 Failure or Lack of Consideration

Defendant must deny, in a verified pleading, that the consideration for the written instrument on which the plaintiff bases its action has failed for specific reasons, to be described by the defendant.[38]

Similarly, regarding a complete lack of consideration, defendant must deny, in a verified pleading, that there is no consideration for the written instrument on which the plaintiff bases its claim because of reasons described by the defendant.[39]

14-12 Usurious Contract

The defendant must assert, in a verified pleading, that the contract sued upon is usurious in that the effective interest rate called for in the contract is a certain interest rate that exceeds the maximum rate allowed by law.[40]

14-13 Form of Verified Denial

Personal knowledge is generally required for a verified denial, unless a statute or rule provides that the verified denial may be made on information and belief.[41] The

---

[34] Tex. R. Civ. P. 185; *Stevens Foods, Inc. v. Loggins Meat Co.*, 644 S.W.2d 908, 909 (Tex. App.—Tyler 1983, no writ).
[35] *See* Tex. R. Civ. P. 185.
[36] *Donald v. Bennett*, 415 S.W.2d 450, 454 (Tex. Civ. App.—Fort Worth 1967, writ ref'd n.r.e.).
[37] Tex. R. Civ. P. 93(15); *Burson v. Employers Cas. Co.*, 558 S.W.2d 547, 549 (Tex. App.—Fort Worth 1977, no writ).
[38] Tex. R. Civ. P. 93(9); *1464-Eight, Ltd. v. Joppich*, 154 S.W.3d 101, 103 (Tex. 2004).
[39] Tex. R. Civ. P. 93(9); *Brown v. Aztec Rig Equipment, Inc.*, 921 S.W.2d 835, 845 (Tex. App.—Houston [14th Dist.] 1996, writ denied).
[40] Tex. R. Civ. P. 93(11); *Midgett v. J. Edelstein Furniture Co.*, 700 S.W.2d 332, 333 (Tex. App.—Corpus Christi 1985, no writ).
[41] *Cantu v. Holiday Inns, Inc.*, 910 S.W.2d 113, 116 (Tex. App.—Corpus Christi 1995, no writ).

verified denial must assert that the facts are true, but no particular form of affidavit is required.[42] The verified denial must also be positive, unequivocal, and sufficiently definite to sustain a perjury prosecution if the statement is false.[43] Instead of an affidavit, a party may use an unsworn declaration that complies with statutory requirements.[44]

---

[42] *Cantu v. Holiday Inns, Inc.*, 910 S.W.2d 113, 116 (Tex. App.—Corpus Christi 1995, no writ); *Davis v. Young Californian Shoes, Inc.*, 612 S.W.2d 703, 704 (Tex. App.—Dallas 1981, no writ).

[43] *Dixon v. Mayfield Bldg. Supply Co., Inc.*, 543 S.W.2d 5, 7–8 (Tex. App.—Fort Worth 1976, no writ).

[44] *See* Tex. Civ. Prac. & Rem. Code Ann. § 132.001.

CHAPTER 15
Inferential Rebuttal Defenses*

An inferential rebuttal defense seeks to disprove an essential element of the plaintiff's case by proof of other facts.[1] Unlike an affirmative defense, an inferential rebuttal presents a contrary or inconsistent theory from the claim relied upon for recovery.[2] If multiple inferential rebuttal theories are submitted to the jury, jurors do not need to agree on which theory applies but need only agree that the defendant was not the responsible party.[3] The stacking of multiple inferential rebuttal issues, however, is frowned upon as potentially commenting on the evidence. The purpose of an inferential rebuttal defense instruction is to advise the jurors, in an appropriate case, that "the jurors do not have to place blame on a party to the suit if the evidence shows that conditions beyond the party's control caused the accident in question or that the conduct of some person not a party to the litigation caused it."[4]

15-1 Sole Proximate Cause

The sole proximate cause instruction is given if the occurrence at issue is caused by a person who is not a party to the suit.[5] The Texas Supreme Court in *Dillard v. Texas Electric Cooperative* defined "sole proximate cause" as follows: "There may be more than one proximate cause of an event, but if an act or omission of any person not a party to the suit was the 'sole proximate cause' of an occurrence, then no act or omission of any other person could have been a proximate cause."[6] Furthermore, a person's conduct does not have to be negligent to be the sole proximate cause.[7]

15-2 Superseding Cause (I.E., New, and Independent Cause)

Superseding cause, or new and independent cause, is an inferential rebuttal defense that negates the causation element of the plaintiff's negligence claim by cutting the

---

* The authors thank Kimberly Trimble for her assistance in the updating of this chapter.
[1] *Dillard v. Tex. Elec. Coop.*, 157 S.W.3d 429, 430 (Tex. 2005).
[2] *Select Ins. Co. v. Boucher*, 561 S.W.2d 474, 477 (Tex. 1978).
[3] *Dillard v. Tex. Elec. Coop.*, 157 S.W.3d 429, 434 (Tex. 2005).
[4] *Dillard v. Tex. Elec. Coop.*, 157 S.W.3d 429, 432 (Tex. 2005). See also, *Bed, Bath & Beyond, Inc. v. Urista*, 211 S.W.3d 753 (Tex. 2006).
[5] *Dillard v. Tex. Elec. Coop.*, 157 S.W.3d 429, 432 (Tex. 2005).
[6] *Dillard v. Tex. Elec. Coop.*, 157 S.W.3d 429, 431 (Tex. 2005).
[7] Tex. PJC 3.2; *Plemmons v. Gary*, 321 S.W.2d 625, 626 (Tex. Civ. App.—Beaumont 1959, orig. proceeding).

causal chain by virtue of an unforeseeable act or omission.[8] The issue has also been considered in the context of tortious interference and civil conspiracy claims.[9] A new and independent cause intervenes "between the original wrong and the final injury such that the injury is attributed to the new cause rather than the first and more remote cause."[10] A concurring cause, in contrast, "'concurs with the continuing and co-operating original negligence in working the injury', leaving the causal connection between the defendant's negligence and the plaintiff's harm intact."[11] Both superseding cause and concurring cause involve some intervening cause. The distinction lies in the effect the intervening cause has on the causal connection between the defendant's negligence and the plaintiff's harm.[12] If the intervening cause is a reasonably foreseeable result of the defendant's negligence, the intervening cause is a concurring cause, not a superseding cause.[13] If the intervening cause could not have been reasonably foreseen, except by "prophetic ken," then the intervening cause is a superseding cause.[14] For example, in an auto accident case, the driver's negligence was the superseding cause of an auto accident that also involved negligence of a utility with respect to a traffic signal.[15] By contrast, if an individual is injured such that they require medical care, negligence by the medical provider is a foreseeable consequence of the negligent act.

15-3 Failure to Mitigate

The plaintiff has a duty to mitigate, or minimize, its damages.[16] The plaintiff is required to use reasonable care in minimizing its damages and if the plaintiff fails to do so, it cannot recover the damages that could have been avoided.[17] The duty to mitigate damages arises in contract and tort actions and the purpose of this duty is to "discourage people from wasting their resources, both physical and economic."[18]

Failure to Mitigate is typically considered an affirmative defense; however, the Texas Supreme Court has recognized an exception to this approach in personal injury litigation.[19] *See* Chapter 12, Section 12-1.

---

[8] *Dew v. Crown Derrick Erectors, Inc.*, 208 S.W.3d 448 (Tex. 2006).

[9] *See, e.g., Immobiliere Jeuness Establissement v. Amegy Bank Nat'l Ass'n*, 525 S.W.3d 875, 880 (Tex. App.—Houston [14th Dist.] 2017, no pet.).

[10] *Stanfield v. Neubaum*, 494 S.W.3d 90, 97 (Tex. 2016) (quoting *Dew v. Crown Derrick Erectors, Inc.*, 208 S.W.3d 448, 450 (Tex. 2006) (plurality op.).

[11] *Stanfield v. Neubaum*, 494 S.W.3d 90, 98 (Tex. 2016) (quoting *Gulf, C. & S.F. Ry. Co. v. Ballew*, 66 S.W.2d 659, 661 (Tex. Comm'n App. 1933, holding approved)).

[12] *See also Bell v. Campbell*, 434 S.W.2d 117 (Tex. 1968) (discussing the distinction between concurring and superseding cause).

[13] *Stanfield v. Neubaum*, 494 S.W.3d 90, 98 (Tex. 2016).

[14] *Stanfield v. Neubaum*, 494 S.W.3d 90, 98 (Tex. 2016) (quoting *Texas & P. Ry. Co. v. Bigham*, 38 S.W. 162, 164 (Tex. 1896)).

[15] *Rampersad v. CenterPoint Energy Hous. Elec., LLC*, 554 S.W.3d 29, 40 (Tex. App.—Houston [1st Dist.] 2017, no pet.).

[16] *See Great Am. Ins. v. N. Austin MUD*, 908 S.W.2d 415, 426 (Tex. 1995).

[17] *See Gunn Infiniti, Inc. v. O'Byrne*, 996 S.W.2d 854, 857 (Tex. 1999); *Pinson v. Red Arrow Freight Lines, Inc.*, 801 S.W.2d 14, 15 (Tex. App.—Austin 1990, no writ).

[18] *Pulaski Bank & Tr. Co. v. Tex. Am. Bank*, 759 S.W.2d 723, 735 (Tex. App.—Dallas 1988, writ denied).

[19] *Moulton v. Alamo Ambulance Serv., Inc.*, 414 S.W.2d 444, 448 (Tex. 1967).

15-4 Unavoidable Occurrence and Sudden Emergency

15-4:1 Unavoidable Occurrence

An "unavoidable occurrence" or "unavoidable accident" is an event "proximately caused by an unforeseeable, nonhuman condition, not by the negligence of any party."[20] From *Dillard*, "the unavoidable-accident instruction is ordinarily used to (1) inquire about the causal effect of some physical condition or circumstance, such as fog, snow, sleet, wet or slick pavement, or obstruction of view," or (2) "to resolve a case involving a very young child who is legally incapable of negligence"; but the use of the instruction is not limited to these circumstances.[21]

15-4:2 Sudden Emergency

Recognized by the Texas Supreme Court in *Dillard*,[22] "sudden emergency" is defined and described as follows:

A sudden emergency instruction is appropriate if there is evidence that

- a person was confronted with a situation that arose suddenly and unexpectedly;
- the situation was not proximately caused by any negligence on the part of the person confronted with it;
- a reasonable person would have believed the situation required immediate action without time for deliberation; and
- the person acted as a person of ordinary prudence would have acted under the same or similar circumstances.[23,24]

15-5 Act of God

An Act of God is an intervening event that typically involves the violence of nature rather than a human interaction.[25] Violent winds, rain, hail, etc. may be subject to an Act of God instruction.[26]

---

[20] *See Dillard v. Tex. Elec. Coop.*, 157 S.W.3d 429, 432 (Tex. 2005).
[21] *Dillard v. Tex. Elec. Coop.*, 157 S.W.3d 429, 433 (Tex. 2005).
[22] *Dillard v. Tex. Elec. Coop.*, 157 S.W.3d 429, 432 (Tex. 2005) (citing and quoting *Hill v. Winn Dixie Tex. Inc.*, 849 S.W.2d 802, 802–03 (Tex. 1992)).
[23] Tex. PJC 3.3.
[24] *See McDonald Transit, Inc. v. Moore*, 565 S.W.2d 43, 44 (Tex. 1978) (elements from instruction to jury approved by the court); *see TXI Transp. v. Hughes*, 224 S.W.3d 870, 905 n.42 (Tex. App.—Fort Worth 2007), *rev'd on other grounds*, 306 S.W.3d 230 (Tex. 2010); *Borrego v. City of El Paso*, 964 S.W.2d 954, 959 (Tex. App.—El Paso 1998, pet. denied).
[25] *Scott v. Atchison, T. & S. F. R. Co.*, 572 S.W.2d 273 (Tex. 1978).
[26] *Scott v. Atchison, T. & S. F. R. Co.*, 572 S.W.2d 273 (Tex. 1978).

CHAPTER 16

Affirmative Defenses*

16-1 Pleading Rules and Their Effect

This chapter addresses the substantive elements for the affirmative defenses, including all of those listed in Tex. R. Civ. P. 94. The pleading requirements for affirmative defenses are discussed in Chapter 13, but the general rule is that a general denial will not be sufficient to support evidence and submission of an affirmative defense in the jury charge.

16-2 Payment

Payment, as an affirmative defense, generally refers to the defendant's payment on the debt which is the subject of the lawsuit. The defendant may assert the defense of the plaintiff's voluntary payment, however, to defeat a plaintiff's claim for unjust enrichment.[1]

16-2:1 Elements

(1) The defendant paid the plaintiff;[2]

(2) Some or all of the debt on which the plaintiff sues.[3]

16-2:2 Elements: Voluntary Payment

(1) The plaintiff made payment to the defendant; and

(2) Such payment was made:

    (a) Voluntarily;

    (b) With full knowledge of all the facts; and

    (c) In the absence of fraud, deception, duress or compulsion.[4]

---

* The authors thank Kimberly Trimble for her assistance in the updating of this chapter.
[1] *BMG Direct Mktg., Inc. v. Peake*, 178 S.W.3d 763, 768 (Tex. 2005).
[2] *First Nat'l Bank in Dallas v. Whirlpool Corp.*, 517 S.W.2d 262, 269 (Tex. 1974).
[3] *First Nat'l Bank in Dallas v. Whirlpool Corp.*, 517 S.W.2d 262, 269 (Tex. 1974).
[4] *BMG Direct Mktg., Inc. v. Peake*, 178 S.W.3d 763, 768 (Tex. 2005).

16-2:3 Other Substantive Issues

When the defendant attempts to prove its own payment as a defense, the defendant must file an account stating distinctly the nature of such payment, and the several items thereof.[5] In other words, the defendant must show what it paid and when to avail itself of the defense and to demonstrate whether the amount paid extinguished all of the sum sued for or just part. Failure to file such an account precludes the availability of the defense unless the payment is so plainly and particularly described in the plea as to give the plaintiff full notice of the character thereof.[6]

16-3 Accord and Satisfaction

The defense of accord and satisfaction is based upon an agreement by the parties that discharges an existing obligation by means of a lesser payment which has been both tendered and accepted.[7] The "accord" represents the new agreement between the parties.[8] The "satisfaction" represents the performance of that agreement.[9] An accord and satisfaction constitutes a complete bar to any action on the original obligation.[10] The defense of accord and satisfaction has its origins in common law, but has also been codified in the UCC. The main differences between the two are that, under the statutory defense, there are requirements that the debt be disputed or unliquidated[11] and that the satisfaction may only be obtained through actual payment.[12]

16-3:1 Elements—Common Law

(1) An express or implied contract between the parties;[13]

    (a) The agreement must be supported by consideration;[14]

---

[5] Tex. R. Civ. P. 95.
[6] Tex. R. Civ. P. 95.
[7] *Lopez v. Munoz, Hockema & Reed, L.L.P.*, 22 S.W.3d 857, 863 (Tex. 2000).
[8] *Melendez v. Padilla*, 304 S.W.3d 850, 852–53 (Tex. App.—El Paso 2010, no pet.).
[9] *Melendez v. Padilla*, 304 S.W.3d 850, 853 (Tex. App.—El Paso 2010, no pet.).
[10] *Harris v. Rowe*, 593 S.W.2d 303, 306 (Tex. 1979).
[11] *Compare Pickering v. First Greenville Nat'l Bank*, 495 S.W.2d 16, 19 (Tex. Civ. App.—Dallas 1973, writ ref'd n.r.e.) (common law accord and satisfaction may be supported based upon an unliquidated debt if the defendant provides additional or substitute consideration), *and* Tex. Bus. & Com. Code Ann. § 3.311(a) (debt must be unliquidated or subject to a bona fide dispute).
[12] *Compare Anderson Dev. Co. v. Producers Grain*, 558 S.W.2d 924, 926 (Tex. Civ. App.—Eastland 1977, writ ref'd n.r.e.) (the parties may agree that the new promise itself constitutes satisfaction of the accord), *and* Tex. Bus. & Com. Code Ann. § 3.311(a) ("The claimant obtained payment of the instrument.").
[13] *Lopez v. Munoz, Hockema & Reed, L.L.P.*, 22 S.W.3d 857, 863 (Tex. 2000).
[14] *Pickering v. First Greenville Nat'l Bank*, 495 S.W.2d 16, 19 (Tex. Civ. App.—Dallas 1973, writ ref'd n.r.e.). In most cases, the consideration element is satisfied when the original debt is either unliquidated or otherwise disputed. *Hycarbex, Inc. v. Anglo-Suisse, Inc.*, 927 S.W.2d 103, 110 (Tex. App.—Houston [14th Dist.] 1996, no writ). However, the consideration element may also be satisfied if the defendant furnishes additional or substitute consideration. (*Pickering v. First Greenville Nat'l Bank*, 495 S.W.2d 16, 19 (Tex. Civ. App.—Dallas 1973, writ ref'd n.r.e.)).

AFFIRMATIVE DEFENSES

(2) In which the parties agree to the discharge of an existing obligation by means of a lesser payment tendered and accepted;[15] and

(3) Which agreement is performed.[16]

16-3:2 Elements—Statutory

(1) The defendant tenders an instrument or an accompanying written communication containing a conspicuous statement to the effect that the instrument was tendered as full satisfaction of the claim;[17]

(2) The defendant in good faith tendered an instrument to the claimant as full satisfaction of the claim;[18]

(3) The amount of the claim was unliquidated or subject to a bona fide dispute;[19] and

(4) The claimant obtained payment of the instrument.[20]

16-3:3 Other Substantive Issues

The most difficult part of proving an accord and satisfaction is showing that an agreement existed between the parties. The agreement may be either express or implied,[21] but in either event, the language which sets out the accord must be "so clear, full, and explicit that it is not susceptible of any other interpretation."[22]

Because an accord may be implied, a plaintiff may unwittingly enter into an accord. Courts routinely hold that a plaintiff who accepts payment which is clearly conditioned as an accord and satisfaction has impliedly agreed to the accord and satisfaction[23] even if the plaintiff crossed out the language creating the condition or included protest language on the endorsement of the check.[24] The rule is the same under the UCC.[25]

---

[15] *Lopez v. Munoz, Hockema & Reed, L.L.P.*, 22 S.W.3d 857, 863 (Tex. 2000).

[16] In some instances, the parties may agree that the new promise itself constitutes satisfaction of the accord. *See Anderson Dev. Co. v. Producers Grain*, 558 S.W.2d 924, 926 (Tex. Civ. App.—Eastland 1977, writ ref'd n.r.e.).

[17] Tex. Bus. & Com. Code Ann. § 3.311(b).

[18] Tex. Bus. & Com. Code Ann. § 3.311(a).

[19] Tex. Bus. & Com. Code Ann. § 3.311(a).

[20] Tex. Bus. & Com. Code Ann. § 3.311(a).

[21] *Lopez v. Munoz, Hockema & Reed, L.L.P.*, 22 S.W.3d 857, 863 (Tex. 2000).

[22] *American Nat'l Ins. Co. v. Gifford-Hill & Co.*, 673 S.W.2d 915, 921 (Tex. App.—Dallas 1984, writ ref'd n.r.e.).

[23] *Pileco, Inc. v. HCI, Inc.*, 735 S.W.2d 561, 562–63 (Tex. App.—Houston [1st Dist.] 1987, writ ref'd n.r.e.).

[24] *Pileco, Inc. v. HCI, Inc.*, 735 S.W.2d 561, 562–63 (Tex. App.—Houston [1st Dist.] 1987, writ ref'd n.r.e.) (protest language); *Hixson v. Cox*, 633 S.W.2d 330, 331–32 (Tex. App.—Dallas 1982, writ ref'd n.r.e.) (crossing out the language creating the condition and adding protest language).

[25] Tex. Bus. & Com. Code Ann. § 3.311, UCC Comment 1–3.

16-4 Arbitration and Award

Parties who have submitted to a valid arbitration proceeding resulting in an award are not allowed to later attempt to litigate the same issue in court.[26] The issues covered by the defense of arbitration and award include those which were submitted to the arbitrator or those which the arbitrator made an award based upon.[27] An arbitration and award defense does not apply if the award was based upon fraud, misconduct, or such gross mistake as would imply bad faith or failure to exercise an honest judgment.[28]

16-4:1 Elements

(1) A dispute which was submitted to arbitration;[29]

(2) An award was made upon the submitted dispute;[30] and

(3) Such award was not based upon fraud, misconduct, or such gross mistake as would imply bad faith or failure to exercise an honest judgment.[31]

16-5 Release

A release is a contractual agreement between parties which extinguishes any claim to liability the plaintiff may have.[32] The scope of the release may be determined based upon the language of the release itself.[33] In some circumstances, the scope of the release is to be determined by the language of the release itself and the information available to both parties.[34] A release may cover both known and unknown injuries.[35] However, a release does not cover claims that existed at the time of the release if the claims do not fall clearly within the release's subject matter.[36] As a contractual agreement, a release may be subject to further avoidance defenses, such as mutual mistake or fraud.[37]

16-5:1 Elements

(1) The parties enter into a contract;[38] and

(2) The contract releases the defendant from liability.[39]

---

[26] *Alderman v. Alderman*, 296 S.W.2d 312, 315 (Tex. App.—San Antonio 1956, writ ref'd).

[27] *Albert v. Albert*, 391 S.W.2d 186, 189 (Tex Civ. App.—San Antonio 1965, writ ref'd n.r.e.).

[28] *Albert v. Albert*, 391 S.W.2d 186, 188 (Tex. Civ. App.—San Antonio 1965, writ ref'd n.r.e.).

[29] *Albert v. Albert*, 391 S.W.2d 186, 189 (Tex. Civ. App.—San Antonio 1965, writ ref'd n.r.e.).

[30] *Albert v. Albert*, 391 S.W.2d 186, 189 (Tex. Civ. App.—San Antonio 1965, writ ref'd n.r.e.).

[31] *Albert v. Albert*, 391 S.W.2d 186, 188 (Tex. Civ. App.—San Antonio 1965, writ ref'd n.r.e.).

[32] *Williams v. Glash*, 789 S.W.2d 261, 264 (Tex. 1990).

[33] *Williams v. Glash*, 789 S.W.2d 261, 264 (Tex. 1990).

[34] *Williams v. Glash*, 789 S.W.2d 261, 264 (Tex. 1990).

[35] *Williams v. Glash*, 789 S.W.2d 261, 264 (Tex. 1990).

[36] *City of Brownsville ex rel. Pub. Utils. Bd. v. AEP Tex. Cent. Co.*, 348 S.W.3d 348, 354–56 (Tex. App.—Dallas 2011, pet. denied).

[37] *Williams v. Glash*, 789 S.W.2d 261, 264 (Tex. 1990).

[38] *Williams v. Glash*, 789 S.W.2d 261, 264 (Tex. 1990).

[39] *Williams v. Glash*, 789 S.W.2d 261, 264 (Tex. 1990).

AFFIRMATIVE DEFENSES 465

16-5:2 Other Substantive Issues

A plaintiff may avoid a release based upon a contractual-avoidance theory.[40] There are also situations in which a plaintiff or a health care provider may avoid a release because the health care provider's statutory lien has not been properly paid.[41]

16-6 Waiver

The defense of waiver is often referenced alongside an estoppel defense.[42] Waiver can either be express or implied under the circumstances.[43] Waiver can never operate as an offensive sword.[44] Waiver can only operate as a defensive shield.[45] A waiver operates as a complete bar to the enforcement of the waived right.[46]

16-6:1 Elements

(1) The plaintiff held an existing right, benefit, or advantage;[47]

(2) The plaintiff had actual knowledge of its existence;[48] and

(3) The plaintiff had actual intent to relinquish the right, or intentional conduct inconsistent with the right.[49]

Even a non-waiver provision in a contract may be waived, but the waiver may not "be anchored in the same conduct the parties specifically agreed would not give rise to a waiver of contract rights."[50] For example, a landlord's acceptance of late rental payments does not waive the non-waiver provision of the underlying commercial lease or the requirement that rent is due on the date specified in the lease and, therefore, the landlord was still able to enforce other rights in the lease agreement and prohibit the tenant from extending the lease under another provision based upon timely payment of rent.[51]

16-7 Res Judicata and Collateral Estoppel

Res judicata and collateral estoppel seek to prevent the relitigation of issues or claims. Res judicata, or claim preclusion, seeks to prevent the relitigation of claims which

---

[40] *Williams v. Glash*, 789 S.W.2d 261, 264 (Tex. 1990).
[41] Tex. Prop. Code Ann. § 55.007(a); *McAllen Hosps., L.P. v. State Farm Cty. Mut. Ins. Co.*, 433 S.W.3d 535, 538 (Tex. 2014).
[42] *Ulico Cas. Co. v. Allied Pilots Ass'n*, 262 S.W.3d 773, 778 (Tex. 2008).
[43] *Motor Vehicle Bd. of Texas Dep't of Transp. v. El Paso Indep. Auto. Dealers Ass'n, Inc.*, 1 S.W.3d 108, 111 (Tex. 1999).
[44] *Washington Nat'l Ins. Co. v. Craddock*, 109 S.W.2d 165, 166 (Tex. Comm'n App. 1937).
[45] *Washington Nat'l Ins. Co. v. Craddock*, 109 S.W.2d 165, 166 (Tex. Comm'n App. 1937) (insurance company's initial payment of a claim outside of the insurance policy could not support the creation of a right of payment in favor of the insured).
[46] *See Motor Vehicle Bd. of Tex. Dep't of Transp. v. El Paso Indep. Auto. Dealers Ass'n, Inc.*, 1 S.W.3d 108, 111 (Tex. 1999).
[47] *Ulico Cas. Co. v. Allied Pilots Ass'n*, 262 S.W.3d 773, 778 (Tex. 2008).
[48] *Ulico Cas. Co. v. Allied Pilots Ass'n*, 262 S.W.3d 773, 778 (Tex. 2008).
[49] *Ulico Cas. Co. v. Allied Pilots Ass'n*, 262 S.W.3d 773, 778 (Tex. 2008).
[50] *Shields, LP v. Bradberry*, No. 15-0803, 2017 WL 2023602 (Tex. May 12, 2017).
[51] *Shields, LP v. Bradberry*, No. 15-0803, 2017 WL 2023602 (Tex. May 12, 2017).

were actually brought, or could have been actually brought, in a prior lawsuit. The doctrine of res judicata reflects the fact that, upon the entry of judgment, the plaintiff's causes of action merge into the judgment and any attempt to relitigate the claim is barred.[52] Collateral estoppel, or issue preclusion, seeks to prevent the relitigation of issues which have already been decided for or against a party.[53] Collateral estoppel can be used as either an offensive sword or a defensive shield.[54]

16-7:1 Elements—Res Judicata

(1) A prior final judgment on the merits by a court of competent jurisdiction;[55]

(2) Identity of parties or those in privity with them;[56] and

(3) A second action based on the same claims as were raised or could have been raised in the first action.[57]

16-7:2 Elements—Collateral Estoppel

(1) The facts sought to be litigated in the second action were fully and fairly litigated in the first action;[58]

(2) Those facts were essential to the judgment in the first action;[59] and

(3) The parties were cast as adversaries in the first action.[60]

16-7:3 Other Substantive Issues

The main thrust of res judicata is the scope of the doctrine. Simply speaking, the doctrine prohibits bringing any claims which were brought or arise out of the same subject matter and could have been brought if the plaintiff had exercised due diligence.[61]

Collateral estoppel bars relitigation of issues which are common to separate causes of action. Therefore, if two or more causes of action have similar discrete issues, collateral estoppel prevents the relitigation of the issue after one has been decided.[62]

A judicial decision applies retroactively to pending cases, even those pending on appeal, but res judicata precludes a collateral attack on a judgment that has become final in order to bring litigation to an end and avoid the possibility of reopening litigation that is the subject of a final judgment because the governing law later changes.[63]

---

[52] *Jeanes v. Henderson*, 688 S.W.2d 100, 103 (Tex. 1985).
[53] *Sysco Food Servs., Inc. v. Trapnell*, 890 S.W.2d 796, 801 (Tex. 1994).
[54] *See Eagle Props., Ltd. v. Scharbauer*, 807 S.W.2d 714, 722 (Tex. 1990).
[55] *Amstadt v. U.S. Brass Corp.*, 919 S.W.2d 644, 652 (Tex. 1996).
[56] *Amstadt v. U.S. Brass Corp.*, 919 S.W.2d 644, 652 (Tex. 1996).
[57] *Amstadt v. U.S. Brass Corp.*, 919 S.W.2d 644, 652 (Tex. 1996).
[58] *Sysco Food Servs., Inc. v. Trapnell*, 890 S.W.2d 796, 801 (Tex. 1994).
[59] *Sysco Food Servs., Inc. v. Trapnell*, 890 S.W.2d 796, 801 (Tex. 1994).
[60] *Sysco Food Servs., Inc. v. Trapnell*, 890 S.W.2d 796, 801 (Tex. 1994).
[61] *Texas Water Rights Commc'n v. Crow Iron Works*, 582 S.W.2d 768, 772 (Tex. 1979); *Abbott Labs. v. Gravis*, 470 S.W.2d 639, 642 (Tex. 1971).
[62] *See Bonniwell v. Beech Aircraft Corp.*, 663 S.W.2d 816, 818–20 (Tex. 1984).
[63] *Engelman Irrigation Dist. v. Shields Bros., Inc.*, No. 15-0188, 2017 WL 1042933, *3 (Tex. Mar. 17, 2017) ("For any rational and workable judicial system, at some point litigation must

16-8 Discharge in Bankruptcy

Following the completion of a bankruptcy proceeding, certain debtors are entitled to a discharge of their debts.[64] Once discharged, a debtor is protected from a creditor's attempt to collect a discharged debt.[65]

16-8:1 Elements

(1) A debtor in bankruptcy;[66]

(2) Was granted a discharge;[67]

(3) The debt which the plaintiff wishes to collect is covered by the discharge.[68]

16-8:2 Other Substantive Issues

If the plaintiff alleges that the defendant's debt has been discharged in bankruptcy, the defendant is not required to affirmatively plead discharge.[69] However, a plaintiff's mere allegations that the defendant has filed for bankruptcy, without specifying whether the defendant's debt to the plaintiff was discharged, does not relieve the defendant of his obligation to affirmatively plead discharge.[70] A defendant may revive a debt which has been discharged if, after the discharge, the defendant makes a legally binding obligation to pay the debt.[71]

16-9 License

License is a consent based defense to a trespass to real property claim.[72] When the plaintiff has pleaded and proven its ownership to land and the defendant's entry upon the land, the defendant must then establish that it had a license to enter the land to avoid liability.[73] A license may either arise from actual or apparent consent.[74]

---

come to an end, so that parties can go on with their lives and the system can move on to other disputes.").

[64] *E.g.*, 11 U.S.C.A. §§ 727, 1141, 1228(a), 1228(b), 1328(b).

[65] 11 U.S.C.A. § 524(a).

[66] 11 U.S.C.A. § 524(a).

[67] 11 U.S.C.A. § 524(a).

[68] Certain statutes except debts from discharge. *E.g.*, 11 U.S.C.A. § 523(a).

[69] *Seiffert v. Bowden*, 556 S.W.2d 406, 409 (Tex. Civ. App.—Corpus Christi 1977, no writ).

[70] *Seiffert v. Bowden*, 556 S.W.2d 406, 409 (Tex. Civ. App.—Corpus Christi 1977, no writ).

[71] *Moore v. Dilworth*, 179 S.W.2d 940, 942 (Tex. 1944).

[72] *Stone Res., Inc. v. Barnett*, 661 S.W.2d 148, 151 (Tex. App.—Houston [1st Dist.] 1983, no writ).

[73] *Stone Res., Inc. v. Barnett*, 661 S.W.2d 148, 151 (Tex. App.—Houston [1st Dist.] 1983, no writ).

[74] *General Mills Rests., Inc. v. Tex. Wings, Inc.*, 12 S.W.3d 827, 835 (Tex. App.—Dallas 2000, no pet.).

16-9:1 Elements

(1) The plaintiff gave its consent for the defendant to enter:[75]

   (a) Actual consent;[76] or

   (b) Apparent consent;[77] and

(2) The defendant's entry was within the scope of the plaintiff's consent.[78]

16-10 Assumption of The Risk and Contributory Negligence

Express assumption of the risk is a complete bar to recovery.[79] Contributory negligence, on the other hand, generally only proportionately reduces the plaintiff's recovery.[80] In cases where the plaintiff's contributory negligence is greater than 50 percent, the plaintiff's recovery is completely barred.[81]

16-10:1 Elements—Express Assumption of the Risk

(1) The plaintiff consented to the dangerous activity;[82] and

(2) The plaintiff's consent was:

   (a) Knowing;[83] and

   (b) Express.[84]

16-10:2 Elements—Contributory Negligence

(1) The plaintiff's fault;[85]

---

[75] *General Mills Rests., Inc. v. Tex. Wings, Inc.*, 12 S.W.3d 827, 835 (Tex. App.—Dallas 2000, no pet.). Consent may be manifested by the conduct of the owner or the condition of the property.

[76] *General Mills Rests., Inc. v. Tex. Wings, Inc.*, 12 S.W.3d 827, 835 (Tex. App.—Dallas 2000, no pet.).

[77] *General Mills Rests., Inc. v. Tex. Wings, Inc.*, 12 S.W.3d 827, 835 (Tex. App.—Dallas 2000, no pet.). Apparent, or implied consent, only exists when "the owner (i) has actual knowledge that people have been entering the land and (ii) fails to take reasonable steps to prevent or discourage those persons from entering the land."

[78] *Loftus v. Maxey*, 11 S.W. 272, 273 (Tex. 1889) (plaintiff's consent to allow the defendant to enter onto her property and remove personal property would not encompass the defendant's forcible entry).

[79] *Farley v. M M Cattle Co.*, 529 S.W.2d 751, 758 (Tex. 1975).

[80] Tex. Civ. Prac. & Rem. Code Ann. § 33.012(a).

[81] Tex. Civ. Prac. & Rem. Code Ann. § 33.001.

[82] *Farley v. M M Cattle Co.*, 529 S.W.2d 751, 758 (Tex. 1975).

[83] *Farley v. M M Cattle Co.*, 529 S.W.2d 751, 758 (Tex. 1975).

[84] *Farley v. M M Cattle Co.*, 529 S.W.2d 751, 758 (Tex. 1975). The plaintiff's express consent must clearly and unequivocally list the risk to be assumed. *Newman v. Tropical Visions, Inc.*, 891 S.W.2d 713, 719 (Tex. App.—San Antonio 1994, writ denied).

[85] Tex. Civ. Prac. & Rem. Code Ann. § 33.003(a). "Fault" includes any negligent act or omission, or any conduct that violates an applicable legal standard. "Fault" also includes the former concept of implied assumption of the risk. (*Farley v. M M Cattle Co.*, 529 S.W.2d 751, 758 (Tex. 1975)).

AFFIRMATIVE DEFENSES

(2) Contributed to the plaintiff's injury.[86]

For a discussion of the Texas Comparative Fault scheme, *see* Chapter 18.

16-10:3 Other Substantive Issues

Implied assumption of the risk is not a viable defense, and therefore cannot be a strict bar to recovery.[87] Any evidence of the plaintiff's implied assumption of risk may be considered when apportioning the plaintiff's fault under Civil Practice and Remedies Code Chapter 33.[88]

16-11 Duress

Duress is an avoidance defense to a contract action.[89] Generally, duress exists when a person threatens another in such a manner as to destroy the free will of the party against whom the threat was issued, thereby causing him to do what he would not otherwise have done.[90] Duress does not make a contract void, but rather makes a contract voidable by the party who experienced the duress.[91]

16-11:1 Elements

(1) The opposing party threatens to do something he has no legal right to do;[92]

(2) The threat was of such a character as to destroy the free will of the party against whom it was issued and thereby overcome his will and cause him to do what he would not otherwise have done;[93]

(3) The threatened injury was imminent;[94] and

(4) The party against whom the threat was issued had no immediate means of protection.[95]

16-11:2 Other Substantive Issues

Generally, the activity must threaten physical violence or wrongful execution on property. However, an economic threat may constitute duress if the threatening party is the cause of the defendant's economic duress.[96] Additionally, the threat must be immi-

---

[86] Tex. Civ. Prac. & Rem. Code Ann. § 33.003(a).
[87] *Farley v. M M Cattle Co.*, 529 S.W.2d 751, 758 (Tex. 1975).
[88] *Farley v. M M Cattle Co.*, 529 S.W.2d 751, 758 (Tex. 1975); *see* Tex. Civ. Prac. & Rem. Code Ann. § 33.003 (requiring the parties' "fault" to be apportioned).
[89] *See Country Cupboard, Inc. v. Texstar Corp.*, 570 S.W.2d 70, 74 (Tex. Civ. App.—Dallas 1978, writ ref'd n.r.e.).
[90] *Dale v. Simon*, 267 S.W. 467, 470 (Tex. Comm'n App. 1924).
[91] *Country Cupboard, Inc. v. Texstar Corp.*, 570 S.W.2d 70, 74 (Tex. Civ. App.—Dallas 1978, writ ref'd n.r.e.).
[92] *Dale v. Simon*, 267 S.W. 467, 470 (Tex. Comm'n App. 1924).
[93] *Dale v. Simon*, 267 S.W. 467, 470 (Tex. Comm'n App. 1924).
[94] *Dale v. Simon*, 267 S.W. 467, 470 (Tex. Comm'n App. 1924).
[95] *Dale v. Simon*, 267 S.W. 467, 470 (Tex. Comm'n App. 1924).
[96] *First Tex. Sav. Ass'n of Dallas v. Dicker Ctr.*, 631 S.W.2d 179, 185–86 (Tex. App.—Tyler 1982, no writ).

nent so that the party against whom the duress is exerted does not presently have protection.[97] Therefore, if the party exerting the duress must go to the courts to enforce the threat, duress is ordinarily not present.[98]

16-12 Estoppel

The defense of estoppel is composed of several different forms of estoppel. Each form of estoppel is an equitable defense which attempts to prevent unfairness because the opposing party has taken an inconsistent position, attitude or course of conduct. Additionally, a party asserting estoppel must not have "unclean hands."[99]

16-12:1 Elements—Equitable Estoppel

(1) A false representation or concealment of material facts;[100]

(2) Made with knowledge, actual or constructive, of those facts;[101]

(3) With the intention that it should be acted on;[102]

(4) To a party without knowledge, or the means of knowledge of those facts;[103]

(5) Who detrimentally relied upon the misrepresentation.[104]

16-12:2 Elements—Promissory Estoppel

(1) The defendant promises to sign a writing that would satisfy the statute of frauds;[105]

(2) The defendant should have expected that his promise would lead the plaintiff to experience a definite and substantial injury;[106]

(3) Such an injury occurred;[107] and

(4) The court must enforce the promise to avoid injustice.[108]

---

[97] *See Tower Contracting Co., Inc. of Tex. v. Burden Bros., Inc.*, 482 S.W.2d 330, 336 (Tex. App.—Dallas 1972, writ ref'd n.r.e.).
[98] *Ward v. Scarborough*, 236 S.W. 434, 437 (Tex. Comm'n App. 1922, judgm't adopted).
[99] *El Paso Nat. Bank v. S.W. Numismatic Inv. Grp., Ltd.*, 548 S.W.2d 942, 949 (Tex. App.—El Paso 1977, no writ).
[100] *Schroeder v. Tex. Iron Works, Inc.*, 813 S.W.2d 483, 489 (Tex. 1991).
[101] *Schroeder v. Tex. Iron Works, Inc.*, 813 S.W.2d 483, 489 (Tex. 1991).
[102] *Schroeder v. Tex. Iron Works, Inc.*, 813 S.W.2d 483, 489 (Tex. 1991).
[103] *Schroeder v. Tex. Iron Works, Inc.*, 813 S.W.2d 483, 489 (Tex. 1991).
[104] *Schroeder v. Tex. Iron Works, Inc.*, 813 S.W.2d 483, 489 (Tex. 1991).
[105] *Nagle v. Nagle*, 633 S.W.2d 796, 800 (Tex. 1982).
[106] *Nagle v. Nagle*, 633 S.W.2d 796, 800 (Tex. 1982).
[107] *Nagle v. Nagle*, 633 S.W.2d 796, 800 (Tex. 1982).
[108] *Nagle v. Nagle*, 633 S.W.2d 796, 800 (Tex. 1982).

16-12:3 Elements—Judicial Estoppel

(1) A litigant successfully maintains one position in a judicial proceeding;[109] and

(2) Attempts to maintain a clearly inconsistent position in another proceeding to obtain an unfair advantage.[110]

Judicial estoppel is not applicable if the inconsistent statements were made either under duress, by mistake, or inadvertently.[111]

The Texas Supreme Court has created the "acceptance of benefits doctrine" based on the principle of estoppel. This doctrine applies when a party accepts the benefits of a judgment while simultaneously complaining about the judgment on appeal. The Texas Supreme Court has applied the doctrine only twice in two divorce cases. In 1950, the court concluded that a husband could not prosecute an appeal of a divorce decree after having already accepted $7,700 that had been awarded to him under the judgment he appealed.[112] The Court's second application of the doctrine came in 2017 when the court narrowed the doctrine as it applies to appeals of divorce decrees, saying "merely using, holding, controlling, or securing possession of community property awarded in a divorce decree does not constitute clear intent to acquiesce in the judgment and will not preclude an appeal absent prejudice to the nonappealing party."[113] The court also discussed its narrowing of the related voluntary payment rule—a doctrine that may prevent a judgment debtor from appealing a judgment he has already paid. The court explained: "Under the modern view of the voluntary-payment rule, payment of a judgment does not bar prosecution of appeal unless the judgment debtor clearly misled the opposing party regarding the judgment debtor's intent to pursue an appeal."[114]

16-13 Illegality

The law will not enforce an agreement that is illegal or against public policy. Such contracts may include gambling debts,[115] unreasonable restraints on trade,[116] or contracts which further criminal activity.[117]

---

[109] *Ferguson v. Bldg. Materials Corp.*, 295 S.W.3d 642, 643 (Tex. 2009). The person must intentionally take this first position. If the person takes the position because of mere inadvertence, fraud or mistake, another party may not claim judicial estoppel. (*Moore v. Neff*, 629 S.W.2d 827, 829 (Tex. App.—Houston [14th Dist.] 1982, writ ref'd n.r.e.)).

[110] *Ferguson v. Bldg. Materials Corp.*, 295 S.W.3d 642, 643 (Tex. 2009).

[111] *Moore v. Neff*, 629 S.W.2d 827, 829 (Tex. App.—Houston [14th Dist.] 1982, writ ref'd n.r.e.).

[112] *Kramer v. Kastleman*, 508 S.W.3d 211, 218 (Tex. 2017) (citing *Carle v. Carle*, 234 S.W.2d 1002, 1002–5).

[113] *Kramer v. Kastleman*, 508 S.W.3d 211, 228 (Tex. 2017).

[114] *Kramer v. Kastleman*, 508 S.W.3d 211, 228 (Tex. 2017) (citing *BMG Direct Mktg., Inc. v. Peake*, 178 S.W.3d 763, 770 (Tex. 2005).

[115] *Tanner v. Jackson*, 246 S.W.2d 319, 321 (Tex. Civ. App.—Amarillo 1952, no writ) ("The courts do not recognize the legality of a gambling debt.").

[116] *See* Tex. Bus. & Com. Code Ann. §§ 15.50-15.52 (covenants not to compete).

[117] *Lewkowicz v. El Paso Apparel Corp.*, 625 S.W.2d 301, 304 (Tex. 1981) (criminal statute prohibiting the compounding of a criminal offense).

16-13:1 Elements

(1) A contract is:

- Illegal;[118] or

- Against public policy.[119]

16-13:2 Other Substantive Issues

The defendant need not affirmatively plead the illegality of a document if the document's illegality is apparent from the plaintiff's pleadings.[120] A contract's illegality may turn on a penal statute[121] or a civil statute.[122] An agreement which is illegal in Texas is unenforceable even if the agreement would not be illegal in the jurisdiction in which it was entered into.[123]

An exception to the statute of frauds is a counter-defense to the defense of statute of frauds and the burden falls on the plaintiff to establish it.[124]

16-14 Failure of Consideration

Failure of consideration and a total lack of consideration are two separate concepts. Failure of consideration occurs when the promised performance fails.[125] A lack of consideration occurs when, at inception, the contract does not impose obligations upon both parties.[126] A failure of consideration must be affirmatively pleaded.[127] A defendant may only allege a lack of consideration to a written contract if the defendant submits a verified pleading to that affect.[128]

16-14:1 Elements

(1) The parties entered into an agreement;[129]

---

[118] *Lewkowicz v. El Paso Apparel Corp.*, 625 S.W.2d 301, 304 (Tex. 1981).
[119] *Lewkowicz v. El Paso Apparel Corp.*, 625 S.W.2d 301, 304 (Tex. 1981).
[120] *Phillips v. Phillips*, 820 S.W.2d 785, 789 (Tex. 1991).
[121] *Lewkowicz v. El Paso Apparel Corp.*, 625 S.W.2d 301, 304 (Tex. 1981) (criminal statute prohibiting the compounding of a criminal offense).
[122] *Mabry v. Priester*, 338 S.W.2d 704, 706 (Tex. 1960) (violation of statute regulating practice of architecture).
[123] *Lewkowicz v. El Paso Apparel Corp.*, 625 S.W.2d 301, 304 (Tex. 1981).
[124] *Gilbert Tex. Constr., L.P. v. Underwriters at Lloyd's London*, 327 S.W.3d 118, 124 (Tex. 2010).
[125] *Cheung-Loon, LLC v. Cergon, Inc.*, 392 S.W.3d 738, 747 (Tex. App.—Dallas 2012, no pet.).
[126] *Cheung-Loon, LLC v. Cergon, Inc.*, 392 S.W.3d 738, 747 (Tex. App.—Dallas 2012, no pet.).
[127] Tex. R. Civ. P. 94.
[128] Tex. R. Civ. P. 93.
[129] *Cheung-Loon, LLC v. Cergon, Inc.*, 392 S.W.3d 738, 747 (Tex. App.—Dallas 2012, no pet.) ("[A] failure of consideration occurs when, because of some supervening cause arising after the contract is formed, the promised performance fails."); *Stewart v. U.S. Leasing Corp.*, 702 S.W.2d 288, 290 (Tex. App.—Houston [1st Dist.] 1985, no writ) (same); *O'Shea v. Coronado Transmission Co.*, 656 S.W.2d 557, 563 (Tex. App.—Corpus Christi 1983, writ ref'd n.r.e.) (same).

AFFIRMATIVE DEFENSES

(2) The consideration consisted of promises for future performance;[130] and

(3) The plaintiff does not fulfill its promise to perform.[131]

16-14:2 Other Substantive Issues

Where a total failure of consideration is a total bar to recovery,[132] a partial failure of consideration allows for the enforcement of part of the contract to the extent that the consideration did not fail.[133] If a defendant pleads a total failure of consideration, the defendant may be allowed present evidence of a partial failure of consideration.[134] There is a presumption that a written contract is supported by consideration.[135]

16-15 Fraud

The defense of fraud is a total bar to recovery under a contract. Additionally, a party's fraudulent conduct may serve as the basis for an independent cause of action,[136] grounds for rescission of a contract,[137] and grounds for recovery under an unjust enrichment theory.[138] Fraud is not presumed, but rather there is a presumption of fairness for transactions until fraud is proven.[139]

16-15:1 Elements

(1) A material representation was made;[140]

(2) The representation was false;[141]

---

[130] *Cheung-Loon, LLC v. Cergon, Inc.*, 392 S.W.3d 738, 747 (Tex. App.—Dallas 2012, no pet.) ("[A] failure of consideration occurs when, because of some supervening cause arising after the contract is formed, the promised performance fails."); *Stewart v. U.S. Leasing Corp.*, 702 S.W.2d 288, 290 (Tex. App.—Houston [1st Dist.] 1985, no writ) (same); *O'Shea v. Coronado Transmission Co.*, 656 S.W.2d 557, 563 (Tex. App.—Corpus Christi 1983, writ ref'd n.r.e.) (same).

[131] *Cheung-Loon, LLC v. Cergon, Inc.*, 392 S.W.3d 738, 747 (Tex. App.—Dallas 2012, no pet.) ("[A] failure of consideration occurs when, because of some supervening cause arising after the contract is formed, the promised performance fails."); *Stewart v. U.S. Leasing Corp.*, 702 S.W.2d 288, 290 (Tex. App.—Houston [1st Dist.] 1985, no writ) (same); *O'Shea v. Coronado Transmission Co.*, 656 S.W.2d 557, 563 (Tex. App.—Corpus Christi 1983, writ ref'd n.r.e.) (same).

[132] *Cheung-Loon, LLC v. Cergon, Inc.*, 392 S.W.3d 738, 748 (Tex. App.—Dallas 2012, no pet.).

[133] *Huff v. Speer*, 554 S.W.2d 259, 263 (Tex. Civ. App.—Houston [1st Dist.] 1977, writ ref'd n.r.e.); *Milner v. Boswell*, 377 S.W.2d 763, 764 (Tex. Civ. App.—Fort Worth 1964, no writ).

[134] *Milner v. Boswell*, 377 S.W.2d 763, 764 (Tex. Civ. App.—Fort Worth 1964, no writ).

[135] *See Wright v. Robert & St. John Motor Co.*, 58 S.W.2d 67, 68–69 (Tex. 1933); *Tripp Vill. v. MBank Lincoln Ctr.*, 774 S.W.2d 746, 749 (Tex. App.—Dallas 1989, writ denied).

[136] *See* Chapter 1—Common Law Fraud.

[137] *See* Chapter 3—Suit for Rescission.

[138] *See* Chapter 3—Unjust Enrichment.

[139] *Neuhaus v. Kain*, 557 S.W.2d 125, 136 (Tex. App.—Corpus Christi 1977, writ ref'd n.r.e.).

[140] *Formosa Plastics Corp. U.S.A. v. Presidio Eng'rs & Contractors, Inc.*, 960 S.W.2d 41, 47 (Tex. 1998).

[141] *Formosa Plastics Corp. U.S.A. v. Presidio Eng'rs & Contractors, Inc.*, 960 S.W.2d 41, 47 (Tex. 1998).

(3) When the speaker made the representation, he knew it was false or made it recklessly without knowledge of the truth and as a positive assertion;[142]

(4) The speaker made it with the intention that it should be acted upon by the party;[143]

(5) The party acted in reliance upon it;[144] and

(6) The party thereby suffered injury.[145]

16-15:2 Other Substantive Issues

When asserted as a defense, fraud is not subject to a statute of limitations.[146]

16-16 Statute of Frauds

The statute of frauds renders certain promises unenforceable unless the promise is memorialized in a writing and signed by the party against whom it is to be enforced. In addition to the statute of frauds, the parol evidence rule operates to exclude extraneous evidence regarding contract interpretation.[147]

16-16:1 Elements

(1) An agreement falls within the statute of frauds; and

    (a) A promise by an executor or administrator to answer out of his own estate for any debt or damage due from his testator or intestate;[148]

    (b) A promise by one person to answer for the debt, default or miscarriage of another person;[149]

    (c) An agreement made on consideration of marriage or on consideration of nonmarital conjugal cohabitation;[150]

    (d) A contract for the sale of real estate;[151]

    (e) A lease of real estate for a term longer than one year;[152]

---

[142] *Formosa Plastics Corp. U.S.A. v. Presidio Eng'rs & Contractors, Inc.*, 960 S.W.2d 41, 47 (Tex. 1998).

[143] *Formosa Plastics Corp. U.S.A. v. Presidio Eng'rs & Contractors, Inc.*, 960 S.W.2d 41, 47 (Tex. 1998).

[144] *Formosa Plastics Corp. U.S.A. v. Presidio Eng'rs & Contractors, Inc.*, 960 S.W.2d 41, 47 (Tex. 1998).

[145] *Formosa Plastics Corp. U.S.A. v. Presidio Eng'rs & Contractors, Inc.*, 960 S.W.2d 41, 47 (Tex. 1998).

[146] *Bodovsky v. Texoma Nat'l Bank of Sherman*, 584 S.W.2d 868, 874 (Tex. Civ. App.—Dallas 1979, writ ref'd n.r.e.).

[147] *David J. Sacks, P.C. v. Haden*, 266 S.W.3d 447, 450 (Tex. 2008).

[148] Tex. Bus. & Com. Code Ann. § 26.01(b).

[149] Tex. Bus. & Com. Code Ann. § 26.01(b).

[150] Tex. Bus. & Com. Code Ann. § 26.01(b).

[151] Tex. Bus. & Com. Code Ann. § 26.01(b).

[152] Tex. Bus. & Com. Code Ann. § 26.01(b).

(f) An agreement which is not to be performed within one year from the date of making the agreement;[153]

(g) A promise or agreement to pay a commission for the sale or purchase of:

   (i) an oil or gas mining lease;

   (ii) an oil or gas royalty;

   (iii) minerals; or

   (iv) a mineral interest;[154]

(h) An agreement, promise, contract or warranty of cure relating to medical care or results thereof made by a physician or health care provider as defined in Section 74.001, Civil Practice and Remedies Code;[155]

(i) Loan agreements in which the amount involved exceeds $50,000;[156]

(j) Sales of goods over $500;[157] and

(k) Leases of goods for a total payment of $1,000 or more.[158]

(2) The statute of frauds is not satisfied unless:

(a) The contract is in writing and signed by the party against whom it will be enforced;[159] or

(b) Promissory estoppel.

16-16:2 Other Substantive Issues

If a plaintiff attempts to artfully plead around the statute of frauds, a court will look to the substance of the plaintiff's allegations in determining whether damages are recoverable.[160] A plaintiff alleges fraud and seeks to recover benefit-of-the-bargain damages which would be barred by the statute of frauds.[161] A plaintiff would be similarly barred from pursuing a negligent misrepresentation claim.[162] A contract is not declared void "merely because it could have been performed illegally or contrary to public policy."[163] For example, a provision in a rental agreement that is so broad as to permit illegal activities was not void because it also permitted performance of the duty in a legal

---

[153] Tex. Bus. & Com. Code Ann. § 26.01(b).
[154] Tex. Bus. & Com. Code Ann. § 26.01(b).
[155] Tex. Bus. & Com. Code Ann. § 26.01(b).
[156] Tex. Bus. & Com. Code Ann. § 26.02.
[157] Tex. Bus. & Com. Code Ann. § 2.201(a).
[158] Tex. Bus. & Com. Code Ann. § 2A.201(a).
[159] Tex. Bus. & Com. Code Ann. § 26.01(a).
[160] *Baylor Univ. v. Sonnichsen*, 221 S.W.3d 632, 636 (Tex. 2007).
[161] *Baylor Univ. v. Sonnichsen*, 221 S.W.3d 632, 636 (Tex. 2007).
[162] *Lam v. Phuong Nguyen*, 335 S.W.3d 786, 790 (Tex. App.—Dallas 2011, pet. denied).
[163] *Philadelphia Indem. Ins. Co. v. White*, 490 S.W.3d 468, 483 (Tex. 2016). *See also In re Kasschau*, 11 S.W.3d 305, 312 (Tex.App.–Houston [14th Dist.] 1999, orig. proceeding) (quoting *Lewis v. Davis*, 145 Tex. 468, 199 S.W.2d 146, 148–149 (1947)).

manner.[164] A provision would be unenforceable per se only if it could not be performed without violating a legal duty.[165]

16-17 Statute of Limitations

See Chapter 17—Statutes of Limitations and Repose.

16-18 Laches

Laches is a similar concept to the statute of limitations. However, whereas the statute of limitations presents a hard deadline within which the plaintiff must bring suit, laches operates as an equitable device limiting the availability of equitable causes of action. Because of its equitable nature, laches does not impose a hard deadline within which the plaintiff must bring suit. Furthermore, a defendant may not assert laches when the plaintiff is pursuing a purely legal right.[166] Whether a right is "purely legal" looks to the substance, rather than the form of the right.[167]

16-18:1 Elements

(1) Unreasonable delay in asserting a legal or equitable right;[168] and

(2) A good faith change in position by the defendant because of the delay.[169]

16-18:2 Other Substantive Issues

Generally, laches will not bar a suit which is brought within the limitations period.[170] However, there are extraordinary circumstances where laches would prohibit the plaintiff's suit even if brought within the limitations period.[171] These instances include where allowing the action would work a "grave injustice."[172]

Although the Supreme Court of Texas has stated that a finding of laches requires a "change in position," the true scope of the doctrine is broader. A defendant who has been injured will prevail even if the defendant hasn't changed position.[173]

---

[164] *Philadelphia Indem. Ins. Co. v. White*, 490 S.W.3d 468, 483 (Tex. 2016).
[165] *Philadelphia Indem. Ins. Co. v. White*, 490 S.W.3d 468, 483 (Tex. 2016).
[166] *Dillard v. Broyles*, 633 S.W.2d 636, 645 (Tex. App.—Corpus Christi 1982, writ ref'd n.r.e.).
[167] *See Callahan v. Giles*, 155 S.W.2d 793, 795 (Tex. 1941) (the common law writ of mandamus is subject to laches because the proceeding is "largely controlled by equitable principles").
[168] *Caldwell v. Barnes*, 975 S.W.2d 535, 538 (Tex. 1998).
[169] *Caldwell v. Barnes*, 975 S.W.2d 535, 538 (Tex. 1998).
[170] *Caldwell v. Barnes*, 975 S.W.2d 535, 538 (Tex. 1998).
[171] *Caldwell v. Barnes*, 975 S.W.2d 535, 538 (Tex. 1998).
[172] *Culver v. Pickens*, 176 S.W.2d 167, 170 (Tex. 1943).
[173] *De Benavides v. Warren*, 674 S.W.2d 353, 362 (Tex. App.—San Antonio 1984, writ ref'd n.r.e.) (finding that when a plaintiff waited seven years to assert its rights, defendant proved laches by showing that it would be "more difficult to retrieve evidence").

16-19 Parental Immunity

The doctrine of parental immunity restricts the rights of children to bring tort actions against their parents.[174] The purpose of the doctrine is to prevent the judicial system from being used to disrupt the wide sphere of reasonable discretion which is necessary in order for parents to properly exercise their responsibility to provide nurture, care, and discipline for their children."[175]

The scope of the doctrine is limited. The doctrine does not extend to suits arising out of the parent's business activities[176] or to automobile accidents involving parents.[177] Even in these cases, however, there is no immunity for ordinary acts of negligence that "involve a reasonable exercise of parental authority or the exercise of ordinary parental discretion with respect to provisions for the care and necessities of the child."

Parental immunity survives the death of the child; thus, parents may plead the defense even in wrongful death cases.[178]

Parental immunity is an affirmative defense that must be specifically pleaded or it is waived.[179]

---

[174] *Shoemake v. Fogel, Ltd.*, 826 S.W.2d 933, 935 (Tex. 1992).
[175] *Shoemake v. Fogel, Ltd.*, 826 S.W.2d 933, 935 (Tex. 1992) (quoting *Felderhoff v. Felderhoff*, 473 S.W.2d 928, 933 (Tex. 1971)).
[176] *Felderhoff v. Felderhoff*, 473 S.W.2d at 933 (Tex. 1971).
[177] *Jilani v. Jilani*, 767 S.W.2d 671 (Tex. 1988).
[178] *Shoemake v. Fogel, Ltd.*, 826 S.W.2d 933, 937 (Tex. 1992).
[179] *Shoemake v. Fogel, Ltd.*, 826 S.W.2d 933, 937 (Tex. 1992).

CHAPTER 17

Statutes of Limitations and Repose*

This chapter discusses statutes of limitations and statutes of repose. The Texas Legislature establishes statutes of limitations within which a cause of action must be brought. A claimant's failure to bring the cause of action within the applicable limitations bars the cause of action. The applicable limitations period begins to run when the cause of action accrues[1]. A statute of repose, by contrast, bars certain causes of action after a certain time period has elapsed, whether or not the cause of action has accrued.

17-1 One-Year Statute of Limitations

The Texas Civil Practice and Remedies Code provides that the following causes of action are governed by the one-year statute of limitations:[2]

- Malicious prosecution
- Libel
- Slander
- Breach of promise to marry
- Setting aside sale of real property seized for nonpayment of ad valorem taxes

The Texas Agriculture Code provides a one-year limitations period for nuisance actions brought against an agricultural operation.[3] The Code provides: "No nuisance action may be brought against an agricultural operation that has lawfully been in operation for one year or more prior to the date on which the action is brought, if the conditions or circumstances complained of as constituting the basis for the nuisance action have existed substantially unchanged since the established date of operation."[4]

---

[*] The authors thank Kimberly Trimble for her assistance in the updating of this chapter.
[1] Notably, this book was being updated during the COVID-19 pandemic. During this time, the Texas Supreme Court by order tolled the statute of limitations across the board.
[2] Tex. Civ. Prac. & Rem. Code § 16.002.
[3] Tex. Agric. Code Ann. § 251.004.
[4] *Id.*

17-2 Two-Year Statute of Limitations

The Texas Civil Practice and Remedies Code provides that the following causes of action are governed by the two-year statute of limitations:[5]

- trespass for injury to the estate or to the property of another
- conversion of personal property
- taking or detaining the personal property of another
- personal injury
- forcible entry and detainer
- forcible detainer
- wrongful death

The two-year statute of limitations is broadly applicable to all tort actions, except for fraud actions, which are governed by the four-year limitations period,[6] including intentional infliction of emotional distress,[7] tortious interference with a business relationship,[8] tortious interference with contract,[9] civil conspiracy claims,[10] invasion of privacy,[11] legal malpractice,[12] an insurer's breach of duty of good faith and fair dealing,[13] and claims under the DTPA.[14]

---

[5] Tex. Civ. Prac. & Rem. Code Ann. § 16.003.

[6] Vol 5, Dorsaneo, Texas Litigation Guide, 72.02[1][b] (Matthew Bender); *Church v. Ortho Diagnostic Sys., Inc.*, 694 S.W.2d 552, 555–56 (Tex. App.—Corpus 1985, writ ref'd n.r.e.).

[7] *Bhalli v. Methodist Hosp.*, 896 S.W.2d 207, 211 (Tex. App.—Houston [1st Dist.] 1995, writ denied) (citing *Twyman v. Twyman*, 855 S.W.2d 619, 625 (Tex. 1993) (describing intentional infliction of emotional distress as a claim for personal injury falling within Section 16.003 of the Texas Civil Practice & Remedies Code)).

[8] If the underlying tort in the tortious interference claim is a defamatory remark, the statute of limitations may be one year. Defamation is subject to a one-year statute of limitations, Tex. Civ. Prac. & Rem. Code § 16.002(a), while tortious interference is subject to at least a two-year statute of limitations, *First Nat'l Bank of Eagle Pass v. Levine*, 721 S.W.2d 287, 289 (Tex. 1986). *See also Hurlbut v. Gulf Atl. Life Ins. Co.*, 749 S.W.2d 762, 766 (Tex. 1987) ("Likewise, we have applied a one-year statute of limitations to business disparagement claims when the gravamen of the complaint is defamatory injury to reputation and there is no evidence of special damages.").

[9] *First Nat'l Bank of Eagle Pass v. Levine*, 721 S.W.2d 287, 289 (Tex. 1986) (citing *Atomic Fuel Extraction Corp. v. Estate of Slick*, 386 S.W.2d 180 (Tex. Civ. App.—San Antonio 1964), writ ref'd n.r.e. (per curiam), 403 S.W.2d 784 (Tex. 1965)).

[10] *Cathey v. First City Bank of Aransas Pass*, 758 S.W.2d 818, 821–22 (Tex. App.—Corpus Christi 1988, writ denied).

[11] *Stevenson v. Koutzarov*, 795 S.W.2d 313, 319 (Tex. App.—Houston [1st Dist.] 1990, writ denied); *Covington v. Houston Post*, 743 S.W.2d 345, 347–48 (Tex. App.—Houston [14th Dist.] 1987, no writ).

[12] *Willis v. Maverick*, 760 S.W.2d 642, 644 (Tex. 1988) ("A cause of action for legal malpractice is in the nature of a tort and is thus governed by the two-year limitations statute.").

[13] *Wilson v. John Daugherty Realtors, Inc.*, 981 S.W.2d 723, 727 (Tex. App.—Houston [1st Dist.] 1998, no pet.).

[14] *Id.*; Tex. Bus. & Com. Code Ann. § 17.565 (Vernon 1987).

17-3 Three-Year Statute of Limitations

The Texas Business and Commerce Code provides a three-year statute of limitations for certain suits related to negotiable instruments. The following actions must be brought within three years:

- An action to enforce the obligation of a party to an unaccepted draft to pay the draft (or 10 years after the date of the draft, whichever period expires first)[15]

- An action to enforce the obligation of the acceptor of a certified check or the issuer of a teller's check, cashier's check or traveler's check must be commenced within three years after demand for payment is made to the acceptor or issuer[16]

- An action for conversion of an instrument, unless governed by other law regarding claims for indemnity or contribution[17]

The Texas Securities Act also provides a three-year limitations period for suits against an investment advisor or his representative for a violation of Section 12 of the Act (advisor registration and notice requirements) or an order under Section 23B or 23-2 of the Act (Cease and Desist Orders).[18] The Texas Civil Practice & Remedies Code applies a three-year limitations period to most suits against carriers of property for compensation or hire[19] and to suits against a person holding property in peaceable and adverse possession under title or color of title.[20]

17-4 Four-Year Statute of Limitations

The Texas Civil Practice & Remedies Code applies a four-year limitations period to the following causes of action:[21]

- Specific performance of a contract for the conveyance of real property
- Penalty or damages on the penal clause of a bond to convey real property
- Contract for a debt
- Fraud
- Breach of fiduciary duty
- Suit on the bond of an executor, administrator or guardian (four years from the death, resignation, removal or discharge)
- Suit against partner for settlement of partnership accounts
- Suit on an open or stated account or a mutual and current account concerning the trade of merchandise between merchants or their agents.

---

[15] Tex. Bus. & Com. Code Ann. § 3.118(c).
[16] *Id.* at § 3.118(d).
[17] *Id.* at § 3.118(g)(1) (This section also provides a three-year limitation period for an action for breach of warranty governed by the UCC.).
[18] Tex. Sec. Act § 33-1(D)(1).
[19] Tex. Civ. Prac. & Rem. Code Ann. § 16.006(a)–(c).
[20] Tex. Civ. Prac. & Rem. Code Ann. § 16.024.
[21] Tex. Civ. Prac. & Rem. Code Ann. § 16.004.

17-4:1 The Residual Four-Year Limitations Period

Section 16.051 of the Texas Civil Practice & Remedies Code provides a residual limitations period of four years for "every action for which there is no express limitations period." Actions that fall within the four-year residual period include:

- Action to reform a deed[22]
- Action to enforce partnership's debt against individual partners[23]
- Suit to set aside a default judgment[24]
- Suit for recession of a written instrument on the grounds of fraud.[25]

17-5 Five-Year Statute of Limitations

A five-year statute of limitations applies to suits for personal injuries if the injuries arise as a result of conduct that violates the following provisions of the Texas Penal Code:[26]

- Section 22.011(a)(1) (Sexual Assault)
- Section 22.021(a)(1)(A) (Aggravated Sexual Assault)
- Section 20A.02 (Trafficking of Persons)
- Section 43.05(a)(1) (Compelling Prostitution)

A suit against an investment advisor or his representative for fraud or fraudulent practices is also governed by a five-year limitations period.[27] Such suits may not be brought more than "five years after the violation occurs or more than three years after the person knew or should have known, by the exercise of reasonable diligence, of the occurrence of the violation."[28]

A five year limitations period applies to suits against a sheriff or other officer for the failure to return an execution issued in the person's favor.[29]

A five-year limitations period applies to suits against a person who holds real property in peaceable and adverse possession and who (1) cultivates, uses, or enjoys the property; (2) pays applicable taxes on the property; and (3) claims the property under a duly registered deed.[30]

---

[22] *Brown v. Havard*, 593 S.W.2d 939, 943 (Tex. 1980); *Trahan v. Mettlen*, 428 S.W.3d 905, 909 (Tex. App.—Texarkana 2014, no pet.) (applying residual four-year period to cause of action for reformation of deed to determine if mineral interests conveyed).

[23] *American Star Energy and Minerals Corp. v. Stowers*, 405 S.W.3d 905, 910 (Tex. App.—Amarillo 2013, pet. granted).

[24] *Klemm v. Schroeder*, 204 S.W.2d 675, 676-7 (Tex. Civ. App.—1947, no writ).

[25] *Smith v. Am. Econ. Ins. Co.*, 794 S.W.2d 574, 577 (Tex. App.—Fort Worth 1990, writ denied); *Johnston v. Barnes*, 717 S.W.2d 164, 165–66 (Tex. App.—Houston [14th Dist.] 1986, no writ) (applying four-year statute to action to set aside a settlement agreement on grounds of fraud); *Gwinn v. Associated Empr's Lloyds*, 280 S.W.2d 624 (Tex. Civ. App.—Fort Worth 1955, writ ref'd n.r.e.).

[26] Tex. Civ. Prac. & Rem. Code Ann. § 16.0045(b).

[27] Tex. Sec. Act § 33-1(D)(1).

[28] *Id.*

[29] Tex. Civ. Prac. & Rem. Code Ann. § 16.007.

[30] *Id.* at § 16.025(a).

17-6 Six-Year Statute of Limitations

The Texas Business & Commerce Code applies a six-year limitations period to the following actions related to negotiable instruments:

- Action to enforce the obligation of a party to pay a note payable at a definite time must be commenced within six years after the due date or dates stated in the note, or, if a due date is accelerated, within six years after the accelerated due date[31]
- Action to enforce the obligation of a party to pay the note if demand for payment is made to the maker of a note payable on demand[32]
- An action to enforce the obligation of a party to a certificate of deposit to pay the instrument (runs from the date demand is paid unless the instrument states a due date, in which case it runs from the due date)[33]
- Action to enforce the obligation of a party to pay an accepted draft, other than a certified check (runs from the due date or dates stated in the draft or acceptance if the obligation of the acceptor is payable at a definite time but runs from the date of the acceptance if the obligation of the acceptor is payable on demand).[34]

17-7 Ten-Year Statute of Limitations

A person must bring suit against another who holds real property in peaceable and adverse possession who cultivates, uses, or enjoys the property.[35]

A 10-year limitations period applies to enforcing judgments. A writ of execution must be issued, generally, within 10 years of the rendition of the judgment on which it is based.[36]

17-8 Fifteen-Year Statute of Limitations

A 15-year statute of limitations applies to suits for personal injuries if the injuries arise as a result of conduct that violates the following provisions of the Texas Penal Code:[37]

- Section 22.011(a)(2) (Sexual Assault of a Child)
- Section 22.021(a)(1)(B) (Aggravated Sexual Assault of a Child)
- Section 21.02 (Continuous Sexual Abuse of Young Child or Children)
- Section 20A.02(a)(7)(A), (B), (C), (D), or (H) or Section 20A.02(a)(8) (Various crimes against children being trafficked)
- Section 43.04(a)(2) (compelling prostitution by a child); or
- Section 21.11 (Indecency with a Child).

---

[31] Tex. Bus. & Com. Code Ann. § 3.118(a).
[32] *Id.* at § 3.118(b).
[33] *Id.* at § 3.118(e).
[34] Tex. Bus. & Com. Code Ann. § 3.118(f).
[35] Tex. Civ. Prac. & Rem. Code Ann. § 16.026.
[36] *Id.* at § 34.001.
[37] *Id.* at §16.0045(a).

17-9 Limitations Established or Modified by Agreement

Parties may agree to modify or extend the limitations period so long as the modification is "specific and for a reasonable time."[38] Parties may not agree to permanently waive the limitations period.[39] The agreement must modify the limitations period to a predetermined and reasonable period of time.[40]

17-10 Commencement of Limitation Period

Generally, a limitation period commences when the cause of action accrues.[41] Accrual can be said to occur, generally, when "the wrongful act effects an injury, regardless of when the plaintiff learned of such injury."[42] Examples of the general accrual date of some common causes of action include:

- *Breach of contract:* "[A] breach of contract claim accrues when the contract is breached"[43]

- *Personal Injury:* the date of the plaintiff's injury[44]

- *Debt Actions:* the date of maturity for a note payable at a specific time;[45] or, in the case of a note due on demand, the date of the note's making;[46] or, if demand is subject to a condition precedent, upon demand[47]

- *Breach of Fiduciary Duty:* upon the defendant's breach of duty[48]

- *Fraud:* upon the defendant's fraudulent misrepresentation or omission[49]

- *Conversion:* upon the defendant's successful conversion of personal property[50]

- *Trespass to Real Property:*
  - for a permanent trespass, upon the discovery of the injury;[51] or

---

[38] *Squyres v. Christian*, 253 S.W.2d 470, 472 (Tex. Civ. App.—Fort Worth 1952, writ ref'd n.r.e).

[39] *Id.*

[40] *American Alloy Steel v. Armco, Inc.*, 777 S.W.2d 173, 177 (Tex. App.—Houston [14th Dist.] 1989, no writ).

[41] *See, e.g.*, Tex. Civ. Prac. & Rem. Code Ann. § 16.002 (one-year limitation period begins to run "on the day the cause of action accrues"); § 16.003 (two-year limitation period expires "not later than two years after the day the cause of action accrues"); § 16.004 (four year limitation period expires "not later than four years after the day the cause of action accrues").

[42] *Moreno v. Sterling Drug, Inc.*, 787 S.W.2d 348, 351 (Tex. 1990).

[43] *Stine v. Stewart*, 80 S.W.3d 586, 592 (Tex. 2002).

[44] *Childs v. Haussecker*, 974 S.W.2d 31, 36 (Tex. 1998). However, the discovery rule might apply to certain injuries.

[45] *Loomis v. Republic Nat'l Bank of Dallas*, 653 S.W.2d 75, 77 (Tex. App.—Dallas 1983, writ ref'd n.r.e.).

[46] *Id.*

[47] *Id.*

[48] *Trousdale v. Henry*, 261 S.W.3d 221, 233 (Tex. App.—Houston [14th Dist.] 2008, pet. denied).

[49] *Quinn v. Press*, 140 S.W.2d 438, 440–41 (Tex. 1940).

[50] *Marathon Oil Co. v. Gulf Oil Corp.*, 130 S.W.2d 365 (Tex. Civ. App.—El Paso 1939), *rev'd in part Gulf Oil Corp. v. Marathon Oil Co.*, 152 S.W.2d 711 (1941).

[51] *Bayouth v. Lion Oil Co.*, 671 S.W.2d 867, 868 (Tex. 1984).

- for a temporary trespass, damages for any injury occurring two years prior to suit are recoverable[52]
- *Legal Malpractice:*
  - A cause of action for legal malpractice begins to run when the plaintiff discovers or should have discovered the facts establishing the elements of the plaintiff's cause of action.[53]
  - The cause of action is tolled until all appeals of the underlying suit are finalized.[54]

This general rule for accrual can be modified by statute. The following are examples of statutes defining accrual for certain types of actions:

- A healthcare liability claim (i.e., medical malpractice) must be commenced within two years from the occurrence of the breach or tort, unless the date of the negligence cannot be ascertained, in which case it runs from the date the medical or health care treatment that is the subject of the claim or the hospitalization for which the claim is made is completed.[55]
- A wrongful death action must be brought within two years of the date of death.[56]
- In cases involving negotiable instruments under the Texas Business & Commerce Code, the limitation period begins to run from the date defined in the statute.
- DTPA Actions.[57]
- Suits for accounting or suits on certain accounts.[58]

---

[52] *Id.*
[53] *Willis v. Maverick*, 760 S.W.2d 642, 646 (Tex. 1988).
[54] *Hughes v. Mahaney & Higgens*, 821 S.W.2d 154, 157 (Tex. 1991) ("when an attorney commits malpractice in the prosecution or defense of a claim that results in litigation, the statute of limitations on the malpractice claim against the attorney is tolled until all appeals on the underlying claim are exhausted"); *but see Apex Towing Co. v. Tolin*, 997 S.W.2d 903 ("Apex contends their claim was timely filed because of two tolling provisions. They first rely upon the tolling principle announced in Hughes . . . However, the Court has subsequently narrowed the tolling provision to situations where the client is continuing to use the same lawyer in the pending litigation."). *See also Murphy v. Campbell*, 964 S.W.2d 265, 272 (Tex. 1997).
[55] Tex. Civ. Prac. & Rem. Code Ann. § 74.251; *Earle v. Ratliff*, 998 S.W.2d 882, 886 (Tex. 1999).
[56] Tex. Civ. Prac. & Rem. Code Ann. § 16.003(b) (providing that the cause of action accrues on the date of death).
[57] Tex. Bus. & Com. Code Ann. § 17.565 ("All actions brought under this subchapter must be commenced within two years after the date on which the false, misleading, or deceptive act or practice occurred or within two years after the consumer discovered or in the exercise of reasonable diligence should have discovered the occurrence of the false, misleading, or deceptive act or practice.").
[58] Tex. Civ. Prac. & Rem. Code Ann. § 16.004 ("[T]he cause of action accrues on the day that the dealings in which the parties were interested together cease."). To establish when dealings have ceased, a defendant must prove more than the date of last payment. (*Capital One Bank (U.S.A.), N.A. v. Conti*, 345 S.W.3d 490, 492 (Tex. App.—San Antonio 2011, no pet.). A defendant's proof that it had stopped advertising with the plaintiff and had made a final payment was sufficient to establish that the dealings between the parties had "ceased"

17-11 Suspending and Extending the Limitations Period

17-11:1 Fraudulent Concealment

A party may not rely upon a statute of limitations defense to avoid liability where the party has committed fraud to prevent another from seeking redress within the limitations period. Fraudulent concealment is an affirmative defense to the statute of limitations defense.[59] A party must plead and prove fraudulent concealment in order to rely on it to avoid the limitations defense either at trial or at summary judgment. The limitations period is tolled until the defrauded party discovers or should have discovered the injury.[60]

The elements of the fraudulent concealment defense are:

- the existence of the underlying tort;
- the defendant's knowledge of the tort;
- the defendant's use of deception to conceal the tort; and
- the plaintiff's reasonable reliance on the deception.[61]

The following have been held to constitute legally sufficient evidence of fraudulent concealment:

- When a conversion plaintiff twice asked the defendant company whether it had any relationship with the production of the converted property, and the defendant twice fraudulently denied any such relationship.[62]

- When there was conflicting evidence as to whether a defendant-doctor informed the plaintiff that he had left a surgical needle inside of the plaintiff's body following surgery.[63]

- When a wrongdoer who was not named as a defendant in a lawsuit retained the same counsel of the two named defendants, and the counsel filed misleading discovery responses that precluded the plaintiff from ascertaining who the proper defendant was.[64]

(*Livingston Ford Mercury, Inc. v. Haley*, 997 S.W.2d 425, 429 (Tex. App.—Beaumont 1999, no pet.).

[59] *Markwardt v. Tex. Indus., Inc.*, 325 S.W.3d 876, 894 (Tex. App.—Houston [14th Dist.] 2010, no pet.) (citing *KPMG Peat Marwick*, 988 S.W.2d at 749; *Ponder v. Brice & Mankoff*, 889 S.W.2d 637, 645 (Tex. App.—Houston [14th Dist.] 1994, writ denied)).

[60] *Ponder v. Brice & Mankoff*, 889 S.W.2d 637, 645 (Tex. App.—Houston [14th Dist.] 1994, writ denied).

[61] *Id.*

[62] *Santanna Nat. Gas Corp. v. Hamon Operating Co.*, 954 S.W.2d 885, 891 (Tex. App.—Austin 1997, pet. denied).

[63] *Borderlon v. Peck*, 661 S.W.2d 907, 909 (Tex. 1983).

[64] *Barnhill v. Integrated Health Servs., Inc.*, 21 S.W.3d 321, 324 (Tex. App.—San Antonio 1999, no pet.).

17-11:2 Discovery Rule

As a general rule, a cause of action accrues when a wrongful act causes injury, even if the injured party does not discover the injury. The discovery rule is an exception to this general rule and defers accrual of the cause of action until the injured party discovered or reasonably should have discovered the injury. The party seeking to benefit from the discovery rule has the burden to plead and prove its elements.[65]

The discovery rule can be distinguished from fraudulent concealment in that the discovery rule addresses situations in which the failure to discover the injury is not due to the fraudulent acts of the defendant. The discovery rule applies when two elements are met—(1) the injury must be inherently undiscoverable and (2) evidence of the injury must be objectively verifiable.[66] An injury is inherently undiscoverable when it is difficult for the injured party to learn of the negligent act or omission.[67] For example, a person does not learn he has been defamed by a false credit report until he applies for credit.[68] A person cannot discover that a vasectomy was improperly performed until a pregnancy occurs or until a test reveals fertility.[69] That a foreign object was left in the incision has been held to implicate the discovery rule because the patient would not discover the foreign object or the problems it may cause for a long time after surgery.[70] In contrast, in 2017 the Texas Supreme Court held that the discovery rule did not defer accrual of a claim for soil contamination because, although soil contamination is objectively verifiable, it is not undiscoverable within the limitations period.[71] The court went on to say that application of the discovery rule to nuisance cases in general is rare because "plaintiffs typically learn of unreasonable discomfort or annoyance promptly."[72]

The discovery rule has been frequently applied to cases of latent onset diseases, such as:

- asbestosis[73]
- mesothelioma[74]
- silicosis[75]

---

[65] *Woods v. William M. Mercer, Inc.*, 769 S.W.2d 515, 515–16 (Tex. 1988).
[66] *Computer Assocs. Int'l, Inc. v. Altai, Inc.*, 918 S.W.2d 453 (Tex. 1996).
[67] *Id.* (citing *Willis v. Maverick*, 760 S.W.2d 642, 645 (Tex. 1988); *see Kelley v. Rinkle*, 532 S.W.2d 947, 949 (Tex. 1976)).
[68] *Kelley v. Rinkle*, 532 S.W.2d 947, 949 (Tex. 1976).
[69] *Hays v. Hall*, 488 S.W.2d 412, 414 (Tex. 1972).
[70] *Gaddis v. Smith*, 417 S.W.2d 577, 578 (Tex. 1967). *Gaddis* has since been superseded by the Medical Liability Act, which abolished the discovery rule and instituted a repose period for health care liability claims governed by the Act. *See* Tex. Civ. Prac. & Rem. Code § 74.251; *see also Walters v. Cleveland Reg'l Med. Ctr.*, 307 S.W.3d 292, 298 (Tex. 2010).
[71] *ExxonMobil Corp. v. Lazy R Ranch, LP*, 511 S.W.3d 538, 544 (Tex. 2017).
[72] *Id.*
[73] *Fibreboard Corp. v. Pool*, 813 S.W.2d 658, 679 (Tex. App.—Texarkana 1991, writ denied).
[74] *Pecorino v. Raymark Indus.*, 763 S.W.2d 561, 568 (Tex. App.—Beaumont 1988, writ denied).
[75] *Sowell v. Dresser Indus., Inc.*, 866 S.W.2d 803, 808 (Tex. App.—Beaumont 1993, writ denied).

- HIV contracted by a healthcare professional from a patient[76]
- health problems related to chemical exposure.[77]

The discovery rule has also been applied to legal malpractice and accounting malpractice cases because the injured party often does not possess the knowledge necessary to discovery the problem.[78] Additionally, the Texas Supreme Court has applied a tolling of the limitations until all appeals of the underlying claim are exhausted when an attorney allegedly commits malpractice while providing legal services in the prosecution or defense of a claim which results in litigation.[79]

17-11:3 Disabilities

If a person is under a legal disability at the time the cause of action accrues, the time the person is under the disability does not count against the limitations period.[80] A disability that arises after the limitations period begins to run, however, does not suspend the running of the limitations period.[81] A person may not tack one legal disability on to another in order to extend a limitations period.[82] A person is under a legal disability if they are younger than the age of 18, even if married, or of unsound mind.[83]

In medical malpractice cases, the limitations period for a minor who was injured before the age of twelve is tolled only until he or she reaches the age of 14.[84] It is likely, however, that the general tolling provision for minors will apply because the Texas Supreme Court found a similar tolling provision unconstitutional as violating the Open Courts provision of the Texas Constitution.[85] Indeed, the San Antonio Court of Appeals has already held that this more limited tolling provision for a minor in healthcare liability cases is unconstitutional.[86]

17-11:4 Death of Claimant

The limitation period is suspended for twelve months upon the death of a claimant.[87] If an executor or administrator of a decedent's estate qualifies before the expiration of

---

[76] *Casarez v. NME Hosps., Inc.*, 883 S.W.2d 360, 365 (Tex. App.—El Paso 1994, writ dism'd).

[77] *Allen v. Roddis Lumber & Veneer Co.*, 796 S.W.2d 758, 761 (Tex. App.—Corpus Christi 1990, writ denied).

[78] *Murphy v. Campbell*, 964 S.W.2d 265, 270 (Tex. 1997) (accounting malpractice); *Willis v. Maverick*, 760 S.W.2d 642, 646 (Tex. 1988) (legal malpractice). *Aduddell v. Parkhill*, 821 S.W.2d 158, 159 (Tex. 1991); *see also Hughes*, 821 S.W.2d at 157; *Gulf Coast Inv. Corp. v. Brown*, 821 S.W.2d 159, 160 (Tex. 1991).

[79] Hughes v. Mahaney & Higgins, 821 S.W.2d 154, 157 (Tex. 1991).

[80] Tex. Civ. Prac. & Rem. Code Ann. § 16.001(b) ("If a person entitled to bring a personal action is under a legal disability when the cause of action accrues, the time of the disability is not included in a limitations period.").

[81] *Id.* at § 16.001(d).

[82] *Id.* at § 16.001(c).

[83] *Id.* at § 16.001(a).

[84] *Id.* at Tex. Civ. Prac. & Rem. Code Ann. § 74.251(a).

[85] *Weiner v. Wasson*, 900 S.W.2d 316, 317–18 (Tex. 1995).

[86] *Adams v. Gottwald*, 179 S.W.3d 101, 103 (Tex. App.—San Antonio 2005, no pet.). *See also Montalvo v. Lopez*, 466 S.W.3d 290, 292 (Tex. App.—San Antonio 2015, no pet.).

[87] Tex. Civ. Prac. & Rem. Code Ann. § 16.062(a).

the one-year suspension, then the statute of limitations begins to run at the time of the qualification.[88] This rule applies to survival actions but not to wrongful death actions because it applies only to causes of action existing at the time of death.[89] The provision does not apply to healthcare liability claims.[90]

17-11:5 Military Service

Pursuant to a federal statute—the Soldier's and Sailor's Civil Relief Act—the running of a limitations period is tolled during the period of a person's military service.[91] This provision applies to actions in both state and federal court.[92] For example, Texas courts have applied the provision to toll actions by service members to recover money deposited in a bank,[93] to recover money due on a promissory note,[94] and to recover property from another in adverse possession of it.[95]

The federal statute also tolls the limitations period in actions against the service member's heirs, administrators, executors or assigns.[96]

The federal tolling provision applies even if it benefits the party adverse to the service member. For example, the period of time during which a person is in military service is not counted as part of the time during which the defendant service member was allegedly in adverse possession of property.[97]

Courts disagree as to whether or not the provision applies to career military personnel. The Fifth Circuit Court of Appeals has held that that the provision does not apply to career service members in the absence of a showing that military service prevented the person from pursuing the right.[98] One Texas court of appeals refused to follow the Fifth Circuit rule and held that the provision applies to all military personnel, including career personnel.[99]

---

[88] Tex. Civ. Prac. & Rem. Code Ann. § 16.062(b).
[89] *Rigo Mfg. Co. v. Thomas*, 458 S.W.2d 180, 181 (Tex. 1970).
[90] Tex. Civ. Prac. & Rem. Code Ann. § 74.251.
[91] 50 U.S.C. § 526(a).
[92] 50 U.S.C. § 526(a) ("The period of a servicemember's military service may not be included in computing any period limited by law, regulation, or order for the bringing of any action or *proceeding in a court, or in any board, bureau, commission, department, or other agency of a State (or political subdivision of a State)* or the United States by or against the servicemember or the servicemember's heirs, executors, administrators, or assigns.") (emphasis added); *Crawford v. Adams*, 213 S.W.2d 721, 722 (Tex. Civ. App.—Galveston 1948, writ ref'd n.r.e.) ("It is, we think, the established law of this state 'that the benefit extended to soldiers and sailors under Section 10322 was intended to apply to actions in state courts as well as those in federal courts', and that Congress had power to pass said act, and that it applies to state courts.") (internal citations omitted).
[93] *First Nat'l Bank of Hico v. English*, 240 S.W.2d 503, 506 (Tex. Civ. App.—Waco 1951, no writ).
[94] *Crawford v. Adams*, 213 S.W.2d 721, 722 (Tex. Civ. App.—Galveston 1948, writ ref'd n.r.e.).
[95] *Easterling v. Murphy*, 11 S.W.2d 329, 333 (Tex. Civ. App.—Waco 1928, writ ref'd).
[96] 50 U.S.C. § 526(a); *Easterling v. Murphy*, 11 S.W.2d 329, 333 (Tex. Civ. App.—Waco 1928, writ ref'd) (applying tolling provision to heir of servicemember).
[97] *Scruggs v. Troncalli*, 307 S.W.2d 300, 304 (Tex. Civ. App.—Waco 1957, writ ref'd n.r.e.).
[98] *Pannell v. Cont'l Can Co., Inc.*, 554 F.2d 216, 225 (5th Cir. 1977) (refusing to apply the tolling provision to a colonel who was career military).
[99] *Barstow v. State*, 742 S.W.2d 495, 500 (Tex. Civ. App.—Austin 1987, writ denied).

17-11:6 Absence from Texas

The Texas Civil Practice & Remedies Code provides that the absence of a person from Texas against whom a cause of action may be maintained suspends the running of the limitations period during the period of the person's absence.[100] In other words, the time during which a defendant is absent from the state does not count against the applicable limitations period.

The most recent Supreme Court of Texas case on this statute seems to substantially limit the applicability of the tolling provision.[101] The court clarified the meaning of the term "absence" in the statute. A person is present (i.e., not absent) if they are amenable to service under the general Texas long arm statute.[102] The court said that in most cases "presence" will be established because the Texas long arm statute authorizes the exercise of jurisdiction to the maximum extent permitted by the Due Process Clause of the 14th Amendment.[103] The Supreme Court's decision overruled its prior decision on the issue, in which it had held that the tolling provision applied even if the defendant was amenable to process under the long arm statute.[104]

17-11:7 Savings Statute for Jurisdictional Dismissals

An action dismissed for lack of subject matter jurisdiction may be re-filed within 60 days of the date the dismissal becomes final, even if the limitations period has otherwise run out.[105] This rule does not apply if, in the second action, the adverse party can demonstrate that the first filing was made with intentional disregard of proper jurisdiction.[106]

17-12 Satisfying the Statute of Limitations

This section discusses how a plaintiff satisfies the statute of limitations. The mere filing of a petition within the limitations period does not satisfy the statute of limitations unless it is accompanied by the plaintiff's due diligence in securing issuance and service of the citation and petition on the defendant or defendants.[107] If the plaintiff exercises due diligence in securing issuance and service of the citation and petition, the date of service relates back to the time of the filing of the petition.[108]

At summary judgment, once the defendant has pled limitations and affirmatively demonstrated that service occurred after the limitations period expired, the burden shifts to the plaintiff to explain the delay.[109] The inquiry is "whether the plaintiff acted

---

[100] Tex. Civ. Prac. & Rem. Code Ann. § 16.063.
[101] *Ashley v. Hawkins*, 293 S.W.3d 175, 178–79 (Tex. 2009).
[102] *Id.*
[103] *Id.*
[104] *Vaughn v. Deitz*, 430 S.W.2d 487 (Tex. 1968).
[105] Tex. Civ. Prac. & Rem. Code Ann. § 16.064(a).
[106] Tex. Civ. Prac. & Rem. Code Ann. § 16.064(b).
[107] *Prouix v. Wells*, 235 S.W.3d 213, 215 (Tex. 2007) (citing *Murray v. San Jacinto Agency, Inc.*, 800 S.W.2d 826, 830 (Tex. 1990); *Rigo Mfg. Co. v. Thomas*, 458 S.W.2d 180, 182 (Tex. 1970)).
[108] *Rigo Mfg. Co. v. Thomas*, 458 S.W.2d 180, 182 (Tex. 1970) (citing *Gant v. DeLeon*, 786 S.W.2d 259, 260 (Tex. 1990)).
[109] *Rigo Mfg. Co. v. Thomas*, 458 S.W.2d 180, 182 (Tex. 1970) (citing *Murray v. San Jacinto Agency, Inc.*, 800 S.W.2d 826, 830 (Tex. 1990)).

as an ordinarily prudent person would have acted under the same or similar circumstances and was diligent up until the time the defendant was served."[110] The plaintiff's diligence is a question of fact and, if the plaintiff, at summary judgment, raises a fact issue as to diligence, the burden shifts back to the defendant to conclusively establish why the explanation is insufficient as a matter of law.[111] Some explanations for delay are insufficient as a matter of law.[112]

17-12:1 Misnomer and Misidentification of Defendants

When a plaintiff names the wrong party in the petition, the issue is often whether or not the filing of such a suit tolls the statute of limitations. The statute of limitations is tolled when the plaintiff commits a "misnomer."[113] The statute of limitations is generally not tolled when the plaintiff commits a "misidentification." A plaintiff commits a misnomer when it sues the correct party, but misnames the defendant in the petition.[114] A plaintiff commits a misidentification when two separate legal entities actually exist and a plaintiff mistakenly sues the entity with a name similar to that of the correct entity.[115]

Generally, a misidentification does not toll the statute of limitations.[116] However, the plaintiff's misidentification of the defendant will toll the statute of limitations if the correct defendant:

- Knew or should have known of the lawsuit within the limitations period;[117]
- Maintained a business relationship with the named defendant;[118]
- Chose to operate under a confusing set of names with the named defendant;[119]
- Would not be prejudiced by tolling; and[120]
- Both the named and correct defendants were entities.[121]

---

[110] *Rigo Mfg. Co. v. Thomas*, 458 S.W.2d 180, 182 (Tex. 1970) (citing *Tate v. Beal*, 119 S.W.3d 378, 381 (Tex. App.—Fort Worth 2003, pet. denied); *Hodge v. Smith*, 856 S.W.2d 212, 215 (Tex. App.—Houston [1st Dist.] 1993, writ denied).
[111] *Hodge v. Smith*, 856 S.W.2d 212, 215 (Tex. App.—Houston [1st Dist.] 1993, writ denied).
[112] *See, e.g., Gant v. DeLeon*, 786 S.W.2d 259, 260 (Tex. 1990) (no explanation for 38 month delay); *see also Webster v. Thomas*, 5 S.W.3d 287, 291 (Tex. App.—Houston 1999 [14th Dist.], no pet.) (four month delay without action designed to procure issuance and service of citation); *Butler v. Ross*, 836 S.W.2d 833, 836 (Tex. App.—Houston [1st Dist.] 1992, no writ) (five-and-a-half months of inactivity between failed attempts constituted a lack of due diligence); *Hansler v. Mainka*, 807 S.W.2d 3, 5 (Tex. App.—Corpus Christi 1991, no writ) (requesting service five months after suit was filed was lack of due diligence).
[113] *Abilene Indep. Tel. Co. v. Williams*, 111 Tex. 102, 105, 229 S.W. 847, 848 (1921).
[114] *Chilkewitz v. Hyson*, 22 S.W.3d 825, 828 (Tex. 1999).
[115] *Id.*
[116] *Enserch Corp. v. Parker*, 794 S.W.2d 2, 4–5 (Tex. 1990).
[117] *Id.*
[118] *Id.*
[119] *Id.*
[120] *Id.*
[121] *Cortinas v. Wilson*, 851 S.W.2d 324, 327 (Tex. App.—Dallas 1993, no writ).

17-12:2 Suit Against Defendant in Assumed or Common Name

Texas Rule of Civil Procedure 28 allows for any partnership, unincorporated association, private corporation or individual doing business under an assumed or common name to sue or be sued in its partnership, assumed or common name.[122] If the defendant has adopted a partnership, assumed or common name which alludes to an existing entity, a plaintiff may sue the defendant in that name regardless of whether such an alluded to entity exists.[123] The effect of suing a defendant under a partnership, assumed or common name is to satisfy the statute of limitations.[124] The only recourse a defendant sued under a partnership, assumed or common name has is to have its legal name substituted for its assumed name.[125]

17-13 Statutes of Repose

A statute of repose provides "a definitive date beyond which an action cannot be filed."[126] A statute of repose differs from a statute of limitations in that it begins to run from a specified date, rather than from accrual of a cause of action.[127] Consequently, a statute of repose can bar actions before a statute of limitations expires and even before a cause of action accrues.[128]

17-13:1 Ten-Year Repose for Suits Against Architects, Engineers, Designers, Inspectors, and Surveyors

Suits for injury or damage to real or personal property, personal injury, wrongful death, contribution or indemnity against a registered or licensed architect, engineer, interior designer or landscape architect in Texas, who designs, plans or inspects the construction of an improvement to real property or equipment attached to real property, must be brought not later than 10 years after the substantial completion of the improvement or the beginning of operation of the equipment in an action arising out of a defective or unsafe condition of the real property, the improvement or the equipment.[129]

This 10-year statute of repose can be extended under certain circumstances. If the claimant has presented a written claim for damages, contribution or indemnity to a per-

---

[122] Tex. R. Civ. P. 28.
[123] *Chilkewitz v. Hyson*, 22 S.W.3d 825, 828–29 (Tex. 1999) (For example, a plaintiff could effectively bring suit against an individual doing business as "Widgets International, Inc." by naming Widgets International, Inc. as the defendant. The Rule would allow the plaintiff to bring suit against the individual even if the plaintiff mistakenly thought that a company under that name legally existed and identified the defendant in his original petition as "Widgets International, Inc., a corporation.").
[124] *Chilkewitz v. Hyson*, 22 S.W.3d 825, 830 (Tex. 1999).
[125] Tex. R. Civ. P. 28.
[126] *Galbraith Eng'g Consultants, Inc. v. Pochucha*, 290 S.W.3d 853, 866 (Tex. 2009) (citing *Holubec v. Brandenberger*, 111 S.W.3d 32, 37 (Tex. 2003)).
[127] *Id.*
[128] *Id.* ("Repose then differs from limitations in that repose not only cuts off rights of action after they accrue, but can cut off rights of action before they accrue.").
[129] Tex. Civ. Prac. & Rem. Code Ann. § 16.008(a), (b).

son who performed the work during the 10-year period, then the period is extended for two years from the date the claim was presented.[130] In actions based on a defective or unsafe condition of real property or a deficiency in the construction or repair of the improvement against a person who constructed or repaired an improvement to real property, the claim must be brought within 10 years of substantial completion of the improvement.[131] If the damage, injury or death occurs in the tenth year of the period, the claim may be brought within two years of the date the cause of action accrued.[132] If the claimant presents a written claim for damages within the 10 years, the period is extended for two years from the date the claim was presented.[133] The statute of repose does not bar the following actions.

- An action on a written warranty, guaranty or other contract that expressly provides for a longer effective period.

- An action against a person in actual possession or control of the real property at the time that the damage, injury or death occurs; or

- An action based on willful misconduct or fraudulent concealment in connection with the performance of the construction or repair.[134]

An action against a surveyor must be brought within 10 years of the completion of the survey unless written demand is made within the 10 year period, in which case the action must be brought within two years of the written demand.[135]

17-13:2 Fifteen-Year Repose for Product Liability Actions

A product liability action, as a general rule, must be commenced within 15 years of the date the defendant sold the product.[136] A product liability action is defined as any action against a manufacturer or seller of a product for any harm caused by the defective product, whether the cause of action alleged is strict liability, negligence, misrepresentation, breach of warranty or any other theory of liability.[137]

In the following circumstances, the 15-year limit is extended.

- The manufacturer or seller expressly warrants in writing that the product has a useful life longer than 15 years, in which case the action must be commenced within the time stated in the written warranty.[138]

- The plaintiff was exposed to the product within the 15 years of the date of first sale; the exposure caused the plaintiff's disease; and the symptoms did not manifest themselves within the 15 year period to a degree that would notify the plaintiff of the injury.[139]

---

[130] *Id.* at § 16.008(c).
[131] *Id.* at § 16.009(a).
[132] Tex. Civ. Prac. & Rem. Code Ann. § 16.009(d).
[133] *Id.* at § 16.009(c).
[134] *Id.* at § 16.009(e).
[135] *Id.* at § 16.011.
[136] *Id.* at § 16.012(b).
[137] Tex. Civ. Prac. & Rem. Code Ann. § 16.012(a)(2).
[138] *Id.* at § 16.012(c).
[139] Tex. Civ. Prac. & Rem. Code Ann. § 16.012(d).

- A cause of action that accrues within the 15 year period may be brought within the period prescribed by the statute of limitations (e.g., a tort cause of action accruing in the fifteenth year may be brought within two years of accrual).[140]

17-13:3 Healthcare Liability Claims

Healthcare liability claims, as a general rule, must be brought within 10 years of the date of the act or omission that gives rise to the claim.[141] The Supreme Court of Texas has held that this provision does not violate the Open Courts provision of the Texas Constitution generally,[142] even as applied to minors.[143]

---

[140] *Id.* at § 16.012(d)(1).
[141] Tex. Civ. Prac. & Rem. Code Ann. § 74.251(b).
[142] *Methodist Healthcare Sys. of San Antonio Ltd, LLP v. Rankin*, 307 S.W.3d 283, 292 (Tex. 2010).
[143] *Tenet Hosps. Ltd. v. Rivera*, 445 S.W.3d 698 (Tex. 2014).

CHAPTER 18

Proportionate Responsibility, Contribution, and Indemnity*

Generally, Chapter 33 of the Civil Practice & Remedies Code governs proportionate responsibility and sets out Texas's comparative fault scheme. Chapter 33 requires the trier of fact to determine the percentage of responsibility of each claimant, defendant, settling person, and any responsible third party who has been designated in compliance with the statute. Damages are thereafter apportioned according to those comparative-fault findings.[1] Texas follows a modified comparative fault scheme, providing that a claimant may not recover if he or she is more than 50% responsible for the harm for which recovery is sought.[2] This section discusses proportionate responsibility under Chapter 33.

18-1 Scope of Chapter 33

Chapter 33 applies to any cause of action based on tort and in actions under the Deceptive Trade Practices Act ("DTPA") in which "a defendant, settling person or responsible third party is found responsible for a percentage of the harm for which relief is sought."[3]

Whether a cause of action is "based on tort," as required for Chapter 33 to apply, is not always easily determined. The focus of the inquiry seems to be on the nature of the damages sought and the nature of the wrong alleged, rather than whether the cause of action sounds in tort or contract.

For example, a breach of implied warranty claim for personal injury or wrongful death caused by a defective product is an action "based on tort" and is subject to Chapter 33.[4] By contrast, Chapter 33 does not apply to a claim for breach of an express warranty where the damages sought are not personal injury or wrongful death damages.[5] Chapter 33 likewise would not apply to an action for conversion of a negotiable

---

* The authors thank Robyn Leatherwood for her assistance in the updating of this chapter.
[1] *In re Xerox Corp.*, 555 S.W.3d 518, 523 (Tex. 2018).
[2] Tex. Civ. Prac. & Rem. Code Ann. § 33.001.
[3] Tex. Civ. Prac. & Rem. Code Ann. § 33.002(a)(1), (2).
[4] *JCW Elec., Inc. v. Garza*, 257 S.W.3d 701, 707 (Tex. 2008).
[5] *GB Tubulars, Inc. v. Union Gas Operating Co.*, 527 S.W.3d 563, 576 (Tex. App.—Houston [14th Dist.] 2017, pet. denied); *Cressman Tubular Prods. Corp. v. Kurt Wiseman Oil & Gas, Ltd.*, 322 S.W.3d 453, 459–60 (Tex. App.—Houston [14th Dist.] 2010, pet denied).

instrument under Article 3 of the Uniform Commercial Code.[6] The application of Chapter 33, however, is not limited to tort causes of action seeking personal injury or wrongful death damages.[7]

If the cause of action is governed by a statutory scheme that cannot be reconciled with the apportionment scheme of Chapter 33, then Chapter 33 does not apply.[8]

Chapter 33 expressly excludes certain actions from its scope. Chapter 33 does not apply to actions to recover workers' compensation benefits or an action against an employer to recover exemplary damages based on the death of the employee,[9] nor does it apply to certain claims for damages based on the manufacture of methamphetamine.[10]

Importantly, Chapter 33 does not apply to claims for exemplary or punitive damages even in an action to which Chapter 33 otherwise applies.[11]

18-2 Determination of Percentage of Responsibility

The trier of fact must determine the percentage of responsibility "with respect to each person's causing or contributing to cause in any way the harm for which recovery of damages is sought" for each claimant, each defendant, each settling person and each responsible third party.[12]

18-2:1 Determination Made as to "Each Cause of Action"

Chapter 33 requires this determination to be made as to "each cause of action asserted."[13] Despite the reference to "cause of action," this provision does not require a separate apportionment question following each question on a legal theory of recovery.[14] In other words, it does not require the jury to "compare all parties alleged to

---

[6] *Southwest Bank v. Info. Support Concepts, Inc.*, 149 S.W.3d 104, 108 (Tex. 2004).

[7] *See, e.g., JCW Elecs., Inc. v. Garza*, 257 S.W.3d 701, 707 (Tex. 2008); *Villarreal v. Wells Fargo Brokerage Servs., LLC*, 315 S.W.3d 109, 125–26 (Tex. App.—Houston [1st Dist.] 2010, no pet.) (applying Chapter 33 *but see Challenger Gaming Sols., Inc. v. Earp*, 402 S.W.3d 290, 299 (Tex. App.—Dallas 2013, no pet.) (holding that Chapter 33 does not apply to a claim under the Uniform Fraudulent Transfer Act).

[8] *See, e.g., Villarreal v. Wells Fargo Brokerage Servs., LLC*, 315 S.W.3d 109, 125–26 (Tex. App.—Houston [1st Dist.] 2010, no pet.) (could not reconcile Uniform Fraudulent Transfer Act with Chapter 33); *Southwest Bank v. Info. Support Concepts, Inc.*, 149 S.W.3d 104, 105 (Tex. 2004) (could not reconcile UCC fault allocation scheme with Chapter 33).

[9] Tex. Civ. Prac. & Rem. Code Ann. § 33.002(c)(1).

[10] Tex. Civ. Prac. & Rem. Code Ann. § 33.002(c)(3).

[11] Tex. Civ. Prac. & Rem. Code Ann. § 33.002(c)(2); *Pemex Exploracion y Produccion v. BASF Corp.*, No. 4:10cv1997, 2011 WL 9523407, at *12 (S. D. Tex. Feb. 8, 2011). *See also Olin Corp. v. Dyson*, 709 S.W.2d 251, 253–54 (Tex. App.—Houston [14th Dist.] 1986, no writ); *Anderson v. Trent*, 685 S.W.2d 712, 714 (Tex. App.—Dallas 1984, writ ref'd n.r.e.).

[12] Tex. Civ. Prac. & Rem. Code Ann. § 33.003(a)(1)–(4); *In re Cambell*, 577 S.W.3d 293, 305 (Tex. App.—Houston [14th Dist.] 2019, no pet.).

[13] Tex. Civ. Prac. & Rem. Code Ann. § 33.003(a).

[14] *In re Sunpoint Sec., Inc.*, 377 B.R. 513, 569 (Bankr. E.D. Tex. 2007) (citing Gregory J. Lensing, *Proportionate Responsibility and Contribution Before and After the Tort Reform of 2003*, 35 Tex. Tech. L. Rev. 1125, 1132 (2004)).

have been negligent in one question, compare all parties alleged to have distributed a defective product in a separate question, and so on."[15]

Instead, "cause of action" in the statute refers to "the entire set of facts giving rise to a single right of recovery, regardless of the specific legal theory of recovery."[16] The practice in Texas is to submit a series of liability questions (if more than one theory of recovery is alleged) followed by a single apportionment question.[17] This includes any pre-occurrence conduct which, under Sec. 33.003(a) caused or contributed to cause the personal injuries sought or under 33.011(4) caused or contributed to cause the death.[18]

18-2:2 Determination Made as to Each Claimant, Defendant, Settling Person, and Responsible Third Party

The apportionment question must include a line for each claimant, defendant, settling person and responsible third party.[19]

A claimant is defined as "a person seeking recovery of damages," including a "plaintiff, counterclaimant, cross-claimant, or third-party plaintiff."[20] In a case in which a party seeks recovery of damages on behalf of another person (e.g., suits on behalf of a minor and wrongful death actions), the term includes both the person who was injured, died, or whose property was damaged and the person seeking recovery on his or his behalf.[21]

A person who seeks recovery on behalf of another is barred from recovery if the person on behalf of whom recovery is sought is more than 50% responsible.[22] Although the Texas Supreme Court has not answered the question, it appears that, where the total fault of both the person seeking recovery and the fault of the person through whom the plaintiff claims exceeds 50%, recovery may also be barred.[23]

A defendant is defined as "any person from whom, at the time of the submission of the case to the trier of fact, a claimant seeks recovery of damages."[24]

---

[15] Gregory J. Lensing, *Proportionate Responsibility and Contribution Before and After the Tort Reform of 2003*, 35 Tex. Tech. L. Rev. 1125, 1132 (2004).

[16] Gregory J. Lensing, *Proportionate Responsibility and Contribution Before and After the Tort Reform of 2003*, 35 Tex. Tech. L. Rev. 1125, 1132 (2004).

[17] Gregory J. Lensing, *Proportionate Responsibility and Contribution Before and After the Tort Reform of 2003*, 35 Tex. Tech. L. Rev. 1125, 1132 (2004) (citing Comm. on Pattern Jury Charges, State Bar of Tex., Texas Pattern Jury Charges Pjc 4.1, 71.3B, 71.11 (2002)).

[18] Nabors Well Services, Ltd. v. Romero, 456 S.W.3d 553 (Tex. 2015).

[19] Tex. Civ. Prac. & Rem. Code Ann. § 33.003(a)(1)–(4).

[20] Tex. Civ. Prac. & Rem. Code Ann. § 33.011(1).

[21] Tex. Civ. Prac. & Rem. Code Ann. § 33.011(1)(A), (B).

[22] *In re Xerox Corp.*, 555 S.W.3d 518, 524 (Tex. 2018).

[23] *Smith v. East*, 411 S.W.3d 519, 529 (Tex. App.—Austin 2013, pet. denied) ("The supreme court's precedents also compel us to conclude that where, as here, the fact-finder apportions more than 50% of responsibility collectively to the derivative plaintiff and the person through whom she claims, Section 33.001 likewise bars the plaintiff's recovery on the cause of action. Although the high court has yet to answer that question directly, this conclusion follows from its jurisprudence addressing settlement credits under Chapter 33.").

[24] Tex. Civ. Prac. & Rem. Code Ann. § 33.011(2).

A settling person is one "who has, at any time, paid or promised to pay money or anything of monetary value to a claimant in consideration of potential liability with respect to the personal injury, property damage, death, or other harm for which recovery of damages is sought."[25]

A responsible third party is "any person who is alleged to have caused or contributed to causing in any way the harm for which recovery of damages is sought."[26] The designation of a non-party as a responsible third party is discussed in Chapter 18, Section 18-5. Whether or not a third-party defendant (made a party under Texas Rule of Civil Procedure 38) is a defendant, a responsible third party, or neither is not entirely clear from the definitions.

A party wishing to ensure that the fault of an impleaded third-party defendant is determined with respect to the plaintiff's cause of action, for example, and not simply with respect to a separate cause of action for contribution or indemnity, should designate the third-party defendant as a responsible third party.

18-2:3 Percentage of Responsibility

In the apportionment question, the jury must determine the percentage of responsibility for each claimant, defendant, settling person and responsible third party.[27] The jury's assignment of percentage of responsibility must be stated in whole numbers totaling 100%.[28]

18-3 Determining Amount of Recovery

A claimant's maximum recovery is determined by, first, reducing the amount of damages by the percentage of responsibility assigned to the claimant.[29] In other words, if a plaintiff's percentage of responsibility is 50% or less, the court will reduce the plaintiff's recovery by that percentage.[30] This number must then be further reduced by the sum of the dollar amounts of all settlements.[31] In a medical malpractice case, the defendants have the option of reducing the plaintiff's maximum amount of recovery by the total percentage of fault of all settling persons, rather than the total dollar amount of the settlements.[32] Generally, the burden is on the defendant to prove the amount of the settlement, but the plaintiff must prove any portion of the settlement that is allocated to punitive damages (as there is no offset for punitive damages).[33] Similarly, it appears that the burden is on the plaintiff to prove what portion of a set-

---

[25] Tex. Civ. Prac. & Rem. Code Ann. § 33.011(5).
[26] Tex. Civ. Prac. & Rem. Code Ann. § 33.011(6).
[27] Tex. Civ. Prac. & Rem. Code Ann. § 33.003(a)(1)–(4).
[28] Tex. Civ. Prac. & Rem. Code Ann. § 33.003(a).
[29] Tex. Civ. Prac. & Rem. Code Ann. § 33.012(a).
[30] *Nabors Well Services, Ltd. v. Romero*, 456 S.W.3d 553, 559 (Tex. 2015).
[31] Tex. Civ. Prac. & Rem. Code Ann. § 33.012(b).
[32] Tex. Civ. Prac. & Rem. Code Ann. § 33.012(c).
[33] *Crown Life Ins. Co. v. Casteel*, 22 S.W.3d 378, 391–92 (Tex. 2000); *Farmers Tex. Cty. Mut. Ins. Co. v. Okelberry*, 525 S.W.3d 786, 795 (Tex. App.—Houston [14th Dist.] 2017, no pet.). *See also* Tex. Civ. Prac. & Rem. Code Ann. § 33.002(c)(2) (providing that Chapter 33 does not apply to "a claim for exemplary damages included in an action to which this chapter otherwise applies").

tlement that did not benefit him (e.g., was for the benefit of another, such as a spouse or child).[34]

A plaintiff may not be able to recover his maximum amount because his recovery may be independently limited by the maximum amount of liability for a defendant.[35] Unless a defendant is jointly and severally liable (defendant's responsibility is greater than 50%[36] or his conduct constitutes certain crimes under the Texas penal code[37]), the maximum amount of liability for a defendant is "the percentage of the damages found by the trier of fact equal to that defendant's percentage of responsibility."[38] For example, where damages are $400,000 and a defendant's percentage of responsibility is 25%, the defendant's maximum amount of liability is $100,000.

Even if the plaintiff's maximum amount of recovery is greater than the defendant's maximum amount of liability, the plaintiff cannot recover from the defendant more than the maximum amount of liability.[39] Where such a case involves multiple plaintiffs, the plaintiffs will recover pro rata shares of the maximum amount of liability from the defendant or defendants.[40]

18-4 Joint and Several Liability

Where a defendant is determined to be jointly and severally liable for the claimants' damages, a plaintiff may recover all damages from that defendant.[41] A defendant is jointly and severally liable if the jury assigns greater than 50% of responsibility to that defendant.[42]

A defendant is also jointly and severally liable if with specific intent to do harm to others he or she acted in concert with another person and engaged in conduct that was the proximate cause of the damages recoverable by the claimant and such conduct constituted any one of the following crimes as defined by the Texas Penal Code: murder; capital murder; aggravated kidnapping; aggravated assault; sexual assault; aggravated sexual assault; injury to a child, the elderly or disabled; forgery; commercial bribery; misapplication of fiduciary property or property of financial institu-

---

[34] *Farmers Tex. Cty. Mut. Ins. Co. v. Okelberry*, 525 S.W.3d 786, 795 (Tex. App.—Houston [14th Dist.] 2017, no pet.) (holding that a plaintiff filing suit for UIM benefits on his auto policy had the burden to prove what portion of an earlier settlement was allocated to his children by analogizing to the Texas Supreme Court's decision in *Ellender* regarding burden as to allocation of punitive damages under Chapter 33).

[35] Gregory J. Lensing, *Proportionate Responsibility and Contribution Before and After the Tort Reform of 2003*, 35 Tex. Tech. L. Rev. 1125, 1132 (2004); Tex. Civ. Prac. & Rem. Code Ann. § 33.013. *See, e.g., Pilgrim's Pride v. Cernat*, 205 S.W.3d 110, 115–18 (Tex. App.—Texarkana 2006) (demonstrating that plaintiff's maximum amount of recovery and defendant's maximum amount of liability may be independent limits on recovery).

[36] Tex. Civ. Prac. & Rem. Code Ann. § 33.013(b)(1).

[37] Tex. Civ. Prac. & Rem. Code Ann. § 33.013(b)(2).

[38] Tex. Civ. Prac. & Rem. Code Ann. § 33.013(a).

[39] *See, e.g., Pilgrim's Pride*, 205 S.W.3d 110, 118 (Tex. App.—Texarkana 2006) ("the two sections set independent limits on recoveries").

[40] *Pilgrim's Pride v. Cernat*, 205 S.W.3d 110, 118–19 (Tex. App.—Texarkana 2006).

[41] Gregory J. Lensing, *Proportionate Responsibility and Contribution Before and After the Tort Reform of 2003*, 35 Tex. Tech. L. Rev. 1125, 1132 (2004).

[42] Tex. Civ. Prac. & Rem. Code Ann. § 33.013(b)(1).

tion; securing execution of document by deception; fraudulent destruction, removal or concealment of writing; continuous sexual abuse of a child or children; and theft constituting a third degree felony or higher.[43]

In order for a defendant to be jointly and severally liable based on certain violations of the penal code, the defendant must have acted with specific intent to do harm to others.[44] This standard is met when it is the defendant's "conscious effort or desire to engage in the conduct for the purpose of doing substantial harm to others."[45] The jury may not be told that the conduct is based on violation of the penal code.

18-5 Procedure for Designation of Responsible Third Parties

Chapter 33 requires the jury to assess the percentage of responsibility for any and all responsible third parties. This section discusses the pleading and proof requirements for designating a person a responsible third party as well as the associated deadlines.

18-5:1 Motion for Leave to Designate a Responsible Third Party

A defendant, and only a defendant, may seek leave to designate a person as a responsible third party.[46] A defendant must seek leave from the court to designate a person as a responsible third party by filing a motion.[47] The motion must be filed on or before the 60th day before the date set for trial unless the party seeking leave can show good cause for the delay.[48] It is wise to designate co-defendants as responsible third parties. A trial court does not abuse its discretion in denying leave to designate within 60 days of trial where a plaintiff nonsuits a co-defendant because all defendants understand that the nonsuit of a co-defendant is a possibility.[49] Typically, the defendant must designate the responsible third party or, at a minimum, identify that party in response to a Rule 194.2 Request for disclosure, prior to the expiration of limitations.[50] This allows the plaintiff the opportunity to add as a party the person alleged to have caused or contributed to cause the injury. If, however, the plaintiff files suit so close to the expiration of the statute of limitations that the defendant cannot designate or disclose prior to limitations running, the Court does not have leave to deny the designation of the responsible third party.[51]

---

[43] Tex. Civ. Prac. & Rem. Code Ann. § 33.013(b)(2)(A)–(N).
[44] Tex. Civ. Prac. & Rem. Code Ann. § 33.013(b)(2).
[45] Tex. Civ. Prac. & Rem. Code Ann. § 33.013(e) ("The jury may not be made aware through voir dire, introduction into evidence, instruction, or any other means that the conduct to which Subsection (b)(2) refers is defined by the Penal Code.").
[46] Tex. Civ. Prac. & Rem. Code Ann. § 33.004(a).
[47] Tex. Civ. Prac. & Rem. Code Ann. § 33.004(a).
[48] Tex. Civ. Prac. & Rem. Code Ann. § 33.004(a).
[49] *In re Unitec Elevator Sers. Co.*, 178 S.W.3d 53, 59 (Tex. App.—Houston [1st Dist.] 2005, no pet.).
[50] In re: Mobile Mini, Inc., ___ S.W.3d ___ (Tex. 2020).
[51] In re: Mobile Mini, Inc., ___ S.W.3d ___ (Tex. 2020).

18-5:2 Objection to a Motion for Leave to Designate a Responsible Third Party

An objection to the motion for leave to designate a responsible third party attacks the sufficiency of the defendant's pleadings as to the responsibility of the responsible third party.

The trial court must grant leave to designate a responsible third party unless another party files an objection to the motion on or before the 15th day after the date the motion is served.[52] Despite the objection, leave will be granted unless the objecting party establishes that the defendant (1) failed to plead "sufficient facts concerning the alleged responsibility of the person to satisfy the pleading requirement of the Texas Rules of Civil Procedure"; and (2) the defendant failed to plead sufficient facts concerning the alleged responsibility after having been granted leave to replead.[53]

18-5:3 Motion to Designate Unknown Criminal as Responsible Third Party

The standard for designating an unknown person who has committed a criminal act as a responsible third party is somewhat more onerous. For one, the defendant must file the motion for leave to designate such a person much earlier in the litigation. The motion for leave must be filed within 60 days of the filing of his original answer.[54]

In his motion for leave, the defendant must satisfy the pleading requirements of the Texas Rules of Civil Procedure, just as he must for designations generally, but, in addition he must:

- plead facts sufficient for the court to determine that there is a reasonable probability that the act of the unknown person was criminal; and

- identify all characteristics of the unknown person, known at the time.[55]

If the court grants leave, the unknown person will be designated a "Jane Doe" or "John Doe" until the person's identify is known.[56]

18-5:4 Motion to Strike the Designation of a Responsible Third Party

While an objection to a motion for leave attacks the allegations in the motion, a motion to strike attacks the evidentiary support for the designation. The procedure set out is essentially the same as that for a no-evidence motion for summary judgment, placing the designating defendant in a position akin to that of a plaintiff who must raise a genuine issue of material fact as to the responsibility of the designated person.

Any party may move to strike the designation of a responsible third party on the ground that there is "no evidence that the designated person is responsible for any

---

[52] Tex. Civ. Prac. & Rem. Code Ann. § 33.004(f).
[53] Tex. Civ. Prac. & Rem. Code Ann. § 33.004(g).
[54] Tex. Civ. Prac. & Rem. Code Ann. § 33.004(j); *In re Echols*, 569 S.W.3d 776, 782–83 (Tex. App.—Dallas 2018, no pet.), reh'g denied (Feb. 8, 2019).
[55] Tex. Civ. Prac. & Rem. Code Ann. § 33.004(j) (1)–(3).
[56] Tex. Civ. Prac. & Rem. Code Ann. § 33.004(k).

portion of the claimant's alleged injury or damage."[57] Just as with a no-evidence motion for summary judgment, the motion to strike may only be made "after adequate time for discovery."[58]

The court will strike the designation unless the designating party can raise a genuine issue of fact regarding the responsibility of the person designated.[59]

18-5:5 Effect of Designation of Responsible Third Party

The granting of the motion for leave designates the person named in the motion as a responsible third party without any further action by the court or defendant.[60] The designation of a responsible third party does not make the person designated a party to the suit or otherwise replace third-party practice under joinder rules in the Texas Rules of Civil Procedure.[61] The designation does not impose liability on the person, nor may it be used in another proceeding to establish liability under the doctrines of *res judicata* or collateral estoppel.[62]

18-6 Contribution and Indemnity

18-6:1 Right of Contribution for Jointly and Severally Liable Defendants

A right of contribution arises under Chapter 33 where a jointly and severally liable defendant pays a percentage of damages greater than the percentage of responsibility apportioned by the jury to that jointly and severally liable defendant.[63] For example, a jointly and severally liable defendant who was apportioned 60% of responsibility and who has paid the full $1 million judgment has a $400,000 right of contribution.

The jointly and severally liable defendant has this right of contribution against each of the other defendants found liable by the jury.[64] However, the jointly and severally liable defendant has this right of contribution against the other liable defendants only to the extent that the other liable defendants have not paid the percentage of damages apportioned to them by the jury.[65]

If, in the example above, two other defendants had been assigned 20% responsibility each, and defendant 1 had already paid $200,000 of the damages, the jointly and severally liable defendant would have no right of contribution against defendant 1. If, on the other hand, defendant 2 had only paid $100,000 in damages, the jointly and severally liable defendant could recover $100,000 in contribution from defendant 2.

---

[57] Tex. Civ. Prac. & Rem. Code Ann. § 33.004(l).
[58] Tex. Civ. Prac. & Rem. Code Ann. § 33.004(l).
[59] Tex. Civ. Prac. & Rem. Code Ann. § 33.004(l).
[60] Tex. Civ. Prac. & Rem. Code Ann. § 33.004(h).
[61] Tex. Civ. Prac. & Rem. Code Ann. § 33.004(b) ("Nothing in this section affects the third-party practice as previously recognized in the rules and statutes of this state with regard to the assertion by a defendant of rights to contribution or indemnity. Nothing in this section affects the filing of crossclaims or counterclaims.").
[62] Tex. Civ. Prac. & Rem. Code Ann. § 33.004(i).
[63] Tex. Civ. Prac. & Rem. Code Ann. § 33.015(a).
[64] Tex. Civ. Prac. & Rem. Code Ann. § 33.015(a).
[65] Tex. Civ. Prac. & Rem. Code Ann. § 33.015(a).

No defendant has a right of contribution against a settling person, irrespective of any responsibility assigned to that settling person by the jury.[66]

18-6:2 Right of Contribution for Other Liable Defendants; Claim Against Contribution Defendant

All liable defendants, including those who are not jointly and severally liable, may have a right of contribution under Chapter 33. A liable defendant (any defendant against whom a judgment can be entered for at least a portion of the damages awarded to the claimant[67]) may assert this right against a "contribution defendant" and may do so in the claimant's action (e.g., the plaintiff's action).[68]

A "contribution defendant" is a defendant, counter-defendant or third-party defendant from whom any party seeks contribution but from whom the claimant seeks no relief at the time of submission.[69] A contribution defendant, therefore, would include a third-party defendant from whom the third-party plaintiff seeks contribution and against whom the plaintiff asserts no claim. It would also include a co-defendant the plaintiff nonsuited but against whom a claim for contribution had already been made by crossclaim.

In a separate question (i.e., separate from the question apportioning responsibility between claimants, defendants, settling persons and responsible third parties), the jury will determine each contribution defendant's percentage of responsibility as compared to the collective responsibility of the liable defendants.[70] The responsibility would be reapportioned based upon the liable defendants' pro rata share of the fault attributed to them in the separate apportionment question that included the contribution defendant.[71]

For example, in a case with two defendants, each of whom was found to have 40% responsibility in the initial apportionment question, and where their collective responsibility was 50% as compared to 50% for the contribution defendant, the liable defendants would be have a right of contribution against the contribution defendant for 50%, or 25% each.

18-6:3 Indemnity

Chapter 33 does not affect statutory, contractual or common law rights to indemnity.[72] Rights to indemnity prevail over the provisions of Chapter 33 to the extent of any conflict.[73]

---

[66] Tex. Civ. Prac. & Rem. Code Ann. § 33.015(d).
[67] Tex. Civ. Prac. & Rem. Code Ann. § 33.011(3).
[68] Tex. Civ. Prac. & Rem. Code Ann. § 33.016(a), (b).
[69] Tex. Civ. Prac. & Rem. Code Ann. § 33.016(a).
[70] Tex. Civ. Prac. & Rem. Code Ann. § 33.016(c); Gregory J. Lensing, *Proportionate Responsibility and Contribution Before and After the Tort Reform of 2003*, 35 Tex. Tech. L. Rev. 1125, 1172 (2004).
[71] Tex. Civ. Prac. & Rem. Code (for a detailed example of the calculation).
[72] Tex. Civ. Prac. & Rem. Code Ann. § 33.017.
[73] Tex. Civ. Prac. & Rem. Code Ann. § 33.017.

SECTION IV
Special Pleading Issues

CHAPTER 19

Texas Pleading Standards*

19-1 Necessity of Pleadings to Support the Charge

"Begin with the end in mind."[1] When representing the plaintiff, draft the anticipated jury charge for a case before drafting the pleadings. This will provide you with a clear picture of what you will need to prove to the jury, and by working backward from the charge, it will ensure that your pleadings provide the legal support to entitle you to the charge questions, definitions, and instructions you need.

The trial court is required to submit controlling factual issues to the jury when those issues have been raised in both the written pleadings and the evidence.[2] The court is not bound to the exact language of the pleadings in forming the questions and instructions to submit to the jury,[3] but to support submission of a jury question, the pleadings must give the opposing party "fair notice" of the claim.[4] (Standards governing the sufficiency of pleadings in Texas are discussed in Chapter 19, Sections 19-3, 19-4, and 19-5 below.) "In determining whether a cause of action was pleaded, plaintiff's pleadings must be adequate for the court to be able, from an examination of the plaintiff's pleadings alone, to ascertain with reasonable certainty and without resorting to outside information the elements of plaintiff's cause of action and the relief sought with sufficient information upon which to base a judgment."[5] Although this basic rule is subject to exceptions based upon an opponent's failure to specially except

---

* The authors thank Robyn Leatherwood for her assistance in the updating of this chapter.
[1] Habit #2 from Stephen R. Covey, The Seven Habits of Highly Effective People New York: Free Press (1989).
[2] Tex. R. Civ. P. 278; *Rosenboom Mach. & Tool, Inc. v. Machala*, 995 S.W.2d 817, 823 (Tex. App.—Houston [1st Dist.] 1999, pet. denied), citing *Elbaor v. Smith*, 845 S.W.2d 240, 243 (Tex. 1992).
[3] *Porter v. Reaves*, 728 S.W.2d 948, 950 (Tex. App.—Fort Worth 1987, no writ) (court not bound to use same language describing contractual breach as used in pleadings).
[4] Tex. R. Civ. P. 45(b), 47(a); *Rosenboom Mach. & Tool, Inc. v. Machala*, 995 S.W.2d 817, 823 (Tex. App.—Houston [1st Dist.] 1999, pet. denied), citing *Murray v. O & A Express, Inc.*, 630 S.W.2d 633, 636 (Tex. 1982).
[5] *Wright v. Modern Grp., Ltd.*, No. 13-12-00293-CV, 2013 WL 4714930, at *8 (Tex. App.—Corpus Christi-Edinburg Aug. 30, 2013, pet. denied).

to pleadings before trial,[6] engagement in trial by consent,[7] or failure to object to submission in the charge of an unpleaded matter,[8] it serves as a good guide for drafting pleadings at the outset of the case.

19-2 Texas Pattern Jury Charges and Other Sources for the Charge

Texas Pattern Jury Charges[9] is the primary source for anticipating and drafting a proposed charge to the jury in a Texas state court case. "Although we are aware that the Texas Pattern Jury Charges are not 'law', they are heavily relied upon by both the bench and bar. The recommendations made in the Texas Pattern Jury Charges are based on what the committee 'perceives the present law to be.' We were able to locate only one case in which a Texas court has expressly altered a Pattern Jury Charge."[10]

In addition to generally applicable instructions, Texas Pattern Jury Charges provides pattern questions and instructions relevant to multiple categories of business tort and contract litigation, including:

- Chapter 10 Agency and Special Relationships
- Chapter 18 Property Damages
- Chapters 60–61 Nonmedical Professional Malpractice
- Chapter 72 Joint and Several Liability
- Chapter 83 Property Damages
- Chapter 84 Economic Damages
- Chapter 85 Exemplary Damages
- Chapter 101 Contracts

---

[6] Tex. R. Civ. P. 90; *In Interest of M.I.W.*, 04-17-00207-CV, 2018 WL 1831678, at *2 (Tex. App.—San Antonio Apr. 18, 2018, no pet.).

[7] Tex. R. Civ. P. 67; *Scott v. Atchison, T. & S. F. R. Co.*, 572 S.W.2d 273, 277 (Tex. 1978) (pleadings of the parties furnish blueprint for the charge, and in the absence of trial by consent, a judgment not supported by the pleadings is erroneous); *Ingram v. Deere*, 288 S.W.3d 886, 892–93 (Tex. 2009) (because both parties presented conflicting testimony on the subject and allowed the issue to be raised in the jury charge, the contract's ambiguity was tried by consent).

[8] Tex. R. Civ. P. 274; *Murray v. O & A Express, Inc.*, 630 S.W.2d 633, 636–37 (Tex. 1982).

[9] Texas Pattern Jury Charges is a multi-volume set of pattern jury charges prepared by the Committee on Pattern Jury Charges of the State Bar of Texas and published by the State Bar of Texas.

[10] *H.E. Butt Grocery Co. v. Bilotto*, 928 S.W.2d 197, 199 (Tex. App.—San Antonio 1996), *aff'd*, 985 S.W.2d 22 (Tex. 1998) (citations omitted). Although the disapproval of a charge submission which was based upon the recommendation of Texas Pattern Jury Charges is relatively rare, it would not be correct to still state today that only one "Texas court has expressly altered a Pattern Jury Charge." In addition to the authority cited by the San Antonio Court of Appeals in 1996, *see, e.g., St. Joseph Hosp. v. Wolff*, 94 S.W.3d 513, 525–30 (Tex. 2002) (disapproving of definition of "joint enterprise" which Austin Court of Appeals had previously approved from Texas Pattern Jury Charges).

TEXAS PLEADING STANDARDS

- Chapter 102 The Texas Deceptive Trade Practices Act and Chapter 541 of the Texas Insurance Code
- Chapter 103 Good Faith and Fair Dealing
- Chapter 104 Fiduciary Duty
- Chapter 105 Fraud and Negligent Misrepresentation
- Chapter 106 Interference with Existing and Prospective Contract
- Chapter 107 Employment
- Chapter 108 Piercing the Corporate Veil
- Chapter 109 Civil Conspiracy
- Chapter 110 Defamation, Business Disparagement and Invasion of Privacy
- Chapter 115 Damages

Despite the prevalence and broad acceptance of Texas Pattern Jury Charges, the Committee on Pattern Jury Charges of the State Bar of Texas acknowledges that "[t]he infinite combinations of possible facts in contract, consumer, employment, and other business cases make it impracticable for the Committee to offer questions suitable for every occasion" and "occasions will arise for the use of questions and instructions not specifically addressed [in Texas Pattern Jury Charges.]"[11]

Ultimately, any source which sets forth the legal elements, defenses or definitions applicable to a particular set of facts and cause of action is a potential source of language for the court's charge. Examples of wording for the charge drawn from sources other than Texas Pattern Jury Charges include statutory language,[12] case law,[13] Restatement authority,[14] and language tailored to fit the evidence presented to the jury.[15] Nevertheless, be aware that the Texas Supreme Court actively discourages embellishment beyond the language suggested by Texas Pattern Jury Charges,[16] and Texas trial courts are justifiably reluctant to utilize charge language which differs from the recommended wording.

---

[11] Texas Pattern Jury Charges—*Business, Consumer, Insurance & Employment*, Section 2 of Introduction at p. xxxv (2016).

[12] *Borneman v. Steak & Ale of Tex., Inc.*, 22 S.W.3d 411, 413 (Tex. 2000) (generally the charge should track the language of the statute as closely as possible when a statutory cause of action is submitted).

[13] *See, e.g., Keetch v. Kroger Co.*, 845 S.W.2d 262, 266–67 (Tex. 1992).

[14] *St. Joseph Hosp. v. Wolff*, 94 S.W.3d 513, 525–30 (Tex. 2002) (disapproving of definition of "joint enterprise" from Texas Pattern Jury Charges and utilizing wording from Restatement 2d of Torts).

[15] *Garza v. Cantu*, 431 S.W.3d 96 n.4 (Tex. App.—Houston [14th Dist.] 2013, pet. denied) (damages instructions in contract suits are necessarily fact-specific and must be rewritten to fit the particular damages raised by the pleadings and proof).

[16] *Lemos v. Montez*, 680 S.W.2d 798, 800–01 (Tex. 1984) (judgment reversed due to the addition of language beyond that suggested by Texas Pattern Jury Charges).

19-3 Texas "Fair Notice" Standard for Pleadings

Tex. R. Civ. P. 47(a) requires the plaintiff to provide "a short statement of the cause of action sufficient to give fair notice of the claim involved." Tex. R. Civ. P. 45(b) clarifies this requirement by stating "[t]hat an allegation be evidentiary or be of legal conclusion shall not be grounds for an objection when fair notice to the opponent is given by the allegations as a whole."

The Texas "fair notice" standard for pleading "looks to whether the opposing party can ascertain from the pleading the nature and basic issues of the controversy and what testimony will be relevant."[17] In the absence of special exceptions, if the factual allegations provide the opponent with notice of the intended claim so that the opponent is enabled to prepare a defense, the sufficiency of the pleading will be upheld despite a failure to actually label the cause of action or plead all elements of the cause of action.[18] Likewise, at the opposite extreme, if the pleading states one or more elements of the claim in the form of legal conclusions rather than pleading factual allegations, the pleading is nevertheless sufficient (at least in the absence of special exception) if it gives "fair notice to the defendant of the basis of [the] complaint."[19] Both of these situations are consistent with the statement in Tex. R. Civ. P. 45(b) that pleadings will not be objectionable for being "evidentiary" or "of legal conclusion" when "fair notice" is "given by the allegations as a whole."

Special exceptions are available to point out pleading defects and omissions,[20] but they are not intended as a substitute for the discovery tools provided by the Texas Rules of Civil Procedure.[21] "When evaluating special exceptions, the trial court must accept as true all material factual allegations and all factual statements reasonably inferred from the allegations in the pleadings being challenged. Consistent with the trial court's discretion, pleadings are to be construed liberally. [The court is] to ignore any factual propositions outside the petition that tend to contradict the petition. The rule on special exceptions does not require that a plaintiff set out in his pleadings the evidence upon which he relies to establish his asserted cause of action. It is not a valid objection to complain that the pleading does not set out enough factual details, if fair notice of the claim is given. Similarly, complaining that a petition does not state a cause of action is inadequate, unless the defendant also specifically points out the defect or the reason the claim is invalid. If a plaintiff does not plead all elements of a cause of action, a defendant may file special exceptions requesting a more specific

---

[17] *Horizon/CMS Healthcare Corp. v. Auld*, 34 S.W.3d 887, 896 (Tex. 2000); *Texas Mut. Ins. Co. v. Ledbetter*, 251 S.W.3d 31, 37 (Tex. 2008).

[18] *Roark v. Allen*, 633 S.W.2d 804, 809–10 (Tex. 1982) (factual allegations held sufficient despite failure to specifically state cause of action for negligence); *In re Lipsky*, 460 S.W.3d 579, 590 (Tex. 2015) (fair notice pleading may exist despite omission of an element from the pleading or absence of supporting evidence in the pleading).

[19] *In re Lipsky*, 460 S.W.3d 579, 590 (Tex. 2015) (quoting *Paramount Pipe & Supply Co., Inc. v. Muhr*, 749 S.W.2d 491, 494–95 (Tex. 1988)).

[20] Tex. R. Civ. P. 90, 91.

[21] *Moore v. Dallas Entm't Co., Inc.*, 496 S.W.2d 711, 713 (Tex. Civ. App.—Tyler 1973, no writ) (when the petition adequately advises the defendant of the nature of the cause of action, the plaintiff is not required to plead evidence in detail in response to special exceptions since the factual basis of the claim is available through the discovery processes).

pleading, but in doing so must specifically identify any alleged missing elements."[22] If the pleading of legal conclusions does not mislead the opposing party, a special exception should not be sustained, but if pure legal conclusions without facts are not sufficient to apprise the defendant of the factual basis for a cause of action, a special exception is appropriate.[23]

There are occasions when the facts adduced at trial differ from the pleaded facts. Not all variances between pleading and proof are legally problematic.[24] As a general rule, a plaintiff "must recover, if at all, on the cause of action as it has been alleged"; nevertheless, "to be fatal, a variance must be substantial, misleading, constitute surprise, and be a prejudicial departure from the pleadings."[25] Even when a variance between pleading and proof is not legally preclusive, however, keep in mind that pleadings (including pleadings superseded by subsequent amendment) are generally admissible into evidence (subject to other potential objections) as party admissions.[26] Substantial variances between what has been alleged previously and what is being proven at trial can be problematic for credibility. Plead with care.

19-4 Comparing Texas and Federal Pleading Requirements

In the years since 2007, federal pleading standards have experienced a sea change. In light of this change, how do Texas pleading standards compare with current federal pleading standards?

The *Twombly*[27] and *Iqbal*[28] cases are the two U.S. Supreme Court opinions most instrumental in revising federal pleading requirements. Prior to *Twombly*, federal courts had analyzed challenges to pleadings based on "the accepted rule that a complaint should not be dismissed for failure to state a claim unless it appears beyond doubt that the plaintiff can prove no set of facts in support of his claim which would entitle him to relief."[29] *Twombly* retired this rule[30] and announced a "plausibility" standard for pleadings as "[t]he need at the pleading stage for allegations plausibly suggesting (not merely consistent with)" an entitlement to relief.[31] "While a complaint attacked by a Rule 12(b)(6) motion to dismiss does not need detailed factual allegations, a plaintiff's obligation to provide the 'grounds' of his 'entitle[ment] to relief' requires more than labels and conclusions, and a formulaic recitation of the elements of a cause of action will not do."[32]

To evaluate compliance with the federal plausibility standard, federal pleadings are analyzed in a two-step process. First, factual allegations are distinguished from con-

---

[22] *Guerrero v. Salinas*, 13-05-323-CV, 2006 WL 2294578, at *4 (Tex. App.—Corpus Christi Aug. 10, 2006, no pet.) (omitting inclusion of cited authorities).
[23] *Hubler v. City of Corpus Christi*, 564 S.W.2d 816, 823 (Tex. Civ. App.—Corpus Christi 1978, writ ref'd n.r.e.).
[24] *Ward v. Ladner*, 322 S.W.3d 692, 696–97 (Tex. App.—Tyler 2010, pet. denied).
[25] *Ward v. Ladner*, 322 S.W.3d 692, 696–97 (Tex. App.—Tyler 2010, pet. denied).
[26] *Bay Area Healthcare Grp., Ltd. v. McShane*, 239 S.W.3d 231 (Tex. 2007).
[27] *Bell Atl. Corp. v. Twombly*, 550 U.S. 544, 127 S. Ct. 1955, 167 L. Ed. 2d 929 (2007).
[28] *Ashcroft v. Iqbal*, 556 U.S. 662, 129 S. Ct. 1937, 173 L. Ed. 2d 868 (2009).
[29] *Conley v. Gibson*, 355 U.S. 41, 45–46, 78 S. Ct. 99, 2 L. Ed. 2d 80 (1957).
[30] *Bell Atl. Corp. v. Twombly*, 550 U.S. 544, 563, 127 S. Ct. 1955, 167 L. Ed. 2d 929 (2007).
[31] *Bell Atl. Corp. v. Twombly*, 550 U.S. 544, 557, 127 S. Ct. 1955, 167 L. Ed. 2d 929 (2007).
[32] *Bell Atl. Corp. v. Twombly*, 550 U.S. 544, 555, 127 S. Ct. 1955, 167 L. Ed. 2d 929 (2007).

clusory allegations, and only factual allegations are accepted as true for purposes of the second step.[33] Second, the factual allegations, accepted as true, are assessed to determine whether they show a plausible entitlement to relief rising beyond mere speculation or a mere inference of the possibility of misconduct.[34] Complaints that do not pass this analysis do not survive.

Is this federal "plausibility standard" for pleadings potentially applicable to Texas pleadings? Although the Texas Supreme Court has not yet fully addressed the question,[35] some Texas courts of appeals have suggested the answer is yes,[36] equating standards for the new Texas rule governing motions to dismiss[37] with standards for a federal 12(b)(6) motion to dismiss.[38]

On the other hand, differences in language between the Texas and federal rules suggest an argument to the contrary.[39] The U.S. Supreme Court emphasizes the wording of Fed. R. Civ. P. 8(b), which requires "showing that the pleader is entitled to relief" as justification for the necessity of evaluating plausibility of the claim at the pleading stage.[40] The Texas rule bearing the greatest similarity in wording is Tex. R. Civ. P. 47(a), requiring "a short statement of the cause of action sufficient to give fair notice of the claim involved" with no mention of "showing that the pleader is entitled to relief." And Texas, unlike the federal rules, further clarifies the Texas "fair notice" pleading standard by stating that pleadings will not be objectionable for being "evidentiary" or "of legal conclusion" when "fair notice" is "given by the allegations as a whole."[41] The potential distinction between state and federal pleading standards is the

---

[33] *Ashcroft v. Iqbal*, 556 U.S. 662, 678, 129 S. Ct. 1937, 173 L. Ed. 2d 868 (2009).

[34] *Ashcroft v. Iqbal*, 556 U.S. 662, 679, 129 S. Ct. 1937, 173 L. Ed. 2d 868 (2009).

[35] The Texas Supreme Court has recently stated: "We review the merits of a Rule 91a motion de novo because the availability of a remedy under the facts alleged is a question of law and the rule's factual-plausibility standard is akin to a legal-sufficiency review." *City of Dall. v. Sanchez*, 494 S.W.3d 722, 724 (Tex. 2016), *referring to Wooley v. Schaffer*, 447 S.W.3d 71, 74–76 (Tex. App.—Houston [14th Dist.] 2014, pet. denied), which analyzes 91a and 12(b)(6).

[36] *Dallas County Republican Party v. Dallas County Democratic Party*, 05-18-00916-CV, 2019 WL 4010776, at *4 (Tex. App.—Dallas Aug. 26, 2019, pet. denied) ("Though not identical to the Rule 12(b)(6) standard, the Texas Courts of Appeals have interpreted Rule 91a as essentially calling for a Rule 12(b)(6)-type analysis and have relied on the Rule 12(b)(6) case law in applying Rule 91a.").

[37] Tex. R. Civ. P. 91a (motion to dismiss claim with no basis in law or fact).

[38] Fed. R. Civ. P. 12(b)(6) (motion to dismiss for failure to state a claim upon which relief can be granted).

[39] *See In re Butt*, 495 S.W.3d 455, 461–62 (Tex. App.—Corpus Christi-Edinburg 2016, no pet. h.) (the federal rules are based on a more stringent pleading standard than the Texas rules, and Rule 91a did not revoke Texas's established "fair notice" pleading standard); *Reaves v. City of Corpus Christi*, 518 S.W.3d 594, 610–11 (Tex. App.—Corpus Christi-Edinburg 2017, no pet.) ("We cannot agree that rule 91a replaced Texas's notice pleading standard. Certain fundamental features of Texas law make it impracticable to incorporate *Iqbal's* standard into this state's pleading requirements.").

[40] *Bell Atl. Corp. v. Twombly*, 550 U.S. 544, 554–55, 127 S. Ct. 1955, 167 L. Ed. 2d 929 (2007); *Ashcroft v. Iqbal*, 556 U.S. 662, 677–78, 129 S. Ct. 1937, 173 L. Ed. 2d 868 (2009).

[41] Tex. R. Civ. P. 45(b).

TEXAS PLEADING STANDARDS

reason why the Fifth Circuit has required pleadings in removal cases to be evaluated according to the federal standards.[42]

In particular circumstances, Texas courts have routinely identified and disregarded conclusory (as distinguished from factual) allegations when the pleadings are serving an evidentiary function, such as supporting a default judgment for liquidated damages,[43] providing summary judgment evidence,[44] or being verified to serve as affidavit evidence for other purposes.[45] These are situations in which the pleadings are purporting to do more than to simply provide fair notice of a claim or defense.

19-5 Additional Pleading Requirements for Equitable Remedies

"Fair notice" of a request for equitable relief necessarily requires more specific pleadings since equity exists as the exceptional alternative only when there is no adequate remedy at law. At a minimum, a pleading seeking an equitable remedy must specifically allege grounds for the equitable remedy and must specifically pray for the requested equitable relief, in addition to alleging no adequate remedy at law.[46]

---

[42] *International Energy Ventures Mgmt., L.L.C. v. United Energy Grp., Ltd.*, 818 F.3d 193, 200–02 (5th Cir. 2016).

[43] *Willacy Cty. Appraisal Review Bd. v. South Padre Land Co.*, 767 S.W.2d 201, 203–04 (Tex. App.—Corpus Christi 1989, no writ).

[44] *Rizkallah v. Conner*, 952 S.W.2d 580, 586–87 (Tex. App.—Houston [1st Dist.] 1997, no pet.).

[45] *Holt Atherton Indus., Inc. v. Heine*, 835 S.W.2d 80, 82–83 (Tex. 1992).

[46] *See, e.g., Ryan v. Collins*, 496 S.W.2d 205, 209–10 (Tex. Civ. App.—Tyler 1973, writ ref'd n.r.e.).

CHAPTER 20

Pleading Texas State Court Discovery Level*

20-1 The Requirement to Plead Discovery Level

Every case filed in a Texas district or county court must be governed by a discovery control plan.[1] "A plaintiff must allege in the first numbered paragraph of the original petition whether discovery is intended to be conducted under Level 1, 2, or 3 of [Rule 190]." Immediately following the preamble paragraph of the Plaintiff's original petition, paragraph number one should state: "plaintiff intends to conduct discovery in this case under Level [1, 2, or 3] of Texas Rule of Civil Procedure 190."

The allegation language is very simple, but the considerations are potentially more complex.

Level 1 is the discovery control plan set forth in Tex. R. Civ. P. 190.2 for a category of small cases, specifically:

"Any suit that is governed by the expedited actions process in Rule 169,"[2] which essentially means any suit seeking only monetary relief (i.e. seeking no equitable or other non-monetary relief) of $100,000 or less (including damages of any kind, penalties, costs, expenses, prejudgment interest and attorney fees), but not including any suit with a claim governed by the Family Code, the Property Code, the Tax Code, or Chapter 74 of the Civil Practice & Remedies Code.[3]

"Any suit for divorce not involving children in which a party pleads that the value of the marital estate is more than zero but not more than $50,000," unless the parties agree that Level 2 should apply or the court orders a Level 3 discovery control plan.[4]

Note that changes are upcoming due to the passage of Texas Senate Bill 2342 and its requirement that the Supreme Court of Texas adopt expedited rules "to promote the prompt, efficient, and cost-effective resolution of civil actions."[5] Effective September 1, 2020, the Supreme Court of Texas shall adopt rules to promote the prompt,

---

* The authors thank Kimberly Trimble for her assistance in the updating of this chapter.
[1] Tex. R. Civ. P. 190.1.
[2] Tex. R. Civ. P. 190.2(a)(1), referencing Tex. R. Civ. P. 169.
[3] *See* Tex. R. Civ. P. 169(a). The Texas expedited actions process is discussed further in Chapter 20, Section 20-2.
[4] Tex. R. Civ. P. 190.2(a)(2).
[5] Tex. S.B. 2342, 86th Leg., R.S. (2019).

efficient, and cost-effective resolution of civil actions filed in county courts at law in which the amount in controversy does not exceed $250,000.[6]

Level 2 is the default discovery control plan set forth in Tex. R. Civ. P. 190.3 to govern all other cases unless a party requests the court to customize a Level 3 discovery control plan (or the court decides to do so on its own motion).[7]

Level 3 is the customizable discovery control plan tailored to fit the circumstances of a particular case.[8] Although many cases ultimately are controlled by Level 3, there is a potential advantage for plaintiffs who initially plead into a Level 2 discovery control plan, as explained in Section 20-3.

20-2 Considerations Before Pleading Level 1

Since this book is addressed specifically to Texas business tort and contract litigation, our focus for Level 1 is directed to expedited actions in business cases seeking only monetary relief of $100,000 or less. Expedited actions were first introduced in Texas in 2013.[9] Before pleading into this category of relief under Tex. R. Civ. P. 47(c)(1) and specifying this discovery level under Tex. R. Civ. P. 190.2, be aware of the potential advantages and disadvantages.[10]

> *Mandatory for Defendants.* A Level 1 discovery plan is mandatory for actions seeking only monetary relief of $100,000 or less (except for cases governed by the Family Code, the Property Code, the Tax Code, or Chapter 74 of the Civil Practice & Remedies Code).[11] A party does not have the ability to simply opt out of Level 1 by filing a request for a Level 3 discovery control plan, although the plaintiff can opt out of the expedited actions process by filing a timely amended pleading seeking non-monetary relief or damages greater than $100,000.[12] It is also possible for any party, including a defendant, to be removed from the expedited actions process on a motion and showing of good cause.[13] For the plaintiff, this means that the highly limited and less costly discovery permitted by Level 1 may aid in getting the case to trial sooner and more affordably, and it may still be

---

[6] Tex. Gov't Code Ann. §22.004 (h-1) (effective September 1, 2020).

[7] Tex. R. Civ. P. 190.3(a), unless superseded as provided by Tex. R. Civ. P. 190.4(a). Level 2 is discussed in Chapter 20, Section 20-3.

[8] Tex. R. Civ. P. 190.4.

[9] There are primarily three rules to consider: Tex. R. Civ. P. 169 (detailing the process), Tex. R. Civ. P. 47 (requiring plaintiffs to plead into or out of the process through categorization of relief sought), and Tex. R. Civ. P. 190 (limiting discovery).

[10] These advantages and disadvantages are discussed in greater detail by Michael Morrison, James Wren, & Chris Galeczka, *Expedited Civil Actions in Texas and the U.S.: A Survey of State Procedures and a Guide to Implementing Texas' New Expedited Actions Process*, 65 Baylor L. Rev. 824, 860–88 (2013), from which these excerpts are drawn.

[11] Tex. R. Civ. P. 169(a) and Tex. R. Civ. P. 169(d)(1).

[12] Tex. R. Civ. P. 169(c)(1)(B) and Tex. R. Civ. P. 190.2(c).

[13] Tex. R. Civ. P. 169(c)(1)(A). In addition, the court is authorized to reopen discovery whenever a pleading amendment or a supplemental discovery response is made so close to the discovery deadline that there is no opportunity to conduct discovery regarding the new material and the adverse party would be unfairly prejudiced without additional discovery. *See* Tex. R. Civ. P. 190.5(a) and Comment (2013) to Tex. R. Civ. P. 190.5.

possible to revert to Level 2 or 3 if the need for more discovery becomes obvious while still in the discovery process.

Short Discovery Period. Level 1 restricts the parties to a relatively short discovery period, starting on the day suit is filed (which means discovery requests can be served with the petition) and continuing "until 180 days after the date the first request for discovery of any kind is served on a party"[14] (allowing the 180-day discovery period to start running on the day the defendant is served with the suit). Keep in mind that parties must serve discovery requests far enough in advance of the deadline to allow for a response within the discovery time period.[15]

Restrictions on Discovery. Level 1 restricts each party to "no more than six hours in total to examine and cross-examine all witnesses in oral depositions," expandable to ten hours by agreement or additional hours by court order.[16] There are also restrictions on the number of interrogatories,[17] requests for production,[18] and requests for admissions[19] allowed, although one additional request for disclosure is allowed to obtain discovery of "all documents, electronic information, and tangible items that the disclosing party has in its possession, custody, or control and may use to support its claims or defenses."[20]

One-Sided Limit on Recovery. A plaintiff who opts in to the expedited actions process will be limited to a maximum recovery of $100,000, even if the jury were to return a verdict for more than that amount.[21] (It may be possible, however, to ask the jury to assess more than $100,000 in damages, as long as the net recovery after reduction for the plaintiff's percentage of responsibility does not exceed $100,000.).[22] A defendant who files a counterclaim for more than $100,000 is not subject to the same limitation on recovery.[23] (Due to this one-sided limitation on recovery, we recommend that plaintiff clients provide written acknowledgement of their understanding and authorization to proceed.)[24] Although it is possible for a plaintiff to amend the petition to plead out of the mandatory process, any such amendment must be filed by the earlier of 30 days after the end of the discovery period or 30 days before trial; after that date, amendment may only be done with leave of court, to be granted only if good cause is shown that outweighs any prejudice to an opponent.[25] A case for breach of contract, or any

---

[14] Tex. R. Civ. P. 190.2(b)(1).
[15] Comment 4 (2013) to Tex. R. Civ. P. 190.
[16] Tex. R. Civ. P. 190.2(b)(2).
[17] Tex. R. Civ. P. 190.2(b)(3).
[18] Tex. R. Civ. P. 190.2(b)(4).
[19] Tex. R. Civ. P. 190.2(b)(5).
[20] Tex. R. Civ. P. 190.2(b)(6).
[21] Tex. R. Civ. P. 169(b); *see* Comment 4 (2013) to Rule 169.
[22] *Cross v. Wagner*, 497 S.W.3d 611 (Tex. App.—El Paso 2016, no pet. h.).
[23] *See* Tex. R. Civ. P. 169(a)(1) and Comment 4 (2013) to Tex. R. Civ. P. 169.
[24] *See* recommended wording for obtaining informed consent of clients at Michael Morrison, James Wren, & Chris Galeczka, *Expedited Civil Actions in Texas and the U.S.: A Survey of State Procedures and a Guide to Implementing Texas' New Expedited Actions Process*, 65 Baylor L. Rev. 824, 866–67 (2013).
[25] Tex. R. Civ. P. 169(c)(2).

case for which attorney fees are recoverable by the prevailing party,[26] highlights the potential effect of a one-sided cap of $100,000 for recovery by the plaintiff. Even if the actual damages are clearly less than $100,000, the verdict limitation set forth in Tex. R. Civ. P. 169(a)(1) constricts "damages of any kind, penalties, costs, expenses, prejudgment interest, and attorney fees." This means that, in an expedited case, a ceiling exists on recovery of attorney fees by a prevailing plaintiff but not by a prevailing defendant, which may have an effect on settlement leverage as attorney fees continue to climb for both sides in a litigated case.[27] Note, however, that recovery for plaintiffs is limited on a per-claimant rather than per-side basis,[28] meaning that a defendant may face a judgment exceeding $100,000 when faced with multiple claimants.[29]

Expert Witness Considerations. If the case is one for which either side will need expert testimony, be aware of the early expert designation deadlines in effect. The expedited action rules do not alter the stated time periods for designation of experts provided by Tex. R. Civ. P. 195, but the shortened Level 1 schedule does effectively alter how quickly the parties will need to be prepared to make expert designations. According to Tex. R. Civ. P. 195.2, experts are to be designated according to the following schedule unless otherwise ordered by the court:

with regard to all experts testifying for a party seeking affirmative relief, 90 days before the end of the discovery period;

with regard to all other experts, 60 days before the end of the discovery period.

The Level 1 discovery period expires 180 days after the first discovery request is served, therefore the plaintiff's expert designation deadline in an expedited case occurs only 90 days after the first service of a discovery request. Also, pursuant to Tex. R. Civ. P. 195.3, the plaintiff will need to produce an expert report for a retained expert or be prepared to produce the expert within 15 days after designation. These early deadlines work to the benefit of the party best prepared to meet them. In addition, the rules for expedited actions decrease the filing of Daubert[30] motions attacking expert testimony. Before trial, unless the party sponsoring the expert requests other-

---

[26] *See, e.g.*, Tex. Civ. Prac. & Rem. Code Ann. § 38.001.

[27] In this scenario, the plaintiff would have the right to amend the petition (if filed by the earlier of 30 days after the end of the discovery period or 30 days before trial) to seek total monetary relief in excess of $100,000, and thereby remove the case from the expedited action process, but the result would be to reopen discovery, including the retaking of depositions, further increasing costs.

[28] Tex. R. Civ. P. 169(b).

[29] Although the language of Tex. R. Civ. P. 169(a) could possibly be read to limit all claimants together to an aggregate total of $100,000 ("The expedited actions process in this rule applies to a suit in which all claimants, other than counter-claimants, affirmatively plead that they seek only monetary relief aggregating $100,000 or less"), Comment 3 to Rule 169 does not support that interpretation, since it instructs courts, in determining whether good cause exists to remove a case from the expedited action process, to consider "whether the damages sought by multiple claimants against the same defendant exceed in the aggregate the relief allowed under 169(a)(1)."

[30] *See Daubert v. Merrell Dow Pharms., Inc.*, 509 U.S. 579, 113 S. Ct. 2786, 125 L. Ed. 2d 469 (1993).

wise, the only way to challenge the admissibility of expert testimony (other than for late designation[31]) is by means of an objection to summary judgment evidence.[32]

Early Trial Setting. The decision to plead the case as an expedited action under Level 1 improves the opportunity for an early trial setting. Tex. R. Civ. P. 169 specifies that "[o]n any party's request, the court must set the case for a trial date that is within 90 days after the [end of the] discovery period."[33] Presumably, either party could secure a future trial setting at the outset of the case, provided the request is made in compliance with any appropriate requirements set forth by local rules. Of course, a setting does not guarantee the case will be reached for trial, but the rule also purports to limit the court's discretion to grant continuances: "The court may continue the case twice, not to exceed a total of 60 days."[34]

Short Trial. Trials are also shorter in expedited action cases. Each side has eight hours "to complete jury selection, opening statements, presentation of evidence, examination and cross-examination of witnesses, and closing arguments."[35] However, time spent "on objections, bench conferences, bills of exception, and challenges for cause to a juror . . . [is] not included in the time limit."[36] For good cause, this time limit per side may be extended to not more than twelve hours on motion of any party.[37] If twelve hours would still not be sufficient time to adequately present the case, the alternative motion would be a motion to remove the case from the expedited action process for good cause, as the court lacks discretion to extend time beyond twelve hours per side.[38]

Jurisdictional Considerations. The decision of whether or not to plead into Level 1 discovery and the expedited actions process can have effects on court jurisdiction, which may be important in some cases. First, if the decision is made to plead out of Level 1 by stating that more than $100,000 in monetary relief is being sought, the requisite amount in controversy for federal removal jurisdiction has been stated and federal diversity jurisdiction potentially exists.[39] Second, most statutory county courts in Texas now have jurisdictional limits of $200,000 and subject matter jurisdiction for counterclaims must be independently, rather than derivatively, established,[40] a plaintiff filing an expedited actions case with Level 1 discovery in a statutory county court can at least limit the extent of counterclaim exposure to $200,000 (although the defendant can still file a separate claim in district court seeking a higher recovery). Third, since an expedited actions

---

[31] *See* Tex. R. Civ. P. 193.6.

[32] Tex. R. Civ. P. 169(d)(5).

[33] Tex. R. Civ. P. 169(d)(2). The party's request for a trial setting would still need to comply with Tex. R. Civ. P. 245 (requiring notice of at least 45 days prior to a first trial setting).

[34] Tex. R. Civ. P. 169(d)(2); pursuant to Tex. R. Civ. P. 245, resetting of a trial date simply requires "reasonable notice."

[35] Tex. R. Civ. P. 169(d)(3).

[36] Tex. R. Civ. P. 169(d)(3)(B).

[37] Tex. R. Civ. P. 169(d)(3).

[38] Tex. R. Civ. P. 169(c)(1)(A).

[39] *See* 28 U.S.C. §§ 1332, 1441.

[40] *Smith v. Clary Corp.*, 917 S.W.2d 796, 798 (Tex. 1996) (county court at law must not only have jurisdiction over amount in controversy, but must also have subject matter jurisdiction over counterclaim).

process can be filed in either a statutory county court or a district court, the decision can be made regarding whether or not to trigger Section 31.004 of the Texas Civil Practice and Remedies Code, which limits the res judicata and collateral estoppel effects of a case litigated in a Texas lower court when other issues from the same transaction or occurrence are subsequently litigated in district court.[41] This can be a consideration for cases in which the possibility exists that an issue litigated in an expedited case could provide the basis for issue preclusion in another case involving larger stakes.[42]

20-3 Considerations Before Pleading Level 2

Level 2 is underutilized by plaintiff attorneys, probably based in part on the knowledge that a defendant can automatically opt out of Level 2 in favor of Level 3, combined with the seeming complexity of computing Level 2 deadlines. Yet Level 2 should be pleaded by plaintiffs far more often than it is, for one simple reason: It is often the plaintiff who wants to press forward with the case, and by pleading Level 2 at the outset of the case the plaintiff is communicating a willingness to the court to be ready for trial within approximately one year from filing of the case. This gives the plaintiff a stronger position for negotiation of a Level 3 order than if the plaintiff had ceded the need for something other than Level 2 deadlines from the outset. It is true that the court must create a Level 3 order if requested to do so by any party,[43] but there is nothing that prevents the court from ordering deadlines which essentially track Level 2 when the plaintiff has already expressed a willingness and need for compliance with Level 2.

Of course, this presumes that the plaintiff truly does understand how to compute Level 2 deadlines and is honestly prepared to comply with them. That's why the remainder of this section explains the computation of Level 2 deadlines and the limits on Level 2 discovery.

Discovery Deadline. The discovery deadline is the first deadline to calendar for Level 2, but its computation is completely different from and more complex than Level 1. Although the discovery period starts with the filing of the suit[44] (which allows discovery requests to be served with the petition), the discovery deadline can't be computed until one of three possible events occurs: (1) written discovery is served by any party, triggering a due date for that discovery; (2) an oral deposition is taken by any party; or (3) a trial date is set. The discovery deadline is then computed as the earliest of these three possibilities:

(i) 30 days before the date set for trial, or

(ii) nine months after the date of the first oral deposition, or

---

[41] *See* Tex. Civ. Prac. & Rem. Code Ann. § 31.004; *Kizer v. Meyer, Lytton, Alen & Whitaker, Inc.*, 228 S.W.3d 384 (Tex. App.—Austin 2007, no pet.) (invoking Tex. Civ. Prac. & Rem. Code § 31.004 to allow second suit for negligence and breach of contract arising out of same transaction for which a prior take-nothing judgment had been rendered).

[42] For discussion of issue preclusion generally, *see, e.g., Barnes v. United Parcel Serv., Inc.*, 395 S.W.3d 165, 174 (Tex. App.—Houston [1 Dist.] 2012, pet. denied).

[43] *See* Tex. R. Civ. P. 190.4.

[44] Tex. R. Civ. P. 190.3(b)(1).

(iii) nine months after the due date (not the service date, and not the actual answer date) of the first response to written discovery.

Practically speaking, in many cases a party will initiate an oral deposition or send written discovery requests well before there is any trial setting, which allows calendaring of a tentative discovery deadline. The discovery deadline is only tentative because it is still subject to be trumped by a trial setting which is less than 30 days after the tentative discovery deadline, meaning that a new discovery deadline is created 30 days before the trial setting. One way to deal with this, consistent with the philosophy that the plaintiff should pursue the case as the ethical aggressor, is to serve discovery with the petition and then promptly obtain a trial setting as soon as the defendant answers, for approximately ten months later. This allows a complete calculation of the discovery deadline, which is necessary for computation of other deadlines, especially the expert designation deadline.

Expert Designation Deadlines. Pursuant to Tex. R. Civ. P. 195.2, experts are to be designated according to the following schedule unless otherwise ordered by the court:

with regard to all experts testifying for a party seeking affirmative relief, 90 days before the end of the discovery period;

with regard to all other experts, 60 days before the end of the discovery period.

This means that, as soon as the discovery deadline can be computed, the plaintiff's expert designation can likewise be computed to expire 90 days before the discovery deadline, and with the defendant's expert designation deadline following 30 days thereafter.

Limits on Discovery. Level 2 allows substantially greater discovery than Level 1, but limits are still imposed. "Each side [meaning all the litigants with generally common interests in the litigation] may have no more than 50 hours in oral depositions to examine and cross-examine parties on the opposing side, experts designated by those parties, and persons who are subject to those parties' control. If one side designates more than two experts, the opposing side may have an additional six hours of total deposition time for each additional expert designated. The court may modify the deposition hours and must do so when a side or party would be given unfair advantage."[45] Additionally, interrogatories (but not the other forms of written discovery) are limited in number.[46] Other forms of discovery including requests for production, and requests for disclosure, and requests for admission are not limited in number under Level 1 and Level 2.[47]

Deadline to Initiate Written Discovery. Since Level 2 deadlines are not spelled out by a court order, it is also important to be aware of the last date on which written discovery requests can be effectively served. The rules governing requests for disclosure,[48] requests for production,[49] interrogatories,[50] and requests for admis-

---

[45] Tex. R. Civ. P. 190.3(b)(2).
[46] Tex. R. Civ. P. 190.3(b)(3).
[47] Comment 5 (2013) to Tex. R. Civ. P. 190.
[48] *See* Tex. R. Civ. P. 194.1.
[49] *See* Tex. R. Civ. P. 196.1(a).
[50] *See* Tex. R. Civ. P. 197.1.

sions[51] all state that the written discovery instrument must be served "no later than 30 days before the end of any applicable discovery period." (These limitations also apply to Level 1 discovery.)

Supplementation of Discovery Responses. There is a continuing duty to amend or supplement an incorrect or incomplete response to written discovery "reasonably promptly" after learning of the need for such, but there is also a presumption "that an amended or supplemental response made less than 30 days before trial was not made reasonably promptly."[52] Based on this, we recommend calendaring a deadline to completely review the accuracy and completeness of written discovery responses more than 30 days before trial. Note that there is also a duty to supplement the report (if any) and oral deposition answers of an expert who "is retained by, employed by, or otherwise under the control of a party with regard to the expert's mental impressions or opinions and the basis for them."[53] (This duty and deadline also apply in Level 1 discovery.)

Amendment of Pleadings. Since there is generally no scheduling order with Level 2 discovery, the default rule for amendment of pleadings will typically apply. Pursuant to Tex. R. Civ. P. 63, absent a scheduling order of the court setting a different deadline, a party may amend pleadings without leave of court up to seven days before the date set for trial, which effectively means that amended pleadings can be filed without leave of court as late as the Monday preceding a trial setting for the next Monday.[54]

Reopening Discovery. In part due to the liberal allowance for amendment of pleadings, Tex. R. Civ. P. 190.5 allows additional discovery to be conducted in response to "new, amended or supplemental pleadings, or new information disclosed in a discovery response or in an amended or supplemental response, if (1) the pleadings or responses were made after the deadline for completion of discovery or so nearly before that deadline that an adverse party does not have an adequate opportunity to conduct discovery related to the new matters, and (2) the adverse party would be unfairly prejudiced without such additional discovery." In a similar vein and based on the same principle, case law extends the opportunity to designate experts after a designation deadline in response to an opponent's amended pleadings raising new allegations.[55] Also, when the trial date is more than three months after the discovery deadline, additional discovery is permitted "regarding matters that have changed materially after the discovery cutoff."[56]

Trial Settings. Unlike Level 1, there is no stated rule or expectation for trials to be set within a specific period of time. This means that it is up to the parties to initiate a trial setting, unless the court sets trial on its own initiative. There are also no stated time limits for the conduct of trial under Level 2, as there are under Level 1.

---

[51] *See* Tex. R. Civ. P. 198.1.
[52] Tex. R. Civ. P. 193.5(b).
[53] Tex. R. Civ. P. 195.6.
[54] *See Sosa v. Cent. Power & Light*, 909 S.W.2d 893 (Tex. 1995) (explaining the counting of days for application of Tex. R. Civ. P. 63).
[55] *Frazin v. Hanley*, 130 S.W.3d 373, 378 (Tex. App.—Dallas 2004, no pet.).
[56] Tex. R. Civ. P. 190.5.

20-4 Considerations Before Pleading Level 3

As expressed at the outset of the preceding section, we believe plaintiffs unnecessarily surrender negotiating leverage for pushing a case to trial within a year when the case is pleaded as a Level 3 case in the original petition. Undoubtedly any party, including both the defendant as well as the plaintiff in a subsequent pleading, can compel the court to fashion a Level 3 order on request, but the plaintiff's argument for a trial setting sooner rather than later is strengthened when the plaintiff has already stated a willingness to abide by Level 2 deadlines.

If a Level 3 discovery control plan is requested, plan to negotiate proposed dates and deadlines with opposing counsel. Parties are expected to cooperate for discovery and are expected to make reasonably necessary agreements. Further, parties must include a certificate with discovery motions and requests for hearings regarding discovery that the party filing the discovery motion has made reasonable effort to resolve the matter without court intervention and has failed.[57] Recognize that, at a minimum, the court must address the following scheduling matters pursuant to Tex. R. Civ. P. 190.4(b):

(1) Trial date, or date for a conference to determine a trial setting;

(2) Discovery period and discovery deadline;

(3) Appropriate limits on the amount of discovery; and

(4) Deadlines for joining additional parties, amending or supplementing pleadings, and designating expert witnesses.

Although not required, there are other scheduling matters including those listed below which are also commonly addressed in a Level 3 scheduling order, and which you will want to be prepared to negotiate with opposing counsel for recommendation to the court:

Deadline for filing dispositive motions (often with deadline for hearing date)

Deadline to file motions challenging expert qualifications or testimony (often with deadline for hearing date)

Deadline for filing designations of trial witnesses and trial exhibit lists

Deadline for filing designations of deposition testimony

Deadline for filing objections to deposition testimony

Deadline for filing pretrial motions (often with specified hearing date)

Deadline for alternative dispute resolution (mediation)

Level 3 may be used in more complex cases to allow for additional discovery. However, there is no requirement for the court to provide for discovery that is in excess of the discovery provided in Level 1 and Level 2. For example, a Level 3 discovery level can be used to limit the amount of discovery to prevent excessive discovery.[58]

---

[57] Tex. R. Civ. P. 191.2.
[58] *See* Comment 1 (2013) to Tex. R. Civ. P. 190.

20-5 Responding to Pleading of Discovery Level

As previously discussed, the defendant cannot simply opt out of a Level 1 discovery control plan when it is part of the mandatory expedited actions process, but there are options available to a defendant who does not believe a Level 1 plan is appropriate. Conversely, when Level 2 has been pleaded by the plaintiff, the defendant has the right to have the court provide a Level 3 plan.

Responding to Level 1. There are at least five types of motions made available under the rules in response to the pleading of Level 1 as an expedited actions process case:

Motion to remove the case from the expedited actions process for good cause, pursuant to Tex. R. Civ. P. 169(c)(1)(A) and Tex. R. Civ. P. 190.2(c).

Motion to reopen discovery after removal of case from expedited action process, to be granted as a matter of right pursuant to Tex. R. Civ. P. 169(c)(3) and Tex. R. Civ. P. 190.2(c).

Motion to enlarge time for depositions, to be granted in the discretion of the court pursuant to Tex. R. Civ. P. 190.2(b)(2).

Motion for additional discovery based on late amendment of pleadings or supplementation of discovery, to be granted in the discretion of the court pursuant to Tex. R. Civ. P. 190.5(a) and the accompanying comment to the rule.

Motion to extend the time limit for trial may be granted for good cause pursuant to Tex. R. Civ. P. 169(d)(3).

Responding to Level 2. In response to a Level 2 pleading by the plaintiff, the defendant may file a motion requesting rendition of a Level 3 discovery control plan, which triggers a mandatory duty by the trial court to provide a "discovery control plan tailored to the circumstances of the specific suit."[59] In addition, if late amendment of pleadings or late production of discovery necessitates the need for additional discovery, a party may obtain additional discovery pursuant to Tex. R. Civ. P. 190.5.

Also, if parties make agreements regarding discovery, the parties must file documentation to the extent needed to comply with the requirements of Tex. R. Civ. P. 11.[60]

---

[59] Tex. R. Civ. P. 190.4(a).
[60] Tex. R. Civ. P. 191.4(b); Tex. R. Civ. P. 11.

CHAPTER 21

Pleading Subject Matter Jurisdiction in Texas State Trial Courts*

21-1 The Subject Matter Jurisdiction of Texas Trial Courts

21-1:1 Justice Courts

Justice Courts have jurisdiction over civil actions where the amount in controversy does not exceed $10,000 (increasing to $20,000 effective September 1, 2020), exclusive of interest, unless exclusive jurisdiction is granted to the county or district courts.[1] A justice court has jurisdiction over cases of forcible entry and detainer (with no statutory limit on amount in controversy) and over foreclosure of mortgages and enforcement of liens on personal property so long as the amount in controversy is within the $10,000 limit (increasing to $20,000 effective September 1, 2020).[2]

Justice Courts do not have jurisdiction over the following cases, irrespective of the amount in controversy.

- A suit on behalf of the state to recover a penalty, forfeiture, or escheat;
- A suit for divorce;
- A suit to recover damages for slander or defamation of character;
- A suit for trial of title to land; or
- A suit for the enforcement of a lien on land.[3]

21-1:2 Constitutional County Courts

The Texas Constitution establishes a constitutional county court in every county in Texas.[4] The constitutional county courts have concurrent jurisdiction with justice courts in civil cases in which the matter in controversy exceeds $200 in value but does not exceed $10,000 (increasing to $20,000 effective September 1, 2020), exclusive of

---

* The authors thank Max Moran for his assistance in the updating of this chapter.
[1] Tex. Gov't Code Ann. § 27.031(a)(1).
[2] Tex. Gov't Code Ann. § 27.031(a)(2), (3).
[3] Tex. Gov't Code Ann. § 27.031(b)(1)–(5).
[4] Tex. Const. Art. 5, § 15.

interest.[5] The constitutional county courts also have appellate jurisdictions in cases over which the justice courts have original jurisdiction and the amount in controversy exceeds $250, exclusive of costs.[6]

A constitutional county court does not have jurisdiction over the following cases.

- A suit to recover damages for slander or defamation of character;
- A suit for the enforcement of a lien on land;
- A suit in behalf of the state for escheat;
- A suit for divorce;
- A suit for the forfeiture of a corporate charter;
- A suit for the trial of the right to property valued at $500 or more and levied on under a writ of execution, sequestration, or attachment;
- An eminent domain case; and
- A suit for the recovery of land.[7]

A constitutional county court may grant writs of mandamus, injunction, sequestration, attachment, garnishment, certiorari, and supersedeas and all other writs necessary to the enforcement of its jurisdiction so long as the case otherwise falls within its subject matter jurisdiction.[8]

Though a constitutional county court may, under certain circumstances, exercise probate jurisdiction, these cases are typically adjudicated in other trial courts.

21-1:3 Statutory County Courts

Statutory county courts (commonly known as "county courts at law") have jurisdiction over all causes and proceedings prescribed by law for constitutional county courts.[9] In addition, the statutory county courts have jurisdiction over civil actions in which the amount in controversy exceeds $500 but does not exceed $200,000 (increasing to $250,000 effective September 1, 2020), excluding interest, statutory or punitive damages and penalties, and attorney's fees and costs.[10]

In addition, the statutory county court has jurisdiction over appeals of final rulings and decisions of the Division of Workers' Compensation of the Texas Department

---

[5] Tex. Gov't Code Ann. § 26.042(a).
[6] Tex. Gov't Code Ann. § 26.042(e).
[7] Tex. Gov't Code Ann. § 26.043.
[8] Tex. Gov't Code Ann. § 26.051; *City of Beaumont v. West*, 484 S.W.2d 789, 792 (Tex. App.—Beaumont 1972, writ ref'd n.r.e.) ("It is only after that jurisdiction has been invoked in the manner prescribed by law and has thus become active that the court may act to enforce or protect the same."); *see also Medina v. Benkiser*, 262 S.W.3d 25, 27 (Tex. App.—Houston [1st Dist.] 2008, no pet.) ("... neither type of county court has jurisdiction to issue a writ of injunction unless the court already has jurisdiction over the controversy, either because of the subject matter or because of the amount in controversy.").
[9] Tex. Gov't Code Ann. § 25.0003(a).
[10] Tex. Gov't Code Ann. § 25.0003(c)(1).

of Insurance regarding workers' compensation claims, regardless of the amount in controversy.[11]

A statutory county court has probate jurisdiction, concurrent with the constitutional county court, except in counties with a statutory probate court, in which case probate matters must be heard in the statutory probate court.[12]

The statutory county court has equitable power to issue writs of injunction, mandamus, sequestration, attachment, garnishment, certiorari, supersedeas and all writs necessary for the enforcement of the jurisdiction of the court, but only if the case otherwise falls within the court's subject matter jurisdiction.[13]

A number of statutory county courts have had their subject matter jurisdiction significantly modified and/or expanded beyond that generally granted to such courts. The precise subject matter jurisdiction of the statutory county courts in each county can be found in the Texas Government Code,[14] and a good practice is to check the appropriate provision before making a presumption about what the jurisdiction of a particular statutory county court. For example, a county civil court at law in Harris County has jurisdiction over condemnation proceedings.[15]

21-1:4 District Courts

District courts are the principal trial courts in Texas and have no upper limit on the amount in controversy in civil cases.[16] For a time, the lower jurisdictional limit was unclear, being either in excess of $200[17] or in excess of $500.[18] The Supreme Court of Texas had not ruled on the issue.[19] An amendment to the statute defining the jurisdiction of district courts, however, appears to have resolved the question. In 2012, the legislature amended the statute to explicitly state that the minimum jurisdictional amount in controversy for civil actions in district court is in excess of $500.[20] In addition, the district courts may hear cases in which the only remedy sought is equitable.[21]

---

[11] Tex. Gov't Code Ann. § 25.0003(c)(2).

[12] Tex. Gov't Code Ann. § 25.0003(d), (e).

[13] *Medina v. Benkiser*, 262 S.W.3d 25, 27 (Tex. App.—Houston [1st Dist.] 2008, no pet.) (holding that statutory county courts do not have jurisdiction over cases where the only relief sought is equitable although they can issue injunctive relief once jurisdiction has attached based on the amount in controversy alleged for a legal remedy).

[14] Tex. Gov't Code Ann. §§ 25.0041-25.2512 (providing subject matter jurisdiction for statutory county courts alphabetically for each county).

[15] Tex. Gov't Code Ann. § 25.1032.

[16] Tex. Gov't Code Ann. § 24.007.

[17] Holding that the lower limit is in excess of $200. *Arteaga v. Jackson*, 994 S.W.2d 342, 342 (Tex. App.—Texarkana 1999, pet. denied); *Arnold v. West Bend Co.*, 983 S.W.2d 365, 366 n.1 (Tex. App.—Houston [1st Dist.] 1998, no pet.).

[18] Holding that the lower limit is in excess of $500, exclusive of interest. *Chapa v. Spivey*, 999 S.W.2d 833, 835-6 (Tex. App.—Tyler 1999, no pet.).

[19] *Peek v. Equip. Serv. Co.*, 779 S.W.2d 802, 804 n.4 (Tex. 1989).

[20] Tex. Gov't Code Ann. § 24.007 (amended 2012 to add "more than $500").

[21] Tex. Gov't Code Ann. § 24.008 ("The district court may hear and determine any cause that is cognizable by courts of law or equity and may grant any relief that could be granted by either courts of law or equity.").

21-1:5 Statutory Probate Courts

In counties with a statutory probate court, the statutory probate court has exclusive jurisdiction over probate and guardianship proceedings.[22] Although other trial courts have probate jurisdiction, contested probate cases are often ultimately heard in probate court because of transfer rules.[23]

The probate courts may exercise jurisdiction over matters related to a probate proceeding, including claims brought by or against a personal representative who is representing an estate.[24] Therefore, a proceeding related to a probate matter would include an action for wrongful death where the estate is the subject of a probate action in probate court.[25]

The statutory probate court has concurrent jurisdiction with the district court over personal injury, wrongful death, and survival actions brought by or against a person in that person's capacity as a personal representative.[26] The general statutory provisions for venue in personal injury, wrongful death, and survival actions govern venue for such matters,[27] despite the provision that venue for causes of action related to a probate proceeding is proper in the statutory probate court in which the estate is pending. In short, the fact that the probate court has subject matter jurisdiction over the tort action is not a substitute for establishing proper venue.[28]

21-2 Pleading and Determining Amount in Controversy

Generally, a pleading invokes the court's jurisdiction by pleading facts that fall within the subject matter jurisdiction of the court.[29] Absent an indication of fraud, jurisdictional allegations in the petition control.[30]

21-2:1 Aggregation of Claims

The claims of multiple plaintiffs are aggregated for the purpose of determining whether or not the suit falls within the amount in controversy of the court.[31] This

---

[22] Tex. Estates Code Ann. § 32.005 ("In a county in which there is a statutory probate court, the statutory probate court has exclusive jurisdiction of all probate proceedings, regardless of whether contested or uncontested."); Tex. Estates Code Ann. § 1022.005 ("In a county in which there is a statutory probate court, the statutory probate court has exclusive jurisdiction of all guardianship proceedings, regardless of whether contested or uncontested.").

[23] Tex. Estates Code Ann. §§ 32.002–.004.

[24] Tex. Estates Code Ann. § 31.002(a)(3), (4).

[25] Tex. Civ. Prac. & Rem. Code Ann. §§ 71.004, 71.021.

[26] Tex. Estates Code Ann. § 32.007(1).

[27] Tex. Estates Code Ann. § 33.003; Tex. Civ. Prac. & Rem. Code Ann. § 15.007.

[28] *Gonzalez v. Reliant Energy, Inc.*, 159 S.W.3d 615, 622 (Tex. 2005) (probate court was not proper venue for wrongful death and survival action even though it had jurisdiction over the action because it was related to the probate proceeding).

[29] *Peek v. Equip. Serv. Co.*, 779 S.W.2d 802, 804 (Tex. 1989).

[30] *Continental Coffee Prod. Co. v. Cazarez*, 937 S.W.2d 444, 449 (Tex. 1996).

[31] Tex. Gov't Code Ann. § 24.009.

PLEADING SUBJECT MATTER JURISDICTION

provision regarding aggregation of the claims of multiple plaintiffs applies only to plaintiffs, not those of other parties, such as multiple counterclaimants.[32]

A single plaintiff's multiple claims are aggregated for purposes of determining the amount in controversy.[33] Where the plaintiff asserts a single claim by way of multiple alternate theories, the amount in controversy is determined by the theory that would yield the largest award.[34] These rules for aggregation of a single claimant's multiple claims also apply to counter, cross, and third-party claimants.[35]

21-2:2 Presumption in Favor of Jurisdiction

District courts presume in favor of jurisdiction unless the absence of jurisdiction is affirmatively demonstrated by the pleadings.[36] This presumption has even been applied to cases filed in statutory county court, a court of limited jurisdiction.[37] Even if the pleadings never establish a jurisdictional amount, the amount may be established during trial.[38]

With respect to determining whether immunity deprives the court of subject matter jurisdiction, the jurisdictional analysis can be more rigorous, as the Texas Supreme Court explained in a 2018 decision:

> Immunity from suit may be asserted through a plea to the jurisdiction or other procedural vehicle, such as a motion for summary judgment. A jurisdictional plea may challenge the pleadings, the existence of jurisdictional facts, or both. When a jurisdictional plea challenges the pleadings, we determine if the plaintiff has alleged facts affirmatively demonstrating subject matter jurisdiction. If, however, the plea challenges the existence of jurisdictional facts, we must move beyond the pleadings and consider evidence when necessary to resolve the jurisdictional issues, even if the evidence implicates both subject matter jurisdiction and the merits of a claim.[39]

---

[32] *Smith v. Clary Corp.*, 917 S.W.2d 796, 799 (Tex. 1996) ("The courts have not and should not apply aggregation to divest a court of jurisdiction on counterclaims asserted by multiple defendants, whose joinder normally is not voluntary, and who have not chosen the forum.").

[33] *French v. Moore*, 169 S.W.3d 1, 7 (Tex. App.—Houston [1st Dist.] 2004, no pet.) (citing *Tejas Toyota, Inc. v. Griffin*, 587 S.W.2d 775, 776 (Tex. App.—Waco 1979, writ ref'd n.r.e.)).

[34] *French v. Moore*, 169 S.W.3d 1, 7 (Tex. App.—Houston [1st Dist.] 2004, no pet.) (citing *Lucey v. Se. Texas Emergency Physicians Assoc.*, 802 S.W.2d 300, 302 (Tex. App.—El Paso 1990, writ denied)).

[35] *See French v. Moore*, 169 S.W.3d 1, 7–8 (Tex. App.—Houston [1st Dist.] 2004, no pet.).

[36] *Peek v. Equip. Serv. Co.*, 779 S.W.2d 802, 804 (Tex. 1989).

[37] *Continental Coffee Prods. Co. v. Cazarez*, 937 S.W.2d 444, 449 (Tex. 1996) (applying presumption to case filed in statutory county court and stating "where the plaintiff's original and amended petitions do not affirmatively demonstrate an absence of jurisdiction, a liberal construction of the pleadings in favor of jurisdiction is appropriate").

[38] *Peek v. Equip. Serv. Co.*, 779 S.W.2d 802, 804 (Tex. 1989).

[39] *Alamo Heights Indep. Sch. Dist. v. Clark*, 544 S.W.3d 755, 770–71 (Tex. 2018). *See also Shamrock Psychiatric Clinic, P.A. v. Tex. Dep't of Health & Human Serv.*, 540 S.W.3d 553 (Tex. 2018).

If the plea challenges the jurisdictional facts, the inquiry resembles the summary judgment procedure. If the plaintiff's jurisdictional facts are challenged with evidence, the plaintiff must respond with evidence raising a genuine issue of material fact with respect to the jurisdictional matter or else face dismissal.[40]

21-2:3 Judgment in Excess of Jurisdictional Maximum

The courts of limited jurisdiction are not prohibited from rendering judgment in excess of their jurisdictional maximum. Even where an amendment increases the allegations beyond the maximum jurisdictional limit of the court, the court will maintain jurisdiction so long as the additional damages accrued due to the passage of time.[41] In cases governed by the Expedited Action Procedures (suits seeking only monetary relief of $100,000 or less), however, the court may not render judgment in excess of $100,000.[42]

A 2013 amendment to the Texas Rules of Civil Procedure requires plaintiffs to categorize the amount in controversy in their pleadings. Except in cases governed by the Family Code, any party seeking affirmative relief must allege that the damages sought are within the jurisdictional limits of the court, make a demand for judgment for any other relief the party may be entitled, as well as pleading into one of five ranges of damages:[43]

(1) only monetary relief of $100,000 or less, including damages of any kind, penalties, costs, expenses, prejudgment interest, and attorney fees; or

(2) monetary relief of $100,000 or less and non-monetary relief; or

(3) monetary relief over $100,000 but not more than $200,000; or

(4) monetary relief over $200,000 but not more than $1,000,000; or

(5) monetary relief over $1,000,000.

If a party fails to satisfy this rule, the rule prohibits the party from conducting discovery until the pleading is amended to comply.[44]

21-3 Subject Matter Jurisdiction for Counter, Cross, and Third-Party Claims

Counter, cross, and third-party claims may not exceed the maximum jurisdictional limits of the Texas justice, constitutional county, statutory probate, and statutory county courts.[45] Where the claim exceeds the maximum jurisdictional limit of the court, the court is without jurisdiction over the claim.[46] The claims of multiple cross, counter, and third-party claimants are not aggregated for purposes of determining if

---

[40] *Alamo Heights Indep. Sch. Dist. v. Clark*, 544 S.W.3d 755, 770–71(Tex. 2018).
[41] *Continental Coffee Prods. Co. v. Cazarez*, 937 S.W.2d 444, 449 (Tex. 1996).
[42] Tex. R. Civ. P. 169(b).
[43] Tex. R. Civ. P. 47(c).
[44] Tex. R. Civ. P. 47.
[45] *See Smith v. Clary Corp.*, 917 S.W.2d 796, 798–99 (Tex. 1996).
[46] *Smith v. Clary Corp.*, 917 S.W.2d 796 (Tex. 1996); *Kondos v. Carrico*, No. 2-05-374-CV, 2007 WL 704587, at *4 (Tex. App.—Fort Worth Mar. 8, 2007, pet. denied).

PLEADING SUBJECT MATTER JURISDICTION

the amount in controversy exceeds the court's maximum jurisdictional limit.[47] However, the claims of a single claimant are aggregated to determine the amount in controversy.[48]

21-4 Case or Controversy Requirement

Texas courts do not have subject matter jurisdiction where there is no case or controversy.[49] Texas courts apply justiciability doctrines, including mootness, ripeness, and standing, to determine if a case or controversy exists.[50]

21-5 Ecclesiastical Disputes

The First Amendment Establishment and Free Exercise Clauses deprive courts of subject matter jurisdiction to resolve ecclesiastical disputes. Texas courts have declined to exercise subject matter jurisdiction in cases requiring an entanglement in the affairs of the church.[51]

21-6 Exclusive Jurisdiction Lying with Agency

Where a statute grants an agency exclusive jurisdiction over a claim or cause of action, the district court is without jurisdiction of the cause.[52] Where the agency is granted original, but not exclusive, jurisdiction over a claim or cause of action, the doctrine of primary jurisdiction determines whether the case will be heard in a court or in the agency, but the trial court is not deprived of subject matter jurisdiction when the agency is granted only original jurisdiction rather than original and exclusive jurisdiction.[53]

21-7 Exclusive Jurisdiction in Federal Court

Texas state courts lack jurisdiction over cases for which Congress has granted exclusive jurisdiction to the federal courts. For example, federal courts have exclusive jurisdiction over admiralty[54] and bankruptcy cases[55] as well as suits against foreign diplomats,[56] suits for the recovery of a fine, penalty, or forfeiture under an Act of Con-

---

[47] *Smith v. Clary Corp.*, 917 S.W.2d 796, 799 (Tex. 1996).
[48] *French v. Moore*, 169 S.W.3d 1, 7 (Tex. App.—Houston [1st Dist.] 2004, no pet.).
[49] *See Patterson v. Planned Parenthood*, 971 S.W.2d 439 (Tex. 1998).
[50] *Patterson v. Planned Parenthood*, 971 S.W.2d 439 (Tex. 1998).
[51] *Westbrook v. Penley*, 231 S.W.3d 389 (Tex. 2007).
[52] *In re Accident Fund Gen. Ins. Co.*, 543 S.W.3d 750, 752 (Tex. 2017) (holding that the Division of Workers' Compensation has exclusive jurisdiction over statutory and tort claims that the bona fide worker process was used to fabricate grounds for terminating employment, saying "[w]hen an agency has exclusive jurisdiction and the plaintiff has not exhausted administrative remedies, the trial court lacks subject-matter jurisdiction and must dismiss any claim within the agency's exclusive jurisdiction."); *Subaru v. David McDavid Nissan*, 84 S.W.3d 212 (Tex. 2002).
[53] *Subaru v. David McDavid Nissan*, 84 S.W.3d 212 (Tex. 2002).
[54] 28 U.S.C. § 1333.
[55] 28 U.S.C. § 1334.
[56] 28 U.S.C. § 1351.

gress,[57] non-maritime seizure cases,[58] and direct actions against insurers of diplomats and their families.[59]

21-8 Sovereign Immunity

In the past, the Texas Supreme Court has stated that Texas courts have no subject matter jurisdiction over claims against a sovereign unless the sovereign has consented to the lawsuit, such as by means of the Texas Tort Claims Act.[60] The Tort Claims Act waives sovereignty in only three areas: (1) use of publicly owned automobiles; (2) premises defects: and (3) injuries arising out of conditions or use of property.[61]

The Texas Supreme Court has subsequently clarified this previous statement:

> "It is true we have stated that sovereign immunity is a jurisdictional bar. For example, we stated in a frequently cited decision, *Texas Department of Parks and Wildlife v. Miranda*, 'In Texas, sovereign immunity deprives a trial court of subject matter jurisdiction for lawsuits in which the state or certain governmental units have been sued unless the state consents to suit'. But more recently, we have been more guarded in our description of the interplay of jurisdiction and sovereign immunity in three decisions: *Houston Belt & Terminal Railway Co. v. City of Houston*; *Manbeck v. Austin Independent School District*; and *Rusk State Hospital v. Black*. We stated in these cases, quite deliberately, that sovereign immunity 'implicates' the trial court's subject matter jurisdiction. We did not hold that sovereign immunity equates to a lack of subject matter jurisdiction for all purposes or that sovereign immunity so implicates subject matter jurisdiction that it allows collateral attack on a final judgment."[62]

21-9 Attacking Subject Matter Jurisdiction

A plea to the jurisdiction challenges a Texas court's subject matter jurisdiction. A plea to the jurisdiction may be presented at any time before final judgment because subject matter jurisdiction cannot be waived prior to final judgment. A challenge to the court's subject matter jurisdiction may be raised for the first time on appeal.[63]

Where a plea to the jurisdiction challenges the pleadings, the court must determine whether the pleader has affirmatively alleged facts demonstrating that the court has subject matter jurisdiction.[64] Where the pleadings do not contain sufficient facts to affirmatively demonstrate the trial court's jurisdiction, the trial court should pro-

---

[57] 28 U.S.C. § 1355.
[58] 28 U.S.C. § 1356.
[59] 28 U.S.C. § 1364.
[60] *Texas Dep't of Parks & Wildlife v. Miranda*, 133 S.W.3d 217, 224 (Tex. 2004); Tex. Civ. Prac. & Rem. Code Ann. §§ 101.001-101.109.
[61] *Texas Dep't of Parks & Wildlife v. Miranda*, 133 S.W.3d 217, 224–25 (Tex. 2004).
[62] *Engelman Irrigation Dist. v. Shields Bros.*, 514 S.W.3d 746, 750–51 (Tex. 2017).
[63] *Henry v. Cox*, 520 S.W.3d 28, 35 (Tex. 2017) (citing *Clint Indep. Sch. Dist. v. Marquez*, 487 S.W.3d 538, 558 (Tex. 2016)); *Rusk State Hosp. v. Black*, 392 S.W.3d 88, 103 (Tex. 2012).
[64] *Texas Dep't of Parks & Wildlife v. Miranda*, 133 S.W.3d 217, 226 (Tex. 2004).

vide an opportunity to amend the pleadings, unless the pleading affirmatively demonstrated a lack of jurisdiction.[65]

In cases where the plea to the jurisdiction attacks the evidence, as is often the case with claims of sovereign immunity, the trial court may consider evidence submitted by the parties.[66] If the evidence raises a fact question with respect to subject matter jurisdiction, the trial court will deny the plea and the fact issue will be resolved by the jury.[67] The Supreme Court of Texas has stated that this procedure mirrors that for summary judgment motions.[68] The burden is on the defendant to establish a lack of subject matter jurisdiction.[69] Only then does the burden shift to the plaintiff to raise a fact issue regarding jurisdiction.[70]

---

[65] *Texas Dep't of Parks & Wildlife v. Miranda*, 133 S.W.3d 217, 226–27 (Tex. 2004).
[66] *Texas Dep't of Parks & Wildlife v. Miranda*, 133 S.W.3d 217, 227 (Tex. 2004).
[67] *Texas Dep't of Parks & Wildlife v. Miranda*, 133 S.W.3d 217, 227 (Tex. 2004).
[68] *Texas Dep't of Parks & Wildlife v. Miranda*, 133 S.W.3d 217, 227 (Tex. 2004).
[69] *Texas Dep't of Parks & Wildlife v. Miranda*, 133 S.W.3d 217, 228 (Tex. 2004).
[70] *Texas Dep't of Parks & Wildlife v. Miranda*, 133 S.W.3d 217, 228 (Tex. 2004).

CHAPTER 22

Pleading Texas Venue*

22-1 Presumptions Accorded to Pleaded Venue Facts

"A party who seeks to maintain venue of the action in a particular county . . . has the burden to make proof . . . that venue is maintainable in the county of suit."[1] The first layer of venue proof requires that venue facts and the cause of action for which the venue is appropriate (if venue is based upon a specific cause of action) are properly pleaded.

"All venue facts [as distinguished from mere conclusions] when properly pleaded, shall be taken as true unless specifically denied by the adverse party."[2] This places a premium on carefully delineating the factual basis for venue, specifically pleading the basis for venue in the venue section of the plaintiff's original petition, and specifically pleading all facts needed to support venue in the body of the original petition (such as the facts demonstrating how all or a substantial part of the events or omissions giving rise to the claim occurred in the county of suit).[3]

Many venue provisions depend upon the existence of a specific cause of action. For example, Texas Civil Practice and Remedies Code Section 15.017 provides for mandatory venue in the plaintiff's county of residence in a suit for libel, slander, or invasion of privacy. Tex. R. Civ. P. 87(2)(b) states that "the existence of a cause of action, when pleaded properly, shall be taken as established as alleged by the pleadings." The key language, however, is "pleaded properly." When the plaintiff's petition does not allege sufficient facts, even though accepted as true, to establish the existence of the cause of action, the cause of action has not been "pleaded properly" and therefore will not support the plaintiff's choice of venue.[4]

---

* The authors thank Max Moran for his assistance in the updating of this chapter.
[1] Tex. R. Civ. P. 87(2)(a).
[2] Tex. R. Civ. P. 87(3)(a); *see Union Carbide Corp. v. Loftin*, 256 S.W.3d 869 (Tex. App.—Beaumont 2008, pet. dism'd) (plaintiff failed to plead venue facts supporting conclusion that all or a substantial part of events or omissions giving rise to claim occurred in county of suit based on disease caused by cumulative exposures to defendants' benzene-containing products that resulted in each plaintiff suffering an indivisible injury).
[3] *See, e.g., Siemens Corp. v. Bartek*, No. 03-04-00613-CV, 2006 WL 1126219 (Tex. App.—Austin Apr. 28, 2006, no pet.).
[4] *In re Dole Food Co.*, 256 S.W.3d 851, 856–58 (Tex. App.—Beaumont 2008, no pet.).

The plaintiff is not required to prove the validity of venue by a preponderance of the evidence. Once the plaintiff provides "any probative evidence"[5] to support the existence of "proper venue,"[6] the trial court is required to accept the plaintiff's venue choice[7] (except when a transfer for convenience is appropriate, as discussed in Chapter 22, Section 22-3). Following judgment, the entire trial record is reviewable to confirm that the plaintiff's choice of venue was in fact supported by "any probative evidence."[8]

This burden of simply providing "any probative evidence" to support venue provides an advantage to the plaintiff, but only if the plaintiff is careful to detail the probative evidence in the pleadings. To properly plead the venue section in the original petition, first ascertain the basis (or multiple bases) for venue, and then specifically plead the venue facts (not just conclusions) required to demonstrate that the venue provision is applicable to the case.

22-2 Overview of the Texas Venue Scheme

Most of the Texas venue provisions are codified in Chapter 15 of the Texas Civil Practice & Remedies Code, but not all.[9] Chapter 15[10] does set forth the basic venue scheme, starting with the definition of "proper venue":

- "Proper venue" means:

---

[5] If the defendant specifically denies the truth of a pleaded venue fact, the plaintiff is then required to provide an affidavit in support of the pleaded venue fact, which is then accepted as prima facie proof of the fact. Tex. R. Civ. P. 87(3)(a).

[6] "Proper venue" is defined by Tex. Civ. Prac. & Rem. Code § 15.001(b), and the meaning of "proper venue" is discussed throughout this chapter.

[7] *Double Diamond-Del., Inc. v. Alfonso,* 487 S.W.3d 265, 270–71 (Tex. App.—Corpus Christi–Edinburg 2016, *reh'g denied*) (venue must be upheld if the record contains any probative evidence that the plaintiff's choice of venue was proper, even if the preponderance of the evidence is to the contrary); *Moveforfree.com, Inc. v. David Hetrick, Inc.,* 288 S.W.3d 539, 541–42 (Tex. App.—Houston [14th Dist.] 2009, no pet.) ("We look for any probative evidence to support the plaintiff's choice of venue, even if the evidence preponderates to the contrary. If any probative evidence supports the plaintiff's choice, then transferring venue is reversible error, mandating a new trial."); *but see Spin Doctor Golf, Inc. v. Paymentech, L.P.,* 296 S.W.3d 354, 357 (Tex. App.—Dallas 2009, pet. denied) ("In reviewing a venue decision, the appellate court must conduct an independent review of the entire record, including the trial on the merits if applicable, to determine whether any probative evidence supports the trial court's venue decision" to transfer venue, apparently ruling contra to *Wilson v. Texas Parks and Wildlife Dept.,* 886 S.W.2d 259, 260–61 (Tex. 1994)).

[8] *Nalle Plastics Family v. Porter,* 406 S.W.3d 186, 195 (Tex. App.—Corpus Christi–Edinburg 2013, pet. denied).

[9] For examples of venue provisions outside of Chapter 15 of the Texas Civil Practice & Remedies Code, *see* Tex. Bus. & Com. Code Ann. § 17.46(b)(23) (making it an unlawful deceptive trade practice to file suit based on a consumer transaction in any county other than in the county in which the defendant resides at the time of the commencement of the action or in the county in which the defendant in fact signed the contract); Tex. Civ. Prac. & Rem. Code Ann. § 65.023 (establishing venue for injunctive relief); Tex. Civ. Prac. & Rem. Code Ann. § 101.102(a) (establishing venue for Texas Tort Claims Act violations).

[10] Tex. Civ. Prac. & Rem. Code Ann. §§ 15.001 et seq.

- the venue required by the mandatory provisions of Subchapter B or another statute prescribing mandatory venue; or

- if Subdivision (1) does not apply, the venue provided by this subchapter or Subchapter C.[11]

This means that mandatory venue provisions (both from Subchapter B of Chapter 15 and from elsewhere) take precedence over the permissive general venue provisions of Subchapter A and the alternative permissive venue provisions of Subchapter C. But the proper venue analysis goes further than that, in three primary respects:

- When two permissive venue provisions provide for conflicting venue, which venue prevails? The case law establishes that the plaintiff's choice of permissive venue controls,[12] unless the court determines that another venue is more convenient,[13] as discussed in Chapter 22, Section 22-3.

- When two mandatory venue provisions provide for conflicting venue, which venue prevails? The case law is unclear, as discussed in Chapter 22, Section 22-4.

- When venue of a plaintiff's claim against at least one defendant has been established based on the foregoing principles, under what circumstances does that determination establish derivative venue over other parties and claims? Principles of derivative venue are discussed in Chapter 22, Section 22-6.

22-3 General Venue Options

The general rule of venue (commonly referred to as general venue) exists to assure a Texas resident of at least one venue choice in Texas, subject to the right of the court to overrule a permissive choice of venue on grounds of convenience.[14] As a result, the general venue options are often utilized.

General venue essentially provides four options to the plaintiff and a potential fifth option to the defendant. The plaintiff may choose to bring suit:[15]

- in the county in which all or a substantial part of the events or omissions giving rise to the claim occurred;

- in the county of defendant's residence at the time the cause of action accrued if defendant is a natural person;

---

[11] Tex. Civ. Prac. & Rem. Code Ann. § 15.001(b).

[12] *Hiles v. Arnie & Co., P.C.*, 402 S.W.3d 820, 825 (Tex. App.—Houston [14th Dist.] 2013, pet. denied) ("In general, plaintiffs are allowed to choose venue first, and when the county in which the plaintiff files suit is at least a permissive venue and no mandatory provision applies, the plaintiff's venue choice should not be disturbed.").

[13] Tex. Civ. Prac. & Rem. Code Ann. § 15.002(b), (c); *Garza v. Garcia*, 137 S.W.3d 36 (Tex. 2004).

[14] *See* Tex. Civ. Prac. & Rem. Code Ann. § 15.002.

[15] Tex. Civ. Prac. & Rem. Code Ann. § 15.002(a). Although the language of Tex. Civ. Prac. & Rem. Code § 15.002(a) speaks in mandatory terms ("all lawsuits shall be brought"), it is clear both from the definition of "proper venue" in Tex. Civ. Prac. & Rem. Code § 15.001(b) and from the introductory clause of Tex. Civ. Prac. & Rem. Code § 15.002(a) ("Except as otherwise provided by this subchapter or Subchapter B or C") that general venue does not take mandatory precedence over other venue provisions.

- in the county of the defendant's principal office in this state, if the defendant is not a natural person; or
- if Subdivisions (1), (2), and (3) do not apply, in the county in which the plaintiff resided at the time of the accrual of the cause of action.

The defendant may respond ("concurrently with or before the filing of the answer") by filing a motion to transfer the case "[f]or the convenience of the parties and witnesses and in the interest of justice" to another county.[16] "A court's ruling or decision to grant or deny a transfer under Subsection (b) is not grounds for appeal or mandamus and is not reversible error."[17]

The case law helps explain each of these general venue options and their proper pleading:

- *Where all or a substantial part of the events or omissions occurred.*[18] This venue provision requires showing more than a "tangential and insubstantial" connection with the county of suit,[19] but the plaintiff is not required to show that the county is where a majority of the events or omissions occurred or that the county has the most substantial connection to the events or omissions giving rise to the claim.[20] The test is whether the pleaded venue facts show that the events or omissions at issue in the county of venue are materially connected to the cause of action,[21] i.e., to the essential elements of the plaintiff's claim.[22]

- *Defendant's residence if defendant is a natural person.*[23] Although an individual may have only one domicile, he may establish more than one county of residence for venue purposes.[24] "Even a rented room may qualify and the intent to make a permanent home is not necessary to the establishment of a second residence away from the domicile."[25] The Texas Supreme Court has set forth a three-element test to determine whether a second residence away from a domicile has been established. The proof must show that (1) the defendant possesses a fixed place of abode, (2) occupied or intended to be occupied consistently over a substantial period of time, (3) which is permanent rather than temporary.[26]

- *Defendant's principal office in this state if defendant is not a natural person.*[27] "'Principal office' means a principal office of the corporation, unincorporated association, or partnership in this state in which the decision makers for the

---

[16] *See* Tex. Civ. Prac. & Rem. Code Ann. § 15.002(b).
[17] Tex. Civ. Prac. & Rem. Code Ann. § 15.002(c).
[18] Tex. Civ. Prac. & Rem. Code Ann. § 15.002(a)(1).
[19] *Chiriboga v. State Farm Mut. Auto. Ins. Co.*, 96 S.W.3d 673, 680–83 (Tex. App.—Austin 2003, no pet.).
[20] *Moveforfree.com, Inc. v. David Hetrick, Inc.*, 288 S.W.3d 539, 542–43 (Tex. App.—Houston [14th Dist.] 2009, no pet.).
[21] *Moveforfree.com, Inc. v. David Hetrick, Inc.*, 288 S.W.3d 539, 542 (Tex. App.—Houston [14th Dist.] 2009, no pet.).
[22] *Chiriboga v. State Farm Mut. Auto. Ins. Co.*, 96 S.W.3d 673, 680 (Tex. App.—Austin 2003, no pet.).
[23] Tex. Civ. Prac. & Rem. Code Ann. § 15.002(a)(2).
[24] *GeoChem Tech Corp. v. Verseckes*, 962 S.W.2d 541, 543–44 (Tex. 1998).
[25] *Mijares v. Paez*, 534 S.W.2d 435, 436 (Tex. App.—Amarillo 1976, no writ).
[26] *Snyder v. Pitts*, 150 Tex. 407, 241 S.W.2d 136, 140 (1951).
[27] Tex. Civ. Prac. & Rem. Code Ann. § 15.002(a)(3).

organization within this state conduct the daily affairs of the organization. The mere presence of an agency or representative does not establish a principal office."[28] A business entity can have more than one principal office in Texas, but a principal office cannot be an office that is "clearly subordinate to and controlled by another Texas office," nor can it be one that conducts "relatively common, low-level managerial decisions."[29] It must involve "officials who run the company day to day," and for there to be more than one principal office, there must be "decision makers of substantially equal responsibility and authority in different offices in the state."[30] "Necessarily, courts must look at the corporation's structure to determine a company's principal office or offices. The titles of the company officials in a particular office are not as informative as a description of their responsibility and authority, relative to other company officials within the state."[31]

- *If first three not applicable, where plaintiff resided.*[32] This fall-back venue provision is intended to provide Texas residents with a Texas venue choice when other venue choices don't apply. It applies to both individual and non-natural (e.g., corporate) plaintiffs.[33]

- *For the convenience of parties and witnesses and in the interest of justice.*[34] This convenience venue provision applies only on the motion of a defendant.[35] It makes sense for defendants to routinely plead to transfer venue for convenience when the plaintiff has asserted general or permissive venue, because a trial court's granting of a convenience transfer is not appealable or reversible in that situation.[36] If the trial court denies the motion to transfer for convenience, that denial is not appealable, but the denial does not affect the ability to review other asserted grounds for transfer of venue,[37] making a motion to transfer for convenience a "no-lose" proposition for defendants. By the terms of Texas Civil Practice and Remedies Code Section 15.002(b), a convenience transfer is not available when the plaintiff has properly pleaded a mandatory venue provision,[38] and

---

[28] Tex. Civ. Prac. & Rem. Code Ann. § 15.001(a).
[29] *In re Missouri Pac. R.R. Co.*, 998 S.W.2d 212, 217–20 (Tex. 1999).
[30] *In re Missouri Pac. R.R. Co.*, 998 S.W.2d 212, 220 (Tex. 1999).
[31] *In re Missouri Pac. R.R. Co.*, 998 S.W.2d 212, 220 (Tex. 1999).
[32] Tex. Civ. Prac. & Rem. Code Ann. § 15.002(a)(4).
[33] *In re Transcontinental Realty Inv'rs, Inc.*, 271 S.W.3d 270 (Tex. 2008).
[34] Tex. Civ. Prac. & Rem. Code Ann. § 15.002(b).
[35] *Chiriboga v. State Farm Mut. Auto. Ins. Co.*, 96 S.W.3d 673, 683 (Tex. App.—Austin 2003, no pet.).
[36] Tex. Civ. Prac. & Rem. Code Ann. § 15.002(c); *Garza v. Garcia*, 137 S.W.3d 36, 39 (Tex. 2004) ("Hypothetically, a trial judge could state there was no evidence for a convenience transfer, but grant it nonetheless, and (except for perhaps reporting it to the Judicial Conduct Commission) there is very little we could do about it.").
[37] *Garza v. Garcia*, 137 S.W.3d 36, 39 (Tex. 2004) ("When a defendant files a motion based on both convenience and another venue ground . . . the judge may deny both, in which case we may review only the latter.").
[38] Tex. Civ. Prac. & Rem. Code Ann. § 15.002(b) applies only when venue would otherwise be established under Subchapter A or Subchapter C, neither of which include mandatory venue provisions.

a convenience transfer order is non-reversible only when it is rendered under Subsection (b).[39]

22-4 Mandatory Venue Options

Although the Texas Supreme Court has said that a plaintiff is entitled to choose between two counties of proper venue and it is reversible error to overrule the plaintiff's choice by transferring venue to another county of proper venue,[40] it is unclear whether this principle is necessarily applicable when choosing between mandatory venue provisions.

Some of the more commonly invoked mandatory venue provisions include those relating to:

- *Land cases:* Actions relating to an interest in real property shall be brought in the county in which all or a part of the property is located.[41]

- *Landlord-tenant cases:* Except as provided by another statute prescribing mandatory venue, a suit between a landlord and a tenant arising under a lease shall be brought in the county in which all or a part of the real property is located.[42]

- *Mandamus against state government:* An action for mandamus against the head of a department of the state government shall be brought in Travis County.[43]

- *Suit against county:* An action against a county shall be brought in that county.[44]

- *Suit against small county political subdivision:* Except as provided by a law not contained in this chapter, an action against a political subdivision that is located in a county with a population of 100,000 or less shall be brought in the county in which the political subdivision is located.[45]

- *Libel, slander or invasion of privacy:* A suit for damages for libel, slander, or invasion of privacy shall be brought in the county in which the plaintiff resided at the time of the accrual of the cause of action, or in the county in which the defendant resided at the time of filing suit, or in the county of the residence of defendants, or any of them, or the domicile of any corporate defendant, at the election of the plaintiff.[46]

---

[39] Tex. Civ. Prac. & Rem. Code Ann. § 15.002(c).
[40] *Wilson v. Tex. Parks & Wildlife Dep't.*, 886 S.W.2d 259, 260–61 (Tex. 1994). This holding predated the legislative authorization of a convenience transfer set forth in Tex. Civ. Prac. & Rem. Code § 15.002(b), which states that a convenience transfer has no application when mandatory venue is involved.
[41] Tex. Civ. Prac. & Rem. Code Ann. § 15.011; *see In re Applied Chem. Magnesias Corp.*, 206 S.W.3d 114 (Tex. 2006) (defining scope of mandatory venue provision relating to interest in land).
[42] Tex. Civ. Prac. & Rem. Code Ann. § 15.0115.
[43] Tex. Civ. Prac. & Rem. Code Ann. § 15.014.
[44] Tex. Civ. Prac. & Rem. Code Ann. § 15.015.
[45] Tex. Civ. Prac. & Rem. Code Ann. § 15.0151.
[46] Tex. Civ. Prac. & Rem. Code Ann. § 15.017.

- *Major transaction:* An action arising from a major transaction shall be brought in a specified county if the party against whom the action is brought has agreed in writing that a suit arising from the transaction may be brought in that county.[47]
- *Injunction:* Except to stay proceedings in a suit or execution on a judgment, a writ of injunction against a party who is a resident of this state shall be tried in a district or county court in the county in which the party is domiciled.[48]
- *Texas Tort Claims Act:* A suit under this chapter shall be brought in state court in the county in which the cause of action or a part of the cause of action arises.[49]
- *Arbitration:* An application to enforce arbitration shall be filed in counties specified by agreement.[50]

When the same mandatory venue provision could support venue in more than one county, the plaintiff's venue decision between two counties of proper venue is determinative, and it constitutes reversible error for the trial court to transfer venue to the other county.[51]

But what happens when more than one mandatory venue provision could apply to a case, and the defendant challenges the plaintiff's pleading of venue with an alternative mandatory venue provision?

- One possibility is to simply apply the previously stated rule, that the plaintiff's venue decision between two counties of proper venue is determinative, and it constitutes reversible error for the trial court to transfer venue to the other county.[52] "Venue may be proper in multiple counties under mandatory venue rules, and the plaintiff is generally afforded the right to choose venue when suit is filed."[53]

But the holdings of various Texas courts have utilized varying rationales[54] to reach different and sometimes conflicting results on this question:

- When venue has been established by written agreement in a major transaction, the major transaction statute will prevail over a conflicting mandatory venue provision in the Texas Civil Practice and Remedies Code.[55]

---

[47] Tex. Civ. Prac. & Rem. Code Ann. § 15.020; *see In re Great Lakes Dredge & Dock Co. LLC*, 251 S.W.3d 68 (Tex. App.—Corpus Christi-Edinburg 2008, no pet.) (written venue selection agreement not enforceable because not in compliance with major transaction requirements); *In re Togs Energy, Inc.*, No. 05-09-01018-CV, 2009 WL 3260910 (Tex. App.—Dallas Oct. 13, 2009, no pet.) (written venue agreement must have stated value of at least $1 million to be enforceable as major transaction).

[48] Tex. Civ. Prac. & Rem. Code Ann. § 65.023.

[49] Tex. Civ. Prac. & Rem. Code Ann. § 101.102(a).

[50] Tex. Civ. Prac. & Rem. Code Ann. § 171.096.

[51] *Wilson v. Tex. Parks & Wildlife Dep't*, 886 S.W.2d 259, 260–61 (Tex. 1994).

[52] *Marshall v. Mahaffey*, 974 S.W.2d 942, 947–50 (Tex. App.—Beaumont 1998, pet. denied) (where there is a conflict between two mandatory venue provisions, general scheme of the venue statute allows plaintiff to choose between two proper venues).

[53] *In re Fisher*, 433 S.W.3d 523, 533 (Tex. 2014), quoting *Wilson v. Tex. Parks & Wildlife Dep't*, 886 S.W.2d 259, 260 (Tex. 1994).

[54] *See* James E. Wren and Cody L. Hill, *Resolving the Quandary of Conflicting, Mandatory-Venue Statutes in Texas*, 68 Baylor L. Rev. 85 (Winter 2016).

[55] *In re Fisher*, 433 S.W.3d 523 (Tex. 2014).

- When injunctive relief is the primary relief being sought by plaintiff (based on the pleading for permanent relief and the statement in the pleadings that damages cannot be ascertained by any certain pecuniary standard), then mandatory venue under Texas Civil Practice and Remedies Code Section 65.023 prevails over the mandatory venue asserted by the plaintiff.[56]

- When an applicable mandatory venue provision originates outside of Chapter 15 of the Texas Civil Practice & Remedies Code, it takes precedence over a mandatory venue provision relied upon by the plaintiff which originates from within Chapter 15.[57]

- When suit has been brought against a county, the mandatory venue provision of Texas Civil Practice and Remedies Code Section 15.015 takes precedence over the mandatory venue provision relied upon by the plaintiff, based upon long established case law, even when the plaintiff's alternative mandatory venue provision originates from outside of Chapter 15 of the Texas Civil Practice & Remedies Code.[58]

- When plaintiff seeks injunctive relief in the face of an arbitration agreement providing for venue, the more specific, later enacted statute of mandatory venue in Texas Civil Practice and Remedies Code Section 171.096(b) controls over the prior enacted statute of mandatory venue in Texas Civil Practice and Remedies Code Section 65.023(a).[59]

22-5 Permissive Venue Options

Permissive venue provisions are found both in Subchapter C of Chapter 15 of the Texas Civil Practices and Remedies Code and in various statutes outside of Chapter 15. Texas Civil Practice and Remedies Code Section 15.038 specifically acknowledges the authority of permissive venue provisions found in statutes outside of Chapter 15.

Some of the more commonly invoked permissive venue provisions provide favorable options to plaintiffs, including those relating to:

- *Suit against an executor, administrator, or guardian:* In the county where the estate is administered or county in which the negligent act of the person whose estate is being administered occurred.[60]

- *Suit against insurance company:* In the county where loss occurred, where policyholder or beneficiary resided, or where company's principal office in state is located.[61]

---

[56] *In re Dole Food Co.*, 256 S.W.3d 851, 854–55 (Tex. App.—Beaumont 2008, no pet.) (citing to *Brown v. Gulf Tel. Co.*, 157 Tex. 607, 306 S.W.2d 706, 708 (1957)).

[57] *In re Dole Food Co.*, 256 S.W.3d 851, 856 (Tex. App.—Beaumont 2008, no pet.) (citing to the language of Tex. Civ. Prac. & Rem. Code Ann. § 15.016 and *In re Texas Dep't of Transp.*, 218 S.W.3d 74, 76 (Tex. 2007) (orig. proceeding)).

[58] *In re Fort Bend Cty.*, 278 S.W.3d 842 (Tex. App.—Houston [14th Dist.] 2009, no pet.) (citing to *City of Tahoka v. Jackson*, 115 Tex. 89, 276 S.W. 662, 663 (1925)).

[59] *In re Sosa*, 370 S.W.3d 79 (Tex. App.—Houston [14th Dist.] 2012, no pet.).

[60] Tex. Civ. Prac. & Rem. Code Ann. § 15.031.

[61] Tex. Civ. Prac. & Rem. Code Ann. § 15.032.

- *Breach of warranty by manufacturer:* In a suit for breach of warranty by a manufacturer of consumer goods, options for venue include the county where the plaintiff resides.[62]
- *Contract in writing:* In the county where a contracting party has agreed in writing to perform an obligation, except suit on a consumer transaction contract is limited to where the consumer signed the contract or resides when the action is commenced.[63]
- *DTPA violations:* In any county authorized by Chapter 15 of the Texas Civil Practice and Remedies Code, or in a county in which the defendant or an authorized agent of the defendant solicited the transaction made the subject of the action.[64]

These permissive venue options can provide favorable venue not only on single claims, but as a basis to establish venue over other claims and defendants when used in conjunction with derivative venue.

22-6 Derivative Venue Options

Derivative venue allows multiple claims and parties to go forward in a single case in order to avoid a multiplicity of suits by allowing the venue of one claim against one party to derivatively fix venue for other properly joined claims and parties.

The most basic rule of derivative venue comes from case law rather than statute, and has been referenced by many cases[65] as the Middlebrook doctrine due to its 1894 application by the Texas Supreme Court in *Middlebrook v. David Bradley Manufacturing. Co.*[66] "This rule is that a plaintiff who in good faith asserts joinable claims against the same defendant can maintain venue upon all those claims in a county where venue is proper as to one claim."[67]

Statutory derivative venue provisions build on this basic rule (allowing a single venue for joinder of multiple claims against one defendant) by providing venue rules for joinder of multiple defendants and third-party defendants, joinder of multiple claims between parties, and (to a limited extent) joinder of multiple plaintiffs.

The key statutory derivative venue provisions to understand for pleading purposes are:

- *Texas Civil Practice and Remedies Code Section 15.004:* Derivative Mandatory Venue for Multiple Claims. This statute builds on the Middlebrook doctrine by explicitly stating that mandatory venue for one claim will establish venue for all

---

[62] Tex. Civ. Prac. & Rem. Code Ann. § 15.033.
[63] Tex. Civ. Prac. & Rem. Code Ann. § 15.035; a violation of this permissive venue provision by filing suit on a consumer transaction in a county other than where the contract was signed or where the consumer resides is made actionable under the DTPA pursuant to Tex. Bus. & Com. Code Ann. § 17.46(b)(23).
[64] Tex. Bus. & Com. Code Ann. § 17.56 (second).
[65] *See, e.g., Brazos Valley Harvestore Sys., Inc. v. Beavers*, 535 S.W.2d 797, 802 (Tex. App.—Tyler 1976, writ dism'd).
[66] *Middlebrook v. David Bradley Mfg. Co.*, 86 Tex. 706, 26 S.W. 935 (1894).
[67] *Brazos Valley Harvestore Sys., Inc. v. Beavers*, 535 S.W.2d 797, 802 (Tex. App.—Tyler 1976, writ dism'd).

other claims of the plaintiff properly joined and arising out of the same transaction, occurrence, or series of transactions or occurrences.

- *Texas Civil Practice and Remedies Code Section 15.005:* Derivative Venue for Multiple Defendants. This statute expands derivative venue by extending venue as to one defendant to all additional defendants for claims of the plaintiff arising out of the same transaction, occurrence, or series of transactions or occurrences.

- *Texas Civil Practice and Remedies Code Section 15.0641:* Venue Rights of Multiple Defendants. This statute limits the potential reach of Texas Civil Practice and Remedies Code Section 15.005 by preventing one defendant's waiver of venue rights from derivatively establishing venue against other defendants.

- *Texas Civil Practice and Remedies Code Section 15.062:* Derivative Venue for Counterclaims, Crossclaims, and Third-Party Claims. This statute extends derivative venue over properly joined counterclaims, crossclaims, and third-party claims.

- *Texas Civil Practice and Remedies Code Section 15.003:* Limited Derivative Venue for Multiple Plaintiffs. The ability of multiple plaintiffs to join in one case is limited to situations in which each plaintiff can independently establish venue against the defendant(s), except in the rare circumstance where a plaintiff (who cannot independently establish venue) is nevertheless able to establish that (1) her joinder or intervention is proper under the Texas Rules of Civil Procedure, (2) maintaining venue for that plaintiff will cause no unfair prejudice to another party, (3) there is an essential need to have that plaintiff's claim tried in the county in which the suit is pending, and (4) the venue is fair and convenient for that plaintiff and all persons against whom the suit is brought.[68]

22-7 Pleadings Attacking and Supporting Venue

Tex. R. Civ. P. 86 sets forth the procedure for filing a motion to transfer venue, including the requirement that the motion be "filed prior to or concurrently with any other plea, pleading or motion except a special appearance motion provided in Rule 120a."[69]

The motion to transfer venue may be included as part of the original answer, or it may be set forth in a separate instrument[70] provided it is not waived by being filemarked at a time later than the filemark shown on the answer. The motion is not required to be verified.[71] Supporting affidavits may be attached with the motion,[72] and will ultimately be needed when controverted venue facts must be established. "All venue facts, when properly pleaded, shall be taken as true unless specifically denied by the adverse party. When a venue fact is specifically denied, the party pleading the

---

[68] *See Surgitek. v. Abel*, 997 S.W.2d 598 (Tex. 1999) (a need to pool resources against common experts and issues was insufficient to establish that it was indispensably necessary to try plaintiffs' claims in county where other two plaintiffs established venue).

[69] Tex. R. Civ. P. 86(1); *see* Chapter 13, Section 13-2 on due order of pleading defenses.

[70] Tex. R. Civ. P. 86(2).

[71] Tex. R. Civ. P. 86(3).

[72] Tex. R. Civ. P. 86(3).

venue fact must make prima facie proof of that venue fact [other than the existence of a cause of action properly pleaded]."[73]

The movant (defendant) has the burden to request a setting on the motion to transfer venue, which must be heard promptly but with at least 45 days notice of hearing.[74] The plaintiff's response to the motion to transfer venue, with any supporting affidavits, must be filed at least 30 days prior to the hearing.[75]

If the movant (defendant) elects to file a reply to the plaintiff's response, the reply and any further affidavits must be filed at least seven days before the hearing, unless leave of court for a later filing is granted.[76]

---

[73] Tex. R. Civ. P. 87(3)(a).
[74] Tex. R. Civ. P. 87(1).
[75] Tex. R. Civ. P. 87(1).
[76] Tex. R. Civ. P. 87(1).

CHAPTER 23

Pleading Parties and Methods of Service*

23-1 Pleading Requirements for Parties

Tex. R. Civ. P. 79 requires that "[t]he petition shall state the names of the parties and their residences, if known." In the initial pleading filed on behalf of an individual party to a suit, whether in the original petition on behalf of the plaintiff or in the original answer on behalf of the defendant (or in an original third-party pleading), "each party or the party's attorney shall include in its initial pleading:

- the last three numbers of the party's driver's license number, if the party has been issued a driver's license; and

- the last three numbers of the party's social security number, if the party has been issued a social security number."[1]

In addition, "each party or the party's attorney must provide the clerk of the court with written notice of the party's name and current residence or business address."[2] In years past, it was common for the petition to simply name parties and list their county of residence, without providing a specific address; but full addresses are now commonly provided in the pleadings to obviate the need for a separate filing and to simplify the issuance and service of process.

All domestic and foreign filing entities (corporations, limited partnerships, limited liability companies, professional associations, cooperatives, real estate investment trusts, and foreign entities that register or are required to register pursuant to state law[3]) are required to maintain a registered agent for service of process,[4] and financial institutions may also maintain a registered agent.[5] When a business entity with a Texas registered agent is named as a party, it is routine to include the name and address of the registered agent with the identification of the business party to facilitate service of process.

---

* The authors thank Max Moran for his assistance in the updating of this chapter.
[1] Tex. Civ. Prac. & Rem. Code Ann. § 30.014(a).
[2] Tex. Civ. Prac. & Rem. Code Ann. § 30.015(a).
[3] For filing requirements of foreign entities, see Tex. Bus. Org. Code Ann. § 9.001.
[4] Tex. Bus. Orgs. Code Ann. § 5.201.
[5] Tex. Fin. Code Ann. § 201.103.

The Texas Business Organizations Code also specifies additional agents for service of process on business entities:[6]

- The president and each vice president of a domestic or foreign corporation is an agent of that corporation;

- Each general partner of a domestic or foreign limited partnership and each partner of a domestic or foreign general partnership is an agent of that partnership;

- Each manager of a manager-managed domestic or foreign limited liability company and each member of a member-managed domestic or foreign limited liability company is an agent of that limited liability company;

- Each person who is a governing person of a domestic or foreign entity, other than an entity listed in Subdivisions (1)–(3), is an agent of that entity; and

- Each member of a committee of a nonprofit corporation authorized to perform the chief executive function of the corporation is an agent of that corporation.

In addition, if a filing entity fails to maintain a registered agent, the secretary of state is statutorily appointed as an agent of the entity for purposes of service of process.[7] When this form of substituted service is relied upon, however, the record (through factual allegations in the petition or through a return of citation on file for attempted service of process) must reflect the facts justifying substituted service on the secretary of state in order to support a default judgment.[8]

Parties may sue and be sued in Texas in their legal names, or in their business assumed names or common names.[9] Although a party is required to comply with the assumed name filing requirements set forth by Chapter 71 of the Texas Business and Commerce Code in order to be entitled to maintain suit in an assumed name,[10] the failure to have a current assumed name certificate on file does not prevent parties from defending suits brought against them arising out of a contract or act for which an assumed name was used,[11] nor does it prevent a plaintiff from suing a defendant in that assumed name.[12] If the failure of a defendant to maintain a current assumed name certificate results in difficulty locating the defendant, the court may award the plaintiff "expenses incurred, including attorney's fees, in locating and effecting service of process on the defendant."[13]

Tex. R. Civ. P. 28 permits a plaintiff to effectively bring suit against an individual doing business under the name of an association, partnership, or corporation, even if the association, partnership, or corporation does not actually exist, and even if the plaintiff mistakenly thinks a company under that name legally exists and identifies

---

[6] Tex. Bus. Orgs. Code Ann. § 5.255.
[7] Tex. Bus. Orgs. Code Ann. § 5.251.
[8] *National Multiple Sclerosis Soc'y-N. Tex. Chapter v. Rice*, 29 S.W.3d 174, 176–78 (Tex. App.—Eastland 2000, no pet.).
[9] Tex. R. Civ. P. 28.
[10] Tex. Bus. & Com. Code Ann. § 71.201(a).
[11] Tex. Bus. & Com. Code Ann. § 71.201(a).
[12] *Broemer v. Houston Lawyer Referral Serv.*, 407 S.W.3d 477, 482 (Tex. App.—Houston [14th Dist.] 2013, no pet.).
[13] Tex. Bus. & Com. Code § 71.201(b).

the defendant in the original petition as a corporation.[14] The converse is also true. A plaintiff can effectively sue a business entity operating in the assumed name of an individual, even when the plaintiff thinks an individual is being sued and states such in the petition.[15] Evidence of a defendant's adoption of an assumed name may be produced from signage, billing statements,[16] contractual agreements,[17] phone books,[18] stationery letterhead,[19] signature blocks,[20] or any source identifying usage of the assumed name by the defendant. The judgment rendered against a defendant in an assumed name is binding on the true defendant.[21]

Tex. R. Civ. P. 29 provides that service of process on a dissolved corporation may be made on the president, directors, general manager, trustee, assignee, or other persons who were in charge of the corporation at the time it was dissolved, if no receiver has been appointed.

23-2 Addressing the Mispleading of Parties

Despite efforts to correctly name adverse parties in pleadings, on occasion a defendant or third-party defendant will contend that a pleading has not correctly named the party. The consequences of using a name other than the legal name of a party can range from being of no consequence at all to being fatal to a claim.

If, in response to a claim of misidentification or misnomer, it can be shown that a party has in fact been sued in an assumed name,[22] then there is no adverse consequence. Tex. R. Civ. P. 28 expressly permits a defendant to be sued in an assumed name. When a defendant has been correctly sued in an assumed name, the filing has the same legal effect as utilizing the legal name of the defendant.[23]

As a second alternative, if it can be shown that service was actually accomplished on the correct party, albeit using an incorrect name, then the rules of misnomer apply.[24] Assuming the defendant has not been misled by the misnomer, then the statute of limitations are tolled as of the date of filing of the suit, and correction of the pleadings to reflect the defendant's true name will relate back to the original date of filing.[25] A

---

[14] *Chilkewitz v. Hyson*, 22 S.W.3d 825, 828–29 (Tex. 1999).
[15] *Chilkewitz v. Hyson*, 22 S.W.3d 825, 829 (Tex. 1999).
[16] *Broemer v. Houston Lawyer Referral Serv.*, 407 S.W.3d 477, 483 (Tex. App.—Houston [14th Dist.] 2013, no pet.).
[17] *Broemer v. Houston Lawyer Referral Serv.*, 407 S.W.3d 477, 483 (Tex. App.—Houston [14th Dist.] 2013, no pet.).
[18] *Chilkewitz v. Hyson*, 22 S.W.3d 825, 829 (Tex. 1999).
[19] *Chilkewitz v. Hyson*, 22 S.W.3d 825, 829 (Tex. 1999).
[20] *Broemer v. Houston Lawyer Referral Serv.*, 407 S.W.3d 477, 483 (Tex. App.—Houston [14th Dist.] 2013, no pet.).
[21] *Old Republic Ins. Co. v. EX-IM Servs. Corp.*, 920 S.W.2d 393, 396 (Tex. App.—Houston [1st Dist.] 1996, no writ).
[22] *See* the discussion of assumed name filings in the preceding section.
[23] *Chilkewitz v. Hyson*, 22 S.W.3d 825, 829 (Tex. 1999).
[24] *In re Greater Houston Orthopaedic Specialists, Inc.*, 295 S.W.3d 323, 325–26 (Tex. 2009) ("When an intended defendant is sued under an incorrect name, the court acquires jurisdiction after service with the misnomer if it is clear that no one was misled or placed at a disadvantage by the error . . . Courts are flexible in these cases because the party intended to be sued has been served and put on notice that it is the intended defendant.").
[25] *In re Greater Houston Orthopaedic Specialists, Inc.*, 295 S.W.3d 323, 325–26 (Tex. 2009).

misnamed defendant who simply ignores the suit based on the misnomer does so at the risk of default judgment.[26]

The separate classification of misidentification occurs when an incorrect defendant has been named and served, and the correct defendant has therefore been left out of the suit.[27] As a general rule, misidentification does nothing to toll the running of limitations.[28] An equitable exception to this general rule exists in the situation where the unnamed and unserved business entity which should have been joined is related to and has a similar name to the business entity which was incorrectly named and served,[29] and had actual knowledge of the suit so that it was not prejudiced by the mistake.[30] Equitable tolling for misidentification has been held to be applicable only to business entities and not to individuals.[31]

To aid in early identification of a misidentification or misnomer, a request for disclosure can be served on each defendant asking the defendant to disclose the correct names of the parties to the lawsuit and the name, address, and telephone number of any potential parties.[32]

23-3 Pleading Personal Jurisdiction over Nonresident Defendants

When defendants residing outside of Texas are being sued, special pleading requirements come into play to establish personal jurisdiction. The Texas rule relating to proof of personal jurisdiction differs from the federal rule, placing the burden on the defendant to negate personal jurisdiction rather than placing the burden on the plaintiff to establish personal jurisdiction over the defendant.[33] Nevertheless, the plaintiff in a Texas state court still effectively has two pleading burdens relating to a nonresident defendant.

First, "[t]he plaintiff bears the initial burden of pleading allegations sufficient to bring a nonresident defendant within the provisions of the long-arm statute,"[34] if service is being accomplished through the long-arm statute. Second, the plaintiff has the burden to plead the bases for asserting personal jurisdiction, because the defendant's burden of proof is to "negate all the bases of personal jurisdiction alleged by the plaintiff."[35]

---

[26] *Abilene Indep. Tel. & Tel. Co. v. Williams,* 111 Tex. 102, 229 S.W. 847 (Tex. 1921).

[27] *Enserch Corp. v. Parker,* 794 S.W.2d 2, 4–5 (Tex. 1990).

[28] *Enserch Corp. v. Parker,* 794 S.W.2d 2, 5 (Tex. 1990).

[29] *Flour Bluff Indep. Sch. Dist. v. Bass,* 133 S.W.3d 272, 274 (Tex. 2004).

[30] *Torres v. Johnson,* 91 S.W.3d 905, 909 (Tex. App.—Fort Worth 2002, no pet.).

[31] *Cortinas v. Wilson,* 851 S.W.2d 324 (Tex. App.—Dallas 1993, no writ).

[32] Tex. R. Civ. P. 194.2(a), (b).

[33] *Kawasaki Steel Corp. v. Middleton,* 699 S.W.2d 199, 203 (Tex. 1985) ("In a Rule 120a special appearance, the non-resident defendant has the burden of proof to negate all bases of personal jurisdiction."); *compare with Stuart v. Spademan,* 772 F.2d 1185, 1192 (5th Cir. 1985) ("When a nonresident defendant presents a motion to dismiss for lack of personal jurisdiction, the plaintiff bears the burden of establishing the district court's jurisdiction over the nonresident.").

[34] *American Type Culture Collection, Inc. v. Coleman,* 83 S.W.3d 801, 807 (Tex. 2002).

[35] *American Type Culture Collection, Inc. v. Coleman,* 83 S.W.3d 801, 807 (Tex. 2002).

PLEADING PARTIES AND METHODS OF SERVICE

With regard to the first pleading burden, a nonresident defendant is not required to be served through use of a Texas long-arm statute, since service through Tex. R. Civ. P. 108 (service in another state) or 108a (service of process in foreign countries) is a viable alternative. But if service via a Texas long-arm statute is employed, it is necessary to plead the specifics as to why the particular long-arm statute is applicable to the particular nonresident defendant, since each long-arm statute is only applicable to a specified category of nonresident defendants.[36] For example, Texas Civil Practice and Remedies Code Section 17.044 authorizes substituted service on the secretary of state for nonresident defendants who qualify for any one of several specified reasons, but not for all nonresident defendants generally.[37] The Texas Supreme Court has held that when a long-arm statute is relied upon for service without a recitation of facts in the petition demonstrating why the long-arm statute applies to the specific defendant, there is a lack of jurisdiction apparent on the face of the record.[38] The proper facts can be alleged by simply tracking the statutory grounds set forth in the statute. Of course, since issues of both personal jurisdiction and proper service can be waived by the defendant, a failure to plead facts showing why a long-arm statute is applicable will not be a problem if the defendant simply answers the lawsuit.

The second pleading burden, to allege the bases for personal jurisdiction over a nonresident defendant, essentially requires pleading the facts which show sufficient minimum contacts to support general or specific personal jurisdiction.[39] This pleading burden applies regardless of what form of service is being utilized.[40] If the plaintiff alleges no facts regarding minimum contacts, a nonresident defendant merely has to prove his nonresident status in order to "negate all bases of personal jurisdiction."[41]

23-4 Pleading Method of Service

Multiple methods exist under the Texas rules and statutes for service of original process, including service by personal delivery or mail to Texas residents[42] or nonresidents,[43] service on nonresidents through various long-arm statutes,[44] substituted

---

[36] *McKanna v. Edgar*, 388 S.W.2d 927, 930 (Tex. 1965).
[37] For a list of Texas statutes designating the secretary of state as process agent, *see* the Texas secretary of state website at http://www.sos.state.tx.us/corp/statutes-service-of-process.shtml. The secretary of state is not the only state official who can be appointed by statute to receive service for a defendant; *see, e.g.*, Tex. Civ. Prac. & Rem. Code Ann. § 17.062 (designating chairman of the Texas Transportation Commission as agent for service of process on nonresident growing out of a collision while operating a motor vehicle in this state).
[38] *McKanna v. Edgar*, 388 S.W.2d 927 (Tex. 1965).
[39] *See e.g. American Type Culture Collection, Inc. v. Coleman*, 83 S.W.3d 801 (Tex. 2002).
[40] *Paramount Pipe & Supply Co. v. Muhr*, 749 S.W.2d 491, 495–96 (Tex. 1988) (necessary to plead bases for personal jurisdiction sufficient to demonstrate compliance with federal due process requirements when service accomplished through a valid procedural service alternative).
[41] *Siskind v. Villa Found. for Educ., Inc.*, 642 S.W.2d 434, 438 (Tex. 1982).
[42] Tex. R. Civ. P. 106(a).
[43] Tex. R. Civ. P. 108 (service in another state); Tex. R. Civ. P. 108a (service in foreign countries).
[44] *See, e.g.*, Tex. Civ. Prac. & Rem. Code Ann. §§ 17.026, 17.041-17.045, 17.061-17.069.

service when normal methods of service have not been effective,[45] and service by publication when the defendant cannot be located.[46]

As a general rule, there is not a necessity to plead in the original petition the desired method of service of citation. (As discussed in the preceding sections, an exception exists when a nonresident defendant is served via substituted service on the secretary of state through a long-arm statute or because a filing entity has failed to maintain a registered agent; a statutory method of substituted service must be supported by a record of all facts necessary to support that method of service.)[47] Instead, the plaintiff is expected to continue to pursue whichever methods of service are likely to be successful.[48] The duty of plaintiff's counsel is to monitor the efforts directed toward service of process and take all steps reasonably necessary to accomplish service with due diligence.[49]

In pursuing the completion of service of process, plaintiff's counsel can demonstrate diligence by seeking an order for substituted service under Tex. R. Civ. P. 106(b) if multiple attempts by other methods of service have been unsuccessful.[50] To obtain this order, a verified motion must be filed detailing the prior attempts at service and explaining why the requested form of substituted service is anticipated to be successful at providing actual notice of suit to the defendant.[51]

Once service of process has been obtained, if the defendant fails to answer and a default judgment becomes necessary, the officer's return of service of citation should be reviewed for completeness and accuracy[52] and filed with the clerk of the court,[53] to be sure the facts of service are part of the record.

---

[45] Tex. R. Civ. P. 106(b).
[46] Tex. R. Civ. P. 109.
[47] *Redwood Grp., L.L.C. v. Louiseau*, 113 S.W.3d 866, 868–70 (Tex. App.—Austin 2003, no pet.).
[48] *Taylor v. State*, 293 S.W.3d 913, 915–16 (Tex. App.—Austin 2009, no pet.) (methods of service under Rule 106(a) continue to be available as options after rendition of Rule 106(b) order for substituted service).
[49] *Webster v. Thomas*, 5 S.W.3d 287 (Tex. App.—Houston [14th Dist.] 1999, no pet.).
[50] *See e.g. Proulx v. Wells*, 235 S.W.3d 213 (Tex. 2007).
[51] Tex. R. Civ. P. 106(b); *Wilson v. Dunn*, 800 S.W.2d 833, 836 (Tex. 1990).
[52] *See* Tex. R. Civ. P. 107. For amendment of an officer's return already on file with the clerk, *see* Tex. R. Civ. P. 118.
[53] Tex. R. Civ. P. 107(h) (requiring the officer's return of service of citation to be on file with the clerk of the court ten days before default judgment can be granted, exclusive of the day of filing and the day of judgment).

CHAPTER 24

Pleading Choice of Law*

24-1 General Principles Governing Choice of Law in Texas

24-1:1 Texas Procedural Rules Applicable

Though Texas follows the approach of the Restatement (Second) of Conflicts in applying the most significant relationship test to determine what substantive law to apply, Texas applies its own procedural laws, even when the substantive law of another state must be applied.[1]

Some bodies of law may appear procedural, but are substantive for purposes of the choice of law analysis. Although the admissibility of evidence is a procedural question, generally, for choice of law purposes,[2] the laws governing privileges are substantive; and Texas applies the law of the state with the most significant relationship to the privilege (usually the state where the communication was made).[3] Similarly, witness competency rules as well as the parol evidence rule and statute of frauds are substantive rules to which the most significant relationship test applies.

24-1:2 Necessity of a Conflict

The first step in a choice of law analysis is to determine if the laws of the competing jurisdictions are in conflict. If there is no conflict, then there is no need to conduct a choice of law analysis.[4]

---

* The authors thank Max Moran for his assistance in the updating of this chapter.
[1] *Creative Thinking Sources, Inc. v. Creative Thinking, Inc.*, 74 S.W.3d 504, 510 (Tex. App.—Corpus Christi-Edinburg 2002, no pet.); *Intevep, S.A. Research & Tech. Support Establishment v. Sena*, 41 S.W.3d 391, 394 (Tex. App.—Dallas 2001, no pet.). *See also State of California v. Copus*, 309 S.W.2d 227, 230–31 (Tex. 1958).
[2] *HealthTronics, Inc. v. Lisa Laser U.S.A, Inc.*, 382 S.W.3d 567, 580 (Tex. App.—Austin 2012, no pet.).
[3] *Ford Motor Co. v. Leggat*, 904 S.W.2d 643, 647 (Tex. 1995).
[4] *Duncan v. Cessna Aircraft Co.*, 665 S.W.2d 414, 421 (Tex. 1984); *St. Paul Surplus Lines Ins. Co. v. Geo Pipe Co.*, 25 S.W.3d 900, 903 n.2 (Tex. App.—Houston [1st Dist.] 2000, no pet.) ("In the absence of a true conflict of law, we do not undertake choice of law analysis.").

24-1:3 The Most Significant Relationship Test

With respect to the substantive law to be applied to a dispute, Texas follows the most significant relationship test in all cases (except those controlled by a valid choice of law clause)[5] as set forth in the Restatement (Second) of Conflicts,[6] and applies the law with the most significant relationship to the dispute.

Texas courts must follow a statutory directive as to the resolution of a choice of law issue. In the absence of a statutory directive, however, and regardless of whether the case sounds in contract or tort, the most significant relationship test of the Restatement (Second) of Conflicts begins with an analysis of the factors listed in Section 6. The factors the court must consider are:

- the needs of the interstate and international systems;
- the relevant policies of the forum;
- the relevant policies of other interested states and the relative interests of those states in the determination of the particular issue;
- the protection of justified expectations;
- the basic policies underlying the particular field of law;
- certainty, predictability and uniformity of result; and
- ease in the determination and application of the law to be applied.[7]

24-1:4 Most Significant Relationship Test in Tort Cases

In a tort case, Section 145 sets forth the contacts to be taken into account in determining the state with the most significant relationship to the dispute under the principles stated in Section 6.[8] The use of the word "include" indicates that the contacts listed in Section 145 are not necessarily exclusive, but the listed contacts are:

- the place where the injury occurred;
- the place where the conduct causing the injury occurred;
- the domicile, residence, nationality, place of incorporation and place of business of the parties; and
- the place where the relationship, if any, between the parties is centered.

Although Texas has abandoned the *lex loci delecti* rule (the law of the place of the injury), this contact is still the most important under Texas case law. Texas courts will

---

[5] *Duncan v. Cessna Aircraft Co.*, 665 S.W.2d 414, 421 (Tex. 1984) (case superseded by statute on other grounds not related to the citation here).

[6] *Duncan v. Cessna Aircraft Co.*, 665 S.W.2d 414, 421 (Tex. 1984) (holding that most significant relationship test applies in all cases). *See also DeSantis v. Wackenhut*, 793 S.W.2d 670 (Tex. 1990) (holding that the most significant relationship test applies in contract cases) (case superseded by statute on other grounds not related to the citation here); *Gutierrez v. Collins*, 583 S.W.2d 312, 318 (Tex. 1979) (holding that most significant relationship test applies in tort cases); Restatement (Second) of Conflicts, §§ 6 and 145.

[7] Restatement (Second) of Conflicts § 6.

[8] Restatement (Second) of Conflicts § 145.

typically apply the law of the place of the injury,[9] but have not done so where the accident occurred in another state but involved residents of Texas[10] or where the accident occurred in Texas but involved residents of another state.[11]

In fraud and misrepresentation cases, as a general rule, the law of the state where both the misrepresentation and reliance occurred will apply.[12] Where the reliance occurred in a state different from where the false statement was made, the court should apply a number of factors to determine the governing law.[13]

In defamation cases, the law of the state where the publication occurred generally applies.[14] In multistate defamation cases, such as with the publication of a book, periodical, etc., the law of the state of the plaintiff's domicile will often apply.[15]

24-1:5 Most Significant Relationship Test in a Contract Case

In a contract case, Section 188 sets forth the contacts to be taken into account in determining the state with the most significant relationship to the dispute under the principles stated in Section 6.[16]

- The place of contracting;
- The place of negotiation of the contract;
- The place of performance;
- The location of the subject matter of the contract; and
- The domicile, residence, nationality, place of incorporation and place of business of the parties.

---

[9] Restatement (Second) of Conflicts §§ 146 (injury to person) and 147 (injury to property). *See, e.g., Vizcarra v. Roldan*, 925 S.W.2d 89, 92 (Tex. App.—El Paso 1996, no writ) (applying the law of Mexico where the car wreck occurred in Mexico, even though the defendant was a Texan).

[10] *Gutierrez v. Collins*, 583 S.W2d 319 (Tex. 1979).

[11] *Robertson v. McKnight*, 609 S.W.2d 534, 537 (Tex. 1980) (applying New Mexico law on interspousal tort immunity in an airplane crash case that occurred in Texas but involved residents of New Mexico who had departed from New Mexico). *But see Torrington Co. v. Stutzman*, 46 S.W.3d 829, 849 (Tex. 2000) (applying the law of Texas to a military helicopter crash involving domiciliaries of various states).

[12] Restatement (Second) of Conflicts § 148(1).

[13] Restatement (Second) of Conflicts at § 148(2)(a)–(f) ((a) the place, or places, where the plaintiff acted in reliance upon the defendant's representations; (b) the place where the plaintiff received the representations; (c) the place where the defendant made the representations; (d) the domicile, residence, nationality, place of incorporation and place of business of the parties; (e) the place where a tangible thing which is the subject of the transaction between the parties was situated at the time; and (f) the place where the plaintiff is to render performance under a contract which he has been induced to enter by the false representations of the defendant.).

[14] Restatement (Second) of Conflicts at § 149.

[15] Restatement (Second) of Conflicts at § 150.

[16] Restatement (Second) of Conflicts at § 188(2).

Section 188 also provides that where the state of performance and the state of negotiation are the same, that state's law should ordinarily govern.[17] The place of performance is ordinarily the most significant contact in a contract for services.[18] Contracts for the repayment of money lent are generally governed by the law where repayment is required to be made.[19] Contracts for the transportation of goods or persons are generally governed by the law of the state from which the goods or passengers depart.[20]

24-1:6 Most Significant Relationship Test in Property Cases

Texas also follows the Restatement approach in property cases and in cases to determine a person's personal status. Generally, the law of the location of the land governs in actions involving real property.[21] Personal property choice of law questions are governed generally by the Uniform Commercial Code choice of law rules, discussed in Chapter 24, Section 24-3:2.

24-1:7 Choice of Law Under the Uniform Commercial Code

The Uniform Commercial Code sets out a choice of law rule that applies generally to cases governed by the Code. It also sets out a number of choice of law provisions that govern particular issues under the Code.

The General choice of law rule under the Texas Uniform Commercial Code is that Texas law will apply to any transaction "bearing an appropriate relation" to Texas.[22]

The Code also provides the following provisions that govern choice of law with respect to certain particular issues.

- *Rights of Seller's Creditor Against Sold Goods:* A creditor of the seller may treat a sale or an identification of goods to a contract for sale as void if as against him a retention of possession by the seller is fraudulent under any rule of law of the state where the goods are situated.[23]

- *Goods Covered by Certificate of Title:* Compliance or noncompliance with such a certificate is governed generally by the law of the issuing state.[24]

---

[17] Restatement (Second) of Conflicts at § 188(e).
[18] *Maxus Expl. v. Moran Brothers*, 817 S.W.2d 50, 53 (Tex. 1991) (citing Restatement (Second) of Conflicts § 196). *See also Castilleja v. Camero*, 414 S.W.2d 424, 425 (Tex. 1967) ("A contract which is made in one jurisdiction but which relates to and is to be performed in another jurisdiction is governed by the law of the place of performance..."); *Gorsalitz v. Olin Mathieson Chem. Corp.*, 429 F.2d 1033, 1048 (5th Cir. 1970) ("the interpretation of a contract executed in Texas but to be performed wholly outside the state is governed by the law of the place of performance").
[19] Restatement (Second) of Conflicts § 196.
[20] Restatement (Second) of Conflicts § 197.
[21] Restatement (Second) of Conflicts § 223.
[22] Tex. Bus. & Com. Code Ann. § 1.301(a).
[23] Tex. Bus. & Com. Code Ann. § 2.402(c).
[24] Tex. Bus. & Com. Code Ann. § 2A.105.

- *Choice of Law Clauses in a Consumer Lease:* Choice of law clause in a consumer lease agreement choosing the law of a state other than the state of the lessee's residence is generally unenforceable.[25]

Additionally, the UCC provides choice of law provisions governing bank deposits and collections,[26] fund transfers,[27] letters of credit,[28] investment securities,[29] and perfection of a security interest.[30]

24-1:8 Other Texas Statutes Affecting Choice of Law

By statute, Texas law generally applies to any contract of insurance payable to any Texas resident and issued by a company doing business in Texas.[31]

Contracts made over the Internet between a person located in Texas and a person located outside Texas who does not maintain an office or agent in Texas are also governed by statute. The statute provides that Texas law applies to such contracts unless each Texan who is a party to the contract is given notice of a choice of law provision

---

[25] Tex. Bus. & Com. Code Ann. § 2A.106.

[26] Tex. Bus. & Com. Code Ann. § 4.102 ("The liability of a bank for action or non-action with respect to an item handled by it for purposes of presentment, payment, or collection is governed by the law of the place where the bank is located. In the case of action or non-action by or at a branch or separate office of a bank, its liability is governed by the law of the place where the branch or separate office is located.").

[27] Tex. Bus. & Com. Code Ann. § 4A.507 (law of receiving bank governs generally).

[28] Tex. Bus. & Com. Code Ann. § 5.116 (In the absence of a choice of law provision, "the liability of an issuer, nominated person, or adviser for action or omission is governed by the law of the jurisdiction in which the person is located.").

[29] Tex. Bus. & Com. Code Ann. § 8.110(a) (the law of the issuer's jurisdiction governs the validity of a security; the rights and duties of the issuer with respect to registration of transfer, the effectiveness of the registration of transfer, whether the issuer owes any duties to an adverse claimant, whether an adverse claim can be asserted against a person to whom transfer of a certificated or uncertificated security is registered or a person who obtains control of an uncertificated security); 8.110(b) (The local law of the securities intermediary's jurisdiction governs acquisition of a security entitlement from the securities intermediary, the rights and duties of the securities intermediary and entitlement holder arising out of a security entitlement, whether the securities intermediary owes any duties to an adverse claimant to a security entitlement, and whether an adverse claim can be asserted against a person who acquires a security entitlement from the securities intermediary or a person who purchases a security entitlement or interest therein from an entitlement holder.); 8.110(c) (The local law of the jurisdiction in which a security certificate is located at the time of delivery governs whether an adverse claim can be asserted against a person to whom the security certificate is delivered).

[30] Tex. Bus. & Com. Code Ann. §§ 9.301-9.307 (applying different choice of law rules depending on the nature of the security interest).

[31] Tex. Ins. Code Art. 21.42 ("Any contract of insurance payable to any citizen or inhabitant of this State by any insurance company or corporation doing business within this State shall be held to be a contract made and entered into under and by virtue of the laws of this State relating to insurance, and governed thereby, notwithstanding such policy or contract of insurance may provide that the contract was executed and the premiums and policy (in case it becomes a demand) should be payable without this State, or at the home office of the company or corporation issuing the same.").

and agrees to the application of that other state's law.[32] This provision does not apply to high value contracts with an aggregate value of at least $1 million.[33]

By statute, a resident of a foreign state or nation may bring an action for personal injury or wrongful death based on an act, neglect or default that occurred in a foreign state or nation so long as the action is brought within the time provided by both the applicable Texas statute of limitations or repose as well as within the time provided by the foreign state or nation where the act, neglect or default occurred.[34] In addition, the foreign state or nation must have equal treaty rights with the United States on behalf of its citizens.[35]

24-1:9 The "Internal Affairs" Doctrine

Consistent with the commands of the Texas Business Organizations Code, Texas courts apply the law of an entity's state of formation to disputes involving its formation or internal affairs.[36] An entity's internal affairs include the rights, powers, and duties of the entity's owners and members and matters relating to its membership or ownership interests.[37] The law of the state of formation also governs the liability of an owner, a member, or a managerial official of the entity in such capacity for an obligation, including a debt or other liability, of the entity for which the owner, member, or managerial official is not otherwise liable by contract by law other than the Business Organizations Code.[38]

24-1:10 Application of Law Contrary to Fundamental Public Policy

Texas courts will not apply a law that is contrary to fundamental Texas public policy, even when the choice of law rule would otherwise require its application.[39] Generally, application of another state's law is not against fundamental Texas policy, even when

---

[32] Tex. Bus. & Com. Code Ann. § 274.003.
[33] Tex. Bus. & Com. Code Ann. § 274.003; Tex. Bus. & Com. Code Ann. §§ 271.001-271.011.
[34] Tex. Civ. Prac. & Rem. Code Ann. § 71.031(a)(1)–(3).
[35] Tex. Civ. Prac. & Rem. Code Ann. § 71.031(a)(4).
[36] *Grynberg v. Grynberg*, 535 S.W.3d 229, 233–34 (Tex. App.—Dallas 2017, no pet.). *See also* Tex. Bus. Orgs. Code Ann. § 1.101 ("The law of this state governs the formation and internal affairs of an entity if the entity's formation occurs when a certificate of formation filed in accordance with Chapter 4 takes effect."); Tex. Bus. Orgs. Code Ann. § 1.102 ("If the formation of an entity occurs when a certificate of formation or similar instrument filed with a foreign governmental authority takes effect, the law of the state or other jurisdiction in which that foreign governmental authority is located governs the formation and internal affairs of the entity."); Tex. Bus. Orgs. Code Ann. § 1.103 ("If the formation of an entity does not occur when a certificate of formation or similar instrument filed with the secretary of state or with a foreign governmental authority takes effect, the law governing the entity's formation and internal affairs is the law of the entity's jurisdiction of formation.").
[37] Tex. Bus. Orgs. Code Ann. § 1.105. *See also In re Dexterity Surgical, Inc.*, 365 B.R. 690, 695 (Bankr. S.D. Tex. 2007).
[38] Tex. Bus. Orgs. Code Ann. § 1.104.
[39] *DeSantis v. Wackenhut*, 793 S.W.2d 670, 681 (Tex. 1990) (refusing to enforce a non-compete agreement with a Florida choice of law clause); *Nexen, Inc. v. Gulf Interstate Eng'g Co.*, 224 S.W.3d 412, 421 (Tex. App.—Houston [1st Dist.] 2006, no pet.).

it is materially different from the law of Texas and would lead to a different result.[40] If the policies in both Texas and the other jurisdiction are the same but the laws at issue take different approaches to the policy, Texas will apply the law of the other jurisdiction.[41] This doctrine is no silver bullet for those seeking to avoid the application of another jurisdiction's law. Texas courts have rarely refused to apply the law of a foreign jurisdiction on this ground.[42]

24-2 Enforcing a Choice of Law Clause

Under the rule of party autonomy, Texas courts will generally enforce the parties' choice of law agreements. Texas will enforce such agreements so long as the clause does not choose the law of a jurisdiction with no relationship whatsoever to them or their agreement and so long as the agreement does not thwart or offend the law of the state that would otherwise apply.[43]

A choice of law clause in an agreement governed by the Texas Uniform Commercial Code will be enforced so long as the transaction bears a reasonable relation to the jurisdiction whose law is chosen.[44] High value transactions (those with an aggregate value of $1 million or more) are governed by separate provisions of the Texas Business and Commerce Code, the purpose of which are to grant greater freedom to choose the governing law.[45]

In other cases, Texas looks to Section 187 of the Restatement (Second) of Conflicts to determine whether or not to enforce a choice of law clause.[46] That section of the Restatement provides that "[t]he law of the state chosen by the parties to govern their contractual rights and duties will be applied if the particular issue is one which the parties could have resolved by an explicit provision in their agreement directed to that issue."[47] If the issue could not have been resolved by an explicit provision in the agreement, then the law chosen by the agreement will be enforced unless:

(a) the chosen state has no substantial relationship to the parties or the transaction and there is no other reasonable basis for the parties' choice; or

(b) application of the law of the chosen state would be contrary to a fundamental policy of a state which has a materially greater interest than the chosen state in the determination of the particular issue and which, under the rule of The Restatement (Second) of Conflicts 188, would be the state of the applicable law in the absence of an effective choice of law by the parties.

---

[40] *DeSantis v. Wackenhut*, 793 S.W.2d 670 (Tex. 1990).
[41] *DeSantis v. Wackenhut*, 793 S.W.2d 670, 681 (Tex. 1990) (applying the repose law of Alberta, Canada even though different from the repose law of Texas because both laws reflected a similar policy).
[42] *See Castilleja v. Camero*, 414 S.W.2d 424, 427 (Tex. 1967) (enforcing contract to divide Mexican lottery winnings); *but see DeSantis v. Wackenhut*, 793 S.W.2d 670, 681 (Tex. 1990) (refusing to enforce a non-compete agreement with a Florida choice of law clause); *Lodge v. Lodge*, 368 S.W.2d 40, 41 (Tex. App.—Austin 1963, no writ) (refusing to enforce agreement providing for permanent alimony).
[43] *DeSantis v. Wackenhut*, 793 S.W.2d 670, 677 (Tex. 1990).
[44] Tex. Bus. & Com. Code Ann. § 1.301(a).
[45] Tex. Bus. & Com. Code Ann. §§ 271.001-271.011.
[46] Tex. Bus. & Com. Code Ann. §§ 271.001-271.011.
[47] Restatement (Second) of Conflicts, § 187.

The Supreme Court of Texas refused, for example, to enforce a choice of law clause choosing Florida law in a non-compete agreement that would preclude a Texas resident from opening a competing business in Texas.[48] To do so would have violated the fundamental policy of Texas.[49]

It is possible to avoid the operation of a choice of law clause in an adhesion contract. Texas courts will not enforce a choice of law clause in an adhesion contract "if to do so would result in substantial injustice to the adherent."[50]

24-3 Pleading and Proving Choice of Law

A party cannot assume that a court will automatically determine and apply the law of another jurisdiction, even where the most significant relationship test would require it. This section discusses the procedural requirements for securing application of the law of another jurisdiction.

24-3:1 Presumption in Favor of Texas Law

Texas courts will presume that the law of another jurisdiction is the same as that of Texas unless the party seeking application of another jurisdiction's law brings the issue to the attention of the court and provides the court the law of the other jurisdiction.[51] The party seeking application of law other than that of Texas bears the burden of establishing that it is different than Texas law.[52] In the absence of such proof, Texas courts presume that the outcome would be the same under both Texas law and the law of the other jurisdiction.[53]

24-3:2 Pleading and Proving Law of Other Jurisdiction

To secure application of law other than that of Texas, a party must (1) clearly request application of the law and (2) provide the court with the law of the other jurisdiction.[54]

---

[48] *DeSantis v. Wackenhut*, 793 S.W.2d 670, 681 (Tex. 1990) ("... the law governing enforcement of noncompetition agreements is fundamental policy in Texas, and that to apply the law of another state to determine the enforceability of such an agreement in the circumstances of a case like this would be contrary to that policy").

[49] *DeSantis v. Wackenhut*, 793 S.W.2d 670, 681 (Tex. 1990).

[50] *CMA-CGM (Am.), Inc. v. Empire Truck Lines, Inc.*, 416 S.W.3d 495, 522 n.3 (Tex. App.—Houston [1st Dist.] 2013, pet. pending).

[51] *Excess Underwriters at Lloyd's, London v. Frank's Casing Crew & Rental Tools, Inc.*, 246 S.W.3d 42, 53 (Tex. 2008) (refusing to apply Louisiana law to reimbursement issue in a reimbursement case following a coverage dispute where the insurers never clearly requested application of Louisiana law and never provided authority to demonstrate how Louisiana law would resolve the issue).

[52] *Excess Underwriters at Lloyd's, London v. Frank's Casing Crew & Rental Tools, Inc.*, 246 S.W.3d 42, 53 (Tex. 2008).

[53] *Excess Underwriters at Lloyd's, London v. Frank's Casing Crew & Rental Tools, Inc.*, 246 S.W.3d 42, 53 (Tex. 2008).

[54] *Excess Underwriters at Lloyd's, London v. Frank's Casing Crew & Rental Tools, Inc.*, 246 S.W.3d 42, 53 (Tex. 2008); Tex. R. Evid. 202 (providing that a court may and, upon motion of a party, must take judicial notice of the laws of another jurisdiction within the United States so long as the court is supplied with the law of the other jurisdiction); Tex. R. Evid. 203 ("A

Texas Rules of Evidence 202 and 203 govern the judicial notice of the laws of other U.S. jurisdictions and the laws of foreign countries, respectively.[55] Rule 202 provides that a court may take judicial notice of the law of another U.S. jurisdiction on its own motion but shall take judicial notice of such law when raised by motion of a party and supplied with sufficient information to comply with the request.[56] Rule 203 requires the requesting party to "provide notice in the pleadings or other reasonable written notice" in order to have the court take judicial notice of the law of a foreign country.[57]

The notice and translation provisions of Rule 203 do not apply to the recognition or enforcement of a judgment or arbitration award based on foreign law in a suit involving a marriage or parent-child relationship under the Family Code or to actions brought under the International Child Abduction Remedies Act (22 U.S.C. § 9001 et seq.) concerning rights under the Hague Convention on the Civil Aspects of International Child Abduction.[58] Instead, in these actions, the translation and notice requirements are governed by Texas Rule of Evidence 308b(d) and (f).[59]

Whether requesting notice of a foreign country's law or the law of another U.S. jurisdiction, the party must provide the court with sufficient information to allow it to comply with the request.[60] If the sources were originally written in a language other than English, the party must provide the court and all other parties both the original foreign language version and an English translation of the source.[61]

Rule 203 explicitly provides that, in determining the law of a foreign nation, the court may consider any other source whether or not submitted by the parties or admissible under the rules of evidence, including but not limited to affidavits, testimony and briefs.[62] Despite the evidentiary nature of the hearing, the court's determination of foreign law is a question of law for the court, not for the jury.[63]

---

party who intends to raise an issue concerning the law of a foreign country shall give notice in the pleadings or other reasonable written notice . . .").

[55] Tex. R. Evid. 202, 203.
[56] Tex. R. Evid. 202.
[57] Tex. R. Evid. 203.
[58] Tex. R. Evid. 203(e); Tex. R. Evid. 308b(c).
[59] Tex. R. Evid. 308b(d)(1) ("Party Seeking Enforcement of a Judgment or Arbitration Award Based on Foreign Law. Within 60 days of filing an original pleading, the party seeking enforcement must give written notice to the court and all parties that describes the court's authority to enforce or decide to enforce the judgment or award."); Tex. R. Evid. 308b(d)(2) ("Party Seeking Enforcement of a Judgment or Arbitration Award Based on Foreign Law. Within 60 days of filing an original pleading, the party seeking enforcement must give written notice to the court and all parties that describes the court's authority to enforce or decide to enforce the judgment or award."); Tex. R. Evid. 308b(e) ("Pretrial Conference. Within 75 days of the date that a notice under (d)(1) is served, the court must conduct a pretrial conference to set deadlines and make other appropriate orders regarding: (1) the submission of materials for the court to consider in determining foreign law; (2) the translation of foreign-language documents; and (3) the designation of expert witnesses.").
[60] Tex. R. Evid. 202, 203.
[61] Tex. R. Evid. 203.
[62] Tex. R. Evid. 202.
[63] Tex. R. Evid. 203; *Long Distance Int'l, Inc. v Telefonos de Mexico*, 49 S.W.3d 347, 351 (Tex. 2001).

CHAPTER 25

Pleading to Avoid or Compel Arbitration*

25-1 Choice of Arbitration Law

As a threshold matter in any effort to compel arbitration, the parties must determine the law of arbitration that applies to the issue. Federal law as well as Texas statutory and common law might govern arbitration issues, depending on the circumstances of the case.

25-1:1 The Federal Arbitration Act

The Federal Arbitration Act FAA governs any written arbitration agreement that affects interstate commerce, and it preempts contrary state law.[1] The FAA extends to the maximum extent of congressional power under the Commerce Clause.[2] The Supreme Court of Texas has held that the FAA "applies to all suits in state and federal court when the dispute concerns a 'contract evidencing a transaction involving commerce.'"[3]

Transporting goods across state lines pursuant to the contract, for example, is a transaction involving interstate commerce,[4] as are loan agreements between Texas and non-Texas residents,[5] construction contracts between residents of different states and/or where supplies were shipped across state lines,[6] and contracts for the pur-

---

* The authors thank Max Moran for his assistance in the updating of this chapter.
[1] 9 U.S.C. § 2; *Jack B. Anglin Co., Inc. v. Tipps*, 842 S.W.2d 266, 261 (Tex. 1992) (recognizing that FAA preempts conflicting provisions in the Texas DTPA).
[2] *Allied-Bruce Terminix Co. v. Dobson*, 513 U.S. 265, 263 (1995).
[3] *Jack B. Anglin Co., Inc. v. Tipps*, 842 S.W.2d 266, 269–70 (Tex. 1992) (quoting *Perry v. Thomas*, 482 U.S. 483, 489 (1987)).
[4] *Jack B. Anglin Co., Inc. v. Tipps*, 842 S.W.2d 266, 261 (Tex. 1992).
[5] *In re First Merit Bank, N.A.*, 52 S.W.3d 749, 754 (Tex. 2001).
[6] *Electronic & Missile Facilities, Inc. v. U.S.*, 306 F.2d 554 (5th Cir. 1962), *rev'd on other grounds sub-nom.*, *Mosley v. Elec. & Missile Facilities, Inc.*, 374 U.S. 167, 83 S. Ct. 1815, 10 L. Ed. 2d 818 (1963); *Blanks v. Midstate Constructors, Inc.*, 610 S.W.2d 220, 225 (Tex. 1980) ("This Court has concluded under the facts of this case that the contract in question evidenced a transaction 'involving commerce' in view of the interstate flow of materials, supplies, services, and personnel in connection with the construction of the project. It is true that no diversity of citizenship exists, but diversity is not all-determinative.").

chase and sale of goods across state lines.[7] Moreover, the FAA applies where parties have agreed that the FAA will govern their arbitration agreement, regardless of the connection with interstate commerce.[8]

Even where the FAA applies in Texas state court, Texas contract law governs the issue of whether or not the arbitration provision is enforceable.[9]

25-1:2 The Texas Arbitration Act

If the transaction is wholly intrastate, the FAA does not apply. For example, the FAA did not apply to a service contract between Texas residents performed entirely within Texas.[10]

For wholly intrastate transactions, Texas arbitration law applies. Generally, the Texas Arbitration Act ("TAA") applies to written agreements to arbitrate disputes that either exist at the time of the agreement or arise thereafter.[11]

The TAA does not apply to a collective bargaining agreement between an employer and a labor union.[12] The TAA does not apply to the purchase of relatively inexpensive property or services or the acquisition of relatively small amounts of credit[13] or to claims for personal injuries unless (1) there is an agreement in writing to arbitrate and (2) each party and his attorney signs the agreement.[14] Importantly, the FAA has no such signature requirement; and therefore, it would preempt this provision in cases involving interstate commerce.[15]

25-1:3 Texas Common Law of Arbitration

In cases where neither the FAA nor the TAA apply, arbitration is governed by Texas common law principles. An example of an agreement that may fall under the common law include those agreements not governed by the FAA that the TAA requires to be signed by the parties and their attorneys.[16]

---

[7] *In re HEB Grocery Co., L.P.*, 299 S.W.3d 393, 396 (Tex. App.—Corpus Christi 2009, orig. proceeding).

[8] *Unit Tex. Drilling, LLC v. Morales*, No. 13-10-00247-CV, 2010 WL 2968046, *3 (Tex. App.—Corpus Christi July 29, 2010, pet. denied); *In re ReadyOne Indus.*, 294 S.W.3d 764, 769 (Tex. App.—El Paso 2009, orig. proceeding).

[9] *In re Palm Harbor Homes, Inc.*, 195 S.W.3d 672, 676 (Tex. 2006); *In re ReadyOne Indus., Inc.*, 294 S.W.3d 764, 768 (Tex. App.—El Paso 2009, orig. proceeding).

[10] *See, e.g., Porter & Clements, L.L.P. v. Stone*, 935 S.W.2d 217, 219 (Tex. App.—Houston [1st Dist.] 1996, no writ) (attorney fee agreement between Texas residents).

[11] Tex. Civ. Prac. & Rem. Code Ann. § 171.001(a).

[12] Tex. Civ. Prac. & Rem. Code Ann. § 171.002(a)(1).

[13] Tex. Civ. Prac. & Rem. Code Ann. § 171.002(b) (TAA does not apply, in the absence of an agreement to arbitrate signed by all parties and their attorneys, to "[a]n agreement for the acquisition by one or more individuals of property, services, money, or credit in which the total consideration to be furnished by the individual is not more than $50,000.").

[14] Tex. Civ. Prac. & Rem. Code Ann. § 171.002(b), (c).

[15] *Forged Components, Inc. v. Guzman*, 409 S.W.3d 91, 98 (Tex. App.—Houston [1st Dist.] 2013, no pet.) (holding that the FAA preempted the TAA provision that requires parties to sign certain arbitration agreements).

[16] *See, e.g., Gerdes v. Tygrett*, 584 S.W.2d 350, 351 (Tex. App.—Texarkana 1979, writ ref'd n.r.e.) ("Where the formal requirements of a binding statutory arbitration are not met, the

25-2 Compelling Arbitration

The procedure for compelling arbitration is similar under both the FAA and TAA. If suit is brought and it is referable to arbitration, a party may compel arbitration with a motion (or application) to compel arbitration.[17] Both the FAA[18] and TAA[19] require the court to stay trial court proceedings that are subject to an arbitration agreement.

Where a lawsuit subject to an arbitration agreement has not already been filed, suit may be filed seeking an order to compel arbitration.[20]

The application to compel arbitration should:

- Show the jurisdiction of the court;
- Have attached a copy of the agreement to arbitrate;
- Define the issue subject to arbitration between the parties under the agreement;
- Specify the status of the arbitration before the arbitrators; and
- Show the need for the court order sought by the applicant.[21]

When a trial court erroneously denies a party's motion to compel arbitration, mandamus is available to correct the error in suits governed by the FAA.[22] Mandamus ordinarily is unnecessary in suits governed by the TAA, as the TAA provides a right to immediate interlocutory appeal.[23]

A court may also seek Texas trial court assistance during a pending arbitration to enforce an arbitrator's order.[24]

---

settlement of the disputed claim by common law arbitration may still be effected where an appropriate agreement to submit the issue to arbitration is shown."). *See also L. H. Lacy Co. v. City of Lubbock*, 559 S.W.2d 348 (Tex. 1977); *Carpenter v. N. River Ins. Co.*, 436 S.W.2d 549 (Tex. App.—Houston [14th Dist.] 1968, writ ref'd n. r. e.).

[17] 9 U.S.C. § 3 (providing that, upon application, any suit involving an issue referable to arbitration will be stayed); Tex. Civ. Prac. & Rem. Code Ann. § 171.021 (providing that the court shall order arbitration upon an application showing an agreement to arbitrate and a party's refusal to arbitrate).

[18] 9 U.S.C. § 3.

[19] Tex. Civ. Prac. & Rem. Code Ann. §§ 171.021(c), 171.025.

[20] 9 U.S.C. § 4 ("A party aggrieved by the alleged failure, neglect, or refusal of another to arbitrate ... may petition any United States district court ... for an order directing that such arbitration proceed in the manner provided for in such agreement."); Tex. Civ. Prac. & Rem. Code Ann. §§ 171.081-171.085.

[21] Tex. Civ. Prac. & Rem. Code Ann. § 171.085.

[22] *In re First Merit Bank, N.A.*, 52 S.W.3d 749, 753 (Tex. 2001); *EZ Pawn Corp. v. Mancias*, 934 S.W.2d 87, 88 (Tex. 1996).

[23] Tex. Civ. Prac. & Rem. Code Ann. § 171.098(a); *In re AIU*, 148 S.W.3d 109, 115 (Tex. 2004) (recognizing the distinction between the use of mandamus and interlocutory appeal for denied motions to compel arbitration depending on whether FAA or TAA applies).

[24] Tex. Civ. Prac. & Rem. Code Ann. § 171.086.

25-3 Resisting Arbitration

This section discusses bases for resisting an arbitration provision. A court may not order arbitration of a dispute that the parties did not agree to arbitrate,[25] nor may a court enforce an arbitration agreement where performance is excused by principles of contract law, such as an unconscionable agreement or one that is the subject of fraud, or where the arbitration agreement has been waived.

25-3:1 Dispute Outside the Scope of the Agreement

A party is not required to arbitrate disputes outside the scope of the arbitration agreement.[26] Because state and federal policies favor arbitration, however, a presumption exists in favor of arbitration, and all doubts regarding the scope of the agreement are resolved in favor of arbitration.[27] In determining whether claims fall within the scope of the arbitration clause, the court focuses on the factual basis of the allegations rather than the legal theories asserted.[28]

"A party seeking to compel arbitration must establish the existence of a valid arbitration agreement and that the claims at issue fall within the scope of that agreement. If the party seeking to compel arbitration meets this burden, the burden then shifts, and to avoid arbitration, the party opposing it must prove an affirmative defense to the provision's enforcement, such as waiver."[29] The advantage in meeting these burdens, however, rests with the party asserting arbitration. "The presumption in favor of arbitration 'is so compelling that a court should not deny arbitration *"unless it can be said with positive assurance* that an arbitration clause is *not* susceptible of an interpretation which would cover the dispute at issue.""[30]

Generally, suit against an employee of a party to an arbitration agreement falls within the scope of the agreement.[31] Where the decedent was a party to an arbitration agreement with his employer, his wrongful death beneficiaries were bound by the agreement to arbitrate.[32] Claims against entities affiliated with a party to an arbitration agreement do not fall within the scope of the agreement where the affiliated entities

---

[25] *In re AdvancePCS Health, LP*, 172 S.W.3d 603, 605 (Tex. 2005); *In re Oakwood Mobile Homes*, Inc., 987 S.W.2d 571, 573 (Tex. 1999), *abrogated on other grounds by In re Haliburton Co.*, 80 S.W.3d 566, 572 (Tex. 2002); *Cantella & Co. v. Goodwin*, 924 S.W.2d 943, 944 (Tex. 1996).

[26] *In re First Merit Bank, N.A.*, 52 S.W. 749, 753 (Tex. 2001).

[27] *In re First Merit Bank, N.A.*, 52 S.W.3d 749, 753 (Tex. 2001); *In re Poly-Am., L.P.*, 262 S.W.3d 337, 348 (Tex. 2008).

[28] *In re First Merit Bank, N.A.*, 52 S.W.3d 749, 753 (Tex. 2001).

[29] *Henry v. Cash Biz, LP*, 551 S.W.3d 111, 115 (Tex. 2018) (citations omitted).

[30] *Henry v. Cash Biz, LP*, 551 S.W.3d 111, 115 (Tex. 2018) (citations omitted, emphasis in original). *See also Ellis v. Schlimmer*, 337 S.W.3d 860, 862 (Tex. 2011).

[31] *In re Merrill Lynch Tr. Co.*, 235 S.W.3d 185, 188–89 (Tex. 2007) ("If a plaintiff's choice between suing the corporation or suing the employees determines whether an arbitration agreement is binding, then such agreements have been rendered illusory on one side.").

[32] *In re Labatt Food Serv.*, L.P., 269 S.W.3d 640 (Tex. 2009). *See also In re Weekley Homes, L.P.*, 180 S.W.3d 126, 131 (Tex. 2005) (recognizing that equitable principles may bind a non-signatory to an arbitration agreement).

are not mentioned in the agreement.[33] Whether the parties have agreed to arbitrate is a matter for the court, not the arbitrator, and whether a claim involving a nonsignatory is arbitrable is a question for the trial court, not the arbitrator.[34] The parties can, however, agree to arbitrate arbitrability.[35]

25-3:2 Resisting on Grounds Agreement Is Unconscionable

A party may avoid arbitration if the arbitration clause is unconscionable, or is the product of duress or fraud. However, to avoid arbitration, these defenses must specifically relate to the arbitration clause itself and not the agreement as a whole.[36] If the defense relates to the entire agreement, the arbitrator will adjudicate the defense.[37]

A court may not enforce an agreement to arbitrate if it was unconscionable at the time it was made.[38] An arbitration agreement may be unconscionable if the expense of arbitration is prohibitive.[39] The party resisting arbitration must prove that the arbitration that would actually be conducted is cost prohibitive "with specific information of future cost."[40] Citing the costs associated with a particular arbitration provider without proving that the arbitration would be conducted with that provider is insufficient.[41]

An arbitration agreement is not unconscionable simply because it requires one party to arbitrate and allows another party to litigate, even if the party with the option to litigate was in the stronger bargaining position.[42]

25-3:3 Resisting on Ground of Fraud

To successfully resist arbitration on the ground of fraud, the party must establish that the fraud pertains specifically to the arbitration agreement, rather than to the agreement as a whole.

Establishing fraud as to the arbitration agreement requires (1) a material representation about the arbitration agreement, rather than the agreement as a whole; (2) the representation was false; (3) when the representation was made, the speaker knew it was false or made it recklessly without any knowledge of the truth; (4) the speaker made the representation with the intent that the other party should act upon it; (5) the party acted in reliance on the representation; and (6) the party thereby suffered

---

[33] *In re Weekley Homes, L.P.*, 180 S.W.3d 126, 131 (Tex. 2005) at 191 ("Unlike a corporation and its employees, corporate affiliates are generally created to separate the businesses, liabilities, and contracts of each. Thus, a contract with one corporation—including a contract to arbitrate disputes—is generally not a contract with any other corporate affiliates.").

[34] *Jody James Farms, JV v. Altman Grp., Inc.*, 547 S.W.3d 624, 632 (Tex. 2018).

[35] *Jody James Farms, JV v. Altman Grp., Inc.*, 547 S.W.3d 624, 632 (Tex. 2018).

[36] *In re First Merit Bank, N.A.*, 52 S.W.3d 749, 756 (Tex. 2001).

[37] *In re First Merit Bank, N.A.*, 52 S.W.3d 749, 756 (Tex. 2001).

[38] Tex. Civ. Prac. & Rem. Code Ann. § 171.022.

[39] *In re First Merit Bank, N.A.*, 52 S.W.3d 749, 756 (Tex. 2001) (citing *Green Tree Fin. Corp. v. Randolph*, 531 U.S. 79, 91 (2000)).

[40] *In re First Merit Bank, N.A.*, 52 S.W.3d 749, 756 (Tex. 2001) (internal citation omitted).

[41] *Green Tree Fin. Corp. v. Randolph*, 531 U.S. 79, 522 (2000); *In re First Merit Bank, N.A.*, 52 S.W.3d 749, 756 (Tex. 2001).

[42] *Green Tree Fin. Corp. v. Randolph*, 531 U.S. 79, 522 (2000); *In re First Merit Bank, N.A.*, 52 S.W.3d 749, 757 (Tex. 2001).

injury.[43] Where there is no evidence of fraud with respect to the arbitration agreement itself, courts will not invalidate the arbitration agreement.[44]

25-3:4 Waiver of Right to Arbitrate

A party to an arbitration agreement can waive their rights under the agreement by "substantially invoking the judicial process to the other party's detriment" and when doing so causes prejudice to the other party.[45] There is a strong presumption against waiver that controls in close cases.[46]

Merely filing suit and seeking initial discovery does not waive the right to arbitrate.[47] In 2018, the Texas Supreme Court held that it has "declined to conclude that the right to arbitrate was waived in all but the most unequivocal of circumstances."[48] On the other hand, parties waive their contractual rights to arbitration when they "conduct full discovery, file motions going to the merits, and seek arbitration only on the eve of trial."[49] A party does not waive an arbitration agreement with respect to a claim against a party with whom it has an arbitration agreement by litigating a distinct claim against an opponent.[50] Conduct short of this standard may or may not constitute waiver under the case law; so, the party seeking to arbitrate is well-advised to do so early on in the litigation.

Factors the court considers in determining waiver include "whether the party asserting the right to arbitrate was plaintiff or defendant in the lawsuit, how long the party waited before seeking arbitration, the reasons for any delay in seeking to arbitrate, how much discovery and other pretrial activity the party seeking to arbitrate conducted before seeking arbitration, whether the party seeking to arbitrate requested the court to dispose of claims on the merits, whether the party seeking to arbitrate asserted affirmative claims for relief in court, the amount of time and expense the parties have expended in litigation, and whether the discovery conducted would be unavailable or useful in arbitration."[51]

25-4 Post-arbitration Proceedings

A party may file suit to have their arbitration award confirmed as a Texas state court judgment.[52] Conversely, a party may file suit seeking to vacate, modify or correct an arbitration award.

---

[43] *Green Tree Fin. Corp. v. Randolph*, 531 U.S. 79, 522 (2000); *In re First Merit Bank, N.A.*, 52 S.W.3d 749, 758 (Tex. 2001).

[44] *Green Tree Fin. Corp. v. Randolph*, 531 U.S. 79, 522 (2000); *In re First Merit Bank, N.A.*, 52 S.W.3d 749, 758 (Tex. 2001).

[45] *In re Citigroup Global Mkts.*, 258 S.W.3d 623, 625 (Tex. 2008) (quoting *Perry Homes v. Cull*, 258 S.W.3d 580, 589–90 (Tex. 2007)).

[46] *RSL Funding, LLC v. Pippins*, 499 S.W.3d 423, 430 (Tex. 2016).

[47] *Henry v. Cash Biz, LP*, 551 S.W.3d 111, 116 (Tex. 2018) (citing *Perry Homes v. Cull*, 258 S.W.3d 580, 590 (Tex. 2008)).

[48] *Henry v. Cash Biz, LP*, 551 S.W.3d 111, 116 (Tex. 2018).

[49] *In re Citigroup Global Mkts.*, 258 S.W.3d 623, 625 (Tex. 2008).

[50] *RSL Funding, LLC v. Pippins*, 499 S.W.3d 423, 430 (Tex. 2016) (citing *Hodges v. Gobellan*, 433 S.W.3d 542, 545 (Tex. 2014)).

[51] *RSL Funding, LLC v. Pippins*, 499 S.W.3d 423, 430 (Tex. 2016).

[52] Tex. Civ. Prac. & Rem. Code Ann. § 171.081.

25-4:1 Confirmation of an Award

The pleading procedure to confirm an award is similar to the procedure to compel arbitration.

The application should:

- Show the jurisdiction of the court;
- Have attached a copy of the agreement to arbitrate;
- Define the issue subject to arbitration between the parties under the agreement;
- Specify the status of the arbitration before the arbitrators; and
- Show the need for the court order sought by the applicant.[53]

Unless the adverse party offers grounds for vacating, modifying, or correcting the award, the trial court shall confirm the award.[54]

25-4:2 Vacating an Award

A party seeking to vacate an arbitration award generally must make its application within 90 days of receiving the award, unless the grounds for vacating the award is based on corruption, fraud or other undue means, in which case the application must be made within 90 days of the date such grounds were discovered or should have been discovered.[55]

There are four grounds for vacating an arbitration award. The grounds for vacating an arbitration award in the TAA are exhaustive. The Texas Supreme Court has held that "a party may avoid confirmation only by demonstrating a ground expressly listed in section 171.088 [of the TAA]."[56] The court may vacate the award if:

- The award was obtained by corruption, fraud or other undue means;
- The rights of a party were prejudiced by (a) evident partiality by an arbitrator appointed as a neutral arbitrator; (b) corruption in an arbitrator; or (c) misconduct or wilful misbehavior of an arbitrator;
- The arbitrators (a) exceeded their powers; (b) refused to postpone the hearing after a showing of sufficient cause for the postponement; or (c) refused to hear evidence material to the controversy; or (d) conducted the hearing, contrary to in a manner that substantially prejudiced the rights of a party; or
- There was no agreement to arbitrate, the issue was not adversely determined, and the party did not participate in the arbitration hearing without raising the objection.[57]

If the court denies the application to vacate the award, and a motion to correct or modify is not pending, the court must confirm the award.[58] Where the court vacates

---

[53] Tex. Civ. Prac. & Rem. Code Ann. § 171.085.
[54] Tex. Civ. Prac. & Rem. Code Ann. § 171.087.
[55] Tex. Civ. Prac. & Rem. Code Ann. § 171.088(b).
[56] *Hoskins v. Hoskins*, 497 S.W.3d 490, 495 (Tex. 2016).
[57] Tex. Civ. Prac. & Rem. Code Ann. § 171.088(a).
[58] Tex. Civ. Prac. & Rem. Code Ann. § 171.088(c).

the award, other than on grounds that there was no agreement to arbitrate, the court may order a rehearing before the arbitrators,[59] or new arbitrators chosen either by the court or according to the terms of the agreement.[60]

25-4:3 Modifying or Correcting an Award

The trial court may modify or correct an award if the award contains an evident miscalculation of numbers, or an evident mistake in the description of a person, thing or property referred to in the award.[61] The court may also modify or correct an award if arbitrators have ruled on a matter not submitted to them so long as the modification or correction can be made without affecting the ruling on the merits of matters that were submitted to them,[62] or if the award is incorrect in a manner not affecting the merits of the award.[63]

---

[59] Tex. Civ. Prac. & Rem. Code Ann. § 171.089(b).
[60] Tex. Civ. Prac. & Rem. Code Ann. § 171.089(a).
[61] Tex. Civ. Prac. & Rem. Code Ann. § 171.091(a)(1).
[62] Tex. Civ. Prac. & Rem. Code Ann. § 171.091(a)(2).
[63] Tex. Civ. Prac. & Rem. Code Ann. § 171.091(a)(3).

CHAPTER 26

Pleading to Resist or Enforce a Forum Selection Clause*

This chapter discusses enforcing and resisting forum selection clauses.

26-1 Enforcing a Forum Selection Clause

This section discusses enforcing forum selection clauses.

26-1:1 Enforceability of Forum Selection Clauses Generally

Forum selection clauses are presumptively valid, and are routinely enforced in Texas courts.[1] The Supreme Court of Texas has consistently held that mandamus will lie to correct a trial court's refusal to enforce a forum selection clause.[2]

A trial court may not refuse to enforce a forum selection clause unless the party opposing its enforcement demonstrates "(1) enforcement would be unreasonable or unjust, (2) the clause is invalid for reasons of fraud or overreaching, (3) enforcement would contravene a strong public policy of the forum where the suit was brought, or (4) the selected forum would be seriously inconvenient for trial."[3]

A party seeking to resist a forum selection clause bears a "heavy burden of proof" and must show that trial in the chosen forum is so "gravely difficult and inconvenient" that he will be deprived of his day in court.[4]

---

[*] The authors thank Max Moran for his assistance in the updating of this chapter.

[1] *In re International Profit Assocs., Inc.*, 274 S.W.3d 672, 675 (Tex. 2009) (orig. proceeding); *In re Nationwide Ins. Co. of Am.*, 494 S.W.3d 708, 712 (Tex. 2016). *See also Pinto Tech. Ventures, L.P. v. Sheldon*, 526 S.W.3d 428, 432 (Tex. 2017) ("Subject to public-policy constraints, forum-selection clauses are generally enforceable in Texas.").

[2] *In re ADM Inv'r Servs., Inc.*, 304 S.W.3d 371 (Tex. 2010) (orig. proceeding); *In re International Profit Assocs.*, 274 S.W.3d 672, 675, 680 (Tex. 2009) (orig. proceeding); *In re Lyon Fin. Servs., Inc.*, 257 S.W.3d 228 (Tex. 2008) (orig. proceeding); *In re AutoNation, Inc.*, 228 S.W.3d 663 (Tex. 2007) (orig. proceeding); *In re Automated Collection Techs., Inc.*, 156 S.W.3d 557 (Tex. 2004) (orig. proceeding); *In re AIU Ins. Co.*, 148 S.W.3d 109 (Tex. 2004) (orig. proceeding).

[3] *In re ADM Inv'r Servs.*, 304 S.W.3d 371, 375 (Tex. 2010); *In re Nationwide Ins. Co. of Am.*, 494 S.W.3d 708, 712 (Tex. 2016).

[4] *In re AIU Ins. Co.*, 148 S.W.3d 109, 113 (Tex. 2004).

Enforcement may be unreasonable or unjust when the forum selected is a "remote alien forum,"[5] though the Supreme Court of Texas has never seen a "remote alien forum,"[6] or where the clause is the product of fraud.

Whether or not the selection clause applies to the particular claims asserted depends upon whether or not the substance of the claims arises from the contract containing the clause.[7] Tort claims between the contracting parties such as fraud and negligent misrepresentation,[8] tortious interference,[9] and breach of fiduciary duty and securities claims related to the contract with the clause[10] have all been held to be subject to the selection clause.

26-1:2 Distinguishing Forum Selection Clauses from Venue Selection Clauses

In the case of *In re Great Lakes Dredge & Dock Co. L.L.C.*, the Corpus Christi Court of Appeals held that the Texas Supreme Court's recent decisions regarding the enforcement of forum selection clauses did not "supplant firmly established Texas law regarding the enforcement of *venue*-selection agreements that contravene a mandatory venue statute."[11]

The court recognized that although Texas case law has sometimes muddled the distinction, "forum" and "venue" each have a distinct legal meaning. "Forum" generally refers to a sovereign or a state. Conversely, "[a]t common law, venue meant the neighborhood, place, or county in which the injury is declared to have been done or in fact declared to have happened." In Texas, the court noted, "venue" refers to the county in which suit is proper within the forum state. Therefore, a "forum" selection agreement is one that chooses another state or sovereign as the location for trial, whereas a "venue" selection agreement chooses a particular county or court within that state or sovereign.[12]

The court then analyzed "nearly a hundred years of Texas case law"[13] establishing that Texas courts will not enforce venue selection agreements that contradict mandatory venue statutes, as a matter of strong, established public policy.[14] As a result, in Texas the fixing of venue by contract, except in instances specifically permitted by

---

[5] *In re AIU Ins. Co.*, 148 S.W.3d 109, 113 (Tex. 2004).
[6] *See, e.g.*, cases at note 2.
[7] *In re Fisher*, 433 S.W.3d 523, 529–30 (Tex. 2014); *see also In re Lisa Laser USA, Inc.*, 310 S.W.3d 880, 886 (Tex. 2010); *In re International Profit Assocs.*, 274 S.W.3d 672, 677 (Tex. 2009).
[8] *In re International Profit Assocs., Inc.*, 274 S.W.3d 672, 677–78 (Tex. 2009).
[9] *In re Lisa Laser U.S.A., Inc.*, 310 S.W.3d 880, 887 (Tex. 2010) (orig. proceeding).
[10] *In re Fisher*, 433 S.W.3d 523, 530–31 (Tex. 2014).
[11] *In re Great Lakes Dredge & Dock Co.*, 251 S.W.3d 68, 77 (Tex. App.—Corpus Christi 2008, no pet.) (emphasis in original).
[12] *In re Great Lakes Dredge & Dock Co.*, 251 S.W.3d 68, 73–74 (Tex. App.—Corpus Christi 2008, no pet.).
[13] *In re Great Lakes Dredge & Dock Co.*, 251 S.W.3d 68, 79 n.11 (Tex. App.—Corpus Christi 2008, no pet.).
[14] *In re Great Lakes Dredge & Dock Co.*, 251 S.W.3d 68, 74–79 (Tex. App.—Corpus Christi 2008, no pet.).

statute, is invalid.[15] One of these instances, where the fixing of venue by contract has been specifically permitted by statute, can be found in section 15.020 of the Texas Civil Practice and Remedies Code. This exception has led Texas courts to find that "venue-selection clauses are generally unenforceable in Texas unless the contract evinces a 'major transaction' as defined in the venue rules."[16]

By Texas statute, "major transactions" may contain venue selection agreements, and the enforcement of these clauses are governed by the statute.[17] A "major transaction" is a transaction evidenced by a writing with a consideration of $1 million or more.[18] However, these transactions do not include transactions entered into for personal, family, or household purposes, or the settlement of wrongful death or personal injury claims.[19]

The statute provides that disputes arising out of major transactions "shall be brought in a county if the party against whom the action is brought has agreed in writing that a suit arising from the transaction may be brought in that county."[20]

The statute also spells out situations in which an action may not be brought in a county. The statute provides that an action may not be brought in a county if "the party bringing the action has agreed in writing that an action arising from the transaction may not be brought in that county, and the action may be brought in another county of this state or in another jurisdiction."[21] In other words, a venue agreement in a written contract for a major transaction may exclude a venue or venues.

The statute also explicitly states that if the writing provides that the action must be brought in a particular county or jurisdiction, then it may not be brought in any other county.[22]

26-2 Resisting a Forum Selection Clause

A forum selection clause will not be enforced if it is the product of fraud or if the party seeking enforcement has waived the clause.

26-2:1 Fraud

Fraud can invalidate a forum selection clause, but such a showing is difficult as it is the same standard as that applied to arbitration clauses, discussed in Chapter 25.[23] The clause itself must be the product of fraud, rather than the agreement as a whole

---

[15] *See, e.g., Fleming v. Ahumada*, 193 S.W.3d 704, 712–13 (Tex. App.—Corpus Christi 2006, *reh'g denied*) (holding that a contractual provision attempting to fix venue in a settlement agreement was invalid because "[i]n general, the fixing of venue by contract, except in such instances as specifically permitted by statute, is invalid and cannot be the subject of private contract").

[16] *Hiles v. Arnie & Co.*, 402 S.W.3d 820, 828 (Tex. App.—Houston [14th Dist.] 2013, pet. denied).

[17] Tex. Civ. Prac. & Rem. Code Ann. § 15.020(a), (b).

[18] Tex. Civ. Prac. & Rem. Code Ann. § 15.020(a).

[19] Tex. Civ. Prac. & Rem. Code Ann. § 15.020(a).

[20] Tex. Civ. Prac. & Rem. Code Ann. § 15.020(b).

[21] Tex. Civ. Prac. & Rem. Code Ann. § 15.020(c)(1).

[22] Tex. Civ. Prac. & Rem. Code Ann. § 15.020(c)(2).

[23] *See* Chapter 25, Section 3:3, discussing fraud as a defense to an arbitration clause.

or in general.[24] A general allegation of fraud directed at the entire agreement will not invalidate the clause.[25]

A forum selection clause is invalidated where a party conceals a forum selection clause with the intent to defraud.[26] Failing to point out the clause standing alone, however, does not constitute fraud; and the fact that a party is unaware of the clause does not make it invalid.[27]

26-2:2 Waiver

The standard for the waiver of a forum selection clause is the same as the standard for the waiver of an arbitration agreement. A party waives a "forum selection clause" by substantially invoking the litigation process and prejudicing the opposing party.[28] *See* Chapter 25-3:4 Waiver of Right to Arbitrate.

---

[24] *In re Lyon Fin. Servs., Inc.*, 257 S.W.3d 228, 232 (Tex. 2008) (orig. proceeding); *see also In re Prudential Ins. Co. of Am.*, 148 S.W.3d 124, 134 (Tex. 2004) (orig. proceeding).

[25] *In re Prudential Ins. Co. of Am.*, 148 S.W.3d 124, 134 (Tex. 2004).

[26] *In re International Profit Assocs., Inc.*, 286 S.W.3d 921, 923 (Tex. 2009) ("Evidence that a party concealed a forum-selection clause combined with evidence proving that concealment was part of an intent to defraud a party may be sufficient to invalidate the clause ...").

[27] *In re International Profit Assocs., Inc.*, 286 S.W.3d 921 (Tex. 2009).

[28] *In re Nationwide Ins. Co. of Am.*, 494 S.W.3d 708, 712–13 (Tex. 2016) ("[W]e have borrowed a different standard from the jurisprudence applicable to arbitration clauses, an analogous type of forum-selection clause.").

CHAPTER 27

Pleading Removal and Remand*

27-1 Removal Generally

As a general rule, any case filed in state court over which the federal district courts would have had original jurisdiction may be removed to federal court.[1] In other words, a case may be removed to federal court if it could have been filed originally in federal court. Put yet another way, subject to exceptions, any case over which the federal district court has subject matter jurisdiction is removable to federal court if first filed in state court.

27-2 Removal on Federal Question Grounds

A case may be removed from state to federal court if it presents a federal question because district courts have original (though not exclusive) jurisdiction over federal question cases.[2]

27-2:1 Federal Question Jurisdiction Defined

District courts have federal question jurisdiction over "all civil actions arising under the Constitution, laws, or treaties of the United States."[3] To determine whether or not a case "arises under" federal law, federal courts apply the well-pleaded complaint rule.[4] Under this rule, the existence of a federal question is determined by resort to the face of the plaintiff's well-pleaded complaint and to the statement of the plaintiff's cause of action.[5] Federal question jurisdiction may not be predicated upon the existence of a federal defense or federal response to a defense.[6] Instead, the cause of action itself must raise a federal question.

---

* The authors thank Max Moran for his assistance in the updating of this chapter.
[1] 28 U.S.C. § 1441(a).
[2] 28 U.S.C. § 1331.
[3] 28 U.S.C. § 1331.
[4] *Louisville & N.R. Co. v. Mottley*, 211 U.S. 149, 152 (1908).
[5] *Louisville & N.R. Co. v. Mottley*, 211 U.S. 149, 152 (1908) ("... a suit arises under the Constitution and laws of the United States only when the plaintiff's statement of his own cause of action shows that it is based upon those laws or that Constitution").
[6] *Louisville & N.R. Co. v. Mottley*, 211 U.S. 149, 152 (1908).

As a general rule, the cause of action arises under the law that creates it.[7] Thus, federally created causes of action present federal questions. State created causes of action, as a general rule, do not. The vast majority of cases can be resolved with application of this straightforward test, also known as the Holmes Test.[8]

In relatively rare cases, a state created cause of action may arise under federal law, thereby presenting a federal question. These rare cases occur when an issue of federal law is an element of the plaintiff's state created cause of action.[9] It is not enough, however, merely for the federal issue to be an element of the state cause of action.[10] Though federal courts, including the Supreme Court, have had difficulty articulating a satisfactory and predictable definition of this strain of federal question jurisdiction, for a state cause of action to constitute a federal question, resolution of the federal issue must be (1) necessary to resolution of the dispute, (2) the federal issue must be substantial in that there is a substantial interest in providing a federal forum for resolution of such disputes, and (3) declaring the state cause of action a federal question will not disrupt the division of labor between the state and federal courts.[11]

27-2:2 Joinder of Federal and State Law Claims

Where a civil action includes both a claim that constitutes a federal question and an otherwise non-removable claim (e.g., state law claim), the entire action may be removed so long as the action would have been removable in the absence of the state law claim.[12]

If the otherwise non removable claim falls within the federal court's supplemental jurisdiction, the court will retain jurisdiction over the entire case, including the otherwise non removable claim. Claims fall within the district court's supplemental jurisdiction when they form part of the same case or controversy as the claim over which the court has original jurisdiction.[13] The "same case or controversy" requirement is satisfied if both claims arise from "a common nucleus of operative fact" (i.e., the same transaction or occurrence).[14] For example, a federal court would retain jurisdiction over a state law claim that arises out of the same or similar operative facts as the federal law claim over which the court has federal question jurisdiction.

If the federal court does not have supplemental jurisdiction over the otherwise non removable claim (e.g., a state law claim that does not arise from a nucleus of operative

---

[7] *Merrell Dow Pharm., Inc. v. Thompson*, 478 U.S. 804, 808 (1986) ("The 'vast majority' of cases that come within this grant of jurisdiction are covered by Justice Holmes' statement that a 'suit arises under the law that creates the cause of action.'").

[8] *Merrell Dow Pharm., Inc. v. Thompson*, 478 U.S. 804, 809 n.5 (1986).

[9] *Grable & Sons Metal Prods., Inc. v. Darue Eng. & Mfg.*, 545 U.S. 308, 312 (2005) ("There is, however, another longstanding, if less frequently encountered, variety of federal 'arising under' jurisdiction, this Court having recognized for nearly 100 years that in certain cases federal-question jurisdiction will lie over state-law claims that implicate significant federal issues.").

[10] *Grable & Sons Metal Prods., Inc. v. Darue Eng. & Mfg.*, 545 U.S. 308, 313 (2005).

[11] *Grable & Sons Metal Prods., Inc. v. Darue Eng. & Mfg.*, 545 U.S. 308, 313–14 (2005).

[12] 28 U.S.C. § 1441(c)(1).

[13] 28 U.S.C. § 1367(a).

[14] *Halmekangas v. State Farm Fire & Cas. Co.*, 603 F.3d 290, 293 (5th Cir. 2010) (citing *Mendoza v. Murphy*, 532 F.3d 342, 346 (5th Cir. 2008)).

PLEADING REMOVAL AND REMAND 577

fact common to the federal question claim) or the claim, although a federal claim, has been made non removable by statute, the federal court will retain jurisdiction over the claim constituting a removable federal question, but the court will sever and remand the state law and non removable federal claims.[15] In this circumstance, only the defendants against whom the removable federal claim is asserted (i.e., the removable federal question) must consent to the removal.[16]

27-3 Removal on Diversity of Citizenship Grounds

Subject to exceptions, a case may be removed to federal court if the case is one over which the federal courts would have diversity of citizenship jurisdiction. A federal court has diversity of citizenship jurisdiction where the amount in controversy exceeds $75,000, exclusive of interest and costs, and there is complete diversity of citizenship.

27-3:1 Determining the Amount in Controversy Requirement

The amount in controversy must exceed the sum or value of $75,000 exclusive of interest and costs.[17] In general, the amount claimed by the plaintiff in good faith in the state court petition is the amount in controversy.[18] However, when the plaintiff seeks injunctive relief, when state law does not permit demand for a specific sum, or when state law allows recovery of damages in excess of the amount alleged—the defendant may allege the amount in controversy in the notice of removal.[19] Even where the plaintiff alleges an amount in controversy below the jurisdictional threshold of $75,000, information in the record of the state court proceeding as well as in discovery responses regarding the true amount in controversy can trigger the defendant's right of removal.[20]

27-3:2 The Complete Diversity Requirement

Though not explicitly required by the statute, the Supreme Court read the statute to require *complete* diversity of citizenship more than 200 years ago.[21] Complete diversity means that no plaintiff may share citizenship with any defendant.[22]

27-3:3 Determining the Citizenship of the Parties

Determining the citizenship of the parties requires, as a threshold matter, identifying the type of person or entity the party is. The tests for citizenship differ based upon whether the party is a human, a corporation, or an unincorporated association.

---

[15] 28 U.S.C. § 1441(c)(2).
[16] 28 U.S.C. § 1441(c)(2).
[17] 28 U.S.C. § 1332(a).
[18] 28 U.S.C. § 1446(c)(2).
[19] 28 U.S.C. § 1446(c)(2).
[20] 28 U.S.C. § 1446(c)(3)(A).
[21] *Strawbridge v. Curtiss*, 7 U.S. 267 (1806).
[22] *Strawbridge v. Curtiss*, 7 U.S. 267 (1806).

27-3:3.1 Citizenship for Natural Persons

A human who is a U.S. citizen is a citizen of the U.S. state in which he is domiciled. Domicile is defined as the person's true, fixed and permanent home and the place to which they intend to return when absent.[23] Domicile has also been defined in more mathematical terms: residency in a state plus intent to remain in the state indefinitely.[24] A natural person may have only one domicile, even if they have several residences.[25]

Parents or guardians establish the domicile of a minor child.[26] Once domicile has been established, either by a parent or by the party himself, the party does not change his domicile unless and until he resides in another state or nation and does so with the intent to remain there indefinitely.[27]

Thus, a party does not change his domicile simply by intending to move away from the current domicile (such as when they have merely decided to move but have not yet done so), nor does a party change domicile by establishing a temporary residency outside the state of domicile. The party must change his residency and intend to remain indefinitely before a new domicile is established. Parties that frequently reside in a state other than the state of domicile include military personnel,[28] college students,[29] and prisoners.[30]

Non-U.S. citizens are considered citizens or subjects of a foreign state under the diversity statute.[31] Even if the non-U.S. citizen has been admitted as a permanent legal resident alien and is domiciled in a U.S. state, he is a citizen or subject of the foreign state for diversity purposes.[32]

However, there is no diversity of citizenship between a citizen of a U.S. state and a permanent legal resident alien who is domiciled in the same state.[33] At first blush, the effect of the rule may seem to be no different than state citizenship for the alien in the state of domicile.

Nothing in this provision, however, states that an alien is a citizen of his state of domicile, which would affect the operation of the forum state defendant rule, discussed in Section 27-3:4. A permanent legal resident alien domiciled in the forum state would not be a forum state defendant for purposes of removal because he is not a citizen of the forum state, even though there would be no diversity between the alien and another citizen of the forum state.

The legal representative of the estate of a decedent, a minor or an incompetent is deemed to be a citizen only of the same state as the decedent, minor or incompetent.[34]

---

[23] *Mas v. Perry*, 489 F.2d 1396, 1399 (5th Cir. 1974).
[24] *Preston v. Tenet Healthsystem Mem'l Med. Ctr. Inc.*, 485 F.3d 793, 798 (5th Cir. 2007).
[25] *Williamson v. Osenton*, 232 U.S. 619 (1914).
[26] *See, e.g., Mas v. Perry*, 489 F.2d 1396, 1399 (5th Cir. 1974).
[27] *Hollinger v. Home State Mut. Ins. Co.*, 654 F.3d 564 (5th Cir. 2011).
[28] *See, e.g., Beers v. North American Van Lines, Inc.*, 836 F.2d 910 (5th Cir. 1988).
[29] *See, e.g., Scoggins v. Pollock*, 727 F.2d 1025, 1027 (11th Cir. 1984).
[30] *See, e.g., Taylor v. Slatkin*, No. 3:02-CV-2404-R, 2003 WL 21662825 (N.D. Tex. May 13, 2003).
[31] Pub. L. No. 112-63 (H.R. 394), 125 Stat. 758 (2011) (eliminating language making permanent legal resident aliens citizens of the state of domicile).
[32] Pub. L. No. 112-63 (H.R. 394), 125 Stat. 758 (2011).
[33] 28 U.S.C. § 1332(a)(2).
[34] 28 U.S.C. § 1332(c)(2).

The representative's citizenship therefore is the result of the test described above but as applied to the decedent, minor or incompetent. This rule prevents parties from manufacturing or destroying diversity through the selection of the nominal party who represents the estate, minor or incompetent.

A natural person who is a U.S. citizen and who is domiciled outside of the United States is neither an alien nor a citizen of a state.[35] These American expatriates cannot sue or be sued in federal court on diversity grounds.[36]

27-3:3.2 Citizenship for Corporations

Corporations are citizens of every state or nation in which they are incorporated and of the state or nation in which it has its principal place of business.[37] This test routinely results in the corporation being a citizen of multiple jurisdictions—at least one based on its place(s) of incorporation and one based on its principal place of business.

The "nerve" test determines the corporation's principal place of business.[38] The corporation's principal place of business is the location of "the place where the corporation maintains its headquarters," which is the "actual center of direction, control, and coordination."[39] The "nerve center" is "not simply an office where the corporation holds its board meetings (for example, attended by directors and officers who have traveled there for the occasion)."[40]

A different test for citizenship applies to insurers (whether or not incorporated) in direct actions on a liability insurance policy where the insured is not a party. In such actions, the insurer is deemed a citizen of (1) every state and foreign state of which the insured is a citizen; (2) all states and nations in which the insurer is incorporated; and (3) the state or foreign state in which the insurer has its principal place of business.[41]

27-3:3.3 Citizenship for Unincorporated Business Entities

Congress has not created a test for unincorporated business entities—such as LLCs, LLPs, LPs and partnerships—except in class actions and mass actions under the Class Action Fairness Act.[42] In all other cases, there is no test for citizenship for unincorpo-

---

[35] *Coury v. Prot*, 85 F.3d 244, 248 (5th Cir. 1996) ("An American national, living abroad, cannot sue or be sued in federal court under diversity jurisdiction, 28 U.S.C. § 1332, unless that party is a citizen, i.e. domiciled, in a particular state of the United States.").

[36] *Coury v. Prot*, 85 F.3d 244, 248 (5th Cir. 1996).

[37] 28 U.S.C. § 1332(c)(1).

[38] *Hertz Corp. v. Friend*, 559 U.S. 77, 91–93 (2010) (abandoning various tests from the courts of appeals—including "locus of operations" and "center of corporate activities" tests—in favor of the "nerve-center" test).

[39] *Hertz Corp. v. Friend*, 559 U.S. 77, 93 (2010).

[40] *Hertz Corp. v. Friend*, 559 U.S. 77, 93 (2010).

[41] 28 U.S.C. § 1332(c)(1)(A)–(C).

[42] 28 U.S.C. § 1332(d)(10) (In class and mass actions, the unincorporated business entity is "deemed to be a citizen of the State where it has its principal place of business and the State under whose laws it is organized.").

rated business entities.[43] Despite acknowledging problems that would result from its decision, the United States Supreme Court refused to create such a test as a matter of common law.[44]

The result of this inaction on the part of Congress and the U.S. Supreme Court is that unincorporated business entities share citizenship with all of their members, be they partners, general partners or limited partners.[45]

27-3:3.4 Citizenship Determined at the Time the Complaint Is Filed

The time-of-filing rule provides that the citizenship of the parties is determined based on the facts as they exist at the time the complaint is filed.[46] Thus, if the parties are completely diverse at the time of filing, a post-complaint change of citizenship will not deprive the court of jurisdiction.[47] Similarly, once diversity jurisdiction is established, the post-complaint addition of a non-diverse party will not deprive the court of subject matter jurisdiction,[48] at least where the additional non-diverse part was not an indispensable party at the time the complaint was filed.[49] Conversely, where the parties are not completely diverse at the time of filing, a post-complaint change of citizenship will not cure the defect.[50]

One exception to the time of filing rule is found in the Supreme Court's *Caterpillar, Inc. v. Lewis* decision.[51] The case was removed to federal court while a diversity destroying defendant was still a party to the suit. Plaintiff's motion to remand was denied by the trial court.[52] Following removal, the diversity-destroying defendant was dropped from the case following settlement.[53] The case proceeded to trial and judg-

---

[43] 28 U.S.C. § 1332(c) (containing no standard for determining citizenship of unincorporated associations created by state law). *See generally, Carden v. Arkoma Assocs.*, 499 U.S. 185 (1990).

[44] *Carden v. Arkoma Assocs.*, 499 U.S. 185, 195 (1990).

[45] *Carden v. Arkoma Assocs.*, 499 U.S. 185, 195–96 (1990).

[46] *Grupo Dataflux v. Atlas Glob. Grp., L.P.*, 541 U.S. 567, 574–75 (2004) ("To our knowledge, the Court has never approved a deviation from the rule articulated by Chief Justice Marshall in 1829 that '[w]here there is no change of party, a jurisdiction depending on the condition of the party is governed by that condition, as it was at the commencement of the suit.'") (internal citation omitted).

[47] *Mollan v. Torrance*, 9 Wheat. 537, 6 L. Ed. 154 (1824); *Clarke v. Mathewson*, 12 Pet. 164, 171, 9 L. Ed. 1041 (1838); *Wichita Railroad & Light Co. v. Public Util. Comm'n of Kansas*, 260 U.S. 48, 54, 43 S. Ct. 51, 53, 67 L. Ed. 124 (1922).

[48] *Freeport-McMoran, Inc. v. KN Energy, Inc.*, 498 U.S. 426, 428–29 (1991) (the addition of a non-diverse party following transfer of interest in contract to the non-diverse party did not deprive the court of subject matter jurisdiction).

[49] *Freeport-McMoran, Inc. v. KN Energy, Inc.*, 498 U.S. 426, 428–29 (1991) ("The additional party" was not an "indispensable" party at the time the complaint was filed; in fact, it had no interest whatsoever in the outcome of the litigation until sometime after suit was commenced).

[50] *Grupo Dataflux v. Atlas Glob. Grp., L.P.*, 541 U.S. 567, 574–75 (2004) (the fact that a party's citizenship changed during the course of the proceedings did not cure a lack of diversity that existed at the time of filing).

[51] *Caterpillar Inc. v. Lewis*, 519 U.S. 61, 65 (1996).

[52] *Caterpillar Inc. v. Lewis*, 519 U.S. 61, 65 (1996).

[53] *Caterpillar Inc. v. Lewis*, 519 U.S. 61, 65 (1996).

ment for the defendant.[54] The Supreme Court held that, though diversity did not exist at the time of filing nor at the time of removal, the dismissal of the diversity destroying defendant meant that subject matter jurisdiction existed at the time of judgment and that following a full trial on the merits "considerations of finality, efficiency, and economy become overwhelming."[55] Despite *Caterpillar*, a party's change in citizenship (as opposed to a change in party) cannot cure a defect in subject matter jurisdiction following removal.[56]

Though removability is generally determined based on the facts at the time of the notice of removal, the parties must be completely diverse both at the time the action is filed in state court and at the time the case is removed to federal court.[57] The requirement that the parties be diverse at both points in time, rather than only at the time of the notice of removal, prevents a defendant from manufacturing removal jurisdiction by changing his citizenship during the course of the lawsuit.

27-3:4 The Forum State Defendant Rule

A case may not be removed to federal court on diversity grounds where any defendant "properly joined and served" is a citizen of the forum state.[58] This limitation does not apply to removal of federal question cases.[59]

The result of the forum state defendant rule is that some suits are not removable, even though the plaintiff could have filed the suit in federal court. For example, an Oklahoma plaintiff could file a $100,000 breach of contract action against a Texas defendant in a federal district court in Texas. That same case, however, is not removable if first filed in Texas state court because the defendant is a citizen of the forum state. Only one forum state defendant is required to preclude removal. The statute makes clear that the case is not removable if *any* defendant is a citizen of the forum state.[60]

27-3:5 The Improperly (Also Known as Fraudulently) Joined Defendant

Defendants may remove a case despite the presence of a forum state or diversity destroying defendant based on the allegation that the defendant is fraudulently joined

---

[54] *Caterpillar Inc. v. Lewis*, 519 U.S. 61, 65 (1996).

[55] *Caterpillar Inc. v. Lewis*, 519 U.S. 61, 75 (1996). *See also Newman-Green, Inc. v. Alfonzo-Larrain*, 490 U.S. 826 (1989) (applying a similar "cure" rule in a case first filed in federal court).

[56] *Grupo Dataflux v. Atlas Glob. Grp., L.P.*, 541 U.S. 567, 574–75 (2004) (rejecting the argument to expand *Caterpillar* to the case of a change of citizenship rather than a change of party).

[57] *Gibson v. Bruce*, 108 U.S. 561, 2 S. Ct. 873, 27 L. Ed. 825 (1883); *Texas Wool & Mohair Mktg. Ass'n v. Standard Acc. Ins. Co.*, 175 F.2d 835, 838 (5th Cir. 1949) ("In order to sustain removal on the ground here asserted, diversity of citizenship must be shown to have existed both when the crossclaim was instituted and when the petition for removal was filed.").

[58] 28 U.S.C. § 1441(b)(2) ("A civil action otherwise removable solely on the basis of the jurisdiction under Section 1332(a) of this title may not be removed if any of the parties in interest properly joined and served as defendants is a citizen of the State in which such action is brought.").

[59] 28 U.S.C. § 1441(b)(2).

[60] 28 U.S.C. § 1441(b)(2).

and that; therefore, his presence should not be considered for purposes of determining the propriety of removal.[61] In an en banc opinion, the Fifth Circuit Court of Appeals used the term "improper joinder" rather than the more commonly used "fraudulent joinder,"[62] much to the dismay of the dissenting judges.[63]

There are two ways to establish fraudulent joinder: (1) fraud in the pleading of the jurisdictional facts and (2) the inability of the plaintiff to establish a cause of action against the non-diverse or forum state defendant in state court.[64] Cases of the first type, those involving allegations of actual fraud in the pleading of jurisdictional facts, are rare.

With respect to the second method, the burden is on the defendant to establish that there is "no possibility of recovery by the plaintiff against an in-state defendant, which stated differently means that there is no reasonable basis for the district court to predict that the plaintiff might be able to recover against an in-state defendant."[65]

Ordinarily, this determination is made based upon the pleadings alone akin to the determination of a Rule 12(b)(6) motion for failure to state a claim.[66] Given the heightened pleading standard in federal court following *Twombly*,[67] at least one federal court has concluded that this requires a plaintiff to plead facts sufficient to show that recovery against the diversity destroying or forum defendant is plausible.[68]

Where the pleadings omit facts that would determine the propriety of joinder, the trial court may pierce the pleadings and consider the evidence.[69] If the trial court uses a summary judgment type inquiry, it is "appropriate only to identify the presence of discrete and undisputed facts that would preclude plaintiff's recovery against the in-state defendant."[70] The Fifth Circuit, sitting en banc, has warned that hearings on the issue should not be substantial and discovery "should not be allowed, except on a tight judicial tether, sharply tailored to the question at hand, and only after a showing

---

[61] *See, e.g., Smallwood v. Illinois Cent. R. Co.*, 385 F.3d 568, 572 (5th Cir. 2004) (defendant removed case to federal court alleging fraudulent joinder despite the presence of a defendant who shared citizenship with both the plaintiff and the forum state).

[62] *Smallwood v. Illinois Cent. R. Co.*, 385 F.3d 568, 572 (5th Cir. 2004).

[63] *Smallwood v. Illinois Cent. R. Co.*, 385 F.3d 568, 585 (5th Cir. 2004) ("And finally, in a remarkable showing of euphemistic chutzpah, the majority has renamed 'fraudulent joinder' as 'improper joinder', upsetting decades of nomenclature without apparent reason.") (J. Smith, dissenting).

[64] *Smallwood v. Illinois Cent. R. Co.*, 385 F.3d 568, 573 (5th Cir. 2004) (citing *Travis v. Irby*, 326 F.3d 644, 646–47 (5th Cir. 2003)).

[65] *Smallwood v. Illinois Cent. R. Co.*, 385 F.3d 568, 573 (5th Cir. 2004).

[66] *Smallwood v. Illinois Cent. R. Co.*, 385 F.3d 568, 573 (5th Cir. 2004).

[67] *See generally, Bell Atl. Corp. v. Twombly*, 550 U.S. 544, 127 S. Ct. 1955, 167 L. Ed. 2d 929 (2007) (requiring plaintiff's allegations to show that recovery is plausible).

[68] *Beavers v. DePuy Orthopaedics, Inc.*, No. 1:11 dp 20275, 2012 WL 1945603, at *5 (N.D. Ohio May 30, 2012) (holding that defendant was fraudulently joined because the plaintiff's allegations "fall well below the threshold required to meet the plausibility standard required under *Twombly*").

[69] *Smallwood v. Illinois Central Ry. Co.*, 385 F.3d 568, 573–74 (5th Cir. 2004).

[70] *Smallwood v. Illinois Central Ry. Co.*, 385 F.3d 568, 573–74 (5th Cir. 2004).

of its necessity."[71] The plaintiff's motive in joining the defendant is not relevant to the inquiry.[72]

Examples of defendants fraudulently joined because of the plaintiff's inability to establish a cause of action include the innocent retailer in a strict product liability case[73] and employees who have committed a tort in the course of their employment with another defendant.[74]

27-3:6 Prohibition on Removal on Diversity Grounds After One Year

A case may not be removed on the basis of diversity of citizenship more than one year after commencement of the action, "unless the district court finds that the plaintiff has acted in bad faith in order to prevent a defendant from removing the action."[75] A plaintiff's refusal to disclose the true amount in controversy to prevent removal is deemed bad faith.[76]

27-4 Cases Made Non Removable by Statute

By statute, the following actions, even if otherwise removable, may not be removed.[77]

- An action against a railroad or its receivers or trustees under 45 U.S.C. 51–54, 55–60 (injuries to employees);

- A civil action against a carrier or its receivers or trustees to recover damages for delay, loss or injury of shipments, arising under Section 11706 or 14706 of title 49, unless the matter in controversy exceeds $10,000, exclusive of interest and costs;

---

[71] *Smallwood v. Illinois Central Ry. Co.*, 385 F.3d 568, 573–74 (5th Cir. 2004).
[72] *Smallwood v. Illinois Central Ry. Co.*, 385 F.3d 568, 573–74 (5th Cir. 2004).
[73] *Ayala v. Enerco Grp., Inc.*, No. 13-30532, 2014 WL 2200642, at *3 (5th Cir. May 28, 2014) (holding that in a strict liability claim for wrongful death against the retailer of a propane heater where Louisiana substantive law applied, the retailer was improperly joined because a Louisiana statute prohibits a consumer from holding a non-manufacturer liable in a wrongful death case). *See also*, Tex. Civ. Prac. & Rem. Code § 82.003 (generally prohibiting liability against non-manufacturers in product liability cases); *but see Reynolds v. Ford Motor Co.*, No. 5:04-CV-085-C, 2004 WL 2870079, at *4 (N.D. Tex. Dec. 13, 2004) (where plaintiffs alleged defendants actual knowledge of the defect (an exception to the general prohibition on non-manufacturer liability) and the only evidence on the issue before the court was conflicting, remand was proper). *See also Watkins v. Gen. Motors, LLC*, No. H-11-2106, 2011 WL 3567017, at *2–3 (S. D. Tex. Aug. 12, 2011); *Salazar v. Merck & Co., Inc.*, No. 05-445, 2005 WL 2875332, at *3 (S.D. Tex. Nov. 2, 2005); *Norris v. Bombardier Recreational Prods., Inc.*, No. 1:08-CV-525, 2009 WL 94531, at *5 (E.D. Tex. Jan. 12, 2009).
[74] *See, e.g., Allen v. Home Depot U.S.A., Inc.*, No. SA-04-CA-703-XR, 2004 WL 2270001, at *3 (W.D. Tex. Oct. 6, 2004); *Bueno v. Cott Beverages, Inc.*, No. SA-04-CA-24-XR, 2004 WL 1124927, at *4 (W.D. Tex. Mar. 15, 2004); *Palmer v. Wal-Mart Stores, Inc.*, 65 F. Supp. 2d 564, 567 (S.D. Tex. 1999); *but see Valdes v. Wal-Mart Stores, Inc.*, 199 F.3d 290, 292 (5th Cir. 2000) (joinder of general manager of Wal-Mart was not improper but Wal-Mart's removal based on allegation of his improper joinder did not warrant sanctions).
[75] 28 U.S.C. § 1446(c)(1).
[76] 28 U.S.C. § 1446(c)(3)(B).
[77] 28 U.S.C. § 1445.

- A civil action in any state court arising under the workmen's compensation laws;
- A civil action in any state court arising under Section 40302 of the Violence Against Women Act of 1994.

27-5 Removal Procedure

27-5:1 Removal Venue

A case must be removed to the federal court for the district and division embracing the location of the state court.[78] This requirement is a venue provision, and venue is proper in the federal court even if the court would not have been a proper venue had the case been first filed there rather than removed.[79]

A case may be transferred to another district court following removal, but the transfer must be pursuant to Section 1404(a) for the convenience of the parties and witnesses—rather than under Section 1406 for improper venue.[80]

The defendant's failure to remove the case to the proper district and division is a procedural defect, meaning that it is waived if not raised in a timely motion to remand.

27-5:2 The Contents of the Notice of Removal

Federal statutes set forth what amount to pleading requirements for the notice of removal. The notice must:[81]

- Be signed pursuant to Federal Rule of Civil Procedure 11, which can subject the defendant and his attorney to sanctions for unsubstantiated allegations in the notice;
- Must be accompanied by all process, pleadings and orders served upon the defendant at the time of the removal; and
- Contain a short and plain statement of the grounds for removal.

Generally, the amount alleged by the plaintiff in his initial pleading determines the amount in controversy,[82] but the notice of removal may allege the amount in controversy if the plaintiff seeks non-monetary relief or the state rules do not permit the pleader to allege a specific sum or permits recovery in excess of the amount alleged.[83] If the notice alleges the amount in controversy, the district court will determine whether or not the amount in controversy requirement is met by a preponderance of the evidence.[84]

---

[78] 28 U.S.C. § 1446(a).
[79] *Polizzi v. Cowles Magazines, Inc.*, 345 U.S. 663, 73 S. Ct. 900, 97 L. Ed. 1331 (1953).
[80] *Kreimerman v. Casa Veerkamp, S.A. de C.V.*, 22 F.3d 634 (5th Cir. 1994) (removal of case to wrong division of correct district was a procedural defect).
[81] 28 U.S.C. § 1446(a).
[82] 28 U.S.C. § 1446(c)(2).
[83] 28 U.S.C. § 1446(c)(2)(B).
[84] 28 U.S.C. § 1446(c)(2)(B).

27-5:3 Deadline to Remove

If the original petition in Texas state court shows an action that is removable, the defendant has 30 days from service to remove the case to federal court.[85]

If the original petition does not show that the action is removable, the action may later become removable due to a change in parties (e.g., dropping from the action a diversity spoiling or forum state defendant), a change in the theories of recovery (e.g., the addition of a federal cause of action constituting a federal question), or a change in the allegations regarding amount in controversy.

The defendant will have 30 days from receipt of a copy of an amended pleading, motion, order or other paper from which it may first be ascertained that the case is one which is or has become removable.[86]

For cases that are not removable based upon the initial petition, whether or not the case later becomes removable will often turn upon application of the voluntary-involuntary rule. Where a plaintiff voluntarily dismisses a diversity-destroying or forum state defendant, the case becomes removable upon receipt by the defendants of a pleading, motion or other paper that shows that the party has been dismissed.[87] For example, a dismissal following settlement or the plaintiff's nonsuit will make the action removable. On the other hand, where the dismissal of the party is the result of action by the court or another defendant, the case does not become removable.[88]

Each defendant has 30 days from receipt of the original petition to remove the case.[89] An earlier-served defendant may join in the notice of removal of a later-served defendant even if the earlier served defendant's time to remove has expired.[90] This rule from the statute overturns the Fifth Circuit's first-served defendant rule, which stated that the deadline for removal for all defendants began to run from the date on which the first defendant was served.[91]

27-5:4 Unanimity of Consent Rule

The unanimity of consent rule requires that all defendants, except for those alleged to be improperly joined, must join in the notice of removal.[92] As discussed earlier Section 27-5:3, an earlier served defendant may join in the notice of removal of a later served defendant even if his time for removal has expired.

27-5:5 Deadline to Answer Following Removal

A defendant who has filed an answer in state court before removal need not file another in federal court unless the court orders it. A defendant who has not filed an

---

[85] 28 U.S.C. § 1446(b)(1).
[86] 28 U.S.C. § 1446(b)(3).
[87] *Weems v. Louis Dreyfus Corp.*, 380 F.2d 545, 547 (5th Cir. 1967) (citing *Powers v. Chesapeake & O. Ry.*, 169 U.S. 92 (1898)); 28 U.S.C. § 1446(b)(3).
[88] *Weems v. Louis Dreyfus Corp.*, 380 F.2d 545, 547 (5th Cir. 1967).
[89] 28 U.S.C. § 1446(b)(2)(B).
[90] 28 U.S.C. § 1446(b)(2)(C).
[91] *Brown v. Demco, Inc.*, 792 F.2d 478, 481–82 (5th Cir.1986) (establishing the first served defendant rule).
[92] 28 U.S.C. § 1446(b)(2)(A).

answer must file his answer or present other defenses or objections under the federal rules (e.g., 12(b) motions) by the later of: 21 days after receipt of the original petition, through service or otherwise, or seven days after the notice of removal is filed.[93]

27-6 Remand

A motion to remand the case based on any defect other than lack of subject matter jurisdiction must be made within 30 days of the filing of the notice of removal.[94] Failure to file the motion within 30 days waives all procedural defects in removal. The prudent plaintiff will assume that procedural defects include the presence of a forum state (but not diversity destroying) defendant, removal to the wrong district or division, untimely removal, and lack of unanimity of consent amongst the defendants.[95] A motion to remand based on a lack of subject matter jurisdiction may be made at any time before final judgment.[96]

---

[93] Fed. R. Civ. P. 81(c).
[94] 28 U.S.C. § 1447(c).
[95] *In re Shell Oil Co.*, 932 F.2d 1518 (5th Cir. 1991) (holding that the presence of a forum state defendant is a waivable procedural defect in removal and saying "we are persuaded by the language of the House report and the commentators that 'any defect in removal procedure' includes all non-jurisdictional defects existing at the time of removal").
[96] 28 U.S.C. § 1447(c).

CHAPTER 28

Motions and Responses to Motions Attacking Pleadings*

28-1 Motions to Dismiss Baseless Causes of Action

Texas Rule of Civil Procedure 91a became effective on March 1, 2013 and authorizes a motion to dismiss a cause of action on the grounds that it has no basis in law or fact.

28-1:1 Scope of Application

Rule 91a authorizes a motion to dismiss in all cases, except for those brought under the Family Code or those brought pursuant to Chapter 14 of the Texas Civil Practice and Remedies Code. A Chapter 14 action under the Texas Civil Practice and Remedies Code is an action brought by an inmate in which an affidavit or unsworn declaration of inability to pay costs is filed by the inmate.[1]

28-1:2 No Basis in Law or Fact

Rule 91a authorizes a party to move to dismiss a cause of action on the grounds that it has no basis in law or fact. A cause of action has no basis in law if "the allegations, taken as true, together with inferences reasonably drawn from them do not entitle the claimant to the relief sought."[2] A cause of action has no basis in fact if no reasonable person could believe the facts pleaded.[3]

The Beaumont Court of Appeals has compared the Rule 91a motion to dismiss to the federal motion to dismiss for failure to state a claim under Federal Rule 12(b)(6).[4] The court used the comparison to import the federal plausibility pleading standards to the determination of whether or not a pleading passes muster under Rule 91a.[5]

---

* The authors thank Max Moran for his assistance in the updating of this chapter.
[1] Tex. Civ. Prac. & Rem. Code Ann. § 14.002.
[2] Tex. R. Civ. P. 91a.1.
[3] Tex. R. Civ. P. 91a.1.
[4] *GoDaddy.com, LLC v. Toups*, 429 S.W.3d 752, 754 (Tex. App.—Beaumont 2014, pet. denied) ("While not identical, Rule 91a is analogous to Rule 12(b)(6).").
[5] *GoDaddy.com, LLC v. Toups*, 429 S.W.3d 752, 754 (Tex. App.—Beaumont 2014, pet. denied) ("For a complaint to survive a Rule 12(b)(6) motion to dismiss, it must contain 'enough facts to state a claim to relief that is plausible on its face.'" (quoting *Bell Atl. Corp. v. Twombly*, 550 U.S. 544, 570 (2007)).

The Beaumont court said, "in determining whether the trial court erred in denying a defendant's motion to dismiss, we take all plaintiff's allegations as true and consider whether a plaintiff's petition contains 'enough facts to state a claim to relief that is plausible on its face.'"[6] The San Antonio Court of Appeals has cited to federal pleading case law and described the standard for dismissal in language similar to that found in federal case law interpreting the plausibility standard.[7] In particular, the court has said that it accepts the plaintiff's factual allegations as true but does not provide the same deference to the plaintiff's legal conclusions or conclusory statements. Other courts of appeals have incorporated Texas's traditional fair notice pleading standard into the standard for ruling on a Rule 91a motion and have largely ignored the federal plausibility standard.[8] Prudence demands compliance with the plausibility standard until the Supreme Court of Texas or other courts of appeals provide clarification.

28-1:3 Contents of Motion

The motion to dismiss must meet the following requirements:

- State that it is made pursuant to Rule 91a;
- Identify each cause of action to which it is addressed; and
- State the reasons the cause of action has no basis in law, no basis in fact, or both.[9]

28-1:4 Timing of Motion, Response, and Hearing

The motion must be filed within 60 days after the first pleading that contains the challenged cause of action is served on the movant.[10] It must be filed at least 21 days before the motion is heard.[11] The response must be filed no later than 7 days before the date of the hearing.[12] The term hearing includes both submission and an oral hearing.[13] Each party is entitled to at least 14 days notice of the hearing on the motion to dismiss, though the trial court need not conduct an oral hearing on the motion.[14]

---

[6] *GoDaddy.com, LLC v. Toups*, 429 S.W.3d 752, 754 (Tex. App.—Beaumont 2014, pet. denied) (citing *Bell Atl. Corp. v. Twombly*, 550 U.S. 544, 570 (2007)).

[7] *Vasquez v. Legend Nat. Gas III, LP*, 492 S.W.3d 448, 451 (Tex. App.—San Antonio 2016, pet. denied) (citing *Ashcroft v. Iqbal*, 556 U.S. 662, 678 (2009)).

[8] *In the Guardianship of Peterson*, No. 01-15-00567-CV, 2016 WL 4487511, at *6 (Tex. App.—Houston [1st Dist.] 2016, no pet.). *See also Wooley v. Schaffer*, 447 S.W.3d 71, 76 (Tex. App.—Houston [14th Dist.] 2014, pet. denied) (In ruling on a motion to dismiss under Rule 91a, "we apply the fair notice pleading standard applicable in Texas to determine whether the allegations of the petition are sufficient to allege a cause of action.").

[9] Tex. R. Civ. P. 91a.2.

[10] Tex. R. Civ. P. 91a.3(a).

[11] Tex. R. Civ. P. 91a.3(b).

[12] Tex. R. Civ. P. 91a.4.

[13] Comment to 2013 Change to Tex. R. Civ. P. 91.

[14] Comment to 2013 Change to Tex. R. Civ. P. 91a.6.

28-1:5 Ruling on the Motion

Rule 91a sets a deadline for the trial court to rule on the motion. The trial court must grant or deny the motion within 45 days after the motion is filed.[15]

The trial court may not consider evidence in ruling on the motion but must decide the motion based solely on the pleading.[16] The court may consider exhibits that were made part of the pleadings under Texas Rule of Civil Procedure 59.[17]

The trial court may not rule on the motion if the respondent nonsuits the challenged cause of action at least three days before the date of the hearing.[18] The trial court may not rule on the motion to dismiss if the movant files a withdrawal of the motion.[19]

The respondent may amend the challenged causes at least three days before the date of the hearing.[20] In response, the movant may withdraw the motion or file an amended motion directed at the amended cause of action. If an amended motion is filed, the amended motion restarts the time periods in the rule.[21]

The court must rule on the motion, despite a nonsuit or amendment, if a nonsuit or amendment was not filed in compliance with the rule (i.e., not at least three days before the hearing).[22] Denials of motions to dismiss under Rule 91a may be reviewed at the time of denial by writ of mandamus or permissive interlocutory appeal.[23]

28-1:6 Award of Costs and Attorney Fees Required

Rule 91a.7 requires the trial court to award the prevailing party on the motion all costs and reasonable and necessary attorney fees incurred with respect to the challenged cause of action. Both a movant and a respondent can be awarded costs and attorney fees under this rule as the rule benefits the "prevailing party." Rule 91a leaves the trial court no discretion to award costs and reasonable attorney fees. The trial court must award them to the prevailing party. A party who prevails later on another motion, such

---

[15] Comment to 2013 Change to Tex. R. Civ. P. 911a.3(c).
[16] Comment to 2013 Change to Tex. R. Civ. P. 91a.6.
[17] Comment to 2013 Change to Tex. R. Civ. P. 91a.6. Tex. R. Civ. P. 59 ("Notes, accounts, bonds, mortgages, records, and all other written instruments, constituting, in whole or in part, the claim sued on, or the matter set up in defense, may be made a part of the pleadings by copies thereof, or the originals, being attached or filed and referred to as such, or by copying the same in the body of the pleading in aid and explanation of the allegations in the petition or answer made in reference to said instruments and shall be deemed a part thereof for all purposes.").
[18] Comment to 2013 Change to Tex. R. Civ. P. 91a.5(a).
[19] Comment to 2013 Change to Tex. R. Civ. P. 91a.5(a).
[20] Comment to 2013 Change to Tex. R. Civ. P. 91a.5(b).
[21] Comment to 2013 Change to Tex. R. Civ. P. 91a.5(d).
[22] Comment to 2013 Change to Tex. R. Civ. P. 91a.5(c).
[23] *ConocoPhillips Co. v. Koopmann*, 547 S.W.3d 858, 880 (Tex. 2018) (citing *In re Essex Ins. Co.*, 450 S.W.3d 524, 526 (Tex. 2014) (by writ of mandamus) and *GoDaddy.com, LLC v. Toups*, 429 S.W.3d 752, 753–54 (Tex. App.—Beaumont 2014, pet. denied) (permissive interlocutory appeal)).

as a motion for summary judgment, is not entitled to attorney fees and costs under Rule 91a.[24]

28-1:7 Effect on Venue and Personal Jurisdiction

Rule 91a modifies the due order of hearing rules for special appearances and motions to transfer venue. As discussed in Chapter 22, Section 22-3, a party may waive a special appearance or a motion to transfer venue by seeking relief inconsistent with the objection to jurisdiction or venue, including by seeking a ruling on the merits of the case. Filing and seeking a ruling on a motion to dismiss under Rule 91a, however, does not waive a special appearance or a motion to transfer venue.

Rule 91a also states: "By filing a motion to dismiss, a party submits to the court's jurisdiction only in proceedings on the motion and is bound by the court's ruling, including an award of attorney fees and costs against the party."

Does this mean that a party can file a motion to dismiss before a special appearance without waiver of the special appearance? To complicate matters, the rule also states that it is not an exception to the pleading requirements for special appearances and motions to transfer venue.

Whether or not this language in the rule is referring to the due order of pleading requirements in Rules 120a and 86 is not entirely clear. What is clear is that the prudent approach is to file special appearances and motions to transfer venue before or at the same time as a motion to dismiss because the motion to dismiss is certainly not waived if it follows one of the other defenses.

28-2 Special Exceptions

Special exceptions are used to challenge defects in the pleadings. Rule 90 provides that "every defect, omission or fault in a pleading either of form or of substance" must be specifically pointed out in writing or it is waived. The special exception is the procedural device used to avoid waiver of the pleading defect.

A special exception must be in writing and point out "intelligibly and with particularity the defect, omission, obscurity, duplicity, generality, or other insufficiency in the allegations in the pleading excepted to."[25] The party specially excepting must obtain a ruling on the exception or the defect is waived.

The special exception has been used to challenge defects of form in the pleadings, such as where the pleading is vague or ambiguous, and to challenge the substance of the pleading, more along the lines of a motion to dismiss,[26] such as where the pleader

---

[24] *ConocoPhillips Co. v. Koopmann*, 547 S.W.3d 858, 880 (Tex. 2018) (holding that a party who prevailed on a motion for summary judgment after its motion to dismiss was denied was not entitled to attorney fees, even though its motion for summary judgment was based on same grounds as the motion to dismiss).

[25] Comment to 2013 Change to Tex. R. Civ. P. 91.

[26] *Baylor Univ. v. Sonnichsen*, 221 S.W.3d 632, 635 (Tex. 2007).

has pled facts that show he can never recover[27] or where the pleading establishes the existence of an affirmative defense.[28]

Normally, if the trial court sustains the special exception, the trial court must give the pleader an opportunity to replead, but the trial court need not provide this opportunity if the defect cannot be cured by amendment, such as where the pleader has demonstrated he can never recover or established an affirmative defense in his petition.[29]

28-3 Pleas in Abatement

A plea in abatement is "a special plea which establishes a matter that may be properly urged to defeat the action or suspend the right to prosecute it."[30] While special exceptions are used to point out deficiencies that appear in a pleading, a plea in abatement is used to raise a defect that exists outside the pleading it attacks.[31] Special exceptions raising evidence outside the pleadings are impermissible "speaking demurrers."[32]

A plea in abatement may not be used to challenge personal jurisdiction or venue; but, otherwise, may be used to raise any matter not in the petition that provides a reason to abate the proceedings.[33] A plea in abatement is used, for example, to raise a party's lack of standing,[34] to challenge a plaintiff's legal capacity to sue,[35] to show that a defendant is not liable in the capacity in which he is sued,[36] and the pendency of another action involving the same parties and claim.[37]

A plea in abatement may be contained in a separate instrument or be made a part of the answer.[38] Pleas in abatement should also be verified.[39]

---

[27] *Baylor Univ. v. Sonnichsen*, 221 S.W.3d 632, 635 (Tex. 2007) (pleading that written contract sued on was never delivered).

[28] *Baylor Univ. v. Sonnichsen*, 221 S.W.3d 632, 635–36 (Tex. 2007) (pleading demonstrated that claim on oral contract did not comply with the statute of frauds).

[29] *Baylor Univ. v. Sonnichsen*, 221 S.W.3d 632, 634 (Tex. 2007).

[30] *Augustine v. Nusom*, 671 S.W.2d 112, 114 (Tex. App.—Houston [14th. Dist.] 1984, writ ref'd n.r.e.).

[31] *Augustine v. Nusom*, 671 S.W.2d 112, 114 (Tex. App.—Houston [14th. Dist.] 1984, writ ref'd n.r.e.).

[32] *Augustine v. Nusom*, 671 S.W.2d 112, 114 (Tex. App.—Houston [14th. Dist.] 1984, writ ref'd n.r.e.).

[33] McDonald, Tex. Civ. Prac., Vol. II, 159 (1982) ("Any matter of fact arising outside the face of the petition, which challenges neither the venue of the action nor the jurisdiction of the court, but which presents a reason why the pending suit should be suspended or dismissed, may form the subject of a plea in abatement.").

[34] Though standing is perhaps more properly raised in a plea to the court's jurisdiction, pleas in abatement have also been used. See, e.g., *Texas Indus. Traffic League v. R.R. Comm'n Tex.*, 633 S.W.2d 821 (Tex. 1982), overruled on other grounds by *Tex. Ass'n of Bus. v. Tex. Air Control Bd.*, 852 S.W.2d 440 (Tex. 1993); *Austin Neighborhoods Council v. Bd. of Adjustment of City of Austin*, 644 S.W.2d 560, 564 n.17 (Tex. App.—Austin 1982, writ ref'd n.r.e.).

[35] *M & M Constr. Co. v. Great Am. Ins. Co.*, 747 S.W.2d 552, 554 (Tex. App.—Corpus 1988, no writ).

[36] *Flowers v. Steelcraft Corp.*, 406 S.W.2d 199, 199 (Tex. 1966).

[37] *Wyatt v. Shaw Plumbing Co.*, 760 S.W.2d 245 (Tex. 1988).

[38] Tex. R. Civ. P. 85.

[39] Tex. R. Civ. P. 93; *Sparks v. Bolton*, 335 S.W.2d 780, 785 (Tex. App.—Dallas 1960, no writ).

28-4 Texas Anti-SLAPP Act

The Texas Citizens Participation Act (an Anti-SLAPP "strategic lawsuits against public participation" act) authorizes a party to make a motion to dismiss an action that is "based on, relates to, or is in response to a party's exercise of the right of free speech, right to petition, or right of association."[40] The Texas Supreme Court has explained that the purpose of the Act is to "identify and summarily dispose of lawsuits designed only to chill First Amendment rights, not to dismiss meritorious lawsuits."[41] Motions to dismiss under the Act are routine in cases involving defamation claims,[42] but the law reaches beyond such suits as well.[43] The Act is not limited to public communications, but can apply to private ones, such as emails,[44] and to any case involving statements connected to a "matter of public concern."[45] The act defines a "matter of public concern" to include an issue related to health or safety; environmental, economic, or community well-being; the government; a public official or public figure; or a good, product, or service in the marketplace.

The movant bears the burden to establish applicability of the Act by a preponderance of the evidence.[46] To avoid dismissal in actions to which the Act applies, the non-movant must establish "by clear and specific evidence a prima facie case for each essential element of the claim in question."[47] This requires evidence sufficient "as a matter of law to establish a given fact if it is not rebutted or contradicted" as to each essential element.[48] The Act does not elevate the burden of proof the plaintiff must meet at trial, and the Texas Supreme Court has rejected the line of cases in the court of appeals that required direct evidence of each essential element of the claim.[49] The motion to dismiss must be filed within 60 days of service of the legal action, unless the court finds good cause for extending the time.[50] The filing of the motion suspends all

---

[40] Tex. Civ. Prac. & Rem. Code Ann. § 27.003(a).
[41] *In re Lipsky*, 460 S.W.3d 579, 589 (Tex. 2015).
[42] *See, e.g., Lippincott v. Whisenhunt*, 462 S.W.3d 507, 509 (Tex. 2015).
[43] Geoff Gannaway, "Does the Texas Anti-SLAPP Statute Apply to Your Lawsuit? You Might be Surprised," 74 *The Advocate* (Texas) 98 (2015) ("Many lawyers who have not yet handled a case involving the statute assume (incorrectly) that the law applies only to suits for slander or libel based on statements made to the general public. That assumption is reasonable because 'SLAPP' stands for 'Strategic Lawsuits Against Public Participation,' and SLAPP suits have been described as those 'filed against politically and socially active individuals—not with the goal of prevailing on the merits but, instead, of chilling those individuals' First Amendment activities.' Yet while defamation actions are certainly impacted by the Anti-SLAPP statute, the law is already reaching well beyond such suits.").
[44] *Lippincott v. Whisenhunt*, 462 S.W.3d 507, 509 (Tex. 2015).
[45] *Lippincott v. Whisenhunt*, 462 S.W.3d 507, 509 (Tex. 2015).
[46] *Lippincott v. Whisenhunt*, 462 S.W.3d 507, 509 (Tex. 2015).
[47] *In re Lipsky*, 460 S.W.3d 579, 590 (Tex. 2015); Tex. Civ. Prac. & Rem. Code Ann. § 27.005(c).
[48] *In re Lipsky*, 460 S.W.3d 579, 590 (Tex. 2015).
[49] *In re Lipsky*, 460 S.W.3d 579, 591 (Tex. 2015) ("Though [the Act] initially demands more information about the underlying claim, the Act does not impose an elevated evidentiary standard or categorically reject circumstantial evidence. In short, it does not impose a higher burden of proof than that required of the plaintiff at trial. We accordingly disapprove those cases that interpret the TCPA to require direct evidence of each essential element of the underlying claim to avoid dismissal.").
[50] Tex. Civ. Prac. & Rem. Code Ann. § 27.003(b).

discovery in the action until the court has ruled on the motion,[51] unless the court finds good cause to allow for limited discovery relevant to the motion to dismiss.[52] Generally, the hearing on the motion must occur within 60 days of the filing of the motion, but may occur no later than 90 days after the filing of the motion if the court's docket conditions require a later hearing, or upon a showing of good cause, or by agreement of the parties.[53] If the court grants limited discovery related to the motion, the hearing must occur no later than 120 days from the date of the motion.[54]

The court must rule on the motion within 30 days of the hearing,[55] and a failure in timely to rule on the motion results in the motion being overruled by operation of law, and immediate interlocutory appeal is available to the movant.[56] If the motion is granted, the court must award to the moving party court costs, attorney fees, and other costs incurred in defending the action and sanctions against the party who brought the action sufficient to deter the party from bringing similar actions.[57]

The Act does not apply to:

- enforcement actions brought in the name of the State or a political subdivision by the attorney general, a district attorney, a criminal district attorney, or a county attorney;
- a legal action brought against a person primarily engaged in the business of selling or leasing goods or services, if the statement or conduct arises out of the sale or lease of goods, services, or an insurance product, insurance services, or a commercial transaction in which the intended audience is an actual or potential buyer or customer;
- a legal action seeking recovery for bodily injury, wrongful death, or survival or to statements made regarding that legal action; or
- a legal action brought under the Insurance Code or arising out of an insurance contract.[58]

---

[51] Tex. Civ. Prac. & Rem. Code Ann. § 27.003(c).
[52] Tex. Civ. Prac. & Rem. Code Ann. § 27.006(b).
[53] Tex. Civ. Prac. & Rem. Code Ann. § 27.004(a).
[54] Tex. Civ. Prac. & Rem. Code Ann. § 27.004(c).
[55] Tex. Civ. Prac. & Rem. Code Ann. § 27.005(a).
[56] Tex. Civ. Prac. & Rem. Code Ann. § 27.008(a).
[57] Tex. Civ. Prac. & Rem. Code Ann. § 27.009(a).
[58] Tex. Civ. Prac. & Rem. Code Ann. § 27.010(a)–(d).

CHAPTER 29

Amendment of Pleadings*

29-1 Distinguishing Between Amended and Supplemental Pleadings

When we speak of "amending pleadings," the term is often used generically to encompass amended pleadings, supplemental pleadings, and trial amendments, and sometimes even trial by consent, but these are not synonymous terms.

Supplemental pleadings supplement rather than replace a prior pleading, and their function is limited to responding to a new allegation of another party.[1] "Ordinarily, a plaintiff's supplemental petition will assert special exceptions, general denials and allegations of new matters not before alleged, in reply to allegations made by the defendant. However, an exception to this rule exists if the necessity of adding a new party arises from facts pled in a defendant's 'defensive pleading.'"[2] The prior pleading that is being supplemented and the new supplemental pleading together constitute the "live pleadings" of the party.[3]

In contrast, amended pleadings are not limited to being responsive to something pleaded by an opponent, and they replace rather than simply supplement a prior pleading.[4] The purpose of an amended pleading is to perfect a prior pleading by adding or withdrawing or correcting something, or to plead an additional claim or defense[5] or add a new party.[6] Since an amended pleading is expected to be entire and complete in

---

* The authors thank Max Moran for his assistance in the updating of this chapter.

[1] Tex. R. Civ. P. 69 ("Each supplemental petition or answer . . . shall be a response to the last preceding pleading by the other party, and shall not repeat allegations formerly pleaded further than is necessary.").

[2] *Tex-Hio P'ship v. Garner*, 106 S.W.3d 886, 890 (Tex. App.—Dallas 2003, no pet.); *see* Tex. R. Civ. P. 80, 98.

[3] Tex. R. Civ. P. 69 ("These instruments, to wit, the original petition and its several supplements, and the original answer and its several supplements, shall respectively, constitute separate and distinct parts of the pleadings of each party."); Tex. R. Civ. P. 78 ("The pleading of plaintiff shall consist of an original petition, and such supplemental petitions as may be necessary in the course of pleading by the parties to the suit."); Tex. R. Civ. P. 83 ("The answer of defendant shall consist of an original answer, and such supplemental answers as may be necessary.").

[4] Tex. R. Civ. P. 65 (substituted instrument takes place of original).

[5] Tex. R. Civ. P. 62 (defining an amended pleading).

[6] *Tex-Hio P'ship v. Garner*, 106 S.W.3d 886, 890 (Tex. App.—Dallas 2003, no pet.).

itself, it should repeat any information from the pleading being superseded which the pleader desires to continue in effect.[7] This is particularly important for plaintiffs with regard to continuing to include any party defendants in the pleading; the omission of a party defendant from an amended pleading can effectively nonsuit the omitted defendant, which can be fatal to the claim if limitations have already expired.[8]

"While an amended pleading must be complete within itself and is substituted for the pleading amended, *Rule 64, Texas Rules of Civil Procedure*, a trial amendment is for the purpose of enlarging the pleadings to meet objections to evidence as not being within the scope of the pleadings and to cure any defect, fault or omission in a pleading, either of form or substance, which is called to the attention of the court during the trial, *Rule 66, Texas Rules of Civil Procedure*, and is supplemental to and in amplification of the current pleading of the party filing such trial amendment."[9]

Trial by consent refers to the circumstance where one party has effectively acquiesced in the trial of an unpleaded issue and thereby entitled the other party to a trial amendment and submission of the issue to the jury.[10]

If a supplemental pleading is misnamed as an amended pleading, or an amended pleading is misnamed as a supplemental pleading, the court will look to the substance of the pleading rather than to the title.[11] This is most likely to matter when a party needs to respond to a newly-filed pleading of an opponent and erroneously files an instrument titled as an amended pleading after the deadline for amended pleadings has expired.

29-2 Effect of Amendment on Superseded Pleadings

An amended pleading, as distinguished from a supplemental pleading, supersedes prior pleadings "[u]nless the [amended pleading] shall be set aside on exceptions" or "unless it be necessary to look to the superseded pleading upon a question of limitation."[12]

The latter exception refers to the relation-back rule set forth in Texas Civil Practice and Remedies Code Section 16.068: "If a filed pleading relates to a cause of action, cross action, counterclaim, or defense that is not subject to a plea of limitation when the pleading is filed, a subsequent amendment or supplement to the pleading that changes the facts or grounds of liability or defense is not subject to a plea of limitation unless the amendment or supplement is wholly based on a new, distinct, or different transaction or occurrence." This relation-back rule allows new theories of liability and defense to be raised for the first time in amended pleadings and avoid a limitations bar if the new theory has some factual overlap with what had been previously pleaded before limitations expired. The fact that the theory of liability changes from tort to

---

[7] Tex. R. Civ. P. 64 ("shall amend by filing a substitute therefor, entire and complete in itself").
[8] *See Johnson v. Coca-Cola Co.*, 727 S.W.2d 756 (Tex. App.—Dallas 1987, writ ref'd n.r.e.) (party defendant nonsuited after expiration of limitations as a result of omission from amended pleading).
[9] *Miller v. Keyes*, 206 S.W.2d 120, 121 (Tex. App.—Austin 1947, writ ref'd n.r.e.).
[10] Tex. R. Civ. P. 67.
[11] Tex. R. Civ. P. 71 (court will treat misnamed pleading as if it had been properly designated).
[12] Tex. R. Civ. P. 65.

AMENDMENT OF PLEADINGS

contract,[13] or that the plaintiff intentionally chose not to pursue the second claim in the initial filing,[14] doesn't matter as long as both theories come from a related set of facts.[15] The relation-back rule does not apply to the joinder of new parties as opposed to the pleading of new causes of action or defenses.[16]

Although a superseded pleading has no continued legal effect beyond application of the relation-back rule, it can continue to be highly useful to an adversary for its evidentiary effect. The superseded status of the pleading doesn't prevent it from being introduced into evidence by an opportunistic opponent who wants to demonstrate how a plaintiff or defendant originally made a statement or took a position that has now been abandoned or shown to be false.[17] It is not necessary to prove that the superseded pleading constitutes a prior inconsistent statement to overcome a hearsay objection.[18] The prior pleading is admissible as a party admission,[19] unless other evidentiary objections[20] succeed in blocking its admission.

29-3 Time Limits for Amendment of Pleadings

The time limits for amendment of pleadings vary depending on which discovery level governs the case.[21]

For an expedited actions case governed by Discovery Level 1,[22] any "pleading, amended pleading, or supplemental pleading that removes a suit from the expedited actions process may not be filed without leave of court unless it is filed before the earlier of 30 days after the discovery period is closed or 30 days before the date set for trial. Leave to amend may be granted only if good cause for filing the pleading outweighs any prejudice to an opposing party."[23] Other amended and supplemental pleadings (which do not have the effect of removing the suit from the expedited actions process) continue to be governed by Tex. R. Civ. P. 63, requiring leave of court for any amended pleading offered within seven days of trial.

Discovery Level 2[24] makes no explicit provision for amended pleadings, thus Tex. R. Civ. P. 63 applies, requiring leave of court for any amended pleading offered within

---

[13] *See Leonard v. Texaco, Inc.*, 422 S.W.2d 160 (Tex. 1967).
[14] *See Lexington Ins. Co. v. Daybreak Express, Inc.*, 393 S.W.3d 242 (Tex. 2013).
[15] *But see Christus Health Gulf Coast v. Carswell*, 505 S.W.3d 528, 537–39 (Tex. 2016) (no "relation back" when the original claims (1) are separated in time from the facts underlying the newly-pleaded claim, (2) are based on facts different and distinct from those underlying the newly-pleaded claim, and (3) involve a different set of occurrences from that underlying the newly-pleaded claim).
[16] *Chavez v. Andersen*, 525 S.W.3d 382, 386–87 (Tex. App.—Houston [14th Dist.] 2017, no pet.).
[17] *See Bay Area Healthcare Grp., Ltd. v. McShane*, 239 S.W.3d 231 (Tex. 2007).
[18] *Bay Area Healthcare Grp., Ltd. v. McShane*, 239 S.W.3d 231 (Tex. 2007).
[19] *Bay Area Healthcare Grp., Ltd. v. McShane*, 239 S.W.3d 231, 235 (Tex. 2007).
[20] *Bay Area Healthcare Grp., Ltd. v. McShane*, 239 S.W.3d 231, 235 n.3 (Tex. 2007).
[21] *See* Chapter 20.
[22] *See* Tex. R. Civ. P. 190.2.
[23] Tex. R. Civ. P. 169(c)(2).
[24] *See* Tex. R. Civ. P. 190.3.

seven days of trial.[25] This means that the last day to file a pleading without leave of court is the Monday preceding a setting for the next Monday.[26]

For cases governed by Discovery Level 3, the court is required to provide a stated deadline for the amendment or supplementation of pleadings,[27] after which leave of court will be required.

Although amended pleadings filed more than seven days before trial (for pleadings governed by Rule 63 rather than by a scheduling order) are still subject to the first requirement of Rule 63 that "an amendment must be made 'at such time as not to operate as a surprise to the opposite party,' a party may file an amended pleading outside seven days of the trial date freely, without leave of court."[28] Even if the trial court does not have discretion to deny the filing of an amendment made before the deadline,[29] if evidence of surprise or prejudice is provided by an opposing party due to the timing of the amendment, the court does have the power to charge a continuance of the case to the party who has filed the amendment or supplementation, including costs and attorney's fees.[30]

For cases in which the pleading deadline is set by a scheduling order, the court has the discretion to deny a pleading amendment offered months before trial when it violates the terms of the scheduling order and the opponent provides evidence of surprise or prejudice.[31]

29-4 Motion for Leave to Amend Pleadings

Once the point in time is reached when leave of court is required for the filing of amended pleadings, an amending party who fails to first seek leave of court does so at his own risk. A court has full discretion to reject the filing of an amended pleading by a party who fails to seek leave at a time when leave of court is required.[32]

Nevertheless, assuming leave to file an amended pleading is requested, the burden remains on the objecting party to provide evidence of surprise[33] or prejudice,[34] and absent such a showing the court has no discretion to deny the opportunity to

---

[25] *See* discussion in the next section regarding a motion for leave to amend pleadings.
[26] *Sosa v. Central Power & Light*, 909 S.W.2d 893 (Tex. 1995).
[27] Tex. R. Civ. P. 190.4(b)(4).
[28] *Mensa-Wilmot v. Smith Int'l, Inc.*, 312 S.W.3d 771, 778 (Tex. App.—Houston [1st Dist.] 2009, no pet.); Tex. R. Civ. P. 63 ("Parties may amend their pleadings . . . at such time as not to operate as a surprise to the opposite party.").
[29] *G.R.A.V.I.T.Y. Enters., Inc. v. Reece Supply Co.*, 177 S.W.3d 537, 542 (Tex. App.—Dallas 2005, no pet.) (trial court must allow the parties to amend their pleadings up to the deadline for amending pleadings).
[30] Tex. R. Civ. P. 70.
[31] *See, e.g., Hakemy Bros., Ltd. v. State Bank & Tr. Co.*, 189 S.W.3d 920, 924–25 (Tex. App.—Dallas 2006, pet. denied) (denying pleading amendment approximately three months before trial).
[32] *Jones v. Pesak Bros. Constr., Inc.*, 416 S.W.3d 618, 632–33 (Tex. App.—Houston [1st Dist.] 2013, no pet.) (trial court does not abuse its discretion by refusing to consider an amended petition filed fewer than seven days before trial if the party fails to seek leave of court).
[33] Tex. R. Civ. P. 63 references "surprise."
[34] Tex. R. Civ. P. 66 references "prejudice."

AMENDMENT OF PLEADINGS

amend.[35] This is true even when the court has provided a scheduling order with a specified deadline for filing; the trial court abuses its discretion in denying leave to file an amended pleading unless the party opposing the amendment presents evidence of surprise or prejudice, or objects to an amendment that asserts a new cause of action or defense that is prejudicial on its face.[36] Additionally, Texas courts have held that in the absence of a sufficient showing of surprise by the opposing party, the failure to obtain leave of court when filing a late pleading may be cured by evidence in the record that the trial court actually treated the amended pleading in a manner consistent with considering it to be filed.[37]

Not all changes to a cause of action or defense are prejudicial on their face. When the change to a cause of action or defense amounts only to a procedural formality that does not change any substantive issue for trial, it is not prejudicial on its face, and evidence of surprise or prejudice instead of a mere objection will be required to deny the amendment.[38] "An amendment adding a new cause of action or defense operates as a surprise and is prejudicial on its face if it: (1) reshapes the nature of the case; (2) could not have been anticipated; and (3) prejudices a party's presentation of the case."[39]

If leave of court is required for filing, a pleading offered for filing electronically is not deemed filed until the date on which a motion for leave is granted by the court.[40]

Obviously, any kind of pleading amendment requested in the midst of trial will be offered in conjunction with a motion to the court for leave to amend, although the court's extent of discretion will vary depending on whether the offer is based on trial by consent, a trial amendment other than for trial by consent, or a supplementation of pleadings in response to allowance of an opponent's trial amendment. Distinctions between these categories are discussed in the next sections.

29-5 Trial Amendment to Pleadings

A trial amendment must be filed as a written pleading; an oral statement at trial is insufficient to modify the pleadings.[41]

Although a trial amendment is only "supplemental to and in amplification of the current pleading of the party filing such trial amendment"[42] (and therefore does not have to repeat all of the allegations in the prior pleading[43]), the entitlement to a trial amendment requested pursuant to Tex. R. Civ. P. 66 is evaluated by the same standard

---

[35] *Smith Detective Agency & Nightwatch Serv., Inc. v. Stanley Smith Sec., Inc.*, 938 S.W.2d 743, 747–48 (Tex. App.—Dallas 1996, writ denied).

[36] *First State Bank of Mesquite v. Bellinger & Dewolf, LLP*, 342 S.W.3d 142, 145–46 (Tex. App.—El Paso 2011, no pet.).

[37] *Hill v. Tx-An Anesthesia Mgmt., LLP*, 443 S.W.3d 416, 422–23 (Tex. App.—Dallas 2014, no pet.).

[38] *Chapin & Chapin v. Tex. Sand & Gravel Co.*, 844 S.W.2d 664 (Tex. 1992).

[39] *Karam v. Brown*, 407 S.W.3d 464, 476 (Tex. App.—El Paso 2013, no pet.).

[40] Tex. R. Civ. P. 21(f)(5)(B).

[41] *City of Fort Worth v. Zimlich*, 29 S.W.3d 62, 73 (Tex. 2000).

[42] *Miller v. Keyes*, 206 S.W.2d 120, 121 (Tex. Civ. App.—Austin 1947, writ ref'd n.r.e.).

[43] 2 McDonald & Carlson Tex. Civ. Prac. § 10:14 (2d. ed.), fn 1 ("A trial amendment supersedes that portion of the pleading that it amends and supplements the balance.").

as a pretrial motion for leave to file a pleading amendment.[44] "Under the rule, a trial court has no discretion to refuse a trial amendment unless: (1) the opposing party presents evidence of surprise or prejudice, or (2) the amendment is prejudicial on its face because it asserts a new cause of action or defense, and the opposing party objects to the amendment."[45] The burden is still on the objecting party "to satisfy the court that the allowance of such amendment would prejudice him in maintaining his action or defense upon the merits,"[46] and when the objecting party fails to satisfy that burden the court is to freely grant the amendment "when the presentation of the merits of the action will be subserved thereby."[47] "Trial amendments that are procedural in nature, such as conforming the pleadings to the evidence at trial, are mandatory,"[48] which effectively means that it is sometimes easier to obtain a trial amendment than a pretrial pleading amendment.

29-6 Trial by Consent

Trial by consent occurs when evidence directed to an unpleaded issue is presented to the judge or jury for determination, without objection by the opposing party.[49]

When unpleaded issues "are tried by the express or implied consent of the parties, they shall be treated in all respects as if they had been raised in the pleadings."[50] A determination of trial by consent is committed to the court's discretion to be made in the exceptional case, and never in a doubtful situation.[51] "The rule of trial by consent should not be applied in doubtful cases, but only when the record makes it clear that the parties understood the non-pleaded matter to be an issue in the case. There can be no trial by consent when the evidence on the non-pleaded matter is relevant to the issues pleaded, and for that reason would not be calculated to elicit an objection when offered."[52] Evidence relevant to a pleaded issue does not, standing alone, support an argument that an unpleaded issue has been tried by consent.[53]

When the court finds that trial by consent has occurred, a requested trial amendment to conform the pleadings to the evidence and support submission of the charge to the jury should be granted pursuant to Tex. R. Civ. P. 67.[54] When the court finds that

---

[44] *Dallas City Limits Prop. Co., L.P. v. Austin Jockey Club, Ltd.*, 376 S.W.3d 792, 797 (Tex. App.—Dallas 2012, pet. denied) (court may not refuse a trial amendment unless the opposing party presents evidence of surprise or prejudice, or the amendment asserts a new cause of action or defense that is prejudicial on its face).

[45] *Crosstex N. Tex. Pipeline, L.P. v. Gardiner*, 505 S.W.3d 580, 617 (Tex. 2016); *Zarate v. Rodriguez*, 542 S.W.3d 26, 37 (Tex. App.—Houston [14th Dist.] 2017, pet. denied).

[46] Tex. R. Civ. P. 66.

[47] Tex. R. Civ. P. 66.

[48] *Tanglewood Homes Ass'n, Inc. v. Feldman*, 436 S.W.3d 48, 64 (Tex. App.—Houston [14th Dist.] 2014, pet. denied).

[49] *Maswoswe v. Nelson*, 327 S.W.3d 889, 895 (Tex. App.—Beaumont 2010, no pet.).

[50] Tex. R. Civ. P. 67.

[51] *Compass Bank v. MFP Fin. Servs., Inc.*, 152 S.W.3d 844, 854 (Tex. App.—Dallas 2005, pet. denied).

[52] *City of San Antonio v. Lopez*, 754 S.W.2d 749, 751 (Tex. App.—San Antonio 1988, writ denied).

[53] *Born v. Virginia City Dance Hall and Saloon*, 857 S.W.2d 951, 956 (Tex. App.—Houston [14th Dist.] 1993, writ denied).

[54] *McFadden v. Hale*, 615 S.W.2d 345, 348 (Tex. App.—Waco 1981, no writ).

AMENDMENT OF PLEADINGS

trial by consent has not occurred, a requested trial amendment may still be directed to the court's discretion pursuant to Tex. R. Civ. P. 63 and 66.[55]

29-7 Post-Verdict Amendment of Pleadings

A post-verdict amendment to the pleadings may be granted before judgment, absent surprise or prejudice.[56] Neither Tex. R. Civ. P. 63 nor 66 make any distinction between a pre-verdict and a post-verdict amendment.[57] The standard for a post-verdict amendment remains the same as for pretrial and trial amendments: "A court may not refuse a [post-verdict] trial amendment unless (1) the opposing party presents evidence of surprise or prejudice, or (2) the amendment asserts a new cause of action or defense, and thus is prejudicial on its face."[58]

Once judgment has been rendered, a trial court can no longer grant a trial amendment.[59] But post-trial amendments have been granted in a variety of circumstances, including to conform the pleadings to the amount of the judgment,[60] to permit recovery of prejudgment interest,[61] to incorporate a matter tried by consent,[62] to add a new cause of action,[63] to plead a specific basis for punitive damages,[64] to allow the addition of a specific denial to support a defensive issue,[65] to delete a severable claim in order to bring a case within the jurisdictional limits of the trial court,[66] and to add a personal representative of the patient's estate as plaintiff for a survival claim after limitations.[67]

The general rule allowing a post-trial amendment to conform the pleadings to the damages found by the jury, based on the Texas Supreme Court's *Greenhalgh* opinion,[68] is not applicable to expedited actions governed by Discovery Level 1.[69] Since the amount of a judgment in an expedited action is capped for a plaintiff at $100,000,[70] and

---

[55] *Wendell v. Cent. Power & Light Co.*, 677 S.W.2d 610, 618 (Tex. App.—Corpus Christi 1984, writ ref'd n.r.e.).

[56] *Krishnan v. Ramirez*, 42 S.W.3d 205, 225 (Tex. App.—Corpus Christ 2001, pet. denied).

[57] *Wal-mart Stores, Inc. v. McKenzie*, 997 S.W.2d 278, 280 (Tex. 1999).

[58] *Libhart v. Copeland*, 949 S.W.2d 783, 797 (Tex. App.—Waco 1997, no writ) (citing *State Bar of Tex. v. Kilpatrick*, 874 S.W.2d 656, 658 (Tex. 1994)).

[59] *Mitchell v. La Flamme*, 60 S.W.3d 123, 132 (Tex. App.—Houston [14th Dist.] 2000, no pet.).

[60] *Greenhalgh v. Serv. Lloyds Ins. Co.*, 787 S.W.2d 938, 939 (Tex. 1990) (defendant unable to show that pretrial amendment to increase damages being sought would have altered defense strategy).

[61] *Benavides v. Isles Constr. Co.*, 726 S.W.2d 23, 26 (Tex. 1987) (post-verdict amendment causes no surprise or prejudice because recovery of prejudgment interest does not require any evidentiary proof at trial).

[62] *Libhart v. Copeland*, 949 S.W.2d 783, 797–98 (Tex. App.—Waco 1997, no writ).

[63] *State Bar of Tex. v. Kilpatrick*, 874 S.W.2d 656, 658 (Tex. 1994) (trial amendment did not impair defendant's ability to present his defense).

[64] *Whole Foods Market Sw., L.P. v. Tijerina*, 979 S.W.2d 768, 775–76 (Tex. App.—Houston [14th Dist.] 1998, pet. denied).

[65] *State Farm Lloyd's Ins. Co. v. Ashby AAA Auto. Supply Co., Inc.*, No. 05-92-01354-CV, 1995 WL 513363, at *18–19 (Tex. App.—Dallas Aug. 28, 1995, writ denied).

[66] *Failing v. Equity Mgmt. Corp.*, 674 S.W.2d 906, 908–09 (Tex. App.—Houston [1st Dist.] 1984, no writ).

[67] *Pratho v. Zapata*, 157 S.W.3d 832, 842 (Tex. App.—Fort Worth 2005, no pet.).

[68] *Greenhalgh v. Serv. Lloyds Ins. Co.*, 787 S.W.2d 938, 939 (Tex. 1990).

[69] Tex. R. Civ. P. 169(d)(1) ("Discovery is governed by Rule 190.2.").

[70] Tex. R. Civ. P. 169(b).

since plaintiffs have time limits on when they can plead out of the expedited actions process,[71] the *Greenhalgh* rule is not available to plaintiffs to allow a post-trial amendment for increasing the pleaded amount of damages in an expedited action.[72] Presumably the *Greenhalgh* rule continues to be available to counter-claimants since they are not limited by a $100,000 cap.[73]

---

[71] Tex. R. Civ. P. 169(c)(2).

[72] *See* 2013 Comment 4 to Tex. R. Civ. P. 169 ("the rule in *Greenhalgh* ... does not apply if a jury awards damages in excess of $100,000 to the party"). *But see Cross v. Wagner*, 497 S.W.3d 611, 614 (Tex. App.—El Paso 2016, no pet. h.) ("By its clear and unambiguous terms then, Rule 169 did not require the trial court to cap the jury's award at $100,000, but rather only required the trial court to cap its judgment to prevent an ultimate recovery of over $100,000. Further, there is nothing in the language of Rule 169 requiring the trial court to cap the jury's award at $100,000 before reducing that award by the proportionate responsibility of the parties.").

[73] *See* 2013 Comment 4 to Tex. R. Civ. P. 169 ("... [t]he limitation in 169(b) does not apply to a counter-claimant that seeks relief other than that allowed under 169(a)(1)").

CHAPTER 30

Making and Responding to Motions for Summary Judgment*

Upon motion, a trial court shall grant summary judgment when there is no genuine issue of material fact and the movant is entitled to judgment as a matter of law. This section discusses both the traditional and no-evidence motions for summary judgment as well as how to respond to such motions.

30-1 The Traditional Motion for Summary Judgment

This section discusses what is known as the traditional motion for summary judgment in Texas practice.

30-1:1 Timing of Motion and Response

Texas Rule of Civil Procedure 166a provides a time period within which motions for summary judgment may be made. A party seeking to recover on a claim, counterclaim, or crossclaim or to obtain a declaratory judgment may move for summary judgment at any time after the adverse party has appeared or answered.[1] A party against whom such a claim is asserted may move for summary judgment at any time.[2]

The motions and any supporting evidence must be filed at least 21 days before the hearing.[3] The response, including any supporting evidence, is due at least seven days before the hearing.[4] The rule provides that the nonmovant may file a late response with leave of court.[5] Alternatively, a nonmovant may seek a continuance of the hearing date and file the response at least seven days before the new hearing date.[6] While Rule 166a does not specify a time for the movant to file a reply to the response or object to the nonmovant's summary judgment evidence, both local rule practice and Tex. R. Civ. P. 21a suggest that the reply must be filed at least 3 days before the hearing.

---

* The authors thank Max Moran for his assistance in the updating of this chapter.
[1] Tex. R. Civ. P. 166a(a).
[2] Tex. R. Civ. P. 166a(b).
[3] Tex. R. Civ. P. 166a(c).
[4] Tex. R. Civ. P. 166a(c).
[5] Tex. R. Civ. P. 166a(c).
[6] *Wil-Roye Inv. Co. II v. Washington Mut. Bank, FA*, 142 S.W.3d 393, 400 (Tex. App.—El Paso 2004, no pet.); *Thomas v. Med. Arts Hosp. of Texarkana, Inc.*, 920 S.W.2d 815, 818 (Tex. App.—Texarkana 1996, writ denied) (where trial court reset hearing, nonmovant could file a timely response even though time to file a timely response based on original setting had passed before the trial court reset the hearing).

If the hearing is continued, notice of the next setting may be made based on reasonable notice rather than another 21 days, assuming the nonmovant had at least 21 days' notice of the initial setting.[7] Reasonable notice generally means at least 7 days before the hearing, but less than 7 days may be sufficient.[8] The Court has discretion to shorten the time limits.[9]

30-1:2 Burden of Persuasion

The summary judgment movant has the burden of persuasion at summary judgment.[10] His burden is to persuade the court that there is no genuine issue of material fact and that the movant is entitled to judgment as a matter of law.[11] The movant may establish either that there is no genuine issue of material fact as to an essential element of a claim on which the movant does not have the burden of proof or may conclusively establish each element of a claim on which he does have the burden of proof.

30-1:3 Movant's Burden of Pleading

Per Rule 166a(c), the motion for summary judgment must state the specific grounds for summary judgment. This requirement is a pleading burden at the summary judgment stage, and must be specific enough to put the nonmovant on notice of the grounds for the motion.[12]

The grounds must be stated in the motion.[13] Where the motion states no grounds, the motion is legally insufficient as a matter of law and must be denied.[14] Even if the supporting brief states the grounds for summary judgment, if the motion does not state the grounds, the motion must be denied.[15]

---

[7] *Skelton v. Commission for Lawyer Discipline*, 56 S.W.3e 687, 691 (Tex. App.—Houston [14th Dist.] 2001, no pet.).

[8] *Brown v. Capital Bank*, 703 S.W.2d 231, 233–34 (Tex. App.—Houston [14th Dist.] 1985, writ ref'd n.r.e.).

[9] Tex. R. Civ. P. 166a(c).

[10] *Smith v. City of Sweeney*, No. 13-05-233-CV, 2006 WL 2371344, at *1 (Tex. App.—Corpus Christi-Edinburg Aug. 17, 2006, pet. denied) ("In a traditional summary judgment motion, the burden of proof falls to the movant to establish as a matter of law that there is no genuine issue of material fact as to one or more of the essential elements of the non-movant's cause of action."); *Chhim v. Univ. of Hous.*, 76 S.W.3d 210, 221 (Tex. App.—Texarkana 2002, pet. denied) ("In deciding a motion for summary judgment, the burden of persuasion remains always on the movant to demonstrate entitlement to judgment as a matter of law."); *Lawler v. Collin Cty.*, No. 05-95-00487-CV, 1996 WL 403986, at *2 (Tex. App.—Dallas 1996, writ denied) ("The movant has the burden of proof to show that no genuine issues of material fact exist and that it is entitled to summary judgment as a matter of law."); Tex. R. Civ. P. 166a(c).

[11] *Smith v. City of Sweeny*, No. 13-05-233-CV, 2006 WL 2371344, at *1 (Tex. App.—Corpus Christi-Edinburg Aug. 17, 2006).

[12] *Timpte Industries, Inc. v Gish*, 286 S.W.3d 306 (Tex. 2009); *Jose Fuentes Co., Inc. v Alfaro*, 418 S.W.3d 280 (Tex. App.—Dallas 2013, pet. denied).

[13] Tex. R. Civ. P. 166a(c) ("The motion for summary judgment shall state the specific grounds therefor."). See *Stiles v. Resolution Trust Corp.*, 867 S.W.3d 24 (Tex. 1993).

[14] See *McConnell v. Southside ISD*, 858 S.W.2d 337, 339–40 (Tex. 1993) (citing *Moody v. Temple Nat'l Bank*, 545 S.W.2d 289, 290 (Tex. App.—Austin 1977, no writ)).

[15] See *McConnell v. Southside ISD*, 858 S.W.2d 337, 339–40 (Tex. 1993).

MAKING AND RESPONDING TO MOTIONS FOR SUMMARY JUDGMENT

A motion that fails to state the grounds for summary judgment is insufficient as a matter of law and must be denied, even if the nonmovant does not object or except to this defect in the motion at the trial court.[16]

To complain on appeal, however, that the grounds in the motion are ambiguous or unclear, the nonmovant must except or object to the motion.[17] The practical effect of a failure to object to grounds in the motion that are unclear or ambiguous "is that the non-movant loses his right to have the grounds for summary judgment narrowly focused, thereby running the risk of having an appellate court determine the grounds it believes were expressly presented in the summary judgment."[18]

A movant may seek summary judgment both on traditional and no evidence grounds in the same motion,[19] but the movant must specify which grounds in the motion are traditional and which are no evidence. Otherwise, the motion fails to give fair notice of the grounds for summary judgment[20]. In this type of hybrid motion, the Court will typically consider the no evidence portion of the motion first.[21]

30-1:4 Movant's Burden of Production

The movant bears the initial burden of production at summary judgment, but what this burden requires depends upon whether the movant would bear at trial the burden of proof on the claim or defense that is the subject of the motion.

If the movant bears the burden of proof at trial on the claim or defense, the movant must support his motion with evidence conclusively establishing every element of the claim or the affirmative defense.[22] A rebuttable presumption may affect the burden of production at trial, but it does not affect the burden of production at summary judgment. As the Texas Supreme Court recently explained, "a presumption operates to establish a fact until rebutted . . . but not in summary judgment proceedings."[23] Thus, the movant must establish the fact with evidence in summary judgment proceedings, even though the movant may rely on the presumption to establish the fact (at least initially) at trial.

If the movant does not bear the burden of proof at trial on the claim or defense, he may satisfy his burden of production with evidence that affirmatively negates at least

---

[16] *See McConnell v. Southside ISD*, 858 S.W.2d 337, 342 (Tex. 1993).
[17] *See McConnell v. Southside ISD*, 858 S.W.2d 337, 342 (Tex. 1993) (citing *Lochabay v. Sw. Bell Media, Inc.*, 828 S.W.2d 167, 170 n.2 (Tex. App.—Austin 1992, no writ).
[18] *See McConnell v. Southside ISD*, 858 S.W.2d 337, 342 (Tex. 1993).
[19] *Neely v. Wilson*, 418 S.W.3d 52, 59 (Tex. 2013).
[20] *Waite v. Woodard, Hall & Primm, P.C.*, 137 S.W.3d 277, 281 (Tex. App.—Houston [1st Dist.] 2004, no pet.).
[21] *Community Health Sys. Prof'l Servs. v. Hansen*, 525 S.W.3d 671, 680 (Tex. 2017).
[22] *Amedisys, Inc. v. Kingwood Home Health Care, LLC*, 437 S.W.3d 507, 510 (Tex. 2014) ("When a movant meets that burden of establishing each element of the claim or defense on which it seeks summary judgment, the burden then shifts to the non-movant to disprove or raise an issue of fact as to at least one of those elements."); *City of Hous. v. Clear Creek Basin Auth.*, 589 S.W.2d 671, 678 (Tex. 1979) ("The movant still must establish his entitlement to a summary judgment on the issues expressly presented to the trial court by conclusively proving all essential elements of his cause of action or defense as a matter of law.").
[23] *Chavez v. Kan. City S.*, 520 S.W.3d 898, 899 (Tex. 2017).

one essential element of the claim or defense.[24] Alternatively, where the movant does not bear the burden of proof at trial, he may use a no-evidence motion for summary judgment under Rule 166a(i), discussed in Section 2 of this chapter.[25]

30-1:5 Effect of a Legally Insufficient Motion

Where the movant fails to carry either his burden of pleading or his burden of production, the motion is insufficient as a matter of law.[26] The nonmovant is not required to object to the legal insufficiency of the motion in order to raise the point on appeal and urge reversal on this basis.[27] In fact, a legally insufficient motion should be denied in the trial court, even if the nonmovant does not respond.[28]

30-1:6 Nonmovant's Burden of Pleading

The nonmovant must "expressly present to the trial court, by written answer or response, any issues defeating the movant's entitlement" to summary judgment.[29] The one exception to this rule is that a nonmovant need not object to the legal sufficiency of the movant's motion in order to argue reversal on this ground on appeal.[30] Special exceptions should be filed at least 7 days before the hearing as they constitute part of the nonmovant's response. The nonmovant may wish to file the special exceptions earlier and seek a hearing on the exception so that the issue is resolved before the time the nonmovant must respond. Special exceptions may be heard with only 3 days' notice of the hearing, affording a window for earlier resolution.[31]

If the movant believes the grounds presented in the response to avoid summary judgment are ambiguous or unclear, he must object and get a ruling in the trial court in order to complain about the issue on appeal.[32]

30-1:7 Nonmovant's Burden of Production

Assuming the movant makes a legally sufficient motion for summary judgment, the nonmovant must raise a genuine issue of material fact with his response and sup-

---

[24] *Science Spectrum, Inc. v. Martinez*, 941 S.W.2d 910, 911 (Tex. 1997).
[25] Tex. R. Civ. P. 166a(i).
[26] *Amedisys, Inc. v. Kingwood Home Health Care, LLC*, 437 S.W.3d 507, 510 (Tex. 2014) (citing *McConnell v. Southside ISD*, 858 S.W.2d 337, 343 (Tex. 1993)).
[27] *McConnell v. Southside ISD*, 858 S.W.2d 337, 343 (Tex. 1993).
[28] *McConnell v. Southside ISD*, 858 S.W.2d 337, 342 (Tex. 1993); *Amedisys Inc. v. Kingwood Home Health Care, LLC*, 437 S.W.3d 507, 511 (Tex. 2014) (If the movant does not satisfy its initial burden, the burden does not shift and the non-movant need not respond or present any evidence. This is because "summary judgments must stand or fall on their own merits, and the non-movant's failure to answer or respond cannot supply by default the summary judgment proof necessary to establish the movant's right" to judgment.) (internal citations omitted).
[29] *McConnell v. Southside ISD*, 858 S.W.2d 337, 343 (Tex. 1993).
[30] *McConnell v. Southside ISD*, 858 S.W.2d 337, 343 (Tex. 1993).
[31] Tex. R Civ. P. 21(b).
[32] *See McConnell v. Southside ISD*, 858 S.W.2d 337, 342–43 (Tex. 1993). ("Any confusion regarding what issues are expressly presented by the non-movant can also be resolved by exception.").

MAKING AND RESPONDING TO MOTIONS FOR SUMMARY JUDGMENT

porting evidence.[33] The nonmovant need only raise a genuine issue of material fact. He need not marshal all his proof or produce that quantum of evidence that would carry his burden of persuasion at trial.[34] Evidence favorable to the nonmovant must be accepted as true and every reasonable inference indulged in the nonmovant's favor.[35]

If the nonmovant bears the burden of persuasion at trial on the claim or defense, then he must support his response with evidence that raises a genuine issue of material fact as to each and every element that the movant conclusively established in support of his motion.[36] Alternatively, the nonmovant can avoid judgment by raising a genuine issue of material fact as to an affirmative defense (including a defense to a defense) that confesses and avoids the effect of the claim or defense that was the subject of the motion.[37]

If the nonmovant does not bear the burden of persuasion at trial on the claim or defense, then he must support his response with evidence that raises a genuine issue of material fact as to at least one of the essential elements of the claim or defense.[38]

30-2 The No-Evidence Motion for Summary Judgment

This section discusses Rule 166a(i)'s no-evidence motion for summary judgment as well as responses thereto.

30-2:1 Timing of Motion and Response

Unlike a traditional motion for summary judgment, a no-evidence motion may be made only "after adequate time for discovery." The rule does not define what constitutes adequate time for discovery, although the comments and subsequent case law provide guidance. Where a pretrial order prescribes the length of the discovery period or sets a date before which a no-evidence motion may not be filed, the pretrial order will ordinarily control the appropriate timing of the motion.[39] While filing a no-evidence motion before the end of the discovery period in the pretrial order generally would not be permitted,[40] the Court can consider other deadlines such as whether expert discovery has been concluded, whether all requested discovery has taken place, and whether the parties sought a shorter discovery period than that which was ordered by the Court. Under such circumstances, a no-evidence motion made before

---

[33] *Amedisys Inc. v. Kingwood Home Health Care*, 437 S.W.3d 507, 517 (Tex. 2014) (citing *Centeq Realty, Inc. v. Siegler*, 899 S.W.2d 195, 197 (Tex. 1995) ("Once the defendant produces sufficient evidence to establish the right to summary judgment, the plaintiff must present evidence sufficient to raise a fact issue.")).

[34] *Centeq Realty v. Siegler*, 899 S.W.2d 195, 197 (Tex. 1995); *Niemann v. Refugio Cty. Mem'l Hosp.*, 855 S.W.2d 94, 97 (Tex. App.—Corpus Christi-Edinburg 1993, no writ).

[35] *Nixon v. Mr. Prop. Mgmt. Co.*, 690 S.W.2d 546, 549 (Tex. 1985).

[36] *Centeq Realty v. Siegler*, 899 S.W.2d 195, 197 (Tex. 1995).

[37] *Ryland Grp., Inc. v. Hood*, 924 S.W.2d 120, 121 (Tex. 1996) (fraudulent concealment was defense to the defense of repose).

[38] *Centeq Realty v. Siegler*, 899 S.W.2d 195, 197 (Tex. 1995).

[39] Comment to 1997 amendment to Tex. R. Civ. P. 166a(i).

[40] Comment to 1997 amendment to Tex. R. Civ. P. 166a(i) ("A discovery period set by pretrial order should be adequate opportunity for discovery unless there is a showing to the contrary, and ordinarily a motion under paragraph (i) would be permitted after the period but not before.").

the completion of discovery may be appropriate, including situations where discovery has dragged on for an extended period of time[41] or when additional discovery would not affect the outcome.[42]

To complain that there has been an inadequate time for discovery, the nonmovant must notify the Court of its complaint either by filing a verified motion for continuance or an affidavit explaining the need for further discovery.[43] Failing to do so waives any complaint that the no-evidence motion is premature or that additional discovery is needed.[44] The Motion and/or affidavit should identify what discovery is needed and why, including any previous efforts to have obtained the needed discovery.

30-2:2 Availability of No-Evidence Motion

A party may make a no-evidence motion for summary judgment only as to a claim or defense on which the nonmovant will bear the burden of proof at trial.[45] The defendant may make a no-evidence motion for summary judgment attacking the plaintiff's negligence claim, for example. The party with the burden of proof at trial may not file a no evidence motion for summary judgment as this would effectively shift the burden of proof on the party's own claim or affirmative defense.[46]

30-2:3 Movant's Burden of Pleading

The no-evidence motion has been called a "pre-trial motion for directed verdict," as it simply points out that the nonmovant has no evidence of one or more essential elements of his claim or defense.[47] The nonmovant must state in the motion the element or elements as to which there is no evidence.[48] The motion need not be so specific as to attack the evidentiary components that may prove an element.[49] While the movant may attach evidence to his motion, he may simply notify the Court in the motion that there is no evidence of a specific element, at which point the burden shifts to the nonmovant to bring forth more than a mere scintilla of evidence on that element. If

---

[41] *In re Mohawk Rubber Co.*, 982 S.W.2d 494, 498 (Tex. App.—Texarkana 1998, no pet.) (no-evidence motion was made "after adequate time for discovery" where discovery was ongoing but case had been pending for 10 years).

[42] *Carter v. McFadyen*, 93 S.W.3d 307, 311 (Tex. App.—Houston [14th Dist.] 2002, pet. denied) ("Obviously, additional discovery is a waste of time and expense if it will make no difference.").

[43] *Tenneco Inc. v. Enterprise Prods.*, 925 S.W.2d 640, 647 (Tex. 1996); *Brown v. Brown*, 145 S.W.3d 745, 749 (Tex. App.—Dalas, 2004, pet. denied).

[44] *Blanche v. First Nationwide Mortg. Corp.*, 74 S.W.3d 444, 450–51 (Tex. App.—Dallas 2002, no pet.) (citing *Tenneco Inc. v. Enter. Prods. Co.*, 925 S.W.2d 640, 647 (Tex. 1996); *McClure v. Attebury*, 20 S.W.3d 722, 729 (Tex. App.—Amarillo 1999, no pet.)).

[45] Tex. R. Civ. P. 166a(i).

[46] *See, e.g., Nowak v. DAS Inv. Corp.*, 110 S.W.3d 677, 680 (Tex. App.—Houston [14th Dist.] 2003, no pet.) (defendant made no-evidence motion for summary judgment on limitations defense).

[47] *Timpte Indus., Inc. v. Gish*, 286 S.W. 3d 306, 310–11 (Tex. 2009).

[48] *Timpte Indus., Inc. v. Gish*, 286 S.W. 3d 306, 310–11 (Tex. 2009); *Rust v. Tex. Farmers Ins.*, 341 S.W.3d 541, 551 (Tex. App.—El Paso 2011, no pet.); *In re Mohawk Rubber Co.*, 982 S.W.2d 494, 497 (Tex. App.—Texarkana 1998, no pet.).

[49] *Rogers v. Zanetti*, 517 S.W.3d 123, 129 (Tex. App.—Dallas 2015), aff'd, 518 S.W.3d 394 (Tex. 2017).

MAKING AND RESPONDING TO MOTIONS FOR SUMMARY JUDGMENT 609

the nonmovant fails to respond to a legally appropriate no evidence motion, the Court must grant judgment—effectively a post-answer default judgment.[50]

30-2:4 Nonmovant's Burden of Production

The nonmovant must support his response with evidence raising a genuine issue of material fact as to each and every element attacked in the no-evidence motion.[51] The nonmovant need not produce evidence that conclusively establishes the existence of the element. Instead, he need only produce evidence raising a genuine issue of material fact, i.e., evidence from which a reasonable juror could conclude that the element was factually so. Put another way, the nonmovant need only produce "more than a scintilla" of probative evidence in order to avoid summary judgment.[52] The court must view the evidence in the light most favorable to the nonmovant.[53] More than a scintilla of evidence exists if the evidence would allow reasonable people to differ as to their conclusions.[54]

30-3 Summary Judgment Evidence

Summary judgment evidence, whether adduced by the movant or the non-movant, must set forth facts that would be admissible at trial. This section discusses this requirement for the various types of summary judgment evidence and objections to summary judgment evidence.

30-3:1 Prohibition on Oral Testimony

Summary judgment evidence must be written and filed with the Court unless submitted pursuant to Tex. R. Civ. P. 166a(d). No oral testimony will be allowed at the hearing.[55]

30-3:2 Deadlines for Filing Summary Judgment Evidence

The movant's summary judgment evidence must be filed at least 21 days before the date of the hearing, and the nonmovant's proof must be filed at least seven days before the hearing if opposing the motion.[56] The Court may consider (and either party may rely on) any evidence on file as summary judgment proof.[57]

---

[50] *Humphrey v. Pelican Isle Owners Ass'n*, 238 S.W. 3d 811 (Tex. App.—Waco 2007, no pet.); *Cuyler v. Minns*, 60 S.W.3d 209 (Tex. App.—Houston [14th Dist.] 2001, pet. denied).

[51] *See, e.g., Nelson v. Regions Mortg., Inc.*, 170 S.W.3d 858, 862 (Tex. App.—Dallas 2005, no pet.) (no-evidence motion not improper even though it was "global" and attacked every element of the plaintiff's cause of action).

[52] *Forbes Inc. v. Granada Biosciences, Inc.*, 124 S.W.3d 167, 172 (Tex. 2003) (citing *King Ranch v. Chapman*, 118 S.W.3d 742, 750 (Tex. 2003); *Wal-Mart Stores, Inc. v. Rodriguez*, 92 S.W.3d 502, 506 (Tex. 2002)).

[53] *Wal-Mart Stores, Inc. v. Rodriguez*, 92 S.W.3d 502, 506 (Tex. 2002).

[54] *Wal-Mart Stores, Inc. v. Rodriguez*, 92 S.W.3d 502, 506 (Tex. 2002).

[55] Tex. R. Civ. P. 166a(c) ("No oral testimony shall be received at the hearing."); *Martin v. Martin, Martin, & Richards, Inc.*, 989 S.W.2d 357, 359 (Tex. 1998).

[56] Tex. R. Civ. P. 166a(c).

[57] *See Schlumberger Tech. v. Pasko*, 544 S.W.3d 830, 835 (Tex. 2018).

30-3:3 Affidavits: Personal Knowledge Requirement

Affidavits, whether supporting or opposing summary judgment, must be based on personal knowledge (unless the affiant is an expert) and must set forth facts that would be admissible in evidence.[58] The affidavit must also show affirmatively that the affiant is competent to testify.[59]

Texas now allows the use of unsworn declarations in lieu of affidavits,[60] but otherwise the requirements applicable to affidavits apply equally to unsworn declarations.

An affidavit must be based on personal knowledge, not speculation or belief about the facts.[61] Affidavits based on the "best of the person's knowledge"[62] or based on knowledge gained after "inquiry" have been held to be insufficient.[63] An affidavit showing no basis for personal knowledge is also insufficient summary judgment proof.[64] The affiant should state the facts showing that the affiant was in a position to have personal knowledge (i.e., the affidavit must credit the witness with personal knowledge using facts).[65] The statements in the affidavit "need factual specificity such as place, time, and exact nature of the alleged facts."[66] Conclusory statements, without factual support, provide no evidence.[67]

30-3:4 Affidavits: Requirement to Set Forth Facts Admissible at Trial

An affidavit must set forth facts that would be admissible at trial.[68] Thus, if what is stated in the affidavit would be objectionable coming from the witness stand, it is objectionable at the summary judgment stage.[69] Statements that are speculative, that address subsequent remedial measures, or which are not the best evidence, are objectionable.

---

[58] Tex. R. Civ. P. 166a(f).
[59] Tex. R. Civ. P. 166a(f).
[60] Tex. Civ. Prac. & Rem. Code Ann. § 132.001.
[61] *Ryland Grp., Inc. v. Hood*, 924 S.W.2d 120, 122 (Tex. 1996); *Brownlee v. Brownlee*, 665 S.W.2d 111, 112 (Tex. 1984).
[62] *Geiselman v. Cramer Fin. Grp., Inc.*, 965 S.W.2d 532, 537 (Tex. App.—Houston [14th Dist.] 1997, no writ).
[63] *Humphreys v. Caldwell*, 888 S.W.2d 469, 471 (Tex. 1994).
[64] *Kerlin v. Arias*, 274 S.W.3d 666, 668 (Tex. 2008).
[65] *Kerlin v. Arias*, 274 S.W.3d 666, 668 (Tex. 2008); *Valenzuela v. State & Cty. Mut. Fire Ins. Co.*, 317 S.W.3d 550, 553 (Tex. App.—Houston [14th Dist.] 2010, no pet.) ("The affidavit must explain how the affiant has personal knowledge.") (citing *Radio Station KSCS v. Jennings*, 750 S.W.2d 760, 762 (Tex. 1988) (per curiam); *SouthTex 66 Pipeline Co., Ltd. v. Spoor*, 238 S.W.3d 538, 543 (Tex. App.—Houston [14th Dist.] 2007, pet. denied).
[66] *Valenzuela v. State & Cty. Mut. Fire Ins. Co.*, 317 S.W.3d 550, 553 (Tex. App.—Houston [14th Dist.] 2010, no pet.).
[67] *Brownlee v. Brownlee*, 665 S.W.2d 111,112 (Tex. 1984); *Elizondo v. Krist*, 415 S.W.3d 259, 264 (Tex. 2013).
[68] Tex. R. Civ. P. 166a(c).
[69] *United Blood Serv. v. Longoria*, 938 S.W.2d 29, 30 (Tex. 1997) ("[N]o difference obtains between the standards for evidence that would be admissible in a summary judgment proceeding and those applicable at a regular trial.") (citing *Hidalgo v. Surety Savings & Loan Ass'n*, 462 S.W.2d 540, 545 (Tex. 1971)).

Affidavits of an expert that do not establish the qualifications of the expert[70] or that contain unsupported conclusions without an explanation of the basis of the opinion or the methodology used to reach the opinion are objectionable.[71] Similarly, affidavits that contain hearsay without establishing an applicable exception are objectionable.[72]

30-3:5 Affidavits: Interested Witnesses

Rule 166a(c) provides that summary judgment may be based on the uncontroverted testimonial evidence of an interested witness so long as the evidence is "clear, positive and direct, otherwise credible and free from contradictions and inconsistencies, and could have been readily controverted."[73] The same rule applies to the affidavit of an expert witness as to "subject matter concerning which the trier of fact must be guided solely by the opinion testimony of experts."[74]

Affidavits of an interested witness (or their employees) or expert may raise a genuine issue of material fact, even if controverted, when used in support of a response to a motion for summary judgment. Rule 166a(c) governs the situation in which the affidavit is used to support the motion for summary judgment.

Interested witness affidavits can provide a basis for summary judgment as long as they meet the requisites of Rule 166a(c) that the contents of the affidavit could have been readily controverted.[75] "Could have been readily controverted" does not mean that the "evidence could have been easily and conveniently rebutted, but rather indicates that the testimony could have been effectively countered by opposing evidence."[76]

The party claiming that the affidavit cannot be readily controverted should object on this ground or the error is waived.[77] Similarly, if additional discovery would be needed to controvert the affidavit, the party so claiming must notify the Court either through a request for continuance or affidavit.

30-3:6 Affidavits: Exhibits to Affidavits

Rule 166a(f) requires that sworn or certified copies of all papers referred to in the affidavit shall be attached thereto or served along with the affidavit. The affidavit should state that attached documents are true and correct copies in order to authenticate them.[78] The affidavit should also establish that the documents are admissible under the hearsay rule by establishing an exception or showing that they are not hearsay.[79]

---

[70] *Surety Savings & Loan Ass'n*, 462 S.W.2d 540, 545 (Tex. 1971).
[71] *Burrow v. Arce*, 997 S.W.2d 229 (Tex. 1999); *Wadewitz v. Montgomery*, 951 S.W.2d 464, 466–67 (Tex. 1997) (expert's unsupported conclusions regarding qualified immunity defense).
[72] *Kerlin v. Arias*, 274 S.W.3d 666, 667–68 (Tex. 2008).
[73] Tex. R. Civ. P. 166a(c).
[74] Tex. R. Civ. P. 166a(c).
[75] *See, e.g., Mathis v. Bocell*, 982 S.W.2d 52, 58 (Tex. App.—Houston [1st Dist.] 1998, no pet.).
[76] *Trico Techs. Corp. v. Montiel*, 949 S.W.2d 308, 310 (Tex. 1997) (citing *Casso v. Brand*, 776 S.W.2d 551, 558 (Tex. 1989)).
[77] *Blancett v. Lagniappe Ventures, Inc.*, 177 S.W.3d 584, 589 (Tex. App.—Houston [1st Dist.] 2005, no pet.).
[78] *Republic Nat'l Leasing Corp. v. Schindler*, 717 S.W.2d 606, 607 (Tex. 1986).
[79] *Kerlin v. Arias*, 274 S.W.3d 666, 667–68 (Tex. 2008).

Documents attached to an expert's affidavit need not be admissible under the hearsay rule so long as they are "information of a type reasonably relied upon by experts in the field."[80]

30-3:7 Sham and Bad Faith Affidavits

Affidavits made in bad faith solely for purposes of delay may result in sanctions including attorney's fees and costs against the party or attorney utilizing the affidavit.[81]

A sham affidavit cannot defeat or support summary judgment. A sham affidavit is one which is executed after witness position, and contradicts the earlier testimony on a material point without a reasonable explanation for the change.[82] A sham affidavit is executed to create a fact issue and avoid summary judgment.[83]

30-3:8 Use of Discovery

Summary judgment may be based on depositions, transcripts, interrogatory answers and other discovery responses referenced or set forth in the motion or response.[84] If the summary judgment evidence is not on file with the clerk, copies of the material or a notice containing specific references to the discovery or specific references to other instruments must be filed and served on all parties.[85]

The notice must contain "specific references" to the discovery.[86] The notice must contain a statement of intent to use the discovery specified in the notice as summary judgment proof.[87] The notice must be filed at least 21 days before the hearing if used to support the motion and at least seven days before the hearing if used to oppose the motion.[88] A party may not rely its own discovery responses as summary judgment evidence.

Deposition excerpts need not be authenticated to constitute proper summary judgment evidence.[89] "Specific references" to deposition transcripts requires the party to

---

[80] Tex. R. Evid. 703 ("The facts or data in the particular case upon which an expert bases an opinion or inference may be those perceived by, reviewed by, or made known to the expert at or before the hearing. If of a type reasonably relied upon by experts in the particular field in forming opinions or inferences upon the subject, the facts or data need not be admissible in evidence.").

[81] Tex. R. Civ. P. 166a(h).

[82] *Lujan v. Navistar, Inc.*, 555 S.W.3d 79, 86 (Tex. 2018).

[83] *Farroux v. Denny's Rests., Inc.*, 962 S.W.2d 108, 111 (Tex. App.—Houston [1st Dist. 1997, no pet.).

[84] Tex. R. Civ. P. 166a(c).

[85] Tex. R. Civ. P. 166a(d).

[86] Tex. R. Civ. P. 166a(d).

[87] Tex. R. Civ. P. 166a(d).

[88] Tex. R. Civ. P. 166a(d).

[89] *McConathy v. McConathy*, 869 S.W.2d 341, 341 (Tex. 1994) (per curiam) ("We conclude that deposition excerpts submitted as summary judgment evidence need not be authenticated.").

show the court the testimony relied on in the deposition; mere reference to names and page and line numbers may not be sufficiently specific.[90]

30-3:9 Pleadings as Summary Judgment Evidence

The court may consider the pleadings on file at the time of the summary judgment hearing.[91] There are limits to the uses for pleadings as summary judgment evidence. A party may not use his own pleadings as evidence to support or oppose a motion for summary judgment.[92] A pleading may be used against the pleader, however, if the document constitutes an admission against interest or a judicial admission.[93] The Court may also take judicial notice of operative facts such as the date the pleading was filed for proof as to whether a matter was filed within the applicable statute of limitations.[94]

30-3:10 Objecting to Summary Judgment Evidence

In general, objections to summary judgment evidence must be made before the trial court rules on the motion or the objections are waived.[95] If an objection is sustained in the trial court, a party may be given an opportunity to cure the defect in an affidavit.[96] If the Court sustains an objection to formal defects in the affidavit, the ruling will provide a basis for reversal of the judgment only if the proponent of the evidence was given an opportunity to amend but refused to do so.[97]

Even without objection, a party may complain of a defect of substantive in summary judgment evidence, as opposed to a defect of form.[98] Substantive defects have been defined as those that either have no probative value or do not relate to a controlling fact.[99] This would include objections that the evidence was conclusory and therefore constituted no evidence.

---

[90] *E.B. Smith Co. v. U.S. Fidelity and Guar. Co.*, 850 S.W.2d 621, 624 (Tex. App.—Corpus Christi-Edinburg 1993, writ denied).

[91] Tex. R. Civ. P. 166a(c).

[92] "Pleadings do not constitute summary judgment evidence." *MGA Ins. Co. v. Charles R. Chesnutt, P.C.*, 358 S.W.3d 808, 815 (Tex. App.—Dallas 2012, no pet.); *Americana Motel, Inc. v. Johnson*, 610 S.W.2d 143, 143 (Tex. 1980); *Welch v. Milton*, 185 S.W.3d 586, 594 (Tex. App.—Dallas 2006, pet. denied) (holding that pleadings are not summary judgment proof).

[93] *Mackie v. Guthrie*, 78 S.W.3d 462, 468 (Tex. App.—Tyler 2001, pet. denied).

[94] *Jones v. Jones*, 888 S.W.2d 849, 852–53 (Tex. App.—Houston [1st Dist.] 1994, no writ).

[95] Tex. R. Civ. P. 166a(f) ("Defects in the forum of affidavits or attachments will not be grounds for reversal unless specifically pointed out by objection by an opposing party with opportunity, but refusal, to amend."); *McConnell v. Southside ISD*, 858 S.W.2d 337, 343 (Tex. 1993).

[96] *McConnell v. Southside ISD*, 858 S.W.2d 337, 343 (Tex. 1993). (Defects are not reversible error without objection and "opportunity, but refusal, to amend."); *Wyatt v. McGregor*, 855 S.W.2d 5, 18 (Tex. App—Corpus Christi-Edinburg 1993, writ denied).

[97] Tex. R. Civ. P. 166a(f).

[98] *Mathis v. Bocell*, 982 S.W.2d 52, 60 (Tex. App.—Houston [1st Dist.] 1998, no pet.) ("Formal defects may be waived by failure to object, and if waived, the evidence is considered. Substantive defects are never waived because the evidence is incompetent and cannot be considered under any circumstances.").

[99] *Mathis v. Bocell*, 982 S.W.2d 52, 60 (Tex. App.—Houston [1st Dist.] 1998, no pet.) (citing Address by Justice Sarah B. Duncan at 26 ("If evidence is incompetent, it necessarily has no probative value because it either does not relate to a controlling fact, or, if material, does not tend to make the existence of that fact more or less probable; therefore, there is no need to

The case law is not consistent regarding the definitions of and distinctions between form and substance defects.[100] The best practice, therefore, is to object to every defect, whether it appears to be one of form or substance.

30-4 The Ruling

30-4:1 Written

The Court's ruling should be in writing, state whether it is intended to be final or partial.

30-4:2 Final Judgment

If the Court grants summary judgment, disposing of all claims and parties, the order granting summary judgment is final order and appealable.[101]

If the Court grants relief which disposes of less than all claims and all parties, the case continues to trial on the remaining issues or the party can nonsuit the remaining claims or parties, converting the interlocutory judgment to a final judgment.

---

object to the erroneous introduction of incompetent evidence either to preserve the error in its admission or to ensure it is not treated as 'some evidence.'")).

[100] *Compare Laidlaw Waste Sys. v. City of Wilmer*, 904 S.W.2d 656, 661 (Tex. 1995) (conclusory statements disregarded even without objection) and *Geiselman v. Cramer Fin. Grp., Inc.*, 956 S.W.2d 532, 539–40 (Tex. App.—Houston [14th Dist.] 1997, no writ) (waived complaint about conclusory statements in affidavit by failing to object).

[101] *Lehmann v. Har-Con Corp.*, 39 S.W.3d 191, 192–93 (Tex. 2001).

Table of Cases

3 Kids, Inc. v. Am. Jewel, LLC,
   3:18-MC-096-S (BH), 2019 WL 462781, at *2 (N.D. Tex. Jan. 15, 2019)   8-7:2

1464-Eight, Ltd. v. Joppich,
   154 S.W.3d 101, 103 (Tex. 2004)   14-11

1717 Bissonnet, LLC v. Loughhead,
   500 S.W.3d 488 (Tex. App.—Houston [14th Dist.] 2016)   8-2:1.1

4415 W Lovers Lane, LLC v. Stanton,
   05-17-01363-CV, 2018 WL 3387384, at *3
   (Tex. App.—Dallas July 12, 2018, no pet.)   8-1:2

8305 Broadway Inc. v. J&J Martindale Ventures, LLC,
   No. 04-16-00447-CV, 2017 Tex. App. LEXIS 5926,
   at *6–7 (App.—San Antonio June 28, 2017)   3-1:3.1a

17090 Parkway, Ltd. v. McDavid,
   80 S.W.3d 252, 256 (Tex. App.—Dallas 2002, pet. denied)   3-1:2

A to Z Rental Ctr. v. Burris,
   714 S.W.2d 433, 435 (Tex. App.—Austin 1986, writ ref'd. n.r.e.)   3-12:2.1

A.G. Servs., Inc. v. Peat, Marwick, Mitchell & Co.,
   757 S.W.2d 503 (Tex. App.—Houston [1st Dist.] 1988, writ denied)   9-16:2

A.H. Belo Corp. v. Sanders,
   632 S.W.2d 145 (Tex. 1982)   7-10:2, 7-10:3.1

Abalos v. Oil Dev. Co. of Tex.,
   544 S.W.2d 627 (Tex. 1976)   7-11:4.3

Abbott Labs. v. Gravis,
   470 S.W.2d 639 (Tex. 1971)   16-7:3

Abell v. Potomac Ins. Co.,
   858 F.2d 1104 (5th Cir. 1988), *cert. granted, judgment
   vacated sub nom. Fryar v. Abell*, 492 U.S. 914 (1989)   2-4:3.1, 2-4:3.2

Abilene Indep. Tel. & Tel. Co. v. Williams,
   111 Tex. 102, 105, 229 S.W. 847 (Tex. 1921)   17-12:1, 23-2

Abraham v. Alpha Chi Omega,
   708 F.3d 614 (5th Cir. 2013)   1-13:4.5

ACS Investors v. McLaughlin,
   943 S.W.2d 426, 430 (Tex. 1997)   1-1:1.1

Adams v. Gottwald,
   179 S.W.3d 101, 103 (Tex. App.—San Antonio 2005, no pet.)   17-11:3

Adams v. Petrade Intern., Inc.,
   754 S.W.2d 696 (Tex. App.—Houston [1st Dist.] 1988, writ denied)   3-5:2.1, 9-5:1

Aduddell v. Parkhill,
   821 S.W.2d 158, 159 (Tex. 1991)   17-11:2

Affordable Power, L.P. v. Buckeye Ventures, Inc.,
   347 S.W.3d 825, 830 (Tex. App.—Dallas 2011, no pet.)   1-7:1

Aiken v. Hancock,
   115 S.W.3d 26 (Tex. App.—San Antonio 2003, pet. denied)   4-1:1

Aikens v. State of Wis.,
   195 U.S. 194 (1904)   9-16:1

Air Park-Dallas Zoning Comm. v. Crow Billingsley Airpark, Ltd.,
   109 S.W.3d 900, 911 (Tex. App.—Dallas 2003, no pet.)   8-3:4.2

Alameda Corp. v. TransAm. Nat. Gas Corp.,
   950 S.W.2d 93 (Tex. App.—Houston [14th Dist.] 1997, writ denied)   7-13:4.1

Alamo Heights Indep. Sch. Dist. v. Clark,
   544 S.W.3d 755, 770–71 (Tex. 2018)   21-2:2

Alan Reuber Chevrolet, Inc. v. Grady Chevrolet, Ltd.,
   287 S.W.3d 877, 889 (Tex. App.—Dallas 2009, no pet.)   1-3:3.1

Albert v. Albert,
   391 S.W.2d 186 (Tex. Civ. App.—San Antonio 1965,
   writ ref'd n.r.e.)   16-4, 16-4:1

Albright v. Lay,
   474 S.W.2d 287 (Tex. Civ. App.—Corpus Christi 1971, no writ)   3-13:3.5

Albright v. Regions Bank,
   13-08-262-CV, 2009 WL 3489853, at *2
   (Tex. App.—Corpus Christi 2009, no pet.)   8-8:2.1

Alderman v. Alderman,
   296 S.W.2d 312 (Tex. Civ. App.—San Antonio 1956, writ ref'd)   16-4

Alexander v. Turtur & Assocs., Inc.,
   146 S.W.3d 113 (Tex. 2004)   4-1:2

All Am. Builders, Inc. v. All Am. Siding of Dallas, Inc.,
   991 S.W.2d 484 (Tex. App.—Fort Worth 1999, no pet.)   1-12:1, 1-12:2, 1-14:1.1,
                                                                                                 1-14:2

Allan v. Nersesova,
   307 S.W.3d 564, 576–78 (Tex. App.—Dallas 2010, no pet.)   10-6

Allen v. Am. Gen. Fin., Inc.,
   251 S.W.3d 676 (Tex. App.—San Antonio 2007,
   pet. granted, judgm't vacated w.r.m.)   3-1:2, 12-1

Allen v. Home Depot U.S.A., Inc.,
   No. SA-04-CA-703-XR, 2004 WL 2270001, at *3
   (W.D. Tex. Oct. 6, 2004)   27-3:5

Allen v. Roddis Lumber & Veneer Co.,
   796 S.W.2d 758, 761 (Tex. App.—Corpus Christi 1990, writ denied)   17-11:2

TABLE OF CASES

Allen v. Wilkerson,
    396 S.W.2d 493 (Tex. Civ. App.—Austin 1965,
    writ ref'd n.r.e.)   2-1:4.3, 2-2:4.4, 2-11:4.1

Allen-Pieroni v. Pieroni,
    535 S.W.3d 887 (Tex. 2017)   7-10:1

Allianz Risk Transfer (Bermuda), Ltd. v. S.J. Camp & Co.,
    117 S.W.3d 92, 96–97 (Tex. App.—Tyler 2003, no pet.)   13-2:1

Allied-Bruce Terminix Co. v. Dobson,
    513 U.S. 265, 263 (1995)   25-1:1

Allison v. Harrison,
    137 Tex. 582, 156 S.W.2d 137 (Tex. Comm'n App. 1941)   3-13:4.1

Allright Auto Parks, Inc. v. Moore,
    560 S.W.2d 129 (Tex. Civ. App.—San Antonio 1977,
    writ ref'd n.r.e.)   3-9:2, 3-10:2.1

Allstate Ins. Co. v. Jordan,
    503 S.W.3d 450, 456 (Tex. App.—Texarkana 2016, no pet.)   5-4:1.1

Allstate Ins. Co. v. Watson,
    876 S.W.2d 145, 149 (Tex. 1994)   5-2:3

Allstate Ins. v. Bonner,
    51 S.W.3d 289, 291 (Tex. 2001)   5-1:1.2, 5-2:3, 5-4:1.1

Allstate Ins. v. Kelly,
    680 S.W.2d 595, 606 (Tex. App.—Tyler 1984, writ n.r.e.)   5-7:3.1

Alpert v. Crain, Caton & James, P.C.,
    178 S.W.3d 398 (Tex. App.—Houston [1st Dist.]
    2005, pet. denied)   9-20:1.1, 9-20:2

Al-Wahban v. Hamdan,
    10-19-00026-CV, 2019 WL 2479894, at *3
    (Tex. App.—Waco June 12, 2019, no pet.)   8-1:2

Amarillo Oil Co. v. Energy-Agri Prods.,
    794 S.W.2d 20 (Tex. 1990)   7-10:2

Ambrosio v. Carter's Shooting Ctr., Inc.,
    20 S.W.3d 262 (Tex. App.—Houston [14th Dist.] 2000, pet denied)   1-11:2

Amedisys, Inc. v. Kingwood Home Health Care, LLC,
    437 S.W.3d 507, 510 (Tex. 2014)   30-1:4, 30-1:5, 30-1:7

Amelia's Auto., Inc. v. Rodriguez,
    921 S.W.2d 767, 771 (Tex. App.—San Antonio 1996, no pet.)   1-3:3.1c

American Alloy Steel v. Armco, Inc.,
    777 S.W.2d 173, 177 (Tex. App.—Houston [14th Dist.]
    1989, no writ)   17-9

American Centennial Ins. Co. v. Canal Ins. Co.,
    843 S.W.2d 480, 484 (Tex. 1992)   4-1:2

American Hous. Resources Inc. v. Slaughter,
   597 S.W.2d 13, 15 (Tex. Civ. App.—Dallas 1980, writ ref'd n.r.e.)   8-3:3.1

American Indem. Co. v. Baumgart,
   840 S.W.2d 634, 639 (Tex. App.—Corpus Christi 1992, no writ)   3-13:2

American Mortg. Corp. v. Samuell,
   130 Tex. 107, 111–12, 108 S.W.2d 193, 196 (1937)   11-5:8

American Nat'l Bank & Tr. Co. v. First Wis. Mortg. Tr.,
   577 S.W.2d 312 (Tex. Civ. App.—Beaumont 1979, writ ref'd n.r.e.)   7-10:3.3

American Nat'l Ins. Co. v. Gifford-Hill & Co.,
   673 S.W.2d 915 (Tex. App.—Dallas 1984, writ ref'd n.r.e.)   16-3:3

American Nat'l Petroleum Co. v. Transcon. Gas Pipe Line Corp.,
   798 S.W.2d 274, 278 (Tex. 1990)   1-1:3.1a, 1-2:3.1a

American Physicians Ins. Exch. v. Garcia,
   876 S.W.2d 842, 846, 848, 849 (Tex. 1994)   5-6:2, 5-7:1.1, 5-7:2, 5-7:4.2

American Star Energy and Minerals Corp. v. Stowers,
   405 S.W.3d 905, 910 (Tex. App.—Amarillo 2013,
   pet. granted)   17-4:1

American Type Culture Collection, Inc. v. Coleman,
   83 S.W.3d 801, 807 (Tex. 2002)   23-3

Americana Motel, Inc. v. Johnson,
   610 S.W.2d 143, 143 (Tex. 1980)   30-3:9

AmeriPath, Inc. v. Hebert,
   447 S.W.3d 319, 342 (Tex. App.—Dallas 2014, pet. denied)   1-1:2

Amoco Prod. Co. v. Alexander,
   622 S.W.2d 563 (Tex. 1981)   7-11:4.2, 7-12:1, 7-12:1.1, 7-12:2, 7-12:3.2, 7-14:1

Amoco Prod. Co. v. Smith,
   946 S.W.2d 162 (Tex. App.—El Paso 1997, no writ)   3-6:3.1, 3-6:4.1

Amstadt v. U.S. Brass Corp.,
   919 S.W.2d 644 (Tex. 1996)   2-8:5.3, 16-7:1

Anadarko Petroleum Corp. v. Thompson,
   94 S.W.3d 550 (Tex. 2002)   7-5:1.1, 7-5:2, 7-5:3.2, 7-11:3.1, 7-12:3.4, 7-13:3.2

Anchor Cas. Co. v. Robertson Transp. Co.,
   389 S.W.2d 135 (Tex. Civ. App.—Corpus Christi 1965,
   writ ref'd n.r.e.)   3-9:3.2

Andersen & Co. v. Perry Equipment Corp.,
   945 S.W.2d 812, 818 (Tex. 1997)   8-11:3.3

Anderson Dev. Co. v. Producers Grain,
   558 S.W.2d 924 (Tex. Civ. App.—Eastland 1977, writ ref'd n.r.e.)   16-3, 16-3:1

Anderson, Greenwood & Co. v. Martin,
   44 S.W.3d 200 (Tex. App.—Houston [14th Dist.] 2001,
   pet. denied)   1-6:2

TABLE OF CASES

Anderson v. Durant,
  550 S.W.3d 605, 614 (Tex. 2018) — 1-4:3.1

Anderson v. Griffith,
  501 S.W.2d 695 (Tex. Civ. App.—Fort Worth 1973, writ ref'd n.r.e) — 3-13:3.4

Anderson v. Trent,
  685 S.W.2d 712, 714 (Tex. App.—Dallas 1984, writ ref'd n.r.e.) — 18-1

Anderton v. City of Cedar Hill,
  583 S.W.3d 188, 195 (Tex. App.—Dallas 2018, no pet.) — 8-10:3.2

Andrews v. Allen,
  724 S.W.2d 893 (Tex. App.—Austin 1987) — 3-9:2

Angroson, Inc. v. Indep. Commc'ns, Inc.,
  711 S.W.2d 268 (Tex. App.—Dallas 1986, writ ref'd n.r.e.) — 3-12:4.2, 3-12:4.3

Antonio v. Marino,
  910 S.W.2d 624, 628, 629 (Tex. App.—Houston [14th Dist.] 1995, no writ) — 13-2:1, 13-2:4

Antwine v. Reed,
  199 S.W.2d 482 (Tex. 1947) — 3-1:4.4

Apex Towing Co. v. Tolin,
  997 S.W.2d 903 — 17-10

Aranda v. Ins. Co. of N. Am.,
  748 S.W.2d 210, 215 (Tex. 1988) — 5-3:2

Archer v. Anderson,
  556 S.W.3d 228 (Tex. 2018) — 1-2:3.1

Archer v. Griffith,
  390 S.W.2d 735 (Tex. 1964) — 3-2:2.1

Archer v. Tregellas,
  566 S.W.3d 281, 287 n.8 (Tex. 2018) — 11-5:4.2

Archon Invs. v. Great Am. Lloyds Ins.,
  174 S.W.3d 334, 339 (Tex. App.—Houston [1st Dist.] 2005, pet. denied) — 5-6:2

Armstrong v. Am. Home Shield Corp.,
  333 F.3d 566 (5th Cir. 2003) — 1-4:4.2, 1-6:4.2, 1-7:4.4

Armstrong v. Armstrong,
  570 S.W.3d 783, 792 (Tex. App.—El Paso 2018, pet. denied) — 8-5:2

Arnold v. Nat'l Cty. Mut. Fire Ins.,
  725 S.W.2d 165, 167 (Tex. 1987) — 5-3:2

Arnold v. West Bend Co.,
  983 S.W.2d 365, 366 n.1 (Tex. App.—Houston [1st Dist.] 1998, no pet.) — 21-1:4

Arteaga v. Jackson,
  994 S.W.2d 342, 342 (Tex. App.—Texarkana 1999, pet. denied) — 21-1:4

Arthur Andersen & Co. v. Perry Equip. Corp.,
   945 S.W.2d 812, 816–17, 818 (Tex. 1997)   8-10:3.2, 10-5, 11-2, 11-3

Ashcroft v. Iqbal,
   556 U.S. 662, 129 S. Ct. 1937, 173 L. Ed. 2d 868 (2009)   13-5:2, 19-4, 28-1:2

Ashley v. Hawkins,
   293 S.W.3d 175, 178–79 (Tex. 2009)   17-11:6

Astoria Indus. of Iowa, Inc. v. SNF, Inc.,
   223 S.W.3d 616 (Tex. App.—Fort Worth 2007, pet. denied)   1-8:2

Atlantic Richfield Co. v. Gruy,
   720 S.W.2d 121 (Tex. App.—San Antonio 1986, writ ref'd n.r.e.)   7-14:2

Atomic Fuel Extraction Corp. v. Estate of Slick,
   386 S.W.2d 180 (Tex. Civ. App.—San Antonio 1964)   17-2

Atrium Cos., Inc. v. ESR Assocs., Inc.,
   No. CIV.A. H-11-1288, 2012 WL 5355754, at *10–11
   (S.D. Tex. Oct. 29, 2012, no pet.)   12-3

Atrium Med. Ctr., LP v. Houston Red C LLC,
   595 S.W.3d 188, 190, 193 (Tex. 2020)   3-1:3.4, 11-4

Augillard v. Madura,
   257 S.W.3d 494, 500–03 n.15 (Tex. App.—Austin 2008, no pet.)   1-3:2

Augustine v. Nusom,
   671 S.W.2d 112, 114 (Tex. App.—Houston [14th. Dist.]
   1984, writ ref'd n.r.e.)   28-3

Austin v. HealthTr., Inc.—The Hosp. Co.,
   967 S.W.2d 400 (Tex. 1998)   9-22:1.1, 9-22:2

Austin Hill Country Realty, Inc. v. Palisades Plaza, Inc.,
   948 S.W.2d 293, 298 (Tex. 1997)   12-1

Austin Lake Estates, Inc. v. Meyer,
   557 S.W.2d 380, 383 (Tex. Civ. App.—Austin 1977, no writ)   8-5:4.1

Austin Neighborhoods Council v. Bd. of Adjustment of City of Austin,
   644 S.W.2d 560, 564 n.17 (Tex. App.—Austin 1982, writ ref'd n.r.e.)   28-3

Austin Nursing Ctr., Inc. v. Lovato,
   171 S.W.3d 845, 848–49 (Tex. 2005)   14-1

Automek, Inc. v. Orandy,
   105 S.W.3d 60, 63–64 (Tex. App.—Houston [1st Dist.] 2003, no pet.)   1-3:2

Autozone, Inc. v. Reyes,
   272 S.W.3d 644 (Tex. App.—Corpus Christi 2006)
   judgment rev'd on other grounds, 272 S.W.3d 588 (Tex. 2008)   6-3:3.1

Ayala v. Enerco Grp., Inc.,
   No. 13-30532, 2014 WL 2200642, at *3 (5th Cir. May 28, 2014)   27-3:5

AZZ Inc. v. Morgan,
   462 S.W.3d 284, 289 (Tex. App.—Fort Worth 2015, no pet.)   3-1:2, 10-5

TABLE OF CASES

B. A. Mortg. Co. v. McCullough,
   590 S.W.2d 955, 957 (Tex. App.—Fort Worth 1979, no writ)   12-2:2

B.D. Holt Co. v. OCE Inc.,
   971 S.W.2d 618 (Tex. App.—San Antonio 1998, pet. denied)   3-2:2.1

Bagwell v. Ridge at Alta Vista Invs. I, LLC,
   440 S.W.3d 287 (Tex. App.—Dallas 2014)   3-1:4.17

Bailey v. Smith,
   581 S.W.3d 374, 399 (Tex. App.—Austin 2019, pet. filed)   8-10:3.2

Baker Hughes Oilfield Operations, Inc. v. Hennig Prod. Co., Inc.,
   164 S.W.3d 438 (Tex. App.—Houston [14th Dist.] 2005, no pet.)   7-11:3.1

Baker v. Energy Transfer Co.,
   No. 10-09-00214-CV, 2011 WL 4978287
   (Tex. App.—Waco Oct. 19, 2011, no pet. h.)   7-6:2

Bank of Am. v. Jeff Taylor LLC,
   358 S.W.3d 848 (Tex. App.—Tyler 2012, no pet.)   3-7:2, 3-8:2.1, 3-8:3.1

Bank of N. Am. v. Bluewater Maint., Inc.,
   578 S.W.2d 841 (Tex. Civ. App.—Houston [1st Dist.]
   1979, writ ref'd n.r.e.)   3-1:4.18

Bank One, Tex., N.A. v. Stewart,
   967 S.W.2d 419 (Tex. App.—Houston [14th Dist.]
   1998, pet. denied)   3-9:2, 3-10:2.1

Bank One, Tex., N.A. v. Sunbelt Sav.,
   F.S.B., 824 S.W.2d 557, 558 (Tex. 1992)   8-8:1

Bankers Life Ins. Co. of Neb. v. Scurlock Oil Co.,
   447 F.2d 997 (5th Cir. 1971)   7-8:2

Baptist Mem'l Hosp. Sys. v. Sampson,
   969 S.W.2d 945 (Tex. 1998)   3-11:2.1

Baptist Missionary & Educ. Convention of State of Tex. v. Knox,
   23 S.W.2d 781, 784 (Tex. Civ. App.—Fort Worth 1929, no writ)   8-9:2.2

Barbara Techs. Corp. v. State Farm Lloyds,
   589 S.W.3d 806, 819 (Tex. 2019)   5-1:1.2, 5-1:2

Barcelo v. Elliott,
   923 S.W.2d 575 (Tex. 1996)   4-1:2

Barham v. McGraw,
   342 S.W.3d 716, 718 (Tex. App.—Amarillo 2011, pet. denied)   8-3:2

Barker v. Eckman,
   213 S.W.3d 306 (Tex. 2006)   3-9:3.1, 3-9:4.1, 3-10:3.1, 3-10:4.1

Barnes v. United Parcel Serv., Inc.,
   395 S.W.3d 165, 174 (Tex. App.—Houston [1 Dist.] 2012, pet. denied)   20-2

Barnhill v. Integrated Health Servs., Inc.,
   21 S.W.3d 321, 324 (Tex. App.—San Antonio 1999, no pet.)   17-11:1

Barr v. Resolution Tr. Corp.,
  837 S.W.2d 627 (Tex. 1992) — 3-3:4.4

Barry v. Jackson,
  309 S.W.3d 135 (Tex. App.—Austin 2010, no pet.) — 3-1:3.1a

Barstow v. State,
  742 S.W.2d 495, 500 (Tex. Civ. App.—Austin 1987, writ denied) — 17-11:5

Bartoo v. Dallas Area Rapid Transit,
  05-02-00828-CV, 2003 WL 751812, at *2
  (Tex. App.—Dallas Mar. 6, 2003, no pet.) — 8-10:2

Bartush-Schnitzius Foods Co. v. Cimco Refrigeration, Inc.,
  518 S.W.3d 432 (Tex. 2017) — 3-1:4.9

Bashara v. Baptist Mem'l Hosp. Sys.,
  685 S.W.2d 307 (Tex. 1985) — 3-3:1.1, 3-3:2, 11-5:8

Basic Energy Serv., Inc. v. D-S-B Props., Inc.,
  367 S.W.3d 254 (Tex. App.—Tyler 2011, no pet.) — 7-11:3.1, 14-1

Basic Inc. v. Levinson,
  485 U.S. 224, 108 S. Ct. 978, L. Ed. 2d 194 (1988) — 2-4:1.1

Bauer v. Valley Bank of El Paso,
  560 S.W.2d 520 (Tex. Civ. App.—El Paso 1977) — 3-10:4.3

Bashara v. Baptist Mem'l Hosp. Sys.,
  685 S.W.2d 307, 310 (Tex. 1985) — 11-5:8

Basley v. Adoni Holdings, LLC,
  373 S.W.3d 577, 588 (Tex. App.—Texarkana 2012, no pet.) — 8-10:2

Bay Area Healthcare Grp., Ltd. v. McShane,
  239 S.W.3d 231 (Tex. 2007) — 10-6, 19-3, 29-2

Bay Area Thoracic & Cardiovascular Surgical Ass'n P.A. v. Nathanson,
  908 S.W.2d 10 (Tex. App.—Houston [1st Dist.] 1995, no writ) — 2-9:3.3

Bay Rock Operating Co. v. St. Paul Surplus Lines Ins. Co.,
  298 S.W.3d 216 (Tex. App.—San Antonio 2009, pet. denied) — 7-11:2

Baylor Univ. v. Sonnichsen,
  221 S.W.3d 632, 636 (Tex. 2007) — 1-4:4.4, 1-6:4.4, 6-1:4.3, 10-5, 11-3, 16-16:2, 28-2

Bayouth v. Lion Oil Co.,
  671 S.W.2d 867, 868 (Tex. 1984) — 17-10

BCOWW Holdings, LLC v. Collins,
  SA-17-CA-00379-FB, 2017 WL 3868184, at *18
  (W.D. Tex. Sept. 5, 2017) — 2-10:4.2, 2-10:4.3, 2-11:4.2

Beard Family P'ship v. Commercial Indem. Ins. Co.,
  116 S.W.3d 839 (Tex. App.—Austin 2003, no pet.) — 3-1:3.15

Beavers v. DePuy Orthopaedics, Inc.,
  No. 1:11 dp 20275, 2012 WL 1945603, at *5
  (N.D. Ohio May 30, 2012) — 27-3:5

TABLE OF CASES

Bed, Bath & Beyond, Inc. v. Urista,
   211 S.W.3d 753, 756–57 (Tex. 2006)   13-6:2

Beers v. North American Van Lines, Inc.,
   836 F.2d 910 (5th Cir. 1988)   27-3:3.1

Bell Atl. Corp. v. Twombly,
   550 U.S. 544, 127 S. Ct. 1955, 167 L. Ed. 2d 929 (2007)   13-5:2, 19-4, 27-3:5, 28-1:2

Bell v. Campbell,
   434 S.W.2d 117 (Tex. 1968)   15-2

Benavides v. Isles Constr. Co.,
   726 S.W.2d 23, 25 (Tex. 1987)   11-13:1, 29-7

Bendalin v. Youngblood & Assocs.,
   381 S.W.3d 719 (Tex. App.—Texarkana 2012, pet. filed)   2-16:1.1

Benefield v. State,
   266 S.W.3d 25, 31 (Tex. App.—Houston [1st Dist.] 2008, no pet.)   8-9:2.1

Benevides v. Lucio,
   13 S.W.2d 71, 72 (Tex. Comm'n App. 1929)   8-11:2.1

Bennett v. Copeland,
   235 S.W.2d 605, 609 (Tex. 1951)   8-3:2

Bennett v. Reynolds,
   315 S.W.3d 867 (Tex. 2010)   1-10:3.2, 1-11:3.2, 3-11:3.2

Bentley v. Bunton,
   94 S.W.3d 561, 605 (Tex. 2002)   11-9:3

Berryman's S. Fork, Inc. v. J. Baxter Brinkmann Intern. Corp.,
   418 S.W.3d 172, 188 (Tex. App.—Dallas 2013, pet. denied)   8-3:2

Best Buy Co. v. Barrera,
   248 S.W.3d 160 (Tex. 2007)   3-4:4.3, 3-5:4.2, 3-6:1.1, 3-6:4.2

Berry v. Encore Bank,
   No. 01-14-00246-CV, 2015 Tex. App. LEXIS 5551
   (Tex. App.—Houston [1st Dist.] 2015, no pet. h.)   3-1:3.11

Better Bus. Bureau of Metro. Houston, Inc. v.
   John Moore Servs., Inc., 441 S.W.3d 345, 361
   (Tex. App.—Houston [1st Dist.] 2013, pet. denied)   1-1:2

Bexar-Medina-Atascosa Ctys. Water Control &
   Improvement Dist. No. 1 v. Medina Lake Prot. Ass'n,
   640 S.W.2d 778, 779–80 (Tex. App.—San Antonio 1982,
   writ ref'd n.r.e.)   5-5:2, 8-10:2

Bhalli v. Methodist Hosp.,
   896 S.W.2d 207, 211 (Tex. App.—Houston [1st Dist.] 1995,
   writ denied)   17-2

Bill Bell, Inc. v. Ramsey,
   284 S.W.2d 244 (Tex. Civ. App.—Waco 1955, no writ)   3-9:2, 3-10:2.1

Birnbaum v. Newport Steel Corp.,
193 F.2d 461 (2d Cir. 1952) — 2-4:2.1

Bishop v. Miller,
412 S.W.3d 758, 779 n.32 (Tex. App.—Houston [14th Dist.] 2013, no pet.) — 11-6:2

Bituminous Cas. Corp. v. Commercial Standard Ins. Co.,
639 S.W.2d 25, 26 (Tex. App.—Tyler 1982, no writ) — 14-4

Blakenship v. Brown,
399 S.W.3d 303 (Tex. App.—Dallas 2013. pet. denied) — 9-1:2

Blancett v. Lagniappe Ventures, Inc.,
177 S.W.3d 584, 589 (Tex. App.—Houston [1st Dist.] 2005, no pet.) — 30-3:5

Blanche v. First Nationwide Mortg. Corp.,
74 S.W.3d 444, 450–51 (Tex. App.—Dallas 2002, no pet.) — 11-9:1, 30-2:1

Blankinship v. Brown,
399 S.W.3d 303, 308 (Tex. App—Dallas 2013, pet. denied) — 1-7:2

Blanks v. Midstate Constructors, Inc.,
610 S.W.2d 220, 225 (Tex. 1980) — 25-1:1

Blue Chip Stamps v. Manor Drug Stores,
421 U.S. 723 (1975) — 2-4:2.1

BMG Direct Mktg., Inc. v. Peake,
178 S.W.3d 763 (Tex. 2005) — 3-4:4.2, 3-4:4.3, 3-5:4.2, 3-6:4.2, 16-2, 16-2:2, 16-12:3

Board of Supervisors for Louisiana State Univ. Agric. & Mech. Coll. v. Smack Apparel Co.,
550 F.3d 465 (5th Cir. 2008) — 1-12:4.6, 1-14:4.6

Board of Water Eng'rs v. City of San Antonio,
283 S.W.2d 722 (Tex. 1955) — 7-9:4.2

Bodovsky v. Texoma Nat'l Bank of Sherman,
584 S.W.2d 868 (Tex. Civ. App.—Dallas 1979, writ ref'd n.r.e.) — 16-15:2

Bohatch v. Butler & Binion,
977 S.W.2d 543 (Tex. 1998) — 9-14:1, 9-14:1.1, 9-14:2

Bohnsack v. Varco, L.P.,
668 F.3d 262 (5th Cir. 2012) — 1-15:3

Bolle, Inc. v. Am. Greetings Corp.,
109 S.W.3d 827 (Tex. App.—Dallas 2003, pet. denied) — 3-1:3.12

Bonham State Bank v. Beadle,
907 S.W.2d 465, 467 (Tex. 1995) — 5-5:2

Bonniwell v. Beech Aircraft Corp.,
663 S.W.2d 816 (Tex. 1984) — 16-7:3

Borderlon v. Peck,
661 S.W.2d 907, 909 (Tex. 1983) — 17-11:1

TABLE OF CASES

Borders v. KRLB, Inc.,
    727 S.W.2d 357, 360 (Tex. App.—Amarillo 1987, writ ref'd n.r.e.)   13-5:1

Born v. Virginia City Dance Hall and Saloon,
    857 S.W.2d 951, 956 (Tex. App.—Houston [14th Dist.]
    1993, writ denied)   29-6

Borneman v. Steak & Ale of Tex., Inc.,
    22 S.W.3d 411, 413 (Tex. 2000)   19-2

Borrego v. City of El Paso,
    964 S.W.2d 954, 959 (Tex. App.—El Paso 1998, pet. denied)   15-4:2

Bossier Chrysler Dodge II, Inc. v. Rauschenberg,
    201 S.W.3d 787 (Tex. App.—Waco 2006)   14-1

Bossier Chrysler-Dodge II, Inc. v. Riley,
    221 S.W.3d 749, 752 (Tex. App.—Waco 2007, pet. denied)   11-10

Bossier Country v. Rauschenberg,
    238 S.W.3d 376 (Tex. 2007)   14-1

Bourque v. Powell Elec. Mfg. Co.,
    617 F.2d 61 (5th Cir.1980)   6-2:2

Bowen v. Robinson,
    227 S.W.3d 86, 94–95 (Tex. App.—Houston [1st Dist.]
    2006, pet. denied)   11-5:7

Bowles v. Fickas,
    167 S.W.2d 741 (Tex. 1943)   3-1:4.4

Boyce Iron Works v. Sw. Bell Tel.,
    747 S.W.2d 785, 787 (Tex. 1988)   12-2:1, 12-2:2

Boyles v. Kerr,
    855 S.W.2d 593 (Tex. 1993)   9-11:1, 9-11:1.1, 9-11:2

BP Am. Prod. Co. v. Red Deer Res., LLC,
    526 S.W.3d 389, 394–95 (Tex. 2017)   7-5:2

BP Am. Prod. Co. v. Zaffirini,
    419 S.W.3d 485, 506 (Tex. App—San Antonio 2013, pet. denied)   1-6:2

Bradford v. Vento,
    48 S.W.3d 749, 757 (Tex. 2001)   1-2:2

Brainard v. Trinity Universal Ins. Co.,
    216 S.W.3d 809 (Tex. 2006)   5-4:1.1, 5-4:3.2

Bramblett v. El Paso County,
    EP-11-CV-167-PRM, 2011 WL 11741275, at *2
    (W.D. Tex. June 13, 2011)   13-2:1

Brantley v. Etter,
    662 S.W.2d 752, 757 (Tex. App.—San Antonio 1983)   8-3:3.1

Brazos River Auth. v. City of Graham,
    163 Tex. 167, 184, 354 S.W.2d 99, 111 (1961)   12-1

Brazos Valley Harvestore Sys., Inc. v. Beavers,
   535 S.W.2d 797, 802 (Tex. App.—Tyler 1976, writ dism'd) 22-6

Breakwater Advanced Mfg., LLC v. E. Tex. Mach. Works, Inc.,
   No. 12-19-00013-CV, 2020 Tex. App. LEXIS 1437, at *11–12
   (Tex. App.—Tyler Feb. 19, 2020, no pet. h.) 3-8:2.2

Breceda v. Whi,
   224 S.W.3d 237, 239–40 (Tex. App.—El Paso 2005, no pet.) 8-11:4.2

Brennen v. Lehn,
   No. X10UWYCV044010222S, 2006 WL 2949111
   (Conn. Super. Ct. Sept. 28, 2006) 2-14:2

Bristol-Myers-Squibb Co. v. Goldston,
   957 S.W.2d 671 (Tex. App.—Fort Worth 1997, pet. denied) 3-1:4.7

Broemer v. Houston Lawyer Referral Serv.,
   407 S.W.3d 477, 482 (Tex. App.—Houston [14th Dist.]
   2013, no pet.) 23-1

Brooks v. Northglen Ass'n.,
   141 S.W.3d 158, 164 (Tex. 2004) 8-10:2

Brookshire Bros, Ltd. v. Aldridge,
   438 S.W.3d 9 (Tex. 2014) 9-19:1, 9-19:2

Brown & Brown v. Omni Metals, Inc.,
   317 S.W.3d 361 (Tex. App.—Houston [1st Dist.] 2010, pet. denied) 1-7:2

Brown v. Aztec Rig Equipment, Inc.,
   921 S.W.2d 835, 845 (Tex. App.—Houston [14th Dist.]
   1996, writ denied) 14-11

Brown v. Brown,
   145 S.W.3d 745, 749 (Tex. App.—Dalas, 2004, pet. denied) 30-2:1

Brown v. Capital Bank,
   703 S.W.2d 231, 233–34 (Tex. App.—Houston [14th Dist.]
   1985, writ ref'd n.r.e.) 30-1:1

Brown v. Demco, Inc.,
   792 F.2d 478, 481–82 (5th Cir.1986) 27-5:3

Brown v. Gilmore,
   267 S.W.2d 908 (Tex. Civ. App.—El Paso 1954, writ dism'd) 7-7:5.1

Brown v. Gulf Tel. Co.,
   157 Tex. 607, 306 S.W.2d 706, 708 (1957) 22-4

Brown v. Havard,
   593 S.W.2d 939, 943 (Tex. 1980) 17-4:1

Browning v. Prostok,
   165 S.W.3d 336 (Tex. 2005) 9-15:2

Browning-Ferris, Inc. v. Reyna,
   852 S.W.2d 540, 549 (Tex. App.—San Antonio 1992) 1-1:3.1, 1-2:3.1

TABLE OF CASES

Brownlee v. Brownlee,
665 S.W.2d 111, 112 (Tex. 1984) — 30-3:3

Brush v. Reata Oil & Gas Corp.,
984 S.W.2d 720, 730 (Tex. App.—Waco 1998, pet. denied) — 8-10:4.2

Bryan v. Citizens Nat'l Bank in Abilene,
628 S.W.2d 761 (Tex. 1982) — 3-4:4.3, 3-5:4.2, 3-6:4.2

Bueno v. Cott Beverages, Inc.,
No. SA-04-CA-24-XR, 2004 WL 1124927, at *4
(W.D. Tex. Mar. 15, 2004) — 27-3:5

Bufkin v. Bufkin,
259 S.W.3d 343, 356–58 (Tex. App.—Dallas 2008, pet. denied) — 11-13:1

Bunker v. Strandhagen,
No. 03-14-00510-CV, 2017 Tex. App. LEXIS 1803, at *18 n.14
(Tex. App.—Austin Mar. 3, 2017) — 11-5:5

Burbage v. Burbage,
447 S.W.3d 249 (Tex. 2014) — 1-8:3.1

Burch v. Hancock,
56 S.W.3d 257 (Tex. App.—Tyler 2001, no pet.) — 3-12:2.1

Burges v. Mosley,
304 S.W.3d 623 (Tex. App.—Tyler 2010, no pet.) — 3-1:3.10

Burlington N.R.R. Co. v. Sw. Elec. Power Co.,
925 S.W.2d 92, 96–97 (Tex. App.—Texarkana 1996,
affirmed by, 966 S.W.2d 467) — 11-11:2

Burnap v. Linnartz,
914 S.W.2d 142 (Tex. App.—San Antonio 1995, writ denied) — 4-1:2

Burns v. Rochon,
190 S.W.3d 263, 271 (Tex. App.—Houston [1st Dist.]
2006, no pet.) — 1-3:4.2

Burris v. Hastert,
191 S.W.2d 811, 814 (Tex. Civ. App.—San Antonio
1945, writ ref'd) — 8-3:2

Burrow v. Arce,
997 S.W.2d 229 (Tex. 1999) — 2-11:3.3, 3-13:3.4, 4-2:3.1, 11-11:5, 30-3:4

Burrus v. Reyes,
516 S.W.3d 170, 188 (Tex. App.—El Paso 2017, pet. denied) — 8-3:2

Burson v. Employers Cas. Co.,
558 S.W.2d 547, 549 (Tex. App.—Fort Worth 1977, no writ) — 13-4:3, 14-10

Burton v. Cravey,
759 S.W.2d 160 (Tex. App.—Houston [1st Dist.]
1988, no writ), *disapproved of on other grounds by*
Huie v. DeShazo, 922 S.W.2d 920 (Tex. 1996) — 2-12:3.1

Butler v. Cont'l Oil Co.,
 182 S.W.2d 843 (Tex. Civ. App.—Galveston 1944, no writ)   3-12:4.1

Butler v. Ross,
 836 S.W.2d 833, 836 (Tex. App.—Houston [1st Dist.]
 1992, no writ)   17-12

Butnaru v. Ford Motor Co.,
 84 S.W.3d 198, 204 (Tex. 2002)   8-1:1.1, 8-1:2, 8-1:5.6, 8-2:2

C.A. May Marine Supply Co. v. Brunswick Corp.,
 649 F.2d 1049, 1053 (5th Cir. 1981)   12-2:1

C.S.C.S., Inc. v. Carter,
 129 S.W.3d 584 (Tex. App.—Dallas 2003, no pet.)   6-1:2

Cabot Corp. v. Brown,
 754 S.W.2d 104 (Tex. 1987)   7-13:2

Cadle Co. v. Int'l Bank of Commerce,
 No. 04-06-00456-CV, 2007 Tex. App. LEXIS 1952
 (App.—San Antonio Mar. 14, 2007)   3-1:3.12

Cage Bros. v. Whiteman,
 163 S.W.2d 638 (Tex. Comm'n App. 1942)   9-4:1, 9-4:1.1, 9-4:2

Cain v. Hearst Corp.,
 878 S.W.2d 577 (Tex. 1994)   9-9:1, 9-9:1.1, 9-9:2

Caldwell v. Barnes,
 975 S.W.2d 535 (Tex. 1998)   16-18:1, 16-18:2

Caldwell v. Wright,
 No. 10-14-00244-CV, 2016 WL 4249136, at *3–4
 (Tex. App.—Waco Aug. 10, 2016, no pet. h.)   12-3

Caller-Times Publ'g Co. v. Triad Commc'ns, Inc.,
 855 S.W.2d 18 (Tex. App.—Corpus Christi 1993, no writ)   1-2:2

Callahan v. Giles,
 155 S.W.2d 793 (Tex. 1941)   16-18

Cambridge Cos., Inc. v. Williams,
 602 S.W.2d 306 (Tex. Civ. App.—Texarkana 1980),
 aff'd, 615 S.W.2d 172 (Tex. 1981)   3-2:2.1

Campbell v. Hamilton,
 632 S.W.2d 633 (Tex. App.—Dallas 1982, writ ref'd n.r.e.)   3-11:2.2

Camunes v. Frontier Enters.,
 61 S.W.3d 579 (Tex. App.—San Antonio 2011, pet. denied)   6-2:2

Canion v. Tex. Cycle Supply, Inc.,
 537 S.W.2d 510 (Tex. Civ. App.—Austin 1976,
 writ ref'd n.r.e.)   2-11:4.2, 2-11:4.3

Cannon v. ICO Tubular Servs.,
 905 S.W.2d 380 (Tex. App.—Houston [1st Dist.] 1995, no writ)   6-1:3.4

TABLE OF CASES

Cantella & Co. v. Goodwin,
924 S.W.2d 943, 944 (Tex. 1996) — 25-3

Cantu v. Holiday Inns, Inc.,
910 S.W.2d 113, 116 (Tex. App.—Corpus Christi
1995, writ denied) — 13-4:2, 13-4:4, 13-4:5, 14-3, 14-13

Capital One Bank (U.S.A.), N.A. v. Conti,
345 S.W.3d 490, 492 (Tex. App.—San Antonio
2011, no pet.) — 3-7:2, 3-8:1.1, 17-10

Carbonit Houston, Inc. v. Exch. Bank,
628 S.W.2d 826, 828 (Tex. App.—Houston [14th Dist.]
1982, writ ref'd n.r.e.) — 13-2:2

Carden v. Arkoma Assocs.,
499 U.S. 185 (1990) — 27-3:3.3

Carl M. Archer Trust v. Tregellas,
566 S.W.3d 281, 288 (Tex.2018) — 1-1:4.1, 1-2:4.1, 6-1:4.1

Carpenter v. Carpenter,
476 S.W.2d 469, 470 (Tex. Civ. App.—Dallas 1972,
no writ) — 8-7:5.6

Carpenter v. N. River Ins. Co.,
436 S.W.2d 549 (Tex. App.—Houston [14th Dist.]
1968, writ ref'd n. r. e.) — 25-1:3

Carr v. Hunt,
651 S.W.2d 875 (Tex. App.—Dallas 1983,
writ ref'd n.r.e.) — 3-11:2.1, 3-11:2.2, 3-12:2.1, 3-13:2

Carr v. Weiss,
984 S.W.2d 753 (Tex. App.—Amarillo 1999, pet. denied) — 7-7:4.1

Carter v. Cookie Coleman Cattle Co., Inc.,
271 S.W.3d 856, 859–60 (Tex. App.—Amarillo 2008, no pet.) — 1-3:4.3

Carter v. McFadyen,
93 S.W.3d 307, 311 (Tex. App.—Houston [14th Dist.]
2002, pet. denied) — 30-2:1

Carter v. Walton,
469 S.W.2d 462 (Tex. Civ. App.—Corpus Christi 1971,
writ ref'd n.r.e.) — 3-12:2.1, 3-12:2.3

Casarez v. NME Hosps., Inc.,
883 S.W.2d 360, 365 (Tex. App.—El Paso 1994, writ dism'd) — 17-11:2

Cass v. Stephens,
156 S.W.3d 38, 68–69 (Tex. App.—El Paso 2004, pet. denied) — 7-8:4.1, 12-3

Casso v. Brand,
776 S.W.2d 551 (Tex. 1989) — 30-3:5

Casstevens v. Smith,
   269 S.W.3d 222, 230 n.3 (Tex. App.—Texarkana 2008,
   pet. denied)   3-4:5.1, 11-4

Castilleja v. Camero,
   414 S.W.2d 424, 425, 427 (Tex. 1967)   24-1:5, 24-1:10

Castle Tex. Prod. Ltd. P'ship v. Long Trs.,
   134 S.W.3d 267 (Tex. App.—Tyler 2003,
   pet. denied)   12-3

Castleberry v. Branscum,
   721 S.W.2d 270 (Tex. 1986)   2-13:1.1, 2-13:2.1, 2-13:2.2, 2-13:5.1

Cate v. Woods,
   299 S.W.3d 149, 152–53 (Tex. App.—Texarkana 2009)   8-3:4.3

Caterpillar Inc. v. Lewis,
   519 U.S. 61, 65 (1996)   27-3:3.4

Cathey v. First City Bank of Aransas Pass,
   758 S.W.2d 818, 821–22 (Tex. App.—Corpus Christi
   1988, writ denied)   17-2

CCD, L.C. v. Millsap,
   2005 UT 42, 116, P.3d 366 (2005)   2-14:2

CCE, Inc. v. PBS&J Constr. Servs., Inc.,
   461 S.W.3d 542 (Tex. App.—Houston [1st Dist.] 2011)   1-7:3.1

CDB Software, Inc. v. Kroll,
   992 S.W.2d 31 (Tex. App.—Houston [1st Dist.] 1999)   3-1:4.18

Celtic Life Ins. v. Coats,
   885 S.W.2d 96, 98 (Tex. 1994)   3-11:1.1, 3-11:2.2, 5-2:3

Centeq Realty, Inc. v. Siegler,
   899 S.W.2d 195, 197 (Tex. 1995)   30-1:7

Center for Biological Diversity v. U.S. Dep't of Interior,
   563 F.3d 466 (D.C. Cir. 2009)   7-9:4.2

Centex Corp. v. Dalton,
   840 S.W.2d 952 (Tex. 1992)   3-1:3.16

Certain Underwriters at Lloyd's v. Prime Nat. Res., Inc.,
   No. 01-17-00881-CV, 2019 Tex. App. LEXIS 10275,
   at *64 (Tex. App.—Houston [1st Dist.] Nov. 26, 2019)   5-1:3.3

Cervantes v. Ocwen Loan Servicing, L.L.C.,
   749 Fed. Appx. 242, 245 (5th Cir. 2018)   2-8:4.2

Ceshker v. Bankers Commercial Life Ins. Co.,
   568 S.W.2d 128, 129 (Tex. 1978)   5-2:3

Cessna Aircraft Co. v. Aircraft Network, L.L.C.,
   213 S.W.3d 455, 464–65 (Tex. App.—Dallas 2006,
   pet. denied)   3-9:2, 3-10:2.1, 11-7:1, 12-2:1

TABLE OF CASES

Chaffin v. Transamerica Ins. Co.,
731 S.W.2d 728, 731 (Tex. App.—Houston [14th Dist.]
1987, writ ref'd n.r.e.) — 5-2:3

Challenger Gaming Sols., Inc. v. Earp,
402 S.W.3d 290, 293–99 (Tex. App.—Dallas 2013, no pet.) — 1-3:4.6, 18-1

Champion v. Wright,
740 S.W.2d 848, 856 (Tex. App.—San Antonio 1987, writ denied) — 1-2:3.1d

Chapa v. Spivey,
999 S.W.2d 833, 835–6 (Tex. App.—Tyler 1999, no pet.) — 21-1:4

Chapin & Chapin v. Tex. Sand & Gravel Co.,
844 S.W.2d 664 (Tex. 1992) — 3-8:4.2, 29-4

Chapman Custom Homes, Inc. v. Dallas Plumbing Co.,
445 S.W.3d 716 (Tex. 2014) — 12-3

Chase Commercial Corp. v. Datapoint Corp.,
774 S.W.2d 359 (Tex. App.—Dallas 1989, no writ) — 1-6:2

Chase Manhattan Bank v. Bowles,
52 S.W.3d 871, 880 (Tex. App.—Waco 2001, no pet.) — 8-9:3.2

Chavco Inv. Co., Inc. v. Pybus,
613 S.W.2d 806 (Tex. Civ. App.—Houston
[14th Dist.] 1981, writ ref'd n.r.e.) — 2-12:2.1, 2-12:2.2, 2-12:2.3, 2-12:2.4, 2-12:4.1

Chavez v. Andersen,
525 S.W.3d 382, 386–87 (Tex. App.—Houston
[14th Dist.] 2017, no pet.) — 29-2

Chavez v. Kan. City S.,
520 S.W.3d 898, 899 (Tex. 2017) — 30-1:4

CHCA East Houston, L.P. v. Henderson,
99 S.W.3d 630, 633 (Tex. App.—Houston [14th Dist.] 2003) — 14-3

Checker Bag Co. v. Wash.,
27 S.W.3d 625, 641–42 (Tex. App.—Waco 2000, pet. denied) — 11-7:1, 12-2:1

Chenault v. Cty. of Shelby,
320 S.W.2d 431 (Tex. Civ. App.—Austin 1959, writ ref'd n.r.e.) — 3-2:2.1

Cheniere Energy, Inc. v. Parallax Enters., LLC,
585 S.W.3d 70, 76 (Tex. App.—Houston [14th Dist.] 2019) — 8-2:2

Cheung-Loon, LLC v. Cergon, Inc.,
392 S.W.3d 738 (Tex. App.—Dallas 2012, no pet.) — 3-1:3.9, 3-1:3.10, 16-14, 16-14:1, 16-14:2

Chhim v. Univ. of Hous.,
76 S.W.3d 210, 221 (Tex. App.—Texarkana 2002, pet. denied) — 30-1:2

Childs v. Haussecker,
974 S.W.2d 31, 36 (Tex. 1998) — 17-10

Chilkewitz v. Hyson,
    22 S.W.3d 825, 828–29 (Tex. 1999)   17-12:1, 17-12:2, 23-1, 23-2

Chinyere v. Wells Fargo Bank, N.A.,
    440 S.W.3d 80, 85 (Tex. App.—Houston [1st Dist.] 2012)   7-4:1

Chiriboga v. State Farm Mut. Auto. Ins. Co.,
    96 S.W.3d 673, 680–83 (Tex. App.—Austin 2003, no pet.)   22-3

Christus Health v. Quality Infusion Care, Inc.,
    359 S.W.3d 719 (Tex. App.—Houston [1st Dist.] 2011, no pet.)   3-1:3.3, 3-3:4.2

Christus Health Gulf Coast v. Carswell,
    505 S.W.3d 528, 537–39 (Tex. 2016)   29-2

Church v. Ortho Diagnostic Sys., Inc.,
    694 S.W.2d 552, 555–56 (Tex. App.—Corpus 1985,
    writ ref'd n.r.e.)   17-2

Citizens Ins. Co. of Am. v. Daccach,
    217 S.W.3d 430 (Tex. 2007)   2-8:4.2

Citizens Nat'l Bank at Brownwood v. Ross Const. Co.,
    206 S.W.2d 593 (Tex. 1947)   3-5:2.2

Citizens' Nat'l Bank of Jasper v. Ratcliff & Lanier,
    253 S.W. 253 (Tex. Comm'n App. 1923)   3-9:2

Citizens Nat'l Bank v. Allen Rae Inves., Inc.,
    142 S.W.3d 459 (Tex. App.—Fort Worth 2004)   1-4:4.2, 1-6:4.2, 1-7:4.4

City of Abilene v. Walker,
    309 S.W.2d 494, 495 (Tex. Civ. App.—Eastland 1958, no writ)   11-8:1, 12-2:1

City of Alton v. Sharyland Water Supply Corp.,
    277 S.W.3d 132, 152–53 (Tex. App.—Corpus Christi 2009)   12-3

City of Austin v. Gifford,
    824 S.W.2d 735 (Tex. App.—Austin 1992, no writ)   6-3:3.2

City of Beaumont v. West,
    484 S.W.2d 789, 792 (Tex. App.—Beaumont 1972, writ ref'd n.r.e.)   21-1:2

City of Carrollton v. RIHR, Inc.,
    308 S.W.3d 444, 452–53 (Tex. App.—Dallas 2010, pet. denied)   11-8:1

City of Dall. v. Sanchez,
    494 S.W.3d 722, 724 (Tex. 2016)   19-4

City of Dallas v. Early,
    281 S.W. 883 (Tex. Civ. App.—Dallas 1926, writ dism'd)   7-9:4.1

City of Dallas v. Ellis,
    No. 05-16-00348-CV, 2017 Tex. App. LEXIS 1408,
    at *9–10 (App.—Dallas Feb. 17, 2017); *Culver v. Pickens*,
    176 S.W.2d 167 (Tex. 1943)   8-1:4.2

City of Fort Worth v. Zimlich,
    29 S.W.3d 62, 73 (Tex. 2000)   29-5

TABLE OF CASES

City of Harker Heights v. Sun Meadows Land, Ltd.,
  830 S.W.2d 313, 317 (Tex. App.—Austin 1992, no writ) — 11-11:2, 11-11:3

City of Harlingen v. Estate of Sharboneau,
  48 S.W.3d 177, 182–83 (Tex. 2001) — 11-6:2, 11-7:2

City of Hous. v. Clear Creek Basin Auth.,
  589 S.W.2d 671, 678 (Tex. 1979) — 30-1:4

City of Ingleside v. Stewart,
  554 S.W.2d 939 (Tex. Civ. App.—Corpus Christi
  1977, writ ref'd n.r.e.) — 3-2:2.3, 3-2:3.2, 3-3:3.1, 3-3:4.3

City of McAllen v. Casso,
  13-11-00749-CV, 2013 WL 1281992, at *15
  (Tex. App.—Corpus Christi Mar. 28, 2013, no pet.) — 8-3:5.3

City of Palmview v. Agua Special Util. Dist.,
  13-18-00416-CV, 2019 WL 1066423, at *7
  (Tex. App.—Corpus Christi Mar. 7, 2019, no pet.) — 8-1:5.5

City of San Antonio v. Greater San Antonio Builders Ass'n,
  04-12-00745-CV, 2013 WL 2247468, at *3
  (Tex. App.—San Antonio May 22, 2013, no pet.) — 8-10:2

City of San Antonio v. Guidry,
  801 S.W.2d 142, 150 (Tex. App.—San Antonio 1990, no writ) — 12-2:1

City of San Antonio v. Lopez,
  754 S.W.2d 749, 751 (Tex. App.—San Antonio 1988, writ denied) — 29-6

City of Tahoka v. Jackson,
  115 Tex. 89, 276 S.W. 662, 663 (1925) — 22-4

City of The Colony v. N. Tex. Mun. Water Dist.,
  272 S.W.3d 699 (Tex. App.—Fort Worth 2008, pet. dism'd) — 3-1:2, 3-1:4.3

City of Tyler v. Likes,
  962 S.W.2d 489, 496 (Tex. 1997) — 11-9:3

City of Waco v. Lopez,
  259 S.W.3d 147 (Tex. 2008) — 6-3:4.2

Claflin v. Hillock Homes, Inc.,
  645 S.W.2d 629, 633 (Tex. App.—Austin 1983) — 8-3:2

Clark v. Perez,
  679 S.W.2d 710 (Tex. App.—San Antonio 1984, no writ) — 7-5:2

Clarke v. Mathewson,
  12 Pet. 164, 171, 9 L. Ed. 1041 (1838) — 27-3:3.4

Classic Superoof LLC v. Bean,
  No. 05-12-00941-CV, 2014 Tex. App. LEXIS 11365
  (App.—Dallas Oct. 14, 2014) — 3-1:3.1a

Classical Vacations, Inc. v. Air France,
  No. 01-01-01137-CV, 2003 WL 1848247
  (Tex. App.—Houston [1st Dist.] Apr. 10, 2003, no pet.) — 12-3

Clayton Williams Energy, Inc. v. BMT O&G TX, L.P.,
  473 S.W.3d 341, 354 (Tex. App.—El Paso 2015) 7-10:2

Cleveland v. San Antonio Bldg. & Loan Ass'n,
  223 S.W.2d 226, 228–29 (Tex. 1949) 8-7:2

Clifton v. Koontz,
  305 S.W.2d 782, 788 (Tex. Civ. App.—Fort Worth 1957),
  aff'd by 325 S.W.2d 684 (Tex. 1959) 7-14:2

Clifton v. Koontz,
  325 S.W.2d 684, 690–91 (Tex. 1959) 7-11:3.1, 7-12:2, 7-14:1, 7-14:1.1,
  7-14:2, 9-23:1.1, 9-23:2

Clint Indep. Sch. Dist. v. Marquez,
  487 S.W.3d 538 (Tex. 2016) 21-9

CMA-CGM (Am.), Inc. v. Empire Truck Lines, Inc.,
  416 S.W.3d 495, 522 n.3 (Tex. App.—Houston
  [1st Dist.] 2013, pet. pending) 24-2

Coastal Oil & Gas Corp. v. Garza Energy Tr.,
  268 S.W.3d 1 (Tex. 2008) 7-5:3.1, 7-8:4.2, 7-12:2, 7-12:3.1, 7-14:3.1

Coastal Transp. Co., Inc. v. Crown Cent. Petroleum Corp.,
  136 S.W.3d 227, 235 (Tex. 2004) 12-2:2

COC Servs. v. Comp. U.S.A., Inc.,
  150 S.W.3d 654, 679 (Tex. App.—Dallas 2004,
  pet. denied) 1-2:2

Coe v. Sienna Fin. Servs., LLC,
  No. 14-18-00338-CV, 2019 Tex. App. LEXIS 7054
  (Tex. App. Aug. 13, 2019) 6-2:2

Coffin v. Finnegan's, Inc.,
  No. 06-01-00171-CV, 2003 WL 21756653, at *2
  (Tex. App.—Texarkana July 31, 2003, no pet.) 13-4:1

Cohen v. Cohen,
  632 S.W.2d 172, 173 (Tex. App.—Waco 1982, no writ) 8-10:3.1

Coinmach Corp. v. Aspenwood Apartment Corp.,
  417 S.W.3d 909, 923 (Tex. 2013) 1-2:2

Collins v. Lewis,
  283 S.W.2d 258 (Tex. Civ. App.—Galveston 1955,
  writ ref'd n.r.e.) 2-15:4.2

Colvin v. Baskett,
  407 S.W.2d 19 (Tex. Civ. App.—Amarillo 1966, no writ) 3-2:2.1

Columbia Rio Grande Healthcare, L.P. v. Hawley,
  284 S.W.3d 851 (Tex. 2009) 13-6:4

Comer v. Murphy Oil U.S.A.,
  585 F.3d 855 (5th Cir. 2009) 7-9:1.1, 7-9:4.2, 7-9:4.6

TABLE OF CASES

Comer v. Murphy Oil U.S.A.,
839 F. Supp. 2d 849 (S.D. Miss. 2012),
aff'd, 718 F.3d 460 (5th Cir. 2013) 7-9:1.1, 7-9:4.3, 7-9:4.4

Commonwealth of Mass. v. Davis,
140 Tex. 398, 168 S.W.2d 216 (1942) 2-8:2, 2-8:3.1

Community Health Sys. Prof'l Servs. Corp. v. Hansen,
525 S.W.3d 671, 689 (Tex. 2017) 1-1:2, 3-11:2.1, 3-11:2.2, 30-1:3

Community Initiatives, Inc. v. Chase Bank of Tex.,
153 S.W.3d 270 (Tex. App—El Paso 2004, no pet.) 1-8:2

Community Mut. Ins. Co. v. Owen,
804 S.W.2d 602 (Tex. App.—Houston [1st Dist.] 1991, writ denied) 3-2:2.1

Compaq Comput. Corp. v. Lapray,
135 S.W.3d 657 (Tex. 2004) 3-1:3.1b

Compass Bank v. MFP Fin. Servs., Inc.,
152 S.W.3d 844, 854 (Tex. App.—Dallas 2005, pet. denied) 29-6

Composite Cooling Sols., L.P. v. Larrabee Air Conditioning, Inc.,
No. 02-17-00006-CV, 2017 WL 2979918, at *5
(Tex. App.—Fort Worth July 13, 2017, no pet.) 13-2:4

Computer Assocs. Int'l, Inc. v. Altai, Inc.,
918 S.W.2d 453 (Tex. 1996) 1-15:3.1, 17-11:2

Comstock Silversmiths, Inc. v. Carey,
894 S.W.2d 56, 57 n.2 (Tex. App.—San Antonio 1995, no writ) 1-1:3.1b, 1-2:3.1b

Concept Gen. Contracting, Inc. v. Asbestos Maint. Servs., Inc.,
346 S.W.3d 172 (Tex. App.—Amarillo 2011, pet. denied) 3-3:2, 3-3:4.5

Condom Sense, Inc. v. Alshalabi,
390 S.W.3d 734 (Tex. App.—Dallas 2012,
no pet.) 1-12:1, 1-12:4.2, 1-12:4.3, 1-13:1.1, 1-13:4.4, 1-14:4.2, 1-14:4.3

Condovest Corp. v. John Street Builders,
662 S.W.2d 138, 140 (Tex. App.—Austin 1983, writ ref'd n.r.e.) 8-3:2

Condra v. Quinoco Petroleum, Inc.,
954 S.W.2d 68 (Tex. App.—San Antonio 1997, pet. denied) 7-13:2

Condry v. Mantooth,
460 S.W.2d 513, 516 (Tex. Civ. App.—Houston
[1st Dist.] 1970, no writ) 14-8

Cone v. Fagadau Energy Corp.,
68 S.W.3d 147 (Tex. App.—Eastland 2001, pet. denied) 7-12:3.3, 7-12:5.1

Conley v. Gibson,
355 U.S. 41, 45–46, 78 S. Ct. 99, 2 L. Ed. 2d 80 (1957) 19-4

ConocoPhillips Co. v. Koopmann,
547 S.W.3d 858, 880 (Tex. 2018) 28-1:5, 28-1:6

Consolidated Gas & Equip. Co. of Am. v. Thompson,
   405 S.W.2d 333 (Tex. 1966) 7-7:1.1, 7-7:2

Consolidated Tex. Fin. v. Shearer,
   739 S.W.2d 477 (Tex. App.—Fort Worth 1987, writ ref'd) 3-2:2.3

Continental Coffee Prod. Co. v. Cazarez,
   937 S.W.2d 444, 449 (Tex. 1996) 21-2, 21-2:2, 21-2:3

Continental Holdings, Ltd. v. Leahy,
   132 S.W.3d 471, 475 (Tex. App.—Eastland 2003, no pet.) 10-3

Continental Oil Co. v. Doornbos,
   402 S.W.2d 879, 883 (Tex. 1966) 11-5:8

Cook v. Brundidge, Fountain, Elliott & Churchill,
   533 S.W.2d 751 (Tex. 1976) 4-1:2

Cortinas v. Wilson,
   851 S.W.2d 324 (Tex. App.—Dallas 1993, no writ) 17-12:1, 23-2

Cosgrove v. Grimes,
   744 S.W.2d 662 (Tex. 1989) 4-1:1, 4-1:2, 4-3:1

Cote v. Texcan Ventures II,
   271 S.W.3d 450, 454 (Tex. App.—Dallas 2008, no pet.) 11-11:1

Country Cupboard, Inc. v. Texstar Corp.,
   570 S.W.2d 70 (Tex. Civ. App.—Dallas 1978, writ ref'd n.r.e.) 16-11

Coury v. Prot,
   85 F.3d 244, 248 (5th Cir. 1996) 27-3:3.1

Covington v. Houston Post,
   743 S.W.2d 345, 347–48 (Tex. App.—Houston
   [14th Dist.] 1987, no writ) 17-2

Cox Operating, L.L.C. v. St. Paul Surplus Lines Ins. Co.,
   No. H-07-2724, 2013 U.S. Dist. LEXIS 116098,
   at *8 (S.D. Tex. 2013) 5-1:3.2

Cox Tex. Newspapers, L.P. v. Wootten,
   59 S.W.3d 717 (Tex. App.—Austin 2001, pet. denied) 9-11:1.1

Craddock v. Goodwin,
   54 Tex. 578 (1881) 7-8:3.2

Craddock v. McAfee,
   151 S.W.2d 936 (Tex. Civ. App.—El Paso 1941, no writ) 6-1:4.4

Crawford v. Adams,
   213 S.W.2d 721, 722 (Tex. Civ. App.—Galveston 1948,
   writ ref'd n.r.e.) 17-11:5

Creative Thinking Sources, Inc. v. Creative Thinking, Inc.,
   74 S.W.3d 504, 510 (Tex. App.—Corpus Christi-Edinburg 2002,
   no pet.) 24-1:1

TABLE OF CASES

Cressman Tubular Prods. Corp. v. Kurt Wiseman Oil & Gas, Ltd.,
   322 S.W.3d 453, 459–60 (Tex. App.—Houston [14th Dist.]
   2010, pet denied) 18-1

Crim Truck & Tractor Co. v. Navistar Int'l Transp. Corp.,
   823 S.W.2d 591 (Tex. 1992) 7-7:2

Cross v. Wagner,
   497 S.W.3d 611 (Tex. App.—El Paso 2016, no pet. h.) 20-2, 29-7

Crossroads Hospice, Inc. v. FC Compassus, LLC,
   No. 01-19-00008-CV, 2020 Tex. App. LEXIS 2216, at *25–26
   (Tex. App.—Houston [1st Dist.] Mar. 17, 2020, no pet. h.) 3-11:3.2

Crosstex North Texas Pipeline, L.P. v. Gardiner,
   505 S.W.3d 580, 595 (Tex. 2016) 7-9:2, 29-5

Crowder v. Tri-C Res., Inc.,
   821 S.W.2d 393 (Tex. App.—Houston [1st Dist.] 1991, no writ) 7-7:2

Crowley v. Coles,
   760 S.W.2d 347 (Tex. App.—Houston [1st Dist.] 1988, no writ) 2-8:4.2

Crown Life Ins. Co. v. Casteel,
   22 S.W.3d 378 (Tex. 2000) 5-2:1.1, 5-2:3, 18-3

Crowson v. Wakeham,
   897 S.W.2d 779, 783 (Tex. 1995) 8-4:5.2

Culver v. Pickens,
   176 S.W.2d 167, 170–71 (Tex. 1943) 8-5:4.2

Cruikshank v. Consumer Direct Mortg., Inc.,
   138 S.W.3d 497 (Tex. App.—Houston [14th Dist.]
   2004, pet. denied) 6-1:2

Curtis v. Ziff Energy Grp., Ltd.,
   12 S.W.3d 114 (Tex. App.—Houston [14th Dist.] 1999, no pet.) 6-1:2

Cushman & Wakefield, Inc. v. Fletcher,
   915 S.W.2d 538 (Tex. App.—Dallas 1995, writ denied) 6-1:2, 6-1:4.2

Cruz v. Andrews Restoration, Inc.,
   364 S.W.3d 817 (Tex. 2012) 3-1:3.7

Cytogenix, Inc. v. Waldroff,
   213 S.W.3d 479, 488 (Tex. App.—Houston [1st Dist.]
   2006, pet. denied) 3-1:3.12, 8-3:2, 11-13:3

D. Houston, Inc. v. Love,
   92 S.W.3d 450, (Tex. 2002) 7-11:2

D.S.A., Inc. v. Hillsboro Indep. Sch. Dist.,
   973 S.W.2d 662 (Tex. 1998) 1-7:1.1, 1-7:2, 1-7:3.1, 1-7:3-2,
                                                      1-7:4.2, 9-8:1, 9-8:1.1, 9-8:2

DaimlerChrysler Motors Co., LLC v. Manuel,
   362 S.W.3d 160, 191 (Tex. App.—Fort Worth 2012, no pet.) 11-6:1

Dairyland Cty. Mut. Ins. Co. v. Roman,
498 S.W.2d 154, 157 (Tex. 1973) — 13-4:6

Dale v. Simon,
267 S.W. 467 (Tex. Comm'n App. 1924) — 3-2:2.1, 16-11, 16-11:1

Dallas City Limits Prop. Co., L.P. v. Austin Jockey Club, Ltd.,
376 S.W.3d 792, 797 (Tex. App.—Dallas 2012, pet. denied) — 29-5

Dallas County Republican Party v. Dallas County Democratic Party,
05-18-00916-CV, 2019 WL 4010776, at *4 (Tex. App.—Dallas Aug. 26, 2019, pet. denied) — 19-4

Dallas Cty. Tax Collector v. Andolina,
303 S.W.3d 926, 930 (Tex. App.—Dallas 2010, no pet.) — 8-10:3.1

Dallas Farm Mach. Co. v. Reaves,
307 S.W.2d 233 (Tex. 1957) — 3-2:2.1

Dallas Fire Ins. Co. v. Texas Contractors Sur. & Cas. Agency,
159 S.W.3d 895, 897 (Tex. 2004) — 5-2:3

Dallas Power & Light Co. v. Cleghorn,
623 S.W.2d 310 (Tex. 1981) — 7-14:4.1

Danciger Oil & Ref. Co. of Tex. v. Powell,
154 S.W.2d 632 (Tex. 1941) — 7-12:4.2

Daniel v. Falcon Interest Realty Corp.,
190 S.W.3d 177 (Tex. App.—Houston [1st Dist.] 2005, no pet.) — 3-13:4.2

Daniels v. Empty Eye, Inc.,
368 S.W.3d 743 (Tex. App.—Houston [14th Dist.] 2012, pet. denied) — 9-1:1

Daubert v. Merrell Dow Pharms., Inc.,
509 U.S. 579, 113 S. Ct. 2786, 125 L. Ed. 2d 469 (1993) — 20-2

Daugherty v. Highland Capital Mgmt.,
L.P., No. 05-14-01215-CV, 2016 WL 4446158, at *3 (Tex. App.—Dallas Aug. 22, 2016, reh'g denied) — 10-2

David H. v. Spring Branch Indep. Sch. Dist.,
569 F. Supp. 1324, 1340 (S.D. Tex. 1983) — 12-1

David J. Sacks, P.C. v. Haden,
266 S.W.3d 447 (Tex. 2008) — 16-16

David McDavid Nissan, Inc. v. Subaru of Am., Inc.,
10 S.W.3d 56 (Tex. App.—Dallas 1999), *aff'd in part, rev'd in part on other grounds,* 84 S.W.3d 212 (Tex. 2002) — 3-5:2.1

David v. Bache Hlasey Stuart Shields, Inc.,
630 S.W.2d 754, 757 (Tex. App.—Houston [1st Dist.] 1982, no writ) — 8-2:2

Davis v. Chaparro,
431 S.W.3d 717 (Tex. App.—El Paso 2014) — 3-12:1.1

TABLE OF CASES

Davis v. OneWest Bank N.A.,
No. 02-14-00264-CV, 2015 Tex. App. LEXIS 3470, at *1–3
(Tex. App.—Fort Worth Apr. 9, 2015, pet. denied) 11-4, 11-11:2

Davis v. Sheerin,
754 S.W.2d 375 (Tex. App.—Houston [1st Dist.] 1988,
writ denied), *disapproved of on other grounds by*
Ritchie v. Rupe, 443 S.W.3d 856 (Tex. 2014) 2-7:5.1, 9-7:1

Davis v. Young Californian Shoes, Inc.,
612 S.W.2d 703, 704 (Tex. App.—Dallas 1981, no writ) 14-13

Dawson-Austin v. Austin,
968 S.W.2d 319, 322 (Tex. 1998) 13-2:2, 13-2:4

Day Cruises Mar., L.L.C v. Christus Spohn Health Sys.,
267 S.W.3d 42, 53 (Tex. App.—Corpus Christi 2008,
pet. denied) 14-9

Day v. Fed'n of State Med. Bds. of the U.S., Inc.,
579 S.W.3d 810, 823–24 (Tex. App.—San Antonio 2019,
no pet. h.) 1-2:2

Day v. State,
489 S.W.2d 368, 371 (Tex. App.—Austin 1972, writ ref'd n.r.e.) 14-2

De Benavides v. Warren,
674 S.W.2d 353 (Tex. App.—San Antonio 1984,
writ ref'd n.r.e.) 16-18:2

De Monet v. PERA,
877 S.W.2d 352 (Tex. App.—Dallas 1994, no writ) 3-2:2.1

Deaton v. United Mobile Networks, L.P.,
926 S.W.2d 756 (Tex. App.—Texarkana 1996),
rev'd on other grounds, 939 S.W.2d 146 (Tex. 1997) 9-3:2

DeClaire v. G & B Mcintosh Family Ltd. P'ship,
260 S.W.3d 34 (Tex. App.—Houston [1st Dist.] 2008, no pet.) 3-1:2

DeGroot v. DeGroot,
369 S.W.3d 918, 926–27 (Tex. App.—Dallas 2012, no pet.) 11-13:1

Delfingen US-Tex., L.P. v. Valenzuela,
407 S.W.3d 791 (Tex. App.—El Paso 2013, no pet.) 3-1:4.19

Dennett v. First Cont'l Inv. Corp.,
559 S.W.2d 384, 385–86 (Tex. App.—Dallas 1977, no writ) 13-2:2

Dennis v. Allison,
698 S.W.2d 94 (Tex. 1985) 9-21:1

DePuy v. Bodine,
509 S.W.2d 698 (Tex. Civ. App.—San Antonio 1974,
writ ref'd n.r.e.) 3-2:4.3

DeSantis v. Wackenhut,
793 S.W.2d 670 (Tex. 1990) 24-1:3, 24-1:10, 24-2

Deutsch v. Hoover, Bax & Slovacek, L.L.P.,
   97 S.W.3d 179, 196 (Tex. App.—Houston
   [14th Dist.] 2002, no pet.) 11-11:5

Dew v. Crown Derrick Erectors, Inc.,
   208 S.W.3d 448, 450–51 (Tex. 2006) 13-6:2, 15-2

Diep Tuyet Vo v. Vu,
   No. 02-15-00188-CV, 2016 WL 2841286, at *6–7
   (Tex. App.—Fort Worth May 12, 2016, no pet.) 12-2:1

DiGiuseppe v. Lawler,
   269 S.W.3d 588 (Tex. 2008) 3-1:3.6, 8-3:1.1, 8-3:2, 8-3:4.6, 11-5:4.2, 11-5:8

Dillard Dep't Stores, Inc. v. Silva,
   148 S.W.3d 370, 372–73 (Tex. 2004) 1-1:3.2, 1-2:3.2

Dillard v. Broyles,
   633 S.W.2d 636 (Tex. App.—Corpus Christi
   1982, writ ref'd n.r.e.) 16-18

Dillard v. Tex. Elec. Co-Op,
   157 S.W.3d 429 (Tex. 2005) 13-6:1, 13-6:2, 13-6:3, 15, 15-1, 15-4:1, 15-4:2

Dillon v. Legg,
   441 P.2d 912 (Cal. 1968) 9-11:1

Dirks v. S.E.C.,
   463 U.S. 646, 103 S. Ct. 3255, 77 L. Ed. 2d 911 (1983) 2-4:1.1, 2-4:2.2, 2-4:2.3

Ditta v. Conte,
   298 S.W.3d 187 (Tex. 2009) 7-1:4.1

Dittmar v. Alamo Nat'l Co.,
   132 Tex. 44, 118 S.W.2d 298 (1938) 7-1:4.2

Dixon v. Mayfield Bldg. Supply Co., Inc.,
   543 S.W.2d 5, 7–8 (Tex. App.—Fort Worth 1976, no writ) 14-13

Doe v. Boys Clubs of Greater Dallas, Inc.,
   907 S.W.2d 472 (Tex. 1995) 1-9:2

Donald v. Bennett,
   415 S.W.2d 450, 454 (Tex. Civ. App.—Fort Worth
   1967, writ ref'd n.r.e.) 14-9

Donnelly v. JP Morgan Chase, NA,
   CIV.A. H-13-1376, 2014 WL 429246, at *3
   (S.D. Tex. Feb. 4, 2014) 8-4:4.4

Dormady v. Dinero Land & Cattle Co., L.C.,
   61 S.W.3d 555, 557 (Tex. App.—San Antonio 2001,
   pet. dism'd w.o.j.) 8-11:2.2

Dorman v. Boehringer,
   195 S.W. 669, *rev'd on reh'g*, 195 S.W. 1183
   (Tex. Civ. App.—San Antonio 1917, no writ) 3-12:2.1

TABLE OF CASES

Double Diamond-Del., Inc. v. Alfonso,
 487 S.W.3d 265, 270–71
 (Tex. App.—Corpus Christi-Edinburg 2016, *reh'g denied*)   22-1

Douglas v. Aztec Petroleum Corp.,
 695 S.W.2d 312 (Tex. App.—Tyler 1985, no writ)   3-13:2

Douglas v. Delp,
 987 S.W.2d 879 (Tex. 1999)   4-1:3.4

Douglas v. Neill,
 545 S.W.2d 903 (Tex. Civ. App.—Texarkana 1977, writ ref'd n.r.e.)   1-4:2

Douglas v. Walker,
 707 S.W.2d 733 (Tex. App.—Beaumont 1986, no writ)   1-14:3.1

Dowell, Inc. v. Cichowski,
 540 S.W.2d 342 (Tex. Civ. App.—San Antonio 1976, no writ)   7-11:1.1, 7-11:3.1

Dowlen v. C.W. Georgs Mfg. Co.,
 59 Tex. Civ. App. 124, 125 S.W. 931 (1910)   3-13:3.5

DP Sols., Inc. v. Rollins, Inc.,
 34 Fed. Appx. 150 (5th Cir. 2002)   1-1:3.3

Dresser Ind., Inc. v. Page Petroleum, Inc.,
 853 S.W.2d 505 (Tex. 1993)   7-11:3.1

Drury Sw., Inc. v. Louie Ledeaux No. 1, Inc.,
 No. 04-12-0087-CV, 2013 WL 5812989, at *11
 (Tex. App.—San Antonio Oct. 30, 2013, no pet.)   10-2

Dryden v. Dairyland Cty. Mut. Ins. Co.,
 633 S.W.2d 912, 914 (Tex. App.—Beaumont 1982, no pet.)
 (Elements 1—3)   5-4:1.1, 5-4:2

Duerr v. Brown,
 262 S.W.3d 63 (Tex. App.—Houston [14th Dist.] 2008, no pet.)   9-1:1

Dulong v. Citibank (South Dakota), N.A.,
 261 S.W.3d 890 (Tex. App.—Dallas 2008, no pet.)   3-7:2

Duncan v. Cessna Aircraft Co.,
 665 S.W.2d 414, 421 (Tex. 1984)   24-1:2, 24-1:3

Duncan Land & Expl., Inc. v. Littlepage,
 984 S.W.2d 318 (Tex. App.—Fort Worth
 1998, pet. denied)   7-1:3.1, 7-1:3.2, 7-1:5.2, 7-10:1.1,
 7-10:2, 7-10:3.1, 7-10:3.3, 7-10:4.2

Dunmore v. Chicago Title Ins. Co.,
 400 S.W.3d 635, 641 (Tex. App.—Dallas 2013)   7-7:4.1, 7-11:4.1

Dunn v. S. Farm Bur. Cas. Ins.,
 991 S.W.2d 467, 478–79 (Tex. App.—Tyler 1999, pet. denied)   5-1:3.3

Dunnagan v. Watson,
 204 S.W.3d 30, 41 (Tex. App.—Fort Worth 2006, pet. denied)   2-10:1.1, 2-10:3.1,
 2-10:3.9, 2-15:1.1, 2-15:2, 2-15:4.1, 8-1:4.1

Dupuy v. Dupuy,
　511 F.2d 641 (5th Cir. 1975) 2-4:2.1, 2-4:2.2

Duval Cty. Ranch Co. v. Wooldridge,
　674 S.W.2d 332, 336 (Tex. App.—Austin 1984, no writ) 11-9:1

Dwyer v. Sabine Mining Co.,
　890 S.W.2d 140 (Tex. App.—Texarkana 1994, writ denied) 1-8:4.4

Dyer v. Shafer, Gilliland, Davis, McCollum & Ashley, Inc.,
　779 S.W.2d 474, 477 (Tex. App.—El Paso 1989, writ denied) 2-11:2

Eagle Mfg. Co. v. Hannaway,
　40 S.W. 13, 13–14 (Tex. 1897) 8-4:5.5

Eagle Props., Ltd. v. Scharbauer,
　807 S.W.2d 714 (Tex. 1990) 16-7

Earle v. Ratliff,
　998 S.W.2d 882, 886 (Tex. 1999) 17-10

East Line & R.R.R. Co. v. Scott,
　10 S.W. 99 (Tex. 1888) 6-2:1

Easterling v. Murphy,
　11 S.W.2d 329, 333 (Tex. Civ. App.—Waco 1928, writ ref'd) 17-11:5

Eaves v. Unifund CCR Partners,
　301 S.W.3d 402 (Tex. App.—El Paso 2009, no pet.) 3-7:2, 3-8:2.1

E.B. Smith Co. v. U.S. Fidelity and Guar. Co.,
　850 S.W.2d 621, 624 (Tex. App.—Corpus Christi-Edinburg
　1993, writ denied) 30-3:8

Ed Hoffman Motors v. G.F.C. Corp.,
　304 S.W.2d 216 (Tex. Civ. App.—San Antonio 1957,
　writ ref'd n.r.e.) 3-2:2.2

Ed Rachal Found. v. D'Unger,
　117 S.W.3d 348 (Tex. App.—Corpus Christi 2003),
　judgment rev'd on other grounds, 207 S.W.3d 330 (Tex. 2006) 6-2:2, 6-2:3.1

Edmunds v. Sanders,
　2 S.W.3d 697, 703–04 (Tex. App.—El Paso 1999, pet. denied) 1-3:4.1

Edwards v. Hefley,
　22 S.W. 659 (Tex. Civ. App.—Austin 1893, no writ) 7-4:1

E.E. Maxwell Co. v. Arti Decor, Ltd.,
　638 F. Supp. 749, 753 (N.D. Tex. 1986) 8-7:1

EEOC v. Courtesy Bldg. Serv., Inc.,
　No. 3:10-CV-1911-D, 2011 WL 208408
　(N.D. Tex. Jan. 21, 2011) 13-5:2

Efremov v. GeoSteering, LLC,
　01-16-00358-CV, 2017 WL 976072, at *2
　(Tex. App.—Houston [1st Dist.] Mar. 14, 2017, pet. denied) 8-1:5.5

TABLE OF CASES

El Paso Mktg., L.P. v. Wolf Hollow I, L.P.,
  383 S.W.3d 138 (Tex. 2012) — 12-3

El Paso Nat. Gas Co. v. Minco Oil & Gas Co.,
  964 S.W.2d 54 (Tex. App.—Amarillo 1997),
  rev'd on other grounds, 8 S.W.3d 309 (Tex. 1999) — 3-1:4.19

E.L. Wilson Hardware Co. v. Anderson Knife & Bar Co.,
  54 S.W. 928, 929 (Tex. Civ. App. 1899, writ ref'd) — 8-8:2.1

Elbaor v. Smith,
  845 S.W.2d 240, 243 (Tex. 1992) — 12-1, 19-1

Electronic & Missile Facilities, Inc. v. U.S.,
  306 F.2d 554 (5th Cir. 1962) — 25-1:1

Electronic Data Sys. Corp. v. Kinder,
  360 F. Supp. 1044, 1051 (N.D. Tex. 1973) — 8-3:2

Elgaghil v. Tarrant Cty. Junior Coll.,
  45 S.W.3d 133 (Tex. App.—Fort Worth 2000, pet. denied) — 6-3:2, 6-3:4.3

Elijah Ragira/Vip Lodging Grp., Inc. v. Vip Lodging Grp., Inc.,
  301 S.W.3d 747 (Tex. App.—El Paso 2009, pet. denied) — 7-1:3.2

Elizondo v. Krist,
  415 S.W.3d 259 (Tex. 2013) — 4-1:2

Elledge v. Friberg-Cooper Water Supply Corp.,
  240 S.W.3d 869, 870 (Tex. 2007) — 3-4:4.1, 3-6:4.1

Elliff v. Texon Drilling Co.,
  210 S.W.2d 558 (Tex. 1948) — 7-11:1.1, 7-11:2

Elliott v. Weatherman,
  396 S.W.3d 224, 228 (Tex. App.—Austin 2013, no pet.) — 8-9:2.1

Ellis v. Schlimmer,
  337 S.W.3d 860, 862 (Tex. 2011) — 25-3:1

Ellis v. Waldrop,
  656 S.W.2d 902, 905 (Tex. 1983) — 11-5:4.1, 11-5:7

Elloway v. Pate,
  238 S.W.3d 882 (Tex. App.—Houston
  [14th Dist.] 2007, no pet.) — 2-1:2.1, 2-1:4.1, 2-1:4.2, 2-2:2.1, 2-2:4.1

Elsas v. Yakkassippi, L.L.C.,
  746 Fed. Appx 344 (5th Cir. 2018) — 3-1:3.1a

Elvis Presley Enters., Inc. v. Capece,
  141 F.3d 188, 206 (5th Cir. 1998) — 1-12:2, 1-12:4.4, 1-12:4.5, 1-14:2, 1-14:4.4

EMC Mortg. Corp. v. Jones,
  252 S.W.3d 857, 872 (Tex. App.—Dallas 2008,
  no pet.) — 5-3:3.1b

Employers Cas. Co. v. Glens Falls Ins.,
  484 S.W.2d 570, 575 (Tex. 1972) — 5-6:4.2

Energy Reserves Grp., Inc. v. Tarina Oil Co.,
   664 S.W.2d 169 (Tex. App.—San Antonio 1983, no writ)   7-7:5.1

Enernational Corp. v. Exploitation Eng'rs., Inc.,
   705 S.W.2d 749, 750–51 (Tex. App.—Houston [1st Dist.]
   1986, writ ref'd n.r.e.)   11-5:6

EnerQuest Oil & Gas, LLC v. Plains Expl. & Prod. Co.,
   No. SA:12-CV-542-DAE, 2013 WL 5951952
   (W.D. Tex. Nov. 7, 2013)   7-6:4.1

Engelman Irrigation Dist. v. Shields Bros.,
   514 S.W.3d 746, 750–51 (Tex. 2017)   16-7:3, 21-8

English v. Dhane,
   294 S.W.2d 709 (Tex. 1956)   3-9:2, 3-10:2.1

English v. Fischer,
   660 S.W.2d 521 (Tex. 1983)   3-4:1.1, 3-5:2.1, 9-5:1, 9-5:2

Ennis v. Interstate Distribs., Inc.,
   598 S.W.2d 903 (Tex. Civ. App.—Dallas 1980, no writ)   3-2:2.1

Enserch Corp. v. Parker,
   794 S.W.2d 2, 4–5 (Tex. 1990)   17-12:1, 23-2

Envision Realty Group, LLC v. Chuan Chen,
   05-18-00613-CV, 2020 WL 1060698, at *4
   (Tex. App.—Dallas Mar. 5, 2020, no pet. h.)   8-10:2, 8-10:3.1

Equistar Chem., L.P. v. Dresser-Rand Co.,
   240 S.W.3d 864, 867–68 (Tex. 2007)   12-3

ERI Consulting Eng'rs, Inc. v. Swinnea,
   318 S.W.3d 867 (Tex. 2010)   2-11:3.4, 3-13:3.2, 3-13:3.3, 11-11:5

Erica P. John Fund, Inc. v. Halliburton Co.,
   563 U.S. 804 (2011)   2-4:2.1

Ernst & Young, L.L.P. v. Pac. Mut. Life Ins. Co.,
   51 S.W.3d 5731 (Tex. 2001)   1-4:2

Ervin v. Mann Frankfort Stein & Lipp CPAS,
   234 S.W.3d 172, 176–77 (Tex. App.—San Antonio
   2007, no pet.)   1-7:2

Escalante v. Luckie,
   77 S.W.3d 410, 418 (Tex. App.—Eastland 2002, pet. denied)   14-5

Essenburg v. Dallas Cty.,
   988 S.W.2d 188 (Tex. 1998)   6-1:4.6

Estate of Farmer,
   09-18-00314-CV, 2018 WL 5660339
   (Tex. App.—Beaumont Nov. 1, 2018, no pet.)   8-4:5.2

Etan Indus., Inc. v. Lehmann,
   359 S.W.3d 620, 624–25 (Tex. 2011)   8-10:2

TABLE OF CASES

Eubank v. Twin Mountain Oil Corp.,
   406 S.W.2d 789 (Tex. Civ. App.—Eastland 1966, writ ref'd n.r.e.)   7-1:4.3

Eun Bok Lee v. Ho Chang Lee,
   411 S.W.3d 95, 111–12 (Tex. App.—Houston
   [1st Dist.] 2013, no pet.)   11-4

Evans v. Henry,
   230 S.W.2d 620 (Tex. Civ. App.—San Antonio 1950, no writ)   3-1:4.5

Evanston Ins. v. ATOFINA Pets., Inc.,
   256 S.W.3d 660, 674 (Tex. 2008)   5-1:2

Everett v. TK-Taito, L.L.C.,
   178 S.W.3d 844, 859 (Tex. App.—Fort Worth 2005, no pet.)   8-5:3.2

Ex parte Hodges,
   625 S.W.2d 304, 306 (Tex. 1981)   8-9:1

Excess Underwriters at Lloyd's, London v.
Frank's Casing Crew & Rental Tools, Inc.,
   246 S.W.3d 42, 53 (Tex. 2008)   3-4:3.1, 24-3:1, 24-3:2

Exito Elecs. Co., Ltd. v. Trejo,
   142 S.W.3d 302, 304 (Tex. 2004)   13-2:1, 13-2:4

Exploracion De La Estrella Soloataria Incorporacion v. Birdwell,
   858 S.W.2d 549 (Tex. App.—Eastland 1993, no writ)   7-1:3.2, 7-1:4.4

Expro Ams., LLC v. Sanguine Gas Expl., LLC,
   351 S.W.3d 915 (Tex. App. Houston [14th Dist.]
   2011, pet. denied)   3-1:2

Exxon Corp. v. Allsup,
   808 S.W.2d 648 (Tex. App.—Corpus Christi 1991, writ denied)   1-1:2, 1-1:3.1b, 1-1:3.2, 1-2:3.1b

Exxon Corp. v. Emerald Oil & Gas Co.,
   348 S.W.3d 194 (Tex. 2011)   1-4:2

Exxon Mobil Corp. v. Kinder Morgan Operating L.P.,
   192 S.W.3d 120, 126–28 (Tex. App.—Houston
   [14th Dist.] 2006, no pet.)   1-3:2

ExxonMobil Corp. v. Lazy R Ranch,
   LP, 511 S.W.3d 538, 544 (Tex. 2017)   17-11:2

Eye Site, Inc. v. Blackburn,
   796 S.W.2d 160 (Tex. 1990)   2-8:2

EZ Pawn Corp. v. Mancias,
   934 S.W.2d 87, 88 (Tex. 1996)   25-2

Failing v. Equity Mgmt. Corp.,
   674 S.W.2d 906, 908–09 (Tex. App.—Houston [1st Dist.] 1984, no writ)   29-7

Fairfield Ins. Co. v. Stephens Martin Paving, LP,
   246 S.W.3d 653, 666 (Tex. 2008)   5-3:3.2, 5-7:3.2

Farkas v. Wells Fargo Bank, N.A.,
  No. 03-14-00716-CV, 2016 Tex. App. LEXIS 12956,
  at *28–29 (App.—Austin Dec. 8, 2016) — 8-2:2

Farley v. M M Cattle Co.,
  529 S.W.2d 751 (Tex. 1975) — 16-10, 16-10:1, 16-10:2, 16-10:3

Farmers Ins. Exch. v. Rodriguez,
  366 S.W.3d 216, 219 (Tex. App.—Houston
  [14th Dist.] 2012, rev. denied) — 5-4:1.1

Farmers Tex. Cty. Mut. Ins. Co. v. Okelberry,
  525 S.W.3d 786, 795 (Tex. App.—Houston
  [14th Dist.] 2017, no pet.) — 18-3

Farnsworth v. Massey,
  365 S.W.2d 1 (Tex. 1963) — 2-9:1.1, 2-9:3.4, 2-9:3.5, 2-9:5.4

Farroux v. Denny's Rests., Inc.,
  962 S.W.2d 108, 111 (Tex. App.—Houston
  [1st Dist.] 1997, no pet.) — 30-3:7

Faucette v. Chantos,
  322 S.W.3d 901, 915 (Tex. App.—Houston
  [14th Dist.] 2010, no pet.) — 1-2:2

FCLT Loans, L.P. v. Estate of Bracher,
  93 S.W.3d 469, 482 (Tex. App.—Houston
  [14th Dist.] 2002, no pet.) — 1-3:2

F.D. Stella Products Co. v. Scott,
  875 S.W.2d 462, 464 (Tex. App.—Austin 1994,
  no writ) — 8-3:4.1

F.D.I.C. v. Benson,
  867 F. Supp. 512 (S.D. Tex. 1994) — 2-1:2.1, 2-2:2.1

F.D.I.C. v. Howse,
  736 F. Supp. 1437 (S.D. Tex. 1990) — 2-1:4.3, 2-2:4.4, 2-11:4.1, 3-13:4.3

F.D.I.C. v. Niblo,
  821 F. Supp. 441 (N.D. Tex. 1993) — 2-1:2.1, 2-2:2.1

F.D.I.C. v. Perry Bros.,
  854 F. sup. 1248 (E.D. Tex. 1994) — 1-8:3.1b

F.D.I.C. v. Schreiner,
  892 F. Supp. 869 (W.D. Tex. 1995) — 2-1:2.1, 2-2:2.1

Federal Land Bank Ass'n of Tyler v. Sloane,
  825 S.W.2d 439 (Tex. 1991) — 1-7:3.1, 1-7:4.3

Felderhoff v. Felderhoff,
  473 S.W.2d 928 (Tex. 1971) — 16-19

Ferguson v. Bldg. Materials Corp.,
  295 S.W.3d 642 (Tex. 2009) — 16-12:3

TABLE OF CASES

Ferguson v. Ferguson,
  327 S.W.2d 787, 789 (Tex. Civ. App.—Fort Worth 1959) — 8-4:3.2

Ferguson v. Mounts,
  281 S.W. 616 (Tex. Civ. App.—Amarillo 1926, writ dism'd w.o.j.)
  disapproved of on other grounds by United States Fid. &
  Guar. Co. v. Bimco Iron & Metal Corp., 464 S.W.2d 353 (Tex. 1971) — 3-2:2.1

Ferrous Prods. Co. v. Gulf States Trading Co.,
  323 S.W.2d 292 (Tex. Civ. App.—Houston 1959),
  aff'd, 160 Tex. 399, 332 S.W.2d 310 (1960) — 3-6:3.2

Fibreboard Corp. v. Pool,
  813 S.W.2d 658, 679 (Tex. App.—Texarkana 1991, writ denied) — 17-11:2

Fincher v. B & D Air Conditioning and Heating Co.,
  816 S.W.2d 509, 512 (Tex. App.—Houston [1st Dist.] 1991) — 14-4

Firemen's Ins. Co. v. Burch,
  442 S.W.2d 331, 332 (Tex. 1969) — 5-6:3.1

Firestone Steel Prods. Co. v. Barajas,
  927 S.W.2d 608 (Tex. 1996) — 1-10:2

First City Bank of Plano, N.A.,
  794 S.W.2d 537 (Tex. App.—Dallas 1990, writ denied) — 3-6:4.1

First Nat'l Bank in Dallas v. Whirlpool Corp.,
  517 S.W.2d 262 (Tex. 1974) — 16-2:1

First Nat. Bank of Fabens v. Pac. Cotton Agency,
  329 S.W.2d 504, 505 (Tex. Civ. App.—San Antonio 1959, no writ) — 8-8:4.5

First Nat'l Bank of Eagle Pass v. Levine,
  721 S.W.2d 287, 288–89 (Tex. 1986) — 1-1:4.1, 1-2:4.1, 17-2

First Nat'l Bank of Mineola, Tex. v. Farmers &
Merchs. State Bank of Athens, Tex.,
  417 S.W.2d 317 (Tex. Civ. App.—Tyler 1967, writ ref'd n.r.e.) — 3-6:2

First Nat'l Bank of Hico v. English,
  240 S.W.2d 503, 506 (Tex. Civ. App.—Waco 1951, no writ) — 17-11:5

First State Bank, N.A. v. Morse,
  227 S.W.3d 820, 827 (Tex. App.—Amarillo 2007, no pet.) — 1-3:2

First Nat'l Bank v. Levine,
  721 S.W.2d 287 (Tex. 1986) — 1-1:4.1, 1-2:4.1

First State Bank of Mesquite v. Bellinger & Dewolf, LLP,
  342 S.W.3d 142, 145–46 (Tex. App.—El Paso 2011, no pet.) — 29-4

First State Bank of Roby v. Hilbun,
  61 S.W.2d 521 (Tex. Civ. App.—Eastland 1933, no writ) — 3-12:2.5

First Tech Fed. Credit Union v. Fisher,
  No. 14-18-00140-CV, 2020 Tex. App. LEXIS 1424, at *10
  (Tex. App.—Houston [14th Dist.] Feb. 20, 2020, no pet. h.) — 3-6:2

First Tex. Sav. Ass'n of Dallas v. Dicker Ctr.,
631 S.W.2d 179 (Tex. App.—Tyler 1982, no writ) 3-1:4.11, 16-11:2

First United Pentecostal Church of Beaumont v. Parker,
No. 15-0708, 60 Tex. Sup. Ct. J. 608, 2017 WL 1032754,
at *5 (Mar. 17, 2017) 4-2:3.1, 11-11:5

First Virginia Bankshares v. Benson,
559 F.2d 1307 (5th Cir. 1977) 2-4:2.1

FLCT, Ltd. v. City of Frisco,
493 S.W.3d 238, 256–60 (Tex. App.—Fort Worth 2016, pet. denied) 8-10:4.4

Fleming v. Ahumada,
193 S.W.3d 704, 712–13 (Tex. App.—Corpus Christi
2006, *reh'g denied*) 26-1:2

Florey v. Estate of McConnell,
212 S.W.3d 439 (Tex. App.—Austin 2006, pet. denied) 7-1:3.2

Flores v. Medline Indus., Inc.,
No. 13-14-00436-CV, 2015 Tex. App. LEXIS 12719
(App.—Corpus Christi 2015, no pet. h.) 3-1:3.13

Flour Bluff Indep. Sch. Dist. v. Bass,
133 S.W.3d 272, 274 (Tex. 2004) 23-2

Flowers v. Steelcraft Corp.,
406 S.W.2d 199, 199 (Tex. 1966) 28-3

Floyd v. Hefner, No. CIV.A. H03-5693, 2006 WL 2844245
(S.D. Tex. Sept. 29, 2006), *on reconsideration in part*,
556 F. Supp. 2d 617 (S.D. Tex. 2008) 2-1:2.1, 2-2:2.1

Fluor Enters., Inc. v. Conex Int'l Corp.,
273 S.W.3d 426, 447 (Tex. App.—Beaumont 2008, pet. denied) 1-1:3.1d

Fogel v. White,
745 S.W.2d 444, 446 (Tex. App.—Houston
[14th Dist.] 1988, no writ) 8-8:2.1, 8-8:2.2, 11-5:8

Forbes Inc. v. Granada Biosciences, Inc.,
124 S.W.3d 167, 172 (Tex. 2003) 1-8:1, 1-8:2, 30-2:4

Ford Motor Co. v. Ledesma,
242 S.W.3d 32, 46 (Tex. 2007) 5-2:3

Ford Motor Co. v. Leggat,
904 S.W.2d 643, 647 (Tex. 1995) 24-1:1

Ford v. City State Bank of Palacios,
44 S.W.3d 121 (Tex. App.—Corpus Christi 2001, no pet.) 3-5:2.2

Ford v. Exxon Mobil Chem. Co.,
235 S.W.3d 615 (Tex. 2007) 7-1:4.1

Forest Oil Corp. v. McAllen,
268 S.W.3d 51, 60 (Tex. 2008) 1-4:4.2

TABLE OF CASES

Forged Components, Inc. v. Guzman,
   409 S.W.3d 91, 98 (Tex. App.—Houston [1st Dist.] 2013, no pet.)   25-1:2

Formosa Plastics Corp., USA v. Kajima Intern., Inc.,
   216 S.W.3d 436, 459 (Tex. App.—Corpus Christi-Edinburg
   2006, pet. denied)   12-1

Formosa Plastics Corp. U.S.A. v. Presidio Eng'rs & Contractors, Inc.,
   960 S.W.2d 41, 44–47 (Tex. 1998)   1-4:1.1, 1-4:2, 1-4:3.1a, 9-8:1, 10-5, 11-2, 12-3, 16-15:1

Fort Bend Cty. v. Martin-Simon,
   177 S.W.3d 479, 483 (Tex. App.—Houston [1st Dist.] 2005)   8-10:2

Fortinberry v. Freeway Lumber Co.,
   453 S.W.2d 849, 851–52 (Tex. Civ. App.—Houston
   [1st Dist.] 1970, no writ)   13-3:2

Fortitude Energy, LLC v. Sooner Pipe LLC,
   564 S.W.3d 167 (Tex. App.—Houston [1st Dist.] 2018, no pet.)   3-1:4.9

Fortune Prod. Co. v. Conoco, Inc.,
   52 S.W.3d 671 (Tex. 2000)   1-4:4.3, 3-3:4.2, 1-6:4.3, 3-4:4.2

Four Bros. Boat Works, Inc. v. Tesoro Petroleum Cos., Inc.,
   217 S.W.3d 653 (Tex. App.—Houston [14th Dist.]
   2006, pet. denied)   1-6:2, 1-6:3.1

Fox v. Tropical Warehouses, Inc.,
   121 S.W.3d 853 (Tex. App.—Fort Worth 2003, pet. denied)   8-1:2, 8-2:2

FPL Energy, LLC v. TXU Portfolio Mgmt. Co., L.P.,
   426 S.W.3d 59 (Tex. 2014)   3-1:3.4

Franco v. Allstate Ins. Co.,
   505 S.W.2d 789 (Tex. 1974)   5-4:4.1

Fraud-Tech, Inc. v. Choicepoint, Inc.,
   102 S.W.3d 366, 380 n.43 (Tex. App.—Fort Worth 2003,
   pet. denied)   11-6:1, 11-7:1

Frazin v. Hanley,
   130 S.W.3d 373, 378 (Tex. App.—Dallas 2004, no pet.)   20-3

Freeman v. Harleton Oil & Gas, Inc.,
   528 S.W.3d 708, 740 (Tex. App.—Texarkana 2017, pet. denied)   11-11:2

Freeport-McMoran, Inc. v. KN Energy, Inc.,
   498 U.S. 426, 428–29 (1991)   27-3:3.4

French v. Moore,
   169 S.W.3d 1, 7 (Tex. App.—Houston [1st Dist.] 2004, no pet.)   21-2:1, 21-3

Frequent Flyer Depot, Inc. v. Am. Airlines, Inc.,
   281 S.W.3d 215, 229 (Tex. App.—Fort Worth 2009, pet. denied)   8-2:2

Frey v. DeCordova Bend Estates Owners Ass'n,
   647 S.W.2d 246, 248 (Tex. 1983)   8-2:2

Friberg-Cooper Water Supply Corp. v. Elledge,
   197 S.W.3d 826 (Tex. App—Fort Worth 2006),
   rev'd on other grounds, 240 S.W.3d 869 (Tex.2007)   3-4:5.1

Friedman Oil Corp. v. S. Oil Ref. Co.,
   73 S.W.2d 137 (Tex. Civ. App.—Waco 1934, writ dism'd)   7-2:2

Fulgham v. Fischer,
   349 S.W.3d 153 (Tex. App.—Dallas 2011)   3-1:3.2

Fun Time Ctrs., Inc. v. Cont'l Nat'l Bank,
   517 S.W.2d 877 (Tex. Civ. App. 1974, writ ref'd n.r.e.)   3-4:2

Furr's Supermarkets, Inc. v. Bethune,
   53 S.W.3d 375, 376–77 (Tex. 2001)   11-13:2

G.A. Stowers Furniture Co. v. Am. Indem. Co.,
   15 S.W.2d 544, 547 (Tex. Comm'n App. 1929, holding approved)   5-7:1.1, 5-7:2, 5-7:4.2

Gaddis v. Smith,
   417 S.W.2d 577, 578 (Tex. 1967)   17-11:2

Gage v. Wimberley,
   476 S.W.2d 724, 731 (Tex. Civ. App.—Tyler 1972)   8-3:2

Gaines v. Kelly,
   235 S.W.3d 179, 183-84 (Tex. 2007)   3-11:2.1

Galbraith Eng'g Consultants, Inc. v. Pochucha,
   290 S.W.3d 853, 866 (Tex. 2009)   17-13

Galleria Bank v. Sw. Props., Inc.,
   498 S.W.2d 5, 7 (Tex. Civ. App.—Houston [1st Dist.] 1973, no writ)   13-4:1

Gant v. DeLeon,
   786 S.W.2d 259, 260 (Tex. 1990)   17-12

Garcia v. Corpus Christi Indep. Sch. Dist.,
   866 F. Supp. 2d 646, 659 (S.D. Tex. 2011)   6-1:2

Garden Ridge, L.P. v. Advance Int'l, Inc.,
   403 S.W.3d 432 (Tex. App.—Houston [14th Dist.] 2013)   3-1:3.1

Garner v. Corpus Christi Nat'l Bank,
   944 S.W.2d 469 (Tex. App.—Corpus Christi 1997, writ denied),
   holding modified by Allied Capital Corp. v. Cravens,
   67 S.W.3d 486 (Tex. App.—Corpus Christi 2002, no pet.)   9-5:1, 9-5:1.1, 9-5:2

Garza v. Cantu,
   431 S.W.3d 96 n.4 (Tex. App.—Houston [14th Dist.]
   2013, pet. denied)   19-2

Garza v. Garcia,
   137 S.W.3d 36 (Tex. 2004)   22-2, 22-3

GB Tubulars, Inc. v. Union Gas Operating Co.,
   527 S.W.3d 563, 576 (Tex. App.—Houston [14th Dist.]
   2017, pet. denied)   18-1

TABLE OF CASES

Case	Reference
Gearhart Indus., Inc. v. Smith Intern., Inc., 741 F.2d 707, 720 (5th Cir. 1984)	2-1:1.1, 2-1:2.1, 2-2:1.1
Gehan Homes, Ltd. v. Emp'rs Mut. Cas. Co., 146 S.W.3d 833, 838 (Tex. App.—Dallas 2004, pet. denied)	5-6:2
Geiselman v. Cramer Fin. Grp., Inc., 956 S.W.2d 532, 539–40 (Tex. App.—Houston [14th Dist.] 1997, no writ)	30-3:3, 30-3:10
General Elec. Capital Corp. v. ICO, Inc., 230 S.W.3d 702, 705 (Tex. App.—Houston [14th Dist.] 2007, pet. denied)	8-8:4.4
General Mills Rests., Inc. v. Tex. Wings, Inc., 12 S.W.3d 827 (Tex. App.—Dallas 2000, no pet.)	16-9, 16-9:1
General Motors Acceptance Corp./Crenshaw, Dupree & Milam, L.L.P. v. Crenshaw, Dupree & Milam, L.L.P./Gen. Motors Acceptance Corp., 986 S.W.2d 632 (Tex. App.—El Paso 1998, pet. denied)	3-13:2
Gentry v. Tucker, 891 S.W.2d 766, 768 (Tex. App.—Texarkana 1995, no writ)	13-2:5
GeoChem Tech Corp. v. Verseckes, 962 S.W.2d 541, 543–44 (Tex. 1998)	22-3
Gerdes v. Tygrett, 584 S.W.2d 350, 351 (Tex. App.—Texarkana 1979, writ ref'd n.r.e.)	25-1:3
Ghosh v. Grover, 412 S.W.3d 749 (Tex. App.—Houston [14th Dist.] 2013, no pet.)	1-4:3.1b
Gibson v. Bruce, 108 U.S. 561, 2 S. Ct. 873, 27 L. Ed. 825 (1883)	27-3:3.4
Gilbane Bldg. Co. v. Keystone Structural Concrete, Ltd., 263 S.W.3d 291 (Tex. App.—Houston [1st Dist.] 2007)	1-4:3.3a, 1-6:3.3b
Gilbert Tex. Constr., L.P. v. Underwriters at Lloyd's London, 327 S.W.3d 118, 124 (Tex. 2010)	5-6:2, 16-13:2
Gilbert Wheeler, Inc. v. Enbridge Pipelines (E. Tex.), L.P., 449 S.W.3d 474 (Tex. 2014)	7-9:4.1, 11-8:1, 11-8:2
Gill v. Oak Cliff Bank & Trust Co., 331 S.W.2d 832, 834 (Tex. Civ. App.—Amarillo 1959, no writ)	8-8:2.1
Ginther Davis Constr. Co. v. Bryant Curington, Inc., 614 S.W.2d 923, 925 (Tex. App.—Waco 1981, no writ)	13-4:1
Ginther v. Taub, 675 S.W.2d 724, 728 (Tex. 1984)	8-5:2
Givens v. Dougherty, 671 S.W.2d 877 (Tex. 1984)	3-2:2.2

Glass v. Anderson,
  596 S.W.2d 507, 514 (Tex. 1980) — 8-3:2

Glass v. Gilbert,
  No. 01-14-00643-CV, 2015 Tex. App. LEXIS 6494
  (Tex. App.—Houston [1st Dist.] 2015, no pet. h.) — 3-1:3.3

Glasstex, Inc. v. Arch Aluminum & Glass Co. Inc.,
  13-07-00483-CV, 2016 WL 747893, at *5
  (Tex. App.—Corpus Christi Feb. 25, 2016, no pet.) — 8-9:1

Glendon Invs., Inc. v. Brooks,
  748 S.W.2d 465 (Tex. App.—Houston [1st Dist.] 1988, writ denied) — 3-12:2.6

Glob. Paragon Dallas, LLC v. SBM Realty, LLC,
  448 S.W.3d 607, 613 (Tex. App.—Houston [14th Dist.] 2014, no pet.) — 13-2:4

GoDaddy.com, LLC v. Toups,
  429 S.W.3d 752, 754 (Tex. App.—Beaumont 2014, pet. denied) — 28-1:2, 28-1:5

Goggins v. Leo,
  849 S.W.2d 373, 375 (Tex. App.—Houston [14th Dist.]
  1993, no writ) — 8-11:2.2, 8-11:5.2

Goidl v. Advance Neckwear Co.,
  123 S.W.2d 865, (Tex. 1939) — 1-14:2

Gold v. Exxon Corp.,
  960 S.W.2d 378 (Tex. App.—Houston [14th Dist.] 1998,
  no pet.) — 6-2:2, 6-3:1.1, 6-3:2

Golden Spread Council, Inc. v. Akins,
  926 S.W.2d 287 (Tex. 1996) — 1-10:2

Goldthorn v. Goldthorn,
  242 S.W.3d 797, 798 (Tex. App.—San Antonio 2007, no pet.) — 8-1:5.5

Gonzales Motor Co. v. Buhidar,
  348 S.W.2d 376 (Tex. Civ. App.—Eastland 1961,
  writ ref'd n.r.e.) — 3-6:2

Gonzales v. Gutierrez,
  694 S.W.2d 384, 390 (Tex. App.—San Antonio 1985, no writ) — 1-1:3.1d, 1-2:3.1d

Gonzalez v. Reliant Energy, Inc.,
  159 S.W.3d 615, 622 (Tex. 2005) — 21-1:5

Good v. Baker,
  339 S.W.3d 260, 266 (Tex. App.—Texarkana 2011, pet. denied) — 11-13:3

Goodyear Tire & Rubber Co. v. Mayes,
  236 S.W.3d 754 (Tex. 2007) — 3-11:2.2

Goodyear Tire & Rubber Co. v. Portilla,
  879 S.W.2d 47 (Tex. 1994) — 6-1:2

Gordin v. Shuler,
  704 S.W.2d 403, 408 (Tex. App.—Dallas 1985, writ ref'd n.r.e.) — 8-3:2

TABLE OF CASES

Gordon v. Leasman,
365 S.W.3d 109 (Tex. App.—Houston
[1st Dist.] 2011, no pet.)   3-12:1.1, 3-12:2.1, 3-12:2.2, 3-12:2.3

Gorman v. Life Ins. Co. of N. Am.,
811 S.W.2d 542, 546 (Tex. 1991)   13-5, 13-5:1

Gorsalitz v. Olin Mathieson Chem. Corp.,
429 F.2d 1033, 1048 (5th Cir. 1970)   24-1:5

GPA Holding, Inc. v. Baylor Health Care Sys.,
344 S.W.3d 467, 475 (Tex. App.—Dallas 2011, pet. denied)   11-5:5

Grable & Sons Metal Prods., Inc. v. Darue Eng. & Mfg.,
545 U.S. 308, 312 (2005)   27-2:1

Graham v. Mary Kay Inc.,
25 S.W.3d 749, 755 (Tex. App.—Houston [14th Dist.]
2000, pet. denied)   1-1:3.3

Granberry v. Tex. Pub. Serv. Co.,
171 S.W.2d 184 (Tex. Civ. App.—Amarillo 1943, no writ)   3-9:2

Grand Prairie Indep. Sch. Dist. v. Missouri Pac. R.R. Co.,
730 S.W.2d 761, 762 (Tex. App.—Dallas 1986, writ ref'd n.r.e.)   11-7:2

Grandfalls Mut. Irr. Co. v. White,
131 S.W. 233, 235 (Tex. Civ. App. 1910, no writ)   8-9:2.1

Grant Thornton LLP v. Prospect High Income Fund,
314 S.W.3d 913, 920 (Tex. 2010)   1-4:1.1, 1-4:2, 1-7:1.1, 1-7:2

G.R.A.V.I.T.Y. Enters., Inc. v. Reece Supply Co.,
177 S.W.3d 537, 542 (Tex. App.—Dallas 2005, no pet.)   29-3

Gray & Wallace v. Steedman Bros.,
63 Tex. 95, 99 (1885)   8-7:2

Grayson v. Crescendo Res., L.P.,
104 S.W.3d 736 (Tex. App.—Amarillo 2003, pet. denied)   7-14:1, 7-14:2

Great Am. Ins. v. N. Austin MUD,
908 S.W.2d 415, 426 (Tex. 1995)   15-3

Great Am. Ins. Co. v. Primo,
512 S.W.3d 890 (Tex. 2017)   5-6:2

Great Glob. Assurance Co. v. Keltex Props.,
904 S.W.2d 771 (Tex. App.—Corpus Christi 1995)   3-8:3.3

Greater Houston Transp. Co. v. Phillips,
801 S.W.2d 523 (Tex. 1990)   1-10:2

Greathouse v. Charter Nat'l Bank Sw.,
851 S.W.2d 173 (Tex. 1992)   1-6:2

Green Tree Fin. Corp. v. Randolph,
531 U.S. 79, 522 (2000)   25-3:2

Green v. Morris,
  43 S.W.3d 604 (Tex. App.—Waco 2001, no pet.) — 3-1:3.12, 3-2:2.1

Greene v. Bearden Enters., Inc.,
  598 S.W.2d 649, 652 (Tex. App.—Fort. Worth 1980,
  writ ref'd n.r.e.) — 12-2:2

Greenhalgh v. Serv. Lloyds Ins. Co.,
  787 S.W.2d 938, 939 (Tex. 1990) — 29-7

Greenspun v. Greenspun,
  145 Tex. 374, 198 S.W.2d 82 (1946) — 2-8:4.3

Grizzle v. Tex. Commerce Bank, N.A.,
  38 S.W.3d 265 (Tex. App.—Dallas 2001),
  rev'd in part on other grounds, 96 S.W.3d 240 (Tex. 2002) — 9-3:2

Gronberg v. York,
  568 S.W.2d 139, 144–45 (Tex. Civ. App.—Tyler 1978,
  writ ref'd n.r.e.) — 1-3:4.7

Grozier v. L-B Sprinkler & Plumbing Repair,
  744 S.W.2d 306, 310 (Tex. App.—Fort Worth 1988, writ denied) — 13-2:5

Grupo Dataflux v. Atlas Glob. Grp., L.P.,
  541 U.S. 567, 574–75 (2004) — 27-3:3.4

Grynberg v. Grynberg,
  535 S.W.3d 229, 233–34 (Tex. App.—Dallas 2017, no pet.) — 24-1:9

Grynberg v. M-I, LLC,
  398 S.W.3d 864, 876 (Tex. App.—Corpus 2012) — 13-2:1

Guaranty Bank v. Lone Star Life Ins. Co.,
  568 S.W.2d 431 (Tex. Civ. App.—Dallas 1978, writ ref'd n.r.e.) — 3-5:3.1

Guardian Bank v. San Jacinto Sav. Ass'n,
  593 S.W.2d 860, 862–63 (Tex. Civ. App.—Houston
  [1st Dist.] 1980, writ ref'd n.r.e.) — 14-6

Guardian Life Ins. Co. v. Kinder,
  663 F. Supp. 2d 544, 552 (S.D. Tex. 2009) — 5-2:3

Guerrero v. Salinas,
  13-05-323-CV, 2006 WL 2294578, at *4
  (Tex. App.—Corpus Christi Aug. 10, 2006, no pet.) — 19-3

GuideOne Elite Ins. Co. v. Fielder Rd. Baptist Church,
  197 S.W.3d 305, 308 (Tex. 2006) — 5-6:2

Gulf, C. & S.F. Ry. Co. v. Ballew,
  66 S.W.2d 659, 661 (Tex. Comm'n App. 1933, holding approved) — 15-2

Gulf Atl. Life Ins. Co. v. Hurlbut,
  696 S.W.2d 83 (Tex. App.—Dallas 1985),
  rev'd on other grounds, 749 S.W.2d 762 (Tex. 1987) — 1-8:3.1c

Gulf Coast Inv. Corp. v. Brown,
  821 S.W.2d 159, 160 (Tex. 1991) — 17-11:2

TABLE OF CASES

Gulf Consol. Intern., Inc. v. Murphy,
   658 S.W.2d 565, 566 (Tex. 1983) — 6-1:3.1, 6-1:4.5

Gulf Oil Corp. v. Marathon Oil Co.,
   152 S.W.2d 711 (1941) — 17-10

Gulf Oil Corp. v. Southland Royalty Co.,
   496 S.W.2d 547 (Tex. 1973) — 7-5:2

Gulf Prod. Co. v. Kishi,
   103 S.W.2d 965 (Tex. Comm'n App. 1937) — 7-14:4.1

Gulf States Paint Co. v. Kornblee Co.,
   390 S.W.2d 356 (Tex. Civ. App.—Texarkana
   1965, writ ref'd n.r.e.) — 3-11:2.1, 3-11:2.2, 3-12:2.1, 3-13:2

Gulley v. Davis,
   321 S.W.3d 213 (Tex. App.—Houston [1st Dist.]
   2010, pet. denied) (*reh'g op.*) — 7-2:2

Gumpert v. ABF Freight Sys., Inc.,
   312 S.W.3d 237, 240–42 (Tex. App.—Dallas 2010, no pet.) — 11-13:2

Gunn Infiniti, Inc. v. O'Byrne,
   996 S.W.2d 854, 857 (Tex. 1999) — 12-1, 15-3

Gutierrez v. Collins,
   583 S.W.2d 312, 318 (Tex. 1979) — 24-1:3, 24-1:4

Gutierrez v. Mobil Oil Corp.,
   798 F. Supp. 1280 (W.D. Tex. 1992) — 7-9:4.4

Guzman v. Ugly Duckling Car Sales,
   63 S.W.3d 522, 526 (Tex. App.—San Antonio 2001, pet. denied) — 5-4:3.3

Gwinn v. Associated Empr's Lloyds,
   280 S.W.2d 624 (Tex. Civ. App.—Fort Worth 1955,
   writ ref'd n.r.e.) — 17-4:1

Haas v. George,
   71 S.W.3d 904 (Tex. App.—Texarkana 2002, no pet.) — 4-1:4.1c

Haase v. Glazner,
   62 S.W.3d 795 (Tex. 2001) — 1-4:2

Hahn v. Love,
   321 S.W.3d 517, 533 (Tex. App.—Houston [1st Dist.]
   2009, pet. denied) — 11-11:1

Hakemy Bros., Ltd. v. State Bank & Tr. Co.,
   189 S.W.3d 920, 924–25 (Tex. App.—Dallas 2006, pet. denied) — 29-3

Haley v. Pearson,
   14 S.W.2d 313, 315 (Tex. Civ. App.—Dallas 1929, no writ) — 8-7:5.5

Hall v. Robbins,
   790 S.W.2d 417, 418 (Tex. App.—Houston [14th Dist.]
   1990, no writ) — 11-8:1

Halmekangas v. State Farm Fire & Cas. Co.,
   603 F.3d 290, 293 (5th Cir. 2010)   27-2:2

Haltom v. Haltom's Jewelers, Inc.,
   691 S.W.2d 823 (Tex. App.—Fort Worth 1985, writ ref'd n.r.e.)   1-14:4.3

Hamblet v. Coveney,
   714 S.W.2d 126, 130 (Tex. App.—Houston [1st Dist.]
   1986, writ ref'd n.r.e.)   11-11:1

Hamman v. Ritchie,
   547 S.W.2d 698, 706 (Tex. Civ. App.—Fort Worth 1977,
   writ ref'd n.r.e.)   8-4:2.1

Hamon v. Allen,
   457 S.W.2d 384, 391 (Tex. Civ. App.—Corpus Christi 1970, no writ)   8-3:5.3

Hanover Mfg. Co. v. Ed Hanover Trailers, Inc.,
   434 S.W.2d 109 (Tex. 1968)   1-14:2

Hansler v. Mainka,
   807 S.W.2d 3, 5 (Tex. App.—Corpus Christi 1991, no writ)   17-12

Hardin-Simmons Univ. v. Hunt Cimarron Ltd. P'ship,
   No. 07-15-00303-CV, 2017 WL 3197920
   (Tex. App.—Amarillo July 25, 2017)   7-14:1

Harper v. Wellbeing Genomics Pty Ltd.,
   03-17-00035-CV, 2018 WL 6318876, at *11
   (Tex. App.—Austin Dec. 4, 2018, pet. denied)   10-3

Harrington v. Texaco, Inc.,
   339 F.2d 814 (5th Cir. 1964)   7-8:1.1, 7-8:3.1

Harris Cty. Dist. 156 v. United Somerset,
   274 S.W.3d 133, 139–40 (Tex. App.—Houston
   [1st Dist.] 2008, no pet)   8-10:2

Harris v. Archer,
   134 S.W.3d 411, 435-41 (Tex. App.—Amarillo 2004, pet. denied)   11-12

Harris v. Rowe,
   593 S.W.2d 303 (Tex. 1979)   3-1:3.17, 16-3

Harstan, Ltd. v. Si Kyu Kim,
   441 S.W.3d 791 (Tex. App.—El Paso 2014, no pet.)   1-5:3.1b

Hart v. Moore,
   952 S.W.2d 90, 97 (Tex. App.—Amarillo 1997, pet. denied)   12-2:1

Hartford Cas. Ins. Co. v. Walker Cty. Agency, Inc.,
   808 S.W.2d 681 (Tex. App.—Corpus Christi 1991, no writ)   3-13:2, 3-13:3.1

Hartley v. Schwab,
   564 S.W.2d 829 (Tex. Civ. App.—Amarillo 1978, writ ref'd n.r.e.)   11-8:2, 12-2:2

Harwell v. State Farm Mut. Auto. Ins.,
   896 S.W.2d 170, 173–74 (Tex. 1995)   5-6:2

TABLE OF CASES

Hastings Oil Co. v. Tex. Co.,
234 S.W.2d 389 (Tex. 1950)   3-1:3.11, 7-8:1

Hatfield v. Solomon,
316 S.W.3d 50, 66 (Tex. App.—Houston [14th Dist.]
2010, no pet.)   11-13:2

Hatton v. Turner,
622 S.W.2d 450, 458 (Tex. Civ. App.—Tyler 1981, no writ)   11-11:1

Hawkins v. Tex. Oil and Gas Corp.,
724 S.W.2d 878, 891 (Tex. App.—Waco 1987, writ ref'd n.r.e.)   8-10:4.2, 8-10:4.3

Hawkins v. Walker,
233 S.W.3d 380 (Tex. App.—Fort Worth 2007, pet. denied)   1-5:4.3

Hawthorne v. Guenther,
917 S.W.2d 924 (Tex. App.—Beaumont 1996, writ denied)   2-10:3.10

Hawthorne v. Star Enter., Inc.,
45 S.W.3d 757 (Tex. App.—Texarkana 2001, pet. denied)   6-2:2

Hays v. Hall,
488 S.W.2d 412, 414 (Tex. 1972)   17-11:2

H.E. Butt Grocery Co. v. Bilotto,
928 S.W.2d 197, 199 (Tex. App.—San Antonio 1996)   19-2

Headington Oil Co., L.P. v. White,
287 S.W.3d 204, 212 (Tex. App.—Houston [14th Dist.]
2009, no pet.)   11-13:2

HealthTronics, Inc. v. Lisa Laser U.S.A, Inc.,
382 S.W.3d 567, 580 (Tex. App.—Austin 2012, no pet.)   24-1:1

H.E.B., L.L.C. v. Ardinger,
369 S.W.3d 496 (Tex. App.—Fort Worth 2012)   3-6:1.1, 3-6:2

HECI Expl. Co. v. Neel,
982 S.W.2d 881, 891 (Tex. 1998)   3-4:2, 7-5:4.2, 7-12:4.2, 7-12:4.3,
7-12:5.2, 7-14:4.1, 11-5:8, 11-11:2

Hegwer v. Edwards,
527 S.W.3d 337, 341 (Tex. App.—Dallas 2017, no pet.)   13-2:1

Heil Co. v. Polar Corp.,
191 S.W.3d 805 (Tex. App.—Fort Worth 2006, pet. denied)   1-4:2

Heldenfels Bros., Inc. v. City of Corpus Christi,
832 S.W.2d 39 (Tex. 1992)   3-4:1.1, 3-4:2

Helena Chem. Co. v. Wilkins,
47 S.W.3d 486, 504 (Tex. 2001)   11-6:1

Henderson v. Hall,
174 S.W.2d 985 (Tex. Civ. App.—Galveston 1943, writ ref'd w.o.m.)   7-2:3.1

Hendricks v. Thornton,
973 S.W.2d 348 (Tex. App.—Beaumont 1998, pet. denied)   1-7:4.1

Henriquez v. Cemex Mgmt.,
   177 S.W.3d 241 (Tex. App.—Houston [1st Dist.]
   2005, pet. denied)   6-1:2

Henry v. Carrington Mortgage Services, LLC,
   CV H-18-4414, 2019 WL 2491950, at *4
   (S.D. Tex. June 14, 2019)   8-4:2.1

Henry v. Cash Biz, LP,
   551 S.W.3d 111, 115 (Tex. 2018)   25-3:1, 25-3:4

Henry v. Cox,
   520 S.W.3d 28, 35 (Tex. 2017)   21-9

Henry I. Siegel Co., Inc. v. Holliday,
   663 S.W.2d 824 (Tex. 1984)   2-3:1.1, 2-3:5.1

Henry Schein v. Stromboe,
   102 S.W.3d 675 (Tex. 2002)   3-5:2.1

Henson v. S. Farm Bureau Cas. Ins. Co.,
   17 S.W.3d 652 (Tex. 2000)   5-4:1

Hernandez v. Martinez,
   04-19-00076-CV, 2019 WL 5580261
   (Tex. App.—San Antonio Oct. 30, 2019, no pet.)   8-11:2.2

Hernandez v. Truck Ins. Exch.,
   553 S.W.3d 689, 702 (Tex. App.—Fort Worth 2018)   5-7:4.1

Hertz Corp. v. Friend,
   559 U.S. 77, 91–93 (2010)   27-3:3.2

Hertz Rental Corp. v. Barousse,
   365 S.W.3d 46 (Tex. App.—Houston [1st Dist.] 2011, pet. denied)   6-1:4.5

Hidalgo v. Surety Savings & Loan Ass'n,
   462 S.W.2d 540, 545 (Tex. 1971)   30-3:4

Hideca Petroleum Corp. v. Tampimex Oil Int'l, Ltd.,
   740 S.W.2d 838 (Tex. App.—Houston [1st Dist.] 1987, no writ)   7-5:3.3

Hiles v. Arnie & Co.,
   402 S.W.3d 820, 828 (Tex. App.—Houston [14th Dist.]
   2013, pet. denied)   22-2, 26-1:2

Hill v. Heritage Res.,
   Inc. 964 S.W.2d 89 (Tex. App.—El Paso 1997, pet. denied)   1-1:2, 1-1:4.1, 1-2:2, 1-2:4.1, 7-10:2

Hill v. Shamoun & Norman, LLP,
   544 S.W.3d 724, 732–33 (Tex. 2018)   3-1:3.2

Hill v. Tx-An Anesthesia Mgmt., LLP,
   443 S.W.3d 416, 422-23 (Tex. App.—Dallas 2014, no pet.)   29-4

Hill v. Winn Dixie Tex. Inc.,
   849 S.W.2d 802, 802–03   15-4:2

TABLE OF CASES

Hillman v. Nueces County,
579 S.W.3d 354, 358 (Tex. 2019) — 6-1, 6-2:2, 6-2:4.2

Hixson v. Cox,
633 S.W.2d 330 (Tex. App.—Dallas 1982, writ ref'd n.r.e.) — 16-3:3

Hodge v. Smith,
856 S.W.2d 212, 215 (Tex. App.—Houston [1st Dist.] 1993, writ denied) — 17-12

Hodges v. Gobellan,
433 S.W.3d 542 (Tex. 2014) — 25-3:4

Hoelscher v. Kilman,
No. 03-04-00440-CV, 2006 Tex. App. LEXIS 1351, at *16 (Tex. App.—Austin 2006, no pet.) — 5-3:3.3, 5-7:3.4

Hoggett v. Brown,
971 S.W.2d 472 (Tex. App.—Houston [14th Dist.] 1997, pet. denied) — 1-6:2

Holladay v. Storey,
2013 UT App 158, 307 P.3d 584 (2013) — 2-14:5.1

Holland v. Thompson,
338 S.W.3d 586 (Tex. App—El Paso 2010, pet. denied) — 1-6:2

Hollinger v. Home State Mut. Ins. Co.,
654 F.3d 564 (5th Cir. 2011) — 27-3:3.1

Hollingsworth v. Nw Nat'l Ins. Co.,
522 S.W.2d 242 (Tex. Civ. App.—Texarkana 1975, no writ) — 3-7:2

Hollis v. Gallagher,
No. 03-11-00278-CV, 2012 Tex. App. LEXIS 7547 (Tex. App.—Austin 2012, no pet.) — 3-1:3.16

Holloway v. Guild Mortgage Co.,
05-19-00491-CV, 2020 WL 582284, at *1 (Tex. App.—Dallas Feb. 6, 2020, no pet.) — 8-11:3.1

Holloway v. Skinner,
898 S.W.2d 793, 795–96 (Tex. 1995) — 1-1:2

Holt Atherton Indus., Inc. v. Heine,
835 S.W.2d 80, 82–83 (Tex. 1992) — 11-6:1, 11-6:2, 19-4

Holt v. JTM Indus., Inc.,
89 F.3d 1224 (5th Cir. 1996) — 9-18:1.1, 9-18:2

Holubec v. Brandenberger,
111 S.W.3d 32, 37 (Tex. 2003) — 17-13

Home Loan Corp. v. Tex. Am. Title Co.,
191 S.W.3d 728 (Tex. App.—Houston [14th Dist.] 2006, pet. denied) — 3-13:2

Hong Kong Dev., Inc. v. Nguyen,
229 S.W.3d 415, 433 (Tex. App.—Houston [1st Dist.] 2007, no pet.) — 8-11:1, 8-11:1.1, 8-11:5.2

Hoodye v. Wells Fargo Bank,
No. 2:12-CV-402, 2013 U.S. Dist. LEXIS 25438, at *4
(S.D. Tex. 2013)   8-4:2.1

Hooks v. Samson Lone Star,
Ltd. P'Ship, 457 S.W.3d 52 (Tex. 2015),
reh'g denied (May 1, 2015)   1-4:4.1

Horizon Health Corp. v. Acadia Healthcare Co.,
520 S.W.3d 848, 859–60 (Tex. 2017)   1-1:3.1d, 1-2:3.1d, 3-1:3.13, 11-6:1

Horizon/CMS Healthcare Corp. v. Auld,
34 S.W.3d 887, 896–97 (Tex. 2000)   10-2, 13-5:2, 19-3

Horner v. Bourland,
724 F.2d 1142, 1144–45 (5th Cir. 1984)   8-3:2

Horowitz v. Berger,
377 S.W.3d 115, 123 (Tex. App.—Houston
[14th Dist.] 2012, no pet.)   13-2:2, 13-2:3, 13-2:4,

Horseshoe Bay Resort Sales Co. v. Lake Lyndon B. Johnson Imp. Corp.,
53 S.W.3d 799 (Tex. App.—Austin 2001, pet. denied)   1-12:2, 1-12:4.1, 1-13:1.1, 1-13:4.2, 1-14:2, 1-14:4.1

Hoskins v. Hoskins,
497 S.W.3d 490, 495 (Tex. 2016)   25-4:2

Hot-Hed, Inc. v. Safehouse Habitats (Scotland), Ltd.,
333 S.W.3d 719 (Tex. App.—Houston [1st Dist.] 2010, pet. denied)   1-12:1

Hous. Auth. of City of Harlingen v. Valdez,
841 S.W.2d 860, 864 (Tex. App.—Corpus Christi 1992, writ denied)   5-5:1

Houston Chronicle Publ'g Co. v. City of Houston,
531 S.W.2d 177, 183 (Tex. App.—Houston [14 th Dist.] 1975,
writ ref'd n.r.e.)   13-5:1

Houston Nat'l Bank v. Biber,
613 S.W.2d 771, 774–75 (Tex. App.—Houston [14th Dist.]
1981, writ ref'd n.r.e.)   1-3:2

Houston Unlimited, Inc. Metal Processing v. Mel Acres Ranch,
443 S.W.3d 820, 831 (Tex. 2014)   11-8:1

Howard v. INA Cty. Mut. Ins. Co.,
933 S.W.2d 212 (Tex. App.—Dallas, 1996, writ denied)   5-4:1

Hubbard v. Goode,
P.2d 1063 (N.M. 1959)   3-10:3.1, 3-10:3.4

Hubbard v. Shankle,
138 S.W.3d 474, 485 (Tex. App.—Fort Worth 2004, pet. denied)   8-5:2

Hubler v. City of Corpus Christi,
564 S.W.2d 816, 823 (Tex. Civ. App.—Corpus Christi 1978,
writ ref'd n.r.e.)   19-3

TABLE OF CASES

Huddleston v. Herman & MacLean,
  640 F.2d 534 (5th Cir. 1981), *aff'd in part, rev'd in part on other grounds,* 459 U.S. 375 (1983) — 2-4:2.1, 2-4:2.2, 2-4:2.3

Hudspeth v. Enter. Life Ins.,
  358 S.W.3d 373, 389 (Tex. App.—Houston [1st Dist.] 2011, no pet.) — 5-3:2

Huff v. Speer,
  554 S.W.2d 259 (Tex. Civ. App.—Houston [1st Dist.] 1977, writ ref'd n.r.e.) — 16-14:2

Huffington v. Upchurch,
  532 S.W.2d 576 (Tex. 1976) — 2-10:1.1, 2-10:3.6, 2-10:4.2, 2-11:4.2

Hughes v. Mahaney & Higgens,
  821 S.W.2d 154, 157 (Tex. 1991) — 4-1:4.1c, 17-10, 17-11:2

Hughes v. Marshall Nat. Bank,
  538 S.W.2d 820, 824 (Tex. Civ. App.—Tyler 1976, writ dism'd w.o.j.) — 8-9:2.1

Huie v. DeShazo,
  922 S.W.2d 920 (Tex. 1996) — 3-13:1.1, 3-13:2

Hull v. S. Coast Catamarans, L.P.,
  365 S.W.3d 35 (Tex. App.—Houston [1st Dist.] 2011, pet. denied) — 3-12:2.4, 3-12:2.6

Humble Oil & Ref. Co. v. Luckel,
  171 S.W.2d 902 (Tex. Civ. App.—Galveston 1943, writ ref'd w.o.m.) — 7-10:4.2

Humphrey v. Camelot Ret. Cmty.,
  893 S.W.2d 55, 59 (Tex. App.—Corpus Christi 1994, no pet.) — 3-2:2.3, 11-5:8

Humphrey v. Pelican Isle Owners Ass'n,
  238 S.W.3d 811 (Tex. App.—Waco 2007, no pet.) — 30-2:3

Humphreys v. Caldwell,
  888 S.W.2d 469, 471 (Tex. 1994) — 30-3:3

Hunt v. State,
  48 S.W.2d 466, 468 (Tex. Civ. App.—Austin 1932, no writ) — 8-9:5.1

Hur v. City of Mesquite,
  893 S.W.2d 227 (Tex. App.—Amarillo 1995, writ denied) — 3-12:2.5

Hurlbut v. Gulf Atl. Life Ins. Co.,
  749 S.W.2d 762 (Tex. 1987) — 1-8:1, 1-8:2, 1-8:3.1, 1-8:3.1a, 1-8:4.1, 1-8:4.2, 17-2

Huynh v. Nguyen,
  180 S.W.3d 608 (Tex. App.—Houston [14 Dist.] 2005, no pet.) — 13-2:4

Hygeia Dairy Co. v. Gonzalez,
  994 S.W.2d 220, 224 (Tex. App.—San Antonio 1999, no pet.) — 12-1

Immobiliere Jeuness Establissement v. Amegy Bank Nat'l Ass'n,
525 S.W.3d 875, 880 (Tex. App.—Houston [14th Dist.]
2017, no pet.) 15-2

Imperial Grp. (Tex.), Inc. v. Scholnick,
709 S.W.2d 358 (Tex. App.—Tyler 1986, writ ref'd n.r.e.) 2-2:4.2, 2-11:2

Imperial Sugar Co. v. Torrans,
604 S.W.2d 73, 74 (Tex. 1980) 1-3:3.1a

In Interest of M.I.W.,
04-17-00207-CV, 2018 WL 1831678, at *2
(Tex. App.—San Antonio Apr. 18, 2018, no pet.) 19-1

In re Accident Fund Gen. Ins. Co.,
543 S.W.3d 750, 752 (Tex. 2017) 21-6

In re ADM Inv'r Servs., Inc.,
304 S.W.3d 371 (Tex. 2010) 26-1:1

In re AdvancePCS Health, LP,
172 S.W.3d 603, 605 (Tex. 2005) 25-3

In re AIU Ins. Co.,
148 S.W.3d 109 (Tex. 2004) 25-2, 26-1:1

In re Applied Chem. Magnesias Corp.,
206 S.W.3d 114 (Tex. 2006) 22-4

In re Argyll Equities, LLC,
227 S.W.3d 268, 273 (Tex. App.—San Antonio 2007, no pet.) . . . 11-5:8

In re Automated Collection Techs., Inc.,
156 S.W.3d 557 (Tex. 2004) 26-1:1

In re Baerg Real Prop. Tr.,
585 B.R. 373, 391 (Bankr. N.D. Tex. 2018) 8-3:2

In re Butt,
495 S.W.3d 455, 461–62 (Tex. App.—Corpus
Christi-Edinburg 2016, no pet. h.) 19-4

In re Capco Energy, Inc.,
669 F.3d 274 (5th Cir. 2012) 3-1:2

In re Cambell,
577 S.W.3d 293, 305 (Tex. App.—Houston
[14th Dist.] 2019, no pet.) 18-2

In re Citigroup Global Mkts.,
258 S.W.3d 623, 625 (Tex. 2008) 25-3:4

In re Dexterity Surgical, Inc.,
365 B.R. 690, 695 (Bankr. S.D. Tex. 2007) 24-1:9

In re Dole Food Co.,
256 S.W.3d 851, 854–55 (Tex. App.—Beaumont 2008,
no pet.) 22-1, 22-4

TABLE OF CASES

In re E. I. Du Pont de Nemours & Co.,
  476 F.2d 1357, 1361 (Cust. & Pat. App 1973) — 1-13:2.1

In re Eastman Chem. Co.,
  13-18-00268-CV, 2019 WL 2529042
  (Tex. App.—Corpus Christi June 20, 2019, no pet.) — 13-2:6

In re Echols,
  569 S.W.3d 776, 782–83 (Tex. App.—Dallas 2018, no pet.) — 18-5:3

In re Essex Ins. Co.,
  450 S.W.3d 524, 527 (Tex. 2014) — 8-10:2

In re Estate of Bateman,
  528 S.W.2d 86, 89 (Tex. Civ. App.—Tyler 1975, writ ref'd n.r.e.) — 8-4:2.1

In re Estate of Bessire,
  399 S.W.3d 642, 651 (Tex. App.—Amarillo 2013, pet. denied) — 8-10:2

In re Estate of Denman,
  362 S.W.3d 134 (Tex. App.—San Antonio 2011, pet. granted) — 7-3:4.1

In re Estate of Melchior,
  365 S.W.3d 794, 798–801 (Tex. App.—San Antonio 2012,
  pet. denied) — 8-5:4.1

In re First Merit Bank, N.A.,
  52 S.W.3d 749, 754 (Tex. 2001) — 25-1:1, 25-2, 25-3:1, 25-3:2

In re Fisher,
  433 S.W.3d 523, 529–30 (Tex. 2014) — 22-4, 26-1:1

In re Fort Bend Cty.,
  278 S.W.3d 842 (Tex. App.—Houston [14th Dist.] 2009,
  no pet.) — 22-4

In re Fox River Real Estate Holdings,
  Inc., 18-0913, 2020 WL 501702, at *4
  (Tex. Jan. 31, 2020), *reh'g denied* (Apr. 17, 2020) — 8-1:5.2

In re Great Lakes Dredge & Dock Co.,
  251 S.W.3d 68, 77 (Tex. App.—Corpus Christi 2008, no pet.) — 22-4, 26-1:2

In re Greater Houston Orthopaedic Specialists, Inc.,
  295 S.W.3d 323, 325–26 (Tex. 2009) — 23-2

In re Green Tree Servicing LLC,
  275 S.W.3d 592 (Tex. App.—Texarkana 2008, no pet.) — 3-1:2

In re Gupta,
  394 F.3d 347, 351 (5th Cir. 2004) — 2-10:2

In re Haliburton Co.,
  80 S.W.3d 566, 572 (Tex. 2002) — 25-3

In re HEB Grocery Co., L.P.,
  299 S.W.3d 393, 396 (Tex. App.—Corpus Christi 2009,
  orig. proceeding) — 25-1:1

In re High Pointe Investments, LLC,
552 S.W.3d 384, 388 (Tex. App.—Waco 2018, no pet.)   8-11:1

In re H.V.,
252 S.W.3d 319 (Tex. 2008)   3-1:4.5

In re International Profit Assocs., Inc.,
274 S.W.3d 672, 675 (Tex. 2009)   26-1:1, 26-2:1

In re Kasschau,
11 S.W.3d 305 (Tex. App.—Houston [14th Dist.] 1999, orig. proceeding)   16-16:2

In re Labatt Food Serv.,
L.P., 269 S.W.3d 640 (Tex. 2009)   25-3:1

In re Life Partners Holdings, Inc.,
No. DR-11-CV-43-AM, 2015 WL 8523103
(W.D. Tex. Nov. 9, 2015) (Texas law)   2-1:2.1, 2-2:2.1

In re Lipsky,
460 S.W.3d 579, 589 (Tex. 2015)   1-8:2, 1-8:4.5, 19-3, 28-4

In re Lisa Laser USA, Inc.,
310 S.W.3d 880, 886 (Tex. 2010)   26-1:1

In re Lyon Fin. Servs., Inc.,
257 S.W.3d 228, 232 (Tex. 2008)   26-1:1, 26-2:1

In re Magnum Hunter Res. Corp. Sec. Litig.,
26 F. Supp. 3d 278, 291 (S.D.N.Y. 2014), aff'd,
616 Fed. Appx. 442 (2d Cir. 2015)   2-4:2.1, 2-4:2.2, 2-4:2.3

In re Merrill Lynch Tr. Co.,
235 S.W.3d 185, 188–89 (Tex. 2007)   3-11:1.1, 25-3:1

In re Missouri Pac. R.R. Co.,
998 S.W.2d 212, 217–20 (Tex. 1999)   22-3

In re Mohawk Rubber Co.,
982 S.W.2d 494, 498 (Tex. App.—Texarkana 1998, no pet.)   30-2:1, 30-2:3

In re Moore,
379 B.R. 284 (Bankr. N.D. Tex. 2007)   2-13:4.1

In re M.V.,
343 S.W.3d 543, 550 (Tex. App.—Dallas 2011, no pet.)   13-2:5

In re Nationwide Ins. Co. of Am.,
494 S.W.3d 708, 712 (Tex. 2016)   26-1:1, 26-2:2

In re Oakwood Mobile Homes,
Inc., 987 S.W.2d 571, 573 (Tex. 1999)   25-3

In re Olshan Found. Repair Co., LLC,
328 S.W.3d 883 (Tex. 2010)   3-1:4.19

In re Palm Harbor Homes, Inc.,
195 S.W.3d 672, 676 (Tex. 2006)   25-1:1

TABLE OF CASES

In re Poly-Am., L.P.,
   262 S.W.3d 337, 348 (Tex. 2008) 25-3:1

In re Prudential Ins. Co. of Am.,
   148 S.W.3d 124, 134 (Tex. 2004) 26-2:1

In re ReadyOne Indus., Inc.,
   294 S.W.3d 764, 768 (Tex. App.—El Paso 2009,
   orig. proceeding) 25-1:1

In re Schmitz,
   285 S.W.3d 451 (Tex. 2009) 2-8:2, 2-8:4.1, 2-8:5.4

In re Shell Oil Co.,
   932 F.2d 1518 (5th Cir. 1991) 27-6

In re Sosa,
   370 S.W.3d 79 (Tex. App.—Houston [14th Dist.] 2012, no pet.) ... 22-4

In re Staley,
   320 S.W.3d 490 (Tex. App.—Dallas 2010, no pet.) 3-1:2

In re Structural Software, Inc.,
   67 Fed. Appx. 253 (5th Cir. 2003) 2-11:2, 2-11:3.1

In re Sunpoint Sec., Inc.,
   377 B.R. 513, 569 (Bankr. E.D. Tex. 2007) 18-2:1

In re Texas Dep't of Transp.,
   218 S.W.3d 74, 76 (Tex. 2007) 22-4

In re Texas. Educ. Agency,
   442 S.W.3d 753 (Tex. App.—Austin 2014) 8-1:5.3

In re Texas Nat. Res. Conservation Comm'n,
   85 S.W.3d 201, 205 (Tex. 2002) 8-1:3.2

In re Togs Energy, Inc.,
   No. 05-09-01018-CV, 2009 WL 3260910
   (Tex. App.—Dallas Oct. 13, 2009, no pet.) 22-4

In re Transcontinental Realty Inv'rs, Inc.,
   271 S.W.3d 270 (Tex. 2008) 22-3

In re Unitec Elevator Sers. Co.,
   178 S.W.3d 53, 59 (Tex. App.—Houston [1st Dist.] 2005, no pet.) . 18-5:1

In re United Services Auto. Ass'n,
   307 S.W.3d 299, 308 (Tex. 2010) 6-3:1

In re Warrior Energy Services Corp.,
   14-19-01010-CV, 2020 WL 1679344 (Tex. App.—Houston
   [14th Dist.] Apr. 7, 2020) 8-7:4.2

In re Weekley Homes, L.P.,
   180 S.W.3d 126, 131 (Tex. 2005) 25-3:1

In re Xerox Corp.,
   555 S.W.3d 518, 523 (Tex. 2018) 18-2:2

In the Guardianship of Peterson,
No. 01-15-00567-CV, 2016 WL 4487511, at *6
(Tex. App.—Houston [1st Dist.] 2016, no pet.)   28-1:2

In the Interest of B.N.L.-B.,
375 S.W.3d 557 (Tex. App.—Dallas 2012)   3-1:14.18

Ingram v. Deere,
288 S.W.3d 886, 892–93 (Tex. 2009)   19-1

Instone Travel Tech. Marine & Offshore v. Int'l Shipping Partners, Inc.,
334 F.3d 423 (5th Cir. 2003)   3-12:2.2, 3-12:2.4

Interceramic, Inc. v. S. Orient R.R. Co., Ltd.,
999 S.W.2d 920, 927–28
(Tex. App.—Texarkana 1999, pet. denied)   11-6:1

International & G.N. Ry. Co. v. Davis,
29 S.W. 483 (Tex. Civ. App.—1895, writ ref'd)   7-9:4.1

International Bankers Life Ins. Co. v. Holloway,
368 S.W.2d 567 (Tex. 1963)   2-1:3.3, 2-1:4.3, 2-2:1.1, 2-2:3.3, 2-2:4.4,
2-11:1.1, 2-11:2, 2-11:3.7, 2-11:4.1, 8-5:3.3

International Energy Ventures Mgmt., L.L.C. v. United Energy Grp., Ltd.,
818 F.3d 193, 200–02 (5th Cir. 2016)   19-4

International Freight Forwarding, Inc. v. Am. Flange,
993 S.W.2d 262 (Tex. App.—San Antonio 1999, no pet.)   3-9:3.2, 3-9:3.6, 3-10:3.5

International Paper Co. v. Ouellette, 479 U.S. 481 (1987)   7-9:5.1

International Piping Sys., Ltd. v. M.M. White & Assoc., Inc.,
831 S.W.2d 444, 452–53 (Tex. App.—Houston [14th Dist.]
1992, writ denied)   11-5:8

International Realty, Inc. v. 2005 RP W., Ltd.,
449 S.W.3d 512 (Tex. App.—Houston [1st Dist.] 2014,
pet. denied)   3-1:3.1a

International Turbine Serv., Inc. v. Lovitt,
881 S.W.2d 805, 809 (Tex. App.—Fort Worth 1994, writ denied)   13-2:4

Intevep, S.A. Research & Tech. Support Establishment v. Sena,
41 S.W.3d 391, 394 (Tex. App.—Dallas 2001, no pet.)   24-1:1

Int'l Bus. Machs. Corp. v. Lufkin Indus. LLC,
573 S.W.3d 224, 229 n.4 (Tex. 2019)   1-4:4.2

IRA Res., Inc. v. Griego,
221 S.W.3d 592 (Tex. 2007)   3-11:2.1, 3-11:2.2, 3-12:2.1, 3-13:2

Isaacs v. Bishop,
249 S.W.3d 100 (Tex. App.—Texarkana 2008, pet. denied)   3-2:4.4

Italian Cowboy Partners, Ltd. v. Prudential Ins. Co. of Am.,
341 S.W.3d 323, 337 (Tex. 2011)   1-4:1.1, 1-4:2, 1-4:3.3a, 1-4:4.2, 1-5:4.2,
1-6:3.3a, 1-6:4.2, 1-7:4.4, 10-4

TABLE OF CASES

J & D Towing, LLC v. Am. Alt. Ins. Corp.,
478 S.W.3d 649, 655–56 (Tex. 2016) — 6-1:3.2, 11-8:2, 12-2:2

Jack B. Anglin Co., Inc. v. Tipps,
842 S.W.2d 266, 261 (Tex. 1992) — 25-1:1

Jackson v. Axelrad,
221 S.W.3d 650 (Tex. 2007) — 1-10:2

Jackson v. Textron Fin. Corp.,
No. 14-07-01011-CV, 2009 WL 997484, at *5
(Tex. App.—Houston [14th Dist.] 2009, no pet.) — 13-3:3

Jackson v. Urban Coolidge, Pennington & Scott,
516 S.W.2d 948 (Tex. App.—Houston [1st Dist.] 1974,
writ ref'd n.r.e.) — 4-1:2

James J. Flanagan Shipping vs. Del Monte Fresh Produce,
403 S.W.3d 360 (Tex. App.—Houston [1st Dist.] 2013, no pet.) — 1-4:3.1a, 12-3

James v. Meinke,
778 F.2d 200 (5th Cir. 1985) — 2-4:3.1, 2-4:3.6

Jarvis v. Feild,
327 S.W.3d 918, 925 (Tex. App.—Corpus Christi 2010, no pet.) — 13-2:5

Jay Petroleum, L.L.C. v. EOG Resources, Inc.,
332 S.W.3d 534, 540–41 (Tex. App.—Houston [1st Dist.]
2009, pet. denied) — 8-10:5.2

JCW Elec., Inc. v. Garza,
257 S.W.3d 701, 707 (Tex. 2008) — 18-1

Jeanes v. Henderson,
688 S.W.2d 100 (Tex. 1985) — 16-7

Jeffrey v. Larry Plotnick Co., Inc.,
532 S.W.2d 99 (Tex. Civ. App.—Dallas 1975, no writ) — 3-8:4.3

Jelinis, LLC v. Hiran,
557 S.W.3d 159, 166 (Tex. App.—Houston [14th Dist.] 2018) — 8-11:1

J.E.M. v. Fidelity & Cas. Co. of N.Y.,
928 S.W.2d 688 (Tex. App.-Houston [1st Dist.] 1996, no writ) — 5-6:3.1

Jenkins v. Jenkins,
991 S.W.2d 440 (Tex. App.—Fort Worth 1999, pet. denied) — 3-1:4.3

Jetall Cos. v. Four Seasons Distribs.,
474 S.W.3d 780, 784 (Tex. App.—Houston [14th Dist.] 2014,
no pet.) — 1-1:4.4, 1-2:4.4

Jewett State Bank v. Evans,
129 S.W.2d 1202, 1203 (Tex. Civ. App.—Waco 1939, no writ) — 8-7:4.2

Jilani v. Jilani,
767 S.W.2d 671 (Tex. 1988) — 16-19

Jimenez v. McGeary,
    542 S.W.3d 810, 814 (Tex. App.—Fort Worth 2018, pet. denied)   8-11:2.2

J.M. Radford Grocery Co. v. Estelline State Bank,
    66 S.W.2d 1110 (Tex. Civ. App.- Amarillo
    1933, writ dism'd)   3-11:2.1, 3-11:2.2, 3-12:2.1, 3-13:2

Jody James Farms, JV v. Altman Grp., Inc.,
    547 S.W.3d 624, 632 (Tex. 2018)   25-3:1

John C. Flood of DC, Inc. v. SuperMedia, L.L.C.,
    408 S.W.3d 645, 650 (Tex. App.—Dallas 2013,
    rehearing overruled)   14-1

John Paul Mitchell Sys. v. Randalls Food Mkts., Inc.,
    17 S.W.3d 721, 730–31 (Tex. App.—Austin
    2000, pet. denied)   1-1:2

Johnson & Higgins of Tex., Inc. v. Kenneco Energy, Inc.,
    962 S.W.2d 507, 528–33 (Tex. 1998, *superseded by
    statute on other grounds*, Tex. Fin. Code Ann.
    § 304.1045)   5-3:3.3, 5-7:3.4, 11-13:1

Johnson v. Brewer & Pritchard, P.C.,
    73 S.W.3d 193, 200 (Tex. 2002)   3-13:1.1, 3-13:2, 11-11:5

Johnson v. Buck,
    540 S.W.2d 393 (Tex. Civ. App.—Corpus Christi 1976,
    writ ref'd n.r.e.)   2-10:3.4

Johnson v. Coca-Cola Co.,
    727 S.W.2d 756 (Tex. App.—Dallas 1987, writ ref'd n.r.e.)   29-1

Johnson v. Johnson,
    275 S.W.2d 146 (Tex. Civ. App.—Texarkana 1955, writ ref'd n.r.e.)   7-2:2

Johnson v. Miller,
    173 S.W.2d 280 (Tex. Civ. App.—Galveston 1943),
    aff'd, 177 S.W.2d 249 (Tex. 1944)   7-1:2

Johnson v. Mohammed,
    No. 03-10-00763-CV, 2013 Tex. App. LEXIS 5808, at *10–12
    (App.—Austin May 10, 2013)   8-11:1

Johnson v. Newberry,
    267 S.W. 476 (Tex. Comm'n App. 1924, holding approved)   3-1:4.5

Johnston v. Barnes,
    717 S.W.2d 164, 165–66 (Tex. App.—Houston [14th Dist.]
    1986, no writ)   17-4:1

Johnston v. Del Mar Distributing Co.,
    776 S.W.2d 768 (Tex. App.—Corpus Christi 1989, writ denied)   6-2:2

Johnston v. McKinney Am., Inc.,
    9 S.W.3d 271, 279 (Tex. App.—Houston [14th Dist.] 1999,
    pet. denied)   13-5:1

TABLE OF CASES

Jones v. Chester,
    363 S.W.2d 150 (Tex. Civ. App.—Austin 1962, writ ref'd n.r.e.)   3-2:2.3

Jones v. Jones,
    888 S.W.2d 849, 852–53 (Tex. App.—Houston [1st Dist.] 1994, no writ)   30-3:9

Jones v. Pesak Bros. Constr., Inc.,
    416 S.W.3d 618, 632–33 (Tex. App.—Houston [1st Dist.] 2013, no pet.)   29-4

Jones v. Whatley,
    No. 13-09-00355-CV, 2011 Tex. App. LEXIS 4380,
    at *9 (Tex. App.—Corpus Christi June 9, 2011)   8-1:4.1

Jose Fuentes Co., Inc. v Alfaro,
    418 S.W.3d 280 (Tex. App.—Dallas 2013, pet. denied)   30-1:3

JPMorgan Chase Bank, N.A. v. Orca Assets, G.P., LLC,
    546 S.W.3d 648, 660 (Tex. 2018)   1-4:4.5

J.P. Morgan Chase Bank, N.A. v. Tex. Contract Carpet, Inc.,
    302 S.W.3d 515 (Tex. App-Austin 2009, no pet.)   1-10:2

Juliette Fowler Homes, Inc. v. Welch Assocs.,
    793 S.W.2d 660, 664–65 (Tex. 1990)   1-1:1.1, 1-1:2

K.A. West, LLC v. GK Invs., Inc.,
    No. 05-11-00617-CV, 2013 WL 5270861
    (Tex. App.—Dallas Sept. 17, 2013, no pet.)   1-6:3.1a

Kansas v. Nebraska,
    135 S. Ct. 1042 (2015)   3-1:3.8

Kaplan v. City of Sugar Land,
    525 S.W.3d 297, 302 (Tex. App.—Hous. [14th Dist.] 2017)   6-3:2

Karam v. Brown,
    407 S.W.3d 464, 476 (Tex. App.—El Paso 2013, no pet.)   29-4

Kawasaki Steel Corp. v. Middleton,
    699 S.W.2d 199, 203 (Tex. 1985)   23-3

KCM Fin. LLC v. Bradshaw,
    457 S.W.3d 70, 87–8 (Tex. 2015)   8-5:1.1, 8-5:2, 8-5:4.3

Keane v. Fox Tel. Stations, Inc.,
    297 F. Supp. 2d 921 (S.D. Tex. 2004), *aff'd*,
    129 Fed. Appx. 874 (5th Cir. 2005)   1-12:1

Keck, Mahin & Cate v. Nat'l Union Fire Ins. Co., of Pittsburgh, Pa.,
    20 S.W.3d 692 (Tex. 2000)   4-1:2, 4-1:3.1

Keene v. Reed,
    340 S.W.2d 859, 860 (Tex. Civ. App.—Waco 1960, writ ref'd)   8-1:4.2

Keetch v. Kroger Co.,
    845 S.W.2d 262, 266–67 (Tex. 1992)   19-2

Kegans v. White,
    131 S.W.2d 990 (Tex. Civ. App.—Eastland 1939, writ ref'd)   7-4:1

Kelley v. Rinkle,
  532 S.W.2d 947, 949 (Tex. 1976) 17-11:2

Kellogg Co. v. Nat'l Biscuit Co.,
  305 U.S. 111 (1938) 1-12:2

Kendziorski v. Saunders,
  191 S.W.3d 395 (Tex. App.—Austin 2006) 3-2:2.1

Kennedy v. Gen. Geophysical Co.,
  213 S.W.2d 707 (Tex. Civ. App.—Galveston 1948,
  writ ref'd n.r.e) 7-6:2

Kerlin v. Arias,
  274 S.W.3d 666, 667–68 (Tex. 2008) 30-3:3, 30-3:4, 30-3:6

Kerr v. Cotton,
  23 Tex. 411, 1859 WL 6291 (1859) 3-13:3.5

Khan v. Chaudhry,
  No. 09-14-00479-CV, 2016 Tex. App. LEXIS 3035
  (App.—Beaumont Mar. 24, 2016) 3-1:3.6

Kidd v. Hoggett,
  331 S.W.2d 515 (Tex. Civ. App.—San Antonio 1959,
  writ ref'd n.r.e.) 7-10:1.1, 7-10:2, 7-10:4.1

Kilpatrick v. McKenzie,
  230 S.W.3d 207 (Tex. App.—Houston [14th Dist.] 2006, no pet.) 7-2:2

King Ranch v. Chapman
  118 S.W.3d 742 (Tex. 2003) 30-2:4

King v. Acker,
  725 S.W.2d 750, 754 (Tex. App.—Houston [1st Dist.] 1987,
  no writ) 1-2:3.1

King v. Dallas Fire Ins.,
  85 S.W.3d 185, 188 (Tex. 2002) 5-6:2

King v. Lyons,
  457 S.W.3d 122, 126 (citing *Roark v. Allen,*
  633 S.W.2d 804, 809–10 (Tex. 1982) 8-2:3

Kinney v. Barnes,
  443 S.W.3d 87 (Tex. 2014) 1-8:4.2

Kinsel v. Lindsey,
  526 S.W.3d 411, 426 (Tex. 2017) 8-5:2

Kinzbach Tool Co. v. Corbett-Wallace Corp.,
  138 Tex. 565, 573–74, 160 S.W.2d 509, 514 (1942) 11-4

Kirby Forest Indus., Inc. v. Dobbs,
  743 S.W.2d 348, 352 (Tex. App.—Beaumont 1987, writ denied) 14-4

Kissman v. Bendix Home Sys., Inc.,
  587 S.W.2d 675, 677 (Tex. 1979) 10-2

TABLE OF CASES

Kizer v. Meyer, Lytton, Alen & Whitaker, Inc., 228 S.W.3d 384 (Tex. App.—Austin 2007, no pet.)	20-2
Klemm v. Schroeder, 204 S.W.2d 675, 676–7 (Tex. Civ. App.—1947, no writ)	17-4:1
Knandel v. Cameron, 263 S.W.2d 184 (Tex. Civ. App.—San Antonio 1953, no writ.)	3-1:4.5
Knox v. Taylor, 992 S.W.2d 40, 60 (Tex. App.—Houston [14th Dist.] 1999, no pet.)	1-1:3.1c, 1-2:3.1c
Kodiak Res., Inc. v. Smith, 361 S.W.3d 246 (Tex. App.—Beaumont 2012, no pet.)	7-3:5.2
Kondos v. Carrico, No. 2-05-374-CV, 2007 WL 704587, at *4 (Tex. App.—Fort Worth Mar. 8, 2007, pet. denied)	21-3
Koral Indus. v. Security-Conn. Life Ins., 802 S.W.2d 650, 651 (Tex. 1990)	5-3:4.3
Kosa v. Dall. Lite & Barricade, Inc., 228 S.W.3d 428 (Tex. App.—Dallas 2007, no pet.)	6-2:2
Kotis v. Nowlin Jewelry, Inc., 844 S.W.2d 920, 922 (Tex. App.—Houston [14th Dist.] 1992, no writ)	1-3:4.3
KPMG Peat Marwick v. Harrison Cty. Hous. Fin. Corp., 988 S.W.2d 746 (Tex. 1999)	1-10:4.1
Krabbe v. Andarko Petroleum Corp., 46 S.W.3d 308 (Tex. App.—Amarillo, 2001, pet. denied)	7-5:4.1
Kraft v. Langford, 565 S.W.2d 223, 227 (Tex. 1978)	11-8:1, 12-2:2
Kramer v. Kastleman, 508 S.W.3d 211 (Tex. 2017)	16-12:3
Krayem v. USRP (PAC), L.P., 194 S.W.3d 91 (Tex. App.—Dallas 2006, pet denied)	3-1:2
Kreimerman v. Casa Veerkamp, S.A. de C.V., 22 F.3d 634 (5th Cir. 1994)	27-5:1
Kress v. Soules, 152 Tex. 595, 597, 261 S.W.2d 703, 704 (1953)	8-3:2
Krishnan v. Ramirez, 42 S.W.3d 205, 225 (Tex. App.—Corpus Christ 2001, pet. denied)	29-7
Krumnow v. Krumnow, 174 S.W.3d 820, 828 (Tex. App.—Waco 2005, pet. denied)	8-9:5.1
Kshatrya v. Tex. Workforce Commc'n, 97 S.W.3d 825, 832 (Tex. App.—Dallas 2003, no pet.)	13-2:5

L. H. Lacy Co. v. City of Lubbock,
    559 S.W.2d 348 (Tex. 1977)   25-1:3

L Series, L.L.C. v. Holt,
    571 S.W.3d 864, 876 (Tex. App.—Fort Worth 2019, pet. denied)   8-3:2

Laidlaw Waste Sys. v. City of Wilmer,
    904 S.W.2d 656, 661 (Tex. 1995)   30-3:10

Lam v. Phuong Nguyen,
    335 S.W.3d 786 (Tex. App.—Dallas 2011, pet. denied)   16-16:2

Lamajak, Inc. v. Frazin,
    230 S.W.3d 786 (Tex. App.—Dallas 2007, no pet.)   3-3:4.1

Lamar Homes, Inc. v. Mid-Continent Cas. Co.,
    242 S.W.3d 1 (Tex. 2007)   5-1:1.2

LandAmerica Commonwealth Title Co. v. Wido,
    No. 05-14-00036-CV, 2015 Tex. App. LEXIS 11201, at *14
    (Tex. App.—Dallas Oct. 29, 2015, no pet.)   3-11:2.1

Lance v. Robinson,
    543 S.W.3d 723, 735 (Tex. 2018)   7-2:1

Landmark Org., L.P. v. Delphini Constr. Co.,
    No. 13-04-371-CV, 2005 Tex. App. LEXIS 8414, at *15
    (Tex. App.—Corpus Christi 2005, pet. denied)   3-1:3.9, 5-3:3.3, 5-7:3.4, 6-1:3.2

Landon v. S & H Mktg. Grp., Inc.,
    82 S.W.3d 666 (Tex. App.—Eastland 2002, no pet.)   2-11:4.3

Landry's Seafood House-Addison, Inc. v. Snadon,
    233 S.W.3d 430, 436 (Tex. App.—Dallas 2007, pet. denied)   12-1

Landscape Design & Const., Inc. v. Warren,
    566 S.W.2d 66, 66 (Tex. Civ. App.—Dallas 1978, no writ)   13-4:4

Lang v. Lee,
    777 S.W.2d 158 (Tex. App.-Dallas 1989)   3-13:2

Langston v. Eagle Publ'g Co.,
    719 S.W.2d 612 (Tex. App.—Waco 1986, writ ref'd n.r.e.)   2-8:4.2

LAN/STV v. Constr. Co.,
    435 S.W.3d 234 (Tex. 2014)   1-7:4.2

LAN/STV v. Martin K. Eby Constr. Co.,
    435 S.W.3d 234, 235–36 (Tex. 2014)   1-7:1.1, 1-7:2, 12-3

Laredo Med. Grp. Corp. v. Mireles,
    155 S.W.3d 417 (Tex. App.—San Antonio 2004, pet. denied)   6-2:2

Larson v. Family Violence & Sexual Assault Prevention Ctr.,
    64 S.W.3d 506, 517 (Tex. App.—Corpus Christi 2001,
    pet. denied)   1-2:2

Latch v. Gratty, Inc.,
    107 S.W.3d 543 (Tex. 2003)   3-12:3.1

TABLE OF CASES

Latham v. Burgher,
320 S.W.3d 602 (Tex. App.—Dallas 2010, no pet.)   2-13:2.1, 2-13:2.2

Lawler v. Collin Cty.,
No. 05-95-00487-CV, 1996 WL 403986, at *2
(Tex. App.—Dallas 1996, writ denied)   30-1:2

Lazer Spot, Inc. v. Hiring Partners, Inc.,
387 S.W.3d 40, 51 (Tex. App.—Texarkana 2012, pet. denied)   1-1:2

Lechuga v. Tex. Emp'rs Ins. Assoc.,
791 S.W.2d 182, 184 (Tex. App.—Amarillo 1990, writ denied)   13-4:5

Ledig v. Duke Energy Corp.,
193 S.W.3d 167 (Tex. App.—Houston [1st Dist.] 2006, no pet.)   3-1:3.3

Lee v. Catlin Specialty Ins.,
766 F. Supp. 2d 812, 825–26 (S.D. Tex. 2011)   5-1:2

Lee v. Hasson,
286 S.W.3d 1 (Tex. App.—Houston [14th Dist.] 2007, pet. denied)   1-6:2

Lee v. Key West Towers, Inc.,
783 S.W.2d 586, 588 (Tex. 1989)   13-3:4

Lee-Wright, Inc. v. Hall,
840 S.W.2d 572 (Tex. App.—Houston [1st Dist.] 1992, no writ)   6-1:4.2

Lehmann v. Har-Con Corp.,
39 S.W.3d 191, 192–93 (Tex. 2001)   30-4:2

Lemos v. Montez,
680 S.W.2d 798, 800–01 (Tex. 1984)   19-2

Leonard v. Eskew,
731 S.W.2d 124, 131–33 (Tex. App.—Austin 1987, writ ref'd n.r.e.)   11-11:3

Leonard v. Texaco, Inc.,
422 S.W.2d 160 (Tex. 1967)   29-2

Lerma v. Border Demolition & Envtl., Inc.,
459 S.W.3d 695, 507 (Tex. App.—El Paso 2015, pet. denied)   3-1:3.2

Lesikar v. Rappeport,
33 S.W.3d 282, 310 (Tex. App.—Texarkana 2000, pet. denied)   8-5:3.3

Lewis v. Bank of Am. NA,
343 F.3d 540 (5th Cir. 2003)   1-4:2

Lewis v. Davis,
145 Tex. 468, 199 S.W.2d 146 (1947)   16-16:2

Lewkowicz v. El Paso Apparel Corp.,
625 S.W.2d 301 (Tex. 1981)   16-13, 16-13:1, 16-13:2

Lexington Ins. Co. v. Daybreak Express, Inc.,
393 S.W.3d 242 (Tex. 2013)   29-2

Liberty Mut. Ins. Co. v. Garrison Contractors,
966 S.W.2d 482, 487 (Tex. 1998)   5-2:3

Libhart v. Copeland,
    949 S.W.2d 783, 797 (Tex. App.—Waco 1997, no writ)   29-7

Lifshutz v. Lifshutz,
    199 S.W.3d 9 (Tex. App.—San Antonio 2006, pet. denied)   2-11:2, 2-11:4.4

Lighthouse Church of Cloverleaf v. Tex. Bank,
    889 S.W.2d 595 (Tex. App.—Houston [14th Dist.] 1994, writ denied)   9-4:1, 9-4:2

Lilani v. Noorali,
    No. H-09-2617, 2011 U.S. Dist. LEXIS 440, at *36–38 (S.D. Tex. Jan. 3, 2011)   11-4, 11-11:2

Limestone Grp., Inc. v. Sai Thong, L.L.C.,
    107 S.W.3d 793, 796–97 (Tex. App.—Amarillo 2003, no pet.)   8-3:4.4

Lincoln General Ins. Co. v. U.S. Auto Ins. Servs.,
    892 F. Supp. 2d 787 (N.D. Tex. 2012)   1-3:2, 8-5:2

Lindsey v. Williams,
    228 S.W.2d 243, 250 (Tex. Civ. App.—Texarkana 1950, no writ)   8-6:5.5

Lippincott v. Whisenhunt,
    462 S.W.3d 507, 509 (Tex. 2015)   1-8:4.5, 28-4

Lisitsa v. Flit,
    419 S.W.3d 672, 678 (Tex. App.—Houston [14th Dist.] 2013, pet. filed)   13-2:4

Little v. Clark,
    592 S.W.2d 61 (Tex. Civ. App.—Fort Worth 1979, writ ref'd n.r.e.)   3-11:4.1

Little v. Smith,
    943 S.W.2d 414 (Tex. 1997)   1-4:4.1

Livingston Ford Mercury, Inc. v. Haley,
    997 S.W.2d 425, 429 (Tex. App.—Beaumont 1999, no pet.)   14-7, 17-10

Livingston v. Livingston,
    537 S.W.3d 578, 588 (Tex. App.—Houston [1st Dist.] 2017, no pet.)   8-2:2

Lloyd v. Holland,
    659 S.W.2d 103, 105–06 (Tex. App.—Houston [14th Dist.] 1983)   8-3:2

Lochabay v. Sw. Bell Media, Inc.,
    828 S.W.2d 167 (Tex. App.—Austin 1992, no writ)   30-1:3

Lockheed Martin Corp. v. Gordon,
    16 S.W.3d 127 (Tex. App.—Houston [1st Dist.] 2000, pet. denied)   9-13:1, 9-13:2

Lodge v. Lodge,
    368 S.W.2d 40, 41 (Tex. App.—Austin 1963, no writ)   24-1:10

Loftus v. Maxey,
    11 S.W. 272 (Tex. 1889)   16-9:1

Logan v. Mullis,
    686 S.W.2d 605, 607–08 (Tex. 1985)   11-8:2

TABLE OF CASES

London v. London,
   192 S.W.3d 6 (Tex. App.—Houston [14th Dist.] 2005, pet. denied)   3-6:2

Long Distance Int'l, Inc. v Telefonos de Mexico,
   49 S.W.3d 347, 351 (Tex. 2001)   24-3:2

Long v. Miken Oil, Inc.,
   No. 12-13-00252-CV, 2014 Tex. App. LEXIS 9189
   (App.—Tyler Aug. 20, 2014)   3-7:2

Long v. Tanner,
   170 S.W.3d 752 (Tex. App.—Waco 2005, pet. denied)   9-15:1.1, 9-15:2

Longoria v. Exxon Mobil Corp.,
   255 S.W.3d 174, 180 (Tex. App.—San Antonio 2008, pet. denied)   8-10:4.1

Longview Energy Co. v. Huff Energy Fund LP,
   533 S.W.3d 866, 873 (Tex. 2017)   8-5:2

Loomis v. Republic Nat'l Bank of Dallas,
   653 S.W.2d 75, 77 (Tex. App.—Dallas 1983, writ ref'd n.r.e.)   17-10

Lopez v. Bucholz,
   No. 03-15-00034-CV, 2017 Tex. App. LEXIS 3071
   (Tex. App.—Austin Apr. 7, 2017)   3-1:2

Lopez v. Munoz, Hockema & Reed, L.L.P.,
   22 S.W.3d 857 (Tex. 2000)   3-1:3.17, 16-3, 16-3:1, 16-3:3

Louisiana v. Rowan Cos. Inc.,
   728 F. Supp. 2d 896 (S.D. Tex. 2010)   7-9:2, 7-9:4.5

Louisville & N.R. Co. v. Mottley,
   211 U.S. 149, 152 (1908)   27-2:1

LPMG Peat Marwick v. Harrison Cty. Hous. Fin. Corp.,
   988 S.W.2d 746 (Tex. 1999)   1-9:4.1, 1-10:4.1, 1-11:4.1

Lubel v. J.H. Uptmore & Assocs.,
   680 S.W.2d 518, 520 (Tex. App.—San Antonio 1984, no writ)   8-3:2

Lucey v. Se. Texas Emergency Physicians Assoc.,
   802 S.W.2d 300, 302 (Tex. App.—El Paso 1990, writ denied)   21-2:1

Lucio v. John G. & Marie Stella Kenedy Mem'l Found.,
   298 S.W.3d 663, 672 (Tex. App.—Corpus
   Christi-Edinburg 2009, pet. denied)   1-3:2, 9-4:1, 9-4:1.1, 9-4:2

Lufkin Indus., Inc. v. Mission Chevrolet, Inc.,
   614 S.W.2d 596 (Tex. App.—Waco 1981)   3-9:2

Lujan v. Defs. of Wildlife,
   504 U.S. 555 (1992)   7-9:4.2

Lujan v. Navistar, Inc.,
   555 S.W.3d 79, 86 (Tex. 2018)   30-3:7

Luna v. N. Star Dodge Sales, Inc.,
   667 S.W.2d 115, 119 (Tex. 1984)   1-3:3.1b, 12-2:1

Lynd v. Bass Pro Outdoor World, Inc.,
   05-12-00968-CV, 2014 WL 1010120, at *8
   (Tex. App.—Dallas Mar. 12, 2014, pet. denied) ... 8-2:2

Lynn v. First Nat'l Bank,
   40 S.W. 228 (Tex. Civ. App. 1897, no writ) ... 8-9:1

Lyons v. Millers Cas. Ins.,
   866 S.W.2d 597, 601 (Tex. 1993) ... 5-3:4.2

Lyons v. Ortego,
   01-17-00092-CV, 2018 WL 4014218, at *5
   (Tex. App.—Houston [1st Dist.] Aug. 23, 2018, pet. denied) ... 8-3:2

M & A Technology, Inc. v. iValue Grp., Inc.,
   295 S.W.3d 356, 366–67 (Tex. App.—El Paso 2009, pet. denied) ... 11-6:1

M & M Constr. Co. v. Great Am. Ins. Co.,
   747 S.W.2d 552, 554 (Tex. App.—Corpus 1988, no writ) ... 28-3

Mabry v. Priester,
   338 S.W.2d 704 (Tex. 1960) ... 16-13:2

MacDonald v. Bank of Kerrville,
   849 S.W.2d 371, 372 (Tex. App.—San Antonio 1993, writ dism'd) ... 13-3:2

Mack v. Newton,
   737 F.2d 1343, 1363 (5th Cir. 1984) ... 2-1:3.3, 2-2:3.3

Mackie v. Guthrie,
   78 S.W.3d 462, 468 (Tex. App.—Tyler 2001, pet. denied) ... 30-3:9

Madera Prod. Co. v. Atl. Richfield Co.,
   107 S.W.3d 652 (Tex. App.—Texarkana 2003,
   pet. denied) ... 7-1:5.1, 7-2:5.1, 7-3:5.1, 7-5:5.1, 7-6:5.1, 7-10:5.1

Maddux v. Reid,
   No. 10-13-00174-CV, 2015 Tex. App. LEXIS 6245
   (App.—Waco June 18, 2015) ... 3-9:1.1, 3-10:2.1

Magee v. Young,
   198 S.W.2d 883 (Tex. 1946) ... 7-7:3.1

Maldonado v. Franklin,
   04-18-00819-CV, 2019 WL 4739438, at *3
   (Tex. App.—San Antonio Sept. 30, 2019, no pet.) ... 8-1:3.2

Man Engines & Components, Inc. v. Shows,
   434 S.W.3d 132, 57 Tex. Sup. Ct. J. 661 (Tex. 2014) ... 13-5:1

Mandell & Wright v. Thomas,
   441 S.W.2d 841 (Tex. 1969) ... 3-1:4.5, 3-2:2.1

Mandril v. Kasishke,
   620 S.W.2d 238 (Tex. Civ. App.—Amarillo 1981
   writ ref'd n.r.e.) ... 3-1:4.20

TABLE OF CASES

Mansfield Heliflight, Inc. v. Bell/Agusta Aero. Co.,
No. 4:06-CV-425-A, 2007 U.S. Dist. LEXIS 79548, at *15
(N.D. Tex. Oct. 26, 2007) — 6-1:3.2

Marathon Oil Co. v. Gulf Oil Corp.,
130 S.W.2d 365 (Tex. Civ. App.—El Paso 1939) — 7-8:4.1, 17-10

Marin v. IESI TX Corp.,
317 S.W.3d 314, 332 (Tex. App.—Houston [1st Dist.] 2010, pet. denied) — 11-12

Markwardt v. Tex. Indus., Inc.,
325 S.W.3d 876, 894 (Tex. App.—Houston [14th Dist.] 2010, no pet.) — 17-11:1

Marrs & Smith P'ship v. D.K. Boyd Oil & Gas Co., Inc.,
223 S.W.3d 1 (Tex. App.—El Paso, 2005) — 7-10:1, 7-10:2

Marsh v. Orville Carr Assocs., Inc.,
433 S.W.2d 928 (Tex. Civ. App.—San Antonio 1968, writ ref'd n.r.e.) — 3-2:2.2

Marshall v. Mahaffey,
974 S.W.2d 942, 947–50 (Tex. App.—Beaumont 1998, pet. denied) — 22-4

Marsoft, Inc. v. United LNG, L.P.,
CIV.A. H-13-2332, 2014 WL 5386094, at *9 (S.D. Tex. Oct. 21, 2014) — 8-8:4.2

Martin v. Amerman,
133 S.W.3d 262 (Tex. 2004) — 7-1:3.2, 7-2:1, 7-2:1.1, 7-3:1.1

Martin v. Martin, Martin, & Richards, Inc.,
989 S.W.2d 357, 359 (Tex. 1998) — 30-3:1

Martin v. Trevino,
578 S.W.2d 763 (Tex. Civ. App.—Corpus Christi 1978) — 9-16:1, 9-16:1.1, 9-16:2

Martinez v. ACCC Ins.,
343 S.W.3d 924, 929 (Tex. App.—Dallas 2011, no pet.) — 5-6:4.3

Martinez v. Hays Constr., Inc.,
355 S.W.3d 170 (Tex. App.—Houston [1st Dist.] 2011, no pet.) — 1-9:2

Marx v. Elec. Data Sys. Corp.,
418 S.W.3d 626 (Tex. App.—Amarillo 2009, no pet.) — 6-2:1.1, 6-2:2

Mary Kay, Inc. v. Weber,
601 F. Supp. 2d 839 (N.D. Tex. 2009) — 1-12:4.1, 1-14:4.1

Mas v. Perry,
489 F.2d 1396, 1399 (5th Cir. 1974) — 27-3:3.1

Mason v. Mason,
07-12-00007-CV, 2014 WL 199649, at *17
(Tex. App.—Amarillo Jan. 13, 2014, no pet.) — 11-13:1

Mastrogiovanni Schorsch & Mersky, P.C. v. Mandel,
139 S. Ct. 1333, 203 L. Ed. 2d 568 (2019) — 8-9:3.1

Maswoswe v. Nelson,
327 S.W.3d 889, 895 (Tex. App.—Beaumont 2010, no pet.) — 29-6

Matagorda Cty. Appraisal Dist. v. Coastal Liquids Partners, L.P.,
  165 S.W.3d 329 (Tex. 2005) — 6-1:4.6

Matal v. Tam — 1-13:4.2

Mathis v. Bocell,
  982 S.W.2d 52, 58 (Tex. App.—Houston [1st Dist.] 1998, no pet.) — 30-3:5, 30-3:10

Matrixx Initiatives, Inc. v. Siracusano,
  563 U.S. 27, 38 (2011) — 2-4:2.1, 2-4:2.2, 2-4:2.3

Matter of Bennett,
  989 F.2d 779, 790 (5th Cir. 1993) — 2-10:3.5

Matter of Mandel,
  747 Fed. Appx. 955, 961 (5th Cir. 2018) — 8-9:3.1

Matter of UTSA Apartments 8, L.L.C.,
  886 F.3d 473, 492 (5th Cir. 2018) — 2-10:2

Matthews Constr. Co., Inc. v. Rosen,
  796 S.W.2d 692 (Tex. 1990) — 2-13:4.1

Matz v. Bennion,
  961 S.W.2d 445 (Tex. App.—Houston [1st Dist.] 1997, pet. denied) — 2-15:5.2

Mauriceville Nat'l Bank v. Zernial,
  880 S.W.2d 282 (Tex. App.—Beaumont 1994),
  rev'd on other grounds, 892 S.W.2d 858 (Tex. 1995) — 7-8:3.2

Maxus Expl. v. Moran Brothers,
  817 S.W.2d 50, 53 (Tex. 1991) — 24-1:5

Mayfield v. Lockheed Eng'g & Scis. Co.,
  970 S.W.2d 185, 187 (Tex. App.—Houston [14th Dist.] 1998,
  pet. denied) — 6-2:2

Mays v. Pierce,
  203 S.W.3d 564 (Tex. App.—Houston [14th Dist.] 2006, pet. denied) — 3-1:3.1b

MBM Fin. Corp. v. Woodlands Operating Co.,
  292 S.W.3d 660 (Tex. 2009) — 3-1:3.5

McAllen Hospitals, L.P. v. State Farm Cty. Mut. Ins. Co. of Tex.,
  No. 12-0983, 2014 WL 1998245 (Tex. May 16, 2014) — 16-5:2

McCaig v. Wells Fargo Bank, N.A.,
  788 F.3d 463, 474–75 (5th Cir. 2015) — 12-3

McCamish, Martin, Brown & Loeffler v. F.E. Appling Interests,
  991 S.W.2d 787 (Tex. 1999) — 1-7:1.1, 1-7:2, 9-1:1, 9-1:1.1, 9-1:2

McCammon v. Ischy,
  No. 03-06-00707-CV, 2010 Tex. App. LEXIS 3642
  (Tex. App.—Austin May 12, 2010, pet. filed) — 7-2:5.4

McClure v. Attebury,
  20 S.W.3d 722, 729 (Tex. App.—Amarillo 1999, no pet.) — 30-2:1

TABLE OF CASES

McCollum v. Dollar,
   213 S.W. 259 (Tex. Comm'n App. 1919)   2-1:2.1

McConathy v. McConathy,
   869 S.W.2d 341, 341 (Tex. 1994)   30-3:8

McConnell v. Southside ISD,
   858 S.W.2d 337, 339–40 (Tex. 1993)   30-1:3, 30-1:5, 30-1:6,
                                                                                 30-1:10, 30-3:10

McCormick v. Hines,
   498 S.W.2d 58, 64
   (Tex. Civ. App.—Amarillo 1973, writ dism'd)   8-3:2

McCullough-Baroid Petroleum Serv. NL Indus. v. Sexton,
   618 S.W.2d 119, 120 (Tex. App.—Corpus Christi 1981,
   writ ref'd n.r.e.)   12-2:2

McDonald Transit, Inc. v. Moore,
   565 S.W.2d 43, 44 (Tex. 1978)   15-4:2

McDonnell Douglas Corp. v. Green,
   411 U.S. 792 (1973)   6-3:1.1, 6-3:2

McFadden v. Hale,
   615 S.W.2d 345, 348 (Tex. App.—Waco 1981, no writ)   29-6

McFarland v. Sanders,
   932 S.W.2d 640, 645–46 (Tex. App.—Tyler 1996, no writ)   3-1:3.2, 11-4, 11-11:4

McGowan & Co., Inc. v. Bogan,
   No. CIV.A. H-12-1716, 2015 WL 3422366 n.6
   (S.D. Tex. May 27, 2015)   1-2:3.2

McGuired, Craddock, Strother & Hale, P.C. v. Transcon. Rlty. Inv'rs, Inc.,
   251 S.W.3d 890 (Tex. App.—Dallas 2008, pet. denied)   4-1:1

McJam, Inc. v. CD Auto Serv.,
   No. 04-17-00849-CV, 2018 Tex. App. LEXIS 9966, at *6
   (Tex. App.—San Antonio Dec. 5, 2018, no pet.)   3-8:2.1

McKanna v. Edgar,
   388 S.W.2d 927 (Tex. 1965)   23-3

McKinney/Pearl Rest. Partners, L.P. v. Metro. Life Ins. Co.,
   241 F. Supp. 3d 737, 774 (N.D. Tex. 2017)   8-3:2

McShan v. Pitts,
   554 S.W.2d 759 (Tex. App.—San Antonio 1977, no writ)   7-2:4.2

McVea v. Verkins,
   587 S.W.2d 526 (Tex. Civ. App.—Corpus Christi 1979, no writ)   3-9:3.10

Mead v. Johnson Grp., Inc.,
   615 S.W.2d 685, 688 (Tex. 1981)   3-1:2, 3-1:3.1, 5-3:3.1b, 11-9:1

Meadows v. Bierschwale,
   516 S.W.2d 125, 128 (Tex. 1974)   8-5:2

Medina v. Benkiser,
   262 S.W.3d 25, 27 (Tex. App.—Houston [1st Dist.] 2008, no pet.)   21-1:2, 21-1:3

MEI, Inc. v. Griffin,
   No. 05-10-00071-CV, 2012 WL 1537460, at *1 n.1
   (Tex. App.—Dallas May 1, 2012, no pet.)   13-3:3

Melendez v. Padilla,
   304 S.W.3d 850 (Tex. App.—El Paso 2010, no pet.)   16-3

Mellon Mortg. Co. v. Holder,
   5 S.W.3d 654 (Tex. 1999)   1-10:2

Melody Home Mfg. Co. v. Barnes,
   741 S.W.2d 349 (Tex. 1987)   9-21:2

Mensa-Wilmot v. Smith Int'l, Inc.,
   312 S.W.3d 771, 778 (Tex. App.—Houston [1st Dist.] 2009, no pet.)   29-3

Mercedes-Benz of N. Am., Inc. v. Dickenson,
   720 S.W.2d 844 (Tex. App.—Fort Worth 1986, no writ)   3-12:4.1

Mercedes-Benz USA, LLC v. Carduco, Inc.,
   583 S.W.3d 553, 558–59 (Tex. 2019)   1-4:4.5, 1-6:2

Merck & Co. v. Reynolds,
   559 U.S. 633 (2010)   2-4:4.3

Merit Mgmt. Partners I, L.P. v. Noelke,
   266 S.W.3d 637 (Tex. App.—Austin, 2008)   7-4:1

Merrell Dow Pharm., Inc. v. Thompson,
   478 U.S. 804, 808 (1986)   27-2:1

Methodist Healthcare Sys. of San Antonio Ltd, LLP v. Rankin,
   307 S.W.3d 283, 292 (Tex. 2010)   17-13:3

Metro Ford Truck Sales, Inc. v. Davis,
   709 S.W.2d 785 (Tex. App.—Fort Worth 1986)   12-2:2

Meyer v. Cathey,
   167 S.W.3d 327 (Tex. 2005)   1-6:2

Meyers v. Moody,
   693 F.2d 1196 (5th Cir. 1982)   2-1:1.1, 2-1:2.1, 2-1:3.1, 2-1:3.2, 2-1:5.1,
   2-2:2.1, 2-2:3.1, 2-2:3.2, 2-2:5.1, 2-11:3.5

MGA Ins. Co. v. Charles R. Chesnutt, P.C.,
   358 S.W.3d 808, 815 (Tex. App.—Dallas 2012, no pet.)   30-3:9

Mid-Century Ins. Co. v. Barclay,
   880 S.W.2d 807, 813 (Tex. App.—Austin 1994, writ denied)   5-1:3.4

Mid-Century Ins. Co. v. Childs,
   15 S.W.3d 187, 189–90 (Tex. App.—Texarkana 2000, no pet.)   5-7:4.3

Mid-Continent Ins. Co. v. Liberty Mut. Ins. Co.,
   236 S.W.3d 765 (Tex. 2007)   9-10:1, 9-10:1.1, 9-10:2

TABLE OF CASES

Middlebrook v. David Bradley Mfg. Co.,
86 Tex. 706, 26 S.W. 935 (1894) — 22-6

Midgett v. J. Edelstein Furniture Co.,
700 S.W.2d 332, 333 (Tex. App.—Corpus Christi 1985, no writ) — 14-12

Midland Judicial Dist. Cmty. Supervision & Corr. Dep't v. Jones,
92 S.W.3d 486, 487 (Tex. 2002) — 6-1

Midwest Emp'rs Cas. Co. v. Harpole,
293 S.W.3d 770 (Tex. App.—San Antonio 2009, no pet.) — 1-10:2

Midwest Oil Corp. v. Winsauer,
323 S.W.2d 944 (1959) — 7-5:4.1

Midwestern Cattle Mktg., L.L.C. v. Legend Bank, N. A.,
800 Fed. Appx. 239, 247 (5th Cir. 2020) — 2-10:3.6

Mijares v. Paez,
534 S.W.2d 435, 436 (Tex. App.—Amarillo 1976, no writ) — 22-3

Milam v. Nat'l Ins. Crime Bureau,
989 S.W.2d 126, 132 (Tex. App.—San Antonio 1999, no pet.) — 1-2:2

Miller v. Keyes,
206 S.W.2d 120, 121 (Tex. App.—Austin 1947, writ ref'd n.r.e.) — 29-1, 29-5

Miller v. Recovery Sys., Inc.,
No. 02-12-00468-CV, 2013 WL 5303060, at *26–27
(Tex. App.—Fort Worth Sept. 19, 2013, pet. denied) — 11-11:3

Mitchell v. La Flamme,
60 S.W.3d 123, 132 (Tex. App.—Houston [14th Dist.] 2000, no pet.) — 11-13:1, 29-7

Mobil Producing Tex. & New Mexico, Inc. v. Cantor,
93 S.W.3d 916, 920 (Tex. App.—Corpus Christi 2002, no pet.) — 11-13:1

Mollan v. Torrance,
9 Wheat. 537, 6 L. Ed. 154 (1824) — 27-3:3.4

Mondragon v. Austin,
954 S.W.2d 191 (Tex. App.—Austin 1997, pet. denied) — 12-1, 12-2:2

Monk v. Pomberg,
263 S.W.3d 199, 207–08 (Tex. App.—Houston [1st Dist.] 2007, no pet.) — 8-10:2

Montalvo v. Lopez,
466 S.W.3d 290, 292 (Tex. App.—San Antonio 2015, no pet.) — 17-11:3

Montgomery Cty. Hosp. Dist. v. Brown,
965 S.W.2d 501, 502 (Tex. 1998) — 6-1, 6-1:2, 6-2:2

Montgomery v. Browder,
930 S.W.2d 772, 779 (Tex. App.—Amarillo 1996) — 8-3:2

Moody v. Temple Nat'l Bank,
545 S.W.2d 289, 290 (Tex. App.—Austin 1977, no writ) — 30-1:3

Moore v. Bushman,
   559 S.W.3d 645 (Tex. App.—Houston [14th Dist.] 2018, no pet.)   1-1:2

Moore v. Dallas Entm't Co., Inc.,
   496 S.W.2d 711, 713 (Tex. Civ. App.—Tyler 1973, no writ)   19-3

Moore v. Elektro-Mobil Tecknik GmbH,
   874 S.W.2d 306 (Tex. App.—El Paso 1994, writ denied)   13-2:1, 13-2:4

Moore v. Trevino,
   94 S.W.3d 723, 729 (Tex. App.—San Antonio 2002, pet. denied)   11-13:2

Moreno v. Sterling Drug, Inc.,
   787 S.W.2d 348, 351 (Tex. 1990)   17-10

Morris v. Collins,
   881 S.W.2d 138, 140 (Tex. App.—Houston [1st Dist.] 1994,
   pet. denied)   8-2:2

Morris v. N. Fort Worth State Bank,
   300 S.W.2d 314, 315 (Tex. Civ. App.—Fort Worth 1957, no writ)   8-9:2.2

Morton v. Nguyen,
   412 S.W.3d 506, 510 (Tex. 2013)   11-11:3

Mosley v. Elec. & Missile Facilities, Inc.,
   374 U.S. 167, 83 S. Ct. 1815, 10 L. Ed. 2d 818 (1963)   25-1:1

Moulton v. Alamo Ambulance Serv., Inc.,
   414 S.W.2d 444, 448 (Tex. 1967)   12-1, 13-6:2, 15-3

Moveforfree .com, Inc. v. David Hetrick, Inc.,
   288 S.W.3d 539, 541–42 (Tex. App.—Houston [14th Dist.]
   2009, no pet.)   22-1, 22-3

Mowbray v. Avery,
   76 S.W.3d 663, 680–81 (Tex. App.—Corpus
   Christi 2002, pet. denied)   3-4:3.1, 3-4:5.1, 7-7:4.1, 11-11:2

M.R. Champion, Inc. v. Mizell,
   904 S.W.2d 617 (Tex. 1995)   2-10:2

Mun. Power Agency v. Pub. Util. Comm'n of Tex.,
   253 S.W.3d 184, 200 (Tex. 2007)   8-10:4.2

Murphy v. Campbell,
   964 S.W.2d 265, 270 (Tex. 1997)   17-10, 17-11:2

Murray v. O & A Express, Inc.,
   630 S.W.2d 633, 636–37 (Tex. 1982)   19-1

Murray v. San Jacinto Agency, Inc.,
   800 S.W.2d 826, 829 (Tex. 1990)   5-7:2, 17-12

Murray v. U.S. Bank Nat'l Ass'n,
   411 S.W.3d 926, 928 (Tex. App.—El Paso 2013)   8-11:2.2

Musterman v. Acme Engine Rebuilding Co.,
   383 S.W.2d 620, 622 (Tex. Civ. App.—Houston 1964)   8-6:4.2

TABLE OF CASES

Meyers v. JDC/Firethorne, LTD.,
548 S.W.3d 477, 485 (Tex. 2018) — 7-9:4.2

Myers v. Walker,
61 S.W.3d 722, 729–30 (Tex. App.—Eastland 2001, pet. denied) — 11-5:7

Nabers v. Nabers,
14-18-00968-CV, 2020 WL 830025, at *3
(Tex. App.—Houston [14th Dist.] Feb. 20, 2020, no pet. h.) — 8-10:3.2

Nabors Drilling, U.S.A. Inc. v. Escoto,
288 S.W.3d 401 (Tex. 2009) — 1-10:2

Nabors Well Services Ltd. v. Romero,
456 S.W.3d 553 (Tex. 2015) — 12-1, 18-2:2, 18-3

Nacogdoches Cty. v. Marshall,
469 S.W.2d 633 (Tex. Civ. App.—Tyler 1971, no writ) — 2-8:4.2

Naegeli Transp. v. Gulf Electroquip, Inc.,
853 S.W.2d 737, 739 (Tex. App.—Houston
[14th Dist.] 1993, writ denied) — 11-5:4.1, 11-5:4.2, 11-5:7, 11-6:3

Nagle v. Nagle,
633 S.W.2d 796 (Tex. 1982) — 3-5:2.2, 3-5:3.2, 16-12:2

Nalle Plastics Family v. Porter,
406 S.W.3d 186, 195 (Tex. App.—Corpus Christi-Edinburg
2013, pet. denied) — 22-1

Nash v. Conatser,
410 S.W.2d 512, 520 (Tex. Civ. App.—Dallas 1966, no writ) — 3-1:3.16, 8-3:2

Nassar v. Liberty Mut. Fire Ins. Co.,
508 S.W.3d 254, 257 (Tex. 2017) — 5-5:1

Nath v. Tex. Children's Hosp.,
446 S.W.3d 355, 370 (Tex. 2014) *reh'g denied* (Nov. 21, 2014) — 1-1:4.1, 1-2:4.1

National Bankers Life Ins. Co. v. Adler,
324 S.W.2d 35 (Tex. Civ. App.—San Antonio 1959, no writ) — 2-8:5.2

National Convenience Stores, Inc. v. T.T. Barge Cleaning Co.,
883 S.W.2d 684 (Tex. App.—Dallas 1994, writ denied) — 3-10:2.2

National Multiple Sclerosis Soc'y-N. Tex. Chapter v. Rice,
29 S.W.3d 174, 176–78 (Tex. App.—Eastland 2000, no pet.) — 23-1

National Union Fire Ins. v. Crocker,
246 S.W.3d 603, 608 (Tex. 2008) — 5-6:2

National Union v. Reyna,
897 S.W.2d 777, 779 (Tex. 1995) — 13-4:3

Nationwide Bi-Weekly Admin., Inc. v. Belo Corp.,
512 F.3d 137, 146–47 (5th Cir. 2007) — 1-1:4.1, 1-2:4.1, 7-2:2, 7-4:1

Nationwide Dist. Serv., Inc. v. Jones,
496 S.W.3d 221, 228 (Tex. App.—Houston [1st Dist.]
2016, no pet.) — 13-2:4

Nat'l County Mut. Fire Ins. Co. v. Johnson,
   829 S.W.2d 322, 324 (Tex. App.—Austin 1992), aff'd,
   879 S.W.2d 1 (Tex. 1993) 5-6:1.1

Natural Gas Pipeline Co. of Am. v. Pool,
   124 S.W.3d 188 (Tex. 2003) 7-4:1

Natural Gas Pipeline Co. of Am. v. Justiss,
   397 S.W.3d 150, 155 (Tex. 2012) 3-1:3.13, 11-8:1

Nears v. Holiday Hosp. Franchising, Inc.,
   295 S.W.3d 787 (Tex. App.—Texarkana 2009, no pet.) 3-11:1.1, 3-11:2.1

Neeley v. W. Orange-Cove Consol. Indep. Sch. Dist.,
   176 S.W.3d 746, 799 (Tex. 2005) 8-10:3.2

Neely v. Wilson,
   418 S.W.3d 52, 59 (Tex. 2013) 30-1:3

Nelson v. Britt,
   241 S.W.3d 672 (Tex. App.—Dallas 2007, no pet.) 13-3:3

Nelson v. Data Terminal Sys., Inc.,
   762 S.W.2d 744, 747–48 (Tex. App.—San Antonio
   1988, writ denied) 11-7:1, 11-7:3, 12-2:1

Nelson v. Regions Mortg., Inc.,
   170 S.W.3d 858, 862 (Tex. App.—Dallas 2005, no pet.) 30-2:4

Nelson Cash Register, Inc. v. Data Terminal Sys., Inc.,
   671 S.W.2d 594, 500 (Tex. App.—San Antonio 1984, no writ) 6-1:2

Neuhaus v. Kain,
   557 S.W.2d 125 (Tex. Civ. App.—Corpus Christi 1977,
   writ ref'd n.r.e.) 1-4:2

Newman v. Tropical Visions, Inc.,
   891 S.W.2d 713 (Tex. App.—San Antonio 1994,
   writ denied) 16-10:1

Newman-Green, Inc. v. Alfonzo-Larrain,
   490 U.S. 826 (1989) 27-3:3.4

Nexen, Inc. v. Gulf Interstate Eng'g Co.,
   224 S.W.3d 412, 421 (Tex. App.—Houston [1st Dist.]
   2006, no pet.) 24-1:10

Nichols v. Loral Vought Sys. Corp.,
   81 F.3d 38 (5th Cir. 1996) 6-2:2, 6-3:1.1, 6-3:2

Niemann v. Refugio Cty. Mem'l Hosp.,
   855 S.W.2d 94 (Tex. App.—Corpus Christi 1993, no writ) 30-1:7

Nixon v. Mr. Prop. Mgmt. Co.,
   690 S.W.2d 546, 549 (Tex. 1985) 1-10:2, 1-11:1.1, 30-1:7

Norman v. Apache Corp.,
   19 F.3d 1017 (5th Cir. 1994) 7-7:2

TABLE OF CASES

Norris v. Bombardier Recreational Prods., Inc.,
No. 1:08-CV-525, 2009 WL 94531, at *5 (E.D. Tex. Jan. 12, 2009) — 27-3:5

Northwest Austin Mun. Util. Dist. No. 1 v. City of Austin,
274 S.W.3d 820, 836 (Tex. App.—Austin 2008) — 5-5:4.1

Nortman v. Itex Engery Corp.,
84 C 421, 1986 WL 9564, at *8 (N.D. Ill. Aug. 26, 1986);
Mamlin v. Fairfield-Noble Corp., 433 F. Supp. 317, 319
(N.D. Tex. 1977) — 8-4:5.3

Noteboom v. Farmers Tex. Cty. Mut. Ins. Co.,
406 S.W.3d 381, 384–85 (Tex. App.—Fort. Worth 2013, no pet.) — 11-8:2, 12-2:1

Nowak v. DAS Inv. Corp.,
110 S.W.3d 677, 680 (Tex. App.—Houston [14th Dist.] 2003,
no pet.) — 30-2:2

Nowlin v. Davis,
03-18-00694-CV, 2019 WL 2440103, at *2 (Tex. App.—Austin
June 12, 2019 no pet.) — 8-10:3.2

Ogletree v. Glen Rose ISD,
314 S.W.3d 450 (Tex. App.—Waco 2010, pet. denied) — 6-1:4.6

Ohrt v. Union Gas Corp.
398 S.W.3d 315, 333 (Tex, App.—Corpus Christi-Edinburg 2012,
pet. denied) — 7-5:3.3

Old Republic Ins. Co. v. EX-IM Servs. Corp.,
920 S.W.2d 393, 396 (Tex. App.—Houston [1st Dist.] 1996, no writ) — 23-1

Old Tin Roof Steakhouse, LLC v. Haskett,
No. 04-12-00363-CV, 2013 Tex. App. LEXIS 2874, at *27
(Tex. App.—San AntonioMar. 20, 2013, no pet.) — 3-5:2.2

Olin Corp. v. Dyson,
709 S.W.2d 251, 253–54 (Tex. App.—Houston [14th Dist.] 1986,
no writ) — 18-1

Olivas v. State Farm Mut. Auto. Ins. Co.,
850 S.W.2d 564, 565–66 (Tex. App.—El. Paso 1993, writ denied) — 5-4:3.1

Omega Energy Corp. v. Gulf States Petroleum Corp.,
No. 13-03-275-CV, 2005 WL 977573, at *3 (Tex. App.—Corpus
Christi-Edinburg Apr. 28, 2005, pet. denied) — 11-5:8

Omohundro v. Matthews,
341 S.W.2d 401, 410 (Tex. 1960) — 8-1:4.1

O'Neal v. Tex. Bank & Trust Co. of Sweetwater,
118 Tex. 133, 137, 11 S.W.2d 791, 792 (Tex. Comm'n App. 1929) — 13-2:5

OneBeacon Ins. Co. v. T. Wade Welch & Assocs.,
841 F.3d 669 (5th Cir. 2016) — 5-7:1.1

Ortiz v. State Farm Lloyds,
589 S.W.3d 127 (Tex. 2019) — 5-1:1.2, 5-2:1.1, 5-4:4.2

O'Shea v. Coronado Transmission Co.,
  656 S.W.2d 557 (Tex. App.-Corpus Christi 1983, writ ref'd n.r.e.)   16-14:1

Overall v. Sw. Bell Yellow Pages, Inc.,
  869 S.W.2d 629, 632 (Tex. App.—Houston [14th Dist.] 1994,
  pet. denied)   14-6

Overton v. Bengel,
  139 S.W.3d 754 (Tex. App.—Texarkana 2004, no pet.)   1-1:2

Owen v. Empr's Mut. Cas. Co.,
  2008 U.S. Dist. LEXIS 24893 at *5 (N. D. Tex. Mar. 28, 2008)   5-4:1.1

Oxford Fin. Cos., Inc. v. Velez,
  807 S.W.2d 460 (Tex. App.—Austin 1991, writ denied)   3-4:2, 3-4:3.1

Padilla v. NCJ Dev., Inc.,
  218 S.W.3d 811, 814 (Tex. App.—El Paso 2007,
  pet. dism'd w.o.j.)   8-11:2.2, 8-11:3.3, 8-11:4.1

Pagayon. v. ExxonMobil Corp.,
  536 S.W.3d 499, 504–06 (Tex. 2017)   1-9:1

Palla v. Bio-One, Inc.,
  424 S.W.3d 722, 726 (Tex. App.—Dallas 2014, no pet.)   1-1:2

Palmer v. Wal-Mart Stores, Inc.,
  65 F. Supp. 2d 564, 567 (S.D. Tex. 1999)   27-3:5

Pampell Interests v. Wolle,
  797 S.W.2d 392 (Tex. App.—Austin 1990, no writ)   7-1:5.2

Pan Am. Petroleum Corp. v. Long,
  340 F.2d 211 (5th Cir. 1964)   7-8:1.1, 7-8:2

Pan Am. Petroleum Corp. v. Orr,
  319 F.2d 612 (5th Cir. 1963)   7-8:4.1

Pannell v. Cont'l Can Co., Inc.,
  554 F.2d 216, 225 (5th Cir. 1977)   17-11:5

Paramount Pipe & Supply Co., Inc. v. Muhr,
  749 S.W.2d 491, 494–95 (Tex. 1988)   19-3, 23-3

Parks v. Developers Sur. & Indem. Co.,
  302 S.W.3d 920, 923-4 (Tex. App.—Dallas 2010, no pet.)   13-5:1

Parkway Co. v. Woodruff,
  901 S.W.2d 434, 441 (Tex. 1995)   11-8:1, 11-9:3

Parr v. Duval Cty.,
  304 S.W.2d 957, 958–59
  (Tex. Civ. App.—Eastland 1957, writ ref'd n.r.e.)   8-5:3.1

PAS, Inc. v. Engel,
  350 S.W.3d 602 (Tex. App.—Houston [14th Dist.] 2011, no pet.)   1-6:2

Pasadena State Bank v. Isaac,
  149 Tex. 47, 228 S.W.2d 127, 129 (1950)   12-2:2

TABLE OF CASES

Paschal v. Great W. Drilling Ltd.,
  215 S.W.3d 437 (Tex. App.—Eastland 2006, pet. denied) — 11-11:1

Patel v. Hussain,
  485 S.W.3d 153 (Tex. App.—Houston [14th Dist.] 2016, no pet.) — 9-11:1

Patel v. St. Luke's Sugar Land P'ship, L.L.P.,
  No. 01-13-00273-CV, 2013 WL 5947500 (Tex. App.—Houston [1st Dist.] Nov. 7, 2013, pet. filed) — 8-1:2

Pathfinder Oil & Gas, Inc. v. Great W. Drilling, Ltd.,
  574 S.W.3d 882, 890 (Tex. 2019) — 7-5:2, 8-3:2

Patterson v. Planned Parenthood,
  971 S.W.2d 439 (Tex. 1998) — 21-4

Patton v. Nicholas,
  279 S.W.2d 848 (Tex. 1955) — 2-7:1, 9-7:2

Peacock v. Harrison,
  189 S.W.2d 500 (Tex. Civ. App.—Austin 1945, writ dism'd) — 3-1:4.4

Pebble Beach Co. v. Tour 18 I Ltd.,
  155 F.3d 526 (5th Cir. 1998) — 1-12:4.6, 1-14:4.6

Pecorino v. Raymark Indus.,
  763 S.W.2d 561, 568 (Tex. App.—Beaumont 1988, writ denied) — 17-11:2

Peek v. Equip. Serv. Co. of San Antonio,
  779 S.W.2d 802, 804 (Tex. 1989) — 8-4:5.1, 21-1:4, 21-2, 21-2:2

Peeler v. Hughes & Luce,
  909 S.W.2d 494 (Tex. 1995) — 4-1:2

Pegasus Energy Grp., Inc. v. Cheyenne Petroleum Co.,
  3 S.W.3d 112, 124 (Tex. App.—Corpus Christi 1999, pet. denied) — 11-13:1

Pegues v. Miss. State Emp't Serv.,
  899 F.2d 1449 (5th Cir. 1990) — 6-3:3.2

Pelto Oil Co. v. CSX Oil & Gas Corp.,
  804 S.W.2d 583 (Tex. App.—Houston [1st Dist.] 1991, writ denied) — 3-6:4.1

Pemex Exploracion y Produccion v. BASF Corp.,
  No. 4:10cv1997, 2011 WL 9523407, at *12 (S. D. Tex. Feb. 8, 2011) — 18-1

Pepi Corp. v. Galliford,
  254 S.W.3d 457, 460 (Tex. App.—Houston [1st Dist.] 2007, pet. denied) — 11-4, 11-5:8, 11-11:2

Perdue v. Pfeifer,
  No. 04-16-00396-CV, 2017 WL 1337645, at *3 (Tex. App.—San Antonio Apr. 12, 2017) — 1-3:3.1a

Perry Homes v. Cull,
  258 S.W.3d 580, 590 (Tex. 2008) — 25-3:4

Perry v. S.N.,
  973 S.W.2d 301 (Tex. 1998) — 1-11:1.1, 1-11:2

Petroleum Synergy Grp., Inc. v. Occidental Permian, Ltd.,
  331 S.W.3d 14 (Tex. App.—Amarillo 2010, pet. denied) 7-12:2

Philadelphia Indem. Ins. Co. v. White,
  490 S.W.3d 468 (Tex. 2016) 16-16:2

Phillips Petroleum Co. v. Bivins,
  423 S.W.2d 340 (Tex. Civ. App.—Amarillo 1967,
  writ ref'd n.r.e.) 7-3:2, 7-3:4.2

Phillips Petroleum Co. v. Cowden,
  241 F.2d 586 (5th Cir.1957) 7-5:3.1, 7-6:1.1, 7-6:2, 7-6:3.1, 7-13:1, 7-13:3.1, 7-13:4.1, 7-13:5.1

Phillips v. Carlton Energy Grp., LLC,
  475 S.W.3d 265, 280 (Tex. 2015) 11-7:1

Phillips v. Phillips,
  820 S.W.2d 785, 788–90 (Tex. 1991) 3-1:3.4, 11-5:5, 13-5:1, 16-13:2

Pickering v. First Greenville Nat'l Bank,
  495 S.W.2d 16 (Tex. Civ. App.—Dallas 1973, writ ref'd n.r.e.) 16-3, 16-3:1

Pierson v. GFH Fin. Servs. Corp.,
  829 S.W.2d 311, 314 (Tex. App.—Austin 1992, no writ) 1-3:2

Pileco, Inc. v. HCI, Inc.,
  735 S.W.2d 561 (Tex. App.—Houston [1st Dist.] 1987,
  writ ref'd n.r.e.) 16-3:3

Pilgrim's Pride v. Cernat,
  205 S.W.3d 110, 115–18 (Tex. App.—Texarkana 2006) 18-3

Pilot Travel Ctrs v. McCray,
  416 S.W.3d 168, 178 (Tex. App—Dallas 2013, no pet.) 13-4:3

Pinnacle Anesthesia Consultants v. Fisher,
  309 S.W.3d 93 (Tex. App.—Dallas 2009, pet. denied) 6-1:4.2

Pinnacle Data Servs., Inc. v. Gillen,
  104 S.W.3d 188 (Tex. App.—Texarkana 2003, no pet.),
  disapproved of on other grounds by Ritchie v. Rupe,
  443 S.W.3d 856 (Tex. 2014) 2-11:2

Pinson v. Odom,
  250 S.W.2d 609 (Tex. Civ. App.—Eastland 1952, no writ) 3-2:2.2

Pinson v. Red Arrow Freight Lines, Inc.,
  801 S.W.2d 14, 15 (Tex. App.—Austin 1990, no writ) 15-3

Pinter v. Dahl,
  486 U.S. 622, 633 (1988) 2-4:4.2

Pinto Tech. Ventures, L.P. v. Sheldon,
  526 S.W.3d 428, 432 (Tex. 2017) 26-1:1

Pipe Linings, Inc. v. Inplace Linings, Inc.,
  349 S.W.2d 279 (Tex. Civ. App.—Fort Worth 1961, writ ref'd n.r.e.) 1-14:2

TABLE OF CASES

Pitman v. Lightfoot,
937 S.W.2d 496 (Tex. App.—San Antonio 1996) — 3-11:2.1

Placer Energy Corp. v. E & S Oil Co., Inc.,
692 S.W.2d 197, 200 (Tex. App.—Fort Worth 1985, no writ) — 8-5:3.2

Placemaker, Inc. v. Greer,
654 S.W.2d 830 (Tex. App.—Tyler 1983) — 3-11:2.1

PlainsCapital Bank v. Martin,
459 S.W.3d 550 (Tex. 2015) — 11-8:1

Plains Expl. & Prod. Co. v. Torch Energy Advisors Inc.,
473 S.W.3d 296, 302 n.4 (Tex. 2015) — 11-11:6

Pleasant v. Bradford,
260 S.W.3d 546 (Tex. App.—Austin 2008, pet. denied) — 1-4:2

Plemmons v. Gary,
321 S.W.2d 625, 626 (Tex. Civ. App.—Beaumont 1959, orig. proceeding) — 15-1

Polizzi v. Cowles Magazines, Inc.,
345 U.S. 663, 73 S. Ct. 900, 97 L. Ed. 1331 (1953) — 27-5:1

Ponder v. Brice & Mankoff,
889 S.W.2d 637, 645 (Tex. App.—Houston [14th Dist.] 1994, writ denied) — 17-11:1

Pont de Nemours & Co.,
118 S.W.3d 60 (Tex. App.—Houston[14th Dist.] 2003, pet. denied) — 3-1:3.16

Porter & Clements, L.L.P. v. Stone,
935 S.W.2d 217, 219 (Tex. App.—Houston [1st Dist.] 1996, no writ) — 25-1:2

Porter v. Reaves,
728 S.W.2d 948, 950 (Tex. App.—Fort Worth 1987, no writ) — 19-1

Portland Sav. & Loan Ass'n v. Bernstein,
716 S.W.2d 532, 534–35 (Tex. App.—Corpus Christi 1985, writ ref'd n.r.e.) — 13-2:3

Portwood v. Portwood,
109 S.W.2d 515 (Tex. Civ. App.—Eastland 1937, writ dism'd) — 3-2:2.1

Poteet v. City of Palestine,
620 S.W.2d 181, 184 (Tex. Civ. App.—Tyler 1981, no writ) — 6-3:4.5

Poth v. Roosth,
202 S.W.2d 442 (Tex. 1947) — 7-2:3.1

Powell v. Forest Oil Corp.,
392 S.W.2d 549 (Tex. Civ. App.—Texarkana 1965, no writ) — 7-8:5.1

Power Reps, Inc. v. Cates,
No. 01-13-00856-CV, 2015 Tex. App. LEXIS 8384 (Tex. App.—Houston [1st Dist.] 2015, no pet. h.) — 6-1:3.3

Powers v. Adams,
 2 S.W.3d 496 (Tex. App.—Houston [14th Dist.] 1999, no pet.)   3-7:1.1, 3-7:5.1, 3-8:2.1, 3-8:2.2

Powers v. Chesapeake & O. Ry.,
 169 U.S. 92 (1898)   27-5:3

Pratho v. Zapata,
 157 S.W.3d 832, 842 (Tex. App.—Fort Worth 2005, no pet.)   29-7

Prestige Ford Garland Ltd. P'ship v. Morales,
 336 S.W.3d 833 (Tex. App.—Dallas 2011, no pet.)   3-5:4.1

Preston v. Tenet Healthsystem Mem'l Med. Ctr. Inc.,
 485 F.3d 793, 798 (5th Cir. 2007)   27-3:3.1

Prewitt v. Branham,
 643 S.W.2d 122 (Tex. 1982)   1-3:3.1a

Prime Prods., Inc. v. S.S.I. Plastics, Inc.,
 97 S.W.3d 631 (Tex. App.—Houston [1st Dist.] 2002, pet. denied)   3-9:1.1, 3-9:2, 3-10:2.1

Primrose Operating Co. v. Senn,
 161 S.W.3d 258, 261 (Tex. App.—Eastland 2005, no pet.)   12-2:2

Pringle v. Nowlin,
 629 S.W.2d 154, 157 (Tex. App.—Fort Worth 1982, writ ref'd n.r.e.)   10-3

Procter & Gamble Co. v. Amway Corp.,
 90 F. Supp. 2d 639 (S.D. Tex 1999), *aff'd in part, rev'd in part on other grounds*, 242 F.3d 539 (5th Cir. 2001)   1-8:4.3

Professional Servs., Inc. v. Amaitis,
 592 S.W.2d 396 (Tex. Civ. App.—Dallas 1979, writ ref'd n.r.e.)   6-1:4.5

Proportionate Responsibility and Contribution Before and After the Tort Reform of 2003, 35 Tex. Tech. L. Rev. 1125, 1132 (2004)   18-2:1, 18-3, 18-4, 18-6:2

Prostok v. Browning,
 112 S.W.3d 876 (Tex. App.—Dallas 2003), *aff'd in part, rev'd in part*, 165 S.W.3d 336 (Tex. 2005)   9-15:1.1, 9-15:2

Prouix v. Wells,
 235 S.W.3d 213, 215 (Tex. 2007)   17-12, 23-4

Provident Am. Ins. Co. v. Castaneda,
 988 S.W.2d 189, 193 (Tex. 1998)   5-2:3, 5-3:2, 5-3:4.2

Providential Inv. Corp. v. Dibrell,
 320 S.W.2d 415 (Tex. Civ. App.—Houston 1959, no writ)   2-8:2

Providian Nat'l Bank v. Ebarb,
 180 S.W.3d 898 (Tex. App.—Beaumont 2005, no pet.)   3-11:2.1, 3-12:2.5, 3-13:4.1

Prudential Ins. Co. of Am. v. Fin. Rev. Servs., Inc.,
 29 S.W.3d 74, 77 (Tex. 2000)   1-1:1.1

TABLE OF CASES

Prudential Secs., Inc. v. Haughland,
  973 S.W.2d 394 (Tex. App.—El Paso 1998, pet. denied) — 6-1:2

Prudential Securities Inc. v. Shoemaker,
  981 S.W.2d 791, 793–94 (Tex. App.—Houston [1st Dist.] 1998, no pet.) — 11-13:2

Pulaski Bank & Tr. Co. v. Tex. Am. Bank,
  759 S.W.2d 723, 735 (Tex. App.—Dallas 1988, writ denied) — 12-1, 15-3,

Purvis v. Prattco, Inc.,
  595 S.W.2d 103 (Tex. 1980) — 3-11:3.2

Qaddura v. Indo-European Foods, Inc.,
  141 S.W.3d 882 (Tex. App.—Dallas 2004, pet. denied) — 3-1:3.1a

Quantum Chem. Corp. v. Toennies,
  47 S.W.3d 473 (Tex. 2001) — 6-3:2

Quigley v. Bennett,
  256 S.W.3d 356 (Tex. App.—San Antonio 2008, no pet.) — 3-3:4.1

Quinn v. Press,
  140 S.W.2d 438, 440–41 (Tex. 1940) — 1-4:4.1, 17-10

Qwest Commc'n Corp. v. AT&T Corp.,
  24 S.W.3d 334, 337 (Tex. 2000) — 8-1:3.1

Radford v. Snyder Nat'l Farm Loan Ass'n,
  121 S.W.2d 478 (Tex. Civ. App.—Austin 1938, no writ) — 3-2:2.1

Radio Station KSCS v. Jennings,
  750 S.W.2d 760, 762 (Tex. 1988) — 30-3:3

Rampersad v. CenterPoint Energy Hous. Elec., LLC,
  554 S.W.3d 29, 40 (Tex. App.—Houston [1st Dist.] 2017, no pet.) — 15-2

Ran Ken, Inc. v. Schlapper,
  963 S.W.2d 102 (Tex. App.—Austin 1998, pet. denied) — 6-2:2

Rankin v. Naftalis,
  557 S.W.2d 940 (Tex. 1977) — 7-7:1.1, 7-7:2

Rasa Floors, L.P. v. Spring Vill. Partners, Ltd.,
  No. 01-08-00918-CV, 2010 Tex. App. LEXIS 9253 (App.—Houston [1st Dist.] Nov. 18, 2010) — 3-3:4.3

Rauscher Pierce Refsnes, Inc. v. Great Sw. Savs., F.A.,
  923 S.W.2d 112, 117 (Tex. App.—Houston [14th Dist.] 1996, no pet.) — 12-1

Rawlings v. Gonzalez,
  407 S.W.3d 420, 425–26 (Tex. App.—Dallas 2013, no pet.) — 8-10:2

Reagan Nat'l Advert. v. Vanderhoof Family Trust,
  82 S.W.3d 366, 369 (Tex. App.—Austin 2002, no pet.) — 1-2:3.3

Reaugh v. McCollum Expl. Co.,
  139 Tex. 485, 163 S.W.2d 620 (1942) — 7-10:3.1

Reaves v. City of Corpus Christi,
   518 S.W.3d 594, 610–11 (Tex. App.—Corpus Christi-Edinburg
   2017, no pet.) 19-4

Redwood Grp., L.L.C. v. Louiseau,
   113 S.W.3d 866, 868–70 (Tex. App.—Austin 2003, no pet.) 23-4

Reed v. White, Weld & Co., Inc.,
   571 S.W.2d 395, 397 (Tex. Civ. App.—Texarkana 1978, no writ) 1-3:3.1a

Reeder v. Wood County Energy, LLC,
   395 S.W.3d 789, 796–97 (Tex. 2012) 7-11:3.2

Regional Props., Inc. v. Fin. & Real Estate Consulting Co.,
   678 F.2d 552 (5th Cir. 1982) 2-4:3.4

Reid Road Mun. Util. Dist. No. 2 v. Speedy Stop Food Stores,
   337 S.W.3d 846, 853–54 (Tex. 2011) 11-8

Reiter v. Coastal States Gas Producing Co.,
   382 S.W.2d 243 (Tex. 1964) 7-2:2

Renger Mem'l Hosp. v. State,
   674 S.W.2d 828 (Tex. App.—Austin 1984, no writ) 2-3:1.1, 2-3:5.1

Republic Bankers Life Ins. Co. v. Jaeger,
   551 S.W.2d 30 (Tex. 1976) 11-6:2

Republic Nat'l Bank v. Northwest Nat'l Bank,
   578 S.W.2d 109, 116–17 (Tex. 1978) 11-13:1

Republic Nat'l Leasing Corp. v. Schindler,
   717 S.W.2d 606, 607 (Tex. 1986) 30-3:6

Republic Underwriters Ins. Co. v. Mex-Tex, Inc.,
   150 S.W.3d 423, 426 (Tex. 2004) 5-1:3.1

Rescar, Inc. v. Ward,
   60 S.W.3d 169 (Tex. App.—Houston [1st Dist.]
   2001, pet. granted, judgm't vacated w.r.m.) 6-2:3.1, 6-2:3.2

Resolution Tr. Corp. v. Acton,
   844 F. Supp. 307 (N.D. Tex. 1994), *aff'd*, 49 F.3d 1086
   (5th Cir. 1995) 2-1:2.1, 2-2:2.1

Restrepo v. All. Riggers & Constructors, Ltd.,
   538 S.W.3d 724 (Tex. App.—El Paso, 2017) 1-12:1

Retamco Operating, Inc. v. Republic Drilling Co.,
   278 S.W.3d 333, 339 (Tex. 2009) 7-5:5.1, 7-6:5.1

Reyelts v. Cross,
   968 F. Supp. 2d 835, 845 n.3 (N.D. Tex. 2013) 11-10

Reyna v. First Nat'l Bank in Edinburg,
   55 S.W.3d 58 (Tex. App.—Corpus 2001, no pet.) 6-1:2

Reyna v. Nat'l Union Fire Ins. Co. of Pittsburgh,
   Pa., 883 S.W.2d 368, 370–73 (Tex. App.—El Paso 1994) 13-4:2, 13-4:3

TABLE OF CASES

Reynolds v. Ford Motor Co.,
  No. 5:04-CV-085-C, 2004 WL 2870079, at *4
  (N.D. Tex. Dec. 13, 2004)   27-3:5

Rhey v. Redic,
  408 S.W.3d 440, 456 (Tex. App.—El Paso 2013, no pet.)   1-5:3.1a, 14-1

Rhodes v. Batilla,
  848 S.W.2d 833 (Tex. App.—Houston [14th Dist.]
  1993, writ denied)   4-1:2, 4-1:3.5

Rhodes v. Kelly,
  No. 05-16-00888-CV, 2017 WL 2774452
  (Tex. App.—Dallas June 27, 2017)   7-1:2

Rice v. Pinney,
  51 S.W.3d 705, 709
  (Tex. App.—Dallas 2001, no pet.)   8-11:2.2, 8-11:5.2, 8-11:4.1, 8-11:5.4

Richardson v. First Nat'l Life Ins. Co.,
  419 S.W.2d 836, 838 (Tex. 1967)   8-4:2.1, 11-11:6

Richardson-Eagle, Inc. v. William M. Mercer, Inc.,
  213 S.W.3d 469, 475–76 (Tex. App.—Houston [1st Dist.]
  2006, pet. denied)   1-2:2

Richmond v. Wells,
  395 S.W.3d 262 (Tex. App.—Eastland 2012, no pet.)   7-3:1.1, 7-3:2, 7-3:4.3

Ridge Oil Co., Inc. v. Guinn Inves., Inc.,
  148 S.W.3d 143 (Tex. 2004)   7-5:4.1

Rigo Mfg. Co. v. Thomas,
  458 S.W.2d 180, 181 (Tex. 1970)   17-11:4, 17-12

Riley v. Meriwether,
  780 S.W.2d 919 (Tex. App.—El Paso 1989, no writ)   7-5:3.2

Ritchie v. Rupe,
  339 S.W.3d 275 (Tex. App.—Dallas 2011, pet. granted)   2-9:3.1

Ritchie v. Rupe,
  443 S.W.3d 856 (Tex. 2014)   2-7:1, 2-7:1.1, 2-7:3.1, 2-7:2, 8-9:1,
  8-9:1.1, 9-7:1.1, 9-7:2

Rizk v. Fin. Guardian Ins. Agency, Inc.,
  584 S.W.2d 860, 862 (Tex. 1979)   3-7:3.2, 11-5:6

Rizkallah v. Conner,
  952 S.W.2d 580, 586–87 (Tex. App.—Houston [1st Dist.]
  1997, no pet.)   19-4

R.J. Suarez Enters. Inc. v. PNYX L.P.,
  380 S.W.3d 238, 249 (Tex. App.—Dallas 2012, no pet.)   1-3:3.2

Roark v. Allen,
  633 S.W.2d 804, 809–10 (Tex. 1982)   19-3

Roberts v. Geosource Drilling Servs., Inc.,
  757 S.W.2d 48 (Tex. App.—Houston [1st Dist.] 1988, no writ)   9-5:1

Robertson v. Church of God, Intern.,
  978 S.W.2d 120 (Tex. App.—Tyler 1997, pet. denied)   1-9:2

Robertson v. Jacobs Cattle Co.,
  285 Neb. 859, 830 N.W.2d 191 (Neb. 2013)   2-14:2

Robertson v. McKnight,
  609 S.W.2d 534, 537 (Tex. 1980)   24-1:4

Robin Singh Educ. Servs., Inc. v. Test Masters Educ. Servs., Inc.,
  401 S.W.3d 95, 97–98 (Tex. App.—Houston [14th Dist.] 2011, no pet.)   1-3:2

Robinson v. Granite Equip. Leasing Corp.,
  553 S.W.2d 633 (Tex. Civ. App.—Houston [1st Dist.] 1977, writ ref'd n.r.e.)   3-10:3.2

Robinson v. Parker,
  353 S.W.3d 753, 756 (Tex. 2011)   8-10:2

Rocor Int'l v. Nat'l Union Fire Ins. Co.,
  77 S.W.3d 253 (Tex. 2002)   5-2:1.1

Rogers v. Alexander,
  244 S.W.3d 370, 385–87 (Tex. App.—Dallas 2007, pet. denied)   11-3

Rogers v. Daniel Oil & Royalty Co.,
  130 Tex. 386, 392, 110 S.W.2d 891, 894 (1937)   11-5:8

Rogers v. Ricane Enters., Inc.,
  772 S.W.2d 76 (Tex. 1989)   7-5:1.1, 7-5:3.1, 7-5:3.2

Rogers v. Ricane Enters., Inc.,
  884 S.W.2d 763 (Tex. 1994)   7-2:1, 7-2:2

Rogers v. Zanetti,
  517 S.W.3d 123, 129 (Tex. App.—Dallas 2015)   30-2:3

Rogers v. Zanetti,
  518 S.W.3d 394 (Tex. 2017)   4-1:2

Rojas v. Duarte,
  393 S.W.3d 837, 845–46 (Tex. App.—El Paso 2012, pet. denied)   11-7:1

Rosenboom Mach. & Tool, Inc. v. Machala,
  995 S.W.2d 817, 823 (Tex. App.—Houston [1st Dist.] 1999, pet. denied)   19-1

Rowan Companies, Inc. v. Transco Expl. Co., Inc.,
  679 S.W.2d 660, 665–66 (Tex. App.—Houston [1st Dist.] 1984, writ ref'd n.r.e., *cert. denied,* 474 U.S. 822, 106 S.Ct. 74, 88 L.Ed.2d 61)   10-2, 11-5:5

Rowe v. Rowe,
  887 S.W.2d 191 (Tex. App.—Fort Worth 1994, writ denied)   2-1:4.3, 2-2:4.4, 2-11:4.1, 3-13:4.3

TABLE OF CASES

Royal Typewriter Co. v. Vestal,
    572 S.W.2d 377, 378 (Tex. App.—Houston [14th Dist.] 1978,
    no writ) 13-5

RSL Funding, LLC v. Pippins,
    499 S.W.3d 423, 430 (Tex. 2016) 25-3:4

Rudasill v. Rudasill,
    206 S.W. 983 (Tex. Civ. App.—Dallas 1918, no writ) 8-9:3.1

Rus-Ann Dev., Inc. v. ECGC, Inc.,
    222 S.W.3d 921, 927 (Tex. App.—Tyler 2007, no pet.) 8-3:2

Rusk State Hosp. v. Black,
    392 S.W.3d 88 (Tex. 2012) 21-9

Russell v. Am. Real Estate Corp.,
    89 S.W.3d 204 (Tex. App.—Corpus Christi 2002) 3-10:2.1

Russell v. Campbell,
    725 S.W.2d 739 (Tex. App.—Houston [14th Dist.] 1987,
    writ ref n.r.e.) 2-15:5.2

Rust v. Tex. Farmers Ins.,
    341 S.W.3d 541, 551 (Tex. App.—El Paso 2011, no pet.) 30-2:3

Ryan v. Collins,
    496 S.W.2d 205 (Tex. Civ. App.—Tyler 1973,
    writ refused n.r.e.) 11-5:8, 19-5

Ryder Integrated Logistics, Inc. v. Fayette Cty.,
    453 S.W.3d 922 (Tex. 2015) 1-10:2

Ryland Grp., Inc. v. Hood,
    924 S.W.2d 120, 121 (Tex. 1996) 30-1:7, 30-3:3

S. Plains Switching, Ltd. Co. v. BNSF Ry. Co.,
    255 S.W.3d 690, 703 (Tex. App.—Amarillo 2008, pet. denied) ... 8-3:2

Sabine Pilot Serv., Inc. v. Hauck,
    687 S.W.2d 733 (Tex. 1985) 6-1:2, 6-2:1, 6-2:1.1, 6-2:2, 6-2:3.3, 6-2:3.4

Sackheim v. Lynch,
    CV SA-11-CA-794-FB, 2013 WL 12394007, at *5
    (W.D. Tex. Mar. 8, 2013) 8-5:2

Sacks v. Dallas Gold & Silver Exch. Inc.,
    720 S.W.2d 177 (Tex. App.—Dallas 1986, no writ) 3-1:4.7

Saden v. Smith,
    415 S.W.3d 450, 469 (Tex. App.—Houston [1st Dist.]
    2013, pet. denied) 2-11:3.3, 3-1:3.13

Sadler v. Duvall,
    815 S.W.2d 285 (Tex. App.—Texarkana 1991, writ denied) 7-10:1

Safeshred, Inc. v. Martinez,
    365 S.W.3d 655 (Tex. 2012) 6-2:3.5

Safway Scaffolds Co. of Hous. v. Sharpstown Realty Co.,
  409 S.W.2d 883 (Tex. Civ. App.—Waco 1966, no writ) ... 3-9:4.3

Salay v. Baylor Univ.,
  115 S.W.3d 625 (Tex. App.—Waco 2003, pet. denied) ... 9-17:1.1, 9-17:2

Salazar v. Merck & Co., Inc.,
  No. 05-445, 2005 WL 2875332, at *3 (S.D. Tex. Nov. 2, 2005) ... 27-3:5

Salomon v. Lesay,
  369 S.W.3d 540, 553 (Tex. App.—Houston [1st Dist.] 2012, no pet.) ... 11-5:7

Sample v. Freeman,
  873 S.W.2d 470 (Tex. App.—Beaumont 1994, writ denied) ... 4-1:3.2

San Antonio River Auth. v. Garrett Bros.,
  528 S.W.2d 266, 274 (Tex. Civ. App.—San Antonio 1975, writ ref'd n.r.e.) ... 11-8:1

San Saba Energy, L.P. v. McCord,
  167 S.W.3d 67 (Tex. App.—Waco 2005, pet. denied) ... 9-3:1, 9-3:1.1, 9-3:2

Sanchez v. Jary,
  768 S.W.2d 933, 936 (Tex. App.—San Antonio 1989, no writ) ... 14-7

Sandare Chem. Co. v. WAKO Int'l,
  820 S.W.2d 21, 24 (Tex. App.—Fort Worth 1991, no writ) ... 1-1:3.1d, 1-2:3.1d

Sanders v. City of Grapevine,
  218 S.W.3d 772 (Tex. App.—Fort Worth 2007, pet. denied) ... 1-6:4.5

Sanroc Co. Intern. v. Roadrunner Transp., Inc.,
  596 S.W.2d 320 (Tex. Civ. App.—Houston [1st Dist.] 1980, no writ) ... 3-9:2, 3-10:2.1

Santa Fe Petroleum, L.L.C. v. Star Canyon Corp.,
  156 S.W.3d 630, 641 (Tex. App.—Tyler 2004, no pet.) ... 14-3

Santanna Nat. Gas Corp. v. Hamon Operating Co.,
  954 S.W.2d 885, 891 (Tex. App.—Austin 1997, pet. denied) ... 17-11:1

Santos v. Mid-Continent Refrigerator Co.,
  471 S.W.2d 568 (Tex. 1971) ... 3-2:5.1

Sarandos v. Dave Seline Roofing Co.,
  498 S.W.2d 393, 394 (Tex. Civ. App.—Houston [1st Dist.] 1973, no writ) ... 11-5:6

Sauceda v. Kerlin,
  164 S.W.3d 892 (Tex. App.—Corpus Christi 2005) ... 8-4:1.1, 8-4:3.3

Sawyer v. Fitts,
  630 S.W.2d 872, 874–75 (Tex. App.—Fort Worth 1982, no writ) ... 11-6:1, 11-7:1, 11-7:2, 12-2:1

SBG Dev. Servs., L.P. v. Nurock Grp., Inc.,
  No. 02-11-00008-CV, 2011 WL 5247873, at *3 (Tex. App.—Fort Worth Nov. 3, 2011, no pet.) ... 13-2:4

TABLE OF CASES

Scarborough v. New Domain Oil & Gas Co.,
  276 S.W. 331 (Tex. Civ. App.—El Paso 1925, writ dism'd w.o.j.)   7-5:4.1

Scherer v. Angell,
  253 S.W.3d 777 (Tex. App.—Amarillo 2007, no pet.)   1-7:2

Schlumberger Tech. v. Swanson,
  959 S.W.2d 171 (Tex. 1997)   1-5:2, 1-6:1, 1-6:1.1

Schlumberger Tech. v. Pasko,
  544 S.W.3d 830, 835 (Tex. 2018)   30-3:2

Schneider Nat. Carriers, Inc. v. Bates,
  147 S.W.3d 264, 284 (Tex. 2004)   7-9:4.1, 8-2:2, 11-8:1

Schneider v. Esperanza Transmission Co.,
  744 S.W.2d 595 (Tex. 1987)   3-10:2.2, 3-10:3.1, 3-10:3.6

Schreiber v. Burlington N., Inc.,
  472 U.S. 1, 7 (1985)   2-4:2.1

Schriver v. Tex. Dep't of Transp.,
  293 S.W.3d 846 (Tex. App.—Fort Worth 2009, no pet.)   3-1:2

Schroeder v. Tex. Iron Works, Inc.,
  813 S.W.2d 483 (Tex. 1991), *overruled on other grounds*,
  307 S.W.3d 299 (2010)   6-3:4.2, 16-12:1

Schucht v. Stidham,
  37 S.W.2d 214 (Tex. Civ. App.—Fort Worth 1930, no writ)   3-8:2.1, 3-8:2.2

Science Spectrum, Inc. v. Martinez,
  941 S.W.2d 910, 911 (Tex. 1997)   30-1:4

Scoggins v. Pollock,
  727 F.2d 1025, 1027 (11th Cir. 1984)   27-3:3.1

Scott v. Atchison, T. & S. F. R. Co.,
  572 S.W.2d 273 (Tex. 1978)   13-6:2, 15-5, 19-1

Scott v. Hewitt,
  90 S.W.2d 816, 818–19 (Tex. 1936)   8-11:5.4

Scott v. Sebree,
  986 S.W.2d 364 (Tex. App.—Austin 1999, pet. denied)   1-4:2, 1-5:1, 1-5:2, 1-5:3.1, 1-5:3.4, 3-1:3.6

Scruggs v. Troncalli,
  307 S.W.2d 300, 304 (Tex. Civ. App.—Waco 1957, writ ref'd n.r.e.)   17-11:5

Scurlock Permian Corp. v. Brazos Cty.,
  869 S.W.2d 478, 483–84 (Tex. App.—Houston [1st Dist.] 1993,
  writ denied)   13-5:1

Searcy v. Hunter,
  17 S.W. 372 (Tex. 1891)   3-1:4.5

Sec. & Commc'ns Sys., Inc. v. Hooper,
  575 S.W.2d 606, 608 (Tex. Civ. App.—Dallas 1978, no writ)   14-5

S.E.C. v. Zandford,
    535 U.S. 813, 819, 122 S. Ct. 1899, 1903, 153 L. Ed. 2d 1 (2002)   2-4:2.1

Seiffert v. Bowden,
    556 S.W.2d 406 (Tex. Civ. App.—Corpus Christi 1977, no writ)   16-8:2

Seger v. Yorkshire Ins. Co., Ltd.,
    503 S.W.3d 388, 395 (Tex. 2016)   5-5:2.1, 5-7:1.1, 5-7:2

Select Ins. Co. v. Boucher,
    561 S.W.2d 474, 477 (Tex. 1978)   13-6:1, 13-6:2, 13-6:3, 15

Senter v. Shanafelt,
    233 S.W.2d 202 (Tex. Civ. App.—Fort Worth
    1950, no writ)   7-14:2

Service Empls. Int'l Union Local 5 v. Prof'l Janitorial Serv. of Hous., Inc.,
    481 S.W. 3d 210 (Tex. 2014, mem. op.)   1-8:4.6

Severs v. Mira Vista Homeowners Ass'n,
    559 S.W.3d 684, 701 (Tex. App.—Fort Worth 2018, pet denied.)   3-5:3.1

Shamrock Hilton Hotel v. Caranas,
    488 S.W.2d 151 (Tex. Civ. App.—Houston [14th Dist.] 1972,
    writ ref'd n.r.e.)   3-9:2

Shamrock Psychiatric Clinic, P.A. v. Tex. Dep't of Health & Human Serv.,
    540 S.W.3d 553 (Tex. 2018)   21-2:2

Shannon v. Barbee,
    No. 10-06-00414-CV, 2008 WL 802266 (Tex. App.—Waco
    Mar. 26, 2008, pet. denied)   7-3:2

Sharifi v. Steen Auto., LLC,
    370 S.W.3d 126, 146 (Tex. App.—Dallas 2012)   8-3:4.5, 11-2, 11-3, 12-2:1

Sharyland Water Supply Corp. v. City of Alton,
    354 S.W.3d 407 (Tex. 2011)   11-1, 12-3, 12-3

Sherer v. Sherer,
    393 S.W.3d 480, 491 n.22 (Tex. App.—Texarkana 2013, pet. denied)   11-4

Sherrod v. Bailey,
    580 S.W.2d 24, 28 (Tex. App.—Houston [1st Dist.] 1979,
    writ red'd n.r.e.)   10-3, 10-4

Shields, LP v. Bradberry,
    No. 15-0803, 2017 WL 2023602 (Tex. May 12, 2017)   16-6:1

Shioleno v. Sandpiper Condo. Council of Owners, Inc.
    No. 13-07-00312-CV, 2008 WL 2764530
    (Tex. App.—Corpus Christi July 17, 2008, no pet.)   2-12:3.1

Shoemaker v. Fogel, Ltd.,
    826 S.W.2d 933, 937 (Tex. 1990)   13-5:1, 16-19

Shor v. Pelican Oil & Gas Mgt., LLC,
    405 S.W.3d 737, 750 (Tex. App.—Hous. [1st Dist.] 2013)   8-1:2

TABLE OF CASES

Shwiff v. Priest,
  650 S.W.2d 894, 903 (Tex. App.—San Antonio 1983, writ ref'd n.r.e.)   8-4:4.3

Siam v. Mt. Vista Builders,
  544 S.W.3d 504, 516 (Tex. App.—El Paso 2018, no pet.)   3-1:3.1b, 3-1:3.10

Siemens Corp. v. Bartek,
  No. 03-04-00613-CV, 2006 WL 1126219 (Tex. App.—Austin
  Apr. 28, 2006, no pet.)   22-1

Silbaugh v. Ramirez,
  126 S.W.3d 88, 93 (Tex. App.—Houston [1st Dist.] 2002, no pet.)   13-2:4

Simmons Airlines v. Lagrotte,
  50 S.W.3d 748 (Tex. App.—Dallas 2001, pet. denied)   6-2:2

Simmons v. Compania Financiera Libano, S.A.,
  830 S.W.2d 789, 792 (Tex. App.—Houston [1st Dist.] 1992, writ denied)   13-5

Singh v. Skibicki,
  01-14-00825-CV, 2015 WL 7785566, at *6 (Tex. App.—Houston
  [1st Dist.] Dec. 3, 2015, no pet.)   8-3:5.1

Siskind v. Villa Found. for Educ., Inc.,
  642 S.W.2d 434, 438 (Tex. 1982)   23-3

Sister Initiative, LLC v. Broughton Maint. Ass'n, Inc.,
  02-19-00102-CV, 2020 WL 726785, at *29 (Tex. App.—Fort Worth
  Feb. 13, 2020, pet. filed)   2-14:4.1

SJW Prop. Commerce, Inc. v. Sw. Pinnacle Props., Inc.,
  328 S.W.3d 121, 151–52 (Tex. App.—Corpus Christi-E dinburg 2010,
  pet. denied)   1-1:2

Skelton v. Commission for Lawyer Discipline,
  56 S.W.3e 687, 691 (Tex. App.—Houston [14th Dist.] 2001, no pet.)   30-1:1

Slaughter v. Cities Serv. Oil Co.,
  660 S.W.2d 860 (Tex. App.—Amarillo 1983, no writ)   7-14:3.2, 7-14:4.2, 7-14:5.2

Smallwood v. Illinois Cent. R. Co.,
  385 F.3d 568, 572 (5th Cir. 2004)   27-3:5

Smith Detective Agency & Nightwatch Serv., Inc. v. Stanley Smith Sec., Inc.,
  938 S.W.2d 743, 747–48 (Tex. App.—Dallas 1996, writ denied)   29-4

Smith v. Am. Econ. Ins. Co.,
  794 S.W.2d 574, 577 (Tex. App.—Fort Worth 1990, writ denied)   17-4:1

Smith v. Bolin,
  271 S.W.2d 93 (Tex. 1954)   7-7:2

Smith v. Chapman,
  897 S.W.2d 399 (Tex. App.—Eastland 1995, no writ)   2-3:1.1, 2-3:5.1

Smith v. City of Sweeney,
  No. 13-05-233-CV, 2006 WL 2371344, at *1 (Tex. App.—Corpus
  Christi-E dinburg Aug. 17, 2006, pet. denied)   30-1:2

Smith v. Clary Corp.,
   917 S.W.2d 796, 798–99 (Tex. 1996) — 20-2, 21-2:1, 21-3

Smith v. East,
   411 S.W.3d 519, 529 (Tex. App.—Austin 2013, pet. denied) — 18-2:2

Smith v. Maximum Racing, Inc.,
   136 S.W.3d 337, 341–42 (Tex. App.—Austin 2004, no pet.) — 1-3:4.5, 9-4:1

Smith v. Miller,
   298 S.W.2d 845, 847 (Tex. Civ. App.—Galveston 1957, writ ref'd n.r.e.) — 8-7:5.2, 8-8:5.1

Smith v. Nat'l Resort Cmtys., Inc.,
   585 S.W.2d 655 (Tex. 1979) — 3-2:2.3

Smith v. Radam, Inc.,
   51 S.W.3d 413 (Tex. App.—Houston [1st Dist.] 2001) — 3-9:2

Smith v. Rogers,
   147 S.W.2d 934, 935 (Tex. Civ. App.—San Antonio 1941, no writ) — 8-8:1

Smith v. Sinclair Ref. Co.,
   77 S.W.2d 894, 895 (Tex. Civ. App.—Fort Worth 1934, no writ) — 8-11:2.1

Smith v. Smith,
   541 S.W.3d 251, 257 (Tex. App.—Houston [14th Dist.] 2017, no pet.) — 13-2:5, 13-2:6

Smith v. Van Gorkom,
   488 A.2d 858 (Del. 1985), *overruled on other grounds by Gantler v. Stephens*, 965 A.2d 695 (Del. 2009) — 2-1:2.1, 2-2:2.1

Smith-Hamm, Inc. v. Equip. Connection,
   946 S.W.2d 458 (Tex. App.-Houston [14th Dist.] 1997, no writ) — 3-9:3.5

Smolowe v. Delendo Corp.,
   136 F.2d 231 (2d Cir. 1943) — 2-4:3.3

Sneed v. Webre,
   465 S.W.3d 169 (Tex. 2015) (recognizing double-derivative standing) — 2-8:2

Snyder v. Pitts,
   150 Tex. 407, 241 S.W.2d 136, 140 (1951) — 22-3

Socony Mobil Oil Corp. v. Belveal,
   430 S.W.2d 529 (Tex. Civ. App.—El Paso 1968, writ ref'd n.r.e.) — 7-2:4.3, 7-2:5.3a

Solutioneers Consulting, Ltd. v. Gulf Greyhound Partners, Ltd.,
   237 S.W.3d 379 (Tex. App.—Houston [14th Dist.] 2007, no pet.) — 1-6:3.1b

Sorbus, Inc. v. UHW Corp.,
   855 S.W.2d 771, 775 (Tex. App.—El Paso 1993, writ denied) — 13-5:1

Sosa v. Central Power & Light,
   909 S.W.2d 893 (Tex. 1995) — 20-3, 29-3

TABLE OF CASES 701

Soukup v. Sedgwick Claims Mgmt. Servs., Inc.,
   No. 01-11-00871-CV, 2012 WL 3134223, at *6–7
   (Tex. App.—Houston [1st Dist.] Aug. 2, 2012, pet. dism'd)   11-9:3

South Plains Switching, Ltd. v. BNSF Ry.,
   255 S.W.3d 690, 703 (Tex. App.—Amarillo 2008)   8-3:3.1

South Tex. Water Auth. v. Lomas,
   223 S.W.3d 304, 307–09 (Tex. 2007)   8-10:2, 8-10:4.3

Southeastern Pipe Line Co. v. Tichacek,
   997 S.W.2d 166 (Tex. 1999)   7-12:4.1

Southern Cty. Mut. Ins. Co. v. Ochoa,
   19 S.W.3d 452, 461 (Tex. App.—Corpus Christi 2000)   14-2

Southland Lloyds Ins. Co. v. Cantu,
   399 S.W.3d 558, 580 (Tex. App.—San Antonio 2011, pet. denied)   5-3:3.3

Southland Lloyd's Ins. v. Tomberlain,
   919 S.W.2d 822, 830 (Tex. App.—Texarkana 1996, writ denied)   5-2:4.1a, 5-2:4.1b

SouthTex 66 Pipeline Co., Ltd. v. Spoor,
   238 S.W.3d 538, 543 (Tex. App.—Houston [14th Dist.] 2007,
   pet. denied)   30-3:3

Southwell v. Univ. of the Incarnate Word,
   974 S.W.2d 351 (Tex. App.—San Antonio 1998, pet. denied)   3-1:2

Southwest Bank & Trust Co. v. Exec. Sportsman Ass'n,
   477 S.W.2d 920, 929 (Tex. Civ. App.—Dallas 1972, writ ref'd n.r.e.)   11-7:1, 11:7:3

Southwest Bank v. Info. Support Concepts, Inc.,
   149 S.W.3d 104, 105 (Tex. 2004)   1-3:4.6, 18-1

Southwest Livestock & Trucking Co. v. Dooley,
   884 S.W.2d 805, 810 (Tex. App.—San Antonio 1994, writ denied)   8-4:3.1

Southwestern Bell Media, Inc. v. Lyles,
   825 S.W.2d 488, 499 (Tex. App.—Houston [1st Dist.] 1992, writ denied)   11-6:2

Southwestern Bell Tel. Co. v. DeLanney,
   809 S.W.2d 493, 494–95 (Tex. 1991)   12-3

Southwestern Bell Tel. Co. v. John Carlo Tex., Inc.,
   843 S.W.2d 470, 472 (Tex. 1992)   1-1:2

Southwestern Elec. Power Co. v. Burlington N. R.R. Co.,
   966 S.W.2d 467 (Tex. 1998)   3-4:4.2

Southwestern Energy Prod. Co. v. Berry-Helfand,
   491 S.W.3d 699 (Tex. 2016)   1-15:3, 1-15:3.1, 11-4

Sowell v. Dresser Indus., Inc.,
   866 S.W.2d 803, 808 (Tex. App.—Beaumont 1993, writ denied)   17-11:2

Spangle v. McGee,
   No. 03-08-00054-CV, 2009 Tex. App. LEXIS 312, at *10
   (App.—Austin Jan. 15, 2009)   8-2:2

Specialty Retailers, Inc. v. DeMoranville,
  933 S.W.2d 490 (Tex. 1996)   6-3:4.1

Spin Doctor Golf, Inc. v. Paymentech, L.P.,
  296 S.W.3d 354, 357 (Tex. App.—Dallas 2009, pet. denied)   22-1

Spitzberg v. Houston Am. Energy Corp.,
  758 F.3d 676, 691 (5th Cir. 2014)   2-4:2.1

Spoljaric v. Percival Tours, Inc.,
  708 S.W.2d 432 (Tex. 1986)   1-6:2

Spring Garden 79U, Inc. v. Stewart Title Co.,
  874 S.W.2d 945 (Tex. App.—Houston [1st Dist.] 1994, no writ)   3-11:1.1, 3-11:2.1

Spurlock v. Johnson,
  94 S.W.3d 655 (Tex. App.—San Antonio 2002, no pet.)   9-15:2

Squyres v. Christian,
  253 S.W.2d 470, 472 (Tex. Civ. App.—Fort Worth 1952,
  writ ref'd n.r.e)   17-9

SSP Partners v. Gladstrong Invs. (U.S.A.) Corp.,
  275 S.W.3d 444 (Tex. 2008)   2-13:1.1, 2-13:2.3

St. Elizabeth Hosp. v. Garrard,
  730 S.W.2d 649 (Tex. 1987) *overruled* by *Boyles v. Kerr,*
  855 S.W.2d 593 (Tex. 1993)   9-11:1

St. Joseph Hosp. v. Wolff,
  94 S.W.3d 513, 525–30 (Tex. 2002)   19-2

St. Paul Surplus Lines Ins. Co. v. Dal-Worth Tank Co.,
  974 S.W.2d 51, 53 (Tex. 1998)   5-2:4.1c, 5-2:4.5, 5-3:3.1c

St. Paul Surplus Lines Ins. Co. v. Geo Pipe Co.,
  25 S.W.3d 900, 903 n.2 (Tex. App.—Houston [1st Dist.]
  2000, no pet.)   24-1:2

Staats v. Miller,
  243 S.W.2d 686 (Tex. 1951)   3-6:2

Stafford v. S. Vanity Magazine, Inc.,
  231 S.W.3d 530 (Tex. App.—Dallas 2007)   8-3:1.1, 8-3:2

Stanfield v. Neubaum,
  494 S.W.3d 90, 97 (Tex. 2016)   15-2

Stanolind Oil & Gas Co. v. Newman Bros. Drill. Co.,
  305 S.W.2d 169 (Tex. 1957)   7-5:4.2

Starkey v. Graves,
  448 S.W.3d 88 (Tex. App.—Houston [14th Dist.] 2014, no pet.)   3-1:3.1b

State Bar of Tex. v. Kilpatrick,
  874 S.W.2d 656, 658 (Tex. 1994)   29-7

State Farm Fire & Cas. Co. v. Miller,
  713 S.W.2d 700, 704 (Tex. App.—Dallas 1986, writ ref'd n.r.e.)   5-2:3

TABLE OF CASES

State Farm Life Ins. Co. v. Beaston,
907 S.W.2d 430, 436 (Tex. 1995) — 5-2:4.1d

State Farm Lloyd's Ins. Co. v. Ashby AAA Auto. Supply Co., Inc.,
No. 05-92-01354-CV, 1995 WL 513363, at *18–19
(Tex. App.—Dallas Aug. 28, 1995, writ denied) — 29-7

State Farm Lloyds Ins. v. Maldonado,
963 S.W.2d 38, 41 (Tex. 1998) — 5-7:2

State of California v. Copus,
309 S.W.2d 227, 230–31 (Tex. 1958) — 24-1:1

State v. Clear Channel Outdoor, Inc.,
463 S.W.3d 488, 493 (Tex. 2015) — 11-8:2

State v. Morello,
547 S.W.3d 881, 887 (Tex. 2018) — 3-12:2.6

Statewide Bank & SN Servicing Corp. v. Keith,
301 S.W.3d 776, 786 (Tex. App.—Beaumont 2009, petition for review abated) — 10-5

Stegall & Stegall v. Cohn,
592 S.W.2d 427, 429 (Tex. App.—Fort Worth 1979, no writ) — 13-2:2

Sterling v. Apple,
513 S.W.2d 255, 257 (Tex. Civ. App.—Houston [1st Dist.] 1974, writ ref'd n.r.e.) — 8-3:5.2

Sterner v. Marathon Oil Co.,
767 S.W.2d 686, 688 (Tex. 1989) — 1-1:2

Stevens Foods, Inc. v. Loggins Meat Co.,
644 S.W.2d 908, 909 (Tex. App.—Tyler 1983, no writ) — 14-9

Stevens v. Vowell,
343 F.2d 374 (10th Cir. 1965) — 2-4:2.1, 2-4:2.2

Stevenson v. Koutzarov,
795 S.W.2d 313, 319 (Tex. App.—Houston [1st Dist.] 1990, writ denied) — 17-2

Stewart & Stevenson Servs., Inc. v. Kratochvil,
737 S.W.2d 65 (Tex. App.—San Antonio 1987, no writ) — 3-9:2, 3-10:2.1

Stewart Title Guar. Co. v. Mims,
405 S.W.3d 319 (Tex. App.—Dallas 2013, no pet.) — 3-4:2

Stewart Title Guar. Co. v. Sterling,
822 S.W.2d 1, 7 (Tex. 1991) — 12-2:1

Stewart v. U.S. Leasing Corp.,
702 S.W.2d 288 (Tex. App.—Houston [1st Dist.] 1985, no writ) — 16-14:1

Stiles v. Resolution Trust Corp.,
867 S.W.3d. 24 (Tex. 1993) — 30-1:3

Stine v. Stewart,
    80 S.W.3d 586, 592 (Tex. 2002)　　　　　　　　　　　　　　　3-1:4.2, 17-10

Stone Res., Inc. v. Barnett,
    661 S.W.2d 148 (Tex. App.—Houston [1st Dist.] 1983, no writ)　　　16-9

Stoneridge Inv. Partners, LLC v. Sci.-Atlanta,
    552 U.S. 148, 159 (2008)　　　　　　　　　　　　　　　　　　2-4:2.1

Stoyer v. State Farm Mut. Auto. Ins. Co.,
    2009 U.S. Dist. LEXIS 15571 at *5 (N. D. Tex. Feb. 24, 2009)　　　5-4:1.1

Strawbridge v. Curtiss,
    7 U.S. 267 (1806)　　　　　　　　　　　　　　　　　　　　　27-3:2

Strebel v. Wimberly,
    371 S.W.3d 267 (Tex. App.—Houston [1st Dist.] 2012, pet. denied)　2-10:2

Street v. Second Ct. of Appeals,
    756 S.W.2d 299, 301 (Tex. 1988)　　　　　　　　　　　　　　5-7:4.1

Stroud v. VBFSB Holding Corp.,
    917 S.W.2d 75 (Tex. App.—San Antonio 1996, writ denied)　　　6-2:4.1

Stuart v. Bayless,
    964 S.W.2d 920, 921 (Tex. 1998)　　　　　　　　　　　　　　10-5

Stubblefield v. Belco Mfg. Co., Inc.,
    931 S.W.2d 54 (Tex. App.—Austin 1996, no pet.)　　　　　　　2-8:4.3

Subaru v. David McDavid Nissan,
    84 S.W.3d 212 (Tex. 2002)　　　　　　　　　　　　　　　　21-6

Sun Expl. & Prod. Co. v. Jackson,
    783 S.W.2d 202 (Tex. 1989)　　　　7-14:1.1, 7-14:2, 7-14:5.1, 9-23:1, 9-23:1.1

Sun Oil Co. v. Whitaker,
    424 S.W.2d 216, 218 (Tex. 1968)　　　　　　　　　　　　　　8-1:5.5

Sunbelt Const. Corp., Inc. v. S & D Mech. Contractors, Inc.,
    668 S.W.2d 415 (Tex. App.—Corpus 1983, writ ref'd n.r.e.)　　　13-4:6

Sunshine v. Manos,
    496 S.W.2d 195 (Tex. Civ. App.—Tyler 1973)　　　　　　　　3-1:4.4

Super Starr Int'l, LLC v. Fresh Tex Produce, LLC,
    531 S.W.3d 829, 849 (Tex. App.—Corpus Christi 2017, no pet.)　　8-1:3.2

Surety Savings & Loan Ass'n,
    462 S.W.2d 540, 545 (Tex. 1971)　　　　　　　　　　　　　　30-3:4

Surgitek. v. Abel,
    997 S.W.2d 598 (Tex. 1999)　　　　　　　　　　　　　　　　22-6

Sustala v. North Side Ready-Mix Concrete Co.,
    317 S.W.2d 64, 67–68 (Tex. Civ. App.—Houston [1st Dist.] 1958, no writ)　13-5

Sutherland v. Sutherland,
    560 S.W.2d 531, 533 (Tex. Civ. App.—Texarkana 1978, writ ref'd n.r.e.)　8-10:3.1

TABLE OF CASES

S.V. v. R.V.,
   933 S.W.2d 1, 4 (Tex. 1996)   3-2:4.1

SW Loan A, L.P. v. Duarte-Viera,
   487 S.W.3d 697, 707 (Tex. App.—San Antonio 2016, no pet.)   8-10:4.2

Swank v. Sverdlin,
   121 S.W.3d 785, 800 (Tex. App.—Houston [1st Dist.] 2003, pet. denied)   1-1:2

Sysco Food Servs., Inc. v. Trapnell,
   890 S.W.2d 796 (Tex. 1994)   16-7, 16-7:2

Taiwan Shrimp Farm Vill. Ass'n v. U.S.A. Shrimp Farm Dev., Inc.,
   915 S.W.2d 61, 65 (Tex. App.—Corpus Christi 1996, writ denied)   1-3:3.3

Talley v. Howsley,
   176 S.W.2d 158, 160 (Tex. 1943)   8-5:3.1

Tamuno Ifiesimama v. Haile,
   522 S.W.3d 675, 685 (Tex. App.—Houston [1st Dist.] 2017, pet. denied)   8-3:1

Tanglewood Homes Ass'n, Inc. v. Feldman,
   436 S.W.3d 48, 64 (Tex. App.—Houston [14th Dist.] 2014, pet. denied)   29-5

Tanglewood Terrace, Ltd. v. City of Texarkana,
   996 S.W.2d 330 (Tex. App.—Texarkana 1999, no pet.)   3-6:4.1

Tanner v. Jackson,
   246 S.W.2d 319 (Tex. Civ. App.—Amarillo 1952, no writ)   16-13

Tarrant Cty. Hosp. Dist. v. GE Automation Servs.,
   156 S.W.3d 885, 895 (Tex. App.—Fort Worth 2005, no pet.)   11-1, 12-3

Tate v. Beal,
   119 S.W.3d 378, 381 (Tex. App.—Fort Worth 2003, pet. denied)   17-12

Taylor v. Allstate Ins. Co.,
   356 S.W.3d 92 (Tex. App.—Houston [1st Dist.] 2011, pet. denied)   9-20:1.1, 9-20:2

Taylor v. Slatkin,
   No. 3:02-CV-2404-R, 2003 WL 21662825 (N.D. Tex. May 13, 2003)   27-3:3.1

Taylor v. State,
   293 S.W.3d 913, 915–16 (Tex. App.—Austin 2009, no pet.)   23-4

TecLogistics, Inc. v. Dresser-Rand Grp. Inc.,
   527 S.W.3d 589 (Tex. App.—Houston [14th Dist.] 2017, no pet. h.)   2-13:2.4

Tejas Toyota, Inc. v. Griffin,
   587 S.W.2d 775, 776 (Tex. App.—Waco 1979, writ ref'd n.r.e.)   21-2:1

Teledyne Isotopes, Inc. v. Bravenec,
   640 S.W.2d 387 (Tex. App.—Houston [1st Dist.] 1982, writ ref'd n.r.e.)   7-1:4.4

Telephone Equip. Network, Inc. v. TA/Westchase Place, Ltd.,
   80 S.W.3d 601, 607 (Tex. App.—Houston [1st Dist.] 2002, no pet. h.)   8-1:5.5

Tellabs, Inc. v. Makor Issues & Rights, Ltd.,
   551 U.S. 308, 319 (2007)   2-4:2.1

Tenet Hosps. Ltd. v. Rivera, 445 S.W.3d 698 (Tex. 2014)	17-13:3
Tenneco Inc. v. Enterprise Prods., 925 S.W.2d 640, 647 (Tex. 1996)	30-2:1
Teon Mgmt., LLC v. Turquoise Bay Corp., 357 S.W.3d 719 (Tex. App.—Eastland 2011, pet. denied)	7-2:2
Tex. Beef Group v. Winfrey, 201 F.3d 680 (5th Cir. 2000)	1-8:1.1
Tex. Campaign for the Env't v. Partners Dewatering Int'l, LLC, 485 S.W.3d 184 (Tex. App.—Corpus Christi 2016, no pet.)	1-1:2
Tex. Dep't of Pub. Safety v. Alexander, 300 S.W.3d 62, 78 (Tex. App.—Austin 2009, pet. denied)	8-10:3.2
Tex. Sting, Ltd. v. R.B. Foods, Inc., 82 S.W.3d 644, 650 n.7 (Tex. App.—San Antonio 2002, pet denied)	13-3:3
Tex. Tax Sols., LLC v. City of El Paso, 593 S.W.3d 903, 909 (Tex. App.—El Paso 2019, no pet.)	13-5
Texas & P. Ry. Co. v. Bigham, 38 S.W. 162, 164 (Tex. 1896)	15-2
Texas & P. Ry. Co. v. Gay, 26 S.W. 599, 601–02 (Tex. 1894)	8-9:2.1
Texas Ass'n of Bus. v. Tex. Air Control Bd., 852 S.W.2d 440, 446 (Tex. 1993)	5-5:1.1, 5-5:2, 28-3
Texas Beef Cattle Co. v. Green, 921 S.W.2d 203, 210 (Tex. 1996)	1-1:3.2
Texas Co. v. State, 281 S.W.2d 83 (Tex. 1955)	3-2:2.1
Texas Commerce Bank Reagan v. Lebco Constructors, Inc., 865 S.W.2d 68 (Tex. App.—Corpus Christi 1993, writ denied)	1-5:2
Texas Comm'n on Human Rights v. Morrison, 346 S.W.3d 838 (Tex. App.—Austin 2011), review granted, *judgm't rev'd on other ground,* 381 S.W.3d 533 (Tex. 2012)	6-3:3.5
Texas Dep't of Cmty. Affairs v. Burdine, 450 U.S. 248 (1981)	6-3:2
Texas Dep't of Human Servs. of State of Tex. v. Hinds, 904 S.W.2d 629 (Tex. 1995)	6-2:2
Texas Dep't of Parks & Wildlife v. Miranda, 133 S.W.3d 217, 224 (Tex. 2004)	21-8, 21-9
Texas Dep't of Transp. v. Able, 35 S.W.3d 608 (Tex. 2000)	2-13:2.3
Texas Disposal Sys. Landfill, Inc. v. Waste Mgmt. Holdings, Inc., 219 S.W.3d 563, 590–91 (Tex. App.—Austin 2007, pet. denied)	1-2:2, 3-1:2

TABLE OF CASES

Case	Reference
Texas Farm Bureau Mut. Ins. Cos. v. Sears, 84 S.W.3d 604 (Tex. 2002)	9-12:1.1, 9-12:2
Texas Farmers Ins. v. Cameron, 24 S.W.3d 386, 399 (Tex. App.—Dallas 2000, pet. denied)	5-1:3.3
Texas Farmers Ins. v. Soriano, 881 S.W.2d 312, 316 n.4 (Tex. 1994)	5-7:2
Texas Gas Expl. Corp. v. Broughton Offshore Ltd. II, 790 S.W.2d 781, 789 (Tex. App.—Houston [14th Dist.] 1990, no writ)	12-1
Texas Gas Util. Co. v. Barrett, 460 S.W.2d 409 (Tex. 1970)	3-2:2.2
Texas Indus. Traffic League v. R.R. Comm'n Tex., 633 S.W.2d 821 (Tex. 1982)	28-3
Texas Instruments, Inc. v. Teletron Energy Mgmt., Inc., 877 S.W.2d 276, 279 (Tex. 1994)	11-6:1
Texas Int'l Airlines v. Nat'l Airlines, Inc., 714 F.2d 533 (5th Cir. 1983)	2-4:4.4
Texas Mut. Ins. Co. v. Ledbetter, 251 S.W.3d 31, 37 (Tex. 2008)	19-3
Texas Mut. Ins. v. Ruttiger, 381 S.W.3d 430 (Tex. 2012)	5-3:2
Texas Oil & Gas Corp. v. U.S., 466 F.2d 1040, 1047–48 (5th Cir. 1972)	8-7:4.3
Texas Pacific Coal & Oil Co. v. Barker, 6 S.W.2d 1031 (Tex. 1928)	7-14:3.1
Texas Parks & Wildlife Dep't v. Sawyer Trust, 354 S.W.3d 384, 389–90 (Tex. 2011)	8-10:2
Texas Water Rights Comm'n v. Crow Iron Works, 582 S.W.2d 768 (Tex. 1979)	16-7:3
Texas Wool & Mohair Mktg. Ass'n v. Standard Acc. Ins. Co., 175 F.2d 835, 838 (5th Cir. 1949)	27-3:3.4
Tex-Hio P'ship v. Garner, 106 S.W.3d 886, 890 (Tex. App.—Dallas 2003, no pet.)	29-1
T.F.W. Mgmt., Inc. v. Westwood Shores Prop. Owners Ass'n, 79 S.W.3d 712 (Tex. App.—Houston [14th Dist.] 2002, pet. denied)	8-4:1.1, 8-4:2.1
Thelander v. Moore, 684 S.W.2d 192, 194 (Tex. App.—Houston [14th Dist.] 1984, no writ)	8-4:2.1
Thigpen v. Locke, 363 S.W.2d 247, 251 (Tex. 1962)	1-4:4.5, 3-2:2.1, 7-7:2

Thomas, Tr. of Performance Products, Inc. v. Hughes,
SA-16-CV-00951-DAE, 2020 WL 773444, at *3
(W.D. Tex. Feb. 18, 2020)　　　　　　　　　　　　　　　　　　　2-11:3.2

Thomas v. Med. Arts Hosp. of Texarkana, Inc.,
920 S.W.2d 815, 818 (Tex. App.—Texarkana 1996, writ denied)　　30-1:1

Thomas, Richardson, Runden & Co., Inc. v. State,
683 S.W.2d 100 (Tex. App.—Tyler 1984,
writ ref'd n.r.e.)　　　　　　1-12:4.1, 1-14:2, 1-14:4.1, 3-12:2.5

Thomas v. Thomas,
902 S.W.2d 621, 626 (Tex. App.—Austin 1995, writ denied)　　　8-10:4.2

Thomas v. Uzoka,
290 S.W.3d 437 (Tex. App.—Houston [14th Dist.] 2009,
pet. denied)　　　　　　　　　　　　　　　　　　　　　　　　　1-11:3.1c

Thompson v. Cherokee Water Co.,
6 S.W.3d 343, 347–48 (Tex. App.—Texarkana 1999, no pet.)　　　6-2:2

Thompson v. Thompson Air Conditioning & Heating, Inc.,
884 S.W.2d 555 (Tex. App.—Texarkana 1994, no writ)　　　　　　1-13:4.1

Thomson Oil Royalty, LLC v. Graham,
351 S.W.3d 162 (Tex. App.—Tyler 2011, no pet.)　　　　3-13:3.4, 3-13:4.1

Timpte Industries, Inc. v Gish,
286 S.W.3d 306 (Tex. 2009)　　　　　　　　　　　　　　　　30-1:3, 30-2:3

TLC Hosp., LLC v. Pillar Income Asset Mgmt., Inc.,
570 S.W.3d 749, 768 (Tex. App.—Tyler 2018, pet. denied)　　　8-3:2

Tony Gullo Motors I, L.P. v. Chapa,
212 S.W.3d 299, 304 (Tex. 2006)　　　1-4:3.1d, 1-4:3.2, 1-6:3.1d, 2-4:3.5, 11-9:3

Torres v. Johnson,
91 S.W.3d 905, 909 (Tex. App.—Fort Worth 2002, no pet.)　　　23-2

Torrington Co. v. Stutzman,
46 S.W.3d 829, 849 (Tex. 2000)　　　　　　　　　　　　　　　　24-1:4

Town of Flower Mound v. Eagleridge Operating, LLC,
02-18-00392-CV, 2019 WL 3955197, at *3
(Tex. App.—Fort Worth Aug. 22, 2019, no pet.)　　　　　　　　8-1:5.5

Tractebel Energy Mktg., Inc. v. E.I. Du Pont de Nemours & Co.,
118 S.W.3d 60 (Tex. App.—Houston [14th Dist.] 2003, pet. denied)　3-1:3.15

Trahan v. Mettlen,
428 S.W.3d 905, 909 (Tex. App.—Texarkana 2014, no pet.)　　　17-4:1

Trammell v. Whitlock,
150 Tex. 500, 242 S.W.2d 157 (1951)　　　　　　　　　　　　　3-9:2

Transitional Entity LP v. Elder Care LP,
No. 05-14-01615-CV, 2016 Tex. App. LEXIS 5711 (App.—Dallas
May 27, 2016)　　　　　　　　　　　　　　　　　　　　　　　3-1:3.1a

TABLE OF CASES

Transp. Ins. Co. v. Moriel,
   879 S.W.2d 10, 22 (Tex. 1994)   2-1:2.1, 2-2:2.1

Transport Ins. v. Faircloth,
   898 S.W.2d 269, 279 (Tex. 1995)   5-3:2

Transportation Ins. Co. v. Franco,
   821 S.W.2d 751, 754–55 (Tex. App.—Amarillo 1992, writ denied)   8-10:4.5

Trantham v. Isaacks,
   218 S.W.3d 750, 753 (Tex. App.—Fort Worth 2007, pet. denied)   8-10:2

Travis v. City of Mesquite,
   830 S.W.2d 94 (Tex. 1992)   1-9:2, 7-11:2

Travis v. Irby,
   326 F.3d 644 (5th Cir.2003)   27-3:5

Trenholm v. Ratcliff,
   646 S.W.2d 927 (Tex. 1983)   1-4:2, 1-4:3.1c

Trevino v. Ortega,
   969 S.W.2d 950 (Tex. 1998)   9-6:1, 9-6:1.1, 9-6:2, 9-15:2, 9-19:1, 9-19:2

Triantaphyllis v. Gamble,
   93 S.W.3d 398 (Tex. App.—Houston [14th Dist.] 2002, pet. denied)   8-2:1.1

Trico Techs. Corp. v. Montiel,
   949 S.W.2d 308, 310 (Tex. 1997)   30-3:5

Trinity Indus. v. Ashland, Inc.,
   53 S.W.3d 852 (Tex. App.—Austin 2001, pet. denied)   1-5:1

Trinity River Auth. v. URS Consultants, Inc.,
   889 S.W.2d 259 (Tex.1994)   1-15:3.1

Trinity Universal Ins. v. Cowan,
   945 S.W.2d 819, 823 (Tex. 1997)   5-6:2

Triplex Commc'ns, Inc. v. Riley,
   900 S.W.2d 716 (Tex. 1995)   9-3:1

Tripp Vill. v. MBank Lincoln Centre,
   774 S.W.2d 746 (Tex. App.—Dallas 1989, writ denied)   16-14:2

Tri-State Chems. v. W. Organics,
   83 S.W.3d 189 (Tex. App.—Amarillo 2002)   3-6:2

Trousdale v. Henry,
   261 S.W.3d 221 (Tex. App.—Houston [14th Dist.] 2008, pet. denied)   9-1:1, 17-10

Truly v. Austin,
   744 S.W.2d 934 (Tex. 1988)   3-3:1.1, 3-1:3.2, 3-3:2, 3-3:4.2, 3-3:4.5, 11-11:4

Twin City Fire Ins. v. Davis,
   904 S.W.2d 663 (Tex. 1995)   5-3:1

Tubb v. Aspect Int'l, Inc.,
  No. 12-14-00323-CV, 2017 Tex. App. LEXIS 362, at *5–6
  (App.—Tyler Jan. 18, 2017)   3-1:4.3a

Tukua Inves., LLC v. Spenst,
  413 S.W.3d 786 (Tex. App.—El Paso 2013, pet. denied)   1-5:2

Turner v. Houston Agr. Credit Corp.,
  601 S.W.2d 61 (Tex. Civ. App.—Houston [1st Dist.] 1980,
  writ ref'd n.r.e.)   3-2:2.1

Twin City Fire Ins. v. Davis,
  904 S.W.2d 663, 666 (Tex. 1995)   5-3:1

Twist v. Nat'l Bank,
  294 S.W.3d 255, 260 (Tex. App.—Corpus Christi-Edinburgh 2009,
  no writ)   13-4:2

Two Pesos, Inc. v. Gulf Ins.,
  901 S.W.2d 495, 501 (Tex. App.—Houston [14th Dist.] 1995,
  no writ)   5-6:4.4

Twyman v. Twyman,
  855 S.W.2d 619, 625 (Tex. 1993)   17-2

TXI Transp. Co. v. Hughes,
  306 S.W.3d 230 (Tex. 2010)   1-9:2

TXI Transp. v. Hughes,
  224 S.W.3d 870, 905 n.42 (Tex. App.—Fort Worth 2007)   15-4:2

Tyra v. Woodson,
  495 S.W.2d 211, 213 (Tex. 1973)   8-5:3.2

Ulico Cas. Co. v. Allied Pilots Ass'n,
  262 S.W.3d 773 (Tex. 2008)   16-6, 16-6:1

Ulmer v. John Hancock Mut. Life Ins. Co.,
  161 S.W.2d 862 (Tex. Civ. App.—Eastland 1942, writ ref'd w.o.m.)   3-2:2.1

UMLIC VP L.L.C. v. T&M Sales & Envtl. Sys.,
  176 S.W.3d 595 (Tex. App.—Corpus Christi 2005, pet. denied)   1-6:2

Union Carbide Corp. v. Loftin,
  256 S.W.3d 869 (Tex. App.—Beaumont 2008, pet. dism'd)   13-2:5, 22-1

Union Pacific Res. Grp., Inc. v. Hankins,
  111 S.W.3d 69, 71 (Tex. 2003)   7-13:2, 7-14:4.1

Unit Tex. Drilling, LLC v. Morales,
  No. 13–10–00247–CV, 2010 WL 2968046, *3
  (Tex. App.—Corpus Christi July 29, 2010, pet. denied)   25-1:1

United Blood Serv. v. Longoria,
  938 S.W.2d 29, 30 (Tex. 1997)   30-3:4

United Mobile Networks, L.P. v. Deaton,
  939 S.W.2d 146, 147–48 (Tex. 1997)   1-3:3.1a

TABLE OF CASES

Universe Life Ins. Co. v. Giles, 950 S.W.2d 48, 56 (Tex. 1997)	5-3:2, 5-3:3.1a, 5-3:3.2, 5-3:3.4
U.S. Metals, Inc. v. Libert Mut. Grp., 490 S.W.3d 20, 24 (Tex. 2016)	5-6:2
USAA Texas Lloyds Co. v. Menchaca, 545 S.W.3d 479 (Tex. 2018)	5-2:1.1, 5-2:4.1
Valdes v. Wal-Mart Stores, Inc., 199 F.3d 290, 292 (5th Cir. 2000)	27-3:5
Valenzuela v. State & Cty. Mut. Fire Ins. Co., 317 S.W.3d 550, 553 (Tex. App.—Houston [14th Dist.] 2010, no pet.)	30-3:3
Van Der Linden v. Khan, 535 S.W.3d 179 (Tex. App.—Fort Worth 2017, no pet.)	1-2:2
Van Indep. Sch. Dist. v. McCarty, 165 S.W.3d 351 (Tex. 2005)	6-1:4.6
Vandervoort v. Sansom, 293 S.W.2d 271 (Tex. Civ. App.—Fort Worth 1956, writ ref'd n.r.e.)	3-2:4.2
Vargas v. HWC Gen. Maint., LLC, No. H–11–875, 2012 WL 948892, at *2 (S.D. Tex. Mar. 20, 2012)	13-5:2
Various Opportunities, Inc. v. Sullivan Invs., Inc., 677 S.W.2d 115, 118 (Tex. App.—Dallas 1984, no writ)	8-3:3.1
Vasquez v. Legend Nat. Gas III, LP, 492 S.W.3d 448, 451 (Tex. App.—San Antonio 2016, pet. denied)	28-1:2
Vaughn v. Deitz, 430 S.W.2d 487 (Tex. 1968)	17-11:6
Vega v. Compass Bank, No. 04-13-00383-CV, 2014 Tex. App. LEXIS 2709 (App.—San Antonio Mar. 12, 2014)	3-1:2
Vela v. Catlin Specialty Ins. Co., No. 13–13–00475–CV, 2015 Tex. App. LEXIS 3743, at *39–40 (Tex. App.—Corpus Christi 2015, pet. denied)	5-7:3.3
Ventling v. Johnson, 466 S.W.3d 143 (Tex. 2015)	3-1:3.10
Vernon v. Perrien, 390 S.W.3d 47 (Tex. App.—El Paso 2012, pet. denied)	7-1:2
Vermont Info. Processing, Inc. v. Montana Beverage Corp., 227 S.W.3d 846 (Tex. App.—El Paso 2007, no pet.)	3-1:2
Vertex Indus., Inc. v. Allstate Fire & Cas. Ins. Co., No. 12–16–00303-CV, 2017 WL 2464698, at *3 (Tex. App.—Tyler June 7, 2017, no pet.)	13-2:4

Via Net v. TIG Ins.,
   211 S.W.3d 310 (Tex. 2006) — 3-1:4.1, 6-1:4.1

Vick v. Merchants' Fast Motor Lines,
   151 S.W.2d 293, 297 (Tex. Civ. App.—Eastland 1941, no writ) — 8-8:3.3

Vickory v. Summit Nat'l Bank,
   702 S.W.2d 324 (Tex. App.—Fort Worth 1986, writ ref'd n.r.e.) — 3-6:4.1

Victoria v. Schott,
   29 S.W. 681 (Tex. Civ. App.—Houston 1895, no writ) — 7-4:1

Villarreal v. Grant Geophysical, Inc.,
   136 S.W.3d 265, 270 (Tex. App.—San Antonio 2004,
   pet. denied) — 7-6:1.1, 7-6:2, 11-11:2

Villarreal v. Wells Fargo Brokerage Servs., LLC,
   315 S.W.3d 109, 125–26 (Tex. App.—Houston [1st Dist.]
   2010, no pet.) — 18-1

Villiers v. Republic Fin. Servs., Inc.,
   602 S.W.2d 566, 570 (Tex. Civ. App.—Texarkana 1980,
   writ ref'd n.r.e.) — 8-4:5.5, 11-11:6

Violet Rose Holdings, Ltd. v. Spinning Star Energy, LLC,
   No. 01–17–00022–CV, 2018 WL 1526169, at *2
   (Tex. App.—Houston [1st Dist.] Mar. 29, 2018) — 1-3:3.1a

Vizcarra v. Roldan,
   925 S.W.2d 89, 92 (Tex. App.—El Paso 1996, no writ) — 24-1:4

Volume Millwork, Inc. v. W. Hous. Airport Corp.,
   218 S.W.3d 722, 725–26 (Tex. App.—Houston [1st Dist.] 2006) — 8-11:3.2

Vortt Exploration Co., Inc. v. Chevron USA, Inc.,
   787 S.W.2d 942, 944 (Tex. 1990) — 3-1:3.2, 3-3:1.1, 3-3:2, 3-3:3.1, 11-11:2

W & F Transp., Inc. v. Wilhelm,
   208 S.W.3d 32 (Tex. App.-Houston [14th Dist.] 2006) — 1-6:2

Wadewitz v. Montgomery,
   951 S.W.2d 464, 466–67 (Tex. 1997) — 30-3:4

Waffle House, Inc. v. Williams,
   313 S.W.3d 796 (Tex. 2010) — 6-3:4.2

Waisath v. Lack's Stores, Inc.,
   474 S.W.2d 444, 446 (Tex. 1971) — 1-3:2

Waite Hill Servs., Inc. v. World Class Metal Works, Inc.,
   959 S.W.2d 182, 184 (Tex. 1998) — 12-2:1

Waite v. Woodard, Hall & Primm, P.C.,
   137 S.W.3d 277, 281 (Tex. App.—Houston [1st Dist.] 2004,
   no pet.) — 30-1:3

Waldrop v. Waldrop,
   552 S.W.3d 396, 411 (Tex. App.—Fort Worth 2018, no pet.) — 8-10:4.1

TABLE OF CASES

Walker & Assocs. Surveying, Inc. v. Austin,
  301 S.W.3d 909, 918 (Tex. App.—Texarkana 2009, no pet.) — 11-5:7

Walker v. Cotter Properties, Inc.,
  181 S.W.3d 895, 900 (Tex. App.—Dallas 2006, no pet.) — 3-4:5.1, 11-11:2

Walker v. Salt Flat Water Co.,
  128 Tex. 140, 143–44, 96 S.W.2d 231, 232 (1936) — 12-1

Walker v. Walker,
  No. 14-16-00357-CV, 2017 Tex. App. LEXIS 2719 (App.—Houston [14th Dist.] Mar. 30, 2017) — 3-5:1

Wallace v. Briggs,
  162 Tex. 485, 491, 348 S.W.2d 523, 527 (1961) — 11-13:2

Walling v. Metcalfe,
  863 S.W.2d 56, 57 (Tex. 1993) — 8-1:2, 8-1:5.3

Wal-Mart Stores, Inc. v. McKenzie,
  997 S.W.2d 278, 280 (Tex. 1999) — 29-7

Wal-Mart Stores, Inc. v. Rodriguez,
  92 S.W.3d 502, 506 (Tex. 2002) — 30-2:4

Wal-Mart Stores, Inc. v. Sturges,
  52 S.W.3d 711 (Tex. 2001) — 1-1:4.3, 1-2:1.1, 1-2:4.3, 1-2:2

Walnut Equip. Leasing Co. v. J-V Dirt & Loam, a Div. of J-V Marble Mfg., Inc.,
  907 S.W.2d 912, 915 (Tex. App.—Austin 1995, writ denied) — 8-8:1

Walters v. Cleveland Reg'l Med. Ctr.,
  307 S.W.3d 292, 298 (Tex. 2010) — 17-11:2

Wansey v. Hole,
  379 S.W.3d 246 (Tex. 2012) — 1-9:1.1, 1-9:2, 1-9:3.1

Ward v. Ladner,
  322 S.W.3d 692, 696–97 (Tex. App.—Tyler 2010, pet. denied) — 19-3

Ward v. Malone,
  115 S.W.3d 267, 270 (Tex. App.—Corpus Christi 2003, pet. denied) — 8-11:4.1, 8-11:5.2

Ware v. United Fire Lloyds,
  No. 09-12-00061-CV, 2013 Tex. App. LEXIS 5730, at *8–9 (Tex. App.—Beaumont 2013, no pet.) — 5-1:3.5

Warrantech Corp. v. Steadfast Ins.,
  210 S.W.3d 760, 769 (Tex. App.—Fort Worth 2006, pet. denied) — 5-5:3.3, 5-6:3.3

Washburn v. Krenek,
  684 S.W.2d 187, 191 (Tex. App.—Houston [14th Dist.] 1984, writ ref'd n.r.e.) — 14-4

Washington Nat'l Ins. Co. v. Craddock,
  109 S.W.2d 165 (Tex. Comm'n App. 1937) — 16-6

Washington Square Fin., LLC v. RSL Funding, LLC,
    418 S.W.3d 761, 767 (Tex. App.—Houston [14th Dist.] 2013,
    pet. denied)   1-1:2

Waste Mgmt. of Tex., Inc. v. Tex. Disposal Sys. Landfill, Inc.,
    434 S.W.3d 142, 149–51 (Tex. 2014)   1-8:2, 1-8:3.1, 11-9:2, 12-3

Watkins v. Gen. Motors, LLC,
    No. H-11-2106, 2011 WL 3567017, at *2–3 (S. D. Tex. Aug. 12, 2011)   27-3:5

Watson v. Rochmill,
    155 S.W.2d 783 (Tex. 1941)   7-1:4.1, 7-10:2

Wauson & Williams, Architects, Inc. v. Reeder Dev. Corp.,
    572 S.W.2d 24 (Tex. Civ. App.—Houston
    [1st Dist.] 1978, no writ)   3-7:4.1, 3-8:4.1, 3-8:4.2,
                                                            3-8:4.3, 3-8:4.4, 3-8:4.5

W.B. Johnson Drilling Co. v. Lacy,
    336 S.W.2d 230 (Tex. Civ. App.-Eastland 1960, no writ)   7-8:5.1

Webb v. Glenbrook Owners Ass'n, Inc.,
    298 S.W.3d 374 (Tex. App.—Dallas 2009, no pet.)   8-2:1.1

Webb v. Voga,
    316 S.W.3d 809, 813 (Tex. App.—Dallas 2010, no pet.)   8-10:2, 8-10:4.3

Webber v. M.W. Kellogg Co.,
    720 S.W.2d 124 (Tex. App.—Houston [14th Dist.] 1986,
    writ ref'd n.r.e.)   6-1:2

Webster v. Allstate Ins. Co.,
    833 S.W.2d 747, 750 (Tex. App.—Houston [1st Dist.] 1992, no writ)   5-4:4.1

Webster v. Thomas,
    5 S.W.3d 287 (Tex. App.—Houston [14th Dist.] 1999, no pet.)   17-12, 23-4

Weems v. Louis Dreyfus Corp.,
    380 F.2d 545, 547 (5th Cir. 1967)   27-5:3

Weiner v. Wasson,
    900 S.W.2d 316, 317–18 (Tex. 1995)   17-11:3

Weingartens, Inc. v. Price,
    461 S.W.2d 260, 263 (Tex. App.—Houston [14th Dist.] 1970,
    writ ref'd n.r.e.)   10-3

Welch v. McLean,
    191 S.W.3d 147, 154 (Tex. App.—Fort Worth 2005, no pet.)   5-7:3.3, 5-7:3.4

Welch v. Milton,
    185 S.W.3d 586, 594 (Tex. App.—Dallas 2006, pet. denied)   30-3:9

Wells Fargo Bank, N.A. v. Ezell,
    410 S.W.3d 919, 922 (Tex. App.—El Paso 2013, no pet.)   8-11:4.1, 8-11:5.2

Wells Fargo Bank, N.A. v. Murphy,
    458 S.W.3d 912, 915 (Tex. 2015)   11-13:3

TABLE OF CASES

Wells Fargo Bank Nw., N.A. v. RPK Capital XVI, L.L.C.,
   360 S.W.3d 691, 706 (Tex. App—Dallas 2012, no pet.)   1-3:2

Welkener v. Welkener,
   71 S.W.3d 364 (Tex. App.—Corpus Christi 2001, no pet.)   3-1:3.13

Wendell v. Cent. Power & Light Co.,
   677 S.W.2d 610, 618 (Tex. App.—Corpus Christi 1984, writ ref'd n.r.e.)   29-6

Westbrook v. Penley,
   231 S.W.3d 389 (Tex. 2007)   21-5

Westchester Fire Ins. Co. v. Admiral Ins. Co.,
   152 S.W.3d 172, 190 n.9 (Tex. App.—Fort Worth 2004, pet. denied)   5-7:3.2

Western Invs. v. Urena,
   162 S.W.3d 547 (Tex. 2005)   1-10:2

Western Union Tel. Co. v. Chihuahua Exch.,
   206 S.W. 364 (Tex. Civ. App.—El Paso 1918, no writ)   3-13:3.5

Wes-Tex Tank Rental, Inc. v. Pioneer Natural Res. U.S.A., Inc.,
   327 S.W.3d 316 (Tex. App.—Eastland 2010, no pet.)   3-1:3.1a, 3-1:3.1b

Whatley v. City of Dallas,
   758 S.W.2d 301, 310 (Tex. App.—Dallas 1988, writ denied)   5-6:4.1

Wheelbarger v. Landing Council of Co-Owners,
   471 S.W.3d 875, 893 (Tex. App.—Houston [1st Dist.] 2015, pet. denied)   12-2:2

Wheeler v. Blacklands Prod. Credit Ass'n,
   627 S.W.2d 846, 849 (Tex. App.—Fort Worth 1982, no writ)   11-11:1

Wheeler v. White,
   398 S.W.2d 93, 97 (Tex. 1965)   3-5:2.1, 3-5:3.1, 9-5:1, 11-5:8

Whitaker v. Bank of El Paso,
   850 S.W.2d 757, 760 (Tex. App.—El Paso 1993, no writ)   1-3:2

White v. Harrison,
   390 S.W.3d 666, 675 n.5 (Tex. App.—Dallas 2012, no pet.)   12-1

White v. Pei,
   452 S.W.3d 527, 2014 WL 6851585
   (Tex. App.—Houston [14th Dist.] 2014, no pet. h.)   1-6:2

White v. Zhou Pei,
   452 S.W.3d 527, 543 (Tex. App.—Houston [14th Dist.] 2014)   1-1:4.2, 1-2:4.2

Whitworth v. Kuhn,
   734 S.W.2d 108 (Tex. App.—Austin 1987, no pet.)   13-2:6

Whole Foods Market Sw., L.P. v. Tijerina,
   979 S.W.2d 768, 775–76 (Tex. App.—Houston [14th Dist.] 1998, pet. denied)   29-7

Wichita Railroad & Light Co. v. Public Util. Comm'n of Kansas,
   260 U.S. 48, 54, 43 S. Ct. 51, 53, 67 L. Ed. 124 (1922)   27-3:3.4

Wiese v. Pro Am. Servs., Inc.,
   317 S.W.3d 857, 863 (Tex. App.—Houston [14th Dist.] 2010, no pet.)   1-3:3.1c

Wilen v. Falkenstein,
   191 S.W.3d 791 (Tex. App.—Fort Worth 2006, pet. denied)   9-4:2

Willacy Cty. Appraisal Review Bd. v. South Padre Land Co.,
   767 S.W.2d 201, 203–04 (Tex. App.—Corpus Christi 1989, no writ)   19-4

Williams v. City of Midland,
   932 S.W.2d 679, 685 (Tex. App.—El Paso 1996, no writ)   1-7:4.5

Williams v. Dodson,
   976 S.W.2d 861, 864 (Tex. App.—Austin 1998, no pet.)   1-3:3.1a

Williams v. First Tenn. Nat'l Corp.,
   97 S.W.3d 798 (Tex. App.—Dallas 2003, no pet.)   3-1:2, 6-1:2

Williams v. Glash,
   789 S.W.2d 261 (Tex. 1990)   16-5, 16-5:1, 16-5:2

Williams v. Jennings,
   755 S.W.2d 874 (Tex. App.—Houston [14th Dist.]
   1988, writ denied)   7-10:1.1, 7-10:2, 7-10:3.2

Williams v. Khalaf,
   802 S.W.2d 651 (Tex. 1990)   3-2:4.1

Williams v. Unifund CCR Partners Assignee of Citibank,
   264 S.W.3d 231 (Tex. App.—Houston [1st Dist.] 2008, no pet.)   3-1:2, 3-7:2

Williams v. Wells Fargo Bank,
   N.A., 560 Fed. Appx. 233, 243 (5th Cir. 2014)   8-4:3.1

Williamson v. Osenton,
   232 U.S. 619 (1914)   27-3:3.1

Willis v. Maverick,
   760 S.W.2d 642 (Tex. 1988)   4-1:4.1a, 4-1:4.1c, 17-2, 17-10, 17-11:2,

Wil-Roye Inv. Co. II v. Washington Mut. Bank, FA,
   142 S.W.3d 393, 400 (Tex. App.—El Paso 2004, no pet.)   30-1:1

Wilson v. Dunn,
   800 S.W.2d 833, 836 (Tex. 1990)   23-4

Wilson v. John Daugherty Realtors, Inc.,
   981 S.W.2d 723, 727 (Tex. App.—Houston [1st Dist.]
   1998, no pet.)   17-2

Wilson v. Texas Parks and Wildlife Dept.,
   886 S.W.2d 259, 260–61 (Tex. 1994)   22-1, 22-3, 22-4

Wilz v. Flournoy,
   228 S.W.3d 674, 676–77 (Tex. 2007)   8-5:1.1, 8-5:2, 11-11:1

Winchek v. Am. Exp. Travel Related Servs. Co., Inc.,
   232 S.W.3d 197 (Tex. App.—Houston [1st Dist.] 2007, no pet.)   3-1:2

TABLE OF CASES

Wing Aviation, L.L.C. v. Balmanno,
  No. 09-06-022-CV, 2006 Tex. App. LEXIS 7447
  (App.—Beaumont Aug. 24, 2006) — 3-8:1.1

Wingate v. Hajdik,
  795 S.W.2d 717, (Tex. 1990) — 2-8:3.1

Winkle Chevy-Olds-Pontiac, Inc. v. Condon,
  830 S.W.2d 740, 746 (Tex. App.—Corpus Christi 1992,
  writ dism'd) — 1-3:2, 1-3:3.1

Winograd v. Clear Lake City Water Auth.,
  811 S.W.2d 147 (Tex. App.—Houston [1st Dist.] 1991,
  writ denied) — 6-1:2

Winters v. Houston Chronicle Pub. Co.,
  795 S.W.2d 723 (Tex. 1990) — 6-1:2, 6-2:2, 9-22:1.1, 9-22:2

Wise v. Complete Staffing Servs.,
  56 S.W.3d 900 (Tex. App.—Texarkana 2001, no pet.) — 1-9:2

Wise v. SR Dallas, LLC,
  436 S.W.3d 402 (Tex. App.—Dallas 2014, no pet.) — 1-3:2, 1-6:2

Wolfe v. Devon Energy Prod. Co.,
  382 S.W.3d 434 (Tex. App.—Waco 2012, pet. denied) — 7-2:2, 7-3:2, 7-3:4.3

Woodhaven Partners, Ltd. v. Shamoun & Norman, L.L.P.,
  422 S.W.3d 821 (Tex. App.—Dallas 2014, no pet.) — 3-7:1.1, 11-5:6

Woodlands Land Dev. Co. v. Jenkins,
  48 S.W.3d 415 (Tex. App.—Beaumont 2001, no pet.) — 1-5:3.2

Woods v. William M. Mercer, Inc.,
  769 S.W.2d 515, 515–16 (Tex. 1988) — 17-11:2

Wooley v. Schaffer,
  447 S.W.3d 71, 74–76 (Tex. App.—Houston [14th Dist.] 2014,
  pet. denied) — 19-4, 28-1:2

Wrenn v. G.A.T.X. Logistics, Inc.,
  73 S.W.3d 489 (Tex. App—Fort Worth 2002, no pet.) — 1-9:2

Wright v. Matthews,
  26 S.W.3d 575 (Tex. App.—Beaumont 2000, pet. denied) — 7-1:2

Wright v. Modern Grp., Ltd.,
  No. 13-12-00293-CV, 2013 WL 4714930, at *8
  (Tex. App.—Corpus Christi-Edinburg Aug. 30, 2013, pet. denied) — 19-1

Wright v. Robert & St. John Motor Co.,
  58 S.W.2d 67 (Tex. 1933) — 16-14:2

Wyatt v. McGregor,
  855 S.W.2d 5, 18 (Tex. App—Corpus Christi-E dinburg 1993,
  writ denied) — 30-3:10

Wyatt v. Shaw Plumbing Co.,
  760 S.W.2d 245 (Tex. 1988) — 28-3

Yarbrough v. Household Fin. Corp. III,
　455 S.W.3d 277, 280 (Tex, App.—Houston [14th Dist.] 2015, no pet.) 　7-4:1

Yarto v. Gilliland,
　287 S.W.3d 83, 89–94 (Tex. App.—Corpus Christi 2009, no pet.) 　8-11:5.2

Yeng v. Zou,
　407 S.W.3d 485, 491 (Tex. App.—Houston [14th Dist.] 2013, no pet.) 　11-3, 12-2:1

York Group, Inc. v. York S., Inc.,
　CIV.A. H-06-0262, 2006 WL 2883373, at *2 (S.D. Tex. Oct. 10, 2006) 　8-4:4.2

York v. Boatman,
　487 S.W.3d 635, 647 (Tex. App.—Texarkana 2016, no pet.) 　8-5:4.1

Yorkshire Ins. Co. v. Seger,
　279 S.W.3d 755, 772 (Tex. App.—Amarillo 2007, pet. denied) 　5-7:3.1

Young v. J. F. Zimmerman & Sons, Inc.,
　434 S.W.2d 926 (Tex. Civ. App.—Waco 1968, writ dism'd) 　3-9:3.8, 3-9:3.9

Young v. United Parcel Serv., Inc.,
　575 U.S. 206 (2015) 　6-3:2

Yzaguirre v. KCS Res., Inc.,
　47 S.W.3d 532 (Tex. App.—Dallas 2000), *aff'd,*
　53 S.W.3d 368 (Tex. 2001) 　9-8:1, 9-8:1.1

Yzaguirre v. KCS Res., Inc.,
　53 S.W.3d 368 (Tex. 2001) 　7-13:1, 7-13:1.1, 7-13:2, 7-13:3.1, 7-13:4.1

Zapata Corp. v. Zapata Trading Int'l, Inc.,
　841 S.W.2d 45 (Tex. App.—Houston [14th Dist.]
　1992, no writ) 　1-12:1, 1-12:2, 1-13:1.1, 1-13:2.1, 1-14:1.1, 1-14:2

Zapatero v. Canales,
　730 S.W.2d 111 (Tex. App.—San Antonio 1987, writ ref'd n.r.e.) 　3-2:2.1

Zarate v. Rodriguez,
　542 S.W.3d 26, 37 (Tex. App.—Houston [14th Dist.] 2017, pet. denied) 　29-5

Zatarains, Inc. v. Oak Grove Smokehouse, Inc.,
　698 F.2d 786 (5th Cir. 1983) 　1-12:2, 1-14:2

Zavala v. Trujillo,
　883 S.W.2d 242, 248 (Tex. App.—El Paso 1994, writ denied) 　11-13:2

Zeecon Wireless Internet, LLC v. Am. Bank of Tex., N.A.,
　305 S.W.3d 813, 818 (Tex. App.—Austin 2010) 　8-8:4.3

Zenith Star Ins. Co. v. Wilkerson,
　150 S.W.3d 525 (Tex. App.—Austin 2004, no pet.) 　4-1:2

Zorrilla v. Aypco Constr. II, LLC,
　469 S.W.3d 143, 155–58 (Tex. 2015) 　1-1:2, 10-7, 11-2, 13-5:1

Zuider Zee Oyster Bar, Inc. v. Martin,
　503 S.W.2d 292, 299 (Tex. Civ. App.—Fort Worth
　1973, writ ref'd n.r.e.) 　5-3:3.3, 5-7:3.4, 6-1:3.2

Index

A

AB INITIO. *See* **VOID AB INITIO**
ABANDONMENT
  Accountings, abandonment of remedy, 8-4:5.3
  Breach of partnership duty, 2-10:4.3
  Misuse of a trade name defense, 1-14:4.3
  Trademark infringement defense, 1-12:4.3, 1-13:4.3
  Usurpation of business opportunity, 2-11:4.3
ACCESS
  General partnership, 2-12:2.3
ACCORD AND SATISFACTION
  Affirmative defenses
    elements
      common law, 16-3:1
      statutory, 16-3:2
    other issues, 16-3:3
    overview, 16-3
  Breach of contract, 3-1:4.17
  Suits on an account, 3-8:4.3
ACCOUNTANTS
  Breach of duty of care, 2-1:4.1
  Breach of duty of loyalty, 2-2:4.1
  Wrongful distribution of dividends, 2-3:4.1
ACCOUNTING
  Breach of partnership duty, 2-10:3.3, 2-10:4.1
  Damages and remedies
    attorneys' fees, 8-4:3.4
    interest, 8-4:3.3
    judgment for payment, 8-4:3.2
    order requiring accounting, 8-4:3.1
  Defenses
    equitable defenses, 8-4:4.4
    laches, 8-4:4.2
    statute of limitations, 8-4:4.1
    unclean hands, 8-4:4.3
  Elements
    equitable accounting, 8-4:2.1
    statutory grounds, 8-4:2.2
  Overview, 8-4:1, 11-11:6
  Procedural implications
    abandonment of remedy, 8-4:5.3
    appeal, 8-4:5.2
    auditor appointed, 8-4:5.5
    jurisdiction, 8-4:5.1
    separate trial on right of accounting, 8-4:5.4
  Related causes of action, 8-4:1.1

ACT OF GOD
  Inferential rebuttal defenses, 15-5
ADVERSE POSSESSION
  Pleading requirements, 7-2:5.3b
  Surface versus mineral rights, 7-2:2
ADVICE OF COUNSEL
  Slander of title, 7-10:4.2
AFFIRMATIVE DEFENSES
  Accord and satisfaction. *See* **ACCORD AND SATISFACTION**
  Arbitration and award
    elements, 16-4:1
    overview, 16-4
  Assumption of risk. *See* **ASSUMPTION OF RISK**
  Collateral estoppel
    elements, 16-7:2
    other issues, 16-7:2
    overview, 16-7
  Consideration failure. *See* **CONSIDERATION**
  Contributory negligence
    elements, 16-10:2
    overview, 16-10
  Definitions
    duress, 16-11
    release, 16-5
  Discharge in bankruptcy. *See* **BANKRUPTCY**
  Duress. *See* **DURESS**
  Estoppel. *See* **ESTOPPEL**
  Fraud. *See* **FRAUD, GENERALLY**
  Fraudulent concealment, 17-11:1
  General denials compared, 13-3:1
  Illegality. *See* **ILLEGALITY**
  Laches. *See* **LACHES**
  License
    elements, 16-9:1
    overview, 16-9
  Overview, 13-1
  Parental immunity, 16-19
  Payment
    elements
      overview, 16-2:1
      other issues, 16-2:3
      voluntary payment, 16-2:2
    overview, 16-2
  Pleading
    defects in pleading, 13-5:2
    overview, 13-5
    types of, 13-5:1

AFFIRMATIVE DEFENSES (*cont.*)
  Release. *See* **RELEASE**
  Res judicata. *See* **RES JUDICATA**
  Statute of Frauds. *See* **STATUTE OF FRAUDS**
  Statutes of limitations. *See* **STATUTES OF LIMITATIONS**
  Waiver
    elements, 16-6:1
    overview, 16-6
AGENCIES
  Subject matter jurisdiction, 21-6
AGENTS AND AGENCY
  Agent liable to third parties
    damages and remedies
      contractual liability, 3-12:3.1
      tort liability, 3-12:3.2
    defenses
      actual damages, 3-12:4.2
      indemnification, 3-12:4.1
      quantum meruit, 3-12:4.3
    elements
      assumption of liability, 3-12:2.4
      disclosed principals, 3-12:2.2
      non-existent or legally incompetent principal, 3-12:2.3
      partially disclosed or undisclosed principal, 3-12:2.1
      tort liability, 3-12:2.6
      warranty of authority breached, 3-12:2.5
    overview, 3-12:1
    related causes of action, 3-12:1.1
  Agent's actions binding principal
    damages and remedies
      exemplary damages, 3-11:3.2
      overview, 3-11:3.1
    defenses, 3-11:4
    elements
      contractual liability, 3-11:2.1
      tort liability, 3-11:2.2
    overview, 3-11:1
    related causes of action, 3-11:1.1
  Breach of duty
    damages and remedies
      actual damages, 3-13:3.1
      avoidance of contract, 3-13:3.4
      disgorgement, 3-13:3.3
      exemplary damages, 3-13:3.6
      forfeiture of fee, 3-13:3.2
      obedience, breach of duty, 3-13:3.5
    defenses
      estoppel, 3-13:4.2
      ratification, 3-13:4.1
      statute of limitations, 3-13:4.3
    elements, 3-13:2
    overview, 3-13:1
    related causes of action, 3-13:1.1
  Definition, vice principals, 3-11:3.2
  Officers and directors liability. *See* **OFFICERS AND DIRECTORS**

AIDING AND ABETTING
  Suits to compel inspection, 2-12:4.1
ALIENS
  Domicile, 27-3:3.1
AMENDMENT
  Attachment, procedural issues, 8-7:5.6
  Dismissal of baseless cause of action, 28-1:5
  General denials
    within 14 days of trial, 13-3:4
    extension to, 13-3:2
  Jurisdictional defects, 21-9
  Level 1 discovery, 20-2
  Level 2 discovery, 20-3
  Pleadings. *See* **PLEADING**
  Sequestration, procedural issues, 8-6:5.6
  Special appearances, unsworn motions, 13-2:2
  Special exceptions and, 28-2
APPEAL
  Accountings, 8-4:5.2
  Arbitration, motion to compel denial, 25-2
  Injunction
    temporary injunction, 8-1:5.6
  Pleading defects, 13-5:2
  Summary judgment, 30-1:3
APPEARANCES. *See* **PLEADING**
ARBITRATION. *See also* **PLEADING**
  Choice of law
    common law, 25-1:3
    Federal Arbitration Act, 25-1:1
    overview, 25-1
    Texas Arbitration Act, 25-1:2
  Compelling, 25-2
  Post arbitration proceedings
    confirmation of an award, 25-4:1
    modifying or correcting an award, 25-4:3
    overview, 25-4
    vacating an award, 25-4:2
  Resisting, 25-3
    dispute outside the scope of the agreement, 25-3:1
    fraud, 25-3:3
    overview, 25-3
    unconscionable agreement, 25-3:2
    waiver of right to arbitrate, 25-3:4
ARBITRATION AND AWARD
  Affirmative defenses
    elements, 16-4:1
    overview, 16-4
ARCHITECTS. *See* **DESIGN MALPRACTICE**
ASSIGNMENT
  Verified and special denials, 14-6
ASSUMED NAMES
  Verified and special denials, 14-8
ASSUMPSIT. *See* **MONEY HAD AND RECEIVED; OIL AND GAS**
ASSUMPTION OF RISK
  Affirmative defenses
    elements, 16-10:1
    other issues, 16-10:3
    overview, 16-10

INDEX

ATTACHMENT
Damages and remedies
  costs, 8-7:3.4
  interest, 8-7:3.4
  levy upon writ, 8-7:3.2
  perishable personal property sold, 8-7:3.3
  writ issued, 8-7:3.1
Defenses
  exemption from execution, 8-7:4.3
  replevy bond, 8-7:4.1
  strict compliance not met, 8-7:4.2
Elements, 8-7:2
Form of writ, 8-7:3.1
Overview, 8-7:1
Procedural issues
  amendment, 8-7:5.6
  bond posted, 8-7:4.1, 8-7:5.2
  ex parte relief, 8-7:5.3
  joinder, 8-7:5.5
  modification or dissolution of writ, 8-7:5.7
  service, 8-7:5.4
  sworn application requirement, 8-7:5.1
  third party rights, 8-7:5.8
Related causes of action, 8-7:1.1

ATTACKING JUSTIFIABLE RELIANCE
Fraud, common law, 1-4:4.5

ATTORNEYS
Advice of counsel, slander of title, 7-10:4.2
Breach of duty of care, 2-1:4.1
Breach of duty of loyalty, 2-2:4.1
Malpractice. *See* **LEGAL MALPRACTICE**
Opposing attorneys, action against
  overview, 9-1:1
  rejected in Texas, 9-1:2
  related causes of action, 9-1:1.1
Verification by, 13-4:4
Wrongful distribution of dividends, 2-3:4.1

ATTORNEYS' FEES
Accountings, 8-4:3.4
Bailment, 3-9:3.4, 3-10:3.3
Breach of contract, 3-1:3.12, 7-5:3.3
Declaratory judgments, 7-3:3.2, 8-10:3.2
Dismissal of baseless cause of action, 28-1:6
Forcible entry and detainer, 8-11:3.3
Fraud, statutory, 1-5:3.4
Insurance
  deceptive insurance practices, 5-2:4.7
  declaratory judgment on coverage, 5-5:3.3
  declaratory judgment on duty to defend, 5-6:3.3
  late payment of claims, 5-1:3.6
  uninsured/underinsured motorist coverage claims, 5-4:3.3
Judicial winding up of partnership, 2-15:3.3
Legal malpractice, underlying attorney fees recoverable, 4-1:3.1
Level 1 discovery, 20-2
Money had and received, 3-6:3.2
Overview, 11-13:3
Quiet title, 7-1:3.2
Slander of title, 7-10:3.3
Suits on an account, 3-8:3.3
Suits to compel inspection, 2-12:3.1
Trademark infringement, statutory, 1-13:3.5
Wrongful discharge in breach of employment agreement, 6-1:3.4
Wrongful withdrawal of partner, 2-16:3.3

AUDITORS
Accountings, 8-4:5.5, 11-11:6

B

BAD FAITH. *See* **INSURANCE BAD FAITH**

BAILMENT
Bailee liability
  damages and remedies
    acceleration, 3-9:3.9
    actual damages, 3-9:3.2
    attorneys' fees, 3-9:3.4
    exemplary damages, 3-9:3.10
    interest, 3-9:3.6
    liquidated damages, 3-9:3.3
    loss of use, 3-9:3.7
    lost profits, 3-9:3.5
    overview, 3-9:3.1
    repossession, 3-9:3.8
  defenses
    consideration issues, 3-9:4.2
    denial of execution, 3-9:4.3
    statute of limitations, 3-9:4.1
  elements, 3-9:2
  overview, 3-9:1
  related causes of action, 3-9:1.1
Bailor liability
  damages and remedies
    actual damages, 3-10:3.1
    attorneys' fees, 3-10:3.3
    exemplary damages, 3-10:3.6
    interest, 3-10:3.5
    liquidated damages, 3-10:3.2
    lost profits, 3-10:3.4
  defenses
    consideration issues, 3-10:4.2
    denial of execution, 3-10:4.3
    negligent entrustment, 3-10:4.4
    statute of limitations, 3-10:4.1
  elements
    negligent entrustment, 3-10:2.2
    subject of the bailment defects, 3-10:2.1
  overview, 3-10:1
  related causes of action, 3-10:1.1

BANKERS
Breach of duty of care, 2-1:4.1
Breach of duty of loyalty, 2-2:4.1
Wrongful distribution of dividends, 2-3:4.1

BANKRUPTCY
Discharge as affirmative defense
  elements, 16-8:1
  other issues, 16-8:2
  overview, 16-8
Suits on an account, 3-8:4.5

BONA FIDE OCCUPATIONAL QUALIFICATION
  Employment discrimination, 6-3:4.5
BONDS
  Attachment, 8-7:4.1, 8-7:5.2
  Forcible entry and detainer, 8-11:3.1
  Garnishment, 8-8:4.1, 8-8:5.1
  Receivership, 8-9:5.2
  Sequestration, 8-6:4.1, 8-6:5.2
BOOK VALUE
  Loss of value, 11-7:2
BOOKS AND RECORDS
  Inspection. *See* **SUITS TO COMPEL INSPECTION**
BREACH OF CONTRACT
  Conspiracy for
    overview, 9-3:1
    rejected in Texas, 9-3:2
    related causes of action, 9-3:1.1
  Damages and remedies
    actual damages
      expectation damages, 3-1:3.1a
      overview, 3-1:3.1
      reliance damages, 3-1:3.1b
      restitution damages, 3-1:3.1c
    attorneys' fees, 3-1:3.12
    court costs. *See* **COURT COSTS**
    declaratory judgments, 3-1:3.9
    interest, 11-3:1
    liquidated damages, 3-1:3.4
    nominal damages, 3-1:3.5
    quantum meruit, 3-1:3.2
    reformation, 3-1:3.8
    rescission, 3-1:3.7
    specific performance, 3-1:3.6
    unjust enrichment, 3-1:3.3
  Defenses
    accord and satisfaction, 3-1:4.17
    capacity, 3-1:4.5
    condition precedent failure, 3-1:4.15
    consideration issues, 3-1:4.9, 3-1:4.10
    duress, 3-1:4.11
    fraud, 3-1:4.8
    illegality, 3-1:4.6
    impossibility, 3-1:4.16
    limitation of liability
      mutual mistake, 3-1:4.12
      unilateral mistake, 3-1:4.13
    modification, 3-1:4.20
    novation, 3-1:4.18
    plaintiff-repudiated contract, 3-1:4.3a
    public policy, 3-1:4.7
    release, 3-1:4.21
    repudiation, 3-1:4.3
    revocation, 3-1:4.4
    standing, 3-1:4.2
    statute of frauds, 3-1:4.14
    statute of limitations, 3-1:4.1
    unconscionability, 3-1:4.19
  Definition, civil conspiracy, 9-3:1
  Elements, 3-1:2
  Negligent misrepresentation, 1-7:4.2
  Oil and gas. *See* **OIL AND GAS**
  Related causes of action, 3-1:1.1
BREACH OF DUTY OF CARE
  Agents. *See* **AGENTS AND AGENCY**
  Damages and remedies
    actual damages, 2-1:3.1
    exemplary damages, 2-1:3.3
    special damages, 2-1:3.2
  Defenses
    exculpatory clauses, 2-1:4.2
    safe harbor defense, 2-1:4.1
    statute of limitations, 2-1:4.3
  Elements, 2-1:2
    mismanagement, 2-1:2.1
    wrongful distribution of dividends. *See* **WRONGFUL DISTRIBUTION OF DIVIDENDS**
  Overview, 2-1:1
  Related causes of action, 2-1:1.1
  Who may sue, 2-1:5.1
BREACH OF DUTY OF LOYALTY
  Agents. *See* **AGENTS AND AGENCY**
  Damages and remedies
    actual damages, 2-2:3.1
    exemplary damages, 2-2:3.3
    special damages, 2-2:3.2
  Defenses
    exculpatory clauses, 2-2:4.3
    interested transaction/corporate opportunity validity procedure, 2-2:4.2
    safe harbor defense, 2-2:4.1
    statute of limitations, 2-2:4.4
  Definition, gross negligence, 2-2:1.1
  Elements
    mismanagement, 2-2:2.1
    wrongful distribution of dividends. *See* **WRONGFUL DISTRIBUTION OF DIVIDENDS**
  Overview, 2-2:1
  Related causes of action, 2-2:1.1
  Tortious interference with fiduciary duties
    overview, 9-20:1
    rejected in Texas, 9-20:2
    related causes of action, 9-20:1.1
  Who may sue, 2-2:5.1
BREACH OF IMPLIED COVENANT TO MARKET. *See* **OIL AND GAS**
BREACH OF IMPLIED COVENANT TO PROTECT AGAINST DRAINAGE. *See* **OIL AND GAS**
BREACH OF IMPLIED COVENANT TO REASONABLY DEVELOP. *See* **OIL AND GAS**
BREACH OF IMPLIED WARRANTY OF PROFESSIONAL SERVICES
  Overview, 9-21:1
  Rejected in Texas, 9-21:2
  Related causes of action, 9-21:1.1

INDEX

BREACH OF PARTNERSHIP DUTY
Damages and remedies
accounting, 2-10:3.3
actual damages, 2-10:3.1
constructive trusts, 2-10:3.6
exemplary damages, 2-10:3.10
forfeiture of compensation, 2-10:3.7
interest, 2-10:3.2
receivership, 2-10:3.8
rescission, 2-10:3.4
restitution, 2-10:3.5
winding up, 2-10:3.9
Defenses
abandonment, 2-10:4.3
financial incapability, 2-10:4.2
statute of limitations, 2-10:4.1
Elements, 2-10:2
Overview, 2-10:1
Related causes of action, 2-10:1.1
Who may sue, 2-10:5.1
BREACH OF WARRANTY. *See also* **WARRANTIES**
Agency actions, defenses
actual damages, 3-12:4.2
quantum meruit, 3-12:4.3
Permissive venue provisions, 22-5
BUSINESS COMPULSION
Breach of contract, 3-1:4.11
BUSINESS DISPARAGEMENT
Damages and remedies
actual damages
loss of business, 1-8:3.1c
loss of credit, 1-8:3.1b
loss of sale, 1-8:3.1a
overview, 1-8:3.1
court costs, 1-8:3.4, 11-13:2
exemplary damages. *See* **DAMAGES AND REMEDIES**
interest, 1-8:3.3, 11-13:1
Defamation compared, 1-8:1
Defenses
plaintiff's fault. *See* **PROPORTIONATE RESPONSIBILITY**
privilege, 1-8:4.1
statute of limitations
discovery rule, 1-8:4.4
Definition
business disparagement, 1-8:1.2
disparaging statement, 1-8:1.2
Elements, 1-8:2
Related causes of action, 1-8:1.1
BUSINESS JUDGMENT RULE
Breach of duty of care, 2-1:2.1
Breach of duty of loyalty, 2-2:2.1
Breach of partnership duty, 2-10:2
Derivative shareholder suits, dismissal, 2-8:5.6
BUSINESS NECESSITY
Employment discrimination, 6-3:4.4

C

CAPACITY AND INCAPACITY
Agents and agency, 3-12:2.3
Breach of contract, 3-1:4.5
Standing compared, 14-1
Statutes of limitations and, 17-11:3
Verified and special denials, 14-1
CAPITALIZATION RATE OF NET CASH FLOW
Loss of value, 11-7:2
CHOICE OF LAW
Arbitration
common law, 25-1:3
Federal Arbitration Act, 25-1:1
overview, 25-1
Texas Arbitration Act, 25-1:2
Clause enforcement, 24-2
Conflict necessary, 24-1:2
"Internal affairs" doctrine, 24-1:9
Most significant relationship test
contract cases, 24-1:5
overview, 24-1:3
property cases, 24-1:6
tort cases, 24-1:4
UCC, 24-1:7
Overview, 24-1:1
Pleading and proving
other jurisdictions, 24-3:2
overview, 24-3
presumption in favor of Texas law, 24-3:1
Public nuisance, 7-9:5.1
Public policy exception, 24-1:10
Statutes affecting, 24-1:8
CLASS ACTIONS
Breach of implied covenant to market, 7-13:5.1
CLOSELY HELD CORPORATIONS
Derivative shareholder suits, 2-8:5.10
COLLATERAL ESTOPPEL
Affirmative defenses
elements, 16-7:2
other issues, 16-7:2
overview, 16-7
COMMON LAW SHAREHOLDER OPPRESSION
Overview, 9-7:1
Rejected in Texas, 9-7:2
Related causes of action, 9-7:1.1
COMPETENCY. *See* **CAPACITY AND INCAPACITY**
CONDITIONS PRECEDENT
Verified and special denials, 13-4:6, 14-10
CONFESSION OF JUDGMENT
Pre-suit instruments
overview, 9-2:1
rejected in Texas, 9-2:2
CONSIDERATION
Affirmative defenses, failure as
elements, 16-14:1
other issues, 16-14:2
overview, 16-14

CONSIDERATION (*cont.*)
  Agency, 3-11:2.1, 3-12:2.1, 3-13:2
  Bailment, 3-9:4.2, 3-10:4.2
  Breach of contract, 3-1:4.9, 3-1:4.10
  Constructive fraud, 3-2:2.1
  Rescission, 3-2:2.2
  Suits on an account, 3-8:4.4
  Verified and special denials, 14-11
CONSPIRACY TO BREACH CONTRACTS
  Definition, civil conspiracy, 9-3:1
  Overview, 9-3:1
  Rejected in Texas, 9-3:2
  Related causes of action, 9-3:1.1
CONSTRUCTIVE TRUSTS
  Breach of partnership duty, 2-10:3.6
  Damages and remedies
    constructive trusts, 8-5:3.1
    exemplary damages, 8-5:3.3
  Defenses
    equitable defenses, 8-5:4.3
    laches, 8-5:4.2
    statute of limitations, 8-5:4.1
  Elements, 8-5:2
    oil and gas. *See* **OIL AND GAS**
  Overview, 8-5:1, 11-11:1
  Related causes of action, 8-5:1.1
  Scope of constructive trust, 8-5:3.2
  Usurpation of business opportunity, 2-11:3.1
CONTRACTS
  Agents. *See* **AGENTS AND AGENCY**
  Arbitration clauses. *See* **ARBITRATION**
  Breach. *See* **BREACH OF CONTRACT**
  Choice of law. *See* **CHOICE OF LAW**
  Confession of judgment
    overview, 9-2:1
    rejected in Texas, 9-2:2
  Damages. *See* **DAMAGES AND REMEDIES**
  Disclaimers. *See* **DISCLAIMERS**
  Employment. *See* **WRONGFUL DISCHARGE IN BREACH OF EMPLOYMENT AGREEMENT**
  Forum selection clauses. *See* **PLEADING**
  Interference with. *See* **TORTIOUS INTERFERENCE WITH EXISTING CONTRACT**
  Limitation of liability provisions, 3-1:3.4
  Non-consent penalties, 3-1:3.4
  Quantum meruit. *See* **QUANTUM MERUIT**
  Reformation. *See* **REFORMATION**
  Requirements for, 3-1:2
  Rescission. *See* **RESCISSION**
  Specific performance. *See* **SPECIFIC PERFORMANCE**
CONTRIBUTION
  Definitions
    contribution defendant, 18-6:2
    liable defendant, 18-6:2
  Jointly and severally liable defendants, 18-6:1
  Other liable defendants, 18-6:2
  Wrongful distribution of dividends, 2-3:3.3
  Wrongful withdrawal of partner, 2-16:3.1
CONTRIBUTORY NEGLIGENCE
  Affirmative defenses
    elements, 16-10:2
    overview, 16-10
CONVERSION
  Damages and remedies
    actual damages
      loss of use, 1-3:3.1b
      loss of value, 1-3:3.1a
      lost profits, 1-3:3.1c
      overview, 1-3:3.1
    court costs, 11-13:2
    exemplary damages, 1-3:3.2
    injunction, 11-13:1
    interest. *See* **INTEREST**
  Defenses
    buyer in the ordinary course of business, 1-3:4.4
    expressed or implied consent, 1-3:4.7
    good faith purchaser, 1-3:4.3
    immunity. *See* **DEFENSES; IMMUNITY**
    plaintiff's fault. *See* **PROPORTIONATE RESPONSIBILITY**
    possession after repair, 1-3:4.5
    qualified good faith refusal, 1-3:4.1
  Elements, 1-3:2
  Oil and gas. *See* **OIL AND GAS**
  Real property
    overview, 9-4:1
    rejected in Texas, 9-4:2
    related causes of action, 9-4:1.1
  Related causes of action, 1-3:1.1
CORPORATIONS
  Citizenship determination for removal, 27-3:3.2
  Closely held corporations. *See* **CLOSELY HELD CORPORATIONS**
  Derivative shareholder suits. *See* **DERIVATIVE SHAREHOLDER SUITS**
  Dissenting shareholders. *See* **DISSENTING SHAREHOLDERS**
  Domicile, 27-3:3.2
  Inspection of books and records. *See* **SUITS TO COMPEL INSPECTION**
  Minority shareholder oppression. *See* **SHAREHOLDER OPPRESSION**
  Officers and directors. *See* **OFFICERS AND DIRECTORS**
  Piercing the corporate veil. *See* **PIERCING THE CORPORATE VEIL**
  Reputation injury, 11-9:2
  Revocation of corporate status. *See* **STATE REVOCATION OF CORPORATE STATUS**
  Service of process, dissolved corporations, 23-1
  Usurpation of business opportunity. *See* **USURPATION OF BUSINESS OPPORTUNITY**
  Verified and special denials, 14-4

INDEX

COUNTERCLAIMS
  General denials, 13-3:3
  Level 1 discovery, 20-2
  Subject matter jurisdiction, 21-3

COURT COSTS
  Attachment, 8-7:3.4
  Credit file information, statutory late provision, 3-31:3.7
  Definition, court costs, 11-13:2
  Dismissal of baseless cause of action, 28-1:6
  Employment discrimination, 6-3:3.3
  Forcible entry and detainer, 8-11:3.3
  Garnishment, 8-8:3.3
  Insurance
    deceptive insurance practices, 5-2:4.6
    declaratory judgment on coverage, 5-5:3.2
    declaratory judgment on duty to defend, 5-6:3.2
    uninsured/underinsured motorist coverage claims, 5-4:3.4
  Overview, 11-13:2

CREDITOR/DEBTOR
  Bankruptcy. *See* **BANKRUPTCY**
  Garnishment. *See* **GARNISHMENT**

CRIME
  Joint and several liability, 18-4
  Perjury as, 9-15:1

CROSSCLAIMS
  General denials, 13-3:3
  Subject matter jurisdiction, 21-3

CURE
  Breach of implied covenant to reasonably develop, 7-14:4.2, 7-14:5.2

D

DAMAGES AND REMEDIES
  Attorneys' fees, 11-13:3
  Character of versus measure of, 10-2
  Contractual damages and remedies
    liquidated damages, 11-5:5
    pleading
      benefit-of-the-bargain, 11-5:7
      other remedies, 11-5:8
      out-of-pocket damages, 11-5:7
      overview, 11-5:5
      sworn accounts, 11-5:6
    UCC. *See* UCC, *below*
  Court costs. *See* **COURT COSTS**
  Credit reputation damage, 11-9:1
  Definitions
    general damages, 10-3
    measure of damages, 10-2
    special damages, 10-4
    unjust enrichment, 11-11:2
  Double recovery
    benefit-of-the-bargain and out-of-pocket, 11-3
    Overview, 12-2:1
  Economic feasibility, prudent owner standard, 12-2:2
  Economic loss rule, 11-1, 12-3
  Equitable remedies
    accountings, 11-11:6
    constructive trusts, 11-11:1
    disgorgement, 11-11:5
    forfeiture, 11-11:5
    overview, 11-11
    quantum meruit, 11-11:4
    rescission, 11-11:3
    restitution, 11-11:3
    unjust enrichment, 11-11:2
  Excessive damages, 12-2:2
  Exemplary damages, 11-12
  General versus special, 10-5
  Interest, 11-13:1
  Loss of credit, 11-9:1
  Loss of value
    lost profits compared, 11-6:1
    models for, 11-7:2
    pleading, 11-7:3
    when to use, 11-7:1
  Lost profits
    discount rates, 11-6:2
    loss of value compared, 11-6:1
    overview, 11-2
    pleading, 11-6:3
    when to use, 11-6:1
  Mitigation of damages. *See* **MITIGATION OF DAMAGES**
  Models for
    benefit-of-the-bargain, 11-2
    lost profits, 11-2
    out-of-pocket damages, 11-3
    overview, 11-1
    restitution, 11-4
  One satisfaction rule, 12-2:1
  Pleading
    amount category, 10-1
    attorneys' fees, 11-13:3
    court costs, 11-13:2
    economic loss rule, 12-3
    exemplary damages, 11-12
    general damages, 10-3
    interest, 11-13:1
    loss of value, 11-7:3
    lost profits, 11-6:3
    proof must match, 10-2
    requests for disclosure and, 10-6
    special damages, 10-2, 10-4
    statutory damages cap, 10-7
    UCC
      buyer, 11-5:4.2
      seller, 11-5:4.1
  Property valuation
    overview, 11-8
    personal property, 11-8:2
    real property, 11-8:1
  Reputation injury
    corporations, 11-9:2
    credit, 11-9:1
    individuals, 11-9:3

DAMAGES AND REMEDIES (*cont.*)
  Statutory, 11-10
  UCC
    buyer remedies, 11-5:3
    overview, 11-5:1
    pleading
      buyer, 11-5:4.2
      seller, 11-5:4.1
    seller remedies, 11-5:2
DEATH OF CLAIMANT
  Statutes of limitations, 17-11:4
DECEPTIVE INSURANCE PRACTICES
  Damages and remedies
    actual damages
      credit reputation damage, 5-2:4.1c
      lost income, 5-2:4.1b
      lost profits, 5-2:4.1a
      personal injury, 5-2:4.1d
    attorneys' fees, 5-2:4.7
    court costs, 5-2:4.6
    equitable remedies, 5-2:4.4
    injunction, 5-2:4.3
    interest, 5-2:4.5
    treble damages, 5-2:4.2
  Defenses
    settlement offer tendered, 5-2:5.2
    statute of limitations, 5-2:5.1
  Elements, 5-2:3
  Related causes of action, 5-2:1.1
DECLARATORY JUDGMENTS
  Breach of contract, 3-1:3.9
  Damages and remedies
    attorneys' fees, 7-1:3.2, 8-10:3.2
    declaratory judgments, 8-10:3.1
  Defenses
    exclusive remedy available, 8-10:4.4
    justiciable controversy lacking, 8-10:4.1
    other active proceeding pending, 8-10:4.2
    standing lacking, 8-10:4.3
    underlying action defenses, 8-10:4.5
  Definitions
    justiciable controversy, 8-10:2
    ripening seeds of controversy, 8-10:2
  Elements, 8-10:2
  Insurance. *See* **INSURANCE**
  Oil and gas. *See* **OIL AND GAS**
  Overview, 8-10:1
  Procedural issues
    joinder, 8-10:5.1
    subsequent relief, 8-10:5.2
  Related causes of action, 8-10:1.1
  Standing, 8-10:2, 8-10:4.3
DEFAMATION
  Business disparagement compared, 1-8:1
DEFENSES
  Affirmative defenses. *See* **AFFIRMATIVE DEFENSES**
  Definitions
    inferential rebuttal defenses, 13-6:1, 15-1
    sole proximate cause, 15-3
    sudden emergency, 15-4:2
    superseding cause, 15-2
    unavoidable occurrence, 15-4:1
  Inferential rebuttal defenses
    charging the jury on, 13-6:3
    defined, 15-1
    examples, 13-6:2
    mitigation failure, 15-4
    overview, 13-6, 13-6:1, 15-1
    pleading requirements, 13-6:4
    sole proximate cause, 15-3
    superseding cause, 15-2
    unavoidable occurrence or sudden emergency
      elements, 15-4:3
      sudden emergency, 15-4:2
      unavoidable occurrence, 15-4:1
  Pleading burdens compared, 13-1
DEFINITIONS
  Actual fraud, 2-13:2.1, 2-13:2.2
  Actual possession, 8-11:2.1
  Capable of production in paying quantities, 7-11:3.1
  Cause-in-fact, 1-10:2
  Civil conspiracy, 9-3:1
  Claim, 5-1:2
  Claimant, 5-1:2, 18-2:2
  Closely held corporations, 2-8:5.10
  Complete diversity, 27-3:2
  Constructive fraud, 2-13:2.2
  Contractual obligation, 2-13:2.1
  Contribution defendant, 18-6:2
  Court costs, 11-13:2
  Covered records, 2-12:2.1, 2-12:2.2, 2-12:2.4
  Defendant, 18-2:2
  Disparaging statement, 1-8:1.2
  Distribution, 2-3:2
  Domicile, 27-3:3.1
  Duress, 16-11
  Expenses, 2-8:3.2
  Fair value, 2-9:3.1
  Force, 8-11:2.1
  Foreseeability, 1-10:2, 7-11:2
  General damages, 10-3
  General denial, 13-3:1
  Gross negligence, 2-2:1.1
  Independently tortious conduct, 1-2:2
  Inferential rebuttal defenses, 13-6:1, 15-1
  Invalid mark, 1-13:4.2
  Irreparable injury, 8-1:2, 8-2:2
  Justiciable controversy, 5-5:2, 8-10:2
  Legal malice, 7-10:2
  Liable defendant, 18-6:2
  Line of business, 2-11:2
  Liquidated debt, 8-8:2.1
  Major transactions, 26-1:2
  Malice, 6-2:3.5
  Market value, 7-13:2
  Measure of damages, 10-2
  Misidentification, 17-10
  Misnomer, 17-10

INDEX

Motivating factor, 6-3:2
Net assets, 2-3:2
Nonpublic information, 2-4:2.2, 2-4:2.3
"On the basis of", 2-4:2.2
Oppressive conduct, 2-7:2
Paying quantities, 7-12:2, 7-14:2
Person, 5-2:2
Political questions, 7-9:4.3
Pooling, 7-12:4.1
Presence, 17-11:6
Principle office, 22-3
Product liability action, 17-13:2
Protected classes, 6-3:2
Public nuisance, 7-9:1
Release, 16-5
Responsible organization, 2-9:5.5
Responsible third party, 18-2:2
Ripening seeds of controversy, 8-10:2
Secondary meaning, 1-12:2
Settling person, 18-2:2
Single business enterprise theory, 2-13:2.3
Sole proximate cause, 15-3
Special damages, 10-4
Stated accounts, 3-8:2.1, 3-8:2.2
Substantial drainage, 7-12:2
Substantive defect, 30-3:10
Sudden emergency, 15-4:2
Superseding cause, 15-2
Surplus, 2-3:2
Trade secret, 1-15:2
Typicality, 7-13:5.1
Unavoidable occurrence, 15-4:1
Unjust enrichment, 11-11:2
Use (trade secret), 1-15:2
Use (trademark), 1-13:2.1
Venue, 22-2
DEMAND
  Derivative shareholder suits
    stay, 2-8:5.5
    time, 2-8:2, 2-8:5.4
  Dissenting shareholders. *See* **DISSENTING SHAREHOLDERS**
  Suits to compel inspection, 2-12:2.1
DERIVATIVE SHAREHOLDER SUITS
  Breach of duty of care. *See* **BREACH OF DUTY OF CARE**
  Breach of duty of loyalty. *See* **BREACH OF DUTY OF LOYALTY**
  Damages and remedies
    cost shifting, 2-8:3.2
    indemnification, 2-8:3.3
    overview, 2-8:3.1
  Defenses
    defendant third parties, 2-8:4.2
    procedural issues, 2-8:4.1
    against shareholder-plaintiff, 2-8:4.3
  Definitions
    closely held corporations, 2-8:5.10
    expenses, 2-8:3.2
  Elements, 2-8:2
  Overview, 2-8:1
  Procedural issues
    claim joinder, 2-8:5.3
    closely held corporations, 2-8:5.10
    demand, 2-8:5.4
    discovery, 2-8:5.7
    dismissal, 2-8:5.6
    foreign corporations, 2-8:5.9
    forum, 2-8:5.1
    settlement, 2-8:5.8
    stay, 2-8:5.5
    venue, 2-8:5.2
  Related causes of action, 2-8:1.1
  Short swing profits. *See* **SECURITIES FRAUD**
  Wrongful distribution of dividends. *See* **WRONGFUL DISTRIBUTION OF DIVIDENDS**
DESIGN MALPRACTICE
  Damages and remedies
    court costs, 11-13:2
    interest. *See* **INTEREST**
    overview. *See* **DAMAGES AND REMEDIES**
  Statutes of repose, 17-13:1
DETRIMENTAL RELIANCE
  Independent tort claim
    overview, 9-5:1
    rejected in Texas, 9-5:2
    related causes of action, 9-5:1.1
DILUTION. *See* **TRADEMARK INFRINGEMENT, STATUTORY**
DIRECTORS. *See* **OFFICERS AND DIRECTORS**
DISABILITIES. *See* **CAPACITY AND INCAPACITY**
DISCHARGE IN BANKRUPTCY. *See* **BANKRUPTCY**
DISCLAIMERS
  Fraud, common law, 1-4:4.2
  Fraud, statutory, 1-5:4.2
  Fraud by non-disclosure, 1-6:4.2
  Negligent misrepresentation, 1-7:4.4
DISCLOSURE
  Fraud by non-disclosure. *See* **FRAUD BY NON-DISCLOSURE**
DISCOUNTED CASH FLOW ANALYSIS OF PROJECTED FUTURE EARNINGS
  Loss of value, 11-7:2
DISCOVERY
  Amount category not pled, 10-1
  Derivative shareholder suits, 2-8:5.7
  General appearances and, 13-2:4
  Levels. *See* **DISCOVERY LEVELS**
  Loss of value calculations, 11-7:3
DISCOVERY CONTROL PLANS
  Pleading, 10-1
DISCOVERY LEVELS
  Amendment of pleadings
    post-verdict, 29-7
    time limits based on, 29-3

DISCOVERY LEVELS (*cont.*)
  Level 1
    considerations for, 20-2
    overview, 20-1
  Level 2
    considerations for, 20-3
    overview, 20-1
  Level 3
    considerations for, 20-4
    overview, 20-1
  Overview, 20-1
  Responding to, 20-5
DISCOVERY RULE
  Assumpsit, 7-6:4.1
  Breach of contract, 3-1:4.1
  Breach of duty of care, 2-1:4.3
  Breach of duty of loyalty, 2-2:4.4
  Business disparagement, 1-8:4.5
  Constructive trusts, 8-5:4.1
  Fraud, common law, 1-4:4.1
  Fraud, statutory, 1-5:4.1
  Fraud by non-disclosure, 1-6:4.1
  Fraudulent concealment compared, 17-11:2
  Legal malpractice, 4-1:4.1c
  Negligence, 1-10:4.1c
  Overview, 17-11:2
  Securities fraud, 2-4:4.3
  Tortious interference with existing contract, 1-1:4.1
  Tortious interference with prospective business relationship, 1-2:4.1
  Usurpation of business opportunity, 2-11:4.1
  Wrongful discharge in breach of employment agreement, 6-1:4.1
DISCRIMINATION
  Employment. *See* **EMPLOYMENT DISCRIMINATION**
DISGORGEMENT
  Agents and agency, 3-13:3.3
  Overview, 11-11:5
  Securities fraud, 2-4:3.3
  Trademark infringement, statutory, 1-13:3.2
  Usurpation of business opportunity, 2-11:3.4
DISMISSAL
  Baseless causes of action. *See* **PLEADING**
  Derivative shareholder suits, 2-8:5.6
  Special appearances and, 13-2:4
  Subject jurisdiction lacking, time to refile, 17-11:1
DISPARAGEMENT. *See* **BUSINESS DISPARAGEMENT**
DISSENTING SHAREHOLDERS
  Damages and remedies
    costs, 2-9:3.3
    exclusive remedies, 2-9:3.4
    fair value, 2-9:3.1
    fraud, special damages, 2-9:3.5
    prejudgment interest, 2-9:3.2
  Defenses
    perfection lacking, 2-9:4
    procedural issues, 2-9:4.1
  Definitions
    fair value, 2-9:3.1
    responsible organization, 2-9:5.5
  Elements, 2-9:2
  Overview, 2-9:1
  Procedural issues
    fair value determination, 2-9:5.4
    ownership interest status, 2-9:5.2
    responsible organization, 2-9:5.5
    strict compliance necessary, 2-9:5.1
    withdrawal of demand, 2-9:5.3
  Related causes of action, 2-9:1.1
DISSOLUTION OF PARTNERSHIPS
  Judicial expulsion
    breach of partnership duty. *See* **BREACH OF PARTNERSHIP DUTY**
    damages and remedies
      expulsion, 2-14:3.1
      wrongful withdrawal of partner, 2-14:3.2
    defenses, 2-14:4.1
    effective date, 2-14:5.1
    elements, 2-14:2
    overview, 2-14:1
    related causes of action, 2-14:1.1
  Judicial winding up
    damages and remedies
      attorneys' fees, 2-15:3.3
      receivership, 2-15:3.2
      winding up and termination, 2-15:3.1
    defenses
      equitable defenses, 2-15:4.2
      unclean hands, 2-15:4.1
    elements, 2-15:2
    overview, 2-15:1
    parties named, 2-15:5.2
    related causes of action, 2-15:1.1
    venue, 2-15:5.1
  Wrongful withdrawal of partner
    damages and remedies
      actual damages, 2-16:3.2
      attorneys' fees, 2-16:3.3
      bad faith demand or payment of estimated redemption, 2-16:3.7
      interest, 2-16:3.5
      liquidated damages, 2-16:3.2
      prior partnership liability, 2-16:3.4
      redemption/contribution, 2-16:3.1
      setoff, 2-16:3.6
    defenses, 2-16:4.1
    elements, 2-16:2
    overview, 2-16:1
    procedural issues
      issues to litigate, 2-16:5.2
      partnership agreements, 2-16:5.3
      who may sue, 2-16:5.1
    related causes of action, 2-16:1.1
DIVIDENDS
  Wrongful distribution. *See* **WRONGFUL DISTRIBUTION OF DIVIDENDS**

INDEX

DRAINAGE. *See* **OIL AND GAS**
DURESS
  Affirmative defenses
    elements, 16-11:1
    other issues, 16-11:2
    overview, 16-11
  Arbitration, 25-3:2
  Breach of contract, 3-1:4.11
  Rescission, 3-2:2.1
  Unjust enrichment, 3-4:2
DUTY OF CARE BREACH. *See* **BREACH OF DUTY OF CARE**
DUTY OF LOYALTY BREACH. *See* **BREACH OF DUTY OF LOYALTY**

E

ECCLESIASTICAL DISPUTES
  Subject matter jurisdiction, 21-5
ECONOMIC LOSS RULE
  Negligence, 1-10:4.6
  Overview, 11-1, 12-3
EMBRACERY
  Overview, 9-6:1
  Rejected in Texas, 9-6:2
  Related causes of action, 9-6:1.1
EMOTIONAL DISTRESS
  Negligent infliction
    overview, 9-11:1
    rejected in Texas, 9-11:2
    related causes of action, 9-11:1.1
EMPLOYMENT
  Agents. *See* **AGENTS AND AGENCY**
  Constructive discharge, 6-2:2
  Discrimination. *See* **EMPLOYMENT DISCRIMINATION**
  Negligent hiring. *See* **NEGLIGENT HIRING**
  Negligent investigation of employee misconduct
    overview, 9-12:1
    rejected in Texas, 9-12:2
    related causes of action, 9-12:1.1
  Whistleblowers. *See* **WHISTLEBLOWERS**
  Wrongful discharge. *See* **WRONGFUL DISCHARGE FOR REFUSAL TO PERFORM ILLEGAL ACTS; WRONGFUL DISCHARGE IN BREACH OF EMPLOYMENT AGREEMENT**
EMPLOYMENT DISCRIMINATION
  Damages and remedies
    cap on, 6-3:3.5
    compensatory damages, 6-3:3.1
    court costs, 6-3:3.3
    equitable remedies, 6-3:3.3
    exemplary damages, 6-3:3.4
    interest, 6-3:3.2
  Defenses
    bona fide employee benefit plan, 6-3:4.8
    bona fide occupational qualification, 6-3:4.5
    business necessity, 6-3:4.4
    exhaustion of administrative remedies failure, 6-3:4.2
    reliance on commission, 6-3:4.6
    religious organizations, 6-3:4.7
    statute of limitations, 6-3:4.1
    statutory defenses, 6-3:4.10
    undue hardship, 6-3:4.9
    waiver, 6-3:4.3
  Definitions
    motivating factor, 6-3:2
    protected classes, 6-3:2
  Elements, 6-3:2
  Overview, 6-3:1
  Related causes of action, 6-3:1.1
ENGINEERS. *See* **DESIGN MALPRACTICE**
ENTRUSTMENT. *See* **BAILMENT**
ESTOPPEL
  Affirmative defenses
    elements
      equitable estoppel, 16-12:1
      judicial estoppel, 16-12:3
      promissory estoppel, 16-12:2
    overview, 16-12
  Agents, breach of duty, 3-27:4.2
  Agents and agency, 3-27:4.2
  Collateral estoppel as affirmative defense
    elements, 16-7:2
    other issues, 16-7:2
    overview, 16-7
  Promissory estoppel. *See* **PROMISSORY ESTOPPEL**
  Quantum meruit, 3-3:4.5
  Specific performance, 8-3:4.5
EVICTION. *See* **FORCIBLE ENTRY AND DETAINER**
EVIDENCE
  Spoliation of evidence
    overview, 9-19:1
    rejected in Texas, 9-19:2
  Summary judgment. *See* **SUMMARY JUDGMENT**
EXCUSE
  Negligence per se, 1-11:2
EXHAUSTION OF ADMINISTRATIVE REMEDIES
  Employment discrimination, 6-3:4.2
  Wrongful discharge in breach of employment agreement, 6-1:4.6
EXPERTS
  Designation of, 20-2, 20-3
  Summary judgment motions, affidavits for
    facts admissible at trial, 30-3:4
    interested witnesses, 30-3:5
EXPRESS OR IMPLIED CONSENT
  Accord and satisfaction, 3-1:4.17, 16-3:1, 16-3:3
  Conversion, defenses, 1-3:4.7
  Misappropriation of trade secrets, 1-15:2
  Trial by consent, 29-6

F

FAIR USE
  Misuse of trade names, 1-14:4.6
  Trademark infringement, common law, 1-12:4.5
  Trademark infringement, statutory, 1-13:4.6
FALSE LIGHT INVASION OF PRIVACY
  Overview, 9-9:1
  Rejected in Texas, 9-9:2
  Related causes of action, 9-9:1.1
FEDERAL ARBITRATION ACT (FAA)
  Oil and gas. *See* **OIL AND GAS**
  Overview, 25-1:1
  Securities fraud. *See* **SECURITIES FRAUD**
  Tortious interference with fiduciary duties
    overview, 9-20:1
    rejected in Texas, 9-20:2
    related causes of action, 9-20:1.1
  Usurpation of business opportunity. *See*
    USURPATION OF BUSINESS OPPORTUNITY
FIRST AMENDMENT
  Ecclesiastical disputes, 21-5
  Misuse of trade names, 1-14:4.5
  Trademark infringement, statutory, 1-13:4.5
FORCIBLE DETAINER. *See* **FORCIBLE ENTRY AND DETAINER**
FORCIBLE ENTRY AND DETAINER
  Authority, 7-4:1.1
  Damages and remedies
    attorneys' fees, 8-11:3.3
    court costs, 8-11:3.3
    unpaid rent, 8-11:3.2
    writ of possession, 8-11:3.1
  Defenses
    injunction, 8-11:4.2
    title disputes, jurisdiction lacking, 8-11:4.1
  Definitions
    actual possession, 8-11:2.1
    force, 8-11:2.1
  Elements
    forcible detainer, 8-11:2.2
    forcible entry and detainer, 8-11:2.1
  Forcible detainer compared, 8-11:1
  Overview, 7-4:1, 8-11:1
  Procedural issues
    concurrent claims for damages, 8-11:5.4
    jurisdiction, 8-11:5.2
    notice to vacate, 8-11:5.1
    possession bond, 8-11:3.1
    sworn statements, 8-11:5.3
  Related causes of action, 8-11:1.1
FORFEITURE
  Agents, forfeiture of fee, 3-13:3.2
  Breach of partnership duty, 2-10:3.7
  Overview, 11-11:5
  Usurpation of business opportunity, 2-11:3.3
FORUM
  Derivative shareholder suits, 2-8:5.2
  Forum selection clauses. *See* **PLEADING**

FORUM STATE DEFENDANT RULE
  Diversity of citizenship test, 27-3:4
FRAUD, COMMON LAW
  Damages and remedies
    actual damages
      benefit-of-the-bargain, 1-4:3.1a
      mental anguish, 1-4:3.1d
      out-of-pocket damages, 1-4:3.1b
      overview, 1-4:3.1
      personal property repair, 1-4:3.1c
    court costs, 11-13:2
    equitable remedies
      overview, 1-4:3.3
      reformation, 1-4:3.3b
      rescission, 1-4:3.3a
    exemplary damages, 1-4:3.2
    interest. *See* **INTEREST**
  Defenses
    attacking justifiable reliance, 1-4:4.5
    disclaimer of reliance, 1-4:4.2
    ratification, 1-4:4.3
    statute of frauds, 1-4:4.4
    statute of limitations, 1-4:4.1
  Elements, 1-4:2
  Oil and gas. *See* **OIL AND GAS**
  Related causes of action, 1-4:1.1
FRAUD, GENERALLY
  Affirmative defenses
    elements, 16-15:1
    other issues, 16-15:2
    overview, 16-15
  Arbitration, 25-3:2, 25-3:3
  Breach of contract, 3-1:4.7
  Common law. *See* **FRAUD, COMMON LAW**
  Diversity, fraudulently joined defendants, 27-3:5
  Forum selection clauses, 26-2:1
  Fraudulent concealment. *See* **FRAUDULENT CONCEALMENT**
  By non-disclosure. *See* **FRAUD BY NON-DISCLOSURE**
  Rescission, 3-2:2.1
  Securities fraud. *See* **SECURITIES FRAUD**
  Statutory. *See* **FRAUD, STATUTORY**
  Suits on an account, 3-8:4.5
FRAUD, STATUTORY
  Damages and remedies
    actual damages
      benefit-of-the-bargain, 1-5:3.1a
      out-of-pocket damages, 1-5:3.1b
      overview, 1-5:3.1
    attorneys' fees, 1-5:3.4
    court costs, 1-5:3.6
    equitable remedies
      overview, 1-5:3.4
    exemplary damages, 1-5:3.2
    interest. *See* **INTEREST**
  Defenses
    disclaimer of reliance, 1-5:4.2
    statute of frauds, 1-5:4.3
    statute of limitations, 1-5:4.1

INDEX

Elements, 1-5:2
Overview, 1-5:1
Related causes of action, 1-5:1.1
Securities fraud. *See* **SECURITIES FRAUD**
FRAUD BY NON-DISCLOSURE
  Damages and remedies
    actual damages
      benefit-of-the-bargain, 1-6:3.1a
      mental anguish, 1-6:3.1d
      out-of-pocket damages, 1-6:3.1b
      overview, 1-6:3.1
      personal property injury, 1-6:3.1c
    court costs, 1-6:3.5
    equitable remedies
      reformation, 1-6:3.3b
      rescission, 1-6:3.3a
    exemplary damages, 1-6:3.2
    interest. *See* **INTEREST**
  Defenses
    disclaimer in contract, 1-6:4.2
    ratification, 1-6:4.3
    sovereign immunity, 1-6:4.5
    Statute of Frauds, 1-6:4.4
    statute of limitations, 1-6:4.1
  Definition, material fact, 1-6:2
  Elements, 1-6:2
  Overview, 1-6:1
  Related causes of action, 1-6:1.1
FRAUDULENT CONCEALMENT
  Discovery rule compared, 17-11:2
  Statutes of limitations and, 17-11:1
FRAUDULENT INDUCEMENT
  Benefit-of-the-bargain damages, 11-2
  Fraud, common law, 1-4:2, 1-4:4.1
    attacking justifiable reliance, 1-4:4.5
  Economic loss rule, 12-3
  Grossly negligent inducement of contract, 9-8:1, 9-8:1.1
    expressly rejected in Texas, 9-8:2
  Insurance
    bad faith, 5-3:4.3
FRAUDULENT REGISTRATION. *See* **TRADEMARK INFRINGEMENT, STATUTORY**

G

GARNISHMENT
  Damages and remedies
    costs, 8-8:3.3
    execution on writ, 8-8:3.2
    interest, 8-8:3.3
    writ issued, 8-8:3.1
  Defenses
    exemption from execution, 8-8:4.4
    replevy bond, 8-8:4.1
    setoff, 8-8:4.5
    strict compliance not met, 8-8:4.2
    underlying judgment invalid, 8-8:4.3
  Definition, liquidated debt, 8-8:2.1

Elements
  postjudgment, 8-8:2.2
  prejudgment, 8-8:2.1
Overview, 8-8:1
Procedural issues
  answer from garnishee, 8-8:5.4
  bond posted, 8-8:5.1
  ex parte relief, 8-8:5.2
  service, 8-8:5.3
Related causes of action, 8-8:1.1
GENERAL DENIALS
  Overview, 13-1
  Pleading burdens. *See* **PLEADING**
GEOPHYSICAL SUBSURFACE TRESPASS.
  See **OIL AND GAS**
GREENHALGH RULE
  Post-verdict amendment of pleadings, 29-7
GROSSLY NEGLIGENT INDUCEMENT OF CONTRACT
  Overview, 9-8:1
  Rejected in Texas, 9-8:2
  Related causes of action, 9-8:1.1

H

HEALTH CARE PROVIDERS
  Release, 16-5:2
HEALTHCARE LIABILITY
  Amount of recovery determination, 18-3
  Statutes of limitations
    death of claimant, 17-11:4
    minors, 17-11:3
  Statutes of repose, 17-13:3
HIRING. *See* **NEGLIGENT HIRING**

I

ILLEGALITY
  Affirmative defenses
    elements, 16-13:1
    other issues, 16-13:2
    overview, 16-13
  Breach of contract, 3-1:4.6
  Wrongful discharge. *See* **WRONGFUL DISCHARGE FOR REFUSAL TO PERFORM ILLEGAL ACTS**
IMMUNITY
  Fraud
    by non-disclosure, 1-6:4.5
  Legal malpractice, 4-1:4.4b
  Parental immunity, 16-19
  Subject matter jurisdiction, 21-8
    refusal to perform illegal acts, 6-2:4.2
IMPLIED CONSENT. *See* **EXPRESS OR IMPLIED CONSENT**
IMPLIED COVENANT TO FURTHER EXPLORE
  Overview, 9-23:1
  Rejected in Texas, 9-23:2
  Related causes of action, 9-23:1.1

IMPOSSIBILITY
  Breach of contract, 3-1:4.16
  Specific performance, 8-3:2
IN PARI DELICTO
  Securities fraud, 2-4:4.2
INCAPACITY. *See* **CAPACITY AND INCAPACITY**
INCOMPETENCY. *See* **CAPACITY AND INCAPACITY**
INDEMNIFICATION
  Agents and agency, 3-12:4.1
  Breach of contract, statute of limitations, 3-1:4.1
  Derivative shareholder suits, 2-8:3.3
  Proportionate responsibility, 18-6:3
INDORSEMENTS
  Verified and special denials, 14-6
INDUCEMENT OF CONTRACT, GROSSLY NEGLIGENT
  Overview, 9-8:1
  Rejected in Texas, 9-8:2
  Related causes of action, 9-8:1.1
INFERENTIAL REBUTTAL DEFENSES. *See* **DEFENSES**
INFRINGEMENT. *See* **TRADEMARK INFRINGEMENT, COMMON LAW; TRADEMARK INFRINGEMENT, STATUTORY**
INJUNCTION
  Definition, irreparable injury, 8-1:2, 8-2:2
  Forcible entry and detainer, tenant enjoyment of property, 8-11:4.2
  Insurance, deceptive insurance practices, 5-2:4.3
  Misuse of trade names, 1-14:3.1
  Permanent injunction
    elements, 8-2:2
    jurisdiction, 8-1:5.1
    overview, 8-2:1
    pleadings, 8-2:3
    related causes of action, 8-2:1.1
    venue, 8-1:5.2
  Public nuisance, 7-9:3.2
  Temporary injunction
    contents of injunction, 8-1:3.1
    damages and remedies, 8-1:3.1
    defenses
      laches, 8-1:4.2
      unclean hands, 8-1:4.1
    elements, 8-1:2
    jurisdiction, 8-1:5.1
    overview, 8-1:1
    procedural issues
      appeal, 8-1:5.6
      hearing requirement, 8-1:5.5
      notice, 8-1:5.4
      petition contents, 8-1:5.3
    related causes of action, 8-1:1.1
    scope of injunction, 8-1:3.2
    venue, 8-1:5.2
  Trademark infringement
    common law, 1-12:3.1
    statutory, 1-13:3.3
  Wrongful discharge for refusal to perform illegal acts, 6-2:3.3
INJUNCTIVE RELIEF
  Conversion, 1-3:3.3
  Forcible entry and detainer, 8-11:4.2
  Mandatory venue options, 22-4
  Misappropriation of trade secrets, 1-15:2
  Tortious interference with existing contract, 1-1:3.3
  Tortious interference with prospective business relationship, 1-2:3.3
INSIDER TRADING. *See* **SECURITIES FRAUD**
INSOLVENCY. *See* **BANKRUPTCY**
INSPECTION OF BOOKS AND RECORDS. *See* **SUITS TO COMPEL INSPECTION**
INSPECTORS
  Statutes of repose, 17-13:1
INSURANCE
  Deceptive insurance practices. *See* **DECEPTIVE INSURANCE PRACTICES**
  Declaratory judgment on coverage
    damages and remedies
      attorneys' fees, 5-5:3.3
      court costs, 5-5:3.2
      declaratory judgments, 5-5:3.1
    defense, statute of limitations, 5-5:4.1
    elements, 5-5:2
    related causes of action, 5-5:1.1
  Declaratory judgment on duty to defend
    damages and remedies
      attorneys' fees, 5-6:3.3
      court costs, 5-6:3.2
      declaratory judgments, 5-6:3.1
    defenses
      cooperation failure, 5-6:4.3
      known loss at time of purchase, 5-6:4.4
      notice lacking, 5-6:4.2
      statute of limitations, 5-6:4.1
    related causes of action, 5-6:1.1
  Definitions
    claim, 5-1:2
    claimant, 5-1:2
    justiciable controversy, 5-5:2
    person, 5-2:2
  Late payment of claims
    damages and remedies
      actual damages, 5-1:3.1
      attorneys' fees, 5-1:3.6
      court costs, 5-1:3.5, 11-13:2
      interest, 5-1:3.3, 5-1:3.4
      plaintiff's fault. *See* **PROPORTIONATE RESPONSIBILITY**
      statutory, 5-1:3.2
    elements, 5-1:2
    related causes of action, 5-1:1.1

INDEX

Negligent defense of third party claim
   overview, 9-10:1
   rejected in Texas, 9-10:2
   related causes of action, 9-10:1.1
Removal, citizenship determinations, 27-3:3.2
Stowers claims
   damages and remedies
      actual damages, 5-7:3.1
      court costs, 11-13:2
      exemplary damages. *See* **DAMAGES AND REMEDIES**
      interest. *See* **INTEREST**
   defenses
      demand not made, 5-7:4.2
      policy limits exhausted, 5-7:4.3
      statute of limitations, 5-7:4.1
   elements, 5-7:2
   related causes of action, 5-7:1.1
Uninsured/underinsured motorist coverage claims
   damages and remedies
      actual damages, 5-4:3.1
      attorneys' fees, 5-4:3.3
      court costs, 5-4:3.4
      interest, 5-4:3.2
   defenses
      rejection of coverage, 5-4:4.2
      statute of limitations, 5-4:4.1
   elements, 5-4:2
   overview, 5-4:1
   related causes of action, 5-4:1.1
INSURANCE BAD FAITH
Damages and remedies
   actual damages
      credit reputation damage, 5-3:3.1b
      increased business costs, 5-3:3.1c
      mental anguish, 5-3:3.1a
      policy proceeds, 5-3:3.1c
   court costs. *See* **COURT COSTS**
   exemplary damages. *See* **DAMAGES AND REMEDIES**
   interest. *See* **INTEREST**
Defenses
   fraudulent inducement, 5-3:4.3
   plaintiff's fault. *See* **PROPORTIONATE RESPONSIBILITY**
   reasonable basis exists, 5-3:4.2
   statute of limitations, 5-3:4.1
Elements, 5-3:2
Overview, 5-3:1
Related causes of action, 5-3:1.1
INTELLECTUAL PROPERTY
Trade name misuse. *See* **MISUSE OF TRADE NAMES**
Trade secret misappropriation. *See* **TRADE SECRET MISAPPROPRIATION**
Trademark infringement. *See* **TRADEMARK INFRINGEMENT, COMMON LAW**; **TRADEMARK INFRINGEMENT, STATUTORY**

INTEREST
Accountings, 8-4:3.3
Attachment, 8-7:3.4
Bailment, 3-23:3.6, 3-24:3.5
   partnership duties, 2-10:3.2
Dissenting shareholders, 2-9:3.2
Dissolution of partnerships, 2-16:3.5
Employment discrimination, 6-3:3.2
Garnishment, 8-8:3.3
Insurance
   deceptive insurance practices, 5-2:3.5
   late payment of claims, 5-1:3.3, 5-1:3.4
   uninsured/underinsured motorist coverage claims, 5-4:3.2
Legal malpractice, 4-1:3.2
Overview, 11-13:1
Quantum meruit, 3-13:3.2
Rescission, 3-2:2.3, 3-2:3.3
Suits on an account, 3-8:3.2
Wrongful discharge for refusal to perform illegal acts, 6-2:3.2
Wrongful withdrawal of partner, 2-16:3.5
INVASION OF PRIVACY, FALSE LIGHT
Overview, 9-9:1
Rejected in Texas, 9-9:2
Related causes of action, 9-9:1.1
INVERSE CONDEMNATION
Oil and gas. *See* **OIL AND GAS**
INVESTMENT BANKERS. *See* **BANKERS**

J

JOINDER
Amended pleadings, relation back, 29-2
Attachment, 8-7:5.5
Declaratory judgments, 7-3:5.2, 8-10:5.1
Fraudulently joined defendants to defeat diversity, 27-3:5
Sequestration, 8-6:5.5
Specific performance, 8-3:5.2
Verified and special denials, 14-3
JOINT AND SEVERAL LIABILITY
Wrongful distribution of dividends, 2-3:3.3
JOINT ENTERPRISE THEORY
Piercing the corporate veil and, 2-13:2.3
JUDICIAL EXPULSION. *See* **DISSOLUTION OF PARTNERSHIPS**
JUDICIAL NOTICE
Choice of law, 24-3:2
JUDICIAL WINDING UP. *See* **DISSOLUTION OF PARTNERSHIPS**
JURIES, RIGHT TO
Dissenting shareholders, 2-9:5.4
Piercing the corporate veil, 2-13:5.1
JURISDICTION
Accountings, 8-4:5.1
Dismissal of baseless cause of action, 28-1:7
Forcible entry and detainer, 8-11:4.1, 8-11:5.2

JURISDICTION (*cont.*)
  Injunction
    permanent injunction, 8-1:5.1
    temporary injunction, 8-1:5.1
  Removal. *See* **REMOVAL**
  Securities fraud, 2-4:5.2
  Subject matter jurisdiction. *See* **SUBJECT MATTER JURISDICTION**
JURY CHARGES
  Breach of implied covenant to reasonably develop, 7-14:5.1
  Pattern jury charges, 19-2
  Pleading to support, 19-1
JURY TAMPERING
  Overview, 9-6:1
  Rejected in Texas, 9-6:2
  Related causes of action, 9-6:1.1
JUSTIFICATION. *See* **PRIVILEGE AND JUSTIFICATION**

L

LACHES
  Accountings, 8-4:4.2
  Affirmative defenses
    elements, 16-18:1
    other issues, 16-18:2
    overview, 16-18
  Constructive trusts, 8-5:4.2
  Injunction
    temporary injunction, 8-1:4.2
  Misuse of trade names, 1-14:4.2
  Rescission, 3-2:4.2
  Specific performance, 8-3:4.2
  Trademark infringement, common law, 1-12:4.2
  Trademark infringement, statutory, 1-13:4.4
LANDLORD AND TENANT
  Forcible entry and detainer. *See* **FORCIBLE ENTRY AND DETAINER**
LEGAL MALPRACTICE
  Damages and remedies
    actual damages, 4-1:3.1
    court costs. *See* **COURT COSTS**
    exemplary damages, 4-1:3.5
    interest, 4-1:3.2
    mental anguish, 4-1:3.4
  Defenses
    immunity, 4-1:4.4b
    plaintiff's fault, 4-1:4.4c
    statute of limitations
      accrual of claims, 4-1:4.1b
      discovery rule, 4-1:4.1c
      overview, 4-1:4.1a
  Elements, 4-1:2
  Overview, 4-1:1
  Related causes of action, 4-1:1.1
LICENSE
  Affirmative defenses
    elements, 16-9:1
    overview, 16-9

LIMITED LIABILITY COMPANIES (LLCS)
  Citizenship determinations, 27-3:3.3
  Piercing the corporate veil. *See* **PIERCING THE CORPORATE VEIL**
  Suits to compel inspection. *See* **SUITS TO COMPEL INSPECTION**
  Usurpation of business opportunity. *See* **USURPATION OF BUSINESS OPPORTUNITY**

M

MALPRACTICE
  Architects. *See* **DESIGN MALPRACTICE**
  Engineers. *See* **DESIGN MALPRACTICE**
  Legal malpractice. *See* **LEGAL MALPRACTICE**
MANDAMUS
  Arbitration, motion to compel denial, 25-2
  Forum selection clauses, 26-1:1
  Suit to compel inspection, 2-12
  Venue for actions against state government, 22-4
MARKET VALUE BASED ON COMPARABLE BUSINESSES
  Loss of value, 11-7:2
MEDICAL MALPRACTICE. *See* **HEALTHCARE LIABILITY**
MENTAL ANGUISH
  Common law fraud, 1-4:3.1d
  Fraud by non-disclosure, 1-6:3.1d
  Insurance bad faith, 5-3:3.1a
  Legal malpractice, 4-1:3.4
  Pecuniary and intangible damages, 11-9:3
  Statutory damages specific to the cause of action, 11-10
  Tortious interference with existing contract, 1-1:3.1b
  Tortious interference with prospective business relationship, 1-2:3.1b
MERGERS
  Dissenting shareholders. *See* **DISSENTING SHAREHOLDERS**
  Liability of successor for tortious conduct of predecessor
    overview, 9-13:1
    rejected in Texas, 9-13:2
MIDDLEBROOK DOCTRINE
  Derivative venue, 22-6
MILITARY SERVICE
  Statutes of limitations and, 17-11:5
MINERAL ESTATES. *See* **OIL AND GAS**
MINORITY SHAREHOLDER OPPRESSION. *See* **SHAREHOLDER OPPRESSION**
MINORS
  Breach of contract, 3-1:4.5
  Domicile, 27-3:3.1
  Negligence, 1-10:2
  Negligence per se, 1-11:2
  Parental immunity, 16-19
  Statutes of limitations and, 17-11:3

INDEX

MISAPPROPRIATION. *See* **RESTITUTION**
MISTAKE
  Contracts, reformation of. *See* **REFORMATION**
  Reformation of deed, statute of limitations, 3-1:4.1
  Rescission, 3-2:2.1
MISUSE OF TRADE NAMES
  Defenses
    abandonment, 1-14:4.3
    acquiescence, 1-14:4.4
    fair use, 1-14:4.6
    First Amendment, 1-14:4.5
    laches, 1-14:4.2
    statute of limitations, 1-14:4.1
  Elements, 1-14:2
  Overview, 1-14:1
  Related causes of action, 1-14:1.1
  Remedy, injunction, 1-14:3.1
MITIGATION OF DAMAGES
  Employment agreement, 6-1:4.5
  Pleading, 12-1
MONEY HAD AND RECEIVED
  Damages and remedies
    attorneys' fees, 3-6:3.2
    restitution, 3-6:3.1
  Defenses
    equitable defenses, 3-6:4.2
    statute of limitations, 3-6:4.1
  Elements, 3-6:2
  Overview, 3-6:1
  Related causes of action, 3-6:1.1
MOTOR VEHICLES
  Negligent entrustment. *See* **BAILMENT**
MULTIPLE OF BOOK
  Loss of value, 11-7:2
MULTIPLE OF EARNINGS
  Loss of value, 11-7:2

N

NEGLIGENCE
  Contributory negligence as affirmative defense
    elements, 16-10:2
    overview, 16-10
  Damages and remedies
    actual damages
      economic injury, 1-10:3.1c
      personal property injury, 1-10:3.1a
      real property injury, 1-10:3.1b
    court costs, 11-13:2
    exemplary damages, 1-10:3.2
    interest. *See* **INTEREST**
  Defenses
    comparative fault, 1.10:4.2
    economic loss rule, 1-10:4.3
    statutes of limitations, 1-10:4.1
  Definitions
    cause-in-fact, 1-10:2
    foreseeability, 1-10:2
  Elements, 1-10:2

Oil and gas. *See* **OIL AND GAS**
Opposing attorneys, action against, 9-1:2
Related causes of action, 1-10:1.1
NEGLIGENCE PER SE
  Damages and remedies
    actual damages
      economic injury, 1-11:3.1c
      personal property injury, 1-11:3.1a
      real property injury, 1-11:3.1b
    court costs, 11-13:2
    exemplary damages, 1-11:3.2
    interest. *See* **INTEREST**
    limits on, 1-11:3.5
  Defenses
    economic loss rule. *See* **ECONOMIC LOSS RULE**
    release, 1-11:4.2
    statute of limitations, 1-11:4.1
  Elements, 1-11:2
  Related causes of action, 1-11:1.1
NEGLIGENT ENTRUSTMENT. *See* **BAILMENT**
NEGLIGENT HIRING
  Damages and remedies
    actual damages. *See* **DAMAGES AND REMEDIES**
    court costs, 11-13:2
    exemplary damages, 1-9:3.2
    interest. *See* **INTEREST**
  Defenses
    presumption of no negligence, 1-9:4.2
    statute of limitations
  Elements, 1-9:2
  Related causes of action, 1-9:1.1
NEGLIGENT INFLICTION OF EMOTIONAL DISTRESS
  Overview, 9-11:1
  Rejected in Texas, 9-11:2
  Related causes of action, 9-11:1.1
NEGLIGENT INSURANCE DEFENSE OF THIRD PARTY CLAIM
  Overview, 9-10:1
  Rejected in Texas, 9-10:2
  Related causes of action, 9-10:1.1
NEGLIGENT INVESTIGATION OF EMPLOYEE MISCONDUCT
  Overview, 9-12:1
  Rejected in Texas, 9-12:2
  Related causes of action, 9-12:1.1
NEGLIGENT MISREPRESENTATION
  Damages and remedies
    actual damages
      overview, 1-7:3.1
    court costs, 11-13:2
    exemplary damages. *See* **DAMAGES AND REMEDIES**
    interest. *See* **INTEREST**
  Defenses
    breach of contract, 1-7:4.2
    disclaimer of reliance, 1-7:4.4

NEGLIGENT MISREPRESENTATION (*cont.*)
    ratification or waiver, 1-7:4.5
    statute of frauds, 1-7:4.3
  Elements, 1-7:2
  Related causes of action, 1-7:1.1

NOVATION
  Breach of contract, 3-1:4.18

NUISANCE
  Agricultural operations, statute of limitations, 17-2
  Oil and gas. *See* **OIL AND GAS**

O

OBEDIENCE
  Agents. *See* **AGENTS AND AGENCY**

OFFICERS AND DIRECTORS
  Agents, liability as. *See* **AGENTS AND AGENCY**
  Breach of duty of loyalty. *See* **BREACH OF DUTY OF LOYALTY**
  Duty of care breach. *See* **BREACH OF DUTY OF CARE**
  Insider trading. *See* **SECURITIES FRAUD**
  Securities fraud. *See* **SECURITIES FRAUD**
  Short swing profits. *See* **SECURITIES FRAUD**
  Usurpation of business opportunity. *See* **USURPATION OF BUSINESS OPPORTUNITY**
  Wrongful distribution of dividends. *See* **WRONGFUL DISTRIBUTION OF DIVIDENDS**

OFFSET
  Quantum meruit, 3-3:4.3

OIL AND GAS
  Assumpsit
    damages and remedies, 7-6:3.1
    elements, 7-6:2
    overview, 7-6:1
    related causes of action, 7-6:1.1
    statute of limitations, 7-6:4.1
    venue, 7-6:5.1
  Breach of contract
    damages and remedies
      attorneys' fees, 7-5:3.3
      compensatory damages, 7-5:3.1
      lease termination, 7-5:3.2
    defenses
      express lease provisions, 7-5:4.2
      temporary cessation, 7-5:4.1
    elements, 7-5:2
    overview, 7-5:1
    related causes of action, 7-5:1.1
    venue, 7-5:5.1
  Breach of fiduciary duty
    damages and remedies, 7-7:3.1
    elements, 7-7:2
    overview, 7-7:1
    related causes of action, 7-7:1.1
    statute of limitations, 7-7:4.1
    venue, 7-7:5.1
  Breach of implied covenant to market
    class certification, 7-13:5.1
    damages and remedies
      conditional cancellation, 7-13:3.2
      royalty, 7-13:3.1
    defenses
      market value lease, 7-13:4.1
      take-or-pay provisions, 7-13:4.2
    elements, 7-13:2
    overview, 7-13:1
    related causes of action, 7-13:1.1
  Breach of implied covenant to protect against drainage
    cotenancy, 7-12:5.1
    damages and remedies
      conditional cancellation, 7-12:3.4
      exemplary damages, 7-16:3.2
      future drainage, 7-12:3.3
      royalty lost, 7-12:3.1
    defenses
      express lease provisions, 7-12:4.2
      pooling, 7-12:4.1
      statute of limitations, 7-12:4.3
    elements, 7-12:2
    overview, 7-12:1
    reasonable diligence required, 7-12:5.2
    related causes of action, 7-12:1.1
  Breach of implied covenant to reasonably develop
    cure opportunity, 7-14:4.2, 7-14:5.2
    damages and remedies
      cancellation of lease, 7-14:3.2
      royalty lost, 7-14:3.1
    defenses
      cure opportunity, 7-14:4.2
      express lease provisions, 7-14:4.1
    elements, 7-14:2
    jury instructions, 7-14:5.1
    overview, 7-14:1
    related causes of action, 7-14:1.1
  Conversion
    damages and remedies
      exemplary damages, 7-8:3.2
      value of converted property, 7-8:3.1
    defenses
      rule of capture, 7-8:4.2
      statute of limitations, 7-8:4.1
    elements, 7-8:2
    overview, 7-8:1
    related causes of action, 7-8:1.1
    trespass to chattel and personalty compared, 7-8:1
    venue, 7-8:5.1
  Declaratory judgments
    damages and remedies
      attorneys' fees, 7-3:3.2
      judicial declaration, 7-3:3.1
    defenses
      improper use of action, 7-3:4.3
      justiciable controversy lacking, 7-3:4.2
      statute of limitations, 7-3:4.1

INDEX

elements, 7-3:2
joinder, 7-3:5.2
overview, 7-3:1
related causes of action, 7-3:1.1
trespass to try title compared, 7-3:1, 7-3:4.3
venue, 7-3:5.1
Definitions
  capable of production in paying quantities, 7-11:3.1
  foreseeability, 7-11:2
  legal malice, 7-10:2
  market value, 7-13:2
  paying quantities, 7-12:2, 7-14:2
  political questions, 7-9:4.3
  pooling, 7-12:4.1
  public nuisance, 7-9:1
  substantial drainage, 7-12:2
  typicality, 7-13:5.1
Forcible entry and detainer
  authority, 7-4:1.1
  overview, 7-4:1
Geophysical subsurface trespass. *See* Assumpsit, *above*
Implied covenant to further explore
  overview, 9-23:1
  rejected in Texas, 9-23:2
  related causes of action, 9-23:1.1
Negligence
  damages and remedies
    compensatory damages, 7-11:3.1
    exemplary damages, 7-11:3.2
  defenses
    contractual duty, 7-11:4.2
    contributory negligence, 7-11:4.3
    statute of limitations, 7-11:4.1
  elements, 7-11:2
  overview, 7-11:1
  related causes of action, 7-11:1.1
Public nuisance
  choice of law, 7-9:5.1
  damages and remedies
    injunction, 7-9:3.2
    special damages, 7-9:3.1
  defenses
    causation lacking, 7-9:4.6
    particularized injury lacking, 7-9:4.5
    political questions, 7-9:4.3
    preemption, 7-9:4.4
    standing, 7-9:4.2
    statute of limitations, 7-9:4.1
  elements, 7-9:2
  overview, 7-9:1
  related causes of action, 7-9:1.1
Quiet title
  damages and remedies
    attorneys' fees, 7-1:3.2
    judicial declaration, 7-1:3.1
  defenses
    defendant proves title, 7-1:4.2
    equitable defenses, 7-1:4.4
    improvement value claims, 7-1:4.3
    statute of limitations, 7-1:4.1
  elements, 7-1:2
  overview, 7-1:1
  procedural issues
    pleading, 7-1:5.2
    recording of judgment, 7-1:5.3
    venue, 7-1:5.1
  related causes of action, 7-1:1.1
  trespass to try title compared, 7-2:1
Regulatory taking. *See* Inverse condemnation, *above*
Slander of title
  damages and remedies
    attorneys' fees, 7-10:3.3
    exemplary damages, 7-10:3.2
    special damages, 7-10:3.1
  defenses
    advice of counsel, 7-10:4.2
    statute of limitations, 7-10:4.1
  elements, 7-10:2
  overview, 7-10:1
  related causes of action, 7-10:1.1
  venue, 7-10:5.1
Slant-hole drilling
  conversion, 7-8:4.2
  explained, 7-8:4.2
Temporary cessation of production doctrine, 7-5:4.1
Trespass to real property
  conversion compared, 9-4:2
  damages and remedies
    court costs, 11-13:2
    immunity. *See* **IMMUNITY**
    plaintiff's fault. *See* **PROPORTIONATE RESPONSIBILITY**
Trespass to try title
  damages and remedies
    judicial declaration, 7-2:3.1
    special injury, 7-2:3.4
    use and occupation, 7-2:3.3
    writ of possession, 7-2:3.2
  declaratory judgments compared, 7-3:1, 7-3:4.3
  defenses
    defendant has superior title, 7-2:4.3
    improvement value claims, 7-2:4.4
    statute of limitations, 7-2:4.1
    third party proof of title, 7-2:4.2
  elements, 7-2:2
  overview, 7-2:1
  pleading
    defendant, 7-2:5.3a, 7-2:5.3c
    plaintiff, 7-2:5.2
  proof requirements, 7-2:5.4
  quiet title compared, 7-2:1
  related causes of action, 7-2:1.1
  venue, 7-2:5.1

OPEN ACCOUNTS. *See* **SUITS ON AN ACCOUNT; SWORN ACCOUNTS**

OPPOSING ATTORNEYS, ACTION AGAINST. *See* ATTORNEYS

P

PARENTAL IMMUNITY
Affirmative defenses, 16-19
PARODIES
Misuse of trade names, 1-14:4.5
Trademark infringement, common law, 1-12:2
PAROL EVIDENCE RULE
Rescission, 3-2:5.1
PARTIES
Misnomer and misidentification of defendants, 17-10
Pleading
   misnomer and misidentification of defendants, 23-2
   non-resident defendants, 23-3
   partnerships, assumed, or common names, 23-1
   requirements for, 23-1
   service method, 23-4
PARTNERSHIPS
Breach of duty. *See* **BREACH OF PARTNERSHIP DUTY**
Citizenship determinations, 27-3:3.3
Dissolution of partnership. *See* **DISSOLUTION OF PARTNERSHIPS**
Suits to compel inspection. *See* **SUITS TO COMPEL INSPECTION**
Verified and special denials, 14-4
Wrongful expulsion of whistleblowing partners
   overview, 9-14:1
   rejected in Texas, 9-14:2
   related causes of action, 9-14:1.1
PERJURY
Overview, 9-15:1
Rejected in Texas, 9-15:2
Related causes of action, 9-15:1.1
PERMANENT INJUNCTION
Elements, 8-2:2
Jurisdiction, 8-1:5.1
Overview, 8-2:1
Pleadings, 8-2:3
Related causes of action, 8-2:1.1
Venue, 8-1:5.2
PERMANENT LEGAL RESIDENT ALIENS
Domicile, 27-3:3.1
PERSONAL PROPERTY
Damages, 11-8:2
PIERCING THE CORPORATE VEIL
Damages and remedies, 2-13:3.1
Defenses, 2-13:4.1
Definitions
   actual fraud, 2-13:2.1, 2-13:2.2
   constructive fraud, 2-13:2.2
   contractual obligation, 2-13:2.1
   single business enterprise theory, 2-13:2.3

Elements
   contractual obligation, 2-13:2.1
   single business enterprise theory, 2-13:2.3
   tort obligations, 2-13:2.2
Juries, right to, 2-13:5.1
Limited liability companies (LLCS), 2-13:2.4
Overview, 2-13:1
Related causes of action, 2-13:1.1
PLEADING
Affirmative defenses
   defects in pleading, 13-5:2
   overview, 13-5
   types of, 13-5:1
Amendment
   effect of, 29-2
   leave, motion for, 29-4
   post-verdict, 29-7
   relation-back rule, 29-2
   special appearances, unsworn motions, 13-2:2
   special exceptions and, 28-2
   supplemental pleadings compared, 29-1
   time limits, 29-3
   trial amendment, 29-5
   trial by consent, 29-6
Arbitration
   compelling arbitration procedure, 25-2
   post arbitration proceedings
      confirmation of award, 25-4:1
      modification or correction of award, 25-4:3
      overview, 25-4
      vacating award, 25-4:2
   resisting arbitration
      fraud, 25-3:3
      outside scope of agreement, 25-3:1
      overview, 25-3
      unconscionability, 25-3:2
      waiver, 25-3:4
Choice of law
   other jurisdictions, 24-3:2
   overview, 24-3
   presumption in favor of Texas law, 24-3:1
Damages and remedies. *See* **DAMAGES AND REMEDIES**
Definitions
   general denial, 13-3:1
   major transactions, 26-1:2
   principle office, 22-3
   venue, 22-2
Discovery levels. *See* **DISCOVERY LEVELS**
Dismissal of baseless cause of action
   Anti-SLAPP Act 28-4
   attorneys' fees and costs, 28-1:6
   basis in law or fact lacking, 28-1:2
   contents of motion, 28-1:3
   overview, 28-1
   personal jurisdiction, effect on, 28-1:7
   response, 28-1:4
   ruling, 28-1:5
   scope, 28-1:1

INDEX

timing issues, 28-1:4
venue, effect on, 28-1:7
Due-order-of-hearing requirement
  dismissal of baseless cause of action, 28-1:7
  special appearances, 13-2:4
  venue motions, 13-2:6
Due-order-of-pleading requirement
  notice of removal, 13-2:1
  overview, 13-2
  Rule 11 agreements, 13-2:1
  special appearances
    overview, 13-2:1
    "subject to" language lacking, 13-2:3
    unsworn motions, 13-2:2
  venue motions, 13-2:5, 22-7
Equitable remedies, 19-5
Fair notice standard, 19-3, 19-4
Federal versus state requirements, 13-5:2, 19-4
Forum selection clauses
  enforcement
    consumer contracts, 26-1:3
    distinguishing forum selection clauses from venue selection clauses, 26-1:2
    major transactions, 26-1:2
    overview, 26-1:1
  resistance
    fraud, 26-2:1
    waiver, 26-2:2
General appearances
  special appearances not in conformity as, 13-2:1
  what constitutes, 13-2:4
General denials
  affirmative defenses compared, 13-3:1
  amendment, 13-3:2, 13-3:4
  counterclaim or crossclaim, deemed general denials, 13-3:3
  groundless bad faith pleadings rule, 13-3:6
  overview, 13-3:1
  venue motions, 13-3:5
Inferential rebuttal defenses, 13-6:4
Overview, 13-1
Parties
  misnomer and misidentification of defendants, 23-2
  non-resident defendants, 23-3
  partnerships, assumed, or common names, 23-1
  requirements for, 23-1
  service method, 23-4
Pattern jury charges, 19-2
Personal jurisdiction over non-resident defendant, 23-3
Plausibility pleading standard, 13-5:2, 19-4, 28-1:2
Proof and pleading, 19-3, 29-5
Removal
  answer deadline, 27-5:5
  contents of notice, 27-5:2
  deadline for, 27-5:3

unanimity of consent rule, 27-5:4
venue, 27-5:1
Special appearances
  due-order-of-hearing requirement, 13-2:4
  due-order-of-pleading requirement
    overview, 13-2:1
    "subject to" language lacking, 13-2:3
    unsworn motions, 13-2:2
  waiver, 28-1:7
Special exceptions
  overview, 19-3, 28-2
  pleas in abatement compared, 28-3
Subject matter jurisdiction. *See* **SUBJECT MATTER JURISDICTION**
Substantive defenses compared, 13-1
Supporting the charge, 19-1
Venue
  derivative venue, 22-6
  distinguishing forum selection clauses from venue selection clauses, 26-1:2
  general venue, 22-3
  importance of factual basis, 22-1
  mandatory venue, 22-4
  overview, 22-2
  permissive venue, 22-5
  presumptions, 22-1
  transfer motions, 13-2:5, 22-7
Verified and special denials
  conditions precedent, 13-4:6
  matters appearing on the record exception, 13-4:5
  overview, 13-4
  personal knowledge requirement
    exceptions, 13-4:3
    overview, 13-4:2
  what requires, 13-4:1
  who may verify, 13-4:4

PLEAS IN ABATEMENT
Overview, 28-3

PLEAS TO JURISDICTION
Subject matter jurisdiction, 21-9

POLITICAL QUESTIONS
Public nuisance, 7-9:4.3

PREEMPTION
Insurance
Public nuisance, 7-9:4.4
Trade secret misappropriation, 1-15:4.3

PRESUIT DEMAND
Derivative shareholder suits, 2-8:2

PRIMA FACIE TORTS
Overview, 9-16:1
Rejected in Texas, 9-16:2
Related causes of action, 9-16:1.1

PRIVILEGE AND JUSTIFICATION
Business disparagement, 1-8:4.1
Tortious interference with existing contract, 1-1:4.3
Tortious interference with prospective business relationship, 1-2:4.3
Trade secret misappropriation, 1-15:4.2

PROFESSIONAL SERVICES
  Breach of implied warranty of professional services
    overview, 9-21:1
    rejected in Texas, 9-21:2
    related causes of action, 9-21:1.1
PROMISSORY ESTOPPEL
  Affirmative defenses
    overview, 16-12
    elements, 16-12:2
  Damages and remedies
    enforcement of promise, 3-5:3.2
    reliance damages, 3-5:3.1
  Defenses
    equitable defenses, 3-5:4.2
    statute of limitations, 3-5:4.1
  Detrimental reliance and, 9-5:1
  Elements
    cause of action, 3-5:2.1
    Statute of Frauds, 3-5:2.2
  Overview, 3-5:1
  Related causes of action, 3-5:1.1
PROPORTIONATE RESPONSIBILITY
  Amount of recovery determination, 18-3
  Contribution
    jointly and severally liable defendants, 18-6:1
    other liable defendants, 18-6:2
  Definitions
    claimant, 18-2:2
    contribution defendant, 18-6:2
    defendant, 18-2:2
    liable defendant, 18-6:2
    responsible third party, 18-2:2
    settling person, 18-2:2
  Designation of responsible third parties
    effect of, 18-5:5
    leave to designate, 18-5:1
    objections, 18-5:2
    overview, 18-5
    striking designation, 18-5:4
    unknown criminals, 18-5:3
  Indemnity, 18-6:3
  Joint and several liability, 18-4
  Percentage determinations
    each cause of action, 18-2:1
    overview, 18-2
    percentage of responsibility, 18-2:3
    persons liable, 18-2:2
  Scope of statute on, 18-1
PUBLIC FIGURES
  Business disparagement. *See* **BUSINESS DISPARAGEMENT**
PUBLIC NUISANCE
  Oil and gas. *See* **OIL AND GAS**
PUBLIC POLICY
  Breach of contract, 3-1:4.7
  Choice of law, 24-1:10

Q

QUANTUM MERUIT
  Agents and agency, 3-12:4.3
  Breach of contract, 3-1:3.2
  Damages and remedies
    interest, 3-3:3.2
    reasonable value determination, 3-3:3.1
  Defenses
    equitable defenses, 3-3:4.5
    express contract exists, 3-3:4.2
    offset, 3-3:4.3
    res judicata, 3-3:4.4
    statute of limitations, 3-3:4.1
  Elements, 3-3:2
  Overview, 3-3:1, 11-11:4
  Related causes of action, 3-3:1.1
QUIET TITLE
  Oil and gas. *See* **OIL AND GAS**

R

RAILROAD COMMISSION
  Breach of implied covenant to protect against drainage, 7-12:2
  Breach of implied covenant to reasonably develop, 7-14:2
RATIFICATION
  Agents and agency, 3-11:2.1, 3-12:2.5, 3-13:4.1
  Breach of contract
    illegality, 3-1:4.6
    minors, 3-1:4.5
    overview, 3-1:4.21
  Fraud, common law, 1-4:4.3
  Fraud by non-disclosure, 1-6:4.3
  Usurpation of business opportunity, 2-11:4.4
REAL PROPERTY
  Boundary line determinations. *See* **DECLARATORY JUDGMENTS**
  Conversion
    overview, 9-4:1
    rejected in Texas, 9-4:2
    related causes of action, 9-4:1.1
  Damages, 11-8:1
  Forcible entry and detainer. *See* **FORCIBLE ENTRY AND DETAINER**
  Fraud. *See* **FRAUD, STATUTORY**
  Mineral estates. *See* **OIL AND GAS**
  Negligence, 1-10:3.1b
  Negligence per se, 1-11:3.1b
  Reformation of deed, statute of limitations, 3-1:4.1
  Sequestration. *See* **SEQUESTRATION**
  Specific performance. *See* **SPECIFIC PERFORMANCE**
RECEIVERSHIP
  Breach of partnership duty, 2-10:3.8
  Damages and remedies
    appointment of receiver, 8-9:3.1
    fees for receiver, 8-9:3.2

INDEX

Defenses, 8-9:4.1
Elements
  common law appointment, 8-9:2.1
  statutory appointment, 8-9:2.2
Judicial winding up of partnership, 2-15:3.2
Overview, 8-9:1
Procedural issues
  bond posted, 8-9:5.2
  ex parte relief, 8-9:5.1
Related causes of action, 8-9:1.1
Shareholder oppression. *See* **SHAREHOLDER OPPRESSION**
Venue, 8-9:5.3
REDEMPTION
Wrongful withdrawal of partner, 2-16:3.1
REFORMATION
Breach of contract, 3-1:3.8
Fraud by non-disclosure, 1-6:3.3b
REGISTERED AGENTS
Requirements for, 23-1
RELEASE
Affirmative defenses
  elements, 16-5:1
  other issues, 16-5:2
  overview, 16-5
Breach of contract, 3-1:4.21
Health care providers, 16-5:2
Negligence per se, 1-11:4.2
Suits on an account, 3-8:4.5
RELIANCE
Agents and agency, 3-12:2.5
Disclaimers. *See* **DISCLAIMERS**
Employment discrimination, commission interpretation or opinion, 6-3:4.6
Fraud, common law, 1-4:2
  attacking justifiable reliance, 1-4:4.5
Fraud, statutory, 1-5:2
Fraud by non-disclosure, 1-6:2
Negligent misrepresentation, 1-7:2
Promissory estoppel, 3-5:2.1
Securities fraud, 2-4:2.1
Wrongful distribution of dividends, 2-3:4.1
RELIGIOUS BELIEF
Employment discrimination, 6-3:4.7
REMAND
Overview, 27-6
REMOVAL
Definitions
  complete diversity, 27-3:2
  domicile, 27-3:3.1
Discovery levels and, 20-2
Diversity of citizenship grounds
  amount in controversy, 27-3:1
  citizenship determinations
    corporations, 27-3:3.2
    natural persons, 27-3:3.1
    overview, 27-3:3
    time of determination, 27-3:3.4
    unincorporated entities, 27-3:3.3

complete diversity requirement, 27-3:2
forum state defendant rule, 27-3:4
fraudulently joined defendants, 27-3:5
overview, 27-3
time for removal, 27-3:6
Federal question grounds
  joinder of state law claims, 27-2:2
  same case or controversy requirement, 27-2:2
  overview, 27-2
  what constitutes, 27-2:1
Notice of removal not general appearance, 13-2:1
Overview, 27-1
Plausibility pleading standard, 13-5:2
Procedural issues. *See* **PLEADING**
Remand, 27-6
Statutes, cases non-removable by, 27-4
REPOSSESSION
Bailment, 3-23:3.8
RES JUDICATA
Affirmative defenses
  elements, 16-7:1
  other issues, 16-7:2
  overview, 16-7
Declaratory judgments, 8-10:5.2
Derivative shareholder suits, 2-8:4.2
Quantum meruit, 3-3:4.4
RESCISSION
Breach of contract, 3-1:3.7
Breach of partnership duty, 2-10:3.4
Damages and remedies
  exemplary damages, 3-2:2.3, 3-2:3.4
  interest, 3-2:2.3, 3-2:3.3
  rescission, 3-2:3.1
  special damages, 3-2:3.2
Defenses
  equitable defenses, 3-2:4.4
  laches, 3-2:4.2
  ratification, 3-2:4.3,
  statute of limitations, 3-2:4.1
  waiver, 3-2:4.3
Elements
  equitable rescission, 3-2:2.1
  rescission by consent, 3-2:2.2
  rescission by option, 3-2:2.3
Fraud by non-disclosure, 1-6:3.3a
Overview, 3-2:1, 11-11:3
Parol evidence, 3-2:5.1
Related causes of action, 3-2:1.1
Securities fraud, 2-4:3.4
RESIDENCE
Venue, 22-3
RESTATEMENT (SECOND) OF CONFLICTS. *See* **CHOICE OF LAW**
RESTITUTION
Breach of contract, 3-1:3.1c
Breach of partnership duty, 2-10:3.5
Money had and received, 3-6:3.1
Overview, 11-4, 11-11:3
Unjust enrichment, 3-4:3.1

RETALIATORY DISCHARGE
  Perception of participation in protected activities
    overview, 9-17:1
    rejected in Texas, 9-17:2
    related causes of action, 9-17:1.1
  Protected acts of third parties
    overview, 9-18:1
    rejected in Texas, 9-18:2
    related causes of action, 9-18:1.1
RIGHT TO FARM ACT
RULE 10B-5 FRAUD. *See* **SECURITIES FRAUD**
RULE 11 AGREEMENTS
  Due-order-of-pleading requirement, 13-2:1

S

SAFE HARBOR DEFENSE
  Breach of duty of care, 2-1:4.1
  Breach of duty of loyalty, 2-2:4.1
SANCTIONS
  Signature on pleadings, 13-3:6
SCIENTER
  Securities fraud, Rule 10b-5, 2-4:2.1
SECURITIES FRAUD
  Common law fraud. *See* **FRAUD, COMMON LAW**
  Damages and remedies
    benefit-of-the-bargain, 2-4:3.2
    consequential damages, 2-4:3.6
    disgorgement, 2-4:3.3
    exemplary damages, 2-4:3.5
    out-of-pocket damages, 2-4:3.1
    rescission, 2-4:3.4
  Defenses
    10b-5-1 plans, 2-4:4.1
    equitable defenses, 2-4:4.4
    in pari delicto, 2-4:4.2
    statute of limitations, 2-4:4.3
  Definitions
    on the basis of, 2-4:2.2
    nonpublic information, 2-4:2.2, 2-4:2.3
  Elements
    Rule 10b-5 fraud, 2-4:2.1
    Rule 10b-5 insider trading, 2-4:2.2
    Rule 14e-3 tender offers, 2-4:2.3
    short swing profits, 2-4:2.4
  Procedural issues
    jurisdiction, 2-4:5.2
    plaintiff in short swing profits cases, 2-4:5.3
    pleading burden, 2-4:5.1
  Related causes of action, 2-4:1.1
SEQUESTRATION
  Damages and remedies
    levy upon writ, 8-6:3.2
    perishable personal property sold, 8-6:3.3
    reply by plaintiff, 8-6:3.4
    writ issued, 8-6:3.1
  Defenses
    exemption from execution, 8-6:4.3
    replevy bond, 8-6:4.1
    strict compliance not met, 8-6:4.2
  Elements, 8-6:2
  Overview, 8-6:1
  Procedural issues
    amendment, 8-6:5.6
    bond posted, 8-6:5.2
    ex parte relief, 8-6:5.3
    joinder, 8-6:5.5
    modification or dissolution of writ, 8-6:5.7
    service, 8-6:5.4
    sworn application requirement, 8-6:5.1
  Related causes of action, 8-6:1.1
SERVICE OF PROCESS
  Agents for, 23-1
  Dissolved corporations, 23-1
  Due diligence for statute of limitations purposes, 17-12
  Method, pleading of, 23-4
  Substituted service, 23-4
SETOFF
  Garnishment, 8-8:4.5
  Wrongful withdrawal of partner, 2-16:3.6
SETTLEMENT
  Deceptive insurance practices, settlement offer tendered, 5-2:4.2
  Derivative shareholder suits, 2-8:5.8
SHAREHOLDER DERIVATIVE SUITS. *See* **DERIVATIVE SHAREHOLDER SUITS**
SHAREHOLDER OPPRESSION
  Common law
    overview, 9-7:1
    rejected in Texas, 9-7:2
    related causes of action, 9-7:1.1
  Defenses, 2-7:4.1
  Definition, oppressive conduct, 2-7:2
  Elements, 2-7:2
  Fact finder's roles, 2-7:5.1
  Overview, 2-7:1
  Receivership as remedy, 2-7:3.1, 9-7:2
  Related causes of action, 2-7:1.1
SHORT SWING PROFITS. *See also* **SECURITIES FRAUD**
  Liability for securities fraud, 2-4:2.4
    procedural implications, 2-4:5.3
SIGNATURES
  Verified and special denials, 14-6
SINGLE BUSINESS ENTERPRISE THEORY
  Piercing the corporate veil, 2-13:2.3
SLANDER OF TITLE. *See* **OIL AND GAS**
SOLDIER'S AND SAILORS CIVIL RELIEF ACT
  Statutes of limitations and, 17-11:5
SOVEREIGN IMMUNITY. *See* **IMMUNITY**

INDEX

SPECIAL APPEARANCES
  Due-order-of-hearing requirement, 13-2:4
  Due-order-of-pleading requirement
    overview, 13-2:1
    "subject to" language lacking, 13-2:3
    unsworn motions, 13-2:2
  Waiver, 28-1:7
SPECIAL DENIALS. *See* **VERIFIED AND SPECIAL DENIALS**
SPECIAL EXCEPTIONS
  Overview, 19-3, 28-2
  Pleas in abatement compared, 28-3
SPECIFIC PERFORMANCE
  Breach of contract, 3-1:3.6
  Damages and remedies, 8-3:3.1
  Defenses
    contractual defenses, 8-3:4.3
    equitable defenses, 8-3:4.6
    estoppel, 8-3:4.5
    laches, 8-3:4.2
    statute of limitations, 8-3:4.1
    waiver, 8-3:4.4
  Elements, 8-3:2
  Overview, 8-3:1
  Procedural issues
    election of remedies, 8-3:5.3
    express right agreed, 8-3:5.1
    joinder of parties necessary, 8-3:5.2
  Related causes of action, 8-3:1.1
SPOLIATION OF EVIDENCE
  Overview, 9-19:1
  Rejected in Texas, 9-19:2
STANDING
  Breach of contract, 3-1:4.2
  Capacity compared, 14-1
  Declaratory judgments, 8-10:2, 8-10:4.3
  Derivative shareholder suits, 2-8:2
  Duty of care breach, 2-1:5.1
  Duty of loyalty breach, 2-2:5.1
  Partnership dissolution, 2-16:5.1
  Partnership duty breach, 2-10:5.1
  Public nuisance, 7-9:4.2
  Retaliatory discharge for protected acts of third parties, 9-18:2
  Wrongful distribution of dividends, 2-3:5.1
STATE REVOCATION OF CORPORATE STATUS
  Damages and remedies, 2-6:3.1
  Elements
    Attorney General judicial termination, 2-6:2.2
    franchise taxes, failure to pay, 2-6:2.3
    Secretary of State administrative termination, 2-6:2.1
  Overview, 2-6:1
  Reinstatement, 2-6:4.1
STATED ACCOUNTS. *See* **SUITS ON AN ACCOUNT; SWORN ACCOUNTS**
STATUTE OF CONVEYANCES
  Agents and agency, 3-11:4

STATUTE OF FRAUDS
  Affirmative defenses
    elements, 16-16:1
    other issues, 16-16:2
    overview, 16-16
  Breach of contract, 3-1:4.14
  Constructive trusts, 8-5:3.2
  Fraud, common law, 1-4:4.4
  Fraud, statutory, 1-5:4.3
  Fraud by non-disclosure, 1-6:4.4
  Promissory estoppel, 3-5:2.2
  Suits on an account, 3-8:4.5
  Wrongful discharge in breach of employment agreement, 6-1:4.3
STATUTES OF FRAUDS
  Negligent misrepresentation, 1-7:4.3
STATUTES OF LIMITATIONS
  Accountings, 8-4:4.1
  Agents and agency, 3-27:4.3
  Amended pleadings, relation back, 29-2
  Assumpsit, 7-6:4.1
  Bailment, 3-9:4.1, 3-10:4.1
  Breach of contract, 3-1:4.1
  Breach of duty of care, 2-1:4.3
  Breach of duty of loyalty, 2-2:4.4
  Breach of implied covenant to protect against drainage, 7-12:4.3
  Breach of partnership duty, 2-10:4.1
  Business disparagement
    discovery rule, 1-8:4.3
  Constructive trusts, 8-5:4.1
  Conversion
    oil and gas, 7-8:4.1
  Declaratory judgments, 7-3:4.1
  Definitions
    misidentification, 17-12:1
    misnomer, 17-12:1
    presence, 17-11:6
  Derivative shareholder suits, 2-8:4.2
  Discovery rule. *See* **DISCOVERY RULE**
  Employment discrimination, 6-3:4.1
  Express warranty of goods, 3-7:4.3
  Fiduciaries
    breach of fiduciary duty, oil and gas, 7-7:5.1
  Fraud, common law, 1-4:4.1
  Fraud, statutory, 1-5:4.1
  Fraud by non-disclosure, 1-6:4.1
  Insurance
    bad faith, 5-3:4.1
    deceptive insurance practices, 5-2:4.1
    declaratory judgment on coverage, 5-5:4.1
    declaratory judgment on duty to defend, 5-6:4.1
    Stowers claims, 5-7:4.1
    uninsured/underinsured motorist coverage claims, 5-4:4.1
  Legal malpractice
    accrual of claims, 4-1:4.1b
    discovery rule, 4-1:4.1c
    overview, 4-1:4.1a

STATUTES OF LIMITATIONS (*cont.*)
  Misnomer and misidentification of defendants, 23-2
  Misuse of trade names, 1-14:4.1
  Money had and received, 3-6:4.1
  Negligence
    oil and gas, 7-11:4.1
    overview, 1-10:4.1
  Overview
    one year, 17-1
    two years, 17-2
    three years, 17-3
    four years
      overview, 17-4
      residual rule, 17-4:1
    five years, 17-5
    six years, 17-6
    ten years, 17-7
    fifteen years, 17-8
    accrual of claims, 17-10
    agreements to modify or limit, 17-9
    suspending and extending
      absence from state, 17-11:6
      death of claimant, 17-11:4
      disabilities, 17-11:3
      discovery rule, 17-11:2
      fraudulent concealment, 17-11:1
      military service, 17-11:5
      saving statute for jurisdictional dismissals, 17-11:7
  Piercing the corporate veil, 2-13:4.1
  Promissory estoppel, 3-5:4.1
  Public nuisance, 7-9:4.1
  Quantum meruit, 3-3:4.1
  Quiet title, 7-1:4.1
  Rescission, 3-2:4.1
  Satisfaction
    misnomer and misidentification of defendants, 17-12:1
    overview, 17-12
    partnerships, assumed, or common names, 17-12:2
  Securities fraud, 2-4:4.3
  Slander of title, 7-10:4.1
  Specific performance, 8-3:4.1
  Statutes of repose compared, 17-13
  Tolling. *See* suspending and extending
  Tortious interference with existing contract, 1-1:4.1
  Tortious interference with prospective business relationship, 1-2:4.1
  Trade secret misappropriation
    overview, 1-15:4.1
  Trademark infringement, common law, 1-12:4.1
  Trademark infringement, statutory, 1-13:4.1
  Unjust enrichment, 3-4:4.1
  Usurpation of business opportunity, 2-11:4.1
  Wrongful discharge for refusal to perform illegal acts, 6-2:4.1
  Wrongful discharge in breach of employment agreement, 6-1:4.1
  Wrongful distribution of dividends, 2-3:4.3
  Wrongful withdrawal of partner, 2-16:4.1
STATUTES OF REPOSE
  Definition, product liability action, 17-13:2
  Fifteen years, 17-13:2
  Fraudulent transfer, 3-4:4.5
  Healthcare liability, 17-13:3
  Overview, 17-13
  Statutes of limitations compared, 17-13
  Ten years, 17-13:1
STAY
  Arbitration, trial court proceedings and, 25-2
  Derivative shareholder suits, 2-8:5.5
STOCK
  Fraud. *See* **FRAUD, STATUTORY**
***STOWERS* CLAIMS**
  Damages and remedies
    actual damages, 5-7:3.1
    court costs, 11-13:2
    exemplary damages. *See* **DAMAGES AND REMEDIES**
    interest. *See* **INTEREST**
  Defenses
    demand not made, 5-7:4.2
    policy limits exhausted, 5-7:4.3
    statute of limitations, 5-7:4.1
  Elements, 5-7:2
  Related causes of action, 5-7:1.1
SUBJECT MATTER JURISDICTION
  Agencies, 21-6
  Case or controversy requirement, 21-4
  Constitutional county courts, 21-1:2
  Counterclaims, 21-3
  Crossclaims, 21-3
  Dismissal for lack of, time to refile, 17-11:1
  District courts, 21-1:4
  Ecclesiastical disputes, 21-5
  Federal court, 21-7
  Justice courts, 21-1:1
  Plea to jurisdiction to attack, 21-9
  Pleading
    amount in controversy
      aggregation of claims, 21-2:1
      overview, 21-2
    judgment in excess of jurisdictional maximum, 21-2:3
    presumption in favor of, 21-2:2
  Sovereign immunity, 21-8
  Statutory county courts, 21-1:3
  Statutory probate courts, 21-1:5
  Third party claims, 21-3
SUIT IN ASSUMPSIT. *See* **OIL AND GAS**
SUITS ON AN ACCOUNT
  Damages and remedies
    actual damages, 3-8:3.1
    attorneys' fees, 3-8:3.3
    interest, 3-8:3.2

INDEX

Defenses
  accord and satisfaction, 3-8:4.3
  consideration issues, 3-8:4.4
  other defenses, 3-8:4.5
  payment, 3-8:4.2
  pleading, 3-8:5.1
  statute of limitations, 3-8:4.1
Definitions
  just amount, 3-8:2.1, 3-8:2.2
  open accounts, 3-8:2.1
  stated accounts, 3-8:2.1, 3-8:2.2
Elements
  open accounts, 3-8:2.1
  stated accounts, 3-8:2.2
Overview, 3-8:1
Related causes of action, 3-8:1.1

SUITS TO COMPEL INSPECTION
Damages and remedies
  actual damages, 2-12:3.2
  attorneys' fees, 2-12:3.1
  costs, 2-12:3.1
Defenses, 2-12:4.1
Definition, covered records, 2-12:2.1, 2-12:2.2, 2-12:2.4
Elements
  corporations, 2-12:2.1
  general partnerships, 2-12:2.3
  limited liability companies (LLCS), 2-12:2.2
  limited partnerships, 2-12:2.4
  public officers who may compel, 2-12:2.5
Overview, 2-12:1
Related causes of action, 2-12:1.1

SUITS TO PIERCE THE CORPORATE VEIL. *See* **PIERCING THE CORPORATE VEIL**

SUMMARY JUDGMENT
Definition, substantive defect, 30-3:10
Evidence
  affidavits
    exhibits, 30-3:6
    facts admissible at trial, 30-3:4
    interested witnesses, 30-3:5
    personal knowledge requirement, 30-3:3
    sham and bad faith, 30-3:7
  deadlines to file, 30-3:2
  declarations, 30-3:3
  discovery for, 30-3:8
  objections to, 30-3:10
  oral testimony, 30-3:1
  overview, 30-3
  pleadings, 30-3:9
No-evidence motions
  availability, 30-2:2
  movant's burden of pleading, 30-2:3
  nonmovant's burden of production, 30-2:4
  overview, 30-2
  timing of motion and response, 30-2:1
Ruling, 30-4
  final judgment, 30-4:2
  written, 30-4:1

Traditional motions
  burden of persuasion, 30-1:2
  burden of pleading
    movant, 30-1:3
    nonmovant, 30-1:6
  burden of production
    movant, 30-1:4
    nonmovant, 30-1:7
  legally insufficient motions, 30-1:5
  timing of motion and response, 30-1:1

SUPPLEMENTAL PLEADINGS
Amendment compared, 29-1

SURVEYORS
Statutes of repose, 17-13:1

SWORN ACCOUNTS
Damages and remedies
  overview, 3-7:3.1
  pleading, 11-5:6
  verified petitions, effect of, 3-7:3.2
Defenses
  overview, 3-7:4.1
  pleading, 3-7:5.1
Elements, 3-7:2
Overview, 3-7:1
Related causes of action, 3-7:1.1
Verified and special denials, 14-9

T

TAKINGS
Oil and gas. *See* **OIL AND GAS**

TAXES
Corporation failure to pay franchise taxes. *See* **OFFICERS AND DIRECTORS**
State revocation of corporate status. *See* **STATE REVOCATION OF CORPORATE STATUS**

TEMPORARY CESSATION OF PRODUCTION DOCTRINE
Oil and gas, 7-5:4.1

TEMPORARY INJUNCTION
Contents of injunction, 8-1:3.1
Damages and remedies, 8-1:3.1
Defenses
  laches, 8-1:4.2
  unclean hands, 8-1:4.1
Elements, 8-1:2
Jurisdiction, 8-1:5.1
Overview, 8-1:1
Procedural issues
  appeal, 8-1:5.6
  hearing requirement, 8-1:5.5
  notice, 8-1:5.4
  petition contents, 8-1:5.3
Related causes of action, 8-1:1.1
Scope of injunction, 8-1:3.2
Venue, 8-1:5.2

TENDER OFFERS. *See* **SECURITIES FRAUD**

TEXAS ANTI-SLAPP ACT
Overview, 28-4

TEXAS ARBITRATION ACT (TAA)
  Overview, 25-1:2
TEXAS CITIZENS PARTICIPATION ACT (TCPA)
  Overview, 1-8:4.5, 28-4
THIRD PARTY CLAIMS
  Subject matter jurisdiction, 21-3
TIME
  Arbitration, vacating award, 25-4:2
  Breach of contract and statute of frauds, 3-1:4.14
  Credit file information, statutory late provision, 3-31:2
  Derivative shareholder suits
    demand, 2-8:2, 2-8:5.4
    stay, 2-8:5.5
  Designation of responsible third parties
    leave to designate, 18-5:1
    objections, 18-5:2
    unknown criminals, 18-5:3
  Discovery periods
    amendment, 20-2, 20-3
    expert designation, 20-2, 20-3
    limits on time for, 20-3
    overview, 20-2, 20-3
    supplementation of discovery responses and, 20-3
    trial setting, 20-2
  Dismissal for lack of subject matter jurisdiction, time to refile, 17-11:1
  Dismissal of baseless cause of action
    filing, 28-1:4
    response, 28-1:4
    ruling, 28-1:5
  Dissenting shareholders
    demand, 2-9:2
    fair value determination, 2-9:5.4
    interest, 2-9:3.2
  Employment discrimination, back pay, 6-3:3.3
  Forcible entry and detainer, 8-11:2.2, 8-11:3.1, 8-11:3.3
  Insurance, payment of claims
    deadline for, 5-1:2
  Remand, 27-6
  Removal, 27-3:6, 27-5:3, 27-5:5
  Securities fraud
    disgorgement, 2-4:3.3
    short swing profits, 2-4:5.3
  Sequestration, 8-6:3.3, 8-6:3.4
  State revocation of corporate status
    Attorney General judicial termination, 2-6:2.2
    franchise taxes, failure to pay, 2-6:2.3
    Secretary of State administrative termination, 2-6:2.1
  Statutes of limitations. *See* **STATUTES OF LIMITATIONS**
  Statutes of repose. *See* **STATUTES OF REPOSE**
  Suits to compel inspection, 2-12:2.1, 2-12:4.1
  Summary judgment, 30-1:1, 30-3:2, 30-3:7
  Venue, transfer motions, 22-7
  Wrongful withdrawal of partner, 2-16:2
TIME-OF-FILING RULE
  Diversity of citizenship test, 27-3:3.4
TORTIOUS INTERFERENCE WITH EXISTING CONTRACT
  Conspiracy to breach contracts compared, 9-3:1
  Damages and remedies
    actual damages
      injury to reputation, 1-1:3.1c
      lost profits, 1-1:3.1d
      mental anguish, 1-1:3.1b
      overview, 1-1:3.1
      pecuniary loss, 1-1:3.1a
    court costs, 11-13:2
    exemplary damages, 1-1:3.1
    injunction. *See* **INJUNCTION**
    interest. *See* **INTEREST**
  Defenses
    comparative fault, 1-1:4.2
    privilege and justification, 1-1:4.3
    statute of limitations, 1-1:4.1
    void ab initio, 1-1:4.4
  Elements, 1-1:2
  Overview, 1-1:1
  Related causes of action, 1-1:1.1
TORTIOUS INTERFERENCE WITH FIDUCIARY DUTIES
  Overview, 9-20:1
  Rejected in Texas, 9-20:2
  Related causes of action, 9-20:1.1
TORTIOUS INTERFERENCE WITH PROSPECTIVE BUSINESS RELATIONSHIP
  Damages and remedies
    actual damages
      lost profits, 1-2:3.1c
      mental anguish, 1-2:3.1b
      overview, 1-2:3.1
      pecuniary loss, 1-2:3.1a
    court costs, 11-13:2
    exemplary damages, 1-2:3.2
    injunction. *See* **INJUNCTION**
    interest. *See* **INTEREST**
  Defenses
    comparative fault, 1-2:4.2
    privilege and justification, 1-2:4.3
    statute of limitations, 1-2:4.1
    void ab initio, 1-2:4.4
  Definition, independently tortious conduct, 1-2:2
  Elements
    business relationship probable, 1-2:2.1
    causation, 1-2:2.4
    independent tortious conduct, 1-2:2.3
    intentional interference, 1-2:2.2
  Overview, 1-2:1
  Related causes of action, 1-2:1.1
TORTS
  Agency. *See* **AGENTS AND AGENCY**
  Economic loss rule, 12-3

INDEX

Liability of successor for tortious conduct of predecessor
  overview, 9-13:1
  rejected in Texas, 9-13:2
Prima facie torts
  overview, 9-16:1
  rejected in Texas, 9-16:2
  related causes of action, 9-16:1.1
Tortious interference with existing contract. *See* **TORTIOUS INTERFERENCE WITH EXISTING CONTRACT**
Tortious interference with fiduciary duties. *See* **TORTIOUS INTERFERENCE WITH FIDUCIARY DUTIES**
Tortious interference with prospective business relationship. *See* **TORTIOUS INTERFERENCE WITH PROSPECTIVE BUSINESS RELATIONSHIP**

TRACING
  Constructive trusts, 8-5:2

TRADE NAME MISUSE. *See* **MISUSE OF TRADE NAMES**

TRADE SECRET MISAPPROPRIATION
  Damages and remedies
    actual damages, 1-15:3.1
    court costs, 11-13:2
    interest. *See* **INTEREST**
  Defenses
    independent development, 1-15:4.4
    preemption, 1-15:4.3
    privilege, 1-15:4.2
    statute of limitations, 1-15:4.1
    unclean hands, 1-15:4.5
  Definitions
    trade secret, 1-15:2
    use, 1-15:2
  Elements, 1-15:2

TRADEMARK INFRINGEMENT, COMMON LAW
  Damages and remedies, injunction, 1-12:3.1
  Defenses
    abandonment, 1-12:4.3
    acquiescence, 1-12:4.4
    fair use, 1-12:4.5
    laches, 1-12:4.2
    statute of limitations, 1-12:4.1
  Definition, secondary meaning, 1-12:2
  Elements, 1-12:2
  Overview, 1-12:1

TRADEMARK INFRINGEMENT, STATUTORY
  Damages and remedies
    actual damages, 1-13:3.1
    attorneys' fees, 1-13:3.5
    disgorgement, 1-13:3.2
    injunction, 1-13:3.3
    statutory damages, 1-13:3.4
  Defenses
    abandonment, 1-13:4.3
    fair use, 1-13:4.6
    First Amendment, 1-13:4.5
    invalid mark, 1-13:4.2
    laches, 1-13:4.4
    news reporting or commentary, 1-13:4
    non-commercial use, 1-13:4.7
    statute of limitations, 1-13:4.1
  Definitions
    invalid mark, 1-13:4.2
    use, 1-13:2.1
  Elements
    dilution, 1-13:2.2
    fraudulent registration, 1-13:2.3
    infringement, 1-13:2.1
  Overview, 1-13:1
  Related causes of action, 1-13:1.1

TRESPASS TO CHATTEL AND PERSONALTY
  Conversion compared, 7-8:1

TRESPASS TO TRY TITLE. *See* **OIL AND GAS**

TRIAL BY CONSENT
  Overview, 29-6

U

UNCLEAN HANDS
  Accountings, 8-4:4.3
  Covenants not to compete, actions on, 3-5:4.3
  Injunction
    temporary injunction, 8-1:4.1
  Judicial expulsion of partners, 2-14:4.1
  Judicial winding up of partnership, 2-15:4.1
  Money had and received, 3-6:4.2
  Promissory estoppel, 3-5:4.2
  Quantum meruit, 3-3:4.5
  Trade secret misappropriation, 1-15:4.5
  Unjust enrichment, 3-4:4.3

UNCONSCIONABILITY
  Arbitration, 25-3:2
  Breach of contract, 3-1:4.19

UNIFORM COMMERCIAL CODE (UCC)
  Choice of law, 24-1:7
  Damages. *See* **DAMAGES AND REMEDIES**

UNIFORM DECLARATORY JUDGMENT ACT. *See* **DECLARATORY JUDGMENTS**

UNINSURED/UNDERINSURED MOTORIST COVERAGE CLAIMS. *See* **INSURANCE**

UNJUST ENRICHMENT
  Breach of contract, 3-1:3.3
  Damage and remedies, 3-4:3
    restitution, 3-4:3.1
  Defenses
    other defenses, 3-4:4.3
    statute of limitations, 3-4:4.1
    valid contract, 3-4:4.2
  Elements, 3-4:2
  Money had and received. *See* **MONEY HAD AND RECEIVED**
  Overview, 3-4:1, 11-11:2
  Pleading, 3-4:5.1
  Quantum meruit. *See* **QUANTUM MERUIT**
  Related causes of action, 3-4:1.1

USURPATION OF BUSINESS OPPORTUNITY
  Damages and remedies
    actual damages, 2-11:3.5
    constructive trusts, 2-11:3.1
    disgorgement, 2-11:3.4
    exemplary damages, 2-11:3.7
    forfeiture of compensation, 2-11:3.3
    removal from office, 2-11:3.6
    turnover of opportunity, 2-11:3.2
  Defenses
    abandonment, 2-11:4.3
    financial incapability, 2-11:4.2
    ratification, 2-11:4.4
    statute of limitations, 2-11:4.1
  Definition, line of business, 2-11:2
  Elements, 2-11:2
  Overview, 2-11:1
  Related causes of action, 2-11:1.1

V

VENUE
  Conversion, 7-8:5.1
  Declaratory judgments, 7-3:5.1
  Definitions
    principle office, 22-3
    venue, 22-2
  Derivative shareholder suits, 2-8:5.2
  Dismissal of baseless cause of action, 28-1:7
  Dissenting shareholders, 2-9:5.4
  Due-order-of-hearing requirement, 13-2:6
  Due-order-of-pleading requirement, 13-2:5
  General denials, 13-3:5
  Injunction
    permanent injunction, 8-1:5.2
    temporary injunction, 8-1:5.2
  Judicial winding up of partnership, 2-15:5.1
  Oil and gas
    assumpsit, 7-6:5.1
    breach of contract, 7-5:5.1
    breach of fiduciary duty, 7-7:5.1
  Pleading. *See* **PLEADING**
  Quiet title, 7-1:5.1
  Receivership, 8-9:5.3
  Rule of capture, conversion, 7-8:4.2
  Slander of title, 7-10:5.1
  Trespass to try title, 7-2:5.1
  Waiver, 28-1:7
VERIFIED AND SPECIAL DENIALS
  Another suit for same claim pending, 14-2
  Assignment, 14-6
  Assumed names, 14-8
  Capacity lacking, 14-1
  Conditions precedent, 14-10
  Consideration, 14-11
  Corporate status, 14-4
  Execution on written instrument, 14-5
  Indorsement genuineness, 14-6
  Joinder issues, 14-3

  Notice or proof of loss or claim lacking, 14-7
  Partnership, 14-4
  Pleading
    conditions precedent, 13-4:6
    matters appearing on the record exception, 13-4:5
    overview, 13-4
    personal knowledge requirement
      exceptions, 13-4:3
      overview, 13-4:2
    what requires, 13-4:1
    who may verify, 13-4:4
  Sworn accounts, 14-9
VOID AB INITIO
  Oil and gas, 7-1:4.1
  Tortious interference with existing contract, 1-1:4.4
  Tortious interference with prospective business relationship, 1-2:4.4

W

WAIVER
  Affirmative defenses
    elements, 16-6:1
    overview, 16-6
  Arbitration, 25-3:4
  Breach of contract
    illegality, 3-1:4.6
    mistake, 3-1:4.12
  Conversion, qualified good faith refusal, 1-3:4.1
  Defenses. *See* **PLEADING**
  Employment discrimination, 6-3:4.3
  Forum selection clauses, 26-2:2
  Fraud, ratification
    common law, 1-4:4.3
    non-disclosure, 1-6:4.3
  Personal jurisdiction, 23-3
  Pleading burdens. *See* **PLEADING**
  Quantum meruit, 3-3:4.5
  Removal, 27-5:1
  Rescission, 3-2:4.3
  Service of process, 23-3
  Sovereign immunity and subject matter jurisdiction, 21-8
  Special appearances, 28-1:7
  Special exceptions, 28-2
  Specific performance, 8-3:4.4
  Summary judgment, 30-3:5
  Venue, 22-7, 28-1:7
  Verified and special denials. *See* **VERIFIED AND SPECIAL DENIALS**
WARRANTIES
  Agency, warranty of authority, 3-12:2.5
WHISTLEBLOWERS
  Private sector employees
    overview, 9-22:1
    rejected in Texas, 9-22:2
    related causes of action, 9-22:1.1

INDEX

Wrongful expulsion of whistleblowing partners
   overview, 9-14:1
   rejected in Texas, 9-14:2
   related causes of action, 9-14:1.1

WINDING UP
   Breach of partnership duty, 2-10:3.9
   Judicial winding up. *See* **DISSOLUTION OF PARTNERSHIPS**

WRITS OF POSSESSION
   Trespass to try title, 7-2:3.2

WRONGFUL DISCHARGE FOR REFUSAL TO PERFORM ILLEGAL ACTS
   Damages and remedies
     actual damages, 6-2:3.1
     exemplary damages, 6-2:3.5
     injunction, 6-2:3.3
     interest, 6-2:3.2
     reinstatement, 6-2:3.4
   Defenses
     immunity, 6-2:4.2
     statute of limitations, 6-2:4.1
   Definition, malice, 6-2:3.5
   Elements, 6-2:2
   Overview, 6-2:1
   Related causes of action, 6-2:1.1

WRONGFUL DISCHARGE IN BREACH OF EMPLOYMENT AGREEMENT
   Damages and remedies
     actual damages, 6-1:3.1
     attorneys' fees, 6-1:3.4
     court costs, 11-13:2
     interest. *See* **INTEREST**
   Defenses
     exhaustion of administrative remedies failure, 6-1:4.6
     good cause, 6-1:4.2
     mitigation of damages, 6-1:4.5
     payment made, 6-1:4.4
     statute of frauds, 6-1:4.3
     statute of limitations, 6-1:4.1
   Elements, 6-1:2
   Employment-at-will, 6-1
   Overview, 6-1
   Related causes of action, 6-1:1.1

WRONGFUL DISTRIBUTION OF DIVIDENDS
   Breach of the duty of care, 2-1:2.2
   Breach of the duty of loyalty, 2-2:2.2
   Damages and remedies
     contribution, 2-3:3.3
     excess distributions, 2-3:3.1
     joint and several liability, 2-3:3.2
   Defenses
     good faith reliance, 2-3:4.1
     purge through subsequent events, 2-3:4.2
     statute of limitations, 2-3:4.3
   Definitions
     distribution, 2-3:2
     net assets, 2-3:2
     surplus, 2-3:2
   Elements, 2-3:2
   Overview, 2-3:1
   Related causes of action, 2-3:1.1
   Who may sue, 2-3:5.1

WRONGFUL EXPULSION OF WHISTLEBLOWING PARTNERS
   Overview, 9-14:1
   Rejected in Texas, 9-14:2
   Related causes of action, 9-14:1.1

WRONGFUL WITHDRAWAL OF PARTNER. *See* **DISSOLUTION OF PARTNERSHIPS**